2006
Gun Digest®

1944 – 2005

Gun Digest

60th
ANNIVERSARY EDITION

**Edited by
Ken Ramage**

© 2005
by Gun Digest Books

Published by

Our toll-free number to place an order or obtain
a free catalog is (800) 258-0929.

Manuscripts, contributions and inquiries, including first class return postage, should be sent to the
Gun Digest Editorial Offices, KP Books, 700 E. State Street, Iola, WI 54990-0001. All materials re-
cieved will receive reasonable care, but we will not be responsible for their safe return. Material accepted is subject to our requirements for editing and revisions. Author payment covers all rights and
title to the accepted material, including photos, drawings and other illustrations. Payment is at our
current rates.

CAUTION: Technical data presented here, particularly technical data on handloading and on firearms
adjustment and alteration, inevitably reflects individual experience with particular equipment and
components under specific circumstances the reader cannot duplicate exactly. Such data presentations
therefore should be used for guidance only and with caution. KP Books accepts no responsibility for
results obtained using these data.

Library of Congress Catalog Number: 0072-9043

ISBN: 0-89689-168-2

Designed by Patsy Howell & Tom Nelsen

Edited by Ken Ramage

Printed in the United States of America

TWENTY-FOURTH ANNUAL
JOHN T. AMBER LITERARY AWARD
Jim Foral

Jim Foral with his favorite rifle, a sporterized Krag that shoots cast bullets extremely well.

Since a young boy, history has been important to me. Thus, I have a penchant for the historically rooted article and tend to specialize in the often-wordy treatment of obscure or overlooked events, trends, and personalities of our sporting heritage. GUN DIGEST allows me the space I need to give the readers something they've not seen before, and for this I am grateful.

My stories, covering topics from cast-bullet shooting to crypto-zoology, have appeared in an assortment of periodicals, and I've done one book, *Gunwriters Of Yesteryear* (Wolfe Publishing Co.). My work has been published in the following books and magazines: GUN DIGEST, GUNS ILLUSTRATED, HANDLOADER'S DIGEST, and KNIVES. Also: *Rifle, Handloader's Bullet-Making Annual, Rifle's Hunting Annual, Precision Shooting, Precision Shooting Annual, North American Whitetail, Man at Arms, Gun Report, Varmint Hunter, Texas Trophy Hunter, International Bowhunter, Longbows and Recurves, Single-Shot Rifle Journal* and *Bear Hunting.*

My wife Kathy and I live in Lincoln, Nebraska, where I work in the commercial floor-covering field, and bow-fish the area creeks.

The only juried literary award in the firearms field, the John T. Amber Award replaced the Townsend Whelen Award originated by the late John T. Amber and later re-named in his honor. Now, a $1000 prize goes to the winner of this annual award.

Nominations for the competition are made by GUN DIGEST editor Ken Ramage and are judged by a distinguished panel of editors experienced in the firearms field. Entries are evaluated for felicity of expression and illustration, originality and scholarship, and subject importance to the firearms field.

This year's Amber Award nominees, in addition to Foral, were:

Clarence Anderson, *"Ahead of Its Time: The Cummins 'Duplex' Riflescope"*
Toby Bridges, *"Smokeless Muzzleloader Velocities–Without the Smokeless"*
Roderick S. Carman, *" Guns of the Real Indiana Jones"*
George J. Layman, *"The Ballard Single-Shot Rifle..."*
Harvey T. Pennington, *"Cast Bullet Hunting Loads for Deer & Bear"*
Thomas D. Schiffer, *"English Blackpowder Express Rifles"*
Fred Stutzenberger, *"Aperture Sights for Aging Eyes"*
John Walter, *"The Lost Guns of Nepal"*
Terry Wieland, *"Eibar Revisited"*

Serving as judges for this year's competition were John D. Acquilino, editor of *Inside Gun News*; Bob Bell, former editor-in-chief of *Pennsylvania Game News*; James W. Bequette, editorial director of Primedia's outdoor group; David Brennan, editor of *Precision Shooting*; Sharon Cunningham, director of Pioneer Press; Pete Dickey, former technical editor of *American Rifleman*; Jack Lewis, former editor and publisher of *Gun World*; Bill Parkerson, former editor of *American Rifleman*, now director of research and information for the National Rifle Association, and Dave Petzal, deputy editor of *Field & Stream.*

INTRODUCTION

In the Beginning....

During the years preceding World War II, Milton Klein owned a chain of sporting goods stores in the Chicago area. He also had a thriving national mail order business through which he sold many sporting items, including firearms.

After the Pearl Harbor attack in December 1941, production of sporting firearms was stopped as factories shifted their efforts to military arms. Klein's mail order business suffered.

In 1943, believing that if shooters couldn't buy guns, they just might buy a book about guns, he advertised the first edition of GUN DIGEST in his catalog for $1.00. He had no idea if or when a book would be produced, so he offered a free calendar as part of the deal, with the promise of a book to come later. He received tens of thousands of orders—all accompanied by dollar bills—and GUN DIGEST was born.

The Editors.......

The first edition, compiled by Klein's advertising manager, Charles R. Jacobs, was published in 1944. The next three editions, published in 1946, 1947, and 1948, were also edited by Jacobs. However, after receiving criticism about the contents from John T. Amber, an arms expert working at Marshall Field's gun department in Chicago, Klein named Amber to the post of Editor-in-Chief, a position he would hold for the next 28 years.

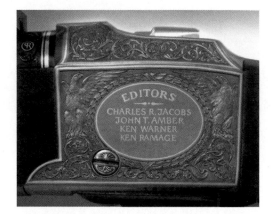

No new edition appeared in 1949 as Amber worked to completely revamp the book's format, but in August 1950, Amber's first edition—the 1951 GUN DIGEST, 5th Edition—made its debut. The book has appeared annually ever since and is acclaimed everywhere as The World's Greatest Gun Book. Amber retired in 1978 and was replaced by Ken Warner, former editor of the *American Rifleman and American Hunter* magazines, both publications of the National Rifle Association.

Warner remained Editor-in-Chief of GUN DIGEST through the 54th Edition, after which the editorship passed to Ken Ramage, a long-time shooter and industry veteran of more than 30 years.

Following service in the Marines and the years spent earning two degrees from the University of Missouri, Ramage joined Lyman Products (Middlefield, Connecticut) in January 1973. In the ensuing years he edited a number of books, predominantly on handloading and muzzleloading topics. Three of those books managed to stay in print for 25 years or longer: *Lyman Blackpowder Handbook* (1975-2000); *Cast Bullet Handbook, 3rd Edition* (1980-present) and the *Lyman Centennial Journal* (1978-present). Other enduring accomplishments from those multi-tasking Lyman days include the Great Plains Rifle, Trade Rifle and the Plains Pistol. In 1986 Ramage joined the staff of *Shooting Times* magazine and, after a number of years, moved back to Connecticut to operate a magazine for the National Shooting Sports Foundation. He joined Krause Publications in December 1997, and his editor's byline appeared for the first time on the cover of the 2001 GUN DIGEST, 55th Edition.

About This Edition.......

The editorial lineup includes several articles that look back over the life of Gun Digest. Unfortunately there just wasn't room to cover all the major arms categories, but be sure to read John Taffin's substantial piece on six-guns and Holt Bodinson's report on ammunition development in the post-war years.

Fans of Holt Bodinson's "Web Directory" will find it relocated to the back of the book; check the table of contents for the specific page.

There is much, much more, including a fully updated arms catalog and directory of the arms trade. Enjoy.

Ken Ramage, Editor
GUN DIGEST

GUN DIGEST Staff

EDITOR
Ken Ramage

CONTRIBUTING EDITORS

Holt Bodinson – Ammunition, Ballistics & Components; Web Directory
Raymond Caranta – The Guns of Europe
J. W. "Doc" Carlson – Blackpowder Review
John Campbell – Single-Shot Rifles
John Haviland – Shotgun Review

John Malloy – Handguns Today: Autoloaders
Larry Sterett – Handloading Update
Layne Simpson – Rifle Review
John Taffin – Handguns Today: Six-guns & Others
Tom Turpin – Engraved & Custom Guns
Wayne van Zwoll – Scopes & Mounts

ABOUT THE COVERS

FRONT COVER

Two new revolvers from Ruger this year are the Super Redhawk Alaskan (top), and the New Vaquero.

The **Alaskan** is a compact version of the stainless steel double-action Super Redhawk fitted with a frame-integral short 2 1/2-inch barrel to enhance portability. This model, weighing only 42 ounces, is available chambered for the 45 Colt/454 Casull or the 480 Ruger cartridges. These potent cartridges do kick, and the Hogue Tamer Monogrips help moderate the recoil, allowing better control of the revolver.

The Alaskan is fitted with a rear sight adjustable for both windage and elevation, and a ramp front blade.

The **New Vaquero** is a smaller version of the Blackhawk family, and replaces the Vaquero model, now discontinued.

Experienced single-action shooters should notice the new revolver feels very much like an original Colt Peacemaker, thanks to the slightly smaller frame and related dimensions. The grips are of simulated black rubber, and the sights are the traditional fixed type: groove-in-frame rear and a blade front.

The New Vaquero is available in either blued/case-colored form, or in polished stainless steel. Both are available chambered for the 357 Magnum or 45 Colt, and in barrel lengths of 4-5/8, 5-1/2 and 7-1/2 inches.

BACK COVER

The GUN DIGEST 60th Anniversary Rifle.

This one-of-a-kind rifle is based on the classic Ruger No. 1 single-shot rifle and was created in Ruger's recently opened Studio of Art and Decoration.

Ruger's master engraver Paul Lantuch designed and executed the engraving and gold inlay. Gunsmith Mitch Schultz (Gunsmithing Ltd., Fairfield, Connecticut) handled all the stock work, metal work, finishing and assembly.

The rifle is chambered for the 38-55 Winchester cartridge and wears a 6x Montana Vintage Arms 28-inch scope with standard crosshairs, mounted in their adjustable Schuetzen mounts.

Come November 2005, some lucky person will be drawn as the winner of this rifle, scope and carrying case. Interested? See entry details on page 6, or visit our web site: www.krause.com.

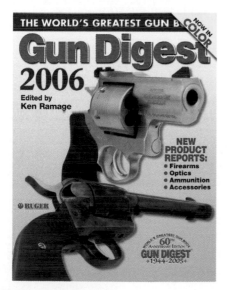

SWEEPSTAKES
Enter to Win

Gun Digest 60th Anniversary Rifle

To commemorate this 60th Anniversary Edition, Sturm, Ruger and Company built a special Ruger No. 1 single-shot rifle for us. This one-of-a-kind rifle will be won by some lucky individual in our open-to-all (*all who are legally able to own firearms*) sweepstakes. Interested? Get your entry in by the end of October 2005. Eligible contestants can enter the free drawing by clicking on the banner ad at www.krausebooks.com and answering a short survey. Or simply send in a post card with name, address, phone number, email and birth date to GUN DIGEST, Ruger Rifle Giveaway, 700 E. State St., Iola, WI 54990-0001. No purchase is necessary.

Entries will be taken until Oct. 26, and the winning entry will be chosen on Nov. 1.

Regular readers of this book are aware of the long-term relationship between GUN DIGEST, the single-shot rifle and Sturm, Ruger and Company. The late John Amber, editor of this book for 28 editions, was an avid collector of single-shot rifles, and one of the founders of the Single Shot Rifle Association. Ruger introduced the classic No. 1 single-shot rifle in 1966, to a ready and appreciative market. Thus, selection of the Ruger No. 1 as our anniversary rifle seemed, well, natural.

The new Ruger Studio of Art and Decoration is a custom gun engraving and decoration department specifically dedicated to the creation of individualized firearms artistry. Ruger's master engraver Paul Lantuch designed and executed the engraving and gold inlay. All the woodwork and metalwork was performed by the well-known Connecticut gunsmith, Mitch Schultz.

The rifle itself is beautiful, and can be seen

▲ *Paul Lantuch, master engraver.*

nearby and on the back cover. It is stocked with premium walnut, in the Alex Henry design, and fitted with a new grip cap designed by the Ruger studio.

The barrel is 26 inches long and is chambered for the 38-55 Winchester cartridge. This is a rare factory barrel that was located by old friend and Ruger executive, Dick Beaulieu. The 6x long-tube scope and mounts are from Montana Vintage Arms. Accompanying the rifle and scope is a compartmented canvas and leather case from Jeff's Outfitters (formerly Cape Outfitters).

Our most sincere thanks to Ruger President Steve Sanetti for accepting this project. And our heart-felt thanks to those who made this rifle happen: Andrew Whitely, manager of the Ruger studio, Dick Beaulieu at the New Hampshire plant, master engraver Paul Lantuch and Mitch Schultz, Gunsmithing Ltd.

CONTENTS

PAGE 10   PAGE 131   PAGE 32

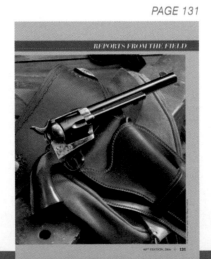

PAGE 175   PAGE 84   PAGE 221   PAGE 74

Magnificent Maverick:
THE 400 BROWN WHELEN

by William V. Woodward

The author's objective was to create an accurate, powerful big bore that looked like it might have come from a London maker. Woodward is happy with the result.

Above the Kalahari, the sun hung like a blood-red ball. As the sun edged toward the horizon, the wind picked up and blew the dust along the desert floor. The last of the kudu cows returned from the water hole and melted into the high grass. Now the bulls came, drifting down the game trail, their spiral horns glistening in the last light of day. A huge bull stole in from the right, the white chevron on his nose luminescent in the fading light. I eased the bolt of the Mauser forward and slid a panatela-sized shell into the chamber....

The best African trophies are the sights and sounds of safari. The memories are endless—the rasp of a leopard at midnight, the sight of an elephant grazing outside the tent, the feel of a classic, well worn rifle.

In 2000, I was planning my third African safari and searching for a big-bore rifle suitable for zebra, kudu and sable—and for Cape buffalo. I had booked an eight-day trip to the highlands of Zimbabwe for plains game and birds, followed by a ten-day hunt for Cape buffalo in the Zambezi Valley. I wanted

On a 2001 safari to Zimbabwe, the battery included the 400 Brown Whelen (left) and a Sako 7mm-08.

an accurate rifle capable of firing a heavy bullet and delivering the 4000-ft/lbs of energy considered minimum for dangerous game. Trajectory was not a consideration, as most shots in the thorn bush of southern Africa are well under 200 yards. The 375 H&H Magnum was an obvious candidate. The 375 has established itself as the all-around cartridge for Africa. Unfortunately, the 375s I had fired were too light,

or poorly stocked—and they kicked!

The book, *Big Bore Rifles and Cartridges*, (Wolfe Publishing Company, February, 1991, Prescott, Arizona), offered some options. I was intrigued by the 40-calibers, but cartridges like the 416 Remington Magnum and 416 Rigby were more than I needed. The 404 Jeffrey, however, was a mild big-bore that looked just right. I had a fine 1950s-era FN Mauser action and decided to use it as the basis for an African rifle. Unfortunately, the 0.537-inch rim and long case of the 404 required significant alterations to the action. I read on, and stumbled on an interesting cartridge—a modern version of the infamous 400 Whelen.

I say "infamous" because the 400 Whelen may be the most cussed and discussed cartridge in the history of wildcatting. One of two cartridges actually developed by Colonel Whelen (the other is the 35 Whelen), the 400 has been steeped in controversy since its invention in the 1920s. The 400 was a favorite of Elmer Keith's, and Griffin and Howe made several 400s. In the 1930s, gun writer Phil Sharpe summed up the 400, citing "a faint indication of a neck" and the danger of failing to establish headspace. The cartridge discussed in *Big Bore Rifles* was an updated Whelen based on the same 30-06 case, but with a well-defined 0.015-inch shoulder. This cartridge is called the 400 Brown Whelen.[1]

In the chapter on the 400 Brown Whelen, author John Kronfeld writes knowledgeably about the history of the cartridge. Kronfeld is the first writer to clearly separate the myth from the reality of the 400 Whelen. After extensive testing, Kronfeld concluded the 400 Brown Whelen was a highly accurate cartridge with "mild recoil." And, he reported, once fire-forming is completed, the cartridge headspaces—every time!

(In recent years several designers have developed 41-caliber cartridges based on the 30-06 case. The list

of designers runs from custom gun makers to magazine editors. Most of these innovations are nothing new under the sun, but variations of the original 400 Whelen and the more efficient 400 Brown Whelen. Little has been written about the performance of these cartridges in Africa. J. D. Jones is an exception to the rule. An innovative designer [and owner of SSK Industries], Jones has developed an extensive line of big-bore cartridges for the T/C Contender and Encore pistols, including a 411 based on the 444 Marlin case, and a 416 based on '06 brass. Jones has hunted extensively in Africa and has taken a wide variety of plains and dangerous game with these cartridges.)[2]

The 400 Brown Whelen uses 30-06 cases to propel 300-grain bullets at 375 H&H velocities (2500 fps). More important, 400-grain bullets approach the ballistics of two British cartridges deemed adequate for everything from eland to elephant. These rounds *(which the Brits refer to as "large medium bores")* are the 404 Jeffrey *(a round for magazine rifles)* and the rimmed 450-400 *(an earlier shell for double and single-shot rifles)*. Both cartridges were popular choices of African and Indian big-game hunters from roughly 1905 to 1960.[3] I read Kronfeld's chapter and promptly fell in love.

I envisioned a rifle that was heavy enough to soak up recoil, but light enough to carry with ease. Reading suggested that 9-1/2 pounds was an optimum weight and that a straight, or "parallel," comb was essential for comfort and recoil reduction. Finally, I wanted a rifle that had all the bells and whistles of an African big bore—and looked like it might have come from a London maker.

I began with a reamer from Pacific Precision, a 411 barrel blank from Shilen and a stock blank from Richard's Microfit Stocks. Brownells provided a Timney trigger, scope mounts by Leupold, a barrel-band front sight, swivels,

1 *Big Bore Rifles and Cartridges*, Wolfe Publishing Company, February 1991, Prescott, Arizona, chapter 37.
2 Telephone conversation with J. D. Jones, May 20, 2004.
3 *Rifles for Africa*, Gregor Woods, Safari Press, Inc., 2002, Long Beach CA, pages 260-262.

Stages for fire-forming the 400 Brown Whelen (from left): 35 Whelen case; 35 Whelen case with neck expanded to 411; loaded and primed expanded case with reversed .410 Hornady 210-grain pistol bullet; first fire-formed case; second fire-formed case; loaded 400 Brown Whelen cartridge; original Kynoch 450-400 round. The Brown Whelen with a 400-grain bullet produces energy comparable to the 450-400.

Top: An old Weaver K-3 scope in Leupold detachable rings added to the utility and appearance of the rifle.
Bottom Left: Woodward shaped the stock for his 400, creating a palm swell that added to the rifle's ergonomics.
Bottom Right: A barrel band front sight provided an important touch.

Some 411 bullets currently available for the 400 Brown Whelen (l-r): 300-grain Hawk; 300-grain Hornady flat nose; 300-grain North Fork; 300-grain Barnes "X"; 350-grain Hawk; 360-grain North Fork; 400-grain Hawk; 400-grain Woodleigh solid.

a Dakota Arms bolt handle and a Pachmayr Decelerator pad.

When the reamer arrived, I sent a copy of the blueprint to RCBS' custom shop and ordered a set of dies. A gun show produced an old Weaver 3x scope *(with no front bell)* that would complement the rifle's classic look.

I planned to assemble the gun by "jobbing out" the work to various specialists. I sent the barrel blank to a barrel specialist with instructions to create a finished profile and a barreled action weighing six pounds. I set about shaping the stock, creating a slender pistol grip with a palm swell that fit my hand exactly. *(I fitted the stock to the floor plate but, because the wood was not inletted for the barreled action, I had no sense of the fit and feel of the completed rifle.)* I fine-sanded the stock, darkened it

with ebony stain and finished it with 12 coats of Tru-Oil. Then I shipped the stock to a retired stockmaker to checker the pistol grip and forend.

When the barrel was finished, I took the action, mounts and accessories to a local gunsmith. It took three months to assemble the rifle, fully inlet the stock, glass the action, install recoil cross bolts and accessories. The bill for parts and labor came to just $1100.

As I waited, it dawned on me that I had overlooked two important factors. First, I neglected to specify taper to the barrel specialist—so he simply turned the entire barrel to an 0.800-inch diameter. Second, I shaped the wood without the barreled action inletted into the stock. Without the barreled action in place, it was impossible to visualize the finished rifle.

Bullets recovered from African game (l-r): (1) 300-grain Hornady flat nose, from Kudu; (2) (3) (4) 325-grain North Fork from wildebeest, sable, and zebra, respectively; (5) 375 300-grain Woodleigh solid that centered a buffalo's heart.

When I walked into the gunsmith's shop I noticed a handsome rifle in a gun vise. "I wish my rifle looked like that," I thought. I looked again. It *WAS* my rifle—trim and classic, with clean lines and a perfect sense of proportion. I released it from the vise and threw it to my shoulder. The rifle handled like a fine shotgun. Pure luck had produced a striking, beautifully balanced rifle.

But, would it shoot?

The first challenge was to fire-form cases. Following Kronfeld's advice, I used 35 Whelen cases instead of '06 brass. *(Whelen brass takes less expansion to reach 40-caliber, and produces a thicker neck.)* I settled on the following procedure:

Run a lightly neck-lubricated case into the sizing die and over the tapered expander ball, enlarging the neck to 40-caliber.

Prime the case and load it with 46 grains of IMR 3031.

Seat a 210-grain Hornady .410 pistol bullet *upside down* in the case. Seat the bullet so that, when the bolt is closed, the bullet *just* touches the lands. *(This step holds the case against*

❦ ● ❦ ● ❦ ● ❦ ● ❦ ● ❦

From left to right: An old sable bull. A zebra taken with the 325-grain North Fork bullet. A Cape buffalo taken with the professional hunter's back-up 375 H&H and a 300-grain Woodleigh solid. Highlight of the Zambezi safari was the frequent appearance of elephant in camp.

the bolt face and ensures ignition).

Fire the cartridge. The result is a case with a discernible but slightly rounded shoulder.

De-prime and resize the case and repeat steps 3 and 4, creating a sharp, fully formed shoulder.

With 20 cases in hand, I was ready to fire my first full-power rounds. Hawk 400-grain round-noses in front of 55 grains of AA 2520 produced a chronographed velocity of 2000 fps and a three-shot cloverleaf at 50 yards. Hornady .411 300-grain bullets *(designed for the 405 Winchester)* loaded ahead of 56 grains of H4895 went into an inch-and-a-half at 100 yards!

Understandably, I wondered if my cases would headspace after each loading. Repeating a test devised by John Kronfeld, I selected twice-fired, fully formed cases, then de-primed and primed them. As Kronfeld suggested, I fired the primed cases *with no powder or bullet.*

Clearly, if the primer fired, the case had headspaced. Pretty slick, huh?

Not so fast. Every one of those primers detonated on the first firing. Unfortunately, when I reloaded the cases *only about a third detonated again!* Were the rumors about the 400 true, after all? Had the curse of the 400 Whelen returned to haunt me?

Gunsmith Ross Billingsley solved the mystery. Billingsley discovered that the strong firing pin spring in my Mauser caused a pin strike that ironed out the shoulder. With

no powder to ignite *(and reform the case through internal pressure)* the shoulders *stayed* ironed out.

I discarded the primer-only test and forged ahead. I found the 0.015-inch shoulder was easily maintained and—thanks to the boys at RCBS—the sizing dies don't set the shoulder back. But there were a few surprises.

I was intrigued by the various 300-grain 0.412-inch bullets designed for the 405 Winchester. I tested one that was constructed with a thick, pure copper jacket. Several reloading gurus assured me that a .412-inch bullet would cause no problems. In a .411-inch bore, however, a soft jacket and a .001-inch increase in diameter made me nervous. So I started at seven grains under maximum. Even at that level, .412-inch bullets produced unacceptably high pressure indications in my .411-inch bore.

The excellent Hawk bullets, available in a number of .411 weights, posed a second challenge. I was unable to push the pure copper-jacketed Hawks as fast as I had hoped. As I learned with other calibers, soft copper jackets or monolithic copper bullets appear to produce lower velocities than comparable-weight cupro-nickel-jacketed bullets.

Based on that experience, my advice to the 400 Brown Whelen reloader: *avoid .412-inch bullets like the plague*—and be content with 100 to 150 fps lower velocity from soft copper bullets that do not have friction-reducing concentric grooves.

Generally speaking, there's very little data available for the 400 Brown Whelen, so I've kept my powder charges conservative. Most of my loads are two or three grains under the maximums listed in Kronfeld's article. At the levels I chose, the 400 Brown Whelen with 300-grain bullets outperforms the 405 Winchester, is easy on the shoulder, and is more than adequate for any of the non-dangerous game on the planet.

For dangerous game, I was able to push the 400-grain Woodleigh solid to 2080 fps—only 20 fps below the velocity of the 450-400 Nitro Express 3-inch. (*I believe the longer bearing surface of the solid keeps it from attaining the same velocity as the Woodleigh 400-grain soft-nose. Kronfeld achieved 404 Jeffrey speeds with the soft-nose [2150 fps].*) To date, with the loads listed in the accompanying chart, my cases have lasted 10 firings with no loosened primer pockets, head separations or failures to headspace. . .

I took the 400 to Africa in 2001, hunting plains game in Zimbabwe's northern highlands and Cape buffalo in the game-rich Zambezi Valley. Two loads were taken: a 325-grain North Fork spire point (at 2400 fps) and a Barnes 400-grain solid (at 2000 fps). The North Fork is a solid, pure copper bullet with a lead insert in the front half. Concentric grooves reduce friction and copper fouling, and produce an exceptionally accurate bullet. In various calibers, the North Fork is noted for excellent expansion and great weight

Author with good (10 1/2-inch) warthog taken with the Hornady 300-grain flat-point.

400 BROWN WHELEN LOAD DATA[5,6,7]

Bullet	Powder	Grains	Velocity (fps)[8]	Remarks
Hornady 300-grain flat nose	IMR 4895	57	1950	Slow
	H 4895	56	2263	Duplicates 405 Winchester; 1.5" groups; light recoil; suitable for warthog, impala, reedbuck, smaller plains game.
	H 4895	60	2511	Maximum. Duplicates 375 H&H velocity with 300-grain bullet; bullet is frangible at this speed.
North Fork 300-grain	H 4895	56	2222	Mild.
	H 4895	58.5	2317	Best all-around plains game load; 1" groups.
Hawk 350-grain	AA 2520	56	2130	Do not exceed.
Woodleigh 400-grain solid	AA 2520	57	2081	Maximum. Dangerous game load; within 20 fps of 450-400 Nitro Express (3") load.

retention. The first animal that fell to the rifle was a 500-pound wildebeest. The bull was facing me at 80 yards, took a frontal chest shot with the North Fork bullet, remained on his feet for ten seconds, then toppled over, dead. A male sable of 450 pounds and a zebra stallion (650 pounds) were also shot with the North Fork.

The sable was shot behind the right shoulder, killing the animal instantly. At 100 yards, the North Fork broke the zebra's upper humerus, but failed to penetrate the body. We followed the stallion for 100 yards and killed him with a second shot to the lungs.

In each of these applications the North Fork expanded brilliantly (to as much as 0.87-inch), but the resulting mushrooms were flat-surfaced, making skeletal penetration difficult. On soft tissue shots—and on smaller animals like impala—full penetration was achieved and killing power was excellent.

My professional hunter was concerned about the expansion of the North Fork, so I used his backup 375 H&H for buffalo.

We tracked a large herd of buffalo for four hours. Finally, the wind shifted and the herd stampeded into an open water hole and turned, facing us. Resting against a sapling, I shot the herd bull at 80 yards. At the shot, the bull turned into the herd then came back toward us, fell and turned over with all four feet in the air. Skinners recovered the 300-grain Woodleigh solid from the paunch, where it came to rest after centering the heart. (Given my limited knowledge of Cape buffalo anatomy, this was the lucky shot of a lifetime.)

Later during the trip, I used the 400-grain Barnes 411 solid to take a second zebra with a high shoulder shot. The animal ran 70 yards and died. As expected, the brass solid penetrated both shoulders and exited.

In 2003 my wife and I hunted plains game in the Kalahari Desert of Namibia, on a safari booked with Wendell Reich of Hunter's Quest. Hornady had just introduced its 300-grain flat nose .411 bullet for the 405 Winchester and I'd tried the bullet on two whitetail. Both animals dropped to shoulder shots that penetrated completely. The bullet was exceptionally accurate loaded to 405 Winchester velocities. I took 40 rounds to Africa.

Anxious to see what effect a lower velocity would have on the North Fork's expansion, I brought 20 rounds of the 325-grain spire point loaded down to 2200 fps

One evening, on a 50,000-acre ranch close to the Botswana border, I watched the dozen kudu bulls mentioned at the beginning of this article. That evening, I encountered more trophy bulls than I'd seen in three previous safaris! I passed on a massive blue-gray bull that would have placed well in the record books—easily 55 inches. The bull never stood broadside, and I had no interest in shooting him in the butt just to hang his horns on my wall.

Soon a consolation prize appeared—an excellent bull that quartered in from my right, looking ghostly in the last light. At 70 yards I placed the thick post of the scope on the leading edge of his shoulder, and squeezed the trigger. The bull turned at the shot, ran 30 yards and dropped. The Hornady 300-grainer had penetrated the lungs but had not exited. Its retained weight was 180 grains (65%).

I shot a 250-pound warthog with this same bullet. I waited in a high

---

4 Recoil and kinetic energy calculated by David Schreiber.

5 **WARNING!** Publisher and author assume no responsibility for these loads. When developing loads in your rifle begin 5 grains **under** listed loads and work up one grain at a time, watching for pressure signs.

6 **WARNING!** Do not substitute 412-inch bullets for 411 bullets. Similar weight bullets of monolithic or soft copper jacket construction may produce increased pressure. Start these bullets 10% under listed loads.

7 Federal GM 215M (magnum large rifle match) primers used in all loads. Accuracy testing consisted of 3-shot groups fired at 100 yards.

8 All velocities computed using a Chrony chronograph.

seat for six hours and saw 74 warthog, but not a single mature boar. On the second day, a fine boar showed up at noon. I was high above him and it took time to figure out the right angle for the shot. I placed the bullet high behind his right shoulder, close to the spine. The bullet exited the chest, near the left front leg. This shot dropped the boar where he stood. He didn't even twitch! His tusks measured an impressive 10-1/2 inches.

The North Fork bullet proved exceptionally flat and effective on 100-pound springbok. Several "cullers" and two trophy rams were shot in the shoulder. All dropped to the shot with bullets that penetrated completely.

Surprisingly, a number of .411 bullets are currently available. Barnes makes a .411 300-grain "X" bullet. Hawk produces several in the caliber, including 300-, 350- and 400-grain bullets in two jacket thicknesses. Woodleigh catalogs a 400-grain soft-nose and solid designed for the 450-400. Hornady makes two 300-grainers for the 405 Winchester: a flat nose and a spire point. North Fork has redesigned their 411 bullet to deliver slow expansion and it is now available in two weights—a 300-grain and 360-grain.

How about recoil? You can't belittle the recoil of a rifle capable of generating close to 4000 foot-pounds. But recoil is a subjective thing, and *perceived* recoil may be vastly different from paper energies.

Fortunately, the 400 Brown Whelen has a kick that resembles a slow "push" rather than a sharp "kick." At 2300 fps, a 300-grain bullet in the Brown Whelen generates 3540 foot-pounds of energy (fpe), and recoil energy of 30.91 foot-pounds. This load is quite comfortable in my rifle, and feels like a 30-06 in an eight-pound rifle. A 350-grain soft-nose at 2130 fps churns up 3544 fpe and 34 foot-pounds of recoil. This load feels like a 35 Whelen. My dangerous game load, the Woodleigh 400-grain solid at 2081 fps tallies 3866 fpe striking force and 41 foot-pounds of recoil—close to the recoil of a 375 H&H Magnum with a 300-grain bullet.

This load resembles the kick of a mid-range 400-grain load in a 45-70.[4]

I shoot this rifle off-hand better than any rifle I own. Recoil is tamed by a 2 1/2-pound trigger, a heavy barrel, a "just-right" weight of 9-1/2 pounds, a straight comb and an eight-ounce mercury recoil suppressor in the forend!

I find, as did John Kronfeld, that the 400 Brown Whelen is the most accurate, comfortable big-bore I've ever fired. Obviously, its trajectory won't compete with the 375 H&H on 300-yard shots. But for 200-yard-and-under shots—the norm in most of Southern Africa—the Brown Whelen is perfect. plains game loads using 300-grain bullets are a joy to shoot and—when sighted in two inches high at 100 yards—they drop only three inches at two hundred.

If there's one lesson Africa teaches the rifleman, it's this: bullet construction and shot placement are much more important than velocity. Whenever possible, a bullet to be used on African game should be evaluated on similar-sized game stateside. My experiences with wildebeest bear this out. Wildebeest are one of the toughest of African plains game. In 2001, I shot a record-book wildebeest with a shoulder shot at 250 yards using a 7mm 150-grain Swift Sirocco. The effect was instantaneous. Both shoulders were broken, and the animal dropped as if hit by a bolt of lightning.

From the performance, you might think this shot had been taken with a 7mm Remington Magnum.

Actually, this wildebeest and several other animals were killed with the tough, accurate 150-grain Swift Sirocco bullet loaded to 2500 fps in a mere 7mm-08.

I'm still testing bullets in the Brown Whelen, but these are my current impressions:

The excellent Hornady 300-grain at 2263 fps is accurate and superb for African game 200 pounds and under. However, this bullet lacks the solid construction required for heavier plains game.

The Hawk 350-grain bullet at 2130 fps is most suitable for game like kudu and wildebeest.

When I return to Africa in 2006 for Cape buffalo, I'll rely on the 400 Woodleigh solid, a tough, accurate bullet at 2080 fps.

Further testing will be required, but I will probably pair the Woodleigh with the 360-grain North Fork soft-nose, which can be driven close to 2300 fps.

My choice for an all-around bullet? The recently redesigned 300-grain North Fork is exceptionally tough, accurate—and shoots flat. If limited to a single bullet for all but dangerous game, this would be my top choice.

Developing a powerful 41-caliber wildcat is no problem. The 416 Taylor and 416 Hoffman both achieved velocities comparable to the 416 Rigby—roughly 2300 fps with a 400-grain bullet. As this is written, Holland and Holland is developing its own 41-caliber cartridge based on the full-length 375 H&H case. The *challenge* is creating a 41-caliber cartridge with *enough* velocity to get the job done—but with tolerable recoil.

That's where the Brown Whelen comes into its own.

With the right bullet, the 400 Brown Whelen is a perfect rifle for any game in southern Africa. The ease with which the case fits and feeds in a standard-length action makes it a natural candidate for a cost-effective custom rifle.

And, yes, Virginia, the Brown Whelen *is* a temperamental maverick. But once tuned, it's a marvelous maverick and the friendliest big-bore around!

SOURCES

Barnes .411 bullets (300-grain) **Barnes Bullets, Inc.** PO Box 215 American Fork, UT 84003 PH: 800-574-9200

Pachmayr recoil pads, Leupold mounts, Timney triggers, barrel band swivels, front sights and stock reinforcing bolts **Brownell's, Inc.** 200 Front Street Montezuma, IA 50171 PH: 818-767-6097

Hornady .411 Bullets (300-grain). **Hornady Mfg Co** PO Box 1848 Grand Island, NE 68802 PH: 800-338-3220

Woodleigh .411 bullets (400-grainsoft-nose and solid) **Huntington Die Specialties** 601 Oro Dam Blvd Oroville, CA 95965 PH: 530-534-1210

North Fork .411 bullets (300- and 360-grain) **North Fork Technologies** PO Box 1689 Glenrock, WY 82637 PH: 307-436-2726

400 Brown Whelen reamers **Pacific Tool & Gauge** 598 Avenue C White City, OR 97503 PH: 541-826-9244

Affordable African safaris custom-tailored to each client **Wendell Reich** Hunters Quest International 6819 Woodland Drive Dallas, TX 75255 PH: 866-209-7346

400 Brown Whelen dies **RCBS** 605 Oro Dam Blvd Oroville, CA 95965 PH: 800-533-5000

96% inletted stocks for a variety of bolt guns **Richards Micro-Fit Stocks** 8331 North San Fernando Avenue Sun Valley, CA 91352 PH: 818-767-6097

.411 barrels **Shilen, Inc.** 205 Metro Park Blvd Ennis, TX 75119 PH: 972-875-5318

FOR TARGETS AND GAME:

MODIFY A RUGER NO. 1 TO 32-40

by Harvey T. Pennington

The author, firing some 32-40 cast-bullet loads from his shooting bench. For load testing and for bench-rest matches, he prefers the external-adjustment scopes, such as this 16-power Unertl.

It was simple: I needed a rifle chambered for the 32-40. Well, perhaps the word "needed" is not entirely accurate, but those of you who enjoy shooting blackpowder cartridge rifles know what I mean. I didn't have a rifle chambered for the 32-40, but I had read such intriguing accounts of the use of that old cartridge—both on the target ranges and in the hunting fields— that I figured it was time to acquire some first-hand experience with it.

A Distinguished History

The 32-40 cartridge was initially introduced in the early 1880s, for use in the Ballard Union Hill single-

Full-length, right-side view of author's 32-40. The Shilen barrel has proven itself to be quite accurate with cast-bullet loads. Before being converted, this Ruger No. 1 was a 243 Win., in the short, lightweight No. 1-A configuration. As a 243, the rifle no longer saw much use, and the author decided to use it as the basis for his custom 32-40.

shot match rifles. With its standard load, using a 165-grain lead-alloy bullet and a powder charge of 40 grains of Fg blackpowder, it quickly gained an enviable reputation as a target cartridge. The velocity of that load was usually given as 1440 feet-per-second (fps). Within a couple of years following its introduction, other manufacturers—including Winchester and Marlin—began chambering their own rifles for the 32-40. In the 200-yard schuetzen matches of that era, the 32-40 was one of the dominant, benchmark cartridges—highly regarded for its accuracy and low recoil.

Although the 32-40 began life as a target cartridge, it also became popular for hunting as well. With its standard blackpowder load, it was generally recognized as having ample power for use on deer and similar game. But, when smokeless powder was introduced, the 32-40 received a very significant ballistic boost. In the early 1900s, Winchester listed the velocity of their ".*32/40 Winchester High Velocity*" load as 1752 fps; later, in 1940, Stoeger Arms advertised Winchester's "*32-40 W.H.V.*" ammo as having a velocity of 1950 fps. An early Marlin catalog in my collection gave the velocity of its ".*32/40 Ballard and Marlin High Power Smokeless*" load to be 2065 fps. Likewise, Remington-UMC offered their "*High-Power*" 32-40 smokeless load at 2065 fps.

These high-velocity factory loads, of course, used jacketed bullets. Significantly, the Marlin catalog warned against the use of these loads in "*...rifles having soft steel barrels and actions made of inferior materials, designed for black powder cartridges only.*" Then it went on to say, "*...The accuracy of this cartridge is surprising,*

considering its high velocity. We have had no difficulty in keeping ten shots in a 2-inch circle at 100 yards or in a 4-inch circle at 200 yards, using an ordinary Marlin hunting repeater. This is the first straight taper shell to be put on the market loaded for high velocity, and we regard it as far superior to any bottle-necked shell made. For antelope, mountain sheep or goats, deer, moose, caribou, elk, bear or similar game, we recommend the 32-40 Marlin, using high power smokeless loads. The regular black powder shells can be used where less power is desired." By today's standards, one would be hard-pressed to find an ammunition company that would recommend a cartridge of those ballistics for such heavy game as moose and elk. Still, when this ad first appeared, I'm sure that it was a very serious recommendation, coming from such a reputable company as Marlin.

Of course, the 32-40 target shooters of the day used much lighter loads, and whatever combination of cast bullet, bullet lube, wad and powder that gave the best accuracy in their individual rifles. Some preferred straight blackpowder loads. Others preferred "duplex loads"—usually, about 4-5 grains of a smokeless powder next to the primer and about 35 grains of blackpowder on top. Still other shooters preferred straight smokeless-powder loads. Some used fixed ammunition—with the bullet seated in the case in the usual manner. But, apparently, the more competitive shooters preferred to fully seat the cast bullet in the barrel, separate from and in front of the cartridge case, either by loading the bullet from the muzzle (*with the aid of a "false muzzle"*), or by "breech-seating" the bullet.

For those who may not be familiar with the breech-seating method, the lubed bullet was placed in the chamber of the rifle; then, using a "dummy cartridge" and a seating tool, the shooter pressed the bullet into the rifling so that the base of the bullet was about 1/32- to 1/16-inch ahead of the point in the rifle's chamber where the mouth of the cartridge case would be. The primed cartridge case, containing the powder, was loaded separately—after the bullet had been seated. When correctly done, this method can lead to much tighter groups than those shot with fixed ammunition.

Selecting the Ruger No. 1 Action

I wanted my 32-40 to serve both as a hunting rifle, and as a 100- and 200-yard schuetzen-style, cast-bullet target rifle. Further, I decided it should be built on a single-shot action. As a serious target rifle, especially if I wanted the option to breech-seat my bullets, only a single-shot would do. In its other role—as a cast-bullet hunting rifle—a single-shot would certainly do just fine for such game as deer and antelope.

Now, the obvious problem was that an original single-shot 32-40—in good enough shape to be put to the uses I had in mind—would be too expensive for my budget. Likewise, the quality reproductions made today would also be a little too costly.

But, I had an ace-in-the-hole. In my gun rack there was a Ruger No. 1 (*in the short, lightweight, 1-A configuration*), chambered for 243 Winchester, that I simply did not use anymore. Although I was very fond of the No. 1 action, I had many different rifles *(including both modern and blackpowder cartridge rifles)* that—in my opinion—were much more effective than the 243 on deer-sized game. As for the 243's use on varmints, I had other modern, flat-shooting rifles that would serve that purpose just as well.

Of course, I was fully aware that if I were to choose the No. 1 action as the basis for the 32-40 rifle that I wanted, there would be some challenges ahead. For instance, I wanted to use a tang-mounted, aperture *(peep)* sight on the rifle, but the No. 1 Ruger has a tang safety which would have to be disengaged or modified to allow such a sight to be mounted. And, since no tang sight base is presently manufactured to fit the contour of the Ruger's tang, I would have to come up with something on my own. Further, since the No. 1 is a modern rifle, its stock is designed, primarily, to be used with a scope sight, and I was concerned that the comb *(top profile)* of the Ruger's buttstock might, perhaps, be too high to permit the comfortable use of iron sights that were attached directly to the barrel. *(Ruger, of course, mounts its factory iron sights—for certain models of the No. 1—to a raised rib, which is attached to the rifle's barrel, thus raising the plane of the iron sights.)*

But, the more I thought about it, the more I became convinced that my idea for using the No. 1 action was workable. Besides, I enjoy the challenge of building my own custom rifle, and the creativity that, inevitably, becomes a part of it. And so, the decision was made, and the project began...

The Conversion Begins: Re-Barreling

Re-barreling the rifle was to be the first order of business. Although I have a small lathe that is capable of handling some work on shorter barrels, the barrel work required for this project would be beyond its capacity. I knew that fitting a long, target-type barrel to my No. 1 would best be accomplished by enlisting the help of a gunsmith who had the proper equipment for such a project, and who would have had a lot of

experience with similar conversions. I knew just such a fellow. So, on our 2003 vacation, my wife and I dropped by to see Dick Kutzler, at his home in Glendive, Montana.

Dick has been a great friend of ours for over 23 years. He is a hunter and an accomplished gunsmith who has built some very fine custom muzzleloading rifles, blackpowder cartridge rifles, and modern rifles as well. During our visit, I explained the project I had in mind, and Dick agreed to give it a try.

Some months passed and, in June of 2004, when Dick had finished his work, my Ruger No. 1 had its new barrel—a Shilen 32-caliber cast-bullet barrel, chambered for 32-40 WCF. The finished barrel was 29 inches long, and round—with a straight taper from 1.150 inches at the breech, to 0.795-inch at the muzzle. I had requested that Dick finish the barrel to these dimensions because I felt it would hold much steadier for me in 200-yard offhand matches. Since I wanted the option of using heavier-than-standard 200-grain bullets for target work, I decided against the one-turn-in-sixteen-inches (1:16) rate of twist for the rifling which is considered standard for the 32-40 and, instead, chose the faster, 1:14 rifling which would better stabilize the longer, heavier bullets. The new Shilen barrel had a groove diameter of 0.320-inch.

Dick had polished the barrel and blued it using "Belgium Blue," a durable and attractive finish. At my request, he cut two 3/8-inch dovetails in the barrel—one for the front sight, and one for an open rear sight on the barrel, should I choose to use one. Also, as I had requested, he did a little hand-engraving at the muzzle end of the barrel.

A Hunting Deadline

So far, so good. But, now, the rest of the work on this project was up to me. And, already, I was beginning to feel the pressure of a new deadline that I had set for myself for the completion of the work. To be more specific, my friend, Steve Geurin, and I had applied for permits for Montana's 2004 antelope season,

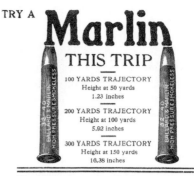

This early Marlin advertisement, promoting its version of the 32-40, is reprinted from the 15th edition of The Ideal Handbook of Useful Information for Shooters. Marlin highly recommended its 32-40 High Power Smokeless loads for hunting—even for use on elk and moose.

❧ ● ❧ ● ❧ ● ❧ ● ❧ ● ❧

and I desperately wanted to finish the new rifle and work up a 32-40 cast-bullet load to use on that hunt.

Mounting Scope Bases And Fitting A New Forend

With only three months to go before the opening of antelope season, my part of the work began. First, since I expected to use a telescopic sight in certain target matches—and for working up target loads—I drilled and tapped the top of the Shilen barrel for two Unertl scope bases. External adjustment scopes, such as the various Unertls and the Lyman Targetspot, have long been my favorites for target work—even on my modern, 1000-yard prone match rifles. And, to me, they look a lot more at home on the old-style, single-shot target rifles than do the more modern internal-adjustment scopes. The centers of the Unertl bases were placed 7-1/2 inches apart, so that one "click" of the scope's external adjustment knobs would give a 1/4-minute adjustment.

Next, when I started to consider trying to fit the No. 1's original forend to the new barrel, I was in for some disappointment. My measurements revealed the Shilen barrel was much too wide to permit re-fitting the slender factory forend, which simply did not have enough wood to permit the barrel channel to be opened up sufficiently to accommodate the newer barrel. Consequently, I would have to shape and fit a new forend.

After some inquiries, I learned that Treebone Carving, a gunstock-supply business run by George Peterson, in Raton, New Mexico, could supply semi-inletted blank forends for the Ruger No. 1. When I telephoned him, Mr. Peterson assured me that he could supply a forend blank wide enough for my barrel, and that he could do it in a short time. He was as good as his word. In only about ten days, a blank forend for my No. 1 arrived in the mail.

As it turned out, the new forend worked out very well indeed. First of all, after I completed inletting it for the new barrel, I decided against drilling the hole for the forend screw at a 45-degree angle and attaching it to the "hanger" under the barrel, which is the method used at the Ruger factory. Instead, I simply attached the forend in the more conventional manner—by drilling the hole for the forend screw at a 90-degree angle to the barrel, and attaching the screw to a matching nut that I dovetailed into the bottom of the barrel in front of the hanger. This arrangement would allow me more flexibility in adjusting the bedding of the forend to the barrel and the receiver.

Pouring a Pewter Forend Tip

Working with a blank forend also permitted me to get a little creative. I have always appreciated the look of a pewter tip on the forestock of a rifle; so, when I had completed shaping the new forend, I decided to go the extra step and try my hand at putting a

pewter tip on it as well. My friend, Dick Kutzler, cooperated by giving me some long-distance guidance, over the phone, from Montana. Also, some additional information accompanied the pound of pewter that I had ordered from Track of the Wolf, Inc., in Elk River, Minnesota, a business that specializes in shooters' accessories.

I began by sketching out a pattern for the pewter tip on a piece of paper, cutting it out, and tracing the pattern onto the tip of the forend. Then, using a knife, I carefully cut into the wood along the lines of the traced pattern. Next, in the area of the tip of the forend, where the pewter would be poured, I removed about 3/32 of an inch from the surface of the wood. (*This was the depth suggested by Dick Kutzler.*) The carved edges of the pattern were then smoothed with a "sanding stick" using a tiny 400-grit sanding belt.

[That sanding-stick is a handy little gadget that was given to me by Steve Rigsby, a local maker of stringed musical instruments (a "luthier"), who lives here in Rowan County, Kentucky. After a visit to Steve's shop, I realized that many of the tools of those who make guitars and fiddles are very similar to those tools used by gunstock-makers.]

Holes were then drilled in the wood where the tip would be located so that the pewter, once in place, would hold firmly to the wood. A chamfering tool was then used to slightly bevel the ends of the drilled holes on the barrel-channel side of the forend, to further ensure stability of the pewter tip.

My next step would be to pour the molten pewter into the form I had carved into the stock. First, I firmly screwed the forend to the barrel. Then, a "dam" around the carved portion of the stock was created by wrapping some tablet backing around that area of the forend and fixing it tightly against the wood with masking tape. The upper point of the "dam" was about one inch above the tip of the forend, and it extended to a point on the forend about one inch below the bottom end of the carved pattern. Any gaps in this dam were plugged with small pieces of tablet backing, to prevent any

Top: For the new 32-40 Shilen barrel, author had to fit and shape a new forend. Here, the tip of the new forend has been carved (to author's pattern) prior to the casting of a pewter tip. The holes were drilled in the tip (before pouring the molten pewter) to ensure that the pewter would not slip once it had hardened.

Bottom: After its final shaping and polishing, the pewter tip on the new forend gave the rifle a distinctive, and pleasing, appearance. To the author, it is reminiscent of the styles that were popular on single-shot rifles of the late 1800s.

leakage of the molten pewter while it was being poured. Of course, once the process of completing the dam was finished, what had been created was, in effect, a "mould" to catch the molten pewter and hold it while it hardened.

Next, with the butt of the rifle resting on the floor, the rifle's barrel was gripped in the jaws of a padded vise, so that the rifle was in an upright position, and could not move. The pewter—which is a metal with a very low melting point—was melted in a small plumber's lead pot, which was heated on an electric hot plate. Once melted, the pewter was poured directly from the lead pot into the open end of the top of the dam on the forend. The entire pouring was completed without interruption. When the metal had hardened and cooled, the masking tape and tablet backing were removed, revealing what at first appeared to be a shapeless mass on the end of my forend.

I then removed the forend from the rifle, and, using various metal files, began the process of slowly and carefully working the pewter tip into the desired shape. It was very pleasing to finally work the excess pewter into the contour that I wanted and watch the pewter and wood gradually meet at the line I had previously carved. After reaching that point with the files, I completed the work by polishing the wood and pewter of the forend with fine crocus cloth and steel wool.

The final result that was achieved by creating the pewter tip was most gratifying to me. Not only did the rifle acquire its own, individual appearance (*separate and distinct from other Ruger No. 1s*), it also acquired a styling feature that was more commonly found on single-shot rifles of the late 1800s—and I liked that.

Next, I decided that the stock of my rifle should have an oil finish. After removing the original (synthetic) factory finish from the buttstock of the rifle, I stained both the new forend and the original buttstock to match, as best I could. "French Red" stock filler (*available from Brownells*) was then used to further stain and fill the pores of both stocks. After the filler had properly cured and been wiped off, I began the process of "wet-sanding" the forend and buttstock using Birchwood Casey "Tru-Oil" and steel wool. I applied about five coats of Tru-Oil—over at least as many days—before considering the job completed.

Selecting and Mounting a Tang Sight

The last major step to be taken in my conversion of the Ruger No. 1 action was to mount a tang sight on the rifle. As I mentioned earlier, there are two major difficulties that must be overcome before a sight can be mounted to the

tang of that action. The first, and most obvious, is that the Ruger's tang safety is located exactly where the tang sight would have to be placed. The second is that there is no tang-sight base that is presently being made which is designed to fit the contour of the tang of the No. 1.

While considering solutions to these problems, I contacted some shooters who are actively engaged in schuetzen-style match competitions who use No. 1s for their shooting, or who were acquainted with others who use them. Some of those shooters did not use a tang sight at all; instead, they used an aperture target sight that was mounted to the receiver of the No. 1, and, therefore, the factory safety could be used. But, this was not an option for me—I wanted the more traditional tang sight.

I also learned that other shooters, who used No. 1 actions, simply disengaged the safety altogether,

The factory Ruger No. 1 safety slide is located on the rifle's tang, making it necessary to reposition the slide in the event a tang sight is to be mounted.

The tang sight author chose to mount on his 32-40 was a C. Sharps Arms mid-range sight. It is adjustable for windage, as well as elevation, and—although intended primarily as a target sight—it can be used for hunting as well. For use on the tang of the No. 1 action, the base of the sight had to be shortened, and then bent, to match the contour of the rifle's tang.

removing the safety slide on the top of the tang. When this method is used, of course, the shooter or hunter simply carries the rifle with its chamber empty, and does not load the rifle, or close the action on a loaded round, until he wishes to fire. In effect, the lever of the rifle—which opens and closes the action—becomes the rifle's safety; and, after all, no rifle is safer than a single-shot rifle that is carried with an empty chamber.

Still, I wanted my completed rifle to have both a tang sight and a working safety, and I thought this could be done. My idea was to modify both the base of the tang sight and the safety itself, so that the sliding button, which would operate the modified safety, could be extended out the right side of the bottom of the sight base. As a matter of fact, two of the people that I contacted while considering this project assured me that they had seen just such modifications to Ruger No. 1 safeties, and that they functioned perfectly.

After examining some of the styles of tang sights and bases that I already had on hand, a mid-range tang sight and base made by C. Sharps Arms, of Big Timber, Montana, seemed to show the most promise for the conversion I had in mind. Since the overall length of the CSA base was too long to be used on the Ruger, my first step was to shorten the base from an overall length of 2.80 inches, to a length of 2.290 inches. Cutting the base to this new length required the removal of the base's front mounting hole, so a new hole for the front mounting screw was drilled. It was positioned about 1.970 inches (*center-to-center*) from the hole for the rear mounting screw.

A new hole also had to be drilled in the shortened base to allow the long leaf spring that attaches to the base to be relocated. Of course, one purpose of this spring is to provide tension to the Vernier sight staff, as it is rotated up into shooting position or rotated down and back so that it is out of the way when not needed. But, the spring also serves the purpose of consistently indexing the sight staff when it is raised into shooting position. More about this later.

First, the CSA sight base had to be modified to match the No. 1's tang. So, using a propane torch and a small ball-peen hammer, I, time and again, heated the sight base to a cherry red and tapped it lightly on the bottom side to try to achieve the same curvature, along its length, as the Ruger tang. While tapping the base, I would hold the base in a set of vise-grip pliers, with each end of the sight base supported by the open jaws of a bench vise. Then, I would let the base cool enough that I could place it against the Ruger's tang to note the progress that I was making. This, of course, was a "heat, tap, and try" procedure, but, in a much shorter period of time than I had expected, the curvature of the base seemed to match that of the rifle's very short tang—not perfectly, but, I thought, as close as I could get it.

With that accomplished, I next drilled and tapped a hole in the tang of my No. 1—just to the rear of the rifle's concave loading port—for the sight base's front mounting screw. Of course, the Ruger's metal tang was far too short to allow both mounting screws for the sight base to be drilled and tapped in it, especially since this sight base had to be long enough, hopefully, to permit the operation of a repositioned, sliding safety button. So, the sight base's rear mounting screw was simply a wood screw which passed through the rear hole of the sight base and was threaded into a hole I drilled in the wrist of the buttstock—in the wood—just behind the end of the metal tang. Of course, prior to drilling the hole, the wood was shaped to fit the bottom of the sight base, and then given a Tru-oil finish to seal it against moisture.

I have used this same method before (*fitting the front mounting screw in the metal tang, and the rear screw in the wood stock*) for mounting sights on other rifles having short metal tangs. Although I would have preferred that each rifle have a metal tang long enough to accommodate the entire sight base, I have discerned no shifting of a sight that was mounted in the manner I have just described.

Making a New Sight-Indexing Spring

As I mentioned earlier, the tapped hole in the sight base—for the screw that held the leaf spring—had to be repositioned once the sight base had been shortened. However, after this repositioning, the original spring was too long to properly index into the groove in the bottom of the sight staff, when the sight was rotated up into the correct position for shooting.

To correct this problem, I made a new spring from the oil-tempered, spring-steel blade of a carpenter's hand-held wood saw. First, I cut out a small piece of the blade, slightly larger than the finished size that would be required. Using a file, I shaped the piece to the correct width, and left it a little longer than I thought necessary. A hole was drilled in one end to accommodate the screw that would attach it to the base. Then the piece was repeatedly heated with a propane torch and shaped, and bent, until its tip would slip into the groove in the bottom of the sight staff when the staff was at, or near, a 90-degree angle to the barrel.

Once the shaping of the work-piece was complete, it had to be re-tempered. For this, I heated the new spring to a cherry-red color and quenched it in oil. The spring was then placed in a small metal container, which contained just enough oil to cover the spring. Next,

Here, an "arm" has been added to the (modified) top of the Ruger safety slide, so that it could be extended out the bottom-right side of the base of the tang sight.

I set the container outside and, using the torch, ignited the small amount of oil in the container. When the oil had burned up completely, the new spring had been properly re-tempered and, after being blued and oiled, it was ready to be put to use.

By the way, for use while hunting, the aperture of the CSA rear sight's eye cup was opened up to .080-inch by using a drill bit. This larger aperture size would permit easier use of the tang sight, especially in low-light hunting situations.

Repositioning the Safety

Once the CSA tang sight had been adapted to the rifle, it was time to reposition the rifle's safety so that it could be used while the tang sight was mounted. First, using my milling machine, I milled the rifle's sliding safety button to dimensions that would allow it to work in the recess in the bottom of the CSA sight base. While doing this, I left a short, square, raised stud on the top of the slide. The purpose of the stud would be to help securely attach an extension to the safety, as explained below.

Next, I cut and shaped a piece of spring-steel saw blade which would become the "arm" that would allow the new safety button to be extended out the bottom-right side of the sight base. A small hole was drilled on one end of the "arm" and, using a four sided jeweler's file, I filed a square hole in the arm that matched the dimensions of the square stud that I had left on the (modified) original safety button during the milling operation. The stud had been left slightly higher than the thickness of the arm, so that—when fitted together—the stud protruded slightly.

To permanently fasten the arm to the stud, I first spread a small amount of JB Weld epoxy where the pieces would join. Then, while the epoxy was still wet, I fitted the square hole in the arm over the square stud of the modified safety button, and lightly peened the top of the stud with a small hammer, so that it spread over the edges of the hole in the arm, riveting the two pieces

together. After allowing 24 hours for the epoxy to harden, I mounted it on the rifle and it worked just fine. The new safety "button"—on the end of the arm that would extend out the right side of the sight base—was simply a socket-head screw that was threaded into a matching 8x32 hole at the end of the arm.

After milling a slot on the bottom-right side of the sight base (just large enough to allow the "arm" of the newly-extended safety to slide back and forth from the "fire" to the "safe" positions), both the safety and the sight were ready for simultaneous use.

Selection of a Front Sight

The front sight that I chose for my rifle was a Lyman 17-A globe sight. With its interchangeable apertures, the 17-A is a fine, inexpensive target sight. Because my eyes can no longer focus on a front sight, I long ago stopped using post- or bead-type front sights when not wearing glasses with corrective lenses. However, since my distance vision is still good, I have found that I can shoot quite well, without glasses, when using an aperture front sight. After all, with an aperture front sight, the shooter does not have to focus on the sight, as would be necessary with a post or bead front sight; instead, the shooter simply looks through it and focuses on the target. I have even found that an aperture front sight makes a good sight for hunting. I presently use aperture front sights on at least two of my small-game rifles, and I saw no reason that such a front sight could not be used for hunting antelope as well.

Another advantage of using the 17-A front sight is that it is available in several different heights. For use on my modified No. 1, I chose to mount one that was quite tall (*0.600-inch from the bottom of the dovetail to the center of the aperture*). This, I believed, would be more compatible with the high profile of the Ruger buttstock. By using a front sight of that height, the plane of the iron sights was raised to a point where I could comfortably assume a sight

This is a close-up view of the altered safety after being installed on the rifle. Also, the modified CSA tang-sight base can be seen. The repositioned safety functions perfectly.

picture. Indeed, after this slight adjustment of the height of the iron sights, I have felt no reason to modify or replace the factory buttstock.

Developing a Cast-Bullet Hunting Load

By this time, the date for our antelope hunt was drawing near, so I began to concentrate on working up a suitable cast-bullet hunting load. Looking forward to the upcoming hunt, I had earlier ordered the RCBS 32-170-FN mould. The bullet cast by this mould is designed to be used with a gas check, which would be necessary to develop the relatively high-velocity load that I had in mind. The added velocity, of course, would further serve to flatten the bullet's trajectory somewhat—a distinct aid when hunting antelope. One of the most important features of the design of the RCBS bullet was its wide, flat nose (meplat), which I consider to be most desirable on a cast bullet intended for hunting.

My goal was to work up a cast-bullet hunting load with a velocity in the neighborhood of 1900 fps, so I chose to use an alloy consisting of one-part tin, to 16 parts of lead (1:16). Bullets used in other hunting rifles, when cast of that alloy, had done well for me when fired at similar velocities; they shot accurately, without leading, and—at those higher velocities—they expanded well on game.

When cast of the 1:16 alloy, the bullet from my RCBS mould

weighed 180 grains, complete with gas check and lubricant. The as-cast diameter of the bullet was 0.323-inch. The lubricant I used was a commercial one, consisting of 50 percent Alox and 50 percent beeswax.

Both the lubricant and a Hornady crimp-on gas check were applied to the bullet using a sizing die in my Lyman 450 Lubri-sizer. I had a choice of using either a .321-inch or .323-inch sizing die. And, since accuracy with cast bullets is usually better for me the less a bullet is sized before shooting, I chose to try the .323-inch die first.

Since the load I wanted to develop

❦ ● ❦ ● ❦ ● ❦ ● ❦ ● ❦

▲ *This is a Lyman 17-A front sight mounted on author's 32-40. This sight comes with numerous types of inserts. The "aperture" style of front sight (shown in this photo) is easier for the author to use than the more common "post" or "bead" front sights, when he is not wearing corrective lenses.*

▶ *Another bullet, intended specifically for target work in the 32-40, is the SAECO #732. This bullet has tapered sides, and is not designed to be loaded into a cartridge case. Instead, the lubed bullet is dropped into the chamber of the rifle and, with the use of a "dummy" cartridge (left), and a seating tool (background), the bullet is pushed into the rifling of the barrel—just ahead of the rifle's chamber.*

would be close to the velocity of the old 32-40 high-velocity, jacketed-bullet loads, I skipped the usual "cast-bullet loads" sections of the loading manuals I have. Those listings usually reference lighter loads, topping out at velocities of about 1500-1600 fps, which have been worked up with the faster-burning powders normally used for pistol loads. Of course, those fast-burning powders—with a burning rate similar to Unique, 2400 and IMR 4227—are appropriate when working up light target loads for the 32-40. But, for hunting antelope, I wanted heavier loads, using medium-burning rifle powders, which would push my cast bullet at essentially the same velocities attained by those old 32-40 high-velocity, factory loads that I mentioned earlier.

My experience with medium-burning powders (such as IMR 3031, 4895 or 4064), with cast-bullet loads in medium-capacity rifle cartridges, has been that they are much easier to work with than the fast powders—when developing high-velocity loads. They definitely give better accuracy with the higher-velocity loads—assuming that an appropriate bullet alloy and lubricant are used. Also, the medium-burning powders usually fill the cartridge case to—or near—the bottom of the bullet, so there is no need to worry about whether to use a "filler" to help keep the powder charge consistently positioned inside the case. And, because they take up so much room in the case, they are safer to work with, since there is less concern about unintentionally throwing two charges of powder in the case ("double-charging"), which can

definitely be a danger when loading small charges of fast-burning powder in medium-capacity rifle cases.

After comparing several reference sources, I found that the jacketed-bullet section of an old (43rd Edition) *Lyman Reloading Handbook* listed several high-velocity loads for the 32-40, using several of the IMR medium-burning powders. One of the powders suggested in that section was IMR 4064. I had several cans of that powder on hand, and I decided to see how it would perform in my 32-40.

[Before continuing, I must remind the reader that the loads I will refer to next are definitely NOT to be used in firearms originally intended for

❦ ● ❦ ● ❦ ● ❦ ● ❦ ● ❦

▲ *Two plain-base cast bullets that show some promise for use on targets—with fixed ammunition—are the classic 165-grain Lyman #319247 (left), and the 200-grain Rapine #321195 (right). New 32-40 Winchester brass cases (center) are once again available.*

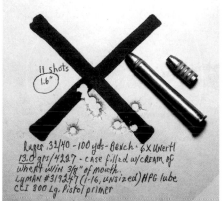

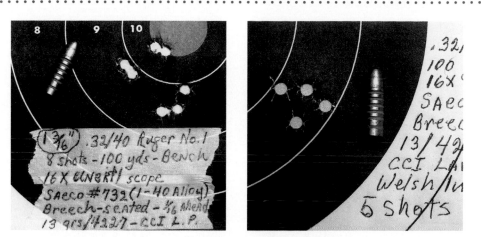

Left: *This 11-shot, 100-yard group was fired using the 165-grain Lyman #319247 cast bullet. This bullet is still useful for developing 32-40 target loads, and also has merit for either blackpowder or low-velocity (1300-1500 fps) hunting loads intended for short-range use on deer-sized game.*
Middle: *The author's hunting load, which gave the RCBS 32-170-FN cast bullet a velocity of 1873 fps, proved to be very accurate. This 100-yard, seven-shot group, was shot from the bench, using iron sights, and measured just 1-7/8 inches.*
Right: *Another group shot with the SAECO #732 breech-seated bullet, this time with a harder (1:25) alloy. This five-shot 100-yard group measured only 3/4-inch.*

✥ ● ✥ ● ✥ ● ✥ ● ✥ ● ✥

blackpowder, nor are they to be used in rifles of weaker design—such as the old Ballards, Stevens Tip-Ups, or Stevens 44 actions. Even in more modern rifles of adequate strength, the reloader should begin testing his loads by decreasing the weight of the listed powder charge by at least 15 percent, and, assuming the absence of any signs of excess pressure, increase his test loads by no more than one grain at a time. Whenever the slightest signs of excess pressure are encountered, that load should immediately be discontinued, and any such remaining loads should be disassembled or discarded.]

The Lyman manual listed a beginning load (*for the 165-grain jacketed bullet*) of 25 grains of 4064, and went to a maximum load of 29 grains. As it turned out, IMR 4064 was nearly perfect for developing the load I had in mind. In combination with the gas-checked RCBS bullet, 1:16 bullet alloy, Tamarack bullet lube (*half Alox,*

and half beeswax), and a CCI 200 Large Rifle primer, 26-28 grains of IMR 4064 powder immediately gave very satisfactory results.

The first load that I chronographed from my rifle used 26 grains of 4064, and gave my 180-grain cast bullet an average velocity of 1685 fps. Accuracy was very good, with groups running about 1-1/2 inches at 100 yards. The load appeared to be quite mild in my rifle. So, slowly, I worked my test loads up to 28 grains of 4064. With that load, I was getting 100-yard groups of 2 inches, or slightly less, and my velocity was at 1873 fps. There were still no signs of excessive pressure. At 200 yards, 5-shot groups were

close to 4 inches. I decided that there was no need for me to test further. This load had both the accuracy level and the velocity level that I had hoped for, and it would be the load I would use. Never before had the development of a suitable cast-bullet hunting load for one of my rifles taken so little time and experimentation.

Before I forget to mention it, all of my loads were assembled in new 32-40 Winchester brass cases. A few years ago, those who shot the old 32-40 had to do some scrounging around to find cartridge cases, since they were no longer being produced by the ammunition companies. Those who could not find the cases had to resort

In certain situations, such as developing target loads, the author prefers to use a telescopic sight. The older-style, external-adjustment scopes are his favorites for target work and, among those, this 16-power Unertl has proven its worth many times over.

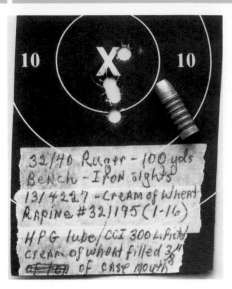

The 200-grain Rapine #321195 has a lot of potential as a target and hunting bullet, as evidenced by this 1.05-inch five-shot group fired at 100 yards.

to forming them from 38/55, 30-30, or 32 Win. Special cases, which had the same case-head size as the 32-40. But, thanks in part to the old cartridge's current popularity with "cowboy-action" shooters, and its continuing use by today's schuetzen competitors, newly manufactured brass is again available. My new 32-40 Winchester brass was simply ordered from a reloader's supply company, and it arrived in just a few days.

Sighting-In For the Hunt

Now that my hunting load had been worked out, I had to decide on the distance to sight-in my rifle for the antelope hunt. Many years ago, I decided that the maximum range that I would attempt to take a big-game animal with a cast-bullet load would be 200 yards. For the most part, this decision was made because of the lower velocity of cast-bullet loads, and their resulting higher trajectories, making good hits beyond that range too difficult over the unknown distances encountered in the field.

But, actually sighting in the cast-bullet rifle for 200 yards would be a mistake. For instance, if I were to sight in my 32-40 (*with the load just mentioned*) at 200 yards, the

bullet would strike about 6 inches above the point of aim at 100 yards. The bullet would be so much above the point of aim, in fact, that if I were to use a normal center-of-the-chest hold on an antelope which appeared at 100 yards, I would run the risk of overshooting the animal, or—even worse—wounding him. And, it would be almost impossible, in a brief hunting situation, to remember to hold the sights 6 inches under where I wanted the bullet to strike. As with most hunters, I simply have not been conditioned to hold lower on close shots.

Thus, it makes much more sense for the hunter to sight in for his "point blank" range. That is, the shooter should sight in for the farthest range for which his rifle (*and load*) can be targeted, without overshooting—at mid-range—the vital zone of the animal being hunted. Should the hunter be required to take a shot beyond the distance for which his rifle is sighted, it is much easier—and more natural—for the hunter to remember to aim slightly higher.

As for me, I chose to sight in my 32-40 for 150 yards. When sighted to strike dead-on at that distance, the bullet was only 3.5 inches high at 100 yards. With the same sight-setting, and a center

hold on a 200-yard target, the bullet would strike about 6 inches low—and I would remember that.

The Aperture Front Sight as a "Range-Finder"

It was while I was shooting my rifle at 200 yards that I made a pleasant—and useful—observation. I had cut out a rectangular piece of cardboard to serve as an "antelope target." The target was plain; there was no bullseye. I had cut the cardboard to a size of 14 x 36 inches, estimating that 14 inches would fairly represent the average measurement from the top of an antelope's back to the bottom of his chest. I hung the target horizontally at 200 yards to simulate a broadside shot on an antelope. While sighting at that target at 200 yards, I realized that the 14 inch height of the cardboard "antelope" almost exactly filled half of the aperture that I was using in my Lyman front sight.

Now, that was a real stroke of luck. Assuming that my estimate of 14 inches was fairly close to the average depth of an antelope's chest, the aperture of my front sight could be used to help determine the distance to an antelope in the field. In other words, if the chest of the antelope completely filled my front aperture, my distance from him should be about 100

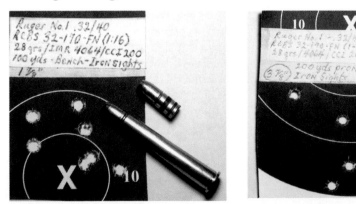

Left: The author's hunting load, which gave the RCBS 32-170-FN cast bullet a velocity of 1873 fps, proved to be very accurate. This 100-yard, seven-shot group, was shot from the bench, using iron sights, and measured just 1-7/8 inches.
Right: The author's hunting load also gave this 3 7/8-inch five-shot group at 200 yards. This group was fired from a prone position using the rifle's iron sights. The trajectory of this load was such that, with the 32-40 sighted in at 150 yards, the bullet was 6 inches low by the time it reached 200 yards—not too bad for a cast-bullet load.

yards; if the chest filled about three-quarters of the aperture, it would be about 150 yards; and (*as on my target*), if it filled only half of the aperture, it would be very close to 200 yards.

Now, this may not seem very exciting to the hunter who uses a modern, scoped magnum, having a point-blank range of 300 yards. But, to those who enjoy the challenge of venturing out each year to hunt with iron-sighted rifles having comparatively high trajectories, being able to make a close estimate of the distance to the game—by using nothing other than the front sight of the rifle—should come in mighty handy at times. Of course, I understand that this method cannot be relied on to give the exact measurement, to the last inch, to a distant antelope. For one thing, adult antelope do come in somewhat different sizes. But, I will state that, based upon my experience, it is a reliable method for the hunter to use, under field conditions, to give him an acceptably close estimate of the distance he is from the game.

With my sighting-in and range-testing completed, there was still one thing I wanted to do to the rifle before the hunt. I decided to mount a front sling-swivel base to the barrel of the rifle. After all, with its long target barrel, my rifle weighed about 10-3/4 pounds, and I knew the chances were good that I would be carrying it on some long walks on the antelope hunt. So, I ordered a set of the Dakota oval, European-style swivel bases sold by Brownells. The bottom of one of the bases was thinned on my milling machine, and quarter-round files were used to give it a concave contour, closely matching the contour of the barrel. After polishing and bluing the swivel base, and drilling and tapping the barrel for the screws that were provided, I mounted it on the bottom of the barrel about 3-1/2 inches in front of the forend. A 3/4-inch-wide, homemade leather carrying-sling was then fitted, and the job was complete.

The Antelope Hunt

Well, on October 10, 2004, my hunting buddy, Steve Geurin, and I

The author used his 32-40 to take two antelope during Montana's 2004 season. In each case, the 32-40 cast-bullet hunting loads proved to be very effective.

were in Jordan, Montana—after a long drive from our homes in eastern Kentucky. There, we joined forces with another friend, Kim Wright, a resident of Jordan, and, for the next few days, the three of us hunted antelope in the wide-open expanse of Garfield County, Montana. Although Steve and I had been unsuccessful in the drawing for buck antelope tags, each of us had been able to purchase a couple of left-over doe tags.

I didn't have to wait very long to get a chance to test my rifle and cartridge on antelope. On the afternoon of the opening day of the season, I saw a small band of antelope disappear over the crest of a hill, and I decided to follow. It was fairly warm that afternoon, and my pursuit of the antelope (*there were about 8-10 of them*) was a long one. I remember thinking how glad I was that I had taken the extra time to equip my rifle with a carrying sling.

As I followed, I would occasionally glimpse a doe and a buck that were bringing up the rear of the group. I would then stop and wait for them to get out of sight before continuing. They were traveling at a walk, and I was simply hoping that they would decide to stop and graze (*or rest*) in a location where I could get

within shooting distance, before they decided to put it in high gear and head for parts unknown.

My pursuit ended on a high, flat area that really offered nothing for me to hide behind, save an occasional, scrawny sagebrush. With my binoculars, I could see that some of the little herd had bedded down, and a few others were feeding on the short, brown grass. The animal nearest me was a doe, but she was still too far away for a shot—definitely beyond 200 yards. So, whenever she would drop her head to feed, or turn her head toward the others, I would slowly advance a few yards. During my last advance in her direction, she turned her head toward me and looked at me with apparent interest. Thinking she might take off at any second, I sank into a sitting position.

The antelope stayed where she was—broadside to me—as I took a breath and tried to relax. (*Only a few moments earlier I had noted that, in the event I would be able to get a shot, there was no wind to worry about—an unusual circumstance for eastern Montana.*) I used a couple of seconds to confirm the distance through my "range-finder" front-sight aperture; it appeared that I was in the neighborhood of 150

For his antelope hunt, the author used a gas-check bullet cast from an RCBS 32-170-FN mould. The wide, flat point of this bullet makes it especially suitable for hunting.

yards from the antelope. That was perfect. Also, the hefty weight of the altered Ruger No. 1 caused the rifle to hold very steadily from my quickly-assumed sitting position. I took one last breath, held my sights for the center of the chest—just behind the front shoulder—and squeezed the trigger.

Almost immediately after the shot, I heard the "plunk" of the bullet's strike. The antelope broke into a desperate, zig-zag run that took her only about 40-50 yards. She fell on her right side, kicked, and lay still. The cast bullet (*which struck a little lower than I intended*) had passed through the antelope's heart and exited the far side of the chest. With the lower strike of the bullet, the actual distance of the shot was probably around 175 yards.

Everything had been perfect for this shot—the distance of the shot, the lack of wind, and the placement of the bullet. I was elated with the performance of both the rifle and the load. But, what would happen when conditions were not so ideal? Well, two days later I would find out....

On the third day of our hunt, Steve and I saw a band of 10 or 12 antelope feeding about a mile-and-a-half away. There was a dry creek bed that wound its way in their direction, and we dropped into it and used it as cover on the first part of our

approach. The creek bed generally ran parallel with the direction the little herd was grazing. But, the closest that it would allow us to get to them was about 600 yards. To close that last distance, Steve and I would have to leave the shelter of the creek bed and travel over open ground.

Luckily, just ahead, we could see a low hill that lay between the creek bed and the small herd of pronghorns. We traveled in the cover of the banks of the creek, until the hill lay between the antelope and us. Then, at a quick walk, we started across the open ground toward the hill.

Reaching the near side of the hill, I carefully edged around to the right of its base until I caught just a glimpse of an antelope. I then backed out of sight a few feet and, signaling to Steve that they were still there, we dropped to our knees and, very slowly, began crawling around the side of the hill.

It was during this part of the stalk that Steve and I both came into much closer contact with the spines of some prickly pear cactus than we wanted. I recall using my teeth to remove some of the spines in my right hand. My right knee and lower leg also met a similar fate, but, since I could do nothing about them at that time, those spines had to remain where they were until later. We continued our crawling stalk until we could just see the antelope through the screen of grass between us.

Since Steve had taken an antelope on the previous day with his 270 Ruger M77, it was now my turn. I managed to slowly assume a sitting position. Using my binoculars, I could see three does ahead. However, the grass on the hill was just tall enough that I had to scoot ahead a few more feet—while still in my sitting position—so that my bullet would pass above the grass when I fired.

Now, if you will remember, I said earlier that I was going to tell about my 32-40's performance when conditions in the field were less than ideal. Well, I wasn't referring to the aggravation of the cactus spines; nor was I thinking about the high grass, which caused me to have to readjust my position just prior to the shot. What I really had in mind when I mentioned the less-

than-ideal conditions was...the wind. The wind had been blowing hard all day, and it seemed to be increasing in intensity. It was the kind of wind that made me thankful for the leather "stampede string" attached to my hat, and the kind of wind that later lifted Kim's baseball cap from his head and carried it 20 yards or so before it hit the ground. By the time I was ready to take my shot, I estimated the wind speed—conservatively, I think—to be about 25 miles per hour.

A flat-point cast bullet, such as mine, traveling at the relatively low muzzle velocity of 1873 fps, was certainly going to be affected by such a strong crosswind. So, for this shot, not only was it necessary to make an estimate of the distance to the antelope—it was also necessary to aim into the wind enough to allow for the amount of lateral drift that it would give the bullet. The conditions surrounding the shot that I was about to attempt reminded me very much of conditions commonly faced in many of the long-range, blackpowder cartridge rifle matches in which I have participated.

The antelope that I selected was standing broadside, and facing to my right. The wind was coming from the left. As I brought the rifle into shooting position, the size of the antelope's chest, as seen through the front sight aperture, indicated that the antelope was just a little less than 200 yards away—close to the visual estimate I had already made.

To compensate for the drop of the bullet, I took aim high on the body—just below where I believed the spine would be located. And, to allow for the drift of the bullet, in this strong wind, I aimed a few inches behind where I imagined the diaphragm to be. Again, I was aware that the hold from my sitting position was very steady, due, in great part, to the weight of the rifle. I took one last breath, relaxed, and squeezed the trigger.

At the shot, the antelope whirled, ran about 25 yards, stood for a few seconds, and, slowly and deliberately, laid down in the short grass. Using the binoculars, I could plainly see blood near the front of the left leg, where the bullet had exited. I walked closer, and fired the finishing shot. The first bullet from my 32-40 had drifted even more than I estimated that it would. The wind had pushed it all the way to the point of the chest—just in front of the right front leg. Still, the antelope could manage to travel no more than a few yards before having to lie down. The flat-pointed cast bullet, even with this hit, had done its job efficiently.

When I later returned to my home in Kentucky, just to satisfy my own curiosity, I referred to the wind-drift tables in the back of the third edition of Lyman's *Cast Bullet Handbook*. Although my specific bullet was not listed, it did give figures for the 170-grain, Lyman #31141, a bullet of very similar design. According to the Lyman chart, this bullet, when fired at a velocity of 1900 fps, at a target 200 yards away, would drift about 19 inches in a 20-mph crosswind—and about 24 inches if the wind were moving at about 25 miles-per-hour. Based upon my experience in Montana, I certainly believed those figures.

I was well satisfied with the performance of the 32-40 on the two antelope. The loads using 28 grains of IMR 4064 powder, and the RCBS 32-170-FN bullet, had proven to be both accurate and powerful. The entrance and exit wounds on the antelope left no doubt of the effectiveness of the flat-nosed RCBS cast-bullet for hunting use.

Some Beginning Target Loads

With my hunting completed, and before the onset of winter, I had a little time to consider developing some 32-40 target loads for future use. Of course, these loads would use plain-base cast bullets. Two of the bullets that I have which show some promise are the Lyman #319247, and the Rapine #321195. Both of these bullets are the traditional, parallel-sided, grooved, cast bullets.

The Lyman #319247 is their standard bullet for the 32-40, weighing about 165 grains with my 1:16 alloy. Although I have not had time to fully develop a target load

for this bullet, it does shoot 10-shot, 100-yard groups of about 1-1/2 inches, when loaded with 13.0 grains of IMR 4227. With this load, after the powder is placed in the case, I fill the case (*to within 3/8-inch of the mouth of the case*) with Cream of Wheat, and then seat the bullet. [*The Cream of Wheat serves to keep the small powder charge consistently positioned in the case, and, being compressed, does not mix with the powder. This was a method used by some of the old schuetzen riflemen.*] The overall length of the cartridge is adjusted so that the bullet just touches the lands of the barrel. With this loading, I have found that the CCI 300 Large Pistol primer seems to give more consistent accuracy than their Large Rifle primer.

The Rapine #321195 bullet weighs about 200 grains, and should prove to be a good 200-yard target bullet. So far, I have only had time to test it at 100 yards with one ten-shot group measuring 1-7/8 inches, and one 5-shot group measuring 1.05 inches. The powder charge was the same as used with the Lyman bullet, above.

With the Lyman and Rapine bullets, I have tried two different homemade lubes, as well as the commercial SPG lube. A lube consisting of 60-percent beeswax and 40-percent Wesson (soybean) Oil did quite well. The bullets were shot as-cast (*without sizing*), and were pan-lubed.

Of course, I also will work to develop blackpowder and duplex loads for these bullets in my rifle. One quick load that I assembled using the Lyman bullet (1:25 alloy) was a duplex load, using 4 grains of IMR 4227 in the bottom of the case, and 35 grains of Cartridge Grade Goex on top. A card wad was placed between the powder and bullet. A homemade lube consisting of 50-percent Vaseline, 50-percent paraffin, and a teaspoon of RCBS case lube per pound of lube, was used. One 10-shot group was fired at 100 yards, giving a 2.4-inch group—but only a 1.9-inch group if the first shot was excluded. This load was shot without cleaning (*and without blowing into the breech of the rifle*) between shots.

Another bullet that is going to be interesting to work with is the SAECO #732. Unlike the Lyman and Rapine bullets just mentioned, this bullet is tapered, and is intended to be breech-seated in the barrel—ahead of the case. It weighs about 200 grains. The bullet from my mould tapers from 0.3155-inch on the front band, to 0.3215-inch on the rear band, when cast of 1:40 alloy. With its base band being 0.0015-inch larger than the groove dimension of my barrel, this bullet is a little difficult to seat.

I use a "dummy" cartridge (*containing a wooden dowel rod that extends about 1/32" out of the mouth of the cartridge case*) to seat this SAECO bullet the proper distance into the barrel. A bullet-seating tool is used to help push the dummy cartridge fully into the chamber so that the bullet is seated to the proper depth. On my first attempt with this bullet, the alloy I used was 1:40. An 8-shot group that I fired with this breech-seated bullet at 100 yards measured 1-3/16 inches. But, the 1:40 alloy seemed too soft for the force required to seat this bullet. So, I changed to a 1:25 alloy, and my first five-shot group measured just 3/4 of an inch. I'm sure the SAECO bullet will be a top-notch performer on targets when I have time to do some proper experimenting with it.

Conclusion

Of course, before the final target loads (*for smokeless powder or blackpowder*) are developed for this specific rifle, I will have much work to do. Many variables will have to be eliminated before the best combination of powder, weight of powder charge, bullet alloy, bullet lube, primer, overall length, etc., can be worked up for each load. But, that work is just part of the charm of developing a good, cast-bullet target cartridge.

And, I look forward to facing the challenge of it—just as soon as the warm, spring weather arrives. After all, if my modified Ruger No. 1 32-40 proves to be as satisfactory as a target rifle as it did as a hunting rifle, then I should be well satisfied.

Photo Courtesy of Winfield Galleries

Above: **Autumn Hunter.** *Winchester calendar artwork, by Robert Robinson, circa 1911.* *Top Right:* **Bring Down the Game.** *Winchester point-of-sale display, art by unknown artist, circa 1920. Bottom Right:* **Father and Son With Bird Dog.** *Winchester calendar artwork by Arthur S. Fulton, circa 1920.*

Photo Courtesy of Winfield Galleries

Photo Courtesy of Winfield Galleries

THE AUTOMATIC QUESTION

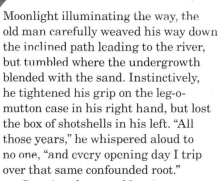

by Jim Foral

*M*oonlight illuminating the way, the old man carefully weaved his way down the inclined path leading to the river, but tumbled where the undergrowth blended with the sand. Instinctively, he tightened his grip on the leg-o-mutton case in his right hand, but lost the box of shotshells in his left. "All those years," he whispered aloud to no one, "and every opening day I trip over that same confounded root."

Crossing the gravel bar in the darkness, the duck hunter arrived at the immense, upturned old cottonwood thirty yards from the east bank of the Platte River. Kneeling in the depression formed behind what remained of the tree's roots, he scraped to one side the spent paper hulls someone expended on the previous year's shoots.

The cottonwood carcass, one of a pair, was a casualty of the 1889 tornado. Its twin was eighty yards upstream. Each was naturally positioned for the finest pass shooting in the Central Flyway, and both were shared communally by townspeople in nearby Hordville, Nebraska. The minutes passed restlessly for the old man. Uncasing his underlifter Parker hammer gun, he eased the barrels onto the frame and snicked the forearm into place. With his back to the massive trunk, he fondled the Parker in his lap as he awaited the first sunrise of the 1906 waterfowling season.

A rustling in the scrub timber disrupted his sense of isolation. The sound of gravel shifting underfoot drew nearer and nearer, until a figure was silhouetted against the orange glow of the eastern sky. "South side's taken. You're very welcome to shoot on the north, though," the old man invited.

"Thank you," replied the shadowy image as he prepared to settle into the vacant pit.

"Frank Kadavy here," the old man announced to the unseen occupant of the north blind. "Who might you be?"

"Nielsen's my name – Wayne Nielsen."

"Nielsen? You are with the Central City Nielsens, are you not?"

"That's right. I've moved to Omaha though–started a legal practice. I'm home for a while… visiting," he explained.

"I remember you as a sprout," Frank said. "Years ago, your uncle Carl and I gunned canvasbacks and greenheads for the Kansas City markets. Yellowlegs too, when there were lots of them. There isn't a day that goes by that I don't think of Carl."

"Certainly I remember you, Sir. My brother and I used to help the pair of you pack all those birds in barrels. I must have been six or seven at the time."

Awaiting shooting light, the two wore down what was left of the pre-dawn grayness reacquainting. As the sun finally peeked over the eastern horizon, Frank broke open his side-by-side and plunked a Winchester ten-gauge blackpowder

shell into each damascus tube. His still-unseen blindmate slid his 12-gauge Remington from its zippered canvas case, and stuffed it full of U.M.C. Nitro Club Shells.

"From the west, Wayne… get ready, here they come!" Frank announced suddenly. As the flock of mallards rocketed past their position, the two hunters stood up and fired. Frank Kadavy cleanly folded a pair of drakes with a pretty left and right. Wayne Nielsen's Remington semi-automatic snapped to his shoulder and barked a staccato sequence of shots, neatly dumping a hen, and dropping the orange foot of another bird. A third struggled frantically to maintain altitude, but cartwheeled out of the sky like a drunken helicopter. It splashed down a quarter-mile upstream.

Triumph and success in competition always benefited the arms maker, and was especially useful to make an advertisable point. Every gun and ammunition maker did it, and Remington was no exception in touting the automatic as a trap gun deluxe in this 1906 ad.

"Automatic!" the old man vented through clenched teeth. Shocked and enraged, he hesitated before turning and facing his young companion for the first time. "Scoundrel!" Frank fumed. "We've few ducks as it is anymore, and it is you culprits and your automatic shotguns that'll finish 'em off."

"No, mister," Wayne retorted. "It is you and your kind that's to blame for the scarcity of birds. You're the ones that shot them to pieces. I intend to get my share while there's still some left to get. Now – let me be to shoot in peace, if you don't mind."

Frank Kadavy gathered his gear and his composure. Looking back over his shoulder he delivered his parting shot: "Think about it, son. You'll realize I'm right."

In the years that were gone for Frank Kadavy, the choice of shotguns was limited to the simpler forms of the single- and double-barrel breechloader. Two successive generations grew accustomed and devoted to the double barrel in the decades that followed the Civil War. In those halcyon days, the only evolutionary design advance of significance was the elimination of the side-by-side's external hammers. Waterfowlers and trapshooters stagnated in their traditional two-shot ways.

Meantime, the world of ordnance became a marvel of progress, and technology invaded the sport of the shotgun shooter. In the 1890s, the quiet little realm of scattergunning was plunged into a headlong state of transition when the repeating shotgun, manipulated by a slide to cycle the mechanism, was introduced. Initially, the pump gun and its capability of loosing the advertised six shots in three seconds met with some rather hearty resistance. There was a time in the early '90s when it required considerable courage for a gunner to show up at the trapshoot or duck marsh packing a twenty-dollar Spencer, Marlin, or Winchester repeater when the field was armed with single- and double-barreled smoothbores. Anyone with the temerity to disregard the traditions of his more conservative fellows committed the ultimate immorality and was invariably the object of derision.

But the pump developed a following and became more and more popular. The gradual acceptance of the American repeating shotgun effectively silenced its critics and somewhat disarmed the prejudice against it. For a little while, the minds of U.S. shooters were receptive and open to accept the innovations of technology. For those who followed the trend of events in the domain of the shotgun, it became increasingly evident that development and perfection would not stop with the pump action. Once the success of the pump had assured a niche for a repeating shotgun, the next logical step was to a self-operating type. Five years into the twentieth century, this step was taken when the Remington Arms Co. released for sale a shotgun whose own recoil reloaded itself.

When first unleashed back in 1905, the Remington automatic was tried out by the curious at the trap ranges, where its novelty quickly wore thin and its effectiveness at this tremendously popular game became apparent. Limited numbers wound up in the duck blinds or stubble fields that fall. But the unexampled advantage of the new contraption did not escape the notice of the Edwardian-era bird hunter. Word of its terrific firepower filtered down, and the obvious potential of the gun was the talk back at the clubhouse, gun store, or wherever sportsmen assembled in the fall of 1905. When the spring came, word of an upsetting number of inappropriate and unsporting episodes involving duck hunters using the new automatic came to light. This reportedly ungentlemanly activity did not escape the scrutiny of the evildoer's better-behaved peers. Inevitably, the news was broadcast in the sporting magazines of the period. Editorial notices were printed, publicly scolding the guilty, and expressing the hope that reoccurrences of these incidents wouldn't extend into the next season.

The automatic shotgun didn't represent the ultimate forward progress of the armsmaker for everyone. The inanimate self-loader was at first perceived by some as fundamentally and intrinsically evil, an infernal device conceived and constructed somewhere in the nether regions. Moreover, by the simple act of brandishing the automatic in public, albeit lawfully, the true nature of the carrier became well known. Any man that could be swayed into acquiring the five-shot Remington shared the same low assessment that those who peopled the New Testament had for their tax collectors. For those tempted and led astray, there could be no forgiveness. This person was regarded with suspicion and contempt by his fellow duck hunters. He was a black-hearted character pre-disposed to mischief and mayhem, automatically branded a scofflaw inclined to nefarious deeds. Without question, the automatic in his hands made him more dangerous and destructive than if he had toted any other type of shotgun. At least, this was the picture that was painted in the sporting press.

Immediately after the Remington's release, public sentiment was in the process of formation. *Forest and Stream*, a bi-weekly, high-browed

A strong selling point for the double-barrel shotgun was its lack of complexity, particularly when contrasted to the automatic. This mid-1910 Fox ad shows how simple a double shotgun could be.

sportsman's journal, first recorded the vocal dissension among its readers, and a controversy invaded the pages of the magazine. In a June 1906 issue, a contributor naively clung to the belief that his comrades should be judged by his own apparently clean-cut standards. Viewing his brother sportsman through rose-colored glasses, he wrote: "The great majority armed with it will not kill game improperly; therefore it would be unjust to the manufacturers to forbid or limit its use." A barrage of disagreement appeared in the issues to follow.

A southern observer was convinced that the decline of the quail supply in his district was due to the local game hogs and their pump guns. When the automatics were turned loose, there would be little chance of the game's recovery. In July 1906, rather early in the squabble, Mr. T.H. Grant wrote the following: "Who cares if the lawful limit is exceeded, or how it is done? Aside from other reasons, humanity alone should be sufficient for prohibiting the use of the deadly automatic, autoloading, or self-loading gun."

G.H. Gould, writing that summer of 1906, hadn't quite made up his mind, but he allowed as how it was "easy to see that very fatal and easily worked killing machines may be undesirable." Another wrote in that it was plain to see that "there is no difference in principle between prohibiting the use of swivel guns or pump guns or automatic guns." Even before its first meaningful autumn in the field, some folks were hard on the untried Remington auto. George Kennedy had this to say: "It is not that the slaughter gun gets so many more birds, but that it kills so many that are not gotten." Yet another wanted to know why anyone would use the automatic. "Is it because, although you get more birds than we old-fashioned double barrels, you have so much more fun wounding the other birds? Is that it?"

The earliest *Forest and Stream* sentiment seemed to be fairly equally divided. A gentleman who signed his name "A Modern Sportsman" defended the newcomer: "Every advancement in firearms must be in ease and rapidity of fire, making the weapons more deadly." Several men stated what they believed to be true; the great majority of sportsmen were responsible law-abiders and did not kill game unethically. M.F. Westover nutshelled their collective thoughts in June 1906: "Do not punish the innocent, honest sportsman, inventor, and manufacturer; smash the actual wrongdoer."

The magazine generally took an editorial stance on controversial matters, such as their universally respected Platform Plank of 1894, which pushed for the cessation of the sale of any and all game. Though *Forest and Stream* traditionally stood in the forefront in support of issues involving game preservation, the expected official position on the automatic shotgun was never announced.

The automatic's detractors foresaw its failure as a rugged waterfowler's weapon, and advanced some smug predictions concerning the unavoidable effects of freezing rain entering the mechanism, through a receiver full of openings, and binding the gun . But by the spring of 1907, the self-loader had proved itself to be virtually element-proof and utterly reliable.

National Sportsman magazine served as the forum for the outdoor enthusiast of modest means. The staff urged and invited the letters, photographs, stories, and opinion sharing of the rural outdoorsman, and this is what comprised the bulk of the magazine's content. In 1907, *NS* circulation consisted of 65,000 subscribers. Certainly, the considerable readership of NS constituted a reliable cross section of small-town U.S. outdoorsmen, and their varied opinion fairly represented the thoughts of the mainstream American sportsman. For the next three years, the columns of *National Sportsman* became a clearinghouse of opinion.

S.B. Ellwell of North Falmouth, Mass., may have been the one to open the NS discussion when he wrote: "I should like to hear through *National Sportsman* how other sportsmen feel on this automatic subject." Many argued that the one-shot single-barrel scattergun was the only sporting weapon. If the automatic was to blame for the scarcity of game, the double gun was a close second. A 1908 episode, recorded in a vintage issue of NS, was offered as proof. That year an enthusiast, sold on his automatic, offered to bet a hundred dollars that he could down a limit of fifteen quail in less time than any man in the state of Indiana, using a double shotgun. A

gunner with the money and confidence was quickly found, and the hunt was on. Both men were to hunt over only one dog, and the two roved the Indiana countryside with an assembly of onlookers in tow. As the competition progressed, each shooter dusted quail bird for bird, until the tally was thirteen bobwhites apiece, at which time tempers flared and the mob's mood suddenly turned sour. The body of spectators, fearing trouble might arise, hastily called the match a draw and concluded the pointless sport.

A Gulf Coast gamehog, far from the prime northern pass and decoy shooting, tried to assure his fellow NS readers that his automatic and "the way it's done in Texas" were warranted. The standard waterfowling method in southern Texas was to crawl up to a

Another Parker Gun Record

Another proof of the wonderful and consistent shooting qualities of the **PARKER GUN**. At Cleveland, April 2, L.S. German shot at 50 pairs and broke 96 out of the 100 targets shot at. A splendid demonstration of the shooting ability of the man and the shooting qualities of the "OLD RELIABLE" PARKER GUN.

Send for catalogue and printed matter relative to 20 gauge guns.

PARKER BROS., Meriden, Conn., N. Y. Salesrooms, 32 Warren St.

Those fearing the automatic shotgun would supplant the double gun predicted the end of the era of the double as an art form. This lavish Parker gun might have gone the way of the passenger pigeon if the foreboding had been accurate.

pond or lake with a good gorge of ducks upon it, and wait until more ducks were attracted, at which time the gunner would "let them light and pump it to them." One really needed the automatic to be efficient at violating ducks on the site, as this Texan explained in 1908: "He gets all he can out of that bunch of ducks and has a good mess; otherwise, with a double barrel, one of each shot is all I can expect to get."

When the locals in western Pennsylvania discovered their grouse were in very short supply in the fall of 1907, they rounded up the usual suspects. Chas. Stevens spoke for his neighbors when he pointed an accusing finger at the dudes from the cities. He'd watched them as they invaded the rural communities, checked into

the hotels, guzzled booze and played cards half the night. In the morning they'd load up the automatic each had brought along and traipse off into the woods. Never mind the fact that the birds were very likely at the ebb of their population cycle; the automatic shotgun had been made the scapegoat. Steven's verdict was in, and the automatic was guilty. In a late 1907 *NS* issue, Mr. Stevens dangled his opinion, and his participles, in front of his fellow readers: "Attacking this country's game the season long, our grouse are being annihilated by these offensive rogues and their automatics. Soon they will kill them all and will go somewhere else."

C.L. Chamberlain found himself in the market for a good shotgun before the 1908 duck opener rolled around. He leaned toward the double, but unlike a lot of men his age, was not so set in his ways that he would exclude the repeater solely on principle. Chamberlain was willing to step into twentieth century shotgunning if he could be shown that the wonders of technology had actually improved upon the side-by-side. Slide-action hammer guns, the old Winchester lever twelve-gauge, and Remington's humpback were all shouldered, swung in front of a mirror, and considered with equal impartiality. As he sighted down the automatic's matted rib, every vilifying word printed in the magazines flooded his unconscious. He imagined pouring in five shots into a bunch of bushwhacked mallards, the buttstock pounding his shoulder time and again. "I could almost feel the bristles begin to grow," he shared with his fellow NS readers. In the end, Chamberlain bought himself a hammerless twelve-gauge double.

An *Outdoor Life* contributor felt he had hit upon the solution to the automatic disagreement. Someone using the pseudonym "A Steady Hold" insisted that it was not especially conducive to the pride of a real sportsman to secure an animal by the use of an arm that belches forth hundreds of pellets. ASH advanced the somewhat scary proposal to prohibit shotguns altogether and issue suitable small-caliber rifles to the duck shooters. Though he may have had a flair for pointing this out, no one was brave enough to go on record as having agreed with him.

If the only criterion to be taken into account by a new gun purchaser was speed of fire, the odds were stacked five to two in favor of the humpback. In 1908, the double-barreled shotgun seemingly had little to recommend it, but other considerations existed. Double gun makers did what they could to defend and justify their goods – and they did this without assaulting the automatic or those who made it their selection. An instant choice of two chokes seemed to make a pretty good argument, even in the face of the Remington's three-shot advantage. With the double, there was a variety of gauges, options in barrel lengths, and a broad spectrum of grades. More importantly, it was pointed out, the double was a beautiful gun, made to scale with its gauge, which had neither a massive rectangular receiver nor bulky forearms. There were no projecting cocking knobs, no rearward moving bolts or barrels to contend with, and no distracting clattering of parts.

But now there was a need to compete with the automatic and be successful at it. The armsmaker touted the double-barrel's simplicity, reliability, proven durability and other virtues.

In the face of the automatic's rocketing popularity, gun manufacturers whose lines included only double shotguns had every reason to be nervous. There were well-founded fears that the glory days of the side-by-side in the U.S. were numbered. The sage marketing people at Remington had, by 1910, discontinued their production of double guns to devote corporate attention to the manufacture of only pump and automatic shotguns. Concerns were expressed that the balance of the trade would see the handwriting that appeared to be on the wall, and abandon the production of double barrels entirely. The artisans

who built the doubles, whether cheap game gatherers or lavishly engraved and checkered masterpieces, were suffering and feared to be a dying breed. Going the same tragic route, it was said, would be the status of the double-barrel bird gun as an art form. The march of progress and the decrees of fashion were clearly headed toward the automatic.

W.L. Colville, a thirty-seven-year veteran contributor to the sporting press lamented that the certain passing of the double gun was near at hand. A fixture in *Forest and Stream*, Mr. Colville preferred to use the pseudonym familiar to two generations of nineteenth century sportsmen – "Dick Swiveler." Colville was granted a rare guest shot in the June 1910 *Outers Book* where his byline appeared above an article entitled "Is the Double Gun Doomed?"

A muzzleloading caplock fowling piece is what Colville grew up with, but he welcomed the innovative breechloaders as they became commonplace in the 1870s. As the years marched on, he watched progress reduce the beloved muzzleloader to an outdated useless relic until the younger generation had not only never shot a percussion shotgun, most, he ventured, had never even laid eyes on one. A similar fate awaited the side-by-side, he was convinced. Colville prophesied the following dire foreboding: "In the course of time there will come a generation of shooters who never saw a double-barrel breechloader." Dick Swiveler's prediction, thankfully, never came to pass, but the generation he represented found the prospects to be deeply troubling.

For the double gunner with the secret desire to modernize and the urge to accelerate the pace of his reloading process, the Rapid Loader Co. sold an equalizer of sorts. This outfit marketed a simple implement known as the Rapid Loader. Clips attached to a ring, held by the middle finger, held two reserve shotshells. When fired cartridges were ejected, both barrels could be quickly reloaded simultaneously. Four shots could be cut loose in two seconds, it was reported. "Makes your double gun as fast as

A truly gentlemanly duck hunter entirely contented with just one duck? Subliminal message or just another double gun ad?

an automatic" was the Rapid Loader Co.'s pitch. These things, presumably shipped in a plain brown wrapper, could be slipped into a coat pocket and be used or not used according to the company in the blind at the time.

In 1908, the uncorrupted double gunner recoiled in disgust when inventors countered with extension magazines for the automatic. Rather than being limited to only five quick

Here is proof that the Remington ad men were reading the magazines. Who could now argue that the much-maligned automatic was not actually a device of conservation, when 60 percent of its magazine capacity was intended to bring cripples into possession, as this December 1909 ad intimates.

❦ ● ❦ ● ❦ ● ❦ ● ❦ ● ❦

shots in succession, the waterfowler with the inclination could stick his long, greedy fingers into the guard of his automatic and rattle off as many as nine loads. Although the magazine extension was billed by one reviewer as "the greatest boon to duck hunters since the invention of repeating guns," its appearance reinforced the argument that the new generation of automatic users was totally devoid of conscience. An early ad for a particular brand of these devices attempted to justify the extra shots by passing off their product as a humane conservationist tool, giving it the illusion of respectability. "Save the Cripples" was its redemptive slogan, intimating that the wounded generated by the first five shots could be polished off with the remaining four. Purchasers were thus handed a guilt-free excuse to rationalize the owning of one. The ad left a conflicting impression of the automatic users as the sort to produce cripples, and as sportsman enough to see to it that they were reduced to possession. In the April of '07 number of NS, W.F.T. of Marshall,

Illinois spoke for them all: "It generally takes all the shots in the automatic to kill them dead." Over in Adams, N.D., P.O.G. was fond of his Remington auto, and he had a talent for explanation. In the July, 1907 issue we find his message: "How many of you have not at different times only wounded a bird after shooting twice at it when with another shot or sometimes two you could still reach it and bring it down?"

Many ordinarily upright citizens shunned the automatic lest they be lured down the same path the disreputable game hog had already taken. Sneers and scoffing oftentimes confronted those striving to remain

pure. Each person with serious misgivings concerning his own vulnerability was forced to ask himself if he could remain a responsible sportsman if he were put to the test. When drugged by the intoxicating sensation of unleashing an ounce and a half of number sixes at a living creature with every bend of the trigger finger, would he be susceptible to the Jekyll and Hyde transformation?

In the September of 1910 number of *NS*, a Michigan subscriber using the *nom-de-plume* "Tall Pine" penned a little narrative about a struggle with the demon, and how it came to pass, that temptation pushed him over the line. In doing so, he made a worthwhile point.

A covey of quail had been discovered and kept track of over the course of a summer, in anticipation of open season. Several hunters were aware of the birds. The covey, it seemed, would belong to whoever flushed them first on opening day. Meantime, our reporter acquired his very own automatic, and had taken it to the edge of town to familiarize himself with the gun. With a full magazine, he unexpectedly bumped into the prettily bunched-up covey. The pious Dominicans who educated me would have classified situations such as this one as "near occasions of sin," by the way. Wild with lust and desire, every evil inclination and craving

Sportsman or game hog? The truth can't be told just by looking, nor by the type of scattergun he swings.

overpowered Tall Pine. Squinting over the bead of the automatic at the tight ball of quail, he teetered on the edge for a second. Disengaging the safety and his conscience with the same motion, he lost all control. He opened up on the covey, and annihilated it to the last bird. Voices in the distance grew nearer until the remark "I'll bet it was Tall Pine cleaning up on the bunch of quail with his new automatic" was audible. Fearing detection, he stuffed the dead birds in his coat. Tall Pine wondered if his friends approaching the scene of the crime would have him prosecuted and use the birds as evidence. While nervously considering the consequences of his actions, Tall Pine was relieved to have his bad dream terminated when a familiar voice called out, "Henry, seven o'clock and breakfast is ready!"

Also included is an element that I like to call the "old fogey factor." The ages of those quarreling were an important consideration. Significantly, there seems to have been some sort of taboo associated with mentioning this in print, and everyone involved did their best to sidestep the issue, though one editor allowed the disparaging terms "whippersnapper," as if it were an expletive, to be seen across the page. This sentiment wasn't expressly stated, but it was certainly understood. Fundamentally, it was a matter of impression.

The invention of the automatic had brought into the marshes and game fields the inevitable influx of undesirables turning themselves loose on the birds. This happened to be the nature of youth, it was inferred. These youngsters were shifty, willingly perverse lads, with a no-holds-barred approach to harvesting ducks. What was worse, they refused to step in line. This appears to be how the old person viewed the young fellow. Collectively, the young person could do nothing to escape the stereotype.

The codger couldn't avoid a similar branding. Older gentlemen, even the indifferent or most progressive, were perceived as mossy old fuds, clinging to archaic habits and practices, unable to adapt and unwilling to catch up to technology. At the same time, this person inflexibly took a stand against

something he didn't understand.

Unmentionable and unmentioned as it was, the mood was real and clear, and it was so obvious that the dullest simpleton could sense it. All the while, a subtle but certain tension in the magazine columns was detectable. In this environment, harmony and unity were seriously threatened. An invisible barrier formed and a wedge was driven between the generations.

When all the words in the world might have failed to make the feuding friends again, a picture helped to salve the wound. In 1911, an insightful Winchester advertising genius locked and loaded one round, aimed in the direction of the rift, made an adjustment for windage, and fired for effect. His shot landed squarely on the split, detonated on impact, and caused both sides to look hard and consider. The artist's two figures, equal yet opposite, were connected by a common thread. The elder was not portrayed as an unyielding, senile old crone, but a kindly, distinguished, patriarchal gentleman, willing to sit still for an explanation. Rather than a disheveled, itchy-fingered miscreant, the clean-cut, slick-haired, every-mother's-son represented the ideal of virtuous youth. He appears to be clarifying an unfortunate misunderstanding to his receptive companion. The two seem to be getting along nicely.

Those who look closely may determine that the presence of the moose head as the room's sole trophy to be powerfully significant, and the background eagle centered between our two players, mounted in this heraldic posture, to be profoundly symbolic. Winchester was selling a rifle here, of course, but we can assume that most individuals were able to transfer the subliminal visual message to the shotgun in general, and the automatic in particular.

For a time, opinions continued to be divided. Before long, the decisive point of the matter was arrived at. More and more people began to put aside their prejudices and accept the pointlessness of further quarreling. Almost everyone came to realize that the wood and steel automatic shotgun was not the true culprit. It was generally agreed upon

Dr. William T. Hornady, the most vocal opponent of the repeating shotgun, and conservationist above the rest.

꧁●꧁●꧁●꧁●꧁●꧁

that the inanimate gun was merely an extension of the man shouldering it, and if this man had greed and evil in his heart, he would no doubt attend to his intended butchery and carnage with any gun he could conveniently access. An individual who identified himself as W.E.G. put this popular thought into words as succinctly as anyone. "It is more the man behind the gun that tells," he wrote in the November 1907 issue of *NS*. Some folks took more convincing than others, and contributors repeatedly restated the same basic opinion in the columns of the various magazines. The repetition was for emphasis. Publishers apparently wanted this important message to sink in, but I suspect that our ancestral gun crank got tired of reading what the great share of them already knew.

Not everyone cared enough to get involved in the magazine row. Texan H.M. Rhompson showed his annoyance in *NS* when he wrote: "If time spent between shots is to be the test – why not return to old muzzleloading cap-and-ball ethics at once and be done with it." Still more, perhaps, were the numbers of the undecided who sought refuge in the neutrality of the sidelines, expecting to be swayed to one side or the other, or determined not to be. In addition, there was the well-populated force of the resistant, the dangerous crowd that was impervious to modern influence, wholly oblivious to the signs of the times, and immune to change. This bunch held fast to their horses and buggies long after the first motorcars roared into town. For their own reasons, they chose to ignore the self-loading shotgun and all the madness associated with it.

And to some men, it mattered not if a hunter extinguished his game with a blunderbuss, pump, or automatic, so long as it was lawfully done. They had grown weary of all the tiresome opinions on the subject, and felt that more hunting and fishing stories would have been a better investment in magazine space. A.M. Stone said it best: "All our subscribers to the *NS* are getting dead sore on all this rot about the automatic." In the January 1909 number of *NS*, Kansan C.S.K. compressed a good many very similar published statements into a very few words – "Kill your birds with the gun you want to and let the next fellow do the same."

New York businessman Arthur Robinson maintained memberships in two exclusive southern ducking clubs. The clubs' 60,000 acres were subjected to a considerable amount of poaching, inflicting terrific damage to the birds. Nearly all the poachers on the grounds shot the new automatic and some of them carried a Remington in each hand, enabling them to rip off a second magazineful into a single flock. At the same time, club members described as "gentlemen and real sportsmen" were also trying out the autoloader and using its potential in an ethical manner. Robinson wasn't opposed to the selfloader in proper hands. Misused, it had terrible possibilities.

His reaction, and he spoke for many who shared the same thought, was that the only safe way to keep the gun from the disreputable element was to abolish it entirely. "The better class," he wrote in 1906, "should be willing to give up this weapon as being the only means of putting a stop to this willful game slaughter."

The League of American Sportsmen, The Camp Fire Club of America, the Boone and Crockett Club, and several other similar organizations adopted strongly worded resolutions condemning the automatic, and recommended enactment of laws against its use. A number of elite sportsman's clubs barred the guns either by rule or code, and lent their support and influence in advocating the model bill these groups had drafted. In a loud, unified, persuasive voice they chanted the oft-proclaimed cry: "No decent man would own one!" This assembly of self-appointeds sought to keep the automatic shotgun out of the lawful reach of the indecent. The movement was on, and a foundation was being laid for removing the automatic by statute.

Supporters of the proposed legislation pointed to other once legitimate examples of the poacher's and game hog's implements being outlawed. Restricting the use of gang-hooks and nets by sport fisherman and barring dynamite sticks from their tackle boxes was entirely proper when the goal was preservation of the resource. Forbidding the use of the punt gun and four-bore swivel gun had been prudent steps towards the defense of the waterfowl. The correspondent summarized in June 1906: "Why should it not be equally just and expedient to

limit the delivery of fire against the rapidly disappearing game?" But even the most radical hater of the self-loader believed that its general prohibition was within realistic grasp. Most dismissed the notion and resigned themselves to just live with the automatic and the vice it occasioned. But the idea had force. It appealed to the sense of the people. It made headway.

The earliest anti-auto sentiment was sufficiently intense and emotionally charged to pressure legislators to hurriedly pass bills barring the gun in some localities. In May of 1907, Pennsylvania lawmakers decided for its citizens what constituted a fair and sporting arm for the taking of the state's wild creatures. They pronounced it to be unlawful "for any person to use what is commonly known as the Automatic gun for the killing of game in the Commonwealth."

Other states followed Pennsylvania's example. Petitioners in Massachusetts called for such a regulation as early as January 1906. New Jersey passed a statute in 1912 requiring a magazine plugged to hold one round, and Ontario went the same way that year. By 1911 the whole of Canada had barred the automatic. Here in Nebraska, a bill went before the Legislature to outlaw it. Several other states were compelled to look the matter over and give it serious consideration. The speed with which laws were passed might be considered a barometer of the country's mood. It was also an indicator of the power their campaigners and lobbyists wielded to effect the change.

Just after 1905, the overall migratory and upland bird shortage was a distressing crisis, and a national shame. Waterfowl were fast going in the wake of the wild pigeon. In many localities, quail were practically extinct, and the woodcock was considered to be a mythical bird. The census of prairie chickens was not encouraging.

The Rapid Loader Co. sold this equalizer for those who couldn't, or wouldn't, spring for the latest automatic. A second of these devices could be used to clean up the cripples.

Winchester's powerful visual ser-monette of 1911. Transferring the inference from rifle to shotgun was left to the beholder.

⁂ ● ⁂ ● ⁂ ● ⁂ ● ⁂ ● ⁂

Ruffed grouse were extremely few. One gunner lamented that he'd "nearly worn out twenty cartridges in his hunting coat" looking for a partridge to shoot at in the autumn of 1907.

Rural people placed the blame on the weekend sports from town, particularly the ones that brought their automatics with them. Also responsible was the well-to-do non-resident with nothing better to do than go and shoot up another district's game. Habitat loss was a key factor, but one that got very little play. Across the country, there was a loud and insistent clamoring for the total abolition of spring duck shooting. Laws had already been implemented in many states, but were largely ignored. In 1908, a half-dozen states afforded ducks no protection at all, and most of them had three to four month seasons with appallingly huge limits. As foreign as the idea was, sensible restrictions needed to be put on the bag if the ducks were to recover. Uniform and reasonable legal shooting hours needed to be established.

Placing bounties on foxes, feral cats, and other vermin was thought to be a step in the right direction. Though it was preconceived that they would become the private hunting preserves of politicians, the establishment of vast game preserves, where the birds could rear their young and killing was prohibited, was wholeheartedly recommended. It would be necessary to zealously apprehend and prosecute violators and poachers, and impose meaningful fines. Putting a price tag on the head of a duck did little to protect it, but still the sale of game was legal almost everywhere in 1908. This practice needed to be rethought. Closing the seasons for two years, giving birds a chance to recover, was given consideration, but could get no real support. "They will not put up their guns."

The hoped-for effectiveness of more restrictive game laws were broadcast in the press and, taken as a whole,

WINCHESTER

.401 Caliber Self-Loading Rifle.

This new Winchester five-shot repeater is the finest and latest example of progress in gun making. It is reloaded by recoil, the repeating as well as the firing mechanism being under control of the trigger finger. A bullet fired from it strikes a blow of 2038 pounds—force enough to topple over the biggest game—penetration enough to reach the innermost vital spot. Tho wonderful in operation and powerful in execution, this rifle is neither complicated in construction nor cumbersome to handle. From butt to muzzle it's a handsome, handy gun.

Don't fail to examine one of these rifles before taking your next hunting trip.

IT HITS LIKE THE HAMMER OF THOR.

PLEASE MENTION NATIONAL SPORTSMAN WHEN WRITING TO ADVERTISERS

the magazines provided and promoted support for these sweeping changes.

About 1909, the readership of *National Sportsmen* admonished the anti-auto agitators to silence themselves and aim their criticism in a more useful and constructive direction. They realized that every howler jabbing the self-loader was taking a thrust at the life of their beloved sport, and that the division in sportsmen's ranks had deteriorated into a dangerous state of affairs. The continual bickering and wrangling in the press might just alert the unwanted attention of citizenry outside of hunting circles. These people would look suspiciously at the divided, the purported innocence of their activities, and the blood sports in general. This is what many people saw developing, and the probable consequences frightened them. The attention and energy of the uneasy brotherhood of *NS* readers, good company prior to the great sadness of 1905, was redirected to more

An advertisement for Remington repeating shotguns, from Outers Book, *August 1914. This is one of the illustrations done by Lynn Bogue Hunt.*

encourage moderation, and publicly shame the game hog and poacher across their pages. They saw to it that the emerging trend to preserve wildlife resources was fostered, and that fair play was at the front of the sporting experience. Newly initiated columns, devoted to conservation, enlightened the readers. The great automatic debate was at least partially responsible for bringing this radical change of direction about.

By the time 1911 rolled around, those who fought the self-loading fowling piece reluctantly accepted the reality that the Remington automatic was simply destined to become part of the fall scenery, and the debate amongst even the most headstrong and contrary waterfowlers was pretty much a withered issue. But when the dispute lost force and stalled to a point just shy of fading entirely, an *Outers Book* feature revved it up and temporarily revitalized the disagreement. In the June 1911 issue, a symposium of opposing viewpoints was published for the benefit of newcomers to the sport and those who hadn't been paying attention for the past five years. Taking the affirmative side in the debate with the somewhat wordy title "Shall the Multi-Loading Gun Be Prohibited?" was William T. Hornady. Mr. Hornady was an author, naturalist, and the director of the New York Zoological Park.

Fundamentally, Hornady's portion of the discussion was a concise rehash of what had been written previously. If future generations were going to be left with more than ragged remnants of feathered game populations, Americans needed to adjust their minds to the necessity of far more drastic protective measures than they'd ever known. Admittedly an alarmist, Hornady advised: "The time to send a fire alarm is before your house is entirely consumed, not after." His recommendation was to

restrictive bags, game preservation and protection, and other roots of the real duck shortage problem.

Capsulizing this new but temporary mood was a fellow who wrote the following: "Instead of a restriction on any particular type of gun, let us place the blame where it belongs – on the bag limit itself. If the automatic ever comes under the ban, let every red-corpuscled sportsman rise up in protest."

Once there was a time when the sportsmen's magazines routinely ran photos depicting lawfully excessive takings of game and fish. Pictures

of wagons and the earliest autos festooned end to end with ducks and prairie chickens were commonsight. The old idea was that nothing succeeds like success, that it was a disgrace to return empty-handed from the chase, and the greatest hunter was the one who killed the most. Before 1900, conservation by name was virtually unknown. A decade later, a new mood was astir. Good sportsmanship meant good conservation. Suddenly, this attitude was very much in vogue. Dutifully, the magazines sought to promote awareness to the cause, reduce both the bag limit and length of the open season by half. Stopping the legal and illegal sale of game was also something that needed to be done immediately. With a directness that some may have found uncomfortable, he then turned the reader's attention to the autoloading scattergun. He began: "There is a very broad line of demarcation between the weapons of the sportsman and those of the pot hunter, and the repeating and automatic shotguns have proven beyond dispute that they are on the wrong side of the line."

Mr. Hornady refused to distinguish lethality between repeating shotguns. The auto happened to be more deadly, but "the 'pump' is quite as bad." His personal objective was to see them both outlawed. Hornady drew his own lines. The pump and the automatic were lumped together in a single foul lot, which was not worthy to be described as "repeating shotguns." Hornady branded them both with a title that had a more sinister ring – machineguns. He was not the sort to pull punches. The machinegun, he maintained, was particularly fearsome when it was in the slippery hands of the lawless "foreigner" or the "songbird-eating Italian." A more detailed attack upon the automatic, and Hornady's determined and continued effort to see it abolished were spelled out in his book *Our Vanishing Wildlife*, distributed in 1913.

P. Emerson Waddell ably countered with the negative viewpoint. Both he and Hornady shared remarkably similar views and goals connected with the game conservation issue, but were at odds as to what constituted a "fair" sporting shotgun. The writer for the opposition reiterated the now familiar contention that the automatic, in and of itself, was not the problem. In Waddell's experience, most of the serious butchery was being perpetrated by a class of unprincipled characters who were little more than vandals with guns. The trouble lay with the man behind the gun, automatic or single barrel. Legislate and police the wrongdoer, the violator, the pot shooter, and the

game will come back. Frame more stringent laws and be vigilant in their enforcement was Waddell's suggestion.

Just as importantly, millions had been invested in the development and perfection of the self-loading concept and mechanism, and it would be the ultimate injustice to throttle this line of advancement "to accomplish some indirect or imaginary results." Waddell wrote: "Laws are easy to pass, but very hard to modify and repeal." The anti-automatic people were like old farm horses with the blinders on, plowing straight ahead and headed for the swamp. To unreasonably brand the automatic the scapegoat for the deeds of a handful of misbehavers might bring serious consequences that would come back to haunt at some future time. Abolishing the automatic would be setting an unwise and dangerous precedent.

A.B. Geikie, editor of the Guns and Ammunition department of *Rod and Gun in Canada*, published a less-than-accurate forecast shortly after the automatic was unleashed. He wrote: "While the repeater, in all its forms, may find special favor as a trap gun, I am of the opinion it will never crowd the double gun for game shooting."

By early 1913, the largest dealer of guns in the Northeast reported that the Remington automatic was outselling all other repeaters by a ratio of six to one. Another merchandiser volunteered that repeating scattergun sales outpaced that of double barrels at a similar rate. Winchester's newest offerings, the 1911 autoloader and Model 1912 pump, were in competition for their fair share of the sportsman's dollars. The automatic arm, as everyone already realized in 1913, was the wave of the near future. Over the next twenty years, side-by-side sales continued to slip, and manufacturers struggled to stay afloat. The companies able to conform developed pumps and autos of their own. The rest foundered one by one.

The fight to rescue the ducks wasn't fairly fought, according to the preservationists. It was thwarted by the millionaire corporations and the 85 percent of American hunters who

really wanted the automatic shotgun. After the initial flurry of law-passing, the Camp Fire Club and its band of idealistic believers surrendered the futile battle. In 1914, they reluctantly elected to pursue other methods of reform to salvage what was left of the ducks, and devoted themselves to sensitizing the literate public to the need for restrictive game laws.

There was enough lasting merit and residual sentiment to the automatic question to inspire and ultimately succeed in passing a Federal regulation that is with us to this day, an enduring legacy to the anti-automatic fray. The verbiage has been revised slightly over the years, but the basic intent remains the same. The provision essentially states that any shotgun used for the taking of migratory birds must have its magazine limited, by the use of a one-piece plug, so that its capacity does not exceed three shells.

When the final straw – the automatic – had been heaped upon the backs of the remaining mallards and the embryonic preservation movement, America's hunters separated themselves into their respective camps.

It is easy to discriminate against a practice in which one does not participate. We have been shown that where there is dissension and a loss of unity, inconstancy and contempt for one's fellowman will surely follow. Critics and faultfinders have always been and will continue to be a vocal influence. Though they do not often deliberately attack those they oppose, discord keeps them aloof. By their silent stares and utter indifference, they actually work against the greater cause.

Today's anti-hunting, anti-gun atmosphere didn't exist in 1906. It is probably a good idea to remain tolerant and mindful of the rights and preferences of each segment of the shooting sports, even the ones we might personally determine to be radical or harmful to a stable, wholesome gun hobbyist image. Patiently making allowances for opinions different than our own leads to harmony within the ranks. This is known as coexistence, by the way.

(Top) George Elgin patent percussion "Cutlass Pistol" with Bowie blade, made by N. P. Ames circa 1873. The pistol is a percussion boxlock with a screw-type barrel of 34-caliber. The 8 1/2-inch blade is integral with the trigger guard. (Center) A unique experimental combination knife/pistol (Charles E. Billings patent of 1868). The single-shot pistol, a 32-caliber rimfire, is built into the handle and crossguard. The blade is a 12-inch clip-point Bowie design. Also shown is a copy of the original patent drawings, and a tintype of a young Charles Billings while he was a Colt Firearms employee, and a member of the Colt company band.

UNSHEATHING AN AMERICAN LEGEND:

THE BOWIE KNIFE

The Bowie Knife in Perspective

by Norm Flayderman

J"*James Bowie*," the name is indelibly fixed in American history and legend. It is usually accorded unmistakable, often admiring recognition by most Americans and, likely, many others worldwide. Although identified for his last stand at the Alamo in the Texan fight for independence from Mexico in 1836, there are still many unknown facets of Bowie's career. His martyrdom at the Alamo with that heroic band of Texans, greatly outnumbered and overwhelmed by opposing Mexican forces, is a well-documented fact. Bowie's name is perhaps best known forever wedded to a fighting knife. Unbiased agreement on the exact origins of

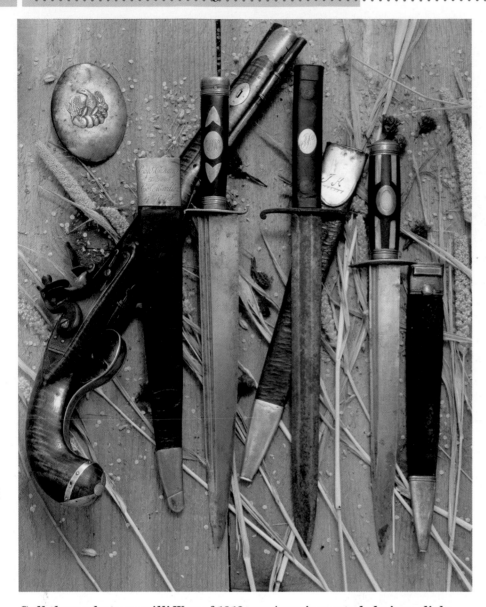

Call them what you will! War of 1812-era American-made knives, dirks and daggers. (Left) Silver-mounted presentation dirk, 14-1/2 inches overall with a 10 1/2-inch tapered single-edge spear-point blade. Horn handles with engraved silver inlays; silver-mounted leather sheath. (Center) This knife measures 15 inches overall, with a 10 1/2-inch straight double-edged spear-point blade. Wood grips with engraved silver inlays. (Right) This silver-mounted knife is well constructed and has a 9-inch single-edge tapered spear-point blade; overall length is 13 inches. Silver-mounted leather sheath. Also shown with these knives are an American infantry officer's oval crossbelt plate circa 1802-1812, and an American Kentucky-style flintlock pistol, with a silver-mounted curly maple stock.

that knife and even its definition have yet to find a consensus. The actual deed for which the knife achieved everlasting fame took less than two minutes, yet it created an enduring image that ultimately caused a man's name and a weapon to become a common phrase in the English language, a feat unique to American heroes. In order to understand the phenomenon, some background on the importance of knives in American culture is relevant.

The Bowie knife was a weapon for close encounter, carried either as a primary weapon or in reserve for possibly ineffective small single shot firearms commonly carried in the first half of the nineteenth century. Not subject to misfires, it was especially important in the era before the introduction and practicality of the percussion revolver, an imposing agent on the American scene. In many parts of the South, the Southwest and the frontiers, most men seldom appeared in public unarmed. Weapons were worn in church, at social functions, at the marketplace and political gatherings; they were part of everyday dress. So much so that it may be said with accuracy that many men from all walks of life felt fully clothed only when wearing a weapon. Similar observations were made by numerous travelers to various sections of America of that century. Col. Edward Stiff in his 1840 guidebook *The Texan Emigrant* described the lawlessness and rough frontier setting of early Houston and quite succinctly characterized the knife's universal appeal:

Perhaps about 3,000 people are to be found at Houston . . . among them are not exceeding forty females. Here may be daily seen parties of traders arriving and departing, composed of every variety of colour from snowy white to sooty, and dressed in every variety of fashion, excepting the savage Bowie-knife, which, as if by common consent, was a necessary appendage to all . . .

Among the most perceptive of European observers in the early nineteenth century was the Frenchman Alexis de Tocqueville. His widely read, often quoted work *Democracy In America* (1835), resulting from his 1831-1832 visit here, in which the expression individualism is said to have been coined, is considered a milestone in the history of democratic thought and is among the very best studies of American life of the era. Although the common phrase *Bowie knife* was obviously not in general use at that early date, if at all, Tocqueville did observe that

". . . quarrels often lead to bloodshed and elections seldom pass without knife blows given and received."

An Ames exhibition hunting or Bowie knife from the early 19th century. The knife is 14-1/2 inches overall, with a ten-inch spear-point blade, fully etched most of its length. The sheath is brass, with gilt finish, and is fully engraved with scroll and floral motifs. The rifle, by the noted maker William Defibaugh, is a relief-carved Bedford County, Pennsylvania, "Kentucky" rifle with engraved silver inlay of an American eagle.

Silver-handled presentation American dirk circa 1800-1830. Fine quality; obviously fashioned by a professional cutler or silversmith. Twelve inches overall, with a 7 1/2-inch double-edge spear-point blade. Matching silver sheath. Also shown is an exceptional Bedford County, Pennsylvania percussion "Kentucky" rifle by Peter White, circa 1810 (Dillon, The Kentucky Rifle, plate 129).

His remarks on the very prevalence of the carrying of weapons are notable: "There is no one here but carries arms under his clothes. At the slightest quarrel, knife or pistol comes to hand. These things happen continually; it is a semi-barbarous state of society."

Nineteenth Century America Learns About The Bowie Knife

To gain an appreciation for how deep-rooted in American life the Bowie knife became, there is no better source than contemporary nineteenth century accounts. Reading these stories firsthand in their original form in newspapers, periodicals and other nineteenth century literature effectively reveals universal awareness of the knife. Clearly, the term *Bowie knife* had become part of the American language. More than a mere compilation of related passages, these stories disclose how the public construed that weapon and how that perception quickly went awry. The thirst for sensational stories and the relatively inadequate ability to satiate that appetite neither overexposed the knife nor desensitized the public's attraction as it might today. Colorful language and overstatements were the rule. The Bowie knife, however vague and imprecise its visualization, had captured the public's imagination.

The Words Make Their Debut

Exactly when *Bowie knife* first appeared in print has yet to come to light. The search for that date offered one of the more fascinating challenges in pursuing this story. As of this writing, 1835 is the earliest year documented. It is reasonably believed that earlier dates will eventually surface. As several makers and dealers were advertising Bowie knives for sale in 1835, it is logical to assume that by offering the availability of such cutlery by name, the public was already familiar with its terminology. Sometime during the eight-year interim between Bowie's use of the knife in the notorious 1827 *"Sandbar Fight,"* and those 1835 advertisements, the words appeared in print. They were sufficiently conspicuous to make a segment of the public aware that there was such a knife! Significantly, Jim Bowie was in fine fettle when that occurred.

Knives of all varieties and sizes were, of course, on the American scene long before the *Bowie knife* arrived. They were just called by other names: belt knives, longknives, hunting knives, daggers, riflemen's knives, dirks, scalping knives, sheath knives and the very popular, all inclusive butcher knives. Self-defense knives and fighting knives were very much a part of everyday life. A contemporary account published by Charles F. Hoffman, in 1835, *A Winter in the West by a New Yorker*, describes a scene in a hotel bar in St. Louis. Reminiscing about an earlier Indian fight, the narrator mentions his ". . . leg knife. . . worn beneath the garter of the leggins [*sic*] and carried in addition to the larger knife which the Western hunter always wears in his girdle."

The ominous-sounding scalping knife was a vaguely defined name for a form of general, all-purpose knife widely sold in frontier areas and trading posts. Its intended use was unlikely for the grisly purpose its name implied. In nineteenth century literature, the term is often used interchangeably with butcher knife. Trading company inventories indicate their purchase and sale in very large quantities. Carl Russell, in the often-cited *Firearms, Traps & Tools of the Mountain Men* (1967), describes them as merely the least expensive form of the butcher knife.

Dirk is another commonly used term whose definition is ambiguous, with numerous possible interpretations, a word more or less "up for grabs" depending on the inclinations of the writer or viewer. Except for its application to a specific type of sailor's knife, *naval dirk*, which takes many dissimilar shapes and forms, and a particular Scottish weapon, *Highland dirk*, the word's usage is customarily generic

Makers of this Bowie, Marks & Rees, of Cincinnati, Ohio are the first (thus far recorded) to advertise the sale of Bowie knives. The knife shown has an 11-inch blade, with a 7-inch false edge. With the knife is an exceptional silver-mounted Kentucky rifle by W. G. Higgins of Monroe County, Georgia, circa 1830.

for a variety of knives that are primarily regarded as weapons.

What's In A Name?

Butcher knife sure lacks dashing image in this modern era. Certainly, use of such an unimaginative weapon would likely diminish the impact today of any romantic tale of Western adventure and gallantry. But, in its day, it represented a very formidable knife. Until the late 1830s and early 1840s it was among the most

commonly applied American term to describe a large, if not ominous, fighting knife, one carried and used as a weapon in hand-to-hand combat with man or beast. Those words dually conveyed all-purpose usage of a utilitarian edged implement as it is recognized in current times. Butcher knife was also the most often used description in contemporary accounts for the knife wielded by Jim Bowie at the fight on the Mississippi River sandbar, the seminal event in the knife's march into legend. The

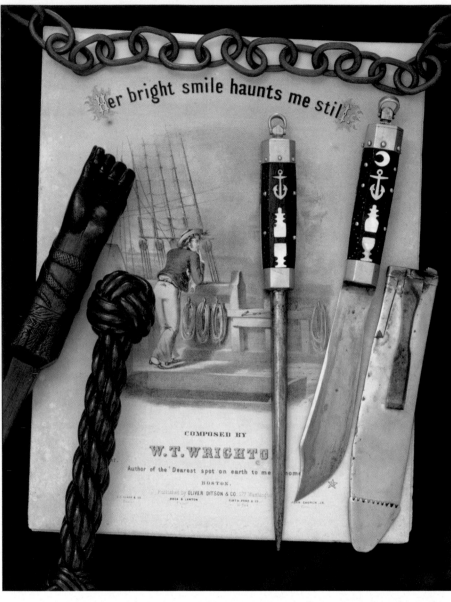

*A sailor's knife and matching fidd (a tool for splicing rope). **The knife measures 10-1/2 inches overall, with a six-inch blade, and is fitted with a German silver sheath. Included in this picture are two typical nautical carvings.***

terminology was practically obligatory for anyone reporting on a large knife of almost any type that was used as a weapon, the phrase of choice to set a menacing tone. Bemoaning the endemic violence then rampant, the *Mississippi Free Trader & Natchez Gazette* of December 8, 1836, related: "[The] many sad consequences resulting from wearing weapons . . . almost a passion throughout the south and southwest … It is almost a strange sight in this section of the country to see a man whose bosom heaves not under a ponderous butcher knife."

The introduction and the acceptance of *Bowie knife* into the American language to describe a fighting weapon, an important moment in etymology, gradually supplanted butcher knife.

An assertion that 1834 was the earliest year to see the words *Bowie knife* in print has received some currency in the knife press in recent years. It appeared on an advertising broadside of one of the earliest known American makers of fine quality Bowie knives, the firms of Joseph English and H. & F. A. Huber & Co. of Philadelphia, c. 1831 or 1832 to c. 1835 or 1836 that operated under the tradename "Sheffield Works." Along with their line of various tools and cutlery, the broadside specifically offered "*Bowie knives*" as an individually inventoried item along with "tomahawks. . . Indian knives. . . hunting knives" and other specialty knives. The 1834 date was not printed on the broadside, but rather, was penciled in the margin by parties unknown. The authenticity of the broadside is unquestioned. However, the penciled date does not represent substantive evidence. It has not been generally accepted by the collecting community to wear the mantle accorded to it.

A Surprising Turn Of Events

Until recently, a letter dated August 29, 1835, to the editor of the Little Rock *Arkansas Advocate* by an Arkansas resident then visiting Boston was considered the earliest mention of Bowie knife. Published almost two months later in the October 16, 1835 Advocate, it had been regarded as the earliest printing of the term as well:

In a few words, little I, this mortal coil of a hundred pounds, would rather live in Arkansas than Massachusetts- - yet the good people here absolutely shudder at the bare mention of Arkansas, Bowie knives, Judge Lynch, Captain Slick, Negro insurrections, duellists, horse thieves, Indian savages, frontiers . . . very awful!

Surprisingly, the very earliest mention of Bowie knives turned up in my own backyard, under my very own nose! It was in a letter dated Philadelphia July 20, 1835, by Nathan P. Ames (of the Ames Mfg. Co., famous sword and cannon makers), written to his brother, James T. Ames in Cabotville, Mass. The letter is cited in *The Ames Sword Company 1829-1935*, (John D. Hamilton, 1983) and, escaping notice of everyone, including myself, appeared and was sold in my own catalog No. 100, October 1976! The patent itself was not actually issued to Elgin until July 5, 1837. In describing the weapon on the patent application the inventor said ". . . the nature of my invention consists in combining the pistol and Bowie knife."

Thus, it is apparent that New England, for all its more moderate, temperate, "kinder and gentler" nature, played a much greater role in the development of the Bowie knife and its entry into the mainstream language than has been reported. As a matter of fact, the entire East was no slouch when it came to manufacturing such weapons for the trade. New York and Philadelphia were prominent players too. But the Ames letters have dual significance. Their early date and discussion of exhibitions clearly demonstrate the rising popularity of Bowie knives and the easy acceptance of the terminology into everyday use. The fact that Jim Bowie was still in the prime of his life when all this was happening obviously accounts for the absence of absurd knife stories. That sport was yet to begin.

The Elgin Bowie knife pistol is an especially fascinating American dual-purpose weapon. Although Ames played a role in its manufacture, it was more widely produced in smaller versions by Morrill, Mosman & Blair of Amherst, Massachusetts, possibly as early as 1836, its first year of operation.

Hypocrisy was obvious in the *Boston Courier's* contradictory article about Morrill, Mosman & Blair in its April 30, 1837 issue (variously reported as August 30th). Its prejudice towards the weapon is unmistakable; stating its purpose to be for hunting, when they quite clearly implied it was primarily designed for more desperate deeds. Describing the Morrill firm and its new operations, the article concluded:

The principal article which it produces is a weapon, which has yet hardly made its appearance, and which will not, probably, for many years, if ever, be much used in New England. It is called the Bowie-knife Pistol, a combination of these two articles, the knife being fixed by means of a spring to the lower side of the pistol barrel. These instruments were intended for the hunter, and the manufacturer has contract for one thousand for a Georgia man who is the patentee. They are made in three sizes. [There is no evidence to indicate the contract was ever fulfilled.]

The Bowie Knife In The American Press – 1835 To Early 1840s

The first advertisement offering Bowie knives for sale, thus far recorded, was by Marks & Rees, Cincinnati, Ohio, makers of surgical instruments. The phrasing clearly indicates the weapons entered public recognition as distinct entities. In the October 21, 1835 edition of the *Cincinnati Daily Gazette*, Marks & Rees offered: ". . . all kinds of Bowie knives on hand, of their own manufacture, finished in a superior style."

By the beginning of the following year, Thomas Gowdey announced, in the January 9, 1836 issue of the Nashville Republican new arrivals at his "fancy store" of . . . "ARKANSAS AND BOOEY [*sic*] KNIVES" among his other weapons, jewelry, liquor and grocery items for sale.

New York City newspapers advised of Bowie knives being available by mid-1836. The *New York Herald* ran an ad by Adam W. Spies, well-known dealer and importer of swords, firearms, military goods and general hardware, in its May 13, 1836, issue informing the public of the availability of ". . . Bowie, Arkansaw [sic] and Texas knives."

By the end of 1836, following Jim Bowie's death, mention of the knife became more frequent. By then there is little question that most of the American public was well aware of the Bowie knife. By the beginning of 1837, the knives were apparently in such demand and supply, that they were advertised as being available in varying blade lengths. This was very possibly the first indication of Sheffield's early and intensified rivalry.

That both names used for the knife were one and the same was clearly implied by a well-known dealer's advertisement in the semiweekly *Missouri Argus* of June 20, 1837. Advising the availability of various guns, powder flasks, gunsmithing materials, special notice was made of ". . . a few Arkansas tooth picks, or as they are sometimes called

Bowie knives, of a superior quality. . . by Henry M. Brown of Olive Street between Main and Church Streets at the sign of Robinson Crusoe."

It did not take long for the words to enter into everyday language. In the same month that the Alamo fell, Bowie knife was already a commonly understood term, as this March 24, 1836 article from the *Greene County Gazette* of Xenia, Ohio clearly shows. In a detailed story headlined "MURDER BY A GAMBLER," a young lawyer taking passage on a Mississippi steamboat got into a discussion about gambling and gamblers. Among those listening was a "sportsman" of that persuasion who did not take kindly to the conversation: "At which the gambling assassin drew from his bosom a tremendous Bowie knife and striking it downward into the breast [*of the lawyer*] nearly laid it open."

By mid-1836 and early 1837, the knife had acquired enough widespread recognition throughout the country to stir up open controversy and lively dispute as to its origins and functions. The seeds of future distortions and misconceptions are immediately evident in the February 3, 1837 issue of the Little Rock *Arkansas Advocate*. The paper had reprinted an article "The Bowie Knife," which they credited only to an undated "New York paper" (*presumed published in May 1836*):

This weapon, of which too much has been said of late, is longer and heavier than a butcher's knife, and equally calculated for cutting or thrusting. It was invented by Col. James Bowie... killed by the Mexicans at the capture of The Alamo... The circumstances which gave rise to this name, was about as creditable as the purposes which it has since subserved. Some twelve or eighteen months ago, three brothers by the name of Bowie, in... Mississippi, had a deadly conflict with seven other persons, armed with every species of weapon, among the rest, with a large knife of which we are now speaking. This was handled by the brothers with such dexterity as to decide the conflict in their favor, although numbers were against them – and it has since been called by their name, "the Bowie Knife." It is made to carry under the coat and is now very generally worn by "gentleman stabbers" in the South and West.

The knife was sufficiently fixed in the popular mind that mere passing reference to it was made in the Niles' issue of April 29, 1837, with a terse entry which left little to the imagination: "Two lads fought at Louisville, a few days since with Bowie knives. One of them died in a few hours after being stabbed."

The latter 1830s saw the knife mentioned in print with increasing frequency. Those years also witnessed the beginnings of ill-conceived attempts by anonymous hack writers to characterize the weapon. Most accounts were likely held in check by Rezin Bowie, who zealously guarded his brother's reputation. The self-proclaimed "authorities" laid low while Rezin still lived. With his passing in 1841 the floodgates opened. From that point on it was anyone's game.

Interesting mention is made of Bowie and his knife by another American legend and fellow hero at the Alamo, Davy Crockett. In the 1837 edition of *Col. Crockett's Exploits and Adventures in Texas. . . Written by Himself,* Crockett himself (!) states:

I found Col. Bowie of Louisiana in the fortress, a man celebrated for having been in more desperate personal conflicts than any other in the country, and whose name has been given to a knife of a peculiar construction, which is now in general use in the south-west". . . [And later, the concocted words uttered at the finale of the Alamo fight.] ". . . the conduct of Col. Bowie was characteristic to the last. When the fort was carried he was sick in bed. He had also one of the murderous butcher knives that bear his name.

That popular book went through many printings during the nineteenth century, including simultaneous publication in England. Regardless of the brazen claim on the title page: "The narrative brought down from the death of Col. Crockett to the battle of San Jacinto by an eyewitness," there is little evidence

to show that Crockett himself ever wrote the book. Of course, the latter section describing what occurred in those final, desperate hours at the Alamo were figments of some other fertile imagination.

Widely published and read in its day, *Davy Crockett's Almanack* [sic] played a role in the Bowie knife story that is seldom, if ever, credited (Chapter XIV). Despite the bold declaration on its cover that it was published in Nashville, Tennessee, the writing, illustrations and printing were quite likely done in Boston by Charles Ellms, notorious for lurid, sensationalistic stories.

Written and published strictly as entertainment, there is no doubt that the fictitious, hairbreadth adventures — in many of which Davy Crockett was the central character (*literally walking on water in the second issue*) — not only amused the Almanack's readership, but also, contributed to the perception of Americans in the less civilized parts of the country. The influence of those Crockett *Almanacks* was likely far greater than is generally acknowledged. First issued in 1835, they enjoyed more than a twenty-year run.

The 1830s and Mayhem in the South

Over one hundred accounts of duels and street fights, fought with a broad variety of weapons from pistols, rifles, knives, whips, umbrellas and even chairs, are seen in a remarkable personal journal kept over the years of 1835-1851. The work, *William Johnson's Natchez…The Ante-Bellum Diary of a Free Negro,* (Louisiana State University, 1951) is considered the ". . . lengthiest, most detailed personal narrative authored by an African-American" of that era. A fascinating record of daily life in that southern city, written by a man whose profession was that of a barber, but whose observant nature and curiosity of all that was happening around him, endowed him with ". . . all the characteristics of a good witness." As to be expected, the Bowie knife was found worthy of special mention; he even purchased one for himself.

The Johnson diary did have a surprise in store. Although I was well aware that Natchez was a popular stomping ground for Jim Bowie, I was singularly unsuspecting that the city harbored quite a number of local residents whose surnames were Bowie, none of whom appear to have been directly related to the knife's namesake. The most prominent of the Natchez Bowies may have been Dr. Alan T. Bowie, whom Johnson mentions in his entry of October 5, 1840, as having delivered a political speech for the Whig party at an important rally. Significantly, Dr. A.T. Bowie was also a duelist.

Another exceptional record of the rampant violence so prevalent in the South and Southwest in the 1830s (*and precursory to many of the antebellum years*) is found in a work which had far reaching influence in its day, published in 1839 by the American Anti-Slavery Society: *American Slavery as it is: A Testimony of One Thousand Witnesses.* Authored by the preeminent abolitionist Theodore Dwight Weld, it is said to have been the inspiration for Harriet Beecher Stowe's *Uncle Tom's Cabin.*

As an account of violence in those years, the Weld book is unique. For Bowie knife students, it offers a mine of reference, a mere handful quoted here. The use of knives is quite evident throughout those many newspaper accounts. They frequently, but not always, mention the Bowie knife by name. It is reasonable to assume that given a few more years, those same stories would use that label in place of other references to dirk, dagger, or knife.

In The Remote Back Woods And Wild Frontiers

There was no equivocating the Bowie knife's notoriety, enviable or despised, on the American frontier. Nor was its dependability and necessity for men of most walks of life and all callings ever in doubt. Both those inherent characteristics recommended the knife as a weapon of choice for most occasions in those remote, little traversed territories.

Remarks in a letter by John Guild, an Ohio-based Indian trader, to his sister in Massachusetts on December 13, 1840 (quoted in full in the *Antique Bowie Knife Journal*, Fall 1999) attest to the weapon's necessity and indispensability. Just returning from an expedition to Wisconsin Territory, where he had some success, he related a harrowing escape while trading among the Indians (*punctuation added*):

We were attacked by three Mexicans and one Indian. One Mexican struck me with a dirk over the left eye. As I was on my knees to rise, I caught his wrist the next blow and drew mine from my belt and gave him the Belly Ache [sic] while Haven, my partner seized the other two Mexicans as they were in the act of taking our guns which stood by the side of a small muskeet [sic] bush. As they wear no hats and long hair [I] gave him a chance with his large hand to hold both until he finished them off with a large Bowie knife. We did not take the trouble [to] bury them in the morning.

Double Exposure: Second Time Around For A Notorious Affair

There are numerous instances in which students have the opportunity to compare differing versions of the same Bowie knife stories that were later to become legendary. The story of the Wilson-Anthony hand-to-hand clash during open session of the Legislature of Arkansas is a classic example. Two accounts—one from 1838, another from 1849—were written within a reasonable time frame to the fracas and have acquired the patina of age. The earliest report abounds with errors, but may be assumed to be closer to actuality. Reading how it was "improved" just a bit over ten years later, on its way into mainstream legend, is as amusing as it is instructive!

At an open session of the Legislature of Arkansas in 1837, during deliberations the speaker of the House of Representatives, John Wilson, took umbrage at words spoken by Representative Joseph J. Anthony. They soon went at each other with Bowie knives, Anthony perishing in the struggle. The Knoxville,

The French made Bowie knives for the American trade, too. Exceptionally fine quality French Bowie knife, circa 1840-50, fashioned directly after the popular pattern of William Butcher of Shefield, including a similar Spanish notch and his splayed (or flared) pommel. The cased French dueling pistols are by noted maker "Devisme/Paris."

Tennessee, *Register* reported the fight and the trial of Wilson with its verdict and aftermath on July 4, 1838, taking it from the earlier edition of the Arkansas *Gazette*.

What a difference a decade makes! Retold by Alfred W. Arrington in his 1849 edition *Lives and Adventures of the Desperadoes of the South-West*, the Wilson – Anthony affair acquired added polish and glaze.

A preacher at eighteen years of age, Arrington's skeptical attitude toward religion caused him to

abandon the ministry for law. First practicing in Missouri, he soon moved to Arkansas where his practice was said to have flourished. At some date during his three or four year residence in Arkansas he was elected to the state legislature. He moved to Texas in 1840. Visiting the East in 1847 and writing under the pseudonym of "Charles Summerfield," he published serially in newspapers a number of articles relating his experiences and observations. All were reprinted in 1849 in his

Desperadoes of the Southwest, "...an eloquently written, but lurid [account] drawn from personal experience" (*Dictionary of American Biography*). Arrington's graphic recounting of the Wilson-Anthony knife fight is, indeed, "lurid." His portrayal of the bloody clash, the principals and the legislator spectators makes entertaining reading. In his introduction to that affair, Arrington wrote, "... the scenes presented ... are not painted from memory alone. They are my experiences..."

In view of having served in the state legislature in that time frame, it is possible that Arrington was witness to the pandemonium. It was unquestionably a spellbinder when first serialized in 1847. In the light of reality, various inconsistencies lend cause to question the author's accuracy. Prominent among them are the incorrect "1836" date and the fact that revolving handguns were unlikely to have been commonly carried weapons at that early year. It is as amusing as it is incongruous that Arrington managed to describe in minute detail the engraved ornamentation on each of the knives used by the battlers in that infamous encounter. No similar motifs have been viewed on any Bowie knife to this day (*and hopefully will not prove the pattern for some enterprising scoundrel in the future!*):

That Wilson-Anthony knock-down-and-drag-out brawl may very well have played a greater role in naming Arkansas "The Toothpick State" than is generally credited. Even the noted English author Charles Dickens twice alluded to the infamous affair in his *American Notes* (1842). William Worthen underscored the unwelcome notoriety heaped upon the ludicrous spectacle in his paper presented to the Arkansas Historical Association: "THE TOOTHPICK STATE:"

The breach of legislative protocol received widespread and long-term attention. Over fifty years after this altercation [in 1889], Frederick Douglass could evoke Anthony's death while talking about Arkansas "... I can remember that a killing occurred in the halls of your legislature, in which an honored citizen was almost dissected by a bowie-knife, and the evil repute cast abroad by that event yet clings around the fair name of your state."

Among the prominent politicians who had a penchant for carrying the Bowie knife was the governor of Mississippi, Hiram G. Runnels. Upon leaving that exalted office, he was entrusted with the presidency of the Union Bank of Mississippi. Following financial reverses to that institution, Runnels' leadership abilities were subjected to censure during an open session of the state legislature. Runnels was in attendance and took personal affront to invective hurled at him. The Natchez *Free Trader* of January 16, 1840 reported:

A disgraceful scene occurred this afternoon near the door of the representatives hall, while the House was in session ... Thomas Kearney ... was roughly assaulted by the ex-Governor Runnels ... in relation to the management of the Union Bank . . . Runnels was ... armed with pistols and a Bowie-knife, told Kearney to go and arm himself [for] a street fight ... Kearney did prepare himself, but was arrested ... Runnels [defied] the sheriff ... one of the members of the House took part in the discreditable fracas.

Bowie Knives and Gamblers, The Law, The Press and Male Coiffure

The year 1837 saw the first laws passed by various states that specifically labeled and attempted to suppress Bowie knives. Subsequently found unconstitutional nine years later, Georgia passed legislation restraining the sale of "Bowie or any other knives, manufactured and sold for the purpose of wearing or carrying the same as arms of offense and defense; pistols, dirks, sword canes, spears, etc." That same year, Alabama taxed Bowie knives while ignoring handguns. It also passed legislation making killing with a Bowie presumptive of premeditated murder. The *Niles National Register* under the caption "USE OF THE BOWIE KNIFE" reported the newly enacted legislation in its Sept. 16, 1837, issue:

. . . if any person carrying the knife or weapon known as Bowie knives, or Arkansas tooth picks on sudden encounter, shall stab or cut another with such a knife by reason of which he dies, it shall be adjudged murder, and the offender shall suffer the same, as if the killing had been by malice and aforethought . . . further enacted, that for every such weapon . . . person selling, giving, or disposing of the same shall pay a tax of one hundred dollars . . . Approved, June 30, 1837. A similar act has passed in the state of Mississippi.

Many other states followed suit, passing anti-Bowie knife legislation with varying degrees of restriction and penalties. Like anti-dueling laws, it did little, if anything, to stem the demand and the use of that weapon. Such ordinances were likely proposed with the most righteous intent, but judging from the almost universal lack of enforcement, their passage appears to have been mostly a sop to the more virtuous.

Evidence that legislation outlawing the carrying and the use of the Bowie knife was not often enforced is quickly grasped from an article reported in the *New York Tribune* February 3, 1843. Such actions on the part of law enforcement were quite common; numerous similar accounts are to be found. Under the bold heading, "A BOWIE-KNIFE STREET FIGHT IN LOUISVILLE," the paper reported names of a local citizen and another Tennessean, each armed with a Bowie knife and firearm: ". . . pistols were discharged and Bowie knives drawn, and both were wounded, but not seriously. It evidences great dereliction of duty on the part of the police of Louisville, but neither of these disturbers of the public peace was arrested, but allowed to leave the City undisturbed."

But not every miscreant using that knife avoided the long arm of the law. Court records clearly show civil and criminal violations of all types. Enforcement, however, was considerably looser, depending on one's station in life, business and blood relationships,

Large, ruggedly made, yet displaying quality craftsmanship, this frontiersman's (possibly Confederate) Bowie knife carries no markings. The knife is 15-1/2 inches overall, with a 10 1/2-inch blade.

Texas-marked knives: (Left) "H. D. Norton & Bro/San Antonio" general utility knife with sheath. (Center) Large, heavy folding Bowie knife with 7-inch single edge blade marked "The Texas Ranger" and "Rough and Ready." (Right) Large Bowie circa 1840-50 marked "Texas Ranger." Unusual copper-finished, one-piece heavy handle. With the knives are a U. S. Model 1842 percussion pistol and a recruiting poster for Texas service following the Civil War.

▶*A remarkable example of an early mid-1830s Sheffield-made Bowie knife. The single-edge blade is 10-1/2 inches long. "The Hunters Companion/My Horse, Knife and Rifle" is etched on the blade. Two-piece ivory grips are fastened by six pins. The silver-mounted Kentucky rifle was made by Jacob Snider of Bedford County, Pennsylvania, circa 1830, and accompanied by a rare early image (courtesy Rick Mack) of a frontiersman wearing an early Bowie knife on his belt.*

Baltimore *Commercial Transcript* of November 16, 1837, noted that: ". . . the *Philadelphia Ledger* insinuates that those who wear those appendages encircling the face are no better than they should be [and] says 'bowie whiskers' are the signs of Bowie knives."

It's doubtful that those sideburns were all the rage for any appreciable amount of time, as the mode does not appear in other fashion columns that have surfaced. But the Bowie made its presence felt in other, unsuspected spheres of daily life too. In all likelihood, its first venture into the humor column was the 1837 comical rendition of the "Arkansas Toothpick" in the earlier mentioned *Davy Crockett Almanack*. By 1861, it is seen in the "Humors of the Day" column of *Harper's Weekly*. The November 23, 1861, edition related a trite, not too funny, story of a schoolmaster and a "patriotic pupil." Following the punch line, such as it was, "The pupil is patted on the hand and presented with a hundred-bladed bowie-knife by way of a prize."

Bowie Momentum Gathers Awareness

The Bowie knife, or at very least, the terminology, was pervasive. With increasing frequency, it was mentioned in news articles throughout America. Just a modest sampling of the press readily bears that out. The widely read New Orleans *Picayune* of August

the locale where the offense took place and, certainly, how heinous the crime. The murder of a newspaper editor, then as now, ranked high on the list of loathsome offenses. Such a homicide was reported in the widely read New Orleans *Picayune* of January 25, 1847 regarding John Chalmers, editor of the Austin, Texas *New Era* and former Secretary of the Treasury of Texas, ". . . killed by a wound in the temple, inflicted by Joshua Holden, with a Bowie knife." The perpetrator was held on a charge of murder and committed to jail awaiting prosecution. It was incongruous that the adjoining column of that same issue ran what it termed, in all solemnity, a "sensible anecdote" of a pistol duel never consummated.

Bowie Whiskers?

Equally indicative that the weapon had become comfortably assimilated into the everyday language of Americans at an early date was its synonymous usage to describe men's muttonchops. The

Unique long-bladed folding dirk, circa 1840-50, featuring a 10 1/2-inch blade, German silver mountings, and original leather sheath.

2, 1838, repeating a secondhand account from a source not given, made special note of a monstrous Bowie used in a dispute in which two men were killed and another suffered the loss of a hand: ". . . a most horrific slaughter with a Bowie knife twenty three inches in length and weighing five pounds took place not long since at St. Marks, Florida."

One wonders if the brusque owner of a Bowie knife and a rifle may have valued them greater than his servant in early days of the Republic of Texas. Handsome recompense was

advertised in the Houston *Telegraph And Texas Register* on May 30, 1838 under the caption: "$50 REWARD. My negro man Bob runaway [sic] from me on the 23'd inst., he . . . took with him a rifle gun, shot pouch and powder horn, the latter is brass mounted, and a strong coarse Bowie knife and a black napsack [sic]".

One generously circulated news article was quick to point out the hypocrisy of another northern state heavily engaged in Bowie knife production. It implied that it was beyond the dignity of the upstanding,

respectable citizens of Pennsylvania to engage in knife-fighting, but conversely, they were only too willing to financially benefit from those so visited by the scourge. The *Natchez Free Trader*, May 30, 1839 retold a story from the Nashville Whig and the Pennsylvanian that took both Pennsylvania and the Bowie knife to task:

These worse than barbarous . . . instruments of human slaughter for sale in Tennessee . . . thanks to the moral firmness [of Tennessee's legislature]. . . we can hardly say the same in Pennsylvania, where, if the Bowie is not much used, it is certainly manufactured and sold in great abundance, for the amusement of the people of other states, whose "combativeness" and "destructiveness," are more largely developed, and who find recreation in unfortunate rencontres thinking that to be killed is no great matter, and that to kill is a very feather in the cap of youth . . . The Bowie knife found a ready market among those new settlers who thought the customs of the country sanctioned its use, but finding our citizens generally, peaceably disposed and unwilling to countenance of violence, they have fallen into disrepute and are seldom seen in the market.

Philadelphia was an important manufacturing source of Bowie knives. That is clearly shown in a story that ran just a few years later in the *New Orleans Commercial Bulletin* on October 14, 1842. The article is notable for its portrayal of the violence rife in America at the time and the implication of the Bowie knife as a contributor to the turbulence:

BOWIE KNIVES. The "PHILADELPHIA EVENING COURIER" states, that the demand for Bowie knives has abated recently, and that a dealer in cutlery in the city has disposed of a quantity bought for the Carthagena Market, $1.50/each, the original price being $20. The inference, therefore, is that the thirst for maiming and killing with these accursed weapons has declined in this country. The desire for murder declines in a ratio to the progress of temperance.

The popularity of the knife, or at least the very commonness of its name and a perception of what it may have represented, was sufficient to cause two Grenada, Mississippi, newspapers, the *Bulletin* and the *Grenadian* to merge and form the newly named *The Bowie Knife.* Issues under that masthead were very short-lived, from March to April 1839, when it was renamed the *Southern Reporter.* Consisting chiefly of advertisements, it is not known if its demise was due to its threatening name or merely to poor circulation.

The Texan War For Independence

Large knives were definitely part of the American scene and were intended for combat. That is obvious from a courageously phrased poster printed at Gonzales, Texas, October 2, 1835, with the opening shots of the Texas War of Independence. Under the blaring headlines "FREE MEN OF TEXAS . . . TO ARMS!!! TO ARMS!!! . . . NOW'S THE DAY AND NOW'S THE HOUR," volunteers were sought among fellow citizens to leave their homes immediately ". . . armed and equipped for war *even to the knife.*" Here, too, there is strong likelihood that "Bowie knife" would have been substituted had the words been more generally recognized. The significance of this broadside is the fact that it was taken for granted that each "fellow citizen" would have normally owned not only a firearm but also a fighting knife as well, one part and parcel of every settler's requisite protective inventory.

There is no doubting the popularity and the widespread use of Bowie knives during those momentous years in Texas. They reflected the first extensive use of the Bowie knife by American volunteers in a large armed conflict. Comprehensive research in literature concerning that heroic struggle, culminating in the birth of the independent Republic of Texas, is certain to reveal many more quotable passages about the Bowie knife than has been undertaken here.

The general interest in Texas was intensified following the formation of the new republic. Articles about it appeared in all manner of publications. A typical example was the series of stories that appeared in the late 1830's in *The Hesperian: A Monthly Miscellany of General Literature*, published in Columbus, Ohio. Its October 1838 issue went to great lengths to describe the coarse, often violent frontier character of the territory.

The *Hesperian's* descriptions of duels and murders were balanced with comment on the sobriety of parishioners attending the first Christian sermon preached in Houston. The Bowie knife and Jim Bowie were duly mentioned in the January 1839 issue in the magazine's continuing series on Texas. In a stirring account of the final moments of the battle at the Alamo, with the Mexicans upon the walls: "The desperate courage of the patriots was, however, too much, at first, for their enemies, and hundreds were either pitched from the walls or put to death by the Bowie knife or bayonet."

Among the legion of subsequent eyewitness claims to Jim Bowie's final moments was the *Hesperian's* account ". . . of a female servant who was [so] fortunate as to escape the general destruction." According to her supposed, unsupported story, the Mexicans rushed into Bowie's room, where he had been confined by sickness: "He was up in time to take his stand in the door; and with the knife which bears his name, he for some time kept the enemy at bay. When his mighty arm was at last tired with the work of death, he fell upon the heaps of the slain which he had thrown around him."

That Bowie knives were taken for granted as an ordinary, normal weapon of those Texas volunteers was demonstrated by their frequent offhand mention in the 1846 (first) edition of *Sam Houston and His Republic* by Charles Edwards Lester.

In 1855, C.E. Lester's book was reissued, under the title *The Life of Sam Houston . . .The Only Authentic Memoir of Him Ever Published*, without crediting the author. It was merely an expanded edition adapted to then U.S. Senator Houston's political campaign. Describing events immediately following the Battle of San Jacinto, the capture and then protest over the contemplated release of Santa Ana, symbolic reference to the famous knife was made as the Mexican general was removed from the vessel about to return him to his country:

Santa Ana remonstrated against the lawless outrage, and . . . declared he would die before he left . . . all other means failing, a military commander ordered him to be put in irons. When the irons were brought . . . the prisoner jumped up, adjusted his collar, put on his hat and stated his readiness to accompany us. And how else could a defenceless prisoner act, with a score of bayonets or bowie-knives at his breast?" . . . [later recounting that battle] " . . . that combat of San Jacinto . . . must forever remain in the catalogue of military miracles. 750 citizens miscellaneously armed with rifles, muskets, belt pistols and knives under a leader who had never seen service, except as a subaltern, march to attack near double their numbers . . . the elite of an invading army.

The Lester volume also offered an interesting early, clear illustration of a classic type, long-bladed, clip point Bowie knife held in the hand of Sam Houston, who is seated before an open fireplace dispassionately whittling wood chips to feed the fire. That innocuous depiction, simply an artist's fancied, unstudied rendering of the room, and the knife, has been occasionally singled out, and with no further documentation, is said to be an exacting representation of Sam Houston's personal knife. Despite such unfounded claims, that knife and all other ill-defined weapons in illustrations throughout the book, remain but artist's renditions of generic types.

An astutely discerning observation, as dispassionate as it was disquieting, was offered in a letter from the office of the British governor of the island of Barbados on July 12, 1840. The British Colonial Office was considering stationing an official government resident in Texas. Leaving no doubt as to the Bowie knife's high profile and pervading presence, it also addressed the unsettled, lawless conditions rampant in the immediate years following the Texan War for Independence:

◄ *Here is an early coffin-handle Ames Bowie knife circa 1830s. Although it is very similar to the one in Wild Bill Hickock's belt (courtesy Kansas State Historical Society), this particular knife has many of the same features of the more ornate knife of Captain Washington Hood and will date to the same early era. The quality of the sheath is almost identical to that of the Washington Hood knife. Shown with the knife, in addition to the Hickock illustration, is a Smith & Wesson Model 2 Army revolver in 32 rimfire.*

❧ ● ❧ ● ❧ ● ❧ ● ❧ ● ❧

The Government is carried on, as in America, and the laws of Texas have, with a very few slight alterations, been copied from those of the United States... the population... are chiefly Americans, a few Germans, and some English and Irish. These are principally bankrupts, swindlers and felons from the United States occasionally diversified with an oasis of respectability which only renders the Desert of Villainy around more conspicuous by contrast . . . murder and every other crime is of great frequency in Texas, and the perpetrators escape with the greatest impunity... it is considered unsafe to walk through the streets of the principal towns without being armed.

The Bowie Knife is the weapon most in vogue and it may not be uninteresting here to state that the greater numbers of these weapons are manufactured in Sheffield and Birmingham and brought over in British ships as a profitable speculation. I have seen one manufactured by 'Bunting & Son' of Sheffield, the blade of which, was 18 inches long and ornamented in beautiful tracery on the steel as "The Genuine Arkansas Tooth Pick" and I have been offered another for sale also of English make, the vendor of which hinted that I ought to pay him a dollar more than he demanded, as he could assure me it had tasted blood.

Following the Texan War for Independence, an influx of settlers and homesteaders headed for the new republic. Among the host of guidebooks, route manuals and other published travel aids for prospective travelers, The Texan Emigrant: Narration of the Adventures of the Author and Texas in a Description of the Soil, Climate, [etc.] (1840) is numbered among the more thorough and inclusive. Not much is known about its author, Col. Edward Stiff. His stay in Texas appears to have been of short duration; he may have been a businessman from Baltimore and his military title is believed honorary or whimsical. Stiff espoused the cause of the "Peace Party" and was not in favor of Texan independence from Mexico; he felt those who fomented the revolution were dishonorable. Despite those obvious prejudices and an irascible nature, his guide proved valuable for accurately portraying the adversities faced by emigrants to the new country. As to be expected, the Bowie knife was found worthy of frequent mention. Col. Stiff was singularly unimpressed with the then seat of government at Houston, a town of but 3,000 inhabitants:

Pick-pockets and every description of bad characters abound here and are in promiscuous confusion mingled with the virtuous part of the community... the police of the City is [sic] entirely worthless . . . [after having possessions stolen] this was the first depredation of the kind I have been made to feel, with the exception of a few dollars picked from my pocket at two different times afterwards, and a Bowie-knife [stolen] out of my bosom when sleeping.

In his travels to backwoods outposts, Stiff mentions his own carrying " . . . of a Bowie knife, about 12 inches long" and visiting a rough-hewn log "hotel"–trading post that " . . . on our arrival was full of men of every color, black excepted, and contained for sale, tomahawks, bowie-knives, powder and lead, Indian trinkets and a quantity of whisky, which last article was being consumed at no slow rate."

Among the more picturesque descriptions found in the *Texan Emigrant* is that of a group of travelers the author came across in the northern prairies: "The men were clothed in Texan costume, and were armed as usual with the deadly rifle and savage Bowie knife, and taken as a whole, were perhaps as forbidding a set of people as even imagination could well picture."

The Bowie knife maintained high profile in Texas in those years. Massive examples were in evidence and openly carried as seen in a short bit of local gossip in the *Texas Sentinel* of Austin February 11, 1841. The editor took a swipe at the errant carrying of the knife. His remarks carried a personal tinge: "A rowdy. . . we noticed a few days since. . . dashing about with a huge Bowie knife protruding from his bosom. We advised him to exchange this weapon for a corn-cob; you will find the latter much lighter and more convenient to wear, than the Bowie knife, and just as useful in a respectable society."

Bowie knives, in all shapes, sizes and forms were widely carried by Americans of all stripes, be they politician, merchant, lawyer, soldier, gambler, or frontiersman . . . and even an occasional member of the fair sex. Often large, occasionally enormous, the knives could be intimidating and fear-inspiring by their mere size. Those Bowies came to symbolize America for many, especially visiting Europeans, a country peopled by a generally uncivilized lot living in a wilderness society. To the often more-urbane Easterner, the knives represented their own untamed, primitive backwoods. Although generally identified with such areas, the Bowie was not purely regional; their manufacture, sale and use was indigenous to just about every part of America. They served everyone equally, upstanding citizens and villains. ✷

Editor's Note: This article is a heavily-edited compilation derived from two chapters appearing in Norm Flayderman's latest book, *The Bowie Knife: Unsheathing an American Legend*. Space constraints required much text and photography be set aside. To read the complete (and most authoritative) history of the Bowie knife ever published, you'll need a copy of this book. It's a big book––512 pages—that contains 245 large color photographs and some 120 b/w photographs of Civil War and 19th century subjects. Order from one of the following: 1) N. Flayderman & Co., P.O. Box 2446, Ft. Lauderdale FL 33303/954-761-8855/Web site: www.flayderman.com. 2) Mowbray Publishers, Inc., P.O. Box 460, Lincoln RI 02865/800-999-4697/Web site: www.manatarmsbooks.com. The book is $79.95, plus $4.50 S&H, from both sources.

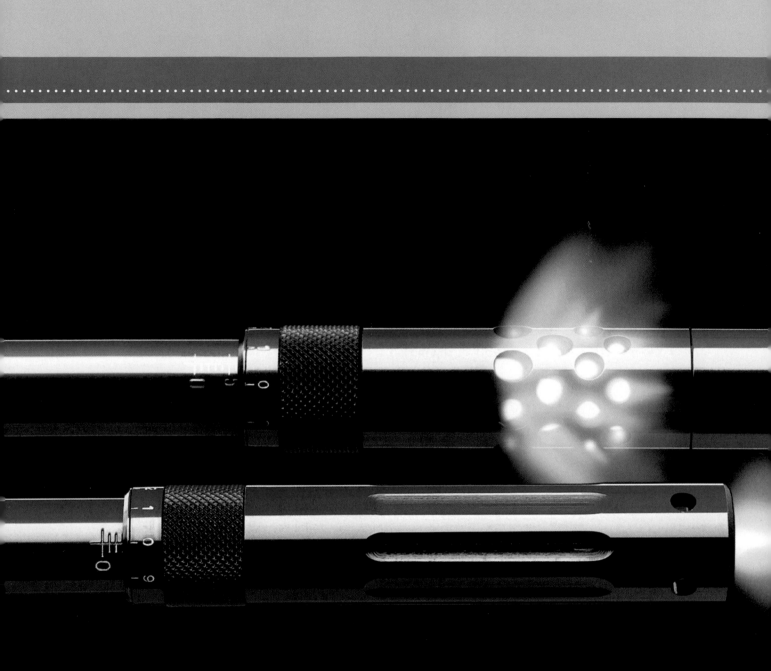

PUTTING BULLETS THROUGH THEIR PACES:
PREMIUM BULLET
PERFORMANCE

by Tom Turpin & Terry Wieland

*O*ver the past 15 years, manufacturers have made a serious effort to improve the performance of their bullets on game. As a result, riflemen today have more bullets available than ever before, and many are truly excellent in terms of both accuracy and terminal ballistics.

Writers Tom Turpin and Terry Wieland have long been engaged in the business of bullet testing, both in expansion boxes and on real animals. In this two-part article, Turpin examines the performance of the current crop of small-caliber (.257 - .338) premium game bullets, while Wieland looks at bullets for dangerous game (.416 and up).

In the case of smaller bullets, accuracy is a prime concern. With dangerous-game bullets, weight retention and penetration are paramount. In the end, however, both our correspondents found that with premium bullets you generally get what you pay for, but you do not necessarily have to pay the most to get the best performance.

BULLETS FOR THE SMALLER STUFF

By Tom Turpin

ACCURACY IS A PRIME CONCERN, AS WELL AS TERMINAL PERFORMANCE

There was a time in this country when bullets were relatively cheap and, by and large, not very good. We demand a lot from our bullet manufacturers. We expect that a bullet will perform outstandingly under any and all circumstances. Bullets in 30-caliber (.308-inch) are good examples. Some of the old-timers leave the muzzle at 2000 fps or less, while some of the new hot rock magnums almost double that velocity. Yet, we expect the same bullet to perform well at both extremes and, if it doesn't, we scream to the high heavens. Actually, the manufacturers have gotten pretty close—but aren't quite there yet.

About ten years ago, perhaps a little longer, I did a story on premium bullets. In fact, I did two of them just a few years apart. At the time, most of the premium bullet makers were small operations, often one-man shops. I guess they made a believer out of the big boys, as these days the major manufacturers have added premium bullets to their lines as well—and thank goodness for that. Some make premium bullets in-house and others buy them from outside sources, and some do both. With all the progress in the technology of bullet design and construction, it is time to do an update to those earlier pieces.

Before getting started on the technical aspects of this piece, a bit

⁂ ● ⁂ ● ⁂ ● ⁂ ● ⁂ ● ⁂

Three generations of Brenneke-designed bullets very popular in Europe, but seldom seen in this country. On the left is the newest Brenneke design, the TOG (Torpedo Optimal Bullet), the brainchild of Wilhelm Brenneke's great grandson Dr. Peter Mank. Middle and right are the better-known TUG and TIG designs.

▶ *Three of the best performers in the author's test. On the left is the newest Barnes offering, the Triple-Shock, in the middle the Speer Trophy Bonded Bear Claw and on the right the Swift A-Frame.*

▶ *Bonded-Core bullets took a long time to catch on in the U.S. and are now spreading to Europe. In addition to the new Brenneke TOG, the respected Norma Company of Sweden is producing a bonded-core bullet called the Oryx. As can be seen, it performed quite well.*

of philosophizing is in order. To me, it seems the height of asininity to spend several hundred dollars–or more, often much more–on a fine rifle; add to that several hundred for optics and mounts; then hook up with a top-notch outfitter to the tune of a few thousand—and then scrimp on the cost of a really premium bullet! That way of thinking simply makes no sense to this country boy.

To my way of thinking, often it is the performance of the bullet that ultimately determines the success or failure of the hunt (*if success is determined by game on the ground*). When viewed in that light, a buck

or two for a bullet that one knows will perform properly seems to be the bargain of the century! This is particularly true when one considers that these days there are lots of really top-quality bullets available to choose from—many of which are loaded into factory ammo. It was not always that way, though. Not all that many years ago, if one did not handload, premium bullets were out of the question. I started using bonded-core bullets to overcome poor bullet performance.

I first learned about bonded-core bullets in 1973. I was stationed with the U.S. Army in Alaska at the time and one of my friends there, who had

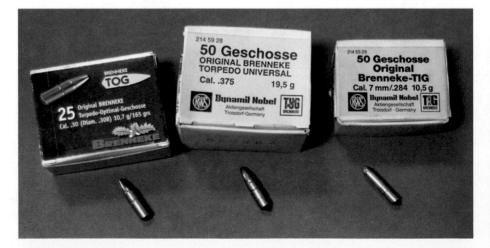

fulfilled his tour requirements and was getting ready to leave, introduced me to a sourdough pal of his who was also a registered guide. My new Alaskan pal, Chris Goll, was a gun nut like me and we hit it off nicely. Among the many other things he added to my education, he introduced me to Bitterroot bullets. One local Anchorage area sporting goods store, Mountain View Sports Center, actually stocked a few of them in the more popular calibers.

To my knowledge, Bill Steigers, the owner and operator of Bitterroot Bullet Company, was the first to bond the lead core of a bullet to the pure copper jacket. I am told that he initially did so by actually soldering the cores to the jackets. These days, as I understand it, most core bonding is done by a chemical process, rather than with heat. Anyway, the only faults I could find with Bitterroot bullets were their cost—and that they were almost impossible to obtain. They also didn't deliver bench-rest accuracy, but I didn't use them for that purpose and they were plenty accurate enough for hunting.

꧁ ● ꧁ ● ꧁ ● ꧁ ● ꧁ ● ꧁

The original bonded-core bullet, the Bitterroot from Bill Steiger's Bitterroot Bullet Company. On the left is a 130-grain 270 bullet taken from the innards of a mule deer buck. The bullet stuck him in the chest as he stood facing the author at about 200 yards. It lost a little over four grains of weight passing through a couple feet of mule deer. On the right is a 338 slug taken from a bullet box. It just doesn't get any better than this.

The newest bullet development from Swift Bullet Company is the Scirocco. It is a bonded-core design but does not feature the partition like the A-Frame. The per-bullet cost is about half that of the older design.

The TOG designer and great-grandson of Wilhelm Brenneke is Dr. Peter Mank, shown here testing the TOG bullet at the range.

As far as I can tell, the second bonded-core bullet to come along was the Trophy Bonded bullet. Texan Jack Carter was a big fan of Bitterroot bullets. However, Jack was an African hunter and the largest bullet available from Bitterroot was the 375 H&H. As a result, Jack developed the Trophy Bonded Bear Claw bullet and manufactured them himself. He made sure that his production was large enough that he overcame Bitterroot's biggest problem, that of availability. The Bear Claw was a fine bullet. The right to produce them was later acquired by Federal Cartridge Company and they are now manufactured by Speer–both ATK companies. However, the 2005 Bear Claw bullet as manufactured by Speer is not exactly the same bullet as turned out by Jack Carter. My colleague–and one of my favorite people–Terry Wieland, covers the differences in the companion piece to this yarn.

Several small bullet makers such as Northern Precision, Grizzly, Jensen, Elkhorn and several others also produced a few bonded-core bullets. Their production was not enough, however, to make much of a dent in the bullet market. I know Northern Precision is still around and making bullets but I'm not sure about the others mentioned. I've not heard of them in quite a long time. A bullet company that did make a dent, though, was Swift Bullet Company and its A-Frame bonded-core design. Not to be outdone by a Yank, Australia's Woodleigh Bullets, run by Geoff McDonald, also offered a line of Weldcore bullets in both large and small calibers. Both the Weldcore and the A-Frame are superb bullets.

It has taken a long time but the advantages of bonded-core bullets have finally taken hold in the industry. Swift came out with a slightly less expensive (than its A-Frame) bonded-core bullet, called the Scirocco. Nosler introduced the Accubond; Hornady the Interbond, Norma the Oryx—and even the Big Green (Remington) developed a bonded-core bullet called the Core-Lokt Ultra. Winchester, on the other hand, has not gone the bonded core route—at least not yet—preferring to stay with the monolithic Fail Safe design instead. I wouldn't keel over in surprise if

Left: The new Brenneke TOG (left), the TIG (center), and the TUG (right). The TIG and TUG were designed by the company founder, Wilhelm Brenneke. The TOG came along two generations later, designed by Brenneke's great-grandson, Dr. Peter Mank.

Right; Nosler's bonded-core bullet is the Accubond. It performed very well in the bullet box and the author used this bullet to take a B&C record book pronghorn in New Mexico last season. Alas, the bullet was not recovered.

the combined technologies of Nosler and Winchester eventually comes out with a version of the Accubond in the CT line. Barnes' "X" bullet, and the latest Triple-Shock designs, are also monolithic hollowpoints.

Another European bullet maker besides Norma has developed a bonded-core bullet. The old and respected firm of Wilhelm Brenneke, designer of the TIG and TUG bullets so popular with European hunters—not to mention the developer of the modern shotgun slug—has recently introduced the TOG bullet. The TIG and TUG designs are from Wilhelm Brenneke himself. Loosely translated, TIG stands for Torpedo International Bullet, and TUG is Torpedo Universal Bullet. TOG stands for, would you believe, Torpedo Optimal Bullet and was designed by Wilhelm Brenneke's great-grandson, Dr. Peter Mank. The TOG is a bonded-core design, whereas the TIG and TUG are not. The word Torpedo in the name stands for the shape of the bullet tail, common to all three of the bullet designs. Last I heard, the new Brenneke design had not yet been marketed in the U.S. Whether it will or not remains to be seen.

I know of no bullet test medium that exactly replicates bullet performance in animal tissue, bone and skin. I'm not sure that such a medium exists. Major manufacturers usually test in ballistic gelatin. I suppose that test medium is as good as any, and better than most. However, for my purposes it is too expensive and too complicated to use. In the past, my test medium has always been wet paper pulp, usually old phone books. For this test, however, I started saving the daily newspapers. Adequately soaked, they serve quite well.

The newsprint will not replicate bullet terminal performance in animal tissue. However, judging on the comparison of the few bullets I have recovered from animal tissue to the same bullet recovered from my bullet box filled with wet paper pulp, the medium is a close approximation. In an accompanying photo shown nearby are two Bitterroot bullets. One was fired into a bullet box and the other into a mule deer buck's chest. The bullet recovered from the bullet box shows more uniform and greater expansion than does the bullet recovered from the buck. One reason

for that is the bullet box bullet was fired into the medium at essentially point-blank range and at full velocity, whereas the bullet recovered from the buck first struck tissue at about 175 - 200 yards. The bullet recovered from game also gives evidence of yawing slightly for some reason. Considering the differences in the situation, their performance is comparable I think.

In addition, wet newsprint provides a consistent medium for the testing of each bullet, is readily available and—essentially—costs nothing. The only downside to using wet paper is that it is miserable to fool with and a pain to dispose of once the testing is finished. After dumping a ton of it in their dumpster, I'm not sure I'll be welcome again at my local range.

As pal Terry mentions in his piece, with the big-bore bullets, gilt-edged accuracy is by no means essential. Minute-of-buffalo accuracy is fine for pretty big targets at proper ranges. In the case of the smaller calibers, however, accuracy is quite important. Match bullet accuracy is not essential, but it is comforting if one can attain it. As previously mentioned, one of the minor problems I experienced with Bitterroot bullets, other that getting them, was that they were not super-accurate. By that I mean that MOA and smaller groups were seldom attained. One and one-half to two MOA groups were common with them, however, and for most hunting applications, that is more than sufficient.

Many—if not most—of today's bonded bullets have overcome that deficiency, and shoot right up there with the best. As we all know, each rifle is somewhat unique and a bullet that will shoot exceptionally well in one rifle, might not shoot as well in others.

For range testing purposes, I decided to use most of the currently available bonded-core bullets. In addition, though this piece is primarily concerned with bonded-core bullets, I included the latest monolithic bullet from Barnes, the Triple Shock, and the Winchester Fail Safe design. Others tested were the Hornady Interbond, the Swift A-Frame, the Nosler Accubond, the Swift Scirocco, the Speer-made Trophy Bonded, the

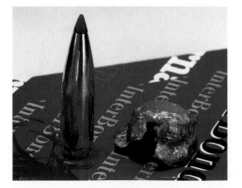

●※●●※●●※●●※●●※●●※●

Hornady entered the bonded-core bullet market with the Interbond. It performs very well, both in the bullet box and in the field. The author used a 130-grain Interbond in his 270 Winchester to take a very good Coues deer buck in Sonora, Mexico. This bullet was also not recovered.

Norma Oryx and the Remington Core-Lokt Ultra. All were handloaded except the Remington offering, which was factory-loaded. I had a small stash of the Brenneke TOG design as well as some field results from Namibia, so decided to include them for comparative purposes. It remains to be seen if and/or when these Brenneke bullets will be made available to U.S. shooters.

Also for comparison purposes, I included the Bitterroot bullet and the Jack Carter-manufactured Trophy Bonded bullet. I still have a lifetime supply of Bitterroots and a very small hoard of pre-Federal Trophy Bonded bullets that Jack gave me. I thought it might be interesting to include them in the test.

I would have liked very much to test the North Fork bullet. However, I just learned of them a short while ago and had no samples to test. Judging from the comments of friends of mine whose assessments I've learned to trust completely, the North Fork is a great bullet.

The test was conducted to determine three things: the weight retention, penetration, and accuracy of each bullet tested. The conclusions reached are not scientifically valid since it would require much more testing, with hundreds if not thousands of shots, to develop scientifically valid statistical data. The logistics of doing such a test program render it practically impossible to accomplish.

Instead, one has to accept the fact that my results are just that, results of a limited test that, at best, gives an idea of how each bullet might perform in the field. The accuracy testing is likewise not statistically valid. The shooting was done by one shooter—me—with my hunting rifles, off a solid bench. I am neither the best nor the worst shooter in the world, and the groups reported here are representative only of my shooting with my rifles; your results may differ.

I had neither the time nor the inclination to shoot group after group using the many different bullets, powders, cases, primers, etc. That was beyond the scope of this article. I was looking only for hunting accuracy, and any significant variances one way or

the other. In most cases, a couple of 3-shot groups were fired with each bullet for accuracy evaluation.

We can pretty much set aside any accuracy questions up front—and very briefly. All the bullets were amply accurate for hunting with my rifles. Some were superbly accurate, and some were…well, let's just say not benchrest quality. From an accuracy perspective, though, I wouldn't hesitate to hunt with any of the bullets I tested.

I can also dispense with any penetration concerns rather quickly. All the bullets I tested provided adequate penetration for hunting purposes. Some writers have been carping about bonded-core bullets not providing adequate penetration. Their hypothesis centers on the concept that since the core is bonded to the jacket, and therefore holds together better than non-bonded-core bullets, the greater expansion of the bonded bullet provides greater resistance passing through animal tissue, and therefore penetrates less. Obviously, there is truth to this argument. However, the crux of the question is not how far a bullet will penetrate, but how much penetration is enough? If total penetration was the key issue, then everyone would be shooting

The author had to fire two Winchester Fail Safe bullets into the bullet box to recover one. The first one apparently shed all its petals and completely penetrated all 44 inches of test medium. The second one shed a couple petals and was recovered after 24.5 inches of penetration.

❧ ● ❧ ● ❧ ● ❧ ● ❧ ● ❧

full metal jacket bullets. Here again, as with the accuracy question, I found that all the tested bullets provided sufficient penetration for most hunting situations.

As mentioned earlier, I use Bitterroot bullets for most of my hunting. In the 30-plus years that I've been using them, I have recovered precious few of them from carcasses; the vast majority having penetrated the target animal completely. One I did

This fine Sonora, Mexico Coues deer buck was taken by the author using his old David Miller custom 270 Winchester. The load was his standard for this rifle, 59.5 grains of H4831, WW brass, CCI 200 primers and, in this case, a 130-grain Hornady Interbond bullet. As can be seen, it worked quite well.

An original Jack Carter-made Trophy Bonded Bear Claw bullet, also taken from the author's bullet box.

	TEST RESULTS			
	Bullet Weight/Grains			
Bullet	**Cartridge**	**Original**	**Recovered**	**Penetration/In.**
Bitterroot	270 Win.	130 grains	125.3	2-1/2 feet/deer
Brenneke TOG	300 Dakota	165 grains	151.4	14.4
Woodleigh	338 Win.	225 grains	194.1	18.5
Old TBBC	338 Win.	250 grains	237.0	19.0
Core-Lokt Ultra	30-06	150 grains	122.5	12.5
Interbond	280 Rem.	139 grains	123.6	13.5
Swift A-Frame	280 Rem.	140 grains	135.0	14.0
Barnes TS	280 Rem.	140 grains	140.0	16.0
Accubond	280 Rem.	140 grains	105.0	15.0
Swift Scirocco	280 Rem.	150 grains	138.4	14.2
Speer® TBBC	280 Rem.	160 grains	155.0	18.0
Norma Oryx	280 Rem.	156 grains	133.5	15.5
Win. Fail Safe	280 Rem.	160 grains	147.6	14.5*

*This was second round fired. The first shot apparently shed its petals and penetrated both bullet boxes completely—over 44 inches in all. All that was found were remnants of the petals. In fairness to Winchester, the Fail Safe bullets used in this test are from a lot several years old. It is possible a different alloy is in use today.

recover was taken from a buck mule deer shot squarely in the chest at about 175 - 200 yards as he stood facing me. The bullet, was a 130-grain 0.277-inch bullet fired from my old 270, that was traveling at 2130 fps. That bullet did not exit, and I found it in the gut pile. It had penetrated over two feet of mule deer and killed the animal in its tracks. In doing this, it lost a total of 4.7 grains of its loaded weight (*125.3 grains vs. 130 grains*). That seems more than adequate penetration to me. I think the penetration issue is largely smoke and mirrors, and grist for the mill of a few outdoor writers although, in fairness, perhaps some have had vastly different experiences than I have.

With all the caveats explained, let's go shooting. In preparation for the range session, I loaded 7mm bullets into the 280 Remington cartridge to simplify the handloading process. For the old Trophy Bonded bullet, I loaded the 250-grain 338 bullet—which was about all I had left from my stash of original Jack Carter bullets. I loaded the 225-grain 338 Woodleigh Weldcore as well for no other reason than I was

An excellent bullet from the Land Down Under is the Woodleigh. This one is a 225-grain 338 Winchester from the bullet box. These bullets perform very well in the field, as well as in the test medium.

loading the TBBC and had the press set up with dies, etc. for the 338. Finally I loaded the new Brenneke TOG 165-grain .308-inch bullet into my 300 Dakota for the test. I had only a small supply of the 30-caliber TOG bullets, and no other caliber was available.

In the 280 I loaded the 150-grain GPA, 139-grain MEN, 139-grain Hornady Interbond, 140-grain Swift A-Frame, 140-grain Barnes Triple Shock, 140-grain Nosler Accubond, 150-grain Swift Scirocco, 160-grain Speer-made Trophy Bonded Bear Claw, 156-grain Norma Oryx and 160-grain Winchester Fail Safe. In all the 280 loads, I used new R-P cases, IMR 4831 powder and CCI 200 primers.

The final bullet for the test is the Remington factory-loaded 150-grain PSP Core-Lokt Ultra for the 30-06. At the time I obtained the Core-Lokt Ultra loads, only factory-loaded ammo was available and the Big Green was using all available bullets in their factory ammo. Presumably, production has caught up and component bullets should be available for reloading.

As can be seen from the results, there are no really bad bullets in this group. All performed plenty well enough to take hunting and be confident in the outcome, assuming proper bullet placement. It is a given that no bullet, regardless of how good it might be, can overcome poor

placement of that bullet in the animal. A bullet could consistently retain 100 percent of its weight, expand to triple its diameter, penetrate an Abrams tank and consistently win 1000-yard matches—yet perform poorly through the guts. The worst performer in the lot through the lungs will outperform this magic (and non-existent) bullet.

Hunters today are truly blessed with a plethora of really good bullets. Also, the prices of really good bullets have come down, rather than go sky-high. The last batch of Bitterroot bullets I bought from Bill Steigers (several years ago) cost me about two dollars per bullet and, I might add, I was happy to pay that just to get them. Many excellent bullets these days cost less than half that amount, some considerably less.

A quick look through my new Midway catalog disclosed many of the bullets used in this test retail for between 30 and 50 cents each. In these days of two dollar per gallon gasoline, today's fine bullets represent the buy of the century and there is no valid excuse for using anything but the best. Find the one that shoots the best in your rifle and go hunting! You can't control the weather or the game, but you can and should control the bullets you use. With the bullets available in 2005, bullet failure can and should be non-existent and inexcusable.

BULLETS FOR THE BIG STUFF

By Terry Wieland

MORE IS DEMANDED OF A BULLET FOR DANGEROUS GAME

Bullets for dangerous game are big and heavy. Typically, they range in caliber from .375 to .600, and in weight from 300 grains to 900 and more. They are intended to put a truculent animal on the ground, and do it quickly. In the most extreme cases, they must stop a charge where failure will mean the death or dismemberment of the hunter. When the hunter is you, interest in bullet performance acquires a whole new dimension.

One of the first authors to take a serious technical interest in bullet performance was the African ivory hunter, John Taylor. In his classic *African Rifles and Cartridges (1948),* Taylor examined various bullets that were loaded in the big English cartridges of the day, and recounted how they performed on elephant, Cape buffalo, rhinoceros, and lesser beasts.

At that time, most British ammunition was proprietary – that is, riflemakers sold ammunition for their own rifles; this ammunition was made to their specifications by Eley-Kynoch, hunters purchased ammunition from the riflemaker, and accepted whatever bullet was offered. Some bullets were good – the steel-clad 410-grain in the 416 Rigby, for example

❧●❧●❧●❧●❧●❧

New Woodleigh 165-grain and old-production Trophy Bonded Bear Claw, recovered from bullet box. The resemblance is uncanny. The Woodleigh retained 155 grains, the Bear Claw 159. Penetration was 14 inches each, from a 30-06.

– while others were not. How the bullet performed determined the reputation of the cartridge, and by extension the rifles that were made for it.

Taylor's observations on bullet performance are still valid after more than half a century and, essentially, they boil down to this: A good soft-nose dangerous-game bullet should expand to a respectable width without disintegrating. If it does so, the retained weight will provide the necessary penetration to reach the vitals and destroy considerable tissue along the way. A poor bullet, on the other hand, either expands too much or not at all, or flies to pieces on impact and fails to penetrate.

When it comes to bullet performance, there are some basic rules that cannot be broken:

1. Striking velocity is a key factor in expansion but not in penetration.
2. The greatest single factor in penetration is bullet weight. The heavier the bullet, generally speaking, the greater the penetration. By comparison, velocity hardly matters and sometimes even works against you. High velocity can cause a bullet to open up too much, too quickly, or even to fly apart, reducing penetration.
3. To penetrate deeply, an expanding bullet must retain as much of its original weight as possible.

A 400-grain bullet that retains 98 percent of its weight will out-penetrate a 500-grain bullet that expands quickly, sheds half its weight, and ends up as a 250-grain shard. With jacketed bullets, the jacket (*usually copper or an alloy*) must be bonded to the core (*usually lead*) if the bullet is to stay in one piece.

Recovered from box, left to right: 400-grain Woodleigh, 400-grain old-production Bear Claw, 400-grain new Bear Claw from Federal, all fired from a 416 Rigby. The difference between the old and new Bear Claw is striking.

❧●❧●❧●❧●❧●❧

Unlike weight retention, penetration must be looked at in context. Sometimes a bullet retains more weight than another but does not penetrate as far. This results from the way the bullet expands, to what diameter, and how quickly. Sometimes a bullet creates so much resistance in front of a broad mushroom that it creates a devastating wound channel but stops an inch or two short of a bullet that does not expand as much, yet sheds more weight and sails on with less resistance. Penetration, therefore, should only be judged in relation to the other major performance factors.

Some bullet-makers have tried to push the idea that a bullet that flies to pieces is deadlier because of the "shrapnel effect" of pieces hitting vital organs. Such performance is wildly unpredictable at best, and no professional hunter I know would recommend such a bullet. It is a desperate attempt to turn a serious fault into a dubious virtue and any hunter of the big stuff should give such bullets a wide berth.

There are two ways of testing bullets. One is on the game animals in question, alive or dead. This is

Professional hunter Derek Hurt, flanked by Masai, and trackers Abedi (left) and Lakina, with deceased Synocerus caffer.

⌘ ● ⌘ ● ⌘ ● ⌘ ● ⌘ ● ⌘

undoubtedly the best way. John Taylor learned what he learned through painful experience and extensive hunting of live game. Even for the independently wealthy, that would be extremely difficult to do today.

The alternative is some sort of test medium in an expansion box. This can be ballistic gelatin, water, multiple thicknesses of lumber, compressed newsprint, the nearest sand bank – you name it, and it has probably been tried. There are drawbacks with each of the above. The best one can hope for is an approximate result showing how a bullet is most likely to perform. More valuable still is learning how one bullet performs in relation to another bullet under identical circumstances.

In the tests I carried out, I wanted to learn several things: First, of course, was how a variety of popular dangerous game bullets performed, both in test boxes and in actual Cape buffalo, alive or dead. Second, I wanted to see how my bullet-box tests, using several feet of thoroughly soaked and compressed newsprint, compared with an actual Cape buffalo. And finally, I wanted to compare older Trophy Bonded Bear Claws against the new bullets made by Federal.

Because this test is aimed at dangerous-game bullets exclusively, I was concerned with only three measurements: Expansion characteristics, weight retention, and penetration. In spite of what some bullet makers insist, accuracy is rarely an important factor with a dangerous-game bullet. Certainly, one would never choose such a bullet for accuracy while ignoring terminal performance. In my experience, such bullets as the Trophy Bonded Bear Claw and Woodleigh WeldCore deliver good to excellent accuracy anyway, and so it was not a concern.

Having chosen the bullets to be tested, I then arrived at suitable loads for each in a 458 Lott, and in a 500 Nitro Express. I shot and chronographed these loads, fired bullets into my bullet boxes and recovered the bullets, and took identical loads to Africa to shoot into Cape buffalo. Altogether, the preparations and testing spanned the better part of a year.

In the 458 Lott, the bullets used were all 500 grain (with one exception), loaded with 79 grains of H4895. This gives muzzle velocity of about 2150 feet per second (fps), duplicating the performance of the great old nitro express cartridges like the 470.

In the 500 NE, I used only Woodleigh 570-grain jacketed bullets, although I also loaded a 515-grain hardened lead bullet at low velocity. The results of that test proved an important point about weight, velocity, and penetration. The Woodleighs were loaded ahead of 110 grains of IMR 4831, delivering about 2000 fps at the muzzle. The lead bullet was loaded with 35 grains of XMP5744, with velocity of 1200 fps.

The 500-grain 458 bullets tested were:
1. Woodleigh WeldCore
2. Trophy Bonded Bear Claw (old production, circa 1991)
3. Trophy Bonded Bear Claw (new production, circa 2004)
4. Hornady Soft Point
5. Speer African Grand Slam
6. Barnes Triple-Shock X-Bullet (450 grains)

While I was in Africa, Robin Hurt (*with whom I was hunting buffalo*) gave

me some new-production 416 Bear Claws he recovered earlier that season from Cape buffalo, along with some factory Federal 416 Rigby ammunition. When I returned home, I tested these in my bullet box, along with some handloaded old-production 416 Trophy Bondeds and a Woodleigh WeldCore.

Finally, Derek Hurt (*Robin's son, also a PH*) gave me a .470 Bear Claw he recovered from a wounded leopard.

The results, I believe, give a valid picture of the performance that can be expected from all these bullets under critical, real-life conditions.

The good news is that of all the bullets I tested, none could be said to have failed. Some performed better than others, but I would use any of them on Cape buffalo with complete confidence.

Since the focus was on the new versus old Trophy Bonded, we should begin with an explanation.

Jack Carter of Houston developed the Trophy Bonded Bear Claw in the 1980s in an attempt to provide hunters with a bonded-core bullet for the largest calibers that would give performance comparable to the legendary Bitterroot bullets. At the time, Bitterroots were hard to get and available only in smaller calibers.

Along the way, Jack taught himself metallurgy. He and I became good friends and I learned a great deal from him about bullets and bullet-testing. In 1990, I went with Jack and Finn Aagard to Tanzania and Botswana to test Trophy Bonded bullets, in both large and small calibers, on a variety of animals including Cape buffalo.

Jack's formula for bullet-making was simple: He used pure lead, which is ductile and holds together tenaciously, like chewing gum; the jacket was pure copper, which shares these qualities. Jacket and core were bonded together using a patented heat treatment – one of three patents Jack held. He sold his company in 1989 and rights to the Trophy Bonded bullets eventually ended up with Federal Cartridge. Federal is part of ATK, along with Speer; today, Federal makes the Trophy Bonded Bear Claw, loads it in some of their premium ammunition, and Speer markets it as a premium game bullet.

Typically, an early TBB will retain up to 95 percent of its weight and expand into a healthy mushroom. In recent years, however, I began receiving reports from hunters, other writers such as Craig Boddington, and custom handloaders like Larry Barnett of Superior Ammunition, of the new Bear Claws coming apart on impact.

"It is not the bullet it used to be," Craig told me bluntly in the spring of 2004. That comment was really the starting point for this whole test. The information I received in Africa from Robin Hurt told exactly the same story.

Gradually, the project expanded to include other bullets. In November, 2004, I went to Tanzania to hunt two Cape buffalo with Robin Hurt, partly for purposes of bullet testing. I shot one with my custom bolt-action 458 Lott, built on a Dakota action, and one with a 500 Nitro Express double made by the new Rigby company in California.

In both cases, the actual hunting was done with Woodleigh bullets, and because I now consider these to be the finest hunting bullets available, we will start with an assessment of their performance.

Woodleigh WeldCore

The accompanying chart gives the retained weight and penetration of all the bullets tested, but numbers do not tell the whole story.

Woodleigh bullets from Australia are unique in several ways. They use a bonding technology that works to perfection and results in high retained weight, as well as near-perfect mushrooming under even the harshest conditions. As well, they are made in many hard-to-find calibers, especially for old Nitro Express rifles. Woodleigh bullets are made to duplicate the ballistic qualities of the original Kynoch bullets for which these rifles were regulated. This allows reloading to original specifications for old doubles.

Woodleighs are imported by Huntington Die Specialties, and available from a number of sources. Non-handloaders can buy factory ammunition loaded with Woodleighs or have it custom-loaded by a company like Superior Ammunition.

My first Tanzania Cape buffalo absorbed four shots from my 458 Lott at a range of 175 yards before he finally went to his reward. The first shot would have killed him in a few minutes, but with darkness approaching, thick bush nearby, and several hundred other buffalo milling around, Derek wanted to make sure. So I kept shooting until his head went down for good. All four bullets were recovered and their performance was exemplary.

Bullet #1 hit the shoulder, took out the top of the heart and lungs, and struck the far shoulder. Bullet #2 was recovered from the paunch, where it entered from the rear. Bullet #3 shattered the hip and toppled the buffalo, and was recovered from the chest cavity. Bullet #4 went into the shoulder beside #1 after the buffalo was down. The first bullet that mangled the shoulder was deformed, but the other three were good mushrooms.

On the second buffalo, I was using the 500 NE with 570-grain Woodleighs. At 25 yards, the first bullet more or less duplicated what the 458 did on the other buff. And, like the first animal, this one would have been dead shortly but we kept shooting as long as he was on his feet.

The accompanying photographs show the Woodleighs recovered from both buffalo, as well as those from my bullet-box. As a group, you could not ask for better performance or prettier mushrooms. To my mind, the Woodleigh WeldCore is, today, the premium dangerous-game bullet against which others should be measured.

As the test progressed, I was struck by the similarity in performance and appearance between today's Woodleigh WeldCores and the original Trophy Bonded Bear Claws. Out of curiosity, I loaded two bullets

◄ 500-grain Woodleigh WeldCores, fired from 458 Lott and recovered from Cape buffalo in Tanzania (2004). The badly mangled bullet (lower left) was the original killing shot that took out the near shoulder, top of the heart, lungs, a rib on each side, and smashed against the inside of the far shoulder, where it was recovered. The bullet (lower right) was also a shoulder shot. The bullet (background right) smashed the hip and penetrated up into the chest cavity, toppling the buffalo. It still retained 469 grains (94 percent) and expanded into an excellent mushroom.

⬩❁⬩❁⬩❁⬩❁⬩❁⬩❁

(165-grain .308) for my 30-06 and tested them in the bullet-box. Each penetrated exactly 14 inches, their retained weight was almost identical (159 grains for the Bear Claw, 155 for the Woodleigh) and their expanded shapes were remarkably similar.

Trophy Bonded Bear Claw (Old)

The old Trophy Bondeds matched the Woodleighs in both box and buffalo, and replicated the performance that I witnessed using them on Cape buffalo in a 416 Weatherby (1990) and a 458 Winchester (1993). Put the old Bear Claw beside the Woodleigh, and they look like twins.

For comparison, I have included a photo of some original 416 Bear Claws recovered from buffalo in 1990, and a 458 from a buffalo in 1993.

Trophy Bonded Bear Claw (New)

The new Trophy Bondeds, however, were disappointing. This requires some explanation.

When Federal began making the bullets under licence, they immediately changed one ingredient: Instead of using pure copper for the jacket, they switched to gilding metal. There were various reasons for this, the main one being that pure copper tends to gum up machinery; it is harder to work with, and therefore more expensive.

New production 500-grain Trophy Bonded Bear Claw, from factory Federal 470 Nitro Express ammunition, recovered from a wounded leopard by Derek Hurt in 2004. The mangled bullet weighs 388 grains (78 percent) which would be decent performance on buffalo but very poor on a soft animal like a leopard. Now, Derek Hurt uses only solids on Cape buffalo.

Gilding metal, a copper alloyed with various levels of zinc or other metals, is easier to work. It is, however, more brittle. Instead of holding together like chewing gum, it tends to shatter or rip apart under stress.

The new 458 Bear Claws broke up – a couple of claws snapped off – in both the bullet-box and the Cape buffalo. As a result, weight was lost. Neither was so dreadful that I would not use the bullet, but it reduces the Bear Claw from excellent to average.

Robin Hurt's experience with new Bear Claws in factory Federal 416 Rigby ammunition was comparable. Two of his recovered bullets had no claws at all. As the picture shows, they were reduced to slugs.

In a letter to me, Robin wrote:

"Enclosed are some 416 Bear Claws which I'm sure you'll agree give cause for concern. All the used bullets came out of buffalo bulls shot on safari with me recently in Maswa (Tanzania).
"I've never seen Bear Claws come apart before – and I'm now worried about recommending them to my clients!
"Can you please bring this to the attention of Federal Cartridge Company. (When we) tested the original Bear Claws in Kigoni-Moyowasi in 1990, they performed perfectly. I believe Federal should worry about this turn of events, and re-examine how their bullets are constructed."

I brought some of Robin's factory Federal ammunition home with me and shot it into my bullet-box; as well, I loaded an original Bear Claw and a Woodleigh in identical 416 Rigby loads. The accompanying image shows the three bullets recovered from the box: the Woodleigh and old Bear Claw are almost identical, while the new Bear Claw has a distinctly different shape (*although it held together admirably*).

Also last season, Derek Hurt used factory Federal 470 Nitro Express ammunition on a wounded leopard at close range. The bullet was quite deformed – far more than one would expect on such a soft animal as a leopard.

As Robin requested, I did inform Federal and had a long discussion about the performance with Larry Head, the chief bullet designer. According to Head, although the jacket was changed to gilding metal for production reasons, the core is still pure lead and the rest of the design is unchanged. He was very concerned to hear about the bullet's performance, and is investigating what might be done to correct the problem.

My overall conclusion is that the changes to the Bear Claw, resulting from its mass production, have turned a superb bullet into one that is merely average.

Speer African Grand Slam

Overall, the Grand Slam is a fine bullet. It retained its weight acceptably, penetrated well, and did not break up. Expansion was good in every case. Considering the price difference with other dangerous-game bullets, the Speer is a bargain (*although, like parachutes, one should not look for bargains in dangerous-game bullets*).

Hornady

Hornady has a dubious distinction: It was the failure of a 458-caliber Hornady that inspired Jack Carter to develop the Trophy Bonded in the first place. Having said that, the Hornady– as it is now made–is hugely improved over what it was 15 years ago.

Craig Boddington said I would be surprised at how well the Hornady performed, and he was right. The bullet turned in a creditable performance in the bullet-box, holding together and retaining 90 percent of its weight. In Tanzania, the test bullet went right through the Cape buffalo and we were unable to find it in the hillside behind. This suggests to me that the bullet shed its petals, but it went through ribs on both sides and the chest cavity in between, and that is good performance regardless. I would not hesitate to hunt dangerous game with the Hornady as it is now made.

Barnes Triple-Shock X

Your correspondent has never been an admirer of the X-bullet, and this exercise only confirmed my reservations about it.

I tested some of the very first X-bullets in 1989, and found them not particularly accurate in a 30-06. Since then, the design and alloy used have been modified several times. The X began as a pure copper bullet, for the metallurgical reasons outlined above; unfortunately, pure copper fouled bores so terribly at high velocities that Barnes began marketing their own aggressive cuprous-fouling solvent.

Since then, the X has evolved into an alloy bullet. In 2001, I used some 400-grain .458s in a 450 Ackley on a greater kudu, and every bullet performed poorly, with almost all the claws snapping off. These bullets were produced around 1996. When I told the people at Barnes about their performance, I was assured the alloy had since been changed to correct that problem. In this most recent test, I used the new Triple-Shock 450-grain bullet. While it performed excellently in the bullet-box, the Cape buffalo provided a sterner test, and two of its four claws snapped off.

This aside, there are other problems with the X-bullet concept.

Because copper is lighter than lead, an X-bullet is long for its weight. A 500-grain X-bullet is simply too long for the 458 Lott and similar cartridges (*although it would be fine in the 460 Weatherby or 450 Dakota*). This being the case, you have a choice of reducing the powder charge (*and hence velocity*), or severely compressing the powder, or seating the bullet farther out. The last option may not be possible, depending on the action and magazine used. If you reduce bullet weight to reduce cartridge length, you sacrifice penetration. Going to a 400-grain bullet, for example, negates much of the value of shooting a 458. These are not choices I relish when loading for dangerous game.

Overall, I found the X-bullet to be the least desirable of all the bullets tested, with problems that are inherent in its concept and, hence, cannot be corrected. I cannot think of a single reason to use an X-bullet on dangerous game, and many good reasons not to.

(*As of February 2005, Barnes says it is once again making the X-Bullet from pure copper, rather than an alloy.*)

Huntington Lead

While I was working with the 500 NE, preparing for the trip to Africa, I loaded some lead bullets in very light loads for practice. The bullet was a 515-grain hardened lead slug from Huntington Die Specialties, at a velocity of 1200 feet per second.

Having a little extra space during one bullet-box session, I decided to see what kind of penetration it gave. The result was quite remarkable. The hardened lead did not mushroom, so it behaved like a solid and penetrated 30 inches-plus of compressed newsprint as well as two thicknesses of half-inch plywood, and then punched on through a two-by-six that was backing it up.

I took one round to Africa and we shot it into the second Cape buffalo after he was down. The bullet penetrated in a straight line through the shoulder and chest cavity, but we were unable to find it in the gore of dismembering the carcass. We do know it penetrated about two feet of buffalo and, while it might not have killed the animal instantly, it would certainly have killed it eventually. This is an extremely mild load in terms of velocity and recoil, yet sheer bullet weight gives it sufficient penetration to handle a large animal.

DANGEROUS GAME BULLET PERFORMANCE IN EXPANSION BOX AND CAPE BUFFALO						
458 Lott						
Ctg. & Bullet		Orig. Wt.	Ret. Wt.%	Penetration	Ret. Wt.	%
Woodleigh .458	500	487	97	20"	394 to 496	79 to 99
Trophy Bonded .458 (old)	500	483	97	21	471	94
Trophy Bonded .458 (new)	500	417	83	25	357	71
Hornady .458	500	451	90	23	Not recovered	
Speer African Grand Slam .458	500	392	78	22	378	76
Barnes Triple-Shock X .458	450	449	99	24	393	79
500 Nitro Express						
Woodleigh WeldCore	570	560	98	25	517 & 556	91 & 98
Huntington Hardened Lead .500	515	N/A	30-plus	Not recovered		
416 Rigby						
Trophy Bonded (old)	400	396	99	23	(a) 276 to 383	69 to 96
Trophy Bonded (new)	400	391	98	23	(b) 247 to 379	62 to 95
Woodleigh WeldCore	400	400	100	21	N/A	N/A
(a) Bullets recovered from a Cape buffalo killed in Botswana in 1990 by Terry Wieland						
(b) Bullets recovered from Cape buffalo killed in Tanzania in 2004 by Robin Hurt's clients						
30-06						
Woodleigh WeldCore	165	155	94	14		
Trophy Bonded (old)	165	159	96	14		
This test was carried out solely to compare the performance of old-production Trophy Bonded Bear Claw with the Woodleigh WeldCore.						

Notes on Solids

If you ever want to witness astonishing penetration, shoot a 500-grain solid into a bullet-box packed with compressed, soaked newsprint.

While this test did not deal with solids, there are some points that should be made.

Solids are rarely used today when hunting buffalo in a herd because of the danger that the bullet will go right through and wound another animal on the far side. Solids are generally reserved for situations where the buffalo might charge. Their other main application is on elephant.

The Trophy Bonded Sledgehammer is a good solid, with a wide meplat that helps ensure straight penetration, whereas round-nosed solids have a tendency to veer off-line. Unfortunately, the flat nose also causes feeding problems, and getting a rifle to feed cartridges loaded with Sledgehammers can be a challenge.

A better solid, in my opinion, is the Speer African Grand Slam Tungsten Core solid. It also has a flat meplat, but it is much smaller and feeds beautifully. As well, because tungsten is heavier than lead, the bullets are actually shorter for weight than one with a lead core, which is all to the good in terms of powder space, magazine length and, ultimately, penetration.

Of all the solids I have tested, the Speer wins the prize, and that's what I carry in ammunition for tight situations.

This is the Elephant Rifle, the first rifle in the Safari Club International "Guns of the Big Five" series. It was built by the David Miller Co. on a then-prototype Winchester Model 70 action that the Miller Co. helped USRAC design. This is now the action found on all the Model 70 Classic (CRF) rifles. The rifle was engraved and gold inlaid by the late Lynton McKenzie. All work on the rifle, accessories and the fitted case with the exception of any engraving, was done in the David Miller Co. shop. Ron Dehn photo.

THE ART OF
ENGRAVED
& CUSTOM
GUNS

by Tom Turpin

Photo courtesy of Barry Lee Hand.

▲ **Above:** *Another example of the fine engraving execution of Barry Lee Hand. This Sharps rifle frame was appropriately embellished for the period rifle. Barry's work is always cleanly cut and very well done.*

▶ *Right: Two views of a Dakota Model 10 single-shot rifle that was engraved by Ed Delorge. Shown are both the right- and left-side views.*

Photos by Ed Delorge.

Photos by Ed Delorge.

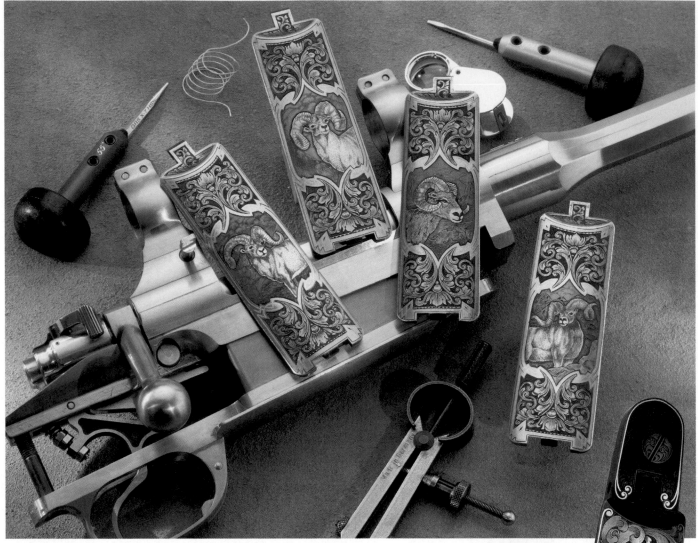

Photo by Michael Wheatly, Camera Arts Studios.

▲ *Over a four-year period, the team of gunmaker John Bolliger and engraver Mike Dubber created a magnificent set of rifles. They were made for the Foundation of North American Wild Sheep (FNAWS) and each had a rendition of one of the four varieties of sheep found on this continent—Big Horn, Desert Big Horn, Dall and Stone sheep. These four rifles were auctioned off at the annual FNAWS Convention, one per year. The project was a resounding success for the organization. FNAWS arranged with Bolliger and Dubber to create a fifth rifle. It included the four floorplates shown in this photo, along with a fifth floorplate depicting the FNAWS logo. Bolliger created a special latching arrangement that permitted the changing of the floorplates easily and without removing the remainder of the bottom metal. This exquisite engraving was executed by Mike Dubber.*

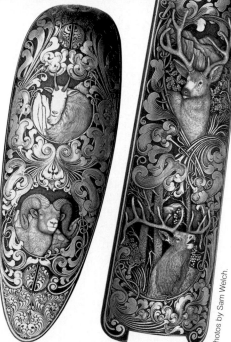

▶ *Two views of some of the engraving for this fund-raising project for 2006. The first view is of the buttplate and the other view is the floorplate. All engraving and inlay work was executed by Sam Welch, a wonderful engraver. Chances on this project will sold during the year and, at the 2006 Exhibition, the winning ticket will be drawn.*

Photos by Sam Welch.

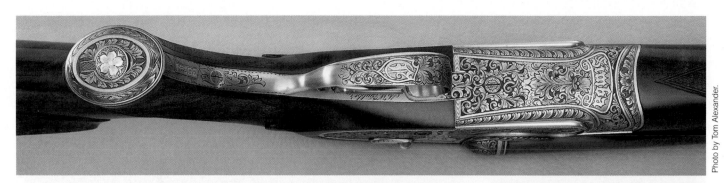

Three views of a magnificent Holland and Holland double rifle as engraved by Hoosier engraver Mike Dubber.

▼ *A beautiful Dakota Model 10 with all metalwork by Ed LaPour, engraving by Bob Evans and stocked in a fine blank of Turkish walnut by Al Lind. The rifle is chambered for the 375 H&H flanged cartridge. Photo by Turk's Head Productions.*

A really wonderful Rigby best-quality sidelock 500NE double rifle. This fine rifle has all the bells and whistles expected of a best quality gun. The outstanding engraving was executed by Barry Lee Hand.

Photos courtesy of Barry Lee Hand.

▶*A really wonderful engraving job on this Parker frame. It is done in the style of the old A1 Special, but better than anything that ever left the Parker factory. The frame is now ready for a superb stocking job and finish work. When completed, it will be a masterpiece.*

Tom Alexander Photography.

▲*One of Doug Turnbull's magnificent restoration jobs on this Winchester Model 1886—but with a twist—he has added some non-traditional engraving patterns from Lee Griffiths. The Griffiths work is unexpected on a period piece like this, but like all of Lee's work, it is exceptional.*

Photo courtesy of Doug Turnbull.

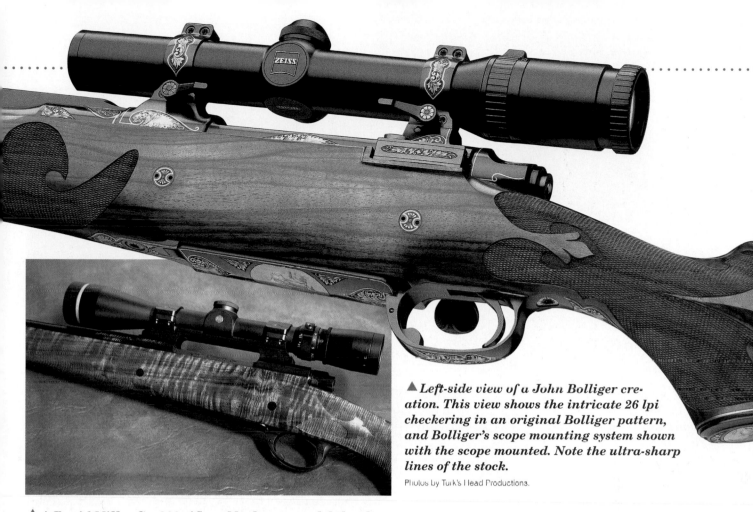

▲ *Left-side view of a John Bolliger creation. This view shows the intricate 26 lpi checkering in an original Bolliger pattern, and Bolliger's scope mounting system shown with the scope mounted. Note the ultra-sharp lines of the stock.*
Photos by Turk's Head Productions.

▲ *A David Miller Co. 338 rifle, a Marksmen model that has been upgraded with a Bastogne walnut stock instead of the "standard" laminate stock. David and Curt build their rifles to hunt with, not to become "vault queens" but, alas, many do. There are substantial and significant differences between the Marksmen and Classic models. Both are the epitome of the gunmaker's art, however.*
Photo by Tom Turpin.

▼ *A magnificent rifle from the Steve Heilmann shop. This rifle won the annual Firearms Marketing Group Award of Excellence at the 2005 ACGG/FEGA Exhibition. This award is judged by members of both the Gunmakers and Engravers Guilds. It is, of all things, a Springfield M2 22LR, obviously substantially modified. Pete Mazur did the metal finish work, and Denis Reece did the engraving. Steve did everything else.* Tom Alexander Photography.

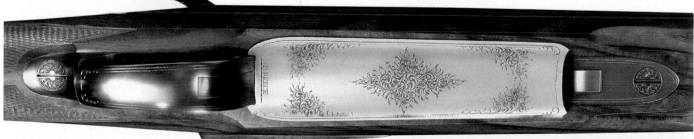

▶ *Engraver supreme Sam Welch engraved this floorplate for the 2006 Guild raffle rifle. Tickets on the rifle will be sold during the year and the winning ticket will be drawn at the annual ACGG/FEGA Exhibition in 2006. In addition to the Welch engraving, Kent Bowerly did the stock, Jim Wisner did the metalwork and Ray Montgomery did the bluing.*
Tom Alexander Photography.

A Craig Click-crafted dangerous game rifle for the author. It features a pre-64 Model 70 action, a Krieger cut rifled barrel, and a fine stock of California English walnut. The rifle is chambered for the 458 Lott cartridge.

▶ **This is the author's idea of ideal open sights on a dangerous game rifle. The H&H style "night sight" front with a large bead coupled with a single standing, shallow "V" rear sight, works great. The multi-folding leaf express sights are fine for show, but impractical in the field. Gunmaker Craig Click did this work for the author.**

Photo by Tom Turpin.

▶ **John Maxon's personal varmint rifle. John started with a Remington 40X action and fitted a Hart 3-groove barrel chambered for the 6BR cartridge. He further fitted an AR-15 extractor and a Jewell trigger. He stocked the rifle in a piece of quarter-sawn American black walnut to suit himself. John holds membership certificate #1 in the American Custom Gunmakers Guild.**

Tom Alexander Photography.

▲ **This was originally a commercial Mauser that has been completely re-worked. Dave Norin did the metal finish work and Al Lofgren did the very Germanic stock, including the ivory inlay.**

Tom Alexander Photography

Gary Goudy's personal Winchester Model 63. Who said the shoemaker's kids never had new shoes? The metalwork is strictly factory on this rifle, but Gary did the lovely stock and Rulph Bone did the engraving. This is a squirrel rifle supreme.

▲ **This rifle began as a 1909 Argentine Model 98 Mauser action, barreled and chambered for the 35 Whelen cartridge. The metal on this rifle was profiled in the 2005 GUN DIGEST custom section. All the work on this rifle was executed by gunmaker Dave Norin in his Waukegan, Illinois shop. The wood is California English which Dave obtained from Paul and Sharon Dressel. He added an ebony forend tip with a widow's peak, a Fisher grip cap and a leather-covered pad. He checkered it in a point pattern at 22 lpi and fashioned a shadow line cheek-piece. As stated, Dave did all the work on this rifle, including rust bluing, nitre bluing and color case-hardening, finish work that is normally farmed out to specialists.**

Photo by Tom Alexander.

A Ruger No. 1 from the shop of Jay McCament. Jay did extensive rework on the metal and crafted the lovely stock, checkering it in a 24 lpi pattern. Bob Evans did the engraving.

A relative newcomer to the business of firearms engraving (not the art of engraving), the work of Denis Reece is starting to pop up all over. Little wonder, he is doing very fine engraving. This is but one example of his work.

Tom Alexander Photography.

A really classy piece of engraving execution on this Ruger No.1 single-shot rifle was done by Barry Lee Hand. Still a young man, it is hard to fathom how he has progressed so far in such a relatively short time. Photo courtesy of Barry Lee Hand.

A lovely AyA sidelock (with hand-detachable locks) shotgun engraved by Bob Strosin. This gun was imported from the manufacturer in Spain in-the-white, as the owner wanted it engraved in this country. Bob obliged him very nicely.

Tom Alexander Photography.

▶ *Two views of the frame of a Hagn action that is chambered for the 416 Rigby cartridge. Engraver Sam Welch engraved a bear on one side of the frame and a Cape buffalo on the other. As is all of Sam's engraving, the work is exquisitely executed.*

Photos by Sam Welch.

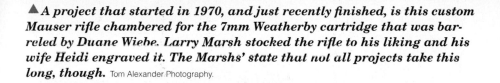

▲ *A project that started in 1970, and just recently finished, is this custom Mauser rifle chambered for the 7mm Weatherby cartridge that was barreled by Duane Wiebe. Larry Marsh stocked the rifle to his liking and his wife Heidi engraved it. The Marshs' state that not all projects take this long, though.* Tom Alexander Photography.

This rather unusual O/U shotgun is a factory original Beretta SO3EELL two-barrel set that was ordered by the current owner's father. Although not custom in the contemporary sense, it certainly is "different" and was ordered with custom features from the factory.

Tom Alexander Photography.

◀ *Ralph Bone has been around the custom gun and knife business for eons now and is still going strong. Shown here is a refurbished Remington #4 rolling block rifle that Ralph restored. It features a new Krieger barrel and all wood, metal and engraving work by Ralph— nothing like a one-stop shop.* Tom Alexander Photography.

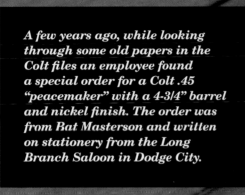

A few years ago, while looking through some old papers in the Colt files an employee found a special order for a Colt .45 "peacemaker" with a 4-3/4" barrel and nickel finish. The order was from Bat Masterson and written on stationery from the Long Branch Saloon in Dodge City.

THE GOOD OLD DAYS:
60 YEARS OF SIX GUNS

by John Taffin

That was then and this is now and these good days are certainly better than the good old days. The GUN DIGEST revolver catalog section requires nearly 20 pages, with small pictures, just to cover currently produced revolvers. Those old Colt and Smith and Wesson revolvers of the 1940s have pretty much disappeared, but have been replaced by many new models. We also find a large supermarket selection from Freedom Arms, Ruger, Taurus, and Wesson Firearms, and replicas of nearly every 19th century six-gun are found...

Oh, for the good old days! Just about everyone, especially those on the sunset side of life, has spent time longing for the good old days. As a writer, I have often talked about the good old days and the great old six-guns of yesteryear. However, if the truth be told, when it comes to medicine, transportation, communication—and especially firearms—these are the good old days!

Consider this. When the first edition of GUN DIGEST appeared in 1944, there were only two revolver manufacturers: Colt and Smith & Wesson. The GUN DIGEST catalog section required only a couple pages to cover their offerings—and occupied that space only by using large pictures. The successful conclusion of World War II was very current history and these two manufacturers were making the switch from wartime to peacetime production. The transition would not be immediate. Colt had moved their machinery for producing big-bore Single Actions and New Services to the parking lot in 1941. It does not take much imagination to realize what Connecticut weather did to the precision machinery during the war years.

Colt did not catalog anything larger than the 38 Special, while Smith & Wesson teased shooters with the 357 Magnum and the 1926 Model 44 Special. Skeeter Skelton joined the Border Patrol around 1950, and would later write about how difficult it was to acquire a 357 Magnum. These magnificent six-guns would not return to civilian production until 1948 and it would be 1952 before Skelton could come up with one.

That was then and this is now and these good days are certainly better than the good old days. The current GUN DIGEST revolver catalog section requires nearly 20 pages, with small pictures, just to cover currently produced revolvers. Those old Colt and Smith & Wesson revolvers of the 1940s have pretty much disappeared but have been replaced by many new models. We also find a large supermarket selection from Freedom Arms, Ruger, Taurus, and Wesson Firearms, and replicas of nearly every 19th-century six-gun are found. Yes, these definitely are the good old days.

Let's take a look at 60 years of great six-guns and how we got from the nostalgic good old days to today—the real good old days. Please realize this is not a complete discourse and all we can do is hit the highlights, basically of only big-bore six-guns. Several large books have been written about Colt, Ruger, and Smith & Wesson—and even these are necessarily incomplete.

During the late 1940s Smith & Wesson teased shooters with images of 357 Magnums and the 44 Special. However, it would be the 1950s before they were available.

Smith & Wesson– Double Action Perfection

As we mentioned, after the end of World War II it took several years for Smith & Wesson to resume production of the 357 Magnum. Pre-war and early post-war six-guns from Smith & Wesson had the old long action; beginning in 1950, that action design was changed to give a shorter hammer fall. Most double-action shooters preferred the smoothness of the older long action; however, it was gone forever. The year 1950 saw several significant revolvers

In the mid-1960s Smith & Wesson introduced their third big-bore Magnum chambering, the 41 Magnum Model 57 in both blue and nickel, with barrel lengths of 4, 6, and 8-3/8 inches.

In the late 1980s, the new wave of Smith & Wesson six-guns arrived with rounded butts and heavy underlug barrels. Shown (counterclockwise from top left): the Model 625 45ACP, Model 625 45 Colt and theModel 686 357 Magnum.

introduced. Though it is not a big bore, the Chiefs Special arrived as the first five-shot J-frame and would set the standard for pocket pistols. The 4th Model 44 Hand Ejector arrived as the 1950 Target Model 44 Special. These were beautifully made six-guns, mostly found with 6 1/2-inch barrels, with a few rare 4- and 5-inch versions also made. A companion six-gun was the 1950 Target Model 45 ACP, also with a 6 1/2-inch barrel, with a few actually being made in 45 Colt. When Smith & Wesson went to model numbers in 1957, these two big-bore revolvers became the Models 24 and 26. The companion fixed-sight Military Model, in 44 Special *(especially rare)* and 45 ACP, was introduced in 1951 and became the Model 21 and 22, respectively.

Relatively speaking, the 357 Magnum was fairly expensive to produce, so in 1954 Smith & Wesson offered the same basic revolver, with a matte blue finish, as the Highway Patrolman. As its name suggests, it became very popular with peace officers and outdoorsmen as a no-frills heavy-duty 357 Magnum. One year later Smith & Wesson upgraded the 1950 Target 45 ACP to the 1955 Target with a heavy bull barrel, target hammer, and target trigger. Later known as the Model 25, it would also be offered in 45 Colt. The year 1955 is also especially significant for two very radical—at the time—new revolvers. The Military & Police 38 Special had been around since 1899 and was very popular with peace officers even after the advent of the heavier 357 Magnum. Border Patrolman Bill Jordan began lobbying Smith & Wesson to build a 357 Magnum on the same size frame as the Military & Police. They listened, and the result was the 357 Combat Magnum, a Military & Police with a heavy bull barrel and an enclosed ejector rod housing. It was widely accepted as the peace officer's dream revolver. By 1957 it was known as the Model 19.

For nearly 30 years Elmer Keith had been trying to convince manufacturers such as Smith & Wesson to bring out a new revolver to house his heavy 44 Special loads. Ammunition manufacturers were

The early 44 Magnums of 1956 are known as pre-29s. Custom stocks are by Roy Fishpaw.

afraid such a load would find its way into older, weaker revolvers so Keith suggested a 44 Special magnum with a cartridge case the same length as the 357 Magnum to preclude it fitting the chambers of 44 Special six-guns. In 1954, Smith & Wesson—in conjunction with Remington—went to work on a new 44 six-gun and cartridge. The 1950 Target Model 44 Special was specially heat-treated and re-chambered to the new, longer 44 Magnum. Keith had asked for a 1200 fps load and received a true magnum with a 240-grain bullet at 1450 fps.

A new era in handgunning had just begun and the increasing popularity of handgun hunting coincides with the arrival of the 44 Magnum. The Smith & Wesson 44 Magnum, complete with full-length cylinder and heavy bull barrel, would become the Model 29 in 1957.

After the 44 Magnum arrived, both Elmer Keith and Bill Jordan began petitioning Smith & Wesson for another new revolver, a 41 to be used by peace officers. Smith & Wesson listened but took a different path and simply chambered the Model 29 for the new 41 Magnum cartridge. It was known as the Model 57 and was accompanied by an oversized Military & Police version, the Model 58. Both six-guns and ammunition were deemed too heavy for police use; however, they did find a special niche with hunters and outdoorsmen.

All of these six-guns are now gone. The Models 21, 22, 24, and 26 were dropped in 1966; the Models 29 and 19 in 1999; Model 25, 1991; Model 57, 1993; and even the original 357 Magnum was gone by 1994, preceded by the 1986 demise of the Highway Patrolman Model 28. It is obvious Smith & Wesson took a new direction in the 1990s.

In 1965 Smith & Wesson introduced the Chief's Special in what would become the material of the future, stainless steel. This was the first successful revolver so constructed and there was some doubt as to whether it could be used with

Top: The early 44 Magnums may stir the emotions; however, the underlug-barreled MagnaClassic and Classic DX are stronger and will usually outshoot the early six-guns.
Above: In the 1980s, S&W briefly resurrected the 44 Special in both the blued Model 24-3 and stainless steel Model 624.
Right: The Smith & Wesson got smaller in the 1990s and early 2000s with the five-shot 44 Special Model 696 and Model 396Ti, and the 12-ounce 340Sc in 357 Magnum.

heavier cartridges. That doubt was removed beginning in 1971 with the stainless steel version of the Model 19 Combat Magnum, the Model 66. This opened doors to the point where the majority of big-bore revolvers are now made of stainless steel. In 1979 the first truly big-bore stainless steel Smith & Wesson arrived, the 44 Magnum Model 629. A significant change had definitely been made.

The year 1980 saw a major change in 357 Magnum production as Smith & Wesson introduced the first L-frame. There were those who complained about the Model 19/66 not holding up with continued use of full-power 357 Magnum ammunition, so Smith & Wesson set about to improve matters, with the result being one of the most accurate 357 Magnums ever offered by the Springfield firm. To arrive at the L-frame, Smith & Wesson maintained the K-frame grip of the Model 66 *(as opposed to the larger N-frame grip of the Model 29 44 Magnum)*, enlarged the cylinder and the front of the frame around the barrel threads. Finally they added weight and stability by using a full under-lug barrel. In stainless steel, this 357 Magnum is known as the Model 686 while the blued version was the 586. The 686, available in both six-shot and seven-shot versions, remains in production and deserves a serious

look by anyone contemplating the purchase of a 357 Magnum.

The 44 Special had been dropped in 1966 and almost immediately people began trying to convince Smith & Wesson to bring it back. At about the same time, a freelance writer by the name of Skeeter Skelton joined the staff of *Shooting Times* magazine and soon began writing about the 44 Special, and urging its return. Smith & Wesson listened and produced a total of 7500 4-inch and 6 1/2-inch Model 24-3s in 1983, followed by a larger run of the same basic six-gun, the Model 624 in stainless steel, from 1985 to 1987.

By now stainless steel was firmly established as the material of the future and the 41 Magnum became the Model 657 in 1986, while the

heavy under-lug Model 625 stainless steel six-guns began emerging in both 45 ACP and 45 Colt in 1989. Standard-contour barrels and square-butt grip frames had pretty much been replaced by heavy under-lug barrels and round-butt grip frames.

In the late 1980s and early 1990s Smith & Wesson made the necessary interior changes to their action, which resulted in the Endurance Package. Action parts were more tightly fitted and cylinder bolt slots were made longer. As a result, the stainless-steel heavy underlug-barreled Model 629s will endure heavier loads longer without shooting loose, as the older Model 29s were wont to do.

In 1996 Smith & Wesson took a new path with the 44 Special, offering it as a five-shot L-frame Model 696, followed three years

Shooting the 4-inch Model 500.

▶ *Far Right: The 4-inch Model 500 S&W dwarfs the Model 29 Mountain Gun in the background*

A half-century of evolution of the Smith and Wesson 44 Magnum: a nickel-plated Model 29, stainless steel Model 629, and Model 629 with built-in muzzle brake. Custom stocks are by BluMagnum, Bear-Hug, and Hogue.

later with the 396Ti lightweight L-frame; partially constructed of the new material for revolvers: titanium. Before the end of the century, S&W revolvers were being fitted with interior locks activated by a key in a small hole above the cylinder release latch.

Titanium was soon joined by scandium and the result, in 2001, was the seven-shot, L-framed Model 386Sc Mountain Lite, an 18 1/2-ounce 357 Magnum. Smith & Wesson did not stop there and also introduced the Chief's Special Model 360Sc and Centennial Model 340Sc, 12-ounce (!) five-shot, J-frame 357 Magnums. Considering these extremely compact 357 Magnums, it is most interesting to go back and read articles about the three pound-plus original 357 Magnum and its recoil, as perceived in the 1930s and 1940s. The 340Sc

kicks to be sure; however, it is quite manageable with 125-grain JHPs and can be carried, virtually unnoticeable, in a pants pocket all day.

As this is written, the latest magnum from Smith & Wesson is the ultralight 26-ounce Model 329PD titanium/scandium 44 Magnum. If the titanium/scandium 357 Magnum kicks, then this one really kicks. Loaded with 44 Specials, it becomes

an easy shooting and very portable big-bore six-gun. Two or three 44 Special rounds, followed by the same number of 44 Magnums, afford a lot of versatility. If you are in territory where a large angry beast could be encountered, load all 44 Magnums.

Smith & Wesson introduced the 357 Magnum in 1935, the 44 Magnum in 1955, the 41 Magnum in 1964, and then faded into the shadows as the 454 Casull, 480 Ruger, and 475 Linebaugh arrived from other manufacturers. However, S&W is once again the King of the Magnum Six-Guns following the introduction of the new X-frame 500 S&W Magnum capable of handling 440-grain bullets at 1600+ fps. Offered in either an 8 3/8- or 4-inch version—both with heavy under-lug ported barrels—this surely represents the ultimate, the apex, the top of the mountain—we simply cannot come up with a more powerful hand-held revolver. Of course, the same was said about the 357 Magnum, and then the 44 Magnum.

We have covered only the high spots and I highly recommend the

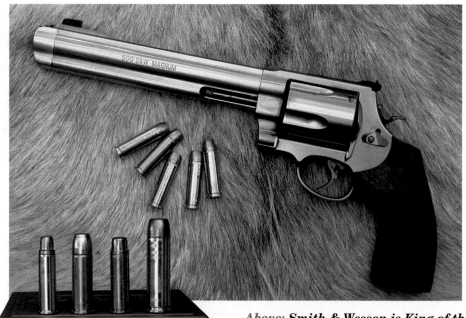

Above: Smith & Wesson is King of the Magnums once again with the X-frame Model 500 chambered in 500 S&W Magnum.

Left: The four big-bore magnum cartridges from S&W: 357 Magnum, 1935; 44 Magnum, 1955; 41 Magnum, 1964; and the 500 Magnum, 2003.

book *Standard Catalog of Smith & Wesson*, *Second Edition* by Supica and Nahas (Krause Publications 2001) for an in-depth study of all Smith & Wesson revolvers and semi-automatics going all the way back to the 1850s.

The Return of Big-Bore Colt Six-Guns

It took a while but in 1955 Colt finally reentered the 357 Magnum market. Prior to World War II, the Colt New Service was offered in 45 Colt, 44 Special, 44-40, 38-40, 45 ACP, 38 Special and 357 Magnum. Now it was gone. However, Colt took a look at their Officers Model Match, added a distinctively shaped and heavy ribbed 6-inch barrel, smoothed the action, and finished the entire six-gun in Royal Blue. It is without doubt the finest double action ever produced by Colt, and some fans will say it is the finest double action ever—period. Over the years it has been offered in blued, nickel, and stainless steel versions, as well as in three other barrel lengths: 2-1/2, 4, and 8 inches.

Never in my life did I lust for a six-gun as much as I did when Colt first started advertising the 4-inch blued Python. The Python, still in production today, is normally in very short supply.

Colt used the Officers Model Match 38 Special as the basic platform to build the 357 Magnum Python in 1955.

The Python, with its action design dating to the 19th century, requires a lot of hand-fitting, leading Colt, in 1986, to begin producing the King Cobra 357 Magnum with 4- and 6-inch barrels. The King Cobra was easier and cheaper to produce than the Python, and was very well known for its accuracy. However, as with so many Colt products the last quarter-century, it proved too expensive to make and so was removed from production.

For 35 years, Colt apparently considered the 44 Magnum a passing fancy. Finally in 1990 their biggest "snake," the Anaconda—sort of an over-sized King Cobra—was chambered in 44 Magnum, making it the first truly big-bore double-action revolver from Colt in 50 years. The Anaconda in stainless steel has been offered in both 44 Magnum and 45 Colt with a choice of 4-, 6- and 8-inch barrels, and 10-inch barrels are at least rumored. The 4-inch barrel version is extremely hard to find. The very early Anacondas had bad barrels; however, that was corrected quickly, and the Anaconda has proven to be a very accurate and very sturdy six-gun. It is still cataloged by Colt today.

Not only was the New Service deep-sixed by Colt in 1941, it was accompanied by the Colt Single Action Army. The New Service never returned, and Colt announced they

An object of Taffin's Shooter's Lust, the 4-inch Colt Python.

The Colt Single Action and the New Frontier were produced in both 2nd Generation runs (top), and 3rd Generation (bottom). These are chambered in 44 Special.

had no plans to ever produce the Single Action Army again. However, after considering the popularity of Western movies on the relatively new medium of television in the early 1950s, coupled with the success of the Ruger Single-Six, Colt changed their mind, re-tooled, and in 1956 brought back the Colt Single Action Army as the 2nd Generation production run. These were offered in both blue/case-colored frame and nickel, and in the three standard barrel lengths of 4-3/4, 5-1/2, and 7-1/2 inches, chambered for the 45 Colt, 44 Special, 38 Special and 357 Magnum. For some reason the 44 Special was never offered with a 4 3/4-inch barrel and the 45 Colt was also offered as a 12-inch Buntline. These 2nd Generation single actions were of excellent quality, at least until the machinery started wearing out in the 1970s.

In 1962 to celebrate or commemorate the New Frontier of John Kennedy, Colt brought out the New Frontier Single Action Army with a flattop frame, adjustable rear sight, and a ramp front sight. These are some of the finest revolvers ever offered by Colt and are mostly found in 45 Colt and 357 Magnum with the three standard Single Action barrel lengths. It is

rarely found in 38 Special and 44 Special, and never found with the 4 3/4-inch barrel in the latter.

In 1974 Colt again removed the Single Action Army from production; however, it returned two years later as the 3rd Generation model run that included a newly designed cylinder ratchet and hand, the absence of a full-length cylinder bushing *(which just recently returned)*, and different barrel threads. With all the old Colts out there going back to 1873 I cannot understand why

they changed the barrel threads when they had a ready market for replacement barrels with the old-style threads. The New Frontier was also resurrected and this time the 44-40 chambering was added, but the 38 Special was dropped. By 1984 all New Frontiers were gone.

The Colt Single Action Army has been an up-and-down, in-and-out, now Custom Shop, now standard catalog item since the 1980s. It remains in production today in the standard barrel lengths, in both blue/case-hardened and nickel finishes, chambered in 45 Colt, 357 Magnum, 38 Special, 38-40, 44-40, 32-20 and finally *(at last)*—the 44 Special is back. Most shooters and collectors hold the 2nd Generation Colt Single Actions in higher esteem than the 3rd Generation examples and they are priced accordingly. A few years ago, 3rd Generation Single Actions had a list price of $1600; however the price has dropped twice in the last five years and now they run about $1200.

Ruger Builds a Six-Gun Dynasty

The decade of the 1950s was the greatest period of six-gun development in the 20th century. Not only did Smith & Wesson introduce the Model 1950 Target and Military, the Highway Patrolman, the 1955

Bill Ruger combined the success of the Mark I and the inspiration of the Colt Single Action in the design of the first Ruger single action, the Single-Six.

Target, the Combat Magnum and the 44 Magnum; and Colt the 357 Python and the return of the Single Action Army; but a whole new source of six-guns arrived on the scene.

In 1949 Sturm, Ruger started business on a small scale with an inexpensive 22 semi-automatic; during the 1950s the company would become a powerful force in the industry. The 22 Mark I from Ruger had been a great success and with so many people asking for the return of a single-action six-gun, Bill Ruger built upon his success with the 22 auto by offering the Single-Six in 1953.

The Single-Six maintained the same size and shape in the grip frame as the old Single Action Army, while the frame itself was downsized commensurate with the 22 Long Rifle cartridge for which the revolver was chambered. In addition to these features, Ruger modernized the action by using all coil springs. The stage was now set for Ruger's entrance into the big-bore six-gun market. In 1955, Bill Ruger took the basic Single-Six, enlarged the frame to Colt Single Action size, flat-topped the frame, added an adjustable rear sight matched with a ramp-style front sight, and the result was the 357 Blackhawk.

The 357 Blackhawk was eagerly accepted for the nearly indestructible, powerful, outdoorsman's six-gun it was. It was promised in 44 Special and 45 Colt soon, however as we related in the section on Smith & Wesson, the most powerful cartridge since 1935—the 357 Magnum—was about to be pushed aside by the advent of the 44 Magnum. Ruger's plans changed as far as chambering the Blackhawk in 44 Special, and instead the frame and cylinder were enlarged to become the 44 Magnum Blackhawk. By 1956, I had all three Ruger single actions: a 5 1/2-inch 22 Single-Six, a 4 5/8-inch 357 Blackhawk, and a 6 1/2-inch 44 Magnum Blackhawk. If neither Ruger nor I had ever advanced past this point I still would have been in pretty good shape for the balance of my six-gunnin' life. However, no gun company has the option of staying the same. They either go forward, or slide back. Ruger went forward.

During the 2nd and 3rd Generation Colt Single Action Army production, the standard barrel lengths were/are 4-3/4, 5-1/2, and 7-1/2 inches; the 12-inch Buntline Special is no longer cataloged.

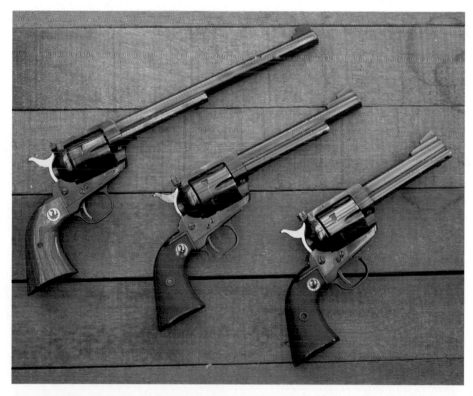

The 357 Flat-Top was offered in the standard barrel lengths of 4-5/8 and 6-1/2 inches, with the 10-inch version being very rare.

▶ *The Flat-Top 357 Blackhawks (left), were produced from 1955-1962; the Old Models (right), from 1963-1972.*

▼ *A new era of single-action six-guns for the outdoorsman began in 1955 with the Ruger 357 Blackhawk.*

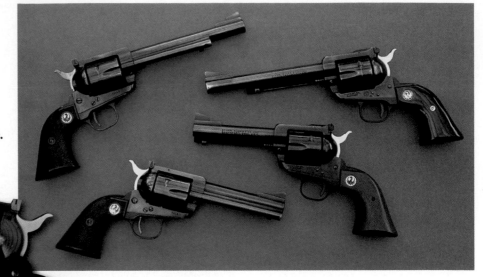

❦ ● ❦ ● ❦ ● ❦ ● ❦ ● ❦

In 1959, Ruger improved their 44 Flat-Top Blackhawk. The barrel length was standardized at 7-1/2 inches, an unfluted cylinder was fitted, protective ears were placed around the rear sight, and an all-steel dragoon-style grip frame with a square-back trigger guard replaced the Colt-style alloy grip frame. The extra weight and larger grip frame helped reduce felt recoil and the new Super Blackhawk was well on its way to becoming the number one six-gun among handgun hunters. The standard 44 Blackhawk would last until 1963, when it was dropped from production. The normal barrel length on the standard 44 was 6-1/2 inches; however, approximately 1000 each were made with 7 1/2- and 10-inch barrels.

In 1963 another change was made. The Flat-Top 357 Magnum became the Old Model following the introduction of a grip frame allowing

❦ ● ❦ ● ❦ ● ❦ ● ❦ ● ❦

▶ *The New Model (left) is safe to carry fully loaded with the hammer down; the Colt Single Action, Great Western, and three-screw Ruger* **MUST** *only be carried with the hammer down on an empty chamber.*

more room between the front strap and the back of the trigger guard, and protective ears around the rear sight as found on the Super Blackhawk. During the 1960s and early 1970s the 357 Magnum, built around a Colt Single Action-sized frame and cylinder, was joined by three other Blackhawks using the same size frame as the Super Blackhawk. The 41 Magnum arrived in 1965, the 30 Carbine in 1968 and the 45 Colt in 1971. This was the first time the 30 Carbine

was offered in a revolver, and for the first time shooters had a 45 Colt revolver capable of handling heavier loads than the Colt Single Action Army. It wasn't long before a 45 Colt load using a 300-grain bullet at 1200 fps became standard fodder for the 45 Colt, turning it into a true hunting handgun.

Since 1836 all single-action six-guns have shared the same basic action and, especially in the case of cartridge-firing revolvers beginning in the early 1870s, were only safe to carry with the hammer down on an empty chamber. This includes all Colt Single Actions, Great Westerns

◀ *Ruger's Bisley Model (top) uses a modification of the hammer, trigger, and grip frame of the original Colt Bisley.*

▼ *A classic single-action hunting handgun is the Ruger Super Blackhawk 44 Magnum.*

and Ruger three-screw models made prior to 1973. Ruger modernized the action of the single-action six-gun in 1953, and then 20 years later made it much safer. The New Model Rugers introduced the transfer bar safety that allowed safe carrying of a fully loaded single action, as the hammer did not contact the firing pin when it was in the *down* position. With the advent of the New Model, the three screws in the right side of the Ruger mainframe were replaced by two pins, the Colt Single Action-sized frame of the 357 Blackhawk was dropped, and all New Model Blackhawks and the Super Blackhawk shared the same large frame size.

By the late 1970s, long-range silhouette was the number one handgun sport, and special revolvers were offered by several companies to meet the long-range requirements of silhouette shooters. In 1979, Ruger's 44 Magnum Super Blackhawk with a 10 1/2-inch barrel was found on firing lines all over the country; my wife and I used a pair of 10 1/2-inch 44 Super Blackhawks for several years. Four years later, the Super Blackhawk, including the 10 1/2-inch version, arrived in stainless steel and, if anything, has proven to be even more accurate than the blued version. Today both blue and stainless steel Super Blackhawks are available with 4 5/8-, 5 1/2-, 7 1/2- and 10 1/2-inch barrels—and they are very popular with hunters and outdoorsmen.

In 1982, one of the finest long-range revolvers ever produced came from Ruger, designed especially for silhouette shooters. The standard 357 Magnum cartridge case was lengthened by 0.30-inch and the result was the 357 Maximum. Ruger's blued Super Blackhawk frame and cylinder were lengthened to accommodate the new cartridge and the combination proved exceptionally accurate. Unfortunately, some writers and shooters who did not understand the concept destroyed the project. The 357 Maximum was made to shoot 180- and 200-grain bullets

◀ *A classic single-action hunting handgun is the Ruger Super Blackhawk 44 Magnum. 3233) The Old Model Blackhawks were offered in (counterclockwise from top right) 357 Magnum, 41 Magnum, 45 Colt, and 30 Carbine. The latter was offered only with a 7 1/2-inch barrel.*

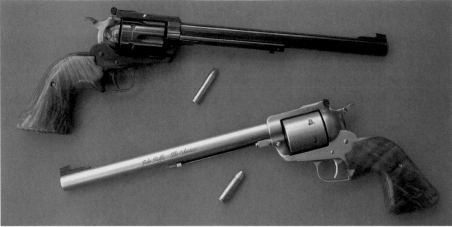

Two of the finest long-range six-guns, both with 10 1/2-inch barrels, from Ruger are the 357 Maximum and the stainless steel 44 Magnum. Custom stocks by BluMagnum.

at the same speed as the 158-grain 357 Magnum. When used this way the Maximum worked fine. However, it did not work well with lighter bullets at high speeds, with one of the problems being flame-cutting on the bottom of the top strap. This did not happen with the heavier bullets. This revolver should still be in production.

Many shooters, me included, did not care for the Super Blackhawk grip frame. For me it accentuates recoil as the angle is wrong and the square-back trigger guard raps my knuckle. Ruger looked at the Colt Bisley grip frame and Elmer Keith's

#5SAA modification that combined the backstrap of the Bisley with the trigger guard of the Single Action Army and came up with their own design—which is probably better than either of the other two. The backstrap rides high in the back, and not quite as high behind the trigger guard on the Colt Bisley and does an excellent job of taming felt recoil. The Bisley Model, except for special runs ordered by Ruger distributors, has only been offered in a blued 7 1/2-inch version in 44 Magnum, 45 Colt, 357 Magnum and 41 Magnum; the latter currently out of production.

In 1959 Ruger developed the Super Blackhawk as the best six-gun for handgun hunters. In 2002 Ruger went several steps farther. The standard 7 1/2-inch stainless steel Super Blackhawk was given a heavy ribbed barrel that accepted Ruger scope rings and the back of the square-back trigger guard was rounded off, the result being the Hunter Model. With its nearly instant removal or installation of the scope it is the number one hunting handgun bargain on the market today. It was improved in 2003 with the introduction of the Bisley Hunter Model; the same six-gun with a Bisley grip frame, hammer and trigger.

By the late 1980s and early 1990s, the number one handgun shooting sport in the country was cowboy action shooting, which required firearms made prior to 1899 or replicas thereof. In 1993 Ruger took their standard Blackhawk, removed the adjustable sights, rounded off the top of the mainframe, added Colt Single Action-style sights, and cowboy action shooters had the Vaquero. Its sales have exceeded all expectations and it is now the single-action six-gun most seen at cowboy action matches.

The Vaquero has been offered in both blue and stainless steel in 45 Colt, 44 Magnum, 357 Magnum and 44-40 with 4 5/8-, 5 1/2- and 7 1/2-inch barrels, however every barrel length has not been available in every caliber. A Bisley Vaquero is also offered with the two shorter barrel lengths, in 45 Colt, 44 Magnum, and 357 Magnum. The Vaquero is not only popular with cowboy action shooters but—especially in stainless steel and chambered in 45 Colt or 44 Magnum—has found a real home with those who spend a lot of time outdoors. Sights are filed-in to hit point of aim with a particular load, then the sights are never touched again.

In 1972 Ruger took another path with their first double-action revolver, the 357 Magnum Security-Six, and in 1985, the GP100 in 357 Magnum replaced the Security Six. Both revolvers have subsequently been made in other chamberings and other versions. The action of the GP100 differs from the Security

One of most popular revolvers with both cowboy action shooters and outdoorsmen is the Ruger Vaquero, here in 45 Colt and stainless steel with leather by The Leather Arsenal.

stainless steel and scope-ready, with the choice of either a 7 1/2- or 9 1/2-inch barrel. It is unique among revolvers in that it has an extended frame that surrounds approximately three inches of the barrel. The Super Redhawk concept is definitely "function over form" as it is not a particularly attractive revolver. It is, however, very strong and very accurate.

The original chambering in 1987 was 44 Magnum. It is now also offered in both 454 Casull and 480 Ruger. The latter two chamberings are easily distinguished from the 44 Magnum model since, instead of a satin-brush stainless steel finish, they exhibit the Target Gray finish, which is achieved by using a different grade of stainless steel to accommodate the higher-pressure cartridges.

Ruger has been offering big-bore six-guns for half a century. They are virtually indestructible when handled with reasonable care, and will last longer than a lifetime.

Dan Wesson Has a Better Six-Gun Idea

In the 1980s, the Dan Wesson six-gun was king when it came to long-range silhouette shooting. Most shooters started with Rugers and Smith & Wessons. However, as Dan Wesson listened to silhouette shooters and provided better sights and longer and heavier barrels, the silhouette crowd migrated heavily to the Dan Wesson six-guns. My first true silhouette six-gun was the Dan Wesson 357 Magnum with a heavy 10-inch barrel. It was incredibly accurate and was followed by other Dan Wesson silhouette six-guns in

Six, as does the grip frame, as it has none. Instead, the GP100 uses a grip frame stud, which the grip wraps around. Between the introductions of the Security Six and the GP100 came the movie *Dirty Harry*. Clint Eastwood's portrayal of the 44 Magnum-carrying San Francisco detective in the early 1970s created a tremendous demand for 44 Magnum revolvers that Smith & Wesson could not meet—even when running their factory to capacity. Ruger looked at the situation and decided to build a 44 Magnum double-action revolver.

In 1980, the extremely strong, six-shot Ruger Redhawk chambered in 44 Magnum arrived. "Extremely strong" means it will probably handle heavier loads and handle them longer than the Super Blackhawk. It has been offered in both blued and stainless steel versions with 5 1/2- and 7 1/2-inch barrels and in 357 Magnum, 41 Magnum, and 45 Colt—in addition to the original 44 Magnum. It remains today only in 45 Colt and 44 Magnum, and in scope-ready models.

Seven years later Ruger introduced their second true big-bore double-action revolver, the Super Redhawk, using the grip frame stud of the GP100. The Super Redhawk is all

◀ *Dan Wesson offered a full line of SuperMag models, here shown in 357SM, 375SM, and 445SM.*

▼ *Two very popular six-guns with silhouette shooters in the 1980s were Dan Wesson's 10-inch Heavy Barrel 357 and 10-inch standard barrel 44 Magnum.*

44 Magnum, 357 SuperMag and the ill-fated 375 SuperMag. The 445 came along too late for me to use in silhouette matches.

Dan Wesson's popularity with the silhouette shooters was a good news/bad news proposition. As long as there were plenty of silhouette shooters, Dan Wesson had a strong market, but once the number of handgun silhouetters started to drop, Wesson was in trouble. Dan Wesson was caught in a squeeze between two factors: the general decline in silhouette shooting clubs across the country and the appearance of the Freedom Arms Silhouette Model chambered in 357 Magnum. Many of the serious shooters that remained in the game took up the Freedom Arms revolver.

Everything caught up with Dan Wesson in the early 1990s and the doors of the factory in Massachusetts closed. The company had gone through several hands, beginning with Dan Wesson; to the family when he passed on and they lost control to an outside group; then in the late 1980s the Wesson family regained control. Unfortunately, it was not to be. When I visited in the early 1990s, it was obvious the company was struggling. It was not too long before the doors were closed and the Dan Wesson revolver was no more. The passing of a truly innovative six-gun saddened many six-gunners.

Dan Wesson's great idea was unique; he planned to offer a basic revolver with interchangeable cylinders and barrels. This concept was revised somewhat and the Wesson revolver emerged in the 1970s as a six-gun that featured interchangeable barrels only. Normally barrels must be removed using a vise and an action wrench. Wesson, by using a barrel and shroud combination with a locking nut at the front of the barrel, made it possible for anyone to change barrels by using the special Wesson wrench supplied with every Dan Wesson six-gun.

The interchangeable barrel system delivered an unexpected bonus: Wesson six-guns were exceptionally accurate. This accuracy is normally attributed to the fact the barrel locked at the front of the shroud and the barrel/cylinder gap was set tightly by the user when

the barrel was installed. Wesson was also the first to offer interchangeable front sight blades. A six-gunner could have his or her choice of black post, or ramp; red, white, or yellow inserts for the front sights–all easily changed with an Allen wrench–and the post front sights were offered in several widths and heights.

Dan Wessons are being produced once again. Not in Massachusetts, but in New York. Using mostly new machinery, Bob Cerva of Wesson Firearms is turning out some beautiful six-guns, probably the best to ever wear the Dan Wesson name. The new Wesson Firearms is not only producing six-guns in the old standby 357 Magnum and 44 Magnum chamberings but also the 41 Magnum, 357 Supermag, 445 SuperMag, 414 SuperMag *(only a very few 414s were originally produced before the factory shut its Massachusetts doors)*, and even the 460 Rowland and 360 DW. The latter is on a case longer than the 357 Magnum but shorter than the 357 SuperMag case.

Editor's Note — *In early February 2005, CZ-USA announced it had purchased Wesson Arms. Manufacturing will continue at the New York location, and CZ will maintain its offices in Kansas City, Kansas.*

Freedom Arms Factory-Built Custom Six-Guns

Since 1983, Freedom Arms revolvers have been virtually custom-built in a small factory in Star Valley, Wyoming on the eastern Idaho border and are, in my opinion, the finest, strongest, factory-built single-action revolvers ever assembled. Every single-action six-gun from Freedom Arms is as close to perfection as it is humanly possible to build a single-action revolver. The first chambering was the 454 Casull, and the six-gun had to be specially built to withstand the tremendous pounding this cartridge affords a revolver.

Available only in stainless steel, Freedom Arms six-guns feature near-perfect cylinder and barrel alignment, and precision fitting of all parts. Tolerances are held to a minimum. Although thoroughly modern, the Freedom Arms offering is a traditionally styled single-action revolver. The cylinders on all full-sized Freedom Arms Model 83 revolvers are chambered for five rounds, providing extra steel between the chambers (in contrast to a six-shot revolver) and locating the cylinder bolt slot between—instead of above—chambers. The cylinder does not have the end shake or side-to-side movement fairly common in

most factory-produced revolvers—the result of tight tolerances throughout. The original 454 Casull chambering has been joined by the 44 Magnum, 357 Magnum, 50 Action Express, 41 Magnum and 475 Linebaugh. Standard barrel lengths are 4-3/4, 6, 7-1/2 and 10-1/2 inches, with other lengths—as well as octagon barrels—offered on a custom basis.

At the Shootists Holiday in 1996, I had the pleasure of test-firing two new Freedom Arms revolvers. Built to about 90 percent of the size of the 454 Casull (slightly smaller than a Colt Single Action Army), one

▲ *For easy packing and portability combined with reasonable power, Freedom Arms offers the Model 97, here shown in 45 Colt and 44 Special.*

▼ *This quartet of 7 1/2-inch Model 83s from Freedom Arms covers everything when it comes to handgun hunting: for small game and turkeys, the 357 Magnum; for deer-sized game, the 44 Magnum; for Africa and Alaska, the 454 and 475. It is also available in 41 Magnum and 50 Action Express.*

▶ *Two of the top candidates for the title of "Perfect Packin' Pistol," the 4 3/4-inch Freedom Arms Model 83 in 454 and 475.*

❀●❀●❀●❀●❀●❀

was chambered in 45 Colt, and the other—the first true six-gun from Freedom Arms—carried six chambers for the 357 Magnum. Although I was able to shoot these prototypes, I had to keep the news under wraps until they were officially unveiled at the 1997 SHOT Show in Las Vegas.

This new six-gun was first called the Mid-Frame, a temporary name until the logical name Model 1997 was applied. The first Model 97s were offered with fixed or adjustable sights, in 357 Magnum with 5 1/2- or 7 1/2-inch barrels. Other chamberings followed, including five-shot versions in 45 Colt, 41 Magnum, and 44 Special; and six-shot convertibles with extra cylinders in 22 Long Rifle/22 Magnum and 32 Magnum/32-20. The Model 97 is built to the same tolerances as its

❀●❀●❀●❀●❀●❀

▼ *Taurus offers the Raging Bull in three serious handgun hunting chamberings: 44 Magnum, 480 Ruger and 454 Casull.*

bigger brother, the Model 83, and of the same high quality materials. If one does not need the muzzle energy of the more powerful chamberings found in the Model 83, the Model 97 makes an excellent and easy-carrying packin' pistol. It is now also available with 4 1/4- and 10-inch barrels, and octagon barrels are a custom option. The latest chambering is the relatively new 17 HMR.

Taurus Bullish about Six-Guns

For several years Taurus was looked upon as a cheaper alternative for those who wanted a 22, 38 Special, or 357 Magnum revolver. This all changed with the coming of the Model 44 in stainless steel, chambered in 44 Magnum, which proved to be an exceptionally accurate revolver. At the 1997 SHOT Show, Taurus became the first major company—other than Freedom Arms—to chamber one of their six-guns for the 454 Casull. The prototype model shown to gunwriters did not cause much excitement; it did not even appear to have a forcing cone. As 1997 progressed, no range-test articles of this gun appeared in any of the gun magazines.

One year later, at SHOT Show 1998, a new Taurus six-gun was unveiled in 454 Casull, along with a presentation by Taurus of the first 454 Casull Raging Bull to the designer of the 454 cartridge, Dick Casull. Taurus had done their homework after SHOT Show 1997, returned to the drawing board, and delivered the best looking double-action six-gun they have ever produced—the Raging Bull Model 454.

Available in both a deep well-polished blue and a frosted matte

stainless finish and in either 6 1/2- or 8 3/8-inch barrel lengths, the Raging Bull features a massive five-shot cylinder, a heavy top strap, a bull barrel with a full underlug and ventilated rib, and user-friendly rubber grips. Today it is also offered in a 5-inch version and also chambered in 44 Magnum and 480 Ruger. All models contain a built-in porting system consisting of a chamber that has four holes on each side of the front sight. This porting is approximately 1-1/4 inches long, so a 6 1/2-inch barreled model is actually slightly over 5 inches as far as the rifling in the barrel goes, while the 8 3/8-inch model is effectively a 7-inch six-gun. Triggers are wide and smooth and the hammers are the semi-target type with user-friendly checkering. The Raging Bull is a sturdy, accurate revolver and good value for the money expended.

The Rise of Replicas

Sometime after the Great Western Frontier six-shooters disappeared in 1964 and before the Colt Single Action Army really began to command high prices, replicas from Italy began to arrive in this country. Those early examples were normally poorly finished, had brass grip frames—and only at a distance resembled the original Colt Single Action Army. They were used in many spaghetti Westerns made in the late 1960s and early 1970s. I have a hard time watching these movies for many reasons including the un-authentic grip frames on the "Colts."

The situation has really changed since the 1970s. Now we have authentic replicas of virtually every percussion revolver, including the Colt Paterson, Walker, Dragoon, 1851 Navy and 1860 Army, and the Remingtons. Cartridge-firing revolvers include copies of the Colt Richards Conversion, Richards-Mason Conversion, 1871-72 Open-Top, 1873 Single Action Army and Bisley Model; the Smith & Wesson Schofield and Model #3 Russian, as well as the 1875 and 1890 Remingtons. All of these replicas came about because increased interest in Western history, mainly due to the popularity of cowboy action shooting, created a demand for more authentically-styled replicas. Companies such as

▲ *Colt cartridge conversion replicas are also offered by Cimarron; grips by Buffalo Brothers.*

❀●❀●❀●❀●❀●❀

Cimarron, EMF, and Navy Arms worked with the Italian gunmakers to turn out more and better replicas. Today, these and other importers bring us truly authentic replicas.

The latest replicas are the 1875 and 1890 Remingtons from Hartford Armory. These are totally American-made revolvers and are basically exact duplicates of the early Remingtons. They are beautifully fitted and finished and chambered in 45 Colt and 44 Magnum. They are capable of handling the heavy 45 Colt loads I normally use in my Ruger 45 Colt Blackhawk.

USFA's Old-Time Single-Action Six-Guns

In the early 1990s I encountered a new source for replica single actions, a source with a gimmick—actually several gimmicks—no one else

❀●❀●❀●❀●❀●❀

◀ *Current examples of replica single actions are shown with these 7 1/2-inch 45 single actions from Cimarron. Grips by Buffalo Brothers.*

was using. The new importer was United States Patent Firearms Co. (USPFA) and they were importing Uberti parts and building the six-guns here in this country in the old Colt factory. Beautifully fitted and finished six-guns, I might add, and a cut above most imported replicas. Their goal was to eventually offer a totally American-made Single Action Army, and that took awhile.

Today, however, United States Firearms Co., now known as USFA, is offering single actions that are totally American-made, including materials sourcing. All the standard Single Action Army barrel lengths are offered, in blue/case-colored, full blue, or nickel. Available chamberings include just about any cartridge ever offered in the pre-war six-guns such as 45 Colt, 44-40, 38-40, 32-20, 41 Colt (the five top chamberings before WW II), as well as 44 Special, 44 Russian and 38 Special. Barrels can be marked the old way, such as "RUSSIAN & S&W SPECIAL 44" or "COLT FRONTIER SIX-SHOOTER" and sights may be the old, small hard-to-see style or the more modern square shape. There really is a practical limit for some of us when it comes to choosing between early authenticity and being able to see the sights. Both the blackpowder-style cylinder pin screw and the more modern spring-loaded catch are offered.

One of the first things noticed about the USFA

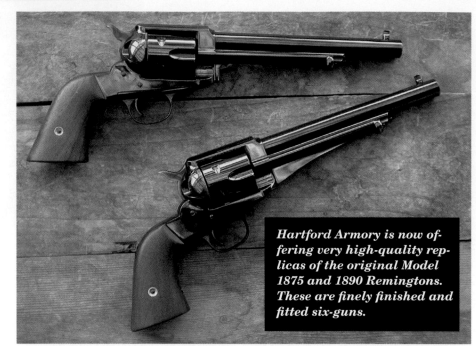

Hartford Armory is now offering very high-quality replicas of the original Model 1875 and 1890 Remingtons. These are finely finished and fitted six-guns.

Single Action Army is the beautiful finish. The frame and the hammer are beautifully case-colored while the balance of the six-gun is finished in a deep, dark Dome Blue. Grips furnished as standard are checkered hard rubber with a "US" molded into the top part of the grip. They are perfectly fitted to the frame and feel very good in the hand.

One of the things I always look for in the fitting and finishing of a single-action six-gun is the radiusing of the lower part of the back of the hammer and the two ears formed by the backstrap where it screws into the frame on both sides of the hammer. A well-made single action will exhibit a smooth contour symmetry of all three. USFA six-guns are very nearly perfect in this respect and the same careful fitting can also be found where the top of the face of the hammer meets the top strap. The fit of the trigger guard to the bottom of the frame is so perfectly done one can run a finger over the area and not feel where one part begins and the other ends. The same is true where the backstrap meets the frame.

The front of both the ejector rod housing and the cylinder is beveled which not only looks good and feels good, but permits easier holstering. Markings on these six-guns include the serial number in three places: the butt, in front of the trigger guard, and on the frame in front of the trigger guard screw—exactly as the original 19th-century Single Action Armies were marked. Cylinders lock up tight both in the hammer-down and hammer-cocked position. In

❦ ● ❦ ● ❦ ● ❦ ● ❦ ● ❦

◀ *These 45 Colt Great Westerns were originally shown on the January 1955 cover of* Guns *Magazine.*

addition to the standard Single Action Army, USFA also offers the old 1890s Flat-Top Target Model in various chamberings and barrel lengths.

Good Gone Six-Guns (GW and TLA)

One year after Ruger introduced the 22 Single-Six, another new gun company in California started building a replica of the Colt Single Action Army. Great Westerns would be pictured on the cover of the first issue of Guns magazine in January 1955. Those two six-guns were chambered in 45 Colt and, 50 years later, I had the pleasure of actually shooting them. Gunsmith Jim Martin of Arizona had to do considerable work to get them in top shooting order and they proved worthy the effort as both are very accurate.

The Great Westerns looked enough like Colts that pictures of real Colts were used in the original advertising; they also incorporated some genuine Colt parts from the Colt factory. At first they were offered with Colt-style firing-pin hammers, or a floating, frame-mounted firing pin. The standard Great Western was a 5 1/2-inch blued and case-colored 45 Colt. Also available were other barrel lengths, 4-3/4 and 7-1/2 inches, as well as other chamberings: 44 Special, 44-40, 38 Special, 357 Magnum, 357 Atomic, 44 Magnum, 44 Special and 22 Long Rifle. There was also a 12 1/2-inch Buntline Special.

Great Western supplied many six-guns to the makers of TV westerns, in fact if one watches those early programs it is easy to spot a Great Western when the hammer is cocked, as there is no firing pin to be seen. When Colt re-entered the Single Action Army market in 1956 the demise of Great Western was certain, even if the Colt sold for a 25-percent premium. By 1964, the Great Western was gone.

For both loading and unloading a Single Action Army, I always switch the six-gun to my left hand, working the ejector rod with my right hand— also using my right hand to reload— and then switch the six-gun back to my right hand for either holstering or shooting. Texas Longhorn Arms had a different way. Bill Grover's idea was to reverse everything; placing both the ejector rod housing and the loading gate on the left side of the six-gun, as well as having the cylinder rotate counterclockwise. This allows the right-handed shooter to hold the gun in his right hand while both loading and unloading operations are performed with the left hand. The six-gun never leaves the shooting hand. It makes sense; however, it does take some getting used to for one who has spent many decades doing it the other way with traditional single actions.

In the early 1980s Bill Grover began building his right-handed single actions. His first offerings were the West Texas Flattop Target and the South Texas Army. The former had a 7 1/2-inch barrel with target style sights, while the latter was a 4 3/4-inch TLA rendition of the standard Single Action Army. In 1987 Grover set out to build a salute to Elmer

Texas Longhorn Arms offered right-handed single actions as the Improved Number Five, the West Texas Flat-Top Target and the South Texas Army. Bottom six-gun has ram's horn stocks by Roy Fishpaw and the holster shown is one of the last George Lawrence #120 Keith holsters made before they close their doors.

Keith with his Improved Number Five. Grover sent me the original Improved Number Five serial number 1 for testing in 1988. Not only was I able to test this Number Five, I also compared it to the original. Although Keith died in 1984, I was able to meet with Elmer's son, Ted, and photograph the two six-guns side-by-side and also hold one in each hand. As expected, the grips felt the same.

There's no doubt the grip frame of the #5SAA inspired Bill Ruger to build the Bisley Model Ruger. However, the Ruger Bisley grip frame is much larger than the Keith design as Elmer had smaller than average hands. The Texas Longhorn "right-handed" single actions were beautifully made, finished, and fitted. Unfortunately TLA closed their doors in the late 1990s and these grand six-guns are now gone the way of the Great Westerns.

BFR—Really Big, Big Bores

The BFR comes from Magnum Research and the revolver is the all-stainless steel "Biggest Finest Revolver." Actually, this revolver started elsewhere and really went nowhere until Magnum Research took it over. The BFR looks very like a Ruger Super Blackhawk; the grip frames will accept the same grips. However, unlike Ruger six-guns, the BFR has a freewheeling cylinder that rotates clockwise or counterclockwise when the loading gate is opened. This is a great advantage if a bullet jumps the crimp and protrudes from the front of the cylinder, preventing it from rotating in the normal direction.

The BFR is offered in two versions: the Short Cylinder chambered in 454 Casull and 480 Ruger/475 Linebaugh; the Long Cylinder is offered in 444 Marlin, 450 Marlin, 45-70 and a special 45 Colt that also accepts 3-inch .410-bore shotgun shells. BFR revolvers are totally American-made with cut-rifled, hand-lapped, recessed muzzle-crowned barrels; tight tolerances; soft brushed stainless steel finish; and are normally equipped with an adjustable rear sight mated with a front sight featuring interchangeable blades of differing heights. I have tested the BFR in 45-70, 475 Linebaugh and 500 S&W Magnum. They are superbly accurate and function perfectly.

Custom Six-Guns

Sixty years ago there were very few custom six-gunsmiths. The coming of the Ruger Blackhawk provided a strong platform for custom work and now gunsmiths such as

Four great custom Ruger three-screws (clockwise from top left): 41 Special by Hamilton Bowen, and 44 Specials by David Clements, Ben Forkin and Andy Horvath. Each is a unique piece of artwork. Custom stocks on the two top six-guns are by BluMagnum and Larry Caudill.

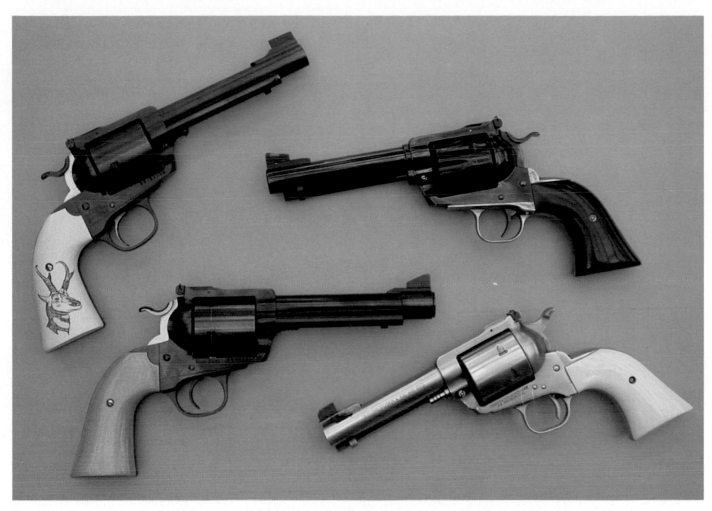

Hamilton Bowen, David Clements, Brian Cosby, Ben Forkin, Andy Horvath, Ken Kelly, John Linebaugh, Milt Morrison, Gary Reeder and Jim Stroh are turning out some of the finest six-guns ever built, with standard calibers being offered in the three-screw Blackhawks and five-shot heavy-duty chamberings—45 Colt and above—on the New Model Bisley. Both the Ruger Redhawk and Super Redhawk offer another solid platform for double-action conversions.

When the first GUN DIGEST came out in 1944, I was too young to pay any attention to six-guns; however, by the time #10 arrived I was wide-awake and shooting. I've seen a great deal of progress over the past half-century and have been able to enjoy all the grand six-guns that have been offered by the various manufacturers and many custom six-guns as well. I won't be around for all of the next 60-year period, but I hope to enjoy a sizable chunk of it. ✸

▲ *Three custom New Model Rugers (counterclockwise from bottom left): 500 Linebaugh by John Linebaugh, five-shot 45 Colt by Jim Stroh, and 357 Magnum by Milt Morrison. The latter is The Chameleon, with interchangeable barrels and cylinders also in 44 Magnum, 41 Magnum, and 45 Colt. The fourth six-gun is an Old Model Super Blackhawk by Mag-Na-Port.*

▲ *Two custom long-range Rugers: a 445 SuperMag built on a 357 Maximum by Ben Forkin, and a 357 Flat-Top by Gary Reeder.*

AMMUNITION, BALLISTICS & COMPONENTS:

A 60-YEAR OVERVIEW

by Holt Bodinson

We were cutting the ends out of tin cans, crushing them, bundling them and turning them in at curbside for wartime tin and steel extraction. Cooking fat was carefully strained off, collected and turned over for industrial recycling as well. Rubber automobile tires were almost impossible to buy. Meat was rationed. Oleomargarine replaced butter on the breakfast table.

You could forget about getting your hands on most calibers of ammunition unless it was hoarded old stock. Manufacture of ammunition for the civilian market virtually ceased. Fresh supplies of bullets, cases and primers? They were simply unavailable to handloaders. It was World War II and, as it ended, the first edition of GUN DIGEST made its debut. We thought the shortage in ammunition and components was over forever, only to watch it dry up again five years later when the Korean War started.

All wars accelerate new developments in the fields of armaments and ammunition. They

Looking back on 60 years... Joyce Hornaday was a tireless experimenter and early pioneer in developing component bullets for handloaders.

also breed generations of new shooters who, once exposed to firearms in the military, return home to enthusiastically pursue the sport in its civilian guise. Ironically, while WWII and the Korean War hit us hard when it came to availability of ammunition and components, those lean years ignited an entrepreneurial spirit that continues to this day to transform the ammunition and components industry.

During the inter-war period, the major manufacturers were pretty strapped themselves. Supplies and allocations of copper, brass and lead were limited so only the most popular calibers were returned to production. While listed in the 1940s editions of the GUN DIGEST, cartridges like the 38-56, 38-72, 40-65, 40-82, 45-90 and 41 Swiss rimfire were progressively weeded out of the lines.

And components? The majors weren't about to sacrifice their scarce slice of basic commodities to supply components to the marketplace, plus they didn't like the idea of handloaders and reloading anyway. They wanted to sell ammunition. The sale and distribution of ammunition at that time was almost entirely through local hardware stores, and hardware stores didn't want to be bothered with stocking components either.

It took some fascinating entrepreneurs in the 1940s to fill the demand for reloading components, men with vision like Fred Huntington, Vernon, Dick and Ray Speer, Joyce Hornady, John Nosler, R.B. Sisk, Fred Barnes, Bruce Hodgdon, P.O. Ackley, Roy Weatherby, Homer Clark, and small, focused bullet companies like Sierra, Western Tool & Copper Works, Arizona Bullet Company, Centrex, the Modern Gun Shop and others.

The vital role these early leaders played in getting the shooting community back on its feet after the wars, and their subsequent influence on developments at

ᘓᘯ●ᘓᘯ●ᘓᘯ●ᘓᘯ●ᘓᘯ●ᘓᘯ

During the war years, production of civilian ammunition virtually ceased. Shooters relied on old ammunition stocks.

Federal, Remington and Winchester, cannot be overemphasized. Much of the innovation and standards of performance in ammunition, ballistics and components over the last 60 years is indeed their legacies.

Huntington, Speer and Hornady got into the component business by using spent or unheaded 22 rimfire cases to form bullet jackets and finished varmint bullets in the 1940s and then branched off to carve out their own niches.

Huntington's early specialty was 22-caliber bullet forming dies

that he marketed to the individual handloader, later broadening off into reloading dies, presses, general tooling, and proprietary wildcat chamberings under the RCBS (Rock Chuck Bullet Swages) label. Today, Huntington "green" is the most common tool color on the reloading bench.

From his plant in Lewiston, Idaho, Vernon Speer grew the business and introduced products like the Hot-Cor hunting bullet, Lawman handgun ammunition, shot capsules and primer-propelled training

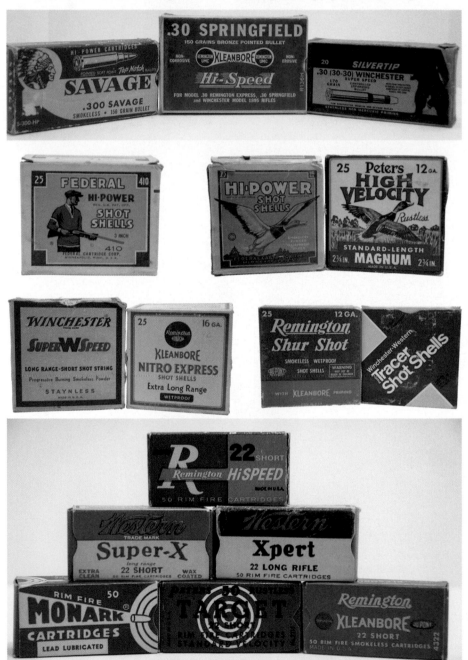

ammunition while his business manager, Ray Speer, compiled the first reloading manual in 1954. In 1975, Vernon sold the company to Omark which subsequently encouraged the development of Gold Dot, Mag-Tip and Grand Slam bullets and ammunition.

Dick Speer began making Newton and Weatherby cases using an impact extrusion process, but post-war brass quality proved unacceptable so he went into the primer and rimfire business. Forming Cascade Cartridge, Inc. (CCI), CCI became a major and reliable source for regular and magnum rifle, pistol and shotgun

primers, and percussion caps. Dick's CCI rimfire business was just as successful with the introduction of the Mini-Magnum. In 1967, Dick sold CCI to Omark, which continued the tradition with the introduction of the hyper-velocity "Stinger" 22 LR cartridge and the radical Berdan-primed, aluminum-cased Blazer centerfire handgun ammunition.

The Speer and CCI traditions continue today under their new owner, ATK.

Joyce Hornady and Vernon Speer were partners briefly in the late 1940s when they designed a machine to

convert spent 22 rimfire cases into jacketed varmint bullets. By 1949, Hornady was already producing 30-caliber bullets on surplus Waterbury Farrell assembly presses. From that point to the present, Hornady bullet selection has done nothing but expand dramatically year-by-year to give us the "Spire Point," the "Secant-Ogive" form, the "InterLock" jacket and "Extreme Terminal Performance (XTP)," "SST," "V MAX," "A-MAX" and "InterBond" bullets—as well as the early Frontier Ammunition line succeeded now by Hornady Custom Ammunition featuring brass drawn in-house by Hornady. An intriguing sidelight to Hornady is its recent involvement in cartridge design and development, giving us the 17 HMR, 17Mach2, 204 Ruger, 376 Steyr, and 450 Marlin.

When you look back over 60 years in ammunition, ballistics and components, there are some intriguing milestones and trends.

▲ *A young Fred Huntington explains the production of his swaging dies while Jack O'Connor examines a finished bullet.*
▶ *Vernon Speer founded Speer Bullets and developed products like the Hot-Cor bullet. Ray Speer, his brother, was the business manager and compiled the first Speer reloading manual in 1954.*

Finally factory components began flowing again.

We Needed the "Triple Deuce"

What really put varmint hunting, reloading, and benchrest shooting back on the map after the war years was the appearance of Remington's little 222 in 1950. Married to the relatively inexpensive Remington Model 722 and the Savage Model 340, the "Triple-Deuce" was an overnight hit and the first, new commercial cartridge to be put into production after WWII.

More importantly, Remington took the basic 222 case, lengthened it to form what we now know as the 222 Remington Magnum for the 1950s U.S. military trials, then modified it again to create the successful 5.56x45mm that was officially adopted by the U.S. in 1964 and subsequently by NATO.

Of course, we know it in its civilian garb as the 223 Remington. Of all the new cartridges, sporting or military, that have been introduced

Top Left & Middle: Over the last six decades, some reloading powders survived, some didn't.
Right: It was war-surplus 4831 that put Hodgdon in business.

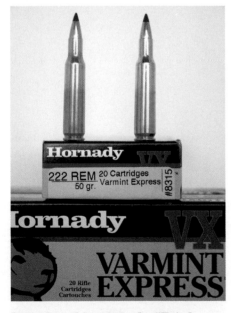

Introduced in 1950, the "Triple Deuce" revived post-war varmint hunting and handloading.

since the first edition of GUN DIGEST, none has had the same impact in the hunting world and on the target range and on the battlefield as the 223 Remington/5.56mm NATO. The "Triple-Deuce" spawned a winner.

Varmint and Dual-Purpose Calibers

In subsequent years, Remington continued to excel in the varmint category with the commercialization of the 6mm Remington, 223 Remington, 17 Remington, 22-250 Remington and the 25-06 Remington. One of the most sensational steps Remington took was to bundle a 55-grain 224-inch bullet in a sabot. Loaded in the 30/30 at 3400 fps and in the 30-'06 at 4080 fps, the "Accelerator" cartridges are still in the line. As successful as the Accelerator was, it is surprising the "sabot" concept didn't go any further in sporting centerfire rifle ammunition.

Winchester stumbled a bit with the introduction of the 225 Winchester, but more than made up for it by fielding the most popular 6mm cartridge ever introduced, the 243 Winchester. Winchester then turned around

and surprised us all with its radical "Super Short Magnums," the 223 WSSM, 243 WSSM, and 25 WSSM.

Curiously, while most gunnies were extolling the virtues of the short, squat 6mm PPC look in modern cartridge design, Hornady and Ruger teamed up in 2004 to design and chamber the long, skinny 204 Ruger, which, together with the 17 Remington, pushed muzzle velocities into the realm previously reserved for the mighty 220 Swift, or 4000 fps plus.

The Velocity Race Heats Up In Centerfire Rifle Cartridges

One of the classic articles in the 5th year of GUN DIGEST was a debate between Roy Weatherby and Elmer Keith entitled "High Velocity vs. Heavy Bullets." Over the next few decades, high velocity and cartridges carrying the name tag "Magnum" won and won big, not only in rifle ammunition but in the handgun, shotgun, and rimfire loadings as well. And the race is still on, it appears.

Weatherby continued to expand his proprietary high-velocity line that started with the 270 Weatherby in 1943, but Weatherby ammunition and rifles were a bit pricey for the average hunter. Remington chambered the 300 H&H in its inexpensive Model 721 as did Winchester in the Model 70, and the 375 H&H as well. It took the appearance of a new commercial case to really get things in motion.

The case was Winchester's 458 Magnum, introduced in 1956. Based on a shortened, belted, H&H case, the new Winchester case was just short enough to fit in a standard 30-'06-length action. It was not a new idea. P.O. Ackley and other wildcatters had done it. Weatherby's earlier 270 and 257 and Sharpe & Hart's 7x61 were based on shortened H&H cases. Winchester's advantage, though, was pricing and marketing, and Winchester quickly necked it down to create the powerful 338 Winchester Magnum and the screaming 264 Winchester Magnum.

Not to let a good thing slip by, Remington picked up the case in 1963 and necked it to 7mm, creating the highly popular 7mm Remington Magnum. Not to be upstaged by Remington, Winchester countered that same year and necked it to 30-caliber, giving us probably the best balanced and most useful cartridge of the lot, the 300 Winchester Magnum.

The magnum race in centerfire rifle cartridges has shown no sign of slowing down with the introduction of cartridges like Norma's 308 and .358 Magnums; Weatherby's 224, 240, 257, 270, 7mm, 300, 30-378, 340, 378, 416, and 460 Magnum series; the 350 Remington Magnum; 6.5mm Remington Magnum; 8mm Remington Magnum; 416 Remington Magnum; Remington's 7mm, 300, 338 and 375 Remington Ultra Magnum family and their 7mm and 300 Short Action Ultra Magnums; Winchester's 270, 7mm, 300 and 325 Short Magnum set and their 223, 243 and 25 Super Short Magnums; and the Dakota and Lazzeroni proprietary magnum cartridges. Might as well throw in the 50 BMG as well, since its popularity is currently soaring among long-distance bullseye shooters.

We even juiced up the older sedate rounds like the 30-'06 to magnum velocities. Hornady the way with its Light and Heavy Magnum loadings and, shortly thereafter, Federal introduced its own line of High Energy ammunition.

Stay tuned though. The velocity race isn't over yet until we get speed-of-light ray guns. In fact, Lazzeroni just announced he's working on the 7.82 (.308-inch) "Battle Star," designed to launch 180-grain bullets at a warp speed of 3850 fps!

Recently, the most significant trend in magnum case design has been the abandonment of the H&H belt in favor of a rimless magnum case, often in a very shortened form. In fact, the day of the magnum symbol, the H&H belted case, is over.

Compact and Balanced

Winchester couldn't have predicted how successful their family of short-action rifle cartridges would become when they introduced the 308 Winchester in 1952. In 1955, they necked it down, to create the 243 Winchester and up, to give us the 358 Winchester. They left a few bases uncovered though and Remington, seeing an opportunity, moved in on the basic case, transforming it into the 7-08 Remington in 1980 and later, the 260 Remington.

On the other hand, the most radical of the early compact, non-belted, short-action cartridges was Winchester's totally original 284 Winchester. Introduced in 1963, sporting a 35-degree shoulder, a rebated rim, and chambered in the Model 100 semi-auto and Model 88 lever gun, the 284 Win's fate was sealed when neither model caught on with the hunting public.

Remington caught us off-guard in 2004 by taking the old 30 Remington case, shortening it a bit, necking it down to 270, and offering it as the 6.8 Remington SPC (Special Purpose Cartridge). Of course, the 6.8 Remington SPC has military purposes since it will fit the action and magazine box of the M16, but nevertheless, it falls neatly into the industry-wide pursuit of "low recoil" ammunition.

The aging 30-'06 case was not forgotten though when, in 1957, Remington altered it slightly and created the ever-popular 280 Remington.

The most interesting trend lately has been the introduction of reduced, "low- or managed-recoil" loadings for old standards like the 270 Winchester, 308 Winchester, 30-'06, 7mm Remington Magnum and 300 Winchester Magnum. Federal, Remington and Winchester see a whole new market for milder loadings that will appeal to younger shooters, women and recoil-sensitive marksmen.

Power to the Levers

One would have thought the lackluster reception given the advanced Winchester Model 88 lever action, chambered in contemporary cartridges like the 243, 284, 308, and 358 Winchester, would have cooled any further interest at Winchester in lever guns and power, but it was not to be so.

In 1978, Winchester rolled out the first of the "Big Bore" chamberings in the Model 94, the 375 Winchester, to be followed by the 307 Winchester (a 308 Winchester clone), 356 Winchester (a 358 Winchester clone) and the distinctive 7-30 Waters; all remarkably good cartridge designs—but the public just wasn't buying into the concept.

Meanwhile, over at Marlin, the story is a bit more positive. Crafted for the Model 1895, the powerful 444 Marlin appeared in 1964, to be followed by the 450 Marlin in 2000. Public acceptance of these big-bore boomers, together with Marlin's successful revival of the 45-70, helped along by Garrett Cartridge's pachyderm-slaying loads, indicate the lever-action crowd likes large-caliber cartridges.

Wild West Guns of Anchorage, Alaska simply confirms this trend with the active business in offering modified Marlin 1895s chambered for their 457 Magnum (a stretched 45-70), 50 Alaskan, and their own "04" lever gun chambered for the 500 S&W and 454 Casull.

The future looks bright for new developments in sporting ammunition. Stay tuned.

A Caseless Future?

Where does rifle ammunition go from here? Probably, the caseless concept will again make its appearance after several abortive attempts. In 1995, I had the pleasure of tagging a nice whitetail buck with a Voere 6mm electronic ignition pistol firing JagerSport caseless ammunition. The pistol, in either 22 or 6mm caliber, grouped caseless JagerSport ammunition into less than an inch at 100 yards. Unfortunately, neither the pistol nor the caseless ammunition was commercially successful. I still think it's the future.

Magnumitis Hits the Handgun Line

Coming out of the war years, the 357 Magnum reigned supreme as the hot handgun load, but there were some persistent and persuasive experimenters like Elmer Keith, Al Goerg, Lee Jurras of Super Vel and Dick Casull who were about to change that.

Introduced in 1955, the 44 Magnum hit the road a-runnin'

and has never slowed down. When introduced, it was considered to be the ultimate big-bore handgun cartridge. It was judged to be just about all a person could handle in terms of recoil and, as a result, Smith & Wesson cooked up the 41 Magnum in 1964 to tone things down a bit. But how things have changed.

Now we have the 41 Magnum, 44 Magnum, 454 Casull, 45 Winchester Magnum, 475 Linebaugh, 460 S&W, 480 Ruger, 50 AE, and 500 S&W on the large end of the scale; the 221 Remington Fireball and 32 H&R Magnum on the small end of the scale; and new cartridges like the 9x23 Winchester, 357 SIG; 356 TSW, 40 S&W, 10mm, and the 45 GAP holding onto the middle. We even jazzed up the sedate old 38 Special with a +P rating.

If you factor in the chamberings available in the T/C Encore and Contender pistols, just about anything goes in handguns these days, including J.D. Jones' 620 JDJ for the Encore that combines a 1000-grain 600 Nitro bullet with a necked-up 577 Nitro case.

Cowboys and Cowgirls

No one predicted it, but the cowboy action sport really caught on across the world. The sport

not only brought in a whole new group of shooters, but it created an entirely new market for lead bullet and reduced velocity loads for rifle and revolvers. Every ammunition maker seems to have a cowboy line, with companies like Black Hills Ammunition even reintroducing cartridges like the 44 Russian, 44 Colt and 45 Schofield. Yahoo!

Shotshells Thrive On Plastic, Non-Toxic Shot and Speed

Shotshells suffered the same fate as metallic cartridges immediately after the war. A selection of loads was difficult to find anywhere and components were as scarce as hens' teeth. Riding to the rescue to bring components back into the market was Homer Clark of Alcan, who imported powder, primers and wads directly from Italy.

WWII had been responsible for some improvements in treating the paper tube to protect it from absorbing moisture and swelling, but Winchester-Western and Remington knew the paper wound-tube had to go. Consequently, they spent millions pursuing a plastic substitute.

It took a German technique, the Reifenhauser process, to successfully

When introduced, the 44 Magnum was considered the ultimate in handgun power, but cartridges like the 454 Casull and 500 S&W have supplanted it.

The new sport of cowboy action shooting has revived many an old cartridge.

❖ ● ❖ ● ❖ ● ❖ ● ❖ ● ❖

bring plastic shotshells to the marketplace in the 1960s. What the Reifenhauser process did was to work the plastic in such a way that both its tensile and radial strength were increased. The end product is known as bi-axial oriented tubing. Cut in shotshell-length segments, the tube and a separate base wad were then securely crimped into a metal head, producing a straight-walled case that was very strong

indeed, and ideal for reloading.

The next significant development in case design was Winchester's compression-formed AA case that appeared in 1965. Polyethylene slugs were placed in a die, heated, and then formed into a case by a punch. Surprisingly, the latest AA case is now produced using the Reifenhauser process. The ultimate example of a plastic case, I suppose, was the Activ design that featured an all-plastic case with a metal-reinforced rim.

Coincidental with development of the plastic case was Remington's invention of the one-piece plastic "Power-Piston" wad. It was a revolutionary design that combined the old over-powder wad, filler wads and plastic shot sleeve into one unit, while adding collapsing ribs that further cushioned the shot charge. It has influenced wad design ever since.

In 1987, Federal developed the 3 1/2-inch 12-gauge magnum shell that was designed specifically for steel shot. It was the product of the U.S. Fish and Wildlife's ruling that non-toxic shot would be mandatory for waterfowl hunting. The non-

toxic shot debate between the USF&WS and the industry was contentious to say the least but, for the industry, the writing was on the wall. It was either adapt or perish.

The introduction of steel shot required new wads, new powders, and harder shotgun barrels. The overall effect hit the average hunter hard in his pocketbook. On the positive side of the ledger, the non-toxic shot requirement stimulated the industry to find better lead substitutes than steel, and we now have bismuth, as well as a variety of new heavier-than-lead types like Hevi-Shot as loaded by Remington, Federal's "Ultra Shok High Density" and "Heavyshot" and Winchester's "Xtended Range High Density" shot.

❖ ● ❖ ● ❖ ● ❖ ● ❖ ● ❖

Below: **Quality control in the manufacture of ammunition is rigorous.**
Inset: **Winchester's lines of plastic shotshells begin with the granular polymers stored in these silos.**

Manufacturers have done an excellent job of developing non-toxic ammunition.

Factories are developing sub-sonic and low recoil loads for urban areas and recoil sensitive shooters.

When the first edition of Gun Digest hit the market, slug gun technology was fairly rudimentary. The soft lead "rifled" Foster slug was the industry standard and shotgun barrels were smooth. Not any more, slug guns now sport rifled bores and fire sabot rounds or aerodynamically designed slug-wad combinations at velocities over 2000 fps. Yet, Federal returned to the old, neglected Foster slug in 2004, placed a round plastic ball in its base which fits a dished-out wad in the case, called it "TruBall," and *voila!*, the old smoothbore slug gun began producing groups that were considered impossible just a year before.

The most intriguing trend in shotshells has been the velocity race, spurred on a bit by the higher velocities generated by steel shot loads. Today, we have 1-1/8 oz/2-3/4"/12ga. field loads

smoking out at 1500 fps+ at normal operating pressures. It will be interesting to see how far shotshell velocity creep will take us.

On the other hand, the major ammunition makers are heading in the opposite direction as well, giving us "managed-recoil" shot and slug loads—and even sub-sonic shot loads for quietly managing urban wildlife; in particular, golf-course geese.

The Rimfire Family Flourishes

When Gun Digest was first published, the rimfire calibers listed included the standard 22 RF, 22 Extra Long, 22 WRF, 22 Automatic, 25 Stevens, 25 Short Stevens, 32 Short, 32 Long and 41 Swiss. The 22 RF series and the 22 WRF survived as standard industry loadings. The others? Only as special runs by companies like the Old Western Scrounger.

If you asked the average farm boy in 1950 what he shot in his twenty-two, he probably would have responded, "Shorts or Longs." Yes, the Long Rifle was considered an expensive and premium cartridge back then. How times have changed. Now we can buy 500 Long Rifle shells for less than ten dollars.

The 22 Long and the 22 Short HP are certainly on the industry's short list these days. Only CCI seems to be keeping them alive. The Long's future is secure in the guise of the quiet, urbane, Long CB cap, but the Short's future is probably assured only in the form of a competition target cartridge.

1959 was a watershed year in rimfire cartridge design with Winchester's release of the highly successful 22 Winchester Magnum Rimfire (WMR). Featuring a 40-grain JHP and FMJ at 1910 fps, the 22 WMR was an instant success in the hunting world, and still is.

In 1969, Remington shook up the rimfire world, too, with the announcement of their 5mm Remington Rimfire Magnum that sent a 38-grain, 20-caliber, jacketed bullet downrange at 2100 fps. Those who tried it, liked it, but Remington made the mistake of chambering it

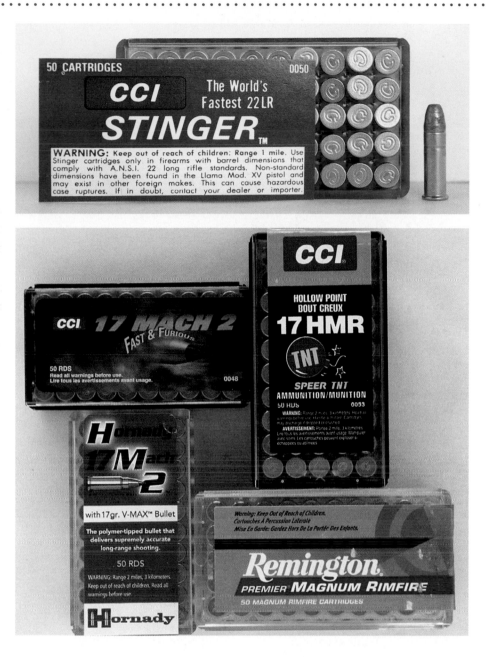

blessed with an endless supply of good components. Yet, factory ammunition is so incredibly accurate and affordable today that fewer of us are taking up the handloading hobby.

PRIMERS: Back in the 1940s and 50s, a primer was a just a primer, except that you needed four different primer seaters for rifle and pistol primers. There were small and large primers, of course, but there were also rounded primers and flat primers. Fortunately, the flat primers won out over time.

The real breakthrough was the development of magnum rifle and pistol primers, lead by CCI with their #250 and Federal—at Weatherby's prompting—with the #215. Now we have a choice of regular or magnum sparkplugs in every primer brand and size.

The next important advance was CCI's discovery that specific workers consistently produced more consistent primers. When those batches of primers were segregated, the result was the dawn of the benchrest-quality primer. CCI's lead has now been followed by Federal with their own benchrest brand.

The only radical revolution in priming has been Remington's electrical "Etronx" #9-1/2 primer, but it doesn't seem like it's burning a new hole in the ammunition world.

POWDER: When Bruce Hodgdon started shoveling war-surplus H4831 out of a boxcar, little could he imagine that his company would one day own Du Pont's old crown jewel, the IMR Powder Company. The acquisition movement in powder again saw another consolidation in 2004 when Western Powders Company, originator of the Ramshot line, bought out Accurate.

The tons of WWII surplus powders that moved into the handloading lines were a godsend.

in cheap rifles with lousy triggers, and the 5mm faded from the scene.

CCI threw the next fast ball in the rimfire world with the introduction of their sensational "Stinger" cartridge in 1977. Featuring an extended Long Rifle case and a 32-grain bullet at 1640 fps, it prompted Winchester to introduce their "Xpediter;" Federal, their "Spitfire;" Remington, their "Yellow Jacket" and "Viper" hyper-velocity loads.

The search was on for even more velocity, and Hornady and CCI gave it to us in the remarkable 17-caliber duo, the 17 HMR and 17 Mach 2. The 17 HMR with its 17-grain jacketed bullets churning up 2550 fps at the muzzle is proving to be the most accurate rimfire cartridge ever introduced, and a sensation in the small-game world. Sub-minute-of-angle groups at 100 yards are almost routine with even modestly-priced rifles. It's the 21st century response to the 22 WRM, and it's breathed new life into the rimfire world in general.

Components Flow Again

Following the dearth in components during the war years, the handloading world today is

Today, handloaders enjoy a wide selection of specialized primers.

❦●❦●❦●❦●❦●❦

The availability of inexpensive powder really did jump-start the whole handloading hobby industry—plus, the war gave us a new type of propellant—ball powder.

The blackpowder industry, too, underwent a revolution when Hodgdon began marketing the Pyrodex substitute and later, Triple Seven, both in granular and pellet form. Not to be left out of the replica race, blackpowder maker, Goex, came up with Clear Shot and recently, Pinnacle. Imported brands like Swiss, Schuetzen, and Elephant gave the blackpowder shooting fraternity a variety of powders to load and test.

The fact is that component powders have never been more available, and it's a worldwide market that includes Winchester, Alliant, IMR, Accurate, Rex, Ramshot, Norma, Vectan, VihtaVuori and others.

BULLETS: They're just getting better and better. While there was a trickling-in of German H-Mantle and Brenneke TIG and TUG bullets following the war years, together with our own Peter's Belted bullet, it was John Nosler who turned up the heat on bullet design with his creation of the Partition bullet, to be followed by Nosler's Ballistic Tip

❦●❦●❦●❦●❦●❦

and now the AccuBond. Meanwhile, Sierra focused on the accurate bullet, particularly for varmint hunting and competition, spurring on other makers to improve their jacket quality and dimensional consistency.

Recently, the most interesting trends have been the development of Barnes solid copper "X"-type bullets, bonded-core bullets, plated-jacket bullets like the Speer's Gold Dot, and environmentally-friendly lead-free or encapsulated bullets of all types and brands.

What has been fascinating is the growth of partnerships between the major ammunition manufacturers and component bullet makers. The leading example of this trend is Winchester and

Nosler working together under the Combined Technology label. Another good example is Federal, that currently loads the Trophy Bonded Sledgehammer and Bear Claw; Woodleigh Weldcore and Solid; Nosler Partition, Solid Base, Ballistic Tip and AccuBond; Barnes Triple-Shock X-Bullet; Sierra GameKing and MatchKing; and Speer Hot-Cor SP in its centerfire rifle lines.

If there is a mega-trend, it's in the direction of lead-free projectiles. We'll see more "green" bullets in the coming years.

BRASS: Winchester, Remington, Norma, Lapua, Hirtenberger and RWS have always supported the component brass market with standard caliber offerings,

The oldest propellant, black-powder, is still in production but alternative substitutes are popular as well.

Handloaders have a choice of over a hundred bullet styles to choose from today.

The colorful ammunition boxes of yesteryear don't hold a candle to the Old Western Scrounger's designs.

꧁●꧁●꧁●꧁●꧁●꧁

but the manufacturing base is rapidly expanding with newcomers like Hornady, Starline, HDS, and Horneber turning out a cornucopia of standard, proprietary and difficult-to-find brass.

Keeping our obsolete guns shooting, Bell and Bertram really deserve a pat on the back for drawing brass that no one else would...like the 351 Winchester, 40-90 Sharps, and 25-21 Stevens. Graf & Sons,

too, deserve our praise for stepping up to the plate to bring us brass, bullets and loaded ammunition for obsolete military cartridges ranging from the 6.5x52 Carcano to the 8x56 Hungarian Mannlicher.

WADS and HULLS: Like the powder market, the shotshell component market today is truly international in scope with components flowing from a number of countries, particularly Italy.

It was Italian hulls, wads and primers imported by Alcan that put shotshell reloading back on the map after WWII, and its Italian firms like Fiocchi where we can still find rarities like 24-gauge and 32-gauge shells. The whole flavor of the international shotshell components market can be savored by reading Ballistic Products' catalog.

Federal, Remington and Winchester have done an outstanding job of bringing to the market the exact same components that go into their best tournament shells. Their R&D in plastics have given us the most durable and reloadable shells ever offered, and they continue to innovate with new hull and wad designs.

SHOT: In the shot business, anything goes. Shotshell loaders now have access to soft shot, hard shot, copper-plated shot, steel shot, bismuth, Hevi-Shot and sabot slugs. If you can shoot it out of a smooth bore, you can buy it.

Looking Back

It's been a busy 60 years in ammunition design, ballistic performance, and the components that made it all possible...but hold on to your seat—it's going to get better, yet! ✺

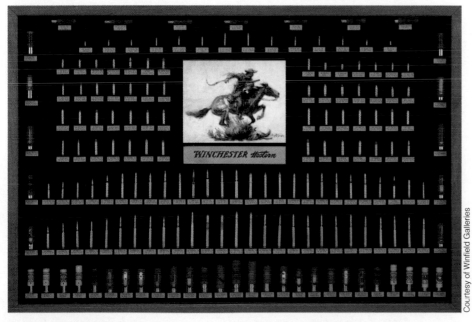

Courtesy of Winfield Galleries

Winchester Ammunition Cartridge Board (circa 1965).

TESTFIRE

◀ Shooting the Nosler rifle.
▼ Inspecting the first three-shot
  grouping fired from
  100 yards.

NOSLER'S
NEW
300 WSM
RIFLE

by Layne Simpson

*I*t is always nice to start off on the right foot when accuracy-testing a new rifle and that's exactly what happened when I fired my very first three-shot group at 100 yards with the new rifle from Bob Nosler and crew. The ammo was Nosler's equally new custom loading of the 300 WSM with the 180-grain AccuBond bullet and that first group measured 0.383-inch. The rifle I shot was no exception, and each one shipped will be guaranteed to shoot three bullets inside a half-inch with Nosler ammo. In the unlikely event the purchaser of one of these rifles is dissatisfied with its accuracy, workmanship or functioning within 30 days after purchase, the company will buy it back at full price—so long as it has undergone no modifications since departing the factory. And yes, this is the same Bob Nosler who makes Partition, AccuBond and Ballistic Tip bullets. The rifle, along with a line of match-grade ammunition and unprimed cases, is available from a subsidiary of Nosler,

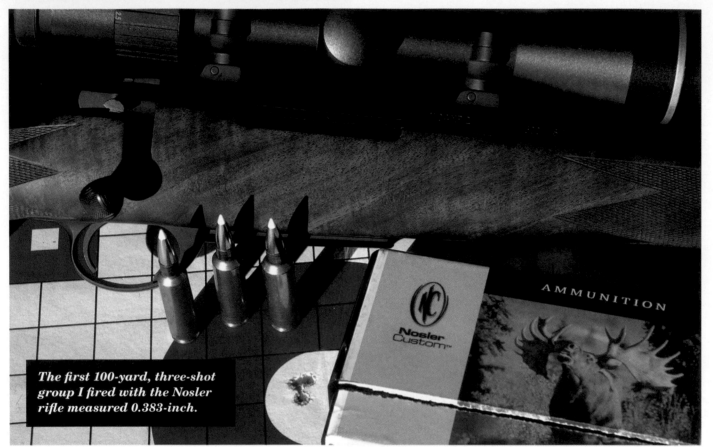

The first 100-yard, three-shot group I fired with the Nosler rifle measured 0.383-inch.

Inc. called Nosler Custom. While the rifle is not actually built by Nosler, each and every one of its component parts is made in America and each rifle is final-inspected and accuracy-proved by Nosler technicians.

Available direct from Nosler, the rifle can be purchased by U.S. mail, by telephone or by Web site (nosler. com), although shipment has to be made to the holder of a federal firearms license. The plan is to build rifles in only one caliber each year, and limit production to 500 units. The 2004 rifle is in 300 WSM and action length will be dedicated to the cartridge the rifle is chambered for. The first 500 rifles will have a short action because they are chambered for a short cartridge. If the next batch of 500 is chambered for the 300 H&H Magnum or some other long cartridge, they obviously will have a long action.

Whereas some riflemakers choose to take the easy route by copying an existing action in this age of expired patents, the Nosler team decided to design its own. The receiver is a classic example of blending the old

with the new. In a perfect world, scope mounts would contain not a single screw to vibrate loose and, while the Nosler rifle does not eliminate them entirely, it does eliminate those that are usually impossible to check for tightness due to their inaccessibility. They accomplished this by making the base of the scope mount an integral part of the receiver and by utilizing a couple of levers from the Leupold Quick-Release mount to hold the rings in place. Think of it as the Leupold quick-detach mount with its two-piece base melted into the receiver and you get the picture. A couple of hardened steel alignment pins protruding from the top of the receiver return the scope to its original zero when it is detached and then reattached.

The dual-opposed locking lugs of the bolt are set back just far enough to allow its nose to rest inside the shank of the barrel. The bolt face is counter-bored so the head of a cartridge resting in the chamber is supported by three rings of steel (*the third being the receiver*). But since the counter-bore rim is notched for a Sako-style

extractor, the support is a bit less than 100 percent. Ejection of spent cases is handled by the ever-familiar spring-loaded, plunger-style ejector housed in the face of the bolt. Longitudinal flat surfaces on the top and sides of the receiver, along with matching flats on the bolt shroud, flow smoothly from fore to aft. Flats on the surface of the shroud give it an octagon shape. The shroud is open at the rear to allow rearward travel of the cocking piece during cocking of the firing pin. Bolt rotation of the rifle I shot was close to effortless, no doubt due to hardened and highly polished firing pin cocking cam surfaces. The bolt stop is retracted by pressing on a spring-loaded tab at the left side of the receiver bridge. The five-panel checkering on the knob of the bolt handle is very nice.

Located at the right-hand side of the receiver, the safety lever has three positions; all the way forward to "Fire," all the way rearward to "Safe;" a middle position allows the bolt to be rotated with the safety engaged. The 24-inch, stainless steel barrel is heavy enough to deliver the consistent half-inch accuracy Nosler promises of the rifle, but not so heavy as to make the rifle overweight. The barrel is match grade and hand-lapped to improve bore and groove diameter uniformity. Rifling twist rate is 1:10 inches, which is standard for the 300 WSM. All metal, including the barrel, has a baked-on Teflon coating with a non-reflective finish.

Magazine capacity is three rounds and, while a couple of rifles from other manufacturers I have tried refused to feed the stubby 300 WSM cartridge smoothly, the Nosler rifle gobbled them up without a hitch. The trigger guard/floorplate assembly, with its straddle-style floorplate, is precision-machined steel and attached to the receiver with a pair of hex-head bolts. The bottom of the floorplate is decorated with the Nosler Custom logo.

Wood-to-metal fit of the rifle I shot was excellent. The stock is a nicely figured piece of European walnut, with 22-line checkering at its wrist and forearm in a point pattern. The buttstock has a straight comb and its cheekrest is shadowline-bordered. Grip cap and forend tip are ebony, while a Pachmayr Decelerator recoil pad out back does a good job of soaking up recoil. Sling swivels

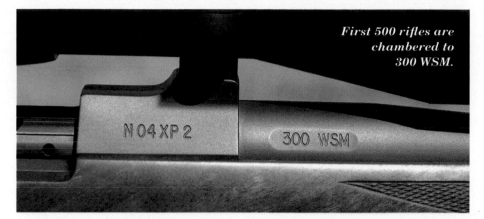

First 500 rifles are chambered to 300 WSM.

are the quick-detachable type. Pull length to the fully adjustable trigger is 13-1/2 inches. Rifle weight will vary slightly due to differences in the densities of walnut stocks, but Nosler gives it a nominal eight-pound rating. Trigger pull was quite crisp with no noticeable creep or over-travel. I had no way to weigh it, but my educated guess is about 2-1/2 pounds.

The Nosler rifle will come with a 2.5 10x Leupold LPS scope attached and zeroed with Nosler ammunition loaded with the 180-grain AccuBond bullet. The serial number of the scope will be the same as the serial number of the rifle wearing it. Subtension between crosshatches on the lower quadrant of the vertical crosshair of

the Boone & Crocket reticle will be correct for the trajectory of the Nosler ammunition (*40 rounds will be shipped with rifle*). A leather sling and a metal case with the buyer's name engraved on it are included in the $3995 price.

The purchaser of a Nosler rifle has its serial number reserved in his or her name and when the next series of 500 rifles in a different caliber is introduced, that person will get first refusal on the same serial number. Five hundred sounds like a lot of rifles, but while shooting one of the first built I became convinced that they will go fast. After all, how many people have the opportunity to shoot Nosler ammunition loaded with Nosler bullets in a Nosler rifle?

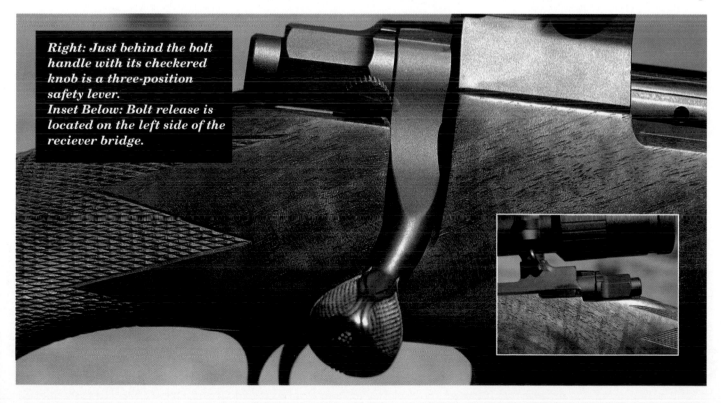

Right: Just behind the bolt handle with its checkered knob is a three-position safety lever.
Inset Below: Bolt release is located on the left side of the reciever bridge.

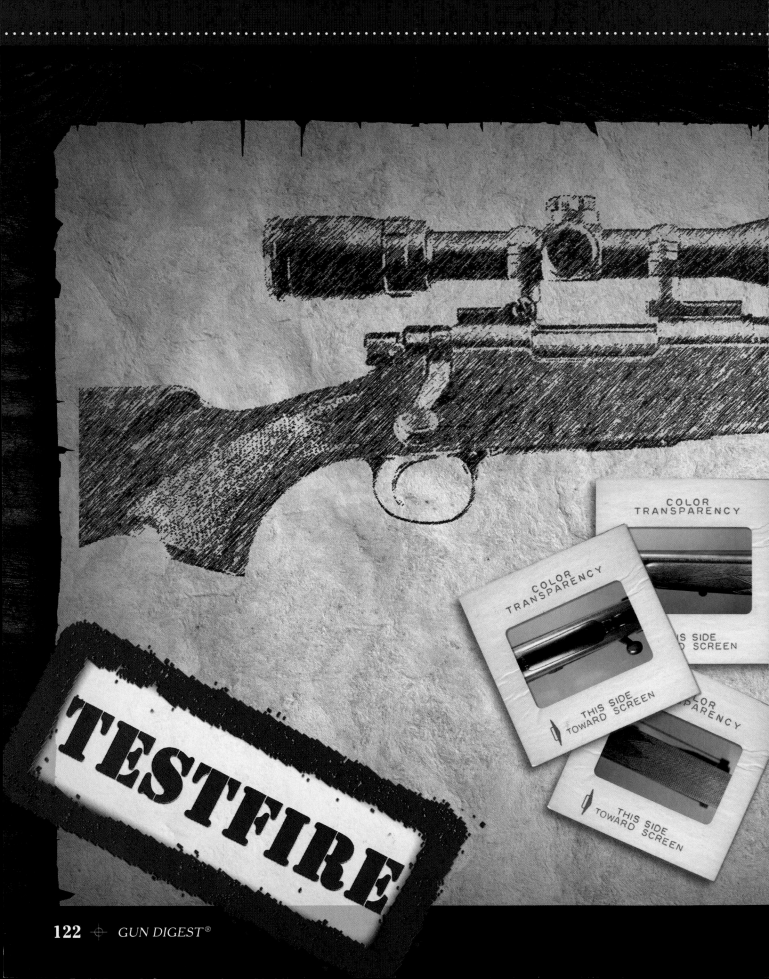

TESTFIRE

COLOR TRANSPARENCY

THIS SIDE TOWARD SCREEN

COLOR TRANSPARENCY

THIS SIDE TOWARD SCREEN

COLOR TRANSPARENCY

THIS SIDE TOWARD SCREEN

REMINGTON'S MODEL 700 CLASSIC IN 8MM MAUSER

by Robert H. VanDenburg, Jr.

This story began a couple of years ago when I was fortunate enough to acquire a near-pristine Model 98K Mauser. I had long been interested in its chambering, the 8x57JS or 8mm Mauser if you prefer, and immediately set about to gather reloading dies, bullets and cases and to retrieve all the 8x57JS data in my library. As a point of reference, I also obtained some Federal and Remington factory ammo.

Both companies refer to the round as the 8mm Mauser and load 170-grain softpoints at a published velocity of 2360 fps not to exceed, I understand, 37,000 C.U.P. This, of course, is in deference to the many older guns in the hands of the

Remington Model 700 Classic in 8mm Mauser.

shooting public and the possibility, however remote, of someone firing a round in one of the older 1888 Commission rifles that has a groove diameter of 0.318-inch rather than the later, and current, 0.323-inch.

I had just gotten my sleeves rolled up when, of all things, Remington announced its 2004 Model 700 Classic rifle would be chambered for the 8mm Mauser. It amazes me how quickly I can react when properly motivated and it was a very short time before I had one of the new Classics of my own.

I am rapidly losing track of all the variations of the famed Model 700 but the one I have most admired over the years has been the annual Classic. Now in its 24th year, with each edition chambered for a different cartridge, the Classic sports a, well, classic-style walnut stock sans cheekpiece, forend tip and, mercifully, white-line spacers. It also omits a pistol grip cap and sights of any kind.

My new Classic has an attractive walnut stock of pleasant color, darker than many, with modest grain. It

has a rubber, rifle-style recoil pad, brown in color with a black base and attached sling swivel studs. The checkering pattern is different from other 700s, based on current catalog pictures, but is identical to that of one of my other 700s, a BDL model made in the '70s. Well, almost identical. The older one has a slightly narrower border, has pointed diamonds and was probably hand-checkered. The Classic has a wider border and the diamonds are flat. How the checkering was applied I can't be sure but it is neatly done. Wood-to-metal fit is not up to custom standards, but it's not bad either.

The stock is well sealed on the inside, with possibly a little sanding taking place on the left side of the magazine well. The recoil shield meets the wood properly. The barrel is free-floated forward of the recoil shield up to a point about two inches from the tip where a 3/4-inch wide boss or raised portion of the stock contacts the barrel. The trigger guard assembly is synthetic. The magazine

follower is metal—at least it's magnetic—with a dull chrome finish.

All recent 700s have a couple of features that my older 700s don't. In all 700s, the safety is mounted on the right rear of the receiver. It is a two-position affair: forward is off, the gun is ready to fire; back is on, the rifle is "safe." In the older guns, placing the safety to the rear locked the bolt and the trigger. This was a good feature in that while hunting and moving through brush, the bolt could not be inadvertently opened, allowing rain, snow or debris to enter the action. It also meant that to open the bolt to remove a round from the chamber, the safety had to be off. Absent proper gun handling, this increased the possibly of an accidental discharge. In the newer guns, the rearward, or "safe" position of the safety does not lock the bolt, meaning the gun can be unloaded without making the gun ready to fire.

The other feature found on newer 700s is a mechanical, key-operated lock built into the bolt. In the "on" position with the bolt retracted, it prevents the bolt from being closed, rendering the gun inoperable. In the "off" position, the gun operates normally.

Overall rifle length is 44-1/2 inches, including a 24-inch barrel, which means it was built on Remington's long action. The barrel tapers from 1.280 inches just forward of the recoil shield to .640-inch at the muzzle. Length of pull is 13-7/8 inches, drop at comb is 1-1/8 inches and drop at heel is 1-3/8 inches. Weight is 7-1/4 pounds. These are all nominal measurements from the Remington catalog but each matches my rifle almost exactly. All in all, it's a very handsome rifle.

I mounted one of the new Ramshot Optics 6x Hunting series scopes. This is a new line of telescopic sights from Western Powder of Miles City, Montana, distributor of the Ramshot line of smokeless propellants. It is made in Japan, has a duplex reticle and a 30mm tube.

In today's world of mass-produced firearms, the final polishing prior to bluing doesn't get the attention it

▶ *The models mechanical, key-activated bolt lock.*
▼ *Trigger guard assembly is synthetic, matches metal well and is nicely fitted.*

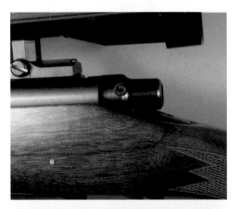

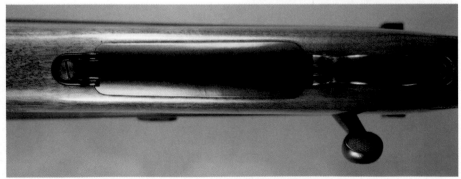

once did. A hand operation requiring a considerable amount of skilled labor is simply too costly for much of today's market. Since the degree of polishing determines the "depth" of the bluing, today's product is often quite shallow and more black than blue. The Remington Classic, while certainly up to modern standards, exhibits this quality. The Ramshot scope, on the other hand, has a matte finish and in most lighting the difference is not readily apparent. A good thing, everything considered.

Before I got to the shooting, I had the opportunity to discuss the project with Tom Dodge, president of Mitchell's Mausers. Most shooters today are probably familiar with this company, which offers World War II-era Mausers in conditions from serviceable to truly pristine, often with period accoutrements. Recently the company has added ammunition, headstamped "Mitchell 8mm Mauser" and loaded to European CIP pressure standards. The ammo is manufactured in Yugoslavia by PPU and is available in four variations: 175-grain PSP BT, 175-grain FMJ HPBT, 198-grain FMJ and 198-grain SWAT, also a FMJ. Mr. Dodge was kind enough to supply me with samples of each. Now I had three brands, three bullet weights and six different loadings to two pressure levels. All would get a workout in the new Remington and, perhaps, the old Mauser as well.

Several trips to the range resulted in the enclosed table. The weather conditions during the shooting were

Checkered bolt knob and safety are standard Remington.

perfect: warm, sunny and no wind. On the other hand, a 6x scope is not the best for wringing the last bit of accuracy out of any gun, and the trigger pull on this one is quite heavy. My gauge only registers to 80 ounces—five pounds. I would guess this one took seven to eight pounds of pressure to release. Still, I'm convinced this gun wants to shoot and I suspect a trigger job will prove it.

At that, the Federal ammo was spectacular, although the velocity was anemic. The Remington ammo, ironically, performed poorly on target but gave velocities that are 82 fps higher than factory published figures. Both Mitchell 175-grain loads were satisfactory, taking into consideration the heavy trigger pull. The only hunting bullet from

Mitchell is the 175-grain PSP, but it is a boattail. The other 175, a FMJ, is best left for paper-punching. The 198-grain FMJ performed well in spite of the trigger pull and I suspect will serve admirably in long-range target work. Much as with the Remington load, the rifle just didn't take to the 198-grain SWAT round.

All the Mitchell ammo gave velocities more in keeping with the higher pressures to which they are loaded, but it would appear even they aren't loaded to European CIP maximums. They did, however, provide valuable information and now, instead of a back-burner interest in this grand old cartridge, I have not one but two rifles chambered for it and a front-burner interest in exploring its potential. Life is good. ✻

REMINGTON MODEL 700 CLASSIC 8MM MAUSER

BRAND	BULLET	VELOCITY	GROUP
Federal	170 SP	2186 fps	3/4 inch
Remington	170 SP	2432	2-1/8
Mitchell	175 PSPBT	2597	1-5/8
Mitchell	175 FMJ HPBT	2543	1-1/2
Mitchell	198 FMJ	2413	1-1/8
Mitchell	198 SWAT	2353	2

NOTES:
Groups are average of three, three-shot groups at 100 yards.
Barrel length is 24 inches.
Federal, Remington loaded to current U.S. pressure limits of <37,000 psi.
Mitchell loaded to European CIP pressure level of <56,350 psi.

Ammo used in tests.

▶Screwing the barrel shroud from the receiver allows the barrel to be removed for switching to another barrel.
▼Outfitting the Fusion with a Shepherd scope and Harris folding bipod makes it a fantastic ground squirrel rifle.

TESTFIRE

VOLQUARTSEN FUSION SWITCH-BARREL RIFLE

by Layne Simpson

Tom Volquartsen makes two types of super-accurate autoloading rifles, both chambered for the 17- and 22-caliber rimfire cartridges. One is a fixed-barrel rifle with its stainless steel barrel screwed into a receiver that is CNC-machined from either stainless steel or hard-anodized, aircraft-grade aluminum. The Superlite version weighs 5-1/2 pounds in 17 HMR and 22 WMR, and a half-pound less in 22 Long Rifle and 17 Hornady Mach 2. The receiver of rifles in 17 HMR and 22 WMR is 0.600-inch longer and, since the rifle is blowback-operated, the greater backthrust generated by those cartridges requires a bolt twice as heavy as the one in rifles in 17 HM2 and 22 LR. Due to a level of hardness considerably higher than is commonly found in the aluminum receivers of run-of-the-mill factory rifles, the aluminum

Due to the extreme hardness of the aluminum stock it is machined from, the receiver of the Fusion is as durable as a stainless steel receiver.

receiver made by Volquartsen is as durable as the stainless steel receiver, or so he claims. Tom went on to say that he introduced the aluminum receiver in 1997 and quite a few of those rifles are owned by ground squirrel shooters who have fired thousands upon thousands of rounds in them; not a single one has been returned with a worn-out receiver.

When making his match-grade, stainless steel barrels, Volquartsen holds a bore and groove diameter tolerance range of plus or minus 0.0001-inch from chamber to muzzle. He keeps all chamber dimensions tight enough to deliver the very best accuracy possible but not so tight as to rule out the use of economy-grade plinking ammunition. All barrels have an outside diameter of 0.950-inch and this takes them out of the lightweight department. Volquartsen also offers drop-in barrels in all the calibers and styles for the Remington 597 as well as Ruger's 10/22, 10/22M, 77/22, 77/22M and 77/17.

For several years now, the barrels of all rifles built by Volquartsen were screwed into their receivers—but his latest creation is quite a departure from that. Called the Fusion, it is a switch-barrel rifle available in either of two combinations, 17 HMR and 22 WMR, or 17 Hornady Mach 2 and 22 Long Rifle. The rifle can be ordered with a pair of interchangeable barrels in two different calibers, or it can be purchased with one barrel only and another barrel ordered later. It does not have to be returned to the factory for fitting of the second barrel. Going from one chambering to another is quick and easy; after the AR-15-style barrel

The Fusion uses Ruger's excellent rotary magazine.

shroud is screwed from the receiver the barrel is removed by pulling it forward. The rifle is now ready for the installation of its other barrel. The 17 HMR and 22 WMR share the same Ruger rotary magazine, and so do the 17 HM2 and 22 LR. The barrel shroud requires only hand-tightening when being reinstalled and once it has been tightened, a spring-loaded ball on the face of the receiver prevents it from vibrating loose as the rifle is being fired.

The Fusion receiver has a different shape than the receiver of Volquartsen's fixed-barrel rifle and

since it is a bit larger, it is available only in hard-anodized aluminum in order to keep weight reasonable. The rifle I am shooting weighs 9-1/4 pounds with a Shepherd 3-9x scope. The shank of the barrel fits inside a hardened steel insert at the front of the receiver so there is no need to worry about wear caused by years of barrel-switching. A Picatinny-style base machined into the top of the receiver accepts scope-mounting rings made by Warne, Burris and others, or you can step a notch above first class and use Nova rings from Volquartsen; they are masterpieces of precision.

Those who are inclined to do such things can utilize a screw-attached Picatinny base at the bottom of the barrel shroud for attaching a flashlight or laser sight, but, since I have no use for either, I removed the base and attached a Harris folding bipod to the sling swivel stud on the shroud. The carbon fiber tension barrel of the Fusion is 18-1/2 inches long for an overall rifle length of 37 inches. Described by Volquartsen as a switch-barrel rifle, "takedown rifle" is equally appropriate since removal of the barrel and scope reduces the length of the package to 19-1/2 inches.

All Volquartsen rifles share the same trigger assembly and it is the same one he sells alone for drop-in installation in the Ruger 10/22. Precision-machined from a solid billet of aircraft-grade aluminum, the housing has an integral trigger guard. The trigger can be adjusted to virtually eliminate the creep that is quite common in the factory 10/22 trigger. The trigger also eliminates the drag-associated inconsistent pulls we commonly experience with triggers on autoloading rifles. The stainless steel hammer is precision-ground and hardened to 58 on the Rockwell C chart. The sear and disconnector are carved from blocks of type A2 hardened steel by the EDM process and held within a tolerance range of plus or minus 0.0002-inch to assure minimum variation in weight of pull. The trigger on the Fusion you see in the photos pulls 30 ounces with zero over-travel and only a slight trace of pre-travel. The fire-control assembly also contains an automatic bolt release and an oversized magazine release, the latter located just forward of the trigger guard. The magazine release is exactly where it needs to be for quick and easy operation, and yet it is not likely to be accidentally bumped in the field.

Tom Volquartsen's accuracy guarantee for all of his autoloading rifles is less than an inch at 100 yards for the 22 WMR, less than 0.75-inch at 100 yards for the 17 HMR and less than 0.375-inch at 50 yards for the 22 Long Rifle, the

VOLQUARTSEN FUSION SWITCH-BARREL RIFLE
100-Yard Accuracy
(Three Five-Shot Group Averages Measured In Inches)

17 HMR BARREL	GROUP	MV
Federal 17-gr. V-Max	0.35	2628
Remington 17-gr. V-Max	0.56	2554
Hornady 20-gr. HP	0.74	2389
Hornady 17-gr. V-Max	0.81	2541
Federal 17-gr. TNT	0.89	2592
CCI 17-gr. TNT	0.92	2569
AVERAGE ACCURACY	0.71	
22 WMR BARREL	**GROUP**	**MV**
Winchester 40-gr. JHP	0.47	1778
CCI 40-gr. JHP	0.54	1893
Remington 33-gr. V-Max	0.61	2022
CCI 40-gr. FMJ	0.63	1807
Winchester 34-gr. JHP	0.65	2074
Winchester 40-gr. FMJ	0.69	1812
CCI 30-gr. +V	0.81	2182
CCI 30-gr. TNT	1.24	2253
Remington 40-gr. JHP	1.26	1822
Remington 40-gr. FMJ	1.27	1792
Federal 30-gr. TNT	1.30	2237
CCI 50-gr. Gold Dot	1.43	1561
Winchester 45-gr. DP	1.61	1553
AVERAGE ACCURACY	0.96	

NOTES:
Volquartsen 17 Hm2 Conversion Kit For The Ruger 10/22

latter with match ammo such as Remington/Eley Match EPS. The Fusion most certainly lives up to its accuracy billing, with room to spare. After boosting scope magnification by replacing its 3-9x Shepherd with a Bushnell 6.5-20x Elite 4200, I waited for a calm day at the range and started shooting quite early in the morning before the wind had a chance to pick up. While wearing its 17 HMR barrel, the little rifle averaged less than a half-inch at 100 yards with three of the six loads I tried, and it did not exceed an inch with either load. The overall average for eighteen five-shot groups fired with six different 17 HMR loads was easy to remember at 0.71-inch. The 22 WMR barrel also performed quite nicely by averaging 0.63-inch with the seven loads it liked best. Overall

Picatinny base machined into the receiver accepts scope-mounting rings available from Volquartsen, Warne and Burris.

❀●❀●❀●❀●❀●❀

accuracy of 39 five-shot groups fired with 13 different loads was .96 inch. This, my friends, is one serious ground squirrel rifle. ❀

SIXGUNS & OTHERS :
HANDGUNS TODAY

by John Taffin

*L*ife used to be so simple! When McDonald's first opened up they had a walk-up window offering two choices: a hamburger or cheeseburger. The choice of the latter was usually predicated on whether one had the extra four cents or not. Today, one has to choose between the drive-through or walk-in, and then be faced with a menu board larger than the square footage in the floor plan of most houses. The same situation now applies to the firearms industry. In 1955, if one wanted a Ruger 357 Blackhawk, the situation was almighty simple; there was only one: blued, with a 4 5/8-inch barrel. One year later, shooters could have any 44 Magnum Blackhawk desired as long as it was a 6 1/2-inch version, also blued. The Super Blackhawk arrived in 1959 and, until well into the 1980s, it was only offered in a blued 7 1/2-inch model.

Over the years, most gun manufacturers have followed McDonald's lead. Ruger alone offers a total of 40 new choices this year, handguns and long guns combined. If we factor in all models from the rest of the major manufacturers I guess there are at least 100 new choices.

It's time to take our annual look at the state of handguns: single-action and double-action six-guns, as well as single-shot pistols.

Ruger

There is good news and bad news from Ruger this year. The bad news: After a dozen years of production and nearly three-quarters of a million units manufactured, the Vaquero has been removed from production. However, the greater good news is that the Vaquero is being replaced by an even better single-action six-gun: the New Vaquero. The original Vaquero was a virtually indestructible single-action six-gun built on the same frame size as the 44 Magnum Super Blackhawk. If there was any complaint about the Vaquero, it was its size and bulkiness. The New Vaquero addresses this "problem."

Several years ago Ruger's Bill Ruger, Jr., Steve Sanetti and Bob Stutler sat down for a brainstorming session and one of the results we are now seeing is the New Vaquero, a much improved, downsized version. The original Vaquero was larger than the traditional Single Action Army; the New Vaquero is basically the same size as the Colt Model P and its replicas. In addition to its smaller,

Production Manager Bob Stutler, with Ruger's latest single action, the New Vaquero.

easier-to-carry size, several other improvements have been made to the New Vaquero. The ejector rod head is now larger, allowing more comfort and positive action when ejecting spent shells, and the cylinder now lines up correctly with the ejector rod. In the old Vaquero, the audible *click* as the cylinder was rotated told us we had gone too far and the cylinder had to be backed up slightly for the ejector rod to enter the chamber mouth; with the New Vaquero the *click* says we are there, and the cylinder is lined up correctly with the ejector rod.

When the first Ruger six-gun, the Single-Six 22, appeared in 1953 the grip frame was virtually identical in size and shape to the 1st Generation Single Action Army. This XR3 frame was carried over to the 357 Blackhawk of 1955 and the 44 Magnum version one year later. In 1963 the grip frame was changed to XR3-RED, allowing more room between the back of the trigger guard and the front of the grip strap. It has taken more than four decades to go back to the original; however, the New Vaquero has the 1950s XR3 size and shape. The New Vaquero grip frame is also slightly narrower than the old and, combined with the checkered rubber grips, which are also slimmer than the original Vaquero's wooden grips, makes it feel awfully good in my hand. In fact, these are the best-feeling Ruger single-action factory stocks I've ever experienced and I've been shooting Ruger single-action six-

guns exactly a half-century this year. Instead of the medallion found in all Ruger stocks since 1953, these new checkered rubber grips have the Ruger Eagle molded into the grip itself.

The New Vaquero will be initially offered in 357 Magnum and 45 Colt, in both blue/case-colored and stainless steel versions in barrel lengths of 4-5/8 and 5-1/2 inches, with the 45 Colt also offered in the longer 7 1/2-inch barrel length. They should be very popular not only with cowboy action shooters but with all six-gunners appreciating traditionally-sized and styled single actions. I certainly hope Ruger will eventually offer it in 44 Special. WARNING: These New Vaqueros are for standard 45 Colt loads only, not the "Heavy Ruger Loads" listed in many loading manuals and articles.

Ruger's other single-action offering, which will probably be sold out by the time you read this, is their 50th Anniversary Model of the 357 Blackhawk. Although it is built on the New Model action instead of the three-screw action of the original, this Anniversary version has the 4 5/8-inch barrel, Micro-style rear sight, and checkered hard rubber grips with a black eagle medallion as did the original Blackhawk in 1955, and it is also the same size as the New Vaquero, having the same old-style XR3 grip frame, and the capability of taking a lot of six-gunners back to their roots. This special Ruger is only to be offered for one year; however, in talking with Ruger President Steve Sanetti I was given hope this basic model could stay in the catalog and also be offered in other chamberings *(hint: 44 Special)*

Ruger's New Vaquero is available in both blued and stainless steel versions, chambered in 357 Magnum or 45 Colt.

and barrel lengths. If you feel the same as I do, a short letter to Ruger would help to influence the decision.

One of the best bargains out there for the handgun hunter has been Ruger's Hunter Model. First introduced in 1992 in 44 Magnum with a 7 1/2-inch solid ribbed heavy barrel cut for Ruger's scope rings, this is a stainless steel six-gun made for heavy-duty outdoor use. Two years ago the Bisley Model version arrived with the Ruger Bisley Model grip frame, hammer, and trigger, and this was then followed one year later by a 22 Single-Six version with an extra cylinder chamber in 22 Magnum. Now for this year Ruger has added the fourth 7 1/2-inch stainless steel, scope-ready Hunter Model to the catalog chambered in 17HMR with an extra cylinder for the 17 Mach 2. With these four Hunter Models, Ruger has covered all the bases when it comes to hunting big game, small game, or varmints.

At the other end of the six-gun spectrum, Ruger is offering something special for those who like truly big-bore packin' pistols. Ruger's Super Redhawk, probably the most durable and strongest double-action revolver ever offered, is now cataloged in a much more convenient carrying version. Until this year the Super Redhawk, whether chambered in 44 Magnum, 480 Ruger or 454 Casull, was offered only in 7 1/2- and 9 1/2-inch barrel lengths, and scope-ready for the handgun hunter. This year Ruger has gone really radical by cutting the barrel even with the extended frame, for a barrel length of only 2-1/2 inches. Known as the Alaskan, this new Super Redhawk will have a rounded trigger guard and trigger, rubber Hogue Monogrip, no cuts in the frame for scope rings, and will be chambered in 480 Ruger and 454 Casull. I expect it to be very popular with those spending a lot of time outdoors and needing a very powerful but portable six-gun.

Smith & Wesson

Two years ago Smith & Wesson introduced the new "world's most powerful revolver" with the X-frame

Two great choices for the handgun hunter are Ruger's Bisley and Super Blackhawk 44 Magnum models.

Top: The 22 LR/22 Magnum and bottom: the 17HMR/17 Mach 2 models have now joined the ranks of handgun hunting choices for hunters

Smith & Wesson's extremely popular X-frame Model 500 is now available with a Hi-Viz front sight.

Now anyone can shoot as fast as Jerry Miculek, or at least dream about it, with S&W's Jerry Miculek Model 625 chambered in 45 ACP and wearing stocks designed by Jerry.

Smith & Wesson is now offering this Airweight with Crimson Trace Laser Grips

Model 500 chambered in 500 S&W Magnum. Now from S&W comes the second chambering in the X-frame: the 460XVR, or X-treme Velocity Revolver. While the 500 in its most powerful loading uses a 440-grain bullet at 1650 fps, the 460 becomes the factory-chambered big-bore revolver velocity king with a 200-grain 45-caliber bullet at 2300 fps.

Smith & Wesson notes this is the most powerful 45-caliber production revolver in the world, with over 2400 ft/lbs of muzzle energy (fpe) and "incredibly low perceived recoil." Several factors come together to help tame the 460: namely, a weight of 73 ounces, a compensated 8 3/8-inch barrel and special recoil-reducing grips made of a rubber-like substance called Sorbothane. One can well imagine what the recoil would feel like in a traditional-sized revolver of 48 ounces. In addition to the 200-grain load, Cor-Bon also offers a 250-grain bulleted load at "only" 1900 fps. The 460 will also accept 454 and 45 Colt loads.

The Model 460XVR comes drilled and tapped for a scope mount base, has a fully adjustable rear sight mated with a black blade front sight with a gold bead, and an interchangeable HI-VIZ green dot front sight is also included. Something new for Smith & Wesson in this revolver is gain-twist rifling, which means the twist becomes faster towards the muzzle. This is not a new idea by any means as it has even been used in muzzle-loading rifles and cap 'n ball revolvers. Like the Model 500, the 460XVR is a double-action six-gun crafted of stainless steel with a satin finish and five-shot cylinder.

Another great old standby revolver, the Model 66, has been dropped from production. However, it has been replaced by the slightly larger L-frame Model 620. It is still stainless steel, with a Model 66-style barrel without the heavy underlug, and has a seven-shot cylinder. The Model 65 has also been upgraded to a fixed sight, seven-shot L-frame 357 Magnum, the Model 619, with a standard barrel without an enclosed ejector rod housing. Smith & Wesson's first stainless steel revolver, the Model 60, is available in a new version having a five-inch barrel with an enclosed ejector rod and adjustable sights. This 357 Magnum five-shooter should be a very popular, relatively lightweight trail gun.

Jerry Miculek, the "World's Fastest Revolver Shooter," a title he holds for such remarkable feats as 12 shots from one six-shot revolver in less than three seconds, now has his name on a standard production gun from Smith & Wesson, the Model 625 Jerry Miculek Professional Series. This is a stainless steel double-action revolver with a 4-inch heavy underlug barrel, adjustable rear sight paired with a gold bead/black post front sight, and chambered in 45 ACP (full-moon clips recommended). Also included are Jerry's specially designed wooden stocks and a wide Miculek Speed trigger.

The 44 Special is also back at Smith & Wesson with the Model 21-4 Thunder Ranch Special. This is the first fixed-sight, 4-inch, blued, six-shot 44 Special since the original Model 21 was dropped 40 years ago. Thanks to Clint Smith's collaboration with Smith & Wesson, we have a real no-nonsense, big-bore fighting six-gun in the Model 21-4. The original run of these "Special" 44 Specials have the Thunder Ranch gold logo on the right side; however, expect later production models to be blued without the logo and chambered in 44 Special, 45 ACP, and 45 Colt. Thank you, Clint Smith and Smith & Wesson.

There was a time I would not even consider laser grips; however, my experience with Crimson Trace Laser Grips has changed my mind and I now find them exceptionally useful. These ingenious grips take the place of regular grips and,

when a small button in the front strap of the grip is depressed as one takes a normal shooting grip, a small red beam appears on the target.

Now Smith & Wesson is offering two J-frame six-guns already equipped with Crimson Trace Laser Grips. The 15-ounce 38 Special stainless steel 2-inch Model 637 and the 13.5-ounce 32 Magnum black matte 2-inch Model 432PD both come

The new high-velocity revolver champion, with a 200-grain bullet at 2300 fps, is Smith & Wesson's 460XVR chambered in 460 S&W Magnum.

It may look a little strange, however, the new 5-inch barreled 357 Magnum chambered J-frame should prove to be very popular on the trail.

S&W's Model 66 K-frame has been replaced by the L-frame, seven-shot Model 620.

The Taurus Gaucho single action (above) is now here in stainless steel or (below) blued steel in 357 Magnum and 45 Colt.

Taurus is now offering the 500 S&W Magnum chambered in the very popular Raging Bull.

Another Raging Bull offering from Taurus is the long-cylinder .410/44-40 revolver.

with Crimson Trace Laser Grips already installed. For those having concealed weapon permits, especially women who do not shoot a lot, either one of these could be very useful.

Taurus

As usual, Taurus has a full line of new six-guns for this year. The single-action Gaucho was prematurely announced last year; however, by now it should be readily available in blue, blue/case-colored, and stainless steel versions. The Gaucho is offered in both 45 Colt and 357 Magnum and barrel lengths of 5-1/2 and 7-1/2 inches, all with fixed sights, black rubber grips, four-click action, half-cock loading notch, and a transfer bar safety. Those I have handled seemed exceptionally smooth.

The Taurus Raging Bull, chambered in 44 Magnum, 454 Casull, and 480 Ruger, has been popular with handgun hunters and big-bore revolver shooters for several years. Joining the lineup is the newest Bull, the 500 Magnum. This 10-inch version features a ported heavy-underlug barrel, adjustable rear sight mated with a black post front, smooth trigger and black rubber finger groove grips with the trademark recoil-reducing red cushion insert along the back strap. Capacity is five shots; weight 4 1/2 pounds.

Taurus also offers an easy-packing big-bore six-gun—the Model 444 Ultralite, a 4-inch Raging Bull-sized, six-shot double-action 44 Magnum with a titanium cylinder. Designed for portability, the 444 Ultralite weighs 28 ounces, and is equipped with fiber-optic sights, smooth trigger and Raging Bull cushioned-insert rubber grips. A second 44 Magnum offered by Taurus is the slightly smaller five-shot Tracker with a 4-inch barrel, Ribber grips, and ported heavy-underlug barrel. Of all steel construction, the Tracker 44 weighs 34 ounces. Both models are offered in either blue or stainless steel.

The last two new big-bore revolvers from Taurus are the Model 44-Ten Tracker and 44-Ten Bull, featuring elongated cylinders to handle the .410 shotgun shell or 44-40 revolver round. Both are available in blue or stainless steel, with a fiber-optic front sight and cushioned insert grips. The Raging Bull version features a ventilated, ribbed barrel. Weights are 32 ounces for the Tracker version and 39 ounces for the Bull model.

Taurus also has several interesting little guns. The very popular 38 Special five-shot Model 85 is now available with Ribber grips, while the IB (Instant Backup) double actions are offered in both blue and stainless versions in either a five-shot 9mm or eight- shot 17 HMR. The Triad Model 85 takes 38 Specials, or 357s plus 9mms with a provided clip. There is also a larger Tracker Triad with a seven-shot cylinder.

All Ruger, Smith & Wesson and Taurus handguns either now have—or soon will have—internal locking devices, which are now required by many cities and states. This is a fact of life in today's society, and whether we like it or not, they are not going to go away.

Colt

What does the Colt Python have in common with the New Service, Official Police, Officers Model Match, Detective Special, King Cobra, and Anaconda? All are great six-guns and all,

including the Python, are now gone. The Python arrived in 1955 and was soon regarded as the Cadillac of double-action revolvers. Now it is gone.

The only revolver left in the Colt catalog is the Single Action Army. It is now offered in barrel lengths of 4-3/4, 5-1/2 and 7-1/2 inches, blue/case hardened or nickel plating and in six chamberings: 32-20, 38 Special, 357 Magnum, 38-40, 44-40 and 45 Colt. The major question is whether or not Colt can continue to compete in the civilian handgun market, offering only the Single Action Army and the 1911 Government Model. They have a very small share of the latter market and must compete with imported replica single actions, as well as American-made single-action six-guns from United States Firearms and Ruger. Most six-gunners would truly be saddened to see Colt disappear from the civilian firearms scene; however, it seems pretty obvious Colt must do more to survive.

With these Freedom Arms Model 83s the handgun hunter can tackle any-thing, anywhere. Top guns are chambered in 454 Casull, while the bottom six-guns are both 475 Linebaughs.

Top: This eye-catching six-gun, the 444 Ultralite, is Taurus' entry into the light-weight 44 Magnum are-na. The red cushion insert along the back strap really helps reduce felt recoil.
Middle: The Taurus IB (Instant Backup) is available in both 17 HMR and 9mm.
Bottom: The Taurus Tracker Triad, with felt recoil-reducing Ribber grips, handles 38 Specials, 357 Magnums, and 9mms—all from the same cylinder.

Freedom Arms

The single-action six-guns from Freedom Arms, whether a full-sized Model 83 or the mid-frame Model 97, are expensive—there is no doubt about that. However, I have yet to hear of any owner of a Freedom Arms revolver saying they are not worth the money.

All of Freedom Arms' six-guns are crafted of stainless steel, and the full-sized Model 83 is offered in both a bright, brushed Premier Grade or less expensive matte finished Field Grade. Whichever finish is chosen, both are built with the same materials and attention to detail and tight tolerances. Premier Grade Model 83s are offered in 475 Linebaugh, 454 Casull and 357, 41 and 44 Magnums, while the Field Grade comes in the same chamberings, plus the 22 Long Rifle. Both models feature adjustable sights with standard barrel lengths of 4-3/4, 6, 7-1/2 and 10 inches; other lengths and octagon barrels are offered on a custom basis. Currently the only fixed-sight Model 83 offered is the Premier Grade chambered in 454.

The Model 97 is available only in the Premier Grade with adjustable-sighted models chambered in 45 Colt, 44 Special, 41 Magnum—all with

▼ *A long cylinder version for such cartridges as the 45-70 or 500 S&W Magnum.*

five-shot cylinders— while the 357 Magnum, 32 H&R Magnum, 22 Long Rifle and 17HMR all have six-shot cylinders. All versions are available with a 4 1/4-, 5 1/2-, or 7 1/2-inch barrel, with 10-inch barrels available on the latter three chamberings. Fixed-sight models are also available in 45 Colt, 357 Magnum, and 32 H&R Magnum.

Freedom Arms also offers auxiliary cylinders in 45 Colt, 45 ACP and 45 Winchester Magnum for the Model 83 in 454 Casull; in 480 Ruger to fit the 475 Linebaugh, and 22 Magnum for the 22 Long Rifle Model 83. Optional cylinders for the Model 97 include 45ACP, 38 Special, 32-20, 22 Match, 22 Magnum and 17

▼ *The Magnum Research BFR is offered in a standard model with a "short" cylinder.*

Mach 2. All Freedom Arms' cylinders have been unfluted; however, they may now be ordered with flutes, and both the Model 83 and Model 97 are now offered with a rounded butt.

Magnum Research

This is the home of the 50 AE Desert Eagle semi-automatic pistol, however Magnum Research also offers the BFR *(Biggest, Finest Revolver)*, a stainless steel single-action six-gun offered in a variety of frame sizes and calibers. With standard "Short Cylinder" and frame, the BFR is found in 454 Casull, 475 Linebaugh/480 Ruger, 50 AE and 22 Hornet, while the Long version is chambered in 45-70, 444 Marlin, 410/45 Colt, 450 Marlin, 30-30, and even in the relatively new 500 S&W.

All BFRs are totally American-made featuring all stainless steel construction, cut-rifle barrels, free-wheeling 5-shot cylinders, adjustable sights, hand-filling grips—and the retail price has just been reduced to $899, making it the least expensive way to get into a really big-bore six-gun. Magnum Research also offers scope mount bases and rings, as well as both leather and

The BFR 475 Linebaugh has proven to be an exceptionally accurate revolver.

Cordura holsters. I have fired BFRs chambered in 475, 500, and 45-70, finding them all to be superbly accurate and smooth-operating.

United States Firearms

USFA is putting out beautiful traditionally styled single-action six-guns! The main frame and the hammer are case-colored in what is described as Armory Bone Case, the balance of the six-gun is finished in a deep, dark Dome Blue color, and the standard grips are checkered hard rubber with a "US" molded into the top part of the grip. On all the USFA single actions I have examined, these stocks are perfectly fitted to the frame and feel exceptionally good in my hand.

One of the things I always look for in the fitting and finishing of single action six-guns is the radiusing of the lower part of the back of the hammer and the two "ears" formed by the backstrap where it screws into the mainframe on both sides of the hammer. A well-made single action will exhibit a smooth mating of the contours of all three. USFA six-guns are very nearly perfect in this area, and the same careful fitting can also be found where the top of the face of the hammer meets the top strap. The fit of the trigger guard to the bottom of the mainframe is so perfectly done one can run a finger over the area and not feel where one part begins and the other ends. The same is true where the backstrap meets the mainframe.

The front of the ejector rod housing as well as the cylinder are both beveled which not only looks good and feels good, it also provides for easier holstering. Markings on these six-guns include the serial number in three places: the butt, in front of the trigger guard and on the mainframe in front of the trigger guard screw. This is exactly as the original 19th-century single action armies were marked. Trigger pulls are set at three pounds. Cylinders lock up tight both in the hammer down or cocked position.

All USFA six-guns are totally American-made and available with

The USFA Single Action is offered in the three standard barrel lengths: 4-3/4, 5-1/2, and 7-1/2inches, with casehardened frame and well-fitted checkered black rubber grips.

a V notch or square-notch rear sight perfectly filled in by a front sight that also has a square profile, rather than tapering to the top. Shooters also have a choice of a cross pin or screw-in "black powder" cylinder pin latch. Chamberings for USFA single

Taffin shooting the USFA 44 Special Flat-Top Target

actions include the 45 Colt, of course; however, other choices include 32 WCF (32-20), 41 Long Colt, 38 Special, 38 WCF (38-40), 44 WCF (44-40), 45 ACP, 44 Russian and 44 Special. The latter can be marked, and properly chambered as "RUSSIAN AND S&W SPECIAL 44" as early Colt single actions were marked, while 38 Specials can also be marked on the left side of the barrel with "COLT AND S&W SPECIAL 38" just as were early 20th-century revolvers.

The less expensive Rodeo is the same basic six-gun as the Single Action Army except it comes with a matte blue finish instead of the beautiful finish of the standard revolver. The Rodeo has proven so popular it is now offered in several chamberings and all three standard barrel lengths. In addition to the Single Action Army that is also offered in an ejectorless Sheriff's Model, USFA offers a Flat-Top Target version patterned after the target models of the 1890s. The Omni-Potent is a special USFA single action with a grip frame reminiscent of the 1878 Colt Double Action. It is available in all calibers and barrel lengths as well as a target version, all with checkered wood grips and a lanyard ring, and what may be the ultimate belly gun—The Snubnose, with a 2-inch barrel *sans* ejector rod housing.

Hartford Armory

Hartford Armory began manufacturing their version of the Remington Models 1875 and 1890, chambered in 45 Colt and capable of handling +P+ loads, last year. As with any new endeavor it is always a slow process getting everything up and running smoothly, however the kinks have been smoothed out and Remingtons are now coming through regularly. These high-quality Remingtons are being produced on thoroughly modern, totally up-to-date machinery using the finest American-made 4130 and 4140 steels with forged mainframes, not cast. Hartford Armory has deviated from the original design in only one way: making the cylinder approximately

1/8-inch longer to allow use of today's 45 Colt ammunition. The original Remington cylinders were even shorter than those in the Colt Single Action Army, and many of the modern rounds offered in 45 Colt are deliberately made long enough to preclude their being used in Colt Single Actions or replica Remingtons as they are simply are not strong enough to handle +P or Heavy Duty 45 Colt hunting loads. However, Hartford Armory's Remingtons are strong enough to handle any factory 45 Colt ammunition currently offered; even strong enough to be chambered in 44 Magnum.

The grip frame of the Remington raises the comfort level considerably when using heavy loads since the backstrap is slightly straighter and also comes up higher, much like the design found on the original Colt Bisley Model and the current Freedom Arms and Ruger Bisley model. Both the 1875 and 1890 Hartford Armory Remingtons come from the factory with smooth actions, easy-to-operate hammers and the trigger pull set at around three pounds. Both models feature a beautifully polished blue finish, with a case-hardened hammer and loading gate, as on the originals. Cylinder lockup is tight with no movement side-to-side or front-to-back. The barrel/cylinder gap will not accept the smallest feeler gauge I have, which is 0.002-inch. Hartford Armory Remingtons are available

only through Taylor's & Co. They are available in blue or stainless steel, with 5 1/2- or 7 1/2-inch barrels and chambered in 45 Colt, 44 Magnum, 44-40 and 357 Magnum.

Gary Reeder

In the 1920s Elmer Keith set about to build the perfect six-gun, the result being his #5SAA, a 5 1/2-inch 44 Special. Gary Reeder is now offering six-guns, built on his frames, of the #5 Improved that is based on Elmer's #5 as it appeared in the 1929 *American Rifleman*. Reeder has made a few changes: better sights, a standard cross-pin cylinder pin latch and a transfer bar safety conversion combined with a standard single-action style action. For loading and unloading, the loading gate is opened and the hammer put on half-cock, even though it has a transfer bar safety.

Reeder's Deluxe Grade all-steel #5 in 44 Special is of polished stainless steel, fully engraved, with an octagonal barrel. Sights are fully adjustable with an interchangeable front sight feature, stocks are elephant ivory, and the grip frame is like no other. Keith had very small hands, which is evident in the design of his #5 grip frame. Reeder has maintained the same basic grip frame while making it more useable by adding 3/8-inch to the length.

The #5 Improved was designed around the 44 Special and will

Gary Reeder is now offering his version of Elmer Keith's #5SAA here shown in the deluxe version chambered in 44 Special and fitted with Mongolian stag stocks.

also be available in 45 Colt. The standard Field Grade #5 with walnut stocks has a base price of $1295, with full engraving, octagon barrel and custom stocks available.

As a companion piece to the #5 Improved, Reeder offers the Improved #6, which is nothing more than a slightly larger #5 Improved that can handle the 44 Magnum, as well as the 41 Magnum and a five-shot version in 454. The Deluxe Grade Improved #6 has a 5 1/2-inch octagon barrel, is also fully engraved, and is fitted with Mongolian stag stocks.

Thompson/Center

For nearly four decades the T/C Contender has been the single-shot pistol by which all other single shots are measured. It was definitely the leading force in long-range silhouetting and remains one of the best choices for the handgun hunter. A few years back, a second version was added to the Thompson/Center lineup: the Encore. The Contender, now in its second stage as the easier-opening G2, handles most revolver and rifle cartridges up to 30-30 pressures, while the Encore is reserved for high-pressure cartridges such as the 454 Casull and the 308 Winchester.

Since the mid-1960s, the Contender has been offered in a long list of chamberings—including just about every six-gun, semi-automatic pistol, and levergun cartridge. It has been especially favored by handgun hunters in 30-30 and 44 Magnum. Current offerings include 22 Match, 22 Hornet, 357 and 44 Magnum, and 45 Colt/.410-bore with 12-inch barrels, while the selection with the Super 14 barrel includes 17HMR, 204 Ruger, 22 Match, 22 Hornet, 223 Remington, 7-30 Waters, 30-30, 375 JDJ, 44 Magnum, 45-70, and 45 Colt/410. When I was participating in long-range silhouetting my favorite chamberings were the 357 and 30-30.

Encores are catalogued with 12-inch barrels in 223, 44 Magnum, 454 Casull, and 45 Colt/410. The longer barrel Encore has a near-rifle length of 15 inches and is offered in a range of rifle cartridges including 204 Ruger,

Top: T/C's G2 Contender is a very popular hunting handgun, especially in the 14-inch version.
Bottom: For high-pressure cartridges such as the 454 Casull, 308, and 30-06, T/C offers the Encore, here in stainless steel.

22 Hornet, 223 Remington, 22-250, 243, 25-06, 270 Winchester, 7mm-08, 308, 30-06, 375 JDJ, 45-70, 45 Colt/.410. Both the Contender and Encore are offered with blued barrels and frames with walnut stocks and forearms, while a few models are offered in stainless steel. The T/C rubber grip is a desirable addition for the harder-kicking Encores.

Thompson/Center has a new owner. Greg Ritz, who has been with T/C for quite a while and may be seen regularly hunting on television, is a true shooter and should prove a very valuable asset not only to Thompson/Center but all shooters.

SSK Industries

It is virtually impossible to mention Thompson/Center single-shot pistols without thinking of SSK Industries and the genius of J.D. Jones. J.D. is one of the world's top handgun hunters using custom SSK T/Cs to take virtually everything. I started handgun hunting with one of SSK's early efforts, the 430 JDJ, nearly 30 years ago; moved up to the 45-70, and then settled on the 375 JDJ for large game and the superb 6.5 JDJ for deer-size game. The latter is

based on the 225 Winchester case expanded and blown out to 6.5mm. It kills all out of proportion to its paper ballistics, especially when loaded with the 120-grain Speer SP at 2400 fps.

With the coming of the Encore, SSK moved up a notch and offers custom barrels in any safe chamberings, including several wildcats such as the 6.5 Dreadnought based on the 30-06 case. Two of the most recent chamberings are the 500 S&W and 460 XVR. In addition to standard Encores chambered in 22-250, 308, and 7mm-08, I also use J.D.'s barrels chambered in the aforementioned Dreadnought and 500 S&W. If it can be done safely, SSK can provide a custom Encore barrel in virtually any rifle chambering. SSK also offers the ONLY scope mounting system for really hard-kicking handguns, the T'SOB. It works and is the only one I recommend for the heavy-hitters.

Mag-Na-Port

Even before J.D. Jones started SSK Industries, his good friend and hunting buddy, Larry Kelly, started helping shooters reduce recoil by the EDM process known as Mag-na-port. The little trapezoidal-shaped ports were cleanly cut into barrels electronically and reduced muzzle flip. Kelly soon began offering not only the Mag-na-port feature but also custom handguns design for the handgun hunter. The Stalker conversions were, and are, accomplished on big bore Ruger, Smith & Wesson, and Freedom Arm six-guns, with specially tuned actions, Mag-na-

Top: The Ruger Super Redhawk becomes a much easier to pack six-gun with the Mag-Na-Port 480 Advantage conversion.
Bottom: Some of the nastiest recoil imaginable is found in the 12-ounce S&W 360Sc 357 Magnum. Mag-na-porting helps tame the muzzle flip.

porting, sling swivels, and scopes mounted using SSK's T-SOB system.

Now Larry Kelly is retired and Mag-na-port is headed up by son Ken who offers several new packages for the new generation of six-guns.

Smith & Wesson's new line of revolvers are traveling in two directions: The 500 and 460 Magnums are two extremely powerful cartridges in very large and heavy revolvers; on the other hand S&W offers the 357 and 44 Magnum in very lightweight revolvers made of scandium and titanium. The answer to help tame recoil, especially on the very lightweight guns, is Mag-na-porting.

European American Armory

EAA has entered the single-shot market. Thor is the latest single-shot pistol from Tanfoglio, via EAA.

Chambered in 45-70, the grip frame is 1911-shaped and Hogue's checkered rubber grips with finger grooves provide a very secure hold. Thor is built heavy-duty with a 1/2-inch block of steel containing the firing pin. To open the action, the hammer is placed on half-cock, the 1911-style "magazine" release button is pushed in and the other hand pushes down on the top of the barrel. A cartridge is inserted, the receiver is pushed down into place and the action locks. To fire, the hammer is fully cocked. There is a thumb safety and grip safety; again, just as on a 1911.

Barrel length, including the entire cartridge, is 14 inches and the top of the massive receiver has a scope mount integrally machined. Thor is finished in matte black, appropriate for a gun with this name, and comes with a matching matte black Leupold M8-4x scope mounted in quick-release rings. Thor is also available in 444 Marlin and 308 Winchester.

Replica Single Actions

I've been hoping and watching for it since Navy Arms first introduced the Schofield Model in the early 1990s. I knew it had to be close when Navy followed with the Model #3 Russian. Now it is here. **Beretta/Uberti** has announced the New Model #3—patterned after the original Smith & Wesson New Model #3 of the 1880s. The original was chambered in 44 Russian, a few in 44-40. For some reason, Beretta/Uberti chose to go with the 45 Colt. The prototype at the SHOT Show was a Target Model hurriedly finished in matte black; production models will be polished blue. It felt very good, with a smooth action, and I hope they chamber it for one of the original cartridges. Beretta/Uberti also displayed nickel-plated Bisley models looking very close to the originals of the 1890s.

By the time you read this, **Cimarron Firearms** hopes to have the cartridge conversion Model 1858 Remington complete with ejector rod housing. They continue to offer the Colt-style cartridge conversions with both the 1851 Navy and 1860 Army grip frame, as well as the 1871-72 Open-Top. The Model P is offered in blue/case-colored, nickel-plated and in a variety of calibers—as well as

The latest entry into the single shot handgun field, here shown chambered in 45-70, is the EAA Thor with a break-open action and a 1911-style grip frame.

stainless steel—in all three standard barrel lengths, chambered in both 357 Magnum and 45 Colt. Their Evil Roy Model P—designed by Gene "Evil Roy" Pearcy with checkered wood stocks, tuned action, and easy-to-see square sights—is proving to be very popular with western action shooters.

EMF continues to offer the Great Western II in blue and nickel finishes and has now added stainless steel models. They also offer a full line of traditionally styled 1873 Colt-style Hartford Models as well as the Pinkerton, Buntline, and Bisley Models—plus the replica Remington Model 1875. EMF's Great Western II is produced by Pietta, which also manufactures the Heritage Single Action. The latter, with a 4 3/4-inch barrel, nickel plating, and well-fitted and shaped American walnut stocks, will retail for only $329.

Navy Arms, as mentioned was the first to offer an S&W single action: the Schofield, followed by the Model #3 Russian. The Schofield, in 45 Colt or 38 Special, is offered in the 7-inch Cavalry, 5-inch Wells Fargo, and 3 1/2-inch Hideout Models, while the Model #3 Russian is offered only in the traditional 6 1/2-inch, and chambered in 44 Russian. In addition to the standard 1873 Single Action, Navy also has The Gunfighter, specially tuned with checkered rubber grips, silver-plated backstrap and trigger guard, all three traditional barrel lengths and chambering choices of 45 Colt, 44-40, and 357 Magnum.

In addition to being the exclusive distributor of the American-made Hartford Armory Remingtons, *Taylor's & Co.* has a full line of traditional-styled 1873 single actions as well as the Bisley Model, round-butted Birdshead, stainless steel Outfitter, and the compact Stallion. New this year is the "TR Presidential" with enhanced photo engraving. Taylor's is the first to offer a specially tuned Ruger New Vaquero as the HandleBar Doc Signature Series. Taylor's also offers a full line of R&D drop-in cylinders to convert cap and ball revolvers to cartridge firing. These include 45 Colt to fit Uberti, Pietta, and ASM Remingtons and Ruger Old Armies as well as 38 Special cylinders for steel frame Pietta or Uberti 36-caliber Remingtons.

Kenny Howell of *R&D* is also doing conversions and offering conversion kits on 1851/1861 and 1860 cap and ball six-guns. These conversions consist of a cartridge cylinder complete with loading gate and a lined barrel to 38LC/38 Special on all models or 44 Colt on the 1860. He is also offering a five-shot 45 Colt cylinder kit, which matches up with the existing barrel on the 1860. These are quality conversions all the way.

Custom Six-Guns On Old Model Ruger Blackhawks

Skeeter started it *(Skeeter Skelton, that is)* with an article in the April 1972 issue of *Shooting Times* about

converting old model Rugers and the S&W Highway Patrolman to 44 Special. Skeeter went Home in 1988 and I have been doing my best to continue to spread the word about the wonders of the 44 Special in general—especially when chambered in a three-screw Ruger, whether it started life as Flat-Top or Old Model 357 Magnum. Unlike the New Model Ruger Blackhawk, which is built on the larger 44 Blackhawk frame, the three-screws manufactured from 1955-1972 all have Colt single action sized frames. Bill Ruger expected to chamber his original Flat-Top Blackhawk in 44 Special; however, the arrival of the 44 Magnum changed all that and he instead brought out a larger-framed 44 Flat-Top in 1956.

Whether starting with a Highway Patrolman or three-screw Ruger for the conversion, it is necessary to re-chamber the cylinder and either re-bore the barrel or use an available

✥✥ ● ✥✥ ● ✥✥ ● ✥✥ ● ✥✥ ● ✥✥

▲ *Mike Harvey of Cimarron Firearms shows an engraved and nickel-plated 1871-72 Open-Top.*
◀ *Some replica single actions available today are,* clockwise from top right, *EMF's Model 1875 Remington, Navy Arms Model #3 Russian, and two from Cimarron—an Original Finish Model P and an 1871-72 Open-Top*

44 Special barrel. This was not a problem with the Smith & Wesson conversion thirty years ago when original 44 Special Model 24 barrels were still available. Today, they are nearly impossible to find. The Ruger conversion is much easier to accomplish since a Ruger 44 Magnum barrel can be used, or one may start with 44 barrel stock, which is much easier to fit to a single action than a double-action revolver requiring a cut out and lock up for the ejector rod.

Here then are ten 44 Special conversions on three-screw Rugers by five different gunsmiths, another custom 44 by a very special friend, and if you look closely you may even catch a glimpse of that other Special, the 41. Feel free to use any of these ideas, or better yet contact one of the four remaining six-gunsmiths, as Bill Grover has been called Home.

HAMILTON BOWEN: Pictured are four 44 Special Blackhawk conversions and one 41 Special Blackhawk with case-colored frame and hammer—all by Hamilton Bowen. Three of the 44s are on Flat-Tops, one on an Old Model, and the 41 on a Flat-Top frame. The latter has to be one of the most beautiful single-action six-guns in existence. Two of the 357 Flat-Tops are now a matched pair of 4 5/8-inch bright blue 44 Specials with stag grips. The third one had been ridden hard and put up wet and although it was mechanically fine, the finish was pitted in places. This has been made into a real workin' 44 Special six-gun with a bead blasted finish. The final 44 Special conversion by Bowen on an Old Model frame is fitted with a 7 1/2-inch barrel, polished grip frame, and black micarta grips by Charles Able.

DAVID CLEMENTS: David Clements is another custom six-gunsmith building many big-bore New Model conversions, however,

❀ • ❀ • ❀ • ❀ • ❀ • ❀

Not a New Frontier but rather a Ruger OM converted to 44 Special, with an auxiliary cylinder in 44-40 and a New Frontier barrel fitted by David Clements. Custom stocks are by Larry Caudill.

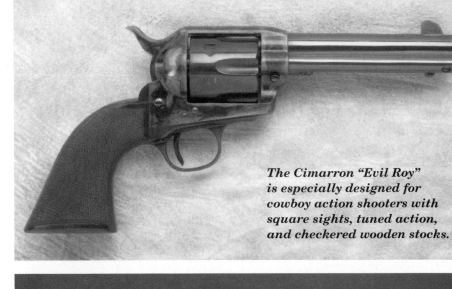

The Cimarron "Evil Roy" is especially designed for cowboy action shooters with square sights, tuned action, and checkered wooden stocks.

Taylor's & Co. now offers the R&D drop-in cylinder, chambered in 45 Colt, for the Ruger Old Army.

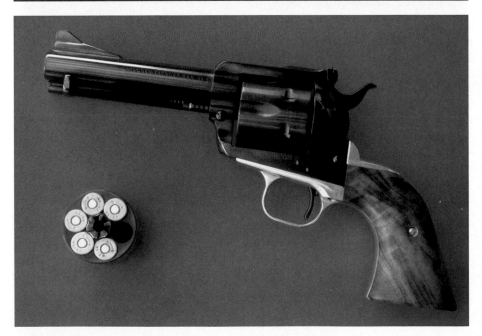

Two easy-packing 44 Specials: the blued version by Andy Horvath and the nickel-plated "Baby" by R.G. Baer.

he also turns out some fine three-screw 44 Special six-guns.

BEN FORKIN: Ben Forkin of Montana began his gunsmithing career the right way, working under Hamilton Bowen. All of the custom three-screw Blackhawks mentioned thus far have 4 5/8- or 7 1/2-inch barrels. Using a recently purchased like-new 6 1/2-inch 44 Magnum Flat-Top barrel, we decided to do a 5 1/2-inch 44 Special complete with case hardened mainframe and hammer. Ben performed his usual action work: smoothing, tuning, and tightening; re-chambered the cylinder to 44 Special cutting it to use .430-inch Keith bullets; cut the 44 Magnum barrel to the proper length and fitted it with a post front sight mated with a Bowen adjustable rear sight. He finished off the package with one of Belt Mountain's #5 base pins.

BILL GROVER: In the late 1980s I saw a very special 44 Special on a Ruger Old Model. The barrel was 4-5/8 inches long, the grip frame was polished bright, and the grips were made from the horns of a bighorn sheep. This special six-gun was shown to me by Bart Skelton as it had belonged to his dad Skeeter before he died and then belonged to gunwriter John Wootters. Two three-screw 357 Blackhawks went off to Bill Grover of Texas Longhorn Arms.

Grover and I put our heads together on this one so a double influence can be seen. The cylinder has been re-chambered to 44 Special tightly to allow the use of .429-inch diameter bullets but kept to minimum dimensions for long case life. Barrel/cylinder gap was set at 0.0025-inch. The Ruger XR3 grip frame and steel ejector housing were not discarded, but put back for use on the other 44 Special Grover was building. In their place Grover fitted steel Colt parts, a Colt backstrap and trigger guard, which now wears one-piece ivories, and a Colt ejector housing along with a bullseye-head ejector rod.

The second 44 Special six-gun from Grover was built with a 7 1/2-inch barrel using a 10 1/2-inch Ruger Super Blackhawk barrel. The XR3 grip frame of #SS4 now resides on this six-gun along with rosewood stocks. This long-range six-gun made to complement the #SS4 packin' pistol also wears a Number Five front sight and a Number Five base pin.

R.G. BAER: Bob Baer is not a working gunsmith but simply a special friend who likes to customize his own six-guns. An Old Model three-screw 357 Ruger Blackhawk was turned over to him with instructions to simply build

me a special gun, his choice of style and caliber. Having seen, handled, and shot many of Baer's creations from short barrels to long barrels, from round butts to lanyard rings, from 22s to 357s to 44s, with all kinds of artistic touches, I knew I would not be disappointed.

Since Baer had a pretty good idea where my heart lies, the conversion is a 44 Special. The front and rear edge of the grip frame are tapered for greater comfort, with no sharp edges to emphasize recoil, and the fancy walnut grips have been expertly fitted to the bright polished aluminum grip frame. The aluminum ejector rod housing is also polished bright while the rest of Baby, as Baer dubbed it, is finished in satin hard nickel plating. To aid in the project, gunsmith Keith DeHart expertly re-chambered the cylinder and furnished the 3 1/4-inch barrel. The total package is a very easy to pack 30 ounces.

ANDY HORVATH: About 20 years ago Horvath was asked if he could do a round-butted, 4-inch barrel 44 built on a Ruger 357 three-screw Blackhawk, a real 44 Special packin' pistol. The answer came back affirmative and off went a 6 1/2-inch 357 three-screw Blackhawk, a 7 1/2-inch Super Blackhawk barrel, and some special items I had been saving for just such a project.

Recently I have had the pleasure of working with one of Horvath's latest 44 Specials. Starting with a Flat-Top 357 Blackhawk, Andy re-chambered it to 44 Special, fitted it with a full-ribbed heavy barrel from a S&W 44 Magnum with an undercut post front sight, re-contoured the front edge of the top strap to blend in perfectly with the ribbed barrel, then fitted it with an abbreviated style #5 base pin. The finish is a deep, high polished blue set off perfectly by a case hardened frame and hammer. It was very difficult to even consider returning this test gun—so I bought it.

Yes, things were much simpler in the old days when so few choices were available. Today's handgunner can sincerely say that sometimes progress can be wonderful. Have a great six-gunnin' year!

AUTOLOADERS:
HANDGUNS TODAY

by John Malloy

The biggest recent news concerning the autoloading handgun scene was probably not mechanical, but political. As those with an interest in firearms know now, the so-called "Assault Weapons Ban" (AWB) was allowed to sunset at its appointed time on September 13, 2004. Then, George W. Bush was reelected President of the United States on November 4, 2004.

This report is not really a place for political commentary. However, some aspects of the political situation affect autoloading handguns directly, so it is perhaps appropriate to discuss them briefly here. The now-defunct AWB was thought by many to deal only with "assault" rifles. However, perhaps most of the effect was actually felt in relation to semiautomatic handguns.

The AWB banned the manufacture of 19 specific firearms, most of them rifles, guns that were deemed to be "assault weapons." Also, "copycat" models were banned if they had any two cosmetic features considered offensive, such as a flash suppressor or a bayonet mount. The false picture presented to the public by the major media was that the rifles that had been banned, such as the semiautomatic AR-15 and AK-47 clones, were really machineguns.

However, semiautomatic handguns, hardly mentioned by the major media, were addressed in greater detail in the law. Only two specific handgun models, the TEC-9 and the SWD M-10 (the "MAC-10") were specifically banned. However, manufacturers were prohibited from making any autoloading pistol that used a detachable magazine and had two or more arbitrary features. Such features included a magazine outside the pistol grip, a threaded muzzle that could accept various accessories, a shroud around the barrel, a weight of 50 ounces or more, or just being a semiautomatic version of a full-automatic firearm.

A major provision of the "Assault Weapon Ban" was the prohibition on the manufacture of "ammunition feeding devices" that held more than 10 rounds. This restriction most affected manufacturers of autoloading handguns. With most rifles that are designed to use extended magazines, the magazine protrudes below the lower line of the rifle. Thus, rifles designed for greater capacity magazines could just substitute a shorter 10-round magazine.

With the sunset of the AWB, Para-Ordnance adds full-capacity offerings back into its 1911 offerings.

The overwhelming majority of automatic pistols, however, have the magazine contained within the pistol's grip frame. The frame is of a size and shape to accommodate a magazine of a certain size and shape. Thus, decreased-capacity pistol magazines had to be redesigned—not only to hold just 10 rounds and fit the pistol and work properly—but to prevent any efforts to later increase the capacity. The innovations in plugged and distorted magazines that resulted might make an interesting historical collection—one that should remind us never to let such legislation become the law of the land again.

It is good that this bad law, which was based largely on emotion, and without any support of facts or logic, has been allowed to sunset. However, the effect of the AWB is not completely gone. A number of laws in different areas essentially duplicated the federal law, and they are still in effect. Since the sunset, anti-gun organizations have made an effort to introduce bills in state legislatures that would, in effect, reestablish the AWB in the affected states.

So, the issue has not gone away. Unfortunately, neither has the federal "Assault Weapons Ban." It was not deleted from federal law; it just remains on the books, dormant, because the sunset clause has removed from it the force of law. We can bet that the antis will continue their efforts to either strike out the sunset language or to write an even more restrictive bill. However, for the present, pistol shooters can legally acquire new magazines that were actually designed for their handguns, and can enjoy "politically-incorrect" features on new guns.

The failure of the anti-gun forces to prevent sunset of the AWB was a prelude to the elections of November 4, 2004. The gun rights issue had been a strong factor in the 2000 elections, and the Democrats' 2004 presidential candidate, John Kerry, made an effort to disguise his two-decade anti-gun voting record. He appeared in TV ads as a hunter and shooter. The facts of his record, coupled with his incredibly bizarre descriptions of his hunting experiences, worked against him. George W. Bush was reelected for a second term as president, and the number of reportedly pro-gun legislators in both the House and Senate increased.

The Bush administration is not perfect, but is basically in accord with firearms rights. The Bush Justice Department released an exhaustively-researched report concluding that the Second Amendment "secures an individual right to keep and bear arms." So, drastic federal anti-gun legislation seems unlikely within the next few years. However, efforts to continue and expand bans of certain firearms and "high-capacity" magazines can be expected to continue at state and local levels. Autoloading pistols always seem to be the objects of such proposed legislation.

Perhaps we should make an effort to dispense with the terminology that the anti-gun forces use. They use the term "high-capacity" as something sinister and evil. A 13-round magazine for a Browning Hi-Power is not really a "high-capacity" magazine—it is the magazine for which the pistol was designed. Thus, it is a "normal-capacity" or "full-capacity" magazine. The 10-round magazines we were forced to use for a decade were "reduced-capacity" or "restricted-capacity" magazines.

Now, then, as far as the guns themselves are concerned: the fighting in Iraq, the threat of terrorism and the continuing need for personal protection have kept interest in autoloading handguns high. Most autoloaders introduced recently are suitable for personal protection, or for police or military use. The 45 ACP cartridge seems still to be king of the hill as far as new introductions are concerned. Several companies have introduced new 45s for the first time.

The tried-and-true Colt/Browning 1911 still reigns as the most-used design. For each of the past few years, a company that had never before made a 1911 brought out its version of the classic design. This year we add another two companies, Taurus and United States Fire Arms.

Old names are returning, and it is good to see them back. To the Detonics and Whitney pistols reintroduced last year, we can now add AMT and AutoMag offerings. The Iver Johnson name is also back, offering, among other things, another new 1911 line!

State and local restrictions, no matter how illogical, have to be considered by the manufacturers. In order to sell their products in all states, some handgun makers have had to add internal locking devices, magazine disconnectors and other mechanical devices, and have to be able to supply restricted-capacity 10-round magazines for those who live in areas where magazine freedom has not reached.

Frame rails have become more popular. More organizations and more shooters seem to like the option of hanging various things from their pistols. With polymer-frame pistols, similar frames may be moulded with or without a rail, and some manufacturers offer both varieties.

Laser sighting devices have also become more popular. If a shooter does not want to attach a laser device to his pistol, he can opt for laser grips. Such grips have the batteries, switches and beam generators contained entirely within the grips. At least one American manufacturer, Smith & Wesson, now offers some handguns that are factory-equipped with laser grips.

As a reason to buy a new pistol, why not a commemorative model to celebrate an anniversary? A number of anniversary models—including anniversaries for pistols and companies and organizations—are offered this year.

Interest in pistol-caliber carbines continues to grow, and the option of larger magazine capacity has perhaps given that category of firearms special favor this year. The pistol-caliber carbines are generally not covered along with traditional hunting and target rifles, so we'll give them at least a little attention here.

Please keep all this in mind, and let's take a look at what the companies are doing:

ADCO

The 45 ACP ADCO TT45 was introduced last year, and it has now been joined by versions in 9mm and 40 S&W. The new pistols were introduced, logically so, as the Models TT9 and TT40. These polymer-frame pistols, made in the Czech Republic and based on the CZ 75 mechanism, weigh 26 ounces. With the federal magazine capacity restrictions lifted, the 9mm has 15+1 capacity, and the 40 holds 12+1. For those in states that still restrict magazine capacity, reduced-capacity 10-round magazines are available.

American Derringer

Almost unnoticed among the variety of derringers and other non-autoloading handguns made by this Texas company, a stainless-steel 25 auto has been in the line for some time. With the increased interest in 25-sized 32 autos, the company investigated revising the pistol into a 32. The prototype apparently worked well, but production of the 32 would have required extensive redesign of the pistol and tooling. A decision was made to drop the work on the 32. The 25, a stainless-steel pistol with wood grips, remains in the line.

AMT/Automag

To the disappointment of many shooters, AMT ceased production of its line of innovative stainless-steel pistols in late 2001. However, in 2004, the Crusader Group acquired the assets, and selected AMT pistols are once more being offered. By early 2005, the double-action-only (DAO) BackUp pistols had been returned to production. They are available in 380 and 45 ACP calibers. The original larger BackUp was also made in five other calibers (40 S&W, 9mm, 38 Super, 357 SIG, and 400 Cor-Bon), and smaller numbers of these additional chamberings are now in the works.

The AutoMag II, the first-ever production autoloading pistol for the 22 Winchester Magnum Rimfire (22 WMR), is now back in production, in three barrel lengths. Lengths offered are the original 6-inch, 4 1/2-inch and 3 3/8-inch variants. A new version in 17 Hornady Magnum Rimfire (17 HMR) was scheduled for late 2005. The AutoMag III, in 30 Carbine, is also being returned to production.

Parts and magazines for AMT and AutoMag pistols will be available, and will work with previously-made guns. Magazines will be available for all models and all calibers. (see also CRUSADER)

Armscor

Armscor offers a line of 45-caliber Philippine-made 1911 pistols, and has recently introduced some changes. All 1911 pistols made under the Armscor name now have external extractors and fully-supported barrels. Guns made under the Rock Island name have the original 1911 features.

Still considered prototypes *(although they made it into the 2005 catalog)* are two new 9mm pistols. Of CZ 75 style, one has a steel frame, and the other has a polymer frame.

Beretta

A number of companies have taken an established pistol design and used it as the basis for a pistol-caliber carbine. Beretta, on the other hand, has taken its successful Storm Cx4 carbine and, with that as a concept, has developed a companion Storm pistol. The new Px4 Storm pistol was shown for the first time at the January 2005 SHOT Show. The new Beretta pistol is a polymer-frame pistol that uses the same magazines as the Storm carbine. It is designed around what Beretta calls a "modular concept."

The emphasis toward potential law-enforcement acceptance is obvious. The Storm pistol can meet just about any specifications a department might have. To fit different hand sizes, the pistol has three interchangeable grip backstraps. Reversible magazine-release buttons—of different sizes—are included to further customize the gun to the shooter. The safety lever also comes in two different interchangeable sizes. Available at first as a conventional double-action (DA), Beretta's vision is that the trigger mechanism can be customized to include the options of conventional DA with or without a manual safety, and two types of double-action-only (DAO) mechanisms.

The locking system is a new rotary barrel arrangement, and the recoil spring is held captive. Takedown is simple, and the pistol frame has a Picatinny accessory rail moulded in. The new Storm pistol is available now in 9mm and 40 S&W, has a barrel length of 4 inches and an overall length of 7-1/2 inches. The 9 weighs 27-1/2 ounces and has 17+1 capacity. The 40 weighs 29 ounces, with 14+1 capacity. Rumors are that a 45-caliber version will also be introduced, and this seems logical, but there was no official confirmation.

The new Beretta Storm Px4 pistol has interchangeable grip backstraps and controls of different sizes to customize a pistol to the shooter's hand.

The action of Browning's Buck Mark rifles is essentially the same as that of the Buck Mark pistols.

The Browning Buck Mark target rifle has a heavy bull barrel and can use a variety of optical or electronic sights.

Browning's Buck Mark Sporter is an open-sight carbine based on the Buck Mark pistols.

The Browning Buck Mark Field Target Rifle has a heavy barrel and laminated stock.

The lightest carbine in Browning's Buck Mark rifle line is the Field Carbon rifle with a carbon composite barrel. Weight is about 3-1/2 pounds.

Bersa

Bersa Thunder 9 and Thunder 40 double-action pistols were designed for larger-capacity magazines, but had to be sold with 10-round magazines. As of January 2005, the Bersa 9mms will be shipped with 17-round, and 40s with 13-round magazines. Extra full-capacity magazines will be available as separate items. Bersa pistols are imported by Eagle Imports.

Browning

Browning has introduced a number of new variants of its popular 22-caliber Buck Mark pistol.

One version is called the Buck Mark Hunter. It features a round, heavy 7 1/4-inch barrel with an integral scope mount base. The pistol has a Pro-Target adjustable rear sight, and a fiber-optic Truglow front sight from Marble. Cocobolo target-type grips are furnished.

The Buck Mark Camper Stainless is a stainless-steel version of the existing Camper pistol, and has a 5 1/2-inch tapered bull barrel.

Two stainless-steel versions of the Buck Mark Standard pistol are now available, one with a flat-sided 5 1/2-inch barrel, and the other as a 4-inch-barrel "Micro" version.

The Buck Mark 5.5 Field pistol has a 5 1/2-inch bull barrel that sports target sights and a full-length mounting rail for optical or electronic sights. The 5.5 Target pistol is similar, and also has the front and rear sights hooded—a potential help when shooting in bright sunlight.

The 22-caliber carbines based on the Buck Mark pistol mechanism *(called "Buck Mark rifles" by Browning)* have proven popular. Several different variants are now available. There is a Sporter with open sights, and also Target and Field Target heavy-barrel variants. A lightweight rifle with a carbon composite barrel weighs only about 3-1/2 pounds. All Buck Mark rifles have 18-inch barrels.

Bushmaster

With the sunset of the "Assault Weapons Ban," Bushmaster is again able to offer models and features not available for a decade. Of interest to us here are the 223-caliber Carbon 15 pistols that Bushmaster offered for the first time last year, which are now freed from weight restrictions.

Recall that Bushmaster acquired Professional Ordnance last year, and thus became a pistol—as well as a rifle—company. Their Carbon 15 pistols feature the same controls as the Bushmaster AR 15-type rifles, but the upper and lower receivers are of Carbon 15 material, bringing the weight down substantially.

The Type 21 pistol, which has a 7 1/4-inch barrel, is now joined by the Type 21S. The new 21S has added a forend/handguard surrounding the barrel, and a full-length optics rail.

The Type 97, with a 7 1/4-inch fluted stainless-steel barrel, is now also offered as the 97S. This new version has a handguard, a full-length upper optics rail, and a lower accessory rail.

A conversion kit to upgrade Type 21 and Type 97 pistols to Type 21S configuration is also available.

Century

Century International Arms carries a line of new Bulgarian Arcus pistols *(based on the Browning "Hi-Power")* in 9mm chambering, and the Bulgarian Makarov pistols in 9x18mm. Century also carries the innovative line of Korean Daewoo "tri-fire" pistols, in 9mm and 40 S&W.

In addition to their newly-manufactured pistols, Century is handling surplus CZ 52 pistols, and has a limited stock of surplus German Lugers and P-38s.

The company recently dropped its line of Philippine-made 45-caliber 1911-type pistols.

Charles Daly

The ZDA pistol, announced by Charles Daly last year, is now a new catalog item. The Zastava-made conventional double-action pistols are available in 9mm or 40 S&W calibers.

The Ultra-X pistol, a very compact double-column polymer-frame 45 of 1911 style, was not approved for importation last year. Charles Daly hoped to have everything worked out so the Ultra-X would be available here by late 2005.

Ciener

Jonathan Arthur Ciener now has in production 22 Long Rifle (22 LR) conversion kits for the Browning Hi-Power pistol and its clones.

Interest in 22 LR conversions for centerfire pistols dates back to the Colt Ace units of the pre-WWII days. In the last fifteen years, Ciener has become a dominant force in such conversions, previously offering kits for 1911, Glock, Beretta and Taurus pistols, as well as for a number of long guns.

22 LR conversion kits obviously let a shooter shoot more for less money. The kits are not firearms, and can generally be purchased without restrictions and shipped directly to a buyer. Use of a conversion kit can extend the usefulness of a pistol in a location that may restrict the number of firearms a person may possess.

Ciener's new Browning kits are offered in two styles, Standard and Hi-Power Plus. The standard unit has fixed sights, while the Plus unit has adjustable sights. Finishes are matte black, gloss black and silver. The units work on both 9mm and 40-caliber Hi-Power pistols.

Cobra

Cobra Enterprises has made a subtle name change, and is now Cobra Enterprises of Utah, Inc. The company still offers pistols similar to those formerly marketed under the Davis, Lorcin, Republic and Talon names. New items now offered are holsters and rebuild kits for older pistols.

Colt

The original Colt 1911, made to World War I specifications, became a catalog item last year, and is now in full production.

The Series 70 pistol is now made in a lightweight Officer's version. The new variant has a 4 1/4-inch barrel, a short "officer's" grip and Novak sights.

A new heavy-barrel 38 Super is being offered. The barrel of the new 38 Super is the same diameter as that of the 45, and fits the 45's barrel bushing.

Crusader

The formation of this new group was announced in September 2004, and although the name may be new to some, to others, the name "Crusader" may evoke memories of the limited-production High Standard Crusader revolver of the late '70s and early '80s. Yes, High Standard is indeed part of the new Crusader Group, which also includes the resurrected AMT and AutoMag lines. Other companies included are Firearms International, Inc., and Arsenal Line Products. (see also AMT / AUTOMAG, and HIGH STANDARD)

CZ

2005 was the 30th anniversary of the CZ 75 pistol, which was introduced in 1975, when Czechoslovakia was still hidden behind the Iron Curtain. Reports of the new pistol at that time were vague, but some thought it to be the best new pistol design introduced. It does seem to have stood the test of time. To commemorate this 30-year milestone, CZ-USA offered a limited run of a special 30th anniversary edition.

The 30th Anniversary pistols will have special serial numbers from 1 to 1000. The pistols are special CZ 75B pistols, chambered for the 9mm cartridge, and featuring high-polish blue, special engraving, inlays, plated controls and blond-finish birch grips. A 15-round magazine comes with each gun.

It is nice to again have design-capacity magazine options, and CZ will now ship full-capacity magazines with the appropriate models.

CZ also introduced a new 40 S&W version of its CZ 75 Compact. The steel frame has an accessory rail, and the pistol has an ambidextrous manual safety. Magazine capacity is 10 rounds. The barrel on the new compact is 3.87 inches, and the gun weighs about 38 ounces.

DETONICS

Detonics USA reintroduced the Detonics pistol last year, and the 45-caliber compact version, the

Top: 2005 was the 30th anniversary of the CZ 75 pistol, and the Czech company has brought out a special commemorative version with engraving, gold-plated parts and special grips.
Bottom: The CZ 75 Compact pistol is now available in a new 40 S&W version.

CombatMaster, is now in production and has been shipping since February 2005. Detonics president Jerry Ahern says that a very few CombatMaster pistols will also be made in 357 SIG, 40 S&W, 38 Super and 9mm.

Eventually the "commander-size" ServiceMaster and then later, the full-size target-ready ScoreMaster will be added to the line.

Before then, though, Detonics had planned a surprise. The new Detonics StreetMaster was scheduled to debut during early 2005. Ahern, a leading authority on concealed carry, felt there was a niche that had not been addressed in the world of concealed carry and personal protection. The new StreetMaster has the same abbreviated frame as the compact CombatMaster, but has a 5-inch barrel and a full-length slide to match. In a number of situations, such a pistol would be easier to carry and conceal than many conventional pistols, while offering the advantages of the longer barrel. With spacers, full-length magazines can be used to offer a full-size grip. The new StreetMaster has been given the trademarked model number 9-11-01.

FNH USA

FNH expanded their FNP line of polymer-frame pistols with two new models in production. The FHP 40 is a 40-caliber pistol with a 4-inch barrel. It is available with 16-round or 10-round magazines, depending on the location of the sale. Interchangeable mainspring housings allow the gun to be fit to the shooter's hand. A rail is made as part of the frame, for attaching lights, lasers or other accessories. Action and controls are the same as the previously-introduced FNP 9.

There is also a new FNP 9. It is a compact version with a 3.8-inch barrel, and an overall length of 7 inches. Weight is about 25 ounces. As with the new 40-caliber pistol, 16- or 10-round magazines are available. The new polymer pistol line now has a magazine disconnector.

The interesting Five-seveN pistol is now available in a new model, the USG. The new refined version of this lightweight polymer pistol has a more

traditionally-shaped trigger guard, reversible magazine release, and a textured grip. The pistol's 5.7x28 cartridge, originally designed for FN's P90 machinegun, had previously been available only to law enforcement. Now, a new sporting round, designated SS196, is available. Because of the small diameter of the cartridge, the magazine capacity is 20 rounds. A 10-round magazine is also available. It will be interesting to follow future sporting interest in this combination.

Glock

The 45 Glock Automatic Pistol (45 G.A.P.) cartridge was introduced two years ago and the Model 37 pistol in that new caliber went into production last year. It was seemingly just a matter of time before compact and subcompact 45 G.A.P. versions were introduced. That time came at the January 2005 SHOT Show, when the new Models 38 and 39 were announced. The compact Model 38 has 8+1 capacity, while the Model 39 subcompact holds 6+1.

Heckler & Koch

2005 was the 25th anniversary of HK's interesting squeeze-cocking P7 pistol. To celebrate, the company brought out a limited commemorative edition of the P7M8, with special engraving and checkered walnut grips. The guns are packaged in wood presentation cases, each with a special commemorative coin. Only 500 of the commemorative P7s will be made.

For 2005, the company offered some of the most popular HK pistols with tan, green or grey frames. These will be offered on a limited basis for five models—the USP 40, the USP 40 Compact, the USP 45, the USP 45 Tactical and the Mark 23.

High Standard

In September 2004, High Standard Manufacturing Company became part of the Crusader Group. Recall that the Crusader revolver was one of the last new products of the old High Standard company before its demise in 1984. Rejuvenated in 1993, High Standard continued its line of 22-caliber

The new Glock Model 38 is a new compact pistol chambered for the 45 G.A.P. cartridge. An accessory rail is molded into the polymer frame.

A new Glock subcompact pistol is chambered for the 45 G.A.P. cartridge. The small Model 39 does not have a rail incorporated into the frame.

target pistols, and added 45-caliber pistols based on the 1911 design.

For 2005, the company has added several new 45s, and two now carry the Crusader name. The Crusader Model 1911 and Crusader Combat pistols are embellished 1911 pistols with 5-inch and 4 1/4-inch barrels, respectively. A shorter version, with a 3 7/8-inch barrel, will also be available. There is also a new military-specification Parkerized 45, the Model of 1911 USA.

One question is sure to be asked, so here is the answer: There is no official word as to whether or not the Crusader revolver will ever be put back into production.

All we know is that it was not a possibility before, and there is at least some possibility now.

High Standard will incorporate the services of a company historian, and will offer factory letters for Hi-Standard pistols. (see also CRUSADER)

Hi-Point

Hi-Point Firearms offers a line of affordable pistols in 380, 9mm, 40 S&W and 45 ACP. The company also produces what is perhaps the most popular line of pistol-caliber carbines in America. Available in 9mm and 40, the carbines have been limited to 10-shot magazines. Now, with the AWB's magazine ban no longer in effect, Hi-Point plans to offer magazines of larger capacity, but none were yet available for inspection at the January 2005 SHOT Show.

Hornady

What is Hornady, a company involved with ammunition and components, doing in this report? Ah, it is here because Hornady has taken an interest in keeping surplus firearms shooting, and has offered a new line of rifle and handgun cartridges and components. The first autoloading pistol cartridge, just made available, is the 9mm Steyr. A lot of nice shootable old 1911/1912 Steyr pistols sit unused now, and fresh new ammunition can get them out and shooting. The new Hornady ammo is distributed by Graf & Sons.

Iver Johnson

The Iver Johnson name has returned, and the new company offers some interesting autoloading pistols. With the name dating back well over a century, Iver Johnson has been located in New England, in Arkansas, and now in Rockledge, Florida. The present company is connected with Essex Arms of Vermont, which acquired the tooling for the Arkansas-made Iver Johnson 30-caliber carbines. Because Essex already made 1911 slides and frames, it seemed a logical move to add complete 1911 pistols to the new Iver Johnson line of M1 carbines and other guns.

The Iver Johnson 1911s are offered in 45 ACP chambering, and also as 22-caliber pistols. 45-caliber guns are made with steel frames and slides, while the 22s have aluminum frames and slides. A pretty extensive line of pistols is offered, with adjustable- and fixed-sight variants, in 5-inch or 4 1/4-inch barrel lengths. Blue or stainless finishes are available, along with two-tone options.

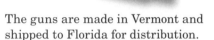

The new Thompson Custom pistol from Kahr has a beavertail tang, extended safety and other custom features.

The guns are made in Vermont and shipped to Florida for distribution.

In addition, the nice little Iver Johnson X300 "Pony" 380 ACP pistol will be offered once again. Initial production was planned for late 2005. This 6+1 capacity 380 pistol goes back a long way, and it will be good to have it available again.

Kahr

Kahr has expanded its lightweight polymer-frame DAO line. Expanded it up to 45-caliber! Kahr's first 45 ACP pistol to actually bear the Kahr name *(we won't count the Auto-Ordnance/Thompson 1911 45s that Kahr also makes)* weighs only a bit over 20 ounces, with magazine. It features a textured black polymer frame with a stainless-steel slide. The barrel is 3-1/2 inches long, and is polygonally rifled. The pistol feels good in the hand, and has a 7 1/2-pound trigger. Capacity is 6+1, and each P45 comes with two magazines.

Kahr also introduced a value-priced pistol to appeal to the concealed-carry market. The CW9 is a 9mm with a 3 1/2-inch barrel and has 7+1 capacity.

In the Thompson 1911 line, Kahr has introduced two new Custom models, one with a stainless-steel frame, and one with an aluminum frame. Both versions have stainless slides, adjustable triggers, beavertail tangs, extended manual safety levers and other features.

Pistol-caliber carbines are popular now, and Malloy tries out what is perhaps the most popular of all, the Hi-Point 9mm carbine. Magazines with capacity of more than 10 rounds are now legal for such carbines.

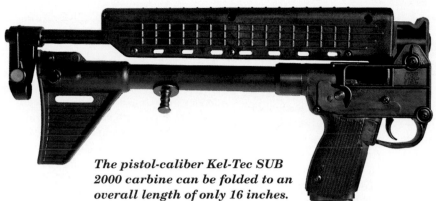

The pistol-caliber Kel-Tec SUB 2000 carbine can be folded to an overall length of only 16 inches.

Kel-Tec

Kel-Tec continues its line of lightweight polymer-frame personal-protection pistols in 9mm, 380 and 32 ACP.

The company has a knack for coming up with interesting model designations for its firearms. Recall that their 380 ACP pistol is the Model P-3AT. I get a kick out of saying that aloud. Their 223 carbine is the SU-16, in which the SU represents a "Sport Utility" rifle.

The company's pistol-caliber carbine, the SUB 2000, has a number of interesting features. For one, it folds in half, with a folded overall length of 16 inches, which is also the barrel length. It is offered in 9mm and 40 S&W calibers. The carbine can be ordered with a number of different frames, to fit standard pistol magazines used in Smith & Wesson, Glock, Beretta, SIG, or Kel-Tec pistols. Thus, a shooter with a favorite 9mm or 40-caliber pistol of one of these types can have a Kel-Tec SUB-2000 carbine that uses the same ammunition—and the same magazines—as his pistol.

Kimber

Interest in 1911 pistols is strong, and Kimber addressed that situation with the introduction of a number of new 1911 variants. Here are some of them.

The 45-caliber LAPD "SWAT" pistol is now available in a stainless-steel version, as the Stainless TLE/RL.

The Stainless Target II is the same as the existing full-size stainless 45 ACP target pistol, but is available in 9mm and 10mm chamberings.

The Pro TLE/RL II in 45 ACP is a blued version with a 4-inch barrel. This shorter variant uses a bushingless barrel-to-slide arrangement. The frame is standard size and includes an accessory rail.

The Stainless Pro TLE/RL is a stainless-steel version of the above pistol.

The Tactical Pro II 9mm, except for caliber, is the same as the 45 ACP version, including lightweight aluminum alloy frame, checkered front strap, and laminated grips.

Two 38 Super pistols have joined the Kimber line. The Stainless II 38 Super is a full-size pistol with polished flats and fixed sights. The Stainless Target II 38 Super is the same basic pistol with adjustable sights.

Kimber claims to be the largest maker of 1911-style pistols. Their goal seems to be to make a variant that will appeal to every individual 1911 shooter, no matter what his preferences.

La Prade

Full-capacity magazines are finally again permissible for ordinary citizens to have, and a number of sources can provide them. Some, like La Prade, can also supply extended magazines. With the growing popularity of pistol-caliber carbines, these can be used to good effect with such carbines, as well as with pistols. The extended magazines can be useful for plinking, law enforcement, for some forms of competition, and for personal protection. La Prade offers Glock magazines in capacities of 33 rounds (9mm), 29 rounds (40 S&W, 357 SIG), 29 rounds (10mm) and 25 rounds (45

ACP). An extended magazine in a Mech-Tech, Kel-Tec or Olympic carbine designed to accept Glock magazines would make an impressive piece of equipment. They will work in the appropriate Glock pistols too, of course.

For those who need one, La Prade also has the last remaining supply of original Bren Ten magazines.

Les Baer

Les Baer Custom has been in business 25 years, and it seemed the appropriate time for a 25th Anniversary Model 1911. The guns will be engraved, and will feature real (legal) ivory grips. White gold inlays of the legend "25th Anniversary" and Baer's signature are on the slide. Only 25 pistols will be made.

A new addition to the Baer line is the "Recon" pistol. A 5-inch 1911 custom pistol, the frame is machined with a Picatinny rail. A SureFire X-200 light comes standard with the pistol.

Llama

The latest Llama catalog does not list any large-capacity pistols, but the Spanish gunmaker has supplied them

La Prade offers new extended Glock magazines that will hold 33 rounds (9mm), 29 rounds (40 or 357 SIG), 29 rounds (10mm) and 25 rounds (45 ACP).

in the past, and the importer has announced that they will again be available. In addition, normal-capacity magazines will be available for those large-capacity pistols previously sold with 10-rounders. The Llama Max-II pistols will be available with 13-round magazines for the 45-caliber Llama Max-II, and 17-rounders for the 9mm version. Import Sports, of New Jersey, imports Llama pistols.

Olympic

The Whitney Wolverine 22-caliber pistol, featured last year as a pre-production item, has advanced to the production stage. By February 2005, the first production run of 5000 pistols was well under way. Seven hundred Whitney pistols had been completed, but the supply of magazines had not kept up with pistol production. By the time you read this, the Wolverine may be on dealers' shelves.

The OA-93, Olympic's big 223-caliber pistol based on the AR-15 design, had been outlawed by the 1994 AWB because of its weight. In response, Olympic had brought out the OA-98, a pistol of similar design, but drastically lightened to get the weight under 50 ounces. The lightening included putting holes in every component possible, giving the big pistol an interesting ventilated appearance. Now, the original OA-93 and the light OA-98 will both be part of Olympic's product line. Barrel length for both pistols is 6-1/2 inches.

The company also makes a variety of pistol-caliber carbines in 9mm,

❧ ● ❧ ● ❧ ● ❧ ● ❧ ● ❧

Top: Para's new LTC pistol is a stainless-steel single-column pistol with a 4 1/4-inch barrel.
Middle: The Colonel is Para's 14+1 steel pistol with a 4 1/4-inch barrel and Para's LDA trigger.
Bottom: The 10+1 Para Nite Hawg is a compact 24-ounce pistol.

40, 10mm and 45 ACP. These guns are all based on the AR-15 design.

Para-Ordnance

Recall that Para-Ordnance was the leader in increased-capacity frames for 1911-type pistols. With the sunset of the AWB, Para adds full-capacity offerings back into its 1911 line.

The company can hardly be said to be lacking for new 1911 offerings. Para has introduced six new models of its PXT (Power Extractor) line. Variants are available with double-action (DA) or single-action (SA) triggers, and with high-capacity or single-column magazines. A Para-Ordnance communication states that the question now is not, "Do I want single-action or double-action, and do I want High Capacity or Single Stack?" but "Which Para do I want?" The company certainly does offer a variety. All the new pistols are in 45 ACP.

The OPS is a single-action, single-column compact pistol. Its 3 1/2-inch barrel gives it an overall length of 7 inches. In stainless steel, it has "Griptor" grasping grooves, other niceties, and Cocobolo stocks.

The stainless-steel Lt. Colonel (LTC) is a single-action, single-column pistol with a 4 1/4-inch barrel and length of 7-3/4 inches. Capacity is 7+1, and the weight is 35 ounces.

The "Hi-Cap LTC" is a similar pistol with a wider frame and 14+1 capacity.

The last of the single-action versions added is the S12.45 Limited. This pistol features a 3 1/2-inch barrel and what Para calls "Sterling" finish—all stainless steel with a black slide that has polished sides. Capacity is 12+1.

Two LDA (Light Double Action) pistols have been introduced. The Stealth Carry is a compact 30-ounce single-column pistol with a 3-inch barrel and a capacity of 6+1.

The Colonel is a high-capacity LDA pistol with a 4 1/4-inch barrel and a weight of 37 ounces. A full 14 + 1 capacity and lots of other niceties.

Para seems to have gone hog-wild with some of its nomenclature. Recall that the "Warthog," a small 10+1 45-caliber pistol with a 3-inch barrel, was introduced last year. This year, the "Nite Hawg" has been added, essentially a Warthog in covert black finish. The "Hawg 9" is a similar pistol in 9mm. The "Slim Hawg" is a new 3-inch 45 with a single-column magazine that gives 6+1 capacity.

Rohrbaugh

The little Rohrbaugh 9mm pistol has been standardized with a revised frame. Pistols with the new frames have fired 5000 rounds without a problem. Serial numbers for the revised-frame pistols now have an "R" prefix. The all-metal pistol weighs 12.8 ounces, and measures 5.2 x 3.7 inches. Carbon-fiber grips are now standard. Still, two models are offered, the Model R9 (without sights) and the Model R9S (with sights). With a capacity of 6+1, the Rohrbaugh is the smallest, lightest, flattest 9mm pistol made. Reportedly, it has received attention from troops going to Iraq—it can be carried inconspicuously and uses the military 9mm ammunition.

Ruger

Sturm, Ruger & Company slipped a mid-year model, the P345, in on us since the last edition. In 45 ACP, this new polymer-frame pistol is available in a blued-slide or stainless-slide manual-safety version, and a stainless-steel "decocker-only" version. The new Ruger 45s are slimmer than the company's previous offerings, and seem to feel good in most hands. With barrel lengths of 4.2 inches, the pistols are 7-1/2 inches in length. Weight for either variant is 29 ounces. Each pistol comes with two 8-round magazines.

The Mark III semiauto, in 22 Long Rifle, is the latest incarnation of the original Ruger Standard pistol of 1949. The magazine release has been moved from the butt to the left side of the frame, and a loaded chamber indicator is on the left side of the receiver. The Mark III series pistols come with Weaver-type scope adapters, as well as new internal locking devices and magazine safeties. A 17 Mach 2 version is now also available. The Mark III 22/45

variant has the controls in the same positions as the 1911-style pistols.

For 2005, the Mark III series offered a special version, the Mark III Hunter. It is of stainless steel, with a 6 7/8-inch barrel, and the barrel is fluted. It features adjustable sights that are a departure from the traditional square-notch type. The rear sight has a V-notch, and the front sight is a round "HiViz" light-gathering sight. Don't like the front-sight color? No problem. Six interchangeable "LitePipes" are included. A scope-mounting base is also included, for which the receiver is already drilled and tapped.

Ruger has made a number of subtle changes on a number of models. Internal locks, magazine disconnectors and other mechanical devices have been added to appropriate models. Such guns now meet the mishmash of state laws, and can now be sold in every state.

Ruger is proud that the company was able to fill a rush order from the U. S. Army for 9mm pistols. The pistols were needed in a hurry, and Ruger was able to deliver an order for 5000 9mm P95 pistols within 30 days.

Ruger 9mm pistols are now supplied with the 15-round magazines for which they were designed. Except, of course, where state or local regulations still limit magazine capacity. There, reduced-capacity magazines can be supplied.

Ruger's pistol-caliber carbines logically use Ruger pistol magazines. The 40-caliber version still comes

Top: The new Ruger P345 is available in a blued version with a manual safety.
Middle: A Ruger P345 with a stainless slide and a decocker is available.
Bottom: Ruger's new Mark III Hunter is in stainless steel, and has a long 6 7/8-inch fluted barrel.

with a 10-round magazine, but the 9mm variant now comes with a 15-round magazine.

Sigarms

Sigarms introduced a number of new pistols this year. One of the most noteworthy is the X-Five. Although SIG has an actual real 1911 in their line now, the X-Five is a stainless-steel P226 pistol modified for single-action firing, and with a 5-inch barrel and with 1911-style controls. The new pistol offers shooters the choice of 9mm or 40 S&W. Magazine capacities are 19 for the 9mm and 14 for the 40. The pistols have fired groups of under 2 inches in factory testing, and the pistol is suited for the Limited category of IPSC (International Practical Shooting Confederation) shooting.

The polymer-frame SP2022 is available in 9mm, 40 and 357 SIG. With slightly modified controls and a standard accessory rail, the pistol was accepted by a U. S. Army unit, which ordered 5000 of the new guns in 9mm chambering. Mechanism is conventional double action, and the standard magazine holds 12 rounds.

The new 22 LR Mosquito pistol was introduced at the January 2005 SHOT Show. With a polymer frame and standard rail, adjustable sights and new locking devices, the 22-caliber Mosquito is about 90 percent the size of the P226. Trigger mechanism is conventional double action. The new blowback 22 has several safety and lock features, and a 10-shot magazine is standard.

The P229 and P226 DAK pistols are double-action-only guns with a new trigger system. Pull is 6-1/2 pounds, and the mechanism allows second-strike capability in case of a misfire. These pistols were available to law enforcement last year, and are now available for commercial sales.

SIG 1911 "commander-size" and "officers-size" pistols will become available in the near future. To be called the GSC (Granite Series Compact) models, the new smaller guns will be made without the accessory rail of the full-size pistol.

Sigarms puts out a number of limited-edition arms each year. It certainly would seem to be a way to keep collectors happy, as they could get at least one new SIG every year. This

Top: The right side view of the Smith & Wesson 410 S.
Bottom: A new stainless-steel SW 1911 factory-equipped with Crimson Trace olive-drab Lasergrips.

Top: 1911 with olive-drab Laser-grips, right view.
Bottom: The 40-caliber S&W 410 S comes from the factory with Crimson Trace Lasergrips.

Top: The Lasergrip-equipped carbon-steel SW 1911 PD, right view.
Bottom: A carbon-steel SW 1911 PD, with a 4 1/4-inch barrel, is fitted with tan Lasergrips.

year, a number of limited editions were offered. Perhaps the most eye-catching were the P239 and P232 pistols with multicolored "rainbow" titanium slides.

Smith & Wesson

All right, S&W brought out another big new headline-stealing revolver, the 460 S&W Magnum, but there were plenty of new items introduced in the autoloading pistol lines.

Three existing pistols are now offered with fitted Crimson Trace Lasergrips. The variants available with these laser grips are the 1911PD 45 ACP with 4 1/4-inch barrel, the standard SW1911 stainless-steel full-size pistol, and the 410S, a double-action, double-column-magazine gun in 40 S&W caliber.

Smith & Wesson, once it decided to make 1911-style pistols, went into it in a big way. Six new 1911 models have now been added to the line. The 1911 scandium-frame full-size pistol with a 5-inch barrel is now available, a larger variant of the original scandium compact pistol that had been recently introduced. A new full-size pistol is now in the line, with frame and slide made of carbon steel, instead of stainless steel.

A special Doug Koenig variant has a blued carbon-steel slide on a stainless frame. Lots of the niceties that many shooters prefer are standard on this model.

A Doug Koenig variant in 38 Super is also available from the S&W Performance Center. This hand-built pistol may perhaps be the company's first handgun in the 38 Super chambering since its experimental big-frame revolver in that caliber back around 1929.

Two additional five-inch-barrel 1911 models are now available. They are similar to the Performance Center models introduced last year, but made of stainless steel. One has a satin finish over its entire surface. The other has the flats polished.

In the 22-caliber line, S&W had added a new Model 22A pistol, this variant with polished sides on the barrel and slide, and a "Hi-Viz" front sight.

Because the Walther PPK does not meet the arbitrary BATF standards for importation, Smith & Wesson, under license from Walther, is now making the PPK here, in 380 ACP. The new gun is smaller and about 3 ounces lighter than the PPK/S that previously replaced the PPK.

Springfield

Springfield's Parkerized military-style 45-caliber 1911-A1 pistols were well-received last year. Now, with the sunset of the AWB, the company has introduced a Parkerized GI-type full-size pistol with a "Hi-Cap" magazine. Specifications are essentially the same as the other military-style pistols, but the frame is wider to house a 13-shot magazine. Other high-capacity competition pistols have also been added to Springfield's line.

In addition, some additional models have been added to the company's line of single-column 45-caliber 1911-style pistols. Most, but not all, are competition variants.

With the acceptance of the 45 G.A.P. cartridge, Springfield last year chambered its XD polymer-frame pistol in that caliber. For 2005, the company thought that those with smaller hands might favor a 1911 with the grip scaled down for that shorter cartridge. The result was the new lightweight 1911 Defender pistol in 45 G.A.P. The new little pistol weighs only 23 ounces, with a grip 1/8-inch shorter front-to-back and 1/4-inch less in circumference.

Steyr

The striking-looking polymer-frame Steyr Model M pistol came on the scene several years ago, then disappeared. For some time, we were unable to learn whether it was even being made any more. This question has now been answered. At the January 2005 SHOT Show, the somewhat redesigned Steyr M-A1 pistol was displayed. The new pistol is available in 9mm and 40S&W *(and 357 SIG on request)*, with a 15-round magazine for the 9 and a 12-rounder for the 40 and 357. The new Steyr pistols still feature

A Smith & Wesson 38 Super, the Doug Koenig Professional Series, is now available.

S&W's new Model 22A pistol has a HI-VIZ front sight and polished sides on the barrel and slide.

The new Defender pistol from Springfield has the grip reduced in length and girth, and is chambered for the new 45 G.A.P. cartridge.

❊●❊●❊●❊●❊●❊

the interesting triangular sight system. Literature accompanying the new pistols listed only an Austrian address, so importation arrangements were still uncertain.

Left: Springfield has introduced a new full-size high-capacity competition pistol, the Loaded Leatham Trophy Match, in 40 S&W. A similar pistol is available in 45 ACP.

Middle: Springfield has added a Hi-Cap pistol to its line of Parkerized GI-style 45-caliber 1911s.

Right: Some new Springfield models are essentially cosmetic changes to the company's 1911 45-caliber line, such as this striking-looking black stainless-steel combat version.

One of Taurus' new 1911 pistols is a blue version with a beavertail tang, ventilated hammer and trigger and other features.

STI

2006 is the 30th anniversary of the International Practical Shooting Confederation (IPSC), and STI International is building special commemorative pistols to celebrate that occasion. Work on the pistols began in 2005 and was scheduled to continue into 2006. The pistols are made in 9mm, 40 S&W and 45 ACP. With 5-inch barrels, the two-tone guns will have "saber tooth" serrations on the slide, and special slide engraving for the IPSC 30th anniversary.

Taurus

The DAO Taurus Model 24/7 was introduced in 9mm and 40 S&W calibers. Now, it has been offered in 45 ACP. The new polymer-frame 45 pistol is available with either a stainless or blued slide. The grip has ergonomic finger-indexing "Memory Pads" that aid in providing a consistent grip. Contrary to competition practice, the magazine release is recessed. The frame extends into an accessory rail that allows attachment of a light or laser. A manual safety lever (not common on a DAO pistol), a firing pin block, and the key-operated Taurus Security System are incorporated in the design. The 45-caliber 24/7 has a 12+1 round capacity. The earlier 9mm and 40 S&W pistols now are available in their full design capacity—17+1 for the 9 and 15+1 for the 40.

Taurus' new PT745 is a new lightweight 45 that comes in under 21 ounces. A polymer-frame pistol, it has a 3 1/4-inch barrel and the single-column magazine holds seven rounds. Similar to the company's Millennium Pro pistol, the PT745 is available with either a blued or stainless slide.

Another new 1911! Taurus displayed two variants of its brand-new PT 1911 at the January 2005 SHOT Show. At that time, the pistols were so new that the two displayed were the only two specimens in the United States. Taurus' new 1911 has the basic Colt/Browning mechanism, and includes other features. Both the blued steel and the stainless versions of the pistol exhibited similar features. Many of the niceties that seem to appeal to modern shooters, such as beavertail tang, ambidextrous safety, Heinie sights and lowered ejection port, are on the Taurus 1911 pistols. The exhibited pistols seemed to have trigger guards that were somewhat thicker than usual, and had rather shallow grasping grooves on both the front and rear of the slide.

The Taurus PT 922, which went through several incarnations and was finally standardized last year, is gone. The 22-caliber autoloader has been dropped from the line and is no longer being produced.

United States Fire Arms

United States Fire Arms Manufacturing Company has made a name for itself by recreating early Colt revolvers. With the continuing current interest in the 1911 semiauto pistol, would it not be logical for the company to pay some attention to the early Colt autoloading pistols? By early 2005, they had done just that.

Two new 45 automatics were introduced by the firm. Mechanically, they are 1911s, but they have a "retro" appearance that makes them look even earlier, and that ties in with the company's other products.

The first one was named the "Model of 1910 Commercial." It has the burr hammer of the older Colt Model 1905 pistol, and also has that earlier pistol's wide, flat walnut grips with small-head grip screws. It has a long trigger, the 1905–type tiny sights, and a commercial-grade high-polish finish. The markings are taken from the 1905, and the caliber is marked, "Calibre 45 Rimless Smokeless."

The "later" version was called the "Model 1911 Military," and has a number of features of the original Model 1911. The gun has a wide hammer spur and a short tang, as did the early 1911s. However, it also sported the 1905 walnut grips and the small grip screws. Each of these 1911 guns will come with a reprint of the 1917 manual, "Description of the Automatic Pistol, Caliber .45 Model of 1911."

The U. S. Fire Arms automatics do not really replicate any particular historical firearm. However, they capture the flavor of the old Colts made in the early days of the automatic pistol in our country.

Walther

The Walther PPK is back. The original PPK fell afoul of the arbitrary BATF point system, and could not be imported. It was replaced by the PPK/S. In early 2005, Walther and Smith & Wesson announced that the little gun would be manufactured by S&W under license in the United States.

Also new in Walther's lineup is the Model P99QA with its polymer frame finished in desert sand color.

Recall that QA stands for "Quick Action" and indicates the striker is partially pre-cocked by the movement of the slide, allowing a short 8-pound pull. The war in Iraq has created some interest in sand-colored pistols, and the new Walther addresses this interest. Strangely, it is available only in 40 S&W chambering. One might have expected it to also be in the NATO-standard 9mm, as are the other series P99QA pistols.

Wildey

The JAWS Viper pistol, a joint venture between Wildey and the country of Jordan, has finalized its design. Parts are now in production, and the initial production run has been sold, even before final production.

Several interesting things were on display by Wildey at the January 2005 SHOT Show. One was the actual pistol used in the "Death Wish 3" motion picture, which starred Charles Bronson.

A Wildey Colt was also displayed. About 5 years or so ago, a small number of Wildey pistols were made by the company for Colt and were so marked. These interesting pistols were reportedly made with three barrels each, for 45 Winchester Magnum, 45 Wildey Magnum and 475 Wildey Magnum. About seven pistols were left undelivered when the arrangement ended. These are interesting collectible items.

Selected Wildey arms, including the Wildey carbine, are now available with a muzzle brake. The 18-inch-barrel Wildey carbine is perhaps taking the concept of the pistol-caliber carbine to its logical extreme. Chambered for 44 AutoMag, 45 Winchester Magnum, 45 Wildey Magnum and 475 Wildey Magnum, it can certainly be considered suitable for a range of game hunting beyond the capability of most traditional pistol cartridges.

Top: A stainless-steel variant of Taurus' new 1911 pistol also has a beavertail tang and other special features, such as an extended manual safety.
Middle: The Walther PPK in 380 ACP is back, made under license in the United States by Smith & Wesson.
Bottom: The JAWS Viper is in final form, and parts are being produced for the first production run.

RIFLES TODAY :

RIFLE REVIEW

by Layne Simpson

The Barrett M468 is an AR-15-style autoloader in 6.8mm Remington SPC. To mention but a few of its features: dual spring extractor system, folding front sight, heavy-duty gas block and two-stage trigger. Overall length, with 16-inch barrel, is 35-1/2 inches and it weighs 7-1/4 pounds.

Benelli

The R-1 rifle I used on a hunt for whitetail deer in 2004 was exactly like the one I carried a few years back while hunting driven boar and stag in the Transylvania Mountains of Romania. At that time its only chambering options were 308 Winchester, 30-06 and 300 Winchester Magnum, but you can now buy one in 270 WSM or 300 WSM as well. It doesn't take a lot to kill a Texas deer, so I stuck with the 308 Winchester and used Fusion ammunition from Federal. I could not have asked for better performance from a bonded-core bullet. Here is the really interesting part: The new line of ammunition will cost the same as Federal Power-Shok ammo, which is a bargain considering it is loaded with bullets of bonded-core design.

We hunted until dark each day and the 3-10x Burris Euro Diamond scope worn by the rifle I hunted with proved to be incredibly bright.

On that same hunt I took a rather large boar with a Benelli turkey gun loaded with Federal's new TruBall version of the 12-gauge rifled slug load. The range was just under 70 yards. The Foster-style slug is the same one Federal has been offering for many years, but a plastic ball and special wad are loaded in the shell behind it to improve accuracy. During the hunt, I did not have an opportunity to seriously check out the accuracy of the new load in the Benelli, but after arriving back home I tried it in two other guns, a Thompson/Center TCR 83 rifle wearing a slug barrel and a Winchester Model 1300 pump gun. Both had smoothbore barrels and both wore scopes. The TCR barrel has a bore diameter of 0.729-inch with no choke constriction, while the bore of the Model 1300 measures 0.733-inch, with 0.003-inch of constriction (Light Skeet). In the Model 1300, the TruBall load averaged 3.31 inches for five, five-shot groups at 50 yards compared to 4.28 inches for the load it has replaced in the Federal ammunition lineup. In

The 2005 Weatherby catalog with a 1950s vintage photo of Roy Weatherby on its cover celebrates the company's 60th anniversary. Everyone who loves Weatherby rifles will have to have a copy.

You can also buy the Benelli R1 in 30-06, 300 Winchester Magnum, 270 WSM and 300 WSM, but since Texas whitetails don't take a lot of killing, I chose one in 308 Winchester to take this buck back in November of 2004. I also used Federal ammo loaded with the new Fusion, bonded-core bullet and it worked great.

the TCR, it was 2.73 inches for the new and 4.66 inches for the old.

The lineup of Uberti rifles imported by Benelli continues to grow, with a copy of the Colt Lightning being the latest addition. It will be offered in 357 Magnum and 45 Colt.

Browning

Since Browning and U.S. Repeating Arms, maker of Winchester rifles, are both owned by the same parent company, and since both have a close working relationship with the other Winchester that makes ammunition, it comes as no surprise to see those two companies first in line to offer rifles with "325 WSM" stamped on their barrels. Simply the 300 WSM case necked up for an 8mm bullet, the new cartridge

is slated to become available in a number of Browning rifles in plenty of time for the 2005 hunting seasons. A-Bolt variants chambered for it will include both right- and left-hand versions of the Hunter, Micro Hunter and Medallion, as well as the Stainless Stalker and Composite Stalker. The year 2005 will also see more A-Bolt variants available in 25 WSSM, a super-short cartridge that duplicates the performance of the 25-06 Remington.

Latest edition of the BLR is the short-action Lightweight with pistol grip stock and 20- or 22-inch barrel in various chamberings ranging in power from the 22-250 to 325 WSM. It weighs 6-1/2 pounds in standard chamberings and a quarter-pound more in the magnums. Moving from big-game rifles to rifles better

The latest version of the short-action, lightweight Browning BLR has a curved grip and is chambered for various cartridges from the old 22-250 to the new 325 WSM.

suited for plinking and small-game hunting, we can now buy the BL-22 in *(surprise!)* 17 HM2. Except in this case it is called the BL-17 and offered in several styles, one with an octagonal barrel and two others with satin-nickeled receivers.

Charles Daly

A real sleeper among small-game rifles, the new Superior II bolt gun has a 22-inch barrel and a walnut stock of classical style with oil finish and cut checkering. The receivers of rifles in 22 LR and 17 HM2 are grooved for scope mounting while those in 22 WMR and 17 HMR are drilled and tapped. The detachable magazine holds five rounds and it weighs six pounds.

Cimarron

Reproductions of several Sharps single-shot rifles are now available from Cimarron. The Texas Ranger Carbine has a 22-inch barrel in 45-70 or 50-70, and is a copy of the 1859 percussion military carbine converted to centerfire. Then we have the Cimarron Big Fifty with a 34-inch barrel in 50-90 or 50-100, either of which Billy Dixon would have been proud to own. Two other Sharps replicas are the Professional Hunter and Pride of Plains, both in 45-70. Also available is a copy of the Winchester Low Wall single shot in 22 LR, 22 Hornet, 30-30, 32-20, 38-40, 357 Magnum, 44-40 and 44 Magnum.

Cooper Arms

Only a very few companies build rifles as accurate as those built by Cooper Arms, and even fewer companies build rifles as handsome. I know of no other company building rifles that are both custom rifle handsome and target rifle accurate. I will go even further by saying that if I had to pick five companies that build the most handsome rifles in America, one of them would have to be Cooper Arms. And since Dan Cooper guarantees his centerfire rifles to shoot three bullets inside half an inch at 100 yards, the beauty of his rifles is more than skin deep. His guarantee for rimfire rifles in 17 HM2, 17 HMR, 22 Long Rifle and 22 WMR is 1/4-inch for five shots at 50 yards.

Three model variations are available in centerfire varmint rifles, Varminter, Montana Varminter and Varminter Extreme. Most of the popular chamberings are available with some of the more interesting being 17 Ackley Hornet, 17 Mach IV, 19 Calhoun, 218 Mashburn Bee, 22 PPC and 220 Weatherby Rocket. I have owned a Varminter Extreme in 17 Remington for several years and it refuses to shoot groups bigger than half an inch at 100 yards with the Berger 25- and 30-grain bullets, and the Hornady 20-grain V-Max. Big-game rifles include the Classic, Custom Classic and Western Classic, the latter with an octagonal barrel and case-colored receiver. Actions range from short enough to be just right for the new 6.8mm Remington SPC to long enough to handle the old 25-06 and Ackley's improved version of same. In addition to the standard chamberings, there are other options such as the 6x45mm, 243 Winchester Improved, 6mm-284, 25x45mm and 257 Roberts Improved. As I write this, all Cooper rifles are single shots––but my crystal ball says I will be writing about the new repeaters next year.

During the 2004 season I took a very nice pronghorn buck while hunting with Mike Ballew of the Whittington Center near Raton, New Mexico and the rifle I used was a Cooper Model 22 Custom Classic in 6.5-284 Norma. Believe me when I say photos do not do its English walnut stock justice. All Cooper rifles come with a test target fired at the Montana factory and, while the one in the box with my rifle was fired at 50 yards, it was still quite impressive since it measured a mere 0.008-inch. That, my friends, is the thickness of two pages in the fine publication you are now holding in your hands. The load used to fire that group consisted of the Federal 210M primer, Hornady case, and 47.0 grains of Reloder 22 behind the 140-grain Sierra MatchKing. Using the same load, I was not able to duplicate

▲ *The Cooper Model 22 in 6.5-284 Norma and Nosler's custom loading of that cartridge with the 120-grain Ballistic Tip bullet, proved to be the perfect combination for taking this very nice New Mexico pronghorn in August of 2004.*

At left is my new Cooper Model 22 in 6.5-284 Norma and at right is my old Cooper Model 21 in 17 Remington. Both will consistently shoot five bullets inside half an inch at 100 yards.

the accuracy of the factory group but I figure the 0.37-inch average I did manage to squeeze off at 100 yards was good enough. In fact, of the dozen handloads I tried in the rifle, only one averaged greater than minute-of-angle, and it came close at 1.08 inches. Five of the loads averaged less than half an inch. One of my three most

accurate recipes was recommended by the folks at Sierra––46.7 grains of IMR-4831 and the 140-grain MatchKing for an average of 0.29-inch. The other two loads were 47.0 grains of VihtaVuori N165 and the Hornady 140-grain A-Max (0.34-inch) and 46.7 grains of IMR-4831 behind the Sierra 142-grain MatchKing for

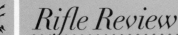

The new Ultra Varmint version of the Handi-Rifle has a stock of radical styling (for H&R) and is available in 204 Ruger, 223 Remington and 22-250.

A reproduction of the Winchester Model 92, the Puma from Legacy is available in a number of interesting chamberings, including 454 Casull and 480 Ruger.

an average of 0.38-inch. The Cooper rifle was also quite accurate with custom ammo loaded by Nosler; the 120-grain Ballistic Tip load I used on the antelope hunt averaged 0.33-inch at 100 yards. Average muzzle velocity of that load was 3025 fps.

CZ-USA

By the time you read this, the CZ 527 should be available in 6.8mm Remington SPC. Over in the rimfire department there is the 542 in 17 HM2 with a 22 1/2-inch barrel and walnut stock. The varmint version has a heavier 21-inch barrel. Both have five-round detachable magazines.

Ed Brown Products

The EBP family of rifles continues to grow. In addition to rifles with serious names like Tactical, Light Tactical and Marine, there is a nine-pound varmint rifle and big-game rifles called Damara (6-1/4 pounds), Denali (seven pounds), Savannah (7-1/2 pounds) and Bushveld at 8-1/2 pounds. All EBP rifles wear McMillan synthetic stocks; a camo finish on the Marine and black on all the rest. Most of the popular chamberings, from 204 Ruger to 458 Lott, are available.

During the 2004 season I took a very nice elk in Utah with a Denali chambered for a cartridge that some say is not big enough to kill an elk, the 270 Winchester. The rifle wore a Zeiss 3-9x scope. The ammo I used was Hornady Light Magnum loaded with the 130-grain InterBond bullet and it averaged about 1-1/2 inches for three shots at 100 yards. I found it interesting that the Hornady loading of the ancient old 270 Winchester is actually faster than Winchester's loadings of the 270 WSM with the same bullet weight. And this is in barrels of the same length. I recently completed a thorough comparison of those two cartridges in a couple of Weatherby Vanguard rifles, both with 24-inch barrels. The Hornady 130-grain Light Magnum load averaged 3218 fps versus 3152 fps for the fastest Winchester load (130-grain Ballistic Silvertip). The pessimist would say the new cartridge is 66 fps slower than the old cartridge. The optimist would say the new cartridge comes within 66 fps of duplicating the performance of one of the finest big-game cartridges ever developed.

Empire Rifles

All rifles from Empire are built around newly-manufactured Mauser 1898 actions in the square bridge style, and they ooze quality from every pore. Stocks are available in synthetic or high-grade walnut. You can get a light rifle in calibers ranging from 257 Roberts to 338 Winchester Magnum, or a heavy rifle in really serious chamberings ranging from 375 H&H Magnum to 505 Gibbs. Five grades are available: Field, Guide, Professional, Express and Empire. The fancier the name the more you pay and you will pay a lot for the Empire with its custom stock and hand engraving. These are very nice rifles and the list of options goes on and on.

Harrington & Richardson

Latest chambering available in the H&R Handi-Rifle is the 500 S&W, a pistol cartridge that behaves like a rifle cartridge when fired in a long barrel. Also new is the Ultra Varmint with a stock of radical styling *(for H&R)* in 204 Ruger, 223 Remington and 22-250.

Kimber

Everybody who is anybody is offering a rifle in 17 Hornady Mach 2, and Kimber is no exception. Called the Kimber 17, several variations are being built. The Classic Varmint has a walnut stock and 20-inch stainless steel barrel with lightening flutes; the Pro Varmint is the same except for its gray laminated wood stock. Weights are six pounds, nine ounces for the former and two ounces more for the latter. Also wearing a walnut stock, another variation called the Hunter has a 22-inch barrel of lighter contour and this lowers its weight to 6-1/2 pounds. The SVT with its high-comb laminated stock and beavertail forearm has an 18 1/2-inch barrel and weighs seven pounds, nine ounces. Like all Kimbers, these have a three-position safety, free-floating barrel and receiver drilled and tapped for scope mounting. As centerfire rifles go, new chamberings are 204 Ruger, 223 Remington and 22-250 in the Model 84M, and the 325 WSM in the Model 8400.

Legacy Sports International

The New Howa Model 1500 Lightning weighs about 7-1/2 pounds and is available in 14 chamberings ranging from 223 Remington to 338 Winchester Magnum. Blued steel and stainless steel barreled actions are available with black and camo synthetic stock options. And now you too can own a lever-action rifle with an oversized finger lever like Chuck Connors once carried on TV. A member of the Puma family of Winchester Model 92 knockoffs, it is called Large Loop Lever and is available in 45 Colt and 357 Magnum. Other Puma variants are available in other interesting chamberings as well, including 480 Ruger and 454 Casull.

The new Model 717M2 autoloader from Marlin is chambered for the 17 Hornady Mach 2.

The Marlin 1894 is now available in 32-20 Winchester, and a very nice little outfit it is.

Marlin

The most handsome rifle I have seen lately, and perhaps the most handsome Marlin ever, is the four-millionth Model 336. Marlin built the rifle and then commissioned the craftsmen at Doug Turnbull Restorations to transform it into a one-of-a-kind, heirloom-quality work of art with styling that takes us back to the turn of the 20th century. It is chambered to 38-55 Winchester. Marlin donated the rifle for auction at the 2005 SHOT Show with the proceeds going to the Hunting & Shooting Sports Heritage Fund and its efforts to protect and enhance America's hunting traditions and firearm freedoms.

Moving on to handsome big-game rifles you and I can afford, Marlin now offers the ever-popular Model 336 in nine different variations, all with cut-checkered wood stocks. Chamberings are 30-30, 35 Remington, 444 Marlin, 45-70 and 450 Marlin and 410 smoothbore. Marlin never describes its Model 336 as the most accurate lever-action rifle available but during the past few years I have shot several in all calibers except 35 Remington, and each one averaged less than two inches at 100 yards for five-shot groups. Some bolt-action rifles are not as accurate.

The Model 1894 family of rifles and carbines also continues to grow and the 32-20 chambering is back in the lineup for 2005. Called the Model 1894CL, its half-length magazine holds six rounds, and its 22-inch

barrel has a rifling twist rate of 1:20 inches. Overall length is 39-1/2 inches and it weighs six pounds. Can the 218 Bee and 25-20 be far behind? Other variations include the Model 1894 (blued steel) and Model 1894SS (stainless) in 44 Magnum, Model 1894FG in 41 Magnum and Model 1894C in 357 Magnum. The "cowboy" versions, with their octagonal barrels in various calibers including 32 H&R Magnum, are quite nice, too.

If your guess is the new Model 717M2 autoloader is chambered for the 17 Mach 2 you are correct. Its detachable magazine holds seven rounds, it has an 18-inch barrel with a 1:9 inch rifling twist rate and it weighs five pounds. Overall length is 37 inches. The Monte Carlo-style stock is described by Marlin as walnut-finished laminated hardwood. This neat little small-game rifle has a last-shot bolt hold-open feature and its receiver is grooved for scope mounting. Also new is the Model 917VSF in the same caliber, a bolt gun with stainless steel-barreled action, laminated wood stock and detachable magazine. It is basically last year's Model 917VS with a fluted barrel.

Nosler

So what is the name Nosler doing in a report on rifles? The rifle I shot had something more than its name in common with Nosler bullets—it was incredibly accurate. To see what such a rifle looks like, you have only to turn to my Testfire report elsewhere in this edition.

Remington

The 6.8mm Special Purpose Cartridge (SPC) was developed as a military cartridge for the AR-16/M-16 rifle and its mission is to deliver quicker stops on bad guys than the 5.6x45mm *(or 223 Remington to us civilians)* is capable of. It is now being promoted by Remington as a low-recoil deer cartridge with the ability to deliver a 115-grain, 270-caliber bullet at about the same level of energy at 200 yards as the 30-30 Winchester does at 100. Of course, this is comparing the performance of a pointed bullet in the 6.8mm to a bluntnose bullet in the 30-30. When loaded to maximum velocity with a 150-grain spitzer and fired in my T/C G2 Contender rifle, the 30-30 equals the 6.8mm in power at all ranges. But that's beside the point to those who do not handload.

The Model Seven AWR now being offered in 6.8mm SPC by Remington was still a long way off back in early September of 2004 when I headed to the far north for caribou so I had to make-do with a short-action Model 700 from Remington's custom shop. I tried all four factory loads in that rifle and the 115-grain Core-Lokt Ultra whipped 'em all in accuracy, including the load with Sierra's MatchKing bullet of the same weight. The CL-U load also accounted for a nice caribou bull. My most accurate handloads consisted of Benchmark powder and two bullets; Hornady's 130-grain SST and Sierra's 135-grain MatchKing. Velocity was around 2400 fps.

I took this caribou in September of 2004 with a Model 700 in 6.8mm Remington SPC and Remington's factory load with the 115-grain Core-Lokt Ultra bullet.

Those of us who have had a few custom rifles built through the years have long known that the extremely rigid Remington XP-100 single-shot action is one of the best available to wrap a varmint rifle around. On top of that, there was a time when the one in 221 Fire Ball was cheap enough to buy and throw away everything except the action. Remington has now made such a rifle available to the shooting masses by introducing its Model XR-100 Rangemaster in 204 Ruger, 223 Remington and 22-250. It is a mixture of XP-100 single-shot action, Model 700 bolt handle and 40-XB trigger, all nestled in gray laminated wood with thumbhole-style buttstock, and beavertail forearm replete with 1955 Buick-style cooling vents. The trigger is adjustable down to about 24 ounces and the medium-heavy barrel is 26 inches long. This one gets my vote as the long-range varmint rifle to be seen in the field with during the next decade or so. I only wish it was available in 220 Swift as well.

I now have two favorite Model 700 variations. When I am in the mood for checkered walnut and blued steel, the Model 700 CDL is the rifle you are likely to see me toting over hill and dale. It reminds me a lot of the old Model 700 Mountain Rifle, but it has a 26-inch barrel for squeezing maximum speed from the magnum cartridges for which it is chambered. I had two bulls on my caribou license so after bumping off one with the 6.8mm SPC, I took the other a few days later with a Model 700 CDL in 7mm Remington Magnum. Back home, it consistently shot inside an inch at 100 yards with Remington's 140- and 160-grain Core-Lokt Ultra factory loads with a number of groups measuring close to half an inch. Its other chamberings are 243 Winchester, 270 Winchester, 7mm-08, 7mm Ultra Mag, 30-06, 300 Winchester Magnum and 300 Ultra Mag. Darned nice rifle, and one of the more handsome ever built by Remington. It and the Model 700 in 6.8mm SPC I used on the caribou hunt wore 2.5-10x Bushnell Elite 4200 scopes with the RainGuard lens coating, and they earned their keep in all that rain. My favorite Model 700 for rough weather hunting, by the way, is the XCR which is short for Xtreme Conditions Rifle.

Last in line and price but certainly not last in value are break-action, single-shot, over-under and side-by-side rifles at unbelievably low prices. All are members of Remington's new Spartan Gunworks line of firearms. The SPR18 single-shot is available in 223 Remington, 243 Winchester, 270 Winchester and 30-06. The SPR94 over-under combination gun is available in 22 LR, 17 HMR and 22 WMR over a 410-bore shotgun barrel or 12-gauge over 223, 308 and 30-06. The SPR22 is a side-by-side double in 30-06 or 45-70. Standard features include chrome-lined, hammer-forged barrels, all-steel receivers, fully adjustable open sights, scope mounting rail atop the receiver, walnut stock and forearm and one-inch carrying sling swivels. Made in Russia, "they strong like bear".

Rogue River Rifle Co.

The Chipmunk is every kid's idea of the perfect rifle and it is now available in 17 HM2 and 22 LR and in a left-hand version as well. TruGlo sights are now standard on all models, and the new stainless steel rifles won't rust as quickly when handled by sticky little hands. The latest variant is called the Barracuda and its stock is unlike anything you have ever seen worn by a Chipmunk.

Rossi

When it comes to break-action, single-shot firearms, nobody offers more choices than Rossi. Inline muzzleloaders, smoothbore shotguns, slug guns with rifled barrels, centerfires, rimfires, you name it and they probably have it. A number of two-barrel sets are available too, with 22-250 and 20-gauge one of the latest additions. The Muzzleloader Plus One pairs offer several combinations, such as a 50-caliber inline barrel matched up with a barrel in 12-gauge or 243 Winchester. The options are so great in number they fill up the latest Rossi catalog.

Ruger

The curved steel buttplate on the stock of the Mini-14 Ranch Rifle has been replaced with a black rubber pad. Also new to this little rifle is a matte finish on the stainless steel and a military-style front sight blade with protective ears. The Mark II Frontier version of the Model 77 rifle is rated at only six pounds. That, along with a barrel length of 16 inches and a stock length-of-pull of only 12-5/8 inches, makes it a compact and lightweight package. Using Ruger rings, you can attach a regular scope to the receiver or, if you are so inclined, you can attach a long-eye relief scope to a quarter-rib out on the barrel. The rib appears to have been robbed from Ruger's No. 1 single-shot rifle. The stock is laminated wood and, like Henry Ford might have said had he built rifles rather than automobiles, you can have any chambering you want so long as the chambering you want is 243 Winchester, 308 Winchester, 300 WSM or 7mm-08. Other news from Prescott includes the 17 HM2 in the Model 77/17, and the 204 Ruger in the No. 1A Light Sporter and Mark II Target Rifle.

Sako

Biggest news from Finland is the Sako Quad, a handsome little bolt-action rifle with 22-inch interchangeable barrels and magazines in 17 HM2, 22 Long Rifle, 17 HMR and 22 WMR. The rifle can be purchased with one barrel or in a combo package with all four barrels. Switching barrels takes mere seconds. The Quad weighs 5-3/4 pounds, has a black synthetic stock and pull weight of its single-stage trigger is adjustable from two to four pounds. I have one of these on the way and will let you know how well it works next year.

Moving on to centerfire rifles, we have a new variation of the Model 75 called Grey Wolf. Its barreled action is stainless steel and as its name might imply, its laminated wood stock is gray in color. Barrel lengths are 22-1/2 inches for standard cartridges ranging from 223 Remington to 30-06, and 24-1/2 inches for Winchester's short magnums in 270, 7mm and 300 calibers. A similar rifle called the Custom Single Shot is offered in 308 Winchester only and one wonders why

it is not also available in various 22-caliber varmint chamberings––and perhaps even 243 Winchester.

Savage

Savage recently brought back the Stevens name with the introduction of an economy-grade knockabout shotgun in side-by-side style and the new Model 200 centerfire rifle is a continuation of that resurrection. Basically a no-frills version of the Savage 110, it is available with both

long and short actions in a variety of calibers. The action is pillar-bedded into a synthetic stock.

Shilen, Inc.

Shilen does not build rifles but the company does make some of the world's most accurate barrels. Something some folks don't realize is the guys at Shilen will rebarrel rifles. I recently had them install a 26-inch benchrest-grade barrel in 257 Weatherby Magnum on a highly

Ruger's Ranch Rifle has undergone a number of upgrades, including a rubber butt pad and a military-style front sight with protective ears.

As its name implies, the Sako Model 75 Gray Wolf has a gray laminated wood stock. It is available in a variety of chamberings from 223 Remington to 300 WSM.

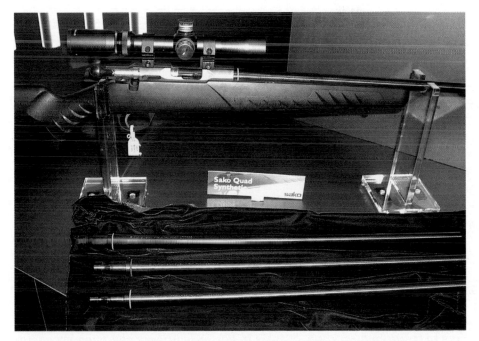

I like switch-barrel rifles and am looking forward to working with the new bolt-action Quad from Sako. It can be bought with one barrel or with four interchangeable barrels and magazines in 17 HM2, 22 LR, 17 HMR and 22 WMR. What fun!

tuned Remington Model 700 action. It consistently averages half an inch for three shots at 100 yards with Weatherby factory ammo loaded with the Nosler 115-grain Ballistic Tip. Shilen offers two types of 257 Weatherby Magnum chambers. One duplicates the freebore of Weatherby factory rifles in that caliber. Another cuts a shorter chamber throat, but factory ammo can still be fired in it. Shilen also offers excellent match-grade triggers for the Model 700. One is for big-game rifles and the other with its two-ounce weight of pull is for use on a target rifle.

Springfield, Inc.

About a week before writing this I watched GUN DIGEST editor Ken Ramage shoot the new Socom II rifle from Springfield and he kept asking for more ammo. The latest variation of the ever-popular M1A1, its 16-1/4 inch barrel is in 7.62mm NATO (or 308 Winchester to we civilians) and it comes with a 10-round magazine (20-rounders are also available). It has a black synthetic stock (what else?) and an extremely loud muzzle brake. Iron sights consist of the standard adjustable aperture at the rear and a tritium-imbedded post with protective ears up front. Four Picatinny rails on the top, bottom and sides of its ventilated forearm (called Cluster Rail System by Springfield) have more than enough room for scopes, red dot sights, lasers, flashlights and other gadgets and gizmos that make a gun like this fun to shoot. Overall length is a compact 37 inches, which is why its manufacturer bills the Socom II as just the ticket for close-quarters work.

Taylor's & Company

This company offers a reproduction of the Winchester Model 92 in three versions, standard, saddle ring carbine and takedown, the latter available with 20- or 24-inch octagon barrel. Chambering options are 32-20, 32 H&R Magnum, 38 Special, 357 Magnum, 38-40, 44-40 and 45 Colt. Stock and forearm are American walnut with an oil finish.

Thompson/Center

The trim little G2 Contender rifle has three new barrel options for 2004. All are 23 inches long. The one in 6.8mm Remington SPC is an excellent choice for a youngster's first centerfire, or for anyone who is looking for a low-recoil rifle capable of taking deer out to 250 yards or so. I have not fired the T/C barrel in this caliber, but the one built by SSK Industries for my G2 Contender rifle will consistently shoot the Hornady 130-grain SST and Sierra 135-grain MatchKing bullets inside three inches at 300 yards. And it is just as accurate with Remington ammo loaded with the 115-grain Core-Lokt Ultra bullet.

Due to its interchangeable barrel design, the G2 Contender has the capability of being many things to many different hunters and when wearing a 45-caliber barrel it is one of my favorite inline muzzleloaders. We all assumed that barrels above 45 caliber are too large in diameter to squeeze into the small G2 receiver but those clever engineers at T/C have now proven us wrong by introducing a 50-caliber barrel for it. They accomplished this by reducing the diameter of the breech of the barrel enough to fit inside the receiver but leaving the rest of the barrel full diameter to keep recoil at a manageable level. The receiver of the prototype I shot a few groups with had a case-colored finish from the T/C custom shop and that along with its excellent accuracy made me want to take it home. The third new barrel is a smoothbore chambered for the 28-gauge shell which is okay by me since I use the 28 for more of my upland hunting than anything else with the possible exception of the .410. It will come with interchangeable chokes in Improved Cylinder, Modifed and Full.

The G2 Contender rifle barrel, by the way, is not the same as the old Contender carbine barrel. It measures 23 inches long and 0.800-inch at the muzzle, compared to 21 inches long and 0.610-inch at the muzzle for the carbine barrel. It will work on both the old and new Contender receivers, but its larger diameter does require the use of a different forearm. On average, I find the heavier barrel to be more accurate and yet, at a weight of about seven pounds, the G2 rifle is plenty light for long-distance walking.

Due to its interchangeable barrels in various calibers, the Thompson/Center G2 rifle can be many different things to many different hunters and in my case, the 30-30 barrel and a handload with the Hornady 150-grain SST bullet was what I needed to harvest this whitetail on a December 2004 hunt in Kansas.

I know this to be true because I used one back in December while hunting deer in Kansas. Many years ago I shot metallic silhouette with a T/C Contender pistol in 30-30 Winchester, but I had never worked with a Contender rifle in that chambering until the Kansas hunt. Unlike rifles with tubular magazines, a single shot is safe to use with pointed bullets so the handload I settled on consisted of the Federal 210M primer, Winchester case and 34.0 grains of H4895 behind the Hornady 150-grain SST. Muzzle velocity averaged close to 2400 fps. Prior to the hunt I shot the G2 rather extensively and it would consistently keep five bullets inside four inches at 300 yards with that load, and it would do the same with the Hornady 150-grain InterBond pushed along by the same powder charge. It shot flat enough too; when zeroed three inches high at 100 yards, either bullet landed just about dead-on my point of aim at 200 yards and halfway between the first and second tick marks of the Ballistic Plex reticle of the Burris 3-10x Euro Diamond scope worn by the rifle. I was prepared to shoot that far but did not have to. With no more than 15 minutes of shooting light left in the day, the buck stepped out of the woods at about 200 yards for his last meal of green winter wheat.

While in Kansas I also had a ball hunting fox squirrels with a prototype of T/C's Classic autoloader in 17 Hornady Mach 2. This particular version is called Model R55 due to design changes necessitated by cycle timing difference of the 17 HM2 cartridge. A floating balance weight riding beneath the barrel is designed to be adjusted at the factory for the 17 HM2 or 22 Long Rifle cartridge. Another new addition is a trapdoor compartment in the buttstock for stowage of an extra magazine, or a small candy bar should you be so inclined. The handsome little rifle I shot functioned perfectly. I did not have the opportunity to ventilate enough paper targets with it to be more specific about its accuracy but I got the impression that you will not believe your eyes when you shoot your first groups with one. The

trajectory of the 17 HM2 is quite flat. With the rifle zeroed dead-on at 50 yards, it was only about an inch low at 100 yards. Inside 40 yards, the Hornady ammo I was shooting seemed to be more effective on body shots to bushytails than 22 Long Rifle hollowpoints, but once it reaches 60 yards or so that tiny 17-grain bullet really begins to run out of steam fast. From that point on you'd best hold those crosshairs on the head.

Tikka

I never cease to be amazed at how much accuracy is available for so few dollars in Tikka rifles. A T3 Lite in 270 Winchester I have been working with will keep a number of factory loads and handloads inside an inch at 100 yards. Some of the groups I fired with the T3 Tactical in 223 Remington measured less than half an inch. For many years I have been telling various firearms manufacturers that a serious varmint rifle needs a stock with a height-adjustable comb due to the great variations in mounting heights among varmint scopes with their various objective diameters. Its adjustable stock is one of the primary reasons I chose the T3 Tactical for most of my varmint shooting during 2004. I

am happy to say that the comb of the fiberglass-reinforced polymer stock of the new-for-2005 Super Varmint is also adjustable for height. The new rifle also inherited the five-round magazine of the Tactical as well as a Picatinny rail atop the receiver that will allow any scope to be positioned to suit the individual shooter. The trigger is easily adjustable in the two to four pounds range, and it can be done without removing the stock. It has a heavy 23 1/2-inch barrel in 223 Remington, 22-250 or 308 Winchester. They claim the Super Varmint is capable of half-inch groups at 100 yards and, since it is basically a civilianized version of the Tactical, I'd say that's probably no brag.

Also new for 2005 is the T3 Big Boar. Its 19-inch barrel is available in 308, 30-06 and 300 WSM; it weighs 6-1/2 pounds.

Ultra Light Arms (New)

Melvin Forbes who, many years ago, raised the performance bar for extremely light big-game rifles, has added the various WSSM chamberings to his already lengthy list of options for the original Model 20 rifle. In case you have not noticed this little company that could, four other centerfire actions are also

This year's Tikka T3 Super Varmint has a lot in common with last year's T3 Tactical which I am shooting here, including a height-adjustable comb and Picatinny rail atop its receiver.

The new Vanguard Compact from Weatherby comes with two stocks, one short enough for a youngster, the other long enough to be used once he or she grows up. The price is no higher than "youth" rifles sold by other companies with one stock.

After the Tribute version is gone, there will be no more Winchester Model 9422 rifles.

available: Model 24 in standard cartridges ranging from 25-06 to 338-06, Model 28 in mid-length magnums from 264 Winchester to 358 Norma; Model 32 in full-length magnums from 7mm STW to 358 STA, and Model 40 in serious stuff such as 416 Rigby and 458 Lott. And as might be expected, the Model 20RF is now available in 17 HM2.

USRAC

If you have been putting off the purchase of a Winchester Model 9422 for the past 33 years you had best not procrastinate any longer because U.S. Repeating Arms is dropping the sweet little rifle from production. That leaves the Marlin 39A as the only high-quality lever-action 22 rimfire being produced in America. USRAC is saying farewell to the 9422 by producing a run of limited-production rifles called the Tribute series. A total of 9,422 will be built and when those along with the 222 Custom Tribute rifles are gone, there will be no more. Rifles in 22 Long Rifle and 22 WMR will be built, some with a 20 1/2-inch barrel and straight-grip stock, others with a 22 1/2-inch barrel and a curved grip. All will have upgraded walnut stocks and special engraving on their receivers.

Moving from bad news to plinkers and small-game hunters to good news for varmint shooters and big-game hunters, there are now even more Model 70 options available. They include the Super Grade III with its handsome walnut stock in both standard and limited-edition Rocky Mountain Elk Foundation versions. The RMEF rifle is available in 300 WSM and 325 WSM, while the other one is offered in those two––plus seven other chamberings ranging from 25-06 to 338 Winchester Magnum. Then we have the Model 70 Ultimate Shadow Blued which is, with one exception, exactly like the Camo Ultimate Shadow Stainless we already had. All seven stubby and super-stubby chamberings from 223 WSSM to 325 WSM are available. Also available in those same calibers is a blued steel version of the old Model 70 Coyote Stainless and the Coyote Lite in both blued and stainless. The latter two have synthetic stocks replete with aluminum bedding block and ventilation slots. And in case you have not noticed, the Model 70 Featherweight and Sporter II are available with left-hand actions. Moving on to rifles that shoot only one time between loadings, the Model 1885 Low Wall is now available in 17 HM2, and you can buy its High Wall mate in three WSM chamberings: 270, 7mm and 300.

Unlike the rimfire version of the Model 94, the centerfire version is still alive and well and available in more than a dozen configurations. Many years ago, the only way to mount a scope on a 94 was over on the left-hand side of its receiver, or out on the barrel. Its top-ejection of spent cases ruled out mounting a scope atop the receiver. Then came 94s with the Angle-Eject feature and suddenly Marlin was not the only company making a lever action rifle with a tubular magazine that ejected cases eastward when you were shooting north. USRAC is now offering a Model 94 designed to be used with a forward-mounted scope which brings everything back full circle. Called the Timber Scout, it has a Weaver-style scope mounting base attached out on its 18-inch barrel and it is available in 30-30 and 44 Magnum. Those who are so inclined have the option of removing the base from the barrel and mounting a scope back on the receiver where it is supposed to go, or you can forego glass sights entirely and use the rifle with its open sights as John Browning meant for it to be used. As Model 94s of current production go, my favorite is the Trails End Hunter Octagon. It has a 20-inch barrel and it is available in 25-35, 30-30 and 38-55. I'd probably buy one in 25-35 if it wore a Marble's tang sight like the one worn by the Legacy series of rifles.

Volquartsen Custom

Tom Volquartsen's goal in designing his new Evolution rifle was to come up with an autoloader in 223 Remington with the accuracy of a match-grade AR15, but one that looks more like a sporting rifle than a battle rifle. He has done just that. The gas-operated Evolution uses AR-15 magazines and is available in 223 Remington and 204 Ruger. Its barrel, and the receiver with its integrally-machined Picatinny scope mounting rail, are stainless steel, and both are made by Volquartsen. Same goes for all other component parts. The rifle is made for varmint-shooting so it is no lightweight at 10 pounds. The relatively heavy barrel is 20 inches long. I will not be surprised to see the Evolution shoot five bullets inside half an inch at 100 yards on a regular basis. Equally interesting is Volquartsen's Fusion takedown rifle in four rimfire calibers. You can learn more about it in my "Testfire" report elsewhere.

Weatherby

Roy Weatherby founded his company in 1945, which makes it 60 years old in 2005. The special catalog the company is printing to celebrate those six decades of fame and success is a must-have item for Weatherby rifle fans. And for those of us who are especially addicted, there are commemorative baseball caps, coffee mugs, t-shirts and embossed tin signs. Mention of the name Weatherby has always brought to mind rifles that are strong, accurate, handsome and chambered for super-quick cartridges but the company has become just as widely known for its shotguns in autoloading, over-under and side-by-side persuasion. And we must not overlook the fact that as hunting clothing goes, Weatherby wool is *"weally"* wonderful. I know this to be true because it has kept my young and tender body warm in terribly cold places ranging from a deer stand on the plains of Iowa in December to the Transylvania mountains of Romania.

The Vanguard family of Weatherby rifles continues to grow in both model variations and chambering options. Whereas the standard Vanguard is guaranteed to keep three bullets inside 1-1/2 inches at 100 yards, the new SUB-MOA version is guaranteed to put three inside minute-of-angle when fed Weatherby factory ammunition or specified premium-grade ammo from Remington, Federal and Winchester. Blued and stainless steel versions are available, both with pillar-bedded, fiberglass/carbon fiber stocks available in six different color patterns. Both rifles have 24-inch barrels in 223 Remington, 22-250, 243 Winchester, 270 Winchester, 308 Winchester or 30-06—or you can choose among seven magnums: the 257 Weatherby, 270 WSM, 7mm Remington, 300 Winchester, 300 WSM, 300 Weatherby or 338 Winchester. As might be expected,

The Weatherby Vanguard is now available in about any chambering your heart might desire, and the one in 270 WSM I used to take this mule deer is new for 2005.

the 270 WSM and 300 WSM are on the same short Vanguard action as the 223 Remington and other short cartridges. The trigger is adjustable for weight of pull and sear engagement. I used one in 270 WSM on a mule deer hunt in Wyoming during the 2004 season and it worked quite nicely.

Weatherby has taken the new Compact version of its Vanguard rifle a step beyond what we have seen from other rifle companies. Youngsters have a tendency to eventually outgrow the extremely short length of pull of the stocks of other so-called "youth" rifles so the better idea from Weatherby comes with two stocks. That way, your son or daughter can start out with the hardwood stock and its 12 1/2-inch pull and then, a few years later, switch to the synthetic stock with its standard 13 1/2-inch pull. The concept also allows Dad to sneak off and hunt with the rifle while junior is in school. Even more good news is the fact that suggested price of the complete package is less than some of the other short-pull rifles that come with only one stock. Its trigger is fully adjustable too. The Vanguard Compact weighs 6-3/4 pounds and has a 20-inch barrel in 22-250, 243

Winchester or 308 Winchester. It is the kind of rifle any kid would absolutely love to grow up with.

So far, Weatherby's best-selling Vanguard has been the Synthetic Package. It comes with a factory-mounted and bore-sighted 3-9x Bushnell banner scope and an Uncle Mike's nylon carrying sling with quick-detach swivels, all in a hard plastic carrying case. Barrel length is 24 inches with the following standard chambering options: 223 Remington, 22-250, 243 Winchester, 270 Winchester, 308 Winchester and 30-06. Magnum chamberings include 257 Weatherby, 270 WSM, 7mm Remington, 300 Weatherby, 300 Winchester, 300 WSM and 338 Winchester. During the 2004 season I took a nice pronghorn buck in Wyoming with the Synthetic Package in 257 Weatherby Magnum and Weatherby factory ammo loaded with the 115-grain Nosler Ballistic Tip bullet. Accuracy averaged 1-1/4 inches at 100 yards.

NOTE: Autographed copies of Layne's full-color, hardback books *Shotguns and Shotgunning, and Rifles,* and *Cartridges For Large Game* are available for $39.95 plus $6 for shipping and handling from High Country Press, 306 Holly Park Lane, Simpsonville, SC 29681. Also available are softcover editions of his *The Custom Model 1911 Pistol and Shooter's Handbook,* either priced at $30.95 plus $4 s&h.

SHOTGUNS TODAY:

SHOTGUN REVIEW

by John Haviland

Shotguns have always been imported into America. This year, though, the number of guns arriving on America's shores have increased substantially, with established American companies putting their names on foreign shotguns. Whether this is a good trend remains to be seen. Certainly these imported guns are taking sales away from American-made shotguns.

Beretta

The Beretta UGB25 Xcel is an inertia-operated autoloading trap gun that breaks open like a hinge action. A Beretta spokesman said the main reason for the break-open feature is to show others the gun is unloaded. A large lever on the left side of the receiver tilts the barrel breech up so the chamber can be loaded. A carrier on the right side of the receiver holds a second shell for shooting doubles. Fired cases eject out the bottom of the gun.

The UGB25 Xcel softens recoil with a stock-mounted spring reducer, GelTek pad and an over-bored barrel with a lengthened forcing cone. The butt pad and comb are adjustable for a custom fit and to move shot pattern impact. The gun weighs

The EELL Diamond Pigeon over/under features a receiver engraved with scenes of the Texas King Ranch and its checkering incorporates the King Ranch's running W brand.

The AL391 Teknys autoloader features a receiver engraved with scenes of the Texas King Ranch and its checkering incorporates the King Ranch's running W brand.

The Charles Daley
Country Squire

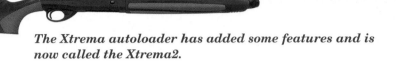

The Kick-off recoil reduction system at least somewhat tames the kick of 3 1/2-inch 12-gauge shells with two hydraulic dampeners incorporated into the recoil pad.

The Beretta UGB25 Xcel is an inertia-operated auto-loading trap gun that breaks open like a hinge action.

The Xtrema autoloader has added some features and is now called the Xtrema2.

to the shot as it leaves the muzzle and results in a wide pattern for jungle shots on quail in the mesquite or ruffed grouse in the alders.

Browning

Browning has further refined its Citori 12- and 20-gauge line with three new models of these over/unders, and two new grades of Lightnings. The Citori Super Lightning combines the styling and weight of the Lightning and Super Light, and wears a blued receiver with gold borders with 26- or 28-inch barrels. The Classic Lightning Feather is pretty much the same style, but with an aluminum receiver that reduces gun weight by about one pound. The Classic Lightning features a silver nitrate receiver and an oil-finished walnut stock with a muted glow. The Grade IV Lightning features a grayed receiver with engraving of various sporting scenes. For example, the 12-gauge model illustrates pheasants on the left side and mallards on the right. The Grade VII features 24-karat gold inlays of pointers and mallards. Both grades are available in .410-bore and 28, 20 and 12 gauges.

The Citori XT Trap has been spiffed up with features like Golden Clays engraving, high-grade wood and Midas Grade choke tubes. It also

eight to nine pounds, depending on barrel length and configuration.

The Xtrema autoloader has added some features and is now called the Xtrema2. The Kick-off recoil reduction system somewhat tames the kick of 3 1/2-inch 12-gauge shells with two hydraulic dampeners incorporated into the recoil pad. The Kick-off system can also adjust length of pull. A new trigger group also provides a shorter trigger travel, crisp pull and quick reset. The gun's forearm is more slender with flutes for the fingertips to grip and rubber inserts to help absorb recoil. All metal of the Xtrema2 is coated to resist corrosion.

Beretta has restyled four of its shotgun models as the King Ranch Shotguns. The Silver Pigeon, EELL Diamond Pigeon and Silver Pigeon IV over/unders and AL391 Teknys autoloaders feature receivers engraved with scenes of the Texas King Ranch, and their checkering incorporates the King Ranch's running W brand.

Bill Hanus Bird Guns

The BSA Royal 20-gauge side-by-side is made in Spain and is available with 26- or 28-inch barrels. The barrels have 3-inch chambers and chrome-lined bores. Three screw-in choke tubes are included. A single selective trigger

and automatic ejectors eliminate the motions of picking a trigger to select a barrel to shoot and pulling fired shells out of the chambers. Wood is Turkish walnut with laser-cut checkering. The sideplates are case-colored and engraved.

Mr. Hanus also sells the Briley Diffusion spreader choke tube for the Royal. Rifling is cut into this skeet tube which imparts a spin

Above: Browning Cynergy 20-gauge with a Texas bobwhite quail.
Inset: Shooting the Browning Cynergy 20-gauge over/under with the blue sky of Texas in the background.

features the Gracoil recoil reduction system and an adjustable comb.

Browning has expanded its line of Gold autoloaders. The Gold Fusion High Grade features a high-grade Turkish walnut stock and forearm and a silver nitride receiver engraved with mallards and a Labrador retriever on the 12-gauge model. The 20-gauge engraving features quail and a pointer. The stock is adjustable with shims that move comb height 1/8 of an inch up and down. A HiViz TriComp sight system keeps the barrel in your peripheral vision.

A Golden Clays version of the Sporting Clays and Ladies Sporting Clays has added. Both guns wear a motif featuring gold enhancements of a pheasant transforming into a clay bird on the right side and a quail changing into a clay bird on the left side. The ladies version wears a stock with slightly smaller dimensions to fit smaller shooters and a somewhat thicker stock to help absorb recoil.

The Cynergy over/under was introduced last year in 12 gauge and is joined this year by 20 and 28 gauges. The Cynergy shotguns feature a trigger system that uses an actuator to reverse the direction of the impact force from the pin to the striker. Browning states this results in a crisper and lighter trigger pull with a greatly reduced lock time and overtravel. The 20- and 28-gauge Cynergy guns each weigh about 6-1/2 pounds.

The new 20-gauge and 28-gauge Cynergys also feature the Browning Inflex Recoil Pad that Browning claims reduces recoil by 25 percent. If you can get past its less than attractive looks, the recoil pad works well. A couple of friends and I shot the 20- and 28-gauge guns at Texas bobwhite quail last winter. Even shooting Winchester Super-X 1 ounce loads in both gauges, the guns recoiled so little I rarely lost the sight picture. That allowed taking a quick second shot. The guns are available in Field and Sporting versions.

Charles Daly

The Charles Daly autoloader is now available in a left-hand model. The Field Grade 12-gauge

The Charles Daly autoloader is now available in a left hand Field Hunter model.

FABARM's left-handed version is now available in the Lion H35 Azur autoloader.

Cosmetic changes made to the Lion H35 Azur autoloader, include a couple of ceramic inlays on the receiver flats and laser-cut checkering patterns that flow along the forearm and through the grip.

The Beta Grade IV is an upgrade of FABARM's side-by-side. The Grade IV includes a wood butt plate, Arabesques and animal motifs on the side plates and titanium coating on the forearm bracket.

wears either a black synthetic stock to match its receiver and barrel, or full camouflage. Barrel lengths are 24, 26, or 28 inches with 3 screw-in choke tubes. The barrel bore is also chrome-lined.

FABARM

The Beta Grade IV is an upgrade of FABARM's side-by-side. The Grade IV includes a wood buttplate, Arabesques and animal motifs on the side plates and titanium coating on the forend bracket.

The Specialists over/under has had a coat of MAX 4 Camouflage added.

Cosmetic changes have been made to the Lion H35 Azur autoloader, including ceramic inlays on the receiver flats and laser-cut checkering patterns that flow along the forearm and through the grip. A green fiber optic insert has been added to the rear top of the receiver to remind

shooters to keep their cheek planted firmly on the comb. A rubber and wood butt pad are included. A left-hand version is also available.

Ithaca

The Turkey Slayer Guide Gun wears the new Accu-Grip pistol grip stock that helps absorb some of the recoil from turkey loads and helps hold the gun still for a long period. A Tasco 30mm Red Dot Sight comes mounted and bore-sighted to help place the tight shot pattern on target when fired through the Triple X Ithaca Turkey choke. A Quake Industries sling and Doskocil hard-side case accompany each gun.

The Home State Shotgun is a limited edition Model 37 Featherlight pump 12-gauge that features the map of an individual state, its banner, name, motto and year of statehood. A stock inlay depicts the official seal of the state. The right side of the receiver carries a flowing banner etched with the edition limit.

The Collector Edition I "One of 100" is limited to 100 guns per state. Grade I will be limited to 100 guns and Grade II to 10 guns. The etchings on both sides of the gun's receiver are plated 24-karat gold. The trigger, safety and magazine cap are also plated with gold.

The Edition II Museum Edition is limited to 10 guns per state. Each of these guns begins as an Edition I gun and from there is hand-engraved over most of the metal, even the muzzle.

The Guide Series Slug gun features a blued finish with a rifled 12- or 20-gauge 20- or 24-inch barrel and Monte Carlo black laminate stock with a ring-tailed forearm. The receiver is drilled and tapped for a scope.

Harrington & Richardson

H&R has started importing a line of autoloading and over/under shotguns.

The Excell Auto 5 autoloading 12-gauge has a 3-inch magnum chamber, 5-shot magazine, magazine cut-off, ventilated recoil pads and ventilated rib barrels. Excell models include the Synthetic, Walnut, Waterfowl with 28-inch ventilated rib barrels, Turkey with a 22-inch barrel and fiber optic sights and Combo with a 28-inch ventilated rib barrel and 24-inch rifled barrel. All come with four screw-in chokes and weigh 7 pounds.

The Pinnacle over/under 12- and 20-gauge models have single selective triggers and selective automatic ejectors. They also feature vent rib barrels and three choke tubes. The stocks are walnut-stained with checkering, curved grips and recoil pads. The 12-gauge gun weighs 6-3/4 pounds and the 20-gauge 6-1/2 pounds.

Kimber

Kimber named its over/under shotgun Augusta after a small town along Montana's Eastern Front of the Rocky Mountains. It is thus only fitting that Kimber's new side-by-side 20-gauge is named after Valier, a town a short distance to the north.

The Valier is a sidelock made in Turkey with 26- or 28-inch barrels and double triggers. A lever on the left plate can be turned out for access to the sideplates. The gun weighs 5 pounds, 14 ounces. The Grade I has no ejectors and wears somewhat plainer Turkish walnut. It retails for $4422. The Grade II has selective automatic ejectors and wears much fancier wood. It costs five grand.

Krieghoff

The K-80 Trap Special Combo has a fully adjustable rib on both its over/under barrels and an "unsingle" barrel for point-of-impact adjustments. Built around the K-80 receiver, the Trap Special comes with 32-inch over/under barrels and 34-inch "unsingle" barrel. A Monte Carlo trap stock with adjustable comb designed for the high-post rib is standard. The rib can be adjusted so the gun shoots from fairly flat (60 percent/40 percent), to a full pattern high (100 percent). The point-of-impact of the over/under barrels can be individually adjusted to different points of impact by changing the front hanger.

Legacy Sports

Legacy's new line of imported Khan shotguns include seven over/unders. The guns include Field models with extractors on the 28-inch barrel of the 12-gauge, and the 26-inch barrel of the 20- and 28-gauge, and .410 bore. Weights run from 5.7 pounds for the .410 to 7.7 pounds for the 12-gauge. The Deluxe and Clays models in 12 and 20 include more brightly finished metal and wood, and ejectors. The .410 wears fixed chokes, while the other gauges come with five screw-in chokes.

The Escort shotguns have several additions. The Escort semi-auto Youth wears a 22-inch barrel and shorter length of pull. Several models have had bores plated with chrome, with outsides coated with black chrome. A 12-gauge 3 1/2-inch magnum is also available. Cantilever scope mounts have also been added to the Slug models.

The Escort pump line has expanded to include a 12-gauge MarineGuard with a nickel-plated 18-inch barrel, and Field Hunter models with multi-chokes in 26-inch barrels. New camo patterns have also been added to several models, as well as HiViz fiber optic front sights.

Marlin

Marlin has owned the famous name of L.C. Smith since 1971 and is now putting the name on over/under and side-by-side guns made by Fausti Stefano of Italy.

The LC12-OU 12-gauge features a 3-inch chamber in 28-inch ventilated

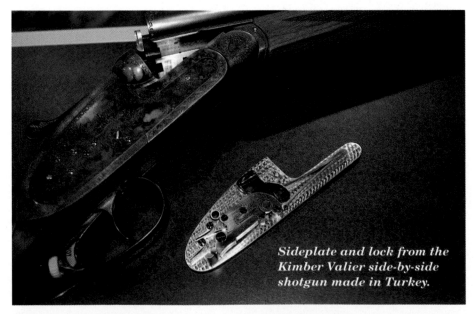

Sideplate and lock from the Kimber Valier side-by-side shotgun made in Turkey.

rib barrels with three screw-in choke tubes, single selective trigger, and selective automatic ejectors. It wears a checkered walnut stock with a fluted comb and recoil pad. The gun weighs 7-1/4 pounds.

The LC12-DB 12-gauge double barrel features a 3-inch chamber, a single trigger, selective automatic ejectors, three choke tubes (IC, M, F), 28-inch barrels with a solid rib and a bead front sight. Its walnut stock is checkered, and has a fluted comb, a beavertail forearm and a recoil pad.

The LC20-DB is pretty much the same gun, but in 20-gauge with 26-inch barrels and a weight of 6 pounds.

Mossberg

Mossberg calls its 935 Magnum the most reliable value-priced 12-gauge 3 1/2-inch autoloader ever made. The gun features an over-bored barrel and a self-regulating gas system to take the sting out of recoil. The gun weighs 7-3/4 pounds and includes 22-, 24-, 26- or 28-inch barrels with a front fiber optic bead and three screw-in choke tubes. Five camo patterns are available.

The 930 autoloader is a 12-gauge 3-inch version of the 935. The 930 weighs 7-1/2 pounds and wears a ported barrel, three choke tubes, receiver drilled and tapped for scope mounts and a cocking indicator.

The 535 All-Terrain Shotgun (ATS) is another inexpensive 3 1/2-inch 12 gauge. The pump shotgun is similar to the established Mossberg 500. With a simple barrel change a hunter can outfit the 535 to hunt upland birds, waterfowl, turkey and deer.

The 500 Bantam pump 20 gauge features a 12-inch length of pull. It also comes with stock spacers and an extra recoil pad that lengthens its synthetic stock to 13 inches. When a young shooter has outgrown that stock, a certificate with the gun is worth 50 percent off the price of a full-size stock. The gun comes in Turkey, Field, Slug and Field/Deer Combo models.

Remington

Remington has added features and improvements to several of

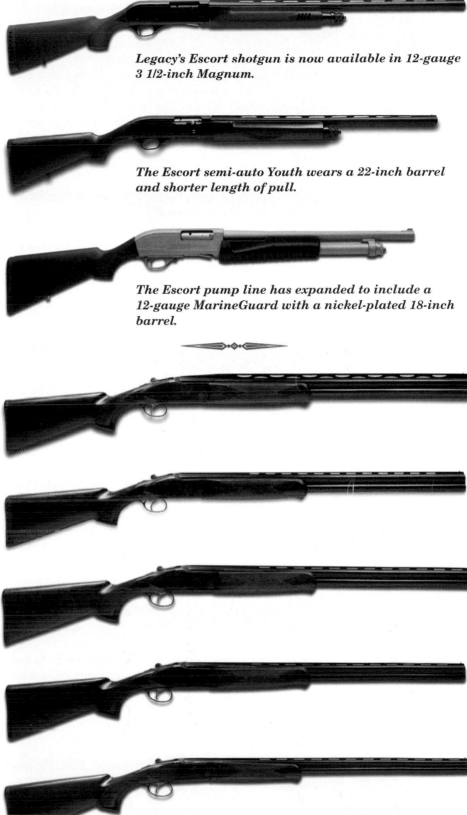

Legacy's Escort shotgun is now available in 12-gauge 3 1/2-inch Magnum.

The Escort semi-auto Youth wears a 22-inch barrel and shorter length of pull.

The Escort pump line has expanded to include a 12-gauge MarineGuard with a nickel-plated 18-inch barrel.

Legacy's new line of imported Khan shotguns include seven over/unders. The guns include Field models with extractors on the 28-inch barrel of the 12-gauge and 26-inch barrel of the 20- and 28-gauge and .410-bore.

Remington's youth Model 870 Express Jr. NWTF Jakes gun is a lightweight 20-gauge pump featuring an 18 3/4-inch ventilated rib barrel, and a synthetic stock with 12-inch length of pull. The stock and forearm are camouflaged in Skyline Excel camo with a "Team NWTF" medallion embedded into the stock.

Remington's Model 11-87 Sportsman slug hunting model has a fully rifled 21-inch barrel and cantilever scope base. Its comb is raised to position the eye behind a scope.

The 11-87 Sportsman comes in 12- and 20-gauge versions with 26- or 28-inch barrels with ventilated ribs and a screw-in Modified choke tube.

Remington's Model 870 Express Super magnum is now covered in Fall Flight camo.

The Model 870 Express Super Magnum Synthetic shoots all lengths of 12-gauge shell. The gun is available with a 26- or 28-inch vent rib barrel with a Modified screw-in choke, matte finish and a black synthetic stock.

The Model 870 Special Purpose Turkey Super Magnum Thumbhole is covered with the same camo. The thumbhole stock makes holding the gun in alignment easier for a longer time when a gobbler is strutting just out of range.

its guns and is importing a line of budget-priced guns made in Russia.

Let's start with the big guns for big birds. The Model SP-10 Magnum is now covered with Mossy Oak Obsession camouflage. The Model 870 Special Purpose Turkey Super Magnum Thumbhole is covered with the same camo. The thumbhole stock makes holding the gun in alignment easier for a longer time when a gobbler is strutting just out of range. The thumbhole stock and R3 recoil pad also take up a lot of the kick from magnum turkey loads. The Model 870 Express Super magnum is now available with a 28-inch barrel and a coat of Fall Flight camo.

The Model 11-87 Sportsman is Remington's most dependable autoloader in a plain wrapper that is easy on the checkbook. The 11-87 Sportsman comes in 12- and 20-gauge versions with 26- or 28-inch barrels with ventilated ribs and a screw in Modified choke tube. The slug hunting model has a fully rifled 21-inch barrel and cantilever scope base. Its comb is raised to position the eye behind a scope.

The youth model 20-gauge wears a 21-inch barrel and 13-inch length of pull. All models include a matte-black metal finish, black synthetic stock and forearm with swivel studs. The youth Model 870 Express Jr. NWTF Jakes gun is a lightweight 20-gauge pump featuring an 18 1/2-inch ventilated rib barrel and a synthetic stock with 12-inch length of pull. The stock and forearm are camouflaged in Skyline Excel camo with a "Team NWTF" medallion embedded into the stock. The receiver and barrel have a black matte finish. A portion of the proceeds from every "Team NWTF" gun will be donated to the National Wild Turkey Federation.

The Model 870 Express Slug Gun wears a fully rifled, heavy contour barrel in either 12 or 20 gauge. The cantilever scope mount base is attached to the barrel and extends back over the receiver. Mounting the scope on the barrel, instead of the receiver, makes for more accurate shooting because the play between the barrel and receiver are removed.

These pump shotguns feature a non-glare matte finish on all exterior metalwork and all-weather black synthetic stocks and fore-ends.

The Model 870 Wingmaster Dale Earnhardt Tribute is the third shotgun in a four-year limited edition series. Earnhardt's love of the shooting sports and his achievements in the world of NASCAR racing are captured in this special edition Model 870 Wingmaster. Remington will donate a portion of the money from each shotgun sold to the Dale Earnhardt Foundation, which supports wildlife initiatives and children's educational programs.

This 12-gauge pump wears a 28-inch light-contour ventilated rib barrel and American walnut stock and forearm with a high gloss finish and cut checkering. Engraved on the polished blued receiver is Earnhardt's likeness, his signature and scrollwork on the left side. On the right side of the frame is engraved "7 Time Winston Cup Champion" banner. The signature and banner are inlayed in 24 karat gold.

The 870 Wingmaster Jr. is a shotgun for young shooters just starting out. The lightweight 20-gauge wears an 18 3/4-inch ventilated rib barrel and an American walnut stock with 12-inch length of pull, cut checkering and high-gloss finish. The barrel features an ivory front sight and steel middle bead, along with Rem Choke tubes for Improved Cylinder, Modified and Full chokes.

The Model 870 Express Super Magnum Synthetic shoots all lengths of 12-gauge shell. The gun is available with a 26- or 28-inch vent rib barrel with a Modified screw-in choke, matte finish and a black synthetic stock. The Model 870 Express Youth Synthetic Combo covers birds and big game. A 20-inch fully rifled barrel with sights is just right for deer, while a 21-inch ventilated rib barrel with a screw-in Modified choke tube and bead sight covers birds and clay targets.

Remington has started importing a variety of break-action guns made in Russia under the Spartan Gunworks name. They include single-shot shotguns that

Remington's Model 870 Wingmaster Tribute is the third shotgun in a four-year limited edition series. Earnhardt's love of the shooting sports and his achievements in the world of NASCAR racing are captured in this special edition Model 870 Wingmaster.

The 870 Wingmaster Jr. is a shotgun for young shooters just starting out. The lightweight 20-gauge wears an 18 3/4-inch ventilated rib barrel and an American walnut stock with 12-inch length of pull, cut checkering and high-gloss finish.

The Athena D'Italia is Weatherby's newest entry into the box lock side-by-side market. The gun is chambered in 12-, 20- and 28-gauge and weighs 6-3/4 to 7-1/4 pounds.

sell for $89 at the local Wal Mart. The Spartan name also includes single-shot rifles, side-by-side and over/under shotguns, rifle/shotgun combinations and side-by-side rifles.

Rossi

The Rossi fully rifled slug gun is ported at the muzzle to help control the punishing recoil of slug rounds. The barrel is equipped with fiber optic sights. The 12- and 20-gauge single shots are drilled and tapped for the installation of an included scope mount base.

Weatherby

The Athena D'Italia is Weatherby's newest entry into the boxlock side-by-side market. The gun is chambered in 12-, 20- and 28-gauge and weighs 6-3/4 to 7-1/4 pounds. The 12- and 20-gauge have a screw-in improved cylinder, modified and full chokes, while the 28 gauge wears fixed

Improved Cylinder and Modified chokes. The chrome-lined barrels are back-bored and have extractors and automatic ejectors. The trigger guard has a rolled edge to eliminate cutting the finger when reaching for the double triggers. The stock has a straight grip and laser-cut checkering of diamond-shaped webs Weatherby calls "New Scottish." Full engraving is included on the false sideplates. The gun stores in a foam-lined hardcase.

Winchester

Now to the Super X2 line is the Super X2 Light Field Model 12-gauge which weighs about 6-1/2 pounds with a 26- or 28-inch barrel.

The new 1300 Practical Defender will rid the garden of carrot-robbing rabbits, and protect against strange things that go bump in the night. The Defender features a composite stock, 22-inch barrel with screw-in chokes, adjustable open sights and an 8-round magazine.

RIFLES TODAY:
SINGLE-SHOT RIFLE REVIEW

by John Campbell

Welcome to the inaugural installment of GUN DIGEST'S single-shot rifle review. For 2006 and subsequent issues of GD, we'll be examining an ever-growing range of single-shot breechloaders. Some will be recreations of classic 19th century rifles. Others will be totally new designs. A few will be a bit of both. But in any case, they're all fun, full of history and tradition, and present a great challenge for the rifleman to make that one shot count. So, let's get started. There's a lot to cover.

Axtell Rifle Co.

For single-shot *cognoscente*, the name Axtell is synonymous with unexcelled quality. This Montana company started out years ago by making precise reproductions of 19th century rifle sights, then expanded into Sharps 1877 rifle recreations. Today, Axtell makes six versions of the 1877, sometimes known as the "English model." This was a sleek evolution of the Sharps 1874, and a very rare iteration of the Sharps "side-hammer" rifles.

Altogether, Axtell offers a Custom Express, No. 1 Creedmoor, No. 2 Long Range, Lower Sporter, Lower Business Rifle and an Overbaugh schuetzen version of their Model 1877. Each rifle features cut rifled Badger barrels plus appropriate features for its application... including a set of renowned Axell iron sights. If you like fine engraving, exhibition English or American black walnut, flawless checkering, or any other custom touch, all you need do is inquire. The sky's the limit at Axtell. Calibers are also appropriate to a rifle's use, and range from the irresistible little 40-50 Sharps bottleneck to the 45-l00... although Axtell unequivocally recommends the 45-70. For any practical use, I wholeheartedly agree. Base prices for the 1877 vary from $2900 to $5200 and delivery time can take about a year. Nonetheless, Axtell

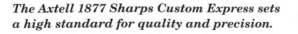

The Axtell 1877 Sharps Custom Express sets a high standard for quality and precision.

Dakota Arms Model 10 is a premium single-shot, mostly targeted toward sporter use. It has sleek lines, a very crisp trigger and fast lock time.

*The Miller action was **long** famous among the target competition crowd, and then Dakota acquired rights to it. Their classic Miller is available in custom configurations, including the sophisticated English style Model F.*

always carries a backlog of orders. And there is good reason. Find out for yourself at www.riflesmith.com

Ballard Rifle Co.

Outside of the Buffalo Bill Historical Museum, one of the best things about Cody, Wyoming, is Ballard Rifle. A visit to their showroom, or web site, will tempt you with fine reproductions of the Ballard, Remington rolling block and Winchester Model 1885 rifles. It's a difficult choice.

First there's the company's namesake: the Ballard. It's available in no less than nine versions including the Schoyen Schuetzen, #8 Union Hill, #7 Long Range, #6 Schuetzen, #5 Pacific, #4 1/2 Midrange, #4 Perfection, #3F Fine Gallery and #1 Silhouette (*not an original Ballard style, of course*). Specifications and calibers vary by model. Base prices range from $3250 to $4155.

Ballard also makes an all-parts-interchange-with-originals reproduction of the classic Winchester Single-Shot. This comes in seven variations including the Special Sporter, Low Wall Special Sporter (paneled side), Low Wall Sporter (flat side), High Wall Express, two levels of High Wall Classic and a High Wall Helm-pattern Schuetzen. Again, calibers and features vary by model and base prices range from $3200 to $4000. But I know from personal experience that these 1885 repros are virtually original for precision and authenticity.

Finally, Ballard makes rolling blocks, too. And, like their Ballard and Winchester products, all parts from these rifles will interchange with originals. Ballard rolling blocks come in #1 Midrange style

This long-range rifle is just one configuration of the Sharps 1878 available from Borchardt Rifle Co. of Silver City, New Mexico.

with pistol grip, plus a straight-grip Heavy Sporter configuration. Prices start at $2400. Specifications and calibers are bewildering.

Ballard also offers a wide array of parts and restoration services for original rifles, too. So spend some quality time with some of the greatest single-shots available today, visit Ballard's web site at www.ballardrifles.com

Borchardt Rifle Co.

Before he created the progenitor of the famous Luger pistol, Hugo Borchardt designed the last single-shot rifle ever made by the Sharps Rifle Co.: the Sharps Model 1878, more commonly known as the Sharps-Borchardt. This was an extremely strong single-shot and was offered in mid- and long-range target versions as well as full-length musket and carbine military configurations. Both military rifles were in 45-70 Govt. But unlike the earlier Sharps, Borchardt's 1878 design utilized a modern, in-line striker for ignition, not a large, slow, aim-jarring hammer.

Most Sharps 1878 rifles were sold in military dress rather than sporter style. And today, any original 1878 sporting rifle comes very dear in the antique gun market. Even a huge number of the once-common military rifles have been stripped for their actions and transmogrified into varmint rifles. As a consequence, most any original Sharps-Borchardt

is a rare commodity these days… unless you know about the Borchardt Rifle Co., of Silver City NM.

There Al Story has literally recreated the Sharps 1878 Borchardt. In fact, Story's actions are so true to the originals that most parts will completely interchange with the Sharps 1878. Story's actions are completely machined from 8620 steel, and Badger barrels are standard. Stocks are select-grade walnut with forearm, grip cap and buttplate exact to original design. Beyond this, your options are wide open because almost every Borchardt that Story builds is a custom order. Prices start at $3100.

For those who want something truly special – and powerful – Story also offers his Al Story falling block rifle in 50 BMG (*not* the Borchardt action). This unique rifle has classic lines, is machined from 4140 steel, nearly five feet long, weighs 32 lbs., and makes a very loud noise. For more information on these precision-crafted rifles, call Al Story at Borchardt Rifle Co., 505-535-2923

Cimarron

If there's one outfit that really caters to aficionados of the Old West, it's Cimarron. And as part of that effort, Cimarron offers no less than eight variants of the Sharps 1874. There's a Billy Dixon model that commemorates this buffalo hunter's famous long shot at the battle of Adobe Walls, as well as a

Borchardt Rifle's Al Story also offers his own design falling block rifle in 50 BMG.

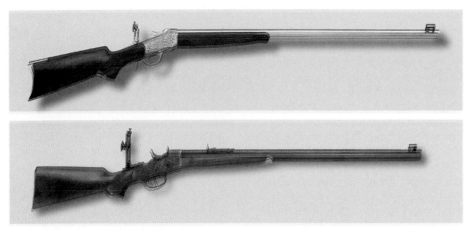

◀ A well-done reproduction of Winchester's Model 1885 flat side low-wall is also in the Cimarron line-up. This one has optional engraving and special wood.

◀ Cimarron's Adobe Walls rolling block features a double-set trigger and recognizes Billy Dixon's personal rifle.

Quigley model that recreates the Sharps rifle used by Tom Selleck in the movie "Quigley Down Under."

From there, you can move on to the 34-inch-barreled Big 50 Sharps, the No. 1 Sporting, the option-laden Pride of The Plains, Texas Ranger Carbine, the Quigley II, or a more austere version of the Billy Dixon. Depending on model, the Cimarron Sharps is available in 45-70, 45-90, 45-120, 45-110, 50-90 and 50-70.

Cimarron also offers an Adobe Walls rolling block with set trigger in 45-70... this to recognize the actual rifle that Billy Dixon owned and used on a daily basis *(he made his famous 1583-yard shot with a borrowed Sharps).*

More recently, Cimarron entered the market with a reproduction of the renowned Winchester Model 1885 Single-Shot; a subject with which I have some passing familiarity. The Cimarron 1885 can be had with either a straight grip or checkered pistol grip buttstock. There is also a Schuetzen double-set trigger available with the early Helm Schuetzen spur lever. These high-walls are available in 45-70, 45-90, 40-65, 38-55, 348 Winchester, and 30-40 Krag.

Finally, Cimarron offers the 1885 flat-side low-wall. It is a fine-looking rifle, and available in 22 LR, 22 Hornet, 30-30 Winchester, 32-20, 38-40, 357 Magnum, 44-40, and 44 Magnum. Check it all out at www.cimarron-firearms.com

CPA Rifles

In the early days of the single-shot's recent revival, one of the few sources for stocks, parts or accurate information on old single-shots was Paul Shuttleworth. Today, Paul heads up the CPA Rifle Co. in Dingman's Ferry, Pennsylvania. It's still one of the best sources you can turn to... especially for CPA's beautiful rendition of the famous Stevens 44 1/2 single-shot rifles. In every case, CPA actions are superior to the originals in material quality and heat treatment.

Since CPA makes virtually all of its rifles to custom order, there's not much you could call a "standard" CPA 44 1/2. But there are three basic models: The Schuetzen, Silhouette, and the Sporting/Varmint Rifle. A host of standard features come with every one. These include a color-cased action, double-set triggers, oil-finished semi-fancy pistol grip stock, a take-down system, and your choice of most any barrel contour in most any chambering from 22 Short to 45-110. Options include additional barrels, checkering, engraving, fancy wood, and more. Base price for a completely finished CPA 44-1/2 rifle ranges from $2225 to $2650. Beyond a modest deposit, you'll have to wait from six to 12 months to have yours delivered. But the quality of these CPA Stevens is worth the wait.

In addition to rifles, CPA offers a large selection of "single-shot stuff" for Stevens, Sharps, Ballard, Remington, Winchester and other classic single-shots. This includes semi-inletted stocks, buttplates, levers, palm rests, scope bases and a whole bunch more. It's worth a trip to the CPA web site just to find out, too. That's www.singleshotrifles.com

C. Sharps Arms Co.

Back in 1975, this was the first company to reproduce the Sharps 1874 rifle. They also offer reproductions of the 1875 and 1877 Sharps as well as their own recreation of the Winchester Model 1885 high-wall.

The heart of C. Sharps' business are five models of the classic 1874 "side-hammer" Sharps. First, there's the 10.5-pound Hartford Sporting Model with 26, 28 or 30-inch tapered octagon barrel double-set triggers, crescent butt and a silver nose-capped forearm. In contrast, the Bridgeport Sporting Rifle has a plain schnabel forend, wider "Bridgeport" steel butt and color-cased receiver. For something really special, there's the Boss Gun upgrade of the Hartford Sporting Rifle. It features a 34-inch barrel, engraved French grey receiver, XXX-figured wood, Hartford-style forend with German silver nose cap, globe front sight, long-range tang rear sight and a lot more. Base price: $4395. There's also a Custom Model Hartford Sporting Rifle available with many of the Boss Gun features. It retails for $3395. But for the ultimate 1874, you must consider the Grade III Boss Gun. It adds a raft of custom features, including a cut-rifled and hand-lapped barrel plus lots of engraving and ultimate wood for $6922. But what a rifle. The 1874 is available in 19 chamberings from 22 LR to 50-140.

C. Sharps also offers the 1875 Sharps in a Sporting Rifle and

Classic Rifle configuration. Both have plain trigger and straight grip stock with an optional pistol grip stock. Pick from 19 calibers here, too.

The elegant 1877 "English" Sharps is also available from C. Sharps. This one is custom production only and comes with a 32 or 34-inch tapered round barrel with Rigby flats at the breech. Calibers are 44-90 Sharps or Remington, 45-70, 45-90 and 45-100 Sharps. It comes with long-range sights, presentation-grade wood, checkering and more. Start saving now. Its base price is $5500.

C. Sharps also introduced one of the first reproductions of the Winchester Model 1885. They still make them in two versions: The Sporting Rifle with single trigger, shotgun butt, straight grip and 26-, 28- or 30-inch tapered octagon barrel, and the Highwall Classic with crescent butt, pistol grip stock and a silver inlay in the forend. You can choose from 19 calibers. The Short Classic highwall is available with an 18-, 20-, 22- or 24-inch tapered octagon barrel at no additional cost.

For the full story on C. Sharps, visit their web site at www.csharpsarms.com

Dakota Arms Inc.

Sturgis, South Dakota, is famous for two things. One is the incomparable sporting arms made by this fine company. And I've forgotten the other thing.

Dakota's Model 10 falling block action is fully machined from steel with a remarkably crisp trigger and fast lock time. The upper and lower tangs are short and straight, allowing for a wide range of stock design. Like the Ruger No. 1 *(which the Model 10 bears a superficial resemblance to)* the Dakota action is attached to the buttstock with a strong through-bolt. Other standard features include XX-wood with hand-rubbed oil finish and checkering, mounts for Talley scope rings and a 23-inch barrel available in most any caliber from 22 LR to 300 Winchester Magnum. The Model 10 Magnum takes you from there all the way up to the 338 Winchester, 375 H&H and 45-70. And because virtually no Model 10 is a "standard" Model 10, you can order any custom feature you want. Base is $4495.

Dakota's "other single-shot" is the famous Miller. Since the early 1970s, this action has been well known to schuetzen riflemen, and is now part of the Dakota line. But the Miller is also one of the best single-shots for a custom sporter. Either way, each Miller is custom built to your specifications. Sporter features include a hand-checkered English style buttstock with XXX- wood and recoil pad. You also get the famous

Miller action with jeweled block and 24-inch round barrel in just about any caliber up to 375 H&H. The Miller Low Boy has a case-colored receiver, half-octagon barrel and more. The Model F is Anglo-inspired with English walnut perch-belly buttstock, Queen Anne grip, stainless receiver, globe front sight and Soule-type rear, plus a 26-inch octagon barrel chambered for any rimmed cartridge up to 45-110. Base price is $6000. The standard Miller starts at $4500. Go to www.millerarms.com and see why these rifles are worth every penny.

Dixie Gun Works

This perennial company needs no introduction when it comes to classic firearms. And these days, that includes a raft of single-shot rifles.

Begin with Steve Meacham's Winchester high-wall reproductions in silhouette and schuetzen configurations. Then add a selection of five Uberti high-walls. From the famous Italian maker, Pedersoli, Dixie offers no less than 16 variations of the Sharps Model 1874 "side-hammer." Pedersoli rolling blocks are also available from Dixie in eight different models, including one to commemorate Col. John Bodine's winning shot in the 1874 Irish-American match. Dixie's Pedersoli line also includes reproductions of the famous

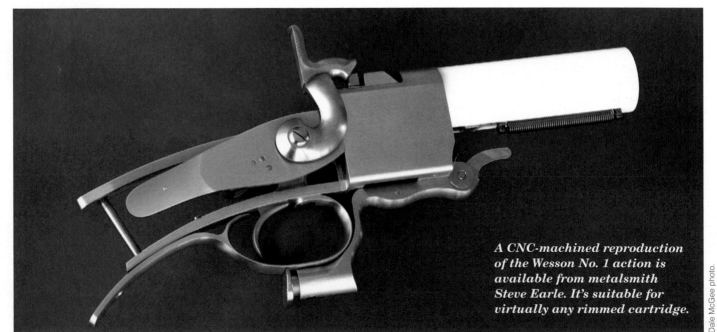

A CNC-machined reproduction of the Wesson No. 1 action is available from metalsmith Steve Earle. It's suitable for virtually any rimmed cartridge.

Dale McGee photo.

For the BPCR silhouette and long-range target enthusiast, S. D. Meacham offers its Silhouette/Long Range model with heavy barrel and straight, recoil-managing buttstock.

The S. D. Meacham Tool & Hardware Co. offers a premiere reproduction of the classic Winchester Single-Shot. This one is the M52 Schuetzen model with prong buttplate for offhand shooting.

Springfield "trapdoor" in rifle, carbine and deluxe "Officer's Model" trim.

And, to be perfectly honest, Dixie prices are some of the best I've seen on any of the single-shots models mentioned above. Worth checking into at www.dixiegunworks.com

Steve Earle

Not many single-shot enthusiasts are familiar with the Wesson No. 1 rifle, and there's a good reason why: Only a handful were ever made. In fact, any original Wesson No. 1 commands a king's ransom on the antique gun market. Even the British Alexander Henry, which the Wesson greatly resembles, is far more numerous. But today, your chances of acquiring a Wesson No. 1 are greatly improved, thanks to Steve Earle of Plympton, Massachusetts.

Steve offers a fully CNC-machined reproduction of the classic Wesson No. 1 action for only $1185. Steve does not offer whole rifles. He sells only in-the-white complete actions. But what actions they are! Steve used an ultra-rare original Wesson No. 1 to measure and back-engineer his reproduction actions. And I kid you not: Each Earle-made Wesson No. 1 is cut from a solid block of 8620 steel and is fitted and finished to tolerances that old man Wesson could only hope to achieve. When you open the box, you'll be delighted with an impressively smooth 400-grit exterior polish.

From a design standpoint, Earle made only two significant changes from the original: The first is a Mann-Niedner style small-diameter firing pin arrangement that's front-loaded into the breechblock. Secondly, Earle eliminated the original Wesson's sear adjustment screw *(which never really worked well anyway)* and replaced it with an adjustment screw in the tumbler that allows reliable sear engagement and elimination of most trigger "creep." While this approach does not strictly allow for trigger pull adjustment, Steve Earle's triggers commonly break at 2 to 2.5 pounds. As for caliber options, Earle's Wesson No. 1 is suitable for any rimmed cartridge with a smaller rim diameter than the 577 Nitro Express. And that's a lot of cartridges.

So, if you're looking to build one of the most enviable single shots on the firing line, you'll find no finer basis than a Steve Earle Wesson No. 1 action. A 30-percent deposit will get you into Steve's production schedule, with final delivery estimated at five to six months. For more information, contact Steve Earle directly at 781-585-6504, or drop him a note at 24 Palmer Rd., Plympton, Massachusetts 02367.

Krieghoff

For those who appreciate life's finer things, there is the Krieghoff Hubertus. This is a break-open single shot made in the finest Old World tradition. It comes with automatic safety, iron-sighted express style quarter-rib milled for scope mounts, a 23 1/2-inch or 21 1/2-inch barrel, hand-checkered European walnut stock with right or left-hand cheekpiece, and a steel or Dural receiver that's nickel-plated for protection. A total of 18 chamberings are available, from the 222 to the 9.3x74R. From there, your options are virtually wide open. For example, you can add a set trigger, wood upgrades, custom-shaped receiver, sideplates, octagon barrel, a recoil reducer, a bewildering range of engraving and receiver finishes, the 7mm Remington Magnum or 300 Winchester Magnum chamberings, and a lot more. In fact, the Hubertus Custom Grade S is one of the finest examples of the gunmaking art anywhere... and good reason to consider a home equity loan.

Meacham Tool & Hardware

This company has operated "below the radar" for years now. And it hasn't hurt Steve Meacham a bit. He seems to have all the orders he can handle for the wonderful Winchester single-shot copies he makes. In fact, I've liked Steve's rifles ever since I first saw one. It was the first dead-on repro of the Model 1885 I'd ever seen. Action, stocks, checkering... virtually the works. Winchester's T. G. Bennett would have been proud of these rifles.

Today Meacham still makes these great rifles in low-wall or high-wall style, and in four basic configurations: Helm Schuetzen, Special Target, Special Sporting, and Silhouette (high-wall only). And unless you're an expert, it would be difficult to tell whether or not these rifles came through some time warp connecting us to the 19th century WRA Co. Every Meacham receiver and block is CNC-machined. Each block is hand-lapped into the frame. Barrels are hand-fitted. Wood is the best American black walnut. And accuracy is outstanding.

Meacham also offers a plethora of options and special features, including your choice of Winchester-style plain, single-set or double-set schuetzen triggers. Base prices for a Meacham high-wall start at around $3300. So check Meacham's web site for one of the best Winchester Single-Shot repros that hardly anyone knows about: www.meachamrifles.com

Montana Vintage Arms

More commonly known as MVA, this firm doesn't make rifles. Instead, it makes some of the finest single-shot sighting equipment you can get. Their mainstay is a host of traditional tang sights based on the windage-adjustable Soule design. But there are also Sharps tang sights and a hunting style Marbles configuration. In front sights, MVA offers Sharps, Stevens and Winchester style globe sights, many with "wind gauge" adjustment. For an aid to older eyes – and an outright better look at the target – you can opt for MVA's traditional straight-tube 6x scope with reproduction Malcolm mounts. It's a sweet piece of equipment.

MVA's product line also includes aperture-adjustable Hadley eyepieces, a Pope style palm rest and precision globe sight inserts. Peruse it all at www.montanavintagearms.com

New England Firearms

For the practical sportsman, this Marlin-owned company offers a line of break-open single-shot rifles that blend unbeatable value with great versatility.

For example, the NEF Handi-Rifle comes in a wide range of calibers from 22 Hornet to the 45-70 and 500

S&W. All have 22-inch barrels. You can also get the Handi-Rifle with a synthetic stock and/or stainless steel barrel and receiver for conditions that demand the ultimate in durability. Another version, called the Sportster, can be had in 17 HMR and with an extra .410-bore shotgun barrel, if you choose. Like I said, if you appreciate choices, check into the NEF Handi-Rifle and its variants. Just visit at www.hr1871.com

Remington

Long before Hollywood or rock-and-roll, one of the most widely recognized American inventions in the world was the Remington rolling block rifle. There was literally no region of the earth that escaped its reach. And although there are no real statistics on the matter, I'd be willing to venture a guess that more American bison fell to the Remington rolling block than to the Sharps model 1874. In addition, Lt. Colonel George Armstrong Custer took a wide variety of Western big game with his rolling block rifle.

But the rolling block was also a nonpareil target arm when properly applied by the best shots of the 19th century. In fact, it played a major role in the famous long-range match between the Irish and U. S. rifle teams in 1875. The Americans won.

Remington makes the No. 1 rolling block available today in two models, both through the Custom Shop. The first is the Mid-Range Sporter with pistol grip buttstock and blued receiver. The 30-inch round barrel is chambered for the 45-70 Govt. cartridge. It's priced at $1450. A set trigger, figured wood, color-cased receiver and other options will add to that base price.

Remington's rolling block Silhouette Target rifle is built to meet all NRA BPCR competition requirements as-delivered. The barrel

is heavy, straight, 30 inches long, and chambered for the 45-70 Govt. A color-cased receiver and single-set trigger are standard equipment as is a pistol grip, checkering and a recoil-absorbing shotgun-style butt. Base price for the Silhouette is $1560. For that, you can be confident that you're getting the real article: A *Remington* rolling block. Get the details at www.remington.com

Shiloh Sharps Rifle Co.

This outfit is one of the originals. For decades, they've grown steadily out in Big Timber, Montana by making faithful copies of the Sharps Model 1863 percussion rifle and the classic "side-hammer" 1874 cartridge rifle. And these products are every bit as good as anything the original Sharps Company ever built. In great measure, this is due to the fact that Shiloh is a vertically integrated concern. In other words, they make virtually all of the components that go into a Shiloh Sharps right there at their own facility. Very little work is farmed out to subcontractors. This approach allows for a high degree of quality control.

This advantage is certainly manifest in Shiloh's 1863 rifles, which are a recreation of the earliest Sharps design that used combustible paper cartridges. They're all offered in 50 or 54-caliber. The Sporting Rifle features a 30-inch octagon barrel with buckhorn rear sight and blade front, plus double-set triggers. The Military Rifle has a 30-inch round barrel and includes a ladder rear sight, military style iron block front sight and single trigger.

As drawn metallic cartridge cases came into widespread use shortly after the Civil War, Sharps adapted the 1863 to handle them and created the Model 1874. This became the classic "buffalo rifle" of the Great Plains, and is the mainstay

The legendary No. 1 rolling block rifle is still available in mid-range Sporter and Silhouette configurations through Remington's Custom Shop.

REPORTS FROM THE FIELD

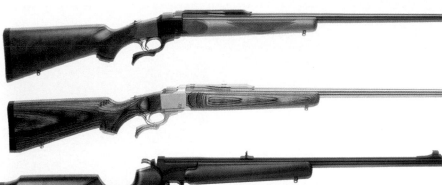

◀ Top Pair: The Ruger No. 1 set a standard, and a trend, in single-shots back in 1966. It's still an icon today.

▼ Bottom: Thompson Center's Encore comes in a variety of models with 24- or 26-inch barrels and in calibers ranging from 22 Hornet to 45-70.

of Shiloh's business today.

Shiloh makes no less than a dozen variants of the 1874, including the Creedmoor Silhouette Rifle, "The Quigley" Model, the Carbine, Hartford Models and more. There's even a Military musket. Prices for the 1874 range from $1547 to $2485 exclusive of extra cost options… of which there is a tempting selection. This includes upgraded wood, cheekpieces, engraving, action finish options, various buttplates, forend tips, grip configurations and virtually any caliber from 30-40 Krag to 50-90 2.5-inch. Thus, you can build your personal Shiloh Sharps pretty much *a la carte.* Get the whole story of Shiloh products at www.shilohrifle.com

Ruger

In 1966, Bill Ruger did something that the "experts" told him wouldn't work. He introduced the Ruger No. 1 single-shot rifle. History has since proven the experts wrong. The No. 1 has been a roaring success for over three decades and is still going strong. In my opinion this is due in great part to the classic styling of its action, which strongly suggests the great British Farquharson.

Today, the No. 1 comes in 10 variations and 23 chamberings, from the 204 Ruger to the 458 Lott. There are even two stainless steel models with laminated stocks. Frankly, I've always lusted for a No. 1 Tropical in 375 H&H. I'd take it anywhere and shoot anything… most of the time, only once.

Thompson Center

While this firm got its start with powerful break-open single-shot pistols, T/C now offers its Encore line of break-open single shot rifles.

The Encore comes with either 24- or 26-inch barrels depending on caliber and with walnut, black composite or a camo composite stock, depending on the options you want. Calibers range from 22 Hornet to 45-70, and barrels will interchange thanks to a removable/interchangeable hinge pin. You can even get an 18-inch carbine barrel with integral muzzle brake in 45-70 or 450 Marlin. That's a lot of power and versatility in one rifle, and worth checking into. So is the Thompson Center web site at www.tcarms.com

Traditions

This outfit isn't just about blackpowder anymore. They sell Pedersoli single-shots, too. And you can choose from two models of rolling blocks repros: A sporting rifle in 30-30 or another version in 45-70 with brass barrel band. And to help feed America's hunger for 1874 Sharps rifles, Traditions offers three Pedersoli-made models, all in 45-70: the standard 1874; the 1874 with engraved silver-satin receiver, 32-inch octagon barrel, double-set trigger, high-grade European walnut and Creedmoor sights. Curiously, there's also a Deluxe model with color-cased receiver, 32-inch barrel, double-set trigger and Creedmoor sights. Of the three, the engraved 1874 seems to be top-of-the-line and retails for just under $2400. A good buy. Visit Traditions website at www.traditionsfirearms.com

Uberti

This Italian manufacturer was one of the first to offer a new version of the Winchester Model 1885 Single-Shot. And while the Uberti design has certain internal differences from the original Winchester "high-wall," it's still a sound and well-made rifle that offers a lot of value for the money.

The foundation of the Uberti High-Wall line is the Sporting and Special Sporting single-shots. They're offered in 45-70 Govt., 45-90, and the bison-blasting 45-120 with 30- or 32-inch tapered octagon barrels that approximate the old Winchester No. 3 contour. The steel frame and lever are color case-hardened. Walnut stocks for the Sporting rifle feature a straight grip buttstock with curved steel buttplate and traditional schnabel forend. The Special Sporting version has a buttstock with a checkered pistol grip.

Those who prefer a slightly more compact rifle can choose Uberti's High-Wall Carbine in 45-70, but with a 28-inch tapered round barrel and a flat, shotgun style buttplate. Check Uberti's web site, www.uberti.com to see the design for yourself.

You can also get a reproduction No. 4 rolling block from Uberti with a 26-inch round or octagon barrel. The carbine model checks in with a round barrel at 22 inches in length. The forged steel frames are color case-hardened, trigger guards and buttplates are brass, and stocks are straight grip walnut. Chamberings available are 22 LR and 22 Magnum. There's even a rolling block pistol available in the same calibers. And the price is a whole lot more reasonable than any original you might find. For a lot of reasons, you might consider Uberti.

TODAY'S MUZZLELOADING: BLACK POWDER REVIEW

by Doc Carlson

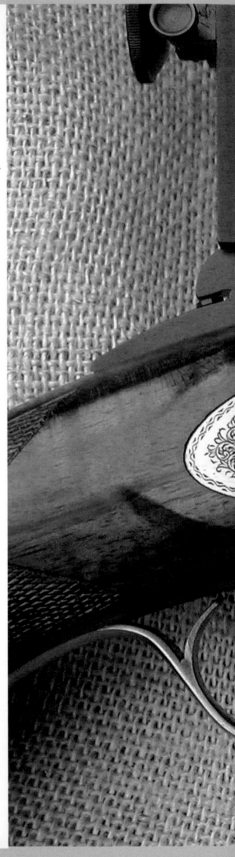

*W*hether one is interested in hunting, target shooting, re-enacting or just plinking, the available selection of blackpowder firearms is such that if an interesting gun can't be found, the person isn't trying very hard. There is bound to be a blackpowder-eating firearm out there to appeal to everyone, regardless of his (or her) area of interest in the sport. There are more types of muzzleloaders available today than a couple of hundred years ago. Now, let's take a quick look at some of the guns and accessories offered in today's marketplace.

One of the myths that has grown up around the muzzleloading firearms of yesterday is the statement that the early Kentucky rifles were of a "small caliber" and that they were the first rifled firearms made. Actually, most of the early long rifles were between 50- and 60-caliber. European rifles were made with rifled barrels well before the Kentucky rifle came on the scene. Why did the "smaller caliber" myth come about? It's probably a matter of semantics. European rifles—English and German primarily—of the time were of rather large caliber, often running well over 60-caliber. So, compared to them, the Kentucky rifle of 55-caliber was smaller. The really small calibers: 36, 40, etc., were made much later, after the golden age of the Kentucky long rifle. They arrived after most of the large game of the East—forest buffalo, bear and such—was gone. After that, most hunting was for small game and the Eastern deer.

The large-caliber English rifles and German Jaegers were fine hunting guns. The stock design handled recoil very well and the large-caliber round ball was a consistent killer. I'm happy to say there is a rekindling of interest in these big-bore guns of yesteryear. If you like to hunt with traditional guns, using patched round ball, bigger is definitely better. Large round balls land with authority—the Brits and Germans knew what they were doing.

James A. Gefroh

James A. Gefroh, a Colorado gunsmith, is one of the custom gunmakers who is keeping the large-

Pedersoli's reproduction of the Gibbs English target rifle.

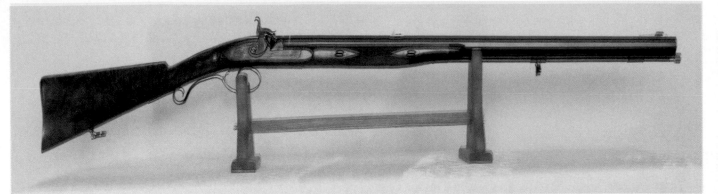

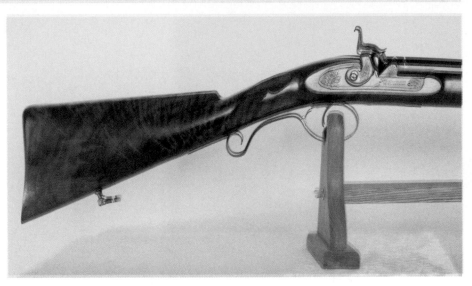

▲ **English half-stock sporting rifle by James Gefroh.**
▶ **Fine-figured black walnut and clean checkering, as well as crisp lines and tight inletting, are typical of Gefroh rifles.**

❧❀❧❀❧❀❧

caliber English and German rifles alive. He builds jaeger- and English-pattern rifles in calibers ranging from 62 (20-bore) through 69 (14-bore), 72 (12-bore), 775 (10-bore)—all the way up to the very impressive 83 (8-bore) for game animals that tend to bite back. The same style can be had in a smoothbore fowler for bird hunting, if the customer desires.

His basic rifle is made with a figured black walnut stock, hooked breech, and tapered barrel utilizing Forsythe-type rifling specifically designed for shooting large round balls. Included are double-set triggers, fixed open sights, ebony nose cap, browned furniture, either flint or percussion ignition in right- or left-hand configurations. No carving or stock embellishments are included in the basic rifle. It is a true working rifle of the period.

However, if one is interested in adding some fancy upgrades,

several options are available. These include more highly figured wood, either American black or English walnut, original-style relief carving, silver wire inlay, or a relief sterling silver animal head set in ivory and surrounded by silver wire inlay. The prices for these upgrades are very reasonable, considering the amount of labor involved. I would certainly add all the upgrades that I could afford;

after all, we look at our firearms more than we actually shoot them. It might as well be pretty, as well as useful. The rifles that Gefroh builds are truly works of art that will become family heirlooms.

Both styles of rifles, English and German, have a stock design that handles the recoil of the large calibers very well. As the rifles are made on a special order basis, stock dimensions are made to fit the owner/shooter. They point like a well-fitted shotgun, allowing fast

Pedersoli's well-made reproduction Gibbs English target rifle—a real match-winner.

▲ *Typical Gefroh German jaeger full-stock flintlock rifle.*

◄ *Fine wire inlay combines with well-executed carving to highlight a James Gefroh jaeger rifle.*

target acquisition, something very important in the hunting field.

Gefroh's rifles have taken large game animals in both Africa and North America. His rifles have been used by very satisfied owners to take the Big Five in Africa. Gefroh, himself, has taken elephant, rhino, Cape buffalo and leopard in Africa, as well as most of the plains game of that country.

Any hunter that enjoys traditional muzzleloading rifles and fowlers for his hunting activities should take a long look at the firearms of James Gefroh.

Pedersoli

The Italian manufacturer, Pedersoli, is one of the top names in the manufacture of traditional-type blackpowder firearms. Their catalog contains an amazing selection of reproduction firearms of the blackpowder era. All periods and countries are represented in a wide range of styles and ignition systems. Civilian and military arms are included.

One of the newest additions to the line of traditional rifles is the Gibbs Target Rifle. This faithful copy of a target rifle made in 1865 by the well-known English gunsmith, George Gibbs, reproduces the peak of the development of the muzzleloading target rifle. The original rifles won many medals and trophies in shooting matches of the time and the Pedersoli reproduction is also winning in competitions around the world.

The rifle is available in 45-caliber utilizing a six land-and-groove barrel with a 1:18 inch twist. It is intended for use with a .451-inch elongated bullet, similar to what one sees being used in the 45/70 cartridge. This highly accurate rifle features an oil-finished walnut pistol grip

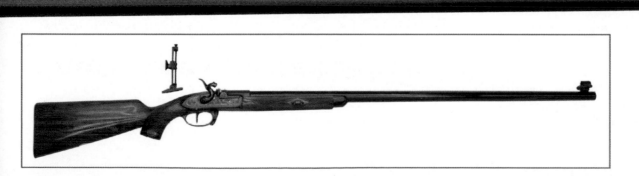

half-stock with an ebony grip cap and forend tip. There is no provision for a ramrod, typical of target rifles of the period. The blued 35 1/4-inch barrel is round, tapered slightly, with an octagon breech area. The percussion bar-type lock shows a pleasing color case-hardened finish. The steel buttplate and trigger guard are blued. Sights are a windage-adjustable front with 15 inserts and spirit level, and a tang-type rear sight, adjustable for elevation.

This outstanding reproduction target rifle has shown very good accuracy at long-range shooting from 100 to 600, 800—or even 1000 yards. The good-looking English style rifle would be a nice addition to any gun cabinet.

Dixie Gun Works

In 1855 Colt Manufacturing brought out their Colt-Root revolving rifle, an attempt to come up with a repeating rifle for both the military and civilian market. They were made in various models and barrel lengths in calibers from 36 through 64, as well as a shotgun version in 10- and 12-gauge. Less than 20,000 were made. Of those, less than 10,000 were the Military Rifle model.

Dixie Gun Works is now marketing a copy of the Colt/Root full stocked military rifle M1855. This six-shot revolving cylinder rifle is 44-caliber, utilizing a .454-inch ball. The blued barrel is 31-1/2 inches long, rifled 1:38 inches and is slightly tapered. The birch military configuration full stock is oil-finished and the furniture is blued steel. The cylinder is full fluted, as were the originals, and the big side-hammer is color case-hardened. Sights are a one-piece blued blade front coupled with a rear sight having two flip-up blades; again, as original. The full-length forearm is held by

two blued steel barrel bands. A steel ramrod is installed under the forearm, and there is a ramrod extension hidden under the middle butt plate screw to extend the ramrod for cleaning. Sling swivels complete the picture of this Civil War military rifle.

The 1855 Colt/Root was issued to Union forces during the War of Northern Aggression, as some call it. It was issued to Berdan's Sharpshooters, the 9th Illinois Volunteer Cavalry, the 21st Ohio Volunteer Infantry and some Wisconsin regiments. This well-made and nicely finished new offering from Dixie will undoubtedly find a home among Civil War re-enactor groups.

Traditions

There are some states that require flintlock ignition for their muzzle-loading hunting seasons and there are folks out there that merely like to hunt with the more primitive ignition system. Up to now, blackpowder was the only useable propellant for these guns since the use of replica blackpowder, such as Pyrodex, was not practical. Traditions Performance Firearms now claims to have an answer. According to Traditions, their PA Pellet Flintlock will fire reliably with Pyrodex—either loose powder or pellets.

The lock, called a "Super Flintlock" by Traditions, has an improved frizzen and a deepened pan. The specially-hardened frizzen throws a massive shower of hot sparks and the deepened pan holds more priming powder for flawless ignition, according to the manufacturer. The specially-designed breech plug directs the fire from the pan through the touchhole and funnels it forward to the base of the Pyrodex pellets for fast, sure ignition. The 26-inch 50-caliber octagonal barrel is rifled with a

1:48 twist to handle patched round ball, sabotted bullets or bore-size slugs. The barrel is easily removable from its hooked breech. The breech plug can be screwed out and the barrel cleaned from the breech, as if it was an inline gun. Sights are the easily seen Tru-Glo fiber optic front and rear. The ramrod is solid aluminum for durability since a broken ramrod in the hunting woods is a real disaster. The rifle is recommended for up to 150-grain loads of Pyrodex or blackpowder.

The rifle is made with a blued finish and hardwood stock in both right- and left-hand models. It is also available with a black synthetic stock and either a nickel or blue barrel. If camo is your interest, the gun is offered with a nickel barrel and Mossy Oak stock or, new this year, an all-camo version with both stock and barrel covered with Hardwoods HD finish.

The focusing of modern technology on the venerable muzzleloader is producing some surprising results. Improvements in powders, primers and bullets, coupled with modern design features of the guns themselves, are rapidly putting the muzzleloader on an equal footing with the modern cartridge rifle-carrying hunter.

Ultimate Firearms

Ultimate Firearms is putting just such a gun on the market. Called the Ultimate Muzzleloader, this bolt-action modern-looking rifle has some serious innovations. The rifle uses a 45 Magnum brass case to carry a Magnum Rifle primer. The case slips over an enlarged nipple in the breech of the rifle and effectively seals against blowback gasses during the firing sequence. The flash of the primer is directed through the

The new Root revolving rifle from Dixie Gun Works.

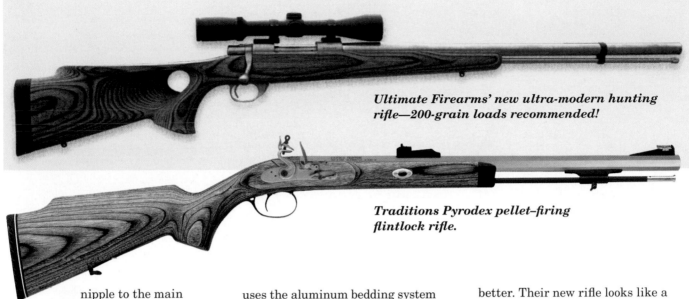

Ultimate Firearms' new ultra-modern hunting rifle—200-grain loads recommended!

Traditions Pyrodex pellet–firing flintlock rifle.

nipple to the main charge (*recommended as four 50-grain pellets of Pyrodex or Triple 7*). The unique nipple-breech system causes a "controlled burn" (called a controlled detonation by the company) that allows 200 grains of Pyrodex or Triple 7 to be consumed in the 50-caliber barrel, resulting in unheard-of velocities and flat trajectories for a muzzle-loading arm. The priming system produces a flame temperature many times hotter than the standard #209 primer.

The gun shoots pretty flat out to 200 yards, with 100-yard and 200-yard groups nearly on top of each other. Accuracy is very good. Groups measuring 1/2-inch at 100 yards and 3-3/4 inches at 500 yards have been shot with sabotted bullets and 200-grain charges, according to the manufacturer. The gun cleans easily. There is no blowback of powder gasses into the action thanks to the sealing characteristics of the primer/nipple system.

The rifle uses a Howa action with a stainless steel barrel and custom trigger system. They are available in three models. The BP Xpress Hunter features a thumbhole stock of laminated wood in one of four colors: Autumn Dawn, Nutmeg, Pepper and a multicolored "Ghost." The BP Xpress Infinity adds an aluminum bedding system with a free-floating barrel and a limb-saver recoil pad. The top-of-the-line BP Xpress Remington 40X Ultra uses the aluminum bedding system in a figured walnut Monte Carlo stock with laser-carved grip and forearm panels, ebony forend tip and the owner's initials carved into the stock.

This new rifle appears to be opening a new era in muzzleloading. The long-range trajectory and accuracy claimed for this rifle is truly eye-opening for this old patched round-ball shooter. We'll be watching this one with interest.

Austin & Halleck

Austin & Halleck, maker of some very nice muzzleloading rifles, both inline and traditional types, is developing a new in-line rifle that is certainly different from the ordinary. Some years ago, Thompson/Center had a rifle they called the Scout Rifle. The little slab-sided rifle had a center-hung hammer and was made with either a 21- or 24-inch round 50-caliber barrel, as I remember. The look and feel of the rifle reminded one of the venerable Model '94 Winchester. It had the same quick handling qualities that have made the Model '94 one of the most popular and recognizable guns in history. Alas, the tooling for the little rifle was lost in a fire at the T/C plant, so the little gun is gone.

Austin & Halleck has gone one better. Their new rifle looks like a Model '94 with a ramrod. The 50-caliber barrel is loaded from the muzzle, the same as any muzzleloader. The lever is cycled to open the bolt, similar to the '94, and a #209 primer is inserted into a cut in the face of the bolt. The bolt is levered closed and firing is accomplished as the center-hung hammer is tripped by pulling the trigger. The result is a front-loading rifle with all the handling characteristics of the Model '94. The fit, finish and quality of this handy rifle are what we have come to expect from the Austin & Halleck folks. Time will tell how this new and very different muzzleloader will be accepted by hunters and shooters—it's certain to attract attention in hunting camp.

Bore-sighting a muzzleloader presents something of a problem because it is difficult to peer through the

LaserLyte laser bore-sighter makes a difficult job easy.

Austin & Halleck 420 LR Monte Carloin-line rifle

Austin & Halleck 320 LR Camo in-line rifle in Real-tree-Hardwoods pattern.

Austin & Halleck Flint-lock Mountain Rifle

bore at a distant object, or collimator screen, since we don't have easy access to the rear end of the bore. Even the in-lines require breech plug removal, to be able to look through the barrel. Further, most of the boresights on the market don't seem to lend themselves to muzzleloaders, due to the higher trajectories of the breed.

A company called **LaserLyte** has a laser boresight that does work very well for the front-loader guns. The laser is projected by a small unit that plugs into the end of the barrel, and is aligned with the bore by expandable plugs. The laser is bright enough to be easily seen at 25 and 50 yards, even on rather bright days. It is even useable at 100 yards when the laser is pointed at a reflective target *(included in the kit)*. The kits are available with expandable stubs

that handle up to 50-caliber, and 20- and 12-gauge stubs are available also. Kits come with either one laser projector for single-barrel guns, or with two to regulate double-barrel rifles and shotguns. I've been using one of these kits in my own shop and find it very accurate. I've used the collimator-type boresight—they work fine, but the laser dot gives a more accurate picture of where the bore is pointing, and makes sight settings easier, in my view. This is a great tool to have—whether you are building guns, installing sights, or just want to check your favorite firearm before going hunting.

Cash Manufacturing

Cash Manufacturing has been making accessories for the muzzleloading crowd since the

'60s. He has always catered to the traditional shooter, making reproductions of accessories that were used in the heyday of the muzzleloader. He recently stepped into the modern world of the inline with two very nice cappers.

The first of these is a straight-line capper for either the four- or six-wing musket caps. It holds 12 caps and has a convenient side-loading slot with a tension spring release. The second is a straight-line capper designed to hold 12 #209 primers. Both these are aimed at the in-line rifles that use either musket caps or the #209 shotgun primer. The straight-line design makes getting the cap or primer into the tight recesses of the inline a much easier job. Both cappers are finely crafted of brass and will probably outlast your rifle.

◄ *Tedd Cash's musket cap inline capper.*

▼ *The #209 capper from Tedd Cash —a needed accessory.*

These new ideas from Tedd Cash make handling the inline just a bit easier and certainly makes carrying the caps and primers very handy.

Hoppe's

Hoppe's, a name that almost every shooter is familiar with, has added to their line a new blackpowder cleaner and solvent. This soap-based solvent is equally effective in removing the residue of blackpowder, Pyrodex, Triple 7—or any of the other replica blackpowders. It also cuts lead and plastic fouling. As it dries, it leaves a microscopic layer of rust inhibitor and dry lube that penetrates into the pores of the steel, protecting the bore and making repeat cleanings easier. It effectively replaces the barrel seasoning and break-in process, according to the Hoppe's folks.

Hoppe's Number 9 solvent was the number one powder fouling cleaner for many, many years. The distinctive, instantly identifiable smell was always associated with fine firearms. I'm told that women who wished to meet hunters and/or gun enthusiasts would put a drop of Hoppe's Number 9 behind their ear instead of perfume. It would draw them like bees to honey.

Goex Powder Products

Goex Powder Products, the continuation of the old DuPont powder company, has some new additions to their product line. They have added a Goex Cowboy grade of black powder specifically designed to provide optimum performance in the blackpowder cartridges used in pistol, rifle and shotgun cowboy action shooting. This is in addition to their regular granulations of 1Fg, 2Fg, 3Fg, 4Fg and Cannon grade—plus Cartridge grade, intended for the large-bore cartridges used in the blackpowder cartridge silhouette competition.

They have a new replica blackpowder also, called Pinnacle. This low-pressure powder is available in 2Fg and 3Fg grades and produces the same velocities and accuracy as blackpowder without the smoke and

smell, while producing less fouling than conventional blackpowder.

Goex also now has a line of blackpowder-loaded cartridges called Black Dawg Cartridges. They are available in a wide range of chamberings for rifle, pistol and shotgun. Long-range cartridges such as 45/70, 45/90, 45/120 and others are loaded for use in the big single-shot rifles. Bullets are cast of a soft alloy, lubed with SPG lube and the cartridges are loaded, of course, with blackpowder. These should find a ready market among cowboy action shooters, and others who like to shoot the old blackpowder loads and don't want to reload.

Hodgdon Powder Company

Triple 7, the very low residue replica blackpowder from the Hodgdon Powder Company, is now available in new packaging that is more convenience to blackpowder hunters. The new 50-grain, 50-caliber pellets come in a pack containing four tubes, each containing six of the pellets. This will allow the hunter to slip one or two

Hodgdon's new packaging for their Triple 7 pellets will be handy for hunters.

of the tubes in his pocket—or possibles bag—and have enough reloads for the average hunt. The tubes protect the pellets from damage until needed and are a handy reloading accessory.

Remington

One of the problems with #209 primers in muzzleloading guns has been the formation of a ring of fouling just above the breech plug where the projectile rests in the loaded barrel. This ring of hard fouling seems to be due to the hot #209 primer. Now Remington is making a #209 primer designed specifically for muzzleloader shooting. Remington promises the new primer will dramatically reduce fouling and make reloading easy, while maintaining velocity and accuracy between shots without swabbing. Remington claims 15 to 20 times less fouling than with the standard #209 primer. Difficulty in reloading for a second shot, without swabbing with a damp patch, has been a problem with the in-lines for some time. It is especially troublesome when using sabbotted bullets. Hopefully, this new Remington Kleenbore primer will reduce this problem.

Modern technology continues to improve the blackpowder field. The lot of the blackpowder shooter and hunter has never been easier. Just when you think nothing can be improved, American ingenuity steps forward. Old Jim Bridger and Daniel Boone would be amazed. ✵

TODAY'S OPTICS:
RIFLEMAN'S GLASS

by Wayne Van Zwoll

*B*inoculars, rifle scopes and spotting scopes these days are so good, you might wonder how their makers can improve them. Though some 2005 sights show only cosmetic changes, there's substance to the increased eye relief and shorter tubes in Burris rifle scopes. Bushnell offers a racier HOLOsight that's also lighter in weight. In upgrading its M8 fixed-power line, Leupold added finger-click adjustments and index-matched coatings. Kahles is offering a scope with an ingenious range-compensating device that allows you to set up to five zeros and bring each up with a quick twist of the elevation dial. Meade has resurrected the Redfield brand and launched a truly new variable under the Simmons label.

The binocular field remains competitive. Brunton, a company that has managed to garner market share despite the odds, has a new variable-power glass in the catalog. Leupold is hawking a Golden Ring binocular priced a notch above its Wind River series. Among the most useful products *(in my view)*: a Minox 6.5x32. It boasts a huge field and great depth of focus. Like the new 24-ounce Minox IF 9.5x42, it is argon-filled. The long-awaited Zeiss Victory FL series includes five models with fluorite glass to all but eliminate color fringing and improve resolution. FL (or APO or ED) lenses appear too in Pentax's PF-65ED, a superb spotting scope for big game hunting that this year accepts 32x, 46x and 20-60x eyepieces.

Truly, there's a remarkable selection of shooting and hunting optics for 2005. Here in more detail is your GUN DIGEST overview.

Aimpoint

Red-dot sights deserve more recognition than they get. The best of the current crop are as reliable, durable and precise as any scope. And, again in the best sights, batteries last a lot longer than they used to.

"Aimpoint's red-dot gives you up to *20,000 hours* on the low setting," Kenneth Mardklint told me five years ago. I'd spoken with Kenneth on a visit to Aimpoint, the Swedish company that built the first red-dot sight back in 1975. Inventor Gunnar Sandberg came up with what he called the single-point sight. You saw the dot with one eye and the target with the other, so you couldn't look through the sight at all!

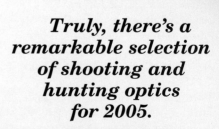

Truly, there's a remarkable selection of shooting and hunting optics for 2005.

New this year are the Weaver ETX spotting scopes like this 73 x125 and (not shown) 48x90 models. Both are camera-adaptable.

Adirondack Optics' three SmartScopes: a 1.5-6x40, 3-10x44 and 6-16x44.

Several renditions, and 20 years later, Aimpoint was producing sophisticated sights that performed like scopes, only faster. In the woods, I used an Aimpoint 7000 to shoot moose. It was the best sight I could have chosen for the thick cover and dark shadows and fleeting shot opportunities. On the target range, the Aimpoint on a Blaser rifle gave me 1 1/2-minute groups. One reason is Aimpoint's front lens, a *compound* glass that corrects for parallax. An ordinary single lens up front will still reflect the dot produced by the diode in the rear bottom of the tube. But Aimpoint's "doublet" always brings the dot to your eye *in a line parallel with the sight's optical axis.* The reflective path of a single-lens sight varies with eye position. If the dot isn't centered in the sight, you get parallax error at distances other than the one for which the sight was parallax-corrected. With an Aimpoint, you'll hit where you see the dot.

Except for models with magnification, Aimpoint red-dot sights offer unlimited eye relief—a real boon for us stock-crawlers. Your eye can be 3 inches back, or 9. You can point as you might with a shotgun bead, both eyes open. Aimpoint's American representative Mike Kingston notes that the company supplies military sights to U.S. and French armies. Its hunting models sell in 40 countries. One of every 10 Swedish hunters using optical sights carries an Aimpoint.

Now there's one more reason to pick this sight: ACET. Advanced Circuit Efficiency Technology reduces power demand, boosting battery life on the new Aimpoint 9000s to 50,000 hours! That's with the brightness set on 7. The highest setting is 10. The 9000 series comprises three models, and you get a choice of 2-minute or 4-minute dot. "Our sights aren't cheap," says Mike. "They're simply the best red dot sights you can get. For low-light deer hunting, they're more effective than ordinary scopes." They're more rugged now than ever, and with battery life

at 50,000 hours, you can stay in the woods all week.

Adirondack Optics

Last year Adirondack Optics, a small company from upstate New York, announced a rifle scope that takes a digital photo. The camera controls are compact and easy to manipulate. Beyond that, it can *automatically* photograph an animal you're going to shoot just as you pull the trigger! The sight picture is there to remind you of the moment of truth— and perhaps tell you why you missed! An ambitious project, SmartScope was designed by Terry Gordon, a young entrepreneur who knew from the start that producing the instrument would be a team project. "It was an expensive effort," he says. "But we had help from many fine and talented people, even the state of New York!"

Adirondack Optics is selling three SmartScopes now: a 1.5-6x40, 3-10x44 and 6-16x44. All have 30mm tubes, and there's a parallax adjustment on the 3-10x and 6-16x. The standard mil-dot reticle is in the front focal plane, so apparent reticle dimensions change with the magnification but not in relation to your target. Terry notes that "There's no way point of impact can shift during power change, because the reticle is stationary, and the lens movement is behind it. Also, you can use the reticle to estimate range without a glance at the magnification dial." European hunters have long favored the advantages of first-plane reticles. It was a design compatible with that of other high-quality scopes in the Czech factory that builds the sight for ADK. Plans are to move all production Stateside: partly to consolidate assembly, partly to shed the 15-percent tariff imposed on imported optics.

SmartScope is in some ways a conventional sight, with quarter-minute adjustments and 3 inches of eye relief. The internal digital camera is what makes this ADK product different. It's powered by a pair of 1.5-volt AA batteries housed at mid-section in a turret compartment. A small screen

atop the ocular bell has the on/off switch and a button that lets you take photos through the scope. The camera uses standard digital cards. "They're Smart Media now," Terry tells me. "But a CD card is coming."

Operating this scope is pretty easy, because SmartScope was designed as a sight first. "We knew hunters wouldn't want to compromise their aim," says Terry. "This is a top-grade rifle scope, with a camera added." To photograph game and shoot it with a bullet at the same time, you need only trigger the rifle. The camera is easy to set to "ready" mode when you begin your hunt. SmartScope takes a picture automatically as your rifle recoils. It's not blurred because software subtracts lock time to record the image as it appeared 7 milliseconds *before* recoil. I've used SmartScope on the range, on rifles of light recoil, and hard kickers. The camera operates reliably, and the photos placed my reticle on the target where the bullets made holes. Frames shot by hunters who've used SmartScope afield show the reticle where you want it — on deer that wound up in the locker. Camera images compare with those you'd expect from a mid-level digital camera. As I found by shooting into deep shadow, SmartScope requires reasonable levels of light, just like any digital camera.

Fully multi-coated lenses make this scope a first-class sight. Resolution and brightness match what you'll get from other high-end scopes. At 22 to 26 ounces, ADK's SmartScope is half again as heavy as many 30mm scopes. It would look out of place on a carbine but is no burden on rifles of average weight. A Picatinny rail increases the limited mounting latitude.

SmartScope is costly: $1500 to start. But there's no other way to hunt with a camera and a rifle at the same time! Phone Adirondack Optics at 800-815-6814.

Alpen Outdoor

In the news the last few years because its products have been so highly rated in the shooting press,

Alpen Outdoors has added another scope to its Apex line of rifle sights. The 4-16x50 AO features parallax correction via a traditional objective collar. It's a 1-inch scope, matte-finished, with fast-focus eyepiece. At 21 ounces, with fully multi-coated optics, this $400 scope is one of the best buys in a high-power variable.

Also new from Alpen: 8x26 and 10x26 Shasta Ridge binoculars, with BaK4 prisms. "They weigh just 13.6 ounces and feature fully multi-coated lenses with pull-up eyecups," says Vickie Gardner. Price: $200. The even more affordable MagnaView series now has a roof prism binocular, a waterproof 10x42. Alpen's line of spotting scopes has doubled in size this year, with a 12-36x50 and two 15-45x60s, offered with straight and angled eyepieces. The 12-36x50 is compact and offers an ideal magnification range for hunters. At just 20 ounces, it's easy to carry, and the wide field of view at 12x gets you on target quickly.

BSA

For 2005, this importer of value-priced optics has announced two new rifle scope lines. The four Panther models feature fully multi-coated lenses, built-in sunshades and finger-adjustable windage and elevation dials. These 1-inch waterproof scopes wear an attractive matte finish. Pick a 3-10x40, 2.5-10x44, 6.5-20x44 or 3.5-10x50. Also recently announced: Sweet 17 Mach II rifle scopes. "They're designed for rimfire rifles," says BSA's John Schild. "There's a trajectory drum on the elevation dial that's calibrated for the 17 Mach II bullet, so you know where to set zero and where to hold at a distance." Sweet 17s come in 2 7x32, 3-9x40 and 4-12x40 versions, all with adjustable objectives.

Browning

A couple of years ago, Browning added optics to its many product lines for sportsmen. Produced under license and marketed by Bushnell, initial Browning offerings included the most popular rifle scope designs:

2-7x32, 3-9x40, 3-9x50 and 5-15x40. For 2005 there's a 4-12x40 and an 8-24x40, priced at $450 and $590. The Browning 15-45x65 spotting scope is of just the right size and power range for western big game hunting, and the company has cataloged a useful selection of roof prism binoculars: 8x32, 8x42 and 10x42. This year you'll find a compact 8x26 as well.

Brunton

"It was a technical hurdle some folks said would be impossible to clear," says John Smithbaker of Brunton's new Epoch Zoom binocular. "Variable power is hard enough to engineer into a compact glass. We've kept the binocular to 32 ounces, and made it waterproof too!" The roof prism design, magnesium alloy frame, lockable twist-out eyecups and fully multi-coated lenses derive from Brunton's top-of-the-line Epoch 10x42. The Zoom, an 8-15x35, offers hunters and birders great versatility. With a 273-foot field of view at 8x, the glass works well for quick spotting. Install it on a tripod, crank it up to 15x, and it serves as a spotting scope. The Brunton Zoom comes in a leather case; list price is $1899.

Also new from the Riverton, Wyoming, optics firm is an Eterna Compact Spotting Scope. The 24-ounce 18-38x50 features fully multi-coated lenses that also boast ED (extra-low dispersion) fluorite glass. "It's the first compact scope to offer ED lenses," John points out. Just 8 inches long, it has a sight tube on the side to speed target acquisition — though with an expansive 141-foot field at 1,000 yards, you might

Brunton's new Epoch Zoom binocular.

not need a sight. The spotting scope comes with a neoprene case and a shoulder strap for $599.

There seems to be an ever-stronger appetite for more power in binoculars. Nowhere is it more justified than among hunting guides. The Eterna 15x51 Outfitter is a 30-ounce, tripod-adaptable binocular that's probably too big and powerful to carry as a hunting glass but is made to order for hunting guides who aren't toting a rifle. They must often look for long periods across long distances, and accurately assess the quality of a trophy. A binocular is much easier to use than a spotting scope; this one combines a wide field (200 feet at 1,000 yards) with enough magnification to spot the ear of a buck a long rifle-shot away. The rubber-armored Outfitter comes with a neoprene vinyl glove and neck strap for $599.

Burris

The focus at Burris has long been on practical scopes for North American hunters. Over the years, the Colorado firm has also aggressively

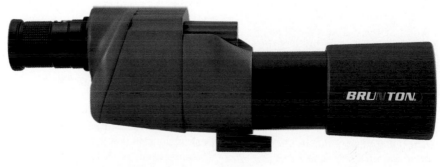

Brunton's Zoom spotting scope.

expanded its lines of optics. In 2005, the company is trotting out a new line of Short Mag scopes, in 1x, 4x, 2-7x, 3-9x and 4.5-14x. These are short-coupled sights with 3 1/2- to 5-inch eye relief and resettable windage and elevation dials. Variables can be ordered with Ballistic Plex reticles. Retail prices range from $316 to $581.

The Signature Select line of rifle scopes introduced last year included several useful refinements to Burris' best-quality 1-inch scopes. More convenient turret location, index-matched lenses, rubber grips on power and AO rings; these improvements—plus resettable windage and elevation dials—are now available in LRS versions that offer lighted reticles with up to 60 hours of battery life. When you don't want a lighted sight, or if the battery does expire, you can aim as with any scope; the black reticle is still there. Signature Select with LRS comes in 1.5-6x, 3-10x and 4-16x configurations.

Another new Burris product is a 32mm Landmark binocular with fully coated lenses. Choose 8x or 10x. These 18.5-ounce binoculars list for $173 and $191. Of interest to riflemen who want their 30mm scopes to hug the receiver is a new medium-height Burris Zee Ring. Signature Zee Rings now have double the original number of attaching screws, to secure scopes on rifles with tooth-rattling recoil.

Like many other optics companies, Burris has been working on tactical sights and related gear. If the men in face-paint don't take them all, my guess is that plenty of civilian

Bushnell's compact 3.2-megapixel camera specifically designed for sportsmen.

shooters will want the newest Burris XTR sights. Xtreme Tactical Rifle scopes in 1.5-6x, 10x and 3-12x feature 30mm tubes with side-mounted parallax adjustments and steel-on-steel target-style windage and elevation knobs. Eyepiece and power ring are integrated. All models feature illuminated reticles but without the bubble of the LRS ocular housings. The Burris Tactical series also includes a SpeedDot sight and Laser flashlight you can mount on the rail of your black gun. If you want the strongest of clamps on your XTR scope, install it in rings of the same name, with six screws each. Available in four heights, from 1/4 inch to 1 inch, Xtreme Tactical Rings are made of aluminum and designed for Picatinny rails.

Bushnell

It's a daunting task to update Bushnell's extensive selection of binoculars and rifle scopes. List prices range from very low to very high; but almost always you get more than you pay for. Perhaps that's why this company sells more sporting optics than any other.

Bushnell is courting the photographer in each of us with a compact 3.2-megapixel camera specifically designed for sportsmen. Its rubber-armored body has buttons that can be manipulated even if you're wearing gloves. It will also shoot movie clips at 20 frames-per-second. Powered by two AA batteries, this $200 camera has 16 MB of storage, a 1.5-inch LCD color monitor and a USB port for downloading images to a computer.

Also in the news: Trail Scout, a camera you set up in the woods to record game activity — maybe catch that big buck whose scrapes you've found. Three versions are cataloged: The VGA offers 640x480 resolution with a passive infrared sensor that detects motion to 60 feet. The 2.1 has 2.1 MP resolution, is useful to 90 feet—both are equipped with an automatic flash that reaches 30 feet. Best of the trio is a 2.1 with night vision technology. All three come with 32 MB SD cards, operate on

Bushnell ImageView binocular/ camera.

four D batteries, and can be set for still or video images. The Trail Scout cameras retail from $312 to $455.

The ImageView binocular/camera line has new entries for 2005. The 8x21 VGA and 10x25 VGA are priced at $74 and $150. There's also an 8x20 monocular at $92.

In rifle sights, Bushnell offers two more "Firefly" models. "The reticle can be illuminated by the blink of a flashlight and give you a bright aiming point just when you need it, without batteries," says Laura Olinger. "The charged reticle fades to black until shooting light grows dim; then it glows." New Elite 4200 scopes, a 1.5-6x36 and a 2.5-10x50, are priced at $604 and $748. All Elite scopes come with RainGuard lens coating that breaks up water droplets so you can see clearly through a wet lens. RainGuard has been improved for 2005. It comes on the company's new Elite 8x43 and 10x43 binoculars; magnesium-framed, 23-ounce beauties that focus as close as 9 feet. Prices reflect their quality: $1459 and $1499. A new Discoverer binocular, 7x42 and 10x42, features BaK 4 prisms and RainGuard for $539 and $599. The Excursion binocular comes in 8x42 and 10x42 for $260 and $280. The Trophy line has new additions too, in 8x, 9x, 10x and 12x magnification, from $249. For the budget-minded, there's a new PowerView stable, with 8x42 roof prism glasses for $90, 10x42s for $110.

Bushnell has another Varmint scope in the 3200 line. The 7-21x40 with front AO sleeve and fast-focus eyepiece boasts 3.7 inches of eye relief. Retail: $550. Another 3200, a 3-10x40, is a versatile sight for big-game hunters who want a bargain. It lists for $298. In the Legend line, you'll find a 4-12x40 with front AO at $266. The Banner Super 17 AO scope includes a bullet drop compensator graduated for 17-caliber bullets — though company literature does not specify a 17 *cartridge*! The Super 17 costs $134, a couple of dollars more than Bushnell's new 1x28 Red/Green Dot Trophy scopes. Choose red or green dot, 3-MOA or 10-MOA, a crosswire or a circle-dot. Instant choice, unlimited eye relief. If you shotgun whitetails or hunt with a handgun, consider the new HOLOsight. It's lighter in weight, lower in profile and, at $300, less costly than previous models. It now uses AAA batteries.

There's a new spotting scope at Bushnell, too: an Image View 15-45x50 that incorporates a digital camera with VGA resolution and 16 MB of internal memory. It comes with shutter cable, tripod, hard case and

PhotoSuite software for $240. For 2005, Bushnell's rangefinder series includes the Elite 1500. It has a 7x eyepiece and 26mm objective. It's waterproof and includes RainGuard lens coating. Powered by a 9-volt battery, it determines yardage to 1500 yards. It costs $574.

Elcan

"We didn't expect such a terrific response at the SHOT Show," mused Rusty Mauldin, who had orchestrated his company's introduction of a digital rifle scope. "Elcan isn't new to optics," he explained to me later. "We've been building infrared scopes for military use since the 1980s." In fact, the firm dates *'way* back – say, to 1849 and Ernst Leitz. "The name Elcan derives from Ernst Leitz of Canada." Rusty added that the company is multi-national, with offices in Midland, Ontario on Lake Huron, and in Malaga, Spain. Rusty works from the U.S. digs in Richardson, Texas, a suburb of Dallas. Part of the enormous Raytheon group, Elcan has been busy with government contracts. This civilian sight is a first-ever departure.

"We had the technology to complete the project earlier," Rusty told me. "But not until recently has it become commercially feasible. Now the components are readily available, and cheap enough that we can keep the cost of our DigitalHunter below $2000.

Well, that may be less than I spent on my pickup, but it's still a tidy sum for a rifle sight. What, I asked, does this scope offer that a traditional scope doesn't? The answer: You can't even compare the two.

Elcan's sight has coated optical lenses up front, in a round housing, and a power range of 2.5-13.5x. Beyond that you have to think digitally. You don't look *through* this scope. You see instead a digital display. The reticle is a device of your own choosing. "You can download four reticles from our website," said Rusty. "Or build your own. Specify different zeroes, even different reticle colors. The SD card you use to install

Bushnell Trail Scout camera.

that information can also register the ballistic properties of your favorite load. Once you install the data, and zero the rifle, you can hold center at any range just by punching in the distance on the scope's keyboard. Software automatically adjusts to compensate for bullet drop."

Zeroing, incidentally, is done as with any other scope – except that instead of mechanical dials, you have electronic buttons with arrows up, down, right, left…. And no, this scope does not have a laser rangefinder. "We could have added that," Rusty told me. "But it would have boosted the cost and weight." As is, the Elcan DigitalHunter scales 28 ounces.

One of the unique features of this scope is its ability to record up to five seconds of video, during a shooting

Bushnell's new spotting scope, the Image View 15-45x50, incorporates a digital camera and 16 MB of internal memory.

One of Bushnell's new Elite 4200 scopes.

Bushnell's new 7-21x40 varmint scope in the 3200 line.

Bushnell's new 1x28 Red/Green Dot Trophy scopes.

Kahles' 3-12x56 CSX Helia illuminated rifle scope.

sequence, if you like. The instrument operates as a still camera too, and can be set for manual or automatic operation. A port allows you to attach a remote screen so, if you're coaching a new shooter, you can see exactly what he or she sees in the sight picture during a shot sequence. Or you can turn on the video and get up to seven five-second clips on a standard 64-mb SD card. A monitor on the top of the sight lets you review the video images right after you record them.

Ordinary scope mounts won't work on this sight, so Elcan is developing its own that will fit to the scope's belly and hook up with a Picatinny rail or Weaver-type base. Key up elcansportsoptics.com.

Famous Maker

The big names in optics all have scope lines more complete than you'll ever need. But I recently found a broad selection of sights, at budget-friendly prices, under the enigmatic banner of "Famous Maker." To be honest, the name is not all that famous. But maybe it should be better known. Its scopes are fogproof and waterproof, with fully multi-coated lens systems. Choose from fixed-power 4x32s to 8-32x44 variables — including specialty scopes for the SKS, slug guns, air rifles and handguns. Red-dot sights, too. Zanders Sporting Goods of Baldwin, Illinois (*gzanders. com*) is handling Famous Maker scopes. They're imported by a sister company, DKG Trading.

Kahles

While Kahles scopes aren't yet as common as Weavers, Leupolds — or even Swarovskis — in whitetail camps or in saddle scabbards, Kahles engineering has long benefited

American hunters. In 1959 Kahles was the first company to use multi-coated lenses. In 1972, it was the first to employ an 0-ring to seal the turret. Kahles has pioneered lightweight, short-coupled 30mm scopes. Kahles' business has quadrupled lately, largely because the company has catered to U.S. tastes. The Kahles line of 1-inch AV scopes includes two personal favorites: a 4x36 and a 2-7x36, ideal sights for deer and elk hunters. The brilliant images in *all* Kahles sights owe a lot to special lens coatings that transmit 99.8-percent of incident light in green/yellow bands (500-540 nanometers). A little red (400 nanometers) is screened, I'm told, because it is less helpful at dawn and dusk.

Recent offerings at Kahles include a 3-12x56 CSX Helia illuminated rifle scope. Batteries are cleverly and unobtrusively housed in the turret. A battery-saving digital mechanism leaves the reticle in stand-by mode. Touch the dial and the reticle instantly brightens to the level you set before. "Because this 30mm scope was designed for the American market, the reticle is in the second image plane," explains Karen Lutto, whose firm represents Kahles stateside. "It does not grow or shrink with changes in magnification." The 56mm objective on this scope brings total weight to just under 19 ounces. If you don't need that much power *(or the list price of $1954 won't fit your budget)*, pick one of three other CSX models: 1.1-4x24, 1.5-6x42 or 2.5-10x50.

The newest Kahles offering is a 1-inch scope series called the CL (Compact Light). With 4 inches of eye relief, these sights deliver 10 percent more than the AVs. A turret-mounted "AO" dial refines focus and eliminates parallax error. Objective-mounted parallax sleeves and now the more convenient mid-section dials remain particularly useful on high-power scopes; but Kahles is offering this feature on *every* CL sight. Kahles marketing manager

Hermann Theisinger points out that parallax *(the apparent shift of the target image against the reticle as you move your eye off the scope's axis)* can be a problem at low power, too. "High magnification shrinks the exit pupil," he says, "forcing your eye onto the optical axis of the sight. At low power, the scope can give you a full field of view when your eye is off-axis. Aiming error results."

Perhaps the most arresting feature of CL scopes is an elevation dial that can be set for multiple zeroes. In fact, you can establish up to five zeroes at distances to 500 yards. "We had a hard time selling this in-house," laughs Hermann. "It's a costly benefit for us, and was devilishly hard to engineer. But we have it perfected now -- and there's nothing like it." A miniature clutch engages to give you normal quarter-minute adjustments; but once you've set a zero, you can disengage it to set another. Each is easily recorded. Once you've finished, all that's needed to change from zero #1 to zero #2 is a twist of the elevation knob to the next detent. You never lose settings unless you deliberately change them. "The CL mechanism is durable, reliable and more accurate than ballistic cams," says Hermann. "The advantage of multiple zeroes is that you won't have to hold over your target at *any* hunting distance." Of course, you can also set zeroes for various loads, or use the settings to lock in point of impact when you switch the scope from one rifle to another.

CL scopes from Kahles: 3-9x42, 3-10x50 and 4-12x52.

Kahles CL scopes are available in three configurations: 3-9x42, 3-10x50 and 4-12x52. Engineered and manufactured in Austria, these sights are assembled at the company's U.S. headquarters and warranty center in Cranston, Rhode Island. They will retail for a little more than the AV scopes. Mike Jensen, sales manager for Kahles in the U.S., points out that CLs have one-piece tubes and an unlimited lifetime warranty. "We consider this series the last step in analog optics. The next few years will bring a trend to digital sights."

I recently tested a CL scope on a 22-250 rifle with zeroes set at 100, 200 and 300 yards. The bullets hit center with center-holds every time. The Kahles factory in Vienna is now running three shifts, seven days a week to stay up with demand. Hermann Theisinger predicts that CL models will keep the factory humming.

Hunter Wicked Optics

A couple of years ago, when I examined the binoculars and rifle scopes that Jim Holzclaw was importing, I was impressed. A 4x40 scope performed as well as some sights costing hundreds more. "We aren't offering much new for 2005," says Jim. "Our goal was–and is–to bring practical, affordable glass to market as we design it. We don't introduce product just to have something new." But there *is* a new line at Hunter this year: red-dot sights with multi-coated lenses and one-piece tubes. If they're as good as the rifle scopes, and priced as reasonably, you'll find them well worth a look at huntercompany.com.

Legacy Sports International

Legacy imports rifles as well as scopes. "We're trying to make American hunters more aware of both," says Janet Davis at Legacy. "Our Howa and Mauser and Nikko-Sterling optics offer high quality at competitive prices." New for 2005 are three Gold Crown rifle scopes: 4x32, 4x32 AO and 3-9x42. "The 4x32 AO is designed for rimfire riflemen who want to zero-out

parallax at short ranges but don't want the bulk or magnification of traditional varmint scopes," Janet says. All three scopes have multi-coated lenses, plex reticles, 1-inch tubes and fast-focus eyepieces. They come with flip-up scope covers too. Prices: under $70! Even easier on budgets are two Reflex Red Dot sights from Nikko-Sterling. New 30mm and 40mm versions with integral mounts have 11 brightness settings and 5 MOA dots.

Leica

Its tradition of supplying only top-quality optics limits the number of new products at Leica. This year, says Eileen Giunta, there are no introductions to report. The recent Ultravid binoculars, lightweight versions of the legendary Trinovids, rank among the best in the world. In my view, they're without peer. Last year's Geovid rangefinding binocular is truly in a class by itself. The earlier Geovid offered superior optics with laser rangefinding capability — but weighed a hefty 47 ounces. It retailed for as much as a living room set, a reflection of that great Leica glass and sophisticated circuitry. Sales were predictably modest.

The new Geovid has an aluminum housing, with a soft rubber jacket. It's waterproof to 16 feet and weighs just 32 ounces — a third less than its forebear. List price is about half: $1800 for the 8x, $1850 for the 10x.

The rangefinder targets reflective objects to 1300 yards with .05 percent accuracy. "You'll read within 2 yards of actual distance out to 800 yards," says Eileen. Leica's LRF Rangemaster series now includes the 800, *(launched in 2000 but since upgraded)*, 900 and 1200 models. Composite bodies measure just 4 inches square and weigh only 11 ounces with battery.

Leupold

Over the last couple of years, Leupold has been overhauling its variable-power hunting scopes. It has introduced the VX-I and VX-IIs with upgraded features, and replaced the Multicoat 4 lens treatment in the Vari-X III with a "matched-lens" system that, in the new VX-III, promises more-light-to-your-eye and a sharper, color-true image with minimal color fringing. Now, after decades of building M8 fixed-power scopes, Leupold is improving that series. The new 4x has the endearing profile of its predecessor: sleek and economical of line, svelte-but-businesslike. It's called the FX-II, a predictable moniker. The FX-II 4x33 weighs 9.3 ounces, same as before. But the lenses feature Multicoat 4 coatings, a step up from the treatment given the old M8s. Coin-slotted quarter-minute click adjustments have replaced traditional friction-fit dials. Available in matte finish or gloss, with wide Duplex or standard Duplex reticle, this scope wears Leupold's new ivory lettering on the left side of the turret. With 4 inches of eye relief, the new 4x33 is to my mind an ideal scope for any lightweight big game rifle — and more versatile than many hunters think.

Of course, Leupold didn't stop with a 4x. The new FX-II 6x36 offers the same improvements. But you can also order this 10-ounce sight with Leupold Dot and Post & Duplex reticles. The slender profile means you can employ low rings. Leupold's other new 6x is the 11-ounce FX-III 6x42. The "III" means that like VX-III variables, it has a matched-lens system. Windage and elevation dials are finger-friendly. Generous objective glass gives you an exit pupil of 7mm. That's about as wide as a healthy young human eye can dilate, even on

Leupold's new lightweight fixed-power scope, the FX-II 4x33.

The new FX-II 6x36 can be ordered with the dot or post & duplex reticle.

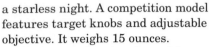

The standard FX-III 6x42 weighs 11 ounces and is also available in a competition model with target knobs and an adjustable objective.

a starless night. A competition model features target knobs and adjustable objective. It weighs 15 ounces.

For longer shooting, Leupold offers an FX-III 12x40 target scope with adjustable objective. For its power, this scope is trim and lightweight: 13 inches and 13 ounces. A good pick for a lightweight varmint rifle. There's plenty of power to quarter small rodents with a crosswire, but field enough for quick pointing. You can read mirage without it destroying your aim.

Deer hunters prowling the woodlots are better equipped with the FX-II Ultralight 2.5x20. At 6.5 ounces, it's lighter than some iron sights and delivers a 40-foot field of view at 100 yards. There's also an FX-II Scout scope, designed for forward mounting. It weighs an ounce more and is a perfect companion to the new Winchester 94 Timber Scout and Ruger 77 Frontier. Leupold has added FXII 2x20 and 4x28 pistol scopes to the stable. Field of view is necessarily smaller than in scopes with shorter

The FX-II Scout scope is designed for forward-mounting on rifles like the new Winchester 94 Timber Scout and the Ruger 77 Frontier.

Leupold's FX-III 12x40 target scope with adjustable objective weighs only 15 ounces.

eye relief: 21 and 9 feet at 100 yards.

The selection of variable scopes from Beaverton has also grown this spring. The VX-I 1-4x20 has a heavy Duplex reticle for quick shooting in dark cover. Both it and a companion 2-7x33 are cataloged as "Shotgun and Muzzleloader," with parallax correction set at a practical 75 yards. New VX-IIs include the Ultralight 2-7x28, at just over 8 ounces, and the 3-9x33 at just under 9. They offer Multicoat 4 lenses. The EFR version of the Ultralight 3-9x33 includes a focusing (AO) sleeve. Also just announced: VX-1 2-7x28 and VX-II 9x33 EFR Rimfire scopes with fine duplex reticles and short-range parallax settings, friction dials and the multi-coating once used on Vari-X II lenses. Choose the FX-I 4x28 if you'd rather scope that 22rf with a fixed-power. For handgunners there's a 2.5-8x32 Leupold VX-III, just 6 ounces 18 inches of eye relief, finger-click adjustments and the best optical coatings the company offers.

Tactical and law enforcement sights from Leupold now include 1.5-5x20 variables. Both feature matched-lens premium-quality lens coatings. The 1-inch "Precision" scope weighs less than 10 ounces. The 30mm Mid Range / Tactical scales 15. A new reticle is designed to permit fine aim at long range but with the up-close-and-urgent speed of a Circle Dot. The 3.5-10x40 Long Range / Tactical Mark 4 gives you a front-plane reticle and choice of tall target knobs and quarter-minute clicks, or compact M3 (bullet drop compensating) dials. The M3 has half-minute windage clicks and elevation clicks a minute apart. These allow quicker sight adjustment to extreme range: "100 yards to 1,000 with a spin of the dial."

Accessory lenses are now available from Beaverton, too. "They thread onto the objective bells of late-model Leupold scopes to enhance specific colors," says the company's Pat Mundy. "The idea is to improve the target image you expect to find, on the range or in the field. There's a lens to coax warm colors out of foliage, so you can better spot game. Other lenses function like tinted shooting glasses to cut glare or brighten your sight picture." Available for most VX scopes *(except some early VX IIs)*; these lenses come in diameters to fit most objective bells. If your scope isn't threaded for the lenses, Leupold will thread it at half the regular cost.

Meade: Simmons, Redfield

Meade Optical Company of Irvine, California, makes astronomical telescopes. Now it also designs and builds rifle scopes. After ATK sold the Redfield, Simmons and Weaver brands to Meade a few years back, the company has been busy charting improvements. Simmons was the first project, and the resulting changes have been implemented in new Redfield products, announced at the 2005 SHOT Show.

Meade CEO Steve Murdock is committed to building rifle scopes that will earn the kind of loyalty commanded by his telescopes. "You need good glass to see stars light years away, and we use the best. You can expect the same in Meade sporting optics."

The Master Series Simmons, just now appearing at market, has a lot to offer sportsmen. Engineers Mark Thomas and Forrest Babcock made the scope simpler. Instead of adding fluff, they improved essential components. The scopes are lighter than their predecessors. The 10.5-ounce 3-9x40 is lighter than most competitive models too. There's up to 17-percent greater windage and elevation range, longer eye relief and a bigger "eye box" so you catch aim as soon as your cheek hits the comb.

Last autumn I installed a prototype Simmons Master Series scope on a Winchester 70 built by Hill Country Rifles. Moving 20 clicks at a time, I fired five groups "around the square." The last struck an inch to 4 o'clock of the first. Net movement was a trifle

The Simmons AETEC 2.8-10 riflescope is available with glossy, matte black or silver finishes.

Simmons ProSport 4-12x variable has an adjustable objective lens.

less than 5 inches laterally; vertical graduations were on the money. But I noted some vertical component to horizontal clicks, and a horizontal shift when I moved only the elevation dial. Run-out, or point-of-impact shift between power settings stayed within 3/4 inch. In scopes with second plane reticles, shift is hard to eliminate and cannot be predicted by looking at the retail price. Any single inexpensive scope can show negligible shift, while a random sample of a costly sight can exhibit 1/2- to 3/4-inch change.

This Simmons scope was a prototype. The Meade folks had obligingly rushed it to me for a tight magazine deadline. "Windage and elevation dials have been refined," said Simmons Product Manager Everett Jones at the time. "Production scopes will be tested to ensure against unwanted impact shift when you change power or use the windage and elevation dials." He said the lens coatings would be tweaked too, though the scope delivered fine optical performance. "Adjustment knobs are getting more surface for easier grip. And we're installing a plex reticle with a finer middle wire."

Inside the Master Series scope, a slotted beryllium and copper ring fitted to the rear of the erector assembly holds that tube tight against the windage and elevation adjustment pegs. Traditionally, the front of the erector tube is pressed against the pegs by a biasing spring on the other side of the tube. The new rear-mounted biasing *ring* eliminates the need for a biasing spring. Result: smoother, more predictable point of impact shift as you turn the dials, and no drag from a forward spring. The new gimbal joint *(the fitting that allows the erector tube 360-degree movement up front)* is simple and sturdy.

A fast-focus ocular housing on helical threads enabled me to get a sharp, clean image of both the target and the reticle. Though the company lists eye relief as 3.75 inches, I found the actual "sweet spot" about 4 inches from the rear lens. There *is* a bigger eyebox. You can move your eye forward and back and slightly off-axis without instant blackout. That means faster aim, quicker second shots. Eye relief is often sacrificed for high magnification or wider field of view. Somehow, Mark and Forrest managed to deliver long eye relief without noticeable compromise.

The 3-9x40 lists for a penny less than $150, a modest tariff indeed for a 3-9x of this quality. "Meade has succeeded in keeping sticker price low," says Sherry Kerr, whose public relations firm represents the Simmons line. "Value is what hunters have come to look for in Simmons scopes. She adds that features on the Master Series will be implemented on other Simmons sights, including the Aetec. Only the entry-level 8-Point scopes will be retained as an entry-level product. They'll get a new name: Blazer.

Steve Murdock emphasizes that Meade is already working on more improvements in rifle scope design. "Our engineers talk about reinventing the rifle scope," he says. "The new erector tube design is just a first step. Our engineers are shooters, too. Their goal is to make sure all Simmons, Weaver and Redfield products enhance your shooting."

Minox

A name well known in Europe, Minox offers U.S. sportsmen binoculars with features found on much more expensive products — Leica's, for instance. "We're an independent company now," says John Bedlion, who has been named general manager for Minox stateside. "But our corporate connection ensures that Minox binoculars will deliver top value." Thorsten Kortemeier, president of the new firm, notes

The ProHunter 3-9x variable comes in several finishes: black gloss, black matte and silver.

Shotgun-only zones will like Simmons' ProDiamond 4x scope.

that Minox GmbH was purchased by Leica in 1996, but in 2001 became an independent company. Separation was completed this April with the formation of Minox USA.

Several new binoculars mark the occasion. The Minox Magnum, a 9.5x42, features individual focus and aspherical lenses. "We use long-lasting argon gas instead of nitrogen for fog-proofing," says John. The rubber-armored, 24-ounce binocular lists for $399. An 8x42 costs $389. So does a 6.5x32 IF binocular that has great depth of focus, plus a very wide field. There's also an 8-14x40 variable binocular, priced at $1198. Minox is also introducing two compact binoculars, 8x25 and 10x25.

Nikon

Several of my favorite hunting scopes hail from the same family. They're Nikon Monarchs, sights with incredibly bright optics and profiles that look good on any hunting rifle. I used a 4x40 Monarch again last year on an elk hunt. A 4-12x on a 243 made it as deadly on distant rockchucks as on deer. In my view, there's not much to improve in the Monarch line. Nikon must have agreed, because it hasn't changed any

Nikon adds the compact 8x20 and 10x25 to the LXL line for 2005.

Nikon's new rangefinder for 2005 is the 1200, available in both black and Realtree camo finishes.

of these first-quality scopes for 2005. But the more affordable Buckmasters have a new look, with rounded objective housings and a quick-focus eyepiece. Long-range shooters will appreciate the new AO models, with the up-front sleeve replaced by a more convenient turret-mounted dial. And, according to C.J. Davis of Chevalier Advertising, "prices are essentially the same as last year."

Nikon has been busier at the binocular bench. Top-ranked LX roof prism glasses are LXLs in the current catalog. The full-size versions (8x42, 10x42, 8x32 and 10x32) have been joined by 8x20 and 10x25 Compacts. List prices start at $500 for the 8x20. "Street prices are lower," C.J. reminds me. "List for our 10x42 is $1500; but MAP, or minimum advertised price, is $1300." All LXLs feature the best components. They're lighter in weight this year, and feature lead-free, arsenic-free glass. A stickier rubber jacket makes them easier to grip in the rain or when your hands are cold.

The ProStaff Compacts in Nikon's ATB line now include 8x, 9x, 10x, and 12x configurations, all with 25mm objectives. Monarch 8x42 and 10x42 glasses have a new 12x42 sibling. It will sell for around $330. In entry-level binoculars, you'll find an EagleView Zoom Compact that affords you instant choice of magnification, from 8 to 24x. The 25mm objectives limit light transmission at the high end. The EagleView will be priced at about $250.

Nikon's 440 and 600 laser rangefinders were joined last year by an 800 model. This spring Nikon is adding a 1200. *(The numbers indicate approximate maximum effective distance, given ideal conditions.)* The 1200 in black will trade for about $430. MAP for the Realtree version is $20 higher.

Pentax

Late in 2004 Pentax announced a new spotting scope, the PF-65ED, a hunting-size, first-quality instrument with both straight and angled eyepieces. Waterproof and lightweight, it's worthy competition for same-size scopes from Leica, Zeiss and

Swarovski. Now there are three new XF-series eyepieces for the PF-65ED: 32x, 46x and 20-60x, all with collet-type attachments. This 37-ounce scope also accepts the XW-series telescope eyepieces and PF-CA35 camera adapter for 35mm SLRs. My latest experience with a Pentax spotting scope came in a Wyoming prairie dog town awash in heavy mirage. I was impressed by the scope's ability to define detail through the soup, it's precise focusing and flat field.

If you're looking close instead of far, and don't want to crease your neck with a heavy binocular, consider the new Papilio 6.5x21 and 8.5x21 compact Porro prism binoculars. "They focus as close as 1.6 feet!" says Pat Lytle, of Pentax. As useful to butterfly enthusiasts as to hunters, they weigh only 10 ounces and provide access to another dimension of the outdoors.

Schmidt & Bender

"Best" is an elusive term, but among rifle scopes, Schmidt &

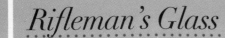

For 2005, the Nikon Buckmasters line has a new look, with a rounded objective and a quick-focus eyepiece. These two are 3-9x40 variables, with matte black and silver finishes.

Benders certainly rank among the best. Some of their features you won't find elsewhere, and overall quality is unsurpassed. When I visited the S&B plant some years ago, it seemed to me more like the surgery wing of a hospital than a factory. In long white cotton coats, intelligent-looking men scurried about gleaming work stations. Parts, in various stages of assembly, could as well have been meant for microscopes or space capsules.

Schmidt & Bender's premier line is the Zenith, represented by 30mm variables in power ranges 1.1-4x24, 1.5-6x42, 2.5-6x56 and 3-12x50. They not only feature resettable windage and elevation dials; the dial faces show where in the range of adjustment you are. You won't run out of inches without warning. If you like, you can use the mount to center the optical axis in the physical axis of the scope. An auxiliary ring under the dial face allows you to record several zeros, for quick return when shooting at various ranges or using different loads.

Also available on Zenith scopes: the FlashDot illuminated reticle. Unlike most lighted reticles, this one will vanish if you want to use the black reticle instead. In dark cover, turn it on and adjust brightness to suit conditions. A beam splitter puts the dot in the exact center of the field – then erases it on command. Forget to turn it off? There's an automatic switch that kills the dot after six hours to save battery. You'll find an extra battery under the windage cap. Incidentally, S&B also offers traditional illuminated reticles in the Classic-series 2.5-10x56, 3-12x50 and 3-12x42, as well as in the fixed 8x56. The 4-16x50, 6x42 and 10x42 come with a broad choice of standard reticles. The firm offers a retrofitting service, too, so shooters using standard reticles can get the illuminated feature on selected S&B scopes they already own.

Schmidt & Bender fixed-power scopes come with 1-inch tubes – and 26mm and 30mm. Variables and fixed sights come with reticles in the first and second focal planes, depending on model. You can also order lens filters

and hoods. S&B guarantees service for 30 years after a scope purchase, free service for 10. But it's unlikely your Schmidt & Bender will ever have to make a return trip to Germany.

Sightron

Shooters have come to appreciate the practical features of Sightron optics," says Alan Orr, who's in charge of Sightron marketing. "And the down-to-earth pricing." New this year is a compact, waterproof binocular that weighs just 12 ounces. Available in 8x and 10x, it has BaK-4 prisms and multicoated glass. Sightron is also adding three variable "SS" scopes with side-mounted parallax adjustments: 3.5-10x44, 4.5-14x44 and 6.5-20x50. Plex, Dot and Mil Dot reticles are cataloged for the high-power models; the 3.5-10x comes with Plex or Mil Dot. All SS scopes are fully multi-coated, waterproof and shipped with sunshades and dust covers. A new 30mm S III-series 6-24x50 offers greater adjustment latitude than do most 1-inch scopes of similar power. Select Plex, Dot or Mil Dot reticle. For whitetail and turkey hunters, Sightron has a new 2.5x32SG scope with more than 4 inches of eye relief. It's an ideal choice for woods rifle or shotgun.

A first-ever Sightron product this year is a hunting-weight spotting scope. It comes with 25x and 20-60x eyepieces, plus a Cordura soft case zippered to allow quick access to the ends. This S II WP2060x63 scope is waterproof and camera-adaptable. It is, of course, fully multi-coated.

Springfield

This is what Springfield's Bill Dermody might call a "catch-up year." The extensive new line of rifle scopes the company trotted out in 2004 didn't reach dealers in quantity until fall. "We had to remind the people who supply our optics that we won't compromise quality to meet shipping deadlines," says Bill. "Springfield's standards are very high, and manufacturers must submit to our inspections." Delivery of the firm's 13 tactical scopes (which

Sightron's new WP 20-60x63 hunting–weight spotting scope is waterproof and camera-adaptable.

include 3-9x42 and 3.5-10x50 hunting sights with 30mm tubes) is now on schedule. In my tests, these scopes performed well. They feature turret-mounted AO dials and an internal bubble level at 6 o'clock to prevent canting. You can specify illuminated reticles on most models. A gear-driven power-change mechanism is standard. "It's 34 times as stout as a slot-and-pin affair," says Bill.

Steiner

Germany's signature supplier of military optics has been ramping up its line of sporting glass, with both big and little binoculars. "The newest Predators, 8.5x26 and 10.5x28 compacts, were announced last year," says Bill Pierce, whose firm represents Steiner in the States. "They have green-tinted lenses that give you an edge spotting deer in the woods. The 10x32 Merlin, also a 2004 introduction, is still one of our new products. But we've just added two compact Merlins – an 8x24 and a 10x26 – plus 8x50 and 10x50 full-size models. All four boast fully multi-coated optics and phase correction. The compacts weigh about 11 ounces, the big binoculars 26. Prices: from $199 to $649.

Also new: an 8.5x50 Peregrine that weighs 30 ounces and focuses down to 6 feet. It is mil-spec waterproof and lists for just shy of $1000. If you're looking for spotting scope performance in a binocular, Steiner offers the new 25x80 Observer. "It weighs 56 ounces, so isn't for neck carry. But on a tripod, it will help you glass comfortably and effectively long after your eye is

Steiner adds two compact Merlins to their binocular line: an 8x24 and 10x26.

Steiner's new 8.5x50 Peregrine is waterproof and focuses down to six feet.

strained to tears in a spotting scope," says Verena Huetteneder, whose firm represents Steiner in the U.S. The Observer is reasonably priced at $650.

Swarovski

Clamping a scope tube in rings is an imperfect way to secure the sight on a rifle. Not only do the rings mar the scope; they can be located only where there's "clear tube" – which may be forward or aft of the rings' position on the base. Also, rings don't index the scope. You can mount any scope cockeyed in a set of rings because you can rotate it freely until you tighten the screws. What looks plumb before you take the final turns with a screwdriver may look anything but when you shoulder the rifle in the field. Finally, a scope can slip in rings during recoil. The inertia of a ponderous variable can pull mightily against the rings jerked suddenly rearward by your 416 Weatherby mountain rifle.

Enter Swarovski's new SR rail scopes. The integral toothed rail on PH 1.25x24, PH 1-6x42 and PH 3-12x50 models eliminates the ring/tube juncture that can fail during heavy recoil. With these scopes, you'll have no ring scars, and no internal damage from tight rings. The tubes are machined from bar stock, so the rail actually strengthens the tube while ensuring that it will never slip. The scope tube looks sleek without rings, too. European hunters have long recognized the advantages of rail-equipped scopes, many of which are imported to the U.S. without rails only in deference to the U.S. market. And until now, there's been a dearth of rail mounts Stateside. Those available for European rifles have been costly, and few are designed to fit rifles popular with American shooters.

So when Swarovski announced that it was going to hawk rail scopes in this country, I naturally thought, "Good, but…." And last year there *was* no practical solution to the mount problem. This spring, however, Jim Morey and the Swarovski crew showed me a stout, simple inexpensive mount that's easy to install on a rail scope and clamps to any Picatinny or Weaver-style base. It looks attractive, too. The front attachment must mate with the rail teeth; the rear clamp is allowed to float slightly so you can position it exactly where you want it. With no ring pressure to threaten the scope's innards, and no chance for tube slippage, Swarvoski SR scopes may well prove the pioneers in a new trend among American shooters.

Tasco

When Bushnell brought the Tasco brand into its business, the idea was to trim the enormous Tasco selection of optics to a more manageable stable of the best models. The 2005 catalog still has many entries. However, according to Chris Lalik at Bushnell, "they represent the better side of Tasco. We're not finished culling yet, but we think current offerings deliver great quality for the money." He points out that though Tasco gets much less exposure in the press than does Bushnell, Leupold, Nikon and carriage-class optics from Germany and Austria, the brand sells in huge volumes to U.S. hunters. Most of them are satisfied with the product. In fact, a $50 Tasco 6x scope I got in a rifle trade some years ago has become a workhorse on test rifles because it gives me a sharp sight picture and holds zero on guns with brutal recoil.

New for 2005: 8x42 and 10x42 binoculars with BaK4 prisms and multi-coated lenses. These roof prism, 26-ounce binoculars list for $70 and $80. There's an illuminated 3-9x40 rifle scope for $84, too. And Tasco has redesigned its 18-36x50 World Class spotting scope. It comes with a window mount, tripod and hard case. The price, remarkably enough, has been reduced to $132.

The current Tasco line includes compact and full-size binoculars, from 8x21 to 9x63. Choose roof or Porro prism models, even variable power. Tasco offers four spotting scopes for shooters. The line of rifle scopes spans fixed and variable power, in magnifications from 1.5x to

Swarovski's integral toothed mounting rail on the new SR scope line eliminates any chance of scope slippage or ring damage.

40x. Tasco's ProPoint red dot sights with 30mm tubes complement the Red Dot series with 38mm tubes. All are 1x (no magnification). Scopes for rimfire rifles include versions with 1-inch and 3/4-inch tubes.

Trijicon

Known for its tritium-illuminated iron sights and optical sights that use both tritium and fiber-optic strands to brighten the reticle, Trijicon lists several new items for 2005. The TR22 2.5-10x56 AccuPoint is a battery-free illuminated scope with a 30mm tube and a delta-shaped, tritium-lit reticle. Fiber-optic assist is adjustable. This year, too, Trijicon will bring to the civilian market its ACOG (*Advanced Combat Optical Gunsight*). Developed for military use, ACOG has been adopted by the USMC. It's compact and rail-mounted.

Weaver

After its transfer to Meade from ATK a few years ago, Weaver's face changed hardly at all. The Grand Slam, T-Series, and Classic scopes remain. To my satisfaction, so do K models. Meade's notable contributions are ETX spotting scopes, 48x90 and 78x125. These look suspiciously like Meade telescopes. They're both camera-adaptable. Magnification is right for long-range target shooting. Classic 20x50 and 15-40x60 spotting scopes are still in production, for those hunters who prefer traditional spotting scopes. An overhaul of Simmons sights, and a revitalized Redfield label, have taken most of Meade's energy lately. With the company's bent to innovation, it wouldn't surprise me to see changes in the Weaver stable. Steve Murdock and his crew at Meade seem committed to building useful scopes, however, and they're careful with properties already serving shooters. So I don't expect any Weaver lines to be discarded.

Zeiss

Following the successful debut of its affordable Conquest rifle scopes a few years ago, Zeiss is still making overtures to American hunters. Now it offers 10 scopes with the rear-plane reticles preferred in the U.S. In the rear plane, a reticle does not change apparent dimensions as you change magnification of a variable scope. Front-plane reticles grow in thickness with power, obscuring small targets that you want to see better at high power. At low magnification, where you set a scope for fast shots in the woods, the reticle becomes less prominent. So why would you want a front-plane reticle? For one thing, there's never a shift in point of impact, one magnification to the next. POI shift is minimal in most second-plane scopes, but to guarantee *no* shift, the reticle must be up front. Secondly, a front-plane reticle stays the same size relative to the target throughout the power range, so when you estimate yardage, magnification doesn't matter. Zeiss caters to European and American tastes in reticle types, too, with range-finding and illuminated versions.

Zeiss currently offers the popular Conquest in 3-9x, 3.5-10x, 4.5-14x and 6.5-20x variations. All have 1-inch tubes. The German optics firm also catalogs the 30mm Diavari VM/V series, costly sights that some experienced riflemen consider the best in the world. The last Diavari I tested beat all competitors optically *and* mechanically.

Consistent with its recent push to win more U.S. market share, Zeiss has invested in building new binoculars to challenge Swarovski's well-received EL models. The Zeiss Victory FL is surely in the same class. This series of lightweight roof prism models incorporates fluorite (FL) glass, for extra-low light dispersion, truer color rendition and brighter, sharper images. As in Zeiss Diascope spotting scopes, edge resolution is remarkable. "Zeiss uses Abbe-König prisms in the 7x42, 8x42 and

Zeiss' popular Conquest 3-9x variable has a one-inch tube.

10x42 versions," says Rich Moncrief, who works at the firm's U.S. headquarters in Virginia. "The 8x32 and 10x32 FLs have Schmidt Pechan prisms with new Zeiss dielectric mirror coatings." All Victory FLs have multilayer lens coatings and phase correction coatings.

"The 32mm binoculars offer very wide fields of view for their size," points out Shannon Jackson, who handles press relations for Zeiss in the U.S. "The 8x delivers 420 feet at 1,000 yards, the 10x 360 feet. Twist-out eyecups have detents so you can lock them at any position for the proper eye relief. All versions focus very close: to about 7 feet." Glass-fiber-reinforced polymer holds the lenses in barrels of magnesium alloy. A steel center shaft with brass bushings ensures smooth focusing; you change diopter setting via a lockable wheel on the front of the hinge. Victory FL binoculars are waterproof. The 42mm versions weigh 26 to 27 ounces, the 8x32 and 10x32 20 ounces. The new FL series retails from $1450 to $1600.

Collimation (barrel alignment) and prism placement are critical, whether you're using Porro-prism or roof-prism binoculars. Competition in the roof-prism arena is keen. To get some idea of the allowable tolerances in Zeiss prisms, consider that if a builder framing a house with a roof span of 40 feet had similar standards, he'd be permitted just half a millimeter difference between left and right rafters. Entrance and exit surfaces on a prism must be parallel to within 1 second of arc. The maximum allowable convergence would put light beams together 8.7 miles from the glass. A glider moving at this angle would sail around the earth if it started just 200 yards from the surface.

HANDLOADING UPDATE

by Larry S. Sterett

Handloaders, particularly ones who have been loading for some years, or who reload a number of different calibers, always seem to be looking for new equipment and/or accessories to make the operation simpler, safer, faster—or all of the above. Such products are available and what follow are some of the newest.

Berry's Manufacturing

Berry's is known for their copper-plated swaged bullets, including two weights for the 50 S&W, but the firm also has a number of other products for handloaders. New are covered loading trays, or blocks. Available in three sizes to fit cases from the 9mm Parabellum and 223 up to cartridges with head sizes just under 0.625-inch, the trays hold 500 rounds and feature clear plastic covers. Other new items include powder funnel inserts to fit 17- and 50-caliber cartridges, and plastic 50-round ammo boxes in smoke and orange colors, in addition to the clear and blue colors previously available. *(Boxes holding 20 and 100 rounds are also available in smoke and orange colors.)* Ten sizes are available to fit most handguns and rifle cartridges from the 380 ACP to the 500 S&W and 50 A.E., including the various WSM and WSSM calibers.

Battenfeld Technologies, Inc.

Battenfeld has a couple of new items in their Frankford Arsenal line. First is a tumbler with up to 600-case capacity and Rotary-7 Media Separator. *(The Rotary 7 Media Separator is available separately, and includes the Separator, bucket adaptor, and a 3-1/2 gallon bucket. Polishing and cleaning*

The Lyman T-Mag II turret press below has been reengineered and upgraded to offer even more versatility and precision. Improvements include: a new hi-tech iron frame, a new turret handle and improved retention system for smoother indexing. With a detachable T-Mag Turret precise set-up with various loading dies (shown right) can be easily maintained while changing calibers.

media in the form of plain or treated corn cobs or walnut hulls is available in quantities from 4-1/2 to 18 pounds, depending on the type.) An easy-to-use Overall Length Gauge to determine the optimum bullet seating depth

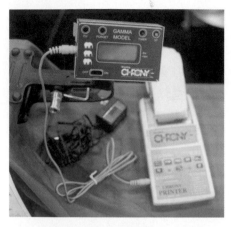

The Gamma Model Shooting Chrony (chronograph) can be attached to a printer to provide a hard copy of your chronographing results, for placement in your handloader's log.

GSI International's Bullet Feed attached to a Dillon XL650 reloading press positions a bullet ready for seating on the downstroke of the press handle. The feed, visible here in the center of the photo, slides into the toolhead slot of the XL650 press.

for reloaded cartridges is also new. All a handloader needs is a cleaning rod of 1/4-inch diameter *(or less)*, calipers, a pencil, and the Frankford gauge, to determine the overall length of the reloaded cartridge so seated bullets just touch the rifling.

GSI International, Inc.

Even when using some progressive reloaders, it's necessary to perform a certain number of manual operations, such as placing a wad when loading shotshells, or inserting a bullet when loading metallic cartridges. GSI International, Inc. has made a portion of the reloading operation easier with their GSI Bullet Feed System for the Dillon XL650 loading press. The GSI System will accept standard 7/8 x 14 dies, and it slides right into the toolhead slot of the XL650 press. *(The Dillon powder system and powder checker fit right in on the GSI toolhead.)* After installation of the GSI System, a bullet is advanced with every pull of the press handle. As the handle moves down, one bullet moves into the seating station, directly above the cartridge case, and a detent ball holds the bullet. Completion of the handle stroke seats the bullet into the cartridge case, without the need to manually position the bullet on top of the case or guide it up to the seating die. Currently, the GSI System, which includes the toolhead, bullet guide, rotary feed wheel and a specially machined seating stem for one caliber, is available in 38/357, 9mm, 40/10mm, 44 and 45 ACP handgun cartridges. *(Originally, the system was to also have been available to handle 223 Remington cartridges.)* It is necessary to keep the hopper filled with bullets.

Hornady Mfg. Company

Hornady always has some items for handloaders, and the latest include trimmer pilots for the 204 Ruger and 500 S&W cartridges, plus a 204 collet for the Cam Lock Bullet Puller. There are Custom-Grade Reloading Dies for the 25 WSSM and 6.8mm Remington SPC cartridges in the Series I sets,

the 338/06 in the Series III sets, 6mm BR in the Match-Grade sets, 8x56mm Hungarian in the Series IV Specialty sets, and 460 S&W in the Series II Three-Die Pistol sets.

Huntington Die Specialties

Huntington, the firm founded by the late Fred Huntington, the R.C.B.S. man, has more standard and hard-to-find reloading products—presses, scales, trimmers, dies, components, bullet moulds, etc.—than any other firm in the business. If reloading dies are available for a specific cartridge, Huntington probably has them or can produce them. From the 17s to the rimmed 3-inch 600-577 Nitro and including the 50 BMG, dies for more than 500 different cartridges are available. It may take awhile for some of the exotics, but they can be obtained. The same comment applies to forming dies, with nearly 300 different ones available. *(More than fifty items, including collets, neck-sizers, die sets, etc., were added to the availability for 2005.)* Huntington currently carries 16 brands of bullets for reloading, and 23 brands of new brass cases, including HDS, Bertram, Norma, Horneber, and RWS. You can even obtain expensive 70 H&H Nitro Express and 4-bore cases, if really needed.

Interest in long-range 50-caliber shooting has increased tremendously in the past five years. Previously, about the only 50 BMG-chambered rifles available to civilian shooters were the Barrett and the L.A.R. Grizzly. Barrett models are available in auto-loading and bolt action single shot and repeater models. The more compact Grizzly is available only as a single shot. At the 2005 SHOT Show there must have been at least a dozen different firms exhibiting 50-caliber rifles of their own design. Most were chambered for the 50 BMG cartridge, and many consisted of upper assemblies which could be attached to AR-15 lower units to produce single-shot, or side-feeding bolt-action rifles.

Not all such rifles were chambered for the 50 BMG cartridge. One of the most interesting fifties is the 510 DTC EUROP developed in Europe five years ago, by Eric Danis, as a solution to the problem of the 50 BMG being prohibited for civilian shooters. Comparable to the 50 BMG, and easily formed from 50 BMG brass, the 510 DTC EUROP is an excellent choice for 1000-yard match competition. *(The 510 is 0.100-inch shorter than the 50 BMG and features an 18 1/2-degree shoulder slope compared to the 15-degree slope for the 50 BMG. Shoulder diameters are 0.760-inch and 0.715-inch, respectively. Thus, the 510 DTC EUROP cartridge will not fit in a 50 BMG chamber and the 50 BMG cartridge is too long to fit the 510 DTC EUROP chamber.)* EDM Arms in Redlands, California, chambers their model 96 Windrunner rifles for both the 50 BMG and 510 DTC EUROP cartridges and guarantees 1 m.o.a. at 1000 yards with match ammunition, which means handloading using Barnes 750-grain solids, or the Hornady A-MAX bullets. Loading dies for the 510 DTC EUROP cartridge are available from C-H Tool & Die Co., and JGS Precision Tool Manufacturing and Dave Manson Precision Reamers have chambering reamers. There are possibly others, as firms producing reamers and/or dies for the 50 BMG

❁●❁●❁●❁●❁●❁

▶ *Some of the new cartridges for which reloading dies and equipment are becoming available. (L/R): 500 Phantom, 6.8mm Remington SPC, 460 Smith & Wesson, 325 Winchester Short Magnum, 50 Spotter (not new, but just becoming popular), 511 DTC EUROPE, 50 BMG (not new, but really coming into its own as a civilian long-range target cartridge) and the 502 Thunder Sabre. The 500 Phantom, .511 DTC EUROP and 50 BMG are loaded with 750-grain Hornady A-MAX bullets, the 50 Spotter with a 750-grain Barnes Solid, and the 502 Thunder Sabre with 325-grain Barnes XPB-Bullet.*

cartridge could produce dies for the 510 DTC EUROP cartridge if there is enough demand, and for the 50 Spotter cartridge as well.

Demand and requests for 50 BMG loading dies were such the Hartford, Wisconsin, firm of Lee Precision decided to introduce a 50 BMG Press Kit for 2005. It consists of the Lee Classic Cast Press, set of 50 BMG loading dies, shell holder, ram prime tool and tube of case sizing die. They manufactured what was anticipated to be a year's supply of dies—and were sold out in the first two weeks following introduction. New dies, which have 1-1/4 x 12 threads, are available separately, as are the 50 BMG shellholder and ram prime tool. *(The Lee Classic Cast Press was introduced in 2004. Its cast iron frame features rigid "O" construction, and is threaded to accept 1-1/4 x 12 dies, but comes with an adapter to handle standard 7/8 x 14 dies. The adjustable handle can be moved from the left to right side, and the hollow ram permits spent primers to be easily discarded via a plastic tube.)*

Other new Lee Precision products include Bottle Neck Pistol Factory Crimp Dies for the 30 Mauser/30 Tokarev, 30 (7.65mm) Luger, 357 SIG, and 400 Cor-Bon cartridges. Lee loading dies for handgun calibers range from the 25 ACP to the 500 S&W Magnum, and include the 455 Webley Mark II, 45 GAP, 480 Ruger, 50 Action Express. Some die sets, such as the 41 A.E., 45 HP Italian, 7mm BR and 7mm TCU are no longer catalogued, but new rifle dies include the 204 Ruger and 6.8mm Remington SPC.

A well-done reproduction of Winchester's Model 1885 flat side low-wall is also in the Cimarron line-up. This one has optional engraving and special wood.

❁●❁●❁●❁●❁

Lee Precision has dropped the wadcutter 208-grain mould for the 44 Special cartridge. New is a double mould to cast a 325-grain flat-nose gas check design for the 480 Ruger and 475 Linebaugh cartridges. Moulds are available to cast 440, 450, and 500-grain bullets for the 500 S&W

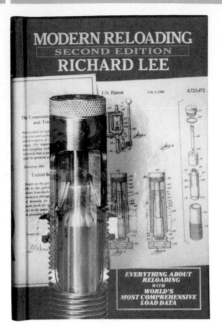

Lee Precision's Modern Reloading manual contains load data for both cast lead and jacket bullets in handgun and rifle loads from the 17 Ackley Bee to the 50 BMG, and much more.

❧ ● ❧ ● ❧ ● ❧ ● ❧ ● ❧

and 50-70 Government cartridges. Missing is a mould to cast a 600-grain gas check 0.511 bullet, similar in shape to the 500-grain 459 3R bullets cast in the #90577 mould for 45-70 cartridges. Maybe next year.

Lyman Products Corporation

Lyman has three new electronic powder measuring devices for handloaders. The 1000 XP Compact has a 1000-grain capacity, and features a hinged fold-back cover, digital readout, and an AC adapter. The larger 1500 XP features a built-in powder trickler, 1500-grain

❧ ● ❧ ● ❧ ● ❧ ● ❧ ● ❧

Right: Lyman's 'top cat' is the 1200 DPS (Digital Powder System), which can store up to 100 loads. Inset: Lyman's new 1500 XP electronic powder measure with hinged cover. (The item to the right of the measure pan is a trickler.) The 1500 is battery or AC powered.

capacity, fold-back dust cover, and a storage tray for scale accessories. Accurate to 0.1-grain, the scales will measure in grains or grams.

The top of the measuring line is the new 1200 DPS II Digital Powder System, with powder hopper and 100-load storage capacity. An optional PC interface is available to permit transfer from, or storage of data on, a computer.

Two other new Lyman accessories include the E-ZEE Powder Funnel, which will handle cases from 22 to 50, and the E-ZEE Flo Universal Powder Trickler. The Trickler works with any beam or electronic scale and is adjustable, up or down, in or out.

MEC

Mayville Engineering Co., Inc., has a new large capacity Progressive Primer Feed to fit the MEC 650, 76 Series, 8567 Grabber and 9000 Series shotshell loaders. The new feed features a self-lubricating plastic tray, which will hold 200+ primers, and pivots flat for easy loading. Other new MEC products for handloaders

include a Bushing Rack that will hold ten powder or shot bushings, a maintenance kit, and jig fixture to permit rapid removal and installation of a MEC reloader on a bench.

MTM

MTM Case-Gard Company usually has something new for handloaders each year; this year is no exception. Their new Universal Powder Funnel Set will handle any case from the 17s to the 500s, and it's packed in a clear storage box. It features two funnels—small multi-caliber and an "Adapto" for use with adaptors and the five included drop tubes.

There never seem to be enough loading blocks of the right size available, but the new MTM Universal Loading Tray will handle handgun and rifle calibers from the 17s to the 500 Smith & Wesson, including the WSM, WSSM and Remington Ultra Mag cases. For bulk storage of empty cases or loaded ammunition, the polypropylene Ammo Can will provide 750 cubic inches of lockable storage. A new version of the R-100

The large capacity progressive primer feed by Mayville Engineering will hold more than 200 (209 size) primers. It will fit many of the MEC shotshell reloading presses.

Rifle Ammo Case, the R-100-MAG for reloaded ammunition, will handle all the WSM, WSSM, SAUM, and similar magnum rifle cartridges—plus the 460 and 500 S&W cartridges. The 64-round P-64-50-10 Ammo Box will handle the 50 A.E. and 502 Thunder Sabre cartridges, plus the 480 Ruger and 475 and 500 Linebaugh.

MTM has a number of other new items, including a new Predator Shooting Table to check out the results of their work. Standing 30 inches tall, the table folds down to less than four inches in thickness for carrying. It's ideal for handloaders wanting to check out the results of their work at the bench.

RCBS

RCBS, a division of ATK (Alliant Techsystems) has a new AmmoMaster 2 Single Stage reloading press, an improvement on the AmmoMaster, consisting of longer support columns and larger toggle block. It's set for standard 7/8 x 14 dies, but will accept 1-1/2 x 12 dies. Thus, with the purchase of a 50 BMG 1-1/2 Die Kit to go with the AmmoMaster-2 press, a handloader is set to load 50 BMG cartridges. *(The 50 BMG Die Kit comes with everything necessary to load for this cartridge,*

including a full-length sizing die, roll crimp seating die, trim die, shellholder, and 50 BMG ram priming unit. The ram priming unit can also be purchased separately.)

New precision mic units in 204 Ruger, 223, 243 and 25 WSSM sizes are available, as are 17, 475, and 500 collets for the Standard Bullet Puller. Case trimmer pilots, reamers, and cutters now include 20 caliber sizes.

To make precision powder weighing easier, two new electronic scales, the RangeMaster 750 *(750-grain capacity)* and ChargeMaster 1500 *(1500 grain capacity)* have been introduced. Available in a choice of 110VAC or 220VAC models, either model will operate on a 9-volt battery. The scales are accurate to ±0.1 grain, and come equipped with two precision calibration/check weights.

For the ultimate weighing convenience, the new ChargeMaster Combo is available. This combines the ChargeMaster 1500 Scale with the ChargeMaster Dispenser. Fill the hopper with a pound+ of the desired powder, enter the desired charge data—in grains or grams—and press the dispense button. A 60-grain charge of smokeless powder will take approximately 20 seconds, and it will be accurate to ±0.1 grain. Up to 30 loads can be stored in the dispenser memory for easy recall, and loads can be from 2.0 to 300.0 grains of ball, flake, or extruded smokeless powder. *(NO BLACKPOWDER)*

A new Competition Powder Measure, for rifle or pistol/small rifle, is available. Based on the Uniflow Measure, but with a baffle and UPM micrometer adjustment screw, the new measure can drop charges weighing from 10 to 110 grains in the rifle size, and from 5 to 40 grains in the pistol size. The new measure is available separately or as a combo item with both drum sizes.

New additions to the RCBS Group A series of reloading

dies include the 204 Ruger, 243 and 25 WSSM, and 6.8mm Remington SPC cartridges. X—never trim again—Dies in the same calibers are now available. The big news in the RCBS die line is the Gold Medal Match Series, available in full-length or neck-sizing sets. *(Neck bushings, available in .001-inch increments, are not included.)* These Gold Medal dies feature a micrometer adjustable, free-floating and self-centering bullet seating system, with a convenient bullet-loading window, Vickerman style. There are 41 calibers currently available, from the 17 Remington to the 338 Lapua. *(The 204 Ruger and 25-06 Remington calibers have been added to the two-die Competition series of dies, and the 6.5mm Remington Magnum and 6.5mm/284 Winchester have been added to the Group D loading dies series.)*

Special reloading dies may be available from RCBS, with a wait time involved and a no-return policy. Custom reloading and case-forming dies are no longer available from RCBS. However, with the specifications for more than a thousand different cartridge reloading

The RCBS ChargeMaster Combo combines the ChargeMaster Dispenser with the Charge-Master 1500 Scale. It can store up to 30 loads in its memory and can dispense charges weighing from 2 to 300 grains with an accuracy of ±0.1 grain.

Getting ready to deprime and resize a 50 BMG case in the RCBS AmmoMaster-2 Single Stage Press. With the adapter, visible just to the rear of the press base, the press can be used with regular 7/8 x 14 loading dies.

and forming sets on file, chances are good RCBS has the one you want.

For those handloaders who cast their own bullets, RCBS has a new wooden mould mallet to help prevent mould damage, plus a new mould to cast a 400-grain SWC bullet for the 500 S&W cartridge. Now, if they will just come out with a mould to cast a 600-grain 0.511-inch bullet similar in design to their 45-500-BPS+, but with a gas check.

Redding Reloading Equipment

Redding now owns Imperial Lubricants, developer and producer of Imperial Sizing Die Wax used to reduce resizing drag. Two container sizes of the wax, bearing the Redding name, plus an Imperial Action Wax syringe and Dry Neck Lube are available. A new Universal Decapping Die, available in small or large size,

should be on every handloader's bench if several different caliber cartridges are reloaded. The small die will accept cases from 22- to 50-caliber up to 2.5 inches in length, with an optional 17- and 20-caliber rod available. The large die will handle cases up to three inches long with neck diameters 7mm or larger. This die will not handle 50 BMG cases.

New Redding products include die sets for the 20 Tactical, 6.8mm Remington SPC, 460 S&W, 500 S&W, with titanium carbide sets for the 45 GAP, 325 WSM, 375/444, 458 Lott, and 6.5/243 WSSM. The number of Type S Match full length and neck die sets, Competition Pro Series in carbide and non-carbide, neck dies sets in series A, B, C, and D, seems almost unlimited, plus a new tapered design on the shellholders makes inserting a case "E-Z Feed." *(Shellholders now include a size 18 for the big Weatherby cases and the 338 Lapua, and "E-Z Feed" shellholder sets are available containing six of the most popular sizes in a hinged plastic case.)*

The T-7 Turret and Big Boss reloading presses have been improved. Both presses feature a ram stroke of 3.8 inches, and the Big Boss will accept 1-1/4 x 12 die sets. *(Redding does not currently catalog 50 BMG reloading dies.)* A slide bar automatic primer feeding system with a capacity of approximately a box of 100 primers will fit both the T-7 and Big Boss presses. *(Big Boss Pro-Paks with all the tools—press, dies, scale, lube, etc. —needed to reload a specific cartridge are available in a number of handguns and rifle calibers.)*

The TR-1400 Case Trimming Lathe has been made longer and stronger. It comes with a universal collet to fit all popular rifle and handgun case head sizes. Unlike most trimmers, the case in the TR-1400 turns against a stationary TiN (titanium nitride)-coated cutter. Featured accessories include six pilots, small and large primer pocket cleaners, and two neck-cleaning brushes that will handle 22- to 30-caliber cases. *(An optional 1/4-inch hex shaft adapter to permit powering with a cordless screwdriver is available.)*

In the SAECO line, Redding now has traditional bullet moulds available in calibers from 309 to 458. Weights range from 140 grains to 525 grains.

Ballistics Products Inc.

Ballistics Products advertises they have everything for shotgunners, and for the reloading of shotshells and slugs this Minnesota firm is well-stocked. There are more reloading manuals and guides for shotshell reloading available from this firm than anywhere else, and new this year is a Shotshell Loading Log. This log consists of a sectioned, organizational binder, with sections for shotguns, ammunition, performance evaluations, load data, and more. *(The ammunition portion provides space for listing the load source, loader adjustments, components required, performance notes, etc.)*

Roll crimping of shotshells is becoming somewhat popular again for special loads, and crimpers are not always readily located. BPI has them to cover every gauge from 8 to 28, and new is one for the .410-bore. Used in a drill press, with the shell held in a Hull Vise, it's easy to turn out perfect crimps, and roll crimps use less case mouth than folded crimps. *(The use of roll crimps allows a bit more space in the case for payload (shot) or powder.)* Another useful new BPI item is the Shotshell Hull I.D. Stamp Kit to mark reloads with the shot size contained. *(The ink is industrial-grade and will dry on metal, plastic, or paper hulls within a minute.)* Several shot size stamps are available from BBB to size 12, plus gauges, either as a kit, or as a single stamp. Why guess? Stamp 'em.

Plastic shotshell hulls, some brands more than others, have a strong crimp memory and, as a result, sometimes catch on the gas-seal of the wad column. A Spin Doctor Hull Conditioner or a Hull Shape-Up can correct this problem by smoothing out the previous crimps.

RUAG Ammotec USA Inc.

This company, distributor of Norma ammunition, powders, unprimed brass, and bullets, has a reloading manual that anyone using

Norma powders should use. It features chapters on ballistics, powders, etc., plus loads for 73 calibers—from the 222 Remington to 505 Gibbs. Naturally, it's for Norma by Norma. (Norma ammunition and unprimed cases are available in calibers not readily available elsewhere.)

Sinclair International

Sinclair now has new 20-caliber neck-turning and expander mandrels for their neck turning tool. Sinclair is also one of the few firms having heavy-duty polyethylene loading blocks to fit 50 BMG cartridges. An inch thick, these blocks have handles on the ends and will hold 30 BMG cartridges, or the same number of 20-gauge shotshells. Although not a new item, Sinclair has an excellent arbor press for those handloaders using hand dies.

Midway USA

Finding heavy 0.511-inch diameter lead bullets for handloading the 50 BMG cartridge is not always as simple as it may sound, nor is finding a suitable mould for casting your own. Midway has a Hoch custom single cavity nose-pour mould that will produce 650-grain 0.512-inch semi-spitzers that should be ideal. Colorado Shooter's Supply can also supply this mould, or can produce a tool room-quality custom design mould to order.

Forster Precision Products

Forster has new full-length loading dies, including the Bench Rest series, for the 204 Ruger, plus the 243 and 25 WSSM cartridges. The 325 WSM and 6.8mm Remington SPC may also be available by the time you read this. For those shooters who pull bullet on surplus military and reload with soft- or hollow-point bullets of equal or lesser weight, Forster has a new 8mm Superfast Bullet Puller. It will even pull the tough lacquered ones. *(Seven other calibers from 224 to 308 are also available.)* Although

not exactly handloading equipment, Forster has new complete 11-piece "Match" headspace gauge sets in 223, 308, and 30-06 sizes. *(Forster has a case trimmer to handle the 50 BMG case, but does not currently produce reloading dies for that cartridge.)*

Meacham T&H, Inc.

Meacham, the firm that specializes in reloading equipment for blackpowder shooters, has new bushing-type neck sizing dies for many blackpowder cartridges. The old 'buffalo hunters' used to reload in the evening, time permitting, for the next

Powder manufacturers keep handloading data up to date by issuing small updated guides and manuals, such as these 2005 editions, on a regular basis; the larger, more inclusive volumes appear on an irregular basis.

day's hunt. They didn't full-length resize every case every time, if ever. They used the same cases in the same rifle, and neck-sized enough to hold the cast bullet in place. You can do the same thing with Meacham dies.

Johnson Design Specialties

This company has a powder measure they claim can charge 100 cases in less than four minutes. Charging directly into the cartridge case, it is said to not cut powder and is simple to use. A powder scale should always be used to check the accuracy of the measure.

Rapine Bullet Moulds

This Pennsylvania company is said to have the world's largest selection of moulds, in a variety of styles, calibers and designs. Many of their current designs have been improved, and they also have a new graphite compound for use in mould preparation.

The Old Western Scrounger

Handloaders unable to find loading dies elsewhere for a specific caliber should check with OWS in Carson City, Nevada. This firm reloads for a number of obsolete cartridges, and handles reloading components and equipment. Available die sets and shellholders currently include such biggies as the 20mm Lahti, 20mm Hispana, and 42mm Hotchkiss. The firm even has dies for wildcats based on the 50 BMG cases, such as the 338/50MMG and 375/50BMG.

Shooting Chrony, Inc.

Handloaders need to use a chronograph if they are to derive the most from their handloads. That 'boom and kick' big bore may be moving faster than you think, or that 'crack and whistle' wildcat may not actually whistle. Check out those handloads on a chronograph. Shooting Chrony has ten models available, from a low of under a C-note to just over two C-notes. They are capable of measuring even low velocity projectiles, such as paintballs, air gun pellets, and arrows. Accessories available include remote controls, indoor light sources, IBM/PC interfaces, and even protective shields—just in case. Some models store a reading until the next shot, others store a series, and readings can even be printed out.

Handloaders should always avail themselves of the loading data provided by the various powder companies every year. The small booklets are complimentary and usually have data on new cartridges long before similar data appears in the larger loading manuals. Check your local dealer for a copy. ✷

THE GUNS OF EUROPE:
THE WALTHER P-22

"If I were allowed only one handgun, it would be this one."

by Raymond Caranta

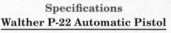

*A*s the American reader is probably aware, European sportsmen are limited in the number of modern cartridge handguns they are allowed to own.

However, in France, our situation is not so bad these days, as target shooters can own a maximum of twelve handguns: seven centerfire, and five rimfire pistols or revolvers. This total has evolved over the last forty years from a low of four, thanks to favorable government policies. In addition, a single handgun for personal protection is allowed for the average citizen. Auto-loading pistols must be smaller than 9mm; revolvers may be any caliber.

The skyrocketing cost of centerfire ammunition––33 cents a round for the cheapest 38 Special, and up to 77 cents a round for the big 44 Magnum–– makes it very expensive to shoot centerfire handguns. Thus, a good 22 Long Rifle multipurpose handgun, operating accurately and reliably with this inexpensive cartridge *(11 cents per round),* is a must for the European shooter.

Another important consideration: The yearly allowance for centerfire ammunition is 1,000 rounds per gun, while unlimited quantities of rimfire ammunition may be purchased by shooters. As a result, it is easily understood why reloading has become a national sport in France, and why the 22 Long Rifle is so popular. For this reason, since 1955, I have kept at least one 22 Long Rifle compact handgun in my battery. Since autoloading pistols are faster to clean than revolvers, and the Walther was the best at that time, I started with an all-steel PPK eight-shot pistol made by Manurhin.

The Basic Walther Line Of Pistols

The original line of modern medium-size police-type Walther pistols began in 1929 with the PP *(Polizei Pistole)* blowback model, available in 32 ACP *(8-shot),* 22 Long Rifle *(9/10-shot),* 380 ACP *(7-shot)* and, for a short time, 25 ACP. The PP is 6-3/4 inches long and weighs 24 oz. empty.

Specifications
Walther P-22 Automatic Pistol

Manufacturer: Carl Walther GmbH, Postfach 2740, Donnerfeld 2, D-5917 Arnsberg, Germany
Chambering: 22 Long Rifle
Magazine capacity: 10-shot
Length overall: 6.25"
Height: 4.72" (w/magazine extension)
Width: 1.18"
Empty weight: 17.14 oz.
Loaded weight: 18.21 oz.
Barrel length: 3.42" (plus 5" optional)
Sight radius: 5.2"
Rear sight: dovetailed on slide, adjustable for windage, with an 0.17" wide x .07" deep square notch between two 0.16" white dots on sides.
Front sight: interchangeable (3 heights). Patridge 0.14" wide, with 0.16" white dot.
SA trigger pull: 3.75 pounds, with slack.
DA trigger pull: 11 pounds.
Safety devices:
— Double action
— Non-decocking firing pin safety
— Magazine safety
— Hammer safety notch
— Inertia firing pin
Receiver: light alloy
Finish: dull black, nickel, green

The elegant streamlined contours and exquisite polishing of the earlier guns were lost, but we now had an entirely functional model at an unbelievably competitive price.

Top: The Manurhin-made Walther PP in 22 Long Rifle.
Middle: The German-made Walther PPK in 22 Long Rifle—even better finish!
Bottom: The Interarms stainless steel TPH in 22 Long Rifle.

Two years after, Walther released a more compact and lighter version of this model, the PPK *(Polizei Pistole Kriminal)* in the same calibers, with a magazine capacity reduced by one shot. The PPK weighs 21 oz. in its all-steel basic configuration, and 16.7 oz. with the light alloy receiver.

These pistols were manufactured in Zella-Mehlis *(Thuringia)* up to the end of World War II. The fixed-barrel PPK, featuring a selective double-action firing mechanism with external hammer and decocking safety, was unquestionably the most accurate of its type at the time. Smartly designed and carefully machined from the best steels, the pre-war PPs and PPKs displayed a splendid workmanship. Trigger pulls were a decent 4-5 pounds in single action and around 12-13 pounds in double action––quite stiff, but at the time considered a major design improvement.

In 1952 the French Manurhin company purchased the license for making these pistols from Fritz Walther *(not allowed to resume handgun production)*, and produced approximately one million of them––in 22 Long Rifle, 32 ACP and 380 ACP––up to 1986.

In 1969 a hybrid PPK/S *(made in both France and Germany)* was introduced, mostly for the American market.

Later, the PPK/S and PPK pistols were manufactured in the U.S.A. for Interarms from 1987 to 2002; subsequently Smith & Wesson partnered with Walther USA to resume and improve their production. Also in 2002, the PP was superseded in Germany by a similar but more economical PPK/E, chambered for the same three cartridges.

The Walther TPH

This was a bantam *(L 5.43"x H 3.7" x D 0.90")* and very light pocket pistol, chambered in 22 Long Rifle and 25 ACP only, with a 6-shot capacity, introduced in 1969 and made at the postwar Ulm factory up to 2001.

With its light alloy receiver, it weighed only 11.0 oz.

The action was similar to that of the PPK, but simplified, with the magazine release under the grip and a less sophisticated twin-notch hammer safety. Also, there was no slide hold-open device.

Trigger pull was a crisp two-pound let-off in single action and a smooth ten pounds in double action! Workmanship was faultless.

In the hands of an expert marksman, this light model displays an outstanding accuracy for short strings at 25 meters (about 28 yards). My best five-shot grouping at this standard range; is 1.65" diameter off-hand (Fiocchi "Maxac") against height 0.82" x width 1.73" for my 22 Long Rifle PP weighing 24 pounds.

However, for 30-round slow-fire scores at 25 meters, the TPH is out-performed––as expected––by both the bigger PPs and PPKs, as it lacks heft *(my record off-hand score on the ISU target featuring a 2-inch ten-ring is only 257/300, while both the PP and PPK scores are ten points higher)*.

The American TPH, made for Interarms from 1987 to 2002, features a stainless steel receiver *(empty weight 14.6 oz.)* and a stronger mainspring, which brings its single-action pull to 3 pounds and the double-action to about 11 pounds. The stainless steel construction is better than the German one for a defense gun, while the stronger spring improves ignition in double action, but the final pistol is less pleasant to shoot.

For summing up, both the 22 Long Rifle PPs and PPKs are beautiful and extremely accurate pistols with a 270/300 potential off-hand on the ISU target at 25 meters, and excellent firepower, thanks to their hold-open devices and respectable magazine capacity––but they are heavy and require an inside-the-waistband holster for concealed carry.

As far as the TPHs are concerned, they are amazingly accurate at 25 meters in slow fire, and faster than the bigger models at short range due to their lighter trigger pulls. They are extremely comfortable to carry in a pocket holster, but their six-shot capacity, without slide hold-open device, makes them less desirable.

Moreover, all these pistols are expensive, as their manufacture requires much precision machining. Therefore, a new and cheaper design was needed that combined the salient features of the earlier models: the Walther P-22.

The Walther P-22

The first time I saw a P-22 pistol at the IWA Show 2001 in Nuremberg, I was flabbergasted! This small pistol looked like a pure "Star War" product. Then, seeing the 259 Euro ($323) price tag, I thought: *"Cheap, indeed!"* and walked on by, thereby missing a major new item in the sport shooting category. Back home, however, when I was able to review its specification sheet, my interest was immediately aroused.

The elegant streamlined contours and exquisite polishing of the earlier guns were lost, but we now had an entirely functional model at an unbelievably competitive price.

Barrels are easily interchangeable, without play.

— The ambidextrous grip is provided with two spare backs for adapting it to the individual shooter.

— The ample ejection port improves reliability by providing greater clearance for fired cases.

— The simple ambidextrous safety does not decock the hammer, but it allows dry firing without risk of breaking the firing pin.

— A standard accessory rail is provided in front of the trigger guard for attaching a laser sight or tactical light.

— The trigger guard bow is square for two-hand shooting.

— The 0.17-inch wide rear sight is windage-adjustable.

— The 0.14-inch square front sight is interchangeable.

— The single-action pull is set at 3.7 pounds, instead of the 4 to 5.5 pounds of a standard PP or PPK; a distinct improvement.

— The double-action pull, just above 10 pounds, is practically as good as that of the German TPH, but with a much stronger hammer strike *(13 pounds on a typical PP or PPK)*.

— There is an external hold-open device on the left side of the receiver.

— Thanks to a light alloy receiver, the empty weight is only 17 oz., against 21 oz. for an all-steel PPK, and 24 oz. for a PP.

— The barrel muzzle is threaded for an excellent *(but expensive)* Stopson silencer, legal in France.

— Dimensions are similar to those of a 22 Long Rifle PPK fitted with a finger-rest extension magazine (*L* 6.25" x *H* 4.72" x *D* 1.18", against *L* 6.18" x *H* 4.6" x *D* 1").

— A 5-inch barrel is available.

Only two minor negative features were noted: The size of the slide rear section requires a holster for carrying the gun if a fast draw capability is required, and the unusual function of the trigger guard lower arm as the magazine release.

Shooting the Walther P-22

It became available in my hometown two years later and, while experienced shooters were reserved at the beginning, the P-22 was quickly accepted by younger people; soon, everybody liked it.

As a matter of fact, the strange-looking but very ergonomic grip is excellent for shooters with small or average hands. However, even with the largest back installed, the grip is quite small for big hands.

Also, in single action, the 2.16 inches between the grip back and trigger is shorter by 0.27-inch than that of the PP and PPK and 0.12-inch shorter than that of the bantam TPH! In double action, this distance of 2.63 inches on the P-22 is much better for fast shooting, falling between the PP and PPK's 2.71 inches and the TPH's 2.6 inches.

The balance is perfect for this kind of pistol. The sights are good, even better than those of a TPH!

The Manurhin-made Walther PPK in 22 Long Rifle. Note the mirror-polish side flats.

The only improvement possible is the fitting of a Hi Viz type front sight for fast target acquisition.

The accuracy potential is very similar to that of the PPs and PPKs, with 30-round offhand groups of 6 inches, and thus a potential score of 270/300 on the ISU P-50 target. My typical 10-round groups under the same conditions are in the 4 inch range *(when I shoot well...)*.

With good ammunition, the reliability is perfect. Even with powerful high-velocity rounds, the 5.2/5.6 fps recoil velocity is mild, just above that of the PPK.

Why the Walther P-22?

In Europe, at least, it is the most cost-effective pistol in its class, highly accurate and reliable, pleasant to shoot, and easy to maintain.

It is a bold, provocative and original design!

Of course, the 22 Long Rifle cartridge is far from being ideal for defense, but it can be legitimately expected that such a gun will never be fired in anger during an owner's life*. Instead, it will be shot recreationally once or twice a week for many, many years, if owned by somebody who likes the shooting game.

In any event, we are talking about a modern 10-shot light double-action pistol more perfected than its competition, and at a better price. What else can we ask?

A left-side view of the basic Walther P-22 in DA shooting configuration.

---

* In France (60 million inhabitants) our 200,000 gendarmes, police and custom officers fired, during calendar year 2003, 709 service rounds in about 100 gunfights, according to the latest available statistics.

AMMUNITION, BALLISTICS & COMPONENTS

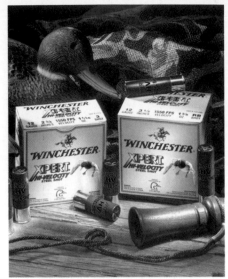

by Holt Bodinson

It's been an active year for acquisitions and consolidations. Western Powder buys Accurate Arms. American Ammunition acquires Triton, and Powerbelt purchases West Coast Bullets.

We needed some new cartridges and we got them. Winchester fielded its "stomper," the 325 WSM while S&W teamed up with Cor-Bon to roll out its "stomper," the 460 S&W. For shooters who don't quite need a "stomper," Remington civilized the mild-mannered 6.8mm Remington.

Speaking about new cartridges, keep an eye on NATEC's polymer-cased 223 and 308 ammunition. There may be a manufacturing revolution in the making.

Green is in. Lead-free bullets and primers continue to make inroads in every major line. Among the more interesting developments was Bismuth's introduction of Bismuth-core 55-grain/223 bullets.

Heavier-than-lead, non-toxic shot is hot. Federal introduced "Heavyshot" while Winchester fielded "Xtended Range High Density" shot. Meanwhile Hevi-Shot introduced "Hevi-Steel" as a lower cost alternative to its original product.

Graf & Sons, teamed with Hornady, is giving the old warhorses a new lease on life with fresh components and loaded ammunition for the 6.5 Carcano, 6.5 Jap, 7.5 Swiss, 7.65 Argentine, 7.7 Jap, 8x56 Hungarian, 9mm Steyr and 455 Webley. For those who own those great old quality Model 99 Savages in 303 Savage, Huntington has arranged with Norma to make a special run of the brass.

Finally, Federal has been tinkering with the internals of shotshells and has commercialized some great design breakthroughs with their new "Flight control" wad and "TruBall" smoothbore slug.

It's been an innovative year indeed in the ammunition, ballistics and components business.

Accurate Arms Company

New owner. Western Powders Company, the largest master distributor of reloading powders in North America and originator of the Ramshot powders, has purchased Accurate Arms and moved it to its home base, Miles City, Montana. Western says the existing line of Accurate Arms powders will be maintained with no disruption of service or availability. www.accuratepowder.com

Aguila

No new products but a great new color catalog this year that is full of photographs and ballistic data. Aguila's 22 rimfire line continues to be outstanding with both the heaviest loading (60 grains) and the highest velocity (1700 fps) loading. www.aguilaammo.com

Alliant

With ten shotgun powders, three pistol powders and six rifle powders in the line, look for a new target shotshell powder from Alliant around mid-year. Until then, it's a corporate secret! www.alliantpowder.com

Ballistic Products

When it comes to shotshell reloading components, Ballistic Products is the place to shop. In stock at all times are all the well-known brands of commercial components, plus Ballistic Products' own designs and the best of the European component lines. To simplify the reloading process, they are even pre-packaging components with instructions for assembling "Master" steel duck/goose, pheasant, sporting clays, and 20-gauge field loads. You just have to add the shot and powder. There's a new slug for rifled bores load this year. The name is LBC BluForce and it's a sabot/slug system that features their hardened 0.650-inch diameter Dangerous Game slug mated with a ribbed, breakaway sabot designed for barrels with a 0.750-inch land diameter. By all means, send for their fascinating catalog. www.ballisticproducts.com

Barnes

Building on the phenomenal success they have had with the performance, accuracy and shooter acceptance of the "Triple-Shock" X-bullet, Barnes is adding fourteen new bullets to the line: a 53-grain 224; 120-grain 6.5mm; 110-grain 6.8mm; 150-grain 270; 120-grain 7mm; 130-grain 308; 180-grain 8mm (325 WSM); 210-grain 338; 225-grain 358; 270-grain 375; 350 and 400-grain 416; and 450- and 500-grain 458. Under the banner of "Barnes Banded Solids," the folks from Utah have carried their grooves over to their dangerous game bullet line with the introduction a 270- and 300-grain 375; 350 and 400-grain 416; and 450- and 500-grain 458. And if that looks like big medicine, there's a new 750-grain 577 Nitro pill in the Coated X-Bullet (XLC) series. Anticipating the unveiling of the 460 S&W, Barnes is producing a new 200-grain 460 (*actually 0.451"*) spitzer boattail bullet in the XPB line. What's interesting is the adoption of the Barnes line by many of the major ammunition makes such as Federal, Cor-Bon, Black Hills, Sako and Sellier & Bellot. "Unleaded" may be the future! www.barnesbullets.com

Berger Bullets

It's catch-up time this year with the focus being the production of Berger's five new 20-caliber pills weighing from 30 to 50 grains. www.bergerbullets.com

Barnes is applying its Triple-Shock technology to a line of big-bore solids carrying the name "Barnes Banded Solids."

Bismuth Cartridge Co.

Bismuth-core 223-caliber varmint bullets? They're here. Bismuth is entering the jacketed rifle bullet world with a 55-grain hollowpoint. Because of their length-to-weight ratio, the new Bismuth bullets require a minimum twist of 1:10. The NATO 1:7 twist is even better. Along the same environmentally friendly lines is a new series of 21-gram 12-, 20-, and 28-gauge shells featuring Eley's "Kleena-Wad" and #8 shot. The Kleena-Wad is made from natural fibers, keeps the barrel virtually residue free, and can be shot in environmentally sensitive areas because it rapidly decomposes. A side benefit of the Bismuth 21-gram load is that it contains the same pellet count as a lead 24-gram loading. Velocity of the 12-gauge, 21-gram load is 1450 fps. www.bismuth-notox.com

Black Hills Ammunition

The Black Hills are famous for gold, and the Black Hills Gold line is famous for being one of the greatest premium hunting ammunition lines ever assembled. Its even better this year with the addition of Nosler AccuBond bullets in the 308, 30-'06, 270 WSM, 300 WSM, 300 WM and 7mm Remington Magnum. Famous for their match-grade ammunition,

Black Hills has matched the 175-grain Sierra MatchKing to the 300 WSM at 2950 fps which should keep the paper punchers and tactical snipers in clover. And speaking of match ammunition, Black Hills has just been awarded the U.S. Army contract for 9mm, 45 ACP and 223 match ammo and continues to furnish the USMC Rifle Team with 77-grain molycoated MatchKing loads. You can buy the exact match load from Black Hills, so be sure to see their complete catalog at www.black-hills.com

Calhoon

While James Calhoon makes his proprietary double hollowpoint, "Slick Silver" varmint bullets in 20- and 22-caliber, his first love remains the 19-caliber. Now there are three Calhoon 19-caliber cartridges: the 19 Calhoon (Hornet) at 3600 fps; the 19-223 at 4000 + fps, and the brand new 19 Badger at 3750 fps. Calhoon can provide complete custom conversions based on the CZ rifle models or re-barrel kits for your own gun. www.jamescalhoon.com

CCI

You've heard of slam-fires occurring in semi-automatic military-style rifles when using ammunition primed with a rather sensitive primer. Or even look at the tiny firing pin sign on chambered, but

Black Hills Ammunition upgrades its premium "Gold" line even further with the addition of AccuBond bullets.

not fired, rounds from firearms like the AR15, AK, and SKS. CCI has a solution—military spec primers that combine a tougher primer cup with a magnum primer charge for military ball powders. Called CCI "Arsenal" primers, the Small and Large Rifle primers use the same reloading data as CCI's 250 and 450 primers and should be on your dealer's shelves as you read this. CCI just improved the 17 HMR with a new 20-grain "GamePoint" bullet that mushrooms just like a big game bullet. The idea is to save game meat and predator hides. The muzzle velocity of the new load is 2375 fps, and it is said to deliver sub-MOA levels of accuracy. www.cci-ammunition.com

Cor-Bon

The Cor-Bon/Smith & Wesson team has done it again. Last year it was the development of the 500 S&W Magnum. This year it's the 460 S&W Magnum with a 200-grain bullet at 2300 fps. If the full-powered 500 S&W is a bit much, Cor-Bon has developed a light target load featuring a 350-grain FMJ at 1,200 fps. Child's play! Expanding their DPX (Deep Penetrating X) line utilizing proprietary Barnes X and Triple Shock bullets, Cor-Bon has added

a new "Hunter" line that includes a variety of handgun and rifle calibers. The light-kicking "Pow'Rball" line offered under the Glaser label has been enhanced with a 165-grain bullet at 1075 fps for the increasingly popular 45 GAP, and oh, yes, the 45 GAP gets a 145-grain Glaser Safety Slug at 1325 fps, too. www.corbon.com

Dakota Arms

Dakota Arms has teamed up with Todd Kindler, founding editor of the *Small Caliber News*, to chamber Kindler's wildcats, the Tac 20, 17 Tactical, 17 VarTag, 20 VarTag, and 22 VarTag. Kindler's 17 and 20 Classics have been renamed the 17 and 20 Dakotas. www.dakotaarms.com

Federal

This is the year for Fusion bullets, super-dense shot, a new concentrator wad, a smoothbore slug that shoots like a sabot round, and some speedy upland loads. Federal's new Fusion rifle bullet is a boattail bonded-core design in which the jacket is plated to the core—plus it's priced at the level of conventional jacketed bullets. Watch for a variety of grain weights in all the popular calibers from 243 Winchester to 300 WSM.

"Heavyshot" is Federal's response to the success of Hevi-Shot. Heavyshot is remarkable stuff. It is 25 percent more dense than Hevi-Shot, 37 percent more dense than lead, and the pellets of this soft tungsten-iron shot are completely round, uniform and consistently sized. It will first appear in Federal's 12-gauge MagnumShok turkey loads featuring a new "Flightcontrol" wad that stays with the shot column longer, separates from it more smoothly, and consequently delivers more highly concentrated patterns. Watch for the Flightcontrol wad in waterfowl loads this year.

Recent slug designs have been focused on sabots and rifled shotgun bores leaving the old smoothbore slug gun to whither on the vine. No longer! Federal has come up with a conventional Foster-type slug that is mated to its driving wad by a plastic ball. Called TruBall, the slug riding on a ball is centered in the wad and the bore. Shooting an open-sighted 18-inch smoothbore slug barrel in a Remington 870, I have achieved 3 1/4 - 3 3/4-inch three-shot groups at 100 yards with the new TruBall ammunition. That's sensational!

Finally, Federal is introducing this year a number of faster upland game loads (1350-1500 fps) for those of us who are a bit slow in getting off a shot at a cackling rooster or a blur of a grouse. www.federalcartridge.com

Fiocchi

"Super Crusher" is a great name for Fiocchi's latest 12-gauge target load consisting of 1 ounce of hi-antimony lead #7.5 and 8 shot at 1400 fps. And then there's the "Paper Crusher"—a paper-hulled version of the same load but a hundred feet slower at 1300 fps.

Fiocchi's 40 S&W offerings have been updated with a 165-grain JHP at 1100 fps and a 165-grain truncated cone encapsulated base projectile at 1140 fps. www.fiocchiusa.com

Garrett Cartridges

If you're pursuing big or dangerous game with a 45-70, you can't do any better than using one of Randy Garrett's superior loads. Two, new

+ P loadings for modern 45-70 rifles are a 500-grain Speer AGS tungsten core solid at 1,530 fps and a 500-grain Woodleigh Weld-Core at 1600. Either one is capable of penetrating a Cape buffalo from stem-to-stern. www.garrettcartridges.com

Goex

Goex is back in the non-corrosive, replica blackpowder business with the introduction of "Pinnacle Black Powder" in FFG and FFFG. We've missed the old Clear Shot brand. Pinnacle looks like blackpowder, shoots consistently with little fouling build up and offers an indefinite shelf life. A new granulation called "Cowboy Action Cartridges" in Goex's standard blackpowder line is designed specifically for 40-grain loads or less. Speaking about cowboy cartridges, GOEX is now marketing a complete line of blackpowder loaded, SPG lubed, Black Dawge cartridges for rifle, pistol and scatterguns. Let the boom begin. www.goexpowder.com

Graf & Sons

There's no excuse for not shooting those old surplus rifles of any nationality. Loaded for them by Hornady, Graf now offers 6.5 Jap, 6.5 Carcano, 7.5 Swiss, 7.65 Argentine, 7.7 Jap, 8x56 Hungarian, 9mm Steyr and 455 Webley ammunition at attractive prices, plus special Hornady

Hodgdon is introducing its "short cut" technology to the IMR powder line.

runs of the component bullets to reload those calibers. Based on my testing, this is premium quality ammunition. Graf is also importing the Privi Partizan brand of ammo in 6.5 Carcano, 7.5 French, 7.5 Swiss and 7.65 Argentine at sensational prices. Stock up while you can. www.grafs.com

Hevi-Shot

Hevi-Shot introduces Hevi-Steel that is 16-20 percent heavier than premium steel shot. Take a 3-inch 12-gauge hull, fill it with 1-1/8 oz. of Hevi-Steel, send it off at 1550 fps and you have Hevi-Steel, aka "Our Fast Little Brother." Two other innovations this year are Hevi-Shot 13, the heaviest shot made to date, and standard 12g/cc Hevi-Shot in the form of T-sized shot for a line of 12-gauge predator shells, named appropriately, "Dead Coyote." www.hevishot.com

Hodgdon Powder

After acquiring the IMR Powder Company last year, Hodgdon is refining the IMR line. The first improvement, which will prove to be a boon for handloaders, is a "super short-cut" version of IMR7828. Grains of the new IMR7828SSC are 35 percent shorter than the older cut length, yield the same burn rate, and run through a powder measure as slick as ball powder. With the reduced size of the grains, IMR7828SSC also yields 4 percent more case capacity, which can be an asset when compressed charges are called for. Great new packaging for Triple Seven 50-caliber/50-grain pellets. They're now offered in a blister pack that contains four clear plastic tubes with six pellets in each tube. Perfect for the hunt. Look for a new complimentary "IMR Smokeless Powder Guide" with updated data for the most recent cartridge introductions like the 204 Ruger and 25 WSSM. www.hodgdon.com

Hevi-Shot's new predator loading for the 12-gauge features T shot.

Hornady's new 300-grain SST bullet churns up 2,050 fps in the 2 3/4"/12-gauge.

Hornady

Smith & Wesson's new 460 Magnum is getting a special 200-grain SST loading from Hornady. The polymer-tipped spitzer SST bullet is loaded to a velocity of 2250 fps, and when sighted-in 3 inches high at 100 yards, drops only 3.8 inches at 200 yards. Flat indeed! The SST bullet design is being carried over to Hornady's shotgun slug line as well with an initial 12-gauge offering with a muzzle velocity of 2050 fps. Look for lots of new Hornady component brass in all of the popular rifle and handgun calibers, plus hard-to-find numbers like 6.5-284, 376 Steyr, 405 Winchester, 458 Lott, and 475 Linebaugh. If you pursue big game, there are three new InterBond (bonded softpoint) bullets being offered this year: 375-caliber/ 300-grain; 416-caliber/400-grain; and a 45-caliber/500-grain. Lots of new rifle, pistol and shotgun additions to Hornady's "TAP" personal defense ammunition line. See them at www.hornady.com.

Huntington

Need some 303 Savage cases? Huntington just had Norma make a run. Here's the one-stop source for common and oddball components for any cartridge you can imagine reloading plus all the RCBS products and parts. Where can you find a complete inventory of Hornebar, Hirtenberger, Norma, Sako, RWS, Walter Gehmann and Dakota cases? Huntington's, of course, and the same can be said for bullets. Don't miss their extensive reference catalog at www.huntington.com

Lapua

Just when you think the 22 Long Rifle can't be improved, it is. Lapua has developed a special 22 Long Rifle bullet design that offers many of the qualities of their coated centerfire bullet line. Named "Signum," the form of the projectile and its lubrication provide decreased bore friction and bullet form integrity. See it at www.lapua.com

Liberty Shooting Supplies

Earlier this year, I was looking for an unplated lead bullet for the 8mm Nambu. Remembering that Liberty Shooting Supplies casts the most extensive array of bullet designs I know of, I went searching there and found exactly what I was looking for. If you enjoy shooting quality cast bullets, sized and lubricated to your specifications, take a look at their catalog. Liberty will also cast from your moulds. www.libertyshootingsupplies.com

Magtech

Magtech's "First Defense" line of 100-percent copper hollowpoint ammunition for law enforcement and personal defense is now available in 38 Special, 357 Magnum and 380 Auto— plus the same bullet technology has been carried over to a new "Hunting" line featuring the larger handgun calibers. For the cost-conscious plinkers, Magtech is offering its most popular handgun calibers in 250-round boxes. www.magtechammunition.com

Meister Bullets

This well-known brand of hard cast bullets is expanding this year to include a 167-grain 30-30 Winchester; 170-grain 32-40 Winchester and 330-grain 500 S&W bullets. www.meisterbullets.com

NATEC

Building on their success with 223 polymer-cased ammunition, NATEC is bringing the technology to bear on the 308 Winchester which will be loaded with a 144-grain tracer, 150-grain FMJBT and Sierra GameKing, and a 168-grain Sierra MatchKing. The claimed benefits for the polymer-cased ammo are reduced weight (*35 percent in the case of the 308 Winchester*) and, because of its insulating qualities, improved propellant combustion and reduced heat transference to the firearm. www.natec-us.com

Norma

If we gave awards for the most beautiful and pro-hunting catalog in the industry, Norma would be this year's winner hands down. Get it. It's a collector's item. Three new cartridges have been added to the line this year: 270 WSM, 7mm-08 Remington and the 470 Nitro Express. Norma's bonded-core Oryx bullet is now being loaded in an expanded list of big-game calibers. Here's something unique, a ballistics software program that can be accessed through the Norma website at www.norma.cc.

Northern Precision

I suspect those long, northern winters in upstate New York give Northern Precision the time to invent the most interesting array of 358, 416-, 429-, 452, and 458-caliber bullets in the industry. Just consider a 200-grain varmint bullet for the 416 Remington for a moment. Northern makes it. This year it's bonded-core spitzers for the 454 Casull and 250-grain bonded-core flat-points for the 356 Winchester. Call for their catalog at (315) 493-1711.

Nosler

This past hunting season, my wife and I shot Nosler AccuBonds exclusively in her 308 Winchester and my 300 WSM. The accuracy and performance of this bonded-core bullet has to be experienced to be appreciated. New in the AccuBond line this year are a 110-grain/257-caliber; 150-grain/30-caliber; 200-grain/8mm (*loaded in the 325 WSM*) and 180-grain/338-caliber. Nosler is also getting into the brass and ammunition businesses. Nosler brass, which is weight-sorted to one-half a grain, deburred and chamfered, is now available for the 223 Remington, 22-250 Remington, 243 Winchester,

Loaded with their own bullets and premium quality brass, Nosler now offers a proprietary line of exacting hunting ammunition.

270 Winchester, 7mm Remington Magnum, 308 Winchester, 30-'06 and 300 Winchester Magnum. The biggest news is that Nosler is offering its own line of precision ammunition direct to the consumer using a variety of components for decimal and metric calibers ranging from 218 Bee to 416 Rigby. www.nosler.com

Old Western Scrounger

When Dangerous Dave states that "we carry the largest and finest inventory of obsolete ammunition, bar-none," you had better believe it. Do you need 20mm Vulcan brass and a press big enough to load it? Or 11mm Mannlicher clips? How about 577 Snyder, 22 Remington Jet, 32 Winchester Self-Loader, 33 Winchester, 9x56 Mannlicher/Schoenauer, 43 Mauser, or 50-140 Sharps ammunition supplied in the most picturesque boxes ever created? The Old Western Scrounger is the place to go. www.ows-ammunition.com

PMC

A big push is on at PMC to bring new calibers into its environmentally friendly PMC Green line featuring frangible copper-polymer bullets and primers made without any heavy metal compounds. Added this year are a 100-grain loading for the 30-'06 and a 77-grain loading for the 380 Auto. The bullets are so frangible they disintegrate harmlessly when fired into steel plate only 3 inches from the muzzle. Over in the rimfire line are an ultra-quiet 22 Super Subsonic featuring a 20-grain bullet at 500 fps, a high-speed 22 Short, and the 17PMC outfitted with a 20-grain bullet at 1800 fps. www.pmcammo.com

Powerbelt

Big news! Powerbelt buys West Coast Bullets and will continue and expand the extensive West Coast cast line under the named "Accura." A few of the new introductions will be hollowpoints and new coatings on top of the standard copper-clad coating. The newer coatings, called "Black Pearl" and "Sterling," permit the use of the cast bullets in Glocks, yielding higher velocities, lower pressures and better accuracy. Also being introduced is a new 40- and 45-caliber frangible line featuring sintered, copper-plated bullets. Powerbelt is expanding its highly popular copper-clad muzzleloading bullet line, that features an attached plastic gas seal, with the introduction of a 45-caliber 175-grain and a 50-caliber 223-grain. Both bullets feature a poly tip named the "Acrotip." www.powerbeltbullets.com

Remington

Tactical goes practical with the rollout of the 6.8mm Remington (Special Purpose Cartridge) and a Model 7 to shoot it in. If it's as successful as Remington's domestication of the 5.56mm in the guise of the 223 Remington, it will be successful indeed. The sporting load consists of a 115-grain PSP Core-Lokt Ultra Bonded bullet at 2775 fps, just right for lightweight rifles and recoil-sensitive shooters. The successful Managed-Recoil line has been extended with a 125-grain PSP Core-Lokt at 2660 fps in the 308 Winchester and a 150-grain loading at 2650 in the 300 Winchester Magnum. There's even a new Premier STS Low-Recoil 12-gauge loading of 1-1/8 oz. of #9s for those extended shoot-offs at Skeet.

A revolutionary new muzzleloading battery-cup primer for in-line and break-action rifles is making its debut. Remington has designed a unique nickel-plated Kleanbore primer that dramatically reduces chamber fouling, permitting more shots to be fired before the need to clean the old smokepole.

The super accurate, green-tipped Premier AccuTip bullet lines keep growing with the introduction of 32- and 40-grain bullets for the 204 Ruger; a 140-grain in the 280 Remington; a 35-grain pill for the 22 Hornet; and a 17-grain green tip for the wee 17 MACH2.

Keeping shooting affordable, Big Green is expanding its UMC lines with a 50-grain JHPs at 3410 fps in the 223 Remington and 3800 fps in the 22-250 Remington, as well as a 230-grain

Remington's new 6.8mm SPC cartridge is ideally matched to lightweight rifles and light big game.

JHP and FMJ at 835 fps in the new 45 GAP. Responding to slug gun hunters who favor a nice light rifled 20-gauge gun, Remington is introducing a 1 oz. Buckhammer slug at 1550 fps.

In shotshells, the old "Heavy Game" load label for shotshells has been replaced by "Pheasant Loads," and at the top of the list is the Nitro Pheasant line featuring copper-plated, 4-percent antimony shot in loads like 1 3/8 oz. of #4, 5, 6 at 1300 fps in the 2 3/4-inch 12 gauge and 1-1/4 oz. of #5, 6 in the 3-inch 20 gauge. To compete with the imports, a new Gun Club line of 12- and 20-gauge shells in #7-1/2, 8, 9 has been created.

Big Green is pushing its reloading components line. Watch for some snappy-looking plastic bags of Remington brass and bullets on your dealer's shelves.

Sierra Bullets

The bulletsmiths are right on top of the latest component market with the addition of 32- and 39-grain BlitzKings for the hot new 20-caliber cartridges—plus there's a super sleek 175-grain 7mm MatchKing that is making its appearance this year. That reminds me, if you haven't tried the 175-grain 308 MatchKing with a BC higher than that of the traditional 180-grain MatchKing, you've been missing out on one of the finest 30-caliber match bullets ever fielded. www.sierrabullets.com

Speer

Building on their successful introduction last year of a 38 Special Gold Dot HP loading for snubbies, Speer has expanded this much-needed concept with loads designed specifically for the short-barreled 9mm, 357 Magnum, 40 S&W, 44 Remington Magnum and 45 Auto. Guess what the line is called? "Short Barrel," of course! www.speer-bullets.com

SSK

JD Jones has finally outdone himself with the 620 JDJ. The new round for the T/C Encore is based on a shortened and fire-formed 577 Nitro case expanded to take a 600 Nitro bullet. JD is getting 1000 fps with a 1000-grain bullet from an Encore with a 12-inch barrel. T-Rex-grade ammunition! www.sskindustries.com

Triton

Whatever happened to Triton? It has been revived by American Ammunition, which recently acquired Triton's assets. Quik-Shok 9mm, 40 S&W and 45 ACP ammunition is once again available featuring the pre-stressed Quik-Shok core bullet that splits into three pieces upon impact. Triton Hi-Vel ammunition may be reintroduced by year's end. www.a-merc.com

Ultramax

Producing quality reloaded ammunition at great savings to the consumer, Ultramax has added three new loadings for the 500 S&W this year. The Ultramax line now includes rifle, pistol and cowboy loadings. www.ultramaxammunition.com

Vihtavuori and Lapua

Vihtavuori and Lapua have expanded their website this year. See their products at www.vihtavuori-lapua.com.

Western Powders

Western Powders buys Accurate Arms! See the comments under Accurate Arms. www.westernpowders.com

Winchester Ammunition

Winchester needed a "thumper" in their short magnum line for game like elk, moose and bear. This year they have it, the 325 WSM. A 325? Actually, it's an 8mm or 323 that combines the velocity of the 300 WSM with the punch of the 338 Winchester Magnum. Two new bullets have been designed for the 325 WSM—a 200-grain AccuBond CT loaded to 2950 fps in the Supreme line and a 220-grain Power-Point at 2840 fps that's been added to the Super-X line. A sleek 180-grain Ballistic Silvertip at 3060 fps fills out the Supreme series for lighter big game. Teamed with super-short-action Winchester Model 70s and Browning A-Bolts, the 325 WSSM is sure to generate a lot of excitement in the big-game hunting field. I've used it on Texas Nilgai, and it's not unusual to break both shoulders of the big bulls with the 200-grain AccuBond. That's performance! Nosler's AccuBond bullet is one of the most consistently accurate bullets ever made.

Given a Lubalox coating by Winchester, it is called an AccuBond CT and this year Winchester is adding a 110-grain loading to the 25-06 and 25 WSSM; and a 140-grain loading to the 7 WSM and 7mm Remington Magnum.

The ever popular 300 WSM is getting some added versatility as well with two new loadings: a 165-grain Fail Safe at 3125 fps and a 150-grain Power-Point at 3250 fps. For the varmint hunting clan, Big Red is adding the 17 HMR and the 204 Ruger to its cartridge offerings while elevating the 22-250 to light big status with the addition of a 64-grain Power-Point loading at 3500 fps.

The powerful 500 S&W is getting quite a play this year, so Winchester will be offering a 400-grain Platinum Tip HP at 1800 fps to the Supreme line for bone-crunching effectiveness.

Winchester continues to upgrade its 500 S&W offerings this year with a Platinum Tip.

Speaking about bone crunching, Winchester's 1 oz. Foster-type 12-gauge Power-Point rifled slug has been redesigned for improved accuracy and given a velocity of 1700 fps. Turkey hunters will be happy with the introduction of Xtended Range High Density shot. That's perfectly round shot that's 10 percent heavier than lead producing denser patterns and higher pellet energy and penetration. The new shot in sizes #5 and #6 will be loaded in the 3 1/2-, 3- and 2 3/4-inch 12-gauge cases. A new 3-inch 20-gauge turkey load consisting of 1-5/16 oz. of #4, #5, #6 lead shot at 1200 fps joins the Supreme High Velocity Turkey line, and it should be a dilly. For those tough old fall roosters, Winchester is pumping up the 3-inch 20 gauge with 1-1/4 oz. of copper-plated #4, #5 and #6 at a sizzling 1250 fps in its Super Pheasant line.

The little .410 is receiving some welcome attention this year with a Super Sport AA sporting clays load consisting of 1/2 oz. of #7-1/2 at 1300 fps; a 3/4 oz. Super-X loading of #4, #6 and #7-1/2 at 1100 fps in the 3-inch case; and a full 1/4 oz. Super-X rifled slug for the 3-inch hull at a sizzling 1800 fps.

Speaking about "sizzling," the full 12-gauge Supreme High-Velocity Buckshot line will be receiving hard copper-plated OO buck roaring out at 1450 fps this year. Keeping the cost of steel shot shells in line, Winchester is introducing a 7/8 oz. loading of #2 and #4 at 1500 fps for the 3-inch 20 gauge in its economical Xpert Steel lineup. It's been a busy year at Winchester Ammunition! www.winchester.com

AVERAGE CENTERFIRE RIFLE CARTRIDGE BALLISTICS AND PRICES

Many manufacturers do not supply suggested retail prices. Others did not get their pricing to us before press time. All pricing can vary dependent on the exact brand and style of ammo selected and/or the retail outlet from which you make your purchase. Pricing has been rounded to the nearest dollar and represents our best estimate of average pricing. An * after the cartridge means these loads are available with Nosler Partition or Swift A-Frame bullets. Listed pricing may or may not reflect this bullet type. ** = these are packed 50 to box, all others are 20 to box. Wea. Mag.= Weatherby Magnum. Spfd. = Springfield. A-A-Sq. = A-Square. N.E.=Nitro Express.

Cartridge	Bullet Wgt. Grs.	VELOCITY (fps)					ENERGY (ft. lbs.)					TRAJ. (in.)				Est. Price/ box
		Muzzle	100 yds.	200 yds.	300 yds.	400 yds.	Muzzle	100 yds.	200 yds.	300 yds.	400 yds.	100 yds.	200 yds.	300 yds.	400 yds.	
17, 22																
17 Remington	25	4040	3284	2644	2086	1606	906	599	388	242	143	+2.0	+1.7	-4.0	-17.0	$17
204 Ruger	32	4225	3632	3114	2652	2234	1268	937	689	500	355	.6	0.0	-4.2	-13.4	NA
204 Ruger	40	3900	3451	3046	2677	2336	1351	1058	824	636	485	.7	0.0	-4.5	-13.9	NA
221 Fireball	50	2800	2137	1580	1180	988	870	507	277	155	109	+0.0	-7.0	-28.0	0.0	$14
22 Hornet	34	3050	2132	1415	1017	852	700	343	151	78	55	+0.0	-6.6	-15.5	-29.9	NA
22 Hornet	35	3100	2278	1601	1135	929	747	403	199	100	67	+2.75	0.0	-16.9	-60.4	NA
22 Hornet	45	2690	2042	1502	1128	948	723	417	225	127	90	+0.0	-7.7	-31.0	0.0	$27**
218 Bee	46	2760	2102	1550	1155	961	788	451	245	136	94	+0.0	-7.2	-29.0	0.0	$16**
222 Remington	40	3600	3117	2673	2269	1911	1151	863	634	457	324	+1.07	0.0	-6.13	-18.9	NA
222 Remington	50	3140	2602	2123	1700	1350	1094	752	500	321	202	+2.0	-0.4	-11.0	-33.0	$11
222 Remington	55	3020	2562	2147	1773	1451	1114	801	563	384	257	+2.0	-0.4	-11.0	-33.0	$12
22 PPC	52	3400	2930	2510	2130	NA	1335	990	730	525	NA	+2.0	1.4	-5.0	0.0	NA
223 Remington	40	3650	3010	2450	1950	1530	1185	805	535	340	265	+2.0	+1.0	-6.0	-22.0	$14
223 Remington	40	3800	3305	2845	2424	2044	1282	970	719	522	371	0.84	0.0	-5.34	-16.6	NA
223 Remington	50	3300	2874	2484	2130	1809	1209	917	685	504	363	1.37	0.0	-7.05	-21.8	NA
223 Remington	52/53	3330	2882	2477	2100	1770	1305	978	722	522	369	+2.0	+0.6	-6.5	-21.5	$14
223 Remington	55	3240	2748	2305	1906	1556	1282	922	649	444	296	+2.0	-0.2	-9.0	-27.0	$12
223 Remington	60	3100	2712	2355	2026	1726	1280	979	739	547	397	+2.0	-0.2	-8.0	-24.7	$16
223 Remington	64	3020	2621	2256	1920	1619	1296	977	723	524	373	+2.0	-0.2	-9.3	-23.0	$14
223 Remington	69	3000	2720	2460	2210	1980	1380	1135	925	750	600	+2.0	+0.8	-5.8	-17.5	$15
223 Remington	75	2790	2554	2330	2119	1926	1296	1086	904	747	617	2.37	0.0	-8.75	-25.1	NA
223 Remington	77	2750	2584	2354	2169	1992	1293	1110	948	804	679	1.93	0.0	-8.2	-23.8	NA
223 WSSM	55	3850	3438	3064	2721	2402	1810	1444	1147	904	704	0.7	0.0	-4.4	-13.6	NA
223 WSSM	64	3600	3144	2732	2356	2011	1841	1404	1061	789	574	1.0	0.0	-5.7	-17.7	NA
222 Rem. Mag.	55	3240	2748	2305	1906	1556	1282	922	649	444	296	+2.0	-0.2	-9.0	-27.0	$14
225 Winchester	55	3570	3066	2616	2208	1838	1556	1148	836	595	412	+2.0	+1.0	-5.0	-20.0	$19
224 Wea. Mag.	55	3650	3192	2780	2403	2057	1627	1244	943	705	516	+2.0	+1.2	-4.0	-17.0	$32
22-250 Rem.	40	4000	3320	2720	2200	1740	1420	980	660	430	265	+2.0	+1.8	-3.0	-16.0	$14
22-250 Rem.	50	3725	3264	2641	2455	2103	1540	1183	896	669	491	0.89	0.0	-5.23	-16.3	NA
22-250 Rem.	52/55	3680	3137	2656	2222	1832	1654	1201	861	603	410	+2.0	+1.3	-4.0	-17.0	$13
22-250 Rem.	60	3600	3195	2826	2485	2169	1727	1360	1064	823	627	+2.0	+2.0	-2.4	-12.3	$19
220 Swift	40	4200	3678	3190	2739	2329	1566	1201	904	666	482	+0.51	0.0	-4.0	-12.9	NA
220 Swift	50	3780	3158	2617	2135	1710	1586	1107	760	506	325	+2.0	+1.4	-4.4	-17.9	$20
220 Swift	50	3850	3396	2970	2576	2215	1645	1280	979	736	545	0.74	0.0	-4.84	-15.1	NA
220 Swift	55	3800	3370	2990	2630	2310	1765	1300	1090	850	650	0.8	0.0	-4.7	-14.4	NA
220 Swift	55	3650	3194	2772	2384	2035	1627	1246	939	694	506	+2.0	+2.0	2.6	-13.4	$19
220 Swift	60	3600	3199	2824	2475	2156	1727	1364	1063	816	619	+2.0	+1.6	-4.1	-13.1	$19
22 Savage H.P.	71	2790	2340	1930	1570	1280	1225	860	585	390	190	+2.0	-1.0	-10.4	-35.7	NA
6mm (24)																
6mm BR Rem.	100	2550	2310	2083	1870	1671	1444	1185	963	776	620	+2.5	-0.6	-11.8	0.0	$22
6mm Norma BR	107	2822	2667	2517	2372	2229	1893	1690	1506	1337	1181	+1.73	0.0	-7.24	-20.6	NA
6mm PPC	70	3140	2750	2400	2070	NA	1535	1175	895	665	NA	+2.0	+1.4	-5.0	0.0	NA
243 Winchester	55	4025	3597	3209	2853	2525	1978	1579	1257	994	779	+0.6	0.0	-4.0	-12.2	NA
243 Winchester	60	3600	3110	2660	2260	1890	1725	1285	945	680	475	+2.0	+1.8	-3.3	-15.5	$17
243 Winchester	70	3400	3040	2700	2390	2100	1795	1435	1135	890	685	1.1	0.0	-5.9	-18.0	NA
243 Winchester	75/80	3350	2955	2593	2259	1951	1993	1551	1194	906	676	+2.0	+0.9	-5.0	-19.0	$16
243 Winchester	85	3320	3070	2830	2600	2380	2080	1770	1510	1280	1070	+2.0	+1.2	-4.0	-14.0	$18
243 Winchester	90	3120	2871	2635	2411	2199	1946	1647	1388	1162	966	1.4	0.0	-6.4	-18.8	NA
243 Winchester*	100	2960	2697	2449	2215	1993	1945	1615	1332	1089	882	+2.5	+1.2	-6.0	-20.0	$16
243 Winchester	105	2920	2689	2470	2261	2062	1988	1686	1422	1192	992	+2.5	+1.6	-5.0	-18.4	$21
243 Light Mag	100	3100	2839	2592	2358	2138	2133	1790	1491	1235	1014	+1.5	0.0	-6.8	-19.8	NA
243 WSSM	55	4060	3628	3237	2880	2550	2013	1607	1280	1013	794	0.6	0.0	-3.9	-12.0	NA
243 WSSM	95	3250	3000	2763	2538	2325	2258	1898	1610	1359	1140	1.2	0.0	-5.7	-16.9	NA
243 WSSM	100	3110	2838	2583	2341	2112	2147	1789	1481	1217	991	1.4	0.0	-6.6	-19.7	NA
6mm Remington	80	3470	3064	2694	2352	2036	2139	1667	1289	982	736	+2.0	+1.1	-5.0	-17.0	$16
6mm Remington	100	3100	2829	2573	2332	2104	2133	1777	1470	1207	983	+2.5	+1.6	-5.0	-17.0	$16
6mm Remington	105	3060	2822	2596	2381	2177	2105	1788	1512	1270	1059	+2.5	+1.1	-3.3	-15.0	$21
6mm Rem. Light Mag.	100	3250	2997	2756	2528	2311	2345	1995	1687	1418	1186	1.59	0.0	-6.33	-18.3	NA
6.17(.243) Spitfire	100	3350	3122	2905	2698	2501	2493	2164	1874	1617	1389	2.4	3.20	0.0	-8.0	NA
240 Wea. Mag.	87	3500	3202	2924	2663	2416	2366	1980	1651	1370	1127	+2.0	+2.0	-2.0	-12.0	$32
240 Wea. Mag.	100	3395	3106	2835	2581	2339	2559	2142	1785	1478	1215	+2.5	+2.8	-2.0	-11.0	$43
25																
25-20 Win.	86	1460	1194	1030	931	858	407	272	203	165	141	0.0	-23.5	0.0	0.0	$32**
25-35 Win.	117	2230	1866	1545	1282	1097	1292	904	620	427	313	+2.5	-4.2	-26.0	0.0	$24
250 Savage	100	2820	2504	2210	1936	1684	1765	1392	1084	832	630	+2.5	+0.4	-9.0	-28.0	$17

Many manufacturers do not supply suggested retail prices. Others did not get their pricing to us before press time. All pricing can vary dependent on the exact brand and style of ammo selected and/or the retail outlet from which you make your purchase. Pricing has been rounded to the nearest dollar and represents our best estimate of average pricing. An * after the cartridge means these loads are available with Nosler Partition or Swift A-Frame bullets. Listed pricing may or may not reflect this bullet type. ** = these are packed 50 to box, all others are 20 to box. Wea. Mag.= Weatherby Magnum. Spfd. = Springfield. A-A-Sq. = A-Square. N.E.=Nitro Express.

Cartridge	Bullet Wgt. Grs.	VELOCITY (fps)					ENERGY (ft. lbs.)					TRAJ. (in.)				Est. Price/ box
		Muzzle	100 yds.	200 yds.	300 yds.	400 yds.	Muzzle	100 yds.	200 yds.	300 yds.	400 yds.	100 yds.	200 yds.	300 yds.	400 yds.	
257 Roberts	100	2980	2661	2363	2085	1827	1972	1572	1240	965	741	+2.5	-0.8	-5.2	-21.6	$20
257 Roberts+P	117	2780	2411	2071	1761	1488	2009	1511	1115	806	576	+2.5	-0.2	-10.2	-32.6	$18
257 Roberts+P	120	2780	2560	2360	2160	1970	2060	1750	1480	1240	1030	+2.5	+1.2	-6.4	-23.6	$22
257 Roberts	122	2600	2331	2078	1842	1625	1831	1472	1169	919	715	+2.5	0.0	-10.6	-31.4	$21
257 Light Mag.	117	2940	2694	2460	2240	2031	2245	1885	1572	1303	1071	+1.7	0.0	-7.6	-21.8	NA
25-06 Rem.	87	3440	2995	2591	2222	1884	2286	1733	1297	954	686	+2.0	+1.1	-2.5	-14.4	$17
25-06 Rem.	90	3440	3043	2680	2344	2034	2364	1850	1435	1098	827	+2.0	+1.8	-3.3	-15.6	$17
25-06 Rem.	100	3230	2893	2580	2287	2014	2316	1858	1478	1161	901	+2.0	+0.8	-5.7	-18.9	$17
25-06 Rem.	117	2990	2770	2570	2370	2190	2320	2000	1715	1465	1246	+2.5	+1.0	-7.9	-26.6	$19
25-06 Rem.*	120	2990	2730	2484	2252	2032	2382	1985	1644	1351	1100	+2.5	+1.2	-5.3	-19.6	$17
25-06 Rem.	122	2930	2706	2492	2289	2095	2325	1983	1683	1419	1189	+2.5	+1.8	-4.5	-17.5	$23
25 WSSM	85	3470	3156	2863	2589	2331	2273	1880	1548	1266	1026	1.0	0.0	-5.2	-15.7	NA
25 WSSM	115	3060	284	2639	2442	2254	2392	2066	1778	1523	1398	1.4	0.0	-6.4	-18.6	NA
25 WSSM	120	2990	2717	2459	2216	1987	2383	1967	1612	1309	1053	1.6	0.0	-7.4	-21.8	NA
257 Wea. Mag.	87	3825	3456	3118	2805	2513	2826	2308	1870	1520	1220	+2.0	+2.7	-0.3	-7.6	$32
257 Wea. Mag.	100	3555	3237	2941	2665	2404	2806	2326	1920	1576	1283	+2.5	+3.2	0.0	-8.0	$32
257 Scramjet	100	3745	3450	3173	2912	2666	3114	2643	2235	1883	1578	+2.1	+2.77	0.0	-6.93	NA

6.5

Cartridge	Bullet Wgt. Grs.	Muzzle	100 yds.	200 yds.	300 yds.	400 yds.	Muzzle	100 yds.	200 yds.	300 yds.	400 yds.	100 yds.	200 yds.	300 yds.	400 yds.	Est. Price/ box
6.5x50mm Jap.	139	2360	2160	1970	1790	1620	1720	1440	1195	985	810	+2.5	-1.0	-13.5	0.0	NA
6.5x50mm Jap.	156	2070	1830	1610	1430	1260	1475	1155	900	695	550	+2.5	-4.0	-23.8	0.0	NA
6.5x52mm Car.	139	2580	2360	2160	1970	1790	2045	1725	1440	1195	985	+2.5	0.0	-9.9	-29.0	NA
6.5x52mm Car.	156	2430	2170	1930	1700	1500	2045	1630	1285	1005	780	+2.5	-1.0	-13.9	0.0	NA
6.5x52mm Carcano	160	2250	1963	1700	1467	1271	1798	1369	1027	764	574	+3.8	0.0	-15.9	-48.1	NA
6.5x55mm Light Mag.	129	2750	2549	2355	2171	1994	2166	1860	1589	1350	1139	+2.0	0.0	-8.2	-23.9	NA
6.5x55mm Swe.	140	2550	NA	NA	NA	NA	2020	NA	NA	NA	NA	0.0	0.0	0.0	0.0	$18
6.5x55mm Swe.*	139/140	2850	2640	2440	2250	2070	2525	2170	1855	1575	1330	+2.5	+1.6	-5.4	-18.9	$18
6.5x55mm Swe.	156	2650	2370	2110	1870	1650	2425	1950	1550	1215	945	+2.5	0.0	-10.3	-30.6	NA
260 Remington	125	2875	2669	2473	2285	2105	2294	1977	1697	1449	1230	1.71	0.0	-7.4	-21.4	NA
260 Remington	140	2750	2544	2347	2158	1979	2351	2011	1712	1448	1217	+2.2	0.0	-8.6	-24.6	NA
6.5-284 Norma	142	3025	2890	2758	2631	2507	2886	2634	2400	2183	1982	1.13	0.0	-5.7	-16.4	NA
6.71 (264) Phantom	120	3150	2929	2718	2517	2325	2645	2286	1969	1698	1440	+1.3	0.0	-6.0	-17.5	NA
6.5 Rem. Mag.	120	3210	2905	2621	2353	2102	2745	2248	1830	1475	1177	+2.5	+1.7	-4.1	-16.3	Disc.
264 Win. Mag.	140	3030	2782	2548	2326	2114	2854	2406	2018	1682	1389	+2.5	+1.4	-5.1	-18.0	$24
6.71 (264) Blackbird	140	3480	3261	3053	2855	2665	3766	3307	2899	2534	2208	+2.4	+3.1	0.0	-7.4	NA
6.8mm Rem.	115	2775	2472	2190	1926	1683	1966	1561	1224	947	723	+2.1	0.0	-3.7	-9.4	NA

27

Cartridge	Bullet Wgt. Grs.	Muzzle	100 yds.	200 yds.	300 yds.	400 yds.	Muzzle	100 yds.	200 yds.	300 yds.	400 yds.	100 yds.	200 yds.	300 yds.	400 yds.	Est. Price/ box
270 Winchester	100	3430	3021	2649	2305	1988	2612	2027	1557	1179	877	+2.0	+1.0	-4.9	-17.5	$17
270 Win. (Rem.)	115	2710	2482	2265	2059	NA	1875	1485	1161	896	NA	0.0	4.8	-17.3	0.0	NA
270 Winchester	130	3060	2776	2510	2259	2022	2702	2225	1818	1472	1180	+2.5	+1.4	-5.3	-18.2	$17
270 Win. Supreme	130	3150	2881	2628	2388	2161	2865	2396	1993	1646	1348	1.3	0.0	-6.4	-18.9	NA
270 Winchester	135	3000	2780	2570	2369	2178	2697	2315	1979	1682	1421	+2.5	+1.4	-6.0	-17.6	$23
270 Winchester*	140	2940	2700	2480	2260	2060	2685	2270	1905	1590	1315	+2.5	+1.8	-4.6	-17.9	$20
270 Win. Light Magnum	130	3215	2998	2790	2590	2400	2983	2594	2246	1936	1662	1.21	0.0	-5.83	-17.0	NA
270 Winchester*	150	2850	2585	2336	2100	1879	2705	2226	1817	1468	1175	+2.5	+1.2	-6.5	-22.0	$17
270 Win. Supreme	150	2930	2693	2468	2254	2051	2860	2416	2030	1693	1402	1.7	0.0	-7.4	-21.6	NA
270 WSM	130	3275	3041	2820	2609	2408	3096	2669	2295	1564	1673	1.1	0.0	-5.5	-16.1	NA
270 WSM	140	3125	2865	2619	2386	2165	3035	2559	2132	1769	1457	1.4	0.0	-6.5	-19.0	NA
270 WSM	150	3120	2923	2734	2554	2380	3242	2845	2490	2172	1886	1.3	0.0	-5.9	-17.2	NA
270 Wea. Mag.	100	3760	3380	3033	2712	2412	3139	2537	2042	1633	1292	+2.0	+2.4	-1.2	-10.1	$32
270 Wea. Mag.	130	3375	3119	2878	2649	2432	3287	2808	2390	2026	1707	+2.5	-2.9	-0.9	-9.9	$32
270 Wea. Mag.*	150	3245	3036	2837	2647	2465	3507	3070	2681	2334	2023	+2.5	+2.6	-1.8	-11.4	$47

7mm

Cartridge	Bullet Wgt. Grs.	Muzzle	100 yds.	200 yds.	300 yds.	400 yds.	Muzzle	100 yds.	200 yds.	300 yds.	400 yds.	100 yds.	200 yds.	300 yds.	400 yds.	Est. Price/ box
7mm BR	140	2216	2012	1821	1643	1481	1525	1259	1031	839	681	+2.0	-3.7	-20.0	0.0	$23
7mm Mauser*	139/140	2660	2435	2221	2018	1827	2199	1843	1533	1266	1037	+2.5	0.0	-9.6	-27.7	$17
7mm Mauser	145	2690	2442	2206	1985	1777	2334	1920	1568	1268	1017	+2.5	+0.1	-9.6	-28.3	$18
7mm Mauser	154	2690	2490	2300	2120	1940	2475	2120	1810	1530	1285	+2.5	+0.8	-7.5	-23.5	$17
7mm Mauser	175	2440	2137	1857	1603	1382	2313	1774	1340	998	742	+2.5	-1.7	-16.1	0.0	$17
7x57 Light Mag.	139	2970	2730	2503	2287	2082	2722	2301	1933	1614	1337	+1.6	0.0	-7.2	-21.0	NA
7x30 Waters	120	2700	2300	1930	1600	1330	1940	1405	990	685	470	+2.5	-0.2	-12.3	0.0	$18
7mm-08 Rem.	120	3000	2725	2467	2223	1992	2398	1979	1621	1316	1058	+2.0	0.0	-7.6	-22.3	$18
7mm-08 Rem.*	140	2860	2625	2402	2189	1988	2542	2142	1793	1490	1228	+2.5	+0.8	-6.9	-21.9	$18
7mm-08 Rem.	154	2715	2510	2315	2128	1950	2520	2155	1832	1548	1300	+2.5	+1.0	-7.0	-22.7	$23
7mm-08 Light Mag.	139	3000	2790	2590	2399	2216	2777	2403	2071	1776	1515	+1.5	0.0	-6.7	-19.4	NA
7x64mm Bren.	140				Not Yet Announced											$17
7x64mm Bren.	154	2820	2610	2420	2230	2050	2720	2335	1995	1695	1430	+2.5	+1.4	-5.7	-19.9	NA
7x64mm Bren.*	160	2850	2669	2495	2327	2166	2885	2530	2211	1924	1667	+2.5	+1.6	-4.8	-17.8	$24
7x64mm Bren.	175				Not Yet Announced											$17

Many manufacturers do not supply suggested retail prices. Others did not get their pricing to us before press time. All pricing can vary dependent on the exact brand and style of ammo selected and/or the retail outlet from which you make your purchase. Pricing has been rounded to the nearest dollar and represents our best estimate of average pricing. An * after the cartridge means these loads are available with Nosler Partition or Swift A-Frame bullets. Listed pricing may or may not reflect this bullet type. ** = these are packed 50 to box, all others are 20 to box. Wea. Mag.= Weatherby Magnum. Spfd. = Springfield. A-A-Sq. = A-Square. N.E.=Nitro Express.

Cartridge	Bullet Wgt. Grs.	VELOCITY (fps)					ENERGY (ft. lbs.)					TRAJ. (in.)				Est. Price/box
		Muzzle	100 yds.	200 yds.	300 yds.	400 yds.	Muzzle	100 yds.	200 yds.	300 yds.	400 yds.	100 yds.	200 yds.	300 yds.	400 yds.	
284 Winchester	150	2860	2595	2344	2108	1886	2724	2243	1830	1480	1185	+2.5	+0.8	-7.3	-23.2	$24
280 Remington	120	3150	2866	2599	2348	2110	2643	2188	1800	1468	1186	+2.0	+0.6	-6.0	-17.9	$17
280 Remington	140	3000	2758	2528	2309	2102	2797	2363	1986	1657	1373	+2.5	+1.4	-5.2	-18.3	$17
280 Remington*	150	2890	2624	2373	2135	1912	2781	2293	1875	1518	1217	+2.5	+0.8	-7.1	-22.6	$17
280 Remington	160	2840	2637	2442	2556	2078	2866	2471	2120	1809	1535	+2.5	+0.8	-6.7	-21.0	$20
280 Remington	165	2820	2510	2220	1950	1701	2913	2308	1805	1393	1060	+2.5	+0.4	-8.8	-26.5	$17
7x61mm S&H Sup.	154	3060	2720	2400	2100	1820	3200	2520	1965	1505	1135	+2.5	+1.8	-5.0	-19.8	NA
7mm Dakota	160	3200	3001	2811	2630	2455	3637	3200	2808	2456	2140	+2.1	+1.9	-2.8	-12.5	NA
7mm Rem. Mag. (Rem.)	140	2710	2482	2265	2059	NA	2283	1915	1595	1318	NA	0.0	-4.5	-1.57	0.0	NA
7mm Rem. Mag.*	139/140	3150	2930	2710	2510	2320	3085	2660	2290	1960	1670	+2.5	+2.4	-2.4	-12.7	$21
7mm Rem. Hvy Mag	139	3250	3044	2847	2657	2475	3259	2860	2501	2178	1890	1.1	0.0	-5.5	-16.2	NA
7mm Rem. Mag.	150/154	3110	2830	2568	2320	2085	3221	2667	2196	1792	1448	+2.5	+1.6	-4.6	-16.5	$21
7mm Rem. Mag.*	160/162	2950	2730	2520	2320	2120	3090	2650	2250	1910	1600	+2.5	+1.8	-4.4	-17.8	$34
7mm Rem. Mag.	165	2900	2699	2507	2324	2147	3081	2669	2303	1978	1689	+2.5	+1.2	-5.9	-19.0	$28
7mm Rem Mag.	175	2860	2645	2440	2244	2057	3178	2718	2313	1956	1644	+2.5	+1.0	-6.5	-20.7	$21
7mm Rem. 3A ULTRA MAG	140	3175	2934	2707	2490	2283	3033	2676	2277	1927	1620	1.3	0.0	-6	-17.7	NA
7mm Rem. SA ULTRA MAG	150	3110	2828	2563	2313	2077	3221	2663	2188	1782	1437	2.5	2.1	-3.6	-15.8	NA
7mm Rem. SA ULTRA MAG	160	2960	2762	2572	2390	2215	3112	2709	2350	2020	1743	2.6	2.2	-3.0	-15.4	NA
7mm Rem. WSM	140	3225	3008	2801	2603	2414	3233	2812	2438	2106	1812	1.2	0.0	-5.6	-16.4	NA
7mm Rem. WSM	160	2990	2744	2512	2081	1883	3176	2675	2241	1864	1538	1.6	0.0	-7.1	-20.8	NA
7mm Wea. Mag.	140	3225	2970	2729	2501	2283	3233	2741	2315	1943	1621	+2.5	+2.0	-3.2	-14.0	$35
7mm Wea. Mag.	154	3260	3023	2799	2586	2382	3539	3044	2609	2227	1890	+2.5	+2.8	-1.5	-10.8	$32
7mm Wea. Mag.*	160	3200	3004	2816	2637	2464	3637	3205	2817	2469	2156	+2.5	+2.7	-1.5	-10.6	$47
7mm Wea. Mag.	165	2950	2747	2553	2367	2189	3188	2765	2388	2053	1756	+2.5	+1.8	-4.2	-16.4	$43
7mm Wea. Mag.	175	2910	2693	2486	2288	2098	3293	2818	2401	2033	1711	+2.5	+1.2	-5.9	-19.4	$35
7.21(.284) Tomahawk	140	3300	3118	2943	2774	2612	3386	3022	2690	2390	2122	2.3	3.20	0.0	-7.7	NA
7mm STW	140	3325	3064	2818	2585	2364	3436	2918	2468	2077	1737	+2.3	+1.8	-3.0	-13.1	NA
7mm STW Supreme	160	3150	2894	2652	2422	2204	3526	2976	2499	2085	1727	1.3	0.0	-6.3	-18.5	NA
7mm Rem. Ultra Mag.	140	3425	3184	2956	2740	2534	3646	3151	2715	2333	1995	1.7	1.60	-2.6	-11.4	NA
7mm Firehawk	140	3625	3373	3135	2909	2695	4084	3536	3054	2631	2258	+2.2	+2.9	0.0	-7.03	NA
7.21 (.284) Firebird	140	3750	3522	3306	3101	2905	4372	3857	3399	2990	2625	1.6	2.4	0.0	-6.0	NA

30

Cartridge	Bullet Wgt. Grs.	Muzzle	100 yds.	200 yds.	300 yds.	400 yds.	Muzzle	100 yds.	200 yds.	300 yds.	400 yds.	100 yds.	200 yds.	300 yds.	400 yds.	Est. Price/box
30 Carbine	110	1990	1567	1236	1035	923	977	600	373	262	208	0.0	-13.5	0.0	0.0	$28**
303 Savage	190	1890	1612	1327	1183	1055	1507	1096	794	591	469	+2.5	-7.6	0.0	0.0	$24
30 Remington	170	2120	1822	1555	1328	1153	1696	1253	913	666	502	+2.5	-4.7	-26.3	0.0	$20
7.62x39mm Rus.	123/125	2300	2030	1780	1550	1350	1445	1125	860	655	500	+2.5	-2.0	-17.5	0.0	$13
30-30 Win.	55	3400	2693	2085	1570	1187	1412	886	521	301	172	+2.0	0.0	-10.2	35.0	$18
30-30 Win.	125	2570	2090	1660	1320	1080	1830	1210	770	480	320	-2.0	-2.6	-19.9	0.0	$13
30-30 Win.	150	2390	1973	1605	1303	1095	1902	1296	858	565	399	+2.5	-3.2	-22.5	0.0	$13
30-30 Win. Supreme	150	2480	2095	1747	1446	1209	2049	1462	1017	697	487	0.0	-6.5	-24.5	0.0	NA
30-30 Win.	160	2300	1997	1719	1473	1268	1879	1416	1050	771	571	+2.5	-2.9	-20.2	0.0	$18
30-30 PMC Cowboy	170	1300	1198	1121			638	474				0.0	-27.0	0.0	0.0	NA
30-30 Win.*	170	2200	1895	1619	1381	1191	1827	1355	989	720	535	+2.5	-5.8	-23.6	0.0	$13
300 Savage	150	2630	2354	2094	1853	1631	2303	1845	1462	1143	886	+2.5	-0.4	-10.1	-30.7	$17
300 Savage	180	2350	2137	1935	1754	1570	2207	1825	1496	1217	985	+2.5	-1.6	-15.2	0.0	$17
30-40 Krag	180	2430	2213	2007	1813	1632	2360	1957	1610	1314	1004	+2.5	-1.4	-13.8	0.0	$18
7.65x53mm Arg.	180	2590	2390	2200	2010	1830	2685	2280	1925	1615	1345	+2.5	0.0	-27.6	0.0	NA
7.5x53mm Argentine	150	2785	2519	2269	2032	1814	2583	2113	1714	1376	1096	+2.0	0.0	-8.8	-25.5	NA
307 Winchester	150	2760	2321	1924	1575	1289	2530	1795	1233	826	554	+2.5	-1.5	-13.6	0.0	Disc.
307 Winchester	180	2510	2179	1874	1599	1362	2519	1898	1404	1022	742	+2.5	-1.6	-15.6	0.0	$20
7.5x55 Swiss	180	2650	2450	2250	2060	1880	2805	2390	2020	1700	1415	+2.5	+0.6	-8.1	-24.9	NA
7.5x55mm Swiss	165	2720	2515	2319	2132	1954	2710	2317	1970	1665	1398	+2.0	0.0	-8.5	-24.6	NA
308 Winchester	55	3770	3215	2726	2286	1888	1735	1262	907	639	435	-2.0	+1.4	0.0	16.0	$22
308 Winchester	150	2820	2533	2263	2009	1774	2648	2137	1705	1344	1048	+2.5	+0.4	-8.5	-26.1	$17
308 Winchester	165	2700	2440	2194	1963	1748	2670	2180	1763	1411	1199	+2.5	0.0	-9.7	-28.5	$20
308 Winchester	168	2680	2493	2314	2143	1979	2678	2318	1998	1713	1460	+2.5	0.0	-8.9	-25.3	$18
308 Win. (Fed.)	170	2000	1740	1510	NA	NA	1510	1145	860	NA	NA	0.0	0.0	0.0	0.0	NA
308 Winchester	178	2620	2415	2220	2034	1857	2713	2306	1948	1635	1363	+2.5	0.0	-9.6	-27.6	$23
308 Winchester*	180	2620	2393	2178	1974	1782	2743	2288	1896	1557	1269	+2.5	-0.2	-10.2	-28.5	$17
308 Light Mag.*	150	2980	2703	2442	2195	1964	2959	2433	1986	1606	1285	+1.6	0.0	-7.5	-22.2	NA
308 Light Mag.	165	2870	2658	2456	2263	2078	3019	2589	2211	1877	1583	+1.7	0.0	-7.5	-21.8	NA
308 High Energy	165	2870	2600	2350	2120	1890	3020	2485	2030	1640	1310	+1.8	0.0	-8.2	-24.0	NA
308 Light Mag.	168	2870	2658	2456	2263	2078	3019	2589	2211	1877	1583	+1.7	0.0	-7.5	-21.8	NA
308 High Energy	180	2740	2550	2370	2200	2030	3000	2600	2245	1925	1645	+1.9	0.0	-8.2	-23.5	NA
30-06 Spfd.	55	4080	3485	2965	2502	2083	2033	1483	1074	764	530	+2.0	+1.9	-2.1	-11.7	$22
30-06 Spfd. (Rem.)	125	2660	2335	2034	1757	NA	1964	1513	1148	856	NA	0.0	-5.2	-18.9	0.0	NA
30-06 Spfd.	125	3140	2780	2447	2138	1853	2736	2145	1662	1279	953	+2.0	+1.0	-6.2	-21.0	$17
30-06 Spfd.	150	2910	2617	2342	2083	1853	2820	2281	1827	1445	1135	+2.5	+0.8	-7.2	-23.4	$17

Many manufacturers do not supply suggested retail prices. Others did not get their pricing to us before press time. All pricing can vary dependent on the exact brand and style of ammo selected and/or the retail outlet from which you make your purchase. Pricing has been rounded to the nearest dollar and represents our best estimate of average pricing. An * after the cartridge means these loads are available with Nosler Partition or Swift A-Frame bullets. Listed pricing may or may not reflect this bullet type. ** = these are packed 50 to box, all others are 20 to box. Wea. Mag.= Weatherby Magnum. Spfd. = Springfield. A-A-Sq. = A-Square. N.E.=Nitro Express.

Cartridge	Bullet Wgt. Grs.	VELOCITY (fps)					ENERGY (ft. lbs.)					TRAJ. (in.)				Est. Price/ box
		Muzzle	100 yds.	200 yds.	300 yds.	400 yds.	Muzzle	100 yds.	200 yds.	300 yds.	400 yds.	100 yds.	200 yds.	300 yds.	400 yds.	
30-06 Spfd.	152	2910	2654	2413	2184	1968	2858	2378	1965	1610	1307	+2.5	+1.0	-6.6	-21.3	$23
30-06 Spfd. *	165	2800	2534	2283	2047	1825	2872	2352	1909	1534	1220	+2.5	+0.4	-8.4	-25.5	$17
30-06 Spfd.	168	2710	2522	2346	2169	2003	2739	2372	2045	1754	1497	+2.5	+0.4	-8.0	-23.5	$18
30-06 Spfd. (Fed.)	170	2000	1740	1510	NA	NA	1510	1145	860	NA	NA	0.0	0.0	0.0	0.0	NA
30-06 Spfd.	178	2720	2511	2311	2121	1939	2924	2491	2111	1777	1486	+2.5	+0.4	-8.2	-24.6	$23
30-06 Spfd. *	180	2700	2469	2250	2042	1846	2913	2436	2023	1666	1362	-2.5	0.0	-9.3	-27.0	$17
30-06 Spfd.	220	2410	2130	1870	1632	1422	2837	2216	1708	1301	988	+2.5	-1.7	-18.0	0.0	$17

30 Mag.

Cartridge	Bullet Wgt. Grs.	Muzzle	100 yds.	200 yds.	300 yds.	400 yds.	Muzzle	100 yds.	200 yds.	300 yds.	400 yds.	100 yds.	200 yds.	300 yds.	400 yds.	Est. Price/ box
30-06 Light Mag.	150	3100	2815	2548	2295	2058	3200	2639	2161	1755	1410	+1.4	0.0	-6.8	-20.3	NA
30-06 Light Mag.	180	2880	2676	2480	2293	2114	3316	2862	2459	2102	1786	+1.7	0.0	-7.3	-21.3	NA
30-06 High Energy	180	2880	2690	2500	2320	2150	3315	2880	2495	2150	1845	+1.7	0.0	-7.2	-21.0	NA
300 REM SA ULTRA MAG	150	3200	2901	2622	2359	2112	3410	2803	2290	1854	1485	1.3	0.0	-6.4	-19.1	NA
300 REM SA ULTRA MAG	165	3075	2792	2527	2276	2040	3464	2856	2339	1898	1525	1.5	0.0	-7	-20.7	NA
300 REM SA ULTRA MAG	180	2960	2761	2571	2389	2214	3501	3047	2642	2280	1959	2.6	2.2	-3.6	-15.4	NA
7.82 (308) Patriot	150	3250	2999	2762	2537	2323	3519	2997	2542	2145	1798	+1.2	0.0	-5.8	-16.9	NA
300 WSM	150	3300	3061	2834	2619	2414	3628	3121	2676	2285	1941	1.1	0.0	-5.4	-15.9	NA
300 WSM	180	2970	2741	2524	2317	2120	3526	3005	2547	2147	1797	1.6	0.0	-7.0	-20.5	NA
300 WSM	180	3010	2923	2734	2554	2380	3242	2845	2490	2172	1886	1.3	0	-5.9	-17.2	NA
308 Norma Mag.	180	3020	2820	2630	2440	2270	3645	3175	2755	2385	2050	+2.5	+2.0	-3.5	-14.8	NA
300 Dakota	200	3000	2824	2656	2493	2336	3996	3542	3131	2760	2423	+2.2	+1.5	-4.0	-15.2	NA
300 H&H Magnum*	180	2880	2640	2412	2196	1990	3315	2785	2325	1927	1583	+2.5	+0.8	-6.8	-21.7	$24
300 H&H Magnum	220	2550	2267	2002	1757	NA	3167	2510	1958	1508	NA	-2.5	-0.4	-12.0	0.0	NA
300 Peterson	180	3500	3319	3145	2978	2817	4896	4401	3953	3544	3172	+2.3	+2.9	0.0	-6.8	NA
300 Win. Mag.	150	3290	2951	2636	2342	2068	3605	2900	2314	1827	1424	+2.5	+1.9	-3.8	-15.8	$22
300 Win. Mag.	165	3100	2877	2665	2462	2269	3522	3033	2603	2221	1897	+2.5	+2.4	-3.0	-16.9	$24
300 Win. Mag.	178	2900	2760	2568	2375	2191	3509	3030	2606	2230	1897	+2.5	+1.4	-5.0	-17.6	$29
300 Win. Mag.*	180	2960	2745	2540	2344	2157	3501	3011	2578	2196	1859	+2.5	+1.2	-5.5	-18.5	$22
300 W.M. High Energy	180	3100	2830	2580	2340	2110	3840	3205	2660	2190	1790	+1.4	0.0	-6.6	-19.7	NA
300 W.M. Light Mag.	180	3100	2879	2668	2467	2275	3840	3313	2845	2431	2068	+1.39	0.0	-6.45	-18.7	NA
300 Win. Mag.	190	2885	1691	2506	2327	2156	3511	3055	2648	2285	1961	+2.5	+1.2	-5.7	-19.0	$26
300 W.M. High Energy	200	2930	2740	2550	2370	2200	3810	3325	2885	2495	2145	+1.6	0.0	-6.9	-20.1	NA
300 Win. Mag.*	200	2825	2595	2376	2167	1970	3545	2991	2508	2086	1742	-2.5	+1.6	-4.7	-17.2	$36
300 Win. Mag.	220	2680	2448	2228	2020	1823	3508	2927	2424	1993	1623	+2.5	0.0	-9.5	-27.5	$23
300 Rem. Ultra Mag.	150	3450	3208	2980	2762	2556	3964	3427	2956	2541	2175	1.7	1.5	-2.6	-11.2	NA
300 Rem. Ultra Mag.	180	3250	3037	2834	2640	2454	4221	3686	3201	2786	2407	2.4	0.0	-3.0	-12.7	NA
300 Wea. Mag.	100	3900	3441	3038	2652	2305	3714	2891	2239	1717	1297	+2.0	+2.6	-0.6	-8.7	$32
300 Wea. Mag.	150	3600	3307	3033	2776	2533	4316	3642	3064	2566	2137	+2.5	+3.2	0.0	-8.1	$32
300 Wea. Mag.	165	3450	3210	3000	2792	2593	4360	3796	3297	2855	2464	+2.5	+3.2	0.0	-7.8	NA
300 Wea. Mag.	178	3120	2902	2695	2497	2308	3847	3329	2870	2464	2104	+2.5	-1.7	-3.6	-14.7	$43
300 Wea. Mag.	180	3330	3110	2910	2710	2520	4430	3875	3375	2935	2540	+1.0	0.0	-5.2	-15.1	NA
300 Wea. Mag.	190	3030	2830	2638	2455	2279	3873	3378	2936	2542	2190	+2.5	+1.6	-4.3	-16.0	$38
300 Wea. Mag.	220	2850	2541	2283	1964	1736	3967	3155	2480	1922	1471	+2.5	+0.4	-8.5	-26.4	$35
300 Warbird	180	3400	3180	2971	2772	2582	4620	4042	3528	3071	2664	+2.59	+3.25	0.0	-7.95	NA
300 Pegasus	180	3500	3319	3145	2978	2817	4896	4401	3953	3544	3172	+2.28	+2.89	0.0	-6.79	NA

31

Cartridge	Bullet Wgt. Grs.	Muzzle	100 yds.	200 yds.	300 yds.	400 yds.	Muzzle	100 yds.	200 yds.	300 yds.	400 yds.	100 yds.	200 yds.	300 yds.	400 yds.	Est. Price/ box
32-20 Win.	100	1210	1021	913	834	769	325	231	185	154	131	0.0	-32.3	0.0	0.0	$23**
303 British	150	2685	2441	2210	1992	1787	2401	1984	1627	1321	1064	+2.5	+0.6	-8.4	-26.2	$18
303 British	180	2460	2124	1817	1542	1311	2418	1803	1319	950	687	+2.5	-1.8	-16.8	0.0	$18
303 Light Mag.	150	2830	2570	2325	2094	1884	2667	2199	1800	1461	1185	+2.0	0.0	-8.4	-24.6	NA
7.62x54mm Rus.	146	2950	2730	2520	2320	NA	2820	2415	2055	1740	NA	+2.5	+2.0	-4.4	-17.7	NA
7.62x54mm Rus.	180	2580	2370	2180	2000	1820	2650	2250	1900	1590	1100	+2.5	0.0	-9.8	-28.5	NA
7.7x58mm Jap.	150	2640	2399	2170	1954	1752	2321	1916	1568	1271	1022	+2.3	0.0	-9.7	-28.5	NA
7.7x58mm Jap.	180	2500	2300	2100	1920	1750	2490	2105	1770	1475	1225	+2.5	0.0	-10.4	-30.2	NA

8mm

Cartridge	Bullet Wgt. Grs.	Muzzle	100 yds.	200 yds.	300 yds.	400 yds.	Muzzle	100 yds.	200 yds.	300 yds.	400 yds.	100 yds.	200 yds.	300 yds.	400 yds.	Est. Price/ box
8x56 R	205	2400	2188	1987	1797	1621	2621	2178	1796	1470	1196	+2.9	0.0	-11.7	-34.3	NA
8x57mm JS Mau.	165	2850	2520	2210	1930	1670	2965	2330	1795	1360	1015	+2.5	+1.0	-7.7	0.0	NA
32 Win. Special	170	2250	1921	1626	1372	1175	1911	1393	998	710	521	+2.5	-3.5	-22.9	0.0	$14
8mm Mauser	170	2360	1969	1622	1333	1123	2102	1464	993	671	476	+2.5	-3.1	-22.2	0.0	$18
325 WSM	180	3060	2841	2632	2432	2242	3743	3226	2769	2365	2009	+1.4	0.0	-6.4	-18.7	NA
325 WSM	200	2950	2753	2565	2384	2210	3866	3367	2922	2524	2170	+1.5	0.0	-6.8	-19.8	NA
325 WSM	220	2840	2605	2382	2169	1968	3941	3316	2772	2300	1893	+1.8	0.0	-8.0	-23.3	NA
8mm Rem. Mag.	185	3080	2761	2464	2186	1927	3896	3131	2494	1963	1525	+2.5	+1.4	-5.5	-19.7	$30
8mm Rem. Mag.	220	2830	2581	2346	2123	1913	3912	3254	2688	2201	1787	+2.5	+0.6	-7.6	-23.5	Disc.

33

Cartridge	Bullet Wgt. Grs.	Muzzle	100 yds.	200 yds.	300 yds.	400 yds.	Muzzle	100 yds.	200 yds.	300 yds.	400 yds.	100 yds.	200 yds.	300 yds.	400 yds.	Est. Price/ box
338-06	200	2750	2553	2364	2184	2011	3358	2894	2482	2118	1796	+1.9	0.0	-8.22	-23.6	NA
330 Dakota	250	2900	2719	2545	2378	2217	4668	4103	3595	3138	2727	+2.3	+1.3	-5.0	-17.5	NA

Many manufacturers do not supply suggested retail prices. Others did not get their pricing to us before press time. All pricing can vary dependent on the exact brand and style of ammo selected and/or the retail outlet from which you make your purchase. Pricing has been rounded to the nearest dollar and represents our best estimate of average pricing. An * after the cartridge means these loads are available with Nosler Partition or Swift A-Frame bullets. Listed pricing may or may not reflect this bullet type. ** = these are packed 50 to box, all others are 20 to box. Wea. Mag.= Weatherby Magnum. Spfd. = Springfield. A-A-Sq. = A-Square. N.E.=Nitro Express.

Cartridge	Bullet Wgt. Grs.	VELOCITY (fps)					ENERGY (ft. lbs.)					TRAJ. (in.)				Est. Price/ box
		Muzzle	100 yds.	200 yds.	300 yds.	400 yds.	Muzzle	100 yds.	200 yds.	300 yds.	400 yds.	100 yds.	200 yds.	300 yds.	400 yds.	
338 Lapua	250	2963	2795	2640	2493	NA	4842	4341	3881	3458	NA	+1.9	0.0	-7.9	0.0	NA
338 Win. Mag.	200	2960	2658	2375	2110	1862	3890	3137	2505	1977	1539	+2.5	+1.0	-6.7	-22.3	$27
338 Win. Mag.*	210	2830	2590	2370	2150	1940	3735	3130	2610	2155	1760	+2.5	+1.4	-6.0	-20.9	$33
338 Win. Mag.*	225	2785	2517	2266	2029	1808	3871	3165	2565	2057	1633	+2.5	+0.4	-8.5	-25.9	$27
338 W.M. Heavy Mag.	225	2920	2678	2449	2232	2027	4259	3583	2996	2489	2053	+1.75	0.0	-7.65	-22.0	NA
338 W.M. High Energy	225	2940	2690	2450	2230	2010	4320	3610	3000	2475	2025	+1.7	0.0	-7.5	-22.0	NA
338 Win. Mag.	230	2780	2573	2375	2186	2005	3948	3382	2881	2441	2054	+2.5	+1.2	-6.3	-21.0	$40
338 Win. Mag.*	250	2660	2456	2261	2075	1898	3927	3348	2837	2389	1999	+2.5	+0.2	-9.0	-26.2	$27
338 W.M. High Energy	250	2800	2610	2420	2250	2080	4350	3775	3260	2805	2395	+1.8	0.0	-7.8	-22.5	NA
338 Ultra Mag.	250	2860	2645	2440	2244	2057	4540	3882	3303	2794	2347	1.7	0.0	-7.6	-22.1	NA
8.59(.338) Galaxy	200	3100	2899	2707	2524	2347	4269	3734	3256	2829	2446	3	3.80	0.0	-9.3	NA
34, 35																
340 Wea. Mag.*	210	3250	2991	2746	2515	2295	4924	4170	3516	2948	2455	+2.5	+1.9	-1.8	-11.8	$56
340 Wea. Mag.*	250	3000	2806	2621	2443	2272	4995	4371	3812	3311	2864	+2.5	+2.0	-3.5	-14.8	$56
330 A-Square	250	3120	2799	2500	2220	1958	5403	4348	3469	2736	2128	+2.5	+2.7	-1.5	-10.5	NA
338-378 Wea. Mag.	225	3180	2974	2778	2591	2410	5052	4420	3856	3353	2902	3.1	3.80	0.0	-8.9	NA
338 Titan	225	3230	3010	2800	2600	2409	5211	4524	3916	3377	2898	+3.07	+3.80	0.0	-8.95	NA
338 Excalibur	200	3600	3361	3134	2920	2715	5755	5015	4363	3785	3274	+2.23	+2.87	0.0	-6.99	NA
338 Excalibur	250	3250	2922	2618	2333	2066	5863	4740	3804	3021	2370	+1.3	0.0	-6.35	-19.2	NA
348 Winchester	200	2520	2215	1931	1672	1443	2820	2178	1656	1241	925	+2.5	-1.4	-14.7	0.0	$42
357 Magnum	158	1830	1427	1138	980	883	1175	715	454	337	274	0.0	-16.2	-33.1	0.0	$25**
35 Remington	150	2300	1874	1506	1218	1039	1762	1169	755	494	359	+2.5	-4.1	-26.3	0.0	$16
35 Remington	200	2080	1698	1376	1140	1001	1921	1280	841	577	445	+2.5	-6.3	-17.1	-33.6	$16
356 Winchester	200	2460	2114	1797	1517	1284	2688	1985	1434	1022	732	+2.5	-1.8	-15.1	0.0	$31
356 Winchester	250	2160	1911	1682	1476	1299	2591	2028	1571	1210	937	+2.5	-3.7	-22.2	0.0	$31
358 Winchester	200	2490	2171	1876	1619	1379	2753	2093	1563	1151	844	+2.5	-1.6	-15.6	0.0	$31
358 STA	275	2850	2562	2292	2039	NA	4958	4009	3208	2539	NA	+1.9	0.0	-8.6	0.0	NA
350 Rem. Mag.	200	2710	2410	2130	1870	1631	3261	2579	2014	1553	1181	+2.5	-0.2	-10.0	-30.1	$33
35 Whelen	200	2675	2378	2100	1842	1606	3177	2510	1958	1506	1145	+2.5	-0.2	-10.3	-31.1	$20
35 Whelen	225	2500	2300	2110	1930	1770	3120	2650	2235	1870	1560	+2.6	0.0	-10.2	-29.9	NA
35 Whelen	250	2400	2197	2005	1823	1652	3197	2680	2230	1844	1515	+2.5	-1.2	-13.7	0.0	$20
358 Norma Mag.	250	2800	2510	2230	1970	1730	4350	3480	2750	2145	1655	+2.5	+1.0	-7.6	-25.2	NA
358 STA	275	2850	2562	229'2	2039	1764	4959	4009	3208	2539	1899	+1.9	0.0	-8.58	-26.1	NA
9.3mm																
9.3x57mm Mau.	286	2070	1810	1590	1390	1110	2710	2090	1600	1220	955	+2.5	-2.6	-22.5	0.0	NA
9.3x62mm Mau.	286	2360	2089	1844	1623	NA	3538	2771	2157	1670	1260	+2.5	-1.6	-21.0	0.0	NA
9.3x64mm	286	2700	2505	2318	2139	1968	4629	3984	3411	2906	2460	+2.5	+2.7	-4.5	-19.2	NA
9.3x74Rmm	286	2360	2089	1844	1623	NA	3538	2771	2157	1670	NA	+2.5	-2.0	-11.0	0.0	NA
375																
38-55 Win.	255	1320	1190	1091	1018	963	987	802	674	587	525	0.0	-23.4	0.0	0.0	$25
375 Winchester	200	2200	1841	1526	1268	1089	2150	1506	1034	714	527	+2.5	-4.0	-26.2	0.0	$27
375 Winchester	250	1900	1647	1424	1239	1103	2005	1506	1126	852	676	+2.5	-6.9	-33.3	0.0	$27
376 Steyr	225	2600	2331	2078	1842	1625	3377	2714	2157	1694	1319	2.5	0.0	-10.6	-31.4	NA
376 Steyr	270	2600	2372	2156	1951	1759	4052	3373	2707	2283	1855	2.3	0.0	0.0	28.0	NA
375 Dakota	300	2000	2316	2051	1004	1579	4502	3573	2800	2167	1661	12.4	0.0	11.0	32.7	NA
375 N.E. 2-1/2"	270	2000	1740	1507	1310	NA	2398	1815	1362	1026	NA	+2.5	-6.0	-30.0	0.0	NA
375 Flanged	300	2450	2150	1886	1640	NA	3998	3102	2369	1790	NA	+2.5	-2.4	-17.0	0.0	NA
375 H&H Magnum	250	2670	2450	2240	2040	1850	3955	3335	2790	2315	1905	+2.5	-0.4	-10.2	-28.4	NA
375 H&H Magnum	270	2690	2420	2166	1928	1707	4337	3510	2812	2228	1747	+2.5	0.0	-10.0	-29.4	$28
375 H&H Magnum*	300	2530	2245	1979	1733	1512	4263	3357	2608	2001	1523	+2.5	-1.0	-10.5	-33.6	$28
375 H&H Hvy. Mag.	270	2870	2628	2399	2182	1976	4937	4141	3451	2150	1845	+1.7	0.0	-7.2	-21.0	NA
375 H&H Hvy. Mag.	300	2705	2386	2090	1816	1568	4873	3793	2908	2195	1637	+2.3	0.0	-10.4	-31.4	NA
375 Rem. Ultra Mag.	270	2900	2558	2241	1947	1678	5041	3922	3010	2272	1689	1.9	2.7	-8.9	-27	NA
375 Rem. Ultra Mag.	300	2760	2505	2263	2035	1822	5073	4178	3412	2759	2210	2.0	0.0	-8.8	-26.1	NA
375 Wea. Mag.	300	2700	2420	2157	1911	1685	4856	3901	3100	2432	1891	+2.5	-.04	-10.7	0.0	NA
378 Wea. Mag.	270	3180	2976	2781	2594	2415	6062	5308	4635	4034	3495	+2.5	+2.6	-1.8	-11.3	$71
378 Wea. Mag.	300	2929	2576	2252	1952	1680	5698	4419	3379	2538	1881	+2.5	+1.2	-7.0	-24.5	$77
375 A-Square	300	2920	2626	2351	2093	1850	5679	4594	3681	2917	2281	+2.5	+1.4	-6.0	-21.0	NA
38-40 Win.	180	1160	999	901	827	764	538	399	324	273	233	0.0	-33.9	0.0	0.0	$42**
405 Win.	300	2200	1851	1545	1296		3224	2282	1589	1119		4.6	0.0	-19.5	0.0	NA
40, 41																
450/400-3"	400	2150	1932	1730	1545	1379	4105	3316	2659	2119	1689	+2.5	-4.0	-9.5	-30.0	NA
416 Dakota	400	2450	2294	2143	1998	1859	5330	4671	4077	3544	3068	+2.5	-0.2	-10.5	-29.4	NA
416 Taylor	400	2350	2117	1896	1693	NA	4905	3980	3194	2547	NA	+2.5	-1.2	15.0	0.0	NA
416 Hoffman	400	2380	2145	1923	1718	1529	5031	4087	3285	2620	2077	+2.5	-1.0	-14.1	0.0	NA
416 Rigby	350	2600	2449	2303	2162	2026	5253	4661	4122	3632	3189	+2.5	-1.8	-10.2	-26.0	NA

Many manufacturers do not supply suggested retail prices. Others did not get their pricing to us before press time. All pricing can vary dependent on the exact brand and style of ammo selected and/or the retail outlet from which you make your purchase. Pricing has been rounded to the nearest dollar and represents our best estimate of average pricing. An * after the cartridge means these loads are available with Nosler Partition or Swift A-Frame bullets. Listed pricing may or may not reflect this bullet type. ** = these are packed 50 to box, all others are 20 to box. Wea. Mag.= Weatherby Magnum. Spfd. = Springfield. A-A-Sq. = A-Square. N.E.=Nitro Express.

Cartridge	Bullet Wgt. Grs.	VELOCITY (fps)					ENERGY (ft. lbs.)					TRAJ. (in.)				Est. Price/ box
		Muzzle	100 yds.	200 yds.	300 yds.	400 yds.	Muzzle	100 yds.	200 yds.	300 yds.	400 yds.	100 yds.	200 yds.	300 yds.	400 yds.	
416 Rigby	400	2370	2210	2050	1900	NA	4990	4315	3720	3185	NA	+2.5	-0.7	-12.1	0.0	NA
416 Rigby	410	2370	2110	1870	1640	NA	5115	4050	3165	2455	NA	+2.5	-2.4	-17.3	0.0	$110
416 Rem. Mag.*	350	2520	2270	2034	1814	1611	4935	4004	3216	2557	2017	+2.5	-0.8	-12.6	-35.0	$82
416 Rem. Mag.*	400	2400	2175	1962	1763	1579	5115	4201	3419	2760	2214	+2.5	-1.5	-14.6	0.0	$80
416 Wea. Mag.*	400	2700	2397	2115	1852	1613	6474	5104	3971	3047	2310	+2.5	0.0	-10.1	-30.4	$96
10.57 (416) Meteor	400	2730	2532	2342	2161	1987	6621	5695	4874	4147	3508	+1.9	0.0	-8.3	-24.0	NA
404 Jeffrey	400	2150	1924	1716	1525	NA	4105	3289	2614	2064	NA	+2.5	-4.0	-22.1	0.0	NA

425, 44

Cartridge	Bullet Wgt. Grs.	Muzzle	100 yds.	200 yds.	300 yds.	400 yds.	Muzzle	100 yds.	200 yds.	300 yds.	400 yds.	100 yds.	200 yds.	300 yds.	400 yds.	Est. Price/ box
425 Express	400	2400	2160	1934	1725	NA	5115	4145	3322	2641	NA	+2.5	-1.0	-14.0	0.0	NA
44-40 Win.	200	1190	1006	900	822	756	629	449	360	300	254	0.0	-33.3	0.0	0.0	$36**
44 Rem. Mag.	210	1920	1477	1155	982	880	1719	1017	622	450	361	0.0	-17.6	0.0	0.0	$14
44 Rem. Mag.	240	1760	1380	1114	970	878	1650	1015	661	501	411	0.0	-17.6	0.0	0.0	$13
444 Marlin	240	2350	1815	1377	1087	941	2942	1753	1001	630	472	+2.5	-15.1	-31.0	0.0	$22
444 Marlin	265	2120	1733	1405	1160	1012	2644	1768	1162	791	603	+2.5	-6.0	-32.2	0.0	Disc.
444 Marlin Light Mag	265	2335	1913	1551	1266		3208	2153	1415	943		2.0	-4.90	-26.5	0.0	NA

45

Cartridge	Bullet Wgt. Grs.	Muzzle	100 yds.	200 yds.	300 yds.	400 yds.	Muzzle	100 yds.	200 yds.	300 yds.	400 yds.	100 yds.	200 yds.	300 yds.	400 yds.	Est. Price/ box
45-70 Govt.	300	1810	1497	1244	1073	969	2182	1492	1031	767	625	0.0	-14.8	0.0	0.0	$21
45-70 Govt. Supreme	300	1880	1558	1292	1103	988	2355	1616	1112	811	651	0.0	-12.9	-46.0	-105.0	NA
45-70 Govt. CorBon	350	1800	1526	1296			2519	1810	1307			0.0	-14.6	0.0	0.0	NA
45-70 Govt.	405	1330	1168	1055	977	918	1590	1227	1001	858	758	0.0	-24.6	0.0	0.0	$21
45-70 Govt. PMC Cowboy	405	1550	1193				1639	1280				0.0	-23.9	0.0	0.0	NA
45-70 Govt. Garrett	415	1850					3150					3.0	-7.0	0.0	0.0	NA
45-70 Govt. Garrett	530	1550	1343	1178	1062	982	2828	2123	1633	1327	1135	0.0	-17.8	0.0	0.0	NA
450 Marlin	350	2100	1774	1488	1254	1089	3427	2446	1720	1222	922	0.0	-9.7	-35.2	0.0	NA
458 Win. Magnum	350	2470	1990	1570	1250	1060	4740	3065	1915	1205	870	+2.5	-2.5	-21.6	0.0	$43
458 Win. Magnum	400	2380	2170	1960	1770	NA	5030	4165	3415	2785	NA	+2.5	-0.4	-13.4	0.0	$73
458 Win. Magnum	465	2220	1999	1791	1601	NA	5088	4127	3312	2646	NA	+2.5	-2.0	-17.7	0.0	NA
458 Win. Magnum	500	2040	1823	1623	1442	1237	4620	3689	2924	2308	1839	+2.5	-3.5	-22.0	0.0	$61
458 Win. Magnum	510	2040	1770	1527	1319	1157	4712	3547	2640	1970	1516	+2.5	-4.1	-25.0	0.0	$41
450 Dakota	500	2450	2235	2030	1838	1658	6663	5544	4576	3748	3051	+2.5	-0.6	-12.0	-33.8	NA
450 N.E. 3-1/4"	465	2190	1970	1765	1577	NA	4952	4009	3216	2567	NA	+2.5	-3.0	-20.0	0.0	NA
450 N.E. 3-1/4"	500	2150	1920	1708	1514	NA	5132	4093	3238	2544	NA	+2.5	-4.0	-22.9	0.0	NA
450 No. 2	465	2190	1970	1765	1577	NA	4952	4009	3216	2567	NA	+2.5	-3.0	-20.0	0.0	NA
450 No. 2	500	2150	1920	1708	1514	NA	5132	4093	3238	2544	NA	+2.5	-4.0	-22.9	0.0	NA
458 Lott	465	2380	2150	1932	1730	NA	5848	4773	3855	3091	NA	+2.5	-1.0	-14.0	0.0	NA
458 Lott	500	2300	2062	1838	1633	NA	5873	4719	3748	2960	NA	+2.5	-1.6	-16.4	0.0	NA
450 Ackley Mag.	465	2400	2169	1950	1747	NA	5947	4857	3927	3150	NA	+2.5	-1.0	-13.7	0.0	NA
450 Ackley Mag.	500	2320	2081	1855	1649	NA	5975	4085	3820	3018	NA	+2.5	-1.2	-15.0	0.0	NA
460 Short A-Sq.	500	2420	2175	1943	1729	NA	6501	5250	4193	3319	NA	+2.5	-0.8	-12.8	0.0	NA
460 Wea. Mag.	500	2700	2404	2128	1869	1635	8092	6416	5026	3878	2969	+2.5	+0.6	-8.9	-28.0	$72

475

Cartridge	Bullet Wgt. Grs.	Muzzle	100 yds.	200 yds.	300 yds.	400 yds.	Muzzle	100 yds.	200 yds.	300 yds.	400 yds.	100 yds.	200 yds.	300 yds.	400 yds.	Est. Price/ box
500/465 N.E.	480	2150	1917	1703	1507	NA	4926	3917	3089	2419	NA	+2.5	-4.0	-22.2	0.0	NA
470 Rigby	500	2150	1940	1740	1560	NA	5130	4170	3360	2695	NA	+2.5	-2.8	-19.4	0.0	NA
470 Nitro Ex.	480	2190	1954	1735	1536	NA	5111	4070	3210	2515	NA	+2.5	-3.5	-20.8	0.0	NA
470 Nitro Ex.	500	2150	1890	1650	1440	1270	5130	3965	3040	2310	1790	+2.5	-4.3	-24.0	0.0	$177
475 No. 2	500	2200	1955	1728	1522	NA	5375	4243	3316	2573	NA	+2.5	-3.2	-20.9	0.0	NA

50, 58

Cartridge	Bullet Wgt. Grs.	Muzzle	100 yds.	200 yds.	300 yds.	400 yds.	Muzzle	100 yds.	200 yds.	300 yds.	400 yds.	100 yds.	200 yds.	300 yds.	400 yds.	Est. Price/ box
505 Gibbs	525	2300	2063	1840	1637	NA	6166	4922	3948	3122	NA	+2.5	-3.0	-18.0	0.0	NA
500 N.E.-3"	570	2150	1928	1722	1533	NA	5850	4703	3752	2975	NA	+2.5	-3.7	-22.0	0.0	NA
500 N.E.-3"	600	2150	1927	1721	1531	NA	6158	4947	3944	3124	NA	+2.5	-4.0	-22.0	0.0	NA
495 A-Square	570	2350	2117	1896	1693	NA	5850	4703	3752	2975	NA	+2.5	-1.0	-14.5	0.0	NA
495 A-Square	600	2280	2050	1833	1635	NA	6925	5598	4478	3562	NA	+2.5	-2.0	-17.0	0.0	NA
500 A-Square	600	2380	2144	1922	1766	NA	7546	6126	4920	3922	NA	+2.5	-3.0	-17.0	0.0	NA
500 A-Square	707	2250	2040	1841	1567	NA	7947	6530	5318	4311	NA	+2.5	-2.0	-17.0	0.0	NA
500 BMG PMC	660	3080	2854	2639	2444	2248	13688		500 yd. zero			+3.1	+3.9	+4.7	+2.8	NA
577 Nitro Ex.	750	2050	1793	1562	1360	NA	6990	5356	4065	3079	NA	+2.5	-5.0	-26.0	0.0	NA
577 Tyrannosaur	750	2400	2141	1898	1675	NA	9591	7633	5996	4671	NA	+3.0	0.0	-12.9	0.0	NA

600, 700

Cartridge	Bullet Wgt. Grs.	Muzzle	100 yds.	200 yds.	300 yds.	400 yds.	Muzzle	100 yds.	200 yds.	300 yds.	400 yds.	100 yds.	200 yds.	300 yds.	400 yds.	Est. Price/ box
600 N.E.	900	1950	1680	1452	NA	NA	7596	5634	4212	NA	NA	+5.6	0.0	0.0	0.0	NA
700 N.E.	1200	1900	1676	1472	NA	NA	9618	7480	5774	NA	NA	+5.7	0.0	0.0	0.0	NA

CENTERFIRE HANDGUN CARTRIDGES — BALLISTICS & PRICES

Notes: Blanks are available in 32 S&W, 38 S&W and 38 Special. "V" after barrel length indicates test barrel was vented to produce ballistics similar to a revolver with a normal barrel-to-cylinder gap. Ammo prices are per 50 rounds except when marked with an ** which signifies a 20 round box; *** signifies a 25-round box. Not all loads are available from all ammo manufacturers. Listed loads are those made by Remington, Winchester, Federal, and others. DISC. is a discontinued load. Prices are rounded to nearest whole dollar and will vary with brand and retail outlet. † = new bullet weight this year; "c" indicates a change in data.

Cartridge	Bullet Wgt. Grs.	VELOCITY (fps)			ENERGY (ft. lbs.)			Mid-Range Traj. (in.)		Bbl. Lgth. (in).	Est. Price/ box
		Muzzle	50 yds.	100 yds.	Muzzle	50 yds.	100 yds.	50 yds.	100 yds.		
22, 25											
221 Rem. Fireball	50	2650	2380	2130	780	630	505	0.2	0.8	10.5"	$15
25 Automatic	35	900	813	742	63	51	43	NA	NA	2"	$18
25 Automatic	45	815	730	655	65	55	40	1.8	7.7	2"	$21
25 Automatic	50	760	705	660	65	55	50	2.0	8.7	2"	$17
30											
7.5mm Swiss	107	1010	NA	NA	240	NA	NA	NA	NA	NA	NEW
7.62mm Tokarev	87	1390	NA	NA	365	NA	NA	0.6	NA	4.5"	NA
7.62 Nagant	97	790	NA	NA	134	NA	NA	NA	NA	NA	NEW
7.63 Mauser	88	1440	NA	NA	405	NA	NA	NA	NA	NA	NEW
30 Luger	93†	1220	1110	1040	305	255	225	0.9	3.5	4.5"	$34
30 Carbine	110	1790	1600	1430	785	625	500	0.4	1.7	10"	$28
30-357/ AeT	123	1992	NA	NA	1084	NA	NA	NA	NA	10"	NA
32											
32 S&W	88	680	645	610	90	80	75	2.5	10.5	3"	$17
32 S&W Long	98	705	670	635	115	100	90	2.3	10.5	4"	$17
32 Short Colt	80	745	665	590	100	80	60	2.2	9.9	4"	$19
32 H&R Magnum	85	1100	1020	930	230	195	165	1.0	4.3	4.5"	$21
32 H&R Magnum	95	1030	940	900	225	190	170	1.1	4.7	4.5"	$19
32 Automatic	60	970	895	835	125	105	95	1.3	5.4	4"	$22
32 Automatic	60	1000	917	849	133	112	96			4"	NA
32 Automatic	65	950	890	830	130	115	100	1.3	5.6	NA	NA
32 Automatic	71	905	855	810	130	115	95	1.4	5.8	4"	$19
8mm Lebel Pistol	111	850	NA	NA	180	NA	NA	NA	NA	NA	NEW
8mm Steyr	112	1080	NA	NA	290	NA	NA	NA	NA	NA	NEW
8mm Gasser	126	850	NA	NA	200	NA	NA	NA	NA	NA	NEW
9mm, 38											
380 Automatic	60	1130	960	NA	170	120	NA	1.0	NA	NA	NA
380 Automatic	85/88	990	920	870	190	165	145	1.2	5.1	4"	$20
380 Automatic	90	1000	890	800	200	160	130	1.2	5.5	3.75"	$10
380 Automatic	95/100	955	865	785	190	160	130	1.4	5.9	4"	$20
38 Super Auto +P	115	1300	1145	1040	430	335	275	0.7	3.3	5"	$26
38 Super Auto +P	125/130	1215	1100	1015	425	350	300	0.8	3.6	5"	$26
38 Super Auto +P	147	1100	1050	1000	395	355	325	0.9	4.0	5"	NA
9x18mm Makarov	95	1000	NA	NA	NA	NA	NA	NA	NA	NA	NEW
9x18mm Ultra	100	1050	NA	NA	240	NA	NA	NA	NA	NA	NEW
9x23mm Largo	124	1190	1055	966	390	306	257	0.7	3.7	4"	NA
9x23mm Win.	125	1450	1249	1103	583	433	338	0.6	2.8	NA	NA
9mm Steyr	115	1180	NA	NA	350	NA	NA	NA	NA	NA	NEW
9mm Luger	88	1500	1190	1010	440	275	200	0.6	3.1	4"	$24
9mm Luger	90	1360	1112	978	370	247	191	NA	NA	4"	$26
9mm Luger	95	1300	1140	1010	350	275	215	0.8	3.4	4"	NA
9mm Luger	100	1180	1080	NA	305	255	NA	0.9	NA	4"	NA
9mm Luger	115	1155	1045	970	340	280	240	0.9	3.9	4"	$21
9mm Luger	123/125	1110	1030	970	340	290	260	1.0	4.0	4"	$23
9mm Luger	140	935	890	850	270	245	225	1.3	5.5	4"	$23
9mm Luger	147	990	940	900	320	290	265	1.1	4.9	4"	$26
9mm Luger +P	90	1475	NA	NA	437	NA	NA	NA	NA	NA	NA
9mm Luger +P	115	1250	1113	1019	399	316	265	0.8	3.5	4"	$27
9mm Federal	115	1280	1130	1040	420	330	280	0.7	3.3	4"V	$24
9mm Luger Vector	115	1155	1047	971	341	280	241	NA	NA	4"	NA
9mm Luger +P	124	1180	1089	1021	384	327	287	0.8	3.8	4"	NA
38											
38 S&W	146	685	650	620	150	135	125	2.4	10.0	4"	$19
38 Short Colt	125	730	685	645	150	130	115	2.2	9.4	6"	$19
39 Special	100	950	900	NA	200	180	NA	1.3	NA	4"V	NA
38 Special	110	945	895	850	220	195	175	1.3	5.4	4"V	$23
38 Special	110	945	895	850	220	195	175	1.3	5.4	4"V	$23
38 Special	130	775	745	710	175	160	120	1.9	7.9	4"V	$22

Notes: Blanks are available in 32 S&W, 38 S&W and 38 Special. "V" after barrel length indicates test barrel was vented to produce ballistics similar to a revolver with a normal barrel-to-cylinder gap. Ammo prices are per 50 rounds except when marked with an ** which signifies a 20 round box; *** signifies a 25-round box. Not all loads are available from all ammo manufacturers. Listed loads are those made by Remington, Winchester, Federal, and others. DISC. is a discontinued load. Prices are rounded to nearest whole dollar and will vary with brand and retail outlet. † = new bullet weight this year; "c" indicates a change in data.

Cartridge	Bullet Wgt. Grs.	VELOCITY (fps)			ENERGY (ft. lbs.)			Mid-Range Traj. (in.)		Bbl. Lgth. (in).	Est. Price/ box
		Muzzle	50 yds.	100 yds.	Muzzle	50 yds.	100 yds.	50 yds.	100 yds.		
38											
38 Special Cowboy	140	800	767	735	199	183	168			7.5" V	NA
38 (Multi-Ball)	140	830	730	505	215	130	80	2.0	10.6	4"V	$10**
38 Special	148	710	635	565	165	130	105	2.4	10.6	4"V	$17
38 Special	158	755	725	690	200	185	170	2.0	8.3	4"V	$18
38 Special +P	95	1175	1045	960	290	230	195	0.9	3.9	4"V	$23
38 Special +P	110	995	925	870	240	210	185	1.2	5.1	4"V	$23
38 Special +P	125	975	929	885	264	238	218	1	5.2	4"	NA
38 Special +P	125	945	900	860	250	225	205	1.3	5.4	4"V	#23
38 Special +P	129	945	910	870	255	235	215	1.3	5.3	4"V	$11
38 Special +P	130	925	887	852	247	227	210	1.3	5.50	4"V	NA
38 Special +P	147/150(c)	884	NA	NA	264	NA	NA	NA	NA	4"V	$27
38 Special +P	158	890	855	825	280	255	240	1.4	6.0	4"V	$20
357											
357 SIG	115	1520	NA	NA	593	NA	NA	NA	NA	NA	NA
357 SIG	124	1450	NA	NA	578	NA	NA	NA	NA	NA	NA
357 SIG	125	1350	1190	1080	510	395	325	0.7	3.1	4"	NA
357 SIG	150	1130	1030	970	420	355	310	0.9	4.0	NA	NA
356 TSW	115	1520	NA	NA	593	NA	NA	NA	NA	NA	NA
356 TSW	124	1450	NA	NA	578	NA	NA	NA	NA	NA	NA
356 TSW	135	1280	1120	1010	490	375	310	0.8	3.50	NA	NA
356 TSW	147	1220	1120	1040	485	410	355	0.8	3.5	5"	NA
357 Mag., Super Clean	105	1650									NA
357 Magnum	110	1295	1095	975	410	290	230	0.8	3.5	4"V	$25
357 (Med.Vel.)	125	1220	1075	985	415	315	270	0.8	3.7	4"V	$25
357 Magnum	125	1450	1240	1090	585	425	330	0.6	2.8	4"V	$25
357 (Multi-Ball)	140	1155	830	665	420	215	135	1.2	6.4	4"V	$11**
357 Magnum	140	1360	1195	1075	575	445	360	0.7	3.0	4"V	$25
357 Magnum	145	1290	1155	1060	535	430	360	0.8	3.5	4"V	$26
357 Magnum	150/158	1235	1105	1015	535	430	360	0.8	3.5	4"V	$25
357 Mag. Cowboy	158	800	761	725	225	203	185				NA
357 Magnum	165	1290	1189	1108	610	518	450	0.7	3.1	8-3/8"	NA
357 Magnum	180	1145	1055	985	525	445	390	0.9	3.9	4"V	$25
357 Magnum	180	1180	1088	1020	557	473	416	0.8	3.6	8"V	NA
357 Mag. CorBon F.A.	180	1650	1512	1386	1088	913	767	1.66	0.0		NA
357 Mag. CorBon	200	1200	1123	1061	640	560	500	3.19	0.0		NA
357 Rem. Maximum	158	1825	1590	1380	1170	885	670	0.4	1.7	10.5"	$14**
40, 10mm											
40 S&W	135	1140	1070	NA	390	345	NA	0.9	NA	4"	NA
40 S&W	155	1140	1026	958	447	362	309	0.9	4.1	4"	$14***
40 S&W	165	1150	NA	NA	485	NA	NA	NA	NA	4"	$18***
40 S&W	180	985	936	893	388	350	319	1.4	5.0	4"	$14***
40 S&W	180	1015	960	914	412	368	334	1.3	4.5	4"	NA
400 Cor-Bon	135	1450	NA	NA	630	NA	NA	NA	NA	5"	NA
10mm Automatic	155	1125	1046	986	436	377	335	0.9	3.9	5"	$26
10mm Automatic	170	1340	1165	1145	680	510	415	0.7	3.2	5"	$31
10mm Automatic	175	1290	1140	1035	650	505	420	0.7	3.3	5.5"	$11**
10mm Auto. (FBI)	180	950	905	865	361	327	299	1.5	5.4	4"	$16**
10mm Automatic	180	1030	970	920	425	375	340	1.1	4.7	5"	$16**
10mm Auto H.V.	180†	1240	1124	1037	618	504	430	0.8	3.4	5"	$27
10mm Automatic	200	1160	1070	1010	495	510	430	0.9	3.8	5"	$14**
10.4mm Italian	177	950	NA	NA	360	NA	NA	NA	NA	NA	NEW
41 Action Exp.	180	1000	947	903	400	359	326	0.5	4.2	5"	$13**
41 Rem. Magnum	170	1420	1165	1015	760	515	390	0.7	3.2	4"V	$33
41 Rem. Magnum	175	1250	1120	1030	605	490	410	0.8	3.4	4"V	$14**
41 (Med. Vel.)	210	965	900	840	435	375	330	1.3	5.4	4"V	$30
41 Rem. Magnum	210	1300	1160	1060	790	630	535	0.7	3.2	4"V	$33
41 Rem. Magnum	240	1250	1151	1075	833	706	616	0.8	3.3	6.5V	NA

Notes: Blanks are available in 32 S&W, 38 S&W and 38 Special. "V" after barrel length indicates test barrel was vented to produce ballistics similar to a revolver with a normal barrel-to-cylinder gap. Ammo prices are per 50 rounds except when marked with an ** which signifies a 20 round box; *** signifies a 25-round box. Not all loads are available from all ammo manufacturers. Listed loads are those made by Remington, Winchester, Federal, and others. DISC. is a discontinued load. Prices are rounded to nearest whole dollar and will vary with brand and retail outlet. † = new bullet weight this year; "c" indicates a change in data.

Cartridge	Bullet Wgt. Grs.	VELOCITY (fps)			ENERGY (ft. lbs.)			Mid-Range Traj. (in.)		Bbl. Lgth. (in).	Est. Price/ box
		Muzzle	50 yds.	100 yds.	Muzzle	50 yds.	100 yds.	50 yds.	100 yds.		
44											
44 S&W Russian	247	780	NA	NA	335	NA	NA	NA	NA	NA	NA
44 S&W Special	180	980	NA	NA	383	NA	NA	NA	NA	6.5"	NA
44 S&W Special	180	1000	935	882	400	350	311	NA	NA	7.5"V	NA
44 S&W Special	200†	875	825	780	340	302	270	1.2	6.0	6"	$13**
44 S&W Special	200	1035	940	865	475	390	335	1.1	4.9	6.5"	$13**
44 S&W Special	240/246	755	725	695	310	285	265	2.0	8.3	6.5"	$26
44-40 Win. Cowboy	225	750	723	695	281	261	242				NA
44 Rem. Magnum	180	1610	1365	1175	1035	745	550	0.5	2.3	4"V	$18**
44 Rem. Magnum	200	1400	1192	1053	870	630	492	0.6	NA	6.5"	$20
44 Rem. Magnum	210	1495	1310	1165	1040	805	635	0.6	2.5	6.5"	$18**
44 (Med. Vel.)	240	1000	945	900	535	475	436	1.1	4.8	6.5"	$17
44 R.M. (Jacketed)	240	1180	1080	1010	740	625	545	0.9	3.7	4"V	$18**
44 R.M. (Lead)	240	1350	1185	1070	970	750	610	0.7	3.1	4"V	$29
44 Rem. Magnum	250	1180	1100	1040	775	670	600	0.8	3.6	6.5"V	$21
44 Rem. Magnum	250	1250	1148	1070	867	732	635	0.8	3.3	6.5"V	NA
44 Rem. Magnum	275	1235	1142	1070	931	797	699	0.8	3.3	6.5"	NA
44 Rem. Magnum	300	1200	1100	1026	959	806	702	NA	NA	7.5"	$17
44 Rem. Magnum	330	1385	1297	1220	1406	1234	1090	1.83	0.00	NA	NA
440 CorBon	260	1700	1544	1403	1669	1377	1136	1.58	NA	10"	NA
45, 50											
450 Short Colt/450 Revolver	226	830	NA	NA	350	NA	NA	NA	NA	NA	NEW
45 S&W Schofield	180	730	NA	NA	213	NA	NA	NA	NA	NA	NA
45 S&W Schofield	230	730	NA	NA	272	NA	NA	NA	NA	NA	NA
45 G.A.P.	185	1090	970	890	490	385	320	1	4.7	5	NA
45 G.A.P.	230	880	842	NA	396	363	NA	NA	NA	NA	NA
45 Automatic	165	1030	930	NA	385	315	NA	1.2	NA	5"	NA
45 Automatic	185	1000	940	890	410	360	325	1.1	4.9	5"	$28
45 Auto. (Match)	185	770	705	650	245	204	175	2.0	8.7	5"	$28
45 Auto. (Match)	200	940	890	840	392	352	312	2.0	8.6	5"	$20
45 Automatic	200	975	917	860	421	372	328	1.4	5.0	5"	$18
45 Automatic	230	830	800	675	355	325	300	1.6	6.8	5"	$27
45 Automatic	230	880	846	816	396	366	340	1.5	6.1	5"	NA
45 Automatic +P	165	1250	NA	NA	573	NA	NA	NA	NA	NA	NA
45 Automatic +P	185	1140	1040	970	535	445	385	0.9	4.0	5"	$31
45 Automatic +P	200	1055	982	925	494	428	380	NA	NA	5"	NA
45 Super	185	1300	1190	1108	694	582	504	NA	NA	5"	NA
45 Win. Magnum	230	1400	1230	1105	1000	775	635	0.6	2.8	5"	$14**
45 Win. Magnum	260	1250	1137	1053	902	746	640	0.8	3.3	5"	$16**
45 Win. Mag. CorBon	320	1150	1080	1025	940	830	747	3.47			NA
455 Webley MKII	262	850	NA	NA	420	NA	NA	NA	NA	NA	NA
45 Colt	200	1000	938	889	444	391	351	1.3	4.8	5.5"	$21
45 Colt	225	960	890	830	460	395	345	1.3	5.5	5.5"	$22
45 Colt + P CorBon	265	1350	1225	1126	1073	884	746	2.65	0.0		NA
45 Colt + P CorBon	300	1300	1197	1114	1126	956	827	2.78	0.0		NA
45 Colt	250/255	860	820	780	410	375	340	1.6	6.6	5.5"	$27
454 Casull	250	1300	1151	1047	938	735	600	0.7	3.2	7.5"V	NA
454 Casull	260	1800	1577	1381	1871	1436	1101	0.4	1.8	7.5"V	NA
454 Casull	300	1625	1451	1308	1759	1413	1141	0.5	2.0	7.5"V	NA
454 Casull CorBon	360	1500	1387	1286	1800	1640	1323	2.01	0.0		NA
460 S&W	200	2300	2042	1801	2350	1851	1441	0	-1.60	NA	NA
460 S&W	250	1900	1640	1412	2004	1494	1106	0	-2.75	NA	NA
460 S&W	395	1550	1389	1249	2108	1691	1369	0	-4.00	NA	NA
475 Linebaugh	400	1350	1217	1119	1618	1315	1112	NA	NA	NA	NA
480 Ruger	325	1350	1191	1076	1315	1023	835	2.6	0.0	7.5"	NA
50 Action Exp.	325	1400	1209	1075	1414	1055	835	0.2	2.3	6"	$24**
500 S&W	275	1665	1392	1183	1693	1184	854	1.5	NA	8.375	NA
500 S&W	400	1675	1472	1299	2493	1926	1499	1.3	NA	8.375	NA
500 S&W	440	1625	1367	1169	2581	1825	1337	1.6	NA	8.375	NA

Note: The actual ballistics obtained with your firearm can vary considerably from the advertised ballistics. Also, ballistics can vary from lot to lot with the same brand and type load.

Cartridge	Bullet Wt. Grs.	Velocity (fps) 22-1/2" Bbl.		Energy (ft. lbs.) 22-1/2" Bbl.		Mid-Range Traj. (in.) 100 yds.	Muzzle Velocity 6" Bbl.
		Muzzle	100 yds.	Muzzle	100 yds.		
17 Aguila	20	1850	1267	NA	NA	NA	NA
17 Hornady Mach 2	17	2100	1530	166	88	0.7	NA
17 HMR	17	2550	1902	245	136	NA	NA
17 HMR	20	2375	1776	250	140	NA	NA
22 Short Blank	—	—	—	—	—	—	—
22 Short CB	29	727	610	33	24	NA	706
22 Short Target	29	830	695	44	31	6.8	786
22 Short HP	27	1164	920	81	50	4.3	1077
22 Colibri	20	375	183	6	1	NA	NA
22 Super Colibri	20	500	441	11	9	NA	NA
22 Long CB	29	727	610	33	24	NA	706
22 Long HV	29	1180	946	90	57	4.1	1031
22 LR Ballistician	25	1100	760	65	30	NA	NA
22 LR Pistol Match	40	1070	890	100	70	4.6	940
22 LR Sub Sonic HP	38	1050	901	93	69	4.7	NA
22 LR Standard Velocity	40	1070	890	100	70	4.6	940
22 LR HV	40	1255	1016	140	92	3.6	1060
22 LR Silhoutte	42	1220	1003	139	94	3.6	1025
22 SSS	60	950	802	120	86	NA	NA
22 LR HV HP	40	1280	1001	146	89	3.5	1085
22 Velocitor GDHP	40	1435	0	0	0	NA	NA
22 LR Hyper HP	32/33/34	1500	1075	165	85	2.8	NA
22 LR Stinger HP	32	1640	1132	191	91	2.6	1395
22 LR Hyper Vel	30	1750	1191	204	93	NA	NA
22 LR Shot #12	31	950	NA	NA	NA	NA	NA
22 WRF LFN	45	1300	1015	169	103	3	NA
22 Win. Mag.	30	2200	1373	322	127	1.4	1610
22 Win. Mag. V-Max BT	33	2000	1495	293	164	0.60	NA
22 Win. Mag. JHP	34	2120	1435	338	155	1.4	NA
22 Win. Mag. JHP	40	1910	1326	324	156	1.7	1480
22 Win. Mag. FMJ	40	1910	1326	324	156	1.7	1480
22 Win. Mag. Dyna Point	45	1550	1147	240	131	2.60	NA
22 Win. Mag. JHP	50	1650	1280	300	180	1.3	NA
22 Win. Mag. Shot #11	52	1000	—	NA	—	—	NA

SHOTSHELL LOADS & PRICES

NOTES: * = 10 rounds per box. ** = 5 rounds per box. Pricing variations and number of rounds per box can occur with type and brand of ammunition. Listed pricing is the average nominal cost for load style and box quantity shown. Not every brand is available in all shot size variations. Some manufacturers do not provide suggested list prices. All prices rounded to nearest whole dollar. The price you pay will vary dependent upon outlet of purchase. # = new load spec this year; "C" indicates a change in data.

Dram Equiv.	Shot Ozs.	Load Style	Shot Sizes	Brands	Avg. Price/box	Velocity (fps)
10 Gauge 3-1/2" Magnum						
4-1/2	2-1/4	premium	BB, 2, 4, 5, 6	Win., Fed., Rem.	$33	1205
Max	2	premium	4, 5, 6	Fed., Win.	NA	1300
4-1/4	2	high velocity	BB, 2, 4	Rem.	$22	1210
Max	18 pellets	premium	00 buck	Fed., Win.	$7**	1100
Max	1-7/8	hevi. shot	4, 5, 6	Rem.	NA	1225
Max	1-7/8	Bismuth	BB, 2, 4	Bis.	NA	1225
Max	1-3/4	hevi. shot	2, 4	Rem.	NA	1300
4-1/4	1-3/4	steel	TT, T, BBB, BB, 1, 2, 3	Win., Rem.	$27	1260
Mag	1-5/8	steel	T, BBB, BB, 2	Win.	$27	1285
Max	1-5/8	Bismuth	BB, 2, 4	Bismuth	NA	1375
Max	1-1/2	steel	T, BBB, BB, 1, 2, 3	Fed.	NA	1450
Max	1-3/8	steel	T, BBB, BB, 1, 2, 3	Fed., Rem.	NA	1500
Max	1-3/8	steel	T, DDD, DD, 2, 3	Fed., Win.	NA	1450
Max	1-3/4	slug, rifled	slug	Fed.	NA	1280
Max	24 pellets	Buckshot	1 Buck	Fed.	NA	1100
Max	54 pellets	Super-X	4 Buck	Win.	NA	1150
12 Gauge 3-1/2" Magnum						
Max	2-1/4	premium	4, 5, 6	Fed., Rem., Win.	$13*	1150
Max	2	Lead	4, 5, 6	Fed.	NA	1300
Max	2	Copper plated turkey	4, 5	Rem.	NA	1300
Max	18 pellets	premium	00 buck	Fed., Win., Rem.	$7**	1100
Max	1-7/8	hevi. shot	4, 5, 6	Rem.	NA	1225
Max	1-7/8	heavyweight	5, 6	Fed.	NA	1300
Max	1-3/4	hevi. shot	4, 5, 6	Rem.	NA	1300
Max	1-7/8	Bismuth	BB, 2, 4	Bis.	NA	1225
Max	1-5/8	high density	BB, 2	Fed.	NA	1450
Max	1-3/8	steel	T, BBB, BB, 2, 4	Fed., Win., Rem.	NA	1450
Max	1-1/2	Supreme H-V	BBB, BB, 2, 3	Win.	NA	1475
Max	1-3/8	H-speed steel	BB, 2	Rem.	NA	1550
Max	24 pellets	Premium	1 Buck	Fed.	NA	1100
Max	54 pellets	Super-X	4 Buck	Win.	NA	1050
12 Gauge 3" Magnum						
4	2	premium	BB, 2, 4, 5, 6	Win., Fed., Rem.	$9*	1175
4	1-7/8	premium	BB, 2, 4, 6	Win., Fed., Rem.	$19	1210
4	1-7/8	duplex	4x6	Rem.	$9*	1210
Max	1-3/4	turkey	4, 5, 6	Fed., Fio., Win., Rem.	NA	1300
Max	1-5/8	high density	BB, 2	Fed.	NA	1450
Max	1-5/8	high velocity	4, 5, 6	Fed.	NA	1350
Max	1-5/8	hevi. shot	4, 5, 6	Rem.	NA	1225
4	1-5/8	premium	2, 4, 5, 6	Win., Fed., Rem.	$18	1290
Max	1-1/2	hevi. shot	4, 5, 6	Rem.	NA	1300
Max	1-5/8	Bismuth	BB, 2, 4, 5, 6	Bis.	NA	1250
4	24 pellets	buffered	1 buck	Win., Fed., Rem.	$5**	1040
4	15 pellets	buffered	00 buck	Win., Fed., Rem.	$6**	1210
4	10 pellets	buffered	000 buck	Win., Fed., Rem.	$6**	1225
4	41 pellets	buffered	4 buck	Win., Fed., Rem.	$6**	1210
Max	1-3/8	heavyweight	5, 6	Fed.	NA	1300
Max	1-3/8	slug	slug	Bren.	NA	1476
Max	1-1/4	slug, rifled	slug	Fed.	NA	1600
Max	1-3/16	saboted slug	copper slug	Rem.	NA	1500
Max	7/8	slug, rifled	slug	Rem.	NA	1875
Max	1-1/8	low recoil	BB	Fed.	NA	850

Dram Equiv.	Shot Ozs.	Load Style	Shot Sizes	Brands	Avg. Price/box	Velocity (fps)
12 Gauge 3" Magnum *(cont.)*						
Max	1-1/8	steel	BB, 2, 3, 4	Fed., Win., Rem.	NA	1550
Max	1	steel	4, 6	Fed.	NA	1330
Max	1-3/8	buckhammer	slug	Rem.	NA	1500
Max	1	slug, rifled	slug, magnum	Win., Rem.	$5**	1760
Max	1	saboted slug	slug	Rem., Win., Fed.	$10**	1550
Max	385 grs.	partition gold	slug	Win.	NA	2000
3-5/8	1-3/8	steel	BBB, BB, 1, 2, 3, 4	Win., Fed., Rem.	$19	1275
Max	1-1/8	steel	BB, 2, 4	Rem.	NA	1500
Max	1-1/8	steel	T, BBB, BB, 2, 4, 5, 6	Fed., Win.	NA	1450
Max	1-1/8	steel	BB, 2	Fed.	NA	1400
4	1-1/4	steel	T, BBB, BB, 1, 2, 3, 4, 6	Win., Fed., Rem.	$18	1400
12 Gauge 2-3/4"						
Max	1-5/8	magnum	4, 5, 6	Win., Fed.	$8*	1250
Max	1-3/8	lead	4, 5, 6	Fiocchi	NA	1485
Max	1-3/8	turkey	4, 5, 6	Fio.	NA	1250
Max	1-3/8	steel	4, 5, 6	Fed.	NA	1400
Max	1-3/8	Bismuth	BB, 2, 4, 5, 6	Bis.	NA	1300
Max	1-3/8	hevi. shot	4, 5, 6	Rem.	NA	1250
3-3/4	1-1/2	magnum	BB, 2, 4, 5, 6	Win., Fed., Rem.	$16	1260
Max	1-1/4	Supreme H-V	4, 5, 6, 7-1/2	Win., Rem.	NA	1400
3-3/4	1-1/4	high velocity	BB, 2, 4, 5, 6, 7-1/2, 8, 9	Win., Fed., Rem., Fio.	$13	1330
Max	1-1/4	hevi. shot	4, 6, 7-1/2	Rem.	NA	1325
3-1/2	1-1/4	mid-velocity	7, 8, 9	Win.	Disc.	1275
3-1/4	1-1/4	standard velocity	6, 7-1/2, 8, 9	Win., Fed., Rem., Fio.	$11	1220
3-1/4	1-1/8	standard velocity	4, 6, 7-1/2, 8, 9	Win., Fed., Rem., Fio.	$9	1255
Max	1-1/8	steel	2, 4	Rem.	NA	1390
Max	1	steel	BB, 2	Fed.	NA	1450
3-1/4	1	standard velocity	6, 7-1/2, 8	Rem., Fed., Fio., Win.	$6	1290
3-1/4	1-1/4	target	7-1/2, 8, 9	Win., Fed., Rem.	$10	1220
3	1-1/8	spreader	7-1/2, 8, 8-1/2, 9	Fio.	NA	1200
3	1-1/8	target	7-1/2, 8, 9, 7-1/2x8	Win., Fed., Rem., Fio.	$7	1200
2-3/4	1-1/8	target	7-1/2, 8, 8-1/2, 9, 7-1/2x8	Win., Fed., Rem., Fio.	$7	1145
2-3/4	1-1/8	low recoil	7-1/2, 8	Rem.	NA	1145
2-1/2	26 grams	low recoil	8	Win.	NA	980
2-1/4	1-1/8	target	7-1/2, 8, 8-1/2, 9	Rem., Fed.	$7	1080
Max	1	spreader	7-1/2, 8, 8-1/2, 9	Fio.	NA	1300
3-1/4	28 grams (1 oz)	target	7-1/2, 8, 9	Win., Fed., Fio.	$8	1290
3	1	target	7-1/2, 8, 8-1/2, 9	Win., Fio.	NA	1205
2-3/4	1	target	7-1/2, 8, 8-1/2, 9	Fed., Rem., Fio.	NA	1180
3-1/4	24 grams	target	7-1/2, 8, 9	Fed., Win., Fio.	NA	1325
3	7/8	light	8	Fio.	NA	1200
3-3/4	8 pellets	buffered	000 buck	Win., Fed., Rem.	$4**	1325
4	12 pellets	premium	00 buck	Win., Fed., Rem.	$5**	1290
3-3/4	9 pellets	buffered	00 buck	Win., Fed., Rem., Fio.	$19	1325
Max	9 pellets	hevi. shot	00 buck	Rem.	NA	1325
3-3/4	12 pellets	buffered	0 buck	Win., Fed., Rem.	$4**	1275

12 Gauge 2-3/4" (cont.)

Dram Equiv.	Shot Ozs.	Load Style	Shot Sizes	Brands	Avg. Price/box	Velocity (fps)
4	20 pellets	buffered	1 buck	Win., Fed., Rem.	$4**	1075
3-3/4	16 pellets	buffered	1 buck	Win., Fed., Rem.	$4**	1250
4	34 pellets	premium	4 buck	Fed., Rem.	$5**	1250
3-3/4	27 pellets	buffered	4 buck	Win., Fed., Rem., Fio.	$4**	1325
Max	1	saboted slug	slug	Win., Fed., Rem.	$10**	1450
Max	1-1/4	slug, rifled	slug	Fed.	NA	1520
Max	1-1/4	slug	slug	Lightfield		1440
Max	1-1/4	saboted slug	attached sabot	Rem.	NA	1550
Max	1	slug, rifled	slug, magnum	Rem., Fio.	$5**	1680
Max	1	slug, rifled	slug	Win., Fed., Rem.	$4**	1610
Max	1	sabot slug	slug	Sauvestre		1640
Max	7/8	slug, rifled	slug	Rem.	NA	1800
Max	400	plat. tip	sabot slug	Win.	NA	1700
Max	385 grains	Partition Gold Slug	slug	Win.	NA	1900
Max	385 grains	Core-Lokt bonded	sabot slug	Rem.	NA	1900
Max	325 grains	Barnes Sabot	slug	Fed.	NA	1900
Max	300 grains	SST Slug	sabot slug	Hornady	NA	2050
3	1-1/8	steel target	6-1/2, 7	Rem.	NA	1200
2-3/4	1-1/8	steel target	7	Rem.	NA	1145
3	1#	steel	7	Win.	$11	1235
3-1/2	1-1/4	steel	T, BBB, BB, 1, 2, 3, 4, 5, 6	Win., Fed., Rem.	$18	1275
3-3/4	1-1/8	steel	BB, 1, 2, 3, 4, 5, 6	Win., Fed., Rem., Fio.	$16	1365
3-3/4	1	steel	2, 3, 4, 5, 6, 7	Win., Fed., Rem., Fio.	$13	1390
Max	7/8	steel	7	Fio.	NA	1440

16 Gauge 2-3/4"

Dram Equiv.	Shot Ozs.	Load Style	Shot Sizes	Brands	Avg. Price/box	Velocity (fps)
3-1/4	1-1/4	magnum	2, 4, 6	Fed., Rem.	$16	1260
3-1/4	1-1/8	high velocity	4, 6, 7-1/2	Win., Fed., Rem., Fio.	$12	1295
Max	1-1/8	Bismuth	4, 5	Bis.	NA	1200
2-3/4	1-1/8	standard velocity	6, 7-1/2, 8	Fed., Rem., Fio.	$9	1185
2-1/2	1	dove	6, 7-1/2, 8, 9	Fio., Win.	NA	1165
2-3/4	1		6, 7-1/2, 8	Fio.	NA	1200
Max	15/16	steel	2, 4	Fed., Rem.	NA	1300
Max	7/8	steel	2, 4	Win.	$16	1300
3	12 pellets	buffered	1 buck	Win., Fed., Rem.	$4**	1225
Max	4/5	slug, rifled	slug	Win., Fed., Rem.	$4**	1570
Max	.92	sabot slug	slug	Sauvestre	NA	1560

20 Gauge 3" Magnum

Dram Equiv.	Shot Ozs.	Load Style	Shot Sizes	Brands	Avg. Price/box	Velocity (fps)
3	1-1/4	premium	2, 4, 5, 6, 7-1/2	Win., Fed., Rem.	$15	1185
3	1-1/4	turkey	4, 6	Fio.	NA	1200
Max	1-1/4	hevi. shot	4, 5, 6	Rem.	NA	1175
Max	1-1/8	hevi. shot	4, 6, 7-1/2	Rem.	NA	1300
Max	18 pellets	buck shot	2 buck	Fed.	NA	1200
Max	24 pellets	buffered	3 buck	Win.	$5**	1150
2-3/4	20 pellets	buck	3 buck	Rem.	$4**	1200
3-1/4	1	steel	1, 2, 3, 4, 5, 6	Win., Fed., Rem.	$15	1330
Max	7/8	steel	2, 4	Win.	MA	1300
Max	1-1/16	Bismuth	2, 4, 5, 6	Bismuth	NA	1250
Mag	5/8	saboted slug	275 gr.	Fed.	NA	1900

20 Gauge 2-3/4"

Dram Equiv.	Shot Ozs.	Load Style	Shot Sizes	Brands	Avg. Price/box	Velocity (fps)
2-3/4	1-1/8	magnum	4, 6, 7-1/2	Win., Fed., Rem.	$14	1175
2-3/4	1	high velocity	4, 5, 6, 7-1/2, 8, 9	Win., Fed., Rem., Fio.	$12	1220
Max	1	Bismuth	4, 6	Bis.	NA	1200
Max	1	hevi-shot	4, 6, 7-1/2	Rem.	NA	1275
Max	1	Supreme H-V	4, 6, 7-1/2	Win. Rem.	NA	1300
Max	7/8	Steel	2, 3, 4	Fio.	NA	1500
2-1/2	1	standard velocity	6, 7-1/2, 8	Win., Rem., Fed., Fio.	$6	1165
2-1/2	7/8	clays	8	Rem.	NA	1200
2-1/2	7/8	promotional	6, 7-1/2, 8	Win., Rem., Fio.	$6	1210
2-1/2	1	target	8, 9	Win., Rem.	$8	1165
Max	7/8	clays	7-1/2, 8	Win.	NA	1275
2-1/2	7/8	target	8, 9	Win., Fed., Rem.	$8	1200
Max	3/4	steel	2, 4	Rem.	NA	1425
2-1/2	7/8	steel - target	7	Rem.	NA	1200
Max	1	buckhammer	slug	Rem.	NA	1500
Max	5/8	Saboted Slug	Copper Slug	Rem.	NA	1500
Max	20 pellets	buffered	3 buck	Win., Fed.	$4	1200
Max	5/8	slug, saboted	slug	Win.,	$9**	1400
2-3/4	5/8	slug, rifled	slug	Rem.	$4**	1580
Max	3/4	saboted slug	copper slug	Fed., Rem.	NA	1450
Max	3/4	slug, rifled	slug	Win., Fed., Rem., Fio.	$4**	1570
Max	.9	sabot slug	slug	Sauvestre		1480
Max	260 grains	Partition Gold Slug	slug	Win.	NA	1900
Max	260 grains	Core-Lokt Ultra	slug	Rem.	NA	1900
Max	260 grains	saboted slug	platinum tip	Win.	NA	1700
Max	3/4	steel	2, 3, 4, 6	Win., Fed., Rem.	$14	1425
Max	1/2	rifled, slug	slug	Rem.	NA	1800

28 Gauge 2-3/4"

Dram Equiv.	Shot Ozs.	Load Style	Shot Sizes	Brands	Avg. Price/box	Velocity (fps)
2	1	high velocity	6, 7-1/2, 8	Win.	$12	1125
2-1/4	3/4	high velocity	6, 7-1/2, 8, 9	Win., Fed., Rem., Fio.	$11	1295
2	3/4	target	8, 9	Win., Fed., Rem.	$9	1200
Max	3/4	sporting clays	7-1/2, 8-1/2	Win.	NA	1300
Max	5/8	Bismuth	4, 6	Bis.	NA	1250

410 Bore 3"

Dram Equiv.	Shot Ozs.	Load Style	Shot Sizes	Brands	Avg. Price/box	Velocity (fps)
Max	11/16	high velocity	4, 5, 6, 7-1/2, 8, 9	Win., Fed., Rem., Fio.	$10	1135
Max	9/16	Bismuth	4	Bis.	NA	1175

410 Bore 2-1/2"

Dram Equiv.	Shot Ozs.	Load Style	Shot Sizes	Brands	Avg. Price/box	Velocity (fps)
Max	1/2	high velocity	4, 6, 7-1/2	Win., Fed., Rem.	$9	1245
Max	1/5	slug, rifled	slug	Win., Fed., Rem.	$4**	1815
1-1/2	1/2	target	8, 8-1/2, 9	Win., Fed., Rem., Fio.	$8	1200
Max	1/2	sporting clays	7-1/2, 8, 8-1/2	Win.	NA	1300
Max		Buckshot	5-000 Buck	Win.		1135

SHOOTER'S MARKETPLACE

PRODUCT NEWS FOR THE ACTIVE SHOOTING SPORTSMAN

The companies represented on the following pages will be happy to provide additional information – feel free to contact them.

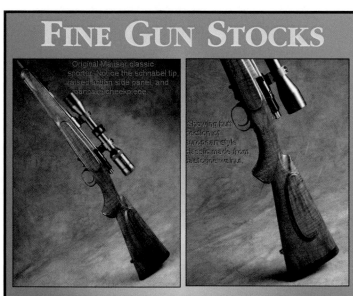
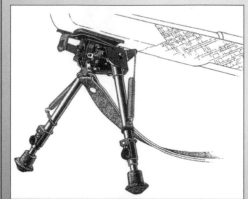

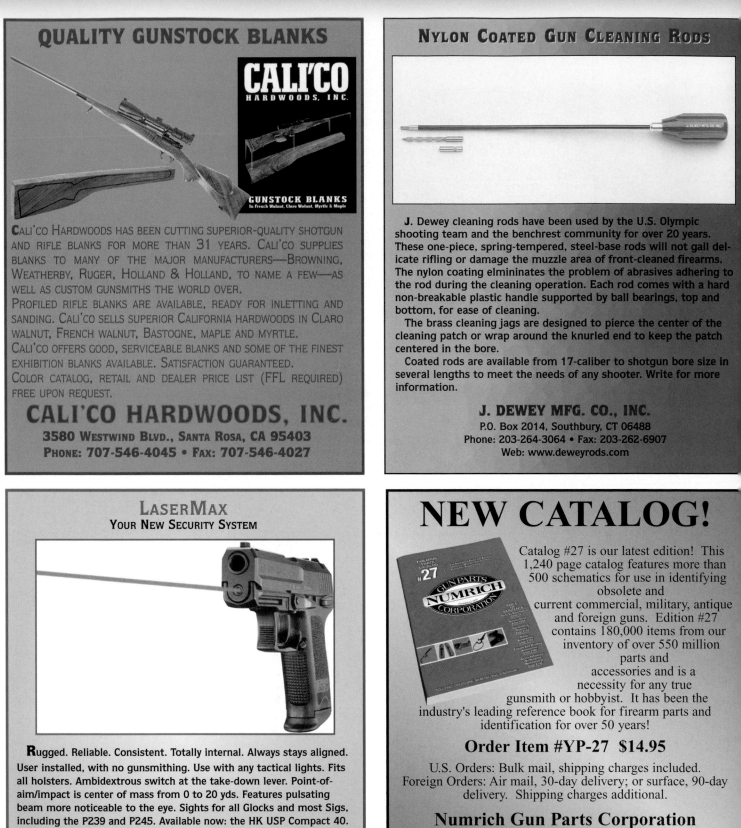

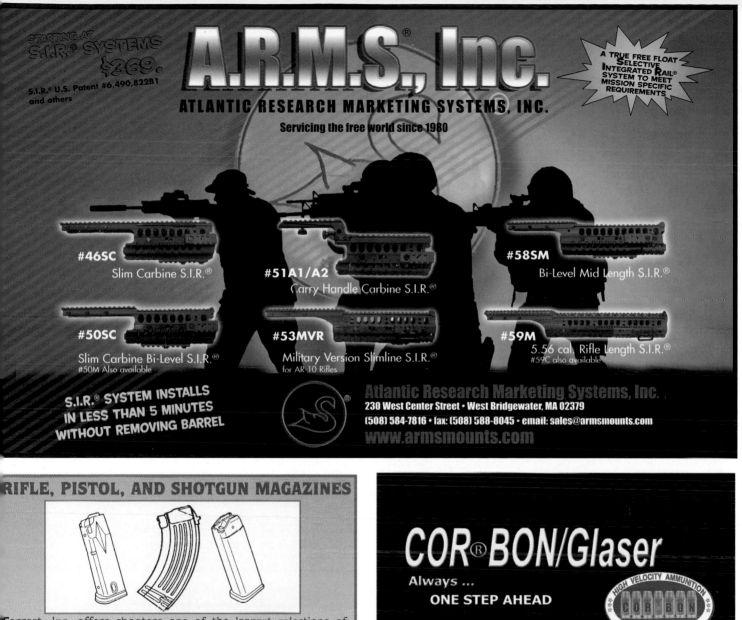
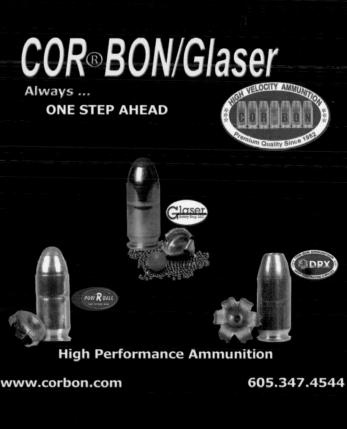

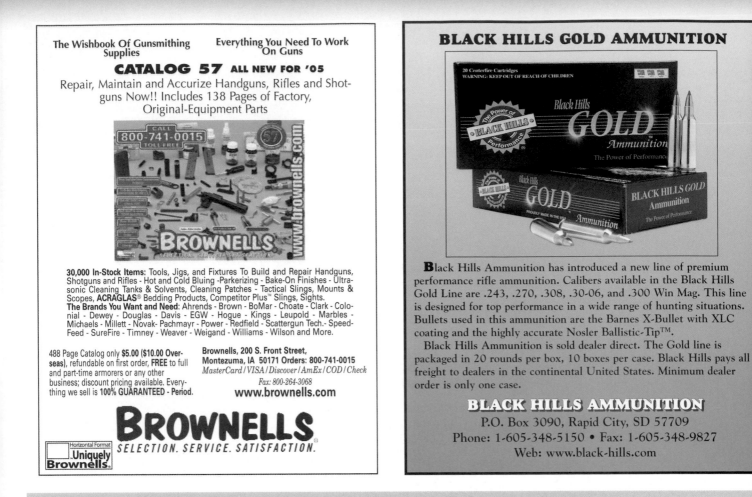

THE BEAR ESSENTIALS
THE RUGER® SUPER REDHAWK® ALASKAN™

The Ruger Super Redhawk has always been the top choice among handgun hunters who want a revolver with the decisive power of the .454 Casull or .480 Ruger cartridge and the confidence of a six-shot cylinder. Now, Sturm, Ruger proudly introduces the perfect revolver for a trek into dangerous game country – the New Super Redhawk Alaskan.

The all-stainless-steel Super Redhawk Alaskan features a Hogue® Monogrip® to help cushion recoil and a 2 1/2" hammer-forged barrel fitted inside the sturdy extended frame, making it the most compact revolver ever offered in these calibers. And, the .454 Casull model allows you to shoot the more economical and lighter-recoiling .45 Colt cartridges at the practice range. With all the power of two of the most potent handgun calibers and a six-shot cylinder, the Super Redhawk Alaskan is essential for trips into dangerous game territory.

New Hogue® Tamer™ Monogrip® helps cushion recoil.

New Ruger
Super Redhawk Alaskan
KSRH-2454
.454 Casull & .45 Colt
Suggested retail price of $819.00
Also available in .480 Ruger

STURM, RUGER & CO., INC.

Southport, CT 06890, U.S.A. • www.ruger.com

All Ruger firearms are designed and built with pride by American workers
at Ruger factories in the United States of America.

FREE Instruction Manuals are available online at www.ruger.com

RUGER®

ARMS MAKERS FOR RESPONSIBLE CITIZENS®

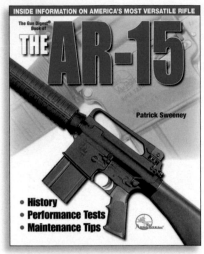
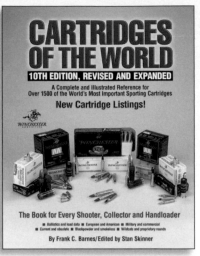
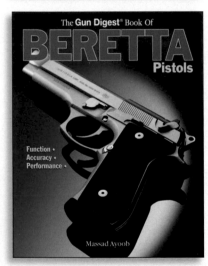

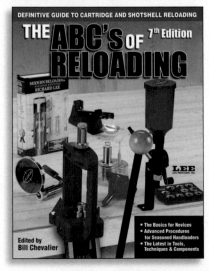
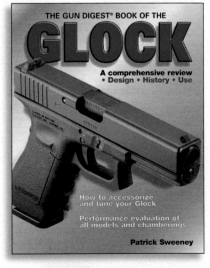

2006 GUN DIGEST Complete Compact CATALOG

GUNDEX

HANDGUNS

RIFLES

SHOTGUNS

BLACKPOWDER

AIRGUNS

ACCESSORIES

REFERENCE

DIRECTORY OF
THE ARMS TRADE

GUNDEX

GUNDEX

GUNDEX

GUNDEX

GUNDEX

GUNDEX

Includes models suitable for several forms of competition and other sporting purposes.

Accu-Tek HC-380

Accu-Tek XL-9

Auto-Ordnance 1911A1 Standard

Baer Custom Carry

Auto-Ordnance Deluxe

Baer Premium II

ACCU-TEK MODEL HC-380 AUTO PISTOL

Caliber: 380 ACP, 10-shot magazine. **Barrel:** 2.75". **Weight:** 26 oz. **Length:** 6" overall. **Grips:** Checkered black composition. **Sights:** Blade front, rear adjustable for windage. **Features:** External hammer; manual thumb safety with firing pin and trigger disconnect; bottom magazine release. Stainless steel construction. Introduced 1993. Price includes cleaning kit and gun lock. Made in U.S.A. by Accu-Tek.
Price: Satin stainless **$249.00**

ACCU-TEK XL-9 AUTO PISTOL

Caliber: 9mm Para., 5-shot magazine. **Barrel:** 3". **Weight:** 24 oz. **Length:** 5.6" overall. **Grips:** Black pebble composition. **Sights:** 3-dot system; rear adjustable for windage. **Features:** Stainless steel construction; double-action-only mechanism. Introduced 1999. Price includes cleaning kit and gun lock, two magazines. Made in U.S.A. by Accu-Tek.
Price: **$267.00**

AMERICAN DERRINGER LM-5 AUTOMATIC PISTOL

Caliber: 25 ACP, 5-shot magazine. **Barrel:** 2-1/4". **Weight:** 15 oz. **Length:** NA. **Grips:** Wood. **Sights:** Fixed. **Features:** Compact, stainless, semi-auto, single-action hammerless design.
Price: **$425.00**

AUTAUGA 32 AUTO PISTOL

Caliber: 32 ACP, 6-shot magazine. **Barrel:** 2". **Weight:** 11.3 oz. **Length:** 4.3" overall. **Grips:** Black polymer. **Sights:** Fixed. **Features:** Double-action-only mechanism. Stainless steel construction.
Price: . . . . **NA**

AUTO-ORDNANCE 1911A1 AUTOMATIC PISTOL

Caliber: 45 ACP, 7-shot magazine. **Barrel:** 5". **Weight:** 39 oz. **Length:** 8-1/2" overall. **Grips:** Checkered plastic with medallion. **Sights:** Blade front, rear adjustable for windage. **Features:** Same specs as 1911A1 military guns-parts interchangeable. Frame and slide blued; each radius has non-glare finish. Made in U.S.A. by Auto-Ordnance Corp.
Price: 45 ACP, blue **$511.00**
Price: 45 ACP, Parkerized **$515.00**
Price: 45 ACP Deluxe (3-dot sights, textured rubber wraparound grips) **$525.00**

AUTOBOND 450

Caliber: 450 Autobond (also 45 ACP). Model 1911-style. **Barrel:** 5".
Price: **$1,150.00**

BAER 1911 CUSTOM CARRY AUTO PISTOL

Caliber: 45 ACP, 7- or 10-shot magazine. **Barrel:** 5". **Weight:** 37 oz. **Length:** 8.5" overall. **Grips:** Checkered walnut. **Sights:** Baer improved ramp-style dovetailed front, Novak low-mount rear. **Features:** Baer forged NM frame, slide and barrel with stainless bushing. Baer speed trigger with 4-lb. pull. Partial listing shown. Made in U.S.A. by Les Baer Custom, Inc.
Price: Standard size, blued **$1,640.00**
Price: Standard size, stainless **$1,690.00**
Price: Comanche size, blued **$1,640.00**
Price: Comanche size, stainless **$1,690.00**
Price: Comanche size, aluminum frame, blued slide **$1,923.00**
Price: Comanche size, aluminum frame, stainless slide **$1,995.00**

BAER 1911 PREMIER II AUTO PISTOL

Caliber: 9x23, 38 Super, 400 Cor-Bon, 45 ACP, 7- or 10-shot magazine. **Barrel:** 5". **Weight:** 37 oz. **Length:** 8.5" overall. **Grips:** Checkered rosewood, double diamond pattern. **Sights:** Baer dovetailed front, low-mount Bo-Mar rear with hidden leaf. **Features:** Baer NM forged steel frame and barrel with stainless bushing, deluxe Commander hammer and sear, beavertail grip safety with pad, extended ambidextrous safety; flat mainspring housing; 30 lpi checkered front strap. Made in U.S.A. by Les Baer Custom, Inc.
Price: Blued **$1,428.00**
Price: Stainless **$1,558.00**
Price: 6" model, blued, from **$1,595.00**

BAER 1911 S.R.P. PISTOL

Caliber: 45 ACP. **Barrel:** 5". **Weight:** 37 oz. **Length:** 8.5" overall. **Grips:** Checkered walnut. **Sights:** Trijicon night sights. **Features:** Similar to the F.B.I. contract gun except uses Baer forged steel frame. Has Baer match barrel with supported chamber, Complete tactical action. Has Baer Ultra Coat finish. Introduced 1996. Made in U.S.A. by Les Baer Custom, Inc.
Price: Government or Comanche length **$2,240.00**

Beretta 96

Beretta U22 Neos

BERETTA MODEL 92FS PISTOL

Caliber: 9mm Para., 10-shot magazine. **Barrel:** 4.9". **Weight:** 34 oz. **Length:** 8.5" overall. **Grips:** Checkered black plastic. **Sights:** Blade front, rear adjustable for windage. Tritium night sights available. **Features:** Double action. Extractor acts as chamber loaded indicator, squared trigger guard, grooved front and backstraps, inertia firing pin. Matte or blued finish. Introduced 1977. Made in U.S.A. and imported from Italy by Beretta U.S.A.
Price: With plastic grips $715.00
Price: Vertec with access rail $760.00
Price: Vertec Inox $825.00

Beretta Model 92FS/96 Brigadier Pistols

Similar to the Model 92FS/96 except with a heavier slide to reduce felt recoil and allow mounting removable front sight. Wraparound rubber grips. 3-dot sights dovetailed to the slide, adjustable for windage. Weighs 35.3 oz. Introduced 1999.
Price: 9mm or 40 S&W, 10-shot $795.00
Price: Inox models (stainless steel) $845.00

Beretta Model 96 Pistol

Same as the Model 92FS except chambered for 40 S&W. Ambidextrous safety mechanism with passive firing pin catch, slide safety/decocking lever, trigger bar disconnect. Has 10-shot magazine. Available with 3-dot sights. Introduced 1992.
Price: Model 96, plastic grips $795.00
Price: Stainless, rubber grips $845.00
Price: Vertec with access rail $760.00
Price: Vertec Inox $825.00

BERETTA MODEL 80 CHEETAH SERIES DA PISTOLS

Caliber: 380 ACP, 10-shot magazine (M84); 8-shot (M85); 22 LR, 7-shot (M87). **Barrel:** 3.82". **Weight:** About 23 oz. (M84/85); 20.8 oz. (M87). **Length:** 6.8" overall. **Grips:** Glossy black plastic (wood optional at extra cost). **Sights:** Fixed front, drift-adjustable rear. **Features:** Double action, quick takedown, convenient magazine release. Introduced 1977. Imported from Italy by Beretta U.S.A.
Price: Model 84 Cheetah, plastic grips $625.00
Price: Model 85 Cheetah, plastic grips, 8-shot $590.00
Price: Model 87 Cheetah, wood, 22 LR, 7-shot $625.00
Price: Model 87 Target, plastic grips $710.00

BERETTA MODEL 21 BOBCAT PISTOL

Caliber: 22 LR or 25 ACP. Both double action. **Barrel:** 2.4". **Weight:** 11.5 oz.; 11.8 oz. **Length:** 4.9" overall. **Grips:** Plastic. **Features:** Available in nickel, matte, engraved or blue finish. Introduced in 1985.
Price: Bobcat, 22 or 25, blue $275.00
Price: Bobcat, 22, stainless $340.00
Price: Bobcat, 22 or 25, matte $275.00

BERETTA MODEL 3032 TOMCAT PISTOL

Caliber: 32 ACP, 7-shot magazine. **Barrel:** 2.45". **Weight:** 14.5 oz. **Length:** 5" overall. **Grips:** Checkered black plastic. **Sights:** Blade front, drift-adjustable rear. **Features:** Double action with exposed hammer; tip-up barrel for direct loading/unloading; thumb safety; polished or matte blue finish. Imported from Italy by Beretta U.S.A. Introduced 1996.
Price: Blue $390.00

Price: Matte $370.00
Price: Stainless $450.00
Price: With Tritium sights $460.00

BERETTA MODEL 9000S COMPACT PISTOL

Caliber: 9mm Para., 40 S&W; 10-shot magazine. **Barrel:** 3.4". **Weight:** 26.8 oz. **Length:** 6.6". **Grips:** Soft polymer. **Sights:** Windage-adjustable white-dot rear, white-dot blade front. **Features:** Glass-reinforced polymer frame; patented tilt-barrel, open-slide locking system; chrome-lined barrel; external serrated hammer; automatic firing pin and manual safeties. Introduced 2000. Imported from Italy by Beretta U.S.A.
Price: 9000S Type F
(single and double action, external hammer) $495.00

BERETTA MODEL U22 NEOS

Caliber: 22 LR, 10-shot magazine. **Barrel:** 4.2"; 6". **Weight:** 32 oz.; 36 oz. **Length:** 8.8"; 10.3". **Sights:** Target. **Features:** Integral rail for standard scope mounts, light, perfectly weighted, 100% American made by Beretta.
Price: $285.00
Price: Inox $335.00
Price: DLX $355.00
Price: Inox $395.00

BERSA THUNDER 45 ULTRA COMPACT PISTOL

Caliber: 45 ACP. **Barrel:** 3.6". **Weight:** 27 oz. **Length:** 6.7" overall. **Grips:** Anatomicaly designed polymer. **Sights:** White outline rear. **Features:** Double action; firing pin safeties, integral locking system. Available in matte, satin nickel, gold, or duo-tone. Introduced 2003. Imported from Argentina by Eagle Imports, Inc.
Price: Thunder 45, matte blue $424.95
Price: Thunder 45, duo-tone $449.95
Price: Thunder 45, satin nickel $466.95

BLUE THUNDER/COMMODORE 1911-STYLE AUTO PISTOLS

Caliber: 45 ACP, 7-shot magazine. **Barrel:** 4-1/4", 5". **Weight:** NA. **Length:** NA. **Grips:** Checkered hardwood. **Sights:** Blade front, drift-adjustable rear. **Features:** Extended slide release and safety, spring guide rod, skeletonized hammer and trigger, magazine bumper, beavertail grip safety. Imported from the Philippines by Century International Arms, Inc.
Price: . . . . $464.80 to $484.80

BROWNING HI-POWER 9mm AUTOMATIC PISTOL

Caliber: 9mm Para., 10-shot magazine. **Barrel:** 4-21/32". **Weight:** 32 oz. **Length:** 7-3/4" overall. **Grips:** Walnut, hand checkered, or black Polyamide. **Sights:** 1/8" blade front; rear screw-adjustable for windage and elevation. Also available with fixed rear (drift-adjustable for windage). **Features:** External hammer with half-cock and thumb safeties. Fixed rear sight model available. Includes gun lock. Imported from Belgium by Browning.
Price: Fixed sight model, walnut grips $628.00
Price: Fully adjustable rear sight, walnut grips $628.00
Price: Mark III, standard matte black finish, fixed sight, molded grips, ambidextrous safety $781.00

**Browning
Buck Mark Standard**

Charles Daly M-1911-A1P

**Browning Buck
Mark Challenge**

Cobra FS380

Browning Hi-Power Practical Pistol
Similar to the standard Hi-Power except has silver-chromed frame with blued slide, wraparound Pachmayr rubber grips, round-style serrated hammer and removable front sight, fixed rear (drift-adjustable for windage). Available in 9mm Para. Includes gun lock. Introduced 1991.
Price: $846.00

BROWNING BUCK MARK STANDARD 22 PISTOL
Caliber: 22 LR, 10-shot magazine. **Barrel:** 5-1/2". **Weight:** 32 oz. **Length:** 9-1/2" overall. **Grips:** Black molded composite with checkering. **Sights:** Ramp front, Browning Pro Target rear adjustable for windage and elevation. **Features:** All steel, matte blue finish or nickel, gold-colored trigger. Buck Mark Plus has laminated wood grips. Includes gun lock. Made in U.S.A. Introduced 1985. From Browning.
Price: Buck Mark Standard, blue $319.00
Price: Buck Mark Stainless, nickel finish with contoured
  rubber grips $345.00
Price: Buck Mark Plus, matte blue with laminated wood grips $390.00
Price: Buck Mark Plus Nickel, nickel finish, laminated wood grips . $427.00

Browning Buck Mark Camper
Similar to the Buck Mark except 5-1/2" bull barrel. Weight is 34 oz. Matte blue finish, molded composite grips. Introduced 1999. From Browning.
Price: $287.00
Price: Camper Nickel, nickel finish, molded composite grips $320.00

Browning Buck Mark Challenge
Similar to the Buck Mark except has a lightweight barrel and smaller grip diameter. Barrel length is 5-1/2", weight is 25 oz. Introduced 1999. From Browning.
Price: $356.00

Browning Buck Mark Micro
Same as the Buck Mark Standard and Buck Mark Plus except has 4" barrel. Available in blue or nickel. Has 16-click Pro Target rear sight. Introduced 1992.
Price: Micro Standard, matte blue finish $319.00
Price: Micro Nickel, nickel finish $390.00
Price: Buck Mark Micro Plus Nickel $427.00

Browning Buck Mark Bullseye
Same as the Buck Mark Standard except has 7-1/4" fluted barrel, matte blue finish. Weighs 36 oz.
Price: Bullseye Standard, molded composite grips $468.00
Price: Bullseye Target, contoured rosewood grips $604.00

Browning Buck Mark 5.5
Same as the Buck Mark Standard except has a 5-1/2" bull barrel with integral scope mount, matte blue finish.
Price: 5.5 Field, Pro-Target adj. rear sight, contoured
  walnut grips $511.00
Price: 5.5 Target, hooded adj. target sights,
  contoured walnut grips $511.00

BROWNING PRO-9
Caliber: 9mm Luger, 10-round magazine. **Barrel:** 4". **Weight:** 30 oz. **Overall length:** 7-1/4". **Features:** Double-action, ambidextrous decocker and safety. Fixed, 3-dot-style sights, 6" sight radius. Molded composite grips with interchangeable backstrap inserts.
Price: $628.00

BROWNING HI-POWER
Caliber: 9mm, 40 S&W. **Barrel:** 4-3/4". **Weight:** 32 to 35 oz. **Overall length:** 7-3/4". **Features:** Blued, matte, polymer or silver-chromed frame; molded, wraparound Pachmayr or walnut grips; Commander-style or spur-type hammer.
Price: Practical model, fixed sights $791.00
Price: Mark II model, epoxy finish $730.00
Price: HP Standard, blued, fixed sights, walnut grips $751.00
Price: HP Standard, blued, adj. sights $805.00

CHARLES DALY M-1911-A1P AUTOLOADING PISTOL
Caliber: 45 ACP, 7- or 10-shot magazine. **Barrel:** 5". **Weight:** 38 oz. **Length:** 8-3/4" overall. **Grips:** Checkered. **Sights:** Blade front, rear drift adjustable for windage; 3-dot system. **Features:** Skeletonized combat hammer and trigger; beavertail grip safety; extended slide release; over-size thumb safety; Parkerized finish. Introduced 1996. Imported from the Philippines by K.B.I., Inc.
Price: $469.95

COBRA ENTERPRISES FS380 AUTO PISTOL
Caliber: 380 ACP, 7-shot magazine. **Barrel:** 3.5". **Weight:** 2.1 lbs. **Length:** 6-3/8" overall. **Grips:** Black composition. **Sights:** Fixed. **Features:** Choice of bright chrome, satin nickel or black finish. Introduced 2002. Made in U.S.A. by Cobra Enterprises, Inc.
Price: $130.00

COBRA ENTERPRISES FS32 AUTO PISTOL
Caliber: 32 ACP, 8-shot magazine. **Barrel:** 3.5". **Weight:** 2.1 lbs. **Length:** 6-3/8" overall. **Grips:** Black composition. **Sights:** Fixed. **Features:** Choice of black, satin nickel or bright chrome finish. Introduced 2002. Made in U.S.A. by Cobra Enterprises, Inc.
Price: $130.00

Cobra CA32

Colt 1991 Model O

Colt 1991 Model O Commander

Colt XSE Model O Commander

Colt XSE Lightweight Commander

Colt Defender

Colt Series 70

Colt 38 Super

COBRA INDUSTRIES PATRIOT PISTOL
Caliber: 380 ACP, 9mm Luger, 10-shot magazine. **Barrel:** 3.3". **Weight:** 20 oz. **Length:** 6" overall. **Grips:** Checkered polymer. **Sights:** Fixed. **Features:** Stainless steel slide with load indicator; double-action-only trigger system. Introduced 2002. Made in U.S.A. by Cobra Enterprises, Inc.
Price: **$279.00**

COBRA INDUSTRIES CA32, CA380
Caliber: 32 ACP, 380 ACP. **Barrel:** 2.8" **Weight:** 22 oz. **Length:** 5.4". **Grips:** Laminated wood (CA32); Black molded synthetic (CA380). **Sights:** Fixed. **Features:** True pocket pistol size. Made in U.S.A. by Cobra Enterprises, Inc.
Price: . . . . **NA**

COLT MODEL 1991 MODEL O AUTO PISTOL
Caliber: 45 ACP, 7-shot magazine. **Barrel:** 5". **Weight:** 38 oz. **Length:** 8.5" overall. **Grips:** Checkered black composition. **Sights:** Ramped blade front, fixed square notch rear, high profile. **Features:** Matte finish. Continuation of serial number range used on original G.I. 1911A1 guns. Comes with one magazine and molded carrying case. Introduced 1991.
Price: **$870.00**
Price: Stainless **$920.00**

Colt Model 1991 Model O Commander Auto Pistol
Similar to the 1991 Model O except has 4-1/4" barrel. Overall length is 7-3/4". Comes with one 7-shot magazine, molded case.
Price: Blue **$870.00**
Price: Stainless steel **$920.00**

COLT XSE SERIES MODEL O AUTO PISTOLS
Caliber: 45 ACP, 8-shot magazine. **Barrel:** 4.25", 5". **Grips:** Checkered, double diamond rosewood. **Sights:** Drift-adjustable 3-dot combat. **Features:** Brushed stainless finish; adjustable, two-cut aluminum trigger; extended ambidextrous thumb safety; upswept beavertail with palm swell; elongated slot hammer. Introduced 1999. From Colt's Mfg. Co., Inc.
Price: XSE Government (5" bbl.) **$1,100.00**
Price: XSE Commander (4.25" bbl.) **$1,100.00**

COLT XSE LIGHTWEIGHT COMMANDER AUTO PISTOL
Caliber: 45 ACP, 8-shot. **Barrel:** 4-1/4". **Weight:** 26 oz. **Length:** 7-3/4" overall. **Grips:** Double diamond checkered rosewood. **Sights:** Fixed, glare-proofed blade front, square notch rear; 3-dot system. **Features:** Brushed stainless slide, nickeled aluminum frame; McCormick elongated slot enhanced hammer, McCormick two-cut adjustable aluminum hammer. Made in U.S.A. by Colt's Mfg. Co., Inc.
Price: Stainless **$1,100.00**

COLT DEFENDER
Caliber: 45 ACP, 7-shot magazine. **Barrel:** 3". **Weight:** 22-1/2 oz. **Length:** 6-3/4" overall. **Grips:** Pebble-finish rubber wraparound with finger grooves. **Sights:** White dot front, snag-free Colt competition rear. **Features:** Stainless finish; aluminum frame; combat-style hammer; Hi Ride grip safety, extended manual safety, disconnect safety. Introduced 1998. Made in U.S.A. by Colt's Mfg. Co., Inc.
Price: **$950.00**

COLT SERIES 70
Caliber: 45 ACP. **Barrel:** 5". **Weight:** NA **Length:** NA **Grips:** Rosewood with double diamond checkering pattern. **Sights:** Fixed. **Features:** Custom replica of the Original Series 70 pistol with a Series 70 firing system, original rollmarks. Introduced 2002. Made in U.S.A. by Colt's Mfg. Co., Inc.
Price: **$990.00**

COLT 38 SUPER
Caliber: 38 Super. **Barrel:** 5" **Weight:** NA. **Length:** 8-1/2" **Grips:** Checkered rubber (stainless and blue models); wood with double diamond checkering pattern (bright stainless model). **Sights:** 3-dot. **Features:** Beveled magazine well, standard thumb safety and service-style grip safety. Introduced 2003. Made in U.S.A. by Colt's Mfg. Co., Inc.
Price: . . . . (Blue) **$950.00** (Stainless steel) **$980.00**
Price: (Bright stainless steel) **$1,200.00**

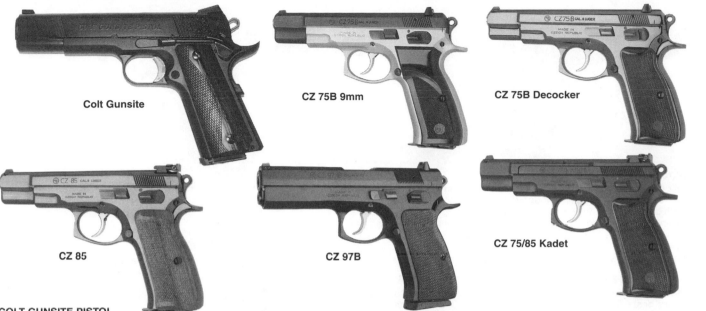

Colt Gunsite

CZ 75B 9mm

CZ 75B Decocker

CZ 85

CZ 97B

CZ 75/85 Kadet

COLT GUNSITE PISTOL

Caliber: 45 ACP **Barrel:** 5". **Weight:** NA. **Length:** NA. **Grips:** Rosewood. **Sights:** Heinie front, Novak rear. **Features:** Contains most all of the Gunsite-school recommended features such as Series 70 firing system, Smith & Alexander metal grip safety w/palm swell, serrated flat mainspring housing. Available in blue or stainless steel. Introduced 2003. Made in U.S.A. by Colt's Mfg. Co., Inc.

Price: . . . . **NA**

CZ 75B AUTO PISTOL

Caliber: 9mm Para., 40 S&W, 10-shot magazine. **Barrel:** 4.7". **Weight:** 34.3 oz. **Length:** 8.1" overall. **Grips:** High impact checkered plastic. **Sights:** Square post front, rear adjustable for windage; 3-dot system. **Features:** Single action/double action design; firing pin block safety; choice of black polymer, matte or high-polish blue finishes. All-steel frame. Imported from the Czech Republic by CZ-USA.

Price: Black polymer **$529.00**
Price: Glossy blue **$559.00**
Price: Dual-tone or satin nickel **$559.00**
Price: 22 LR conversion unit **$399.00**

CZ 75B Decocker

Similar to the CZ 75B except has a decocking lever in place of the safety lever. All other specifications are the same. Introduced 1999. Imported from the Czech Republic by CZ-USA.

Price: 9mm, black polymer **$559.00**
Price: 40 S&W **$569.00**

CZ 75B Compact Auto Pistol

Similar to the CZ 75 except has 10-shot magazine, 3.9" barrel and weighs 32 oz. Has removable front sight, non-glare ribbed slide top. Trigger guard is squared and serrated; combat hammer. Introduced 1993. Imported from the Czech Republic by CZ-USA.

Price: 9mm, black polymer **$559.00**
Price: Dual tone or satin nickel **$569.00**
Price: D Compact, black polymer **$569.00**
Price: CZ2075 Sub-compact RAMI **$559.00**

CZ 75M IPSC Auto Pistol

Similar to the CZ 75B except has a longer frame and slide, slightly larger grip to accommodate new heavy-duty magazine. Ambidextrous thumb safety, safety notch on hammer; two-port in-frame compensator; slide racker; frame-mounted Firepoint red dot sight. Introduced 2001. Imported from the Czech Republic by CZ USA.

Price: 40 S&W, 10-shot mag. **$1,551.00**
Price: CZ 75 Standard IPSC (40 S&W, adj. sights) **$1,038.00**

CZ 85B Auto Pistol

Same gun as the CZ 75 except has ambidextrous slide release and safety levers; non-glare, ribbed slide top; squared, serrated trigger guard; trigger stop to prevent overtravel. Introduced 1986. Imported from the Czech Republic by CZ-USA.

Price: Black polymer **$483.00**
Price: Combat, black polymer **$540.00**
Price: Combat, dual-tone **$487.00**
Price: Combat, glossy blue **$499.00**

CZ 85 Combat

Similar to the CZ 85B (9mm only) except has an adjustable rear sight, trigger adjustable for overtravel, free-fall magazine, extended magazine catch. Does not have the firing pin block safety. Introduced 1999. Imported from the Czech Republic by CZ-USA.

Price: 9mm, black polymer **$540.00**
Price: 9mm, glossy blue **$566.00**
Price: 9mm, dual-tone or satin nickel **$586.00**

CZ 83B DOUBLE-ACTION PISTOL

Caliber: 9mm Makarov, 32 ACP, 380 ACP, 10-shot magazine. **Barrel:** 3.8". **Weight:** 26.2 oz. **Length:** 6.8" overall. **Grips:** High impact checkered plastic. **Sights:** Removable square post front, rear adjustable for windage; 3-dot system. **Features:** Single action/double action; ambidextrous magazine release and safety. Blue finish; non-glare ribbed slide top. Imported from the Czech Republic by CZ-USA.

Price: Blue **$378.00**
Price: Nickel **$397.00**

CZ 97B AUTO PISTOL

Caliber: 45 ACP, 10-shot magazine. **Barrel:** 4.85". **Weight:** 40 oz. **Length:** 8.34" overall. **Grips:** Checkered walnut. **Sights:** Fixed. **Features:** Single action/double action; full-length slide rails; screw-in barrel bushing; linkless barrel; all-steel construction; chamber loaded indicator; dual transfer bars. Introduced 1999. Imported from the Czech Republic by CZ-USA.

Price: Black polymer **$625.00**
Price: Glossy blue **$641.00**

CZ 75/85 KADET AUTO PISTOL

Caliber: 22 LR, 10-shot magazine. **Barrel:** 4.88". **Weight:** 36 oz. **Grips:** High impact checkered plastic. **Sights:** Blade front, fully adjustable rear. **Features:** Single action/double action mechanism; all steel construction. Introduced 1999. Imported from the Czech Republic by CZ-USA.

Price: Black polymer **$486.00**

CZ 100

**Dan Wesson Firearms
Pointman Major**

**Dan Wesson Firearms
Major Aussie**

**Dan Wesson Firearms
Patriot Marksman**

CZ 100 AUTO PISTOL

Caliber: 9mm Para., 40 S&W, 10-shot magazine. **Barrel:** 3.7". **Weight:** 24 oz. **Length:** 6.9" overall. **Grips:** Grooved polymer. **Sights:** Blade front with dot, white outline rear drift adjustable for windage. **Features:** Double action only with firing pin block; polymer frame, steel slide; has laser sight mount. Introduced 1996. Imported from the Czech Republic by CZ-USA.
Price: 9mm Para $405.00
Price: 40 S&W $424.00

DAN WESSON FIREARMS POINTMAN MAJOR AUTO PISTOL

Caliber: 45 ACP. **Barrel:** 5". **Grips:** Rosewood checkered. **Features:** Blued or stainless steel frame and serrated slide; Chip McCormick match-grade trigger group, sear and disconnect; match-grade barrel; high-ride beavertail safety; checkered slide release. **Sights:** High rib; interchangeable sight system; laser engraved. Introduced 2000. Made in U.S.A. by Dan Wesson Firearms.
Price: Model PM1-B (blued) $799.00
Price: Model PM1-S (stainless) $699.00

Dan Wesson Firearms Pointman Seven Auto Pistols

Similar to Pointman Major, dovetail adjustable target rear sight and dovetail target front sight. Available in blued or stainless finish. Introduced 2000. Made in U.S.A. by Dan Wesson Firearms.
Price: PM7 (blued frame and slide) $999.00
Price: PM7S (stainless finish) $799.00

Dan Wesson Firearms Pointman Guardian Auto Pistols

Similar to Pointman Major, more compact frame with 4.25" barrel. Available in blued or stainless finish with fixed or adjustable sights. Introduced 2000. Made in U.S.A. by Dan Wesson Firearms.
Price: PMG-FS, all new frame (fixed sights) $769.00
Price: PMG-AS (blued frame and slide, adjustable sights) $799.00
Price: PMGD-FS Guardian Duce, all new frame
(stainless frame and blued slide, fixed sights) $829.00
Price: PMGD-AS Guardian Duce
(stainless frame and blued slide, adj. sights) $799.00

Dan Wesson Firearms Major Tri-Ops Packs

Similar to Pointman Major. Complete frame assembly fitted to 3 match-grade complete slide assemblies (9mm, 10mm, 40 S&W). Includes recoil springs and magazines that come in hard cases fashioned after high-grade European rifle case. Brass corner protectors, dual combination locks, engraved presentation plate on the lid. Introduced 2002. Made in U.S.A. by Dan Wesson Firearms.
Price: TOP1B (blued), TOP1-S (stainless) $2,459.00

Dan Wesson Firearms Major Aussie

Similar to Pointman Major. Available in 45 ACP. Features Bomar-style adjustable rear target sight, low (1/16" high) sight rib 3/8" wide with lengthwise serrations. Southern Cross flag emblem laser engraved on the sides of the slide. Introduced 2002. Made in U.S.A. by Dan Wesson Firearms.
Price: PMA-B (blued) $799.00
Price: PMA-S (stainless) $799.00

Dan Wesson Firearms Pointman Minor Auto Pistol

Similar to Pointman Major. Full size (5") entry level IDPA or action pistol model with blued carbon alloy frame and round top slide, bead blast matte

finish on frame and slide top and radius, satin-brushed polished finish on sides of slide, chromed barrel, dovetail mount fixed rear target sight and tactical/target ramp front sight, match trigger, skeletonized target hammer, high ride beavertail, fitted extractor, serrations on thumb safety, slide release and magazine release, lowered and relieved ejection port, beveled magazine well, exotic hardwood grips, serrated mainspring housing, laser engraved. Introduced 2000. Made in U.S.A. by Dan Wesson Firearms.
Price: Model PM2-P $599.00

Dan Wesson Firearms Pointman Hi-Cap Auto Pistol

Similar to Pointman Minor. Full-size, high-capacity (10-shot) magazine with 5" chromed barrel, blued finish and dovetail fixed rear sight. Match adjustable trigger, ambidextrous extended thumb safety, beavertail safety. Introduced 2001. From Dan Wesson Firearms.
Price: PMHC (Pointman High-Cap) $689.00

Dan Wesson Firearms Pointman Dave Pruitt Signature Series

Similar to other full-sized Pointman models, customized by Master Pistolsmith and IDPA Grand Master Dave Pruitt. Alloy carbon-steel with black oxide bluing and bead-blast matte finish. Front and rear chevron cocking serrations, dovetail mount fixed rear target sight and tactical/target ramp front sight, ramped match barrel with fitted match bushing and link, match-grade trigger group, serrated ambidextrous tactical/carry thumb safety, high ride beavertail, serrated slide release and checkered mag release, match-grade sear and hammer, fitted extractor, lowered and relieved ejection port, beveled magazine well, full length 2-piece recoil spring guide rod, cocobolo double diamond checkered grips, serrated steel mainspring housing, special laser engraving. Introduced 2001. From Dan Wesson Firearms.
Price: PMDP (Pointman Dave Pruitt) $899.00

DAN WESSON FIREARMS PATRIOT 1911 PISTOL

Caliber: 45 ACP. **Grips:** Exotic exhibition grade cocobolo, double diamond hand cut checkering. **Sights:** New innovative combat/carry rear sight that completely encloses the dovetail. **Features:** The new Patriot Expert and Patriot Marksman are full-size match-grade series 70 1911s machined from steel forgings. Available in blued chome-moly steel or stainless steel. Beveled magazine well, lowered and flared ejection port, high sweep beavertail safety. Introduced June 2002.
Price: Model PTM-B (blued) $797.00
Price: Model PTM-S (stainless) $898.00
Price: Model PTE-B (blued) $864.00
Price: Model PTE-S (stainless) $971.00

Desert Eagle Mark XIX

EAA Witness

Desert Baby Eagle

Ed Brown Commander Bobtail

Ed Brown Kobra Carry

Entréprise Elite P500

DESERT EAGLE MARK XIX PISTOL

Caliber: 357 Mag., 9-shot; 44 Mag., 8-shot; 50 AE, 7-shot. **Barrel:** 6", 10", interchangeable. **Weight:** 357 Mag.-62 oz.; 44 Mag.-69 oz.; 50 AE-72 oz. **Length:** 10-1/4" overall (6" bbl.). **Grips:** Polymer; rubber available. **Sights:** Blade on ramp front, combat-style rear. Adjustable available. **Features:** Interchangeable barrels; rotating three-lug bolt; ambidextrous safety; adjustable trigger. Military epoxy finish. Satin, bright nickel, chrome, brushed, matte or black finishes available. 10" barrel extra. Imported from Israel by Magnum Research, Inc.

Price: 357, 6" bbl., standard pistol **$1,249.00**
Price: 44 Mag., 6", standard pistol **$1,249.00**
Price: 50 Magnum, 6" bbl., standard pistol **$1,249.00**

DESERT BABY EAGLE PISTOLS

Caliber: 9mm Para., 40 S&W, 45 ACP, 10-round magazine. **Barrel:** 3.5", 3.7", 4.72". **Weight:** 26.8-39.8 oz. **Length:** 7.25" to 8.25" overall. **Grips:** Polymer. **Sights:** Drift-adjustable rear, blade front. **Features:** Steel frame and slide; polygonal rifling to reduce barrel wear; slide safety; decocker. Reintroduced in 1999. Imported from Israel by Magnum Research, Inc.

Price: Standard (9mm or 40 cal.; 4.72" barrel, 8.25" overall) **$499.00**
Price: Semi-Compact (9mm, 40 or 45 cal.; 3.7" barrel,
7.75" overall) **$499.00**
Price: Compact (9mm or 40 cal.; 3.5" barrel, 7.25" overall) **$499.00**
Price: Polymer (9mm or 40 cal; polymer frame; 3.25" barrel,
7.25" overall) **$499.00**

EAA WITNESS DA AUTO PISTOL

Caliber: 9mm Para., 10-shot magazine; 38 Super, 40 S&W, 10-shot magazine; 45 ACP, 10-shot magazine. **Barrel:** 4.50". **Weight:** 35.33 oz. **Length:** 8.10" overall. **Grips:** Checkered rubber. **Sights:** Undercut blade front, open rear adjustable for windage. **Features:** Double-action trigger system; round trigger guard; frame-mounted safety. Introduced 1991. Imported from Italy by European American Armory.

Price: 9mm, blue **$449.00**
Price: 9mm, Wonder finish **$459.00**
Price: 9mm Compact, blue, 10-shot **$449.00**
Price: As above, Wonder finish **$459.00**
Price: 38 Super, blue **$449.00**
Price: 38 Super, Wonder finish **$459.00**
Price: 40 S&W, blue **$449.00**
Price: As above, Wonder finish **$459.00**

Price: 40 S&W Compact, 9-shot, blue **$449.00**
Price: As above, Wonder finish **$459.00**
Price: 45 ACP, blue **$449.00**
Price: As above, Wonder finish **$459.00**
Price: 45 ACP Compact, 8-shot, blue **$449.00**
Price: As above, Wonder finish **$459.00**

ED BROWN CLASSIC CUSTOM

Caliber: 45 ACP, 7 shot. **Barrel:** 5". **Weight:** 39 oz. **Stocks:** Cocobolo wood. **Sights:** Bo-Mar adjustable rear, dovetail front. **Features:** Single-action, M1911 style, custom made to order, stainless frame and slide available.

Price: **$2,895.00**
Price: Stainless **$3,095.00**

ED BROWN KOBRA CARRY BOBTAIL

Caliber: 45 ACP, 400 Cor-Bon, 40 S&W, 357 SIG, 38 Super, 9mm Luger, 7-shot magazine. **Barrel:** 4.25". **Weight:** 34 oz. **Grips:** Hogue exotic wood. **Sights:** Customer preference front; fixed Novak low mount rear. Optional night inserts available. **Features:** Checkered forestrap and bobtailed mainspring housing.

Price: Executive Carry . . . . **$2,195.00 to $2,370.00**

ED BROWN KOBRA

Caliber: 45 ACP, 7-shot magazine. **Barrel:** 5" (Kobra); 4.25" (Kobra Carry). **Weight:** 39 oz. (Kobra); 34 oz. (Kobra Carry). **Grips:** Hogue exotic wood. **Sights:** Ramp, front; fixed Novak low-mount night sights, rear. **Features:** Has snakeskin pattern serrations on forestrap and mainspring housing, dehorned edges, beavertail grip safety.

Price: Kobra **$2,095.00**
Price: Kobra Carry **$2,195.00**

ENTRÉPRISE ELITE P500 AUTO PISTOL

Caliber: 45 ACP, 10-shot magazine. **Barrel:** 5". **Weight:** 40 oz. **Length:** 8.5" overall. **Grips:** Black ultra-slim, double diamond, checkered synthetic. **Sights:** Dovetailed blade front, rear adjustable for windage; 3-dot system. **Features:** Reinforced dust cover; lowered and flared ejection port; squared trigger guard; adjustable match trigger; bolstered front strap; high grip cut; high ride beavertail grip safety; steel flat mainspring housing; extended thumb lock; skeletonized hammer; match grade sear, disconnector; Wolff springs. Introduced 1998. Made in U.S.A. by Entréprise Arms.

Price: **$739.90**

Entréprise Boxer P500

Entréprise Tactical 500

Felk MTF 450

Firestorm 45 Gov't

Glock 17C

Firestorm Mini

Entréprise Medalist P500 Auto Pistol

Similar to the Elite model except has adjustable rear sight with dovetailed Patridge front; machined slide parallel rails; front and rear slide serrations; lowered and flared ejection port; full-length one-piece guide rod with plug; National Match barrel and bushing; stainless firing pin; tuned match extractor; oversize firing pin stop; slide lapped to frame. Introduced 1998. Made in U.S.A. by Entréprise Arms.

Price: 45 ACP **$979.00**
Price: 40 S&W **$1,099.00**

Entréprise Boxer P500 Auto Pistol

Similar to the Medalist model except has adjustable Competizione "melted" rear sight with dovetailed Patridge front; high mass chiseled slide with sweep cut; machined slide parallel rails; polished breech face and barrel channel. Introduced 1998. Made in U.S.A. by Entréprise Arms.

Price: **$1,399.00**

Entréprise Tactical P500 Auto Pistol

Similar to the Elite model except has Tactical2 Ghost Ring sight or Novak low-mount sight; ambidextrous thumb safety; front and rear slide serrations; full-length guide rod; throated barrel; tuned match extractor; fitted barrel and bushing; stainless firing pin; slide lapped to frame. Introduced 1998. Made in U.S.A. by Entréprise Arms.

Price: **$979.90**
Price: Tactical Plus (full-size frame, Officer's slide) **$1,049.00**

FELK MTF 450 AUTO PISTOL

Caliber: 9mm Para. (10-shot); 40 S&W (8-shot); 357 Mag, 45 ACP (9-shot magazine). **Barrel:** 3.5". **Weight:** 19.9 oz. **Length:** 6.4" overall. **Grips:** Checkered. **Sights:** Blade front; adjustable rear. **Features:** Double-action only trigger; striker fired; polymer frame; trigger safety, firing pin safety, trigger bar safety; adjustable trigger; fully interchangeable slide/barrel to change calibers. Introduced 1998. Imported by Felk Inc.

Price: **$395.00**
Price: 45 ACP pistol with 9mm and 40 S&W slide/barrel assemblies **$999.00**

FIRESTORM AUTO PISTOL

Features: 7 or 10 rd. double action pistols with matte, duo-tone or nickel finish. Distributed by SGS Importers International.

Price: 22 LR 10 rd, 380 7 rd. matte **$283.95**
Price: Duo-tone **$291.95**
Price: Mini 9mm, 40 S&W, 10 rd. matte **$399.95**
Price: Duo-tone **$408.95**
Price: Nickel **$399.95**
Price: Mini 45, seven-round matte **$408.95**
Price: Duo-tone 45 .... **$416.95**
Price: Nickel 45 .... **$433.95**
Price: 45 Government, Compact, 7-round matte **$308.95**
Price: Duo-tone **$316.95**
Price: Extra magazines .... **$29.95 to $49.95**

GLOCK 17 AUTO PISTOL

Caliber: 9mm Para., 10-shot magazine. **Barrel:** 4.49". **Weight:** 22.04 oz. (without magazine). **Length:** 7.32" overall. **Grips:** Black polymer. **Sights:** Dot on front blade, white outline rear adjustable for windage. **Features:** Polymer frame, steel slide; double-action trigger with "Safe Action" system; mechanical firing pin safety, drop safety; simple takedown without tools; locked breech, recoil operated action. Adopted by Austrian armed forces 1983. NATO approved 1984. Imported from Austria by Glock, Inc.

Price: Fixed sight, extra magazine, magazine loader, cleaning kit . **$624.00**
Price: Adjustable sight **$642.00**
Price: Model 17C, ported barrel (compensated) **$646.00**

Glock 20 10mm Auto Pistol

Similar to the Glock Model 17 except chambered for 10mm Automatic cartridge. Barrel length is 4.60", overall length is 7.59", and weight is 26.3 oz. (without magazine). Magazine capacity is 10 rds. Fixed or adjustable rear sight. Comes with an extra magazine, magazine loader, cleaning rod and brush. Introduced 1990. Imported from Austria by Glock, Inc.

Price: Fixed sight **$701.00**

Glock 21C Auto Pistol

Similar to the Glock 17 except chambered for 45 ACP, 10-shot magazine. Overall length is 7.59", weight is 25.2 oz. (without magazine). Fixed or adjustable rear sight. Introduced 1991.

Price: Fixed sight **$700.00**
Price: Adjustable sight **$730.00**

Glock 22

Glock 26

Glock 30

Glock 31

Glock 35

Glock 22 Auto Pistol

Similar to the Glock 17 except chambered for 40 S&W, 10-shot magazine. Overall length is 7.28", weight is 22.3 oz. (without magazine). Fixed or adjustable rear sight. Introduced 1990.

Price: Fixed sight **$646.00**

Glock 23 Auto Pistol

Similar to the Glock 19 except chambered for 40 S&W, 10-shot magazine. Overall length is 6.85", weight is 20.6 oz. (without magazine). Fixed or adjustable rear sight. Introduced 1990.

Price: Fixed sight **$646.00**

GLOCK 26, 27 AUTO PISTOLS

Caliber: 9mm Para. (M26), 10-shot magazine; 40 S&W (M27), 9-shot magazine. **Barrel:** 3.46". **Weight:** 21.75 oz. **Length:** 6.29" overall. **Grips:** Integral. Stippled polymer. **Sights:** Dot on front blade, fixed or fully adjustable white outline rear. **Features:** Subcompact size. Polymer frame, steel slide; double-action trigger with "Safe Action" system, three safeties. Matte black Tenifer finish. Hammer-forged barrel. Imported from Austria by Glock, Inc. Introduced 1996.

Price: Fixed sight **$624.00**
Price: Adjustable sight **$642.00**

GLOCK 29, 30 AUTO PISTOLS

Caliber: 10mm (M29), 45 ACP (M30), 10-shot magazine. **Barrel:** 3.78". **Weight:** 24 oz. **Length:** 6.7" overall. **Grips:** Integral. Stippled polymer. **Sights:** Dot on front, fixed or fully adjustable white outline rear. **Features:** Compact size. Polymer frame steel slide; double-recoil spring reduces recoil; Safe Action system with three safeties; Tenifer finish. Two magazines supplied. Introduced 1997. Imported from Austria by Glock, Inc.

Price: Fixed sight **$662.00**
Price: Adjustable sight **$680.00**

Glock 31/31C Auto Pistols

Similar to the Glock 17 except chambered for 357 Auto cartridge; 10-shot magazine. Overall length is 7.32", weight is 23.28 oz. (without magazine). Fixed or adjustable sight. Imported from Austria by Glock, Inc.

Price: Fixed sight **$646.00**

Glock 32/32C Auto Pistols

Similar to the Glock 19 except chambered for the 357 Auto cartridge; 10-shot magazine. Overall length is 6.85", weight is 21.52 oz. (without magazine). Fixed or adjustable sight. Imported from Austria by Glock, Inc.

Price: Fixed sight **$646.00**
Price: Adjustable sight **$642.00**

Glock 33 Auto Pistol

Similar to the Glock 26 except chambered for the 357 Auto cartridge; 9-shot magazine. Overall length is 6.29", weight is 19.75 oz. (without magazine). Fixed or adjustable sight. Imported from Austria by Glock, Inc.

Price: Fixed sight **$624.00**
Price: Adjustable sight **$642.00**

GLOCK 34, 35 AUTO PISTOLS

Caliber: 9mm Para. (M34), 40 S&W (M35), 10-shot magazine. **Barrel:** 5.32". **Weight:** 22.9 oz. **Length:** 8.15" overall. **Grips:** Integral. Stippled

Hammerli Trailside

polymer. **Sights:** Dot on front, fully adjustable white outline rear. **Features:** Polymer frame, steel slide; double-action trigger with "Safe Action" system; three safeties; Tenifer finish. Imported from Austria by Glock, Inc.

Price: Model 34, 9mm **$704.00**

GLOCK 36 AUTO PISTOL

Caliber: 45 ACP, 6-shot magazine. **Barrel:** 3.78". **Weight:** 20.11 oz. **Length:** 6.77" overall. **Grips:** Integral. Stippled polymer. **Sights:** Dot on front, fully adjustable white outline rear. **Features:** Polymer frame, steel slide; double-action trigger with "Safe Action" system; three safeties; Tenifer finish. Imported from Austria by Glock, Inc.

Price: Fixed sight **$662.00**
Price: Adjustable sight **$680.00**

Glock 37 Auto Pistol

Similar to the Glock 17 except 45 GAP, has a 4.49" barrel, overall length, 7.32" and weight, 25.95 oz. Magazine capacity is 10 rds. Fixed or adjustable rear sight.

Price: Fixed sight **$639.00**
Price: Adjustable sight **$657.00**
Price: Night sight **$686.00**

HAMMERLI "TRAILSIDE" TARGET PISTOL

Caliber: 22 LR. **Barrel:** 4.5", 6". **Weight:** 28 oz. **Grips:** Synthetic. **Sights:** Fixed. **Features:** 10-shot magazine. Imported from Switzerland by SIGARMS. Distributed by Hammerli U.S.A.

Price: **$579.00**

Heckler & Koch
USP Compact

Heckler & Koch USP45

Heckler & Koch
USP45 Compact

Heckler & Koch
USP45 Tactical

Heckler & Koch
Elite

Heckler & Koch
Mark 23 Special Operations

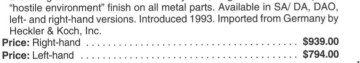

Heckler & Koch P7M8

HECKLER & KOCH USP AUTO PISTOL

Caliber: 9mm Para., 10-shot magazine, 40 S&W, 10-shot magazine, 357 Mag. **Barrel:** 4.25". **Weight:** 28 oz. (USP40). **Length:** 6.9" overall. **Grips:** Non-slip stippled black polymer. **Sights:** Blade front, rear adjustable for windage. **Features:** New HK design with polymer frame, modified Browning action with recoil reduction system, single control lever. Special "hostile environment" finish on all metal parts. Available in SA/ DA, DAO, left- and right-hand versions. Introduced 1993. Imported from Germany by Heckler & Koch, Inc.
Price: Right-hand **$939.00**
Price: Left-hand **$794.00**

Heckler & Koch USP Compact Auto Pistol

Similar to the USP except has 3.58" barrel, measures 6.81" overall, and weighs 1.60 lbs. (9mm). Available in 9mm Para. 357 SIG or 40 S&W with 10-shot magazine. Introduced 1996. Imported from Germany by Heckler & Koch, Inc.
Price: Blue **$874.00**

Heckler & Koch USP45 Auto Pistol

Similar to the 9mm and 40 S&W USP except chambered for 45 ACP, 10-shot magazine. Has 4.13" barrel, overall length of 7.87" and weighs 30.4 oz. Has adjustable 3-dot sight system. Available in SA/DA, DAO, left- and right-hand versions. Introduced 1995. Imported from Germany by Heckler & Koch, Inc.
Price: Right-hand **$839.00**

Heckler & Koch USP45 Compact

Similar to the USP45 except has stainless slide; 8-shot magazine; modified and contoured slide and frame; extended slide release; 3.80" barrel, 7.09" overall length, weighs 1.75 lbs.; adjustable 3-dot sights. Introduced 1998. Imported from Germany by Heckler & Koch, Inc.
Price: With control lever on left, stainless **$874.00**

HECKLER & KOCH USP45 TACTICAL PISTOL

Caliber: 45 ACP, 10-shot magazine. **Barrel:** 4.92". **Weight:** 2.24 lbs. **Length:** 8.64" overall. **Grips:** Non-slip stippled polymer. **Sights:** Blade front, fully adjustable target rear. **Features:** Has extended threaded barrel with rubber O-ring; adjustable trigger; extended magazine floorplate; adjustable trigger stop; polymer frame. Introduced 1998. Imported from Germany by Heckler & Koch, Inc.
Price: **$1,115.00**

HECKLER & KOCH MARK 23 SPECIAL OPERATIONS PISTOL

Caliber: 45 ACP, 10-shot magazine. **Barrel:** 5.87". **Weight:** 43 oz. **Length:** 9.65" overall. **Grips:** Integral with frame; black polymer. **Sights:** Blade front, rear drift adjustable for windage; 3-dot. **Features:** Civilian version of the SOCOM pistol. Polymer frame; double action; exposed hammer; short recoil, modified Browning action. Introduced 1996. Imported from Germany by Heckler & Koch, Inc.
Price: **$2,412.00**

Heckler & Koch USP Expert Pistol

Combines features of the USP Tactical and HK Mark 23 pistols with a new slide design. Chambered for 45 ACP, 40 S&W & 9mm; 10-shot magazine. Has adjustable target sights, 5.20" barrel, 8.74" overall length, weighs 1.87 lbs. Match-grade single- and double-action trigger pull with adjustable stop; ambidextrous control levers; elongated target slide; barrel O-ring seals and centers barrel. Suited to IPSC competition. Introduced 1999. Imported from Germany by Heckler & Koch, Inc.
Price: **$1,356.00**

Heckler & Koch Elite

A long slide version of the USP. 6.2" barrel. Available in 9mm and 45 ACP. Introduced 2003. Imported from Germany by Heckler & Koch, Inc.
Price: **$1,356.00**

HECKLER & KOCH P7M8 AUTO PISTOL

Caliber: 9mm Para., 8-shot magazine. **Barrel:** 4.13". **Weight:** 29 oz. **Length:** 6.73" overall. **Grips:** Stippled black plastic. **Sights:** Blade front, adjustable rear; 3-dot system. **Features:** Unique "squeeze cocker" in front strap cocks the action. Gas-retarded action. Squared combat-type trigger guard. Blue finish. Compact size. Imported from Germany by Heckler & Koch, Inc.
Price: P7M8, blued **$1,515.00**

Hi-Point 9MM Comp

Kahr K9

HECKLER & KOCH P2000 GPM PISTOL

Caliber: 9mmx19; 10-shot magazine. 13- or 16-round law enforcement/military magazines. **Barrel:** 3.62". **Weight:** 21.87 ozs. **Length:** 7". **Grips:** Interchangeable panels. **Sights:** Fixed Patridge style, drift adjustable for windage, standard 3-dot. **Features:** German Pistol Model incorporating features of the HK USP Compact. Introduced 2003. Imported from Germany by Heckler & Koch, Inc.
Price: **$887.00**

HECKLER & KOCK P2000SK SUBCOMPACT

Caliber: 9mm and 40 S&W. **Barrel:** 2.48". **Weight:** 1.49 lbs. (9mm) or 1.61 lbs. (40 S&W). **Sights:** Fixed Patridge style, drift adjustable. **Features:** Standard accessory rails, ambidextrous slide release, polymer frame, polygonal bore profile.
Price: **$929.00**

HI-POINT FIREARMS 9MM COMP PISTOL

Caliber: 9mm, Para., 10-shot magazine. **Barrel:** 4". **Weight:** 39 oz. **Length:** 7.72" overall. **Grips:** Textured plastic. **Sights:** Adjustable; low profile. **Features:** Single-action design. Scratch-resistant, non-glare blue finish, alloy frame. Muzzle brake/compensator. Compensator is slotted for laser or flashlight mounting. Introduced 1998. From MKS Supply, Inc.
Price: Matte black **$159.00**

HI-POINT FIREARMS MODEL 9MM COMPACT PISTOL

Caliber: 9mm Para., 8-shot magazine. **Barrel:** 3.5". **Weight:** 29 oz. **Length:** 6.7" overall. **Grips:** Textured plastic. **Sights:** Combat-style adjustable 3-dot system; low profile. **Features:** Single-action design; frame-mounted magazine release; polymer or alloy frame. Scratch-resistant matte finish. Introduced 1993. Made in U.S.A. by MKS Supply, Inc.
Price: Black, alloy frame **$149.00**
Price: With polymer frame (29 oz.), non-slip grips **$149.00**
Price: Aluminum with polymer frame **$149.00**

Hi-Point Firearms Model 380 Polymer Pistol

Similar to the 9mm Compact model except chambered for 380 ACP, 8-shot magazine, adjustable 3-dot sights. Weighs 29 oz. Polymer frame. Introduced 1998. Made in U.S.A. by MKS Supply, Inc.
Price: **$114.00**

Hi-Point Firearms 380 Comp Pistol

Similar to the 380 Polymer Pistol except has a 4" barrel with muzzle compensator; action locks open after last shot. Includes 10-shot and 8-shot magazine; trigger lock. Introduced 2001. Made in U.S.A. by MKS Supply, Inc.
Price: **$135.00**
Price: With laser sight **$229.00**

HI-POINT FIREARMS 45 POLYMER FRAME

Caliber: 45 ACP (9-shot), 40 S&W. **Barrel:** 4.5". **Weight:** 35 oz. **Sights:** Adjustable 3-dot. **Features:** Last round lock-open, grip mounted magazine release, magazine disconnect safety, integrated accessory rail. Introduced 2002. Made in U.S.A. by MKS Supply, Inc.
Price: **$179.00**

IAI M-2000 PISTOL

Caliber: 45 ACP, 8-shot. **Barrel:** 5", (Compact 4.25"). **Weight:** 36 oz. **Length:** 8.5", (6" Compact). **Grips:** Plastic or wood. **Sights:** Fixed.

Features: 1911 Government U.S. Army-style. Steel frame and slide Parkerized. GI grip safety. Beveled feed ramp barrel. By IAI, Inc.
Price: **$465.00**

KAHR K9, K40 DA AUTO PISTOLS

Caliber: 9mm Para., 7-shot, 40 S&W, 6-shot magazine. **Barrel:** 3.5". **Weight:** 25 oz. **Length:** 6" overall. **Grips:** Wraparound textured soft polymer. **Sights:** Blade front, rear drift adjustable for windage; bar-dot combat style. **Features:** Trigger-cocking double-action mechanism with passive firing pin block. Made of 4140 ordnance steel with matte black finish. Contact maker for complete price list. Introduced 1994. Made in U.S.A. by Kahr Arms.
Price: E9, black matte finish **$425.00**
Price: Matte black, night sights 9mm **$668.00**
Price: Matte stainless steel, 9mm **$638.00**
Price: 40 S&W, matte black **$580.00**
Price: 40 S&W, matte black, night sights **$668.00**
Price: 40 S&W, matte stainless **$638.00**
Price: K9 Elite 98 (high-polish stainless slide flats, Kahr combat trigger), from **$694.00**
Price: As above, MK9 Elite 98, from **$694.00**
Price: As above, K40 Elite 98, from **$694.00**
Price: Covert, black, stainless slide, short grip **$599.00**
Price: Covert, black, Tritium nite sights **$689.00**

Kahr K9 9mm Compact Polymer Pistol

Similar to K9 steel frame pistol except has polymer frame, matte stainless steel slide. Barrel length 3.5"; overall length 6"; weighs 17.9 oz. Includes two 7-shot magazines, hard polymer case, trigger lock. Introduced 2000. Made in U.S.A. by Kahr Arms.
Price: **$599.00**

Kahr MK9/MK40 Micro Pistol

Similar to the K9/K40 except is 5.5" overall, 4" high, with a 3" barrel. Weighs 22 oz. Has snag-free bar-dot sights, polished feed ramp, dual recoil spring system, DA-only trigger. Comes with 6- and 7-shot magazines. Introduced 1998. Made in U.S.A. by Kahr Arms.
Price: Matte stainless **$638.00**
Price: Elite 98, polished stainless, Tritium night sights **$791.00**

KAHR PM9 PISTOL

Caliber: 9x19. **Barrel:** 3", 1:10 twist. **Weight:** 15.9 oz. **Length:** 5.3" overall. **Features:** Lightweight black polymer frame, polygonal rifling, stainless steel slide, DAO with passive striker block, trigger lock, hard case, 6- and 7-round mags.
Price: Matte stainless slide **$622.00**
Price: Tritium night sights **$719.00**

KEL-TEC P-11 AUTO PISTOL

Caliber: 9mm Para., 10-shot magazine. **Barrel:** 3.1". **Weight:** 14 oz. **Length:** 5.6" overall. **Grips:** Checkered black polymer. **Sights:** Blade front, rear adjustable for windage. **Features:** Ordnance steel slide, aluminum frame. Double-action-only trigger mechanism. Introduced 1995. Made in U.S.A. by Kel-Tec CNC Industries, Inc.
Price: Blue **$320.00**
Price: Hard chrome **$375.00**
Price: Parkerized **$362.00**

Kel-Tec P-32

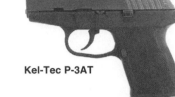

Kel-Tec P-3AT

Kimber Pro Carry II

Kimber Ultra Carry II

Kimber Ten II High Capacity Polymer

Kimber Gold Match II

KEL-TEC P-32 AUTO PISTOL

Caliber: 32 ACP, 7-shot magazine. **Barrel:** 2.68". **Weight:** 6.6 oz. **Length:** 5.07" overall. **Grips:** Checkered composite. **Sights:** Fixed. **Features:** Double-action-only mechanism with 6-lb. pull; internal slide stop. Textured composite grip/frame. Now available in 380 ACP. Made in U.S.A. by Kel-Tec CNC Industries, Inc.

Price: Blue	$306.00
Price: Hard chrome	$362.00
Price: Parkerized	$346.00

KEL-TEC P-3AT PISTOL

Caliber: 380 Auto; 7-rounds. **Weight:** 7.2 oz. **Length:** 5.2". **Features:** Lightest 380 auto made; aluminum frame, steel barrel.

Price: Blue	$311.00
Price: Hard Chrome	$367.00
Price: Parkerized	$351.00

KIMBER CUSTOM II AUTO PISTOL

Caliber: 45 ACP, 40 S&W, 38 Super, 9mm, 10mm. **Barrel:** 5", match grade; 9mm, 10mm, 40 S&W, 38 Super barrels ramped. **Weight:** 38 oz. **Length:** 8.7" overall. **Grips:** Checkered black rubber, walnut, rosewood. **Sights:** Dovetailed front and rear, Kimber low profile adj. or fixed sights. **Features:** Slide, frame and barrel machined from steel or stainless steel. Match grade barrel, chamber and trigger group. Extended thumb safety, beveled magazine well, beveled front and rear slide serrations, high ride beavertail grip safety, checkered flat mainspring housing, kidney cut under trigger guard, high cut grip, match grade stainless steel barrel bushing, polished breech face, Commander-style hammer, lowered and flared ejection port, Wolff springs, bead blasted black oxide or matte stainless finish. Introduced in 1996. Made in U.S.A. by Kimber Mfg., Inc.

Price: Custom II	$768.00
Price: Custom II Walnut (double-diamond walnut grips)	$775.00
Price: Stainless II	$865.00
Price: Stainless II 40 S&W	$884.00
Price: Stainless II Target 45 ACP (stainless, adj. sight)	$983.00
Price: Stainless II Target 38 Super	$1,014.00

Kimber Compact Stainless II Auto Pistol

Similar to Pro Carry II except has stainless steel frame, 4-inch bbl., grip is .400" shorter than standard, no front serrations. Weighs 34 oz. 45 ACP only. Introduced in 1998. Made in U.S.A. by Kimber Mfg., Inc.

Price:	$907.00

Kimber Pro Carry II Auto Pistol

Similar to Custom II, has aluminum frame, 4" bull barrel fitted directly to the slide without bushing. HD with stainless steel frame. Introduced 1998. Made in U.S.A. by Kimber Mfg., Inc.

Price: Pro Carry II	$779.00
Price: Pro Carry II w/night sights	$902.00
Price: Pro Carry II Stainless w/night sights	$985.00
Price: Pro Carry HD II	$906.00

Kimber Ultra Carry II Auto Pistol

Lightweight aluminum frame, 3" match grade bull barrel fitted to slide without bushing. Grips .4" shorter. Low effort recoil. Weighs 25 oz. Introduced in 1999. Made in U.S.A. by Kimber Mfg., Inc.

Price:	$791.00
Price: Ultra Carry II Stainless	$875.00
Price: Ultra Carry II Stainless 40 S&W	$921.00

Kimber Ten II High Capacity Polymer Pistol

Similar to Custom II, Pro Carry II and Ultra Carry II depending on barrel length. Thirteen-round magazine capacity (double stack and flush fitting). Polymer grip frame molded over stainless steel or aluminum (BP Ten pistols only) frame insert. Checkered front strap and belly of trigger guard. All models have fixed sights except Gold Match Ten II, which has adjustable sight. Frame grip dimensions approximately that of the standard 1911. **Weight:** 24 to 34 oz. Improved version of the Kimber Polymer series. Made in U.S.A. by Kimber Mfg., Inc.

Price: Pro Carry Ten II	$794.00
Price: Stainless Ten II	$786.00

Kimber Gold Match II Auto Pistol

Similar to Custom II models. Includes stainless steel barrel with match grade chamber and barrel bushing, ambidextrous thumb safety, adjustable sight, premium aluminum trigger, hand-checkered double diamond rosewood grips. Barrel hand-fitted for target accuracy. Made in U.S.A. by Kimber Mfg., Inc.

Price: Gold Match II	$1,204.00
Price: Gold Match Stainless II 45 ACP	$1,369.00
Price: Gold Match Stainless II 40 S&W	$1,400.00

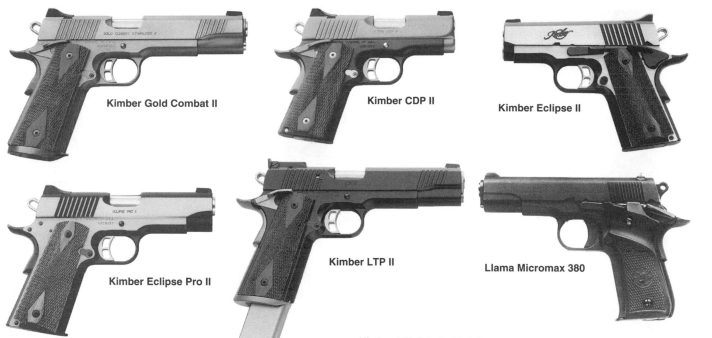

Kimber Gold Combat II

Kimber CDP II

Kimber Eclipse II

Kimber Eclipse Pro II

Kimber LTP II

Llama Micromax 380

Kimber Gold Match Ten II Polymer Auto Pistol
Similar to Stainless Gold Match II. High capacity polymer frame with 13-round magazine. Thumb safety. Introduced 1999. Made in U.S.A. by Kimber Mfg., Inc.
Price: **$1,072.00**

Kimber Gold Combat II Auto Pistol
Similar to Gold Match II except designed for concealed carry. Extended and beveled magazine well, Meprolight Tritium night sights; premium aluminum trigger; 30 lpi front strap checkering; extended magazine well. Introduced 1999. Made in U.S.A. by Kimber Mfg., Inc.
Price: Gold Combat II **$1,733.00**
Price: Gold Combat Stainless II **$1,674.00**

Kimber CDP II Series Auto Pistol
Similar to Custom II, but designed for concealed carry. Aluminum frame. Standard features include stainless steel slide, fixed Meprolight tritium 3-dot (green) dovetail-mounted night sights, match grade barrel and chamber, 30 LPI front strap checkering, two-tone finish, ambidextrous thumb safety, hand-checkered double diamond rosewood grips. Introduced in 2000. Made in U.S.A. by Kimber Mfg., Inc.
Price: Ultra CDP II 40 S&W **$1,215.00**
Price: Ultra CDP II (3" barrel, short grip) **$1,177.00**
Price: Compact CDP II (4" barrel, short grip) **$1,177.00**
Price: Pro CDP II (4" barrel, full length grip) **$1,177.00**
Price: Custom CDP II (5" barrel, full length grip) **$1,177.00**

Kimber Eclipse II Series Auto Pistol
Similar to Custom II and other stainless Kimber pistols. Stainless slide and frame, black oxide, two-tone finish. Gray/black laminated grips. 30 lpi front strap checkering. All models have night sights; Target versions have Meprolight adjustable Bar/Dot version. Made in U.S.A. by Kimber Mfg., Inc.
Price: Eclipse Ultra II (3" barrel, short grip) **$1,085.00**
Price: Eclipse Pro II (4" barrel, full length grip) **$1,085.00**
Price: Eclipse Pro Target II (4" barrel, full length grip,
adjustable sight) **$1,189.00**
Price: Eclipse Custom II (5" barrel, full length grip) **$1,105.00**
Price: Eclipse Target II (5" barrel, full length grip,
adjustable sight) **$1,189.00**
Price: Eclipse Custom II (10mm) **$1,220.00**

Kimber LTP II Auto Pistol
Similar to Gold Match II. Built for Limited Ten competition. First Kimber pistol with new, innovative Kimber external extractor. KimPro premium finish. Stainless steel match grade barrel. Extended and beveled magazine well. Checkered front strap and trigger guard belly. Tungsten full length guide rod. Premium aluminum trigger. Ten-round single stack magazine. Wide ambidextrous thumb safety. Made in U.S.A. by Kimber Mfg., Inc.
Price: **$2,099.00**

Kimber Super Match II Auto Pistol
Similar to Gold Match II. Built for target and action shooting competition. Tested for accuracy, target included. Stainless steel barrel and chamber. KimPro finish on stainless steel slide. Stainless steel frame. 30 lpi checkered front strap, premium aluminum trigger, Kimber adjustable sight. Introduced in 1999.
Price: **$1,986.00**

KORTH PISTOL
Caliber: 40 S&W, 357 SIG (9-shot); 9mm Para, 9x21 (10-shot). **Barrel:** 4" (standard), 5" (optional). **Weight:** 3.3 lbs. (single action), 11 lbs. (double action). **Sights:** Fully adjustable. **Features:** Recoil-operated action, mechanically-locked via large pivoting bolt block. Accessories include sound suppressor for qualified buyers. Imported by Korth U.S.A.
Price: **$7,578.00**

LLAMA MICROMAX 380 AUTO PISTOL
Caliber: 32 ACP (9-shot), 380 ACP (8-shot). **Barrel:** 3-11/16". **Weight:** 23 oz. **Length:** 6-1/2" overall. **Grips:** Checkered high impact polymer. **Sights:** 3-dot combat. **Features:** Single-action. Mini custom extended slide release; mini custom extended beavertail grip safety; combat-style hammer. Introduced 1997. Distributed by Import Sports, Inc.
Price: Matte blue **$281.95**
Price: Satin chrome (380 only) **$299.95**

LLAMA MINIMAX SERIES
Caliber: 40 S&W (8-shot); 45 ACP (7-shot). **Barrel:** 3-1/2". **Weight:** 35 oz. **Length:** 7-1/3" overall. **Grips:** Checkered rubber. **Sights:** 3-dot combat. **Features:** Single action, skeletonized combat-style hammer, extended slide release, cone-style barrel, flared ejection port. Introduced 1996. Distributed by Import Sports, Inc.
Price: Blue **$308.95**
Price: Duo-tone finish (45 only) **$315.95**
Price: Satin chrome **$333.95**

Llama Minimax

Llama Max-1 Government Deluxe

North American Arms Guardian

Para-Ordnance Carry

Para-Ordnance P12.45

Para-Ordnance LDA

Para-Ordnance Limited

Llama Minimax Sub-Compact Auto Pistol
Similar to the Minimax except has 3.14" barrel, weighs 31 oz.; 6.8" overall length; has 10-shot magazine with finger extension; beavertail grip safety. Introduced 1999. Distributed by Import Sports, Inc.
Price: 45 ACP, matte blue **$315.95**
Price: As above, satin chrome **$341.95**
Price: Duo-tone finish (45 only) **$324.95**

LLAMA MAX-I AUTO PISTOLS
Caliber: 45 ACP, 7-shot. **Barrel:** 5-1/8". **Weight:** 36 oz. **Length:** 8-1/2" overall. **Grips:** Polymer. **Sights:** Blade front; 3-dot system. **Features:** Single-action trigger; skeletonized combat-style hammer; steel frame; extended manual and grip safeties, matte finish. Introduced 1995. Distributed by Import Sports, Inc.
Price: 45 ACP, 7-round, Government model **$358.95**
Price: Maxi II, 17-round model **$324.95**

NORTH AMERICAN ARMS GUARDIAN PISTOL
Caliber: 32 ACP, 380 ACP, 32NAA, 6-shot magazine. **Barrel:** 2.1". **Weight:** 13.5 oz. **Length:** 4.36" overall. **Grips:** Black polymer. **Sights:** Fixed. **Features:** Double-action only mechanism. All stainless steel construction. Introduced 1998. Made in U.S.A. by North American Arms.
Price: . . . . **$402.00 to $479.00**

OLYMPIC ARMS OA-93 AR PISTOL
Caliber: 5.56 NATO. **Barrel:** 6.5", chrome-moly steel. **Weight:** 5.8 lbs. **Length:** 26.5". **Sights:** None. **Features:** Black matte finish; flash suppressor; tubular handguard. Introduced 2005. Made in U.S.A. by Olympic Arms, Inc.
Price: **$1,020.00**

Olympic Arms OA-98 AR Pistol
Similar to the OA-93 except has removable 7-shot magazine, weighs 3 lbs. Introduced 1999. Made in U.S.A. by Olympic Arms, Inc.
Price: **$1,020.00**

PARA-ORDNANCE P-SERIES AUTO PISTOLS
Caliber: 9mm Para., 40 S&W, 45 ACP, 10-shot magazine. **Barrel:** 3", 3-1/2", 4-1/4", 5". **Weight:** From 24 oz. (alloy frame). **Length:** 8.5" overall. **Grips:** Textured composition. **Sights:** Blade front, rear adjustable for windage. High visibility 3-dot system. **Features:** Available with alloy, steel or stainless steel frame with black finish (silver or stainless gun). Steel and stainless steel frame guns weigh 40 oz. (P14.45), 36 oz. (P13.45), 34 oz. (P12.45). Grooved match trigger, rounded combat-style hammer. Beveled magazine well. Manual thumb, grip and firing pin lock safeties. Solid barrel bushing. Contact maker for full details. Introduced 1990. Made in Canada by Para-Ordnance.

Price: Steel frame **$855.00**
Price: Alloy frame **$840.00**
Price: Stainless steel **$988.00**

Para-Ordnance Limited Pistols
Similar to the P-Series pistols except with full-length recoil guide system; fully adjustable rear sight; tuned trigger with over-travel stop; beavertail grip safety; competition hammer; front and rear slide serrations; ambidextrous safety; lowered ejection port; ramped match-grade barrel; dove-tailed front sight. Introduced 1998. Made in Canada by Para-Ordnance.
Price: 9mm, 40 S&W, 45 ACP **$1,105.00**

Para-Ordnance LDA Auto Pistols
Similar to P-series except has double-action trigger mechanism. Steel frame with matte black finish, checkered composition grips. Available in 9mm Para., 40 S&W, 45 ACP. Introduced 1999. Made in Canada by Para-Ordnance.
Price: . . . . **$899.00 to $973.00**

Para-Ordnance LDA Limited Pistols
Similar to LDA, has ambidextrous safety, adjustable rear sight, front slide serrations and full-length recoil guide system. Made in Canada by Para-Ordnance.
Price: Black finish **$1,105.00**
Price: Stainless **$1,049.00**

PARA-ORDNANCE 45 LDA PARA CARRY
Caliber: 45 ACP. **Barrel:** 3", 7-shot. **Weight:** 30 oz. **Length:** 6.5". **Grips:** Double diamond checkered cocobolo. **Features:** Stainless finish and receiver. Para LDA trigger system and safeties.
Price: **$988.00**

PARA-ORDNANCE 45 LDA PARA COMPANION
Caliber: 45 ACP. **Barrel:** 3.5", 8-shot. **Weight:** 32 oz. **Length:** 7". **Grips:** Double diamond checkered cocobolo. **Features:** Para LDA trigger system with Para LDA 3 safeties (slide lock, firing pin block and grip safety). Lightning speed, full size capacity.
Price: **$899.00**

Peters Stahl High Capacity

Peters Stahl Trophy Master

Peters Stahl Millennium

Phoenix Arms HP22

Ruger P89

Ruger P90

Rock River Standard Match

PETERS STAHL AUTOLOADING PISTOLS
Caliber: 9mm Para., 45 ACP. **Barrel:** 5" or 6". **Grips:** Walnut or walnut with rubber wrap. **Sights:** Fully adjustable rear, blade front. **Features:** Stainless steel extended slide stop, safety and extended magazine release button; speed trigger with stop, approx. 3-lb. pull; polished ramp. Introduced 2000. Imported from Germany by Phillips & Rogers.
Price: High Capacity (accepts 15-shot magazines in 45 cal.;
  includes 10-shot magazine) **$1,695.00**
Price: Trophy Master (blued or stainless,
  7-shot in 45, 8-shot in 9mm) **$1,995.00**
Price: Millennium Model (titanium coating on receiver and slide) **$2,195.00**

PHOENIX ARMS HP22, HP25 AUTO PISTOLS
Caliber: 22 LR, 10-shot (HP22), 25 ACP, 10-shot (HP25). **Barrel:** 3". **Weight:** 20 oz. **Length:** 5-1/2" overall. **Grips:** Checkered composition. **Sights:** Blade front, adjustable rear. **Features:** Single action, exposed hammer; manual hold-open; button magazine release. Available in satin nickel, polished blue finish. Introduced 1993. Made in U.S.A. by Phoenix Arms.
Price: With gun lock and cable lanyard **$130.00**
Price: HP Rangemaster kit with 5" bbl.,
  locking case and assessories **$171.00**
Price: HP Deluxe Rangemaster kit with 3" and 5" bbls.,
  2 mags., case **$210.00**

ROCK RIVER ARMS STANDARD MATCH AUTO PISTOL
Caliber: 45 ACP. **Barrel:** NA. **Weight:** NA. **Length:** NA. **Grips:** Cocobolo, checkered. **Sights:** Heine fixed rear, blade front. **Features:** Chrome-moly steel frame and slide; beavertail grip safety with raised pad; checkered slide stop; ambidextrous safety; polished feed ramp and extractor; aluminum speed trigger with 3.5 lb. pull. Made in U.S.A. From Rock River Arms.
Price: **$1,025.00**

ROCKY MOUNTAIN ARMS PATRIOT PISTOL
Caliber: 223, 10-shot magazine. **Barrel:** 7", with muzzle brake. **Weight:** 5 lbs. **Length:** 20.5" overall. **Grips:** Black composition. **Sights:** None furnished. **Features:** Milled upper receiver with enhanced Weaver base; milled lower receiver from billet plate; machined aluminum National Match handguard. Finished in DuPont Teflon-S matte black or NATO green. Comes with black nylon case, one magazine. Introduced 1993. From Rocky Mountain Arms, Inc.
Price: With A-2 handle top . . . . **$2,500.00 to $2,800.00**
Price: Flat top model . . . . **$3,000.00 to $3,500.00**

RUGER P89 AUTOLOADING PISTOL
Caliber: 9mm Para., 15-shot magazine. **Barrel:** 4.50". **Weight:** 32 oz. **Length:** 7.84" overall. **Grips:** Grooved black synthetic composition. **Sights:** Square post front, square notch rear adjustable for windage, both with white dot inserts. **Features:** Double action, ambidextrous slide-mounted safety-levers. Slide 4140 chrome-moly steel or 400-series stainless steel, frame lightweight aluminum alloy. Ambidextrous magazine release. Blue, stainless steel. Introduced 1986; stainless 1990.
Price: P89, blue, extra mag and mag loader, plastic case locks . . . **$475.00**
Price: KP89, stainless, extra mag and mag loader,
  plastic case locks **$525.00**

Ruger P89D Decocker Autoloading Pistol
Similar to standard P89 except has ambidextrous decocking levers in place of regular slide-mounted safety. Decocking levers move firing pin inside slide where hammer cannot reach. Blue, stainless steel. Introduced 1990.
Price: P89D, blue, extra mag and mag loader, plastic case locks . **$475.00**
Price: KP89D, stainless, extra mag and mag loader,
  plastic case locks **$525.00**

RUGER P90 MANUAL SAFETY MODEL AUTOLOADING PISTOL
Caliber: 45 ACP, 8-shot magazine. **Barrel:** 4.50". **Weight:** 33.5 oz. **Length:** 7.75" overall. **Grips:** Grooved black synthetic composition. **Sights:** Square post front, square notch rear adjustable for windage, both with white dot. **Features:** Double action; ambidextrous slide-mounted safety-levers. Stainless steel only. Introduced 1991.
Price: KP90 with extra mag, loader, case and gunlock **$565.00**
Price: P90 (blue) **$525.00**

Ruger KP94D

Ruger 22/45-P4

Ruger KP512

Ruger KP90 Decocker Autoloading Pistol

Similar to the P90 except has a manual decocking system. Ambidextrous decocking levers move the firing pin inside the slide where the hammer cannot reach it. Available only in stainless steel. Overall length 7.75", weighs 33.5 oz. Introduced 1991.

Price: KP90D with case, extra mag and mag loading tool **$565.00**

Ruger KP94 Autoloading Pistol

Sized midway between full-size P-Series and compact KP94. 4.25" barrel, 7.5" overall length, weighs about 33 oz. KP94 manual safety model; KP94D is decocker-only in 40-caliber with 10-shot magazine. Slide gripping grooves roll over top of slide. KP94 has ambidextrous safety-levers; KP944D has ambidextrous decocking levers. Matte finish stainless slide, barrel, alloy frame. Also blue. Includes hard case and lock. Introduced 1994. Made in U.S.A. by Sturm, Ruger & Co.

Price: P944, blue (manual safety) **$495.00**
Price: KP944 (40-caliber) (manual safety-stainless) **$575.00**
Price: KP944D (40-caliber)-decocker only **$575.00**

RUGER P95 AUTOLOADING PISTOL

Caliber: 9mm Para., 15-shot magazine. **Barrel:** 3.9". **Weight:** 27 oz. **Length:** 7.25" overall. **Grips:** Grooved; integral with frame. **Sights:** Blade front, rear drift adjustable for windage; 3-dot system. **Features:** Molded polymer grip frame, stainless steel or chrome-moly slide. Suitable for +P+ ammunition. Safety model, decocker or DAO. Introduced 1996. Made in U.S.A. by Sturm, Ruger & Co. Comes with lockable plastic case, spare magazine, loader and lock.

Price: P95D15 decocker only **$425.00**
Price: P9515 stainless steel decocker only **$475.00**
Price: KP9515 safety model, stainless steel **$475.00**
Price: P9515 safety model, blued finish **$425.00**

RUGER MARK II STANDARD AUTOLOADING PISTOL

Caliber: 22 LR, 10-shot magazine. **Barrel:** 4-3/4" or 6". **Weight:** 35 oz. (4-3/4" bbl.). **Length:** 8-5/16" (4-3/4" bbl.). **Grips:** Checkered composition grip panels. **Sights:** Fixed, wide blade front, fixed rear. **Features:** Updated design of original Standard Auto. New bolt hold-open latch. 10-shot magazine, magazine catch, safety and trigger. Introduced 1982.

Price: Blued (MKIII4, MKIII6) **$322.00**

Ruger 22/45 Mark II Pistol

Similar to other 22 Mark II autos except has grip frame of Zytel that matches angle and magazine latch of Model 1911 45 ACP pistol. Available in 4" standard, 4-3/4" and 5-1/2" bull barrels. Comes with extra magazine, plastic case, lock. Introduced 1992.

Price: P4MKIII, 4" standard barrel, adjustable sights **$307.00**
Price: KP512 (5-1/2" bull bbl.), stainless steel, adj. sights **$398.00**
Price: P512 (5-1/2" bull bbl., all blue), adj. sights **$307.00**

SAFARI ARMS ENFORCER PISTOL

Caliber: 45 ACP, 6-shot magazine. **Barrel:** 3.8", stainless. **Weight:** 36 oz. **Length:** 7.3" overall. **Grips:** Smooth walnut with etched black widow spider logo. **Sights:** Ramped blade front, LPA adjustable rear. **Features:** Extended safety, extended slide release; Commander-style hammer; beavertail grip safety; throated, polished, tuned. Parkerized matte black or satin stainless steel finishes. Made in U.S.A. by Safari Arms, Inc.

Price: **$630.00**

SAFARI ARMS GI SAFARI PISTOL

Caliber: 45 ACP, 7-shot magazine. **Barrel:** 5", 416 stainless. **Weight:** 39.9 oz. **Length:** 8.5" overall. **Grips:** Checkered walnut. **Sights:** G.I.-style blade front, drift-adjustable rear. **Features:** Beavertail grip safety; extended thumb safety and slide release; Commander-style hammer. Parkerized finish. Reintroduced 1996.

Price: **$439.00**

SAFARI ARMS CARRIER PISTOL

Caliber: 45 ACP, 7-shot magazine. **Barrel:** 6", 416 stainless steel. **Weight:** 30 oz. **Length:** 9.5" overall. **Grips:** Wood. **Sights:** Ramped blade front, LPA adjustable rear. **Features:** Beavertail grip safety; extended controls; full-length recoil spring guide; Commander-style hammer. Throated, polished and tuned. Satin stainless steel finish. Introduced 1999. Made in U.S.A. by Safari Arms, Inc.

Price: **$714.00**

SAFARI ARMS COHORT PISTOL

Caliber: 45 ACP, 7-shot magazine. **Barrel:** 3.8", 416 stainless. **Weight:** 37 oz. **Length:** 8.5" overall. **Grips:** Smooth walnut with laser-etched black widow logo. **Sights:** Ramped blade front, LPA adjustable rear. **Features:** Combines the Enforcer model, slide and MatchMaster frame. Beavertail grip safety; extended thumb safety and slide release; Commander-style hammer. Satin stainless finish. Introduced 1996. Made in U.S.A. by Safari Arms, Inc.

Price: **$654.00**

SAFARI ARMS MATCHMASTER PISTOL

Caliber: 45 ACP, 7-shot. **Barrel:** 5" or 6", 416 stainless steel. **Weight:** 38 oz. (5" barrel). **Length:** 8.5" overall. **Grips:** Smooth walnut. **Sights:** Ramped blade, LPA adjustable rear. **Features:** Beavertail grip safety; extended controls; Commander-style hammer; throated, polished, tuned. Parkerized matte-black or satin stainless steel. Made in U.S.A. by Olympic Arms, Inc.

Price: 5" barrel **$594.00**
Price: 6" bbl. **$654.00**

Safari Arms Carry Comp Pistol

Similar to the Matchmaster except has Wil Schueman-designed hybrid compensator system. Made in U.S.A. by Olympic Arms, Inc.

Price: **$1,067.00**

SEECAMP LWS 32 STAINLESS DA AUTO

Caliber: 32 ACP Win. Silvertip, 6-shot magazine. **Barrel:** 2", integral with frame. **Weight:** 10.5 oz. **Length:** 4-1/8" overall. **Grips:** Glass-filled nylon. **Sights:** Smooth, no-snag, contoured slide and barrel top. **Features:** Aircraft quality 17-4 PH stainless steel. Inertia-operated firing pin. Hammer fired double-action-only. Hammer automatically follows slide down to safety rest position after each shot, no manual safety needed. Magazine safety disconnector. Polished stainless. Introduced 1985. From L.W. Seecamp.

Price: **$425.00**

SIG-Sauer P220

SIG-Sauer P245 Compact

SIG-Sauer Pro 2009

SIG-Sauer P229 Sport

SIG-Sauer P232

SEMMERLING LM-4 SLIDE-ACTION PISTOL

Caliber: 45 ACP, 4-shot magazine. **Barrel:** 2". **Weight:** 24 oz. **Length:** NA. **Grips:** NA. **Sights:** NA. **Features:** The Semmerling LM-4 is a super compact pistol employing a thumb activated slide mechanism (the slide is manually retracted between shots). From American Derringer Corp.

Price: $2,635.00

SIG-SAUER P220 SERVICE AUTO PISTOL

Caliber: 45 ACP, (7- or 8-shot magazine). **Barrel:** 4-3/8". **Weight:** 27.8 oz. **Length:** 7.8" overall. **Grips:** Checkered black plastic. **Sights:** Blade front, drift adjustable rear for windage. Optional Siglite night sights. **Features:** Double action. Decocking lever permits lowering hammer onto locked firing pin. Squared combat-type trigger guard. Slide stays open after last shot. Imported from Germany by SIGARMS, Inc.

Price: Blue SA/DA or DAO $790.00
Price: Blue, Siglite night sights $880.00
Price: K-Kote or nickel slide $830.00
Price: K-Kote or nickel slide with Siglite night sights $930.00

SIG-Sauer P220 Sport Auto Pistol

Similar to the P220 except has 4.9" barrel, ported compensator, stainless steel frame and slide, adjustable sights, extended competition controls. Overall length is 9.9", weighs 43.5 oz. Introduced 1999. From SIGARMS, Inc.

Price: $1,320.00

SIG-Sauer P245 Compact Auto Pistol

Similar to the P220 except has 3.9" barrel, shorter grip, 6-shot magazine, 7.28" overall length, and weighs 27.5 oz. Introduced 1999. From SIGARMS, Inc.

Price: Blue $780.00
Price: Blue, with Siglite sights $850.00
Price: Two-tone $830.00
Price: Two-tone with Siglite sights $930.00
Price: With K-Kote finish $830.00
Price: K-Kote with Siglite sights $930.00

SIG-Sauer P229 DA Auto Pistol

Similar to the P228 except chambered for 9mm Para., 40 S&W, 357 SIG. Has 3.86" barrel, 7.08" overall length and 3.35" height. Weight is 30.5 oz. Introduced 1991. Frame made in Germany, stainless steel slide assembly made in U.S.; pistol assembled in U.S. From SIGARMS, Inc.

Price: $795.00

Price: With nickel slide $890.00
Price: Nickel slide Siglite night sights $935.00

SIG PRO AUTO PISTOL

Caliber: 9mm Para., 40 S&W, 10-shot magazine. **Barrel:** 3.86". **Weight:** 27.2 oz. **Length:** 7.36" overall. **Grips:** Composite and rubberized one-piece. **Sights:** Blade front, rear adjustable for windage. Optional Siglite night sights. **Features:** Polymer frame, stainless steel slide; integral frame accessory rail; replaceable steel frame rails; left- or right-handed magazine release. Introduced 1999. From SIGARMS, Inc.

Price: SP2340 (40 S&W) $596.00
Price: SP2009 (9mm Para.) $596.00
Price: As above with Siglite night sights $655.00

SIG-Sauer P226 Service Pistol

Similar to the P220 pistol except has 4.4" barrel, and weighs 28.3 oz. 357 SIG or 40 S&W. Imported from Germany by SIGARMS, Inc.

Price: Blue SA/DA or DAO $830.00
Price: With Siglite night sights $930.00
Price: Blue, SA/DA or DAO 357 SIG $830.00
Price: With Siglite night sights $930.00
Price: K-Kote finish, 40 S&W only or nickel slide $830.00
Price: K-Kote or nickel slide Siglite night sights $930.00
Price: Nickel slide 357 SIG $875.00
Price: Nickel slide, Siglite night sights $930.00

SIG-Sauer P229 Sport Auto Pistol

Similar to the P229 except in 357 SIG only; 4.8" heavy barrel; 8.6" overall length; weighs 40.6 oz.; vented compensator; adjustable target sights; rubber grips; extended slide latch and magazine release. Stainless steel. Introduced 1998. From SIGARMS, Inc.

Price: $1,320.00

SIG-SAUER P232 PERSONAL SIZE PISTOL

Caliber: 380 ACP, 7-shot. **Barrel:** 3-3/4". **Weight:** 16 oz. **Length:** 6-1/2" overall. **Grips:** Checkered black composite. **Sights:** Blade front, rear adjustable for windage. **Features:** Double action/single action or DAO. Blowback operation, stationary barrel. Introduced 1997. Imported from Germany by SIGARMS, Inc.

Price: Blue SA/DA or DAO $505.00
Price: In stainless steel $545.00
Price: With stainless steel slide, blue frame $525.00
Price: Stainless steel, Siglite night sights, Hogue grips $585.00

Smith & Wesson 457 TDA

Smith & Wesson 908

Smith & Wesson 4013 TSW

Smith & Wesson 410 DA

Smith & Wesson 910 DA

Smith & Wesson 3913 LadySmith

SIG-SAUER P239 PISTOL

Caliber: 9mm Para., 8-shot, 357 SIG 40 S&W, 7-shot magazine. **Barrel:** 3.6". **Weight:** 25.2 oz. **Length:** 6.6" overall. **Grips:** Checkered black composite. **Sights:** Blade front, rear adjustable for windage. Optional Siglite night sights. **Features:** SA/DA or DAO; blackened stainless steel slide, aluminum alloy frame. Introduced 1996. Made in U.S.A. by SIGARMS, Inc.

Price: SA/DA or DAO **$620.00**
Price: SA/DA or DAO with Siglite night sights **$720.00**
Price: Two-tone finish **$665.00**
Price: Two-tone finish, Siglite sights **$765.00**

SMITH & WESSON MODEL 457 TDA AUTO PISTOL

Caliber: 45 ACP, 7-shot magazine. **Barrel:** 3-3/4". **Weight:** 29 oz. **Length:** 7-1/4" overall. **Grips:** One-piece Xenoy, wraparound with straight backstrap. **Sights:** Post front, fixed rear, 3-dot system. **Features:** Aluminum alloy frame, matte blue carbon steel slide; bobbed hammer; smooth trigger. Introduced 1996. Made in U.S.A. by Smith & Wesson.

Price: Blue finish **$649.00**
Price: Matte finish **$676.00**

SMITH & WESSON MODEL 908 AUTO PISTOL

Caliber: 9mm Para., 8-shot magazine. **Barrel:** 3-1/2". **Weight:** 24 oz. **Length:** 6-13/16". **Grips:** One-piece Xenoy, wraparound with straight backstrap. **Sights:** Post front, fixed rear, 3-dot system. **Features:** Aluminum alloy frame, matte blue carbon steel slide; bobbed hammer; smooth trigger. Introduced 1996. Made in U.S.A. by Smith & Wesson.

Price: Blue finish **$587.00**
Price: Matte finish **$611.00**

SMITH & WESSON MODEL 4013 TSW AUTO

Caliber: 40 S&W, 9-shot magazine. **Barrel:** 3-1/2". **Weight:** 26.8 oz. **Length:** 6 3/4" overall. **Grips:** Xenoy one-piece wraparound. **Sights:** Novak 3-dot system. **Features:** Traditional double-action system; stainless slide, alloy frame; fixed barrel bushing; ambidextrous decocker; reversible magazine catch, equipment rail. Introduced 1997. Made in U.S.A. by Smith & Wesson.

Price: Model 4013 TSW **$973.00**

SMITH & WESSON MODEL 410 DA AUTO PISTOL

Caliber: 40 S&W, 10-shot magazine. **Barrel:** 4". **Weight:** 28.5 oz. **Length:** 7.5". **Grips:** One-piece Xenoy, wraparound with straight backstrap. **Sights:** Post front, fixed rear; 3-dot system. **Features:** Aluminum alloy frame; blued carbon steel slide; traditional double action with left-side slide-mounted decocking lever. Introduced 1996. Made in U.S.A. by Smith & Wesson.

Price: Model 410 . . . . **$649.00**
Price: Model 410S, matte finish **$669.00**
Price: Crimson trace grips **$993.00**

SMITH & WESSON MODEL 910 DA AUTO PISTOL

Caliber: 9mm Para., 10-shot magazine. **Barrel:** 4". **Weight:** 28 oz. **Length:** 7-3/8" overall. **Grips:** One-piece Xenoy, wraparound with straight backstrap. **Sights:** Post front with white dot, fixed 2-dot rear. **Features:** Alloy frame, blue carbon steel slide. Slide-mounted decocking lever. Introduced 1995.

Price: Model 910 . . . . **$587.00**
Price: Model 910, matte finish **$602.00**

SMITH & WESSON MODEL 3913 TRADITIONAL DOUBLE ACTION

Caliber: 9mm Para., 8-shot magazine. **Barrel:** 3-1/2". **Weight:** 24.8 oz. **Length:** 6-3/4" overall. **Grips:** One-piece Delrin wraparound, textured surface. **Sights:** Post front with white dot, Novak LoMount Carry with two dots. **Features:** Aluminum alloy frame, stainless slide (M3913). Bobbed hammer with no half-cock notch; smooth .304" trigger with rounded edges. Straight backstrap. Equipment rail. Extra magazine included. Introduced 1989.

Price: **$834.00**

Smith & Wesson Model 3913-LS Ladysmith Auto

Similar to the standard Model 3913 except has frame that is upswept at the front, rounded trigger guard. Comes in frosted stainless steel with matching gray grips. Grips are ergonomically correct for a woman's hand. Novak LoMount Carry rear sight adjustable for windage. Extra magazine included. Introduced 1990.

Price: **$858.00**

SMITH & WESSON MODEL SW1911

Caliber: 45 ACP, 8 rounds. **Barrel:** 5". **Weight:** 39 oz. **Length:** 8.7". **Grips:** Wood/rubber. **Sights:** Novak Lo-Mount Carry, white dot front.

Price: Stainless steel frame **$960.00**
Price: Adjustable sights, stainless **$1,049.00**
Price: Carbon steel frame **$960.00**
Price: Stainless w/Crimson Trace Lasergrip **$1,281.00**
Price: Doug Koenig Pro Series **$1,213.00**

Smith & Wesson 4006

Smith & Wesson 4566 TSW

Smith & Wesson Sigma SW40V

Springfield, Inc. 1911A1 Standard

Springfield, Inc. Full-Size 1911A1

Springfield, Inc. TRP

SMITH & WESSON MODEL SW1911PD

Caliber: 45 ACP, 8 rounds. **Barrel:** 4-1/4" or 5". **Weight:** 28 oz. **Length:** 7-5/8" or 8.7". **Grips:** Wood. **Sights:** Novak Lo-Mount Carry, white dot front.

Price: 4-1/4" bbl.	$1,029.00
Price: 5"	$1,029.00
Price: Carbon steel frame	$960.00
Price: Scandium alloy w/Crimson Trace Lasergrip	$1,330.00

SMITH & WESSON MODEL 4040PD

Caliber: 40 S&W, 7 rounds. **Barrel:** 3.5". **Weight:** 25.6 oz. **Length:** 6.9". **Grips:** Rubber. **Sights:** Novak Lo-Mount Carry, white dot front.

Price: Scandium alloy frame	$840.00

SMITH & WESSON MODEL SW990L COMPACT

Caliber: 9mm (10 rounds), 40 S&W (8 rounds). **Barrel:** 3.5". **Weight:** 23 oz. **Length:** 6.6". **Grips:** Polymer. **Sights:** Adj. rear, white dot front.

Price:	$694.00
Price: Model 5946 DAO (as above, stainless frame and slide)	$863.00

SMITH & WESSON ENHANCED SIGMA SERIES DAO PISTOLS

Caliber: 9mm Para., 40 S&W, 10-shot magazine. **Barrel:** 4". **Weight:** 24.7 oz. **Length:** 7-1/4" overall. **Grips:** Integral. **Sights:** White dot front, fixed rear; 3-dot system. Tritium night sights available. **Features:** Ergonomic polymer frame; low barrel centerline; internal striker firing system; corrosion-resistant slide; Teflon-filled, electroless-nickel coated magazine, equipment rail. Introduced 1994. Made in U.S.A. by Smith & Wesson.

Price:	$379.00

SMITH & WESSON MODEL CS9 CHIEF'S SPECIAL AUTO

Caliber: 9mm Para., 7-shot magazine. **Barrel:** 3". **Weight:** 20.8 oz. **Length:** 6-1/4" overall. **Grips:** Hogue wraparound rubber. **Sights:** White dot front, fixed 2-dot rear. **Features:** Traditional double-action trigger mechanism. Alloy frame, stainless slide. Ambidextrous safety. Introduced 1999. Made in U.S.A. by Smith & Wesson.

Price: Stainless	$747.00

SMITH & WESSON MODEL CS45 CHIEF'S SPECIAL AUTO

Caliber: 45 ACP, 6-shot magazine. **Weight:** 23.9 oz. **Features:** Introduced 1999. Made in U.S.A. by Smith & Wesson.

Price: Stainless	$787.00

SMITH & WESSON MODEL SW990L

Caliber: 9mm Para. 4" barrel; 40 S&W 4-1/8" barrel; adj. sights. **Features:** Traditional double action satin stainless, black polymer frame, equipment rail, Saf-T-Trigger, interchangeable backstrap.

Price: 9mm, 40 S&W	$694.00
Price: 45 ACP	$736.00

SPRINGFIELD ARMORY FULL-SIZE 1911A1 AUTO PISTOL

Caliber: 9mm Para., 9-shot; 38 Super, 9-shot; 40 S&W, 9-shot; 45 ACP, 7-shot. **Barrel:** 5". **Weight:** 35.6 oz. **Length:** 8-5/8" overall. **Grips:** Cocobolo. **Sights:** Fixed 3-dot system. **Features:** Beveled magazine well; lowered and flared ejection port. All forged parts, including frame, barrel, slide. All new production. Introduced 1990. From Springfield Armory.

Price: Mil-Spec 45 ACP, Parkerized	$640.00
Price: Tactical, 45 ACP, TRP Armory Kote, Novak sights	$1,560.00
Price: Standard, 45 ACP, stainless, Novak sights	$876.00
Price: Lightweight 45 ACP (28.6 oz., matte finish, night sights)	$922.00
Price: 40 S&W, stainless	$1,409.00
Price: 9mm, stainless	$948.00

Springfield Armory TRP Pistols

Similar to 1911A1 except 45 ACP only, checkered front strap and main-spring housing, Novak Night Sight combat rear sight and matching dove-tailed front sight, tuned, polished extractor, oversize barrel link; lightweight speed trigger and combat action job, match barrel and bushing, extended ambidextrous thumb safety and fitted heavertail grip safety. Checkered cocobolo wood grips, comes with two Wilson 7-shot magazines. Frame is engraved "Tactical," both sides of frame with "TRP." Introduced 1998. From Springfield Armory.

Price: Standard with Armory Kote finish	$1,560.00
Price: Standard, stainless steel	$1,409.00
Price: Standard with Operator Light Rail Armory Kote	$1,573.00

Springfield Armory 1911A1 High Capacity Pistol

Similar to Standard 1911A1, available in 45 ACP with 10-shot magazine. Commander-style hammer, walnut grips, beveled magazine well, plastic carrying case. Can accept higher-capacity Para-Ordnance magazines. Introduced 1993. From Springfield Armory.

Price: Mil-Spec 45 ACP	$559.00
Price: 45 ACP Ultra Compact (3-1/2" bbl.)	$922.00

Taurus PT-22

Taurus PT-24

Taurus PT-92

Taurus PT-100

Springfield Armory 1911A1 Champion Pistol

Similar to standard 1911A1, slide is 4". Available in 45 ACP only. Novak Night Sights. Delta hammer and cocobolo grips. Parkerized or stainless. Introduced 1989.

Price: Stainless **$886.00**

Springfield Armory Ultra Compact Pistol

Similar to 1911A1 Compact, shorter slide, 3.5" barrel, beavertail grip safety, beveled magazine well, Novak Low Mount or Novak Night Sights, Videki speed trigger, flared ejection port, stainless steel frame, blued slide, match grade barrel, rubber grips. Introduced 1996. From Springfield Armory.

Price: Stainless 45 ACP, Novak Tritium sights **$922.00**
NEW! Price: Lightweight Bi-Tone stainless **$1,184.00**

Springfield Armory Compact Lightweight Bi-Tone

Mates a Springfield Inc. Champion length slide with the shorter Ultra-Compact forged alloy frame for concealability. In 45 ACP.

Price: **$1,184.00**

Springfield Armory Trophy Match 1911A1 Pistol

Similar to Full Size model, 5" match barrel and slide, fully adjustable sights. From Springfield Armory.

Price: Trophy Match 45 ACP, stainless **$1,049.00**
Price: Trophy Match, 40 S&W, Polymer **$1,409.00**

SPRINGFIELD ARMORY MICRO-COMPACT 1911A1 PISTOL

Caliber: 45 ACP, 40 S&W 6+1 capacity. **Barrel:** 3" 1:16 LH. **Weight:** 24 oz. **Length:** 5.7". **Sights:** Novak LoMount tritium. Dovetail front. **Features:** Forged frame and slide, ambi thumb safety, extreme carry bevel treatment, lockable plastic case, 2 magazines.

Price: . . . . **$922.00 to $1,247.00**

SPRINGFIELD ARMORY DEFENDER

Caliber: 9mm, 40 S&W, 45 GAP. **Barrel:** 3". **Weight:** 23 oz. **Length:** NA **Sights:** Novak low mount. **Features:** Alloy frame, slide and barrel; adjustable trigger; Delta lightweight hammer; loaded chamber indicator.

Price: . . . . **NA**

STEYR M & S SERIES AUTO PISTOLS

Caliber: 9mm Para., 40 S&W, 357 SIG; 10-shot magazine. **Barrel:** 4" (3.58" for Model S). **Weight:** 28 oz. (22.5 oz. for Model S). **Length:** 7.05" overall (6.53" for Model S). **Grips:** Ultra-rigid polymer. **Sights:** Drift-adjustable, white-outline rear; white-triangle blade front. **Features:** Polymer frame; trigger-drop firing pin, manual and key-lock safeties; loaded chamber indicator; 5.5-lb. trigger pull; 111-degree grip. Introduced 2000. Imported from Austria by GSI Inc.

Price: Model M (full-sized frame with 4" barrel) **$609.95**
Price: Model S (compact frame with 3.58" barrel) **$609.95**
Price: Extra 10-shot magazines (Model M or S) **$39.00**

TAURUS MODEL PT-22/PT-25 AUTO PISTOLS

Caliber: 22 LR, 8-shot (PT 22); 25 ACP, 9-shot (PT 25). **Barrel:** 2.75". **Weight:** 12.3 oz. **Length:** 5.25" overall. **Grips:** Smooth rosewood or mother-of-pearl. **Sights:** Fixed. **Features:** Double action. Tip-up barrel for loading, cleaning. Blue, nickel, duo-tone or blue with gold accents. Introduced 1992. Made in U.S.A. by Taurus International.

Price: 22 LR, 25 ACP, blue, nickel or with duo-tone finish with rosewood grips **$219.00**
Price: 22 LR, 25 ACP, blue with gold trim, rosewood grips **$234.00**

Price: 22 LR, 25 ACP, blue, nickel or duo-tone finish with checkered wood grips **$219.00**
Price: 22 LR, 25 ACP, blue with gold trim, mother-of-pearl grips . . **$250.00**

TAURUS MODEL PT-24/7

Caliber: 9mm, 10+1 shot; 40 cal., 10+1 shot. **Barrel:** 4". **Weight:** 27.2 oz. **Length:** 7-18". **Grips:** RIBBER rubber-finned overlay on polymer. **Sights:** Adjustable. **Features:** Accessory rail, four safeties, blue or stainless finish. Introduced 2003. Imported from Brazil by Taurus International.

Price: 9mm **$578.00**
Price: 40 cal. **$594.00**

TAURUS MODEL PT-92 AUTO PISTOL

Caliber: 9mm Para., 10-shot mag. **Barrel:** 5". **Weight:** 34 oz. **Length:** 8.5" overall. **Grips:** Checkered rubber, rosewood, mother-of-pearl. **Sights:** Fixed notch rear. 3-dot sight system. Also offered with micrometer-click adjustable night sights. **Features:** Double action, ambidextrous 3-way hammer drop safety, allows cocked & locked carry. Blue, stainless steel, blue with gold highlights, stainless steel with gold highlights, forged aluminum frame, integral key-lock. .22 LR conversion kit available. Imported from Brazil by Taurus International.

Price: Blue . . . . **$578.00 to $672.00**

Taurus Model PT-99 Auto Pistol

Similar to PT-92, fully adjustable rear sight.

Price: Blue . . . . **$575.00 to $670.00**
Price: 22 Conversion kit for PT 92 and PT99 (includes barrel and slide) **$266.00**

TAURUS MODEL PT-100/101 AUTO PISTOL

Caliber: 40 S&W, 10-shot mag. **Barrel:** 5". **Weight:** 34 oz. **Length:** 8-1/2". **Grips:** Checkered rubber, rosewood, mother-of-pearl. **Sights:** 3-dot fixed or adjustable; night sights available. **Features:** Single/double action with three-position safety/decocker. Reintroduced in 2001. Imported by Taurus International.

Price: PT100 . . . . **$578.00 to $672.00**
Price: PT101 . . . . **$594.00 to $617.00**

TAURUS MODEL PT-111 MILLENNIUM PRO AUTO PISTOL

Caliber: 9mm Para., 10-shot mag. **Barrel:** 3.25". **Weight:** 18.7 oz. **Length:** 6-1/8" overall. **Grips:** Polymer. **Sights:** 3-dot fixed; night sights available. Low profile, 3-dot combat. **Features:** Double action only, polymer frame, matte stainless or blue steel slide, manual safety, integral key-lock. Deluxe models with wood grip inserts.

Price: . . . . **$445.00 to $539.00**

Taurus PT-132 Millennium Pro

Taurus PT-138 Millennium Pro

Taurus PT-140 Millennium Pro

Taurus PT-145 Millennium Pro

Taurus PT-911

Taurus PT-938

Taurus PT-940

Taurus PT-945

Taurus Model PT-111 Millennium Titanium Pistol
Similar to PT-111, titanium slide, night sights.
Price: **$586.00**

TAURUS PT-132 MILLENNIUM PRO AUTO PISTOL
Caliber: 32 ACP, 10-shot mag. **Barrel:** 3.25". **Weight:** 18.7 oz. **Grips:** Polymer. **Sights:** 3-dot fixed; night sights available. **Features:** Double-action-only, polymer frame, matte stainless or blue steel slide, manual safety, integral key-lock action. Introduced 2001.
Price: . . . . **$445.00 to $461.00**

TAURUS PT-138 MILLENNIUM PRO SERIES
Caliber: 380 ACP, 10-shot mag. **Barrel:** 3.25". **Weight:** 18.7 oz. **Grips:** Polymer. **Sights:** Fixed 3-dot fixed. **Features:** Double-action-only, polymer frame, matte stainless or blue steel slide, manual safety, integral key-lock.
Price: . . . . **$445.00 to $461.00**

TAURUS PT-140 MILLENNIUM PRO AUTO PISTOL
Caliber: 40 S&W, 10-shot mag. **Barrel:** 3.25". **Weight:** 18.7 oz. **Grips:** Checkered polymer. **Sights:** 3-dot fixed; night sights available. **Features:** Double action only; matte stainless or blue steel slide, black polymer frame, manual safety, integral key-lock action. From Taurus International.
Price: . . . . **$484.00 to $578.00**

TAURUS PT-145 MILLENNIUM AUTO PISTOL
Caliber: 45 ACP, 10-shot mag. **Barrel:** 3.27". **Weight:** 23 oz. **Stock:** Checkered polymer. **Sights:** 3-dot fixed; night sights available. **Features:** Double-action only, matte stainless or blue steel slide, black polymer frame, manual safety, integral key-lock. From Taurus International.
Price: . . . . **$484.00 to $578.00**

TAURUS MODEL PT-911 AUTO PISTOL
Caliber: 9mm Para., 10-shot mag. **Barrel:** 4". **Weight:** 28.2 oz. **Length:** 7" overall. **Grips:** Checkered rubber, rosewood, mother-of-pearl. **Sights:** Fixed, 3-dot blue or stainless; night sights optional. **Features:** Double action, semi-auto ambidextrous 3-way hammer drop safety, allows cocked & locked carry. Blue, stainless steel, blue with gold highlights, or stainless steel with gold highlights, forged aluminum frame, integral key-lock.
Price: . . . . **$523.00 to $617.00**

TAURUS MODEL PT-938 AUTO PISTOL
Caliber: 380 ACP, 10-shot mag. **Barrel:** 3.72". **Weight:** 27 oz. **Length:** 6.5" overall. **Grips:** Checkered rubber. **Sights:** Fixed, 3-dot. **Features:** Double action, ambidextrous 3-way hammer drop allows cocked & locked carry. Forged aluminum frame. Integral key-lock. Imported by Taurus International.

Price: Blue **$516.00**
Price: Stainless **$531.00**

TAURUS MODEL PT-940 AUTO PISTOL
Caliber: 40 S&W, 10-shot mag. **Barrel:** 3-5/8". **Weight:** 28.2 oz. **Length:** 7" overall. **Grips:** Checkered rubber, rosewood or mother-of-pearl. **Sights:** Fixed, 3-dot blue or stainless; night sights optional. **Features:** Double action, semi-auto ambidextrous 3-way hammer drop safety, allows cocked & locked carry. Blue, stainless steel, blue with gold highlights, or stainless steel with gold hightlights, forged aluminum frame, integral key-lock.
Price: . . . . **$523.00 to $617.00**

TAURUS MODEL PT-945 SERIES
Caliber: 45 ACP, 8-shot mag. **Barrel:** 4.25". **Weight:** 28.2/29.5 oz. **Length:** 7.48" overall. **Grips:** Checkered rubber, rosewood or mother-of-pearl. **Sights:** Fixed, 3-dot; night sights optional. **Features:** Double-action with ambidextrous 3-way hammer drop safety allows cocked & locked carry. Forged aluminum frame, PT-945C has ported barrel/slide. Blue, stainless, blue with gold highlights, stainless with gold highlights, integral key-lock. Introduced 1995. Imported by Taurus International.
Price: . . . . **$563.00 to $641.00**

Taurus PT-957

Walther PPK

Walther PPK/S

Walther P99

Walther P22

Wilkinson Sherry

TAURUS MODEL PT-957 AUTO PISTOL

Caliber: 357 SIG, 10-shot mag. **Barrel:** 4". **Weight:** 28 oz. **Length:** 7" overall. **Grips:** Checkered rubber, rosewood or mother-of-pearl. **Sights:** Fixed, 3-dot blue or stainless; night sights optional. **Features:** Double-action, blue, stainless steel, blue with gold accents or stainless with gold accents, ported barrel/slide, three-position safety with decocking lever and ambidextrous safety. Forged aluminum frame, integral key-lock. Introduced 1999. Imported by Taurus International.
Price: . . . . **$525.00 to $620.00**
Price: Non-ported . . . . **$525.00 to $535.00**

TAURUS MODEL 922 SPORT PISTOL

Caliber: .22 LR, 10-shot magazine. **Barrel:** 6". **Weight:** 24.8 oz. **Length:** 9-1/8". **Grips:** Polymer. **Sights:** Adjustable. **Features:** Matte blue steel finish, machined target crown, polymer frame, single and double action, easy disassembly for cleaning.
Price: . . . . (blue) **$310.00**
Price: . . . . (stainless) **$328.00**

WALTHER PPK/S AMERICAN AUTO PISTOL

Caliber: 380 ACP, 7-shot magazine. **Barrel:** 3.27". **Weight:** 23-1/2 oz. **Length:** 6.1" overall. **Stocks:** Checkered plastic. **Sights:** Fixed, white markings. **Features:** Double action; manual safety blocks firing pin and drops hammer; chamber loaded indicator on 32 and 380; extra finger rest magazine provided. Made in the United States. Introduced 1980.
Price: 380 ACP only, blue **$563.00**
Price: As above, 32 ACP or 380 ACP, stainless **$543.00**

Walther PPK American Auto Pistol

Similar to Walther PPK/S except weighs 21 oz., has 6-shot capacity. Made in the U.S. Introduced 1986.
Price: Stainless, 32 ACP or 380 ACP **$543.00**
Price: Blue, 380 ACP only **$543.00**

WALTHER P99 AUTO PISTOL

Caliber: 9mm Para., 9x21, 40 S&W,10-shot magazine. **Barrel:** 4". **Weight:** 25 oz. **Length:** 7" overall. **Grips:** Textured polymer. **Sights:** Blade front (comes with three interchangeable blades for elevation adjustment), micrometer rear adjustable for windage. **Features:** Double-action mechanism with trigger safety, decock safety, internal striker safety; chamber loaded indicator; ambidextrous magazine release levers; polymer frame with interchangeable backstrap inserts. Comes with two magazines. Introduced 1997. Imported from Germany by Smith & Wesson U.S.A.
Price: **$665.00**

WALTHER P22 PISTOL

Caliber: 22 LR. **Barrel:** 3.4", 5". **Weight:** 19.6 oz. (3.4"), 20.3 oz. (5"). **Length:** 6.26", 7.83". **Grips:** NA. **Sights:** Interchangeable white dot, front, 2-dot adjustable, rear. **Features:** A rimfire version of the Walther P99 pistol, available in nickel slide with black frame, or green frame with black slide versions. Made in Germany and distributed in the U.S. by Smith & Wesson.
Price: From **$295.00**

WILKINSON SHERRY AUTO PISTOL

Caliber: 22 LR, 8-shot magazine. **Barrel:** 2-1/8". **Weight:** 9-1/4 oz. **Length:** 4-3/8" overall. **Grips:** Checkered black plastic. **Sights:** Fixed, groove. **Features:** Crossbolt safety locks the sear into the hammer. Available in all-blue finish or blue slide and trigger with gold frame. Introduced 1985.
Price: **$280.00**

WILKINSON LINDA AUTO PISTOL

Caliber: 9mm Para. **Barrel:** 8-5/16". **Weight:** 4 lbs., 13 oz. **Length:** 12-1/4" overall. **Grips:** Checkered black plastic pistol grip, walnut forend. **Sights:** Protected blade front, aperture rear. **Features:** Semi-auto only. Straight blowback action. Crossbolt safety. Removable barrel. From Wilkinson Arms.
Price: **$675.00**

CONSULT

SHOOTER'S MARKETPLACE

Page 243, This Issue

Includes models suitable for several forms of competition and other sporting purposes.

Baer 1911 Ultimate Master

BF Ultimate

Baer 1911 Bullseye Wadcutter

Browning Buck Mark Target 5.5

Browning Buck Mark Bullseye

BAER 1911 ULTIMATE MASTER COMBAT PISTOL

Caliber: 9x23, 38 Super, 400 Cor-Bon 45 ACP (others available), 10-shot magazine. **Barrel:** 5", 6"; Baer NM. **Weight:** 37 oz. **Length:** 8.5" overall. **Grips:** Checkered rosewood. **Sights:** Baer dovetail front, low-mount Bo-Mar rear with hidden leaf. **Features:** Full-house competition gun. Baer forged NM blued steel frame and double serrated slide; Baer triple port, tapered cone compensator; fitted slide to frame; lowered, flared ejection port; Baer reverse recoil plug; full-length guide rod; recoil buff; beveled magazine well; Baer Commander hammer, sear; Baer extended ambidextrous safety, extended ejector, checkered slide stop, beavertail grip safety with pad, extended magazine release button; Baer speed trigger. Made in U.S.A. by Les Baer Custom, Inc.
Price: Compensated, open sights **$2,476.00**
Price: 6" Model 400 Cor-Bon **$2,541.00**

BAER 1911 NATIONAL MATCH HARDBALL PISTOL

Caliber: 45 ACP, 7-shot magazine. **Barrel:** 5". **Weight:** 37 oz. **Length:** 8.5" overall. **Grips:** Checkered walnut. **Sights:** Baer dovetail front with undercut post, low-mount Bo-Mar rear with hidden leaf. **Features:** Baer NM forged steel frame, double serrated slide and barrel with stainless bushing; slide fitted to frame; Baer match trigger with 4-lb. pull; polished feed ramp, throated barrel; checkered front strap, arched mainspring housing; Baer beveled magazine well; lowered, flared ejection port; tuned extractor; Baer extended ejector, checkered slide stop; recoil buff. Made in U.S.A. by Les Baer Custom, Inc.
Price: **$1,335.00**

Baer 1911 Bullseye Wadcutter Pistol

Similar to National Match Hardball except designed for wadcutter loads only. Polished feed ramp and barrel throat; Bo-Mar rib on slide; full length recoil rod; Baer speed trigger with 3-1/2-lb. pull; Baer deluxe hammer and sear; Baer beavertail grip safety with pad; flat mainspring housing checkered 20 lpi. Blue finish; checkered walnut grips. Made in U.S.A. by Les Baer Custom, Inc.
Price: From **$1,495.00**
Price: With 6" barrel, from **$1,690.00**

BF ULTIMATE SILHOUETTE HB SINGLE SHOT PISTOL

Caliber: 7mm U.S., 22 LR Match and 100 other chamberings. **Barrel:** 10.75" Heavy Match Grade with 11-degree target crown. **Weight:** 3 lbs., 15 oz. **Length:** 16" overall. **Grips:** Thumbrest target style. **Sights:** Bo-Mar/Bond ScopeRib I Combo with hooded post front adjustable for height and width, rear notch available in .032", .062", .080" and .100" widths; 1/2-MOA clicks. **Features:** Designed to meet maximum rules for IHMSA Production Gun. Hand fitted and headspaced. Etched receiver; gold-colored trigger. Introduced 1988. Made in U.S.A. by E. Arthur Brown Co. Inc.
Price: **$669.00**

BF Classic Hunting Pistol

Similar to BF Ultimate Silhouette HB Single Shot Pistol, except no sights; drilled and tapped for scope mount. Barrels from 8" to 15". Variety of options offered. Made in U.S.A. by E. Arthur Brown Co. Inc.
Price: **$599.00**

BROWNING BUCK MARK TARGET 5.5

Caliber: 22 LR, 10-shot magazine. **Barrel:** 5-1/2" barrel with .900" diameter. **Weight:** 35-1/2 oz. **Length:** 9-5/8" overall. **Grips:** Contoured walnut grips with thumbrest, or finger-groove walnut. **Sights:** Hooded sights mounted on scope base that accepts optical or reflex sight. Rear sight is Browning fully adjustable Pro Target, front sight is adjustable post that customizes to different widths, can be adjusted for height. **Features:** Matte blue finish. Introduced 1990. From Browning.
Price: **$496.00**

Browning Buck Mark Field 5.5

Same as Target 5.5, hoodless ramp-style front sight and low profile rear sight. Matte blue finish, contoured or finger-groove walnut stocks. Introduced 1991.
Price: **$496.00**

Browning Buck Mark Bullseye

Similar to Buck Mark Silhouette, 7-1/4" heavy barrel with three flutes per side; trigger adjusts from 2-1/2 to 5 lbs.; specially designed rosewood target or three-finger-groove stocks with competition-style heel rest, or with contoured rubber grip. Overall length 11-5/16", weighs 36 oz. Introduced 1996. Made in U.S.A. From Browning.
Price: With ambidextrous moulded composite stocks **$468.00**
Price: With rosewood stocks, or wraparound finger groove **$604.00**

Colt Special Combat

Competitor Single Shot

EAA Witness Gold Team

COLT DEFENDER XSE
Caliber: 45 ACP. **Barrel:** 3", 4.25" and 5". **Weight:** 23-40 oz. **Sights:** Fixed. **Features:** Rubber wraparound or rosewood grips; single-action; carbon or stainless steel; blue or stainless finish, 7- or 8-round magazines.
Price: Blue **$9500.00**
Price: Stainless **$1,100.00**

COLT GOLD CUP
Caliber: 45 ACP. **Barrel:** 5". **Weight:** 39 oz. **Sights:** Dovetail front, BoMar-style rear; or Colt adjustable staked front. **Features:** Stainless or blue finish; adjustable trigger; furnished with 7- and 8-round magazines.
Price:Blued $1,300.00
Price: Stainless $1,400.00

COLT GUNSITE PISTOL
Caliber: 45 ACP. **Barrel:** 5", 4.5". **Weight:** 38 to 36 oz. **Sights:** Heinie front, Novak rear. **Features:** Brushed stainless or blue finish; short trigger; Wilson safety; grip safety. Furnished with two 6- and 8-round magazines.
Price: $1,400.00

COLT COMBAT GOVERNMENT
Caliber: 45 ACP, 38 Super. **Barrel:** 5". **Weight:** 39 oz. **Sights:** Dovetail front, Bo-Mar-style rear. **Features:** Chromed or blued slide; ambidextrous thumb safety; 8-round standard with bumper magazines.
Price: $2,000.00

COLT MODEL 1991/2991
Caliber: 45 ACP, 28 Super. **Barrel:** 5". **Sight:** Fixed white dot style. **Features:** Stainless or blue finish; furnished with 7-round magazines.
Price: . . . . **$870.00 to $980.00**

COLT GOLD CUP MODEL O PISTOL
Caliber: 45 ACP, 8-shot magazine. **Barrel:** 5", with new design bushing. **Weight:** 39 oz. **Length:** 8-1/2". **Grips:** Checkered rubber composite with silver-plated medallion. **Sights:** Patridge-style front, Bo-Mar-style rear adjustable for windage and elevation, sight radius 6-3/4". **Features:** Arched or flat housing; wide, grooved trigger with adjustable stop; ribbed-top slide, hand fitted, with improved ejection port.
Price: Blue $1,300.00
Price: Stainless $1,400.00

COLT SPECIAL COMBAT GOVERNMENT
Caliber: 45 ACP. **Barrel:** 5". **Weight:** NA. **Length:** 8-1/2". **Grips:** Rosewood w/double diamond checkering pattern. **Sights:** Clark dovetail, front; Bo-Mar adjustable, rear. **Features:** A competition-ready pistol with enhancements such as skeletonized trigger, upswept grip safety, custom tuned action, polished feed ramp. Blue or satin nickel finish. Introduced 2003. Made in U.S.A. by Colt's Mfg. Co.
Price: $2,000.00

COMPETITOR SINGLE SHOT PISTOL
Caliber: 22 LR through 50 Action Express, including belted magnums. **Barrel:** 14" standard; 10.5" silhouette; 16" optional. **Weight:** About 59 oz. (14" bbl.). **Length:** 15.12" overall. **Grips:** Ambidextrous; synthetic (standard) or laminated or natural wood. **Sights:** Ramp front, adjustable rear. **Features:** Rotary canon-type action cocks on opening; cammed ejector; interchangeable barrels, ejectors. Adjustable single stage trigger, sliding thumb safety and trigger safety. Matte blue finish. Introduced 1988. From Competitor Corp., Inc.
Price: 14", standard calibers, synthetic grip $414.95
Price: Extra barrels . . . . From $159.95

CZ 75 CHAMPION COMPETITION PISTOL
Caliber: 9mm Para., 9x21, 40 S&W, 10-shot mag. **Barrel:** 4.49". **Weight:** 35 oz. **Length:** 9.44" overall. **Grips:** Black rubber. **Sights:** Blade front, fully adjustable rear. **Features:** Single-action trigger mechanism; three-port compensator (40 S&W, 9mm have two port) full-length guide rod; extended magazine release; ambidextrous safety; flared magazine well; fully adjustable match trigger. Introduced 1999. Imported from the Czech Republic by CZ-USA.
Price: 9mm Para., 9x21, 40 S&W, dual-tone finish $1,551.00

CZ 75 ST IPSC AUTO PISTOL
Caliber: 40 S&W, 10-shot magazine. **Barrel:** 5.12". **Weight:** 2.9 lbs. **Length:** 8.86" overall. **Grips:** Checkered walnut. **Sights:** Fully adjustable rear. **Features:** Single-action mechanism; extended slide release and ambidextrous safety; full-length slide rail; double slide serrations. Introduced 1999. Imported from the Czech Republic by CZ-USA.
Price: Dual-tone finish $1,038.00

EAA/BAIKAL IZH-35 AUTO PISTOL
Caliber: 22 LR, 5-shot mag. **Barrel:** 6". **Grips:** Walnut; fully adjustable right-hand target-style. **Sights:** Fully adjustable rear, blade front; detachable scope mount. **Features:** Hammer-forged target barrel; machined steel receiver; adjustable trigger; manual slide hold back, grip and manual trigger-bar disconnect safeties; cocking indicator. Introduced 2000. Imported from Russia by European American Armory.
Price: Blued finish $489.00

EAA WITNESS GOLD TEAM AUTO
Caliber: 9mm Para., 9x21, 38 Super, 40 S&W, 45 ACP. **Barrel:** 5.1". **Weight:** 44 oz. **Length:** 10.5" overall. **Grips:** Checkered walnut, competition-style. **Sights:** Square post front, fully adjustable rear. **Features:** Triple-chamber cone compensator; competition SA trigger; extended safety and magazine release; competition hammer; beveled magazine well; beavertail grip. Hand-fitted major components. Hard chrome finish. Match-grade barrel. From E.A.A. Custom Shop. Introduced 1992. From European American Armory.
Price: $1,699.00

EAA Witness Silver Team Auto
Similar to Witness Gold Team with double-chamber compensator, oval magazine release, black rubber grips, double-dip blue finish. Super Sight and drilled and tapped for scope mount. Introduced 1992. From European American Armory Custom Shop.
Price: 9mm Para., 9x21, 38 Super, 40 S&W, 45 ACP $968.00

Freedom Arms 83 22 Silhouette Class

Hammerli SP 20

High Standard Trophy

ED BROWN CLASSIC CUSTOM PISTOL
Caliber: 45 ACP. **Barrel:** 5". **Weight:** 39 oz. **Grips:** Hogue exotic wood. **Sights:** Modified ramp or post, front; fully-adjustable Bo-Mar, rear. **Features:** Highly-polished slide, two-piece guide rod, oversize mag release, ambidextrous safety.
Price: **$2,895.00**

ED BROWN CLASS A LIMITED
Caliber: 45 ACP, 400 Cor-Bon, 10mm, 40 S&W, 357 SIG, 38 Super, 9x23, 9mm Luger, 7-shot magazine. **Barrel:** 4.25", 5". **Weight:** 34 to 39 oz. **Grips:** Hogue exotic wood. **Sights:** Customer preference, front; fixed Novak low-mount or fully-adjustable Bo-Mar, rear. **Features:** Checkered forestrap and mainspring housing, matte finished top sighting surface. Many options available.
Price: **$2,250.00**

ENTRÉPRISE TOURNAMENT SHOOTER MODEL I
Caliber: 45 ACP, 10-shot mag. **Barrel:** 6". **Weight:** 40 oz. **Length:** 8.5" overall. **Grips:** Black ultra-slim double diamond checkered synthetic. **Sights:** Dovetailed Patridge front, adjustable rear. **Features:** Oversized magazine release button; flared magazine well; fully machined parallel slide rails; front and rear slide serrations; serrated top of slide; stainless ramped bull barrel with fully supported chamber; full-length guide rod with plug; stainless firing pin; match extractor; polished ramp; tuned match extractor; black oxide. Introduced 1998. Made in U.S.A. by Entréprise Arms.
Price: **$2,300.00**
Price: TSMIII (Satin chrome finish, two-piece guide rod) **$2,700.00**

EXCEL INDUSTRIES CP-45, XP-45 AUTO PISTOL
Caliber: 45 ACP, 6-shot & 10-shot mags. **Barrel:** 3-1/4". **Weight:** 31 oz. & 25 oz. **Length:** 6-3/8" overall. **Grips:** Checkered black nylon. **Sights:** Fully adjustable rear. **Features:** Stainless steel frame and slide; single action with external hammer and firing pin block, manual thumb safety; last-shot hold open. Includes gun lock and cleaning kit. Introduced 2001. Made in U.S.A. by Excel Industries Inc.
Price: CP-45 .... **$425.00**
Price: XP-45 .... **$465.00**

FEINWERKEBAU AW93 TARGET PISTOL
Caliber: 22. **Barrel:** 6". **Grips:** Fully adjustable orthopaedic. **Sights:** Fully adjustable micrometer. **Features:** Advanced Russian design with German craftmanship. Imported from Germany by Nygord Precision Products.
Price: **$1,495.00**

FREEDOM ARMS MODEL 83 22 FIELD GRADE SILHOUETTE CLASS
Caliber: 22 LR, 5-shot cylinder. **Barrel:** 10". **Weight:** 63 oz. **Length:** 15.5" overall. **Grips:** Black Micarta. **Sights:** Removable Patridge front blade; Iron Sight Gun Works silhouette rear, click adjustable for windage and elevation (optional adj. front sight and hood). **Features:** Stainless steel, matte finish, manual sliding-bar safety system; dual firing pins, lightened hammer for fast lock time, pre-set trigger stop. Introduced 1991. Made in U.S.A. by Freedom Arms.
Price: Silhouette Class **$1,901.75**
Price: Extra fitted 22 WMR cylinder **$264.00**

FREEDOM ARMS MODEL 83 CENTERFIRE SILHOUETTE MODELS
Caliber: 357 Mag., 41 Mag., 44 Mag.; 5-shot cylinder. **Barrel:** 10", 9" (357 Mag. only). **Weight:** 63 oz. (41 Mag.). **Length:** 15.5", 14-1/2" (357 only). **Grips:** Pachmayr Presentation. **Sights:** Iron Sight Gun Works silhouette rear sight, replaceable adjustable front sight blade with hood. **Features:** Stainless steel, matte finish, manual sliding-bar safety system. Made in U.S.A. by Freedom Arms.
Price: Silhouette Models **$1,634.85**

GAUCHER GP SILHOUETTE PISTOL
Caliber: 22 LR, single shot. **Barrel:** 10". **Weight:** 42.3 oz. **Length:** 15.5" overall. **Grips:** Stained hardwood. **Sights:** Hooded post on ramp front, open rear adjustable for windage and elevation. **Features:** Matte chrome barrel, blued bolt and sights. Other barrel lengths available on special order. Introduced 1991. Imported by Mandall Shooting Supplies.
Price: **$425.00**

HAMMERLI SP 20 TARGET PISTOL
Caliber: 22 LR, 32 S&W. **Barrel:** 4.6". **Weight:** 34.6-41.8 oz. **Length:** 11.8" overall. **Grips:** Anatomically shaped synthetic Hi-Grip available in five sizes. **Sights:** Integral front In three widths, adjustable rear with changeable notch widths. **Features:** Extremely low-level sight line; anatomically shaped trigger; adjustable JPS buffer system for different recoil characteristics. Receiver available in red, blue, gold, violet or black. Introduced 1998. Imported from Switzerland by SIGARMS, Inc and Hammerli Pistols USA.
Price: Hammerli 22 LR **$1,668.00**
Price: Hammerli 32 S&W **$1,743.00**

HAMMERLI X-ESSE SPORT PISTOL
An all-steel .22 LR target pistol with a Hi-Grip in a new anatomical shape and an adjustable hand rest. Made in Switzerland. Introduced 2003.
Price: **$710.00**

HARRIS GUNWORKS SIGNATURE JR. LONG RANGE PISTOL
Caliber: Any suitable caliber. **Barrel:** To customer specs. **Weight:** 5 lbs. **Stock:** Gunworks fiberglass. **Sights:** None furnished; comes with scope rings. **Features:** Right- or left-hand benchrest action of titanium or stainless steel; single shot or repeater. Comes with bipod. Introduced 1992. Made in U.S.A. by Harris Gunworks, Inc.
Price: **$2,700.00**

HIGH STANDARD TROPHY TARGET PISTOL
Caliber: 22 LR, 10-shot mag. **Barrel:** 5-1/2" bull or 7-1/4" fluted. **Weight:** 44 oz. **Length:** 9.5" overall. **Stock:** Checkered hardwood with thumbrest. **Sights:** Undercut ramp front, frame-mounted micro-click rear adjustable for windage and elevation; drilled and tapped for scope mounting. **Features:** Gold-plated trigger, slide lock, safety-lever and magazine release; stippled front grip and backstrap; adjustable trigger and sear. Barrel weights optional. From High Standard Manufacturing Co., Inc.
Price: 5-1/2", scope base **$540.00**
Price: 7.25" **$689.00**
Price: 7.25", scope base **$625.00**

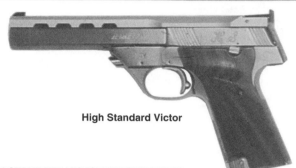

High Standard Victor

Kimber Super Match II

HIGH STANDARD VICTOR TARGET PISTOL

Caliber: 22 LR, 10-shot magazine. **Barrel:** 4-1/2" or 5-1/2"; push-button takedown. **Weight:** 46 oz. **Length:** 9.5" overall. **Stock:** Checkered hardwood with thumbrest. **Sights:** Undercut ramp front, micro-click rear adjustable for windage and elevation. Also available with scope mount, rings, no sights. **Features:** Stainless steel construction. Full-length vent rib. Gold-plated trigger, slide lock, safety-lever and magazine release; stippled front grip and backstrap; polished slide; adjustable trigger and sear. Comes with barrel weight. From High Standard Manufacturing Co., Inc.

Price: 4-1/2" scope base **$564.00**
Price: 5-1/2", sights **$625.00**
Price: 5-1/2" scope base **$564.00**

KIMBER SUPER MATCH II

Caliber: 45 ACP, 7-shot magazine. **Barrel:** 5". **Weight:** 38 oz. **Length:** 18.7" overall. **Sights:** Blade front, Kimber fully adjustable rear. **Features:** Guaranteed shoot 1" group at 25 yards. Stainless steel frame, black KimPro slide; two-piece magazine well; premium aluminum match-grade trigger; 30 lpi front strap checkering; stainless match-grade barrel; ambidextrous safety; special Custom Shop markings. Introduced 1999. Made in U.S.A. by Kimber Mfg., Inc.

Price: **$1,986.00**

KORTH MATCH REVOLVER

Caliber: 357 Mag., 38 Special, 32 S&W Long, 9mm Para., 22 WMR, 22 LR. **Barrel:** 5-1/4", 6". **Grips:** Adjustable match of oiled walnut with matte finish. **Sights:** Fully adjustable rear sight leaves (width of sight notch: 3.4mm, 3.5mm, 3.6mm); undercut Patridge, front. **Trigger:** Equipped with machined trigger shoe. Interchangeable caliber cylinders available as well as a variety of finishes. Made in Germany.

Price: From **$7,619.00**

MORINI MODEL 84E FREE PISTOL

Caliber: 22 LR, single shot. **Barrel:** 11.4". **Weight:** 43.7 oz. **Length:** 19.4" overall. **Grips:** Adjustable match type with stippled surfaces. **Sights:** Interchangeable blade front, match-type fully adjustable rear. **Features:** Fully adjustable electronic trigger. Introduced 1995. Imported from Switzerland by Nygord Precision Products.

Price: **$1,450.00**

PARDINI MODEL SP, HP TARGET PISTOLS

Caliber: 22 LR, 32 S&W, 5-shot magazine. **Barrel:** 4.7". **Weight:** 38.9 oz. **Length:** 11.6" overall. **Grips:** Adjustable; stippled walnut; match type. **Sights:** Interchangeable blade front, interchangeable, fully adjustable rear. **Features:** Fully adjustable match trigger. Introduced 1995. Imported from Italy by Nygord Precision Products.

Price: Model SP (22 LR) **$995.00**
Price: Model HP (32 S&W) **$1,095.00**

PARDINI GP RAPID FIRE MATCH PISTOL

Caliber: 22 Short, 5-shot magazine. **Barrel:** 4.6". **Weight:** 43.3 oz. **Length:** 11.6" overall. **Grips:** Wraparound stippled walnut. **Sights:** Interchangeable post front, fully adjustable match rear. Introduced 1995. Imported from Italy by Nygord Precision Products.

Price: Model GP **$1,095.00**
Price: Model GP-E Electronic, has special parts **$1,595.00**

PARDINI K22 FREE PISTOL

Caliber: 22 LR, single shot. **Barrel:** 9.8". **Weight:** 34.6 oz. **Length:** 18.7" overall. **Grips:** Wrap-around walnut; adjustable match type. **Sights:**

Interchangeable post front, fully adjustable match open rear. **Features:** Removable, adjustable match trigger. Barrel weights mount above the barrel. Upgraded model introduced in 2002. Imported from Italy by Nygord Precision Products.

Price: **$1,295.00**

PARDINI GT45 TARGET PISTOL

Caliber: 45, 9mm, 40 S&W. **Barrel:** 5", 6". **Grips:** Checkered forestrap. **Sights:** Interchangeable post front, fully adjustable match open rear. **Features:** Ambi-safeties, trigger pull adjustable. Fits Helweg Glock holsters for defense shooters. Imported from Italy by Nygord Precision Products.

Price: 5" **$1,050.00**
Price: 6" **$1,125.00**
Price: Frame mount available . . . . **$75.00 extra**
Price: Slide mount available . . . . **$35.00 extra**

PARDINI/NYGORD "MASTER" TARGET PISTOL

Caliber: 22 cal. **Barrel:** 5-1/2". **Grips:** Semi-wraparound. **Sights:** Micrometer rear and red dot. **Features:** Reciprocating internal weight barrel shroud. Imported from Italy by Nygord Precision Products.

Price: **$1,145.00**

RUGER MARK III TARGET MODEL AUTOLOADING PISTOL

Caliber: 22 LR, 10-shot magazine. **Barrel:** 6-7/8". **Weight:** 42 oz. **Length:** 11-1/8" overall. **Grips:** Checkered composition grip panels. **Sights:** .125" blade front, micro-click rear, adjustable for windage and elevation, loaded chamber indicator; integral lock, magazine disconnect. Sight radius 9-3/8". Plastic case with lock included. **Features:** Introduced 1982.

Price: Blued (MK-678) **$382.00**
Price: Stainless models . . . . **$483.00 to $567.00**

Ruger Mark III Government Target Model

Same gun as Mark III Target Model except has 6-7/8" barrel, higher sights and is roll marked "Government Target Model" on right side of receiver below rear sight. Identical in all aspects to military model except markings. Comes with factory test target, also lockable plastic case. Introduced 1987.

Price: Blued (MK-678G) **$425.00**
Price: Stainless (KMK-678G) **$509.00**

Ruger Stainless Competition Model Pistol

Similar to Mark III Government Target Model stainless pistol, 6-7/8" slab-sided barrel; receiver top is fitted with Ruger scope base of blued, chrome-moly steel; has Ruger 1" stainless scope rings for mounting variety of optical sights; checkered laminated grip panels with right-hand thumbrest. Blued open sights with 9-1/4" radius. Overall length 11-1/8", weight 45 oz. Case and lock included. Introduced 1991.

Price: KMK III 678 and 678 GC . . . . **$382.00 to $555.00**

Ruger Mark III Bull Barrel

Same gun as Target Model except has 5-1/2" or 10" heavy barrel. Weight with 5-1/2" barrel is 42 oz. Case with lock included.

Price: Blued (MKIII-512) **$382.00**
Price: Stainless (KMKIII-512) **$483.00**

HANDGUNS — Competition

Smith & Wesson Model 41

Smith & Wesson Model 22A

Smith & Wesson Model 22S

Springfield, Inc. 1911A1
Bullseye Wadcutter

SAFARI ARMS BIG DEUCE PISTOL

Caliber: 45 ACP, 7-shot magazine. **Barrel:** 6", 416 stainless steel. **Weight:** 40.3 oz. **Length:** 9.5" overall. **Grips:** Smooth walnut. **Sights:** Ramped blade front, LPA adjustable rear. **Features:** Beavertail grip safety; extended thumb safety and slide release; Commander-style hammer. Throated, polished and tuned. Parkerized matte black slide with satin stainless steel frame. Introduced 1995. Made in U.S.A. by Safari Arms, Inc.
Price: $714.00

SMITH & WESSON MODEL 41 TARGET

Caliber: 22 LR, 10-shot clip. **Barrel:** 5-1/2", 7". **Weight:** 41 oz. (5-1/2" barrel). **Length:** 10-1/2" overall (5-1/2" barrel). **Grips:** Checkered walnut with modified thumbrest, usable with either hand. **Sights:** 1/8" Patridge on ramp base; micro-click rear adjustable for windage and elevation. **Features:** 3/8" wide, grooved trigger; adjustable trigger stop drilled and tapped.
Price: S&W Bright Blue, either barrel $1,062.00

SMITH & WESSON MODEL 22A TARGET PISTOL

Caliber: 22 LR, 10-shot magazine. **Barrel:** 5-1/2" bull. **Weight:** 39 oz. **Length:** 9-1/2" overall. **Grips:** Dymondwood® with ambidextrous thumbrests and flared bottom or rubber soft touch with thumbrest. **Sights:** Patridge front, fully adjustable rear. **Features:** Sight bridge with Weaver-style integral optics mount; alloy frame, stainless barrel and slide; blue finish. Introduced 1997. Made in U.S.A. by Smith & Wesson.
Price: $407.00
Price: HiViz front sight $429.00
Price: Camo model $367.00
Price: Two-tone model $401.00
Price: Light barrel model $324.00
Price: 4" bbl. $293.00
Price: 7" bbl. $367.00

Smith & Wesson Model 22S Target Pistol

Similar to the Model 22A except has stainless steel frame. Introduced 1997. Made in U.S.A. by Smith & Wesson.
Price: $434.00
Price: HiViz front sight $453.00

SPRINGFIELD ARMORY 1911A1 BULLSEYE WADCUTTER PISTOL

Caliber: 38 Super, 45 ACP. **Barrel:** 5". **Weight:** 45 oz. **Length:** 8.59" overall (5" barrel). **Grips:** Checkered walnut. **Sights:** Bo-Mar rib with undercut blade front, fully adjustable rear. **Features:** Built for wadcutter loads only. Has full-length recoil spring guide rod, fitted Videki speed trigger with 3.5-lb. pull; match Commander hammer and sear; beavertail grip safety; lowered and flared ejection port; tuned extractor; fitted slide to frame; recoil buffer system; beveled and polished magazine well; checkered front strap and steel mainspring housing (flat housing standard); polished and throated National Match barrel and bushing. Comes with two magazines, plastic carrying case, test target. Introduced 1992. From Springfield Armory.
Price: $1,499.00
Price: Adj. Target $1,049.00
Price: M1911SC, Commander-style $1,029.00

Springfield Armory Basic Competition Pistol

Has low-mounted Bo-Mar adjustable rear sight, undercut blade front; match throated barrel and bushing; polished feed ramp; lowered and flared ejection port; fitted Videki speed trigger with tuned 3.5-lb. pull; fitted slide to frame; recoil buffer system; checkered walnut grips; serrated, arched mainspring housing. Comes with two magazines with slam pads, plastic carrying case. Introduced 1992. From Springfield Armory.
Price: 45 ACP, blue, 5" only $1,295.00

CONSULT

SHOOTER'S MARKETPLACE

Page 243, This Issue

Springfield, Inc. Expert

Springfield, Inc. 1911A1 Trophy Match

Springfield, Inc. Distinguished

Springfield, Inc. N.M. Hardball

Springfield Armory Expert Pistol

Similar to the Competition Pistol except has triple-chamber tapered cone compensator on match barrel with dovetailed front sight; lowered and flared ejection port; fully tuned for reliability; fitted slide to frame; extended ambidextrous thumb safety, extended magazine release button; beavertail grip safety; Pachmayr wraparound grips. Comes with two magazines, plastic carrying case. Introduced 1992. From Springfield Armory.

Price: 45 ACP, Duo-tone finish **$1,724.00**
Price: Expert Ltd. (non-compensated) **$1,624.00**

Springfield Armory Distinguished Pistol

Has all the features of the 1911A1 Expert except is full-house pistol with deluxe Bo-Mar low-mounted adjustable rear sight; full-length recoil spring guide rod and recoil spring retainer; checkered frontstrap; S&A magazine well; walnut grips. Hard chrome finish. Comes with two magazines, plastic carrying case. From Springfield Armory

Price: 45 ACP **$2,445.00**
Price: Distinguished Limited (non-compensated) **$2,345.00**

Springfield Armory 1911A1 N.M. Hardball Pistol

Has Bo-Mar adjustable rear sight with undercut front blade; fitted match Videki trigger with 4-lb. pull; fitted slide to frame; throated National Match barrel and bushing; recoil buffer system; tuned extractor; Herrett walnut grips. Comes with two magazines, plastic carrying case, test target. Introduced 1992. From Springfield Armory

Price: 45 ACP, blue **$1,336.00**

Springfield Armory Leatham Legend TGO Series Pistols

Three models of 5" barrel, 45 ACP 1911 pistols built for serious competition. TGO 1 has deluxe low mount Bo-Mar rear sight, Dawson fiber optics front sight, 3.5 lb. trigger pull. TGO 2 has Bo-Mar low mount adjustable rear sight, Dawson fiber optic front sight, 4.5 to 5 lb. trigger pull. TGO 3 has Springfield Armory fully adjustable rear sight with low mount BoMar cut Dawson fiber optic front sight, 4.5 to 5 lb. trigger.

Price: TGO 1 . . . . **$2,999.00**
Price: TGO 2 . . . . **$1,899.00**
Price: TGO 3 . . . . **$1,295.00**

Springfield Armory Trophy Match Pistol

Similar to Springfield Armory's Full Size model, but designed for bullseye and action shooting competition. Available with a Service Model 5" frame with matching slide and barrel in 5" and 6" lengths. Fully adjustable sights, checkered frame front strap, match barrel and bushing. In 45 ACP only. From Springfield Inc.

Price: **$1,248.00**

STI EAGLE 5.0, 6.0 PISTOL

Caliber: 9mm, 9x21, 38 & 40 Super, 40 S&W, 10mm, 45 ACP, 10-shot magazine. Barrel: 5", 6" bull. Weight: 34.5 oz. Length: 8.62" overall. Grips: Checkered polymer. Sights: STI front, Novak or Heine rear. Features: Standard frames plus 7 others; adjustable match trigger; skeletonized hammer; extended grip safety with locator pad. Introduced 1994. Made in U.S.A. by STI International.

Price: . . . . (5.0 Eagle) **$1,794.00**, (6.0 Eagle) **$1,894.00**

STI EXECUTIVE PISTOL

Caliber: 40 S&W. Barrel: 5" bull. Weight: 39 oz. Length: 8-5/8". Grips: Gray polymer. Sights: Dawson fiber optic, front; STI adjustable rear. Features: Stainless mag. well, front and rear serrations on slide. Made in U.S.A. by STI.

Price: **$2,389.00**

STI TROJAN

Caliber: 9mm, 38 Super, 40S&W, 45 ACP. Barrel: 5", 6". Weight: 36 oz. Length: 8.5". Grips: Rosewood. Sights: STI front with STI adjustable rear. Features: Stippled front strap, flat top slide, one-piece steel guide rod.

Price: (Trojan 5") **$1,024.00**
Price: (Trojan 6", not available in 38 Super) **$1,232.50**

WALTHER GSP MATCH PISTOL

Caliber: 22 LR, 32 S&W Long (GSP-C), 5-shot magazine. Barrel: 4.22". Weight: 44.8 oz. (22 LR), 49.4 oz. (32). Length: 11.8" overall. Grips: Walnut. Sights: Post front, match rear adjustable for windage and elevation. Features: Available with either 2.2-lb. (1000 gm) or 3-lb. (1360 gm) trigger. Spare magazine, barrel weight, tools supplied. Imported from Germany by Nygord Precision Products.

Price: GSP, with case **$1,495.00**
Price: GSP-C, with case **$1,595.00**

**Includes models suitable for hunting and
competitive courses of fire, both police and international.**

Comanche III

Dan Wesson Firearms
Model 445 Supermag

ARMSPORT MODEL 4540 REVOLVER
Caliber: 38 Special. **Barrel:** 4". **Weight:** 32 oz. **Length:** 9" overall. **Sights:** Fixed rear, blade front. **Features:** Ventilated rib; blued finish. Imported from Argentina by Armsport Inc.
Price: $140.00

COLT SINGLE-ACTION ARMY
Caliber: 32-20, 38 Special, 357 Magnum, 38-40, 44-4-, 44 Special, 45 Long Colt. **Barrel:** 4.7 5", 5.5", 7.5". **Weight:** 40-44 oz. **Sights:** Blade front, notch rear. **Features:** Available in black powder and sheriff's models; nickel, blued or case-hardened frame; 6-round cylinder.
Price: .... (Blued) $1,380.00; (Stainless) $1,530.00

COMANCHE I, II, III DA REVOLVERS
Features: Adjustable sights. Blue or stainless finish. Distributed by SGS Importers.
Price: I 22 LR, 6" bbl., 9-shot, blue $236.95
Price: I 22LR, 6" bbl., 9-shot, stainless $258.95
Price: II 38 Special, 3", 4" bbl., 6-shot, blue $219.95
Price: II 38 Special, 4" bbl., 6-shot, stainless $236.95
Price: III 357 Mag, 3", 4", 6" bbl., 6-shot, blue $253.95
Price: III 357 Mag, 3", 4", 6" bbl., 6-shot, stainless $274.95
Price: II 38 Special, 3" bbl., 6-shot, stainless steel $236.95

DAN WESSON FIREARMS MODEL 722 SILHOUETTE REVOLVER
Caliber: 22 LR, 6-shot. **Barrel:** 10" vented heavy. **Weight:** 53 oz. **Grips:** Combat style. **Sights:** Patridge-style front, .080" narrow notch rear. **Features:** Single action only. Satin brushed stainless finish. Reintroduced 1997. Made in U.S.A. by Dan Wesson Firearms.
Price: 722 VH10 (vent heavy 10" bbl.) $888.00
Price: 722 VH10 SRS1 (Super Ram Silhouette, Bo-Mar sights, front hood, trigger job) $1,164.00

DAN WESSON FIREARMS MODEL 3220/73220 TARGET REVOLVER
Caliber: 32-20, 6-shot. **Barrel:** 2.5", 4", 6", 8", 10" standard vent, vent heavy. **Weight:** 47 oz. (6" VH). **Length:** 11.25" overall. **Grips:** Hogue Gripper rubber (walnut, exotic hardwoods optional). **Sights:** Red ramp interchangeable front, fully adjustable rear. **Features:** Bright blue (3220) or stainless (73220). Reintroduced 1997. Made in U.S.A. by Dan Wesson Firearms.
Price: 3220 VH2.5 (blued, 2.5" vent heavy bbl.) $643.00
Price: 73220 VH10 (stainless 10" vent heavy bbl.) $873.00

DAN WESSON FIREARMS MODEL 40/740 REVOLVERS
Caliber: 357 Maximum, 6-shot. **Barrel:** 4", 6", 8", 10". **Weight:** 72 oz. (8" bbl.). **Length:** 14.3" overall (8" bbl.). **Grips:** Hogue Gripper rubber (walnut or exotic hardwood optional). **Sights:** 1/8" serrated front, fully adjustable rear. **Features:** Blue or stainless steel. Made in U.S.A. by Dan Wesson Firearms.
Price: Blue, 4" $702.00
Price: Blue, 6" $749.00
Price: Blue, 8" $795.00
Price: Blue, 10" $858.00
Price: Stainless, 4" $834.00
Price: Stainless, 6" $892.00
Price: Stainless, 8" slotted $1,024.00
Price: Stainless, 10" $998.00
Price: 4", 6", 8" Compensated, blue .... $749.00 to $885.00
Price: As above, stainless .... $893.00 to $1,061.00

Dan Wesson Firearms Model 414/7414 and 445/7445 SuperMag Revolvers
Similar size and weight as Model 40 revolvers. Chambered for 414 SuperMag or 445 SuperMag cartridge. Barrel lengths of 4", 6", 8", 10". Contact maker for complete price list. Reintroduced 1997. Made in the U.S.A. by Dan Wesson Firearms.
Price: 4", vent heavy, blue or stainless $904.00
Price: 8", vent heavy, blue or stainless $1,026.00
Price: 10", vent heavy, blue or stainless $1,103.00
Price: Compensated models .... $965.00 to $1,149.00

DAN WESSON FIREARMS MODEL 22/722 REVOLVERS
Caliber: 22 LR, 22 WMR, 6-shot. **Barrel:** 2-1/2", 4", 6", 8" or 10"; interchangeable. **Weight:** 36 oz. (2-1/2"), 44 oz. (6"). **Length:** 9-1/4" overall (4" barrel). **Grips:** Hogue Gripper rubber (walnut, exotic woods optional). **Sights:** 1/8" serrated, interchangeable front, white outline rear adjustable for windage and elevation. **Features:** Built on the same frame as the Wesson 357; wide trigger with over-travel adjustment, wide spur hammer, with short double-action travel. Available in blue or stainless steel. Reintroduced 1997.
Price: 22 VH2.5/722 VH2.5 (blued or stainless 2-1/2" bbl.) $551.00
Price: 22VH10/722 VH10 (blued or stainless 10" bbl.) $750.00

Dan Wesson 722M Small Frame Revolver
Similar to Model 22/722 except chambered for 22 WMR. Blued or stainless finish, 2-1/2", 4", 6", 8" or 10" barrels.
Price: Blued or stainless finish .... $643.00 to $873.00

DAN WESSON FIREARMS MODEL 15/715 and 32/732 REVOLVERS
Caliber: 32-20, 32 H&R Mag. (Model 32), 357 Mag. (Model 15). **Barrel:** 2-1/2", 4", 6", 8" (M32), 2-1/2", 4", 6", 8", 10" (M15); vented heavy. **Weight:** 36 oz. (2-1/2" barrel). **Length:** 9-1/4" overall (4" barrel). **Grips:** Checkered, interchangeable. **Sights:** 1/8" serrated front, fully adjustable rear. **Fea-tures:** New Generation Series. Interchangeable barrels; wide, smooth trigger, wide hammer spur; short double-action travel. Available in blue or stainless. Reintroduced 1997. Made in U.S.A. by Dan Wesson Firearms.
Price: Model 15/715, 2-1/2" (blue or stainless) $551.00
Price: Model 15/715, 8" (blue or stainless) $612.00
Price: Model 15/715, compensated .... $704.00 to $827.00
Price: Model 32/732, 4" (blue or stainless) $674.00
Price: Model 32/732, 8" (blue or stainless) $766.00

DAN WESSON FIREARMS MODEL 41/741, 44/744 and 45/745 REVOLVERS
Caliber: 41 Mag., 44 Mag., 45 Colt, 6-shot. **Barrel:** 4", 6", 8", 10"; interchangeable; 4", 6", 8" compensated. **Weight:** 48 oz. (4"). **Length:** 12" overall (6" bbl.) **Grips:** Smooth. **Sights:** 1/8" serrated front, white outline rear adjustable for windage and elevation. **Features:** Available in blue or stainless steel. Smooth, wide trigger with adjustable over-travel, wide hammer spur. Available in Pistol Pac set also. Reintroduced 1997. Made in U.S.A. by Dan Wesson Firearms.
Price: 41 Mag., 4", vent heavy (blue or stainless) $643.00
Price: 44 Mag., 6", vent heavy (blue or stainless) $689.00
Price: 45 Colt, 8", vent heavy (blue or stainless) $766.00
Price: Compensated models (all calibers) .... $812.00 to $934.00

**Dan Wesson Firearms
Super Ram Silhouette**

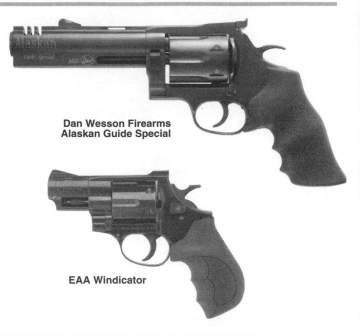

**Dan Wesson Firearms
Alaskan Guide Special**

EAA Windicator

DAN WESSON FIREARMS LARGE FRAME SERIES REVOLVERS
Caliber: 41, 741/41 Magnum; 44, 744/44 Magnum; 45, 745/45 Long Colt; 360, 7360/357; 460, 7460/45. **Barrel:** 2"-10". **Weight:** 49 oz.-69 oz. **Grips:** Standard, Hogue rubber Gripper Grips. **Sights:** Standard front, serrated ramp with color insert. Standard rear, adustable wide notch. Other sight options available. **Features:** Available in blue or stainless steel. Smooth, wide trigger with overtravel, wide hammer spur. Double and single action.
Price: .... **$769.00 to $889.00**

DAN WESSON FIREARMS MODEL 360/7360 REVOLVERS
Caliber: 357 Mag. **Barrel:** 4", 6", 8", 10"; vent heavy. **Weight:** 64 oz. (8" barrel). **Grips:** Hogue rubber finger groove. **Sights:** Interchangeable ramp or Patridge front, fully adjustable rear. **Features:** New Generation Large Frame Series. Interchangeable barrels and grips; smooth trigger, wide hammer spur. Blue (360) or stainless (7360). Introduced 1999. Made in U.S.A. by Dan Wesson Firearms.
Price: 4" bbl., blue or stainless **$735.00**
Price: 10" bbl., blue or stainless **$873.00**
Price: Compensated models .... **$858.00 to $980.00**

DAN WESSON FIREARMS MODEL 460/7460 REVOLVERS
Caliber: 45 ACP, 45 Auto Rim, 45 Super, 45 Winchester Magnum and 460 Rowland. **Barrel:** 4", 6", 8", 10"; vent heavy. **Weight:** 49 oz. (4" barrel). **Grips:** Hogue rubber finger groove; interchangeable. **Sights:** Interchangeable ramp or Patridge front, fully adjustable rear. **Features:** New Generation Large Frame Series. Shoots five cartridges (45 ACP, 45 Auto Rim, 45 Super, 45 Winchester Magnum and 460 Rowland; six half-moon clips for auto cartridges included). Interchangeable barrels and grips. Available with non-fluted cylinder and slotted lightweight barrel shroud. Introduced 1999. Made in U.S.A. by Dan Wesson Firearms.
Price: 4" bbl., blue or stainless **$735.00**
Price: 10" bbl., blue or stainless **$888.00**
Price: Compensated models .... **$919.00 to $1,042.00**

DAN WESSON FIREARMS STANDARD SILHOUETTE REVOLVERS
Caliber: 357 SuperMag/Maxi, 41 Mag., 414 SuperMag, 445 SuperMag. **Barrel:** 8", 10". **Weight:** 64 oz. (8" barrel). **Length:** 14.3" overall (8" barrel). **Grips:** Hogue rubber finger groove; interchangeable. **Sights:** Patridge front, fully adjustable rear. **Features:** Interchangeable barrels and grips, fluted or non-fluted cylinder, satin brushed stainless finish. Introduced 1999. Made in U.S.A. by Dan Wesson Firearms.
Price: 357 SuperMag/Maxi, 8" **$1,057.00**
Price: 41 Mag., 10" **$888.00**
Price: 414 SuperMag., 8" **$1,057.00**
Price: 445 SuperMag., 8" **$1,057.00**

Dan Wesson Firearms Super Ram Silhouette Revolver
Similar to Standard Silhouette except has 10 land and groove Laser Coat barrel, Bo-Mar target sights with hooded front, special laser engraving. Fluted or non-fluted cylinder. Introduced 1999. Made in U.S.A. by Dan Wesson Firearms.
Price: 357 SuperMag/Maxi, 414 SuperMag., 445 SuperMag., 8", blue or stainless **$1,364.00**
Price: 41 Magnum, 44 Magnum, 8", blue or stainless **$1,241.00**
Price: 41 Magnum, 44 Magnum, 10", blue or stainless **$1,333.00**

DAN WESSON FIREARMS ALASKAN GUIDE SPECIAL
Caliber: 445 SuperMag, 44 Magnum. **Barrel:** Compensated 4" vent heavy barrel assembly. **Features:** Stainless steel with baked on, non-glare, matte black coating, special laser engraving.
Price: Model 7445 VH4C AGS **$995.00**
Price: Model 744 VH4C AGS **$855.00**

EAA WINDICATOR REVOLVERS
Caliber: 38 Spec., 6-shot; 357 magnum, 6-shot. **Barrel:** 2", 4". **Weight:** 38 oz. (22 rimfire, 4"). **Length:** 8.5" overall (4" bbl.). **Grips:** Rubber with finger grooves. **Sights:** Blade front, fixed or adjustable on rimfires; fixed only on 32, 38. **Features:** Swing-out cylinder; hammer block safety; blue finish. Introduced 1991. Imported from Germany by European American Armory.
Price: 38 Special 2" **$249.00**
Price: 38 Special, 4" **$259.00**
Price: 357 Magnum, 2" **$259.00**
Price: 357 Magnum, 4" **$279.00**

KORTH COMBAT REVOLVER
Caliber: 357 Mag., 32 S&W Long, 9mm Para., 22 WMR, 22 LR. **Barrel:** 3", 4", 5-1/4", 6", 8". **Sights:** Fully adjustable, rear; Baughman ramp, front. **Grips:** Walnut (checkered or smooth). Also available as a Target model in 22 LR, 38 Spl., 32 S&W Long, 357 Mag. with undercut Patridge front sight; fully adjustable rear. Made in Germany. Imported by Korth USA.
Price: From **$7,203.00**

KORTH TROJA REVOLVER
Caliber: .357 Mag. **Barrel:** 6". **Finish:** Matte blue. **Grips:** Smooth, over-sized finger contoured walnut. Introduced 2003. Imported from Germany by Korth USA.
Price: From **$5,593.00**

**CONSULT
SHOOTER'S
MARKETPLACE
Page 243, This Issue**

Medusa Model 47

Rossi Model 971

Rossi Model 972

Rossi Model 851

Ruger GP-161

Ruger KGP-141

MEDUSA MODEL 47 REVOLVER

Caliber: Most 9mm, 38 and 357 caliber cartridges; 6-shot cylinder. **Barrel:** 2-1/2", 3", 4", 5", 6"; fluted. **Weight:** 39 oz. **Length:** 10" overall (4" barrel). **Grips:** Gripper-style rubber. **Sights:** Changeable front blades, fully adjustable rear. **Features:** Patented extractor allows gun to chamber, fire and extract over 25 different cartridges in the 355 to 357 range without half-moon clips. Steel frame and cylinder; match quality barrel. Matte blue finish. Introduced 1996. Made in U.S.A. by Phillips & Rogers, Inc.

Price: **$899.00**

ROSSI MODEL 351/352 REVOLVERS

Caliber: 38 Special +P, 5-shot. **Barrel:** 2". **Weight:** 24 oz. **Length:** 6-1/2" overall. **Grips:** Rubber. **Sights:** Blade front, fixed rear. **Features:** Patented key-lock Taurus Security System; forged steel frame. Introduced 2001. Imported by BrazTech/Taurus.

Price: Model 351 (blued finish) **$298.00**
Price: Model 352 (stainless finish) **$345.00**

ROSSI MODEL 461/462 REVOLVERS

Caliber: 357 Magnum +P, 6-shot. **Barrel:** 2". **Weight:** 26 oz. **Length:** 6-1/2" overall. **Grips:** Rubber. **Sights:** Fixed. **Features:** Single/double action. Patented key-lock Taurus Security System; forged steel frame. Introduced 2001. Imported by BrazTech/Taurus.

Price: Model 461 (blued finish) **$298.00**
Price: Model 462 (stainless finish) **$345.00**

ROSSI MODEL 971/972 REVOLVERS

Caliber: 357 Magnum +P, 6-shot. **Barrel:** 4", 6". **Weight:** 40-44 oz. **Length:** 8-1/2" or 10-1/2" overall. **Grips:** Rubber. **Sights:** Fully adjustable. **Features:** Single/double action. Patented key-lock Taurus Security System; forged steel frame. Introduced 2001. Imported by BrazTech/Taurus.

Price: Model 971 (blued finish, 4" bbl.) **$345.00**
Price: Model 972 (stainless steel finish, 6" bbl.) **$391.00**

Rossi Model 851

Similar to Model 971/972, chambered for 38 Special +P. Blued finish. 4" barrel. Introduced 2001. From BrazTech/Taurus.

Price: **$298.00**

RUGER GP-100 REVOLVERS

Caliber: 38 Spec., 357 Mag., 6-shot. **Barrel:** 3", 3" full shroud, 4", 4" full shroud, 6", 6" full shroud. **Weight:** 3" barrel-35 oz., 3" full shroud-36 oz., 4" barrel-37 oz., 4" full shroud-38 oz. **Sights:** Fixed; adjustable on 4" full shroud, all 6" barrels. **Grips:** Ruger Santoprene Cushioned Grip with Goncalo Alves inserts. **Features:** Uses action, frame features of both the Security-Six and Redhawk revolvers. Full length, short ejector shroud. Satin blue and stainless steel.

Price: GP-141 (357, 4" full shroud, adj. sights, blue) **$499.00**
Price: GP-160 (357, 6", adj. sights, blue) **$499.00**
Price: GP-161 (357, 6" full shroud, adj. sights, blue), 46 oz. **$499.00**
Price: GPF-331 (357, 3" full shroud) **$495.00**
Price: GPF-340 (357, 4") **$495.00**
Price: GPF-341 (357, 4" full shroud) **$495.00**
Price: KGP-141 (357, 4" full shroud, adj. sights, stainless) **$555.00**
Price: KGP-160 (357, 6", adj. sights, stainless), 43 oz. **$555.00**
Price: KGP-161 (357, 6" full shroud, adj. sights, stainless) 46 oz. . **$555.00**
Price: KGPF-330 (357, 3", stainless) **$555.00**
Price: KGPF-331 (357, 3" full shroud, stainless) **$555.00**
Price: KGPF-340 (357, 4", stainless), KGPF-840 (38 Special) **$555.00**
Price: KGPF-341 (357, 4" full shroud, stainless) **$555.00**
Price: KGPF-840 (38 Special, 4", stainless) **$555.00**

Ruger SP101 Double-Action-Only Revolver

Similar to standard SP101 except double-action-only with no single-action sear notch. Spurless hammer, floating firing pin and transfer bar safety system. Available with 2-1/4" barrel in 357 Magnum. Weighs 25 oz., overall length 7.06". Natural brushed satin, high-polish stainless steel. Introduced 1993.

Price: KSP321XL (357 Mag.) **$495.00**

RUGER SP101 REVOLVERS

Caliber: 22 LR, 32 H&R Mag., 6-shot; 38 Spec. +P, 357 Mag., 5-shot. **Barrel:** 2-1/4", 3-1/16", 4". **Weight:** (38 & 357 mag models) 2-1/4"-25 oz.; 3-1/16"-27 oz. **Sights:** Adjustable on 22, 32, fixed on others. **Grips:** Ruger Cushioned Grip with inserts. **Features:** Compact, small frame, double-action revolver. Full-length ejector shroud. Stainless steel only. Introduced 1988.

Price: KSP-821X (2-1/4", 38 Spec.) **$495.00**
Price: KSP-831X (3-1/16", 38 Spec.) **$495.00**
Price: KSP-241X (4" heavy bbl., 22 LR), 34 oz. **$495.00**
Price: KSP-3231X (3-1/16", 32 H&R), 30 oz. **$495.00**
Price: KSP-321X (2-1/4", 357 Mag.) **$495.00**
Price: KSP-331X (3-1/16", 357 Mag.) **$495.00**
Price: KSP-3241X (32 Mag., 4" bbl.) **$495.00**

Ruger Redhawk

Smith & Wesson Model 10

Ruger Super Redhawk

Smith & Wesson Model 386

Smith & Wesson Model 629 Classic DX

Smith & Wesson Model 36LS

RUGER REDHAWK

Caliber: 44 Rem. Mag., 45 Colt, 6-shot. **Barrel:** 5-1/2", 7-1/2". **Weight:** About 54 oz. (7-1/2" bbl.). **Length:** 13" overall (7-1/2" barrel). **Grips:** Square butt cushioned grip panels. **Sights:** Interchangeable Patridge-type front, rear adjustable for windage and elevation. **Features:** Stainless steel, brushed satin finish, blued ordnance steel. 9-1/2" sight radius. Introduced 1979.
Price: Blued, 44 Mag., 5-1/2" RH-445, 7-1/2" RH-44 .... **$585.00**
Price: Blued, 44 Mag., 7-1/2" RH44R, with scope mount, rings ... **$625.00**
Price: Stainless, 44 Mag., KRH445, 5-1/2", 7-1/2" KRH-44 ...... **$645.00**
Price: Stainless, 44 Mag., 7-1/2", with scope mount,
rings KRH-44R **$685.00**
Price: Stainless, 45 Colt, KRH455, 5-1/2", 7-1/2" KRH-45 ...... **$645.00**
Price: Stainless, 45 Colt, 7-1/2", with scope mount and rings
KRH-45R **$685.00**

Ruger Super Redhawk Revolver

Similar to standard Redhawk except has heavy extended frame with Ruger Integral Scope Mounting System on wide topstrap. Also available in 454 Casull and 480 Ruger. Wide hammer spur lowered for better scope clearance. Incorporates mechanical design features and improvements of GP-100. Choice of 7-1/2" or 9-1/2" barrel, both ramp front sight base with Redhawk-style Interchangeable Insert sight blades, adjustable rear sight. Target gray stainless steel. Introduced 1987.
Price: KSRH-7 (7-1/2"), KSRH-9 (9-1/2"), 44 Mag **$685.00**
Price: KSRH-7454 (7-1/2") 454 Casull, 9-1/2 KSRH-9454 .... **$775.00**
Price: KSRH-7480 (7-1/2") 480 Ruger **$775.00**
Price: KSRH-9480 (9-1/2") 480 Ruger **$775.00**

SMITH & WESSON MODEL 10 M&P HB REVOLVER

Caliber: 38 Spec., 6-shot. **Barrel:** 4". **Weight:** 36 oz. **Length:** 8-7/8" overall. **Grips:** Uncle Mike's Combat soft rubber; square butt. **Sights:** Fixed; ramp front, square notch rear.
Price: Blue **$544.00**

SMITH & WESSON MODEL 325PD

Caliber: 45 ACP, 6-round. **Barrel:** 2-1/2". **Weight:** 21.5 oz. **Length:** 7-1/4". **Grips:** Wood. **Sights:** Adj. rear, HiViz front. **Features:** Alloy large frame, titanium cylinder.
Price: **$939.00**

SMITH & WESSON MODEL 329PD

Caliber: 44 Mag., 44 Spec., 6-round. **Barrel:** 4". **Weight:** 26 oz. **Length:** 9-1/2". **Grips:** Wood. **Sights:** Adj. rear, HiViz front. **Features:** Alloy large frame, titanium cylinder.
Price: **$960.00**

SMITH & WESSON MODEL 386

Caliber: 357 Mag., 38 Spec., 7-round. **Barrel:** 3-1/8". **Weight:** 18.5 oz. **Length:** 8-1/8". **Grips:** Hogue Bantam. **Sights:** Adj. rear, HiViz front. **Features:** Alloy large frame, titanium cylinder.
Price: **$876.00**

SMITH & WESSON MODEL 629 REVOLVERS

Caliber: 44 Magnum, 44 S&W Special, 6-shot. **Barrel:** 4". **Weight:** 45 oz. (6" bbl.). **Length:** 11-5/8" overall (6" bbl.). **Grips:** Soft rubber; wood optional. **Sights:** 1/8" red ramp front, white outline rear, internal lock, adjustable for windage and elevation.
Price: Model 629, 4" **$787.00**
Price: Model 629, 6" **$810.00**

Smith & Wesson Model 629 Classic Revolver

Similar to standard Model 629 with full-lug 5", 6-1/2" or 8-3/8" barrel, chamfered front of cylinder, interchangeable red ramp front sight with adjustable white outline rear, Hogue grips with S&W monogram, drilled and tapped for scope mounting. Factory accurizing and endurance packages. Overall length with 5" barrel is 10-1/2"; weighs 45.5 oz. Introduced 1990.
Price: Model 629 Classic (stainless), 5", 6-1/2" **$843.00**
Price: As above, 8-3/8" **$871.00**
Price: Model 629 Classic with HiViz front sight **$894.00**

SMITH & WESSON MODEL 37 AIRWEIGHT

Caliber: 38 Spec. +P, 5-shot. **Barrel:** 1-7/8". **Weight:** 15.0 oz. **Length:** 6-5/16" (round butt). **Grips:** Round butt soft rubber. **Sights:** Fixed, serrated ramp front, square notch rear. Glass beaded finish.
Price: Model 37 .... **$573.00**

Smith & Wesson Model 637 Airweight Revolver

Similar to the Model 37 Airweight except has alloy frame, stainless steel barrel, cylinder and yoke; rated for 38 Spec. +P; Uncle Mike's Boot Grip. Weighs 15 oz. Introduced 1996. Made in U.S.A. by Smith & Wesson.
Price: **$450.00**

SMITH & WESSON MODEL 36LS, 60LS LADYSMITH

Caliber: .38 S&W Special +P (M36), 357 Mag. (M60LS), 5-shot. **Barrel:** 1-7/8, 2-1/8". **Weight:** 20 oz. **Length:** 6-3/16 overall (1-7/8" barrel). **Grips:** Combat Dymondwood® grips with S&W monogram. **Sights:** Serrated ramp front, fixed notch rear. **Features:** Speedloader cutout. Comes in a fitted carry/storage case. Introduced 1989.
Price: Model 36LS **$568.00**
Price: Model 60LS, 2-1/8" bbl. stainless, 357 Magnum **$621.00**
Price: Model 36LS, 38 Spec **$450.00**

**Smith & Wesson
Model 60 Chief's Special**

**Smith & Wesson
Model 317 AirLite**

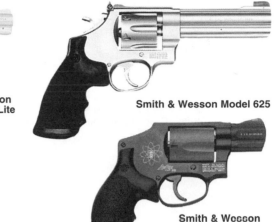

Smith & Wesson Model 625

**Smith & Wesson
Model 340PD Airlite Sc**

SMITH & WESSON MODEL 60 CHIEF'S SPECIAL
Caliber: 357 Magnum, 38 Spec., 5-shot. **Barrel:** 2-1/8", 3" or 5". **Weight:** 24 oz. **Length:** 7-1/2 overall (3" barrel). **Grips:** Rounded butt synthetic grips. **Sights:** Fixed, serrated ramp front, square notch rear. **Features:** Stainless steel construction. 3" full lug barrel, adjustable sights, internal lock. Made in U.S.A. by Smith & Wesson.
Price: 2-1/8" barrel **$594.00**
Price: 3" bbl. **$630.00**
Price: 5" bbl. **$671.00**

SMITH & WESSON MODEL 65
Caliber: 357 Mag. and 38 Spec., 6-shot. **Barrel:** 4". **Weight:** 34 oz. **Length:** 9-5/16" overall (4" bbl.). **Grips:** Uncle Mike's Combat. **Sights:** 1/8" serrated ramp front, fixed square notch rear. **Features:** Heavy barrel. Stainless steel construction. Internal lock.
Price: **$531.00**

SMITH & WESSON MODEL 317 AIRLITE, 317 KIT GUN REVOLVERS
Caliber: 22 LR, 8-shot. **Barrel:** 1-7/8", 3". **Weight:** 10.05 oz. **Length:** 6-3/16" overall. **Grips:** Dymondwood® Boot or Uncle Mike's Boot. **Sights:** Serrated ramp front, fixed notch rear. **Features:** Aluminum alloy, carbon and stainless steels, and titanium construction. Short spur hammer, smooth combat trigger. Clear Cote finish. Introduced 1997. Made in U.S.A. by Smith & Wesson.
Price: With Uncle Mike's Boot grip **$603.00**
Price: With Boot grip, 3" barrel, HiViz front sight, internal lock **$658.00**

SMITH & WESSON MODEL 351PD
Caliber: 22 Mag. **Barrel:** 2". **Features:** Seven-shot, Scandium alloy.
Price: **$625.00**

SMITH & WESSON MODEL 64 STAINLESS M&P
Caliber: 38 Spec. +P, 6-shot. **Barrel:** 3", 4". **Weight:** 36 oz. **Length:** 8-7/16" overall. **Grips:** Soft rubber. **Sights:** Fixed, 1/8" serrated ramp front, square notch rear. **Features:** Satin finished stainless steel, square butt.
Price: 3", 4" bbl. **$583.00**

SMITH & WESSON MODEL 648
Caliber: 22 Mag., 6-round. **Barrel:** 6". **Weight:** 45 oz. **Length:** 11-1/8". Grips: Rubber. **Sights:** Adj. rear, Patridge front. **Features:** Stainless steel frame, satin finish.
Price: **$703.00**

SMITH & WESSON MODEL 619
Caliber: 38 S&W Special; 7 rounds. **Barrel:** 4". **Weight:** 37.5 oz. **Length:** 9-1/2". Grips: Rubber. **Sights:** White outline rear, red ramp front. **Features:** Stainless frame and cylinder.
Price: **$615.00**

SMITH & WESSON MODEL 620
Caliber: 38 S&W Special; 7 rounds. **Barrel:** 4". **Weight:** 37.5 oz. **Length:** 9-1/2". **Grips:** Rubber. **Sights:** White outline rear, red ramp front. **Features:** Stainles frame and cylinder.
Price: **$669.00**

SMITH & WESSON MODEL 686
Caliber: 357 Mag., 38 S&W Special; 6 rounds. **Barrel:** 2-1/2", 4", 6". **Weight:** 40 oz. (4"). **Length:** 9-9/16". **Grips:** Rubber. **Sights:** White outline rear, red ramp front. **Features:** Stainless frame and cylinder.
Price: 2-1/2" bbl. **$667.00**
Price: 4" bbl. **$694.00**
Price: 6" bbl. **$700.00**

SMITH & WESSON MODEL 686 POWERPORT
Caliber: 357 Mag., 38 S&W Special; 6 rounds. **Barrel:** 6". **Weight:** 44 oz. **Length:** 11-3/8". **Grips:** Rubber. **Sights:** Adj. rear, Patridge front. **Features:** Stainless frame and cylinder.
Price: **$747.00**

Smith & Wesson Model 686 Magnum PLUS Revolver
Similar to the Model 686 except has 7-shot cylinder, 2-1/2", 4" or 6" barrel. Weighs 34-1/2 oz., overall length 7-1/2" (2-1/2" barrel). Hogue rubber grips. Internal lock. Introduced 1996. Made in U.S.A. by Smith & Wesson.
Price: 2-1/2" bbl. **$692.00**
Price: 4" bbl. **$716.00**
Price: 6" bbl. **$727.00**

SMITH & WESSON MODEL 625 REVOLVER
Caliber: 45 ACP, 6-shot. **Barrel:** 4", 5". **Weight:** 45 oz. **Length:** 10-3/8" overall. **Grips:** Soft rubber; wood optional. **Sights:** Patridge front on ramp, S&W micrometer click rear adjustable for windage and elevation. **Features:** Stainless steel construction with .400" semi-target hammer, .312" smooth combat trigger; full lug barrel. Glass beaded finish. Introduced 1989.
Price: 5" **$817.00**
Price: 4" with internal lock **$817.00**
Price: 5" Jerry Miculek Pro series **$845.00**

SMITH & WESSON MODEL 640 CENTENNIAL DA ONLY
Caliber: 357 Mag., 38 Spec. +P, 5-shot. **Barrel:** 2-1/8". **Weight:** 23 oz. **Length:** 6-3/4" overall. **Grips:** Uncle Mike's Boot grip. **Sights:** Serrated ramp front, fixed notch rear. **Features:** Stainless steel. Fully concealed hammer, snag-proof smooth edges. Internal lock. Introduced 1995 in 357 Magnum.
Price: **$658.00**

SMITH & WESSON MODEL 617 K-22 MASTERPIECE
Caliber: 22 LR, 6- or 10-shot. **Barrel:** 4", 6". **Weight:** 41 oz. (4" barrel). **Length:** NA. **Grips:** Soft rubber. **Sights:** Patridge front, adjustable rear. Drilled and tapped for scope mount. **Features:** Stainless steel with satin finish; 4" has .312" smooth trigger, .375" semi-target hammer; 6" has either .312" combat or .400" serrated trigger, .375" semi-target or .500" target hammer; 8-3/8" with .400" serrated trigger, .500" target hammer. Introduced 1990.
Price: 4" **$707.00**
Price: 6", target hammer, target trigger **$686.00**
Price: 6", 10-shot **$734.00**

SMITH & WESSON MODEL 340PD AIRLITE Sc CENTENNIAL
Caliber: 357 Magnum, 38 Spec. +P, 5-shot. **Barrel:** 1-7/8". **Grips:** Rounded butt grip. **Sights:** HiViz front. **Features:** Synthetic grip, internal lock. Bluc.
Price: HiViz front **$877.00**
Price: Red ramp front **$862.00**

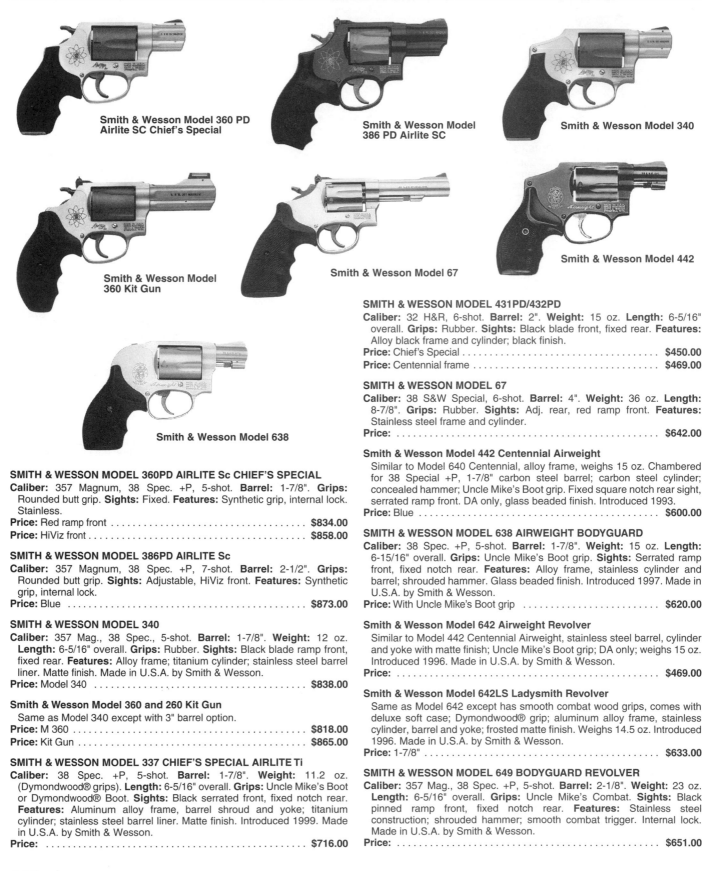

Smith & Wesson Model 360 PD Airlite SC Chief's Special

Smith & Wesson Model 386 PD Airlite SC

Smith & Wesson Model 340

Smith & Wesson Model 360 Kit Gun

Smith & Wesson Model 67

Smith & Wesson Model 442

Smith & Wesson Model 638

SMITH & WESSON MODEL 360PD AIRLITE Sc CHIEF'S SPECIAL

Caliber: 357 Magnum, 38 Spec. +P, 5-shot. **Barrel:** 1-7/8". **Grips:** Rounded butt grip. **Sights:** Fixed. **Features:** Synthetic grip, internal lock. Stainless.

Price: Red ramp front $834.00
Price: HiViz front $858.00

SMITH & WESSON MODEL 386PD AIRLITE Sc

Caliber: 357 Magnum, 38 Spec. +P, 7-shot. **Barrel:** 2-1/2". **Grips:** Rounded butt grip. **Sights:** Adjustable, HiViz front. **Features:** Synthetic grip, internal lock.

Price: Blue $873.00

SMITH & WESSON MODEL 340

Caliber: 357 Mag., 38 Spec., 5-shot. **Barrel:** 1-7/8". **Weight:** 12 oz. **Length:** 6-5/16" overall. **Grips:** Rubber. **Sights:** Black blade ramp front, fixed rear. **Features:** Alloy frame; titanium cylinder; stainless steel barrel liner. Matte finish. Made in U.S.A. by Smith & Wesson.

Price: Model 340 . . . . $838.00

Smith & Wesson Model 360 and 260 Kit Gun

Same as Model 340 except with 3" barrel option.

Price: M 360 . . . . $818.00
Price: Kit Gun $865.00

SMITH & WESSON MODEL 337 CHIEF'S SPECIAL AIRLITE Ti

Caliber: 38 Spec. +P, 5-shot. **Barrel:** 1-7/8". **Weight:** 11.2 oz. (Dymondwood® grips). **Length:** 6-5/16" overall. **Grips:** Uncle Mike's Boot or Dymondwood® Boot. **Sights:** Black serrated front, fixed notch rear. **Features:** Aluminum alloy frame, barrel shroud and yoke; titanium cylinder; stainless steel barrel liner. Matte finish. Introduced 1999. Made in U.S.A. by Smith & Wesson.

Price: $716.00

SMITH & WESSON MODEL 431PD/432PD

Caliber: 32 H&R, 6-shot. **Barrel:** 2". **Weight:** 15 oz. **Length:** 6-5/16" overall. **Grips:** Rubber. **Sights:** Black blade front, fixed rear. **Features:** Alloy black frame and cylinder; black finish.

Price: Chief's Special $450.00
Price: Centennial frame $469.00

SMITH & WESSON MODEL 67

Caliber: 38 S&W Special, 6-shot. **Barrel:** 4". **Weight:** 36 oz. **Length:** 8-7/8". **Grips:** Rubber. **Sights:** Adj. rear, red ramp front. **Features:** Stainless steel frame and cylinder.

Price: $642.00

Smith & Wesson Model 442 Centennial Airweight

Similar to Model 640 Centennial, alloy frame, weighs 15 oz. Chambered for 38 Special +P, 1-7/8" carbon steel barrel; carbon steel cylinder; concealed hammer; Uncle Mike's Boot grip. Fixed square notch rear sight, serrated ramp front. DA only, glass beaded finish. Introduced 1993.

Price: Blue $600.00

SMITH & WESSON MODEL 638 AIRWEIGHT BODYGUARD

Caliber: 38 Spec. +P, 5-shot. **Barrel:** 1-7/8". **Weight:** 15 oz. **Length:** 6-15/16" overall. **Grips:** Uncle Mike's Boot grip. **Sights:** Serrated ramp front, fixed notch rear. **Features:** Alloy frame, stainless cylinder and barrel; shrouded hammer. Glass beaded finish. Introduced 1997. Made in U.S.A. by Smith & Wesson.

Price: With Uncle Mike's Boot grip $620.00

Smith & Wesson Model 642 Airweight Revolver

Similar to Model 442 Centennial Airweight, stainless steel barrel, cylinder and yoke with matte finish; Uncle Mike's Boot grip; DA only; weighs 15 oz. Introduced 1996. Made in U.S.A. by Smith & Wesson.

Price: $469.00

Smith & Wesson Model 642LS Ladysmith Revolver

Same as Model 642 except has smooth combat wood grips, comes with deluxe soft case; Dymondwood® grip; aluminum alloy frame, stainless cylinder, barrel and yoke; frosted matte finish. Weighs 14.5 oz. Introduced 1996. Made in U.S.A. by Smith & Wesson.

Price: 1-7/8" $633.00

SMITH & WESSON MODEL 649 BODYGUARD REVOLVER

Caliber: 357 Mag., 38 Spec. +P, 5-shot. **Barrel:** 2-1/8". **Weight:** 23 oz. **Length:** 6-5/16" overall. **Grips:** Uncle Mike's Combat. **Sights:** Black pinned ramp front, fixed notch rear. **Features:** Stainless steel construction; shrouded hammer; smooth combat trigger. Internal lock. Made in U.S.A. by Smith & Wesson.

Price: $651.00

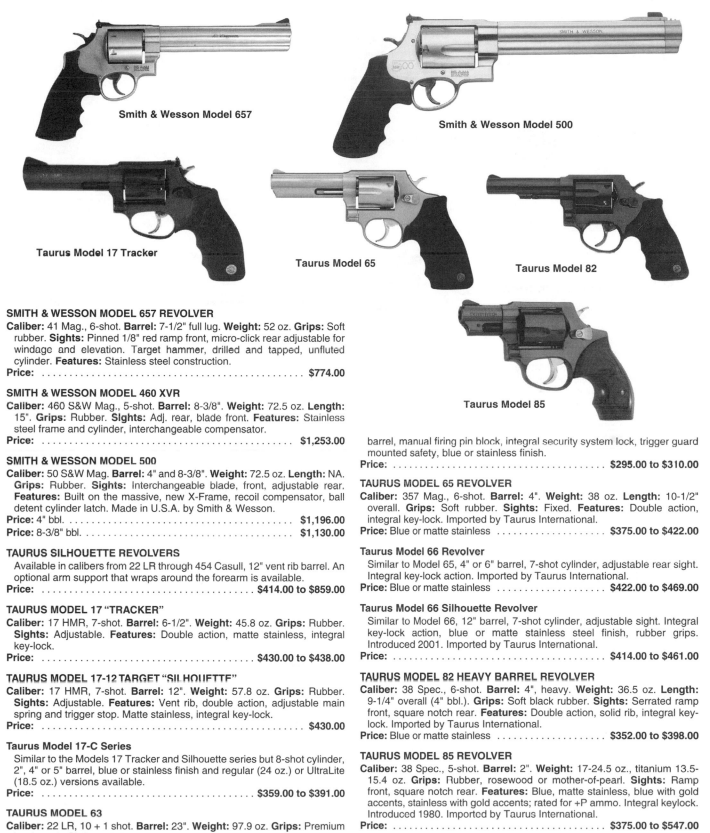

Smith & Wesson Model 657

Smith & Wesson Model 500

Taurus Model 17 Tracker

Taurus Model 65

Taurus Model 82

Taurus Model 85

SMITH & WESSON MODEL 657 REVOLVER
Caliber: 41 Mag., 6-shot. **Barrel:** 7-1/2" full lug. **Weight:** 52 oz. **Grips:** Soft rubber. **Sights:** Pinned 1/8" red ramp front, micro-click rear adjustable for windage and elevation. Target hammer, drilled and tapped, unfluted cylinder. **Features:** Stainless steel construction.
Price: $774.00

SMITH & WESSON MODEL 460 XVR
Caliber: 460 S&W Mag., 5-shot. **Barrel:** 8-3/8". **Weight:** 72.5 oz. **Length:** 15". **Grips:** Rubber. **Sights:** Adj. rear, blade front. **Features:** Stainless steel frame and cylinder, interchangeable compensator.
Price: $1,253.00

SMITH & WESSON MODEL 500
Caliber: 50 S&W Mag. **Barrel:** 4" and 8-3/8". **Weight:** 72.5 oz. **Length:** NA. **Grips:** Rubber. **Sights:** Interchangeable blade, front, adjustable rear. **Features:** Built on the massive, new X-Frame, recoil compensator, ball detent cylinder latch. Made in U.S.A. by Smith & Wesson.
Price: 4" bbl. $1,196.00
Price: 8-3/8" bbl. $1,130.00

TAURUS SILHOUETTE REVOLVERS
Available in calibers from 22 LR through 454 Casull, 12" vent rib barrel. An optional arm support that wraps around the forearm is available.
Price: . . . . $414.00 to $859.00

TAURUS MODEL 17 "TRACKER"
Caliber: 17 HMR, 7-shot. **Barrel:** 6-1/2". **Weight:** 45.8 oz. **Grips:** Rubber. **Sights:** Adjustable. **Features:** Double action, matte stainless, integral key-lock.
Price: . . . . $430.00 to $438.00

TAURUS MODEL 17-12 TARGET "SILHOUETTE"
Caliber: 17 HMR, 7-shot. **Barrel:** 12". **Weight:** 57.8 oz. **Grips:** Rubber. **Sights:** Adjustable. **Features:** Vent rib, double action, adjustable main spring and trigger stop. Matte stainless, integral key-lock.
Price: $430.00

Taurus Model 17-C Series
Similar to the Models 17 Tracker and Silhouette series but 8-shot cylinder, 2", 4" or 5" barrel, blue or stainless finish and regular (24 oz.) or UltraLite (18.5 oz.) versions available.
Price: . . . . $359.00 to $391.00

TAURUS MODEL 63
Caliber: 22 LR, 10 + 1 shot. **Barrel:** 23". **Weight:** 97.9 oz. **Grips:** Premium hardwood. **Sights:** Adjustable. **Features:** Auto loading action, round barrel, manual firing pin block, integral security system lock, trigger guard mounted safety, blue or stainless finish.
Price: . . . . $295.00 to $310.00

TAURUS MODEL 65 REVOLVER
Caliber: 357 Mag., 6-shot. **Barrel:** 4". **Weight:** 38 oz. **Length:** 10-1/2" overall. **Grips:** Soft rubber. **Sights:** Fixed. **Features:** Double action, integral key-lock. Imported by Taurus International.
Price: Blue or matte stainless . . . . $375.00 to $422.00

Taurus Model 66 Revolver
Similar to Model 65, 4" or 6" barrel, 7-shot cylinder, adjustable rear sight. Integral key-lock action. Imported by Taurus International.
Price: Blue or matte stainless . . . . $422.00 to $469.00

Taurus Model 66 Silhouette Revolver
Similar to Model 66, 12" barrel, 7-shot cylinder, adjustable sight. Integral key-lock action, blue or matte stainless steel finish, rubber grips. Introduced 2001. Imported by Taurus International.
Price: . . . . $414.00 to $461.00

TAURUS MODEL 82 HEAVY BARREL REVOLVER
Caliber: 38 Spec., 6-shot. **Barrel:** 4", heavy. **Weight:** 36.5 oz. **Length:** 9-1/4" overall (4" bbl.). **Grips:** Soft black rubber. **Sights:** Serrated ramp front, square notch rear. **Features:** Double action, solid rib, integral key-lock. Imported by Taurus International.
Price: Blue or matte stainless . . . . $352.00 to $398.00

TAURUS MODEL 85 REVOLVER
Caliber: 38 Spec., 5-shot. **Barrel:** 2". **Weight:** 17-24.5 oz., titanium 13.5-15.4 oz. **Grips:** Rubber, rosewood or mother-of-pearl. **Sights:** Ramp front, square notch rear. **Features:** Blue, matte stainless, blue with gold accents, stainless with gold accents; rated for +P ammo. Integral keylock. Introduced 1980. Imported by Taurus International.
Price: . . . . $375.00 to $547.00
Price: Total Titanium $531.00

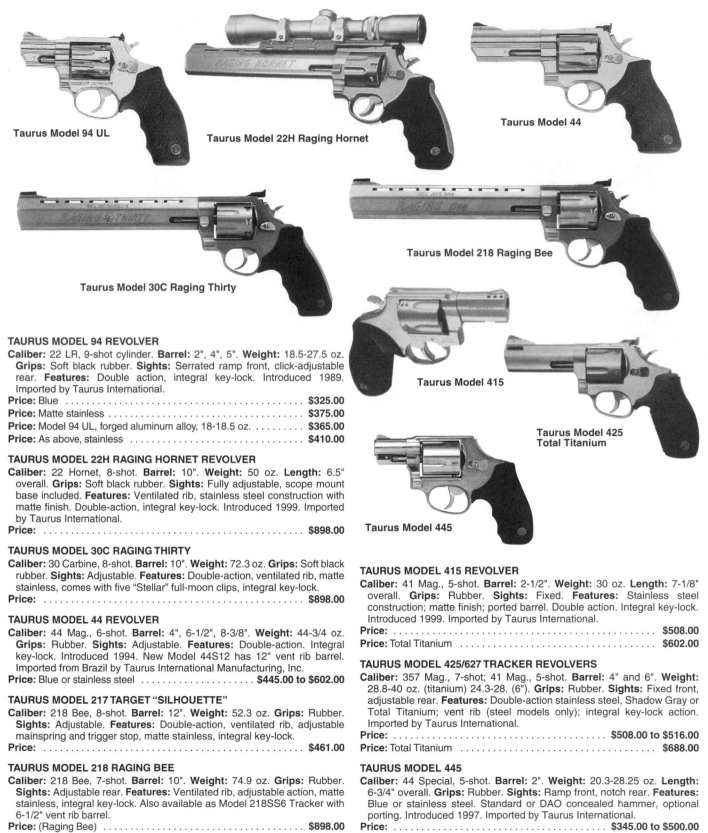

Taurus Model 94 UL

Taurus Model 22H Raging Hornet

Taurus Model 44

Taurus Model 30C Raging Thirty

Taurus Model 218 Raging Bee

Taurus Model 415

Taurus Model 425 Total Titanium

Taurus Model 445

TAURUS MODEL 94 REVOLVER

Caliber: 22 LR, 9-shot cylinder. **Barrel:** 2", 4", 5". **Weight:** 18.5-27.5 oz. **Grips:** Soft black rubber. **Sights:** Serrated ramp front, click-adjustable rear. **Features:** Double action, integral key-lock. Introduced 1989. Imported by Taurus International.

Price: Blue **$325.00**
Price: Matte stainless **$375.00**
Price: Model 94 UL, forged aluminum alloy, 18-18.5 oz. **$365.00**
Price: As above, stainless **$410.00**

TAURUS MODEL 22H RAGING HORNET REVOLVER

Caliber: 22 Hornet, 8-shot. **Barrel:** 10". **Weight:** 50 oz. **Length:** 6.5" overall. **Grips:** Soft black rubber. **Sights:** Fully adjustable, scope mount base included. **Features:** Ventilated rib, stainless steel construction with matte finish. Double-action, integral key-lock. Introduced 1999. Imported by Taurus International.

Price: **$898.00**

TAURUS MODEL 30C RAGING THIRTY

Caliber: 30 Carbine, 8-shot. **Barrel:** 10". **Weight:** 72.3 oz. **Grips:** Soft black rubber. **Sights:** Adjustable. **Features:** Double-action, ventilated rib, matte stainless, comes with five "Stellar" full-moon clips, integral key-lock.

Price: **$898.00**

TAURUS MODEL 44 REVOLVER

Caliber: 44 Mag., 6-shot. **Barrel:** 4", 6-1/2", 8-3/8". **Weight:** 44-3/4 oz. **Grips:** Rubber. **Sights:** Adjustable. **Features:** Double-action. Integral key-lock. Introduced 1994. New Model 44S12 has 12" vent rib barrel. Imported from Brazil by Taurus International Manufacturing, Inc.

Price: Blue or stainless steel . . . . **$445.00 to $602.00**

TAURUS MODEL 217 TARGET "SILHOUETTE"

Caliber: 218 Bee, 8-shot. **Barrel:** 12". **Weight:** 52.3 oz. **Grips:** Rubber. **Sights:** Adjustable. **Features:** Double-action, ventilated rib, adjustable mainspring and trigger stop, matte stainless, integral key-lock.

Price: **$461.00**

TAURUS MODEL 218 RAGING BEE

Caliber: 218 Bee, 7-shot. **Barrel:** 10". **Weight:** 74.9 oz. **Grips:** Rubber. **Sights:** Adjustable rear. **Features:** Ventilated rib, adjustable action, matte stainless, integral key-lock. Also available as Model 218SS6 Tracker with 6-1/2" vent rib barrel.

Price: (Raging Bee) **$898.00**
Price: (Tracker) **$406.00**

TAURUS MODEL 415 REVOLVER

Caliber: 41 Mag., 5-shot. **Barrel:** 2-1/2". **Weight:** 30 oz. **Length:** 7-1/8" overall. **Grips:** Rubber. **Sights:** Fixed. **Features:** Stainless steel construction; matte finish; ported barrel. Double action. Integral key-lock. Introduced 1999. Imported by Taurus International.

Price: **$508.00**
Price: Total Titanium **$602.00**

TAURUS MODEL 425/627 TRACKER REVOLVERS

Caliber: 357 Mag., 7-shot; 41 Mag., 5-shot. **Barrel:** 4" and 6". **Weight:** 28.8-40 oz. (titanium) 24.3-28. (6"). **Grips:** Rubber. **Sights:** Fixed front, adjustable rear. **Features:** Double-action stainless steel, Shadow Gray or Total Titanium; vent rib (steel models only); integral key-lock action. Imported by Taurus International.

Price: . . . . **$508.00 to $516.00**
Price: Total Titanium **$688.00**

TAURUS MODEL 445

Caliber: 44 Special, 5-shot. **Barrel:** 2". **Weight:** 20.3-28.25 oz. **Length:** 6-3/4" overall. **Grips:** Rubber. **Sights:** Ramp front, notch rear. **Features:** Blue or stainless steel. Standard or DAO concealed hammer, optional porting. Introduced 1997. Imported by Taurus International.

Price: . . . . **$345.00 to $500.00**
Price: Total Titanium 19.8 oz. **$600.00**

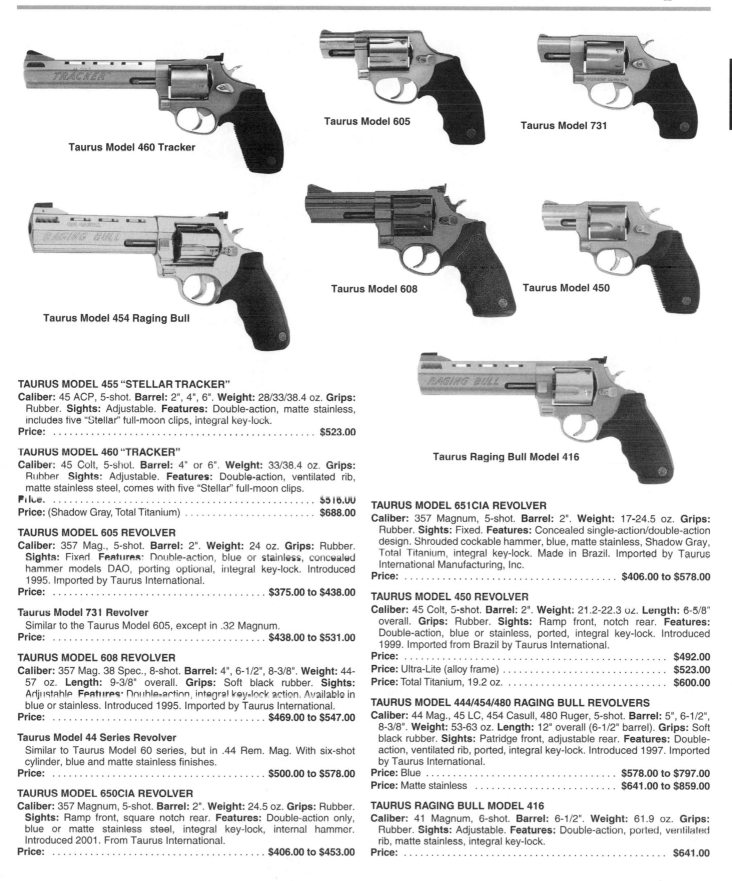

Taurus Model 460 Tracker

Taurus Model 605

Taurus Model 731

Taurus Model 454 Raging Bull

Taurus Model 608

Taurus Model 450

Taurus Raging Bull Model 416

TAURUS MODEL 455 "STELLAR TRACKER"

Caliber: 45 ACP, 5-shot. Barrel: 2", 4", 6". Weight: 28/33/38.4 oz. Grips: Rubber. Sights: Adjustable. Features: Double-action, matte stainless, includes five "Stellar" full-moon clips, integral key-lock.
Price: $523.00

TAURUS MODEL 460 "TRACKER"

Caliber: 45 Colt, 5-shot. Barrel: 4" or 6". Weight: 33/38.4 oz. Grips: Rubber. Sights: Adjustable. Features: Double-action, ventilated rib, matte stainless steel, comes with five "Stellar" full-moon clips.
Price. $516.00
Price: (Shadow Gray, Total Titanium) $688.00

TAURUS MODEL 605 REVOLVER

Caliber: 357 Mag., 5-shot. Barrel: 2". Weight: 24 oz. Grips: Rubber. Sights: Fixed. Features: Double-action, blue or stainless, concealed hammer models DAO, porting optional, integral key-lock. Introduced 1995. Imported by Taurus International.
Price: . . . . $375.00 to $438.00

Taurus Model 731 Revolver

Similar to the Taurus Model 605, except in .32 Magnum.
Price: . . . . $438.00 to $531.00

TAURUS MODEL 608 REVOLVER

Caliber: 357 Mag. 38 Spec., 8-shot. Barrel: 4", 6-1/2", 8-3/8". Weight: 44-57 oz. Length: 9-3/8" overall. Grips: Soft black rubber. Sights: Adjustable. Features: Double-action, integral key-lock action. Available in blue or stainless. Introduced 1995. Imported by Taurus International.
Price: . . . . $469.00 to $547.00

Taurus Model 44 Series Revolver

Similar to Taurus Model 60 series, but in .44 Rem. Mag. With six-shot cylinder, blue and matte stainless finishes.
Price: . . . . $500.00 to $578.00

TAURUS MODEL 650CIA REVOLVER

Caliber: 357 Magnum, 5-shot. Barrel: 2". Weight: 24.5 oz. Grips: Rubber. Sights: Ramp front, square notch rear. Features: Double-action only, blue or matte stainless steel, integral key-lock, internal hammer. Introduced 2001. From Taurus International.
Price: . . . . $406.00 to $453.00

TAURUS MODEL 651CIA REVOLVER

Caliber: 357 Magnum, 5-shot. Barrel: 2". Weight: 17-24.5 oz. Grips: Rubber. Sights: Fixed. Features: Concealed single-action/double-action design. Shrouded cockable hammer, blue, matte stainless, Shadow Gray, Total Titanium, integral key-lock. Made in Brazil. Imported by Taurus International Manufacturing, Inc.
Price: . . . . $406.00 to $578.00

TAURUS MODEL 450 REVOLVER

Caliber: 45 Colt, 5-shot. Barrel: 2". Weight: 21.2-22.3 oz. Length: 6-5/8" overall. Grips: Rubber. Sights: Ramp front, notch rear. Features: Double-action, blue or stainless, ported, integral key-lock. Introduced 1999. Imported from Brazil by Taurus International.
Price: $492.00
Price: Ultra-Lite (alloy frame) $523.00
Price: Total Titanium, 19.2 oz. $600.00

TAURUS MODEL 444/454/480 RAGING BULL REVOLVERS

Caliber: 44 Mag., 45 LC, 454 Casull, 480 Ruger, 5-shot. Barrel: 5", 6-1/2", 8-3/8". Weight: 53-63 oz. Length: 12" overall (6-1/2" barrel). Grips: Soft black rubber. Sights: Patridge front, adjustable rear. Features: Double-action, ventilated rib, ported, integral key-lock. Introduced 1997. Imported by Taurus International.
Price: Blue . . . . $578.00 to $797.00
Price: Matte stainless . . . . $641.00 to $859.00

TAURUS RAGING BULL MODEL 416

Caliber: 41 Magnum, 6-shot. Barrel: 6-1/2". Weight: 61.9 oz. Grips: Rubber. Sights: Adjustable. Features: Double-action, ported, ventilated rib, matte stainless, integral key-lock.
Price: $641.00

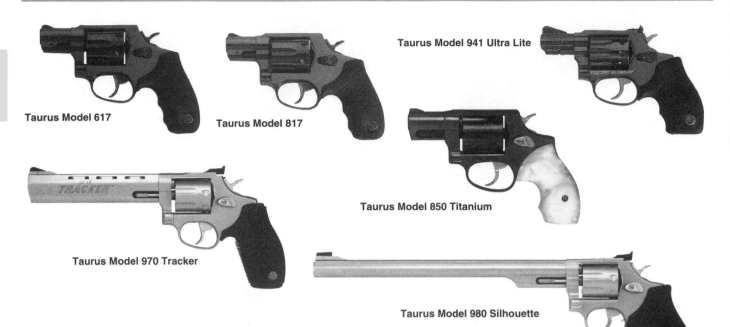

Taurus Model 617

Taurus Model 817

Taurus Model 941 Ultra Lite

Taurus Model 970 Tracker

Taurus Model 850 Titanium

Taurus Model 980 Silhouette

Taurus Model 905

TAURUS MODEL 617 REVOLVER
Caliber: 357 Magnum, 7-shot. **Barrel:** 2". **Weight:** 28.3 oz. **Length:** 6-3/4" overall. **Grips:** Soft black rubber. **Sights:** Fixed. **Features:** Double-action, blue, Shadow Gray, bright spectrum blue or matte stainless steel, integral key-lock. Available with porting, concealed hammer. Introduced 1998. Imported by Taurus International.
Price: . . . . **$391.00 to $453.00**
Price: Total Titanium, 19.9 oz. **$602.00**

Taurus Model 445 Series Revolver
Similar to Taurus Model 617 series except in 44 Spl. with 5-shot cylinder.
Price: . . . . **$389.00 to $422.00**

Taurus Model 617ULT Revolver
Similar to Model 617 except aluminum alloy and titanium components, matte stainless finish, integral key-lock action. Weighs 18.5 oz. Available ported or non-ported. Introduced 2001. Imported by Taurus International.
Price: (5-shot cylinder) . . . . **$530.00 to $545.00**

TAURUS MODEL 817 ULTRA-LITE REVOLVER
Caliber: 38 Spec., 7-shot. **Barrel:** 2". **Weight:** 21 oz. **Length:** 6-1/2" overall. **Grips:** Soft rubber. **Sights:** Fixed. **Features:** Double-action, integral key-lock. Rated for +P ammo. Introduced 1999. Imported from Brazil by Taurus International.
Price: Blue **$375.00**
Price: Blue, ported **$395.00**
Price: Matte, stainless **$420.00**
Price: Matte, stainless, ported **$440.00**

TAURUS MODEL 850CIA REVOLVER
Caliber: 38 Special, 5-shot. **Barrel:** 2". **Weight:** 17-24.5 oz. **Grips:** Rubber, mother-of-pearl. **Sights:** Ramp front, square notch rear. **Features:** Double-action only, blue or matte stainless steel, rated for +P ammo, integral key-lock, internal hammer. Introduced 2001. From Taurus International.
Price: . . . . **$406.00 to $453.00**
Price: Total Titanium **$578.00**

TAURUS MODEL 851CIA REVOLVER
Caliber: 38 Spec., 5-shot. **Barrel:** 2". **Weight:** 17-24.5 oz. **Grips:** Rubber. **Sights:** Fixed-UL/ULT adjustable. **Features:** Concealed single-action/double-action design. Shrouded cockable hammer, blue, matte stainless, Total Titanium, blue or stainless UL and ULT, integral key-lock. Rated for +P ammo.
Price: . . . . **$406.00 to $578.00**

TAURUS MODEL 94, 941 REVOLVER
Caliber: 22 LR (Mod. 94), 22 WMR (Mod. 941), 8-shot. **Barrel:** 2", 4", 5". **Weight:** 27.5 oz. (4" barrel). **Grips:** Soft black rubber. **Sights:** Serrated ramp front, rear adjustable. **Features:** Double-action, integral key-lock. Introduced 1992. Imported by Taurus International.
Price: Blue . . . . **$328.00 to $344.00**
Price: Stainless (matte) . . . . **$375.00 to $391.00**
Price: Model 941 Ultra Lite, forged aluminum alloy, 2" . **$359.00 to $375.00**
Price: As above, stainless . . . . **$406.00 to $422.00**

TAURUS MODEL 970/971 TRACKER REVOLVERS
Caliber: 22 LR (Model 970), 22 Magnum (Model 971); 7-shot. **Barrel:** 6". **Weight:** 53.6 oz. **Grips:** Rubber. **Sights:** Adjustable. **Features:** Double barrel, heavy barrel with ventilated rib; matte stainless finish, integral key-lock. Introduced 2001. From Taurus International.
Price: . . . . **$391.00 to $406.00**

TAURUS MODEL 980/981 SILHOUETTE REVOLVERS
Caliber: 22 LR (Model 980), 22 Magnum (Model 981); 7-shot. **Barrel:** 12". **Weight:** 68 oz. **Grips:** Rubber. **Sights:** Adjustable. **Features:** Double-action, heavy barrel with ventilated rib and scope mount, matte stainless finish, integral key-lock. Introduced 2001. From Taurus International.
Price: (Model 980) **$398.00**
Price: (Model 981) **$414.00**

TAURUS MODEL 905, 405, 455 PISTOL CALIBER REVOLVERS
Caliber: 9mm, .40, .45 ACP, 5-shot. **Barrel:** 2", 4", 6-1/2". **Weight:** 21 oz. to 40.8 oz. **Grips:** Rubber. **Sights:** Fixed, adjustable on Model 455SS6 in .45 ACP. **Features:** Produced as a backup gun for law enforcement officers. Introduced 2003. Imported from Brazil by Taurus International.
Price: . . . . **$383.00 to $523.00**

Both classic six-shooters and modern adaptations for hunting and sport.

Century Model 100

Cimarron Lightning

Cimarron Model P
New Sheriff

Cimarron Bisley

Cimarron Model P Jr.

Cimarron USV

Cimarron Open Top

CENTURY GUN DIST. MODEL 100 SINGLE-ACTION

Caliber: 30-30, 375 Win., 444 Marlin, 45-70, 50-70. **Barrel:** 6-1/2" (standard), 8", 10". **Weight:** 6 lbs. (loaded). **Length:** 15" overall (8" bbl). **Grips:** Smooth walnut. **Sights:** Ramp front, Millett adjustable square notch rear. **Features:** Highly polished high tensile strength manganese bronze frame, blue cylinder and barrel; coil spring trigger mechanism. Introduced 1975. Made in U.S.A. From Century Gun Dist., Inc.
Price: 6-1/2" barrel, 45-70 . . . . **$2,000.00**

CIMARRON LIGHTNING SA

Caliber: 32-20, 32 H&R, 38 Colt, 38 Special. **Barrel:** 3-1/2", 4-3/4", 5-1/2". **Grips:** Smooth or checkered walnut. **Sights:** Blade front. **Features:** Replica of the Colt 1877 Lightning DA. Similar to Cimarron Thunderer™, except smaller grip frame to fit smaller hands. Standard blue, charcoal blue or nickel finish with forged, old model, or color case hardened frame. Introduced 2001. From Cimarron F.A. Co.
Price: . . . . **$499.00 to $559.00**

CIMARRON MODEL P

Caliber: 32 WCF, 38 WCF, 357 Mag., 44 WCF, 44 Spec., 45 Colt, 45LC and 45 ACP. **Barrel:** 4-3/4", 5-1/2", 7-1/2". **Weight:** 39 oz. **Length:** 10" overall (4" barrel). **Grips:** Walnut. **Sights:** Blade front, fixed or adjustable rear. **Features:** Uses "old model" black powder frame with "Bullseye" ejector or New Model frame. Imported by Cimarron F.A. Co.
Price: . . . . **$499.00 to $559.00**
Price: New Sheriff . . . . **$499.00 to $559.00**

Cimarron Bisley Model Single-Action Revolvers

Similar to 1873 Model P, special grip frame and trigger guard, knurled wide-spur hammer, curved trigger. Available in 357 Mag., 44 WCF, 44 Spl., 45 Colt. Introduced 1999. Imported by Cimarron F.A. Co.
Price: **$525.00**

CIMARRON MODEL "P" JR.

Caliber: 32-20, 32 H&R, 38 Special. **Barrel:** 3-1/2", 4-3/4", 5-1/2". **Grips:** Checkered walnut. **Sights:** Blade front. **Features:** Styled after 1873 Colt Peacemaker, except 20 percent smaller. Blue finish with color case-hardened frame; Cowboy Comp® action. Introduced 2001. From Cimarron F.A. Co.
Price: . . . . **$489.00 to $529.00**

CIMARRON U. S. VOLUNTEER ARTILLERY MODEL SINGLE-ACTION

Caliber: 45 Colt. **Barrel:** 5-1/2". **Weight:** 39 oz. **Length:** 11-1/2" overall. **Grips:** Walnut. **Sights:** Fixed. **Features:** U.S. markings and cartouche, case-hardened frame and hammer; 45 Colt only. Imported by Cimarron F.A. Co.
Price: . . . . **$549.00 to $599.00**

CIMARRON 1872 OPEN TOP REVOLVER

Caliber: 38, 44 Special, 44 Colt, 44 Russian, 45LC, 45 S&W Schofield. **Barrel:** 5-1/2" and 7-1/2". **Grips:** Walnut. **Sights:** Blade front, fixed rear. **Features:** Replica of first cartridge-firing revolver. Blue, charcoal blue, nickel or Original® finish; Navy-style brass or steel Army-style frame. Introduced 2001 by Cimarron F.A. Co.
Price: . . . . **$529.00 to $599.00**

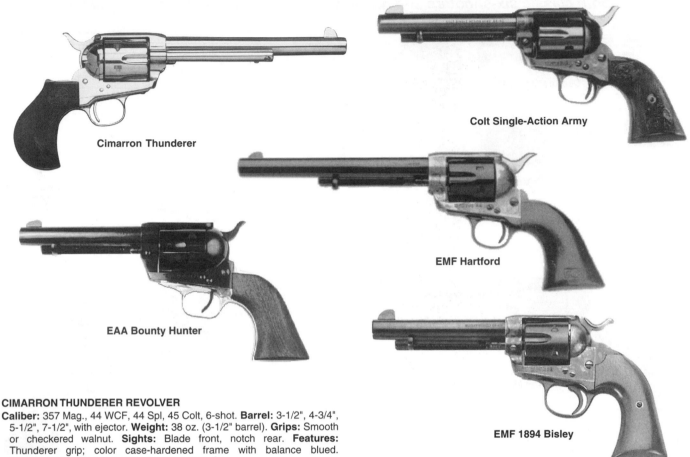

Cimarron Thunderer

Colt Single-Action Army

EMF Hartford

EAA Bounty Hunter

EMF 1894 Bisley

CIMARRON THUNDERER REVOLVER

Caliber: 357 Mag., 44 WCF, 44 Spl, 45 Colt, 6-shot. **Barrel:** 3-1/2", 4-3/4", 5-1/2", 7-1/2", with ejector. **Weight:** 38 oz. (3-1/2" barrel). **Grips:** Smooth or checkered walnut. **Sights:** Blade front, notch rear. **Features:** Thunderer grip; color case-hardened frame with balance blued. Introduced 1993. Imported by Cimarron F.A. Co.

Price: 3-1/2", 4-3/4", smooth grips	**$519.00 to $549.00**
Price: As above, checkered grips	**$564.00 to $584.00**
Price: 5-1/2", 7-1/2", smooth grips	**$519.00 to $549.00**
Price: As above, checkered grips	**$564.00 to $584.00**

COLT SINGLE-ACTION ARMY REVOLVER

Caliber: 357 Mag., 38 Special, .32/20, 44-40, 45 Colt, 6-shot. **Barrel:** 4-3/4", 5-1/2", 7-1/2". **Weight:** 40 oz. (4-3/4" barrel). **Length:** 10-1/4" overall (4-3/4" barrel). **Grips:** Black Eagle composite. **Sights:** Blade front, notch rear. **Features:** Available in full nickel finish with nickel grip medallions, or Royal Blue with color case-hardened frame. Reintroduced 1992.

Price: .... **$1,380.00 to $1,500.00**

EAA BOUNTY HUNTER SA REVOLVERS

Caliber: 22 LR/22 WMR, 357 Mag., 44 Mag., 45 Colt, 6-shot. **Barrel:** 4-1/2", 7-1/2". **Weight:** 2.5 lbs. **Length:** 11" overall (4-5/8" barrel). **Grips:** Smooth walnut. **Sights:** Blade front, grooved topstrap rear. **Features:** Transfer bar safety; 3-position hammer; hammer forged barrel. Introduced 1992. Imported by European American Armory.

Price: Blue or case-hardened	**$369.00**
Price: Nickel	**$399.00**
Price: 22LR/22WMR, blue	**$269.00**
Price: As above, nickel	**$299.00**

EMF MODEL 1873 FRONTIER MARSHAL

Caliber: 357 Mag., 45 Colt. **Barrel:** 4-3/4", 5-1/2, 7-1/2". **Weight:** 39 oz. **Length:** 10-1/2" overall. **Grips:** One-piece walnut. **Sights:** Blade front, notch rear. **Features:** Bright brass trigger guard and backstrap, color case-hardened frame, blued barrel and cylinder. Introduced 1998. Imported from Italy by IAR, Inc.

Price: **$395.00**

EMF HARTFORD SINGLE-ACTION REVOLVERS

Caliber: 357 Mag., 32-20, 38-40, 44-40, 44 Spec., 45 Colt. **Barrel:** 4-3/4", 5-1/2", 7-1/2". **Weight:** 45 oz. **Length:** 13" overall (7-1/2" barrel). **Grips:** Smooth walnut. **Sights:** Blade front, fixed rear. **Features:** Identical to the original Colts with inspector cartouche on left grip, original patent dates and U.S. markings. All major parts serial numbered using original Colt-style lettering, numbering. Bullseye ejector head and color case-hardening on frame and hammer. Introduced 1990. From E.M.F.

Price:	**$500.00**
Price: Cavalry or Artillery	**$390.00**
Price: Nickel plated, add	**$125.00**
Price: Case-hardened New Model frame	**$365.00**

EMF 1894 Bisley Revolver

Similar to the Hartford single-action revolver except has special grip frame and trigger guard, wide spur hammer; available in 38-40 or 45 Colt, 4-3/4", 5-1/2" or 7-1/2" barrel. Introduced 1995. Imported by E.M.F.

Price: Case-hardened/blue	**$400.00**
Price: Nickel	**$525.00**

EMF Hartford Pinkerton Single-Action Revolver

Same as the regular Hartford except has 4" barrel with ejector tube and bird's-head grip. Calibers: 357 Mag., 45 Colt. Introduced 1997. Imported by E.M.F.

Price: **$375.00**

EMF Hartford Express Single-Action Revolver

Same as the regular Hartford model except uses grip of the Colt Lightning revolver. Barrel lengths of 4", 4-3/4", 5-1/2". Introduced 1997. Imported by E.M.F.

Price: **$375.00**

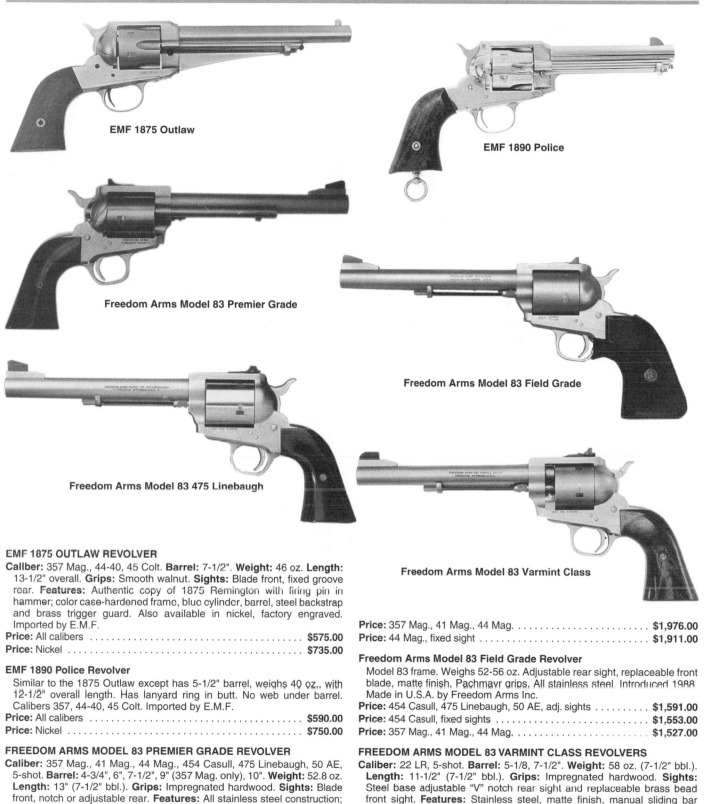

EMF 1875 Outlaw

EMF 1890 Police

Freedom Arms Model 83 Premier Grade

Freedom Arms Model 83 Field Grade

Freedom Arms Model 83 475 Linebaugh

Freedom Arms Model 83 Varmint Class

EMF 1875 OUTLAW REVOLVER
Caliber: 357 Mag., 44-40, 45 Colt. **Barrel:** 7-1/2". **Weight:** 46 oz. **Length:** 13-1/2" overall. **Grips:** Smooth walnut. **Sights:** Blade front, fixed groove rear. **Features:** Authentic copy of 1875 Remington with firing pin in hammer; color case-hardened frame, blue cylinder, barrel, steel backstrap and brass trigger guard. Also available in nickel, factory engraved. Imported by E.M.F.
Price: All calibers **$575.00**
Price: Nickel **$735.00**

EMF 1890 POLICE REVOLVER
Similar to the 1875 Outlaw except has 5-1/2" barrel, weighs 40 oz., with 12-1/2" overall length. Has lanyard ring in butt. No web under barrel. Calibers 357, 44-40, 45 Colt. Imported by E.M.F.
Price: All calibers **$590.00**
Price: Nickel **$750.00**

FREEDOM ARMS MODEL 83 PREMIER GRADE REVOLVER
Caliber: 357 Mag., 41 Mag., 44 Mag., 454 Casull, 475 Linebaugh, 50 AE, 5-shot. **Barrel:** 4-3/4", 6", 7-1/2", 9" (357 Mag. only), 10". **Weight:** 52.8 oz. **Length:** 13" (7-1/2" bbl.). **Grips:** Impregnated hardwood. **Sights:** Blade front, notch or adjustable rear. **Features:** All stainless steel construction; sliding bar safety system. Lifetime warranty. Made in U.S.A. by Freedom Arms, Inc.
Price: 454 Casull, 475 Linebaugh, 50 AE. **$2,058.00**
Price: 454 Casull, fixed sight **$1,979.00**

Price: 357 Mag., 41 Mag., 44 Mag. **$1,976.00**
Price: 44 Mag., fixed sight **$1,911.00**

Freedom Arms Model 83 Field Grade Revolver
Model 83 frame. Weighs 52-56 oz. Adjustable rear sight, replaceable front blade, matte finish, Pachmayr grips. All stainless steel. Introduced 1988. Made in U.S.A. by Freedom Arms Inc.
Price: 454 Casull, 475 Linebaugh, 50 AE, adj. sights **$1,591.00**
Price: 454 Casull, fixed sights **$1,553.00**
Price: 357 Mag., 41 Mag., 44 Mag. **$1,527.00**

FREEDOM ARMS MODEL 83 VARMINT CLASS REVOLVERS
Caliber: 22 LR, 5-shot. **Barrel:** 5-1/8, 7-1/2". **Weight:** 58 oz. (7-1/2" bbl.). **Length:** 11-1/2" (7-1/2" bbl.). **Grips:** Impregnated hardwood. **Sights:** Steel base adjustable "V" notch rear sight and replaceable brass bead front sight. **Features:** Stainless steel, matte finish, manual sliding bar system, dual firing pins, pre-set trigger stop. Made in U.S.A. by Freedom Arms, Inc.
Price: Varmint Class **$1,828.00**
Price: Extra fitted 22 WMR cylinder **$264.00**

Freedom Arms Model 97 Premier Grade

Heritage Rough Rider

Magnum Research Long Cylinder BFR

Navy Arms Flat Top

Navy Arms Bisley

FREEDOM ARMS MODEL 97 PREMIER GRADE REVOLVER
Caliber: 22 LR, 357 Mag., 41 Mag., 44 Special, 45 Colt, 5-shot. **Barrel:** 4-1/2", 5-1/2", 7-1/2", 10". **Weight:** 37 oz. (45 Colt 5-1/2"). **Length:** 10-3/4" (5-1/2" bbl.). **Grips:** Impregnated hardwood. **Sights:** Adjustable rear, replaceable blade front. **Features:** Stainless steel, brushed finish, automatic transfer bar safety system. Introduced in 1997. Made in U.S.A. by Freedom Arms.

Price: 357 Mag., 41 Mag., 45 Colt **$1,668.00**
Price: 357 Mag., 45 Colt, fixed sight **$1,576.00**
Price: Extra fitted cylinders 38 Special, 45 ACP **$264.00**
Price: 22 LR with sporting chambers **$1,732.00**
Price: Extra fitted 22 WMR cylinder **$264.00**
Price: Extra fitted 22 LR match grade cylinder **$476.00**
Price: 22 match grade chamber instead of 22 LR sport chamber . . **$214.00**

HERITAGE ROUGH RIDER REVOLVER
Caliber: 17HMR, 17LR, 32 H&R, 32 S&W, 32 S&W Long, .45LC, 22 LR, 22 LR/22 WMR combo, 6-shot. **Barrel:** 2-3/4", 3-1/2", 4-3/4", 6-1/2", 9". **Weight:** 31 to 38 oz. **Length:** NA. **Grips:** Exotic hardwood, laminated wood or mother-of-pearl; bird's-head models offered. **Sights:** Blade front, fixed rear. Adjustable sight on 4", 6" and 9" models. **Features:** Hammer block safety. High polish blue, black satin, silver satin, case-hardened and nickel finish. Introduced 1993. Made in U.S.A. by Heritage Mfg., Inc.
Price: . . . . **$159.95 to $389.95**

MAGNUM RESEARCH BFR SINGLE-ACTION REVOLVER
(Long cylinder) Caliber: 30/30, 45/70 Government, 444 Marlin, 45 LC/410, 450 Marlin, .500 S&W. **Barrel:** 7.5", 10". **Weight:** 4 lbs., 4.36 lbs. **Length:** 15", 17.5".
(Short cylinder) Caliber: 50AE, 454 Casull, 22 Hornet, BFR 480/475. **Barrel:** 6.5", 7.5", 10". **Weight:** 3.2 lbs, 3.5 lbs., 4.36 lbs. (10"). **Length:** 12.75 (6"), 13.75", 16.25".
Sights: All have fully adjustable rear, black blade ramp front. **Features:** Stainless steel construction, rubber grips, all 5-shot capacity. Barrels are stress-relieved and cut rifled. Made in U.S.A. From Magnum Research, Inc.
Price: **$899.00**

NAVY ARMS FLAT TOP TARGET MODEL REVOLVER
Caliber: 45 Colt, 6-shot cylinder. **Barrel:** 7-1/2". **Weight:** 40 oz. **Length:** 13-1/4" overall. **Grips:** Smooth walnut. **Sights:** Spring-loaded German silver front, rear adjustable for windage. **Features:** Replica of Colt's Flat Top Frontier target revolver made from 1888 to 1896. Blue with color case-hardened frame. Introduced 1997. Imported by Navy Arms.
Price: **$450.00**

NAVY ARMS BISLEY MODEL SINGLE-ACTION REVOLVER
Caliber: 44-40 or 45 Colt, 6-shot cylinder. **Barrel:** 4-3/4", 5-1/2", 7-1/2". **Weight:** 40 oz. **Length:** 12-1/2" overall (7-1/2" barrel). **Grips:** Smooth walnut. **Sights:** Blade front, notch rear. **Features:** Replica of Colt's Bisley Model. Polished blue finish, color case-hardened frame. Introduced 1997. Imported by Navy Arms.
Price: . . . . **$425.00 to $460.00**

Navy Arms 1873

Navy Arms 1875 Schofield

North American Mini

North American Mini-Master

Navy Arms New Model Russian

North American Black Widow

NAVY ARMS 1873 SINGLE-ACTION REVOLVER
Caliber: 357 Mag., 44-40, 45 Colt, 6-shot cylinder. **Barrel:** 4-3/4", 5-1/2", 7-1/2". **Weight:** 36 oz. **Length:** 10-3/4" overall (5-1/2" barrel). **Grips:** Smooth walnut. **Sights:** Blade front, notch rear. **Features:** Blue with color case-hardened frame. Introduced 1991. Imported by Navy Arms.
Price. **$405.00**

NAVY ARMS 1875 SCHOFIELD REVOLVER
Caliber: 44-40, 45 Colt, 6-shot cylinder. **Barrel:** 3-1/2", 5", 7". **Weight:** 39 oz. **Length:** 10-3/4" overall (5" barrel). **Grips:** Smooth walnut. **Sights:** Blade front, notch rear. **Features:** Replica of Smith & Wesson Model 3 Schofield. Single-action, top-break with automatic ejection. Polished blue finish. Introduced 1994. Imported by Navy Arms.
Price: Hideout Model, 3-1/2" barrel **$695.00**
Price: Wells Fargo, 5" barrel **$695.00**
Price: U.S. Cavalry model, 7" barrel, military markings **$695.00**

NAVY ARMS NEW MODEL RUSSIAN REVOLVER
Caliber: 44 Russian, 6-shot cylinder. **Barrel:** 6-1/2". **Weight:** 40 oz. **Length:** 12" overall. **Grips:** Smooth walnut. **Sights:** Blade front, notch rear. **Features:** Replica of the S&W Model 3 Russian Third Model revolver. Spur trigger guard, polished blue finish. Introduced 1999. Imported by Navy Arms.
Price: **$769.00**

NAVY ARMS 1851 NAVY CONVERSION REVOLVER
Caliber: 38 Spec., 38 Long Colt. **Barrel:** 5-1/2", 7-1/2". **Weight:** 44 oz. **Length:** 14" overall (7-1/2" barrel). **Grips:** Smooth walnut. **Sights:** Bead front, notch rear. **Features:** Replica of Colt's cartridge conversion revolver. Polished blue finish with color case-hardened frame, silver plated trigger guard and backstrap. Introduced 1999. Imported by Navy Arms.
Price: **$165.00**

NAVY ARMS 1860 ARMY CONVERSION REVOLVER
Caliber: 38 Spec., 38 Long Colt. **Barrel:** 5-1/2", 7-1/2". **Weight:** 44 oz. **Length:** 13-1/2" overall (7-1/2" barrel). **Grips:** Smooth walnut. **Sights:**

Blade front, notch rear. **Features:** Replica of Colt's conversion revolver. Polished blue finish with color case-hardened frame, full-size 1860 Army grip with blued steel backstrap. Introduced 1999. Imported by Navy Arms.
Price: **$190.00**

NORTH AMERICAN MINI REVOLVERS
Caliber: 22 Short, 22 LR, 22 WMR, 5-shot. **Barrel:** 1-1/8", 1-5/8". **Weight:** 4 to 6.6 oz. **Length:** 3-5/8" to 6-1/8" overall. **Grips:** Laminated wood. **Sights:** Blade front, notch fixed rear. **Features:** All stainless steel construction. Polished satin and matte finish. Engraved models available. From North American Arms.
Price: 22 Short, 22 LR **$193.00**
Price: 22 WMR, 1-1/8" or 1-5/8" bbl. **$193.00**
Price: 22 WMR, 1-1/8" or 1-5/8" bbl. with extra 22 LR cylinder **$193.00**

NORTH AMERICAN MINI-MASTER
Caliber: 22 LR, 22 WMR, 17 HMR, 5-shot cylinder. **Barrel:** 4". **Weight:** 10.7 oz. **Length:** 7.75" overall. **Grips:** Checkered hard black rubber. **Sights:** Blade front, white outline rear adjustable for elevation, or fixed. **Features:** Heavy vented barrel; full-size grips. Non-fluted cylinder. Introduced 1989.
Price: Adjustable sight, 22 WMR, 17 HMR or 22 LR **$301.00**
Price: As above with extra WMR/LR cylinder **$330.00**
Price: Fixed sight, 22 WMR, 17 HMR or 22 LR **$272.00**
Price: As above with extra WMR/LR cylinder **$330.00**

North American Black Widow Revolver
Similar to Mini-Master, 2" heavy vent barrel. Built on 22 WMR frame. Non-fluted cylinder, black rubber grips. Available with Millett Low Profile fixed sights or Millett sight adjustable for elevation only. Overall length 5-7/8", weighs 8.8 oz. From North American Arms.
Price: Adjustable sight, 22 LR, 17 HMR or 22 WMR **$287.00**
Price: As above with extra WMR/LR cylinder **$316.00**
Price: Fixed sight, 22 LR, 17 HMR or 22 WMR **$287.00**
Price: As above with extra WMR/LR cylinder **$287.00**

Ruger "Bird's-Head" Single Six

Ruger SSMBH-4F

Ruger Blackhawk

Ruger Bisley Single-Action

Ruger Super Blackhawk Hunter

Ruger Vaquero

RUGER NEW MODEL SINGLE SIX REVOLVER

Caliber: 32 H&R. **Barrel:** 4-5/8", 6-shot. **Grips:** Black Micarta "bird's-head", rosewood with color case. **Sights:** Fixed. **Features:** High impact case, gun lock standard.
Price: Stainless, KSSMBH-4F, bird's-head **$576.00**
Price: Color case, SSMBH-4F, bird's-head **$576.00**
Price: Color case, SSM-4F-S, rosewood **$576.00**

RUGER NEW MODEL BLACKHAWK AND BLACKHAWK CONVERTIBLE

Caliber: 30 Carbine, 357 Mag./38 Spec., 41 Mag., 45 Colt, 6-shot. **Barrel:** 4-5/8" or 5-1/2", either caliber; 7-1/2" (30 carbine and 45 Colt). **Weight:** 42 oz. (6-1/2" bbl.). **Length:** 12-1/4" overall (5-1/2" bbl.). **Grips:** American walnut. **Sights:** 1/8" ramp front, micro-click rear adjustable for windage and elevation. **Features:** Ruger transfer bar safety system, independent firing pin, hardened chrome-moly steel frame, music wire springs throughout. Case and lock included.
Price: Blue 30 Carbine, 7-1/2" (BN31) **$435.00**
Price: Blue, 357 Mag., 4-5/8", 6-1/2" (BN34, BN36) **$435.00**
Price: As above, stainless (KBN34, KBN36) **$530.00**
Price: Blue, 357 Mag./9mm Convertible, 4-5/8", 6-1/2"
(BN34X, BN36X) includes extra cylinder **$489.00**
Price: Blue, 41 Mag., 4-5/8", 6-1/2" (BN41, BN42) **$435.00**
Price: Blue, 45 Colt, 4-5/8", 5-1/2", 7-1/2" (BN44, BN455, BN45) .. **$435.00**
Price: Stainless, 45 Colt, 4-5/8", 7-1/2" (KBN44, KBN45) **$530.00**
Price: Blue, 45 Colt/45 ACP Convertible, 4-5/8", 5-1/2"
(BN44X, BN455X) includes extra cylinder **$489.00**

Ruger Bisley Single-Action Revolver

Similar to standard Blackhawk, hammer is lower with smoothly curved, deeply checkered wide spur. The trigger is strongly curved with wide smooth surface. Longer grip frame. Adjustable rear sight, ramp-style front. Unfluted cylinder and roll engraving, adjustable sights. Chambered for 357, 44 Mags. and 45 Colt; 7-1/2" barrel; overall length of 13"; weighs 48 oz. Plastic lockable case. Introduced 1985.
Price: RB-35W, 357Mag, RBD-44W, 44Mag, RB-45W, 45 Colt ... **$535.00**

RUGER NEW MODEL SUPER BLACKHAWK

Caliber: 44 Mag., 6-shot. Also fires 44 Spec. **Barrel:** 4-5/8", 5-1/2", 7-1/2", 10-1/2" bull. **Weight:** 48 oz. (7-1/2" bbl.), 51 oz. (10-1/2" bbl.). **Length:** 13-3/8" overall (7-1/2" bbl.). **Grips:** American walnut. **Sights:** 1/8" ramp front, micro-click rear adjustable for windage and elevation. **Features:** Ruger transfer bar safety system, fluted or unfluted cylinder, steel grip and

cylinder frame, round or square back trigger guard, wide serrated trigger, wide spur hammer. With case and lock.
Price: Blue, 4-5/8", 5-1/2", 7-1/2" (S458N, S45N, S47N) **$519.00**
Price: Blue, 10-1/2" bull barrel (S411N) **$529.00**
Price: Stainless, 4-5/8", 5-1/2", 7-1/2" (KS458N, KS45N, KS47N) . **$535.00**
Price: Stainless, 10-1/2" bull barrel (KS411N) **$545.00**

RUGER NEW MODEL SUPER BLACKHAWK HUNTER

Caliber: 44 Mag., 6-shot. **Barrel:** 7-1/2", full-length solid rib, unfluted cylinder. **Weight:** 52 oz. **Length:** 13-5/8". **Grips:** Black laminated wood. **Sights:** Adjustable rear, replaceable front blade. **Features:** Reintroduced Ultimate SA revolver. Includes instruction manual, high-impact case, set 1" medium scope rings, gun lock, ejector rod as standard.
Price: **$639.00**

RUGER VAQUERO SINGLE-ACTION REVOLVER

Caliber: 357 Mag., 44-40, 44 Mag., 45 LC, 6-shot. **Barrel:** 4-5/8", 5-1/2", 7-1/2". **Weight:** 38-41 oz. **Length:** 13-1/8" overall (7-1/2" barrel). **Grips:** Smooth rosewood with Ruger medallion. **Sights:** Blade front, fixed notch rear. **Features:** Transfer bar safety system and loading gate interlock. Blued model color case-hardened finish on frame, rest polished and blued. Stainless has high-gloss. Introduced 1993. From Sturm, Ruger & Co.
Price: 357 Mag. BNV34, KBNV34 (4-5/8"),
BNV35, KBNV35 (5-1/2") **$535.00**
Price: 44-40 BNV40, KBNV40 (4-5/8"). BNV405,
KBNV405 (5-1/2"). BNV407, KBNV407 (7-1/2") **$535.00**
Price: 44 Mag., BNV474, KBNV474 (4-5/8"). BNV475,
KBNV475 (5-1/2"). BNV477, KBNV477 (7-1/2") **$535.00**
Price: 45 LC, BN444, KBNV44 (4-5/8"). BNV455,
KBNV455 (5-1/2"). BNV45, KBNV45 (7-1/2") **$535.00**
Price: 45 LC, BNVBH453, KBNVBH453 3-3/4" with
"bird's-head" grip **$576.00**
Price: 357 Mag., RBNV35 (5-1/2") **$535.00**; KRBNV35 (5-1/2") .. **$555.00**
Price: 45 LC, RBNV44 (4-5/8"), RBNV455 (5-1/2") **$535.00**
Price: 45 LC, KRBNV44 (4-5/8"), KRBNV455 (5-1/2") **$555.00**

Ruger Bisley-Vaquero

Ruger New Bearcat

Ruger Single-Six

Ruger Super Single-Six

Ruger Bisley

Tristar Regulator

Ruger Bisley-Vaquero Single-Action Revolver

Similar to Vaquero model with Bisley-style hammer, grip and trigger, available in 357 Magnum, 44 Magnum and 45 LC only; 4-5/8" or 5-1/2" barrel. Smooth rosewood grips with Ruger medallion. Roll-engraved, unfluted cylinder. Introduced 1997. From Sturm, Ruger & Co.

Price: Color case-hardened frame, blue grip frame, barrel and cylinder, RBNV-475, RBNV-474, 44 Mag. **$535.00**
Price: High-gloss stainless steel, KRBNV-475, KRBNV-474 . . . . . . **$555.00**
Price: For simulated ivory grips, add . . . . **$41.00 to $44.00**

RUGER NEW BEARCAT SINGLE-ACTION

Caliber: 22 LR, 6-shot. **Barrel:** 4". **Weight:** 24 oz. **Length:** 8-7/8" overall. **Grips:** Smooth rosewood with Ruger medallion. **Sights:** Blade front, fixed notch rear. **Features:** Reintroduction of the Ruger Bearcat with slightly lengthened frame, Ruger patented transfer bar safety system. Available in blue only. Introduced 1993. With case and lock. From Sturm, Ruger & Co.

Price: SBC4, blue **$379.00**
Price: KSBC-4, ss **$429.00**

RUGER MODEL SINGLE-SIX REVOLVER

Caliber: 32 H&R Magnum. **Barrel:** 4-5/8", 6-shot. **Weight:** 33 oz. **Length:** 10-1/8". **Grips:** Blue, rosewood, stainless, simulated ivory. **Sights:** Blade front, notch rear fixed. **Features:** Transfer bar and loading gate interlock safety, instruction manual, high impact case and gun lock.

Price: **$576.00**
Price: Blue, SSM4FS **$576.00**
Price: SS, KSSM4FSI **$576.00**

RUGER SINGLE-SIX AND SUPER SINGLE-SIX CONVERTIBLE

Caliber: 22 LR, 6-shot; 22 WMR in extra cylinder; 17 HMR. **Barrel:** 4-5/8", 5-1/2", 6-1/2", 9-1/2" (6-groove). **Weight:** 35 oz. (6-1/2" bbl.). **Length:** 11-13/16" overall (6-1/2" bbl.). **Grips:** Smooth American walnut. **Sights:** Improved Patridge front on ramp, fully adjustable rear protected by integral frame ribs (super single-six); or fixed sight (single six). **Features:** Transfer bar safety system, loading gate interlock, hardened chrome-moly steel frame, wide trigger, music wire springs throughout, independent firing pin.

Price: 4-5/8", 5-1/2", 6-1/2", 9-1/2" barrel, blue,
adjustable sight NR4, NR5, NR6, NR9 . . . . **$399.00**
Price: 5-1/2", 6-1/2" bbl. only, stainless steel, adjustable sight
KNR5, KNR6 . . . . **$485.00**
Price: 5-1/2", 6-1/2" barrel, blue fixed sights **$399.00**
Price: 6-1/2" barrel, NR 617, 17 HMR **$399.00**
Price: Ruger 50th Anniversary Single Six with 4-5/8" barrel and a gold-colored rollmark, "50 years of Single Six 1953 to 2003," blued steel finish, cocobolo wood grips with red Ruger medallions and both 22 LR and 22 WMR cylinders **$599.00**
Price: Stainless Hunter **$650.00**

Ruger Bisley Small Frame Revolver

Similar to Single-Six, frame is styled after classic Bisley "flat-top." Hammer is lower and smoothly curved with deeply checkered spur. Trigger is strongly curved with wide smooth surface. Longer grip frame design, and trigger guard is a large oval. Adjustable dovetail rear sight; front sight base accepts interchangeable square blades. Unfluted cylinder and roll engraving. Weighs 41 oz. Chambered for 22 LR, 6-1/2" barrel only. Plastic lockable case. Introduced 1985.

Price: RB-22AW **$422.00**

TRISTAR/UBERTI REGULATOR REVOLVER

Caliber: 45 Colt. **Barrel:** 4-3/4", 5-1/2". **Weight:** 32-38 oz. **Length:** 8-1/4" overall (4-3/4" bbl.) **Grips:** One-piece walnut. **Sights:** Blade front, notch rear. **Features:** Uberti replica of 1873 Colt Model "P" revolver. Color-case hardened steel frame, brass backstrap and trigger guard, hammer-block safety. Imported from Italy by Tristar Sporting Arms.

Price: Regulator **$335.00**
Price: Regulator Deluxe (blued backstrap, trigger guard) **$367.00**

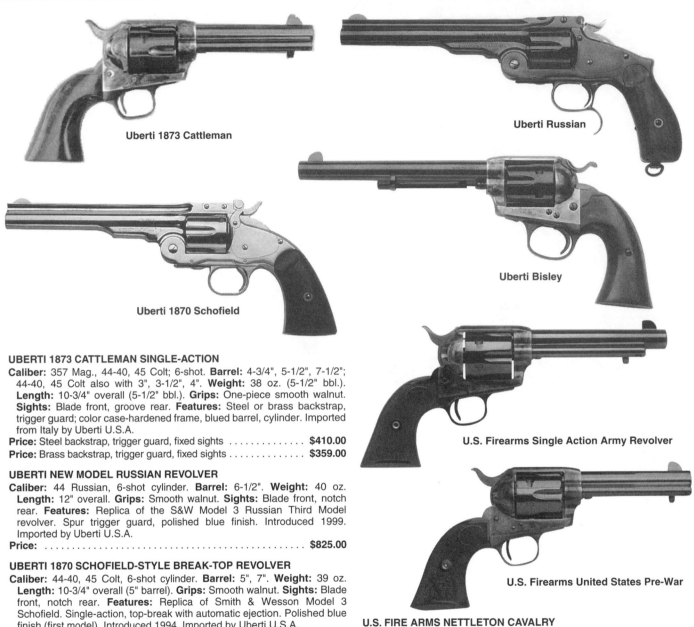

Uberti 1873 Cattleman

Uberti Russian

Uberti 1870 Schofield

Uberti Bisley

U.S. Firearms Single Action Army Revolver

U.S. Firearms United States Pre-War

UBERTI 1873 CATTLEMAN SINGLE-ACTION
Caliber: 357 Mag., 44-40, 45 Colt; 6-shot. **Barrel:** 4-3/4", 5-1/2", 7-1/2"; 44-40, 45 Colt also with 3", 3-1/2", 4". **Weight:** 38 oz. (5-1/2" bbl.). **Length:** 10-3/4" overall (5-1/2" bbl.). **Grips:** One-piece smooth walnut. **Sights:** Blade front, groove rear. **Features:** Steel or brass backstrap, trigger guard; color case-hardened frame, blued barrel, cylinder. Imported from Italy by Uberti U.S.A.
Price: Steel backstrap, trigger guard, fixed sights **$410.00**
Price: Brass backstrap, trigger guard, fixed sights **$359.00**

UBERTI NEW MODEL RUSSIAN REVOLVER
Caliber: 44 Russian, 6-shot cylinder. **Barrel:** 6-1/2". **Weight:** 40 oz. **Length:** 12" overall. **Grips:** Smooth walnut. **Sights:** Blade front, notch rear. **Features:** Replica of the S&W Model 3 Russian Third Model revolver. Spur trigger guard, polished blue finish. Introduced 1999. Imported by Uberti U.S.A.
Price: **$825.00**

UBERTI 1870 SCHOFIELD-STYLE BREAK-TOP REVOLVER
Caliber: 44-40, 45 Colt, 6-shot cylinder. **Barrel:** 5", 7". **Weight:** 39 oz. **Length:** 10-3/4" overall (5" barrel). **Grips:** Smooth walnut. **Sights:** Blade front, notch rear. **Features:** Replica of Smith & Wesson Model 3 Schofield. Single-action, top-break with automatic ejection. Polished blue finish (first model). Introduced 1994. Imported by Uberti U.S.A.
Price: **$775.00**

UBERTI BISLEY MODEL SINGLE-ACTION REVOLVER
Caliber: 357 Mag., 45 Colt, 6-shot cylinder. **Barrel:** 4-3/4", 5-1/2", 7-1/2". **Weight:** 40 oz. **Length:** 12-1/2" overall (7-1/2" barrel). **Grips:** Smooth walnut. **Sights:** Blade front, notch rear. **Features:** Replica of Colt's Bisley Model. Polished blue finish, color case-hardened frame. Introduced 1997. Imported by Uberti U.S.A.
Price: **$460.00**

U.S. FIRE ARMS SINGLE ACTION ARMY REVOLVER
Caliber: 45 Colt (standard); 32 WCF, 38 WCF, 38 S&W, 41 Colt, 44WCF, 44 S&W (optional, additional charge), 6-shot cylinder. **Barrel:** 4-3/4", 5-1/2", 7-1/2". **Weight:** 37 oz. **Length:** NA. **Grips:** Hard rubber. **Sights:** Blade front, notch rear. **Features:** Recreation of original guns; 3" and 4" have no ejector. Available with all-blue, blue with color case-hardening, or full nickel-plate finish. Made in U.S.A. by United States Fire Arms Mfg. Co.
Price: Blue/cased-colors **$949.00**
Price: Nickel **$1,220.00**

U.S. FIRE ARMS NETTLETON CAVALRY
Caliber: 45 Colt, 6-shot cylinder. **Barrel:** 5-1/2" (artillery model), 7-1/2". **Grips:** One-piece walnut. **Features:** Military armory blue and bone case finish. Made in U.S.A. by Fire Arms Mfg. Co.
Price: Blued finish **$1,485.00**
Price: Nickel finish **$1,619.00**

U.S. FIRE ARMS RODEO COWBOY ACTION REVOLVER
Caliber: 45 Colt. **Barrel:** 4-3/4", 5-1/2". **Grips:** Rubber. **Features:** Historically correct Armory bone case hammer, blue satin finish, transfer bar safety system, correct solid firing pin. Entry level basic cowboy SASS gun.
Price: **$649.00**

U.S. FIRE ARMS UNITED STATES PRE-WAR
Caliber: 45 Colt, other caliber available. **Barrel:** 4-3/4", 5-1/2", 7-1/2". **Grips:** Hard rubber. **Features:** Armory bone case/Armory blue finish standard, cross-pin or black powder frame. Introduced 2002. Made in U.S.A. by United States Firearms Mfg. Co.
Price: **$1,345.00**

Specially adapted single-shot and multi-barrel arms.

American Derringer Model 1

American Derringer Model 4

American Derringer Model 6

American Derringer Model 7

American Derringer Lady Derringer

American Derringer DA 38

AMERICAN DERRINGER MODEL 1

Caliber: 22 LR, 22 WMR, 30 Carbine, 30 Luger, 30-30 Win., 32 H&R Mag., 32-20, 380 ACP, 38 Super, 38 Spec., 38 Spec. shotshell, 38 Spec. +P, 9mm Para., 357 Mag., 357 Mag./45/410, 357 Maximum, 10mm, 40 S&W, 41 Mag., 38-40, 44-40 Win., 44 Spec., 44 Mag., 45 Colt, 45 Win. Mag., 45 ACP, 45 Colt/410, 45-70 single shot. **Barrel:** 3". **Weight:** 15-1/2 oz. (38 Spec.). **Length:** 4.82" overall. **Grips:** Rosewood, Zebra wood. **Sights:** Blade front. **Features:** Made of stainless steel with high-polish or satin finish. Two-shot capacity. Manual hammer block safety. Introduced 1980. Available in most pistol calibers. From American Derringer Corp.

Price: 22 LR	CALL
Price: 38 Spec.	CALL
Price: 357 Maximum	CALL
Price: 357 Mag.	CALL
Price: 9mm, 380	CALL
Price: 40 S&W	CALL
Price: 44 Spec.	CALL
Price: 44-40 Win.	CALL
Price: 45 Colt	CALL
Price: 30-30, 45 Win. Mag.	CALL
Price: 41, 44 Mags.	CALL
Price: 45-70, single shot	CALL
Price: 45 Colt, 410, 2-1/2"	CALL
Price: 45 ACP, 10mm Auto	CALL

American Derringer Model 4

Similar to the Model 1 except has 4.1" barrel, overall length of 6", and weighs 16-1/2 oz.; chambered for 357 Mag., 357 Maximum, 45-70, 3" 410-bore shotshells or 45 Colt or 44 Mag. Made of stainless steel. Manual hammer block safety. Introduced 1980.

Price: 3" 410/45 Colt	$425.00
Price: 45-70	$560.00
Price: 44 Mag. with oversize grips	$515.00
Price: Alaskan Survival model (45-70 upper barrel, 410 or 45 Colt lower)	$475.00

American Derringer Model 6

Similar to the Model 1 except has 6" barrel chambered for 3" 410 shotshells or 22 WMR, 357 Mag., 45 ACP, 45 Colt; rosewood stocks; 8.2" o.a.l. and weighs 21 oz. Manual hammer block safety. Introduced 1980.

Price: 22 WMR	$440.00
Price: 357 Mag.	$440.00
Price: 45 Colt/410	$450.00
Price: 45 ACP	$440.00

American Derringer Model 7 Ultra Lightweight

Similar to Model 1 except made of high strength aircraft aluminum. Weighs 7-1/2 oz., 4.82" o.a.l., rosewood stocks. Available in 22 LR, 22 WMR, 32 H&R Mag., 380 ACP, 38 Spec., 44 Spec. Introduced 1980.

Price: 22 LR, WMR	$325.00
Price: 38 Spec.	$325.00
Price: 380 ACP	$325.00
Price: 32 H&R Mag/32 S&W Long	$325.00
Price: 44 Spec.	$565.00

American Derringer Model 10 Ultra Lightweight

Similar to the Model 1 except frame is aluminum, giving weight of 10 oz. Stainless barrels. Available in 38 Spec., 45 Colt or 45 ACP only. Matte gray finish. Introduced 1980.

Price: 45 Colt	$385.00
Price: 45 ACP	$330.00
Price: 38 Spec.	$305.00

American Derringer Lady Derringer

Same as the Model 1 except has tuned action, is fitted with scrimshawed synthetic ivory grips; chambered for 32 H&R Mag. and 38 Spec.; 357 Mag., 45 Colt, 45/410. Deluxe Grade is highly polished; Deluxe Engraved is engraved in a pattern similar to that used on 1880s derringers. All models come in a French-fitted jewelry box. Introduced 1989.

Price: 32 H&R Mag.	$375.00
Price: 357 Mag.	$405.00
Price: 38 Spec.	$360.00
Price: 45 Colt, 45/410	$435.00

American Derringer Texas Commemorative

Model 1 Derringer with solid brass frame, stainless steel barrel and rosewood grips. Available in 38 Spec., 44-40 Win., or 45 Colt. Introduced 1980.

Price: 38 Spec.	$365.00
Price: 44-40	$420.00
Price: Brass frame, 45 Colt	$450.00

AMERICAN DERRINGER DA 38 MODEL

Caliber: 22 LR, 9mm Para., 38 Spec., 357 Mag., 40 S&W. **Barrel:** 3". **Weight:** 14.5 oz. **Length:** 4.8" overall. **Grips:** Rosewood, walnut or other hardwoods. **Sights:** Fixed. **Features:** Double-action only; two shots. Manual safety. Made of satin-finished stainless steel and aluminum. Introduced 1989. From American Derringer Corp.

Price: 22 LR	$435.00
Price: 38 Spec.	$460.00
Price: 9mm Para.	$445.00
Price: 357 Mag.	$450.00
Price: 40 S&W	$475.00

ANSCHUTZ MODEL 64P SPORT/TARGET PISTOL

Caliber: 22 LR, 22 WMR, 5-shot magazine. **Barrel:** 10". **Weight:** 3 lbs. 8 oz. **Length:** 18-1/2" overall. **Stock:** Choate Rynite. **Sights:** None furnished; grooved for scope mounting. **Features:** Right-hand bolt; polished blue finish. Introduced 1998. Imported from Germany by AcuSport.

Price: 22 LR	$455.95
Price: 22 WMR	$479.95

Bond Arms Texas Defender

Bond Arms Century 2000 Defender

Cobra Big Bore

Cobra D-Series

Comanche Super Single Shot

Gaucher GN1 Silhouette

Downsizer WSP Single Shot

BOND ARMS DEFENDER DERRINGER
Caliber: From 22 LR to 45 LC/410 shotshells **Barrel:** 3". **Weight:** 19-20 oz. **Grips:** Rosewood. **Sights:** Blade front, fixed rear. **Features:** Interchangeable barrels, stainless steel firing pins, cross-bolt safety, automatic extractor for rimmed calibers. Stainless steel construction. Right or left hand.
Price: Texas (with removable trigger guard) 3" bbl. $379.00

BOND ARMS CENTURY 200
Caliber: 45LC/410 shotshells. **Barrel:** 3.5". **Weight:** 21 oz. **Features:** Similar to Defender series.
Price: $394.00

BOND ARMS SNAKE SLAYER
Caliber: 45 LC/410 shotshell (2-1/2" or 3"). **Barrel:** 3.5". **Weight:** 21 oz. **Grips:** Extended rosewood. **Sights:** Blade front, fixed rear. **Features:** Single-action; interchangeable barrels; stainless steel firing pin. Introduced 2005.
Price: $445.00

BROWN CLASSIC SINGLE SHOT PISTOL
Caliber: 17 Ackley Hornet through 375x444. **Barrel:** 15" air-gauged match grade. **Weight:** About 3 lbs. 7 oz. **Grips:** Walnut; thumb rest target-style. **Sights:** None furnished; drilled and tapped for scope mounting. **Features:** Falling block action gives rigid barrel-receiver mating; hand fitted and headspaced. Introduced 1998. Made in U.S.A. by E.A. Brown Mfg.
Price: $589.00

COBRA BIG BORE DERRINGERS
Caliber: 22 WMR, 32 H&R Mag., 38 Spec., 9mm Para. **Barrel:** 2.75". **Weight:** 11.5 oz. **Length:** 4.65" overall. **Grips:** Textured black synthetic. **Sights:** Blade front, fixed notch rear. **Features:** Alloy frame, steel-lined barrels, steel breech block. Plunger-type safety with integral hammer block. Chrome or black Teflon finish. Introduced 2002. Made in U.S.A. by Cobra Enterprises.
Price: $98.00
Price: 9mm Para $136.00

COBRA LONG-BORE DERRINGERS
Caliber: 22 WMR, 38 Spec., 9mm Para. **Barrel:** 3.5". **Weight:** 13 oz. **Length:** 5.65" overall. **Grips:** Textured black synthetic. **Sights:** Fixed. **Features:** Chrome or black Teflon finish. Larger than Davis D-Series models. Introduced 2002. Made in U.S.A. by Cobra Enterprises.
Price: $136.00
Price: 9mm Para. $136.00
Price: Big-Bore models (same calibers, 3/4" shorter barrels) $136.00

COBRA STARBIRD-SERIES DERRINGERS
Caliber: 22 LR, 22 WMR, 25 ACP, 32 ACP. **Barrel:** 2.4". **Weight:** 9.5 oz. **Length:** 4" overall. **Grips:** Laminated wood or pearl. **Sights:** Blade front, fixed notch rear. **Features:** Choice of black powder coat, satin nickel or chrome finish; spur trigger. Introduced 2002. Made in U.S.A. by Cobra Enterprises.
Price: $112.00

COMANCHE SUPER SINGLE SHOT PISTOL
Caliber: 45 LC, 410 ga. **Barrel:** 10". **Sights:** Adjustable. **Features:** Blue finish, not available for sale in CA, MA. Distributed by SGS Importers International, Inc.
Price: $174.95
Price: Satin nickel $191.95
Price: Duo-tone $185.95

DOWNSIZER WSP SINGLE SHOT PISTOL
Caliber: 357 Magnum, 45 ACP, 38 Special. **Barrel:** 2.10". **Weight:** 11 oz. **Length:** 3.25" overall. **Grips:** Black polymer. **Sights:** None. **Features:** Single shot, tip-up barrel. Double action only. Stainless steel construction. Measures .900" thick. Introduced 1997. From Downsizer Corp.
Price: $499.00

GAUCHER GN1 SILHOUETTE PISTOL
Caliber: 22 LR, single shot. **Barrel:** 10". **Weight:** 2.4 lbs. **Length:** 15.5" overall. **Grips:** European hardwood. **Sights:** Blade front, open adjustable rear. **Features:** Bolt action, adjustable trigger. Introduced 1990. Imported from France by Mandall Shooting Supplies.
Price: About $525.00
Price: Model GP Silhouette $425.00

Maximum Single Shot

RPM XL Pistol

Thompson/Center G2 Contender

MAXIMUM SINGLE SHOT PISTOL

Caliber: 22 LR, 22 Hornet, 22 BR, 22 PPC, 223 Rem., 22-250, 6mm BR, 6mm PPC, 243, 250 Savage, 6.5mm-35M, 270 MAX, 270 Win., 7mm TCU, 7mm BR, 7mm-35, 7mm INT-R, 7mm-08, 7mm Rocket, 7mm Super-Mag., 30 Herrett, 30 Carbine, 30-30, 308 Win., 30x39, 32-20, 350 Rem. Mag., 357 Mag., 357 Maximum, 358 Win., 375 H&H, 44 Mag., 454 Casull. **Barrel:** 8-3/4", 10-1/2", 14". **Weight:** 61 oz. (10-1/2" bbl.); 78 oz. (14" bbl.). **Length:** 15", 18-1/2" overall (with 10-1/2" and 14" bbl., respectively). **Grips:** Smooth walnut stocks and forend. Also available with 17" finger groove grip. **Sights:** Ramp front, fully adjustable open rear. **Features:** Falling block action; drilled and tapped for M.O.A. scope mounts; integral grip frame/receiver; adjustable trigger; Douglas barrel (interchangeable). Introduced 1983. Made in U.S.A. by M.O.A. Corp.
Price: Stainless receiver, blue barrel **$799.00**
Price: Stainless receiver, stainless barrel **$883.00**
Price: Extra blued barrel **$254.00**
Price: Extra stainless barrel **$317.00**
Price: Scope mount **$60.00**

RPM XL SINGLE SHOT PISTOL

Caliber: 22 LR through 45-70. **Barrel:** 8", 10-3/4", 12", 14". **Weight:** About 60 oz. **Grips:** Smooth Goncalo Alves with thumb and heel rests. **Sights:** Hooded front with interchangeable post, or Patridge, ISGW rear adjustable for windage and elevation. **Features:** Barrel drilled and tapped for scope mount. Visible cocking indicator. Spring-loaded barrel lock, positive hammer-block safety. Trigger adjustable for weight of pull and over-travel. Contact maker for complete price list. Made in U.S.A. by RPM.
Price: XL Hunter model (action only) $1,045.00
Price: Extra barrel, 8" through 10-3/4" $407.50
Price: Extra barrel, 12" through 14" $547.50
Price: Muzzle brake $160.00
Price: Left-hand action, add $50.00

SAVAGE STRIKER BOLT-ACTION HUNTING HANDGUN

Caliber: 223, 243, 7mm-08, 308, 300 WSM 2-shot mag. **Barrel:** 14". **Weight:** About 5 lbs. **Length:** 22-1/2" overall. **Stock:** Black composite ambidextrous mid-grip; grooved forend; "Dual Pillar" bedding. **Sights:** None furnished; drilled and tapped for scope mounting. **Features:** Short left-hand bolt with right-hand ejection; free-floated barrel; uses Savage Model 110 rifle scope rings/bases. Introduced 1998. Made in U.S.A. by Savage Arms, Inc.
Price: Model 503 (blued barrel and action) $285.00
Price: Model 503 R17FSS (stainless barrel and action) $281.00
Price: Model 516FSAK black stock (ss, aMB, 300 WSM) $260.00

Savage Sport Striker Bolt-Action Hunting Handgun

Similar to Striker, but chambered in 22 LR and 22 WMR. Detachable 10-shot magazine (5-shot magazine for 22 WMR). Overall length 19", weighs 4 lbs. Ambidextrous fiberglass/graphite composite rear grip. Drilled and tapped, scope mount installed. Introduced 2000. Made in U.S.A. by Savage Arms Inc.
Price: Model 501F (blue finish, 22 LR) **$236.00**
Price: Model 501FXP with soft case, 1.25-4x28 scope **$258.00**
Price: Model 502F (blue finish, 22 WMR) **$238.00**

SPRINGFIELD M6 SCOUT PISTOL

Caliber: 22 LR/45 LC/410, 22 Hornet, 45 LC/410. **Barrel:** 10". **Weight:** NA. **Length:** NA. **Grips:** NA. **Sights:** NA. **Features:** Adapted from the U.S. Air Force M6 Survival Rifle, also available as a carbine with 16" barrel.
Price: . . . . **$169.00 to $197.00**
Price: Pistol/Carbine . . . . **$183.00 to $209.00**

THOMPSON/CENTER ENCORE PISTOL

Caliber: 22-250, 223, 204 Ruger, 6.8 Rem., 260 Rem., 7mm-08, 243, 308, 270, 30-06, 375 JDJ, 204 Ruger, 44 Mag., 454 Casull, 480 Ruger, 444 Marlin single shot, 450 Marlin with muzzle tamer, no sights. **Barrel:** 12", 15", tapered round. **Weight:** NA. **Length:** 21" overall with 12" barrel. **Grips:** American walnut with finger grooves, walnut forend. **Sights:** Blade on ramp front, adjustable rear, or none. **Features:** Interchangeable barrels; action opens by squeezing the trigger guard; drilled and tapped for scope mounting; blue finish. Announced 1996. Made in U.S.A. by Thompson/Center Arms.
Price: . . . . **$589.00 to $592.00**
Price: Extra 12" barrels $262.00
Price: Extra 15" barrels $270.00
Price: 45 Colt/410 barrel, 12" $292.00
Price: 45 Colt/410 barrel, 15" $299.00

Thompson/Center Stainless Encore Pistol

Similar to blued Encore, made of stainless steel, available with 15" barrel in 223, 22-250, 243 Win., 7mm-08, 308, 30/06 Sprgfld., 45/70 Gov't., 45/410 VR. With black rubber grip and forend. Made in U.S.A. by Thompson/Center Arms.
Price: . . . . **$636.00 to $644.00**

Thompson/Center G2 Contender Pistol

A second generation Contender pistol maintaining the same barrel interchangeability with older Contender barrels and their corresponding forends (except Herrett forend). The G2 frame will not accept old-style grips due to the change in grip angle. Incorporates an automatic hammer block safety with built-in interlock. Features include trigger adjustable for overtravel; adjustable rear sight; ramp front sight blade; blued steel finish.
Price: $570.00

UBERTI ROLLING BLOCK TARGET PISTOL

Caliber: 22 LR, 22 WMR, 22 Hornet, 357 Mag., 45 Colt, single shot. **Barrel:** 9-7/8", half-round, half-octagon. **Weight:** 44 oz. **Length:** 14" overall. **Stock:** Walnut grip and forend. **Sights:** Blade front, fully adjustable rear. **Features:** Replica of the 1871 rolling block target pistol. Brass trigger guard, color case-hardened frame, blue barrel. Imported by Uberti U.S.A.
Price: $410.00

Both classic arms and recent designs in American-style repeaters for sport and field shooting.

Armalite M15A2

Armalite AR-10A4

Armalite AR-180B

ARMALITE M15A2 CARBINE
Caliber: 223, 30-round magazine. **Barrel:** 16" heavy chrome lined; 1:9" twist. **Weight:** 7 lbs. **Length:** 35-11/16" overall. **Stock:** Green or black composition. **Sights:** Standard A2. **Features:** Upper and lower receivers have push-type pivot pin; hard coat anodized; A2-style forward assist; M16A2-type raised fence around magazine release button. Made in U.S.A. by ArmaLite, Inc.
Price: Green **$1,100.00**
Price: Black **$1,100.00**

ARMALITE AR-10A4 SPECIAL PURPOSE RIFLE
Caliber: 308 Win., 10- and 20-round magazine. **Barrel:** 20" chrome-lined, 1:11.25" twist. **Weight:** 9.6 lbs. **Length:** 41" overall. **Stock:** Green or black composition. **Sights:** Detachable handle, front sight, or scope mount available; comes with international style flattop receiver with Picatinny rail. **Features:** Forged upper receiver with case deflector. Receivers are hard-coat anodized. Introduced 1995. Made in U.S.A. by ArmaLite, Inc.
Price: Green **$1,506.00**
Price: Black **$1,506.00**
Price: Green or black with match trigger **$1,606.00**

ArmaLite AR-10(T)
Similar to the ArmaLite AR-10A4 but with stainless steel, barrel, machined tool steel, two-stage National Match trigger group and other features.
Price: AR-10(T) rifle **$2,126.00**
Price: AR-10(T) carbine **$2,126.00**

ArmaLite AR-10A2
Utilizing the same 20" double-lapped, heavy barrel as the ArmaLite AR-10A4 Special Purpose Rifle. Offered in 308 caliber only. Made in U.S.A. by ArmaLite, Inc.
Price: AR-10A2 rifle or carbine **$1,506.00**
Price: AR-10A2 rifle or carbine with match trigger **$1,606.00**

ARMALITE AR-180B RIFLE
Caliber: 223, 10-shot magazine. **Barrel:** 19.8". **Weight:** 6 lbs. **Length:** 38". **Stock:** Synthetic. **Sights:** Rear sight adjustable for windage, small and large apertures. **Features:** Lower receiver made of polymer, upper formed of sheet metal. Uses standard AR-15 magazines. Made in U.S.A. by Armalite.
Price: **$750.00**

ARSENAL USA SSR-56
Caliber: 7.62x39mm. **Barrel:** 16.25". **Weight:** 7.4 lbs. **Length:** 35.5" **Stock:** Black polymer. **Sights:** Adjustable rear. **Features:** An AK-47-style rifle built on a hardened Hungarian FEG receiver with the required six U.S.-made parts to make it legal for use with all extra-capacity magazines. From Arsenal I, LLC.
Price: **$565.00**

ARSENAL USA SSR-74-2
Caliber: 5.45x39mm **Barrel:** 16.25" **Weight:** 7 lbs. **Length:** 36.75" **Stock:** Polymer or wood. **Sights:** Adjustable. **Features:** Built with parts from an unissued Bulgarian AK-47 rifle, it has a Buffer Technologies recoil buffer, enough U.S.-made parts to allow pistol grip stock and use with all extra-capacity magazines. Assembled in U.S.A. From Arsenal I, LLC.
Price: **$499.00**

ARSENAL USA SSR-85C-2
Caliber: 7.62x39mm. **Barrel:** 16.25". **Weight:** 7.1 lbs. **Length:** 35.5". **Stock:** Polymer or wood. **Sights:** Adjustable rear calibrated to 800 meters. **Features:** Built from parts obtained from unissued Polish AK-47 rifles, the gas tube is vented and the receiver cover is plain. Rifle contains enough U.S.-sourced parts to allow pistol grip stock and use with all extra-capacity magazines. Assembled in U.S.A. by Arsenal I, LLC.
Price: **$499.00**

Auto-Ordnance 1927 A-1 Thompson

Barrett Model 82A-1

Browning Mark II Safari

AUTO-ORDNANCE 1927 A-1 THOMPSON
Caliber: 45 ACP. **Barrel:** 16-1/2". **Weight:** 13 lbs. **Length:** About 41" overall (Deluxe). **Stock:** Walnut stock and vertical forend. **Sights:** Blade front, open rear adjustable for windage. **Features:** Recreation of Thompson Model 1927. Semi-auto only. Deluxe model has finned barrel, adjustable rear sight and compensator; Standard model has plain barrel and military sight. From Auto-Ordnance Corp.
Price: Deluxe **$950.00**
Price: 1927A1C lightweight model (9-1/2 lbs.) **$950.00**

Auto-Ordnance Thompson M1/M1-C
Similar to the 1927 A-1 except is in the M-1 configuration with side cocking knob, horizontal forend, smooth unfinned barrel, sling swivels on butt and forend. Matte black finish. Introduced 1985.
Price: M1 semi-auto carbin **$950.00**
Price: M1-C lightweight semi-auto **$925.00**

Auto-Ordnance 1927 A-1 Commando
Similar to the 1927 A-1 except has Parkerized finish, black-finish wood butt, pistol grip, horizontal forend. Comes with black nylon sling. Introduced 1998. Made in U.S.A. by Auto-Ordnance Corp.
Price: **$950.00**

BARRETT MODEL 82A-1 SEMI-AUTOMATIC RIFLE
Caliber: 50 BMG, 10-shot detachable box magazine. **Barrel:** 29". **Weight:** 28.5 lbs. **Length:** 57" overall. **Stock:** Composition with energy-absorbing recoil pad. **Sights:** Scope optional. **Features:** Semi-automatic, recoil operated with recoiling barrel. Three-lug locking bolt; muzzle brake. Adjustable bipod. Introduced 1985. Made in U.S.A. by Barrett Firearms.
Price: From **$7,200.00**

BENELLI RI RIFLE
Caliber: 300 Win. Mag., 30-06, 308, 300 WSM, 270 WSM. **Barrel:** 20", 22", 24". **Weight:** 7.1 lbs. **Length:** 43.75" **Stock:** Select satin walnut. **Sights:** None. **Features:** Auto-regulating gas-operated system, three-lug rotary bolt, interchangeable barrels. Introduced 2003. Imported from Italy by Benelli USA.
Price: **$1,080.00**

BROWNING BAR MARK II SAFARI SEMI-AUTO RIFLE
Caliber: 243, 25-06, 270, 30-06, 308, 270 WSM, 7mm WSM. **Barrel:** 22" round tapered. **Weight:** 7-3/8 lbs. **Length:** 43" overall. **Stock:** French walnut pistol grip stock and forend, hand checkered. **Sights:** Gold bead on hooded ramp front, click adjustable rear, or no sights. **Features:** Has new bolt release lever; removable trigger assembly with larger trigger guard; redesigned gas and buffer systems. Detachable 4-round box magazine. Scroll-engraved receiver is tapped for scope mounting. BOSS barrel vibration modulator and muzzle brake system available only on models without sights. Mark II Safari introduced 1993. Imported from Belgium by Browning.
Price: Safari, with sights **$833.00**
Price: Safari, no sights **$815.00**
Price: Safari, 270 and 30-06, no sights, BOSS **$891.00**

Browning BAR Mark II Safari Rifle (Magnum)
Same as the standard caliber model, except weighs 8-3/8 lbs., 45" overall, 24" bbl., 3-round mag. Cals. 7mm Mag., 300 Win. Mag., 338 Win. Mag. BOSS barrel vibration modulator and muzzle brake system available only on models without sights. Introduced 1993.
Price: Safari, no sights **$908.00**
Price: Safari, no sights, BOSS **$1,007.00**

BROWNING BAR SHORT TRAC/LONG TRAC AUTO RIFLES
Caliber: (Short Trac models) 270 WSM, 7mm WSM, 300 WSM, 243 Win., 308 WIn.; (Long Trac models) 270 Win., 30-06 Sprfld., 7mm Rem. Mag., 300 Win. Mag. **Barrel:** 23". **Weight:** 6 lbs. 10 oz. to 7 lbs. 4 oz. **Length:** 41-1/2" to 44". **Stock:** Satin-finish walnut, pistol-grip, fluted forend. **Sights:** Adj. rear, bead front standard, no sights on BOSS models (optional). **Features:** Designed to handle new WSM chamberings. Gas-operated, blued finish, rotary bolt design (Long Trac models).
Price: Short Trac, WSM calibers **$885.00**
Price: Short Trac, 243, 308 . . . . **$885.00**
Price: Long Trac calibers **$965.00**

Bushmaster M17S Bullpup

Bushmaster XM15 E2S Carbine

Bushmaster Varminter

Colt Match Target Lightweight

BROWNING BAR STALKER AUTO RIFLES

Caliber: 243, 308, 270, 30-06, 7mm Rem. Mag., 300 Win. Mag., 338 Win. Mag., 270 WSM, 7mm WSM. **Barrel:** 20", 22" and 24". **Weight:** 6 lbs., 12 oz. (243) to 8 lbs., 2 oz. (magnum cals.) **Length:** 41" to 45" overall. **Stock:** Black composite stock and forearm. **Sights:** Hooded front and adjustable rear or none. **Features:** Optional BOSS (no sights); gas-operated action with seven-lug rotary bolt; dual action bars; 3- or 4-shot magazine (depending on caliber). Introduced 2001. Imported by Browning.
Price: BAR Stalker, open sights (243, 308, 270, 30-06) **$883.00**
Price: BAR Stalker, open sights (7mm, 300 Win. Mag.,
338 Win. Mag.) **$964.00**

BUSHMASTER M17S BULLPUP RIFLE

Caliber: 223, 10-shot magazine. **Barrel:** 21.5", chrome lined; 1:9" twist. **Weight:** 8.2 lbs. **Length:** 30" overall. **Stock:** Fiberglass-filled nylon. **Sights:** Designed for optics-carrying handle incorporates scope mount rail for Weaver-type rings; also includes 25-meter open iron sights. **Features:** Gas-operated, short-stroke piston system; ambidextrous magazine release. Introduced 1993. Made in U.S.A. by Bushmaster Firearms, Inc./Quality Parts Co.
Price: **$765.00**

BUSHMASTER SHORTY XM15 E2S CARBINE

Caliber: 223, 10-shot magazine. **Barrel:** 16", heavy; 1:9" twist. **Weight:** 7.2 lbs. **Length:** 34.75" overall. **Stock:** A2 type; fixed black composition. **Sights:** Fully adjustable M16A2 sight system. **Features:** Patterned after Colt M-16A2. Chrome-lined barrel with manganese phosphate finish. "Shorty" handguards. Has forged aluminum receivers with pushpin. Made in U.S.A. by Bushmaster Firearms, Inc.
Price: (A2) **$985.00**
Price: (A3) **$1,085.00**

Bushmaster XM15 E2S Dissipator Carbine

Similar to the XM15 E2S Shorty carbine except has full-length "Dissipator" handguards. Weighs 7.6 lbs.; 34.75" overall; forged aluminum receivers with push-pin style takedown. Made in U.S.A. by Bushmaster Firearms, Inc.

Price: (A2 type) **$995.00**
Price: (A3 type) **$1,095.00**

Bushmaster XM15 E25 AK Shorty Carbine

Similar to the XM15 E2S Shorty except has 14.5" barrel with an AK muzzle brake permanently attached giving 16" barrel length. Weighs 7.3 lbs. Introduced 1999. Made in U.S.A. by Bushmaster Firearms, Inc.
Price: (A2 type) $1,005.00
Price: (A3 type) $1,105.00

Bushmaster M4/M4A3 Post-Ban Carbine

Similar to the XM15 E2S except has 14.5" barrel with Mini Y compensator, and fixed telestock. MR configuration has fixed carry handle; M4A3 has removeable carry handle.
Price: (M4) $1,065.00
Price: (M4A3) $1,165.00

BUSHMASTER VARMINTER RIFLE

Caliber: 223 Rem., 5-shot. **Barrel:** 24", 1:9" twist, fluted, heavy, stainless. **Weight:** 8-3/4 lbs. **Length:** 42-1/4". **Stock:** Rubberized pistol grip. **Sights:** 1/2" scope risers. **Features:** Gas-operated, semi-auto, two-stage trigger, slotted free floater forend, lockable hard case.
Price: $1,245.00

COLT MATCH TARGET MODEL RIFLE

Caliber: 223 Rem., 5-shot magazine. **Barrel:** 16.1" or 20". **Weight:** 7.1 to 8-1/2 lbs. **Length:** 34-1/2" to 39" overall. **Stock:** Composition stock, grip, forend. **Sights:** Post front, rear adjustable for windage and elevation. **Features:** 5-round detachable box magazine, flash suppressor, sling swivels. Forward bolt assist included. Introduced 1991. Made in U.S.A. by Colt's Mfg. Co., Inc.
Price: Match Target HBAR, from $1,300.00

DSA SA58 Standard

DSA SA58 Carbine

DSA SA58 Medium Contour Tactical

DSA SA58 Medium Contour

DPMS PANTHER ARMS A-15 RIFLES

Caliber: 223 Rem., 7.62x39. **Barrel:** 16" to 24". **Weight:** 7-3/4 to 11-3/4 lbs. **Length:** 34-1/2" to 42-1/4" overall. **Stock:** Black Zytel® composite. **Sights:** Square front post, adjustable A2 rear. **Features:** Steel or stainless steel heavy or bull barrel; hardcoat anodized receiver; aluminum free-float tube handguard; many options. From DPMS Panther Arms.

Price: Panther Bull A-15 (20" stainless bull bbl.). $915.00
Price: Panther Bull Twenty-Four (24" stainless bull bbl.). $945.00
Price: Bulldog (20" stainless fluted bbl., flattop receiver) $1,219.00
Price: Panther Bull Sweet Sixteen (16" stainless bull bbl.). $885.00
Price: DCM Panther (20" stainless heavy bbl., n.m. sights) $1,099.00
Price: Panther 7.62x39 (20" steel heavy bbl.). $849.00

DSA SA58 CONGO, PARA CONGO

Caliber: 308 Win. **Barrel:** 18" w/short muzzle brake. **Weight:** 8.6 lbs. (Congo); 9.85 lbs. (Para Congo). **Length:** 39.75" **Stock:** Synthetic w/military grade furniture (Congo); Synthetic with non-folding steel para stock (Para Congo). **Sights:** Post, front, windage adjustable peep, rear (Congo); Belgian-style para flip peep, rear (Para Congo). **Features:** Fully-adjustable gas system, high-grade steel upper receiver with carry handle. Made in U.S.A. by DSA, Inc.

Price: . . . . (Congo) $1,695.00; (Para Congo) $1,995.00

DSA SA58 GRAY WOLF

Caliber: 308 Win., 300 WSM. **Barrel:** 21" match-grade bull w/target crown. **Weight:** 13 lbs. **Length:** 41.75". **Stock:** Synthetic. **Sights:** Elevation adjustable post, front; windage adjustable match peep, rear. **Features:** Fully-adjustable gas system, high-grade steel upper receiver, Picatinny scope mount, DuraCoat finish. Made in U.S.A. by DSA, Inc.

Price: $2,120.00

DSA SA58 PREDATOR

Caliber: 260 Rem., 243 Win., 308 Win. **Barrel:** 16" and 19" w/target crown. **Weight:** 9 to 9.3 lbs. **Length:** 36.25" to 39.25". **Stock:** Synthetic. **Sights:** Elevation adjustable post, front; windage adjustable match peep, rear. **Features:** Fully-adjustable gas system, high-grade steel upper receiver, Picatinny scope mount, DuraCoat solid and camo finishes.

Price: . . . . (308 Win.) $1,595.00; (243 Win., 260 Rem.) $1,695.00

DSA SA58 T48

Caliber: 308 Win. **Barrel:** 16.25" with Browning replica flash hider. **Weight:** 9.3 lbs. **Length:** 44.5". **Stock:** European walnut. **Sights:** Adjustable post front, adjustable rear peep. **Features:** Gas-operated semi-auto with fully adjustable gas system, high grade steel upper receiver. DuraCoat finishes. Made in U.S.A. by DSA, Inc.

Price:. $1,795.00

DSA SA58 GI

Similar to the SA58 T48 except has steel bipod cut handguard with hardwood stock and synthetic pistol grip, original GI steel lower receiver with GI bipod. Made in U.S.A. by DSA, Inc.

Price: $1,695.00

DSA SA58 TACTICAL CARBINE, CARBINE

Caliber: 308 Win., limited 243 and 260. **Barrel:** 16.25" with integrally machined muzzle brake. **Weight:** 8.75 lbs. **Length:** 38.25". **Stock:** Fiberglass reinforced synthetic handguard. **Sights:** Adjustable post front, adjustable rear peep. **Features:** Gas-operated semi-auto with fully adjustable gas system, high grade steel or 416 stainless upper receiver. In variety of camo finishes. Made in U.S.A. by DSA, Inc.

Price: Tactical fluted bbl. $1,475.00
Price: Carbine stainless steel bbl. $1,645.00
Price: Carbine high-grade steel bbl. $1,395.00

DSA SA58 MEDIUM CONTOUR

Caliber: 308 Win., limited 243 and 260. **Barrel:** 21" with integrally machined muzzle brake. **Weight:** 9.75 lbs. **Length:** 43". **Stock:** Fiberglass reinforced synthetic handguard. **Sights:** Adjustable post front with match rear peep. **Features:** Gas-operated semi-auto with fully adjustable gas system, high grade steel or 416 stainless upper receiver. In variety of camo finishes. Made in U.S.A. by DSA, Inc.

Price: Chrome-moly $1,475.00
Price: Stainless steel $1,725.00

DSA SA58 Bull

Heckler & Koch USC

DSA SA58 OSW

Hi-Point Carbine

DSA SA58 21" OR 24" BULL BARREL RIFLE
Caliber: 308 Win., 300 WSM. **Barrel:** 21" or 24". **Weight:** 11.1 and 11.5 lbs. **Length:** 41.5" and 44.5". **Stock:** Synthetic, free floating handguard. **Sights:** Elevation adjustable protected post front, match rear peep. **Features:** Gas-operated semi-auto with fully adjustable gas system, high grade steel or stainless upper receiver. Made in U.S.A. by DSA, Inc.
Price: 21", 24" **$1,745.00**
Price: 24" fluted bbl. **$1,795.00**

DSA SA58 MINI OSW
Caliber: 7.62 NATO. **Barrel:** 11" or 13" with muzzle brake. **Weight:** 9 to 9.35 lbs. **Length:** 33". **Stock:** Synthetic. **Features:** Gas-operated semi-auto or select fire with fully adjustable short gas system, optional FAL Rail Interface Handguard, SureFire Vertical Foregrip System, EOTech HOLOgraphic Sight and ITC cheekrest. Made in U.S.A. by DSA, Inc.
Price: **$1,525.00**

EAA/SAIGA SEMI-AUTO RIFLE
Caliber: 7.62x39, 308, 223. **Barrel:** 20.5", 22", 16.3". **Weight:** 7 to 8-1/2 lbs. **Length:** 43". **Stock:** Synthetic or wood. **Sights:** Adjustable, sight base. **Features:** Based on AK Combat rifle by Kalashnikov. Imported from Russia by EAA Corp.
Price: 7.62x39 (syn.) **$239.00**
Price: 308 (syn. or wood) **$429.00**
Price: 223 (syn.) **$389.00**

EAGLE ARMS AR-10 RIFLE
Caliber: 308. **Barrel:** 20", 24". **Weight:** NA. **Length:** NA. **Stock:** Synthetic. **Sights:** Adjustable A2, front, Std. A2, rear; Flattop and Match Rifle have no sights but adjustable Picatinny rail furnished. **Features:** Introduced 2003. Made in U.S.A. by Eagle Arms.
Price: AR-10 Service rifle **$1,055.00**
Price: AR-10 Flattop rifle. **$999.95**
Price: AR-10 Match rifle **$1,480.00**

EAGLE ARMS M15 RIFLE
Caliber: 223. **Barrel:** 16", 20". **Weight:** NA. **Length:** NA. **Stock:** Synthetic. **Sights:** Adjustable A2, front; Std. A2, rear; flattop rifle and carbine

versions, no sights furnished. **Features:** Available in 4 different configurations. Introduced 2003. Made in U.S.A. by Eagle Arms.
Price: A2 Rifle. **$795.00**
Price: A2 carbine **$795.00**
Price: Flattop rifle **$835.00**
Price: Flattop carbine **$835.00**

HECKLER & KOCH USC CARBINE
Caliber: 45 ACP, 10-shot magazine. **Barrel:** 16". **Weight:** 8.6 lb. **Length:** 35.4" overall. **Stock:** Skeletonized polymer thumbhole. **Sights:** Blade front with integral hood, fully adjustable diopter. **Features:** Based on German UMP submachine gun. Blowback operation; almost entirely constructed of carbon fiber-reinforced polymer. Free-floating heavy target barrel. Introduced 2000. From H&K.
Price: **$1,249.00**

HI-POINT 9MM CARBINE
Caliber: 9mm Para., 40 S&W, 10-shot magazine. **Barrel:** 16-1/2" (17-1/2" for 40 S&W). **Weight:** 4-1/2 lbs. **Length:** 31-1/2" overall. **Stock:** Black polymer, camouflage. **Sights:** Protected post front, aperture rear. Integral scope mount. **Features:** Grip-mounted magazine release. Black or chrome finish. Sling swivels. Available with laser or red dot sights. Introduced 1996. Made in U.S.A. by MKS Supply, Inc.
Price: Black or chrome, 9mm **$199.00**
Price: 40 S&W **$225.00**
Price: Camo stock **$210.00**

IAI M-333 M1 GARAND
Caliber: 30-06, 8-shot clip. **Barrel:** 24". **Weight:** 9-1/2 lbs. **Length:** 43.6" overall. **Stock:** Hardwood. **Sights:** Blade front, aperture adjustable rear. **Features:** Parkerized finish; gas-operated semi-automatic; remanufactured to military specifications. From Intrac Arms International, Inc.
Price: **$971.75**

Les Baer Flattop

Les Baer IPSC

IAI M-888 M1 CARBINE SEMI-AUTOMATIC RIFLE
Caliber: 22, 30 carbine. **Barrel:** 18"-20". **Weight:** 5-1/2 lbs. **Length:** 35"-37" overall. **Stock:** Laminate, walnut or birch. **Sights:** Blade front, adjustable rear. **Features:** Gas-operated, air cooled, manufactured to military specifications. 10/15/30 rnd. mag, scope available. From Intrac Arms International, Inc..
Price: 30 cal. . . . . **$556.00 to $604.00**
Price: 22 cal. . . . . **$567.00 to $654.00**

IAI-65 Rifle
A civilian-legal version of the original HKM rifle manufactured in Hungary. Manufactured by Gordon Technologies using an original AMD-65 matching parts kit built on an AKM receiver. The original wire stock is present, but it is welded in the open position as per BATF regulations. Furnished with a 12.6" barrel with large weld-in-place muzzle brake to bring its length over the 16" federal minimum. This rifle accepts all 7.62x39mm magazines and drums. Introduced 2002. From Intrac Arms International, Inc.
Price: **$799.00**

LES BAER CUSTOM ULTIMATE AR 223 RIFLES
Caliber: 223. **Barrel:** 18", 20", 22", 24". **Weight:** 7-3/4 to 9-3/4 lb. **Length:** NA. **Stock:** Black synthetic. **Sights:** None furnished; Picatinny-style flattop rail for scope mounting. **Features:** Forged receiver; Ultra single-stage trigger (Jewell two-stage trigger optional); titanium firing pin; Versa-Pod bipod; chromed National Match carrier; stainless steel, hand-lapped and cryo-treated barrel; guaranteed to shoot 1/2 or 3/4 MOA, depending on model. Made in U.S.A. by Les Baer Custom Inc.
Price: Super Varmint Model **$1,989.00**
Price: M4 flattop model **$2,195.00**
Price: IPSC action model **$2,195.00**

LR 300 SR LIGHT SPORT RIFLE
Caliber: 223. **Barrel:** 16-1/4"; 1:9" twist. **Weight:** 7.2 lbs. **Length:** 36" overall (extended stock), 26-1/4" (stock folded). **Stock:** Folding, tubular steel, with thumbhole-type grip. **Sights:** Trijicon post front, Trijicon rear. **Features:** Uses AR-15 type upper and lower receivers; flattop receiver

with weaver base. Accepts all AR-15/M-16 magazines. Introduced 1996. Made in U.S.A. from Z-M Weapons.
Price: **$2,550.00**

OLYMPIC ARMS CAR-97 RIFLES
Caliber: 223, 7-shot; 9mm Para., 45 ACP, 40 S&W, 10mm, 10-shot. **Barrel:** 16". **Weight:** 7 lbs. **Length:** 34.75" overall. **Stock:** A2 stowaway grip, telescoping-look butt. **Sights:** Post front, fully adjustable aperature rear. **Features:** Based on AR-15 rifle. Post-ban version of the CAR-15. Made in U.S.A. by Olympic Arms, Inc.
Price: 223 . . . . **$780.00**
Price: 9mm Para., 45 ACP, 40 S&W, 10mm. **$840.00**
Price: PCR Eliminator (223, full-length handguards) **$803.00**

OLYMPIC ARMS PCR-4 RIFLE
Caliber: 223, 10-shot magazine. **Barrel:** 20". **Weight:** 8 lbs., 5 oz. **Length:** 38.25" overall. **Stock:** A2 stowaway grip, trapdoor buttstock. **Sights:** Post front, A1 rear adjustable for windage. **Features:** Based on the AR-15 rifle. Barrel is button rifled with 1:9" twist. No bayonet lug. Introduced 1994. Made in U.S.A. by Olympic Arms, Inc.
Price: **$803.00**

OLYMPIC ARMS K-3B RIFLE
Caliber: 5.56 NATO, 10-shot magazine. **Barrel:** Match grade, 16". **Weight:** 7 lbs. **Length:** 34" overall. **Stock:** Collapsible. **Sights:** Adj. front and rear. **Features:** Black matte anodized, flash suppressor and bayonet lug. Carbine or Featherweight models. Introduced in 2005. Made in U.S.A. by Olympic Arms, Inc.
Price: Rifle **$1,012.00**
Price: Carbine **$810.00**

PANTHER ARMS CLASSIC AUTO RIFLE
Caliber: 5.56x45mm. **Barrel:** Heavy 16" to 20" w/flash hider. **Weight:** 7 to 9 lbs. **Length:** 34-11/16" to 38-7/16". **Sights:** Adj. rear and front. **Stock:** Black Zytel w/trap door assembly. **Features:** Gas operated rotating bolt, mil spec or Teflon black finish.
Price:. **$809.00**
Price: Stainless, match sights **$1,099.00**
Price: Southpaw **$875.00**
Price: 16" bbl. **$799.00**
Price: Panther Lite, 16" bbl. **$720.00**
Price: Panther carbine. . . . . **$799.00 to $989.00**
Price: Panther bull bbl. . . . . **$885.00 to $1,199.00**

Remington Model 7400

Ruger Deerfield 99/44 Carbine

Ruger PC4 Carbine

Ruger Ranch Mini 14/5R

REMINGTON MODEL 7400 AUTO RIFLE

Caliber: 243 Win., 270 Win., 308 Win., 30-06, 4-shot magazine. **Barrel:** 22" round tapered. **Weight:** 7-1/2 lbs. **Length:** 42-5/8" overall. **Stock:** Walnut, deluxe cut checkered pistol grip and forend. Satin or high-gloss finish. **Sights:** Gold bead front sight on ramp; step rear sight with windage adjustable. **Features:** Redesigned and improved version of the Model 742. Positive cross-bolt safety. Receiver tapped for scope mount. Introduced 1981.
Price: **$624.00**
Price: Carbine (18-1/2" bbl., 30-06 only) **$624.00**
Price: With black synthetic stock, matte black metal,
  rifle or carbine **$520.00**
Price: Weathermaster, nickel-plated w/synthetic stock and forend,
  270, 30-06 . . . . **$624.00**

ROCK RIVER ARMS STANDARD A2 RIFLE

Caliber: 45 ACP. **Barrel:** NA. **Weight:** 8.2 lbs. **Length:** NA. **Stock:** Thermoplastic. **Sights:** Standard AR-15 style sights. **Features:** Two-stage, national match trigger; optional muzzle brake. Made in U.S.A. From River Rock Arms.
Price: **$925.00**

RUGER DEERFIELD 99/44 CARBINE

Caliber: 44 Mag., 4-shot rotary magazine. **Barrel:** 18-1/2". **Weight:** 6-1/4 lbs. **Length:** 36-7/8" overall. **Stock:** Hardwood. **Sights:** Gold bead front, folding adjustable aperture rear. **Features:** Semi-automatic action; dual front-locking lugs lock directly into receiver; integral scope mount; push-button safety; includes 1" rings and gun lock. Introduced 2000. Made in U.S.A. by Sturm, Ruger & Co.
Price: **$675.00**

RUGER PC4, PC9 CARBINES

Caliber: 9mm Para., 40 cal., 10-shot magazine. **Barrel:** 16.25". **Weight:** 6 lbs., 4 oz. **Length:** 34.75" overall. **Stock:** Black high impact synthetic checkered grip and forend. **Sights:** Blade front, open adjustable rear; integral Ruger scope mounts. **Features:** Delayed blowback action; manual push-button cross bolt safety and internal firing pin block safety automatic slide lock. Introduced 1997. Made in U.S.A. by Sturm, Ruger & Co.
Price: PC9, PC4, (9mm, 40 cal.) **$605.00**
Price: PC4GR, PC9GR, (40 auto, 9mm, post sights, ghost ring) . . **$628.00**

RUGER MINI-14/5 AUTOLOADING RIFLE

Caliber: 223 Rem., 5-shot detachable box magazine. **Barrel:** 18-1/2". Rifling twist 1:9". **Weight:** 6.4 lbs. **Length:** 37-1/4" overall. **Stock:** American hardwood, steel reinforced. **Sights:** Ramp front, fully adjustable rear. **Features:** Fixed piston gas-operated, positive primary extraction. New buffer system, redesigned ejector system. Ruger S100RM scope rings included on Ranch Rifle.
Price: Mini-14/5R, Ranch Rifle, blued, scope rings **$695.00**
Price: K-Mini-14/5R, Ranch Rifle, stainless, scope rings **$770.00**
Price: Mini-14/5, blued **$655.00**
Price: K-Mini-14/5, stainless **$715.00**
Price: K-Mini-14/5P, stainless, synthetic stock **$715.00**
Price: K-Mini-14/5RP, Ranch Rifle, stainless, synthetic stock **$770.00**

Ruger Mini Thirty Rifle

Similar to the Mini-14 Ranch Rifle except modified to chamber the 7.62x39 Russian service round. Weight is about 6-7/8 lbs. Has 6-groove barrel with 1:10" twist, Ruger Integral Scope Mount bases and folding peep rear sight. Detachable 5-shot staggered box magazine. Blued finish. Introduced 1987.
Price: Blue, scope rings **$695.00**
Price: Stainless, scope rings **$770.00**

Springfield M1A

Springfield National Match M1A

Springfield Super Match with Camo M1A

SPRINGFIELD ARMORY M1A RIFLE

Caliber: 7.62mm NATO (308), 5- or 10-shot box magazine. **Barrel:** 25-1/16" with flash suppressor, 22" without suppressor. **Weight:** 9-3/4 lbs. **Length:** 44-1/4" overall. **Stock:** American walnut with walnut-colored heat-resistant fiberglass handguard. Matching walnut handguard available. Also available with fiberglass stock. **Sights:** Military, square blade front, full click-adjustable aperture rear. **Features:** Commercial equivalent of the U.S. M-14 service rifle with no provision for automatic firing. From Springfield Armory

Price: Standard M1A, black fiberglass stock.................. $1,498.00
Price: Standard M1A, black fiberglass stock, stainless $1,727.00
Price: Standard M1A, black stock, carbon barrel $1,379.00
Price: Standard M1A, Mossy Oak stock, carbon barrel $1,507.00
Price: Scout Squad M1A...................... $1,653.00 to $1,727.00
Price: National Match .... $2,049.00 to $2,098.00
Price: Super Match (heavy premium barrel), about $3,149.00
Price: M1A SOCOM II rifle, about......................... $1,948.00
Price: M25 White Feather Tactical rifle $4,648.00

SPRINGFIELD M1 GARAND RIFLE

Caliber: 308, 30-06. **Barrel:** 24". **Weight:** 9.5 lbs. **Length:** 43-3/5". **Stock:** Walnut. **Sights:** Military aperture with MOA adjustments for both windage and elevation, rear; military square post, front. **Features:** Original U.S. government-issue parts on a new walnut stock.

Price: .... $1,348.00 to $1,378.00

STONER SR-15 M-5 RIFLE

Caliber: 223. **Barrel:** 20". **Weight:** 7.6 lbs. **Length:** 38" overall. **Stock:** Black synthetic. **Sights:** Post front, fully adjustable rear (300-meter sight).

Features: Modular weapon system; two-stage trigger. Black finish. Introduced 1998. Made in U.S.A. by Knight's Mfg.

Price: $1,650.00
Price: M-4 Carbine (16" barrel, 6.8 lbs) $1,555.00

STONER SR-25 CARBINE

Caliber: 7.62 NATO, 10-shot steel magazine. **Barrel:** 16" free-floating **Weight:** 7-3/4 lbs. **Length:** 35.75" overall. **Stock:** Black synthetic. **Sights:** Integral Weaver-style rail. Scope rings, iron sights optional. **Features:** Shortened, non-slip handguard; removable carrying handle. Matte black finish. Introduced 1995. Made in U.S.A. by Knight's Mfg. Co.

Price: $3,345.00

WILKINSON LINDA CARBINE

Caliber: 9mm Para. **Barrel:** 16-3/16". **Weight:** 7 lbs. **Stocks:** Fixed tubular with wood pad. **Sights:** Aperture rear sight. **Features:** Aluminum receiver, pre-ban configuration (limited supplies), vent. barrel shroud, small wooden forearm, 18 or 31 shot mag. Many accessories.

Price: $1,800.00

Wilkinson Linda L2 Limited Edition

Manufactured from the last 000 of the original 2,200 pre-ban Linda carbines, includes many upgrades and accessories. New in 2002.

Price: $4,800.00

WILKINSON TERRY CARBINE

Caliber: 9mm Para. **Barrel:** 16-3/16". **Weight:** 7 lbs. **Stocks:** Black or maple. **Sights:** Adjustable. **Features:** Blowback semi-auto action, 31-shot mag., closed breech.

Price: .... NA

CENTERFIRE RIFLES — Lever & Slide

Both classic arms and recent designs in American-style repeaters for sport and field shooting.

Browning Lightning

Cimarron 1866 Winchester Replica

Cimarron 1873 Long Range

Dixie 1873

BROWNING MODEL '81 LIGHTNING LEVER-ACTION RIFLE

Caliber: 22-250, 243, 7mm-08, 308 Win., 270 WSM, 7mm WSM, 300 WSM, 358 Win., 450 Marlin, 270 Win., 30-06 Sprg., 7mm Rem. Mag., 300 Win. Mag. 4-shot detachable magazine. **Barrel:** 20" round tapered. **Weight:** 6 lbs., 8 oz. **Length:** 39-1/2" overall. **Stock:** Walnut. Checkered grip and forend, high-gloss finish. **Sights:** Gold bead on ramp front; low profile square notch adjustable rear. **Features:** Wide, grooved trigger; half-cock hammer safety; fold-down hammer. Receiver tapped for scope mount. Recoil pad installed. Introduced 1996. Imported from Japan by Browning.
Price: **$710.00**

Browning Model '81 Lightning Long Action

Similar to the standard Lightning BLR except has long action to accept 30-06, 7mm Rem. Mag. and 300 Win. Mag. Barrel lengths are 22" for 30-06 and 270, 24" for 7mm Rem. Mag. and 300 Win. Mag. Has six-lug rotary bolt; bolt and receiver are full-length fluted. Fold-down hammer at half-cock. Weighs about 7 lbs., overall length 42-7/8" (22" barrel). Introduced 1996.
Price: **$686.00**

CIMARRON 1860 HENRY REPLICA

Caliber: 44 WCF, 45LC; 13-shot magazine. **Barrel:** 24-1/4" (rifle), 22" (carbine). **Weight:** 9-1/2 lbs. **Length:** 43" overall (rifle). **Stock:** European walnut. **Sights:** Bead front, open adjustable rear. **Features:** Brass receiver and buttplate. Uses original Henry loading system. Copy of the original rifle. Introduced 1991. Imported by Cimarron F.A. Co.
Price: **$1,199.00**

CIMARRON 1866 WINCHESTER REPLICAS

Caliber: 38 Spec., 357, 45LC, 32 WCF, 38 WCF, 44 WCF. **Barrel:** 24-1/4" (rifle), 19" (carbine). **Weight:** 9 lbs. **Length:** 43" overall (rifle). **Stock:** European walnut. **Sights:** Bead front, open adjustable rear. **Features:** Solid brass receiver, buttplate, forend cap. Octagonal barrel. Copy of the original Winchester '66 rifle. Introduced 1991. Imported by Cimarron F.A. Co.
Price: Rifle **$965.00**
Price: Carbine **$950.00**

CIMARRON 1873 SHORT RIFLE

Caliber: 357 Mag., 38 Spec., 32 WCF, 38 WCF, 44 Spec., 44 WCF, 45 Colt. **Barrel:** 20" tapered octagon. **Weight:** 7.5 lbs. **Length:** 39" overall. **Stock:** Walnut. **Sights:** Bead front, adjustable semi-buckhorn rear. **Features:** Has half "button" magazine. Original-type markings, including caliber, on barrel and elevator and "Kings" patent. From Cimarron F.A. Co.
Price: **$1,149.00**

Cimarron 1873 Sporting Rifle

Similar to the 1873 Short Rifle except has 24" barrel with half-magazine.
Price: **$1,149.00**

CIMARRON 1873 LONG RANGE RIFLE

Caliber: 44 WCF, 45 Colt. **Barrel:** 30", octagonal. **Weight:** 8-1/2 lbs. **Length:** 48" overall. **Stock:** Walnut. **Sights:** Blade front, semi-buckhorn ramp rear. Tang sight optional. **Features:** Color case-hardened frame; choice of modern blue-black or charcoal blue for other parts. Barrel marked "Kings Improvement." From Cimarron F.A. Co.
Price: **$1,199.00**

DIXIE ENGRAVED 1873 RIFLE

Caliber: 44-40, 11-shot magazine. **Barrel:** 20", round. **Weight:** 7-3/4 lbs. **Length:** 39" overall. **Stock:** Walnut. **Sights:** Blade front, adjustable rear. **Features:** Engraved and case-hardened frame. Replica of Winchester 1873. Made in Italy. From 21 Gun Works.
Price: **$1,350.00**
Price: Plain, blued carbine **$850.00**

Marlin 336C

Marlin 336Y Spikehorn

E.M.F. 1860 HENRY RIFLE
Caliber: 44-40 or 45 Colt. **Barrel:** 24.25". **Weight:** About 9 lbs. **Length:** About 43.75" overall. **Stock:** Oil-stained American walnut. **Sights:** Blade front, rear adjustable for elevation. **Features:** Reproduction of the original Henry rifle with brass frame and buttplate, rest blued. From E.M.F.
Price: Brass frame $850.00
Price: Steel frame $950.00

E.M.F. 1866 YELLOWBOY LEVER ACTIONS
Caliber: 38 Spec., 44-40. **Barrel:** 19" (carbine), 24" (rifle). **Weight:** 9 lbs. **Length:** 43" overall (rifle). **Stock:** European walnut. **Sights:** Bead front, open adjustable rear. **Features:** Solid brass frame, blued barrel, lever, hammer, buttplate. Imported from Italy by E.M.F.
Price: Rifle $690.00
Price: Carbine $675.00

E.M.F. HARTFORD MODEL 1892 LEVER-ACTION RIFLE
Caliber: 45 Colt. **Barrel:** 24", octagonal. **Weight:** 7-1/2 lbs. **Length:** 43" overall. **Stock:** European walnut. **Sights:** Blade front, open adjustable rear. **Features:** Color case-hardened frame, lever, trigger and hammer with blued barrel, or overall blue finish. Introduced 1998. Imported by E.M.F.
Price: Standard $590.00

E.M.F. MODEL 1873 LEVER-ACTION RIFLE
Caliber: 32/20, 357 Mag., 38/40, 44-40, 44 Spec., 45 Colt. **Barrel:** 24". **Weight:** 8 lbs. **Length:** 43-1/4" overall. **Stock:** European walnut. **Sights:** Bead front, rear adjustable for windage and elevation. **Features:** Color case-hardened frame (blue on carbine). Imported by E.M.F.
Price: Rifle $865.00
Price: Carbine, 19" barrel $865.00

E.M.F. MODEL 1873 REVOLVER CARBINE
Caliber: 357 Mag., 45 Colt. **Barrel:** 18". **Weight:** 4 lbs., 8 oz. **Length:** 34" overall. **Stock:** One-piece walnut. **Sights:** Blade front, notch rear. **Features:** Color case-hardened frame, blue barrel, backstrap and trigger guard. Introduced 1998. Imported from Italy by IAR, Inc.
Price: Standard $490.00

MARLIN MODEL 336C LEVER-ACTION CARBINE
Caliber: 30-30 or 35 Rem., 6-shot tubular magazine. **Barrel:** 20" Micro-Groove®. **Weight:** 7 lbs. **Length:** 38-1/2" overall. **Stock:** Checkered American black walnut, capped pistol grip. Mar-Shield® finish; rubber buttpad; swivel studs. **Sights:** Ramp front with Wide-Scan hood, semi-buckhorn folding rear adjustable for windage and elevation. **Features:** Hammer-block safety. Receiver tapped for scope mount, offset hammer spur; top of receiver sandblasted to prevent glare. Includes safety lock.
Price: $558.00

Marlin Model 336A Lever-Action Carbine
Same as the Marlin 336C except has cut-checkered, walnut-finished hardwood pistol grip stock with swivel studs, 30-30 only, 6-shot. Hammer-block safety. Adjustable rear sight, brass bead front. Includes safety lock.
Price: $477.00
Price: With 4x scope and mount. $527.00

Marlin Model 336SS Lever-Action Carbine
Same as the 336C except receiver, barrel and other major parts are machined from stainless steel. 30-30 only, 6-shot; receiver tapped for scope. Includes safety lock.
Price: $692.00

Marlin Model 336W Lever-Action Rifle
Similar to the Model 336C except has walnut-finished, cut-checkered Maine birch stock; blued steel barrel band has integral sling swivel; no front sight hood; comes with padded nylon sling; hard rubber buttplate. Introduced 1998. Includes safety lock. Made in U.S.A. by Marlin.
Price: $482.00
Price: With 4x scope and mount. $535.00

Marlin Model 336Y "Spikehorn"
Similar to the models in the 336 series except in a compact format with 10-1/2" barrel measuring only 34" in overall length. Weight is 6-1/2 lbs., length of pull 12-1/2". Blued steel barrel and receiver. Chambered for 30/30 cartridge. Introduced 2003.
Price: $586.00

MARLIN MODEL 444 LEVER-ACTION SPORTER
Caliber: 444 Marlin, 5-shot tubular magazine. **Barrel:** 22" deep cut Ballard rifling. **Weight:** 7-1/2 lbs. **Length:** 40-1/2" overall. **Stock:** Checkered American black walnut, capped pistol grip, rubber rifle buttpad. Mar-Shield® finish; swivel studs. **Sights:** Hooded ramp front, folding semi-buckhorn rear adjustable for windage and elevation. **Features:** Hammer-block safety. Receiver tapped for scope mount; offset hammer spur. Includes safety lock.
Price: $654.00

MARLIN MODEL 1894 LEVER-ACTION CARBINE
Caliber: 44 Spec./44 Mag., 10-shot tubular magazine. **Barrel:** 20" Ballard-type rifling. **Weight:** 6 lbs. **Length:** 37-1/2" overall. **Stock:** Checkered American black walnut, straight grip and forend. Mar-Shield® finish. Rubber rifle buttpad; swivel studs. **Sights:** Wide-Scan hooded ramp front, semi-buckhorn folding rear adjustable for windage and elevation. **Features:** Hammer-block safety. Receiver tapped for scope mount, offset hammer spur, solid top receiver sand blasted to prevent glare. Includes safety lock.
Price: $591.00

Marlin Model 1894C Carbine
Similar to the standard Model 1894 except chambered for 38 Spec./357 Mag. with full-length 9-shot magazine, 18-1/2" barrel, hammer-block safety, hooded front sight. Introduced 1983. Includes safety lock.
Price: $591.00

Marlin 1894 Cowboy

Marlin 1894SS

Marlin 1895

Marlin 1895GS

Marlin 1895M

MARLIN MODEL 1894 COWBOY
Caliber: 357 Mag., 44 Mag., 45 Colt, 10-shot magazine. **Barrel:** 20" except .45 Colt which has a 24" tapered octagon, deep cut rifling. **Weight:** 7-1/2 lbs. **Length:** 41-1/2" overall. **Stock:** Straight grip American black walnut, hard rubber buttplate, Mar-Shield® finish. **Sights:** Marble carbine front, adjustable Marble semi-buckhorn rear. **Features:** Squared finger lever; straight grip stock; blued steel forend tip. Designed for Cowboy Shooting events. Introduced 1996. Includes safety lock. Made in U.S.A. by Marlin.
Price: **$849.00**

Marlin Model 1894 Cowboy Competition Rifle
Similar to Model 1894 except 20" barrel, 37-1/2" long, weighs 6 lbs., antique finish on receiver, lever and bolt. Factory-tuned for competitive cowboy action shooting. Available in .38 Spl. and .45 Colt.
Price: **$986.00**

Marlin Model 1894SS
Similar to Model 1894 except has stainless steel barrel, receiver, lever, guard plate, magazine tube and loading plate. Nickel-plated swivel studs.
Price: **$716.00**

MARLIN MODEL 1895 LEVER-ACTION RIFLE
Caliber: 45-70, 4-shot tubular magazine. **Barrel:** 22" round. **Weight:** 7-1/2 lbs. **Length:** 40-1/2" overall. **Stock:** Checkered American black walnut, full pistol grip. Mar-Shield® finish; rubber buttpad; quick detachable swivel studs. **Sights:** Bead front with Wide-Scan hood, semi-buckhorn folding rear adjustable for windage and elevation. **Features:** Hammer-block safety. Solid receiver tapped for scope mounts or receiver sights; offset hammer spur. Includes safety lock.
Price: **$719.00**

Marlin Model 1895G Guide Gun Lever-Action Rifle
Similar to Model 1895 with deep-cut Ballard-type rifling; straight-grip walnut stock. Overall length is 37", weighs 7 lbs. Introduced 1998. Includes safety lock. Made in U.S.A. by Marlin.
Price: **$668.00**

Marlin Model 1895GS Guide Gun
Similar to Model 1895G except receiver, barrel and most metal parts are machined from stainless steel. Chambered for 45-70, 4-shot, 18-1/2" barrel. Overall length is 37", weighs 7 lbs. Introduced 2001. Includes safety lock. Made in U.S.A. by Marlin.
Price: **$805.00**

Marlin Model 1895 Cowboy Lever-Action Rifle
Similar to Model 1895 except has 26" tapered octagon barrel with Ballard-type rifling, Marble carbine front sight and Marble adjustable semi-buckhorn rear sight. Receiver tapped for scope or receiver sight. Overall length is 44-1/2", weighs about 8 lbs. Introduced 2001. Includes safety lock. Made in U.S.A. by Marlin.
Price: **$849.00**

Marlin Model 1895M Lever-Action Rifle
Similar to Model 1895 except has an 18-1/2" barrel with Ballard-type cut rifling. New Model 1895MR variant has 22" barrel, pistol grip. Chambered for 450 Marlin. Includes safety lock.
Price: (Model 1895M) **$719.00**

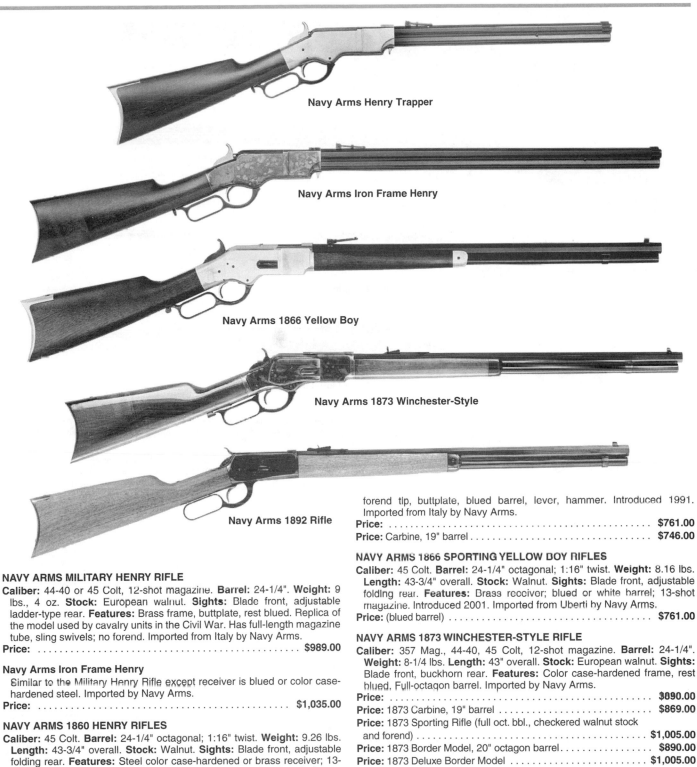

Navy Arms Henry Trapper

Navy Arms Iron Frame Henry

Navy Arms 1866 Yellow Boy

Navy Arms 1873 Winchester-Style

Navy Arms 1892 Rifle

NAVY ARMS MILITARY HENRY RIFLE

Caliber: 44-40 or 45 Colt, 12-shot magazine. **Barrel:** 24-1/4". **Weight:** 9 lbs., 4 oz. **Stock:** European walnut. **Sights:** Blade front, adjustable ladder-type rear. **Features:** Brass frame, buttplate, rest blued. Replica of the model used by cavalry units in the Civil War. Has full-length magazine tube, sling swivels; no forend. Imported from Italy by Navy Arms.
Price: $989.00

Navy Arms Iron Frame Henry

Similar to the Military Henry Rifle except receiver is blued or color case-hardened steel. Imported by Navy Arms.
Price: $1,035.00

NAVY ARMS 1860 HENRY RIFLES

Caliber: 45 Colt. **Barrel:** 24-1/4" octagonal; 1:16" twist. **Weight:** 9.26 lbs. **Length:** 43-3/4" overall. **Stock:** Walnut. **Sights:** Blade front, adjustable folding rear. **Features:** Steel color case-hardened or brass receiver; 13-shot magazine. Introduced 2001. Imported from Uberti by Navy Arms.
Price: (Steel color case-hardened receiver) $984.00
Price: (Brass receiver). $1,035.00

NAVY ARMS 1866 YELLOW BOY RIFLE

Caliber: 38 Spec., 44-40, 45 Colt, 12-shot magazine. **Barrel:** 20" or 24", full octagon. **Weight:** 8-1/2 lbs. **Length:** 42-1/2" overall. **Stock:** Walnut. **Sights:** Blade front, adjustable ladder-type rear. **Features:** Brass frame,

forend tip, buttplate, blued barrel, lever, hammer. Introduced 1991. Imported from Italy by Navy Arms.
Price: $761.00
Price: Carbine, 19" barrel $746.00

NAVY ARMS 1866 SPORTING YELLOW BOY RIFLES

Caliber: 45 Colt. **Barrel:** 24-1/4" octagonal; 1:16" twist. **Weight:** 8.16 lbs. **Length:** 43-3/4" overall. **Stock:** Walnut. **Sights:** Blade front, adjustable folding rear. **Features:** Brass receiver; blued or white barrel; 13-shot magazine. Introduced 2001. Imported from Uberti by Navy Arms.
Price: (blued barrel) $761.00

NAVY ARMS 1873 WINCHESTER-STYLE RIFLE

Caliber: 357 Mag., 44-40, 45 Colt, 12-shot magazine. **Barrel:** 24-1/4". **Weight:** 8-1/4 lbs. **Length:** 43" overall. **Stock:** European walnut. **Sights:** Blade front, buckhorn rear. **Features:** Color case-hardened frame, rest blued. Full-octagon barrel. Imported by Navy Arms.
Price: $890.00
Price: 1873 Carbine, 19" barrel $869.00
Price: 1873 Sporting Rifle (full oct. bbl., checkered walnut stock
and forend) $1,005.00
Price: 1873 Border Model, 20" octagon barrel................ $890.00
Price: 1873 Deluxe Border Model $1,005.00

NAVY ARMS 1892 RIFLE

Caliber: 357 Mag., 44-40, 45 Colt. **Barrel:** 24-1/4" octagonal. **Weight:** 7 lbs. **Length:** 42" overall. **Stock:** American walnut. **Sights:** Blade front, semi-buckhorn rear. **Features:** Replica of Winchester's early Model 1892 with octagonal barrel, forend cap and crescent buttplate. Blued or color case-hardened receiver. Introduced 1998. Imported by Navy Arms.
Price: $545.00

Navy Arms 1892 Short Rifle

Puma Model 92

Remington 7600 Rifle

Ruger Model 96/44

Tristar 1873 Sporting Rifle

Navy Arms 1892 Stainless Carbine
Similar to the 1892 Rifle except stainless steel, has 20" round barrel, weighs 5-3/4 lbs., and is 37-1/2" overall. Introduced 1998. Imported by Navy Arms.
Price: **$585.00**

Navy Arms 1892 Short Rifle
Similar to the 1892 Rifle except has 20" octagonal barrel, weighs 6-1/4 lbs., and is 37-3/4" overall. Replica of the rare, special order 1892 Winchester nicknamed the "Texas Special." Blued or color case-hardened receiver and furniture. Introduced 1998. Imported by Navy Arms.
Price: **$545.00**
Price: (stainless steel, 20" octagon barrel) **$585.00**

NAVY ARMS 1892 STAINLESS RIFLE
Caliber: 357 Mag., 44-40, 45 Colt. **Barrel:** 24-1/4" octagonal. **Weight:** 7 lbs. **Length:** 42". **Stock:** American walnut. **Sights:** Brass bead front, semi-buckhorn rear. **Features:** Designed for the Cowboy Action Shooter. Stainless steel barrel, receiver and furniture. Introduced 2000. Imported by Navy Arms.
Price: **$585.00**

PUMA MODEL 92 RIFLES & CARBINES
Caliber: 38 Spec./357 Mag., 44 Mag., 45 Colt, 454 Casull (20" carbine only), 480 Ruger. **Barrel:** 16". 18", 20" round, 24" octagonal; porting available. **Weight:** 6.1 to 7.7 lbs. **Stock:** Walnut-stained hardwood. **Sights:** Open, buckhorn front & rear; HiViz also available. **Features:** Blue, case-hardened, stainless steel and brass receivers, matching buttplates.

Blued, stainless steel barrels, full-length magazines. Thumb safety. 45 Colt and 454 Casull carbine introduced in 2002. The 480 Ruger version introduced in 2003. Imported from Brazil by Legacy Sports International.
Price: . . . . **$257.00 to $603.00**

REMINGTON MODEL 7600 PUMP ACTION
Caliber: 243, 270, 30-06, 308. **Barrel:** 22" round tapered. **Weight:** 7-1/2 lbs. **Length:** 42-5/8" overall. **Stock:** Cut-checkered walnut pistol grip and forend, Monte Carlo with full cheekpiece. Satin or high-gloss finish. **Sights:** Gold bead front sight on matted ramp, open step adjustable sporting rear. **Features:** Redesigned and improved version of the Model 760. Detachable 4-shot clip. Cross-bolt safety. Receiver tapped for scope mount. Introduced 1981.
Price: **$588.00**
Price: Carbine (18-1/2" bbl., 30-06 only) **$588.00**
Price: With black synthetic stock, matte black metal, rifle or carbine **$484.00**

RUGER MODEL 96/44 LEVER-ACTION RIFLE
Caliber: 44 Mag., 4-shot rotary magazine. **Barrel:** 18-1/2". **Weight:** 5-7/8 lbs. **Length:** 37-5/16" overall. **Stock:** American hardwood. **Sights:** Gold bead front, folding leaf rear. **Features:** Solid chrome-moly steel receiver. Manual cross-bolt safety, visible cocking indicator; short-throw lever action; integral scope mount; blued finish; color case-hardened lever. Introduced 1996. Made In U.S. by Sturm, Ruger & Co.
Price: 96/44M, 44 Mag **$546.00**

TRISTAR/UBERTI 1873 SPORTING RIFLE
Caliber: 44-40, 45 Colt. **Barrel:** 24-1/4", 30", octagonal. **Weight:** 8.1 lbs. **Length:** 43-1/4" overall. **Stock:** Walnut. **Sights:** Blade front adjustable for windage, open rear adjustable for elevation. **Features:** Color case-hardened frame, blued barrel, hammer, lever, buttplate, brass elevator. Imported from Italy by Tristar Sporting Arms Ltd.
Price: 24-1/4" barrel **$925.00**
Price: 30" barrel **$969.00**

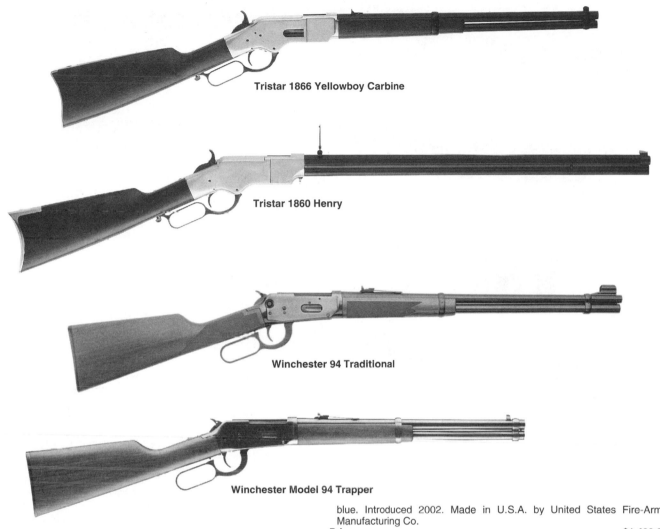

Tristar 1866 Yellowboy Carbine

Tristar 1860 Henry

Winchester 94 Traditional

Winchester Model 94 Trapper

TRISTAR/UBERTI 1866 SPORTING RIFLE, CARBINE
Caliber: 22 LR, 22 WMR, 38 Spec., 44-40, 45 Colt. **Barrel:** 24-1/4", octagonal. **Weight:** 8.1 lbs. **Length:** 43-1/4" overall. **Stock:** Walnut. **Sights:** Blade front adjustable for windage, rear adjustable for elevation. **Features:** Frame, buttplate, forend cap of polished brass, balance charcoal blued. Imported by Tristar Sporting Arms Ltd.
Price: **$779.00**
Price: Yellowboy carbine (19" round bbl.) **$739.00**

TRISTAR/UBERTI 1860 HENRY RIFLE
Caliber: 44-40, 45 Colt. **Barrel:** 24-1/4", half-octagon. **Weight:** 9.2 lbs. **Length:** 43-3/4" overall. **Stock:** American walnut. **Sights:** Blade front, rear adjustable for elevation. **Features:** Frame, elevator, magazine follower, buttplate are brass, balance blue. Imported by Tristar Sporting Arms Ltd. Arms, Inc.
Price: **$989.00**

Tristar/Uberti 1860 Henry Trapper Carbine
Similar to the 1860 Henry Rifle except has 18-1/2" barrel, measures 37-3/4" overall, and weighs 8 lbs. Introduced 1999. Imported from Italy by Tristar Sporting Arms Ltd.
Price: Brass frame, blued barrel **$989.00**

U.S. FIRE ARMS LIGHTNING MAGAZINE RIFLE
Caliber: 45 Colt, 44 WCF, 44 Spl., 38 WCF, 32 WCF, 15-shot. **Barrel:** 26" (rifle); 20" carbine, round or octagonal. **Stock:** Oiled walnut. **Finish:** Dome blue. Introduced 2002. Made in U.S.A. by United States Fire-Arms Manufacturing Co.
Price: **$1,480.00**

WINCHESTER TIMBER CARBINE
Caliber: Chambered for 450 Marlin. **Barrel:** 18" barrel, ported. **Weight:** 6 lbs. **Length:** 36-1/4" overall. **Stock:** Half-pistol grip stock with buttpad; checkered grip and forend. **Sights:** XS ghost-ring sight. **Features:** Introduced 1999. Made in U.S.A. by U.S. Repeating Arms Co., Inc.
Price: **$610.00**

WINCHESTER MODEL 94 TRADITIONAL-CW
Caliber: 30-30 Win., 6-shot; 44 Mag., 11-shot tubular magazine. **Barrel:** 20". **Weight:** 6-1/2 lbs. **Length:** 37-3/4" overall. **Stock:** Straight grip checkered walnut stock and forend. **Sights:** Hooded blade front, semi-buckhorn rear. Drilled and tapped for scope mount. Post front sight on Trapper model. **Features:** Solid frame, forged steel receiver; side ejection, exposed rebounding hammer with automatic trigger-activated transfer bar. Introduced 1984.
Price: 30-30 . . . . **$469.00**
Price: 44 Mag.. . . . . **$492.00**
Price: Traditional (no checkering, 30-30 only) **$435.00**

Winchester Model 94 Trapper
Similar to Model 94 Traditional except has 16" barrel, 5-shot magazine in 30-30, 9-shot in 357 Mag., 44 Magnum/44 Special, 45 Colt. Has stainless steel claw extractor, saddle ring, hammer spur extension, smooth walnut stocks.
Price: 30-30 . . . . **$459.00**
Price: 44 Mag., 357 Mag., 45 Colt **$459.00**

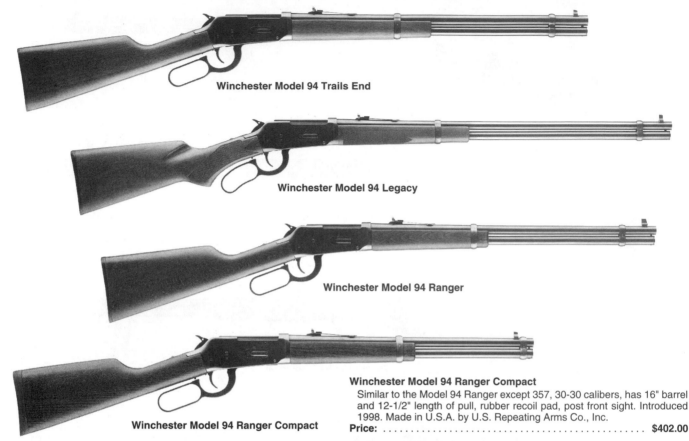

Winchester Model 94 Trails End

Winchester Model 94 Legacy

Winchester Model 94 Ranger

Winchester Model 94 Ranger Compact

Winchester Model 94 Trail's End

Similar to the Model 94 Traditional except octagon-barrel version available, chambered only for 357 Mag., 44-40, 44 Mag., 45 Colt; 11-shot magazine. Available with standard lever loop. Introduced 1997. From U.S. Repeating Arms Co., Inc.
Price: With standard lever loop $474.00

Winchester Model 94 Legacy

Similar to the Model 94 Traditional except has half-pistol grip walnut stock, checkered grip and forend. Chambered for 30-30, 357 Mag., 44 Mag., 45 Colt; 24" barrel. Introduced 1995. Made in U.S.A. by U.S. Repeating Arms Co., Inc.
Price: With 24" barrel. $487.00

Winchester Model 94 Ranger

Similar to the Model 94 Traditional except has a hardwood stock, post-style front sight and hammer-spur extension.
Price: (20" barrel) $379.00
Price: Trail's End octagon $757.00
Price: Trail's End octagon, case color $815.00

Winchester Model 94 Ranger Compact

Similar to the Model 94 Ranger except 357, 30-30 calibers, has 16" barrel and 12-1/2" length of pull, rubber recoil pad, post front sight. Introduced 1998. Made in U.S.A. by U.S. Repeating Arms Co., Inc.
Price: $402.00

WINCHESTER MODEL 1895 LEVER-ACTION RIFLE

Caliber: 405 Win, 4-shot magazine. **Barrel:** 24", round. **Weight:** 8 lbs. **Length:** 42" overall. **Stock:** American walnut. **Sights:** Gold bead front, buckhorn rear adjustable for elevation. **Features:** Re-creation of the original Model 1895. Polished blue finish. Two-piece cocking lever, Schnabel forend, straight-grip stock. Introduced 1995. From U.S. Repeating Arms Co., Inc.
Price: Grade I $1,116.00

Includes models for a wide variety of sporting and competitive purposes and uses.

Anschutz 1733D

Barrett Model 95

Blaser R93 Classic

ANSCHUTZ 1743D BOLT-ACTION RIFLE

Caliber: 222 Rem., 3-shot magazine. **Barrel:** 19.7". **Weight:** 6.4 lbs. **Length:** 39" overall. **Stock:** European walnut. **Sights:** Hooded blade front, folding leaf rear. **Features:** Receiver grooved for scope mounting; single stage trigger; claw extractor; sling safety; sling swivels. Imported from Germany by AcuSport Corp.
Price: **$1,588.95**

ANSCHUTZ 1740 MONTE CARLO RIFLE

Caliber: 22 Hornet, 5-shot clip; 222 Rem., 3-shot clip. **Barrel:** 24". **Weight:** 6-1/2 lbs. **Length:** 43.25" overall. **Stock:** Select European walnut. **Sights:** Hooded ramp front, folding leaf rear; drilled and tapped for scope mounting. **Features:** Uses Match 54 action. Adjustable single stage trigger. Stock has roll-over Monte Carlo cheekpiece, slim forend with Schnabel tip, Wundhammer palm swell on grip, rosewood gripcap with white diamond insert. Skip-line checkering on grip and forend. Introduced 1997. Imported from Germany by AcuSport Corp.
Price: From **$1,439.00**
Price: Model 1730 Monte Carlo, as above except in
22 Hornet.. **$1,439.00**

Anschutz 1733D Rifle

Similar to the 1740 Monte Carlo except has full-length, walnut, Mannlicher-style stock with skip line checkering, rosewood Schnabel tip, and is chambered for 22 Hornet. Weighs 6.4 lbs., overall length 39", barrel length 19.7". Imported from Germany by AcuSport Corp.
Price: **$1,588.95**

BARRETT MODEL 95 BOLT-ACTION RIFLE

Caliber: 50 BMG, 5-shot magazine. **Barrel:** 29". **Weight:** 22 lbs. **Length:** 45" overall. **Stock:** Energy-absorbing recoil pad. **Sights:** Scope optional. **Features:** Bolt-action, bullpup design. Disassembles without tools; extendable bipod legs; match-grade barrel; muzzle brake. Introduced 1995. Made in U.S.A. by Barrett Firearms Mfg., Inc.
Price: From **$4,950.00**

BLASER R93 BOLT-ACTION RIFLE

Caliber: 22-250, 243, 6.5x55, 270, 7x57, 7mm-08, 308, 30-06, 257 Wby. Mag., 7mm Rem. Mag., 300 Win. Mag., 300 Wby. Mag., 338 Win Mag., 375 H&H, 416 Rem. Mag. **Barrel:** 22" (standard calibers), 26" (magnum). **Weight:** 7 lbs. **Length:** 40" overall (22" barrel). **Stock:** Two-piece European walnut. **Sights:** None furnished; drilled and tapped for scope mounting. **Features:** Straight pull-back bolt action with thumb-activated safety slide/cocking mechanism; interchangeable barrels and bolt heads. Introduced 1994. Imported from Germany by SIGARMS.
Price: R93 Classic **$3,680.00**
Price: R93 LX **$1,895.00**
Price: R93 Synthetic (black synthetic stock) **$1,595.00**
Price: R93 Safari Synthetic (416 Rem. Mag. only)............. **$1,855.00**
Price: R93 Grand Lux... **$4,915.00**
Price: R93 Attaché **$5,390.00**

BRNO 98 BOLT-ACTION RIFLE

Caliber: 7x64, 243, 270, 308, 30-06, 300 Win. Mag., 9.3x62. **Barrel:** 23.6". **Weight:** 7.2 lbs. **Length:** 40.9" overall. **Stock:** European walnut. **Sights:** Blade on ramp front, open adjustable rear. **Features:** Uses Mauser 98-type action; polished blue. Announced 1998. Imported from the Czech Republic by Euro-Imports.
Price: Standard calibers **$507.00**
Price: Magnum calibers **$547.00**
Price: With set trigger, standard calibers **$615.00**
Price: As above, magnum calibers............................... **$655.00**
Price: With full stock, set trigger, standard calibers **$703.00**
Price: As above, magnum calibers............................... **$743.00**
Price: 300 Win. Mag., with BOSS............................... **$933.00**

BROWNING A-BOLT RIFLES

Caliber: 223, 22-250, 240, 7mm 08, 308, 25 06, 260, 270, 30-06, 260 Rem., 7mm Rem. Mag., 300 Win. Short Mag., 300 Win. Mag., 338 Win. Mag., 375 H&H Mag, 223 WSSM, 243 WSSM, 270 WSM, 7mm WSM, 300 WSM. **Barrel:** 22" medium sporter weight with recessed muzzle; 26" on mag. cals. **Weight:** 6-1/2 to 7-1/2 lbs. **Length:** 44-3/4" overall (magnum and standard); 41-3/4" (short action). **Stock:** Classic style American walnut; recoil pad standard on magnum calibers. **Features:** Short-throw (60") fluted bolt, three locking lugs, plunger-type ejector; adjustable trigger is grooved and gold-plated. Hinged floorplate, detachable box magazine (4 rounds std. cals., 3 for magnums). Slide tang safety. BOSS barrel vibration modulator and muzzle brake system not available in 375 H&H. Introduced 1985. Imported from Japan by Browning.
Price: Hunter, no sights **$705.00**
Price: Hunter, no sights, magnum calibers..................... **$734.00**
Price: For BOSS add **$80.00**

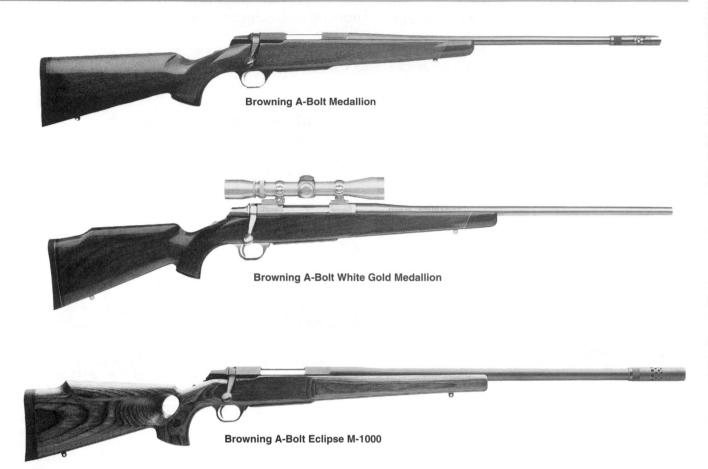

Browning A-Bolt Medallion

Browning A-Bolt White Gold Medallion

Browning A-Bolt Eclipse M-1000

Browning A-Bolt Medallion

Similar to standard A-Bolt except has glossy stock finish, rosewood grip and forend caps, engraved receiver, high-polish blue, no sights. New calibers include 223 WSSM, 243 WSSM, 270 WSM, 7mm WSM.

Price: Short-action calibers **$805.00**
Price: Long-action calibers **$805.00**
Price: Medallion, 375 H&H Mag., open sights **$835.00**
Price: 300 Win. Short Magnum **$835.00**
Price: For BOSS, add **$80.00**

Browning A-Bolt Medallion Left-Hand

Same as the Medallion model A-Bolt except has left-hand action and is available in 270, 30-06, 7mm Rem. Mag., 300 Win. Mag. Introduced 1987.

Price: 270, 30-06 (no sights) **$837.00**
Price: 7mm Mag., 300 Win. Mag. (no sights) **$865.00**
Price: For BOSS, add **$80.00**

Browning A-Bolt White Gold Medallion

Similar to the standard A-Bolt except has select walnut stock with brass spacers between rubber recoil pad and between the rosewood gripcap and forend tip; gold-filled barrel inscription; palm-swell pistol grip, Monte Carlo comb, 22 lpi checkering with double borders; engraved receiver flats. In 270, 30-06, 7mm Rem. Mag. and 300 Win. Mag. Introduced 1988.

Price: 270, 30-06 . . . . **$1,183.00**
Price: 7mm Rem. Mag, 300 Win. Mag. **$1,155.00**
Price: For BOSS, add **$80.00**

BROWNING A-BOLT WHITE GOLD RMEF

Caliber: 7mm Rem. Mag. Similar to the A-Bolt Medallion except has select walnut stock with rosewood forend cap, RMEF-engraved gripcap; continental cheekpiece; gold engraved, stainless receiver and bbl. Introduced 2004. Imported from Japan by Browning.

Price: **$1,261.00**

Browning A-Bolt Eclipse Hunter

Similar to the A-Bolt except has gray/black laminated, thumbhole stock, BOSS barrel vibration modulator and muzzle brake. Available in long and short action with heavy barrel. In 270 Win., 30-06, 7mm Rem. Mag. Introduced 1996. Imported from Japan by Browning.

Price: 270, 30-06, with BOSS. **$1,134.00**
Price: 7mm Rem. Mag, with BOSS **$1,162.00**

Browning A-Bolt Eclipse M-1000

Similar to the A-Bolt Eclipse except has long action and heavy target barrel. Chambered only for 300 Win. Mag. Adjustable trigger, bench-style forend, 3-shot magazine; laminated thumbhole stock; BOSS system standard. Introduced 1997. Imported for Japan by Browning.

Price: **$1,292.00**

Browning A-Bolt Micro Hunter

Similar to the A-Bolt Hunter except has 13-5/16" length of pull, 20" barrel, and comes in 260 Rem., 243, 308, 7mm-08, 223, 22-250, 22 Hornet, 270 WSM, 7mm WSM, 300 WSM. Weighs 6 lbs., 1 oz. Introduced 1999. Imported by Browning. Also available in left-hand version.

Price: (no sights) **$714.00**

Browning A-Bolt Mountain TI

Similar to the A-Bolt Hunter except has low-luster bluing and walnut stock with Monte Carlo comb, pistol grip palm swell, double-border checkering. Available in 223 WSSM, 243 WSSM. Introduced 1999. Imported by Browning.

Price: WSM. **$1,690.00**
Price: WSSM **$1,669.00**

Browning A-Bolt Stalker

Charles Daly Field Mauser

CZ 527 Lux

CZ 550 Lux

Browning A-Bolt Stainless Stalker

Similar to the A-Bolt Hunter model except receiver and barrel are made of stainless steel; other exposed metal surfaces are finished silver-gray matte. Graphite-fiberglass composite textured stock. No sights are furnished. Available in 260, 243, 308, 7mm-08, 270, 280,30-06, 7mm Rem. Mag., 300 WSM, 300 Rem. Ultra Mag., 338 Win. Mag., 338 Rem. Ultra Mag., 375 H&H, 223 WSSM, 243 WSSM, 270 WSM, 7mm WSM. Introduced 1987.

Price: Short-action calibers	$897.00
Price: Magnum calibers	$926.00
Price: 300 Win. Short Magnum	$926.00
Price: For BOSS, add	$80.00
Price: Left-hand, 270, 30-06	$1,005.00
Price: Left-hand, 7mm, 300 Win. Mag., 338 Win. Mag.	$1,034.00
Price: Left-hand, 375 H&H, with sights	$1,034.00
Price: Left-hand, for BOSS, add	$80.00

Browning A-Bolt Composite Stalker

Similar to the A-Bolt Hunter except has black graphite-fiberglass stock with textured finish. Matte blue finish on all exposed metal surfaces. Available in 223, 22-250, 243, 7mm-08, 308, 30-06, 270, 280, 25-06, 7mm Rem. Mag., 300 WSM, 300 Win. Mag., 338 Win. Mag, 223 WSSM, 243 WSSM, 270 WSM, 7mm WSM. BOSS barrel vibration modulator and muzzle brake system offered in all calibers. Introduced 1994.

Price: Standard calibers, no sights	$705.00
Price: WSSM	$755.00
Price: Magnum calibers, no sights	$734.00
Price: For BOSS, add	$80.00

CARBON ONE BOLT-ACTION RIFLE

Caliber: 22-250 to 375 H&H. **Barrel:** Up to 28". **Weight:** 5-1/2 to 7-1/4 lbs. **Length:** Varies. **Stock:** Synthetic or wood. **Sights:** None furnished. **Features:** Choice of Remington, Browning or Winchester action with free-floated Christensen graphite/epoxy/steel barrel, trigger pull tuned to 3 to 3-1/2 lbs. Made in U.S.A. by Christensen Arms.

Price: Carbon One Hunter Rifle, 6-1/2 to 7 lbs.	$1,499.00
Price: Carbon One Custom, 5-1/2 to 6-1/2 lbs., Shilen trigger	$2,750.00
Price: Carbon Ranger, 50 BMG, 5-shot repeater	$4,750.00
Price: Carbon Ranger, 50 BMG, single shot	$3,950.00

CHARLES DALY FIELD MAUSER RIFLE

Caliber: 22-250, 243, 25-06, 270, 308, 30-06 (in 22" barrels); 7mm Rem. Mag. and 300 Win. Mag. in 24" barrels. **Weight:** NA **Sights:** None; drilled and tapped for scope mounts. **Features:** Mauser Model 98-type action; carbon or stainless steel barrels; slide safety; polymer stock; fully adjustable trigger.

Price: Field Grade Mauser	$459.00
Price: Mauser SS	$549.00
Price: Magnum calibers	$579.00

CZ 527 LUX BOLT-ACTION RIFLE

Caliber: 22 Hornet, 222 Rem., 223 Rem., detachable 5-shot magazine. **Barrel:** 23-1/2"; standard or heavy barrel. **Weight:** 6 lbs., 1 oz. **Length:** 42-1/2" overall. **Stock:** European walnut with Monte Carlo. **Sights:** Hooded front, open adjustable rear. **Features:** Improved mini-Mauser action with non-rotating claw extractor; single set trigger; grooved receiver. Imported from the Czech Republic by CZ-USA.

Price:	$566.00
Price: Model FS, full-length stock, cheekpiece	$658.00

CZ 527 American Classic Bolt-Action Rifle

Similar to the CZ 527 Lux except has classic-style stock with 18 lpi checkering; free-floating barrel; recessed target crown on barrel. No sights furnished. Introduced 1999. Imported from the Czech Republic by CZ-USA.
Price: 22 Hornet, 222 Rem., 223 Rem. . . . . . . **$586.00 to $609.00**

CZ 550 LUX BOLT-ACTION RIFLE

Caliber: 22-250, 243, 6.5x55, 7x57, 7x64, 308 Win., 9.3x62, 270 Win., 30-06. **Barrel:** 20.47". **Weight:** 7.5 lbs. **Length:** 44.68" overall. **Stock:** Turkish walnut in Bavarian style or FS (Mannlicher). **Sights:** Hooded front, adjustable rear. **Features:** Improved Mauser-style action with claw extractor, fixed ejector, square bridge dovetailed receiver; single set trigger. Imported from the Czech Republic by CZ-USA.

Price: Lux	$566.00 to $609.00
Price: FS (full stock)	$706.00

CZ 550 American Classic

CZ 550 Magnum

Dakota 76 Classic

Dakota 76 Safari

CZ 550 American Classic Bolt-Action Rifle

Similar to CZ 550 Lux except has American classic-style stock with 18 lpi checkering; free-floating barrel; recessed target crown. Has 25.6" barrel; weighs 7.48 lbs. No sights furnished. Introduced 1999. Imported from the Czech Republic by CZ-USA.

Price: .... $586.00 to $609.00

CZ 550 Medium Magnum Bolt-Action Rifle

Similar to the CZ 550 Lux except chambered for the 300 Win. Mag. and 7mm Rem. Mag.; 5-shot magazine. Adjustable iron sights, hammer-forged barrel, single-set trigger, Turkish walnut stock. Weighs 7.5 lbs. Introduced 2001. Imported from the Czech Republic by CZ-USA.

Price: $621.00

CZ 550 Magnum Bolt-Action Rifle

Similar to CZ 550 Lux except has long action for 300 Win. Mag., 375 H&H, 416 Rigby, 458 Win. Mag. Overall length is 46.45"; barrel length 25"; weighs 9.24 lbs. Hooded front sight, express rear with one standing, two folding leaves. Imported from the Czech Republic by CZ-USA.

Price: 300 Win. Mag. $717.00
Price: 375 H&H $756.00
Price: 416 Rigby $809.00
Price: 458 Win. Mag. $744.00

CZ 700 M1 SNIPER RIFLE

Caliber: 308 Winchester, 10-shot magazine. **Barrel:** 25.6". **Weight:** 11.9 lbs. **Length:** 45" overall. **Stock:** Laminated wood thumbhole with adjustable buttplate and cheekpiece. **Sights:** None furnished; permanently attached Weaver rail for scope mounting. **Features:** 60-degree bolt throw; oversized trigger guard and bolt handle for use with gloves; full-length equipment rail on forend; fully adjustable trigger. Introduced 2001. Imported from the Czech Republic by CZ-USA.

Price: $2,097.00

DAKOTA 76 TRAVELER TAKEDOWN RIFLE

Caliber: 257 Roberts, 25-06, 7x57, 270, 280, 30-06, 338-06, 35 Whelen (standard length); 7mm Rem. Mag., 300 Win. Mag., 338 Win. Mag., 416 Taylor, 458 Win. Mag. (short magnums); 7mm, 300, 330, 375 Dakota Magnums. **Barrel:** 23". **Weight:** 7-1/2 lbs. **Length:** 43-1/2" overall. **Stock:** Medium fancy-grade walnut in classic style. Checkered grip and forend; solid buttpad. **Sights:** None furnished; drilled and tapped for scope mounts. **Features:** Threadless disassembly. Uses modified Model 76 design with many features of the Model 70 Winchester. Left-hand model also available. Introduced 1989. Made in U.S.A. by Dakota Arms, Inc.

Price: Classic $4,495.00
Price: Safari $5,495.00
Price: Extra barrels .... $1,650.00 to $1,950.00

DAKOTA 76 CLASSIC BOLT-ACTION RIFLE

Caliber: 257 Roberts, 270, 280, 30-06, 7mm Rem. Mag., 338 Win. Mag., 300 Win. Mag., 375 H&H, 458 Win. Mag. **Barrel:** 23". **Weight:** 7-1/2 lbs. **Length:** 43-1/2" overall. **Stock:** Medium fancy grade walnut in classic style. Checkered pistol grip and forend; solid buttpad. **Sights:** None furnished; drilled and tapped for scope mounts. **Features:** Has many features of the original Winchester Model 70. One-piece rail trigger guard assembly; steel gripcap. Model 70-style trigger. Many options available. Left-hand rifle available at same price. Introduced 1988. From Dakota Arms, Inc.

Price: $3,595.00

DAKOTA 76 SAFARI BOLT-ACTION RIFLE

Caliber: 270 Win., 7x57, 280, 30-06, 7mm Dakota, 7mm Rem. Mag., 300 Dakota, 300 Win. Mag., 330 Dakota, 338 Win. Mag., 375 Dakota, 458 Win. Mag., 300 H&H, 375 H&H, 416 Rem. **Barrel:** 23". **Weight:** 8-1/2 lbs. **Length:** 43-1/2" overall. **Stock:** XXX fancy walnut with ebony forend tip; point-pattern with wraparound forend checkering. **Sights:** Ramp front, standing leaf rear. **Features:** Has many features of the original Winchester Model 70. Barrel band front swivel, inletted rear. Cheekpiece with shadow line. Steel gripcap. Introduced 1988. From Dakota Arms, Inc.

Price: Wood stock. $4,595.00

Dakota Longbow

Dakota 97 Lightweight Hunter

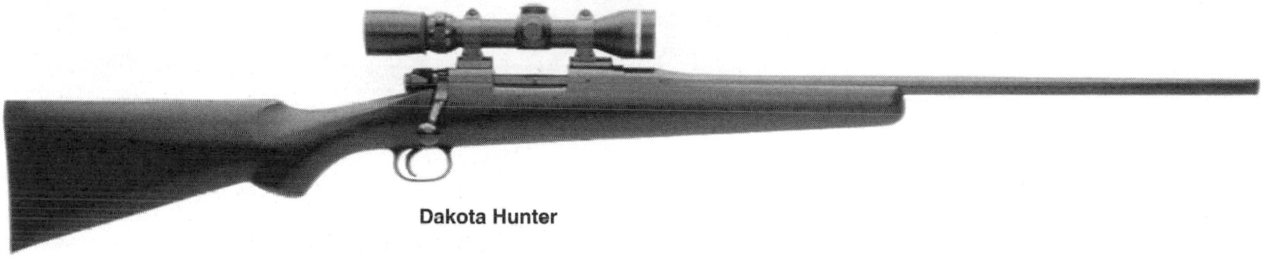

Dakota Hunter

Ed Brown 702 Savanna

Dakota African Grade

Similar to 76 Safari except chambered for 338 Lapua Mag., 404 Jeffery, 416 Rigby, 416 Dakota, 450 Dakota, 4-round magazine, select wood, two stock cross-bolts. 24" barrel, weighs 9-10 lbs. Ramp front sight, standing leaf rear. Introduced 1989.

Price: $4,995.00

DAKOTA LONGBOW TACTICAL E.R. RIFLE

Caliber: 300 Dakota Magnum, 330 Dakota Magnum, 338 Lapua Magnum. Barrel: 28", .950" at muzzle Weight: 13.7 lbs. Length: 50" to 52" overall. Stock: Ambidextrous McMillan A-2 fiberglass, black or olive green color; adjustable cheekpiece and buttplate. Sights: None furnished. Comes with Picatinny one-piece optical rail. Features: Uses the Dakota 76 action with controlled-round feed; three-position firing pin block safety, claw extractor; Model 70-style trigger. Comes with bipod, case tool kit. Introduced 1997. Made in U.S.A. by Dakota Arms, Inc.

Price: $4,250.00

DAKOTA 97 LIGHTWEIGHT HUNTER

Caliber: 22-250 to 330. Barrel: 22" to 24". Weight: 6.1 to 6.5 lbs. Length: 43" overall. Stock: Fiberglass. Sights: Optional. Features: Matte blue finish, black stock. Right-hand action only. Introduced 1998. Made in U.S.A. by Dakota Arms, Inc.

Price: $1,995.00

DAKOTA LONG RANGE HUNTER RIFLE

Caliber: 25-06, 257 Roberts, 270 Win., 280 Rem., 7mm Rem. Mag., 7mm Dakota Mag., 30-06, 300 Win. Mag., 300 Dakota Mag., 338 Win. Mag., 330 Dakota Mag., 375 H&H Mag., 375 Dakota Mag. Barrel: 24", 26", match-quality; free-floating. Weight: 7.7 lbs. Length: 45" to 47" overall. Stock: H-S Precision black synthetic, with one-piece bedding block system. Sights: None furnished. Drilled and tapped for scope mounting. Features: Cylindrical machined receiver controlled round feed; Mauser-style extractor; three-position striker blocking safety; fully adjustable match trigger. Right-hand action only. Introduced 1997. Made in U.S.A. by Dakota Arms, Inc.

Price: $1,995.00

ED BROWN SAVANNA RIFLE

Caliber: 30-06, 300 Win. Mag., 300 Weatherby, 338 Win. Mag. Barrel: 22", 23", 24". Weight: 8 to 8-1/2 lbs. Stock: Fully glass-bedded McMillan fiberglass sporter. Sights: None furnished. Talley scope mounts utilizing heavy duty 8-40 screws. Features: Custom action with machined steel trigger guard and hinged floor plate. Available in left-hand version.

Price: From................................. $2,795.00 to $2,895.00

Ed Brown 702 Ozark

Ed Brown 702 Bushveld

Ed Brown 702 Varmint

Harris Gunworks Alaskan

Ed Brown Model 702 Denali, Ozark

Similar to the Ed Brown Model 702 Savanna but lighter weight, designed specifically for mountain hunting, especially suited to the 270 and 280 calibers. Right-hand only. Weighs about 7.75 lbs. The Model 702 Ozark is made on a short action with a lightweight stock. Ozark calibers are 223, 243, 6mm, 260 Rem., 7mm-08, 308. Weight 6.5 lbs.

Price: From **$2,800.00**

ED BROWN MODEL 702 BUSHVELD

Caliber: 338 Win. Mag., 375 H&H, 416 Rem. Mag., 458 Win. Mag., 458 Lott and all Ed Brown Savanna long action calibers. **Barrel:** 24" medium or heavy weight. **Weight:** 8.25 lbs. **Stock:** Fully bedded McMillan fiberglass with Monte Carlo style cheekpiece, Pachmayr Decelerator recoil pad. **Sights:** None furnished. Talley scope mounts utilizing heavy duty 8-40 screws. **Features:** Options include left-hand action, stainless steel barrel, additional calibers, iron sights.

Price: From . . . . **$2,895.00 to $3,195.00**

ED BROWN MODEL 702 VARMINT

Caliber: 223, 22-250, 220 Swift, 243, 6mm, 308. **Barrel:** Medium weight #5 contour 24"; heavyweight #17 contour 24"; 26" optional. **Weight:** 9 lbs. **Stock:** Fully glass-bedded McMillan fiberglass with recoil pad. **Sights:** None furnished. Talley scope mounts with heavy duty 8-40 screws. **Features:** Fully-adjustable trigger, steel trigger guard and floor plate, many options available.

Price: From **$2,495.00**

HARRIS GUNWORKS SIGNATURE CLASSIC SPORTER

Caliber: 22-250, 243, 6mm Rem., 7mm-08, 284, 308 (short action); 25-06, 270, 280 Rem., 30-06, 7mm Rem. Mag., 300 Win. Mag., 300 Wby. (long action); 338 Win. Mag., 340 Wby., 375 H&H (magnum action). **Barrel:** 22", 24", 26". **Weight:** 7 lbs. (short action). **Stock:** Fiberglass in green, beige, brown or black. Recoil pad and 1" swivels installed. Length of pull up to 14-1/4". **Sights:** None furnished. Comes with 1" rings and bases. **Features:** Uses right- or left-hand action with matte black finish. Trigger pull set at 3 lbs. Four-round magazine for standard calibers; three for magnums. Aluminum floorplate. Wood stock optional. Introduced 1987. From Harris Gunworks, Inc.

Price: **$2,700.00**

Harris Gunworks Signature Classic Stainless Sporter

Similar to Signature Classic Sporter except action is made of stainless steel. Same calibers, in addition to 416 Rem. Mag. Fiberglass stock, right- or left-hand action in natural stainless, glass bead or black chrome sulfide finishes. Introduced 1990. From Harris Gunworks, Inc.

Price: **$2,900.00**

Harris Gunworks Signature Alaskan

Similar to Classic Sporter except match-grade barrel with single leaf rear sight, barrel band front, 1" detachable rings and mounts, steel floorplate, electroless nickel finish. Wood Monte Carlo stock with cheekpiece, palm-swell grip, solid buttpad. Chambered for 270, 280 Rem., 30-06, 7mm Rem. Mag., 300 Win. Mag., 300 Wby., 358 Win., 340 Wby., 375 H&H. Introduced 1989.

Price: **$3,800.00**

Harris Gunworks Signature Titanium Mountain

Harris Gunworks Signature Super Varminter

Harris Gunworks Talon Safari

Howa Lightning

Harris Gunworks Signature Titanium Mountain Rifle
Similar to Classic Sporter except action made of titanium alloy, barrel of chrome-moly steel. Stock is graphite reinforced fiberglass. Weight is 5-1/2 lbs. Chambered for 270, 280 Rem., 30-06, 7mm Rem. Mag., 300 Win. Mag. Fiberglass stock optional. Introduced 1989.
Price: **$3,300.00**
Price: With graphite-steel composite lightweight barrel **$3,700.00**

Harris Gunworks Signature Varminter
Similar to Signature Classic Sporter except has heavy contoured barrel, adjustable trigger, field bipod and special hand-bedded fiberglass stock. Chambered for 223, 22 250, 220 Swift, 243, 6mm Rem., 25-06, 7mm-08, 7mm BR, 308, 350 Rem. Mag. Comes with 1" rings and bases. Introduced 1989.
Price: **$2,700.00**

HARRIS GUNWORKS TALON SAFARI RIFLE
Caliber: 300 Win. Mag., 300 Wby. Mag., 300 Phoenix, 338 Win. Mag., 30/378, 338 Lapua, 300 H&H, 340 Wby. Mag., 375 H&H, 404 Jeffery, 416 Rem. Mag., 458 Win. Mag. (Safari Magnum); 378 Wby. Mag., 416 Rigby, 416 Wby. Mag., 460 Wby. Mag. (Safari Super Magnum). **Barrel:** 24". **Weight:** About 9-10 lbs. **Length:** 43" overall. **Stock:** Gunworks fiberglass Safari. **Sights:** Barrel band front ramp, multi-leaf express rear. **Features:** Uses Harris Gunworks Safari action. Has quick detachable 1" scope mounts, positive locking steel floorplate, barrel band sling swivel. Match-grade barrel. Matte black finish standard. Introduced 1989. From Harris Gunworks, Inc.

Price: Talon Safari Magnum **$3,900.00**
Price: Talon Safari Super Magnum **$4,200.00**

HARRIS GUNWORKS TALON SPORTER RIFLE
Caliber: 22-250, 243, 6mm Rem., 6mm BR, 7mm BR, 7mm-08, 25-06, 270, 280 Rem., 284, 308, 30-06, 350 Rem. Mag. (long action); 7mm Rem. Mag., 7mm STW, 300 Win. Mag., 300 Wby. Mag., 300 H&H, 338 Win. Mag., 340 Wby. Mag., 375 H&H, 416 Rem. Mag. **Barrel:** 24" (standard). **Weight:** About 7-1/2 lbs. **Length:** NA. **Stock:** Choice of walnut or fiber-glass. **Sights:** None furnished; comes with rings and bases. Open sights optional. **Features:** Uses pre-'64 Model 70-type action with cone breech, controlled feed, claw extractor and three-position safety. Barrel and action are of stainless steel; chrome-moly optional. Introduced 1991. From Harris Gunworks, Inc.
Price: **$2,000.00**

HOWA LIGHTNING BOLT-ACTION RIFLE
Caliber: 223, 22-250, 243, 6.5x55, 270, 308, 30-06, 7mm Rem. Mag., 300 Win. Mag., 338 Win. Mag, 300 WSM, 7mm WSM, 270 WSM. **Barrel:** 22", 24" magnum calibers. **Weight:** 7-1/2 lbs. **Length:** 42" overall (22" barrel). **Stock:** Black Bell & Carlson Carbelite composite with Monte Carlo comb; checkered grip and forend; also Realtree camo available. **Sights:** None furnished. Drilled and tapped for scope mounting. **Features:** Three-position thumb safety; hinged floorplate; polished blue/black finish. Introduced 1993. From Legacy Sports International.
Price: Blue, standard calibers **$508.00**
Price: Blue, magnum calibers **$531.00**
Price: Stainless, standard calibers **$620.00**
Price: Stainless, magnum calibers **$649.00**

Howa M-1500 Hunter

Howa M-1500 Ultralight

Howa M-1500 Varmint Supreme

Kimber 84M Classic

Howa M-1500 Hunter Bolt-Action Rifle

Similar to Lightning Model except has walnut-finished hardwood stock, three-position safety. Polished blue finish or stainless steel. Introduced 1999. From Legacy Sports International.

Price: Blue, standard calibers	$574.00
Price: Stainless, standard calibers	$682.00
Price: Blue, magnum calibers	$595.00
Price: Stainless, magnum calibers	$704.00
Price: Blued, camo stock	$545.00
Price: Blued, camo, magnum cal.	$568.00
Price: Stainless, camo, standard cal.	$661.00
Price: Stainless, camo, magnum cal.	$690.00

Howa M-1500 Supreme Rifles

Similar to Howa M-1500 Lightning except stocked with JRS Classic or Thumbhole Sporter laminated wood stocks in Nutmeg (brown/black) or Pepper (gray/black) colors. Barrel: 22"; 24" magnum calibers. Weights are JRS stock 8 lbs., THS stock 8.3 lbs. Three-position safety. Introduced 2001. Imported from Japan by Legacy Sports International.

Price: Blue, standard calibers, JRS stock	$646.00
Price: Blue, standard calibers, THS stock	$704.00
Price: Blue, magnum calibers, JRS stock	$675.00
Price: Blue, magnum calibers, THS stock	$733.00
Price: Stainless, standard calibers, JRS stock	$755.00
Price: Stainless, standard calibers, THS stock	$813.00
Price: Stainless, magnum calibers, JRS stock	$784.00
Price: Stainless, magnum calibers, THS stock	$842.00

Howa M-1500 Ultralight

Similar to Howa M-1500 Lightning except receiver milled to reduce weight; three-position safety; tapered 22" barrel; 1-10" twist. Chambered for 243 Win. Stocks are black texture-finished hardwood. Weighs 6.4 lbs. Length 40" overall.

Price: Blued	$539.00
Price: Stainless model	$658.00

Howa M-1500 Varmint and Varmint Supreme Rifles

Similar to M-1500 Lightning except has heavy 24" hammer-forged barrel. Chambered for 223, 22-250, 308. Weighs 9.3 lbs.; overall length 44.5". Introduced 1999. Imported from Japan by Interarms/Howa. Varminter Supreme has heavy barrel, target crown muzzle; three-position safety. Heavy 24" barrel, laminated wood with raised comb stocks, rollover cheekpiece, vented beavertail forearm; available in 223 Rem., 22-250 Rem., 308 Win. Weighs 9.9 lbs. Introduced 2001. Imported from Japan by Legacy Sports International.

Price: Varminter, blue, polymer stock	$546.00
Price: Varminter, stainless, polymer stock	$664.00
Price: Varminter, blue, wood stock	$610.00
Price: Varminter, stainless, wood stock	$719.00
Price: Varminter Supreme, blued	$711.00 to $733.00
Price: Varminter Supreme, stainless	$820.00 to $842.00
Price: Varminter, blued, camo stock	$582.00
Price: Varminter, stainless, camo stock	$704.00

KIMBER MODEL 8400 BOLT-ACTION RIFLE

Caliber: 270, 7mm, 300 or 325 WSM, 4 shot. **Barrel:** 24". **Weight:** 6 lbs. 3 oz. to 6 lbs 10 oz. **Length:** 43.25". **Stock:** Claro walnut or Kevlar-reinforced fiberglass. **Sights:** None; drilled and tapped for bases. **Features:** Mauser claw extractor, two-position wing safety, action bedded on aluminum pillars and fiberglass, free-floated barrel, match grade adjustable trigger set at 4 lbs., matte or polished blue or matte stainless finish. Introduced 2003. Made in U.S.A. by Kimber Mfg. Inc.

Price: Classic	$1,080.00 to $2,030.00

KIMBER MODEL 84M BOLT-ACTION RIFLE

Caliber: 22-250, 204 Ruger, 223, 243, 260 Rem., 7mm-08, 308, 5-shot. **Barrel:** 22", 24", 26". **Weight:** 5 lbs., 10 oz. to 10 lbs. **Length:** 41" to 45". **Stock:** Claro walnut, checkered with steel gripcap; synthetic or gray laminate. **Sights:** None; drilled and tapped for bases. **Features:** Mauser claw extractor, three-position wing safety, action bedded on aluminum pillars, free-floated barrel, match-grade trigger set at 4 lbs., matte blue finish. Includes cable lock. Introduced 2001. Made in U.S.A. by Kimber Mfg. Inc.

Price: Classic (243, 260, 7mm-08, 308)	$945.00 to $1,828.00
Price: Varmint (22-250)	$1,038.00

Kimber 84M Varmint

L.A.R. Grizzly

Magnum Research Tactical

Raptor Bolt-Action

Remington 673 Guide

L.A.R. GRIZZLY 50 BIG BOAR RIFLE
Caliber: 50 BMG, single shot. **Barrel:** 36". **Weight:** 30.4 lbs. **Length:** 45.5" overall. **Stock:** Integral. Ventilated rubber recoil pad. **Sights:** None furnished; scope mount. **Features:** Bolt-action bullpup design, thumb and bolt stop safety. All steel construction. Introduced 1994. Made in U.S.A. by L.A.R. Mfg., Inc.
Price: **$2,295.00**

MAGNUM RESEARCH MAGNUM LITE TACTICAL RIFLE
Caliber: 223 Rem., 22-250, 308 Win., 300 Win. Mag., 300 WSM. **Barrel:** 26" Magnum Lite™ graphite. **Weight:** 8.3 lbs. **Length:** NA. **Stock:** H-S Precision™ tactical black synthetic. **Sights:** None furnished; drilled and tapped for scope mount. **Features:** Accurized Remington 700 action; adjustable trigger; adjustable comb height. Tuned to shoot 1/2" MOA or better. Introduced 2001. From Magnum Research Inc.
Price: **$2,400.00**

MOUNTAIN EAGLE MAGNUM LITE RIFLE
Caliber: 22-250, 223 Rem. (Varmint); 280, 30-06 (long action); 7mm Rem. Mag., 300 Win. Mag., (magnum action). **Barrel:** 24", 26", free floating.

Weight: 7 lbs., 13 oz. **Length:** 44" overall (24" barrel). **Stock:** Kevlar-graphite with aluminum bedding block, high comb, recoil pad, swivel studs; made by H-S Precision. **Sights:** None furnished; accepts any Remington 700-type base. **Features:** Special Sako action with one-piece forged bolt, hinged steel floorplate, lengthened receiver ring; adjustable trigger. Krieger cut-rifled benchrest barrel. Introduced 1996. From Magnum Research, Inc.
Price: Magnum Lite (graphite barrel) **$2,295.00**

RAPTOR BOLT-ACTION RIFLE
Caliber: 270, 30-06, 243, 25-06, 308, 4-shot magazine. **Barrel:** 22". **Weight:** 7 lbs., 6 oz. **Length:** 42.5" overall. **Stock:** Black synthetic, fiberglass reinforced; checkered grip and forend; vented recoil pad; Monte Carlo cheekpiece. **Sights:** None furnished; drilled and tapped for scope mounts. **Features:** Rust-resistant "Taloncote" treated barreled action; pillar bedded; stainless bolt with three locking lugs; adjustable trigger. Introduced 1997. Made in U.S.A. by Raptor Arms Co., Inc.
Price: **$249.00**

REMINGTON MODEL 673 GUIDE RIFLE
Caliber: 65mm Rem. Mag., 308 Win., 300 Rem. SA Ultra Mag., 350 Rem. Mag. **Barrel:** 22". **Weight:** 7-1/2 lbs. **Length:** 41-3/16". **Stock:** Two-tone wide striped, laminated, weather resistant. **Features:** Magnum contour barrel with machined steel ventilated rib, iron sights.
Price: **$825.00**

Remington 700 Classic

Remington 700 ADL Synthetic

Remington 700 BDL

Remington 700 BDL Left-Hand

REMINGTON MODEL 700 CLASSIC RIFLE
Caliber: 300 Savage. **Barrel:** 24". **Weight:** About 7-1/4 lbs. **Length:** 44-1/2" overall. **Stock:** American walnut, 20 lpi checkering on pistol grip and forend. Classic styling. Satin finish. **Sights:** None furnished. Receiver drilled and tapped for scope mounting. **Features:** A "classic" version of the BDL with straight comb stock. Fitted with rubber recoil pad. Sling swivel studs installed. Hinged floorplate. Limited production in 2003 only.
Price: **$683.00**
Price: Left-hand model .... **$769.00 to $796.00**

REMINGTON MODEL 700 ADL DELUXE RIFLE
Caliber: 270, 30-06. **Barrel:** 22" round tapered. **Weight:** 7-1/4 lbs. **Length:** 41-5/8" overall. **Stock:** Walnut. Satin-finished pistol grip stock with fine-line cut checkering, Monte Carlo. **Sights:** Gold bead ramp front; removable, step-adjustable rear with windage screw. **Features:** Side safety, receiver tapped for scope mounts.
Price: **$580.00**

Remington Model 700 ADL Synthetic
Similar to the 700 ADL except has a fiberglass-reinforced synthetic stock with straight comb, raised cheekpiece, positive checkering, and black rubber buttpad. Metal has matte finish. Available in 22-250, 223, 243, 270, 308, 30-06 with 22" barrel, 300 Win. Mag., 7mm Rem. Mag. with 24" barrel. Introduced 1996.
Price: From .... **$500.00 to $527.00**

Remington Model 700 ADL Synthetic Youth
Similar to the Model 700 ADL Synthetic except has 1" shorter stock, 20" barrel. Chambered for 243, 308. Introduced 1998.
Price: **$500.00**

Remington Model 700 BDL Custom Deluxe Rifle
Same as 700 ADL except chambered for 222, 223 (short action, 24" barrel), 7mm-08, 280, 22-250, 25-06, (short action, 22" barrel), 243, 270, 30-06, skip-line checkering, black forend tip and gripcap with white line spacers. Matted receiver top, quick-release floorplate. Hooded ramp front sight, quick detachable swivels.
Price: **$683.00**
Also available in 17 Rem., 7mm Rem. Mag., 7mm Rem. Ultra Mag., 300 Win. Mag. (long action, 24" barrel); 300 Rem. Ultra Mag. (26" barrel). Overall length 44-1/2", weight about 7-1/2 lbs.
Price: .... **$709.00 to $723.00**

Remington Model 700 BDL Left-Hand Custom Deluxe
Same as 700 BDL except mirror-image left-hand action, stock. Available in 270, 30-06, 7mm Rem. Mag., 300 Rem. Ultra Mag, 338 Rem. Ultra Mag., 7mm Rem. Ultra Mag.
Price: .... **$709.00 to $749.00**

Remington Model 700 BDL DM Rifle
Same as 700 BDL except detachable box magazine (4-shot, standard calibers, 3-shot for magnums). Glossy stock finish, open sights, recoil pad, sling swivels. Available in 270, 30-06, 7mm Rem. Mag., 300 Win. Mag. Introduced 1995.
Price: From .... **$749.00 to $776.00**

Remington 700 BDL SS

Remington 700 BDL SS DM

Remington 700 LSS Mountain

Remington 700 Safari KS

Remington 700 APR African Plains

Remington Model 700 BDL SS Rifle

Similar to 700 BDL rifle except hinged floorplate, 24" standard weight barrel in all calibers; magnum calibers have magnum-contour barrel. No sights supplied, but comes drilled and tapped. Corrosion-resistant follower and fire control, stainless BDL-style barreled action with fine matte finish. Synthetic stock has straight comb and cheekpiece, textured finish, positive checkering, plated swivel studs. Calibers: 270, 30-06; magnums:7mm Rem. Mag., 7mm Rem. UltraMag., 300 Rem. Ultra Mag. (26" barrel) 300 Win. Mag., 338 Rem. Ultra Mag., 7mm Rem. SAUM, 300 Rem. SAUM. Weight: 7-3/8 to 7-1/2 lbs. Introduced 1993.
Price: From . . . . **$735.00 to $775.00**

Remington Model 700 BDL SS DM Rifle

Same as 700 BDL SS except detachable box magazine. Barrel, receiver and bolt made of #416 stainless steel; black synthetic stock, fine-line engraving. Available in 270, 30-06, 7mm Rem. Mag., 300 Win. Mag. Introduced 1995.
Price: From . . . . **$801.00 to $828.00**

Remington Model 700 Custom KS Mountain Rifle

Similar to 700 BDL except custom finished with aramid fiber reinforced resin synthetic stock. Available in left- and right-hand versions. Chambered 270 Win., 280 Rem., 30-06, 7mm Rem. Mag., 7mm STW, 300 Win. Ultra Mag., 338 Rem. Ultra Mag., 300 Win. Mag., 300 Wby. Mag., 35 Whelen, 338 Win. Mag., 8mm Rem. Mag., 375 H&H, with 24" barrel (except 300 Rem. Ultra Mag., 26"), 7mm RUM, 375 RUM. Weighs 6 lbs., 6 oz. Introduced 1986.
Price: Right-hand **$1,314.00**

Price: Left-hand **$1,393.00**
Price: Stainless . . . . **$1,500.00 to $1,580.00**

Remington Model 700 LSS Mountain Rifle

Similar to Model 700 Custom KS Mountain Rifle except stainless steel 22" barrel and two-tone laminated stock. Chambered in 260 Rem., 7mm-08, 270 Winchester and 30-06. Overall length 42-1/2", weighs 6-5/8 oz. Introduced 1999.
Price: **$800.00**

Remington Model 700 Safari Grade

Similar to 700 BDL aramid fiber reinforced fiberglass stock, blued carbon steel bbl. and action, or stainless, w/cheekpiece, custom finished and tuned. In 8mm Rem. Mag., 375 H&H, 416 Rem. Mag. or 458 Win. Mag. calibers only with heavy barrel. Right- and left-hand versions.
Price: Safari KS . . . . **$1,520.00 to $1,601.00**
Price: Safari KS (stainless right-hand only) **$1,697.00**

Remington Model 700 AWR Alaskan Wilderness Rifle

Similar to the 700 BDL except has stainless barreled action and black Teflon 24" bbl. 26" Ultra Mag raised cheekpiece, magnum-grade black rubber recoil pad. Chambered for 7mm RUM, 375 RUM, 7mm STW, 300 Rem. Ultra Mag., 300 Win. Mag., 300 Wby. Mag., 338 Rem. Ultra Mag., 338 Win. Mag., 375 H&H. Aramid fiber reinforced fiberglass stock. Introduced 1994.
Price: . . . . (right-hand) **$1,593.00**; (left-hand) **$1,673.00**

Remington Model 700 APR African Plains Rifle

Similar to Model 700 BDL except magnum receiver and specially contoured 26" Custom Shop barrel with satin blued finish, laminated wood stock with raised cheekpiece, satin finish, black buttpad, 20 lpi cut checkering. Chambered for 7mm Rem. Mag., 7mm RUM, 375 RUM, 300 Rem. Ultra Mag., 300 Win. Mag., 300 Wby. Mag., 338 Win. Mag., 338 Rem. Ultra Mag., 375 H&H. Introduced 1994.
Price: **$1,716.00**

Remington 700 Titanium

Remington 700 VLS

Remington 700 VS

Remington 700 VS SF

Remington 700 Sendero SF

Remington Model 700 LSS Rifle
Similar to 700 BDL except stainless steel barreled action, gray laminated wood stock with Monte Carlo comb and cheekpiece. No sights furnished. Available in (RH) 7mm Rem. Mag., 300 Win. Mag., 300 RUM, 338 RUM, 7mm Rem. Ultra Mag., 375 Rem. Ultra Mag., (LH) 7mm Rem. Ultra Mag., 300 Rem. Ultra Mag., and 338 RUM. Introduced 1996.
Price: From . . . . (Right-hand) **$820.00 to $840.00;** (left-hand) **$867.00**

Remington Model 700 MTN DM Rifle
Similar to 700 BDL except weighs 6-1/2 to 6-5/8 lbs., 22" tapered barrel. Redesigned pistol grip, straight comb, contoured cheekpiece, hand-rubbed oil stock finish, deep cut checkering, hinged floorplate and magazine follower, two-position thumb safety. Chambered for 260 Rem., 270 Win., 7mm-08, 25-06, 280 Rem., 30-06, 4-shot detachable box magazine. Overall length is 41-5/8" to 42-1/2". Introduced 1995.
Price: **$728.00**

Remington Model 700 Titanium
Similar to 700 BDL except has titanium receiver, spiral-cut fluted bolt, skeletonized bolt handle and carbon-fiber and aramid fiber reinforced stock with sling swivel studs. Barrel 22"; weighs 5-1/4 lbs. (short action) or 5-1/2 lbs. (long action). Satin stainless finish. 260 Rem., 270 Win., 7mm-08, 30-06, 308 Win. Introduced 2001.
Price: **$1,239.00**

Remington Model 700 VLS Varmint Laminated Stock
Similar to 700 BDL except 26" heavy barrel without sights, brown laminated stock with beavertail forend, gripcap, rubber buttpad. Available in 223 Rem., 22-250, 6mm, 243, 308. Polished blue finish. Introduced 1995.
Price: From **$705.00**

Remington Model 700 VS Varmint Synthetic Rifles
Similar to 700 BDL Varmint Laminated except composite stock reinforced with aramid fiber reinforced, fiberglass and graphite. Aluminum bedding block that runs full length of receiver. Free-floating 26" barrel. Metal has black matte finish; stock has textured black and gray finish and swivel studs. Available in 223, 22-250, 308. Right- and left-hand. Introduced 1992.
Price: . . . . **$811.00 to $837.00**

Remington Model 700 VS SF Rifle
Similar to Model 700 Varmint Synthetic except satin-finish stainless barreled action with 26" fluted barrel, spherical concave muzzle crown. Chambered for 223, 220 Swift, 22-250 and 204 Ruger. Introduced 1994.
Price: **$1,025.00**

Remington Model 700 EtronX VSSF Rifle
Similar to Model 700 VS SF except features battery-powered ignition system for near-zero lock time and electronic trigger mechanism. Requires ammunition with EtronX electrically fired primers. Aluminum-bedded 26" heavy, stainless steel, fluted barrel; overall length 45-7/8"; weight 8 lbs., 14 oz. Black, Kevlar-reinforced composite stock. Light-emitting diode display on grip top indicates fire or safe mode, loaded or unloaded chamber, battery condition. Introduced 2000.
Price: 220 Swift, 22-250 or 243 Win. **$1,332.00**

Remington Model 700 XCR Rifle
Similar to standard Model 700 except 24" or 26" barrel; black matte finish; stainless steel barrel and receiver; comes in standard, magnum and short/long magnum calibers.
Price: . . . . **$867.00 to $893.00**

REMINGTON MODEL 700 SENDERO SF RIFLE
Caliber: 7mm Rem. SAUM, 300 Rem. SAUM, 7mm Rem. Mag., 7mm STW, 300 Rem. Ultra Mag., 338 Rem. Ultra Mag., 300 Win. Mag., 7mm Rem. Ultra Mag. **Barrel:** 26". **Weight:** 8-1/2 lbs. **Length:** 45-3/4" to 46-5/8" overall. **Stock:** Aramid fiber refinforced fiberglass. **Sights:** NA **Features:** Stainless steel action and fluted stainless barrel. Introduced 1996.
Price: . . . . **$1,003.00 to $1,016.00**

Remington Seven LS

Remington Model Seven LS Mag

Remington Model Seven SS Mag

Remington Model Seven Custom MS

Remington Seven Custom KS

REMINGTON MODEL 710 BOLT-ACTION RIFLE
Caliber: 270 Win., 30-06. **Barrel:** 22". **Weight:** 7-1/8 lbs. **Length:** 42-1/2" overall. **Stock:** Gray synthetic. **Sights:** Bushnell Sharpshooter 3-9x scope mounted and bore-sighted. **Features:** Unique action locks bolt directly into barrel; 60-degree bolt throw; 4-shot dual-stack magazine; key-operated Integrated Security System locks bolt open. Introduced 2001. Made in U.S.A. by Remington Arms Co.
Price: $425.00

REMINGTON MODEL SEVEN LS
Caliber: 223 Rem., 243 Win., 7mm-08 Rem., 308 Win. **Barrel:** 20". **Weight:** 6-1/2 lbs. **Length:** 39-1/4" overall. **Stock:** Brown laminated, satin finished. **Features:** Satin finished carbon steel barrel and action, 4-round magazine, hinged magazine floorplate. Furnished with iron sights and sling swivel studs, drilled and tapped for scope mounts.
Price: $701.00
Price: 7mmRSAUM, 300RSAUM, LS Magnum, 22" bbl. $741.00
Price: AWR model.................................... $1,547.00

Remington Model Seven SS
Similar to Model Seven LS except stainless steel barreled action and black synthetic stock, 20" barrel. Chambered for 243, 260 Rem., 7mm-08, 308. Introduced 1994.

Price: $729.00
Price: 7mmRSAUM, 300RSAUM, Model Seven SS
Magnum, 22" bbl. $769.00

Remington Model Seven Custom MS Rifle
Similar to Model Seven LS except full-length Mannlicher-style stock of laminated wood with straight comb, solid black recoil pad, black steel forend tip, cut checkering, gloss finish. Barrel length 20", weighs 6-3/4 lbs. Available in 222 Rem., 223, 22-250, 243, 6mm Rem., 260 Rem., 7mm-08 Rem., 308, 350 Rem. Mag., 250 Savage, 257 Roberts, 35 Rem. Polished blue finish. Introduced 1993. From Remington Custom Shop.
Price: From $1,332.00

Remington Model Seven Youth Rifle
Similar to Model Seven LS except hardwood stock, 1" shorter length of pull, chambered for 223, 243, 260 Rem., 7mm-08. Introduced 1993.
Price: $547.00

Remington Model Seven Custom KS
Similar to Model Seven LS except gray aramid fiber reinforced stock with 1" black rubber recoil pad and swivel studs. Blued satin carbon steel barreled action. No sights on 223, 260 Rem., 7mm-08, 308; 35 Rem. and 350 Rem. have iron sights.
Price: $1,314.00

Ruger Magnum

Ruger 77/22 Hornet Varmint

Ruger M77 Mark II

Ruger KM77RLFP MKII

Ruger KM77RFP MKII

Price: M77RMKII (no sights) **$716.00**
Price: M77LRMKII (left-hand, 25/06, 270, 30-06, 7mm Rem.
Mag.,300 Win. Mag.). **$716.00**

Ruger M77RSI International Carbine
Same as standard Model 77 except 18" barrel, full-length International-style stock, steel forend cap, loop-type steel sling swivels. Integral base receiver, open sights, Ruger 1" steel rings. Improved front sight. Available in 243, 270, 308, 30-06. Weighs 7 lbs. Length overall is 38-3/8".
Price: M77RSIMKII **$819.00**

Ruger M77 Mark II All-Weather and Sporter Model Stainless Rifle
Similar to wood-stock M77 Mark II except all metal parts are stainless steel, has an injection-molded, glass-fiber-reinforced polymer stock. Laminated wood stock. Chambered for 223, 22/250, 25/06, 260 Rem., 7mm WSM, 7mm/08, 7mm SWM, 280 Rem., 300 WSM, 204 Ruger, 243, 270, 308, 30-06, 7mm Rem. Mag., 300 Win. Mag., 338 Win. Mag. Fixed-blade-type ejector, three-position safety, new trigger guard with patented floorplate latch. Integral Scope Base Receiver, 1" Ruger scope rings, built-in sling swivel loops. Introduced 1990.
Price: K77RFPMKII **$716.00**
Price: K77RLFPMKII Ultra-Light, synthetic stock, rings, no sights . **$716.00**
Price: K77LRBBZMKII, left-hand bolt, rings, no sights, laminated
stock **$773.00**
Price: K77RBZMKII, no sights, laminated wood stock, 223,
22/250, 243, 270, 280 Rem., 7mm Rem. Mag., 30-06,
308, 300 Win. Mag., 338 Win. Mag. **$773.00**
Price: KM77RFPMKII, M77RMKII **$773.00**

Ruger M77RL Ultra Light
Similar to standard M77 except weighs 6 lbs., chambered for 223, 243, 308, 270, 30-06, 257 Roberts, barrel tapped for target scope blocks, 20" Ultra Light barrel. Overall length 40". Ruger's steel 1" scope rings supplied. Introduced 1983.
Price: M77RLMKII **$729.00**

RUGER MAGNUM RIFLE
Caliber: 375 H&H, 416 Rigby, 458 Lott. **Barrel:** 23". **Weight:** 9-1/2 to 10-1/4 lbs. **Length:** 44". **Stock:** AAA Premium Grade Circassian walnut with live-rubber recoil pad, metal gripcap, and studs for mounting sling swivels. **Sights:** Blade, front; V-notch rear express sights (one stationary, two folding) drift-adjustable for windage. **Features:** Floorplate latch secures the hinged floorplate against accidental dumping of cartridges; one-piece bolt has a non-rotating Mauser-type controlled-feed extractor; fixed-blade ejector.
Price: M77RSMMKII **$1,975.00**

RUGER 77/22 HORNET BOLT-ACTION RIFLE
Caliber: 22 Hornet, 6-shot rotary magazine. **Barrel:** 20". **Weight:** About 6 lbs. **Length:** 39-3/4" overall. **Stock:** Checkered American walnut, black rubber buttpad. **Sights:** Brass bead front, open adjustable rear; also available without sights. **Features:** Same basic features as rimfire model except slightly lengthened receiver. Uses Ruger rotary magazine. Three-position safety. Comes with 1" Ruger scope rings. Introduced 1994.
Price: 77/22RH (rings only). **$649.00**
Price: K77/22VHZ Varmint, laminated stock, no sights **$685.00**

RUGER M77 MARK II RIFLE
Caliber: 223, 220 Swift, 22-250, 204 Ruger, 243, 6mm Rem., 257 Roberts, 25-06, 6.5x55 Swedish, 270, 260 Rem., 280 Rem., 308, 30-06, 7mm Rem. Mag., 7mm WSM, 7mm/08, 7mm Rem. Short Ultra Mag., 300 Rem. Short Ultra Mag., 300 WSM, 300 Win. Mag., 338 Win. Mag., 4-shot magazine. **Barrel:** 20", 22"; 24" (magnums). **Weight:** About 7 lbs. **Length:** 39-3/4" overall. **Stock:** Synthetic American walnut; swivel studs, rubber buttpad. **Sights:** None furnished. Receiver has Ruger integral scope mount base, Ruger 1" rings. Some with iron sights. **Features:** Short action with new trigger, 3-position safety. Steel trigger guard. Left-hand available. Introduced 1989.

Ruger M77VT Target

Ruger Frontier

Sako TRG-S

Sako 75 Hunter

Sako 75 Stainless Hunter

Ruger M77 Mark II Compact Rifles

Similar to standard M77 except reduced 16-1/2" barrel, weighs 5-3/4 lbs. Chambered for 223, 243, 260 Rem., 308, and 7mm-08.
Price: M77CR MKII (blued finish, walnut stock) **$675.00**
Price: KM77CRBBZ MkII (stainless finish, black laminated stock). . **$729.00**

RUGER M77VT TARGET RIFLE

Caliber: 22-250, 220 Swift, 223, 204 Ruger, 243, 25-06, 308. **Barrel:** 26" heavy stainless steel with target gray finish. **Weight:** 9-3/4 lbs. **Length:** Approx. 44" overall. **Stock:** Laminated American hardwood with beavertail forend, steel swivel studs; no checkering or gripcap. **Sights:** Integral scope mount bases in receiver. **Features:** Ruger diagonal bedding system. Ruger steel 1" scope rings supplied. Fully adjustable trigger. Steel floorplate and trigger guard. New version introduced 1992.
Price: K77VTMKII **$870.00**

RUGER FRONTIER RIFLE

Caliber: 243, 7mm/08, 308, 300WSM. **Barrel:** 16-1/2". **Weight:** 6-1/4 lbs. **Stock:** Black laminate. **Features:** Front scope mounting rib, blued finish; overall length 35-1/2". Introduced 2005.
Price: **$799.00**

SAKO TRG-42 BOLT-ACTION RIFLE

Caliber: 338 Lapua Mag. and 300 Win. Mag. **Barrel:** 27-1/8". **Weight:** 11-1/4 lbs. **Length:** NA. **Stock:** NA. **Sights:** NA. **Features:** 5-shot magazine, fully adjustable stock and competition trigger. Imported from Finland by Beretta USA.
Price: **$3,589.00**

SAKO 75 HUNTER BOLT-ACTION RIFLE

Caliber: 17 Rem., 222, 223, 22-250, 243, 7mm-08, 308 Win., 25-06, 270, 280, 30-06; 270 Wby. Mag., 7mm Rem. Mag., 7mm STW, 7mm Wby. Mag., 300 Win. Mag., 300 Wby. Mag., 338 Win. Mag., 340 Wby. Mag., 375 H&H, 416 Rem. Mag. **Barrel:** 22", standard calibers; 24", 26" magnum calibers. **Weight:** About 6 lbs. **Length:** NA. **Stock:** European walnut with matte lacquer finish. **Sights:** None furnished; dovetail scope mount rails. **Features:** New design with three locking lugs and a mechanical ejector, key locks firing pin and bolt, cold hammer-forged barrel is free-floating, two position safety, hinged floorplate or detachable magazine that can be loaded from the top, short 70-degree bolt lift. Five action lengths. Introduced 1997. Imported from Finland by Beretta USA.
Price: Standard calibers **$1,419.00**
Price: Magnum calibers **$1,499.00**

Sako 75 Stainless Synthetic Rifle

Similar to 75 Hunter except all metal is stainless steel, synthetic stock has soft composite panels molded into forend and pistol grip. Available in 22-250, 243, 308 Win., 25-06, 270, 30-06 with 22" barrel, 7mm Rem. Mag., 7mm STW, 300 Win. Mag., 338 Win. Mag. and 375 H&H Mag. with 24" barrel and 300 Wby. Mag., 300 Rem. Ultra Mag. with 26" barrel. Introduced 1997. Imported from Finland by Beretta USA.
Price: Standard calibers **$1,499.00**
Price: Magnum calibers **$1,499.00**

Sako 75 Deluxe

Sako 75 Varmint

Savage 110GXP3

Savage 11FXP3

Sako 75 Deluxe Rifle

Similar to 75 Hunter except select wood rosewood gripcap and forend tip. Available in 17 Rem., 222, 223, 25-06, 243, 7mm-08, 308, 25-06, 270, 280, 30-06; 270 Wby. Mag., 7mm Rem. Mag., 7mm STW, 7mm Wby. Mag., 300 Win. Mag., 300 Wby. Mag., 338 Win. Mag., 340 Wby. Mag., 375 H&H, 416 Rem. Mag. Introduced 1997. Imported from Finland by Beretta USA.

Price: Standard calibers **$2,044.00**
Price: Magnum calibers. **$2,044.00**

Sako 75 Varmint Stainless Laminated Rifle

Similar to Sako 75 Hunter except chambered only for 222, 223, 22-250, 22 PPC USA, 6mm PPC, heavy 24" barrel with recessed crown; set trigger; all metal is stainless steel, laminated wood stock with beavertail forend. Introduced 1999. Imported from Finland by Beretta USA.

Price: **$1,959.00**

Sako 75 Varmint Rifle

Similar to Model 75 Hunter except chambered only for 17 Rem., 222 Rem., 223 Rem., 22-250 Rem., 22 PPC and 6mm PPC, 24" heavy barrel with recessed crown; set trigger; beavertail forend. Introduced 1998. Imported from Finland by Beretta USA.

Price: **$1,684.00**

SAUER 202 BOLT-ACTION RIFLE

Caliber: Standard 243, 6.5x55, 270 Win., 308 Win., 30-06; magnum 7mm Rem. Mag., 300 Win. Mag., 300 Wby. Mag., 375 H&H. **Barrel:** 23.6" (standard), 26" (magnum). **Weight:** 7.7 lbs. (standard). **Length:** 44.3" overall (23.6" barrel). **Stock:** Select American Claro walnut with high-gloss epoxy finish, rosewood grip and forend caps; 22 lpi checkering. Synthetic also available. **Sights:** None furnished; drilled and tapped for scope mounting. **Features:** Short 60" bolt throw; detachable box magazine; six-lug bolt; quick-change barrel; tapered bore; adjustable two-stage trigger; firing pin cocking indicator. Introduced 1994. Imported from Germany by SIGARMS, Inc.

Price: Standard calibers, right-hand **$1,035.00**
Price: Magnum calibers, right-hand **$1,106.00**
Price: Standard calibers, synthetic stock **$985.00**
Price: Magnum calibers, synthetic stock **$1,056.00**

SAVAGE MODEL 10GXP3, 110GXP3 PACKAGE GUNS

Caliber: 223 Rem., 22-250 Rem., 243 Win., 7mm-08 Rem., 308 Win., 300 WSM (10GXP3). 25-06 Rem., 270 Win., 30-06 Spfld., 7mm Rem. Mag., 300 Win. Mag., 300 Rem. Ultra Mag. (110GXP3). **Barrel:** 22" 24", 26". **Weight:** 7.5 lbs. average. **Length:** 43" to 47". **Stock:** Walnut Monte Carlo with checkering. **Sights:** 3-9x40mm scope, mounted & bore sighted. **Features:** Blued, free floating and button rifled, internal box magazines, swivel studs, leather sling. Left-hand available.

Price: Accu-trigger **$539.00**

SAVAGE MODEL 11FXP3, 111FXP3, 111FCXP3, 11FYXP3 (Youth) PACKAGE GUNS

Caliber: 223 Rem., 22-250 Rem., 243 Win., 308 Win., 300 WSM (11FXP3). 270 Win., 30-06 Spfld., 25-06 Rem., 7mm Rem. Mag., 300 Win. Mag., 338 Win. Mag., 300 Rem. Ultra Mag. (11FCXPE & 111FXP3). **Barrel:** 22" to 26". **Weight:** 6.5 lbs. **Length:** 41" to 47". **Stock:** Synthetic checkering, dual pillar bed. **Sights:** 3-9X40mm scope, mounted & bore sighted. **Features:** Blued, free floating and button rifled, Top loading internal box mag (except 111FXCP3 has detachable box mag.). Nylon sling and swivel studs. Some left-hand available.

Price: Model 11FXP3 . . . . **$516.00**
Price: Model 111FCXP3. . . . . **$411.00**
Price: Model 11FYXP3, 243 Win., 12.5" pull (youth) **$501.00**

Savage 111FCXP3

Savage Model 10FP

Savage Model 10FPLE1

Savage Model 10FPXP-LE

SAVAGE MODEL 16FXP3, 116FXP3 SS ACTION PACKAGE GUNS

Caliber: 223 Rem., 243 Win., 308 Win., 300 WSM, 270 Win., 30-06 Spfld., 7mm Rem. Mag., 300 Win. Mag., 338 Win. Mag., 375 H&H, 7mm S&W, 7mm Rem. Ultra Mag., 300 Rem. Ultra Mag. **Barrel:** 22", 24", 26". **Weight:** 6.75 lbs. average. **Length:** 41" to 46". **Stock:** Synthetic checkering, dual pillar bed. **Sights:** 3-9X40mm scope, mounted & bore sighted. **Features:** Free floating and button rifled. Internal box mag., nylon sling and swivel studs.
Price: $601.00

SAVAGE MODEL 10FM SIERRA ULTRA LIGHT RIFLE

Caliber: 223, 243, 308. **Barrel:** 20". **Weight:** 6 lbs. **Length:** 41-1/2". **Stock:** "Dual Pillar" bedding in black synthetic stock with silver medallion in gripcap. **Sights:** None furnished; drilled and tapped for scope mounting. **Features:** True short action. Model 10FCM has detachable box magazine. Comes with sling and quick-detachable swivels. Introduced 1998. Made in U.S.A. by Savage Arms, Inc.
Price: $552.00

SAVAGE MODEL 10/110FP LONG RANGE RIFLE

Caliber: 223, 25-06, 308, 30-06, 300 Win. Mag., 7mm Rem. Mag., 4-shot magazine. **Barrel:** 24", heavy; recessed target muzzle. **Weight:** 8-1/2 lbs.

Length: 45.5" overall. **Stock:** Black graphite/fiberglass composition; positive checkering. **Sights:** None furnished. Receiver drilled and tapped for scope mounting. **Features:** Pillar-bedded stock. Black matte finish on all metal parts. Double swivel studs on the forend for sling and/or bipod mount. Right- or left-hand. Introduced 1990. From Savage Arms, Inc.
Price: Right- or left-hand. $601.00

Savage Model 10FP Tactical Rifle

Similar to the Model 110FP except has true short action, chambered for 223, 308; black synthetic stock with "Dual Pillar" bedding. Introduced 1998. Made in U.S.A. by Savage Arms, Inc.
Price: $601.00
Price: Model 10FLP (left-hand) $601.00
Price: Model 10FP-LE1 (20"), 10FPLE2 (26") $601.00
Price: Model 10FPXP-LE w/Burris 3.5-10x50 scope,
Harris bipod package $1,805.00

Savage Model 10FP-LE1A Tactical Rifle

Similar to the Model 110FP except weighs 10.75 lbs. and has overall length of 39.75". Chambered for 223 Rem., 308 Win. Black synthetic Choate™ adjustable stock with accessory rail and swivel studs.
Price: $729.00

Savage Model 111F

Savage Model 11FCNS

Savage Model 11G

Savage Model 10GY

Savage Model 12FV

SAVAGE MODEL 111 CLASSIC HUNTER RIFLES

Caliber: 25-06 Rem., 270 Win., 30-06 Spfld., 7mm Rem. Mag, 300 Win. Mag., 7mm RUM, 300 RUM. **Barrel:** 22", 24", 26" (magnum calibers). **Weight:** 6.5 to 7.5 lbs. **Length:** 42.75" to 47.25". **Stock:** Walnut-finished hardwood (M111G, GC); graphite/fiberglass filled composite. **Sights:** Ramp front, open fully adjustable rear; drilled and tapped for scope mounting. **Features:** Three-position top tang safety, double front locking lugs, free-floated button-rifled barrel. Comes with trigger lock, target, ear puffs. Introduced 1994. Made in U.S.A. by Savage Arms, Inc.
Price: Model 111F (270 Win., 30-06 Spfld., 7mm Rem. Mag., 300 Win.
  Mag.) **$486.00**
Price: Model 111F (25-06 Rem., 338 Win. Mag., 7mm Rem. Ultra Mag, 300
  Rem. Ultra Mag.) **$486.00**
Price: Model 111G
  (wood stock, top-loading magazine, right- or left-hand) **$436.00**
Price: Model 111GNS (wood stock, detachable box magazine, no sights,
  right-hand only) **$518.00**

Savage Model 11 Classic Hunter Rifles, Short Action

Similar to the Model 111F except has true short action, chambered for 22-250, Rem., 243 Win., 7mm-08 Rem., 308 Win.; black synthetic stock with "Dual Pillar" bedding, positive checkering. Introduced 1998. Made in U.S.A. by Savage Arms, Inc.
Price: Model 11F. **$486.00**
Price: Model 11FL (left-hand) **$486.00**
Price: Model 11FCNS (right-hand, no sights). **$507.00**
Price: Model 11G (wood stock). **$496.00**
Price: Model 11GL (as above, left-hand) **$496.00**

Savage Model 10GY

Similar to the Model 111G except weighs 6.3 lbs., is 42-1/2" overall, and the stock is scaled for ladies, small-framed adults and youths. Chambered for 223, 243, 308. Ramp front sight, open adjustable rear; drilled and tapped for scope mounts. Made in U.S.A. by Savage Arms, Inc.
Price: Model 10GY (short action, calibers 223, 243, 308) **$496.00**

SAVAGE MODEL 112 LONG RANGE RIFLES

Caliber: 5-shot magazine. **Barrel:** 26" heavy. **Weight:** 8.8 lbs. **Length:** 47.5" overall. **Stock:** Black graphite/fiberglass filled composite with positive checkering. **Sights:** None furnished; drilled and tapped for scope mounting. **Features:** Pillar-bedded stock. Blued barrel with recessed target-style muzzle. Double front swivel studs for attaching bipod. Introduced 1991. Made in U.S.A. by Savage Arms, Inc.
Price: Model 112BVSS (heavy-prone laminated stock with high comb,
  Wundhammer swell, fluted stainless barrel, bolt handle,
  trigger guard) **$675.00**

Savage Model 12 Long Range Rifles

Similar to the Model 112 Long Range except with true short action, chambered for 223, 22-250, 308. Models 12FV, 12FVSS have black synthetic stocks with "Dual Pillar" bedding, positive checkering, swivel studs; Model 12BVSS has brown laminated stock with beavertail forend, fluted stainless barrel. Introduced 1998. Made in U.S.A. by Savage Arms, Inc.
Price: Model 12FV (223, 22-250, 243 Win., 308 Win., blue) **$549.00**
Price: Model 12FVSS (blue action, fluted stainless barrel) **$667.00**
Price: Model 12FLV (as above, left-hand) **$549.00**
Price: Model 12FVS (blue action, fluted stainless barrel,
  single shot) **$667.00**
Price: Model 12BVSS (laminated stock) **$721.00**
Price: Model 12BVSS-S (as above, single shot) **$721.00**

Savage Model 12VSS

Savage Model 16FCSS

Savage Model 116FSAK

Sigarms SHR 970

Steyr Mannlicher SBS

Savage Model 12VSS Varminter Rifle
Similar to other Model 12s except blue/stainless steel action, fluted stainless barrel, Choate full pistol grip, adjustable synthetic stock, Sharp Shooter trigger. Overall length 47-1/2", weighs appx. 15 lbs. No sights; drilled and tapped for scope mounts. Chambered in 223, 22-250, 308 Win. Made in U.S.A. by Savage Arms, Inc.
Price: **$934.00**

SAVAGE MODEL 116 WEATHER WARRIORS
Caliber: 375 H&H, 300 Rem. Ultra Mag., 308 Win., 300 Rem. Ultra Mag., 300 WSM, 7mm Rem. Ultra Mag., 7mm Rem. Short Ultra Mag., 7mm S&W, 7mm-08 Rem. **Barrel:** 22", 24" for 7mm Rem. Mag., 300 Win. Mag., 338 Win. Mag. (M116FSS only). **Weight:** 6.25 to 6.5 lbs. **Length:** 41" to 47". **Stock:** Graphite/fiberglass filled composite. **Sights:** None furnished; drilled and tapped for scope mounting. **Features:** Stainless steel with matte finish; free-floated barrel; quick-detachable swivel studs; laser-etched bolt; scope bases and rings. Left-hand models available in all models, calibers at same price. Model 116FSS introduced 1991; 116FSAK introduced 1994. Made in U.S.A. by Savage Arms, Inc.
Price: Model 116FSS (top-loading magazine) **$520.00**
Price: Model 116FSAK (top-loading magazine,
Savage adjustable muzzle brake system).................... **$601.00**
Price: Model 16BSS (brown laminate, 24")................... **$668.00**
Price: Model 116BSS (brown laminate, 26")................... **$668.00**

Savage Model 16FCSS Rifle
Similar to Model 116FSS except true short action, chambered for 223, 243, 22" free-floated barrel; black graphite/fiberglass stock, "Dual Pillar" bedding. Also left-hand version available. Introduced 1998. Made in U.S.A. by Savage Arms, Inc.
Price: **$552.00**

SIGARMS SHR 970 SYNTHETIC RIFLE
Caliber: 270, 30-06. **Barrel:** 22". **Weight:** 7.2 lbs. **Length:** 41.9" overall. **Stock:** Textured black fiberglass or walnut. **Sights:** None furnished; drilled and tapped for scope mounting. **Features:** Quick takedown; interchangeable barrels; removable box magazine; cocking indicator; three position safety. Introduced 1998. Imported by SIGARMS, Inc.
Price: Synthetic stock..................................... **$499.00**
Price: Walnut stock.. **$550.00**

STEYR CLASSIC MANNLICHER SBS RIFLE
Caliber: 243, 25-06, 308, 6.5x55, 6.5x57, 270, 7x64 Brenneke, 7mm-08, 7.5x55, 30-06, 9.3x62, 6.5x68, 7mm Rem. Mag., 300 Win. Mag., 8x68S, 4-shot magazine. **Barrel:** 23.6" standard; 26" magnum; 20" full stock standard calibers. **Weight:** 7 lbs. **Length:** 40.1" overall. **Stock:** Hand-checkered fancy European oiled walnut with standard forend. **Sights:** Ramp front adjustable for elevation, V-notch rear adjustable for windage. **Features:** Single adjustable trigger; 3-position roller safety with "safe-bolt" setting; drilled and tapped for Steyr factory scope mounts. Introduced 1997. Imported from Austria by GSI, Inc.
Price: Full-stock, standard calibers **$1,749.00**

Steyr SBS Forester

Steyr SBS Prohunter

Steyr Scout Rifle

Tikka T-3 Hunter

STEYR SBS FORESTER RIFLE

Caliber: 243, 25-06, 270, 7mm-08, 308 Win., 30-06, 7mm Rem. Mag., 300 Win. Mag. Detachable 4-shot magazine. **Barrel:** 23.6", standard calibers; 25.6", magnum calibers. **Weight:** 7.5 lbs. **Length:** 44.5" overall (23.6" barrel). **Stock:** Oil-finished American walnut with Monte Carlo cheekpiece. Pachmayr 1" swivels. **Sights:** None furnished. Drilled and tapped for Browning A-Bolt mounts. **Features:** Three-position ambidextrous roller tang safety. Matte finish on barrel and receiver; adjustable trigger. Rotary cold-hammer forged barrel. Introduced 1997. Imported by GSI, Inc.

Price: Standard calibers **$799.00**
Price: Magnum calibers **$829.00**

Steyr SBS Prohunter Rifle

Similar to the SBS Forester except has ABS synthetic stock with adjustable butt spacers, straight comb without cheekpiece, palm swell, Pachmayr 1" swivels. Special 10-round magazine conversion kit available. Introduced 1997. Imported by GSI.

Price: Standard calibers **$769.00**
Price: Magnum calibers **$799.00**

STEYR SCOUT BOLT-ACTION RIFLE

Caliber: 308 Win., 5-shot magazine. **Barrel:** 19", fluted. **Weight:** NA. **Length:** NA. **Stock:** Gray Zytel. **Sights:** Pop-up front & rear, Leupold M8 2.5x28 IER scope on Picatinny optic rail with Steyr mounts. **Features:** luggage case, scout sling, two stock spacers, two magazines. Introduced 1998. From GSI.

Price: From **$1,969.00**

STEYR SSG BOLT-ACTION RIFLE

Caliber: 308 Win., detachable 5-shot rotary magazine. **Barrel:** 26". **Weight:** 8.5 lbs. **Length:** 44.5" overall. **Stock:** Black ABS Cycolac with spacers for length of pull adjustment. **Sights:** Hooded ramp front adjustable for elevation, V-notch rear adjustable for windage. **Features:** Sliding safety; NATO rail for bipod; 1" swivels; Parkerized finish; single or double-set triggers. Imported from Austria by GSI, Inc.

Price: SSG-PI, iron sights **$1,699.00**
Price: SSG-PII, heavy barrel, no sights **$1,699.00**
Price: SSG-PIIK, 20" heavy barrel, no sights **$1,699.00**
Price: SSG-PIV, 16.75" threaded heavy barrel with flash hider . . . **$2,659.00**

TIKKA T-3 BIG BOAR SYNTHETIC BOLT-ACTION RIFLE

Caliber: 308, 30-06, 300 WSM. **Barrel:** 19". **Weight:** 6 lbs. **Length:** 39.5" overall. **Stock:** Laminated. **Sights:** None furnished. **Features:** Detachable, 3-round. Receiver dove-tailed for scope mounting. Reintroduced 1996. Imported from Finland by Beretta USA.

Price: Left-hand **$719.00**

Tikka T-3 Varmint Rifle

Similar to the standard T-3 rifle except has 23-3/8" heavy stainless or blued barrel. Chambered for 22-250, 223, 308. Reintroduced 2005. Made in Finland by Sako. Imported by Beretta USA.

Price: . . . . **$839.00 to $908.00**

TIKKA T-3 HUNTER

Caliber: 223, 22-250, 243, 308, 25-06, 270, 30-06, 300 Win. Mag., 338 Win. Mag., 270 WSM, 300 WSM, 6.5x55 Swedish Mauser, 7mm Rem. Mag. **Stock:** Walnut. **Sight:** None furnished. **Barrel:** 22-7/16", 24-3/8". **Features:** Detachable magazine, aluminum scope rings. Introduced 2005. Imported from Finland by Beretta USA.

Price: Standard cal. **$759.00**
Price: Magnum calibers **$798.00**
Price: T-3 Lite (synthetic stock) . . . . **$674.00 to $709.00**

Weatherby Mark V Lazermark

Weatherby Mark V Sporter

Weatherby Mark V Stainless

Weatherby Mark V Synthetic

Tikka T-3 Stainless Synthetic
Similar to the T-3 Hunter except stainless steel, synthetic stock. Available in 243, 25-06, 270, 308, 30-06, 270 WSM, 300 WSM, 7mm Rem. Mag., 300 Win. Mag., 338 Win. Mag. Introduced 2005. Imported from Finland by Beretta USA.
Price: Standard calibers **$908.00**
Price: Magnum calibers. **$944.00**

ULTRA LIGHT ARMS BOLT-ACTION RIFLES
Caliber: 17 Rem. to 416 Rigby. **Barrel:** Douglas, length to order. **Weight:** 4-3/4 to 7-1/2 lbs. **Length:** Varies. **Stock:** Kevlar® graphite composite, variety of finishes. **Sights:** None furnished; drilled and tapped for scope mounts. **Features:** Timney trigger, hand-lapped action, button-rifled barrel, hand-bedded action, recoil pad, sling-swivel studs, optional Jewell trigger. Made in U.S.A. by New Ultra Light Arms.
Price: Model 20 (short action). **$2,800.00**
Price: Model 24 (long action) **$2,900.00**
Price: Model 28 (magnum action). **$3,200.00**
Price: Model 40 (300 Wby. Mag., 416 Rigby) **$3,200.00**
Price: Left-hand models, add **$100.00**

WEATHERBY MARK V DELUXE BOLT-ACTION RIFLE
Caliber: All Weatherby calibers plus 22-250, 243, 25-06, 270 Win., 280 Rem., 7mm-08, 30-06, 308 Win. **Barrel:** 24" barrel on standard calibers. **Weight:** 8-1/2 to 10-1/2 lbs. **Length:** 46-5/8" to 46-3/4" overall. **Stock:** Walnut, Monte Carlo with cheekpiece; high luster finish; checkered pistol grip and forend; recoil pad. **Sights:** None furnished. **Features:** Cocking indicator; adjustable trigger; hinged floorplate, thumb safety; quick detachable sling swivels. Made in U.S.A. From Weatherby.
Price: 257, 270, 7mm, 300, 340 Wby. Mags., 26" barrel **$1,767.00**
Price: 416 Wby. Mag. with Accubrake, 28" barrel. **$2,079.00**
Price: 460 Wby. Mag. with Accubrake, 28" barrel. **$2,443.00**
Price: 24" barrel. **$1,715.00**

Weatherby Mark V Lazermark Rifle
Same as Mark V Deluxe except stock has extensive oak leaf pattern laser carving on pistol grip and forend. Introduced 1981.

Price: 257, 270, 7mm Wby. Mag., 300, 340, 26" **$1,923.00**
Price: 378 Wby. Mag., 28" **$2,266.00**
Price: 416 Wby. Mag., 28", Accubrake. **$2,266.00**
Price: 460 Wby. Mag., 28", Accubrake. **$2,661.00**

Weatherby Mark V Sporter Rifle
Same as the Mark V Deluxe without the embellishments. Metal has low-luster blue, stock is Claro walnut with matte finish, Monte Carlo comb, recoil pad. Introduced 1993. From Weatherby.
Price: 22-250, 243, 240 Wby. Mag., 25-06, 7mm-08,
270 WCF, 280, 30-06, 308; 24". **$1,091.00**
Price: 257 Wby., 270, 7 mm Wby., 7mm Rem., 300 Wby.,
300 Win., 340 Wby., 338 Win. Mag., 26" barrel for Wby. calibers;
24" for non-Wby. calibers **$1,143.00**

Weatherby Mark V Stainless Rifle
Similar to the Mark V Deluxe except made of 410-series stainless steel. Also available in 30-378 Wby. Mag. Has lightweight injection-molded synthetic stock with raised Monte Carlo comb, checkered grip and forend, custom floorplate release. Right-hand only. Introduced 1995. Made in U.S.A. From Weatherby.
Price: 22-250 Rem., 243 Win., 240 Wby. Mag., 25-06 Rem.,
270 Win., 280 Rem., 7mm-08 Rem., 30-06 Spfld., 308 Win.,
24" barrel. **$1,018.00**
Price: 257, 270, 7mm, 300, 340 Wby. Mag., 26" barrel **$1,070.00**
Price: 7mm Rem. Mag., 300 Win. Mag., 338 Win. Mag.,
375 H&H Mag., 24" barrel. **$1,070.00**

Weatherby Mark V Synthetic
Similar to the Mark V Stainless except made of matte finished blued steel. Injection molded synthetic stock. Weighs 6-1/2 lbs., 24" barrel. Available in 22-250, 240 Wby. Mag., 243, 25-06, 270, 7mm-08, 280, 30-06, 308. Introduced 1997. Made in U.S.A. From Weatherby.
Price: **$923.00**
Price: 257, 270, 7mm, 300, 340 Wby. Mags., 26" barrel **$975.00**
Price: 7mm STW, 7mm Rem. Mag., 300, 338 Win. Mags **$975.00**
Price: 375 H&H, 24" barrel. **$975.00**
Price: 30-378 Wby. Mag., 338-378 Wby. 28" barrel **$1,151.00**

Weatherby Mark V Accumark

Weatherby Mark V SVR

Weatherby Mark V Fibermark

Weatherby Mark V Dangerous Game Rifle

WEATHERBY MARK V ACCUMARK RIFLE

Caliber: 257, 270, 7mm, 300, 340 Wby. Mags., 338-378 Wby. Mag., 30-378 Wby. Mag., 7mm STW, 7mm Rem. Mag., 300 Win. Mag. **Barrel:** 26", 28". **Weight:** 8-1/2 lbs. **Length:** 46-5/8" overall. **Stock:** Bell & Carlson with full length aluminum bedding block. **Sights:** None furnished. Drilled and tapped for scope mounting. **Features:** Uses Mark V action with heavy-contour stainless barrel with black oxidized flutes, muzzle diameter of .705". Introduced 1996. Made in U.S.A. From Weatherby.

Price: 26". **$1,507.00**

Price: 30-378 Wby. Mag., 338-378 Wby. Mag., 28",
Accubrake **$1,724.00**

Price: 223, 22-250, 243, 240 Wby. Mag., 25-06, 270,
280 Rem., 7mm-08, 30-06, 308; 24" **$1,455.00**

Price: Accumark left-hand 257, 270, 7mm, 300, 340 Wby.
Mag., 7mm Rem. Mag., 7mm STW, 300 Win. Mag. **$1,559.00**

Price: Accumark left-hand 30-378, 333-378 Wby. Mags. **$1,788.00**

Weatherby Mark V Accumark Ultra Lightweight Rifles

Similar to the Mark V Accumark except weighs 5-3/4 lbs., 6-3/4 lbs. in Mag. calibers.; 24", 26" fluted barrel with recessed target crown; hand-laminated stock with CNC-machined aluminum bedding plate and faint gray "spider web" finish. Available in 257, 270, 7mm, 300 Wby. Mags., (26"); 243, 240 Wby. Mag., 25-06, 270 Win., 280 Rem., 7mm-08, 7mm Rem. Mag., 30-06, 338-06 A-Square, 308, 300 Win. Mag. (24"). Introduced 1998. Made in U.S.A. by Weatherby.

Price: . . . . **$1,459.00 to $1,517.00**

Price: Left-hand models **$1,559.00**

Weatherby Mark V SVM/SPM Rifles

Similar to the Mark V Accumark except has 26" fluted (SVM) or 24" fluted Krieger barrel, spiderweb-pattern tan laminated synthetic stock. SVM has a fully adjustable trigger. Chambered for 223, 22-250, 220 Swift (SVM only), 243, 7mm-08 and 308. Made in U.S.A. by Weatherby.

Price: SVM (Super VarmintMaster), repeater or single-shot **$1,517.00**

New! **Price:** SPM (Super Predator Master) **$1,459.00**

Weatherby Mark V Special Varmint Rifle (SVR)

Similar to the Super VarmintMaster and Accumark with 22", #3 contour chrome-moly 4140 steel Krieger Criterion button-rifled barrel with one-degree target crown and hand-laminated composite stock. Available in .223 Rem. (5+1 magazine capacity) and .22-250 Rem. (4+1 magazine capacity) in right-hand models only.

Price: **$999.00**

Weatherby Mark V Fibermark Rifles

Similar to other Mark V models except has black Kevlar® and fiberglass composite stock and bead-blast blue or stainless finish. Chambered for 19 standard and magnum calibers. Introduced 1983; reintroduced 2001. Made in U.S.A. by Weatherby.

Price: Fibermark . . . . **$1,070.00 to $1,347.00**

Price: Fibermark stainless . . . . **$1,165.00 to $1,390.00**

WEATHERBY MARK V DANGEROUS GAME RIFLE

Caliber: 375 H&H, 375 Wby. Mag., 378 Wby. Mag., 416 Rem. Mag., 416 Wby. Mag., 458 Win. Mag., .458 Lott, 460 Wby. Mag. 300 Win. Mag., 300 Wby., Mag., 338 Win. Mag., 340 Wby. Mag., 24" only **Barrel:** 24" or 26". **Weight:** 8-3/4 to 9-1/2 lbs. **Length:** 44-5/8" to 46-5/8" overall. **Stock:** Kevlar® and fiberglass composite. **Sights:** Barrel-band hooded front with large gold bead, adjustable ramp/shallow "V" rear. **Features:** Designed for dangerous game hunting. Black oxide matte finish on all metalwork; Pachmayr Decelerator™ recoil pad, short-throw Mark V action. Introduced 2001. Made in U.S.A. by Weatherby.

Price: . . . . **$2,703.00 to $2,935.00**

Wilderness Explorer

Winchester Model 70 Classic

Winchester Model 70 Classic Stainless

Winchester Model 70 Classic Featherweight

WEATHERBY MARK V SUPER BIG GAMEMASTER DEER RIFLE
Caliber: 240 Wby. Mag., 25-06 Rem., 270 Win., 280 Rem., 30-06 Spfld., 257 Wby. Mag., 270 Wby. Mag., 7mm Rem., Mag., 7mm Wby. Mag., 338-06 A-Square, 300 Win. Mag., 300 Wby. Mag. **Barrel:** 26", target crown. **Weight:** 5-3/4 lbs., (6-3/4 lbs. Magnum). **Stock:** Raised comb Monte Carlo composite. **Features:** Fluted barrel, aluminum bedding block, Pachmayr decelerator, 54-degree bolt lift, adj. trigger.
Price: $1,459.00
Price: Magnum $1,517.00

WEATHERBY MARK V ROYAL CUSTOM RIFLE
Caliber: 257, 270, 7mm, 300, 340 all Wby. Mags. Other calibers available upon request. **Barrel:** 26". **Stock:** Monte Carlo hand-checkered Claro walnut with high gloss finish. **Features:** Bolt and follower are damasconed with checkered knob. Engraved receiver, bolt sleeve and floorplate sport scroll pattern. Animal images on floorplate optional. High gloss blue, 24-karat gold and nickel-plating. Made in U.S.A. From Weatherby.
Price: $5,831.00

WEATHERBY THREAT RESPONSE RIFLES (TRR) SERIES
Caliber: TRR 223 Rem., 300 Win. TRR Magnum and Magnum Custom 300 Win. Mag., 300 Wby. Mag., 30-378 Wby. Mag., 328-378 Wby. Mag. **Barrel:** 22", 26", target crown. **Stock:** Hand-laminated composite. TTR & TRR Magnum have raised comb Monte Carlo style. TRR Magnum Custom adjustable ergonomic stock. **Features:** Adjustable trigger, aluminum bedding block, beavertail forearms dual tapered, flat-bottomed. "Rocker Arm" lockdown scope mounting. 54 degree bolt. Pachmayr decelerator pad. Made in U.S.A.
Price: TRR Magnum Custom 300 .... $2,699.00
Price: 30-378, 338-378 with accubrake $2,861.00

WILDERNESS EXPLORER MULTI-CALIBER CARBINE
Caliber: 22 Hornet, 218 Bee, 44 Magnum, 50 A.E. (interchangeable). **Barrel:** 18", match grade. **Weight:** 5.5 lbs **Length:** 38-1/2" overall. **Stock:** Synthetic or wood. **Sights:** None furnished; comes with Weaver-style mount on barrel. **Features:** Quick-change barrel and bolt face for caliber switch. Removable box magazine; adjustable trigger with side safety; detachable swivel studs. Introduced 1997. Made in U.S.A. by Phillips & Rogers, Inc.
Price: $995.00

WINCHESTER MODEL 70 CLASSIC SPORTER III
Caliber: 25-06, 270 Win., 30-06, 7mm STW, 7mm Rem. Mag., 300 Win. Mag., 338 Win. Mag., 3-shot magazine; 5-shot in 25-06, 270 Win., 30-06. **Barrel:** 24", 26" for magnums. **Weight:** 7-3/4 to 8 lbs. **Length:** 46-3/4" overall (26" bbl.). **Stock:** American walnut with cut checkering and satin finish. Classic style with straight comb. **Sights:** None furnished. Drilled and tapped for scope mounting. **Features:** Uses pre-64-type action with controlled round feeding. Three-position safety, stainless steel magazine follower; rubber buttpad; epoxy bedded receiver recoil lug. From U.S. Repeating Arms Co.
Price: 25-06, 270, 30-06 .... $742.00
Price: Other calibers $810.00
Price: Left-hand, 270 or 30-06 .... $778.00
Price: Left-hand, 7mm Rem. Mag or 300 Win. Mag. $810.00

Winchester Model 70 Classic Stainless Rifle
Same as Model 70 Classic Sporter except stainless steel barrel and pre-64-style action with controlled round feeding and matte gray finish, black composite stock impregnated with fiberglass and graphite, contoured rubber recoil pad. No sights (except in 375 H&H). Available in 270 Win., 30-06, 7mm STW, 7mm Rem. Mag., 300 Win. Mag., 300 Ultra Mag., 338 Win. Mag., 375 H&H Mag. (24" barrel), 3- or 5-shot magazine. Weighs 7-1/2 lbs. Introduced 1994.
Price: 270, 30-06 .... $817.00
Price: 375 H&H Mag., with sights $943.00
Price: Other calibers $847.00

Winchester Model 70 Classic Featherweight
Same as Model 70 Classic except action bedded in standard-grade walnut stock. Available in 22-250, 243, 6.5x55, 308, 7mm-08, 270 Win., 30-06. Drilled and tapped for scope mounts. Weighs 7 lbs. Introduced 1992.
Price: $814.00

Winchester Model 70 Classic Compact

Winchester Model 70 Coyote

Winchester Model 70 Stealth

Winchester Model 70 Classic Super Grade

Winchester Model 70 WSM

Winchester Model 70 Classic Compact
Similar to Model 70 Classic Featherweight except scaled down for smaller shooters. 20" barrel, 12-1/2" length of pull. Pre-'64-type action. Available in 243, 308 or 7mm-08. Introduced 1998. Made in U.S.A. by U. S. Repeating Arms Co.
Price: **$762.00**

Winchester Model 70 Coyote
Similar to Model 70 Classic except laminated wood stock, 24" medium-heavy stainless steel barrel. Available in 223 Rem., 22-250 Rem., 243 Win., or 308 Win.
Price: **$742.00**

WINCHESTER MODEL 70 STEALTH RIFLE
Caliber: 223, 22-250, 308 Win. **Barrel:** 26". **Weight:** 10-3/4 lbs. **Length:** 46" overall. **Stock:** Kevlar/fiberglass/graphite Pillar Plus Accu-Block with full-length aluminum bedding block. **Sights:** None furnished. **Features:** Push-feed bolt design; matte finish. Introduced 1999. Made in U.S.A. by U.S. Repeating Arms Co.
Price: **$886.00**

WINCHESTER MODEL 70 CLASSIC SUPER GRADE
Caliber: 25-06, 270, 30-06, 5-shot magazine; 7mm Rem. Mag., 300 Win. Mag., 338 Win. Mag., 3-shot magazine. **Barrel:** 24", 26" for magnums. **Weight:** 7-3/4 lbs. to 8 lbs. **Length:** 44-1/2" overall (24" bbl.) **Stock:** Walnut with straight comb, sculptured cheekpiece, wraparound cut checkering, tapered forend, solid rubber buttpad. **Sights:** None furnished; comes with scope bases and rings. **Features:** Controlled round feeding with stainless steel claw extractor, bolt guide rail, 3-position safety; all steel bottom metal, hinged floorplate, stainless magazine follower. Introduced 1994. From U.S. Repeating Arms Co.
Price: 25-06, 270, 30-06 .... **$1,036.00**
Price: Other calibers **$1,024.00**

WINCHESTER MODEL 70 CLASSIC SAFARI EXPRESS
Caliber: 375 H&H Mag., 416 Rem. Mag., 458 Win. Mag., 3-shot magazine. **Barrel:** 24". **Weight:** 8-1/4 to 8-1/2 lbs. **Stock:** American walnut with Monte Carlo cheekpiece. Wrap-around checkering and finish. **Sights:** Hooded ramp front, open rear. **Features:** Controlled round feeding. Two steel cross bolts in stock for added strength. Front sling swivel stud mounted on barrel. Contoured rubber buttpad. From U.S. Repeating Arms Co.
Price: **$1,189.00**
Price: Left-hand, 375 H&H only **$1,163.00**

WINCHESTER MODEL 70 WSM RIFLES
Caliber: 300 WSM, 3-shot magazine. **Barrel:** 24". **Weight:** 7-1/4 to 7-3/4 lbs. **Length:** 44" overall. **Stock:** Checkered walnut, black synthetic or laminated wood. **Sights:** None. **Features:** Model 70 designed for the new 300 Winchester Short Magnum cartridge. Short-action receiver, 3-position safety, knurled bolt handle. Introduced 2001. From U.S. Repeating Arms Co.
Price: Classic Featherweight WSM
(checkered walnut stockand forearm)...................... **$892.00**
Price: Classic stainless WSM (black syn. stock, stainless steel bbl.) **$859.00**
Price: Classic laminated WSM (laminated wood stock)......... **$810.00**

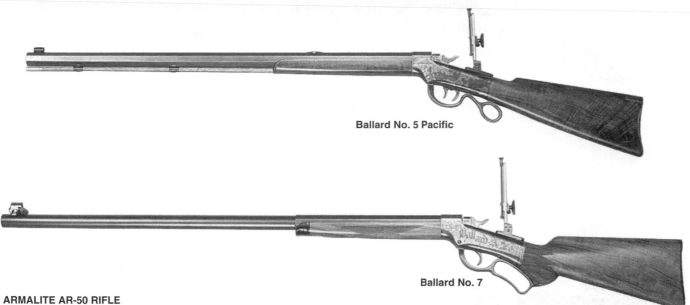

Ballard No. 5 Pacific

Ballard No. 7

ARMALITE AR-50 RIFLE
Caliber: 50 BMG **Barrel:** 31". **Weight:** 33.2 lbs. **Length:** 59.5" **Stock:** Synthetic. **Sights:** None furnished. **Features:** A single-shot bolt action rifle designed for long range shooting. Available in left-hand model. Made in U.S.A. by Armalite.
Price: **$2,885.00**

ARMSPORT 1866 SHARPS RIFLE, CARBINE
Caliber: 45-70. **Barrel:** 28", round or octagonal. **Weight:** 8.10 lbs. **Length:** 46" overall. **Stock:** Walnut. **Sights:** Blade front, folding adjustable rear. Tang sight set optionally available. **Features:** Replica of the 1866 Sharps. Color case-hardened frame, rest blued. Imported by Armsport.
Price: **$865.00**
Price: With octagonal barrel **$900.00**
Price: Carbine, 22" round barrel **$850.00**

BALLARD NO. 1 3/4 FAR WEST RIFLE
Caliber: 22 LR, 32-40, 38-55, 40-65, 40-70, 45-70, 45-110, 50-70, 50-90. **Barrel:** 30" std. or heavyweight. **Weight:** 10-1/2 lbs. (std.) or 11-3/4 lbs. (heavyweight bbl.) **Length:** NA. **Stock:** Walnut. **Sights:** Blade front, Rocky Mountain rear. **Features:** Single or double-set triggers, S-lever or ring-style lever; color case-hardened finish; hand polished and lapped Badger barrel. Made in U.S.A. by Ballard Rifle & Cartridge Co.
Price: **$2,250.00**

BALLARD NO. 4 PERFECTION RIFLE
Caliber: 22 LR, 32-40, 38-55, 40-65, 40-70, 45-70, 45-90, 45-110, 50-70, 50-90. **Barrel:** 30" or 32" octagon, standard or heavyweight. **Weight:** 10-1/2 lbs. (standard) or 11-3/4 lbs. (heavyweight bbl.). **Length:** NA. **Stock:** Smooth walnut. **Sights:** Blade front, Rocky Mountain rear. **Features:** Rifle or shotgun-style buttstock, straight grip action, single or double-set trigger, "S" or right lever, hand polished and lapped Badger barrel. Made in U.S.A. by Ballard Rifle & Cartridge Co.
Price: **$2,250.00**

BALLARD NO. 5 PACIFIC SINGLE-SHOT RIFLE
Caliber: 32-40, 38-55, 40-65, 40-90, 40-70 SS, 45-70 Govt., 45-110 SS, 50-70 Govt., 50-90 SS. **Barrel:** 30", or 32" octagonal. **Weight:** 10-1/2 lbs. **Length:** NA. **Stock:** High-grade walnut; rifle or shotgun style. **Sights:** Blade front, Rocky Mountain rear. **Features:** Standard or heavy barrel; double-set triggers; under-barrel wiping rod; ring lever. Introduced 1999. Made in U.S.A. by Ballard Rifle & Cartridge Co.
Price: **$2,575.00**

BALLARD NO. 7 LONG RANGE RIFLE
Caliber: 32-40, 38-55, 40-65, 40-70 SS, 45-70 Govt., 45-90, 45-110. **Barrel:** 32", 34" half-octagon. **Weight:** 11-3/4 lbs. **Length:** NA. **Stock:** Walnut; checkered pistol grip shotgun butt, ebony forend cap. **Sights:** Globe front. **Features:** Designed for shooting up to 1000 yards. Standard or heavy barrel; single or double-set trigger; hard rubber or steel buttplate. Introduced 1999. Made in U.S.A. by Ballard Rifle & Cartridge Co.
Price: From **$2,475.00**

BALLARD NO. 8 UNION HILL RIFLE
Caliber: 22 LR, 32-40, 38-55, 40-65 Win., 40-70 SS. **Barrel:** 30" half-octagon. **Weight:** About 10-1/2 lbs. **Length:** NA. **Stock:** Walnut; pistol grip butt with cheekpiece. **Sights:** Globe front. **Features:** Designed for 200-yard offhand shooting. Standard or heavy barrel; double-set triggers; full loop lever; hook Schuetzen buttplate. Introduced 1999. Made in U.S.A. by Ballard Rifle & Cartridge Co.
Price: From **$2,500.00**

BALLARD MODEL 1885 HIGH WALL SINGLE SHOT RIFLE
Caliber: 17 Bee, 22 Hornet, 218 Bee, 219 Don Wasp, 219 Zipper, 22 Hi-Power, 225 Win., 25-20 WCF, 25-35 WCF, 25 Krag, 7mmx57R, 30-30, 30-40 Krag, 303 British, 33 WCF, 348 WCF, 35 WCF, 35-30/30, 9.3x74R, 405 WCF, 50-110 WCF, 500 Express, 577 Express. **Barrel:** Lengths to 34". **Weight:** NA. **Length:** NA. **Stock:** Straight-grain American walnut. **Sights:** buckhorn or flattop rear, blade front. **Features:** Faithful copy of original Model 1885 High Wall; parts interchange with original rifles; variety of options available. Introduced 2000. Made in U.S.A. by Ballard Rifle & Cartridge LLC.
Price: From **$2,313.00**
Price: With single set trigger from **$2,355.00**

BARRETT MODEL 99 SINGLE SHOT RIFLE
Caliber: 50 BMG. **Barrel:** 33". **Weight:** 25 lbs. **Length:** 50.4" overall. **Stock:** Anodized aluminum with energy-absorbing recoil pad. **Sights:** None furnished; integral M1913 scope rail. **Features:** Bolt action; detachable bipod; match-grade barrel with high-efficiency muzzle brake. Introduced 1999. Made in U.S.A. by Barrett Firearms.
Price: From **$3,000.00**

BROWN MODEL 97D SINGLE SHOT RIFLE
Caliber: 17 Ackley Hornet through 45-70 Govt. **Barrel:** Up to 26", air gauged match grade. **Weight:** About 5 lbs., 11 oz. **Stock:** Sporter style with pistol grip, cheekpiece and Schnabel forend. **Sights:** None furnished; drilled and tapped for scope mounting. **Features:** Falling block action gives rigid barrel-receiver matting; polished blue/black finish. Hand-fitted action. Many options. Made in U.S.A. by E. Arthur Brown Co., Inc.
Price: From **$699.00**

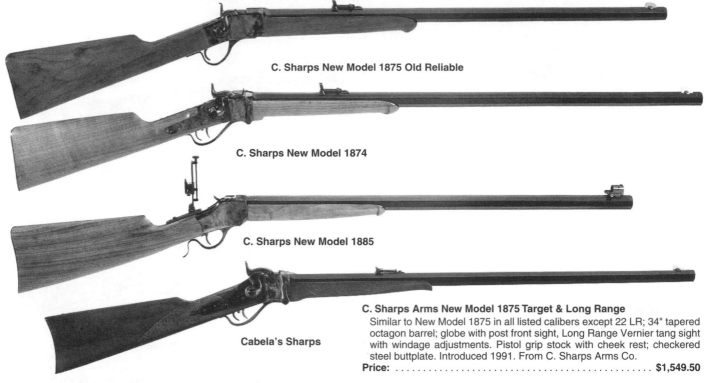

C. Sharps New Model 1875 Old Reliable

C. Sharps New Model 1874

C. Sharps New Model 1885

Cabela's Sharps

BROWNING MODEL 1885 HIGH WALL SINGLE SHOT RIFLE

Caliber: 22-250, 30-06, 270, 7mm Rem. Mag., 454 Casull, 45-70. **Barrel:** 28". **Weight:** 8 lbs., 12 oz. **Length:** 43-1/2" overall. **Stock:** Walnut with straight grip, Schnabel forend. **Sights:** None furnished; drilled and tapped for scope mounting. **Features:** Replica of J.M. Browning's high-wall falling block rifle. Octagon barrel with recessed muzzle. Imported from Japan by Browning. Introduced 1985.
Price: **$1,027.00**

BRNO ZBK 110 SINGLE SHOT RIFLE

Caliber: 222 Rem., 5.6x52R, 22 Hornet, 5.6x50 Mag., 6.5x57R, 7x57R, 8x57JRS. **Barrel:** 23.6". **Weight:** 5.9 lbs. **Length:** 40.1" overall. **Stock:** European walnut. **Sights:** None furnished; drilled and tapped for scope mounting. **Features:** Top tang opening lever; cross-bolt safety; polished blue finish. Announced 1998. Imported from The Czech Republic by Euro-Imports.
Price: Standard calibers **$223.00**
Price: 7x57R, 8x57JRS.................................. **$245.00**
Price: Lux model, standard calibers **$311.00**
Price: Lux model, 7x57R, 8x57JRS **$333.00**

C. SHARPS ARMS NEW MODEL 1875 OLD RELIABLE RIFLE

Caliber: 22LR, 32-40 & 38-55 Ballard, 38-56 WCF, 40-65 WCF, 40-90 3-1/4", 40-90 2-5/8", 40-70 2-1/10", 40-70 2-1/4", 40-70 2-1/2", 40-50 1-11/16", 40-50 1-7/8", 45-90, 45-70, 45-100, 45-110, 45-120. Also available on special order only in 50-70, 50-90, 50-140. **Barrel:** 24", 26", 30" (standard), 32", 34" optional. **Weight:** 8-12 lbs. **Stock:** Walnut, straight grip, shotgun butt with checkered steel buttplate. **Sights:** Silver blade front, Rocky Mountain buckhorn rear. **Features:** Recreation of the 1875 Sharps rifle. Production guns will have case-colored receiver. Available in Custom Sporting and Target versions upon request. Announced 1986. From C. Sharps Arms Co.
Price: 1875 Sporting Rifle (30" tapered oct. bbl.) **$1,185.00**

C. Sharps Arms 1875 Classic Sharps

Similar to New Model 1875 Sporting Rifle except 26", 28" or 30" full octagon barrel, crescent buttplate with toe plate, Hartford-style forend with cast German silver nose cap. Blade front sight, Rocky Mountain buckhorn rear. Weighs 10 lbs. Introduced 1987. From C. Sharps Arms Co.
Price: **$1,470.00**

C. Sharps Arms New Model 1875 Target & Long Range

Similar to New Model 1875 in all listed calibers except 22 LR; 34" tapered octagon barrel; globe with post front sight, Long Range Vernier tang sight with windage adjustments. Pistol grip stock with cheek rest; checkered steel buttplate. Introduced 1991. From C. Sharps Arms Co.
Price: **$1,549.50**

C. SHARPS ARMS NEW MODEL 1874 OLD RELIABLE

Caliber: 40-50, 40-70, 40-90, 45-70, 45-90, 45-100, 45-110, 45-120, 50-70, 50-90, 50-140. **Barrel:** 26", 28", 30" tapered octagon. **Weight:** About 10 lbs. **Length:** NA. **Stock:** American black walnut; shotgun butt with checkered steel buttplate; straight grip, heavy forend with Schnabel tip. **Sights:** Blade front, buckhorn rear. Drilled and tapped for tang sight. **Features:** Recreation of the Model 1874 Old Reliable Sharps Sporting Rifle. Double-set triggers. Reintroduced 1991. Made in U.S.A. by C. Sharps Arms.
Price: **$1,584.00**

C. SHARPS ARMS NEW MODEL 1885 HIGHWALL RIFLE

Caliber: 22 LR, 22 Hornet, 219 Zipper, 25-35 WCF, 32-40 WCF, 38-55 WCF, 40-65, 30-40 Krag, 40-50 ST or BN, 40-70 ST or BN, 40-90 ST or BN, 45-70 2-1/10" ST, 45-90 2-4/10" ST, 45-100 2-6/10" ST, 45-110 2-7/8" ST, 45-120 3-1/4" ST. **Barrel:** 26", 28", 30", tapered full octagon. **Weight:** About 9 lbs., 4 oz. **Length:** 47" overall. **Stock:** Oil-finished American walnut; Schnabel-style forend. **Sights:** Blade front, buckhorn rear. Drilled and tapped for optional tang sight. **Features:** Single trigger; octagonal receiver top; checkered steel buttplate; color case-hardened receiver and buttplate, blued barrel. Many options available. Made in U.S.A. by C. Sharps Arms Co.
Price: From **$1,439.00**

C. SHARPS ARMS CUSTOM NEW MODEL 1877 LONG RANGE TARGET RIFLE

Caliber: 44-90 Sharps/Rem., 45-70, 45-90, 45-100 Sharps. **Barrel:** 32", 34" tapered round with Rigby flat. **Weight:** Appx. 10 lbs. **Stock:** Walnut checkered. Pistol grip/forend. **Sights:** Classic long range with windage. **Features:** Custom production only.
Price: .... **$5,550.00 and up**

CABELA'S SHARPS SPORTING RIFLE

Caliber: 45-70, 45-120, 45-110, 50-70. **Barrel:** 32", tapered octagon. **Weight:** 9 lbs. **Length:** 47-1/4" overall. **Stock:** Checkered walnut. **Sights:** Blade front, open adjustable rear. **Features:** Color case-hardened receiver and hammer, rest blued. Introduced 1995. Imported by Cabela's.
Price: **$999.99**
Price: (Heavy target Sharps, 45-70, 45-120, 50-70) **$1,199.99**
Price: (Quigley Sharps, 45-70, 45-120, 45-110) **$1,499.99**
Price: Sharps Competition 45/70 .... **$1,299.99**

Cimarron Billy Dixon

Cimarron Quigley

Cimarron 1885 High Wall

Cumberland Mountain Plateau

Dakota Single Shot

CIMARRON BILLY DIXON 1874 SHARPS SPORTING RIFLE

Caliber: 40-40, 50-90, 50-70, 45-70. **Barrel:** 32" tapered octagonal. **Weight:** NA. **Length:** NA. **Stock:** European walnut. **Sights:** Blade front, Creedmoor rear. **Features:** Color case-hardened frame, blued barrel. Hand-checkered grip and forend; hand-rubbed oil finish. Introduced 1999. Imported by Cimarron F.A. Co.
Price: $1,670.00

CIMARRON QUIGLEY MODEL 1874 SHARPS SPORTING RIFLE

Caliber: 45-110, 50-70, 50-10, 45-70, 45-90, 45-120. **Barrel:** 34" octagonal. **Weight:** NA. **Length:** NA. **Stock:** Checkered walnut. **Sights:** Blade front, adjustable rear. **Features:** Blued finish; double-set triggers. From Cimarron F.A. Co.
Price: $1,805.00

CIMARRON SILHOUETTE MODEL 1874 SHARPS SPORTING RIFLE

Caliber: 45-70, 50-70. **Barrel:** 32" octagonal. **Weight:** NA. **Length:** NA. **Stock:** Walnut. **Sights:** Blade front, adjustable rear. **Features:** Pistol-grip stock with shotgun-style buttplate; cut-rifled barrel. From Cimarron F.A. Co.
Price: $1,620.00

CIMARRON MODEL 1885 HIGH WALL RIFLE

Caliber: 38-55, 40-65, 45-70, 45-90, 45-120, 30-40 Krag, 348 Winchester. **Barrel:** 30" octagonal. **Weight:** NA. **Length:** NA. **Stock:** European walnut. **Sights:** Bead front, semi-buckhorn rear. **Features:** Replica of the Winchester 1885 High Wall rifle. Color case-hardened receiver and lever, blued barrel. Curved buttplate. Optional double-set triggers. Introduced 1999. Imported by Cimarron F.A. Co.
Price: $995.00
Price: With pistol grip $1,175.00

CUMBERLAND MOUNTAIN PLATEAU RIFLE

Caliber: 40-65, 45-70. **Barrel:** Up to 32"; round. **Weight:** About 10-1/2 lbs. (32" barrel). **Length:** 48" overall (32" barrel). **Stock:** American walnut. **Sights:** Marble's bead front, Marble's open rear. **Features:** Falling block action with underlever. Blued barrel and receiver. Stock has lacquer finish, crescent buttplate. Introduced 1995. Made in U.S.A. by Cumberland Mountain Arms, Inc.
Price: $1,085.00

DAKOTA MODEL 10 SINGLE SHOT RIFLE

Caliber: Most rimmed and rimless commercial calibers. **Barrel:** 23". **Weight:** 6 lbs. **Length:** 39-1/2" overall. **Stock:** Medium fancy grade walnut in classic style. Checkered grip and forend. **Sights:** None furnished. Drilled and tapped for scope mounting. **Features:** Falling block action with underlever. Top tang safety. Removable trigger plate for conversion to single set trigger. Introduced 1990. Made in U.S.A. by Dakota Arms.
Price: $3,595.00
Price: Barreled action $2,095.00
Price: Action only $1,850.00
Price: Magnum calibers $3,595.00
Price: Magnum barreled action $2,050.00
Price: Magnum action only $1,675.00

Dixie 1874 Sharps Silhouette

H&R Ultra Varmint

H&R Ultra Hunter

H&R Buffalo

DIXIE 1874 SHARPS BLACK POWDER SILHOUETTE RIFLE
Caliber: 45-70. **Barrel:** 30"; tapered octagon; blued; 1:18" twist. **Weight:** 10 lbs., 3 oz. **Length:** 47-1/2" overall. **Stock:** Oiled walnut. **Sights:** Blade front, ladder-type hunting rear. **Features:** Replica of the Sharps #1 Sporter. Shotgun-style butt with checkered metal buttplate; color case-hardened receiver, hammer, lever and buttplate. Tang is drilled and tapped for tang sight. Double-set triggers. Meets standards for NRA blackpowder cartridge matches. Introduced 1995. Imported from Italy by Dixie Gun Works.
Price: $1,075.00

Dixie 1874 Sharps Lightweight Hunter/Target Rifle
Same as the Dixie 1874 Sharps Black Powder Silhouette model except has a straight-grip buttstock with military-style buttplate. Based on the 1874 military model. Introduced 1995. Imported from Italy by Dixie Gun Works.
Price: $1,025.00

E.M.F. 1874 METALLIC CARTRIDGE SHARPS RIFLE
Caliber: 45-70, 45/120. **Barrel:** 28", octagon. **Weight:** 10-3/4 lbs. **Length:** NA. **Stock:** Oiled walnut. **Sights:** Blade front, flip-up open rear. **Features:** Replica of the 1874 Sharps Sporting rifle. Color case-hardened lock; double-set trigger; blue finish. Imported by E.M.F.
Price: From $700.00
Price: With browned finish. $1,000.00
Price: Military Carbine. $650.00

HARRINGTON & RICHARDSON ULTRA VARMINT RIFLE
Caliber: 223, 243. **Barrel:** 24", heavy. **Weight:** About 7.5 lbs. **Stock:** Hand-checkered laminated birch with Monte Carlo comb. **Sights:** None furnished. Drilled and tapped for scope mounting. **Features:** Break-open action with side-lever release, positive ejection. Scope mount. Blued receiver and barrel. Swivel studs. Introduced 1993. From H&R 1871, Inc.
Price: $332.00

Harrington & Richardson Ultra Hunter Rifle
Similar to Ultra Varmint rifle except chambered for 25-06 with 26" barrel, or 308 Win., 450 Marlin with 22" barrel. Stock and forend are of cinnamon-colored laminate; hand-checkered grip and forend. Introduced 1995. Made in U.S.A. by H&R 1871, LLC.
Price: $332.00

HARRINGTON & RICHARDSON BUFFALO CLASSIC RIFLE
Caliber: 45-70. **Barrel:** 32" heavy. **Weight:** 8 lbs. **Length:** 52" overall. **Stock:** American black walnut. **Sights:** Williams receiver sight; Lyman target front sight with 8 aperture inserts. **Features:** Color case-hardened Handi-Rifle action with exposed hammer; color case-hardened crescent buttplate; 19th century checkering pattern. Introduced 1995. Made in U.S.A. by H&R 1871, LLC.
Price: About $418.00

Harrington & Richardson 38-55 Target Rifle
Similar to the Buffalo Classic rifle except chambered for 38-55 Win., has 28" barrel. The barrel, steel trigger guard and forend spacer, are highly polished and blued. Color case-hardened receiver and buttplate. Williams receiver sight; Lyman target front sight with 8 aperture inserts. Introduced 1998. Made in U.S.A. by H&R 1871, LLC.
Price: $418.00

HARRIS GUNWORKS ANTIETAM SHARPS RIFLE
Caliber: 40-65, 45-75. **Barrel:** 30", 32", octagon or round, hand-lapped stainless or chrome-moly. **Weight:** 11.25 lbs. **Length:** 47" overall. **Stock:** Choice of straight grip, pistol grip or Creedmoor with Schnabel forend; pewter tip optional. Standard wood is A Fancy; higher grades available. **Sights:** Montana Vintage Arms #111 Low Profile Spirit Level front, #108 mid-range tang rear with windage adjustments. **Features:** Recreation of the 1874 Sharps sidehammer. Action is color case-hardened, barrel satin black. Chrome-moly barrel optionally blued. Optional sights include #112 Spirit Level Globe front with windage, #107 Long Range rear with windage. Introduced 1994. Made in U.S.A. by Harris Gunworks.
Price: $2,400.00

Lonestar Silhouette

Model 1885 High Wall

Mossberg SSi-One Sporter

Mossberg SSi-One Varminter

KRIEGHOFF HUBERTUS SINGLE-SHOT RIFLE

Caliber: 222, 243, 270, 308, 30-06, 5.6x50R Mag., 5.6x52R, 6x62R Freres, 6.5x57R, 6.5x65R, 7x57R, 7x65R, 8x57JRS, 8x75RS, 7mm Rem. Mag., 300 Win. Mag. **Barrel:** 23-1/2". **Weight:** 6-1/2 lbs. **Length:** NA. **Stock:** High-grade walnut. **Sights:** Blade front, open rear. **Features:** Break-open loading with manual cocking lever on top tang; takedown; extractor; Schnabel forearm; many options. Imported from Germany by Krieghoff International Inc.

Price: Hubertus single shot, from $5,950.00
Price: Hubertus, magnum calibers $6,950.00

LONE STAR NO. 5 REMINGTON PATTERN ROLLING BLOCK RIFLE

Caliber: 25-35, 30-30, 30-40 Krag. **Barrel:** 26" to 34". **Weight:** NA. **Length:** NA **Stock:** American walnut. **Sights:** Beech style, Marble bead, Rocky Mountain-style, front; Buckhorn, early or late combination, rear. **Features:** Round, tapered round, octagon, tapered octagon, half octagon-half round barrels; bone-pack color case-hardened actions; single, single set, or double-set triggers. Made in U.S.A. by Lone Star Rifle Co., Inc.

Price: $1,595.00

Lone Star Cowboy Action Rifle

Similar to the Lone Star No. 5 rifle, but designed for cowboy action shooting with 28-33" barrel, buckhorn rear sight.

Price: $1,595.00

Lone Star Custom Silhouette Rifle

Similar to the Lone Star No. 5 rifle but custom made in any caliber or barrel length.

Price: $1,995.00

MEACHAM HIGHWALL SILHOUETTE RIFLE

Caliber: 40-65 Match, 45-70 Match. **Barrel:** 30", 34" octagon. **Stock:** Black walnut with cheekpiece. **Weight:** 11.5 to 11.9 lbs. **Sights:** None. Tang drilled for Win. base, 3/8" dovetail notch, front. **Length of pull:** 13-5/8". **Features:** Parts interchangeable copy of '85 Winchester. Available with single trigger, single set trigger, or Schuetzen-style double-set triggers. Color case-hardened action. Introduced 2002. From Meacham T&H, Inc.

Price: $2,999.00

MERKEL K-1 MODEL LIGHTWEIGHT STALKING RIFLE

Caliber: 243 Win., 270 Win., 7x57R, 308 Win., 30-06, 7mm Rem. Mag., 300 Win. Mag., 9.3x74R. **Barrel:** 23.6". **Weight:** 5.6 lbs. unscoped. **Stock:** Satin-finished walnut, fluted and checkered; sling-swivel studs. **Sights:** None (scope base furnished). **Features:** Franz Jager single-shot break-open action, cocking/uncocking slide-type safety, matte silver receiver, selectable trigger pull weights, integrated, quick detach 1" or 30mm optic mounts (optic not included). Imported from Germany by GSI.

Price: Standard, simple border engraving $3,795.00
Price: Premium, light arabesque scroll. $3,795.00
Price: Jagd, fine engraved hunting scenes $4,395.00

MODEL 1885 HIGH WALL RIFLE

Caliber: 30-40 Krag, 32-40, 38-55, 40-65 WCF, 45-70. **Barrel:** 26" (30-40), 28" to 30" all others. Douglas Premium #3 tapered octagon. **Weight:** 9 lbs, 4 oz. **Length:** 47" overall. **Stock:** Premium American black walnut. **Sights:** Marble's standard ivory bead front, #66 long blade top rear with reversible notch and elevator. **Features:** Receiver with octagon top, thick-wall High Wall with coil spring action. Tang drilled, tapped for High Wall tang sight. Receiver, lever, hammer and breechblock color case-hardened. Available from Montana Armory, Inc.

Price: $1,350.00

MOSSBERG SSi-ONE SINGLE SHOT RIFLE

Caliber: 223 Rem., 22-250 Rem., 243 Win., 270 Win., 308 Rem., 30-06. **Barrel:** 24". **Weight:** 8 lbs. **Length:** 40". **Stock:** Satin-finished walnut, fluted and checkered; sling-swivel studs. **Sights:** None (scope base furnished). **Features:** Frame accepts interchangeable barrels including 12 gauge, fully rifled slug barrel and 12 ga., 3-1/2" chambered barrel with Ulti-Full Turkey choke tube. Lever-opening, break-action design; single-stage trigger; ambidextrous, top-tang safety; internal eject/extract selector. Introduced 2000. From Mossberg.

Price: SSi-One Sporter (standard barrel) or 12 ga., 3-1/2" chamber. $459.00
Price: SSi-One Varmint (bull barrel, 22-250 Rem. only; weighs 10 lbs.) $480.00
Price: SSi-One 12 gauge Slug (fully rifled barrel, no sights, scope base) $480.00

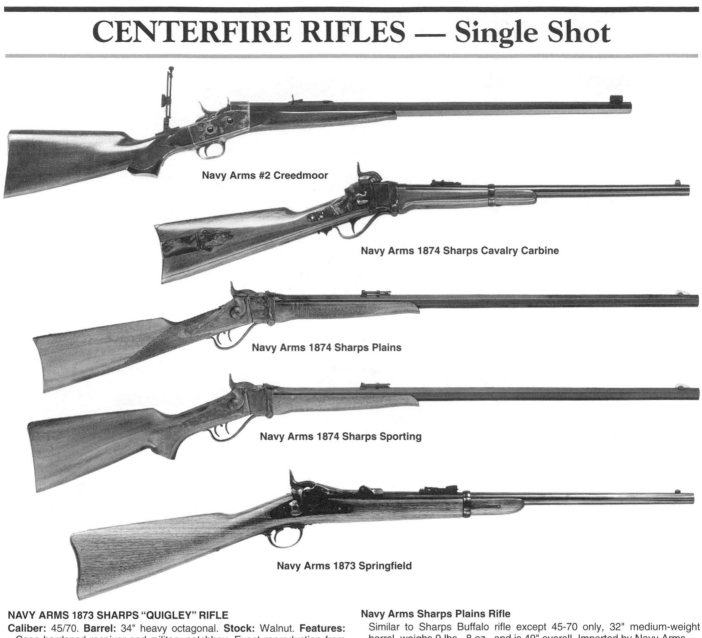

Navy Arms #2 Creedmoor

Navy Arms 1874 Sharps Cavalry Carbine

Navy Arms 1874 Sharps Plains

Navy Arms 1874 Sharps Sporting

Navy Arms 1873 Springfield

NAVY ARMS 1873 SHARPS "QUIGLEY" RIFLE

Caliber: 45/70. **Barrel:** 34" heavy octagonal. **Stock:** Walnut. **Features:** Case-hardened receiver and military patchbox. Exact reproduction from "Quigley Down Under."
Price: $1,390.00

NAVY ARMS 1873 SHARPS NO. 2 CREEDMOOR RIFLE

Caliber: 45/70. **Barrel:** 30" tapered round. **Stock:** Walnut. **Sights:** Front globe, "soule" tang rear. **Features:** Nickel receiver and action. Lightweight sporting rifle.
Price: $1,300.00

NAVY ARMS 1874 SHARPS CAVALRY CARBINE

Caliber: 45-70. **Barrel:** 22". **Weight:** 7 lbs., 12 oz. **Length:** 39" overall. **Stock:** Walnut. **Sights:** Blade front, military ladder-type rear. **Features:** Replica of the 1874 Sharps military carbine. Color case-hardened receiver and furniture. Imported by Navy Arms.
Price: $1,000.00

NAVY ARMS 1874 SHARPS BUFFALO RIFLE

Caliber: 45-70, 45-90. **Barrel:** 28" heavy octagon. **Weight:** 10 lbs., 10 oz. **Length:** 46" overall. **Stock:** Walnut; checkered grip and forend. **Sights:** Blade front, ladder rear; tang sight optional. **Features:** Color case-hardened receiver, blued barrel; double-set triggers. Imported by Navy Arms.
Price: $1,160.00

Navy Arms Sharps Plains Rifle

Similar to Sharps Buffalo rifle except 45-70 only, 32" medium-weight barrel, weighs 9 lbs., 8 oz., and is 49" overall. Imported by Navy Arms.
Price: $1,125.00

Navy Arms Sharps Sporting Rifle

Same as the Navy Arms Sharps Plains Rifle except has pistol grip stock. Introduced 1997. Imported by Navy Arms.
Price: 45-70 only. $1,160.00

NAVY ARMS 1885 HIGH WALL RIFLE

Caliber: 45-70; others available on special order. **Barrel:** 28" round, 30" octagonal. **Weight:** 9.5 lbs. **Length:** 45-1/2" overall (30" barrel). **Stock:** Walnut. **Sights:** Blade front, vernier tang-mounted peep rear. **Features:** Replica of Winchester's High Wall designed by Browning. Color case-hardened receiver, blued barrel. Introduced 1998. Imported by Navy Arms.
Price: 28", round barrel, target sights. $920.00
Price: 30" octagonal barrel, target sights $995.00

NAVY ARMS 1873 SPRINGFIELD CAVALRY CARBINE

Caliber: 45-70. **Barrel:** 22". **Weight:** 7 lbs. **Length:** 40-1/2" overall. **Stock:** Walnut. **Sights:** Blade front, military ladder rear. **Features:** Blued lockplate and barrel; color case-hardened breechblock; saddle ring with bar. Replica of 7th Cavalry gun. Imported by Navy Arms.
Price: $930.00

Navy Arms Rolling Block Buffalo

New England Firearms Handi-Rifle

New England Firearms Super Light

New England Firearms Survivor

NAVY ARMS ROLLING BLOCK RIFLE

Caliber: 45-70. **Barrel:** 26", 30". **Stock:** Walnut. **Sights:** Blade front, adjustable rear. **Features:** Reproduction of classic rolling block action. Available with full-octagon or half-octagon/half-round barrel. Color case-hardened action, steel fittings. From Navy Arms.
Price: Buffalo. **$825.00**
Price: Special Sporting, 26" half round bbl. **$730.00**

NAVY ARMS "JOHN BODINE" ROLLING BLOCK RIFLE

Caliber: 45-70. **Barrel:** 30" heavy octagonal. **Stock:** Walnut. **Sights:** Globe front, "soule" tang rear. **Features:** Double-set triggers.
Price: **$1,385.00**

NAVY ARMS SHARPS NO. 3 LONG RANGE RIFLE

Caliber: 45-70, 45-90. **Barrel:** 34" octagon. **Weight:** 10 lbs., 12 oz. **Length:** 51-1/2". **Stock:** Deluxe walnut. **Sights:** Globe target front and match grade rear tang. **Features:** Shotgun buttplate, German silver forend cap, color case hardenend receiver. Imported by Navy Arms.
Price: **$1,885.00**

NEW ENGLAND FIREARMS HANDI-RIFLE

Caliber: 22 Hornet, 223, 243, 30-30, 270, 280 Rem., 308, 30-06, 357 Mag., 44 Mag., 45-70. **Barrel:** 22", 24"; 26" for 280 Rem. **Weight:** 7 lbs. **Stock:** Walnut-finished hardwood; black rubber recoil pad. **Sights:** Ramp front, folding rear (22 Hornet, 30-30, 45-70). Drilled and tapped for scope mount; 223, 243, 270, 280, 30-06 have no open sights, come with scope mounts.

Features: Break-open action with side-lever release. The 223, 243, 270 and 30-06 have recoil pad and Monte Carlo stock for shooting with scope. Swivel studs on all models. Blue finish. Introduced 1989. From New England Firearms.
Price: **$270.00**
Price: 280 Rem., 26" barrel **$270.00**
Price: Synthetic Handi-Rifle (black polymer stock and forend, swivels, recoil pad) **$281.00**
Price: Handi-Rifle Youth (223, 243) **$270.00**
Price: Stainless Handi-Rifle (223 Rem., 243 Rem.). **$337.00**

New England Firearms Super Light Rifle

Similar to Handi-Rifle except new barrel taper, shorter 20" barrel with recessed muzzle, special lightweight synthetic stock and forend. No sights furnished on 223 and 243 versions, which have factory-mounted scope base and offset hammer spur; Monte Carlo stock; 22 Hornet has ramp front, fully adjustable open rear. Overall length 36", weight is 5.5 lbs. Introduced 1997. Made in U.S.A. by New England Firearms.
Price: 22 Hornet, 223 Rem. or 243 Win. **$281.00**

NEW ENGLAND FIREARMS SURVIVOR RIFLE

Caliber: 223, 308 Win., single shot. **Barrel:** 22". **Weight:** 6 lbs. **Length:** 36" overall. **Stock:** Black polymer, thumbhole design. **Sights:** None furnished; scope mount provided. **Features:** Receiver drilled and tapped for scope mounting. Stock and forend have storage compartments for ammo, etc.; comes with integral swivels and black nylon sling. Introduced 1996. Made in U.S.A. by New England Firearms.
Price: Blue finish. **$284.00**

Remington No. 1 Mid-Range

Ruger No. 1B

Ruger K1-B-BBZ

Ruger No. 1A Light Sporter

Ruger No. 1V Varminter

REMINGTON NO. 1 ROLLING BLOCK MID-RANGE SPORTER
Caliber: 45-70. **Barrel:** 30" round. **Weight:** 8-3/4 lbs. **Length:** 46-1/2" overall. **Stock:** American walnut with checkered pistol grip and forend. **Sights:** Beaded blade front, adjustable center-notch buckhorn rear. **Features:** Recreation of the original. Polished blue metal finish. Many options available. Introduced 1998. Made in U.S.A. by Remington.
Price: **$1,450.00**
Price: Silhouette model with single-set trigger, heavy barrel **$1,560.00**

ROSSI SINGLE SHOT CENTERFIRE RIFLE
Caliber: 308 Win., 270 Win., 30-06 Spfld., 223 Rem., 243 Win. **Barrel:** 23". **Weight:** 6 to 6.5 lbs. **Stock:** Monte Carlo, exotic woods, walnut finish & swivels with white line space and recoil pad. **Sights:** None, scope rails and hammer extension included. **Features:** Break-open, positive ejection, internal transfer bar mechanism and manual external safety. Trigger block system included.
Price: **$179.95**

ROSSI CENTERFIRE/SHOTGUN "MATCHED PAIRS"
Caliber: 12 ga./223 Rem., full size, 20 ga./223 Rem. full & youth, 12 ga./342 Win. full, 20 ga./243 Win., full & youth, 12 ga./308 Win. full, 20 ga./308 Win. full & youth, 12 ga./30-06 Spfld. full, 20 ga./30-06 Spfld. full, 12 ga./270 Win. full, 20 ga./270 Win. full. **Barrel:** 28"/23" full, 22"/22" youth. **Weight:** 5 to 7 lbs. **Stock:** Straight, exotic woods, walnut finish and swivels with white line spacer and recoil pad. **Sights:** Bead front shotgun, fully adjustable rifle, drilled and tapped. **Features:** Break-open, positive

ejection, internal transfer bar mechanism and manual external safety. Trigger block system included.
Price: **$350.00**

RUGER NO. 1B SINGLE SHOT
Caliber: 218 Bee, 22 Hornet, 220 Swift, 22-250, 223, 204 Ruger, 243, 25-06, 270, 30-06, 7mm Rem. Mag., 300 Win. Mag., 308 Win., 338 Win. Mag., 270 Wby., 300 Wby. **Barrel:** 26" round tapered with quarter-rib; with Ruger 1" rings. **Weight:** 8 lbs. **Length:** 42-1/4" overall. **Stock:** Walnut, two-piece, checkered pistol grip and semi-beavertail forend. **Sights:** None, 1" scope rings supplied for integral mounts. **Features:** Under-lever, hammerless falling block design has auto ejector, top tang safety.
Price: 1B **$966.00**
Price: K1-B-BBZ stainless steel, laminated stock 25-06, 7MM mag, 7MM STW, 300 Win Mag., 243 Win., 30-06, 308 Win. **$910.00**

Ruger No. 1A Light Sporter
Calibers: 204 Ruger, 243, 30-06, 270 and 7x57. **Weight:** About 7-1/4 lbs. Similar to the No. 1B Standard Rifle except has lightweight 22" barrel, Alexander Henry-style forend, adjustable folding leaf rear sight on quarter-rib, dovetailed ramp front with gold bead.
Price: No. 1A **$966.00**

Ruger No. 1V Varminter
Similar to the No. 1B Standard Rifle except has 24" heavy barrel. Semi-beavertail forend, barrel ribbed for target scope block, with 1" Ruger scope rings. Calibers 22-250, 220 Swift (w/26" bbl.), 223, 25-06, 6mm Rem. Weight about 9 lbs.
Price: No. 1V **$966.00**
Price: K1-V-BBZ stainless steel, laminated stock 22-250 .... **$998.00**

Ruger No. 1 RSI

Ruger No. 1H Tropical

Ruger No. 1S Medium Sporter

Shiloh 1874 Long Range Express

Shiloh 1874 Quigley

Price: No. 1S. **$966.00**
Price: K1-S-BBZ, S/S, 45-70 . . . . **$998.00**

SHILOH RIFLE CO. SHARPS 1874 LONG RANGE EXPRESS
Caliber: 40-50 BN, 40-70 BN, 40-90 BN, 45-70 ST, 45-90 ST, 45-110 ST, 50-70 ST, 50-90 ST, 38-55, 40-70 ST, 40-90 ST. **Barrel:** 34" tapered octagon. **Weight:** 10-1/2 lbs. **Length:** 51" overall. **Stock:** Oil-finished walnut (upgrades available) with pistol grip, shotgun-style butt, traditional cheek rest, Schnabel forend. **Sights:** Customer's choice. **Features:** Re-creation of the Model 1874 Sharps rifle. Double-set triggers. Made in U.S.A. by Shiloh Rifle Mfg. Co.
Price: **$1,638.00**
Price: Sporting Rifle No. 1 (similar to above except with 30" bbl., blade front, buckhorn rear sight). **$1,638.00**
Price: Sporting Rifle No. 3 (similar to No. 1 except straight-grip stock, standard wood). **$1,547.00**

SHILOH RIFLE CO. SHARPS 1874 QUIGLEY
Caliber: 45-70, 45-110. **Barrel:** 34" heavy octagon. **Stock:** Military-style with patch box, standard grade American walnut. **Sights:** Semi buckhorn, interchangeable front and midrange vernier tang sight with windage. **Features:** Gold inlay initials, pewter tip, Hartford collar, case color or antique finish. Double-set triggers.
Price: **$2,903.00**

Ruger No. 1 RSI International
Similar to the No. 1B Standard Rifle except has lightweight 20" barrel, full-length International-style forend with loop sling swivel, adjustable folding leaf rear sight on quarter-rib, ramp front with gold bead. Calibers 243, 30-06, 270 and 7x57. Weight is about 7-1/4 lbs.
Price: No. 1 RSI. **$998.00**

Ruger No. 1H Tropical Rifle
Similar to the No. 1B Standard Rifle except has Alexander Henry forend, adjustable folding leaf rear sight on quarter-rib, ramp front with dovetail gold bead, 24" heavy barrel. Calibers 375 H&H, 416 Rigby, 458 Lott, 405 Win. and 458 Win. Mag. (weighs about 9 lbs.).
Price: No. 1H. **$966.00**
Price: K1-H-BBZ, S/S, 375 H&H, 416 Rigby. **$998.00**

Ruger No. 1S Medium Sporter
Similar to the No. 1B Standard Rifle except has Alexander Henry-style forend, adjustable folding leaf rear sight on quarter-rib, ramp front sight base and dovetail-type gold bead front sight. Calibers 218 Bee, 45-70 with 22" barrel. Weighs about 7-1/2 lbs. In 45-70.

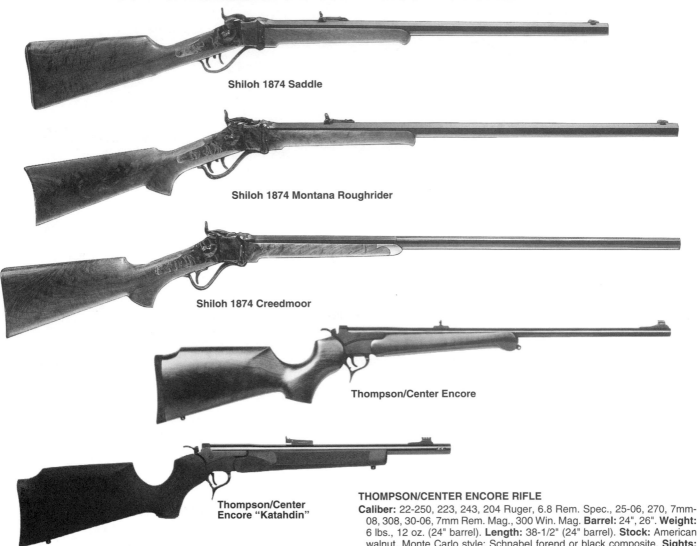

Shiloh 1874 Saddle

Shiloh 1874 Montana Roughrider

Shiloh 1874 Creedmoor

Thompson/Center Encore

Thompson/Center Encore "Katahdin"

SHILOH RIFLE CO. SHARPS 1874 SADDLE RIFLE
Caliber: 38-55, 40-50 BN, 40-65 Win., 40-70 BN, 40-70 ST, 40-90 BN, 40-90 ST, 44-77 BN, 44-90 BN, 45-70 ST, 45-90 ST, 45-100 ST, 45-110 ST, 45-120 ST, 50-70 ST, 50-90 ST. **Barrel:** 26" full or half octagon. **Stock:** Semi fancy American walnut. Shotgun style with cheekrest. **Sights:** Buckhorn and blade. **Features:** Double-set trigger, numerous custom features can be added.
Price: **$1,594.00**

SHILOH RIFLE CO. SHARPS 1874 MONTANA ROUGHRIDER
Caliber: 38-55, 40-50 BN, 40-65 Win., 40-70 BN, 40-70 ST, 40-90 BN, 40-90 ST, 44-77 BN, 44-90 BN, 45-70 ST, 45-90 ST, 45-100 ST, 45-110 ST, 45-120 ST, 50-70 ST, 50-90 ST. **Barrel:** 30" full or half octagon. **Stock:** American walnut in shotgun or military style. **Sights:** Buckhorn and blade. **Features:** Double-set triggers, numerous custom features can be added.
Price: **$1,638.00**

SHILOH RIFLE CO. SHARPS CREEDMOOR TARGET
Caliber: 38-55, 40-50 BN, 40-65 Win., 40-70 BN, 40-70 ST, 40-90 BN, 40-90 ST, 44-77 BN, 44-90 BN, 45-70 ST, 45-90 ST, 45-100 ST, 45-110 ST, 45-120 ST, 50-70 ST, 50-90 ST. **Barrel:** 32", half round-half octagon. **Stock:** Extra fancy American walnut. Shotgun style with pistol grip. **Sights:** Customer's choice. **Features:** Single trigger, AA finish on stock, polished barrel and screws, pewter tip.
Price: **$2,485.00**

THOMPSON/CENTER ENCORE RIFLE
Caliber: 22-250, 223, 243, 204 Ruger, 6.8 Rem. Spec., 25-06, 270, 7mm-08, 308, 30-06, 7mm Rem. Mag., 300 Win. Mag. **Barrel:** 24", 26". **Weight:** 6 lbs., 12 oz. (24" barrel). **Length:** 38-1/2" (24" barrel). **Stock:** American walnut. Monte Carlo style; Schnabel forend or black composite. **Sights:** Ramp-style white bead front, fully adjustable leaf-type rear. **Features:** Interchangeable barrels; action opens by squeezing trigger guard; drilled and tapped for T/C scope mounts; polished blue finish. Introduced 1996. Made in U.S.A. by Thompson/Center Arms.
Price: . . . . **$604.00 to $663.00**
Price: Extra barrels **$277.00**

Thompson/Center Stainless Encore Rifle
Similar to blued Encore except stainless steel with blued sights, black composite stock and forend. Available in 22-250, 223, 7mm-08, 30-06, 308. Introduced 1999. Made in U.S.A. by Thompson/Center Arms.
Price: . . . . **$680.00 to $738.00**

THOMPSON/CENTER ENCORE "KATAHDIN" CARBINE
Caliber: 45-70 Gov't., 450 Marlin. **Barrel:** 18" with muzzle tamer. **Stock:** Composite.
Price: **$619.00**

Thompson/Center G2 Contender Rifle
Similar to the G2 Contender pistol, but in a compact rifle format. Weighs 5-1/2 lbs. Features interchangeable 23" barrels, chambered for 17 HMR, 22LR, 223 Rem., 30/30 Win. and 45/70 Gov't; plus a 45 Cal. Muzzleloading barrel. All of the 16-1/4" and 21" barrels made for the old-style Contender will fit. Introduced 2003. Made in U.S.A. by Thompson/Center Arms.
Price: . . . . **$622.00 to $637.00**

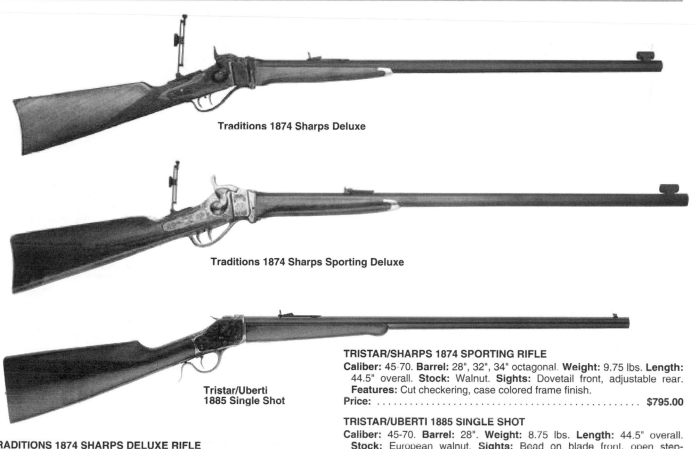

Traditions 1874 Sharps Deluxe

Traditions 1874 Sharps Sporting Deluxe

Tristar/Uberti
1885 Single Shot

TRADITIONS 1874 SHARPS DELUXE RIFLE

Caliber: 45-70. **Barrel:** 32" octagonal; 1:18" twist. **Weight:** 11.67 lbs. **Length:** 48.8" overall. **Stock:** Checkered walnut with German silver nose cap and steel buttplate. **Sights:** Globe front, adjustable Creedmore rear with 12 inserts. **Features:** Color case-hardened receiver; double-set triggers. Introduced 2001. Imported from Pedersoli by Traditions.
Price: $999.00

Traditions 1874 Sharps Sporting Deluxe Rifle

Similar to Sharps Deluxe but custom silver engraved receiver, European walnut stock and forend, satin finish, set trigger, fully adjustable.
Price: $1,999.00

Traditions 1874 Sharps Standard Rifle

Similar to 1874 Sharps Deluxe except has blade front and adjustable buckhorn-style rear sight. Weighs 10.67 pounds. Introduced 2001. Imported from Pedersoli by Traditions.
Price: $769.00

TRADITIONS ROLLING BLOCK SPORTING RIFLE

Caliber: 45-70. **Barrel:** 30" octagonal, 1.10" twist. **Weight:** 11.67 lbs. **Length:** 46.7" overall. **Stock:** Walnut. **Sights:** Blade front, adjustable rear. **Features:** Antique silver, color case-hardened receiver, drilled and tapped for tang/globe sights; brass buttplate and trigger guard. Introduced 2001. Imported from Pedersoli by Traditions.
Price: $769.00

TRADITIONS ROLLING BLOCK SPORTING RIFLE IN 30-30 WINCHESTER

Caliber: 30-30. **Barrel:** 28" round, blued. **Weight:** 8.25 lbs. **Stock:** Walnut. **Sights:** Fixed front, adjustable rear. **Features:** Steel buttplate, trigger guard, barrel band.
Price: $769.00

TRISTAR/SHARPS 1874 SPORTING RIFLE

Caliber: 45-70. **Barrel:** 28", 32", 34" octagonal. **Weight:** 9.75 lbs. **Length:** 44.5" overall. **Stock:** Walnut. **Sights:** Dovetail front, adjustable rear. **Features:** Cut checkering, case colored frame finish.
Price: $795.00

TRISTAR/UBERTI 1885 SINGLE SHOT

Caliber: 45-70. **Barrel:** 28". **Weight:** 8.75 lbs. **Length:** 44.5" overall. **Stock:** European walnut. **Sights:** Bead on blade front, open step-adjustable rear. **Features:** Recreation of the 1885 Winchester. Color case-hardened receiver and lever, blued barrel. Introduced 1998. Imported from Italy by Tristar Sporting Arms Ltd.
Price: .... $850.00 to $1,050.00

UBERTI BABY ROLLING BLOCK CARBINE

Caliber: 22 LR, 22 WMR, 22 Hornet, 357 Mag., single shot. **Barrel:** 22". **Weight:** 4.8 lbs. **Length:** 35-1/2" overall. **Stock:** Walnut stock and forend. **Sights:** Blade front, fully adjustable open rear. **Features:** Resembles Remington New Model No. 4 carbine. Brass trigger guard and buttplate; color case-hardened frame, blued barrel. Imported by Uberti USA Inc.
Price: $535.00
Price: Rolling Block Rifle, 26" bbl. $600.00

WINCHESTER MODEL 1885 HIGH WALL WSM

Caliber: 17 HMR, 17 Mach 2. **Barrel:** 28". **Weight:** 8.5 lbs. **Length:** 44". **Stock:** Walnut. **Features:** Single-shot, Pachmayr recoil pad.
Price:... $1,085.00

DRILLINGS, COMBINATION GUNS, DOUBLE GUNS

Designs for sporting and utility purposes worldwide.

Beretta Express SSO

Beretta Model 455 SxS

Charles Daly Superior

Charles Daly Empire Combo

BERETTA EXPRESS SSO O/U DOUBLE RIFLES
Caliber: 375 H&H, 458 Win. Mag., 9.3x74R. **Barrel:** 25.5". **Weight:** 11 lbs. **Stock:** European walnut with hand-checkered grip and forend. **Sights:** Blade front on ramp, open V-notch rear. **Features:** Sidelock action with color case-hardened receiver (gold inlays on SSO6 Gold). Ejectors, double triggers, recoil pad. Introduced 1990. Imported from Italy by Beretta U.S.A.
Price: SSO6 . . . . **$21,000.00**
Price: SSO6 Gold **$23,500.00**

BERETTA MODEL 455 SxS EXPRESS RIFLE
Caliber: 375 H&H, 458 Win. Mag., 470 NE, 500 NE 3", 416 Rigby. **Barrel:** 23-1/2" or 25-1/2". **Weight:** 11 lbs. **Stock:** European walnut with hand-checkered grip and forend. **Sights:** Blade front, folding leaf V-notch rear. **Features:** Sidelock action with easily removable sideplates; color case-hardened finish (455), custom big game or floral motif engraving (455EELL). Double triggers, recoil pad. Introduced 1990. Imported from Italy by Beretta U.S.A.
Price: Model 455 . . . . **$36,000.00**
Price: Model 455EELL **$47,000.00**

BRNO 500 COMBINATION GUNS
Caliber/Gauge: 12 (2-3/4" chamber) over 5.6x52R, 5.6x50R, 222 Rem., 243, 6.x55, 308, 7x57R, 7x65R, 30-06. **Barrel:** 23.6". **Weight:** 7.6 lbs. **Length:** 40.5" overall. **Stock:** European walnut. **Sights:** Bead front, V-notch rear; grooved for scope mounting. **Features:** Boxlock action; double-set trigger; blue finish with etched engraving. Announced 1998. Imported from The Czech Republic by Euro-Imports.
Price: **$1,023.00**
Price: O/U double rifle, 7x57R, 7x65R, 8x57JRS **$1,125.00**

BRNO ZH 300 COMBINATION GUN
Caliber/Gauge: 22 Hornet, 5.6x50R Mag., 5.6x52R, 7x57R, 7x65R, 8x57JRS over 12, 16 (2-3/4" chamber). **Barrel:** 23.6". **Weight:** 7.9 lbs. **Length:** 40.5" overall. **Stock:** European walnut. **Sights:** Blade front, open adjustable rear. **Features:** Boxlock action; double triggers; automatic safety. Announced 1998. Imported from The Czech Republic by Euro-Imports.
Price: **$724.00**

BRNO ZH Double Rifles
Similar to ZH 300 Combination guns except double rifle barrels. Available in 7x65R, 7x57R and 8x57JRS. Announced 1998. Imported from The Czech Republic by Euro-Imports.
Price: **$1,125.00**

CHARLES DALY SUPERIOR COMBINATION GUN
Caliber/Gauge: 12 ga. over 22 Hornet, 223 Rem., 22-250, 243 Win., 270 Win., 308 Win., 30-06. **Barrel:** 23.5", shotgun choked Imp. Cyl. **Weight:** About 7.5 lbs. **Stock:** Checkered walnut pistol grip buttstock and semi-beavertail forend. **Features:** Silvered, engraved receiver; chrome-moly steel barrels; double triggers; extractors; sling swivels; gold bead front sight. Introduced 1997. Imported from Italy by K.B.I. Inc.
Price: **$1,479.00**

Charles Daly Empire Combination Gun
Same as the Superior grade except has deluxe wood with European-style comb and cheekpiece; slim forend. Introduced 1997. Imported from Italy by K.B.I., Inc.
Price: **$2,189.00**

CZ 584 SOLO COMBINATION GUN
Caliber/Gauge: 7x57R; 12, 2-3/4" chamber. **Barrel:** 24.4". **Weight:** 7.37 lbs. **Length:** 45.25" overall. **Stock:** Circassian walnut. **Sights:** Blade front, open rear adjustable for windage. **Features:** Kersten-style double lump locking system; double-trigger Blitz-type mechanism with drop safety and adjustable set trigger for the rifle barrel; auto safety; dual extractors; receiver dovetailed for scope mounting. Imported from the Czech Republic by CZ-USA.
Price: $851.00

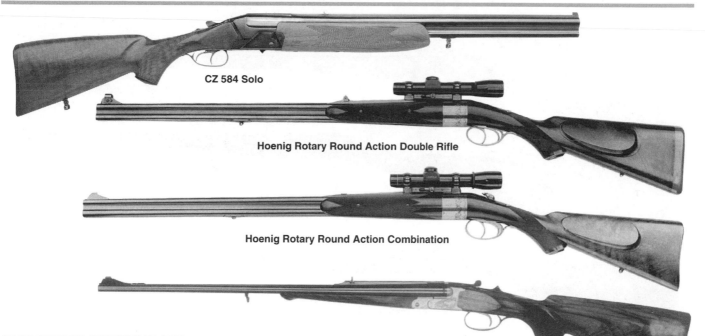

CZ 584 Solo

Hoenig Rotary Round Action Double Rifle

Hoenig Rotary Round Action Combination

Krieghoff Classic Double Rifle

CZ 589 STOPPER OVER/UNDER GUN

Caliber: 458 Win. Magnum. **Barrels:** 21.7". **Weight:** 9.3 lbs. **Length:** 37.7" overall. **Stock:** Turkish walnut with sling swivels. **Sights:** Blade front, fixed rear. **Features:** Kersten-style action; Blitz-type double trigger; hammer-forged, blued barrels; satin-nickel, engraved receiver. Introduced 2001. Imported from the Czech Republic by CZ USA.

Price: $2,999.00
Price: Fully engraved model $3,999.00

DAKOTA DOUBLE RIFLE

Caliber: 470 Nitro Express, 500 Nitro Express. **Barrel:** 25". **Stock:** Exhibition-grade walnut. **Sights:** Express-style. **Features:** Round action; selective ejectors; recoil pad; Americase. From Dakota Arms Inc.

Price: $25,000.00

EAA/BAIKAL IZH-94 COMBINATION GUN

Caliber/Gauge: 12, 3" chamber; 222 Rem., 223, 5.6x50R, 5.6x55E, 7x57R, 7x65R, 7.62x39, 7.62x51, 308, 7.62x53R, 7,62x54R, 30-06. **Barrel:** 24", 26"; imp., mod. and full choke tubes. **Weight:** 7.28 lbs. **Stock:** Walnut; rubber buttpad. **Sights:** Express-style. **Features:** Hammer-forged barrels with chrome-lined bores; machined receiver; single-selective or double triggers. Imported by European American Armory.

Price: Blued finish $549.00
Price: 20 ga./22 LR, 20/22 Mag, 3" $629.00

GARBI EXPRESS DOUBLE RIFLE

Caliber: 7x65R, 9.3x74R, 375 H&H. **Barrel:** 24-3/4". **Weight:** 7-3/4 to 8-1/2 lbs. **Length:** 41-1/2" overall. **Stock:** Turkish walnut. **Sights:** Quarter-rib with express sight. **Features:** Side-by-side double; H&H-pattern sidelock ejector with reinforced action; chopper lump barrels of Boehler steel; double triggers; fine scroll and rosette engraving, or full coverage ornamental; coin-finished action. Introduced 1997. Imported from Spain by Wm. Larkin Moore.

Price: $19,900.00

HOENIG ROTARY ROUND ACTION DOUBLE RIFLE

Caliber: Most popular calibers from 225 Win. to 9.3x74R. **Barrel:** 22" to 26". **Stock:** English Walnut; to customer specs. **Sights:** Swivel hood front with button release (extra bead stored in trap door gripcap), express-style rear on quarter-rib adjustable for windage and elevation; scope mount. **Features:** Round action opens by rotating barrels, pulling forward. Inertia extractor system, rotary safety blocks strikers. Single lever quick-detachable scope mount. Simple takedown without removing forend. Introduced 1997. Made in U.S.A. by George Hoenig.

Price: $24,975.00

HOENIG ROTARY ROUND ACTION COMBINATION

Caliber: 28 ga. **Barrel:** 26". **Weight:** 7 lbs. **Stock:** English Walnut to customer specs. **Sights:** Front ramp with button release blades. Foldable aperture tang sight windage and elevation adjustable. Quarter-rib with scope mount. **Features:** Round action opens by rotating barrels, pulling forward. Inertia extractor; rotary safety blocks strikers. Simple takedown without removing forend. Made in U.S.A. by George Hoenig.

Price: $24,975.00

KRIEGHOFF CLASSIC DOUBLE RIFLE

Caliber: 7x57R, 7x65R, 308 Win., 30-06, 8x57 JRS, 8x75RS, 9.3x74R, 375NE, 500/416NE, 470NE, 500NE. **Barrel:** 23.5". **Weight:** 7.3 to 8 lbs. **Stock:** High grade European walnut. Standard model has conventional rounded cheekpiece, Bavaria model has Bavarian-style cheekpiece. **Sights:** Bead front with removable, adjustable wedge (375 H&H and below), standing leaf rear on quarter-rib. **Features:** Boxlock action; double triggers; short opening angle for fast loading; quiet extractors; sliding, self-adjusting wedge for secure bolting; Purdey-style barrel extension; horizontal firing pin placement. Many options available. Introduced 1997. Imported from Germany by Krieghoff International.

Price: With small Arabesque engraving $8,475.00
Price: With engraved sideplates $11,725.00
Price: For extra barrels $4,950.00
Price: Extra 20-ga., 28" shotshell barrels $3,750.00

Krieghoff Classic Big Five Double Rifle

Similar to the standard Classic except available in 375 Flanged Mag. N.E., 500/416 N.E., 470 N.E., 500 N.E. Has hinged front trigger, non-removable muzzle wedge (models larger than 375 caliber), Universal Trigger System, Combi Cocking Device, steel trigger guard, specially weighted stock bolt for weight and balance. Many options available. Introduced 1997. Imported from Germany by Krieghoff International.

Price: $10,975.00
Price: With engraved sideplates $14,225.00

LEBEAU-COURALLY EXPRESS RIFLE SxS

Caliber: 7x65R, 8x57JRS, 9.3x74R, 375 H&H, 470 N.E. **Barrel:** 24" to 26". **Weight:** 7-3/4 to 10-1/2 lbs. **Stock:** Fancy French walnut with cheekpiece. **Sights:** Bead on ramp front, standing left express rear on quarter-rib. **Features:** Holland & Holland-type sidelock with automatic ejectors; double triggers. Built to order only. Imported from Belgium by Wm. Larkin Moore.

Price: $41,000.00

Merkel 96K Engraved

Merkel 140-1

Rizzini Express

Savage 24F Combination

Springfield M6 Scout

MERKEL DRILLINGS

Caliber/Gauge: 12, 20, 3" chambers, 16, 2-3/4" chambers; 22 Hornet, 5.6x50R Mag., 5.6x52R, 222 Rem., 243 Win., 6.5x55, 6.5x57R, 7x57R, 7x65R, 308, 30-06, 8x57JRS, 9.3x74R, 375 H&H. **Barrel:** 25.6". **Weight:** 7.9 to 8.4 lbs. depending upon caliber. **Stock:** Oil-finished walnut with pistol grip; cheekpiece on 12-, 16-gauge. **Sights:** Blade front, fixed rear. **Features:** Double barrel locking lug with Greener cross bolt; scroll-engraved, case-hardened receiver; automatic trigger safety; Blitz action; double triggers. Imported from Germany by GSI.
Price: Model 96K (manually cocked rifle system), from **$7,495.00**
Price: Model 96K Engraved (hunting series on receiver) **$8,595.00**

MERKEL BOXLOCK DOUBLE RIFLES

Caliber: 5.6x52R, 243 Winchester, 6.5x55, 6.5x57R, 7x57R, 7x65R, 308 Winchester, 30-06 Springfield, 8x57 IRS, 9.3x74R. **Barrel:** 23.6". **Weight:** 7.7 oz. **Length:** NA. **Stock:** Walnut, oil finished, pistol grip. **Sights:** Fixed 100 meter. **Features:** Anson & Deely boxlock action with cocking indicators, double triggers, engraved color case-hardened receiver. Introduced 1995. Imported from Germany by GSI.
Price: Model 140-1, from. **$6,695.00**
Price: Model 140-1.1 (engraved silver-gray receiver), from **$7,795.00**

RIZZINI EXPRESS 90L DOUBLE RIFLE

Caliber: 30-06, 7x65R, 9.3x74R. **Barrel:** 24". **Weight:** 7-1/2 lbs. **Length:** 40" overall. **Stock:** Select European walnut with satin oil finish; English-style cheekpiece. **Sights:** Ramp front, quarter-rib with express sight. **Features:** Color case-hardened boxlock action; automatic ejectors; single selective trigger; polished blue barrels. Extra 20 gauge shotgun barrels available. Imported for Italy by Wm. Larkin Moore.
Price: With case **$3,850.00**

SAVAGE 24F PREDATOR O/U COMBINATION GUN

Caliber/Gauge: 22 Hornet, 223, 30-30 over 12 (24F-12) or 22 LR, 22 Hornet, 223, 30-30 over 20 ga. (24F-20); 3" chambers. **Action:** Takedown, low rebounding visible hammer. Single trigger, barrel selector spur on hammer. **Barrel:** 24" separated barrels; 12 ga. has mod. choke tubes, 20 ga. has fixed Mod. choke. **Weight:** 8 lbs. **Length:** 40-1/2" overall. **Stock:** Black Rynite composition. **Sights:** Blade front, rear open adjustable for elevation. **Features:** Introduced 1989.
Price: 24F-12 . . . . **$661.00**
Price: 24F-20 . . . . **$628.00**

SPRINGFIELD ARMORY M6 SCOUT RIFLE/SHOTGUN

Caliber/Gauge: 22 LR or 22 Hornet over 410 bore. **Barrel:** 18.25". **Weight:** 4 lbs. **Length:** 32" overall. **Stock:** Folding detachable with storage for 15 22 LR, four 410 shells. **Sights:** Blade front, military aperture for 22; V-notch for 410. **Features:** All metal construction. Designed for quick disassembly and minimum maintenance. Folds for compact storage. Introduced 1982; reintroduced 1996. Imported from the Czech Republic by Springfield Armory.
Price: Parkerized **$185.00**
Price: Stainless steel **$219.00**

Designs for hunting, utility and sporting purposes, including training for competition.

Browning Buck Mark Target

Browning Semi-Auto 22

CZ 511 Auto

Henry U.S. Survival

Marlin Model 60

AR-7 EXPLORER CARBINE

Caliber: 22 LR, 8-shot magazine. **Barrel:** 16". **Weight:** 2-1/2 lbs. **Length:** 04 1/2", 16 1/2" stowed. **Stock:** Molded Cycolac; snap on rubber buttpad. **Sights:** Square blade front, aperture rear. **Features:** Takedown design stores barrel and action in hollow stock. Light enough to float. Reintroduced 1999. From AR-7 Industries, LLC.
Price: Black matte finish $150.00
Price: AR-20 Sporter (tubular stock, barrel shroud) $200.00
New! Price: AR-7 camo- or walnut-finish stock $164.95

BROWNING BUCK MARK SEMI-AUTO RIFLES

Caliber: 22 LR, 10-shot magazine. **Barrel:** 18" tapered (Sporter), heavy bull (Target), or carbon composite barrel (Classic Carbon). **Weight:** 4 lbs., 2 oz. (Sporter) or 5 lbs., 4 oz. (Target). **Length:** 34" overall. **Stock:** Walnut stock and forearm with full pistol grip. **Sights:** HiViz adjustable (Sporter). **Features:** A rifle version of the Buck Mark Pistol; straight blowback action; machined aluminum receiver with integral rail scope mount; recessed muzzle crown; manual thumb safety. Introduced 2001. From Browning.
Price: Sporter (adj. sights) $518.00
Price: Target (heavy bbl., no sights) $518.00

BROWNING SEMI-AUTO 22 RIFLE

Caliber: 22 LR, 11-shot. **Barrel:** 19-1/4". **Weight:** 5 lbs., 3 oz. **Length:** 37" overall. **Stock:** Checkered select walnut with pistol grip and semi-beavertail forend. **Sights:** Gold bead front, folding leaf rear. **Features:** Engraved receiver with polished blue finish; cross-bolt safety; tubular magazine in buttstock; easy takedown for carrying or storage. Imported from Japan by Browning.
Price: Grade I $479.00

Browning Semi-Auto 22, Grade VI

Same as the Grade I Auto-22 except available with either grayed or blued receiver with extensive engraving with gold-plated animals: right side pictures a fox and squirrel in a woodland scene; left side shows a beagle chasing a rabbit. On top is a portrait of the beagle. Stock and forend are of high-grade walnut with a double-bordered cut checkering design. Introduced 1987.
Price: Grade VI, blue or gray receiver $1,028.00

BRNO ZKM 611 AUTO RIFLE

Caliber: 22 WMR, 6- or 10-shot magazine. **Barrel:** 20.4". **Weight:** 5.9 lbs. **Length:** 38.9" overall. **Stock:** European walnut. **Sights:** Hooded blade front, open adjustable rear. **Features:** Removable box magazine; polished blue finish; cross-bolt safety; grooved receiver for scope mounting; easy takedown for storage. Imported from The Czech Republic by Euro-Imports.
Price: $475.00

CZ 511 AUTO RIFLE

Caliber: 22 LR, 8-shot magazine. **Barrel:** 22.2". **Weight:** 5.39 lbs. **Length:** 38.6" overall. **Stock:** Walnut with checkered pistol grip. **Sights:** Hooded front, adjustable rear. **Features:** Polished blue finish; detachable magazine; sling swivel studs. Imported from the Czech Republic by CZ-USA.
Price: $351.00

HENRY U.S. SURVIVAL RIFLE .22

Caliber: 22 LR, 8-shot magazine. **Barrel:** 16" steel lined. **Weight:** 2.5 lbs. **Stock:** ABS plastic. **Sights:** Blade front on ramp, aperture rear. **Features:** Takedown design stores barrel and action in hollow stock. Light enough to float. Silver, black or camo finish. Comes with two magazines. Introduced 1990. From Henry Repeating Arms Co.
Price: $205.00

MARLIN MODEL 60 AUTO RIFLE

Caliber: 22 LR, 14-shot tubular magazine. **Barrel:** 19" round tapered. **Weight:** About 5-1/2 lbs. **Length:** 37-1/2" overall. **Stock:** Press-checkered, walnut-finished Maine birch with Monte Carlo, full pistol grip; Mar-Shield® finish. **Sights:** Ramp front, open adjustable rear. **Features:** Matted receiver is grooved for scope mount. Manual bolt hold-open; automatic last-shot hold-open. Model 60C is similar except has hardwood Monte Carlo stock with Mossy Oak Break-Up camouflage pattern. From Marlin.
Price: $185.00
Price: With 4x scope $193.00
Price: (Model 60C) $220.00

Marlin Model 60SSK

Marlin Model 70PSS

Marlin 795

Remington 552 BDL Speedmaster

Remington 597

Marlin Model 60SS Self-Loading Rifle

Same as the Model 60 except breech bolt, barrel and outer magazine tube are made of stainless steel; most other parts are either nickel-plated or coated to match the stainless finish. Monte Carlo stock is of black/gray Maine birch laminate, and has nickel-plated swivel studs, rubber buttpad. Introduced 1993. From Marlin.

Price:	**$297.00**
Price: Model 60SSK (black fiberglass-filled stock)	**$257.00**
Price: Model 60SB (walnut-finished birch stock)	**$235.00**
Price: Model 60SB with 4x scope	**$251.00**

MARLIN 70PSS PAPOOSE STAINLESS RIFLE

Caliber: 22 LR, 7-shot magazine. **Barrel:** 16-1/4" stainless steel, Micro-Groove® rifling. **Weight:** 3-1/4 lbs. **Length:** 35-1/4" overall. **Stock:** Black fiberglass-filled synthetic with abbreviated forend, nickel-plated swivel studs, molded-in checkering. **Sights:** Ramp front with orange post, cut-away Wide Scan™ hood; adjustable open rear. Receiver grooved for scope mounting. **Features:** Takedown barrel; cross-bolt safety; manual bolt hold-open; last shot bolt hold-open; comes with padded carrying case. Introduced 1986. Made in U.S.A. by Marlin.

Price: **$304.00**

MARLIN MODEL 7000 AUTO RIFLE

Caliber: 22 LR, 10-shot magazine **Barrel:** 18" heavy target with 12-groove Micro-Groove® rifling, recessed muzzle. **Weight:** 5-1/2 lbs. **Length:** 37" overall. **Stock:** Black fiberglass-filled synthetic with Monte Carlo combo, swivel studs, molded-in checkering. **Sights:** None furnished; comes with ring mounts. **Features:** Automatic last-shot bolt hold-open, manual bolt hold-open; cross-bolt safety; steel charging handle; blue finish, nickel-plated magazine. Introduced 1997. Made in U.S.A. by Marlin Firearms Co.

Price: **$249.00**

MARLIN MODEL 795 AUTO RIFLE

Caliber: 22. **Barrel:** 18" with 16-groove Micro-Groove® rifling. Ramp front sight, adjustable rear. Receiver grooved for scope mount. **Stock:** Black synthetic. **Features:** 10-round magazine, last shot hold-open feature. Introduced 1997. Made in U.S.A. by Marlin Firearms Co.

Price: **$176.00**

Marlin Model 795SS Auto Rifle

Similar to Model 795 except stainless steel barrel. Most other parts nickel-plated. Adjustable folding semi-buckhorn rear sights, ramp front high-visibility post and removeable cutaway wide scan hood.

Price: **$235.00**

REMINGTON MODEL 552 BDL DELUXE SPEEDMASTER RIFLE

Caliber: 22 S (20), L (17) or LR (15) tubular mag. **Barrel:** 21" round tapered. **Weight:** 5-3/4 lbs. **Length:** 40" overall. **Stock:** Walnut. Checkered grip and forend. **Sights:** Big game. **Features:** Positive cross-bolt safety, receiver grooved for tip-off mount.

Price: **$393.00**

REMINGTON 597 AUTO RIFLE

Caliber: 22 LR, 10-shot clip. **Barrel:** 20". **Weight:** 5-1/2 lbs. **Length:** 40" overall. **Stock:** Black synthetic. **Sights:** Big game. **Features:** Matte black finish, nickel-plated bolt. Receiver is grooved and drilled and tapped for scope mounts. Introduced 1997. Made in U.S.A. by Remington.

Price:	**$169.00**
Price: Model 597 Magnum, 22 WMR, 8-shot clip.	**$335.00**
Price: Model 597 LSS (laminated stock, stainless)	**$279.00**
Price: Model 597 SS	
(22 LR, stainless steel, black synthetic stock)	**$224.00**
Price: Model 597 LS heavy barrel (22 LR, laminated stock)	**$265.00**
Price: Model 597 Magnum LS heavy barrel	
(22 WMR, lam. stock)	**$399.00**
Price: Model 597 Magnum 17 HMR, 8-shot clip	**$361.00**

Ruger 10/22 Deluxe Sporter

Ruger 10/22 Target

Savage Model 64FV

RUGER 10/22 AUTOLOADING CARBINE

Caliber: 22 LR, 10-shot rotary magazine. **Barrel:** 18-1/2" round tapered. **Weight:** 5 lbs. **Length:** 37-1/4" overall. **Stock:** American hardwood with pistol grip and barrel band or synthetic. **Sights:** Brass bead front, folding leaf rear adjustable for elevation. **Features:** Detachable rotary magazine fits flush into stock, cross-bolt safety, receiver tapped and grooved for scope blocks or tip-off mount. Scope base adaptor furnished with each rifle.
Price: Model 10/22 RB (blue) $258.00
Price: Model K10/22RB (bright finish stainless barrel) $304.00
Price: Model 10/22RPF (blue, synthetic stock) $258.00

Ruger 10/22 Deluxe Sporter
Same as 10/22 Carbine except walnut stock with hand checkered pistol grip and forend; straight buttplate, no barrel band, has sling swivels.
Price: Model 10/22 DSP $324.00

Ruger 10/22T Target Rifle
Similar to the 10/22 except has 20" heavy, hammer-forged barrel with tight chamber dimensions, improved trigger pull, laminated hardwood stock dimensioned for optical sights. No iron sights supplied. Introduced 1996. Made in U.S.A. by Sturm, Ruger & Co.
Price: 10/22T $445.00
Price: K10/22T, stainless steel $495.00
Price: K10/22R, 20" bbl. $275.00

Ruger K10/22RPF All-Weather Rifle
Similar to the stainless K10/22/RB except has black composite stock of thermoplastic polyester resin reinforced with fiberglass; checkered grip and forend. Brushed satin, natural metal finish with clear hardcoat finish. Weighs 5 lbs., measures 36-3/4" overall. Introduced 1997. From Sturm, Ruger & Co.
Price: $304.00

RUGER 10/22 MAGNUM AUTOLOADING CARBINE

Caliber: 22 WMR, 9-shot rotary magazine. **Barrel:** 18-1/2". **Weight:** 6 lbs. **Length:** 37-1/4" overall. **Stock:** Birch. **Sights:** Gold bead front, folding rear. **Features:** All-steel receiver has integral Ruger scope bases for the included 1" rings. Introduced 1999. Made in U.S.A. by Sturm, Ruger & Co.
Price: 10/22RBM $536.00

SAVAGE MODEL 64G AUTO RIFLE

Caliber: 22 LR, 10-shot magazine. **Barrel:** 20", 21". **Weight:** 5-1/2 lbs. **Length:** 40", 41". **Stock:** Walnut-finished hardwood with Monte Carlo-type comb, checkered grip and forend. **Sights:** Bead front, open adjustable rear. Receiver grooved for scope mounting. **Features:** Thumb-operated rotating safety. Blue finish. Side ejection, bolt hold-open device. Introduced 1990. Made in Canada, from Savage Arms.
Price: $162.00
Price: Model 64FSS, stainless $202.00
Price: Model 64F, black synthetic stock $135.00
Price: Model 64GXP package gun includes
4x15 scope and mounts $171.00
Price: Model 64FXP (black stock, 4x15 scope) $142.00
Price: Model 64F Camo $135.00

Savage Model 64FV Auto Rifle
Similar to the Model 64F except has heavy 21" barrel with recessed crown; no sights provided, comes with Weaver-style bases. Introduced 1998. Imported from Canada by Savage Arms, Inc.
Price: $135.00
Price: Model 64FSS, stainless $202.00

TAURUS MODEL 63 RIFLE

Caliber: 22 LR, 10-shot tube-fed magazine. **Barrel:** 23". **Weight:** 72 oz. **Length:** 32-1/2". **Stock:** Hand-fitted walnut-finished hardwood. **Sights:** Adjustable rear, fixed front. **Features:** Manual safety, metal buttplate, can accept Taurus tang sight. Charged and cocked with operating plunger at front of forend. Available in blue or polished stainless steel.
Price: 63 . . . . $295.00
Price: 63SS $311.00

THOMPSON/CENTER 22 LR CLASSIC RIFLE

Caliber: 22 LR, 8-shot magazine. **Barrel:** 22" match-grade. **Weight:** 5-1/2 pounds. **Length:** 39-1/2" overall. **Stock:** Satin-finished American walnut with Monte Carlo-type comb and pistol gripcap, swivel studs. **Sights:** Ramp-style front and fully adjustable rear, both with fiber optics. **Features:** All-steel receiver drilled and tapped for scope mounting; barrel threaded to receiver; thumb-operated safety; trigger guard safety lock included. New .22 Classic Benchmark TGT target rifle variant has 18" heavy barrel, brown laminated target stock, blued with matte finish, 10-shot magazine and no sights; drilled and tapped.
Price: T/C 22 LR Classic (blue) $396.00
Price: T/C 22 LR Classic Benchmark $505.00

Browning BL-22

Henry Lever-Action 22

Henry Golden Boy 22

Henry Pump-Action 22

Marlin Model 39A

BROWNING BL-22 LEVER-ACTION RIFLE
Caliber: 22 S (22), L (17) or LR (15), tubular magazine. **Barrel:** 20" round tapered. **Weight:** 5 lbs. **Length:** 36-3/4" overall. **Stock:** Walnut, two-piece straight grip Western style. **Sights:** Bead post front, folding-leaf rear. **Features:** Short throw lever, half-cock safety, receiver grooved for tip-off scope mounts, gold-colored trigger. Imported from Japan by Browning.
Price: Grade I **$415.00**
Price: Grade II (engraved receiver, checkered grip and forend).... **$471.00**
Price: Classic, Grade I (blued trigger, no checkering) **$415.00**
Price: Classic, Grade II (cut checkering, satin wood finish,
polished bluing) **$471.00**

HENRY LEVER-ACTION 22
Caliber: 22 Long Rifle (15-shot). **Barrel:** 18-1/4" round. **Weight:** 5-1/2 lbs. **Length:** 34" overall. **Stock:** Walnut. **Sights:** Hooded blade front, open adjustable rear. **Features:** Polished blue finish; full-length tubular magazine; side ejection; receiver grooved for scope mounting. Introduced 1997. Made in U.S.A. by Henry Repeating Arms Co.
Price: **$279.95**
Price: Youth model (33" overall, 11-round 22 LR) **$279.95**

HENRY GOLDEN BOY 22 LEVER-ACTION RIFLE
Caliber: 22 LR, 22 Magnum, 16-shot. **Barrel:** 20" octagonal. **Weight:** 6.25 lbs. **Length:** 38" overall. **Stock:** American walnut. **Sights:** Blade front, open rear. **Features:** Brasslite receiver, brass buttplate, blued barrel and lever. Introduced 1998. Made in U.S.A. from Henry Repeating Arms Co.
Price: **$409.95**
Price: Magnum **$485.00**

HENRY PUMP-ACTION 22 PUMP RIFLE
Caliber: 22 LR, 15-shot. **Barrel:** 18.25". **Weight:** 5.5 lbs. **Length:** NA. **Stock:** American walnut. **Sights:** Bead on ramp front, open adjustable rear. **Features:** Polished blue finish; receiver groved for scope mount; grooved slide handle; two barrel bands. Introduced 1998. Made in U.S.A. from Henry Repeating Arms Co.
Price: **$309.95**

MARLIN MODEL 39A GOLDEN LEVER-ACTION RIFLE
Caliber: 22, S (26), L (21), LR (19), tubular mag. **Barrel:** 24" Micro-Groove®. **Weight:** 6-1/2 lbs. **Length:** 40" overall. **Stock:** Checkered American black walnut; Mar-Shield® finish. Swivel studs; rubber buttpad. **Sights:** Bead ramp front with detachable Wide-Scan™ hood, folding rear semi-buckhorn adjustable for windage and elevation. **Features:** Hammer block safety; rebounding hammer. Takedown action, receiver tapped for scope mount (supplied), offset hammer spur, gold-plated steel trigger. From Marlin Firearms.
Price: **$552.00**

Remington Model 572 BDL Deluxe Fieldmaster

Ruger Model 96/22

Ruger Model 96/17

Taurus 62R

Taurus 72C-SS

Winchester 9422 Legacy

REMINGTON 572 BDL DELUXE FIELDMASTER PUMP RIFLE
Caliber: 22 S (20), L (17) or LR (15), tubular mag. **Barrel:** 21" round tapered. **Weight:** 5-1/2 lbs. **Length:** 40" overall. **Stock:** Walnut with checkered pistol grip and slide handle. **Sights:** Big game. **Features:** Cross-bolt safety; removing inner magazine tube converts rifle to single shot; receiver grooved for tip-off scope mount.
Price: **$407.00**

RUGER MODEL 96 LEVER-ACTION RIFLE
Caliber: 22 WMR, 9 rounds; 44 Magnum, 4 rounds; 17 HMR 9 rounds. **Barrel:** 18-1/2". **Weight:** 5-1/4 lbs. **Length:** 37-1/4" overall. **Stock:** Hardwood. **Sights:** Gold bead front, folding leaf rear. **Features:** Sliding cross button safety, visible cocking indicator; short-throw lever action. Introduced 1996. Made in U.S.A. by Sturm, Ruger & Co.
Price: 96/22M (22 WMR)................................ **$390.00**
Price: 96/22M (44 Mag.)................................ **$546.00**
Price: 96/17M (17 HMR)................................ **$390.00**

TAURUS MODEL 62 PUMP RIFLE
Caliber: 22 LR, 12- or 13-shot. **Barrel:** 16-1/2" or 23" round. **Weight:** 72 oz. to 80 oz. **Length:** 39" overall. **Stock:** Premium hardwood. **Sights:** Adjustable rear, bead blade front, optional tang. **Features:** Blue, case hardened or stainless, bolt-mounted safety, pump action, manual firing pin block, integral security lock system. Imported from Brazil by Taurus International.
Price: M62C (blue) **$280.00**
Price: M62C-CH (case-hardened, blue) **$280.00**
Price: M62CCH-T (case-hardened, blue) **$358.00**
Price: M62C-SS (stainless steel) **$295.00**
Price: M62CSS-T (stainless steel) **$373.00**
Price: M62C-SS-Y (stainless steel)..................... **$327.00**

Price: M62C-T (blue) **$358.00**
Price: M62C-Y (blue) **$311.00**
Price: M62R (blue) **$280.00**
Price: M62R-CH (case-hardened, blue)................... **$280.00**
Price: M62RCH-T (case-hardened, blue) **$358.00**
Price: M62R-SS (stainless steel) **$295.00**
Price: M62RSS-T (stainless steel)...................... **$373.00**
Price: M62R-T (blue) **$358.00**

Taurus Model 72 Pump Rifle
Same as Model 62 except chambered in 22 Magnum or .17 HMR; 16-1/2" bbl. holds 10-12 shots, 23" bbl. holds 11-13 shots. Weighs 72 oz. to 80 oz. Introduced 2001. Imported from Brazil by Taurus International.
Price: M72C (blue) **$295.00**
Price: M72C-CH (case-hardened, blue)................... **$295.00**
Price: M72CCH-T (case-hardened, blue) **$373.00**
Price: M72C-SS (stainless steel) **$311.00**
Price: M72CSS-T (stainless steel)...................... **$389.00**
Price: M72C-T (blue) **$373.00**
Price: M72R (blue) **$295.00**
Price: M72R-CH (case-hardened, blue)................... **$295.00**
Price: M72RCH-T (case-hardened, blue) **$373.00**
Price: M72R-SS (stainless steel) **$311.00**
Price: M72RSS-T (stainless steel)...................... **$389.00**
Price: M72R-T (blue) **$373.00**

WINCHESTER MODEL 9422 LEVER-ACTION RIFLES
Caliber: 22 LR, 22 WMR, tubular magazine. **Barrel:** 20-1/2". **Weight:** 6-1/4 lbs. **Length:** 37-1/8" overall. **Stock:** American walnut, two-piece, straight grip (Traditional) or semi-pistol grip (Legacy). **Sights:** Hooded ramp front, adjustable semi-buckhorn rear. **Features:** Side ejection, receiver grooved for scope mounting, takedown action. From U.S. Repeating Arms Co.
Price: Traditional, 22 LR 15-shot **$465.00**
Price: Traditional, 22WMR, 11-shot **$487.00**
Price: Legacy, 22 LR 15-shot **$498.00**
Price: Legacy 22 WMR, 11-shot.......................... **$521.00**

Includes models for a variety of sports, utility and competitive shooting.

Anschutz 1710D

Chipmunk Deluxe

CZ 452 Lux

ANSCHUTZ 1416D/1516D CLASSIC RIFLES

Caliber: 22 LR (1416D), 5-shot clip; 22 WMR (1516D), 4-shot clip. **Barrel:** 22-1/2". **Weight:** 6 lbs. **Length:** 41" overall. **Stock:** European hardwood with walnut finish; classic style with straight comb, checkered pistol grip and forend. **Sights:** Hooded ramp front, folding leaf rear. **Features:** Uses Match 64 action. Adjustable single stage trigger. Receiver grooved for scope mounting. Imported from Germany by AcuSport Corp.

Price: 1416D, 22 LR **$755.95**
Price: 1516D, 22 WMR **$779.95**
Price: 1416D Classic left-hand **$679.95**

Anschutz 1416D/1516D Walnut Luxus Rifles

Similar to the Classic models except have European walnut stocks with Monte Carlo cheekpiece, slim forend with Schnabel tip, cut checkering on grip and forend. Introduced 1997. Imported from Germany by AcuSport Corp.

Price: 1416D (22 LR) **$755.95**
Price: 1516D (22 WMR) **$779.95**

ANSCHUTZ 1518D LUXUS BOLT-ACTION RIFLE

Caliber: 22 WMR, 4-shot magazine. **Barrel:** 19-3/4". **Weight:** 5-1/2 lbs. **Length:** 37-1/2" overall. **Stock:** European walnut. **Sights:** Blade on ramp front, folding leaf rear. **Features:** Receiver grooved for scope mounting; single stage trigger; skip-line checkering; rosewood forend tip; sling swivels. Imported from Germany by AcuSport Corp.

Price: **$1,186.95**

ANSCHUTZ 1710D CUSTOM RIFLE

Caliber: 22 LR, 5-shot clip. **Barrel:** 24-1/4". **Weight:** 7-3/8 lbs. **Length:** 42-1/2" overall. **Stock:** Select European walnut. **Sights:** Hooded ramp front, folding leaf rear; drilled and tapped for scope mounting. **Features:** Match 54 action with adjustable single-stage trigger; roll-over Monte Carlo cheekpiece, slim forend with Schnabel tip, Wundhammer palm swell on pistol grip, rosewood gripcap with white diamond insert; skip-line checkering on grip and forend. Introduced 1988. Imported from Germany by AcuSport Corp.

Price: **$1,289.95**

CHARLES DALY SUPERIOR II RIMFIRE RIFLE

Caliber: 22LR, 22MRF, 17HRM. **Barrel:** 22". **Weight:** 6 pounds. **Sights:** None. Drilled and tapped for scope mounts. **Features:** Manufactured by Zastava. Walnut stock, two-position safety; 5-round magazine capacity. Introduced 2005.

Price: 22LR **$259.00**
Price: 22WMR **$299.00**
Price: 17HMR **$334.00**

CHIPMUNK SINGLE SHOT RIFLE

Caliber: 22 LR, 22 WMR, single shot. **Barrel:** 16-1/8". **Weight:** About 2-1/2 lbs. **Length:** 30" overall. **Stocks:** American walnut. **Sights:** Post on ramp front, peep rear adjustable for windage and elevation. **Features:** Drilled and tapped for scope mounting using special Chipmunk base ($13.95). Engraved model also available. Made in U.S.A. Introduced 1982. From Rogue Rifle Co., Inc.

Price: Standard **$194.25**
Price: Standard 22 WMR **$209.95**
Price: Deluxe (better wood, checkering) **$246.95**
Price: Deluxe 22 WMR **$262.95**
Price: Laminated stock **$209.95**
Price: Laminated stock, 22 WMR **$225.95**
Price: Bull barrel models of above, add **$16.00**

CHIPMUNK TM (TARGET MODEL)

Caliber: 22 S, L, or LR. **Barrel:** 18" blue. **Weight:** 5 lbs. **Length:** 33". **Stocks:** Walnut with accessory rail. **Sights:** 1/4 minute micrometer adjustable. **Features:** Manually cocking single shot bolt action, blue receiver, adjustable buttplate and buttpad.

Price: **$329.95**

COOPER MODEL 57-M BOLT-ACTION RIFLE

Caliber: 22 LR, 22 WMR, 17 HMR. **Barrel:** 23-3/4" stainless steel or 41-40 match grade. **Weight:** 6.6 lbs. **Stock:** Claro walnut, 22 lpi hand checkering. **Sights:** None furnished. **Features:** Three rear locking lug, repeating bolt-action with 5-shot mag. Fully adjustable trigger. Many options. Made 100% in the U.S.A. by Cooper Firearms of Montana, Inc.

Price: Classic **$1,295.00**
Price: LVT **$1,395.00**
Price: Custom Classic **$1,995.00**
Price: Western Classic **$2,595.00**

CZ 452 LUX BOLT-ACTION RIFLE

Caliber: 22 LR, 22 WMR, 5-shot detachable magazine. **Barrel:** 24.8". **Weight:** 6.6 lbs. **Length:** 42.63" overall. **Stock:** Walnut with checkered pistol grip. **Sights:** Hooded front, fully adjustable tangent rear. **Features:** All-steel construction, adjustable trigger, polished blue finish. Imported from the Czech Republic by CZ-USA.

Price: 22 LR, 22 WMR **$378.00**

CZ 452 Varmint

CZ 452 American Classic

Henry "Mini" Bolt 22

Kimber 22 Classic

Kimber 22 SuperAmerica

CZ 452 Varmint Rifle
Similar to the Lux model except has heavy 20.8" barrel; stock has beavertail forend; weighs 7 lbs.; no sights furnished. Available only in 22 LR. Imported from the Czech Republic by CZ-USA.
Price: **$407.00**

CZ 452 American Classic Bolt-Action Rifle
Similar to the CZ 452 M 2E Lux except has classic-style stock of Circassian walnut; 22.5" free-floating barrel with recessed target crown; receiver dovetail for scope mounting. No open sights furnished. Introduced 1999. Imported from the Czech Republic by CZ-USA.
Price: 22 LR, 22 WMR. **$420.00**

HARRINGTON & RICHARDSON
ULTRA HEAVY BARREL 22 MAG RIFLE
Caliber: 22 WMR, single shot. **Barrel:** 22" bull. **Stock:** Cinnamon laminated wood with Monte Carlo cheekpiece. **Sights:** None furnished; scope mount rail included. **Features:** Hand-checkered stock and forend; deep-crown rifling; tuned trigger; trigger locking system; hammer extension. Introduced 2001. From H&R 1871 LLC.
Price: **$193.00**

HENRY ACU-BOLT RIFLE
Caliber: 22, 22 Mag., 17HMR; single shot. **Barrel:** 20". **Weight:** 4.15 lbs. **Length:** 36". **Stock:** One-piece fiberglass synthetic. **Sights:** Scope mount and 4x scope included. **Features:** Stainless barrel and receiver, bolt-action.
Price: **$325.00**

HENRY "MINI" BOLT ACTION 22 RIFLE
Caliber: 22 LR, single shot youth gun. **Barrel:** 16" stainless, 8-groove rifling. **Weight:** 3.25 lbs. **Length:** 30", LOP 11-1/2". **Stock:** Synthetic, pistol grip, wraparound checkering and beavertail forearm. **Sights:** William Fire sights. **Features:** One-piece bolt configuration manually operated safety.
Price: **$169.95**

KIMBER 22 CLASSIC BOLT-ACTION RIFLE
Caliber: 22 LR and 17 Mach 2, 5-shot magazine. **Barrel:** 18", 22", 24" match grade; 11-degree target crown. **Weight:** 5 to 8 lbs. **Length:** 35" to 43". **Stock:** Classic Claro walnut, hand-cut checkering, steel gripcap, swivel studs. **Sights:** None, drilled and tapped. **Features:** All-new action with Mauser-style full-length claw extractor, two-position wing safety, match trigger, pillar-bedded action with recoil lug. Introduced 1999. Made in U.S.A. by Kimber Mfg., Inc.
Price: Classic 22. .... **$1,147.00**
Price: Classic Varmint (22 or17M2) **$1,055.00**
Price: Hunter (22) **$809.00**
Price: Hunter (17M2) **$846.00**

Kimber 22 SuperAmerica Bolt-Action Rifle
Similar to 22 Classic except has AAA Claro walnut stock with wraparound 22 lpi hand-cut checkering, ebony forend tip, beaded cheekpiece. Introduced 1999. Made in U.S.A. by Kimber Mfg., Inc.
Price: **$1,865.00**

Kimber 22 SVT

Kimber 22 HS

Marlin 917V

Marlin Model 15YN "Little Buckaroo"

Marlin Model 980S

Kimber 22 SVT Bolt-Action Rifle

Similar to 22 Classic except has 18" stainless steel, fluted bull barrel, gray laminated, high-comb target-style stock with deep pistol grip, high comb, beavertail forend with bipod stud. Weighs 7.5 lbs., overall length 36.5". Matte finish on action. Introduced 1999. Made in U.S.A. by Kimber Mfg., Inc.

Price: 22 model **$1,007.00**
Price: 17M2 model **$1,055.00**

Kimber 22 HS (Hunter Silhouette) Bolt-Action Rifle

Similar to 22 Classic except 24" medium sporter match-grade barrel with half-fluting; high comb, walnut, Monte Carlo target stock with 18 lpi checkering; matte blue metal finish. Introduced 1999. Made in U.S.A. by Kimber Mfg., Inc.

Price: **$915.00**

MARLIN MODEL 917V MAGNUM

Caliber: 17 Magnum, 7-shot. **Barrel:** 22. **Weight:** 6 lbs., stainless 7 lbs. **Length:** 41". **Stock:** Checkered walnut Monte Carlo SS, laminated black/grey. **Sights:** No sights but receiver grooved. **Features:** Swivel studs, positive thumb safety, red cocking indicator, safety lock, SS 1" brushed aluminum scope rings.

Price: $284.00
Price: W/fire control system $450.00

MARLIN MODEL 15YN "LITTLE BUCKAROO"

Caliber: 22 S, L, LR, single shot. **Barrel:** 16-1/4" Micro-Groove®. **Weight:** 4-1/4 lbs. **Length:** 33-1/4" overall. **Stock:** One-piece walnut-finished, press-checkered Maine birch with Monte Carlo; Mar-Shield® finish. **Sights:** Ramp front, adjustable open rear. **Features:** Beginner's rifle with thumb safety, easy-load feed throat, red cocking indicator. Receiver grooved for scope mounting. Introduced 1989.

Price: $221.00
Price: Stainless steel with fire sights $233.00

MARLIN MODEL 980S BOLT-ACTION RIFLE

Caliber: 22 LR, 7-shot clip magazine. **Barrel:** 22" Micro-Groove®. **Weight:** 6 lbs. **Length:** 41" overall. **Stock:** Black fiberglass-filled synthetic with nickel-plated swivel studs and molded-in checkering. **Sights:** Ramp front with orange post and cutaway Wide-Scan™ hood, adjustable semi-buckhorn folding rear. **Features:** Stainless steel barrel, receiver, front breech bolt and striker; receiver grooved for scope mounting. Introduced 1994. Model 880SQ (Squirrel Rifle) is similar but has heavy 22" barrel. Made in U.S.A. by Marlin.

Price: (Model 980S) $333.00

Marlin Model 981T Bolt-Action Rifle

Same as Marlin 980S except blued steel, tubular magazine, holds 17 Long Rifle cartridges. Weighs 6 lbs.

Price: $225.00

Marlin 880V

Marlin 925

Marlin 925C

Marlin 883S

Marlin 983T

Marlin Model 980V

Similar to Model 980S except uses heavy target barrel. Black synthetic stock with molded-in checkering, double bedding screws, matte blue finish. Without sights, no dovetail or filler screws; receiver grooved for scope mount. Weighs 7 lbs. Introduced 2005. Made in U.S.A. by Marlin.
Price: $349.00

Marlin Model 925 Bolt-Action Repeater

Similar to Marlin 980S, except walnut-finished hardwood stock, adjustable open rear sight, ramp front. Weighs 5.5 lbs.
Price: $223.00
Price: With 4x scope and mount $232.00

Marlin Model 925C Bolt-Action Repeater

Same as Model 980S except Mossy Oak® Break-Up camouflage stock. Made in U.S.A. by Marlin. Weighs 5.5 lbs.
Price: $263.00

MARLIN MODEL 982 BOLT-ACTION RIFLE

Caliber: 22 WMR. **Barrel:** 22" Micro-Groove®. **Weight:** 6 lbs. **Length:** 41" overall. **Stock:** Walnut Monte Carlo genuine American black walnut with swivel studs; full pistol grip; classic cut checkering; rubber rifle butt pad; tough Mar-Shield® finish. **Sights:** Adjustable semi-buckhorn folding rear, ramp front sight with brass bead and Wide-Scan™ front sight hood. **Features:** 7-shot clip, thumb safety, red cocking indicator, receiver grooved for scope mount. Made in U.S.A. by Marlin Firearms Co.
Price: $341.00
Price: Model 982L (laminated hardwood stock; weighs 6-1/4 lbs.) . $342.00

Marlin Model 982S Bolt-Action Rifle

Same as the Marlin Model 982 except has stainless steel front breech bolt, barrel, receiver and bolt knob. All other parts are either stainless steel or nickel-plated. Has black Monte Carlo stock of fiberglass-filled polycarbonate with molded-in checkering, nickel-plated swivel studs. Introduced 2005. Made in U.S.A. by Marlin Firearms Co.
Price: $364.00

Marlin Model 982VS Bolt-Action Rifle

Similar to the Model 982S except has selected heavy 22" stainless steel barrel with recessed muzzle, and comes without sights; receiver is grooved for scope mount and 1" ring mounts are included. Weighs 7 lbs. Introduced 1997. Made in U.S.A. by Marlin Firearms Co.
Price: $357.00

Marlin Model 925M/925MC Bolt-Action Rifles

Similar to the Model 982 except chambered for 22 WMR. Has 7-shot clip magazine, 22" Micro-Groove® barrel, checkered walnut-finished Maine birch stock. Introduced 1989.
Price: 25M. $255.00
New! Price: 25MC (Mossy Oak® Break-Up camouflage stock) . . . $294.00

MARLIN MODEL 983 BOLT-ACTION RIFLE

Caliber: 22 WMR. **Barrel:** 22"; 1:16" twist. **Weight:** 6 lbs. **Length:** 41" overall. **Stock:** Walnut Monte Carlo with sling swivel studs, rubber buttpad. **Sights:** Ramp front with brass bead, removable hood; adjustable semi-buckhorn folding rear. **Features:** Thumb safety, red cocking indicator, receiver grooved for scope mount. Made in U.S.A. by Marlin Firearms Co.
Price: $356.00

Marlin Model 983S Bolt-Action Rifle

Same as the Model 983 except front breech bolt, striker knob, trigger stud, cartridge lifter stud and outer magazine tube are of stainless steel; other parts are nickel-plated. Has two-tone brown laminated Monte Carlo stock with swivel studs, rubber buttpad. Introduced 1993.
Price: $377.00

Marlin Model 983T Bolt-Action Rifle

Same as the Model 983 except has a black Monte Carlo fiberglass-filled synthetic stock with sling swivel studs. Weighs 6 lbs., length 41" overall. Introduced 2001. Made in U.S.A. by Marlin Firearms Co.
Price: $273.00

Ruger K77/22 Varmint

Ruger 77/22R

Savage Mark I-G

Savage Mark II-BV

MEACHAM LOW-WALL RIFLE

Caliber: 22 RF Match, 17 HMR. **Barrel:** 28". **Weight:** 10 lbs. **Sights:** None. Tang drilled for Win. base, 3/8" dovetail slot, front. **Stock:** Fancy eastern black walnut with cheekpiece; ebony insert in forend. **Features:** Available with single trigger, single set trigger, or Schuetzen-style double-set triggers. Introduced 2002. From Meacham T&H, Inc.
Price: **$2,999.00**

NEW ENGLAND FIREARMS SPORTSTER™ SINGLE-SHOT RIFLES

Caliber: 22 LR, 22 WMR, 17 HMR, single-shot. **Barrel:** 20". **Weight:** 5-1/2 lbs. **Length:** 36-1/4" overall. **Stock:** Black polymer. **Sights:** None furnished; scope mount included. **Features:** Break open, side-lever release; automatic ejection; recoil pad; sling swivel studs; trigger locking system. Introduced 2001. Made in U.S.A. by New England Firearms.
Price: **$149.00**
Price: Youth model (20" bbl., 33" overall, weighs 5-1/3 lbs.) **$149.00**
Price: Sportster 17 HMR **$180.00**

NEW ULTRA LIGHT ARMS 20RF BOLT-ACTION RIFLE

Caliber: 22 LR, single shot or repeater. **Barrel:** Douglas, length to order. **Weight:** 5-1/4 lbs. **Length:** Varies. **Stock:** Kevlar®/graphite composite, variety of finishes. **Sights:** None furnished; drilled and tapped for scope mount. **Features:** Timney trigger, hand-lapped action, button-rifled barrel, hand-bedded action, recoil pad, sling-swivel studs, optional Jewell trigger. Made in U.S.A. by New Ultra Light Arms.
Price: 20 RF single shot **$800.00**
Price: 20 RF repeater **$850.00**

ROSSI MATCHED PAIR SINGLE-SHOT RIFLE/SHOTGUN

Caliber: 22 LR or 22 Mag. **Barrel:** 18-1/2" or 23". **Weight:** 6 lbs. **Stock:** Hardwood (brown or black finish). **Sights:** Fully adjustable front and rear. **Features:** Break-open breech, transfer-bar manual safety, includes matched 410-, 20 or 12 gauge shotgun barrel with bead front sight. Introduced 2001. Imported by BrazTech/Taurus.
Price: Blue **$139.95**
Price: Stainless steel **$169.95**

RUGER K77/22 VARMINT RIFLE

Caliber: 22 LR, 10-shot, 22 WMR, 9-shot detachable rotary magazine. **Barrel:** 24", heavy. **Weight:** 6-7/8 lbs. **Length:** 43.25" overall. **Stock:** Laminated hardwood with rubber buttpad, quick-detachable swivel studs. **Sights:** None furnished. Comes with Ruger 1" scope rings. **Features:** Stainless steel or blued finish. Three-position safety, dual extractors. Stock has wide, flat forend. Introduced 1993.

Price: K77/22VBZ, 22 LR **$685.00**
Price: K77/22VMBZ, 22 WMR **$685.00**

RUGER 77/22 RIMFIRE BOLT-ACTION RIFLE

Caliber: 22 LR, 10-shot rotary magazine; 22 WMR, 9-shot rotary magazine. **Barrel:** 20". **Weight:** About 6 lbs. **Length:** 39-3/4" overall. **Stock:** Checkered American walnut, laminated hardwood, or synthetic stocks, stainless sling swivels. **Sights:** Plain barrel with 1" Ruger rings. **Features:** Mauser-type action uses Ruger's rotary magazine. Three-position safety, simplified bolt stop, patented bolt locking system. Uses the dual-screw barrel attachment system of the 10/22 rifle. Integral scope mounting system with 1" Ruger rings. Blued model introduced 1983. Stainless steel and blued with synthetic stock introduced 1989.
Price: 77/22R (no sights, rings, walnut stock) **$613.00**
Price: K77/22RP (stainless, no sights, rings, synthetic stock) **$613.00**
Price: 77/22RM (22 WMR, blue, walnut stock) **$613.00**
Price: K77/22RMP (22 WMR, stainless, synthetic stock) **$613.00**
Price: K77/17RM, 17RMP, 17VMBBZ (17 HMR, walnut, synthetic or laminate stocks, no sights, rings, blued or stainless) . **$613.00 to $746.00**

SAVAGE MARK I-G BOLT-ACTION RIFLE

Caliber: 22 LR, single shot. **Barrel:** 20-3/4". **Weight:** 5-1/2 lbs. **Length:** 39-1/2" overall. **Stock:** Walnut-finished hardwood with Monte Carlo-type comb, checkered grip and forend. **Sights:** Bead front, open adjustable rear. Receiver grooved for scope mounting. **Features:** Thumb-operated rotating safety. Blue finish. Rifled or smooth bore. Introduced 1990. Made in Canada, from Savage Arms Inc.
Price: Mark IG, rifled or smooth bore, right- or left-handed **$152.00**
Price: Mark I-GY (Youth), 19" bbl., 37" overall, 5 lbs. **$152.00**
Price: Mark I-LY (Youth), 19" bbl., color laminate **$187.00**
Price: Mark I-GSB (22 LR shot cartridge) **$152.00**

SAVAGE MARK II BOLT-ACTION RIFLE

Caliber: 22 LR, 10-shot magazine. **Barrel:** 20-1/2". **Weight:** 5-1/2 lbs. **Length:** 39-1/2" overall. **Stock:** Walnut-finished hardwood with Monte Carlo-type comb, checkered grip and forend. **Sights:** Bead front, open adjustable rear. Receiver grooved for scope mounting. **Features:** Thumb-operated rotating safety. Blue finish. Introduced 1990. Made in Canada, from Savage Arms, Inc.
Price: Mark II-BV **$264.00**
Price: Mark II Camo **$184.00**
Price: Mark II-GY (youth), 19" barrel, 37" overall, 5 lbs. **$169.00**
Price: Mark II-GL, left-hand **$169.00**
Price: Mark II-GLY (youth) left-hand **$169.00**
Price: Mark II-FXP (as above with black synthetic stock) **$158.00**
Price: Mark II-F (as above, no scope) **$151.00**

Savage Mark II-FXP

Savage Mark II-FSS

Savage Model 93G

Savage Model 93FSS

Savage Model 93FVSS

Thumb-operated rotary safety. Blue finish. Introduced 1994. Made in Canada, from Savage Arms.
Price: **$195.00**
Price: Model 93F (as above with black graphite/fiberglass stock) . . **$187.00**

Savage Model 93FSS Magnum Rifle
Similar to Model 93G except stainless steel barreled action and black synthetic stock with positive checkering. Weighs 5-1/2 lbs. Introduced 1997. Imported from Canada by Savage Arms, Inc.
Price: **$236.00**

Savage Model 93FVSS Magnum Rifle
Similar to Model 93FSS Magnum except 21" heavy barrel with recessed target-style crown, satin-finished stainless barreled action, black graphite/fiberglass stock. Drilled and tapped for scope mounting; comes with Weaver-style bases. Introduced 1998. Imported from Canada by Savage Arms, Inc.
Price: **$267.00**
Price: With scope **$305.00**

Savage Mark II-FSS Stainless Rifle
Similar to the Mark II except has stainless steel barreled action and black synthetic stock with positive checkering, swivel studs, and 20.75" free-floating and button-rifled barrel with detacheable magazine. Weighs 5.5 lbs. Introduced 1997. Imported from Canada by Savage Arms, Inc.
Price: **$213.00**

SAVAGE MODEL 93G MAGNUM BOLT-ACTION RIFLE
Caliber: 22 WMR, 5-shot magazine. **Barrel:** 20-3/4". **Weight:** 5-3/4 lbs. **Length:** 39-1/2" overall. **Stock:** Walnut-finished hardwood with Monte Carlo-type comb, checkered grip and forend. **Sights:** Bead front, adjustable open rear. Receiver grooved for scope mount. **Features:**

Savage Model 30G Stevens "Favorite"

Savage Cub G Youth

Winchester Model 52B

Winchester Model 1885 Low Wall

Price: 22 S, L, LR **$156.00**
Price: 17 Mach 2 . . . . **$165.00**

SAVAGE MODEL 30G STEVENS "FAVORITE"

Caliber: 22 LR, 22WMR Model 30GM, 17 HMR Model 30R17. **Barrel:** 21".
Weight: 4.25 lbs. **Length:** 36.75". **Stock:** Walnut, straight grip, Schnabel
forend. **Sights:** Adjustable rear, bead post front. **Features:** Lever action
falling block, inertia firing pin system, Model 30G half octagonal bbl. Model
30GM full octagonal bbl.
Price: Model 30G **$228.00**
Price: Model 30GM **$266.00**
Price: Model 30R17 . . . . **$292.00**

SAVAGE CUB G YOUTH

Caliber: 22 S, L, LR; 17 Mach 2. **Barrel:** 16.125" **Weight:** 3.3 lbs. **Length:**
33" **Stock:** Walnut finished hardwood. **Sights:** Bead post, front; peep,
rear. **Features:** Mini single shot bolt action, free-floating button-rifled
barrel, blued finish. From Savage Arms.

WINCHESTER MODEL 52B BOLT-ACTION RIFLE

Caliber: 22 Long Rifle, 5-shot magazine. **Barrel:** 24". **Weight:** 7 lbs.
Length: 41-3/4" overall. **Stock:** Walnut with checkered grip and forend.
Sights: None furnished; grooved receiver and drilled and tapped for
scope mounting. **Features:** Adjustable trigger; match chamber;
detachable magazine. Reintroduced 1997. From U.S. Repeating Arms
Co.
Price: **$662.00**

WINCHESTER MODEL 1885 LOW WALL RIMFIRE

Caliber: 17 HMR, single-shot. **Barrel:** 24-1/2"; half-octagon. **Weight:** 8 lbs.
Length: 41" overall. **Stock:** Walnut. **Sights:** Blade front, semi-buckhorn
rear. **Features:** Drilled and tapped for scope mount or tang sight; target
chamber. From U.S. Repeating Arms Co.
Price: Grade I **$1,014.00**

Includes models for classic American and ISU target competition and other sporting and competitive shooting.

Anschutz 1451 Target

Anschutz 2013

ANSCHUTZ 1451R SPORTER TARGET RIFLE

Caliber: 22 LR, 5-shot magazine. **Barrel:** 22" heavy match. **Weight:** 6.4 lbs. **Length:** 39.75" overall. **Stock:** European hardwood with walnut finish. **Sights:** None furnished. Grooved receiver for scope mounting or Anschutz micrometer rear sight. **Features:** Sliding safety, two-stage trigger. Adjustable buttplate; forend slide rail to accept Anschutz accessories. Imported from Germany by AcuSport Corp.
Price: **$549.00**

ANSCHUTZ 1451 TARGET RIFLE

Caliber: 22 LR. **Barrel:** 22". **Weight:** About 6.5 lbs. **Length:** 40". **Sights:** Optional. Receiver grooved for scope mounting. **Features:** Designed for the beginning junior shooter with adjustable length of pull from 13.25" to 14.25" via removable butt spacers. Two-stage trigger factory set at 2.6 lbs. Introduced 1999. Imported from Germany by Gunsmithing, Inc.
Price: **$347.00**
Price: #6834 Match Sight Set **$227.10**

ANSCHUTZ 1808D-RT SUPER RUNNING TARGET RIFLE

Caliber: 22 LR, single shot. **Barrel:** 32-1/2". **Weight:** 9 lbs. **Length:** 50" overall. **Stock:** European walnut. Heavy beavertail forend; adjustable cheekpiece and buttplate. Stippled grip and forend. **Sights:** None furnished. Grooved for scope mounting. **Features:** Designed for Running Target competition. Nine-way adjustable single-stage trigger, slide safety. Introduced 1991. Imported from Germany by Accuracy International, Gunsmithing, Inc.
Price: Right-hand. **$1,364.10**

ANSCHUTZ 1903 MATCH RIFLE

Caliber: 22 LR, single shot. **Barrel:** 25.5", .75" diameter. **Weight:** 10.1 lbs. **Length:** 43.75" overall. **Stock:** Walnut-finished hardwood with adjustable cheekpiece; stippled grip and forend. **Sights:** None furnished. **Features:** Uses Anschutz Match 64 action and #5098 two-stage trigger. A medium weight rifle for intermediate and advanced Junior Match competition. Introduced 1987. Imported from Germany by Accuracy International, Gunsmithing, Inc.
Price: Right-hand. **$720.40**
Price: Left-hand. **$757.90**

ANSCHUTZ 64-MS R SILHOUETTE RIFLE

Caliber: 22 LR, 5-shot magazine. **Barrel:** 21-1/2", medium heavy; 7/8" diameter. **Weight:** 8 lbs. **Length:** 39.5" overall. **Stock:** Walnut-finished hardwood, silhouette-type. **Sights:** None furnished. **Features:** Uses Match 64 action. Designed for metallic silhouette competition. Stock has stippled checkering, contoured thumb groove with Wundhammer swell.

Two-stage #5008 trigger. Slide safety locks sear and bolt. Introduced 1980. Imported from Germany by AcuSport Corp., Accuracy International, Gunsmithing, Inc.
Price: 64-MS R **$704.30**

ANSCHUTZ 2013 BENCHREST RIFLE

Caliber: 22 LR, single shot. **Barrel:** 19.6". **Weight:** About 10.3 lbs. **Length:** 37.75" to 42.5" overall. **Stock:** Benchrest style of European hardwood. Stock length adjustable via spacers and buttplate. **Sights:** None furnished. Receiver grooved for mounts. **Features:** Uses the Anschutz 2013 target action; two-stage adjustable target trigger factory set at 3.9 oz. Introduced 1994. Imported from Germany by Accuracy International, Gunsmithing, Inc.
Price: **$1,757.20**

Anschutz 2007 Match Rifle

Uses same action as the Model 2013, but has a lighter barrel. European walnut stock in right-hand, true left-hand or extra-short models. Sights optional. Available with 19.6" barrel with extension tube, or 26", both in stainless or blue. Introduced 1998. Imported from Germany by Gunsmithing, Inc., Accuracy International.
Price: Right-hand, blue, no sights **$1,766.60**
Price: Right-hand, blue, no sights, extra-short stock **$1,756.60**
Price: Left-hand, blue, no sights. **$1,856.80**

ANSCHUTZ 1827 BIATHLON RIFLE

Caliber: 22 LR, 5-shot magazine. **Barrel:** 21-1/2". **Weight:** 8-1/2 lbs. with sights. **Length:** 42-1/2" overall. **Stock:** European walnut with cheekpiece, stippled pistol grip and forend. **Sights:** Optional globe front specially designed for Biathlon shooting, micromotor rear with hinged snow cap. **Features:** Uses Super Match 54 action and nine-way adjustable trigger; adjustable wooden buttplate, biathlon butthook, adjustable hand-stop rail. Introduced 1982. Imported from Germany by Accuracy International, Gunsmithing, Inc.
Price: Right-hand, with sights, about .... **$1,500.50 to $1,555.00**

Anschutz 1827BT Fortner Biathlon Rifle

Similar to the Anschutz 1827 Biathlon rifle except uses Anschutz/Fortner system straight-pull bolt action, blued or stainless steel barrel. Introduced 1982. Imported from Germany by Accuracy International, Gunsmithing, Inc.
Price: Right-hand, with sights. .... **$1,908.00 to $2,210.00**
Price: Left-hand, with sights. .... **$2,099.20 to $2,395.00**
Price: Right-hand, sights, stainless barrel **$2,045.20**

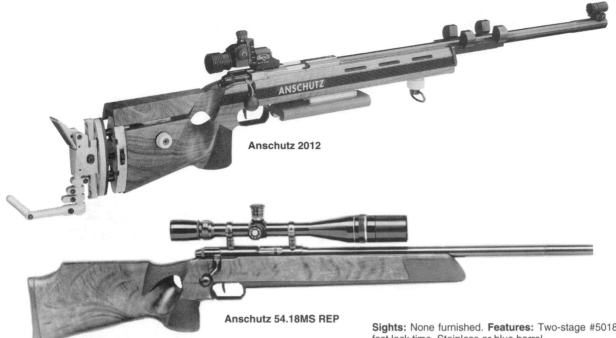

Anschutz 2012

Anschutz 54.18MS REP

ANSCHUTZ SUPER MATCH SPECIAL MODEL 2013 RIFLE

Caliber: 22 LR, single shot. **Barrel:** 25.9". **Weight:** 13 lbs. **Length:** 41.7" to 42.9". **Stock:** A thumbhole version made of European walnut, both the cheekpiece and buttplate are highly adjustable. **Sights:** None furnished. **Features:** Developed by Anschütz for women to shoot in the sport rifle category. Stainless or blue. Introduced in 1997.
Price: Right-hand, blue, no sights, walnut. $2,219.30
Price: Right-hand, stainless, no sights, walnut $2,345.30
Price: Left-hand, blue, no sights, walnut $2,319.50

ANSCHUTZ 2012 SPORT RIFLE

Caliber: 22 LR, 5-shot magazine. **Barrel:** 22.4" match; detachable muzzle tube. **Weight:** 7.9 lbs. **Length:** 40.9" overall. **Stock:** European walnut, thumbhole design. **Sights:** None furnished. **Features:** Uses Anschutz 54.18 barreled action with two-stage match trigger. Introduced 1997. Imported from Germany by Accuracy International, AcuSport Corp.
Price: . . . . $1,425.00 to $2,219.95

ANSCHUTZ 1911 PRONE MATCH RIFLE

Caliber: 22 LR, single shot. **Barrel:** 27-1/4". **Weight:** 11 lbs. **Length:** 46" overall. **Stock:** Walnut-finished European hardwood; American prone-style with adjustable cheekpiece, textured pistol grip, forend with swivel rail and adjustable rubber buttplate. **Sights:** None furnished. Receiver grooved for Anschutz sights (extra). **Features:** Two-stage trigger adjustable from 2.1 to 8.6 oz. Extremely fast lock time. Stainless or blue barrel. Imported from Germany by Accuracy International, Gunsmithing, Inc.
Price: Right-hand, no sights $1,714.20

ANSCHUTZ 1912 SPORT RIFLE

Caliber: 22 LR, single shot. **Barrel:** 25.9". **Weight:** About 11.4 lbs. **Length:** 41.7 to 42.9". **Stock:** European walnut or aluminum. **Sights:** None furnished. **Features:** Lightweight sport rifle version of the 1913 but weighs 1.5 pounds less. Stainless or blue barrel. Introduced 1997.
Price: Right-hand, blue, no sights, walnut. $1,789.50
Price: Right-hand, blue, no sights, aluminum $2,129.80
Price: Right-hand, stainless, no sights, walnut $1,910.30
Price: Left-hand, blue, no sights, walnut $1,879.00

ANSCHUTZ 1913 SUPER MATCH RIFLE

Caliber: 22 LR, single shot. **Barrel:** 27.1". **Weight:** About 14.3 lbs. **Length:** 44.8 to 46". **Stock:** European walnut, color laminate, or aluminum.

Sights: None furnished. **Features:** Two-stage #5018 trigger. Extremely fast lock time. Stainless or blue barrel.
Price: Right-hand, blue, no sights, walnut stock. $2,262.90
Price: Right-hand, blue, no sights, color laminate stock $2,275.10
Price: Right-hand, blue, no sights, aluminum stock $2,262.90
Price: Left-hand, blue, no sights, walnut stock $2,382.20

Anschutz 1913 Super Match Rifle

Same as the Model 1911 except European walnut International-type stock with adjustable cheekpiece, or color laminate, both available with straight or lowered forend, adjustable aluminum hook buttplate, adjustable hand stop, weighs 15.5 lbs., 46" overall. Stainless or blue barrel. Imported from Germany by Accuracy International, Gunsmithing, Inc.
Price: Right-hand, blue, no sights, walnut stock. . . . $2,139.00 to $2,175.00
Price: Right-hand, blue, no sights, color laminate stock $2,199.40
Price: Right-hand, blue, no sights, walnut, lowered forend $2,181.80
Price: Right-hand, blue, no sights, color laminate,
lowered forend $2,242.20
Price: Left-hand, blue, no sights, walnut stock . . . . . $2,233.10 to $2,275.00

Anschutz 54.18MS REP Deluxe Silhouette Rifle

Same basic action and trigger specifications as the Anschutz 1913 Super Match but with removable 5-shot clip magazine, 22.4" barrel extendable to 30" using optional extension and weight set. Weight is 8.1 lbs. Receiver drilled and tapped for scope mounting. Stock is thumbhole silhouette version or standard silhouette version, both are European walnut. Introduced 1990. Imported from Germany by Accuracy International, Gunsmithing, Inc.
Price: Thumbhole stock $1,461.40
Price: Standard stock $1,212.10

Anschutz 1907 Standard Match Rifle

Same action as Model 1913 but with 7/8" diameter 26" barrel (stainless or blue). Length is 44.5" overall, weighs 10.5 lbs. Choice of stock configurations. Vented forend. Designed for prone and position shooting ISU requirements; suitable for NRA matches. Also available with walnut flat-forend stock for benchrest shooting. Imported from Germany by Accuracy International, Gunsmithing, Inc.
Price: Right-hand, blue, no sights,
hardwood stock. . . . . $1,253.40 to $1,299.00
Price: Right-hand, blue, no sights, colored laminated
stock . . . . $1,316.10 to $1,375.00
Price: Right-hand, blue, no sights, walnut stock. $1,521.10
Price: Left-hand, blue barrel, no sights, walnut stock. $1,584.60

Anschutz 1907

Armalite AR-10(T)

Bushmaster A2

Bushmaster DCM

ARMALITE AR-10(T) RIFLE
Caliber: 308, 10-shot magazine. **Barrel:** 24" target-weight Rock 5R custom. **Weight:** 10.4 lbs. **Length:** 43.5" overall. **Stock:** Green or black compostion; N.M. fiberglass handguard tube. **Sights:** Detachable handle, front sight, or scope mount available. Comes with international-style flattop receiver with Picatinny rail. **Features:** National Match two-stage trigger. Forged upper receiver. Receivers hard-coat anodized. Introduced 1995. Made in U.S.A. by ArmaLite, Inc.
Price: Green **$2,126.00**
Price: Black **$2,126.00**

ARMALITE M15A4(T) EAGLE EYE RIFLE
Caliber: 223, 10-round magazine. **Barrel:** 24" heavy stainless; 1:8" twist. **Weight:** 9.2 lbs. **Length:** 42-3/8" overall. **Stock:** Green or black butt, N.M. fiberglass handguard tube. **Sights:** One-piece international-style flattop receiver with Weaver-type rail, including case deflector. **Features:** Detachable carry handle, front sight and scope mount (30mm or 1") available. Upper and lower receivers have push-type pivot pin, hard coat anodized. Made in U.S.A. by ArmaLite, Inc.
Price: Green **$1,378.00**
Price: Black **$1,393.00**

BLASER R93 LONG RANGE RIFLE
Caliber: 308 Win., 10-shot detachable box magazine. **Barrel:** 24". **Weight:** 10.4 lbs. **Length:** 44" overall. **Stock:** Aluminum with synthetic lining. **Sights:** None furnished; accepts detachable scope mount. **Features:** Straight-pull bolt action with adjustable trigger; fully adjustable stock; quick takedown; corrosion resistant finish. Introduced 1998. Imported from Germany by SIGARMS.
Price: **$2,360.00**

BUSHMASTER A2 RIFLE
Caliber: 308, 5.56mm. **Barrel:** 16", 20". **Weight:** 8.3 lbs. **Length:** 38.25" overall (20" barrel). **Stock:** Black composition; A2 type. **Sights:** Adjustable post front, adjustable aperture rear. **Features:** Patterned after Colt M-16A2. Chrome-lined barrel with manganese phosphate exterior. Forged aluminum receivers with push-pin takedown. Available in stainless barrel and camo stock versions. Made in U.S.A. by Bushmaster Firearms Co.
Price: 20" match heavy barrel (A2 type) . . . . **$1,025.00 to $1,185.00**
Price: (A3 type) **$1,135.00**

BUSHMASTER DCM COMPETITION RIFLE
Caliber: 223. **Barrel:** 20" extra-heavy (1" diameter) barrel with 1.8" twist for heavier competition bullets. **Weight:** Appx. 12 lbs. with balance weights. **Length:** NA. **Stock:** NA. **Sights:** A2 rear sight. **Features:** Has special competition rear sight with interchangeable apertures, extra-fine 1/2- or 1/4-MOA windage and elevation adjustments; specially ground front sight post in choice of three widths. Full-length handguards over free-floater barrel tube. Introduced 1998. Made in U.S.A. by Bushmaster Firearms, Inc.
Price: **$1,395.00**

Colt Accurized

Colt Match Target HBAR

Colt Match Target HBAR II

EAA/IZHMASH URAL 5.1

BUSHMASTER VARMINTER RIFLE
Caliber: 5.56mm. **Barrel:** 24", fluted. **Weight:** 8.4 lbs. **Length:** 42.25" overall. **Stock:** Black composition, A2 type. **Sights:** None furnished; upper receiver has integral scope mount base. **Features:** Chrome-lined .950" extra heavy barrel with counter-bored crown, manganese phosphate finish, free-floating aluminum handguard, forged aluminum receivers with push-pin takedown, hard anodized mil-spec finish. Competition trigger optional. Made in U.S.A. by Bushmaster Firearms, Inc.
Price: 20" Match heavy barrel **$1,265.00**
Price: Stainless barrel **$1,265.00**

COLT MATCH TARGET MODEL RIFLE
Caliber: 223 Rem., 8-shot magazine. **Barrel:** 20". **Weight:** 7.5 lbs. **Length:** 39" overall. **Stock:** Composition stock, grip, forend. **Sights:** Post front, aperture rear adjustable for windage and elevation. **Features:** Five-round detachable box magazine, standard-weight barrel, sling swivels. Has forward bolt assist. Military matte black finish. Introduced 1991.
Price: **$1,144.00**
Price: With compensator **$1,150.00**

Colt Accurized Rifle
Similar to the Match Target Model except has 24" barrel. Features flat-top receiver for scope mounting, stainless steel heavy barrel, tubular handguard, and free-floating barrel. Matte black finish. Weighs 9.25 lbs. Made in U.S.A. by Colt's Mfg. Co., Inc.
Price: Model CR6724 . . . . **$1,290.00 to $1,470.00**

Colt Match Target HBAR Rifle
Similar to the Target Model except has heavy barrel, 800-meter rear sight adjustable for windage and elevation, 9-round capacity. Weighs 8 lbs. Introduced 1991.
Price: Model MT6601, MT6601C **$1,300.00**

Colt Match Target Competition HBAR Rifle
Similar to the Match Target except has removeable carry handle for scope mounting, 1:9" rifling twist, 9-round magazine. Weighs 8.5 lbs. Introduced 1991.
Price: Model MT6700, MT6700C **$1,315.00**

Colt Match Target Competition HBAR II Rifle
Similar to the Match Target Competition HBAR except has 16:1" barrel, overall length 34.5", and weighs 7.1 lbs. Introduced 1995.
Price: Model MT6731 . . . . **$1,290.00**

EAA/HW 660 MATCH RIFLE
Caliber: 22 LR. **Barrel:** 26". **Weight:** 10.7 lbs. **Length:** 45.3" overall. **Stock:** Match-type walnut with adjustable cheekpiece and buttplate. **Sights:** Globe front, match aperture rear. **Features:** Adjustable match trigger; stippled pistol grip and forend; forend accessory rail. Introduced 1991. Imported from Germany by European American Armory.
Price: About **$999.00**
Price: With laminate stock **$1,159.00**

EAA/IZHMASH URAL 5.1 TARGET RIFLE
Caliber: 22 LR. **Barrel:** 26.5". **Weight:** 11.3 lbs. **Length:** 44.5". **Stock:** Wood, international style. **Sights:** Adjustable click rear, hooded front with inserts. **Features:** Forged barrel with rifling, adjustable trigger, aluminum rail for accessories, hooked adjustable buttplate. Adjustable comb, adjustable large palm rest. Hand stippling on grip area.
Price: . . . . **NA**

EAA/IZHMASH Biathlon

EAA/IZHMASH Biathlon Target

Ed Brown Model 702 Light Tactical

Ed Brown Model 702 Tactical

Ed Brown 702

EAA/Izhmash Biathlon Target Rifle

Similar to URAL with addition of snow covers for barrel and sights, stock holding extra mags, round trigger block. Unique bolt utilizes toggle action. Designed to compete in 40 meter biathlon event. 22 LR, 19.5" bbl.

Price: **$979.00**

EAA/Izhmash Biathalon Basic Target Rifle

Same action as Biathlon but designed for plinking or fun. Beech stock, heavy barrel with Weaver rail for scope mount. 22 LR, 19.5" bbl.

Price: **$339.00**

ED BROWN MODEL 702 LIGHT TACTICAL

Caliber: 223, 308. **Barrel:** 21". **Weight:** 8.75 lbs. **Stock:** Fully glass-bedded fiberglass with recoil pad. Wide varmint-style forend. **Sights:** None furnished. Talley scope mounts utilizing heavy duty screws.

Price: From **$2,800.00**

ED BROWN MODEL 702 TACTICAL

Caliber: 308, 300 Win. Mag. **Barrel:** 26". **Weight:** 11.25 lbs. **Stock:** Hand bedded McMillan A-3 fiberglass tactical stock with recoil pad. **Sights:**

None furnished. Leupold Mark 4 30mm scope mounts utilizing heavy-duty screws. **Features:** Custom short or long action, steel trigger guard, hinged floor plate, additional calibers available.

Price: From **$2,900.00**

ED BROWN MODEL 702, M40A2 MARINE SNIPER

Caliber: 308 Win., 30-06 Springfield. **Barrel:** Match-grade 24". **Weight:** 9.25 lbs. **Stock:** Hand bedded McMillan GP fiberglass tactical stock with recoil pad in special Woodland Camo molded in colors. **Sights:** None furnished. Leupold Mark 4 30mm scope mounts with heavy-duty screws. **Features:** Steel trigger guard, hinged floor plate, three position safety. Left-hand model available.

Price: From **$2,900.00**

HARRIS GUNWORKS NATIONAL MATCH RIFLE

Caliber: 7mm-08, 308, 5-shot magazine. **Barrel:** 24", stainless steel. **Weight:** About 11 lbs. (std. bbl.). **Length:** 43" overall. **Stock:** Fiberglass with adjustable buttplate. **Sights:** Barrel band and Tompkins front; no rear sight furnished. **Features:** Gunworks repeating action with clip slot, Canjar trigger. Match-grade barrel. Available in right-hand only. Fiberglass stock, sight installation, special machining and triggers optional. Introduced 1989. From Harris Gunworks, Inc.

Price: **$3,500.00**

Harris Gunworks Long Range

Harris Gunworks M-86

Remington 40-XB Rangemaster

HARRIS GUNWORKS LONG RANGE RIFLE

Caliber: 300 Win. Mag., 7mm Rem. Mag., 300 Phoenix, 338 Lapua, single shot. **Barrel:** 26", stainless steel, match-grade. **Weight:** 14 lbs. **Length:** 46-1/2" overall. **Stock:** Fiberglass with adjustable buttplate and cheekpiece. Adjustable for length of pull, drop, cant and cast-off. **Sights:** Barrel band and Tompkins front; no rear sight furnished. **Features:** Uses Gunworks solid bottom single shot action and Canjar trigger. Barrel twist 1:12". Introduced 1989. From Harris Gunworks, Inc.
Price: $3,620.00

HARRIS GUNWORKS M-86 SNIPER RIFLE

Caliber: 308, 30-06, 4-shot magazine; 300 Win. Mag., 3-shot magazine. **Barrel:** 24", Gunworks match-grade in heavy contour. **Weight:** 11-1/4 lbs. (308), 11-1/2 lbs. (30-06, 300). **Length:** 43-1/2" overall. **Stock:** Specially designed McHale fiberglass stock with textured grip and forend, recoil pad. **Sights:** None furnished. **Features:** Uses Gunworks repeating action. Comes with bipod. Matte black finish. Sling swivels. Introduced 1989. From Harris Gunworks, Inc.
Price: $2,700.00

HARRIS GUNWORKS M-89 SNIPER RIFLE

Caliber: 308 Win., 5-shot magazine. **Barrel:** 28" (with suppressor). **Weight:** 15 lbs., 4 oz. **Stock:** Fiberglass; adjustable for length; recoil pad. **Sights:** None furnished. Drilled and tapped for scope mounting. **Features:** Uses Gunworks repeating action. Comes with bipod. Introduced 1990. From Harris Gunworks, Inc.
Price: Standard (non-suppressed) $3,200.00

HARRIS GUNWORKS COMBO M-87 SERIES 50-CALIBER RIFLES

Caliber: 50 BMG, single shot. **Barrel:** 29, with muzzle brake. **Weight:** About 21-1/2 lbs. **Length:** 53" overall. **Stock:** Gunworks fiberglass. **Sights:** None furnished. **Features:** Right-handed Gunworks stainless steel receiver, chrome-moly barrel with 1:15" twist. Introduced 1987. From Harris Gunworks, Inc.
Price: $3,885.00
Price: M87R 5-shot repeater $4,000.00
Price: M-87 (5-shot repeater) "Combo". $4,300.00
Price: M-92 Bullpup (shortened M-87 single shot with bullpup stock) $4,770.00
Price: M-93 (10-shot repeater with folding stock, detachable magazine) $4,150.00

OLYMPIC ARMS PCR-SERVICEMATCH RIFLE

Caliber: 223, 10-shot magazine. **Barrel:** 20", broach-cut 416 stainless steel. **Weight:** About 10 lbs. **Length:** 39.5" overall. **Stock:** A2 stowaway grip and trapdoor buttstock. **Sights:** Post front, E2-NM fully adjustable aperture rear. **Features:** Based on the AR-15. Conforms to all DCM standards. Free-floating 1:8.5" or 1:10" barrel; crowned barrel; no bayonet lug. Introduced 1996. Made in U.S.A. by Olympic Arms, Inc.
Price: $1,062.00

OLYMPIC ARMS PCR-1 RIFLE

Caliber: 223, 10-shot magazine. **Barrel:** 20", 24"; 416 stainless steel. **Weight:** 10 lbs., 3 oz. **Length:** 38.25" overall with 20" barrel. **Stock:** A2 stowaway grip and trapdoor butt. **Sights:** None supplied; flattop upper receiver, cut-down front sight base. **Features:** Based on the AR-15 rifle. Broach-cut, free-floating barrel with 1:8.5" or 1:10" twist. No bayonet lug. Crowned barrel; fluting available. Introduced 1994. Made in U.S.A. by Olympic Arms, Inc.
Price: $1,038.00

Olympic Arms PCR-2, PCR-3 Rifles

Similar to the PCR-1 except has 16" barrel, weighs 8 lbs., 2 oz.; has post front sight, fully adjustable aperture rear. Model PCR-3 has flattop upper receiver, cut-down front sight base. Introduced 1994. Made in U.S.A. by Olympic Arms, Inc.
Price: $958.00

REMINGTON 40-XB RANGEMASTER TARGET CENTERFIRE

Caliber: 15 calibers from 220 Swift to 300 Win. Mag. **Barrel:** 27-1/4". **Weight:** 11-1/4 lbs. **Length:** 47" overall. **Stock:** American walnut, laminated thumbhole or Kevlar with high comb and beavertail forend stop. Rubber non-slip buttplate. **Sights:** None. Scope blocks installed. **Features:** Adjustable trigger. Stainless barrel and action. Receiver drilled and tapped for sights.
Price: Standard single shot . . (right-hand) **$1,636.00**; (left-hand) **$1,761.00**
Price: Repeater. **$1,734.00**

REMINGTON 40-XBBR KS

Caliber: Five calibers from 22 BR to 308 Win. **Barrel:** 20" (light varmint class), 24" (heavy varmint class). **Weight:** 7-1/4 lbs. (light varmint class); 12 lbs. (heavy varmint class). **Length:** 38" (20" bbl.), 42" (24" bbl.). **Stock:** Aramid fiber. **Sights:** None. Supplied with scope blocks. **Features:** Unblued benchrest with stainless steel barrel, trigger adjustable from 1-1/2 lbs. to 3-1/2 lbs. Special two-oz. trigger extra cost. Scope and mounts extra.
Price: Single shot **$1,876.00**

Remington 40-XC KS

Springfield, Inc. M1A Super Match

Springfield, Inc. M1A/M-21

Stoner SR-25

REMINGTON 40-XC KS TARGET RIFLE
Caliber: 7.62 NATO, 5-shot. **Barrel:** 24", stainless steel. **Weight:** 11 lbs. without sights. **Length:** 43-1/2" overall. **Stock:** Aramid fiber. **Sights:** None furnished. **Features:** Designed to meet the needs of competitive shooters. Stainless steel barrel and action.
Price: **$1,821.00**

REMINGTON 40-XR CUSTOM SPORTER
Caliber: 22 LR, 22 WM. **Features:** Model XR-40 Target rifle action. Many options available.
Price: Single shot **$3,383.00**

SAKO TRG-22 BOLT-ACTION RIFLE
Caliber: 308 Win., 10-shot magazine. **Barrel:** 26". **Weight:** 10-1/4 lbs. **Length:** 45-1/4" overall. **Stock:** Reinforced polyurethane with fully adjustable cheekpiece and buttplate. **Sights:** None furnished. Optional quick-detachable, one-piece scope mount base, 1" or 30mm rings. **Features:** Resistance-free bolt, free-floating heavy stainless barrel, 60-degree bolt lift. Two-stage trigger is adjustable for length, pull, horizontal or vertical pitch. Introduced 2000. Imported from Finland by Beretta USA.
Price: Green **$2,898.00**
Price: Model TRG-42, as above except in 338 Lapua Mag or 300 Win. Mag.. **$2,829.00**
Price: Green (new) **$3,243.00**

SPRINGFIELD ARMORY M1A SUPER MATCH
Caliber: 308 Win. **Barrel:** 22", heavy Douglas Premium. **Weight:** About 11 lbs. **Length:** 44.31" overall. **Stock:** Heavy walnut competition stock with longer pistol grip, contoured area behind the rear sight, thicker butt and forend, glass bedded. **Sights:** National Match front and rear. **Features:** Has figure-eight-style operating rod guide. Introduced 1987. From Springfield Armory.
Price: About.. **$2,479.00**

Springfield Armory M1A/M-21 Tactical Model Rifle
Similar to M1A Super Match except special sniper stock with adjustable cheekpiece and rubber recoil pad. Weighs 11.6 lbs. From Springfield Armory.
Price: **$2,975.00**

SPRINGFIELD ARMORY M-1 GARAND AMERICAN COMBAT RIFLES
Caliber: 30-06, 308 Win., 8-shot. **Barrel:** 24". **Weight:** 9.5 lbs. **Length:** 43.6". **Stock:** American walnut. **Sights:** Military square post front, military aperture, MOA adjustable rear. **Features:** Limited production, certificate of authenticity, all new receiver, barrel and stock with remaining parts USGI mil-spec. Two-stage military trigger.
Price: About **$2,479.00**

STONER SR-15 MATCH RIFLE
Caliber: 223. **Barrel:** 20". **Weight:** 7.9 lbs. **Length:** 38" overall. **Stock:** Black synthetic. **Sights:** None furnished; flattop upper receiver for scope mounting. **Features:** Short Picatinny rail, two-stage match trigger. Introduced 1998. Made in U.S.A. by Knight's Mfg.Co.
Price:... **$1,650.00**

STONER SR-25 MATCH RIFLE
Caliber: 7.62 NATO, 10-shot steel magazine, 5-shot optional. **Barrel:** 24" heavy match; 1:11.25" twist. **Weight:** 10.75 lbs. **Length:** 44" overall. **Stock:** Black synthetic AR-15A2 design. Full floating forend of mil-spec synthetic attaches to upper receiver at a single point. **Sights:** None furnished. Has integral Weaver-style rail. Rings and iron sights optional. **Features:** Improved AR-15 trigger, AR-15-style seven-lug rotating bolt. Introduced 1993. Made in U.S.A. by Knight's Mfg. Co.
Price: **$3,345.00**
Price: SR-25 Lightweight Match (20" medium match target contour barrel, 9.5 lbs., 40" overall) **$3,345.00**

Includes a wide variety of sporting guns and guns suitable for various competitions.

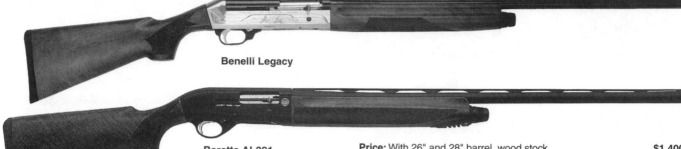

Benelli Legacy

**Beretta AL391
Urika Gold Sporting**

AYA MODEL 4/53 SHOTGUNS
Gauge: 12, 16, 20, 28, 410. **Barrel:** 27" (28 and 410) or 28". **Weight:** To customer specifications. **Length:** To customer specifications. **Features:** Hammerless boxlock action; double triggers; light scroll engraving; automatic safety; straight grip oil finish walnut stock; checkered butt.
Price: **$2,795.00**

BENELLI LEGACY SHOTGUN
Gauge: 12, 20, 2-3/4" and 3" chamber. **Barrel:** 24", 26", 28" (Full, Mod., Imp. Cyl., Imp. Mod., cylinder choke tubes). Mid-bead sight. **Weight:** 5.8 to 7.4 lbs. **Length:** 49-5/8" overall (28" barrel). **Stock:** Select European walnut with satin finish. **Features:** Uses the rotating bolt inertia recoil operating system with a two-piece steel/aluminum etched receiver (bright on lower, blue upper). Drop adjustment kit allows the stock to be custom fitted without modifying the stock. Introduced 1998. Imported from Italy by Benelli USA, Corp.
Price: **$1,435.00**

Benelli Sport II Shotgun
Similar to the Legacy model except has dual tone blue/silver receiver, two carbon fiber interchangeable vent ribs, adjustable butt pad, adjustable buttstock, and functions with ultra-light target loads. Walnut stock with satin finish. Introduced 1997. Imported from Italy by Benelli USA.
Price: **$1,470.00**

BENELLI M2 FIELD SHOTGUNS
Gauge: 12 ga. **Barrel:** 21", 24", 26", 28". **Weight:** 6 lbs., 9 oz. to 7 lbs., 2 oz. **Length:** 14-3/8" overall. **Stock:** Synthetic, Advantage® Max-4 HD™, Advantage® Timber HD™. **Sights:** Red bar. **Features:** Uses the Inertia Driven™ bolt mechanism. Vent rib. Comes with set of five choke tubes. Imported from Italy by Benelli USA.
Price: Timber HD **$1,165.00**
Price: 24" rifled barrel Synthetic **$1,165.00**
Price: 24" rifled barrel Timber HD **$1,165.00**

BENELLI MONTEFELTRO SHOTGUNS
Gauge: 12 and 20 ga. Full, Imp. Mod, Mod., Imp. Cyl. choke tubes. **Barrel:** 24", 26", 28". **Weight:** 6.8 to 7.1 lbs. **Stock:** Checkered walnut with satin finish. **Length:** 14-3/8" overall. **Features:** Uses the Montefeltro rotating bolt system with a simple inertia recoil design. Finish is blue. Introduced 1987.
Price: 24", 26", 28" **$1,070.00**
Price: Left-hand, 26" **$1,080.00**
Price: Grade I, 26" **$1,070.00**
Price: Short stock model **$1,080.00**

BENELLI SUPER BLACK EAGLE II SHOTGUNS
Gauge: 12, 3-1/2" chamber. **Barrel:** 24", 26", 28" (Cyl. Imp. Cyl., Mod., Imp. Mod., Full choke tubes). **Weight:** 7 lbs., 5 oz. **Length:** 49-5/8" overall (28" barrel). **Stock:** European walnut with satin finish, or polymer. Adjustable for drop. **Sights:** Red bar front. **Features:** Uses Montefeltro inertia recoil bolt system. Fires all 12 gauge shells from 2-3/4" to 3-1/2" magnums, vent rib. Introduced 1991. Imported from Italy by Benelli USA.

Price: With 26" and 28" barrel, wood stock **$1,400.00**
Price: Timber HD Camo 24", 26", 28" barrel **$1,455.00**
Price: With 24", 26" and 28" barrel, polymer stock **$1,335.00**
Price: Left-hand, 24", 26", 28", polymer stock **$1,455.00**
Price: Steadygrip Turkey Gun **$1,535.00**

Benelli Super Black Eagle Slug Guns
Similar to the Benelli Super Black Eagle except has 24" rifled barrel with 2-3/4" and 3" chamber, drilled and tapped for scope. Uses the inertia recoil bolt system. Matte finish receiver. Weight is 7.5 lbs., overall length 45.5". Wood or polymer stocks available. Introduced 1992. Imported from Italy by Benelli USA.
Price: With polymer stock **$1,465.00**
Price: 24" barrel, Timber HD camo **$1,585.00**
Price: W/ComforTech stock **$1,035.00**

BENELLI CORDOBA HIGH-VOLUME SHOTGUN
Gauge: 12; 5-round magazine. **Barrel:** 28" and 30", ported, 10mm sporting rib. **Weight:** 7.2 lbs. **Length:** 49.6". **Features:** Designed for high-volume sporting clays and Argentina dove shooting. Inertia-driven action, CrioChokes, ComfortTech stock reduces felt recoil by 49 percent.
Price: **$1,600.00**

BERETTA AL391 TEKNYS SHOTGUNS
Gauge: 12, 20 gauge; 3" chamber, semi-auto. **Barrel:** 26", 28". **Weight:** 5.9 lbs. (20 ga.), 7.3 lbs. (12 ga.). **Length:** NA. **Stock:** X-tra wood (special process wood enhancement). **Features:** Flat 1/4 rib, TruGlo Tru-Bead sight, recoil reducer, stock spacers, overbored bbls., flush choke tubes. Comes with fitted, lined case.
Price: **$1,295.00**
Price: Teknys Gold (green enamel inlays, oil-finished walnut) . . . **$1,595.00**
Price: Teknys Gold Sporting (blue inlays, select walnut) **$1,995.00**

BERETTA AL391 URIKA AUTO SHOTGUNS
Gauge: 12, 20 gauge; 3" chamber. **Barrel:** 22", 24", 26", 28", 30"; five Mobilchoke choke tubes. **Weight:** 5.95 to 7.28 lbs. **Length:** Varies by model. **Stock:** Walnut, black or camo synthetic; shims, spacers and interchangeable recoil pads allow custom fit. **Features:** Self-compensating gas operation handles full range of loads; recoil reducer in receiver; enlarged trigger guard; reduced-weight receiver, barrel and forend; hard-chromed bore. Introduced 2000. Imported from Italy by Beretta USA.
Price: AL391 Urika (12 ga., 26", 28", 30" barrels) **$1,095.00**
Price: AL391 Urika (20 ga., 24", 26", 28" barrels) **$1,095.00**
Price: AL391 Urika Synthetic
(12 ga., 24", 26", 28", 30" barrels) **$1,095.00**
Price: AL391 Urika Camo. (12 ga., Realtree Hardwoods
or Max 4-HD) **$1,195.00**

Beretta AL391 Urika Gold and Gold Sporting Auto Shotguns
Similar to AL391 Urika except features deluxe wood, jewelled bolt and carrier, gold-inlaid receiver with black or silver finish. Introduced 2000. Imported from Italy by Beretta USA.
Price: AL391 Urika Gold Sporting
(12 or 20, black receiver, engraving) **$1,395.00**
Price: AL391 Urika Gold Sporting
(12 ga., silver receiver, engraving **$1,395.00**

Beretta AL391 Urika Sporting

Beretta A391 Xtrema2 3.5

Browning Gold Deer Hunter

Browning Gold Fusion

Beretta AL391 Urika Sporting Auto Shotguns

Similar to AL391 Urika except has competition sporting stock with rounded rubber recoil pad, wide vent rib with white front and mid-rib beads, satin-black receiver with silver markings. Available in 12 and 20 gauge. Introduced 2000. Imported from Italy by Beretta USA.
Price: AL391 Urika Sporting. **$1,195.00**

Beretta AL391 Urika Trap Auto Shotguns

Similar to AL391 Urika except in 12 ga. only, has wide vent rib with white front and mid-rib beads, Monte Carlo stock and special trap recoil pad. Gold Trap features highly figured walnut stock and forend, gold-filled Beretta logo and signature on receiver. Optima bore and Optima choke tubes. Introduced 2000. Imported from Italy by Beretta USA.
Price: AL391 Urika Trap **$1,195.00**

Beretta AL391 Urika Parallel Target RL and SL Auto Shotguns

Similar to AL391 Urika except has parallel comb, Monte Carlo stock with tighter grip radius and stepped vent rib. SL model has same features but with 13.5" length of pull stock. Introduced 2000. Imported from Italy by Beretta USA.
Price: AL391 Urika Parallel Target RL **$1,195.00**
Price: AL391 Urika Parallel Target SL **$1,195.00**

Beretta AL391 Urika Youth Shotgun

Similar to AL391 Urika except has a 24" or 26" barrel with 13.5" stock for youths and smaller shooters. Introduced 2000. From Beretta USA.
Price: **$1,035.00**

BERETTA A391 XTREMA2 3.5 AUTO SHOTGUNS

Gauge: 12 ga. 3-1/2" chamber. **Barrel:** 24", 26", 28". **Weight:** 7.8 lbs. **Stock:** Synthetic. **Features:** Semi-auto goes with two-lug rotating bolt and self-compensating gas valve, extended tang, cross bolt safety, self-cleaning, with case.
Price: Synthetic **$1,295.00**
Price: Realtree Hardwood HD Camo and Max 4-HD **$1,495.00**

BROWNING GOLD HUNTER AUTO SHOTGUN

Gauge: 12, 3" or 3-1/2" chamber; 20, 3" chamber. **Barrel:** 12 ga.-26", 28", 30", Invector Plus choke tubes; 20 ga.-26", 30", Invector choke tubes. **Weight:** 7 lbs., 9 oz. (12 ga.), 6 lbs., 12 oz. (20 ga.). **Length:** 46-1/4" overall (20 ga., 26" barrel). **Stock:** 14"x1-1/2"x2-1/3"; select walnut with gloss finish; palm swell grip. **Features:** Self-regulating, self-cleaning gas system shoots all loads; lightweight receiver with special non-glare deep black finish; large reversible safety button; large rounded trigger guard, gold trigger. The 20 gauge has slightly smaller dimensions; 12 gauge have back-bored barrels, Invector Plus tube system. Introduced 1994. Imported by Browning.
Price: 12 or 20 gauge, 3" chamber. **$894.00**
Price: 12 ga., 3-1/2" chamber **$1,038.00**
Price: Extra barrels . . . . **$336.00 to $415.00**

Browning Gold Rifled Deer Hunter Auto Shotgun

Similar to the Gold Hunter except 12 or 20 gauge, 22" rifled barrel with cantilever scope mount, walnut stock with extra-thick recoil pad. Weighs 7 lbs., 12 oz., overall length 42-1/2". Sling swivel studs fitted on the magazine cap and butt. Introduced 1997. Imported by Browning.
Price: 12 gauge **$1,131.00**
Price: With Mossy Oak® Break-up camouflage **$1,218.00**
Price: 20 ga. (satin-finish walnut stock, 3" chamber) **$1,131.00**

Browning Gold Deer Stalker Shotgun

Similar to the Gold Deer Hunter except has black composite stock and forend, fully rifled barrel, cantilever scope mount. Introduced 1999. Imported by Browning.
Price: 12 gauge **$1,131.00**

Browning Gold Fusion Auto Shotgun

Similar to the Gold Hunter, 12 and 20 gauge with 26", 28" or 30" barrel; front HiViz Pro-Comp and center bead on tapered vent rib; ported and back-bored Invector Plus barrel; 2-3/4" chamber; satin-finished stock with solid, radiused recoil pad with hard heel insert; non-glare black alloy receiver, shim-adj. stock. Introduced 1996. Imported from Japan by Browning.
Price: **$2,095.00**

Browning NWTF Mossy Oak® Break-Up™

Browning Gold Light 10 Gauge

Browning Gold Micro Auto Shotgun
Similar to the Gold Hunter except has a 26" barrel, 13-7/8" pull length and smaller pistol grip for youths and other small shooters. Weighs 6 lbs., 10 oz. Introduced 2001. From Browning.
Price: **$1,329.00**

Browning Gold Stalker Auto Shotgun
Similar to the Gold Hunter except has black composite stock and forend. Choice of 3" or 3-1/2" chamber.
Price: 12 ga. with 3" chamber **$941.00**
Price: With 3-1/2" chamber **$1,148.00**

Browning Gold Mossy Oak® Shadow Grass Shotgun
Similar to the Gold Hunter except 12 gauge only, completely covered with Mossy Oak® Shadow Grass camouflage. Choice of 3" or 3-1/2" chamber and 26" or 28" barrel. Introduced 1999. Imported by Browning.
Price: 12 ga. 3" chamber................................ **$1,127.00**
Price: 12 ga., 3-1/2" chamber **$1,332.00**

Browning Gold Mossy Oak® Break-Up™ Shotguns
Similar to the Gold Hunter except 12 gauge only, completely covered with Mossy Oak® Break-Up™ camouflage. Imported by Browning.
Price: 3" chamber **$1,202.00**
Price: 3-1/2" chamber **$1,332.00**
Price: NWTF model, 3" chamber, 24" bbl. with HiViz sight **$1,202.00**
Price: NWTF model, 3-1/2" chamber, 24" bbl. with HiViz sight .. **$1,440.00**
Price: Gold Rifled Deer (22" rifled bbl., Cantilever scope mount) **$1,218.00**

Browning Gold Field Hunter Auto Shotgun
Similar to the Gold Hunter 3" except has semi-hump back receiver, magazine cut-off, adjustable comb, and satin-finish wood. Introduced 1999. Imported by Browning.
Price: 12 or 20 gauge **$1,025.00**

Browning Gold NWTF Turkey Series Camo Shotgun
Similar to the Gold Hunter except 10- or 12-gauge (3" or 3-1/2" chamber), 24" barrel with extra-full choke tube, HiViz fiber-optic sights and complete gun coverage in Mossy Oak® Break-Up™ camouflage with National Wild Turkey Federation logo on stock. Introduced 2001. From Browning.
Price: 10 gauge.. **$738.00**
Price: 12 gauge, 3-1/2" chamber Ultimate **$1,440.00**
Price: 12 gauge, 3" chamber **$1,202.00**

Browning Gold Upland Special Auto Shotgun
Similar to the Gold Hunter except has straight-grip walnut stock, 12 or 20 gauge, 3" chamber. Introduced 2001. From Browning
Price: 12-gauge model (24" bbl., weighs 7 lbs.) **$1,025.00**
Price: 20-gauge model (26" bbl., weighs 6 lbs., 12 oz.) **$1,025.00**

Browning Gold Light 10 Gauge Auto Shotgun
Similar to the Gold Hunter except has an alloy receiver that is 1 lb. lighter than standard model. Offered in 26" or 28" bbls. With Mossy Oak® Break-Up™ or Shadow Grass coverage; 5-shot magazine. Weighs 9 lbs., 10 oz. (28" bbl.). Introduced 2001. Imported by Browning.
Price: Camo model only **$1,336.00**

Browning Gold Evolve Shotgun
Similar to Gold Auto shotguns with new rib design, HiViz sights, three bbl. lengths (12 ga. only, 26", 28" or 30").
Price: **$1,196.00**

CHARLES DALY FIELD SEMI-AUTO SHOTGUNS
Gauge: 12, 20, 28. **Barrel:** 22", 24", 26", 28" or 30". **Stock:** Synthetic black, Realtree Hardwoods or Advantage Timber. **Features:** Interchangeable barrels handle all loads including steel shot. Slug model has adjustable sights.
Price: Field Hunter **$389.00**
Price: Field Hunter Advantage **$459.00**
Price: Field Hunter TImber **$459.00**
Price: Field Advantage Max **$559.00**

CHARLES DALY SUPERIOR II SEMI-AUTO SHOTGUNS
Gauge: 12, 20, 28. **Barrel:** 26", 28" or 30". **Stock:** Select Turkish walnut. **Features:** Factory ported interchangeable barrels; wide vent rib on Trap and Sport models; fluorescent red sights.
Price: Superior Hunter VR-MC **$539.00**
Price: Superior Sport **$569.00**
Price: Superior Trap **$589.00**

DIAMOND SEMI-AUTO SHOTGUNS
Gauge: 12 ga., 2-3/4" and 3" chambers. **Barrel:** 20" to 30". **Stock:** Walnut, synthetic. **Features:** One-piece receiver, rotary butt, gas ejection, high strength steel. Gold, Silver Marine, Elite and Panther series with vented barrels and all but Silver have 3 chokes. Slug guns available, all but Panther with sights. Imported from Istanbul by Adco Sales, Inc.
Price: Gold, 28", walnut **$549.00**
Price: Gold, 28", synthetic **$499.00**
Price: Gold Slug, 24", w/sights, walnut **$549.00**
Price: Gold Slug, 24", w/sights, synthetic **$499.00**
Price: Silver Mariner, 22", synthetic **$499.00**
Price: Silver Mariner, 20" slug w/sights, synthetic **$479.00**
Price: Elite, 22" Slug, 24"-28", walnut .... **$429.00 to $449.00**
Price: Panther, 22" slug; 26", 28", vent rib w/3 chokes, synthetic .... **$379.00 to $399.00**
Price: Imperial 12, 20 ga., 24" slug w/sights, 26", 28" vent rib w/3 chokes, walnut .... **$479.00 to $499.00**
Price: Imperial, 12 ga., 28" vent rib w/3 chokes, 3.5" chamber, walnut **$499.00**

SHOTGUNS — Autoloaders

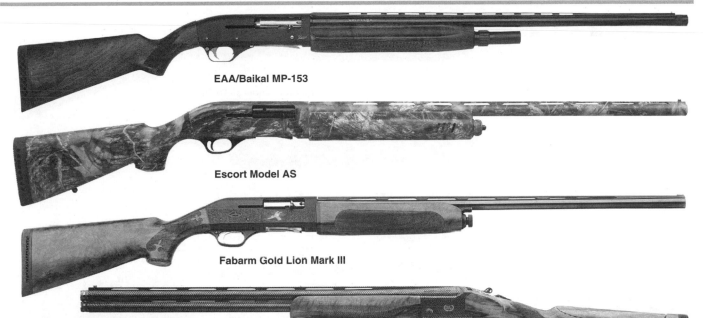

EAA/Baikal MP-153

Escort Model AS

Fabarm Gold Lion Mark III

Fabarm Sporting Clays Extra

EAA BAIKAL MP-153 AUTO SHOTGUNS
Gauge: 12, 3-1/2" chamber. **Barrel:** 24", 26", 28"; Imp., Mod. and Full choke tubes. **Weight:** 7.8 lbs. **Stock:** Walnut. **Features:** Gas-operated action with automatic gas-adjustment valve allows use of light and heavy loads interchangeably; 4-round magazine; rubber recoil pad. Introduced 2000. Imported by European American Armory.
Price: MP-153 (blued finish, walnut stock and forend) $459.00
Price: MP-153 (field grade, synthetic stock) $349.00

EAA SAIGA AUTO SHOTGUN
Gauge: 12, 20, .410, 3" chamber. **Barrel:** 19", 21", 24". **Weight:** 6.6 to 7.6 lbs. **Length:** 40" to 45". **Stock:** Synthetic. **Features:** Retains best features of the AK Rifle by Kalashnikov as the semi-auto shotgun. Magazine fed. Imported from Russia by EAA Corp.
Price: .410 ga. $299.00
Price: 20 ga. $389.00
Price: 12 ga. . . . . $409.00 to $439.00

ESCORT SEMI-AUTO SHOTGUNS
Gauge: 12, 20. **Barrel:** 22", 24", 26", 18" (AimGuard model); 3" chambers. **Weight:** 6 lbs, 4 0. to 7 lbs., 6 oz. **Stock:** Polymer, black, or camo finish; also Turkish walnut. **Features:** Black chrome finish; top of receiver dovetailed for sight mounting. Gold-plated trigger, trigger guard safety, magazine cut-off. Three choke tubes (IC, M, F — except AimGuard); 24" bbl. model comes with turkey choke tube. **Sights:** Optional HiViz Spark and TriViz fiber-optic sights. Introduced 2002. Camo model introduced 2003. Youth, Slug, Obsession Camo models introduced 2005. Imported from Turkey by Legacy Sports International.
Price: Model AS, walnut stock. $421.00
Price: Model PS, black polymer stock $399.00
Price: Camo polymer stock, Spark sight $443.00
Price: Camo, 24" bbl; 3.5 mag.; TriViz sight, turkey choke $523.00
Price: AimGuard, 18" bbl., black stock, cyl bore $392.00
Price: Waterfowl/turkey combo, camo, 2 bbls $574.00

FABARM GOLD LION MARK III AUTO SHOTGUN
Gauge: 12, 3" chamber. **Barrel:** 24", 26", 28", choke tubes. **Weight:** 7 lbs. **Length:** 45.5" overall. **Stock:** European walnut with gloss finish; olive wood grip cap. **Features:** TriBore barrel, reversible safety; gold-plated trigger and carrier release button; leather-covered rubber recoil pad. Introduced 1998. Imported from Italy by Heckler & Koch, Inc.
Price: $939.00

Fabarm Sporting Clays Extra Auto Shotgun
Similar to Gold Lion except 28" TriBore ported barrel with interchangeable colored front-sight beads, mid-rib bead, 10mm channeled vent rib, carbon-fiber finish, oil-finished walnut stock and forend with olive wood gripcap. Stock dimensions are 14.58"x1.58"x2.44". Distinctive gold-colored receiver logo. Available in 12 gauge only, 3" chamber. Introduced 1999. Imported from Italy by Heckler & Koch, Inc.
Price: $1,249.00

FRANCHI 48AL SHOTGUN
Gauge: 20 or 28, 2-3/4" chamber. **Barrel:** 24", 26", 28" (Full, Cyl., Mod., choke tubes). **Weight:** 5.5 lbs. (20 gauge). **Length:** 44" to 48". **Stock:** 14-1/4"x1-5/8"x2-1/2". Walnut with checkered grip and forend. **Features:** Long recoil-operated action. Chrome-lined bore; cross-bolt safety. Imported from Italy by Benelli USA.
Price: 20 ga. $735.00
Price: 28 ga. $1,020.00

Franchi 48AL Deluxe Shotgun
Similar to 48AL but with select walnut stock and forend and high-polish blue finish with gold trigger. Introduced 2000.
Price: (20 gauge, 26" barrel) $970.00
Price: (28 gauge, 26" barrel) $990.00

Franchi 48AL English Shotgun
Similar to 48AL Deluxe but with straight grip English-style stock. 20 ga., 28 ga., 26" bbl, ICMF tubes.
Price: 20 gauge $970.00
Price: 28 gauge $1,020.00

Franchi 48AL Short Stock Shotgun
Similar to 48AL but with stock shortened to 12-1/2" length of pull.
Price: (20 gauge, 26" barrel) $735.00

FRANCHI MODEL 912 SHOTGUNS
Gauge: 12. **Barrel:** 24", 26", 28", 30". **Weight:** 7.5 to 7.8 lbs. **Length:** 46" to 52". **Stock:** Satin walnut; synthetic. **Sights:** White bead front. **Features:** Chambered for 3-1/2" magnum shells with Dual-Recoil-Reduction-System, multi-lugged rotary bolt. Made in Italy and imported by Benelli USA.
Price: Walnut $850.00
Price: Synthetic $790.00
Price: Timber HD & Max-4 . . . . $900.00
Price: Steadygrip Timber HD $850.00

SHOTGUNS — Autoloaders

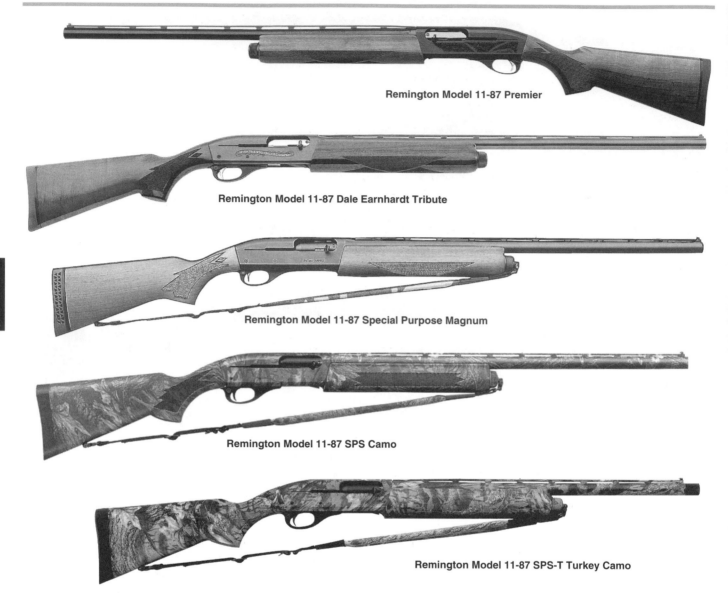

Remington Model 11-87 Premier

Remington Model 11-87 Dale Earnhardt Tribute

Remington Model 11-87 Special Purpose Magnum

Remington Model 11-87 SPS Camo

Remington Model 11-87 SPS-T Turkey Camo

FRANCHI RAPTOR SPORTING CLAYS SHOTGUN
Gauge: 12 and 20; 6-round capacity. **Barrel:** 30" (12 ga.) or 28" (20 ga.); ported; tapered target rib and bead front sight. **Weight:** 7.1 lbs. (Model 712) or 6.2 lbs. (Model 720). **Stock:** Walnut with WeatherCoat (impervious to weather). **Features:** Gas-operated, satin nickel receiver.
Price: **$850.00**

REMINGTON MODEL 11-87 PREMIER SHOTGUNS
Gauge: 12, 20, 3" chamber. **Barrel:** 26", 28", 30" RemChoke tubes. Light Contour barrel. **Weight:** About 7-3/4 lbs. **Length:** 46" overall (26" bbl.). **Stock:** Walnut with satin or high-gloss finish; cut checkering; solid brown buttpad; no white spacers. **Sights:** Bradley-type white-faced front, metal bead middle. **Features:** Pressure compensating gas system allows shooting 2-3/4" or 3" loads interchangeably with no adjustments. Stainless magazine tube; redesigned feed latch, barrel support ring on operating bars; pinned forend. Introduced 1987.
Price: Light contour barrel............................... **$777.00**
Price: Left-hand, 28" barrel **$831.00**
Price: Premier cantilever deer barrel, fully-rifled, 21" sling, swivels, Monte Carlo stock **$859.00**
Price: 3-1/2" Super Magnum, 28" barrel **$865.00**
Price: Dale Earnhardt Tribute, 12 ga., 28" barrel **$972.00**

Remington Model 11-87 Special Purpose Magnum
Similar to the 11-87 Premier except has dull stock finish, Parkerized exposed metal surfaces. Bolt and carrier have dull blackened coloring. Comes with 26" or 28" barrel with RemChokes, padded Cordura nylon sling and quick detachable swivels. Introduced 1987.
Price: With synthetic stock and forend (SPS) **$791.00**

Remington Model 11-87 SPS Special Purpose Synthetic Camo
Similar to the 11-87 Special Purpose Magnum except has synthetic stock and all metal (except bolt and trigger guard) and stock covered with Mossy Oak® Break-Up™ camo finish. In 12 gauge only, 26", RemChoke. Comes with camo sling, swivels. Introduced 1992.
Price: **$925.00**

Remington Model 11-87 SPS-T Turkey Camo
Similar to the 11-87 Special Purpose Magnum except with synthetic stock, 21" vent rib barrel with RemChoke tube. Completely covered with Mossy Oak® Break-Up™ Brown camouflage. Bolt body, trigger guard and recoil pad are non-reflective black.
Price: **$905.00**
Price: Model 11-87 SPS-T Camo CL cantilever............... **$907.00**

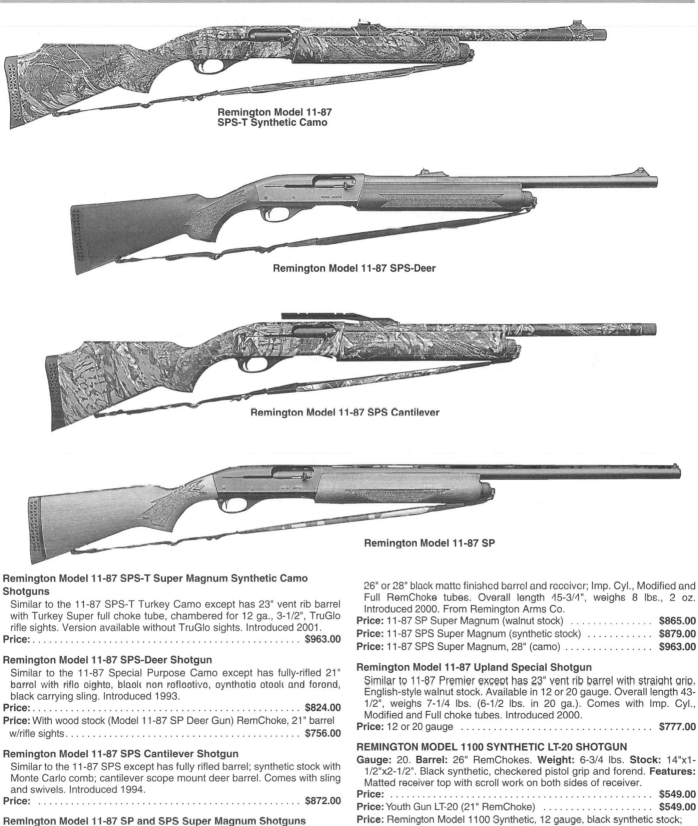

**Remington Model 11-87
SPS-T Synthetic Camo**

Remington Model 11-87 SPS-Deer

Remington Model 11-87 SPS Cantilever

Remington Model 11-87 SP

Remington Model 11-87 SPS-T Super Magnum Synthetic Camo Shotguns

Similar to the 11-87 SPS-T Turkey Camo except has 23" vent rib barrel with Turkey Super full choke tube, chambered for 12 ga., 3-1/2", TruGlo rifle sights. Version available without TruGlo sights. Introduced 2001.
Price: **$963.00**

Remington Model 11-87 SPS-Deer Shotgun

Similar to the 11-87 Special Purpose Camo except has fully-rifled 21" barrel with rifle sights, black non reflective, synthetic stock and forend, black carrying sling. Introduced 1993.
Price: **$824.00**
Price: With wood stock (Model 11-87 SP Deer Gun) RemChoke, 21" barrel w/rifle sights **$756.00**

Remington Model 11-87 SPS Cantilever Shotgun

Similar to the 11-87 SPS except has fully rifled barrel; synthetic stock with Monte Carlo comb; cantilever scope mount deer barrel. Comes with sling and swivels. Introduced 1994.
Price: **$872.00**

Remington Model 11-87 SP and SPS Super Magnum Shotguns

Similar to Model 11-87 Special Purpose Magnum except has 3-1/2" chamber. Available in flat finish American walnut or black synthetic stock,

26" or 28" black matte finished barrel and receiver; Imp. Cyl., Modified and Full RemChoke tubes. Overall length 45-3/4", weighs 8 lbs., 2 oz. Introduced 2000. From Remington Arms Co.
Price: 11-87 SP Super Magnum (walnut stock) **$865.00**
Price: 11-87 SPS Super Magnum (synthetic stock) **$879.00**
Price: 11-87 SPS Super Magnum, 28" (camo) **$963.00**

Remington Model 11-87 Upland Special Shotgun

Similar to 11-87 Premier except has 23" vent rib barrel with straight grip, English-style walnut stock. Available in 12 or 20 gauge. Overall length 43-1/2", weighs 7-1/4 lbs. (6-1/2 lbs. in 20 ga.). Comes with Imp. Cyl., Modified and Full choke tubes. Introduced 2000.
Price: 12 or 20 gauge **$777.00**

REMINGTON MODEL 1100 SYNTHETIC LT-20 SHOTGUN

Gauge: 20. **Barrel:** 26" RemChokes. **Weight:** 6-3/4 lbs. **Stock:** 14"x1-1/2"x2-1/2". Black synthetic, checkered pistol grip and forend. **Features:** Matted receiver top with scroll work on both sides of receiver.
Price: **$549.00**
Price: Youth Gun LT-20 (21" RemChoke) **$549.00**
Price: Remington Model 1100 Synthetic, 12 gauge, black synthetic stock; vent rib 28" barrel, Mod. RemChoke tube. Weighs about 7-1/2 lbs. Introduced 1996 .... **$549.00**

Remington Model 1100 Youth Turkey Camo

Remington 1100 LT-20 Deer

Remington Model 1100 Sporting 28

Remington Model 1100 Classic Trap

Remington Model 1100 Sporting 12

Remington Model SP-10

Remington Model 1100 Youth Synthetic Turkey Camo Shotgun
Similar to the Model 1100 LT-20 except has 1" shorter stock, 21" vent rib barrel with Full RemChoke tube; 3" chamber; synthetic stock and forend are covered with Skyline Excel camo, and barrel and receiver have non-reflective, black matte finish. Introduced 2003.
Price: $612.00

Remington Model 1100 LT-20 Synthetic Deer Shotgun
Similar to the Model 1100 LT-20 except has 21" fully rifled barrel with rifle sights, 2-3/4" chamber, and fiberglass reinforced synthetic stock. Introduced 1997. Made in U.S. by Remington.
Price: $583.00

Remington Model 1100 Sporting 28 Shotgun
Similar to the 1100 LT-20 except in 28 gauge with 25" barrel; comes with skeet, Imp. Cyl., Light Mod., Mod. RemChoke tube. Semi-fancy walnut with gloss finish, Sporting rubber butt pad. Made in U.S. by Remington. Introduced 1996.
Price: $901.00

Remington Model 1100 Sporting 20 Shotgun
Similar to Model 1100 LT-20 except tournament-grade American walnut stock with gloss finish and sporting style recoil pad, 28" RemChoke barrel for skeet, Imp. Cyl., Light Modified and Modified. Introduced 1998.
Price: $868.00

Remington Model 1100 Classic Trap Shotgun
Similar to Standard Model 1100 except 12 gauge with 30", low-profile barrel, semi-fancy American walnut stock, high-polish blued receiver with engraving and gold eagle inlay. Singles, mid handicap and long handicap choke tubes. Overall length 50-1/2", weighs 8 lbs., 4 oz. Introduced 2000. From Remington Arms Co.
Price: $895.00

Remington Model 1100 Sporting 12 Shotgun
Similar to Model 1100 Sporting 20 Shotgun except in 12 gauge, 28" ventilated barrel with semi-fancy American walnut stock, gold-plated trigger. Overall length 49", weighs 8 lbs. Introduced 2000. From Remington Arms Co.
Price: $901.00

SHOTGUNS — Autoloaders

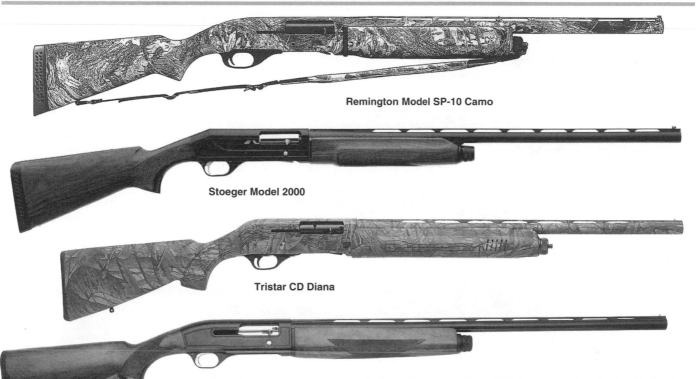

Remington Model SP-10 Camo

Stoeger Model 2000

Tristar CD Diana

Traditions ALS 2100

Remington Model 1100 Synthetic Deer Shotgun
Similar to Model 1100 LT-20 except 12 gauge, 21" fully rifled barrel with cantilever scope mount and fiberglass-reinforced synthetic stock with Monte Carlo comb. Introduced 1997. Made in U.S. by Remington Arms Co.
Price: **$629.00**

REMINGTON MODEL SP-10 MAGNUM SHOTGUN
Gauge: 10, 3-1/2" chamber, 2-shot magazine. **Barrel:** 26", 30" (full and mod. RemChokes). **Weight:** 10-3/4 to 11 lbs. **Length:** 47-1/2" overall (26" barrel). **Stock:** Walnut with satin finish or black synthetic with 26" barrel. Checkered grip and forend. **Sights:** Twin bead. **Features:** Stainless steel gas system with moving cylinder; 3/8" vent rib. Receiver and barrel have matte finish. Brown recoil pad. Comes with padded Cordura nylon sling. Introduced 1989.
Price: **$1,317.00**

Remington Model SP-10 Magnum Camo Shotgun
Similar to SP-10 Magnum except buttstock, forend, receiver, barrel and magazine cap are covered with Mossy Oak® Break-Up™ camo finish; bolt body and trigger guard have matte black finish. RemChoke tube, 26" vent rib barrel with mid-rib bead and Bradley-style front sight, swivel studs and quick-detachable swivels, non-slip Cordura carrying sling in same camo pattern. Introduced 1993.
Price: **$1,453.00**

SARSILMAZ SEMI-AUTOMATIC SHOTGUN
Gauge: 12, 3" chamber. **Barrel:** 26" or 28"; fixed chokes. **Stock:** Walnut or synthetic. **Features:** Handles 2-3/4" or 3" magnum loads. Introduced 2000. Imported from Turkey by Armsport Inc.
Price: With walnut stock **$969.95**
Price: With synthetic stock **$919.95**

STOEGER MODEL 2000 SHOTGUNS
Gauge: 12, 3" chamber, set of five choke tubes. **Barrel:** 24", 26", 28", 30". **Stock:** Walnut, deluxe, synthetic, and Timber HD. **Sights:** White bar.

Features: Inertia-recoil for light target to turkey loads. Single trigger combo 26"/24" pack with optional 24" slug barrel.
Price: Walnut, 26", 28", 30" bbl. **$475.00**
Price: Synthetic, 24", 26", 28" bbl. **$400.00**
Price: Timber HD, 24", 26", 28" bbl. **$475.00**
Price: Slug model **$589.00**

STOEGER P-350 PUMP SHOTGUN
Gauge: 12. **Barrel:** 18.5" to 28". **Weight:** 6.4 to 6.9 lbs. **Features:** Synthethic, Timber HD or Max-4 stock; extended turkey choke available.
Price: .... **$269.00 to $329.00**

TRADITIONS ALS 2100 SERIES SEMI-AUTOMATIC SHOTGUNS
Gauge: 12, 3" chamber; 20, 3" chamber. **Barrel:** 24", 26", 28" (Imp. Cyl., Mod. and Full choke tubes). **Weight:** 5 lbs., 10 oz. to 6 lbs., 5 oz. **Length:** 44" to 48" overall. **Stock:** Walnut or black composite. **Features:** Gas-operated; vent rib barrel with Beretta-style threaded muzzle. Introduced 2001 by Traditions.
Price: Field Model (12 or 20 ga., 26" or 28" bbl., walnut stock) **$479.00**
Price: Youth Model (12 or 20 ga., 24" bbl., walnut stock) **$479.00**
Price: (12 or 20 ga., 26" or 28" barrel, composite stock) **$459.00**

Traditions ALS 2100 Turkey Semi-Automatic Shotgun
Similar to ALS 2100 Field Model except chambered in 12 gauge, 3" only with 26" barrel and Mossy Oak® Break Up™ camo finish. Weighs 6 lbs.; 46" overall.
Price: **$519.00**

Traditions ALS 2100 Waterfowl Semi-Automatic Shotgun
Similar to ALS 2100 Field Model except chambered in 12 gauge, 3" only with 28" barrel and Advantage® Wetlands™ camo finish. Weighs 6.25 lbs.; 48" overall. Multi chokes.
Price: **$529.00**

Traditions ALS 2100 Hunter Combo
Similar to ALS 2100 Field Model except 2 barrels, 28" vent rib and 24" fully rifled deer. Weighs 6 to 6.5 lbs.; 48" overall. Choice TruGlo adj. sights or fixed cantilever mount on rifled barrel. Multi chokes.
Price: Walnut, rifle barrel **$609.00**
Price: Walnut, cantilever **$629.00**
Price: Synthetic **$579.00**

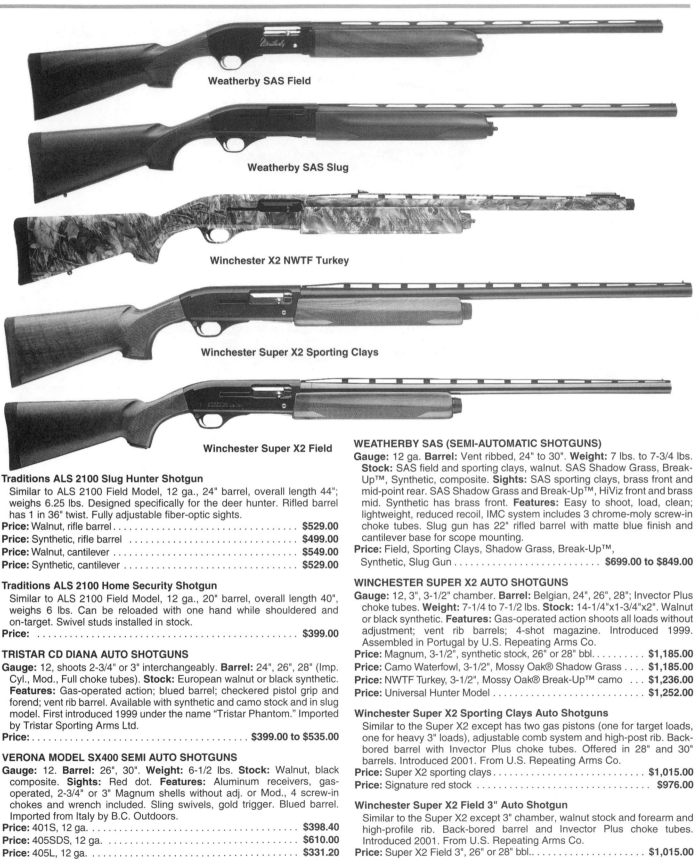

Weatherby SAS Field

Weatherby SAS Slug

Winchester X2 NWTF Turkey

Winchester Super X2 Sporting Clays

Winchester Super X2 Field

Traditions ALS 2100 Slug Hunter Shotgun

Similar to ALS 2100 Field Model, 12 ga., 24" barrel, overall length 44"; weighs 6.25 lbs. Designed specifically for the deer hunter. Rifled barrel has 1 in 36" twist. Fully adjustable fiber-optic sights.

Price: Walnut, rifle barrel **$529.00**
Price: Synthetic, rifle barrel **$499.00**
Price: Walnut, cantilever **$549.00**
Price: Synthetic, cantilever **$529.00**

Traditions ALS 2100 Home Security Shotgun

Similar to ALS 2100 Field Model, 12 ga., 20" barrel, overall length 40"; weighs 6 lbs. Can be reloaded with one hand while shouldered and on-target. Swivel studs installed in stock.

Price: **$399.00**

TRISTAR CD DIANA AUTO SHOTGUNS

Gauge: 12, shoots 2-3/4" or 3" interchangeably. **Barrel:** 24", 26", 28" (Imp. Cyl., Mod., Full choke tubes). **Stock:** European walnut or black synthetic. **Features:** Gas-operated action; blued barrel; checkered pistol grip and forend; vent rib barrel. Available with synthetic and camo stock and in slug model. First introduced 1999 under the name "Tristar Phantom." Imported by Tristar Sporting Arms Ltd.

Price: . . . . **$399.00 to $535.00**

VERONA MODEL SX400 SEMI AUTO SHOTGUNS

Gauge: 12. **Barrel:** 26", 30". **Weight:** 6-1/2 lbs. **Stock:** Walnut, black composite. **Sights:** Red dot. **Features:** Aluminum receivers, gas-operated, 2-3/4" or 3" Magnum shells without adj. or Mod., 4 screw-in chokes and wrench included. Sling swivels, gold trigger. Blued barrel. Imported from Italy by B.C. Outdoors.

Price: 401S, 12 ga. **$398.40**
Price: 405SDS, 12 ga. **$610.00**
Price: 405L, 12 ga. **$331.20**

WEATHERBY SAS (SEMI-AUTOMATIC SHOTGUNS)

Gauge: 12 ga. **Barrel:** Vent ribbed, 24" to 30". **Weight:** 7 lbs. to 7-3/4 lbs. **Stock:** SAS field and sporting clays, walnut. SAS Shadow Grass, Break-Up™, Synthetic, composite. **Sights:** SAS sporting clays, brass front and mid-point rear. SAS Shadow Grass and Break-Up™, HiViz front and brass mid. Synthetic has brass front. **Features:** Easy to shoot, load, clean; lightweight, reduced recoil, IMC system includes 3 chrome-moly screw-in choke tubes. Slug gun has 22" rifled barrel with matte blue finish and cantilever base for scope mounting.

Price: Field, Sporting Clays, Shadow Grass, Break-Up™,
Synthetic, Slug Gun . . . . **$699.00 to $849.00**

WINCHESTER SUPER X2 AUTO SHOTGUNS

Gauge: 12, 3", 3-1/2" chamber. **Barrel:** Belgian, 24", 26", 28"; Invector Plus choke tubes. **Weight:** 7-1/4 to 7-1/2 lbs. **Stock:** 14-1/4"x1-3/4"x2". Walnut or black synthetic. **Features:** Gas-operated action shoots all loads without adjustment; vent rib barrels; 4-shot magazine. Introduced 1999. Assembled in Portugal by U.S. Repeating Arms Co.

Price: Magnum, 3-1/2", synthetic stock, 26" or 28" bbl. **$1,185.00**
Price: Camo Waterfowl, 3-1/2", Mossy Oak® Shadow Grass **$1,185.00**
Price: NWTF Turkey, 3-1/2", Mossy Oak® Break-Up™ camo . . . **$1,236.00**
Price: Universal Hunter Model **$1,252.00**

Winchester Super X2 Sporting Clays Auto Shotguns

Similar to the Super X2 except has two gas pistons (one for target loads, one for heavy 3" loads), adjustable comb system and high-post rib. Back-bored barrel with Invector Plus choke tubes. Offered in 28" and 30" barrels. Introduced 2001. From U.S. Repeating Arms Co.

Price: Super X2 sporting clays **$1,015.00**
Price: Signature red stock **$976.00**

Winchester Super X2 Field 3" Auto Shotgun

Similar to the Super X2 except 3" chamber, walnut stock and forearm and high-profile rib. Back-bored barrel and Invector Plus choke tubes. Introduced 2001. From U.S. Repeating Arms Co.

Price: Super X2 Field 3", 26" or 28" bbl. **$1,015.00**

Includes a wide variety of sporting guns and guns suitable for competitive shooting.

Benelli Nova Pump

Benelli Nova Pump Slug

Browning BPS 10 gauge

Browning BPS 10 gauge
Mossy Oak® Shadow Grass

BENELLI NOVA PUMP SHOTGUNS

Gauge: 12, 20. **Barrel:** 24", 26", 28". **Stock:** Synthetic, Max-4 and Timber H-D (12 ga. and 20 ga). **Sights:** Red bar. **Features:** 2-3/4", 3" chamber (3-1/2" 12 ga. only). Montefeltro rotating bolt design with dual action bars, magazine cut-off, synthetic trigger assembly, 4-shot magazine. Introduced 1999. Imported from Italy by Benelli USA.

Price: Synthetic	**$350.00**
Price: Timber HD	**$435.00**
Price: Max-4	**$425.00**
Price: Youth Model	**$440.00**

Benelli Nova Pump Tactical Shotgun

Similar to the Nova except has 18.5" barrel with adjustable rifle-type or ghost ring sights; weighs 7.2 lbs.; black synthetic stock. Introduced 1999. Imported from Italy by Benelli USA.

Price: With rifle sights	**$315.00**
Price: With ghost-ring sights	**$350.00**

Benelli Nova Pump Rifled Slug Gun

Similar to Nova Pump Slug Gun except has 24" barrel and rifled bore; open rifle sights; synthetic stock; weighs 0.1 lbs.

Price: Synthetic	**$525.00**
Price: Timber HD	**$600.00**
Price: Field/Slug combo, synthetic	**$545.00**

BROWNING BPS PUMP SHOTGUNS

Gauge: 10, 12, 3-1/2" chamber; 12 or 20, 3" chamber (2-3/4" in target guns), 28, 2-3/4" chamber, 5-shot magazine, .410, 3" chamber. **Barrel:** 10 ga.-24" Buck Special, 28", 30", 32" Invector; 12, 20 ga.-22", 24", 26", 28", 30", 32" (Imp. Cyl., Mod. or Full), .410-26" barrel. (Imp. Cyl., Mod. and Full choke tubes.) Also available with Invector choke tubes, 12 or 20 ga.; Upland Special has 22" barrel with Invector tubes. BPS 3" and 3-1/2" have back-bored barrel. **Weight:** 7 lbs., 8 oz. (28" barrel). **Length:** 48-3/4" overall (28" barrel). **Stock:** 14-1/4"x1-1/2"x2-1/2". Select walnut, semi-beavertail forend, full pistol grip stock. **Features:** All 12 gauge 3" guns except Buck Special and game guns have back-bored barrels with Invector Plus choke tubes. Bottom feeding and ejection, receiver top safety, high post vent rib. Double action bars eliminate binding. Vent rib barrels only. All 12 and 20 gauge guns with 3" chamber available with fully engraved receiver flats at no extra cost. Each gauge has its own unique game scene. Introduced 1977. Imported from Japan by Browning.

Price: 12 ga., 3-1/2" Magnum Stalker (black syn. stock)	**$688.00**
Price: 12, 20 ga., Hunter, Invector Plus	**$509.00**
Price: 12 ga. Deer Hunter (22" rifled bbl., cantilever mount)	**$624.00**
Price: 28 ga., Hunter, Invector	**$544.00**
Price: .410, Hunter, Invector	**$544.00**

Browning BPS 10 Gauge Camo Pump Shotgun

Similar to the standard BPS except completely covered with Mossy Oak® Shadow Grass camouflage. Available with 24", 26", 28" barrel. Introduced 1999. Imported by Browning.

Price:	**$688.00**

Browning BPS Waterfowl Camo Pump Shotgun

Similar to the standard BPS except completely covered with Mossy Oak® Shadow Grass camouflage. Available in 12 gauge, with 24", 26" or 28" barrel, 3" chamber. Introduced 1999. Imported by Browning.

Price:	**$688.00**

Browning BPS Game Gun Deer Hunter

Similar to the standard BPS except has newly designed receiver/magazine tube/barrel mounting system to eliminate play, heavy 20.5" barrel with rifle-type sights with adjustable rear, solid receiver scope mount, "rifle" stock dimensions for scope or open sights, sling swivel studs. Gloss or matte finished wood with checkering, polished blue metal. Introduced 1992.

Price:	**$624.00**

Browning BPS Game Gun Turkey Special

Similar to the standard BPS except has satin-finished walnut stock and dull-finished barrel and receiver. Receiver is drilled and tapped for scope mounting. Rifle-style stock dimensions and swivel studs. Has Extra-Full Turkey choke tube. Introduced 1992.

Price:	**$605.00**

EAA Baikal MP-133

Escort AimGuard

Escort Field Hunter

Browning BPS Stalker Pump Shotgun

Same gun as the standard BPS except all exposed metal parts have a matte blued finish and the stock has a durable black finish with a black recoil pad. Available in 10 ga. (3-1/2") and 12 ga. with 3" or 3-1/2" chamber, 22", 28", 30" barrel with Invector choke system. Introduced 1987.

Price: 12 ga., 3" chamber, Invector Plus **$492.00**
Price: 10, 12 ga., 3-1/2" chamber **$579.00**

Browning BPS NWTF Turkey Series Pump Shotgun

Similar to the BPS Stalker except has full coverage Mossy Oak® Break-Up™ camo finish on synthetic stock, forearm and exposed metal parts. Offered in 10 and 12 gauge, 3" or 3-1/2" chamber; 24" bbl. has extra-full choke tube and HiViz fiber-optic sights. Introduced 2001. From Browning.

Price: 10 ga., 3-1/2" chamber **$738.00**
Price: 12 ga., 3-1/2" chamber **$674.00**
Price: 12 ga., 3" chamber **$738.00**

Browning BPS Micro Pump Shotgun

Similar to the BPS Stalker except 20 ga. only, 22" Invector barrel, stock has pistol grip with recoil pad. Length of pull is 13-1/4"; weighs 6 lbs., 12 oz. Introduced 1986.

Price: **$509.00**

CHARLES DALY FIELD PUMP SHOTGUNS

Gauge: 12, 20. **Barrel:** Interchangeable 18-1/2", 24", 26", 28", 30" multi-choked. **Weight:** NA. **Stock:** Synthetic, various finishes, recoil pad. **Receiver:** Machined aluminum. **Features:** Field Tactical and Slug models come with adustable sights; Youth models may be upgraded to full size. Imported from Akkar, Turkey.

Price: Field Tactical **$199.00**
Price: Field Hunter **$289.00**
Price: Field Hunter, Realtree Hardwood **$289.00**
Price: Field Hunter Advantage **$289.00**

CHARLES DALY MAXI-MAG PUMP SHOTGUNS

Gauge: 12 gauge, 3-1/2". **Barrel:** 24", 26", 28"; multi-choke system. **Weight:** NA. **Stock:** Synthetic, Realtree Hardwoods, or Advantage Timber receiver, aluminum alloy. **Features:** Handles 2-3/4", 3" and 3-1/2" loads. Interchangeable ported barrels; Turkey package includes sling, HiViz sights, XX Full choke. Imported from Akkar, Turkey.

Price: Field Hunter **$469.00**
Price: Field Hunter Advantage **$539.00**
Price: Field Hunter Hardwoods **$539.00**
Price: Field Hunter Turkey **$609.00**

DIAMOND 12 GA. PUMP SHOTGUNS

Gauge: 12, 2-3/4" and 3" chambers. **Barrel:** 18"-30". **Weight:** 7 lbs. **Stock:** Walnut, synthetic. **Features:** Aluminum one-piece receiver sculpted for lighter weight. Double locking on fixed bolt. Gold, Elite and Panther series with vented barrels and 3 chokes. All series slug guns available (Gold and Elite with sights). Imported from Istanbul by ADCO Sales.

Price: Gold, 28" vent rib w/3 chokes, walnut **$359.00**
Price: Gold, 28", synthetic **$329.00**
Price: Gold Slug, 24" w/sights, walnut or synthetic . . . . **$329.00 to $359.00**
Price: Silver Mariner 18.5" Slug, synthetic **$399.00**
Price: Silver Mariner 22" vent rib w/3 chokes **$419.00**
Price: Elite, 22" slug w/sights; 24", 28" vent rib w/3 chokes,
walnut . . . . **$329.00 to $349.00**
Price: Panther, 28", 30" vent rib w/3 chokes, synthetic **$279.00**
Price: Panther,18.5", 22" Slug, synthetic . . . . **$209.00 to $265.00**
Price: Imperial 12 ga., 28" vent rib w/3 chokes, 3.5" chamber,
walnut **$399.00**

EAA BAIKAL MP-133 PUMP SHOTGUN

Gauge: 12, 3-1/2" chamber. **Barrel:** 18-1/2", 20", 24", 26", 28"; Imp., Mod. and Full choke tubes. **Weight:** NA. **Stock:** Walnut; checkered grip and grooved forearm. **Features:** Hammer-forged, chrome-lined barrel with vent rib; machined steel parts; dual action bars; trigger-block safety; 4-shot magazine tube; handles 2-3/4" through 3-1/2" shells. Introduced 2000. Imported by European American Armory.

Price: MP-133 (blued finish, walnut stock and forend) **$359.00**

ESCORT PUMP SHOTGUNS

Gauge: 12, 20; 3" chamber. **Barrel:** 18" (AimGuard model); 22" (FH Slug model), 24", 26" and 28" (Field Hunter models), choke tubes (M, IC, F); turkey choke w/24" bbl. **Weight:** 6.4 to 7 lbs. **Stock:** Polymer, black chrome or camo finish. **Features:** Alloy receiver w/dovetail for sight mounting. Two stock adjusting spacers included. Introduced 2003. From Legacy Sports International.

Price: Field Hunter, black stock **$247.00**
Price: Field Hunter, camo stock **$812.00**
Price: Camo, 24" bbl. **$363.00**
Price: AimGuard, 20" bbl., black stock **$211.00**
Price: MarineGuard, nickel finish **$254.00**
Price: Combo (2 bbls.) **$270.00**

Fabarm Field Pump

Ithaca Model 37 Waterfowl

Ithaca Model 37 Deerslayer II

**Mossberg Model 835
Mossy Oak Camo**

FABARM FIELD PUMP SHOTGUN
Gauge: 12, 3" chamber. **Barrel:** 28" (24" rifled slug barrel available). **Weight:** 76.6 lbs. **Length:** 48.25" overall. **Stock:** Polymer. **Features:** Similar to Fabarm FP6 Pump Shotgun. Alloy receiver; twin action bars; available in black or Mossy Oak® Break-Up™ camo finish. Includes Cyl., Mod. and Full choke tubes. Introduced 2001. Imported from Italy by Heckler & Koch Inc.
Price: Matte black finish **$399.00**
Price: Mossy Oak® Break-Up™ finish **$469.00**

ITHACA MODEL 37 DELUXE PUMP SHOTGUNS
Gauge: 12, 16, 20, 3" chamber. **Barrel:** 26", 28", 30" (12 gauge), 26", 28" (16 and 20 gauge), choke tubes. **Weight:** 7 lbs. **Stock:** Walnut with cut-checkered grip and forend. **Features:** Steel receiver; bottom ejection; brushed blue finish, vent rib barrels. Reintroduced 1996. Made in U.S. by Ithaca Gun Co.
Price: **$633.00**
Price: With straight English-style stock **$803.00**
Price: Model 37 New Classic (ringtail forend, sunburst recoil pad, hand-finished walnut stock, 26" or 28" barrel) **$803.00**

Ithaca Model 37 Waterfowl Shotgun
Similar to Model 37 Deluxe except in 12 gauge only with 24", 26", or 30" barrel, special extended steel shot choke tube system. Complete coverage in Advantage Wetlands or Hardwoods camouflage. Storm models have synthetic stock. Introduced 1999. Made in U.S. by Ithaca Gun Co.
Price: . . . . **$499.00 to $549.00**

ITHACA MODEL 37 ULTRALIGHT DELUXE SHOTGUNS
Gauge: 16 ga. 2-3/4" chamber. **Barrel:** 24", 26", 28". **Weight:** 5.25 lbs. **Stock:** Standard deluxe. **Sights:** Raybar. **Features:** Vent rib, drilled and tapped, interchangeable barrel. F, M, IC choke tubes.
Price: Deluxe **$649.00**
Price: Classic/English **$824.00**
Price: Classic/Pistol **$824.00**

ITHACA MODEL 37 DEERSLAYER II PUMP SHOTGUNS
Gauge: 12, 16, 20; 3" chamber. **Barrel:** 24", 26", fully rifled. **Weight:** 11 lbs. **Stock:** Cut-checkered American walnut with Monte Carlo comb. **Sights:** Rifle-type. **Features:** Integral barrel and receiver. Bottom ejection. Brushed blue finish. Introduced 1999. Made in U.S. by Ithaca Gun Co. Reintroduced 1997. Made in U.S. by Ithaca Gun Co.
Price: **$633.00**
Price: Smooth Bore Deluxe **$582.00**

Price: Rifled Deluxe **$582.00**
Price: Storm **$399.00**

ITHACA MODEL 37 DEERSLAYER III PUMP SHOTGUN
Gauge: 12, 20, 2-3/4" and 3" chambers. **Barrel:** 26" free floated. **Weight:** 9 lbs. **Stock:** Monte Carlo laminate. **Sights:** Rifled. **Features:** Barrel length gives increased velocity. Trigger and sear set hand filed and stoned for creep-free operation. Weaver-style scope base. Swivel studs. Matte blue. Made in U.S. by Ithaca Gun Co.
Price: . . . . **Custom order only**

ITHACA MODEL 37 RUFFED GROUSE SPECIAL EDITION SHOTGUN
Gauge: 20 ga. **Barrel:** 22", 24", interchangeable choke tubes. **Weight:** 5.25 lbs. **Stock:** American black walnut. **Features:** Laser engraved stock with line art drawing. Bottom eject. Vent rib and English style. Right- or left-hand through simple safety change. Aluminum receiver. Made in U.S.A. by Ithaca Gun Co.
Price: **$840.00**

ITHACA TURKEYSLAYER STORM SHOTGUN
Gauge: 12 or 20 ga., 3" chamber. **Barrel:** 24" ported. **Stock:** Composite. **Sights:** TruGlo front and rear. **Features:** IthaChoke full turkey choke tube. Matte metal, Realtree Hardwoods pattern, swivel studs.
Price: Storm **$459.00**

MARLIN PARDNER PUMP SHOTGUN
Gauge: 12 ga., 3". **Barrel:** 28" vent rib, screw-in Modified choke tube. **Weight:** 7-1/2 lbs. **Length:** 48-1/2". **Stock:** American walnut, grooved forend, ventilated recoil pad. **Sights:** Bead front. **Features:** Machined steel receiver, double action bars, five-shot magazine.
Price: **$200.00**

MOSSBERG MODEL 835 ULTI-MAG PUMP SHOTGUNS
Gauge: 12, 3-1/2" chamber. **Barrel:** Ported 24" rifled bore, 24", 28", Accu-Mag choke tubes for steel or lead shot. **Weight:** 7-3/4 lbs. **Length:** 48-1/2" overall. **Stock:** 14"x1-1/2"x2-1/2". Dual Comb. Cut-checkered hardwood or camo synthetic; both have recoil pad. **Sights:** White bead front, brass mid-bead; fiber-optic rear. **Features:** Shoots 2-3/4", 3" or 3-1/2" shells. Back-bored and ported barrel to reduce recoil, improve patterns. Ambidextrous thumb safety, twin extractors, dual slide bars. Mossberg Cablelock included. Introduced 1988.
Price: 28" vent rib, hardwood stock **$394.00**
Price: Combos, 24" rifled or smooth bore, rifle sights, 24" vent rib Accu-Mag Ulti-Full choke tube, Mossy Oak® camo finish **$556.00**
Price: RealTree Camo Turkey, 24" vent rib, Accu-Mag extra-full tube, synthetic stock **$460.00**
Price: Mossy Oak® Camo, 28" vent rib, Accu-Mag tubes, synthetic stock **$460.00**
Price: OFM Camo, 28" vent rib, Accu-Mag Mod. tube, synthetic stock **$438.00**

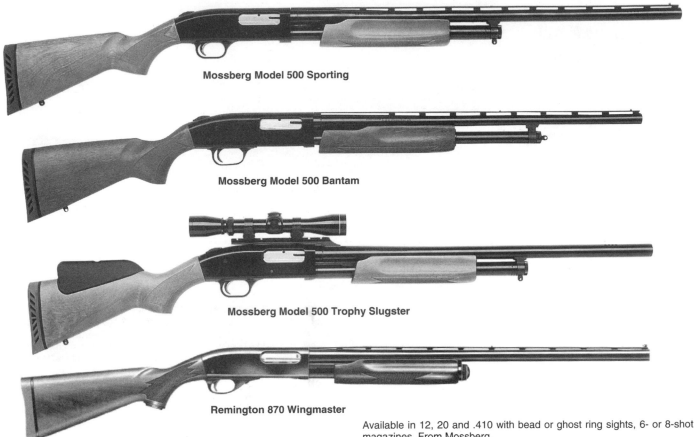

Mossberg Model 500 Sporting

Mossberg Model 500 Bantam

Mossberg Model 500 Trophy Slugster

Remington 870 Wingmaster

Mossberg Model 835 Synthetic Stock Shotgun

Similar to the Model 835, except with 28" ported barrel with Accu-Mag Mod. choke tube, Parkerized finish, black synthetic stock and forend. Introduced 1998. Made in U.S. by Mossberg.
Price: $394.00

MOSSBERG MODEL 500 SPORTING PUMP SHOTGUNS

Gauge: 12, 20, .410, 3" chamber. **Barrel:** 18-1/2" to 28" with fixed or Accu-Choke, plain or vent rib. **Weight:** 6-1/4 lbs. (.410), 7-1/4 lbs. (12). **Length:** 48" overall (28" barrel). **Stock:** 14"x1-1/2"x2-1/2". Walnut-stained hardwood. Cut-checkered grip and forend. **Sights:** White bead front, brass mid-bead; fiber-optic. **Features:** Ambidextrous thumb safety, twin extractors, disconnecting safety, dual action bars. Quiet Carry forend. Many barrels are ported. From Mossberg.
Price: From about $316.00
Price: Sporting Combos (field barrel and Slugster barrel). From . . . $381.00

Mossberg Model 500 Bantam Pump Shotgun

Same as the Model 500 Sporting Pump except 12 or 20 gauge, 22" vent rib Accu-Choke barrel with choke tube set; has 1" shorter stock, reduced length from pistol grip to trigger, reduced forend reach. Introduced 1992.
Price: $316.00
Price: With Realtree Hardwoods camouflage finish (20 ga. only) . . $364.00

Mossberg Model 500 Camo Pump Shotgun

Same as the Model 500 Sporting Pump except 12 gauge only and entire gun is covered with Mossy Oak® Advantage camouflage finish. Receiver drilled and tapped for scope mounting. Comes with quick detachable swivel studs, swivels, camouflage sling, Mossberg Cablelock.
Price: From about $364.00

MOSSBERG MODEL 500 PERSUADER/CRUISER SHOTGUNS

Similar to Mossberg Model 500 except has 18-1/2" or 20" barrel with cylinder bore choke, synthetic stock and blue or Parkerized finish.

Available in 12, 20 and .410 with bead or ghost ring sights, 6- or 8-shot magazines. From Mossberg.
Price: 12 gauge, 20" barrel, 8-shot, bead sight. $391.00
Price: 20 gauge or .410, 18-1/2" barrel, 6-shot, bead sight $353.00
Price: 12 gauge, Parkerized finish, 6-shot, 18-1/2" barrel,
ghost ring sights $468.00
Price: Home Security 410 (.410, 18-1/2" barrel
with spreader choke) $335.00

Mossberg Model 590 Special Purpose Shotgun

Similar to Model 500 except has Parkerized or Marinecote finish, 9-shot magazine and black synthetic stock (some models feature Speed Feed). Available in 12 gauge only with 20", cylinder bore barrel. Weighs 7-1/4 lbs. From Mossberg.
Price: Bead sight, heat shield over barrel $417.00
Price: Ghost ring sight, Speed Feed stock $586.00

MOSSBERG MODEL 500 SLUGSTER SHOTGUN

Gauge: 12, 20, 3" chamber. **Barrel:** 24", ported rifled bore. Integral scope mount. **Weight:** 7-1/4 lbs. **Length:** 44" overall. **Stock:** 14" pull, 1-3/8" drop at heel. Walnut. Dual Comb design for proper eye positioning with or without scoped barrels. Recoil pad and swivel studs. **Features:** Ambidextrous thumb safety, twin extractors, dual slide bars. Comes with scope mount. Mossberg Cablelock included. Introduced 1988.
Price: Rifled bore, integral scope mount, 12 or 20 ga. $361.00
Price: Fiber-optic, rifle sights $361.00
Price: Rifled bore, rifle sights $338.00
Price: 20 ga., Standard or Bantam. From $338.00

REMINGTON MODEL 870 WINGMASTER SHOTGUNS

Gauge: 12 ga., 16 ga., 3" chamber. **Barrel:** 26", 28", 30" (RemChokes). **Weight:** 7-1/4 lbs. **Length:** 46", 48". **Stock:** Walnut, hardwood, synthetic. **Sights:** Single bead (Twin bead Wingmaster). **Features:** Light contour barrel. Double action bars, cross-bolt safety, blue finish.
Price: Wingmaster, walnut, blued, 26", 28", 30" $584.00
Price: 870 Wingmaster Super Magnum, 3-1/2" chamber, 28" $665.00

SHOTGUNS — Slide & Lever Actions

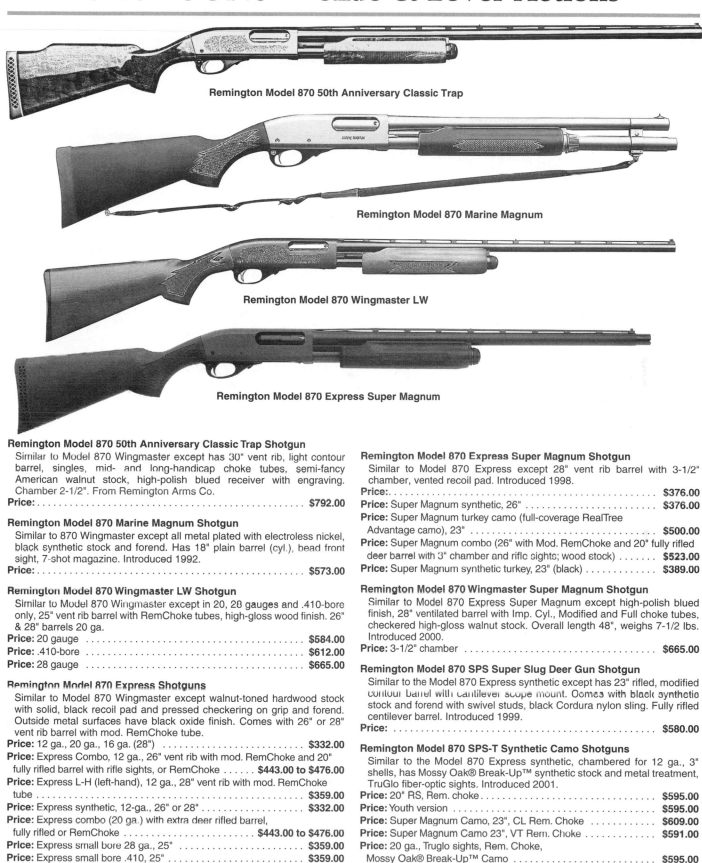

Remington Model 870 50th Anniversary Classic Trap

Remington Model 870 Marine Magnum

Remington Model 870 Wingmaster LW

Remington Model 870 Express Super Magnum

Remington Model 870 50th Anniversary Classic Trap Shotgun
Similar to Model 870 Wingmaster except has 30" vent rib, light contour barrel, singles, mid- and long-handicap choke tubes, semi-fancy American walnut stock, high-polish blued receiver with engraving. Chamber 2-1/2". From Remington Arms Co.
Price: **$792.00**

Remington Model 870 Marine Magnum Shotgun
Similar to 870 Wingmaster except all metal plated with electroless nickel, black synthetic stock and forend. Has 18" plain barrel (cyl.), bead front sight, 7-shot magazine. Introduced 1992.
Price: **$573.00**

Remington Model 870 Wingmaster LW Shotgun
Similar to Model 870 Wingmaster except in 20, 28 gauges and .410-bore only, 25" vent rib barrel with RemChoke tubes, high-gloss wood finish. 26" & 28" barrels 20 ga.
Price: 20 gauge **$584.00**
Price: .410-bore **$612.00**
Price: 28 gauge **$665.00**

Remington Model 870 Express Shotguns
Similar to Model 870 Wingmaster except walnut-toned hardwood stock with solid, black recoil pad and pressed checkering on grip and forend. Outside metal surfaces have black oxide finish. Comes with 26" or 28" vent rib barrel with mod. RemChoke tube.
Price: 12 ga., 20 ga., 16 ga. (28") **$332.00**
Price: Express Combo, 12 ga., 26" vent rib with mod. RemChoke and 20" fully rifled barrel with rifle sights, or RemChoke ...... **$443.00 to $476.00**
Price: Express L-H (left-hand), 12 ga., 28" vent rib with mod. RemChoke tube **$359.00**
Price: Express synthetic, 12-ga., 26" or 28" **$332.00**
Price: Express combo (20 ga.) with extra deer rifled barrel, fully rifled or RemChoke .... **$443.00 to $476.00**
Price: Express small bore 28 ga., 25" **$359.00**
Price: Express small bore .410, 25" **$359.00**

Remington Model 870 Express Super Magnum Shotgun
Similar to Model 870 Express except 28" vent rib barrel with 3-1/2" chamber, vented recoil pad. Introduced 1998.
Price: **$376.00**
Price: Super Magnum synthetic, 26" **$376.00**
Price: Super Magnum turkey camo (full-coverage RealTree Advantage camo), 23" **$500.00**
Price: Super Magnum combo (26" with Mod. RemChoke and 20" fully rifled deer barrel with 3" chamber and rifle sights; wood stock) **$523.00**
Price: Super Magnum synthetic turkey, 23" (black) **$389.00**

Remington Model 870 Wingmaster Super Magnum Shotgun
Similar to Model 870 Express Super Magnum except high-polish blued finish, 28" ventilated barrel with Imp. Cyl., Modified and Full choke tubes, checkered high-gloss walnut stock. Overall length 48", weighs 7-1/2 lbs. Introduced 2000.
Price: 3-1/2" chamber **$665.00**

Remington Model 870 SPS Super Slug Deer Gun Shotgun
Similar to the Model 870 Express synthetic except has 23" rifled, modified contour barrel with cantilever scope mount. Comes with black synthetic stock and forend with swivel studs, black Cordura nylon sling. Fully rifled cantilever barrel. Introduced 1999.
Price: **$580.00**

Remington Model 870 SPS-T Synthetic Camo Shotguns
Similar to the Model 870 Express synthetic, chambered for 12 ga., 3" shells, has Mossy Oak® Break-Up™ synthetic stock and metal treatment, TruGlo fiber-optic sights. Introduced 2001.
Price: 20" RS, Rem. choke **$595.00**
Price: Youth version **$595.00**
Price: Super Magnum Camo, 23", CL Rem. Choke **$609.00**
Price: Super Magnum Camo 23", VT Rem. Choke **$591.00**
Price: 20 ga., Truglo sights, Rem. Choke, Mossy Oak® Break-Up™ Camo **$595.00**

Remington Model 870 Express Deer Gun

Remington Model 870 Express Turkey

Remington Model 870 SPS Super Slug Deer Gun

Remington Model 870 SPS-T Camo

Winchester 1300 Walnut Field Pump

Remington Model 870 Express Youth Gun Shotgun

Same as Model 870 Express except 13" length of pull, 21" barrel with mod. RemChoke tube. Weighs 6.25 lbs. Hardwood stock with low-luster finish. Introduced 1991.

Price: 20 ga. Express Youth (1" shorter stock), from. **$332.00**
Price: 20 ga. Youth Deer 20" FR/RS **$365.00**
Price: 16 ga. Youth Synthetic **$332.00**

Remington Model 870 Express Rifle-Sighted Deer Gun Shotguns

Same as Model 870 Express except 20" barrel with fixed imp. cyl. choke, open iron sights, Monte Carlo stock. Introduced 1991.

Price: **$332.00**
Price: With fully rifled barrel **$365.00**
Price: Express Synthetic Deer
(black synthetic stock, black matte metal) **$372.00**

Remington Model 870 Express Turkey Shotguns

Same as Model 870 Express except 3" chamber, 21" vent rib turkey barrel and extra-full Rem. choke turkey tube; 12 ga. only. Introduced 1991.

Price: **$345.00**
Price: Express Turkey Camo stock has Skyline Excel
camo, matte black metal **$399.00**
Price: Express Youth Turkey camo (as above with 1" shorter
length of pull), 20 ga., Skyline Excel camo **$399.00**

Remington Model 870 Express Synthetic 18" Shotgun

Similar to Model 870 Express with 18" barrel except synthetic stock and forend; 7-shot. Introduced 1994.

Price: **$319.00**

REMINGTON MODEL 870 SPS SUPER MAGNUM CAMO SHOTGUN

Gauge: 12, 3-1/2" chamber. **Barrel:** 26", 28", vent rib, with Full, Mod., Imp. Cyl. RemChoke. **Weight:** 7-1/4 lbs. to 7-1/2 lbs. **Length:** 46" to 481/2" overall. **Stock:** Mossy Oak® Break-Up™ camo finish. **Sights:** Metal bead front. **Features:** Synthetic stock and all metal (except bolt and trigger guard) and stock covered with Mossy Oak® Break-Up™ camo finish. Comes with camo sling, swivels.

Price: **$637.00**

SARSILMAZ PUMP SHOTGUN

Gauge: 12, 3" chamber. **Barrel:** 26" or 28". **Stocks:** Oil-finished hardwood. **Features:** Includes extra pistol-grip stock. Introduced 2000. Imported from Turkey by Armsport Inc.

Price: With pistol-grip stock **$299.95**
Price: With metal stock **$349.95**

WINCHESTER MODEL 1300 WALNUT SPORTING/FIELD PUMP SHOTGUN

Gauge: 12, 20, 3" chamber, 5-shot capacity. **Barrel:** 26", 28", vent rib, with Full, Mod., Imp. Cyl. Winchoke tubes. **Weight:** 6-3/8 lbs. **Length:** 42-5/8" overall. **Stock:** American walnut with deep cut checkering on pistol grip, traditional ribbed forend; high luster finish. **Sights:** Metal bead front. **Features:** Twin action slide bars; front-locking rotary bolt; roll-engraved receiver; blued, highly polished metal; cross-bolt safety with red indicator. Introduced 1984. From U.S. Repeating Arms Co., Inc.

Price: **$439.00**

Winchester 1300 Black Shadow Field Gun

Winchester 1300 Deer Black Shadow Gun

Winchester 1300 Ranger Compact

Winchester 9410

Winchester Model 1300 Upland Pump Shotgun
Similar to Model 1300 Walnut except straight-grip stock, 24" barrel. Introduced 1999. Made in U.S. by U.S. Repeating Arms Co.
Price: **$438.00**

Winchester Model 1300 Black Shadow Field Shotgun
Similar to Model 1300 Walnut except black composite stock and forend, matte black finish. Has vent rib 26" or 28" barrel, 3" chamber, Mod. Winchoke tube. Introduced 1995. From U.S. Repeating Arms Co., Inc.
Price: 12 or 20 gauge **$351.00**

Winchester Model 1300 Deer Black Shadow Shotguns
Similar to Model 1300 Black Shadow Turkey Gun except ramp-type front sight, fully adjustable rear, drilled and tapped for scope mounting. Black composite stock and forend, matte black metal. Smoothbore 22" barrel with one Imp. Cyl. Winchoke tube; 12 gauge only, 3" chamber. Weighs 6-3/4 lbs. Introduced 1994. From U.S. Repeating Arms Co., Inc.
Price: With rifled barrel **$453.00**
Price: Combo (22" rifled and 28" smoothbore bbls.) **$453.00**

WINCHESTER MODEL 1300 RANGER PUMP SHOTGUNS
Gauge: 12, 20, 3" chamber, 5-shot magazine. **Barrel:** 28" vent rib with Full, Mod., Imp. Cyl. Winchoke tubes. **Weight:** 7 to 7-1/4 lbs. **Length:** 48-5/8" to 50-5/8" overall. **Stock:** Walnut-finished hardwood with ribbed forend. **Sights:** Metal bead front. **Features:** Cross-bolt safety, black rubber recoil pad, twin action slide bars, front-locking rotating bolt. From U.S. Repeating Arms Co., Inc.

Price: Vent rib barrel, Winchoke **$366.00**
Price: Model 1300 Compact, 24" vent rib **$366.00**
Price: Compact wood model, 20 ga. **$366.00**

WINCHESTER MODEL 1300 UNIVERSAL HUNTER TURKEY SHOTGUN
Gauge: 12, 3". **Barrel:** 26" vent rib with Extra Long, Extra Full Extended, Full, Mod., Imp. Cyl. Winchoke tubes. **Weight:** 7 lbs. **Length:** 47" overall. **Stock:** Composite. **Sights:** Red dot. **Features:** Rotary bolt action. Durable Mossy Oak® break-up finish. TruGlo® 3-dot sights and stock sling studs also included. From U.S. Repeating Arms Co., Inc.
Price: Universal Hunter **$509.00**

WINCHESTER MODEL 9410 LEVER-ACTION SHOTGUN
Gauge: .410, 2-1/2" chamber. **Barrel:** 24" cyl. bore, also Invector choke system. **Weight:** 6-3/4 lbs. **Length:** 42-1/8" overall. **Stock:** Checkered walnut straight-grip; checkered walnut forearm. **Sights:** Adjustable "V" rear, TruGlo® front. **Features:** Model 94 rifle action (smoothbore) chambered for .410 shotgun. Angle Controlled Eject extractor/ejector; choke tubes, 9-shot tubular magazine; 10 1/2" length of pull. Introduced 2001. From U.S. Repeating Arms Co.
Price: 9410 fixed choke **$626.00**
Price: 9410 Packer w/chokes **$647.00**
Price: 9410 w/Invector, traditional model **$626.00**
Price: 9410 w/Invector, Packer model **$647.00**
Price: 9410 w/Invector, semi-fancy traditional **$626.00**

Includes a variety of game guns and guns for competitive shooting.

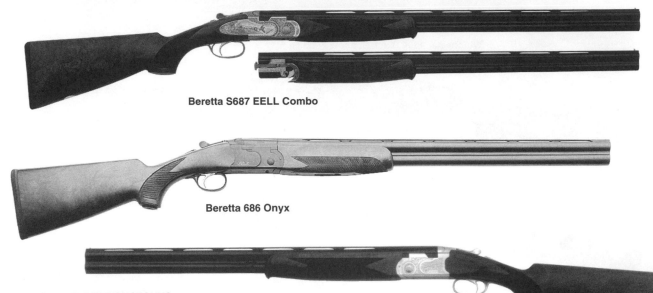

Beretta S687 EELL Combo

Beretta 686 Onyx

Beretta S686 Silver Pigeon

BERETTA DT10 TRIDENT SHOTGUNS

Gauge: 12, 2-3/4", 3" chambers. **Barrel:** 28", 30", 32", 34"; competition-style vent rib; fixed or Optima choke tubes. **Weight:** 7.9 to 9 lbs. **Stock:** High-grade walnut stock with oil finish; hand-checkered grip and forend, adjustable stocks available. **Features:** Detachable, adjustable trigger group, raised and thickened receiver, forend iron has adjustment nut to guarantee wood-to-metal fit. Introduced 2000. Imported from Italy by Beretta USA.

Price: DT10 Trident Trap (selective, lockable single trigger,
   adjustable stock) **$6,995.00**
Price: DT10 Trident Top Single **$6,995.00**
Price: DT10 Trident X Trap Combo
   (single and o/u barrels) **$8,995.00**
Price: DT10 Trident skeet (skeet stock with rounded recoil
   pad, tapered rib) **$6,995.00**
Price: DT10 Trident Sporting (sporting clays stock with
   rounded recoil pad) **$6,495.00**
Price: DT10L Sporting **$7,995.00**

BERETTA SERIES 682 GOLD E SKEET, TRAP, SPORTING O/U SHOTGUNS

Gauge: 12, 2-3/4" chambers. **Barrel:** skeet-28"; trap-30" and 32", Imp. Mod. & Full and Mobilchoke; trap mono shotguns-32" and 34" Mobilchoke; trap top single guns-32" and 34" Full and Mobilchoke; trap combo sets-from 30" O/U, to 32" O/U, 34" top single. **Stock:** Close-grained walnut, hand checkered. **Sights:** White Bradley bead front sight and center bead. **Features:** Receiver has Greystone gunmetal gray finish with gold accents. Trap Monte Carlo stock has deluxe trap recoil pad. Various grades available. Imported from Italy by Beretta USA.

Price: 682 Gold E Trap with adjustable stock **$4,125.00**
Price: 682 Gold E Trap Top Combo **$5,295.00**
Price: 682 Gold E Sporting **$3,595.00**
Price: 682 Gold E skeet, adjustable stock **$3,905.00**
Price: 687 EELL Diamond Pigeon Sporting **$6,495.00**

BERETTA 686 ONYX O/U SHOTGUNS

Gauge: 12, 3" chambers. **Barrel:** 28", 30" (Mobilchoke tubes). **Weight:** 7.7 lbs. **Stock:** Checkered American walnut. **Features:** Intended for the beginning sporting clays shooter. Has wide, vented target rib, radiused recoil pad. Polished black finish on receiver and barrels. Introduced 1993. Imported from Italy by Beretta U.S.A.

Price: White Onyx **$1,795.00**
Price: Onyx Pro **$1,895.00**
Price: Onyx Pro 3.5 . . . . **$2,795.00**

BERETTA 686 SILVER PIGEON O/U SHOTGUNS

Gauge: 12, 20, 28, 3" chambers (2-3/4" 28 ga.). **Barrel:** 26", 28". **Weight:** 6.8 lbs. **Stock:** Checkered walnut. **Features:** Interchangeable barrels (20 and 28 ga.), single selective gold-plated trigger, boxlock action, auto safety, Schnabel forend.

Price: Silver Pigeon S **$1,995.00**
Price: Silver Pigeon S Combo **$2,795.00**

BERETTA ULTRALIGHT O/U SHOTGUNS

Gauge: 12, 2-3/4" chambers. **Barrel:** 26", 28", Mobilchoke tubes. **Weight:** About 5 lbs., 13 oz. **Stock:** Select American walnut with checkered grip and forend. **Features:** Low-profile aluminum alloy receiver with titanium breech face insert. Electroless nickel receiver with game scene engraving. Single selective trigger; automatic safety. Introduced 1992. Imported from Italy by Beretta U.S.A.

Price: **$1,995.00**
Price: Silver Pigeon II **$2,395.00**
Price: Silver Pigeon II Combo **$3,295.00**
Price: Silver Pigeon III **$2,495.00**
Price: Silver Pigeon IV **$2,795.00**
Price: Silver Pigeon V **$3,295.00**
Price: Ultralight Deluxe **$2,495.00**

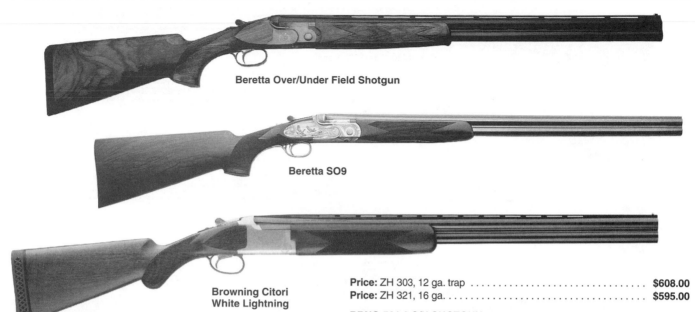

Beretta Over/Under Field Shotgun

Beretta SO9

Browning Citori
White Lightning

Beretta Ultralight Deluxe O/U Shotgun

Similar to the Ultralight except has matte electroless nickel finish receiver with gold game scene engraving; matte oil-finished, select walnut stock and forend. Imported from Italy by Beretta U.S.A.

Price: **$2,495.00**

BERETTA COMPETITION SHOTGUNS

Gauge: 12, 20, 28, and .410 bore, 2-3/4", 3" and 3-1/2" chambers. **Barrel:** 26" and 28" (Mobilchoke tubes). **Stock:** Close-grained walnut. **Features:** Highly-figured, American walnut stocks and forends, and a unique, weather-resistant finish on barrels. Silver designates standard 686, 687 models with silver receivers; 686 Silver Pigeon has enhanced engraving pattern, Schnabel forend; Gold indicates higher grade 686EL, 687EL models with full sideplates; Diamond is for 687EELL models with highest grade wood, engraving. Case provided with Gold and Diamond grades. Imported from Italy by Beretta U.S.A.

Price: S687 EL Gold Pigeon II (deep relief engraving) **$4,795.00**
Price: S687 EELL Gold Pigeon Sporting (D.R. engraving) **$6,495.00**
Price: Gold Sporting Pigeon **$4,971.00**
Price: 28 and 410 combo **$5,520.00**

BERETTA MODEL SO5, SO6, SO9 SHOTGUNS

Gauge: 12, 2-3/4" chambers. **Barrel:** To customer specs. **Stock:** To customer specs. **Features:** SO5-trap, skeet and sporting clays models SO5; SO6-SO6 and SO6 EELL are field models. SO6 has a case-hardened or silver receiver with contour hand engraving. SO6 EELL has hand-engraved receiver in a fine floral or "fine English" pattern or game scene, with bas-relief chisel work and gold inlays. SO6 and SO6 EELL are available with sidelocks removable by hand. Imported from Italy by Beretta U.S.A.

Price: SO5 Trap, skeet, Sporting **$13,000.00**
Price: SO6 Trap, skeet, Sporting **$17,500.00**
Price: SO6 EELL Field, custom specs **$28,000.00**
Price: SO9 (12, 20, 28, .410, 26", 28", 30", any choke) **$31,000.00**

BRNO ZH 300 O/U SHOTGUNS

Gauge: 12, 2-3/4" chambers. **Barrel:** 26", 27-1/2", 29" (skeet, Imp. Cyl., Mod., Full). **Weight:** 7 lbs. **Length:** 44.4" overall. **Stock:** European walnut. **Features:** Double triggers; automatic safety; polished blue finish; engraved receiver. Announced 1998. Imported from the Czech Republic by Euro-Imports.

Price: ZH 301, field **$594.00**
Price: ZH 302, skeet **$608.00**

Price: ZH 303, 12 ga. trap **$608.00**
Price: ZH 321, 16 ga. **$595.00**

BRNO 501.2 O/U SHOTGUN

Gauge: 12, 2-3/4" chambers. **Barrel:** 27.5" (Full & Mod.). **Weight:** 7 lbs. **Length:** 44" overall. **Stock:** European walnut. **Features:** Boxlock action with double triggers, ejectors; automatic safety; hand-cut checkering. Announced 1998. Imported from the Czech Republic by Euro-Imports.

Price: **$850.00**

BROWNING CYNERGY O/U SHOTGUNS

Gauge: 12, 20, 28. **Barrel:** 26", 28", 30", 32". **Stock:** Walnut or composite. **Features:** Mono-Lock hinge, recoil-reducing Inflex recoil pad, silver nitride receiver; ported barrel option.

Price: Cynergy Field, 20 and 28 gauge **$2,062.00**
Price: Cynergy Sporting, 20 and 28 gauge **$3,080.00**
Price: Cynergy Field, 12 gauge **$2,048.00**
Price: Cynergy Field, composite stock **$1,890.00**
Price: Cynergy Sporting, 12 gauge **$3,046.00**
Price: Cynergy Sporting, composite stock **$2,846.00**

BROWNING CITORI O/U SHOTGUNS

Gauge: 12, 20, 28 and .410. **Barrel:** 26", 28" in 28 and .410. Offered with Invector choke tubes. All 12 and 20 gauge models have back-bored barrels and Invector Plus choke system. **Weight:** 6 lbs., 8 oz. (26" .410) to 7 lbs., 13 oz. (30" 12 ga.). **Length:** 43" overall (26" bbl.). **Stock:** Dense walnut, hand checkered, full pistol grip, beavertail forend. Field-type recoil pad on 12 ga. field guns and trap and skeet models. **Sights:** Medium raised beads, German nickel silver. **Features:** Barrel selector integral with safety, automatic ejectors, three-piece takedown. Imported from Japan by Browning.

Price: Lightning, 12 and 20 gauge **$1,645.00**
Price: Lightning, 28 and .410 .... **$1,709.00**
Price: White Lightning, 12 and 20 gauge **$1,714.00**
Price: White Lightning, 28 and .410 Lightning **$1,790.00**
Price: Lightning, 525 Field, 12, 20 .... **$1,981.00**
Price: Lightning, 525 Field, 28 and 410 .... **$2,010.00**
Price: Superlight Feather, 12, 20 .... **$1,938.00**
Price: Super Lightning, Grade I, 12 and 20 gauge **$1,866.00**
Price: Classic Lightning, Grade I, 12 and 20 gauge **$1,891.00**
Price: Classic Lightning Feather, Grade I, 12 and 20 gauge **$1,952.00**

Browning Citori High Grade Shotguns

Similar to standard Citori except has engraved hunting scenes and gold inlays, high-grade, hand-oiled walnut stock and forearm. Introduced 2000. From Browning.

Price: Citori VI Lightning blue or gray
(gold inlays of ducks and pheasants) From **$2,608.00**

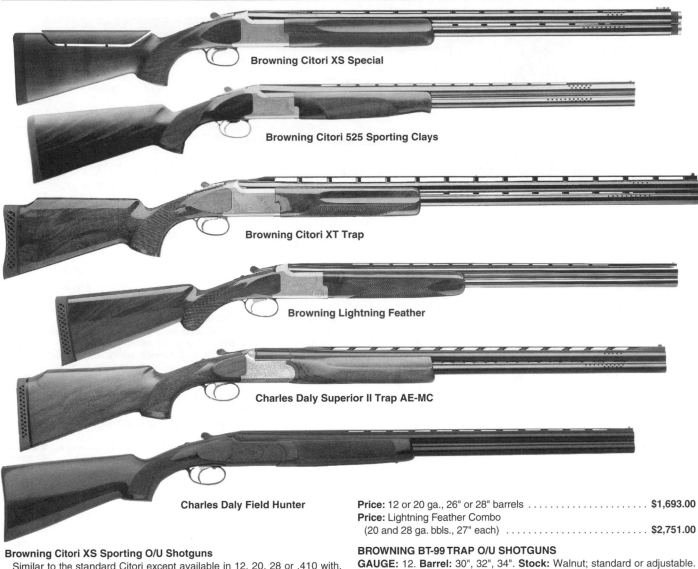

Browning Citori XS Special

Browning Citori 525 Sporting Clays

Browning Citori XT Trap

Browning Lightning Feather

Charles Daly Superior II Trap AE-MC

Charles Daly Field Hunter

Browning Citori XS Sporting O/U Shotguns

Similar to the standard Citori except available in 12, 20, 28 or .410 with, 26" or 28" barrels choked skeet, Cylinder, Imp. Cyl., Mod. and Imp. Mod. Has pistol grip stock, rounded or Schnabel forend. Weighs 7 lbs. 1 oz. to 8 lbs. 10 oz., 15 oz. Introduced 2005.

Price: Citori XS Special, 12 gauge	**$2,727.00**
Price: Citori XS Sporting, 12 or 20 gauge	**$2,472.00**
Price: Citori XS Skeet, 12 or 20 gauge	**$2,434.00**
Price: Citori 525 Sporting, Grade I, 12 gauge	**$2,319.00**
Price: Citori 525 Golden Clays, 12 or 20 gauge	**$3,058.00**
Price: Citori 525 Golden Clays, 28 or .410	**$4,653.00**

Browning Citori XT Trap O/U Shotgun

Similar to the Citori XS Special except has engraved silver nitride receiver with gold highlights, vented side barrel rib. Available in 12 gauge with 30" or 32" barrels, Invector-Plus choke tubes, adjustable comb and buttplate. Introduced 1999. Imported by Browning.

Price:	**$2,275.00 to $4,221.00**
Price: With adjustable-comb stock	**$2,549.00**

Browning Citori Lightning Feather O/U Shotgun

Similar to the 12 gauge Citori Grade I except has 2-3/4" chambers, rounded pistol grip, lightning-style forend, and lightweight alloy receiver. Weighs 6 lbs. 15 oz. with 26" barrels (12 ga.); 6 lbs., 2 oz. (20 ga., 26" bbl.), silvered, engraved receiver. Introduced 1999. Imported by Browning.

Price: 12 or 20 ga., 26" or 28" barrels	**$1,693.00**
Price: Lightning Feather Combo (20 and 28 ga. bbls., 27" each)	**$2,751.00**

BROWNING BT-99 TRAP O/U SHOTGUNS

GAUGE: 12. **Barrel:** 30", 32", 34". **Stock:** Walnut; standard or adjustable. **Weight:** 7 lbs. 11 oz. to 9 lbs. **Features:** Back-bored single barrel; interchangeable chokes; beavertail forearm; extractor only; high rib.

Price: BT-99, adj. comb	**$1,329.00**
Price: BT-99, Golden Clays	**$3,509.00**
Price: BT-99 Micro	**$1,329.00**

CHARLES DALY SUPERIOR II TRAP AE-MC O/U SHOTGUN

Gauge: 12, 2-3/4" chambers. **Barrel:** 30" choke tubes. **Weight:** About 7 lbs. **Length:** 47-3/8". **Stock:** Checkered walnut; pistol grip, semi-beavertail forend. **Features:** Silver engraved receiver, chrome-moly steel barrels; gold single selective trigger; automatic safety, automatic ejectors; red bead front sight, metal bead center; recoil pad. Introduced 1997. Imported from Italy by K.B.I., Inc.

Price:	**$1,699.00**

CHARLES DALY FIELD II HUNTER O/U SHOTGUN

Gauge: 12, 20, 28 and .410 bore (3" chambers, 28 ga. has 2-3/4"). **Barrel:** 28" Mod & Full, 26" Imp. Cyl. & Mod (.410 is Full & Full). **Weight:** About 7 lbs. **Length:** 42-3/4" to 44-3/4". **Stock:** Checkered walnut pistol grip and forend. **Features:** Blued engraved receiver, chrome-moly steel barrels; gold single selective trigger; automatic safety; extractors; gold bead front sight. Introduced 1997. Imported from Italy by K.B.I., Inc.

Price: 12 or 20 ga.	**$1,029.00**
Price: 28 ga., .410 bore	**$1,129.00**

Charles Daly Superior Hunter

Charles Daly Empire II Mono Trap

Charles Daly Empire II EDL Hunter

Charles Daly Empire Sporting O/U

Charles Daly Superior II Hunter AE O/U Shotgun
Similar to the Field Hunter AE except has silvered, engraved receiver. Introduced 1997. Imported from Italy by F.B.I., Inc.
Price: 28 ga., .410 bore **$1,449.00**

Charles Daly Field Hunter AE-MC O/U Shotgun
Similar to the Field Hunter except in 12 or 20 only, 26" or 28" barrels with five multi-choke tubes, automatic ejectors. Introduced 1997. Imported from Italy by K.B.I., Inc.
Price: 12 or 20 ga. **$1,279.00**

Charles Daly Superior II Sporting O/U Shotgun
Similar to the Field Hunter AE-MC except 28" or 30" barrels; silvered, engraved receiver; five choke tubes; ported barrels; red bead front sight. Introduced 1997. Imported from Italy by K.B.I., Inc.
Price: **$1,659.00**

CHARLES DALY EMPIRE II EDL HUNTER AE, AE-MC O/U SHOTGUNS
Gauge: 12, 20, .410, 3" chambers, 28 ga., 2-3/4". **Barrel:** 26", 28" (12, 20, choke tubes), 26" (Imp. Cyl. & Mod., 28 ga.), 26" (Full & Full, .410). **Weight:** About 7 lbs. **Stocks:** Checkered walnut pistol grip buttstock, semi-beavertail forend; recoil pad. **Features:** Silvered, engraved receiver; chrome-moly barrels; gold single selective trigger; automatic safety; automatic ejectors; red bead front sight, metal bead middle sight. Introduced 1997. Imported from Italy by K.B.I., Inc.
Price: Empire II EDL AE-MC (dummy sideplates) 12 or 20 . . . . . **$2,029.00**
Price: Empire II EDL AE, 28 . . . . **$2,019.00**
Price: Empire II EDL AE, .410 . . . . **$2,019.00**

Charles Daly Empire II Sporting AE-MC O/U Shotgun
Similar to the Empire II EDL Hunter except 12 or 20 gauge only, 28", 30" barrels with choke tubes; ported barrels; special stock dimensions. Introduced 1997. Imported from Italy by K.B.I., Inc.
Price: **$2,049.00**

CHARLES DALY EMPIRE II TRAP AE-MC O/U SHOTGUNS
Gauge: 12, 2-3/4" chambers. **Barrel:** 30" choke tubes. **Weight:** About 7 lbs. **Stock:** Checkered walnut; pistol grip, semi-beavertail forend. **Features:** Silvered, engraved, reinforced receiver; chrome-moly steel barrels; gold single selective trigger; automatic safety, automatic ejector; red bead front sight, metal bead center; recoil pad. Imported from Italy by K.B.I., Inc.
Price: **$2,099.00**
Price: Mono AE-MC, adj. comb **$2,999.00**
Price: AE-MC combo set, adj. comb **$3,919.00**

CHARLES DALY DIAMOND REGENT GTX DL HUNTER O/U SHOTGUNS
Gauge: 12, 20, .410, 3" chambers, 28, 2-3/4" chambers. **Barrel:** 26", 28", 30" (choke tubes), 26" (Imp. Cyl. & Mod. in 28, 26" (Full & Full) in .410. **Weight:** About 7 lbs. **Stock:** Extra select fancy European walnut with 24" hand checkering, hand rubbed oil finish. **Features:** Boss-type action with internal side lumps. Deep cut hand-engraved scrollwork and game scene set in full sideplates. GTX detachable single selective trigger system with coil springs; chrome-moly steel barrels; automatic safety; automatic ejectors; white bead front sight, metal bead center sight. Introduced 1997. Imported from Italy by K.B.I., Inc.
Price: 12 or 20 . . . . **Special order only**
Price: 28 . . . . **Special order only**
Price: .410 bore . . . . **Special order only**
Price: Diamond Regent GTX EDL Hunter (as above with engraved scroll and birds, 10 gold inlays), 12 or 20 . . . . **Special order only**
Price: As above, 28 . . . . **Special order only**
Price: As above, .410 . . . . **Special order only**

CHARLES DALY DIAMOND GTX SPORTING O/U SHOTGUN
Gauge: 12, 20, 3" chambers. **Barrel:** 28", 30" with choke tubes. **Weight:** About 8.5 lbs. **Stock:** Checkered deluxe walnut; sporting clays dimensions. Pistol grip; semi-beavertail forend; hand rubbed oil finish. **Features:** Chromed, hand-engraved receiver, chrome-moly steel barrels; GTX detachable single selective trigger system with coil springs, automatic safety; automatic ejectors; red bead front sight; ported barrels. Introduced 1997. Imported from Italy by K.B.I., Inc.
Price: . . . . **Price on request**

CHARLES DALY DIAMOND GTX TRAP AE-MC O/U SHOTGUN
Gauge: 12, 2-3/4" chambers. **Barrel:** 30" (Full & Full). **Weight:** About 8.5 lbs. **Stock:** Checkered deluxe walnut; pistol grip; trap dimensions; semi-beavertail forend; hand-rubbed oil finish. **Features:** Silvered, hand-engraved receiver; chrome-moly steel barrels; GTX detachable single selective trigger system with coil springs, automatic safety, automatic ejectors, red bead front sight, metal bead middle; recoil pad. Imported from Italy by K.B.I., Inc.
Price: . . . . **Price on request**

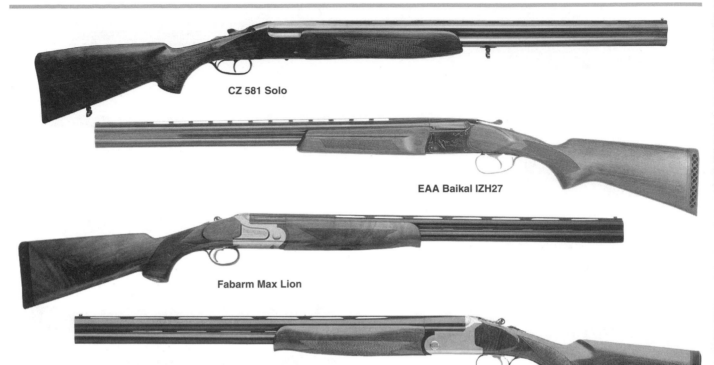

CZ 581 Solo

EAA Baikal IZH27

Fabarm Max Lion

Fabarm Silver Lion Youth

CHARLES DALY DIAMOND GTX DL HUNTER O/U SHOTGUN

Gauge: 12, 20, .410, 3" chambers, 28, 2-3/4" chambers. **Barrel:** 26, 28", choke tubes in 12 and 20 ga., 26" (Imp. Cyl. & Mod.), 26" (Full & Full) in .410-bore. **Weight:** About 8.5 lbs. **Stock:** Select fancy European walnut stock, with 24 lpi hand checkering; hand-rubbed oil finish. **Features:** Boss-type action with internal side lugs, hand-engraved scrollwork and game scene. GTX detachable single selective trigger system with coil springs; chrome-moly steel barrels, automatic safety, automatic ejectors, red bead front sight, recoil pad. Introduced 1997. Imported from Italy by K.B.I., Inc.

Price: . . . . **Special order only**

CZ 581 SOL O/U SHOTGUN

Gauge: 12, 2-3/4" chambers. **Barrel:** 27.6" (Mod. & Full). **Weight:** 7.37 lbs. **Length:** 44.5" overall. **Stock:** Circassian walnut. **Features:** Automatic ejectors; double triggers; Kersten-style double lump locking system. Imported from the Czech Republic by CZ-USA.

Price: **$799.00**

EAA BAIKAL IZH27 O/U SHOTGUN

Gauge: 12 (3" chambers), 16 (2-3/4" chambers), 20 (3" chambers), 28 (2-3/4" chambers), .410 (3"). **Barrel:** 26-1/2", 28-1/2" (imp., mod. and full choke tubes for 12 and 20 gauges; improved cylinder and modified for 16 and 28 gauges; Improved Modified and Full for .410; 16 also offered in Mod. and Full). **Weight:** NA. **Stock:** Walnut, checkered forearm and grip. Imported by European American Armory.

Price: IZH27 (12, 16 and 20 gauge) **$509.00**
Price: IZH27 (28 gauge and .410) **$569.00**

EAA Baikal IZH27 O/U Shotgun

Basic IZH27 with barrel porting, wide vent rib with double sight beads, engraved nickel receiver, checkered walnut stock and forend with palm swell and semi beavertail, 3 screw-in chokes, SS trigger, selectable ejectors, auto tang safety.

Price: 12 ga., 29" bbl. **$589.00**

EAA Baikal Nickel O/U Shotgun

Same as IZH27 but with polished nickel receiver.
Price: **$529.00**

FABARM MAX LION O/U SHOTGUN

Gauge: 12, 3" chambers, 20, 3" chambers. **Barrel:** 26", 28", 30" (12 ga.); 26", 28" (20 ga.), choke tubes. **Weight:** 7.4 lbs. **Length:** 47.5" overall (26"

barrel). **Stock:** European walnut; leather-covered recoil pad. **Features:** TriBore barrel, boxlock action with single selective trigger, manual safety, automatic ejectors; chrome-lined barrels; adjustable trigger. Silvered, engraved receiver. Comes with locking, fitted luggage case. Introduced 1998. Imported from Italy by Heckler & Koch, Inc.

Price: 12 or 20 . . . . **$1,799.00**

FABARM ULTRA CAMO MAG LION O/U SHOTGUN

Gauge: 12, 3-1/2" chambers. **Barrel:** 28" (Cyl., Imp. Cyl., Mod., Imp. Mod., Full, SS-mod., SS-full choke tubes). **Weight:** 7.9 lbs. **Length:** 50" overall. **Stock:** Camo-colored walnut. **Features:** TriBore barrel, Wetlands Camo finished metal surfaces, single selective trigger, non-auto ejectors, leather-covered recoil pad. Locking hard plastic case. Introduced 1998. Imported from Italy by Heckler & Koch, Inc.

Price: **$1,229.00**

FABARM MAX LION PARADOX O/U SHOTGUN

Gauge: 12, 20, 3" chambers. **Barrel:** 24". **Weight:** 7.6 lbs. **Length:** 44.5" overall. **Stock:** Walnut with special enhancing finish. **Features:** TriBore upper barrel, both wood and receiver are enhanced with special finishes, color case-hardened type finish.

Price: 12 or 20 . . . . **$1,129.00**

FABARM SILVER LION O/U SHOTGUN

Gauge: 12, 3" chambers, 20, 3" chambers. **Barrel:** 26", 28", 30" (12 ga.); 26", 28" (20 ga.), choke tubes. **Weight:** 7.2 lbs. **Length:** 47.5" overall (26" barrels). **Stock:** Walnut; leather-covered recoil pad. **Features:** TriBore barrel, boxlock action with single selective trigger; silvered receiver with engraving; automatic ejectors. Comes with locking hard plastic case. Introduced 1998. Imported from Italy by Heckler & Koch, Inc.

Price: 12 or 20 . . . . **$1,229.00**

Fabarm Silver Lion Youth Model O/U Shotgun

Similar to the Silver Lion except has 12.5" length of pull, 12 gauge only, comes with 24" TriBore barrel system. Weight is 6 lbs. Introduced 1999. Imported from Italy by Heckler & Koch, Inc.

Price: **$1,229.00**

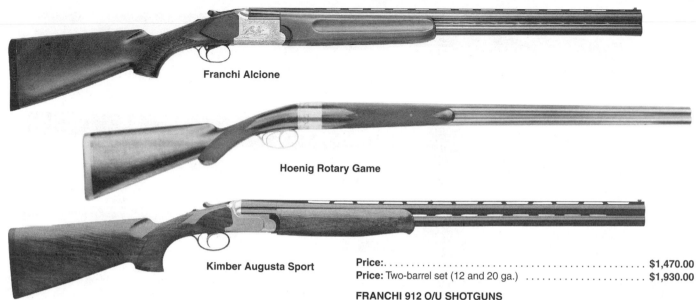

Franchi Alcione

Hoenig Rotary Game

Kimber Augusta Sport

FABARM CAMO TURKEY MAG O/U SHOTGUN

Gauge: 12, 3-1/2" chambers. **Barrel:** 20" TriBore (Ultra-Full ported tubes). **Weight:** 7.5 lbs. **Length:** 46" overall. **Stock:** 14.5"x1.5"x2.29". Walnut. **Sights:** Front bar, Picatinny rail scope base. **Features:** Completely covered with Xtra Brown camouflage finish. Unported barrels. Introduced 1999. Imported from Italy by Heckler & Koch, Inc.
Price: **$1,199.00**

FABARM SPORTING CLAYS COMPETITION EXTRA O/U SHOTGUN

Gauge: 12, 20, 3" chambers. **Barrel:** 12 ga. has 30", 20 ga. has 28"; ported TriBore barrel system with five tubes. **Weight:** 7 to 7.8 lbs. **Length:** 49.6" overall (20 ga.). **Stock:** 14.50"x1.38"x2.17" (20 ga.); deluxe walnut; leather-covered recoil pad. **Features:** Single selective trigger, auto ejectors; 10mm channeled rib; carbon fiber finish. Introduced 1999. Imported from Italy by Heckler & Koch, Inc.
Price: **$1,749.00**

FRANCHI ALCIONE FIELD O/U SHOTGUN

Gauge: 12, 20, 3" chambers. **Barrel:** 26", 28"; IC, M, F tubes. **Weight:** 7.5 lbs. **Length:** 43" overall with 26" barrels. **Stock:** European walnut. **Features:** Boxlock action with ejectors, barrel selector mounted on trigger; silvered, engraved receiver, vent center rib, automatic safety, interchangeable 20 ga. bbls., left-hand available. Imported from Italy by Benelli USA. Hard case included.
Price: **$1,310.00**
Price: (12 or 20 gauge barrel set) **$490.00**

Franchi Alcione SX O/U Shotgun

Similar to Alcione Field model with high grade walnut stock and forend. Gold engraved removeable sideplates, interchangeable barrels.
Price: **$1,855.00**
Price: (12 gauge barrel set) .... **$490.00 to $560.00**
Price: (20 gauge barrel set) **$490.00**

Franchi Alcione Sport SL O/U Shotgun

Similar to Alcione Field except 2-3/4" chambers, elongated forcing cones and porting for sporting clays shooting. 10mm vent rib, tightly curved pistol grip, manual safety, removeable sideplates. Imported from Italy by Benelli USA.
Price: **$1,700.00**

FRANCHI ALCIONE TITANIUM O/U SHOTGUN

Gauge: 12, 20, 3" chambers. **Barrel:** 26", 28"; IC, M, F tubes. **Weight:** 6.8 lbs. **Length:** 43", 45". **Stock:** Select walnut. **Sights:** Front/mid. **Features:** Receiver (titanium inserts) made of aluminum alloy. 7mm vent rib. Fast locking triggers. Left-hand available.

Price: **$1,470.00**
Price: Two-barrel set (12 and 20 ga.) **$1,930.00**

FRANCHI 912 O/U SHOTGUNS

Gauge: 12 ga., 2-3/4", 3", 3-1/2" chambers. **Barrel:** 24" to 30". **Weight:** Appx. 7.6 lbs. **Length:** 46" to 52". **Stock:** Walnut, synthetic, Timber HD, Max-4. **Sights:** White bead front. **Features:** Based on 612 design, magazine cut-off, stepped vent rib, dual-recoil-reduction system.
Price: Satin walnut **$850.00**
Price: Synthetic **$790.00**
Price: Timber HD & Max-4 .... **$900.00**
Price: Steadygrip Timber HD **$850.00**

FRANCHI VELOCE O/U SHOTGUN

Gauge: 20, 28. **Barrel:** 26", 28"; IC, M, F tubes. **Weight:** 5.5 to 5.8 lbs. **Length:** 43" to 45". **Stock:** High grade walnut. **Features:** Aluminum receiver with steel reinforcement scaled to 20 gauge for light weight. Pistol grip stock with slip recoil pad. Imported by Benelli USA. Hard case included.
Price: **$1,470.00**
Price: 28 ga. **$1,545.00**

Franchi Veloce English O/U Shotgun

Similar to Veloce standard model with straight grip English-style stock. Available with 26" barrels in 20 and 28 gauge. Hard case included.
Price: **$1,470.00**
Price: 28 ga. **$1,545.00**

HOENIG ROTARY ROUND ACTION GAME GUN O/U SHOTGUN

Gauge: 20, 28. **Barrel:** 26", 28", solid tapered rib. **Weight:** 6 lbs. and 6-1/4 lbs. **Stock:** English walnut to customer specifications. **Features:** Round action opens by rotating barrels, pulling forward. Inertia extraction system, rotary wing safety blocks strikers. Simple takedown without removing forend. Introduced 1997. Made in U.S.A. by George Hoenig.
Price: **$19,980.00**

KHAN ARTEMIS O/U SHOTGUN

Gauge: 12, 20, 28, 410. **Barrel:** 26", 28". **Stock:** Walnut. **Features:** Engraved receiver, single selective trigger, vent rib; choke tubes and extractors (Fixed IC, M choke on 410 models). Introduced 2005. Imported by Legacy Sports Int.
Price: .... **$617.00 to $791.00**
Price: Sporting clays model **$1,104.00**

KIMBER AUGUSTA O/U SHOTGUNS

Gauge: 12, 3". **Barrel:** 26" to 27-1/2". **Weight:** 7 lbs., 2 oz. **Length:** NA. **Stock:** Checkered AAA-grade European walnut. **Features:** Premium over/under, Boss-type action. Tri-alloy barrel with choke tubes. Back bored, long forcing cones. HiViz sight with center bead on vent rib. Satin or high gloss finish. Imported from Italy by Kimber Mfg., Inc.
Price: Field, Skeeet, Sporting, Trap **$6,000.00**

Kolar Sporting Clays

Krieghoff K-80 Sporting Clays

Ljutic LM-6 Super Deluxe

KOLAR SPORTING CLAYS O/U SHOTGUNS

Gauge: 12, 2-3/4" chambers. **Barrel:** 30", 32", 34"; extended choke tubes. **Stock:** 14-5/8"x2-1/2"x1-7/8"x1-3/8". French walnut. Four stock versions available. **Features:** Single selective trigger, detachable, adjustable for length; overbored barrels with long forcing cones; flat tramline rib; matte blue finish. Made in U.S. by Kolar.

Price: Standard	$7,995.00
Price: Elite	$10,990.00
Price: Elite Gold	$12,990.00
Price: Legend	$13,990.00
Price: Select	$15,990.00
Price: Custom	**Price on request**

Kolar AAA Competition Trap O/U Shotgun

Similar to the Sporting Clays gun except has 32" O/U /34" Unsingle or 30" O/U /34" Unsingle barrels as an over/under, unsingle, or combination set. Stock dimensions are 14-1/2"x2-1/2"x1-1/2"; American or French walnut; step parallel rib standard. Contact maker for full listings. Made in U.S.A. by Kolar.

Price: Over/under, choke tubes, standard	$8,220.00
Price: Unsingle, choke tubes, standard	$8,600.00
Price: Combo (30"/34", 32"/34"), standard	$10,995.00

Kolar AAA Competition Skeet O/U Shotgun

Similar to the Sporting Clays gun except has 28" or 30" barrels with Kolarite AAA sub gauge tubes; stock of American or French walnut with matte finish; flat tramline rib; under barrel adjustable for point of impact. Many options available. Contact maker for complete listing. Made in U.S.A. by Kolar.

| Price: Standard, choke tubes | $8,645.00 |
| Price: Standard, choke tubes, two-barrel set | $10,995.00 |

KRIEGHOFF K-80 SPORTING CLAYS O/U SHOTGUN

Gauge: 12. **Barrel:** 28", 30" or 32" with choke tubes. **Weight:** About 8 lbs. **Stock:** #3 Sporting stock designed for gun-down shooting. **Features:** Standard receiver with satin nickel finish and classic scroll engraving. Selective mechanical trigger adjustable for position. Choice of tapered flat or 8mm parallel flat barrel rib. Free-floating barrels. Aluminum case. Imported from Germany by Krieghoff International, Inc.

| Price: Standard grade with five choke tubes, from | $9,395.00 |

KRIEGHOFF K-80 SKEET O/U SHOTGUNS

Gauge: 12, 2-3/4" chambers. **Barrel:** 28", 30", (skeet & skeet), optional choke tubes). **Weight:** About 7-3/4 lbs. **Stock:** American skeet or straight skeet stocks, with palm-swell grips. Walnut. **Features:** Satin gray receiver finish. Selective mechanical trigger adjustable for position. Choice of

ventilated 8mm parallel flat rib or ventilated 8-12mm tapered flat rib. Introduced 1980. Imported from Germany by Krieghoff International, Inc.

| Price: Standard, skeet chokes | $8,220.00 |
| Price: Skeet Special (28" or 30", tapered flat rib, skeet & skeet choke tubes) | $8,920.00 |

KRIEGHOFF K-80 TRAP O/U SHOTGUNS

Gauge: 12, 2-3/4" chambers. **Barrel:** 30", 32" (Imp. Mod. & Full or choke tubes). **Weight:** About 8-1/2 lbs. **Stock:** Four stock dimensions or adjustable stock available; all have palm-swell grips. Checkered European walnut. **Features:** Satin nickel receiver. Selective mechanical trigger, adjustable for position. Ventilated step rib. Introduced 1980. Imported from Germany by Krieghoff International, Inc.

Price: K-80 O/U (30", 32", Imp. Mod. & Full), from	$8,695.00
Price: K-80 Unsingle (32", 34", Full), standard, from	$9,675.00
Price: K-80 Combo (two-barrel set), standard, from	$13,990.00

Krieghoff K-20 O/U Shotgun

Similar to the K-80 except built on a 20-gauge frame. Designed for skeet, sporting clays and field use. Offered in 20, 28 and .410; 28", 30" and 32" barrels. Imported from Germany by Krieghoff International Inc.

Price: K-20, 20 gauge, from	$9,395.00
Price: K-20, 28 gauge, from	$9,545.00
Price: K-20, .410, from	$9,545.00

L. C. SMITH O/U SHOTGUN

Gauge: 12, 20. **Barrel:** 26", 28". **Stock:** Checkered walnut w/recoil pad. **Features:** 3" chambers; single selective trigger, selective automatic ejectors; vent rib; bead front sight. Imported from Italy by Marlin. Introduced 2005.

| Price: | $1,394.00 |

LEBEAU-COURALLY BOSS-VEREES O/U SHOTGUN

Gauge: 12, 20, 2-3/4" chambers. **Barrel:** 25" to 32". **Weight:** To customer specifications. **Stock:** Exhibition-quality French walnut. **Features:** Boss-type sidelock with automatic ejectors; single or double triggers; chopper lump barrels. A custom gun built to customer specifications. Imported from Belgium by Wm. Larkin Moore.

| Price: From | $96,000.00 |

LJUTIC LM-6 SUPER DELUXE O/U SHOTGUNS

Gauge: 12. **Barrel:** 28" to 34", choked to customer specs for live birds, trap, international trap. **Weight:** To customer specs. **Stock:** To customer specs. Oil finish, hand checkered. **Features:** Custom-made gun. Hollow-milled rib, pull or release trigger, push-button opener in front of trigger guard. From Ljutic Industries.

Price: Super Deluxe LM-6 O/U	$19,995.00
Price: Over/Under combo (interchangeable single barrel, two trigger guards, one for single trigger, one for doubles)	$27,995.00
Price: Extra over/under barrel sets, 29"-32"	$6,995.00

Marocchi Conquista Sporting Clay

Merkel Model 2001EL

Price: Grade III	$3,275.00
Price: Grade III Gold	$3,450.00
Price: Blackgold	$4,150.00
Price: Lodestar	$5,125.00
Price: Brittania	$5,125.00
Price: Diana	$6,350.00

LUGER CLASSIC O/U SHOTGUNS

Gauge: 12, 3" and 3-1/2" chambers. **Barrel:** 26", 28", 30"; Imp. Cyl. Mod. and Full choke tubes. **Weight:** 7-1/2 lbs. **Length:** 45" overall (28" barrel) **Stock:** Select-grade European walnut, hand-checkered grip and forend. **Features:** Gold, single selective trigger; automatic ejectors. Introduced 2000.

| Price: Classic (26", 28" or 30" barrel; 3-1/2" chambers) | $919.00 |
| Price: Classic Sporting (30" barrel; 3" chambers) | $964.00 |

MAROCCHI CONQUISTA SPORTING CLAYS O/U SHOTGUNS

Gauge: 12, 2-3/4" chambers. **Barrel:** 28", 30", 32" (ContreChoke tubes); 10mm concave vent rib. **Weight:** About 8 lbs. **Stock:** 14-1/2"-14-7/8"x2-3/16"x1-7/16"; American walnut with checkered grip and forend; sporting clays butt pad. **Sights:** 16mm luminescent front. **Features:** Lower mono-block and frame profile. Fast lock time. Ergonomically-shaped trigger adjustable for pull length. Automatic selective ejectors. Coin-finished receiver, blued barrels. Five choke tubes, hard case. Available as true left-hand model, opening lever operates from left to right; stock has left-hand cast. Introduced 1994. Imported from Italy by Precision Sales International.

Price: Grade I, right-hand	$1,490.00
Price: Grade I, left-hand	$1,615.00
Price: Grade II, right-hand	$1,828.00
Price: Grade II, left-hand	$2,180.00
Price: Grade III, right-hand, from	$3,093.00
Price: Grade III, left-hand, from	$3,093.00

Marocchi Conquista Trap O/U Shotguns

Similar to Conquista Sporting Clays model except 30" or 32" barrels choked Full & Full, stock dimensions of 14-1/2"-14-7/8"x1-11/16"x1-9/32"; weighs about 8-1/4 lbs. Introduced 1994. Imported from Italy by Precision Sales International.

Price: Grade I, right-hand	$1,490.00
Price: Grade II, right-hand	$1,828.00
Price: Grade III, right-hand, from	$3,093.00

Marocchi Conquista Skeet O/U Shotguns

Similar to Conquista Sporting Clays model except 28" (skeet & skeet) barrels, stock dimensions of 14-3/8"-14-3/4"x2-3/16"x1-1/2". Weighs about 7-3/4 lbs. Introduced 1994. Imported from Italy by Precision Sales International.

Price: Grade I, right-hand	$1,490.00
Price: Grade II, right-hand	$1,828.00
Price: Grade III, right-hand, from	$3,093.00

MAROCCHI MODEL 99 SPORTING TRAP AND SKEET O/U SHOTGUNS

Gauge: 12, 2-3/4", 3" chambers. **Barrel:** 28", 30", 32". **Stock:** French walnut. **Features:** Boss Locking system, screw-in chokes, low recoil, lightweight Monoblock barrels and ribs. Imported from Italy by Precision Sales International.

Price: Grade I	$2,350.00
Price: Grade II	$2,870.00
Price: Grade II Gold	$3,025.00

MAROCCHI CONQUISTA USA MODEL 92 SPORTING CLAYS O/U SHOTGUN

Gauge: 12, 3" chambers. **Barrel:** 30"; back-bored, ported (ContreChoke Plus tubes); 10 mm concave ventilated top rib, ventilated middle rib. **Weight:** 8 lbs. 2 oz. **Stock:** 14-1/4"-14-5/8"x 2-1/8"x1-3/8"; American walnut with checkered grip and forend; sporting clays butt pad. **Features:** Low profile frame; fast lock time; automatic selective ejectors; blued receiver and barrels. Comes with three choke tubes. Ergonomically shaped trigger adjustable for pull length without tools. Barrels are back-bored and ported. Introduced 1996. Imported from Italy by Precision Sales International.

| Price: | $1,490.00 |

MERKEL MODEL 2001EL O/U SHOTGUN

Gauge: 12, 20, 3" chambers, 28, 2-3/4" chambers. **Barrel:** 12-28"; 20, 28 ga.-26-3/4". **Weight:** About 7 lbs. (12 ga.). **Stock:** Oil-finished walnut; English or pistol grip. **Features:** Self-cocking Blitz boxlock action with cocking indicators; Kersten double cross-bolt lock; silver-grayed receiver with engraved hunting scenes; coil spring ejectors; single selective or double triggers. Imported from Germany by GSI, Inc.

Price: 12, 20	$7,295.00
Price: 28 ga.	$7,295.00
Price: Model 2000EL (scroll engraving, 12, 20 or 28)	$5,795.00

Merkel Model 303EL O/U Shotgun

Similar to Model 2001EL except Holland & Holland-style sidelock action with cocking indicators; English-style arabesque engraving. Available in 12, 20, 28 gauge. Imported from Germany by GSI, Inc.

| Price: | $19,995.00 |

Merkel Model 2002EL O/U Shotgun

Similar to Model 2001EL except dummy sideplates, arabesque engraving with hunting scenes; 12, 20, 28 gauge. Imported from Germany by GSI, Inc.

| Price: | $10,995.00 |

PERAZZI MX8/MX8 SPECIAL TRAP, SKEET O/U SHOTGUNS

Gauge: 12, 2-3/4" chambers. **Barrel:** Trap: 29-1/2" (Imp. Mod. & Extra Full), 31-1/2" (Full & Extra Full). Choke tubes optional. Skeet: 27-5/8" (skeet & skeet). **Weight:** About 8-1/2 lbs. (trap); 7 lbs., 15 oz. (skeet). **Stock:** Interchangeable and custom made to customer specs. **Features:** Has detachable and interchangeable trigger group with flat V springs. Flat 7/16" vent rib. Many options available. Imported from Italy by Perazzi U.S.A., Inc.

Price: From	$12,756.00
Price: MX8 Special (adj. four-position trigger) From	$11,476.00
Price: MX8 Special combo (o/u and single barrel sets) From	$15,127.00

Perazzi MX8 Special Skeet O/U Shotgun

Similar to the MX8 Skeet except has adjustable four-position trigger, skeet stock dimensions. Imported from Italy by Perazzi U.S.A., Inc.

| Price: From | $11,166.00 |

SHOTGUNS — Over/Unders

Perazzi MX8

Perazzi MX28

Piotti Boss

Rizzini S790 Emel

PERAZZI MX8 O/U SHOTGUNS

Gauge: 12, 2-3/4" chambers. **Barrel:** 28-3/8" (Imp. Mod. & Extra Full), 29-1/2" (choke tubes). **Weight:** 7 lbs., 12 oz. **Stock:** Special specifications. **Features:** Has single selective trigger; flat 7/16" x 5/16" vent rib. Many options available. Imported from Italy by Perazzi U.S.A., Inc.

Price: Standard **$12,532.00**
Price: Sporting **$11,166.00**
Price: Trap Double Trap (removable trigger group) **$15,581.00**
Price: Skeet **$12,756.00**
Price: SC3 grade (variety of engraving patterns) .... **$23,000.00+**
Price: SCO grade (more intricate engraving, gold inlays) .... **$39,199.00+**

Perazzi MX8/20 O/U Shotgun

Similar to the MX8 except has smaller frame and has a removable trigger mechanism. Available in trap, skeet, sporting or game models with fixed chokes or choke tubes. Stock is made to customer specifications. Introduced 1993. Imported from Italy by Perazzi U.S.A., Inc.
Price: From **$11,166.00**

PERAZZI MX12 HUNTING O/U SHOTGUNS

Gauge: 12, 2-3/4" chambers. **Barrel:** 26-3/4", 27-1/2", 28-3/8", 29-1/2" (Mod. & Full); choke tubes available in 27-5/8", 29-1/2" only (MX12C). **Weight:** 7 lbs., 4 oz. **Stock:** To customer specs; interchangeable. **Features:** Single selective trigger; coil springs used in action; Schnabel forend tip. Imported from Italy by Perazzi U.S.A., Inc.
Price: From **$11,166.00**
Price: MX12C (with choke tubes) From **$11,960.00**

Perazzi MX20 Hunting O/U Shotguns

Similar to the MX12 except 20 ga. frame size. Non-removable trigger group. Available in 20, 28, .410 with 2-3/4" or 3" chambers. 26" standard, and choked Mod. & Full. Weight is 6 lbs., 6 oz. Imported from Italy by Perazzi U.S.A., Inc.
Price: From **$11,166.00**
Price: MX20C (as above, 20 ga. only, choke tubes) From **$11,960.00**

PERAZZI MX10 O/U SHOTGUN

Gauge: 12, 2-3/4" chambers. **Barrel:** 29.5", 31.5" (fixed chokes). **Weight:** NA. **Stock:** Walnut; cheekpiece adjustable for elevation and cast. **Features:** Adjustable rib; vent side rib. Externally selective trigger. Available in single barrel, combo, over/under trap, skeet, pigeon and sporting models. Introduced 1993. Imported from Italy by Perazzi U.S.A., Inc.
Price: MX200410 .... **$18,007.00**

PERAZZI MX28, MX410 GAME O/U SHOTGUN

Gauge: 28, 2-3/4" chambers, .410, 3" chambers. **Barrel:** 26" (Imp. Cyl. & Full). **Weight:** NA. **Stock:** To customer specifications. **Features:** Made on scaled-down frames proportioned to the gauge. Introduced 1993. Imported from Italy by Perazzi U.S.A., Inc.
Price: From **$22,332.00**

PIOTTI BOSS O/U SHOTGUN

Gauge: 12, 20. **Barrel:** 26" to 32", chokes as specified. **Weight:** 6.5 to 8 lbs. **Stock:** Dimensions to customer specs. Best quality figured walnut. **Features:** Essentially a custom-made gun with many options. Introduced 1993. Imported from Italy by Wm. Larkin Moore.
Price: From **$48,000.00**

REMINGTON MODEL 332 O/U SHOTGUN

Gauge: 12, 3" chambers. **Barrel:** 26", 28", 30". **Weight:** 7.75 lbs. **Length:** 42" to 47". **Stock:** Satin-finished American walnut. **Sights:** Twin bead. **Features:** Light-contour, vent rib, RemChoke barrel, blued, traditional M-32 experience with M-300 Ideal performance, standard auto ejectors, set trigger. Proven boxlock action.
Price: **$1,624.00**

RIZZINI S790 EMEL O/U SHOTGUN

Gauge: 20, 28, .410. **Barrel:** 26", 27.5" (Imp. Cyl. & Imp. Mod.). **Weight:** About 6 lbs. **Stock:** 14"x1-1/2"x2-1/8". Extra fancy select walnut. **Features:** Boxlock action with profuse engraving; automatic ejectors; single selective trigger; silvered receiver. Comes with Nizzoli leather case. Introduced 1996. Imported from Italy by Wm. Larkin Moore & Co.
Price: From **$9,725.00**

Rizzini S792 EMEL O/U Shotgun

Similar to S790 EMEL except dummy sideplates with extensive engraving coverage. Nizzoli leather case. Introduced 1996. Imported from Italy by Wm. Larkin Moore & Co.
Price: From **$9,075.00**

SHOTGUNS — Over/Unders

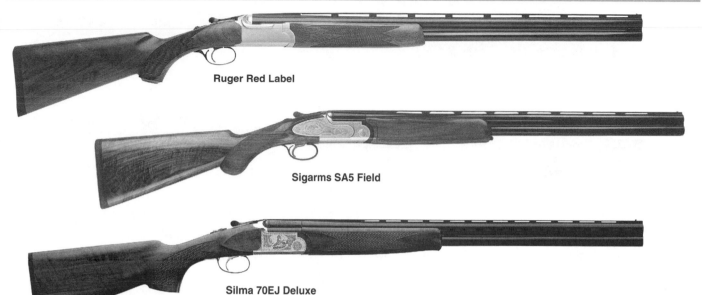

Ruger Red Label

Sigarms SA5 Field

Silma 70EJ Deluxe

RIZZINI UPLAND EL O/U SHOTGUN

Gauge: 12, 16, 20, 28, .410. **Barrel:** 26", 27-1/2", Mod. & Full, Imp. Cyl. & Imp. Mod. choke tubes. **Weight:** About 6.6 lbs. **Stock:** 14-1/2"x1-1/2"x2-1/4". **Features:** Boxlock action; single selective trigger; ejectors; profuse engraving on silvered receiver. Comes with fitted case. Introduced 1996. Imported from Italy by Wm. Larkin Moore & Co.
Price: From **$3,350.00**

Rizzini Artemis O/U Shotgun

Same as Upland EL model except dummy sideplates with extensive game scene engraving. Fancy European walnut stock. Fitted case. Introduced 1996. Imported from Italy by Wm. Larkin Moore & Co.
Price: From **$2,100.00**

RIZZINI S782 EMEL O/U SHOTGUN

Gauge: 12, 2-3/4" chambers. **Barrel:** 26", 27.5" (Imp. Cyl. & Imp. Mod.). **Weight:** About 6.75 lbs. **Stock:** 14-1/2"x1-1/2"x2-1/4". Extra fancy select walnut. **Features:** Boxlock action with dummy sideplates, extensive engraving with gold inlaid game birds, silvered receiver, automatic ejectors, single selective trigger. Nizzoli leather case. Introduced 1996. Imported from Italy by Wm. Larkin Moore & Co.
Price: From **$11,450.00**

RUGER RED LABEL O/U SHOTGUNS

Gauge: 12, 20, 3" chambers; 28 2-3/4" chambers. **Barrel:** 26", 28" (skeet [two], Imp. Cyl., Full, Mod. screw-in choke tubes). Proved for steel shot. **Weight:** About 7 lbs. (20 ga.); 7-1/2 lbs. (12 ga.). **Length:** 43" overall (26" barrels). **Stock:** 14"x1-1/2"x2-1/2". Straight grain American walnut or black synthetic. Checkered pistol grip and forend, rubber butt pad. **Features:** Stainless steel receiver. Single selective mechanical trigger, selective automatic ejectors; serrated free-floating vent rib. Comes with two skeet, one Imp. Cyl., one Mod., one Full choke tube and wrench. Made in U.S. by Sturm, Ruger & Co.
Price: Red Label with pistol grip stock **$1,622.00**
Price: English Field with straight-grip stock **$1,622.00**
Price: All-Weather Red Label with black synthetic stock **$1,622.00**
Price: Sporting clays (30" bbl.) **$1,622.00**

Ruger Engraved Red Label O/U Shotgun

Similar to Red Label except scroll engraved receiver with 24-carat gold game bird (pheasant in 12 gauge, grouse in 20 gauge, woodcock in 28 gauge, duck on All-Weather 12 gauge). Introduced 2000.
Price: Engraved Red Label
(12, 20 and 28 gauge in 26" and 28" barrels) **$1,811.00**

SARSILMAZ O/U SHOTGUNS

Gauge: 12, 3" chambers. **Barrel:** 26", 28"; fixed chokes or choke tubes. **Weight:** NA. **Length:** NA. **Stock:** Oil-finished hardwood. **Features:** Double or single selective trigger, wide vent rib, chrome-plated parts, blued finish. Introduced 2000. Imported from Turkey by Armsport Inc.
Price: Double triggers; mod. and full or imp. cyl.
and mod. fixed chokes **$499.95**
Price: Single selective trigger; imp. cyl. and mod. or mod.
and full fixed chokes **$575.00**
Price: Single selective trigger, five choke tubes and wrench **$695.00**

SIGARMS SA5 O/U SHOTGUNS

Gauge: 12, 20, 3" chamber. **Barrel:** 26-1/2", 27" (Full, Imp. Mod., Mod., Imp. Cyl., Cyl. choke tubes). **Weight:** 6.9 lbs. (12 gauge), 5.9 lbs. (20 gauge). **Stock:** 14-1/2" x 1-1/2" x 2-1/2". Select grade walnut; checkered 20 lpi at grip and forend. **Features:** Single selective trigger, automatic ejectors; hand engraved detachable side plate; matte nickel receiver, rest blued; tapered bolt lock-up. Introduced 1997. Imported by SIGARMS, Inc.
Price: Field, 12 gauge **$2,670.00**
Price: Sporting clays **$2,800.00**
Price: Field 20 gauge **$2,670.00**

SILMA MODEL 70EJ DELUXE O/U SHOTGUNS

Gauge: 12 (3-1/2" chambers), 20, .410 (3" chambers), 28 (2-3/4" chambers). **Barrel:** 28" (12 and 20 gauge, fixed and tubed, 28 and .410 fixed), 26" (12 and 20 fixed). **Weight:** 7.6 lbs 12 gauge, 6.9 lbs, 20, 28 and .410. **Stock:** Checkered select European walnut, pistol grip, solid rubber recoil pad. **Features:** Monobloc construction, chrome-moly blued steel barrels, raised vent rib, automatic safety and ejectors, single selective trigger, gold plated, bead front sight. Brushed, engraved receiver. Introduced 2002. Clays models introduced 2003. Imported from Italy by Legacy Sports International.
Price: 12 gauge **$1,089.00**
Price: 20 gauge **$1,016.00**
Price: 28, .410 .... **$1,140.00**
Price: Sporting clays **$1,387.00**

Silma Model 70EJ Superlight O/U Shotgun

Similar to Silma 70EJ Deluxe except 12 gauge, 3" chambers, alloy receiver, weighs 5.6 lbs.
Price: 12, 20 multi-chokes (IC, M, F) **$1,191.00**

Silma Model 70EJ Standard O/U Shotgun

Similar to Silma 70EJ Deluxe except 12 and 20 gauge only, standard walnut stock, light engraving, silver-plated trigger.
Price: 12 gauge **$1,016.00**
Price: 20 gauge **$944.00**

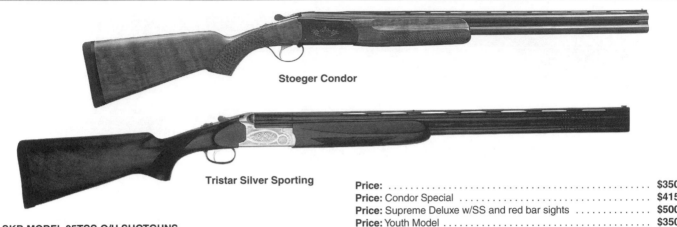

Stoeger Condor

Tristar Silver Sporting

SKB MODEL 85TSS O/U SHOTGUNS

Gauge: 12, 20, .410: 3"; 28, 2-3/4". **Barrel:** Chrome lined 26", 28", 30", 32" (w/choke tubes). **Weight:** 7 lbs., 7 oz. to 8 lbs., 14 oz. **Stock:** Hand-checkered American walnut with matte finish, Schnabel or grooved forend. Target stocks available in various styles. **Sights:** Metal bead front or HiViz competition sights. **Features:** Low profile boxlock action with Greener-style cross bolt; single selective trigger; manual safety. Back-bored barrels with lengthened forcing cones. Introduced 2004. Imported from Japan by G.U. Inc.

Price: Sporting clays, 12 or 20	**$1,949.00**
Price: Sporting clays, 28	**$1,949.00**
Price: Sporting clays set, 12 and 20	**$3,149.00**
Price: Skeet, 12 or 20	**$1,949.00**
Price: Skeet, 28 or .410	**$2,129.00 to $2,179.00**
Price: Skeet, three-barrel set, 20, 28, .410	**$4,679.00**
Price: Trap, standard or Monte Carlo	**$1,499.00**
Price: Trap adjustable comb	**$2,129.00**

SKB MODEL 585 O/U SHOTGUNS

Gauge: 12 or 20, 3"; 28, 2-3/4"; .410, 3". **Barrel:** 12 ga.-26", 28", 30", 32", 34" (InterChoke tubes); 20 ga.-26", 28" (InterChoke tubes); 28-26", 28" (InterChoke tubes); .410-26", 28" (InterChoke tubes). Ventilated side ribs. **Weight:** 6.6 to 8.5 lbs. **Length:** 43" to 51-3/8" overall. **Stock:** 14-1/8"x1-1/2"x2-3/16". Hand checkered walnut with high-gloss finish. Target stocks available in standard and Monte Carlo. **Sights:** Metal bead front (field), target style on skeet, trap, sporting clays. **Features:** Boxlock action; silver nitride finish with field or target pattern engraving; manual safety, automatic ejectors, single selective trigger. All 12 gauge barrels are back-bored, have lengthened forcing cones and longer choke tube system. Sporting clays models in 12 gauge with 28" or 30" barrels available with optional 3/8" step-up target-style rib, matte finish, nickel center bead, white front bead. Introduced 1992. Imported from Japan by G.U., Inc.

Price: Field	**$1,499.00**
Price: Two-barrel field set, 12 & 20	**$2,399.00**
Price: Two-barrel field set, 20 & 28 or 28 & .410	**$2,469.00**

SKB Model 585 Gold Package

Similar to Model 585 Field except gold-plated trigger, two gold-plated game inlays, Schnabel forend. Silver or blue receiver. Introduced 1998. Imported from Japan by G.U. Inc.

Price: 12, 20 ga.	**$1,689.00**
Price: 28, .410	**$1,749.00**

SKB Model 505 O/U Shotgun

Similar to Model 585 except blued receiver, standard bore diameter, standard InterChoke system on 12, 20, 28, different receiver engraving. Imported from Japan by G.U. Inc.

Price: Field, 12 (26", 28"), 20 (26", 28")	**$1,229.00**

STOEGER CONDOR SPECIAL O/U SHOTGUNS

Gauge: 12, 20, 2-3/4" 3" chambers. **Barrel:** 26", 28". **Weight:** 7.7 lbs. **Sights:** Brass bead. **Features:** IC and M screw-in choke tubes with each gun. Oil finished hardwood with pistol grip and forend. Auto safety, single trigger, automatic extractors.

Price:	**$350.00**
Price: Condor Special	**$415.00**
Price: Supreme Deluxe w/SS and red bar sights	**$500.00**
Price: Youth Model	**$350.00**
Price: Competition Model (w/ported bbls.)	**$579.00**

TRADITIONS CLASSIC SERIES O/U SHOTGUNS

Gauge: 12, 3"; 20, 3"; 16, 2-3/4"; 28, 2-3/4"; .410, 3". **Barrel:** 26" and 28". **Weight:** 6 lbs., 5 oz. to 7 lbs., 6 oz. **Length:** 43" to 45" overall. **Stock:** Walnut. **Features:** Single-selective trigger; chrome-lined barrels with screw-in choke tubes; extractors (Field Hunter and Field I models) or automatic ejectors (Field II and Field III models); rubber butt pad; top tang safety. Imported from Fausti of Italy by Traditions.

Price: Field Hunter: Blued receiver; 12 or 20 ga.; 26" bbl. has IC and Mod. tubes, 28" has mod. and full tubes	**$669.00**
Price: Field I: Blued receiver; 12, 20, 28 ga. or .410; fixed chokes (26" has I.C. and mod., 28" has mod. and full)	**$619.00**
Price: Field II: Coin-finish receiver; 12, 16, 20, 28 ga. or .410; gold trigger; choke tubes	**$789.00**
Price: Field III: Coin-finish receiver; gold engraving and trigger; 12 ga.; 26" or 28" bbl.; choke tubes	**$999.00**
Price: Upland II: Blued receiver; 12 or 20 ga.; English-style straight walnut stock; choke tubes	**$839.00**
Price: Upland III: Blued receiver, gold engraving; 20 ga.; high-grade pistol grip walnut stock; choke tubes	**$1,059.00**
Price: Upland III: Blued, gold engraved receiver, 12 ga. Round pistol grip stock, choke tubes	**$1,059.00**
Price: Sporting Clay II: Silver receiver; 12 ga.; ported barrels with skeet, i.c., mod. and full extended tubes	**$959.00**
Price: Sporting Clay III: Engraved receivers, 12 and 20 ga., walnut stock, vent rib, extended choke tubes	**$1,189.00**

TRADITIONS MAG 350 SERIES O/U SHOTGUNS

Gauge: 12, 3-1/2". **Barrel:** 24", 26" and 28". **Weight:** 7 lbs. to 7 lbs., 4 oz. **Length:** 41" to 45" overall. **Stock:** Walnut or composite with Mossy Oak® Break-Up™ or Advantage® Wetlands ™ camouflage. **Features:** Black matte, engraved receiver; vent rib; automatic ejectors; single-selective trigger; three screw-in choke tubes; rubber recoil pad; top tang safety. Imported from Fausti of Italy by Traditions.

Price: (Mag Hunter II: 28" black matte barrels, walnut stock, includes I.C., Mod. and Full tubes)	**$799.00**
Price: (Turkey II: 24" or 26" camo barrels, Break-Up™ camo stock, includes Mod., Full and X-Full tubes)	**$889.00**
Price: (Waterfowl II: 28" camo barrels, Advantage Wetlands camo stock, includes IC, Mod. and Full tubes)	**$899.00**

TRISTAR SILVER SPORTING O/U SHOTGUN

Gauge: 12, 2-3/4" chambers, 20 3" chambers. **Barrel:** 28", 30" (skeet, Imp. Cyl., Mod., Full choke tubes). **Weight:** 7-3/8 lbs. **Length:** 45-1/2" overall. **Stock:** 14-3/8"x1-1/2"x2-3/8". Figured walnut, cut checkering; sporting clays quick-mount buttpad. **Sights:** Target bead front. **Features:** Boxlock action with single selective trigger, automatic selective ejectors; special broadway channeled rib; vented barrel rib; chrome bores. Chrome-nickel finish on frame, with engraving. Introduced 1990. Imported from Italy by Tristar Sporting Arms Ltd.

Price:	**$799.00**

Tristar Silver II

Tristar TR-SC "Emilio Rizzini"

Tristar TR Royal "Emilio Rizzini"

Tristar TR-Mag "Emilio Rizzini"

Tristar TR-Mag "Emilio Rizzini"
Mossy Oak® Shadow Grass Camo

Tristar Silver II O/U Shotgun
Similar to the Silver except 26" barrel (Imp. Cyl., Mod., Full choke tubes, 12 and 20 ga.), 28" (Imp. Cyl., Mod., Full choke tubes, 12 ga. only), 26" (Imp. Cyl. & Mod. fixed chokes, 28 and .410), automatic selective ejectors. Weight is about 6 lbs., 15 oz. (12 ga., 26").
Price: **$669.00**

TRISTAR TR-SC "EMILIO RIZZINI" O/U SHOTGUN
Gauge: 12, 20, 3" chambers. **Barrel:** 28", 30" (Imp. Cyl., Mod., Full choke tubes). **Weight:** 7-1/2 lbs. **Length:** 46" overall (28" barrel). **Stock:** 1-1/2"x2-3/8"x14-3/8". Semi-fancy walnut; pistol grip with palm swell; semi-beavertail forend; black sporting clays recoil pad. **Features:** Silvered boxlock action with Four Locks locking system, auto ejectors, single selective (inertia) trigger, auto safety. Hard chrome bores. Vent 10mm rib with target-style front and mid-rib beads. Introduced 1998. Imported from Italy by Tristar Sporting Arms, Ltd.
Price: Sporting clay model **$1,047.00**
Price: 20 ga. **$1,127.00**

Tristar TR-Royal "Emilio Rizzini" O/U Shotgun
Similar to the TR-SC except has special parallel stock dimensions (1-1/2"x1-5/8"x14-3/8") to give low felt recoil; Rhino ported, extended choke tubes; solid barrel spacer; has "TR-Royal" gold engraved on the silvered receiver. Available in 12 gauge (28", 30") 20 and 28 gauge (28" only). Introduced 1999. Imported from Italy by Tristar Sporting Arms, Ltd.
Price: 12, 20, 28 ga. **$1,319.00**

Tristar TR-L "Emilio Rizzini" O/U Shotgun
Similar to the TR-SC except has stock dimensions designed for female shooters (1-1/2"x3"x13-1/2"). Standard grade walnut. Introduced 1998. Imported from Italy by Tristar Sporting Arms, Ltd.
Price: **$1,063.00**

TRISTAR TR-I, II "EMILIO RIZZINI" O/U SHOTGUNS
Gauge: 12, 20, 3" chambers (TR-I); 12, 16, 20, 28, .410 3" chambers. **Barrel:** 12 ga., 26" (Imp. Cyl. & Mod.), 28" (Mod. & Full); 20 ga., 26" (Imp. Cyl. & Mod.), fixed chokes. **Weight:** 7-1/2 lbs. **Stock:** 1-1/2"x2-3/8"x14-3/8". Walnut with palm swell pistol grip, hand checkering, semi-beavertail forend, black recoil pad. **Features:** Boxlock action with blued finish, Four Locks locking system, gold single selective (inertia) trigger system, automatic safety, extractors. Introduced 1998. Imported from Italy by Tristar Sporting Arms, Ltd.
Price: TR-I. **$779.00**
Price: TR-II (automatic ejectors, choke tubes) 12, 16 ga. **$919.00**
Price: 20, 28 ga., .410 . . . . **$969.00**

Tristar TR-Mag "Emilio Rizzini" O/U Shotguns
Similar to TR-I, 3-1/2" chambers; choke tubes; 24" or 28" barrels with three choke tubes; extractors; auto safety. Matte blue finish on all metal, non-reflective wood finish. Introduced 1998. Imported from Italy by Tristar Sporting Arms, Ltd.
Price: **$799.00**
Price: Mossy Oak® Break-Up™ camo **$969.00**
Price: Mossy Oak® Shadow Grass camo **$969.00**
Price: 10 ga., Mossy Oak® camo patterns **$1,132.10**

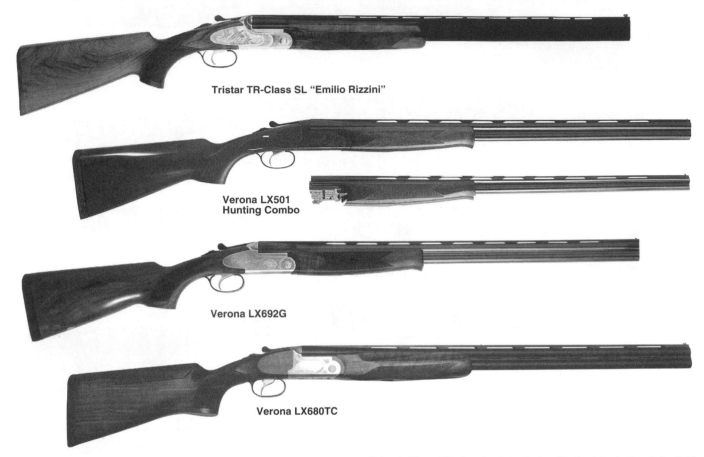

Tristar TR-Class SL "Emilio Rizzini"

Verona LX501 Hunting Combo

Verona LX692G

Verona LX680TC

TRISTAR TR-CLASS SL "EMILIO RIZZINI" O/U SHOTGUN
Gauge: 12, 2-3/4" chambers. **Barrel:** 28", 30". **Weight:** 7-3/4 lbs. **Stock:** Fancy walnut, hand checkering, semi-beavertail forend, black recoil pad, gloss finish. **Features:** Hand-fitted gun. Boxlock action with silvered, engraved sideplates; Four Lock locking system; automatic ejectors; hard chrome bores; vent tapered 7mm rib with target-style front bead. Introduced 1999. Imported from Italy by Tristar Sporting Arms, Ltd.
Price: **$1,775.00**

TRISTAR WS/OU 12 O/U SHOTGUN
Gauge: 12, 3-1/2" chambers. **Barrel:** 28" or 30" (Imp. Cyl., Mod., Full choke tubes). **Weight:** 6 lbs., 15 oz. **Length:** 46" overall. **Stock:** 14-1/8"x1-1/8"x2-3/8". European walnut with cut checkering, black vented recoil pad, matte finish. **Features:** Boxlock action with single selective trigger, automatic selective ejectors; chrome bores. Matte metal finish. Imported by Tristar Sporting Arms Ltd.
Price: **$645.00**

VERONA LX501 HUNTING O/U SHOTGUNS
Gauge: 12, 20, 28, .410 (2-3/4", 3" chambers). **Barrel:** 28"; 12, 20 ga. have Interchoke tubes, 28 ga. and .410 have fixed Full & Mod. **Weight:** 6-7 lbs. **Stock:** Matte-finished walnut with machine-cut checkering. **Features:** Gold-plated single-selective trigger; ejectors; engraved, blued receiver, non-automatic safety; coil spring-operated firing pins. Introduced 1999. Imported from Italy by B.C. Outdoors.
Price: 12 and 20 ga. **$878.08**
Price: 28 ga. and .410 . . . . **$926.72**
Price: .410 . . . . **$907.01**
Price: Combos 20/28, 28/.410 . . . . **$1,459.20**

Verona LX692 Gold Hunting O/U Shotguns
Similar to Verona LX501 except engraved, silvered receiver with false sideplates showing gold inlaid bird hunting scenes on three sides;

Schnabel forend tip; hand-cut checkering; black rubber butt pad. Available in 12 and 20 gauge only, five Interchoke tubes. Introduced 1999. Imported from Italy by B.C. Outdoors.
Price: **$1,295.00**
Price: LX692G Combo 28/.410 . . . . **$2,192.40**

Verona LX680 Sporting O/U Shotgun
Similar to Verona LX501 except engraved, silvered receiver; ventilated middle rib; beavertail forend; hand-cut checkering; available in 12 or 20 gauge only with 2-3/4" chambers. Introduced 1999. Imported from Italy by B.C. Outdoors.
Price: **$1,159.68**

Verona LX680 Skeet/Sporting/Trap O/U Shotgun
Similar to Verona LX501 except skeet or trap stock dimensions; beavertail forend, palm swell on pistol grip; ventilated center barrel rib. Introduced 1999. Imported from Italy by B.C. Outdoors.
Price: **$1,736.96**

Verona LX692 Gold Sporting O/U Shotgun
Similar to Verona LX680 except false sideplates have gold-inlaid bird hunting scenes on three sides; red high-visibility front sight. Introduced 1999. Imported from Italy by B.C. Outdoors.
Price: Skeet/sporting **$1,765.12**
Price: Trap (32" barrel, 7-7/8 lbs.) **$1,594.80**

VERONA LX680 COMPETITION TRAP O/U SHOTGUNS
Gauge: 12. **Barrel:** 30" O/U, 32" single bbl. **Weight:** 8-3/8 lbs. combo, 7 lbs. single. **Stock:** Walnut. **Sights:** White front, mid-rib bead. **Features:** Interchangeable barrels switch from o/u to single configurations. 5 Briley chokes in combo, 4 in single bbl. extended forcing cones, ported barrels 32" with raised rib. By B.C. Outdoors.
Price: Trap Single (LX680TGTSB) **$1,736.96**
Price: Trap Combo (LX680TC) **$2,553.60**

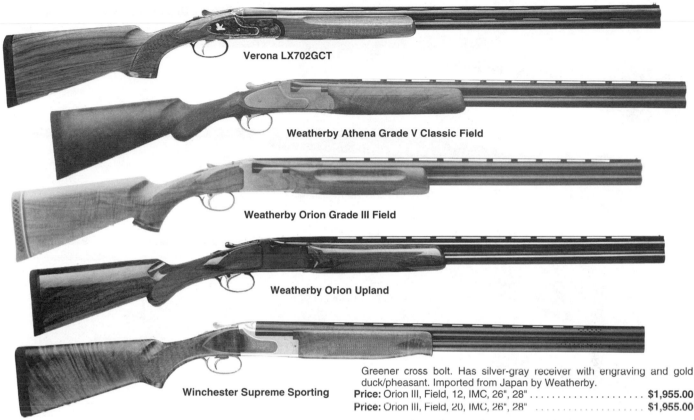

Verona LX702GCT

Weatherby Athena Grade V Classic Field

Weatherby Orion Grade III Field

Weatherby Orion Upland

Winchester Supreme Sporting

VERONA LX702 GOLD TRAP COMBO O/U SHOTGUNS

Gauge: 20/28, 2-3/4" chamber. **Barrel:** 30". **Weight:** 7 lbs. **Stock:** Turkish walnut with beavertail forearm. **Sights:** White front bead. **Features:** 2-barrel competition gun. Color case-hardened side plates and receiver with gold inlaid pheasant. Vent rib between barrels. 5 Interchokes. Imported from Italy by B.C. Outdoors.
Price: Combo **$2,467.84**
Price: 20 ga. **$1,829.12**

Verona LX702 Skeet/Trap O/U Shotguns

Similar to Verona LX702. Both are 12 gauge and 2-3/4" chamber. Skeet has 28" barrel and weighs 7-3/4 lbs. Trap has 32" barrel and weighs 7-7/8 lbs. By B.C. Outdoors.
Price: Skeet **$1,829.12**
Price: Trap **$1,829.12**

WEATHERBY ATHENA GRADE V CLASSIC FIELD O/U SHOTGUN

Gauge: 12, 20, 3" chambers. **Barrel:** 26", 28", IMC multi-choke tubes. **Weight:** 12 ga., 7-1/4 to 8 lbs.; 20 ga. 6-1/2 to 7-1/4 lbs. **Stock:** Oil-finished American Claro walnut with fine-line checkering, rounded pistol grip and slender forend. **Features:** Old English recoil pad. Sideplate receiver has rose and scroll engraving.
Price: **$3,037.00**

Weatherby Athena Grade III Classic Field O/U Shotgun

Similar to Athena Grade V, has Grade III Claro walnut with oil finish, rounded pistol grip, slender forend; silver nitride/gray receiver has rose and scroll engraving with gold-overlay upland game scenes. Introduced 1999. Imported from Japan by Weatherby.
Price: 12, 20, 28 ga. **$2,173.00**

WEATHERBY ORION GRADE III FIELD O/U SHOTGUNS

Gauge: 12, 20, 3" chambers. **Barrel:** 26", 28", IMC multi-choke tubes. **Weight:** 6-1/2 to 8 lbs. **Stock:** 14-1/4"x1-1/2"x2-1/2". American walnut, checkered grip and forend. Rubber recoil pad. **Features:** Selective automatic ejectors, single selective inertia trigger. Top tang safety, Greener cross bolt. Has silver-gray receiver with engraving and gold duck/pheasant. Imported from Japan by Weatherby.
Price: Orion III, Field, 12, IMC, 26", 28" **$1,955.00**
Price: Orion III, Field, 20, IMC, 26", 28" **$1,955.00**

Weatherby Orion Grade II Classic Field O/U Shotgun

Similar to Orion Grade III Field except stock has high-gloss finish, and bird on receiver is not gold. Available in 12 gauge, 26", 28", 30" barrels, 20 gauge, 26" 28", both with 3" chambers, 28 gauge, 26", 2-3/4" chambers. All have IMC choke tubes. Imported from Japan by Weatherby.
Price: **$1,622.00**

Weatherby Orion Upland O/U Shotgun

Similar to Orion Grade III Field. Plain blued receiver, gold W on trigger guard; rounded pistol grip, slender forend of Claro walnut with high-gloss finish; black butt pad. Available in 12 and 20 gauge with 26" and 28" barrels. Introduced 1999. Imported from Japan by Weatherby.
Price: **$1,299.00**

WEATHERBY ORION SSC O/U SHOTGUN

Gauge: 12, 3" chambers. **Barrel:** 28", 30", 32" (skeet, SC1, Imp. Cyl., SC2, Mod. IMC choke tubes). **Weight:** About 8 lbs. **Stock:** 14-3/4"x2-1/4"x1-1/2". Claro walnut with satin oil finish; Schnabel forend tip; sporter-style pistol grip; Pachmayr Decelerator recoil pad. **Features:** Designed for sporting clays competition. Has lengthened forcing cones and back-boring; ported barrels with 12mm grooved rib with mid-bead sight; mechanical trigger is adjustable for length of pull. Introduced 1998. Imported from Japan by Weatherby.
Price: SSC (Super Sporting Clays) **$2,059.00**

WINCHESTER SELECT O/U SHOTGUNS

Gauge: 12, 2-3/4", 3" chambers. **Barrel:** 28", 30", Invector Plus choke tubes. **Weight:** 7 lbs. 6 oz. to 7 lbs. 12. oz. **Length:** 45" overall (28" barrel). **Stock:** Checkered walnut stock. **Features:** Chrome-plated chambers; back-bored barrels; tang barrel selector/safety; deep-blued finish. Introduced 2000. From U.S. Repeating Arms. Co.
Price: Select Field (26" or 28" barrel, 6mm vent rib) **$1,498.00**
Price: Select Energy **$1,950.00**
Price: Select Elegance **$2,320.00**
Price: Select Energy Trap **$1,871.00**
Price: Select Energy Trap adjustable **$2,115.00**
Price: Select Energy Sporting adjustable **$2,115.00**

Variety of models for utility and sporting use, including some competitive shooting.

Charles Daly Superior Hunter

Charles Daly Empire Hunter AE-MC

Charles Daly Diamond DL

Charles Daly Diamond Regent DL

ARRIETA SIDELOCK DOUBLE SHOTGUNS
Gauge: 12, 16, 20, 28, .410. **Barrel:** Length and chokes to customer specs. **Weight:** To customer specs. **Stock:** To customer specs. Straight English with checkered butt (standard), or pistol grip. Select European walnut with oil finish. **Features:** Essentially custom gun with myriad options. H&H pattern hand-detachable sidelocks, selective automatic ejectors, double triggers (hinged front) standard. Some have self-opening action. Finish and engraving to customer specs. Imported from Spain by Wingshooting Adventures.

Price: Model 557, auto ejectors. From **$3,250.00**
Price: Model 570, auto ejectors. From **$3,950.00**
Price: Model 578, auto ejectors. From **$4,350.00**
Price: Model 600 Imperial, self-opening. From **$6,050.00**
Price: Model 601 Imperial Tiro, self-opening. From **$6,950.00**
Price: Model 801. From **$9,135.00**
Price: Model 802. From **$9,135.00**
Price: Model 803. From **$6,930.00**
Price: Model 871, auto ejectors. From **$5,060.00**
Price: Model 872, self-opening. From **$12,375.00**
Price: Model 873, self-opening. From **$8,200.00**
Price: Model 874, self-opening. From **$9,250.00**
Price: Model 875, self-opening. From **$14,900.00**

CHARLES DALY SUPERIOR HUNTER AND SUPERIOR MC DOUBLE SHOTGUNS
Gauge: 12, 20, 3" chambers; 28, 2-3/4" chambers. **Barrel:** 28" (Mod. & Full) 26" (Imp. Cyl. & Mod.). **Weight:** About 7 lbs. **Stock:** Checkered walnut pistol grip buttstock, splinter forend. **Features:** Silvered, engraved receiver; chrome-lined barrels; gold single trigger; automatic safety; extractors; gold bead front sight. Introduced 1997. Imported from Italy by K.B.I., Inc.
Price: Superior Hunter, 28 gauge and .410 . . . . **$1,659.00**
Price: Superior Hunter MC 26"-28" **$1,629.00**

Charles Daly Empire Hunter AE-MC Double Shotgun
Similar to Superior Hunter except deluxe wood English-style stock, game scene engraving, automatic ejectors. Introduced 1997. Imported from Italy by K.B.I., Inc.
Price: 12 or 20 . . . . **$2,119.00**

CHARLES DALY DIAMOND DL DOUBLE SHOTGUN
Gauge: 12, 20, .410, 3" chambers, 28, 2-3/4" chambers. **Barrel:** 28" (Mod. & Full), 26" (Imp. Cyl. & Mod.), 26" (Full & Full, .410). **Weight:** From 5 lbs. to 7 lbs. **Stock:** Select fancy European walnut, English-style butt, beavertail forend; hand-checkered, hand-rubbed oil finish. **Features:** Drop-forged action with gas escape valves; demi-block barrels with concave rib; selective automatic ejectors; hand-detachable double safety sidelocks with hand-engraved rose and scrollwork. Hinged front trigger. Color case-hardened receiver. Introduced 1997. Imported from Spain by K.B.I., Inc.
Price: . . . . **Special order only**

CHARLES DALY DIAMOND REGENT DL DOUBLE SHOTGUN
Gauge: 12, 20, .410, 3" chambers, 28, 2-3/4" chambers. **Barrel:** 28" (Mod. & Full), 26" (Imp. Cyl. & Mod.), 26" (Full & Full, .410). **Weight:** About 5-7 lbs. **Stock:** Special select fancy European walnut, English-style butt, splinter forend; hand-checkered; hand-rubbed oil finish. **Features:** Drop-forged action with gas escape valves; demi-block barrels of chrome-nickel steel with concave rib; selective automatic-ejectors; hand-detachable, double-safety H&H sidelocks with demi-relief hand engraving; H&H pattern easy-opening feature; hinged trigger; coin finished action. Introduced 1997. Imported from Spain by K.B.I., Inc.
Price: Special Custom Order . . . . **NA**

CHARLES DALY FIELD II, AE-MC HUNTER DOUBLE SHOTGUN
Gauge: 12, 20, 28, .410 (3" chambers; 28 has 2-3/4"). **Barrel:** 32" (Mod. & Mod.), 28, 30" (Mod. & Full), 26" (Imp. Cyl. & Mod.) .410 (Full & Full). **Weight:** 6 lbs. to 11.4 lbs. **Stock:** Checkered walnut pistol grip and forend. **Features:** Silvered, engraved receiver; gold single selective trigger in 10, 12, and 20 ga.; double triggers in 28 and .410; automatic safety; extractors; gold bead front sight. Introduced 1997. Imported from Spain by K.B.I., Inc.
Price: 28 ga., .410-bore **$1,189.00**
Price: 12 or 20 AE-MC **$1,099.00**

Charles Daly Field II Hunter

EAA Baikal IZH43K Bounty Hunter

EAA Baikal MP-213

Fabarm Classic Lion

Fabarm Classic Lion Elite

DAKOTA PREMIER GRADE SHOTGUN

Gauge: 12, 16, 20, 28, .410. **Barrel:** 27". **Weight:** NA. **Length:** NA. **Stock:** Exhibition-grade English walnut, hand-rubbed oil finish with straight grip and splinter forend. **Features:** French grey finish; 50 percent coverage engraving; double triggers; selective ejectors. Finished to customer specifications. Made in U.S. by Dakota Arms.

Price: 12, 16, 20 gauge **$13,950.00**
Price: 28 gauge and .410 . . . . **$15,345.00**

Dakota Legend Shotgun

Similar to Premier Grade except has special selection English walnut, full-coverage scroll engraving, oak and leather case. Made in U.S. by Dakota Arms.

Price: 12, 16, 20 gauge **$18,000.00**
Price: 28 gauge and .410 . . . . **$19,800.00**

EAA BAIKAL BOUNTY HUNTER IZH43K SHOTGUN

Gauge: 12, 3" chambers. **Barrel:** 18-1/2", 20", 24", 26", 28", three choke tubes. **Weight:** 7.28 lbs. **Overall length:** NA. **Stock:** Walnut, checkered forearm and grip. **Features:** Machined receiver; hammer-forged barrels with chrome-lined bores; external hammers; double triggers (single, selective trigger available); rifle barrel inserts optional. Imported by European American Armory.

Price: . . . . **$379.00 to 399.00**

EAA BAIKAL IZH43 BOUNTY HUNTER SHOTGUN

Gauge: 12, 3" chambers. **Barrel:** 20", 24", 26", 28"; imp., mod. and full choke tubes. **Stock:** Hardwood or walnut; checkered forend and grip.

Features: Hammer forged barrel; internal hammers; extractors; engraved receiver; automatic tang safety; non-glare rib. Imported by European American Armory.

Price: IZH43 Bounty Hunter (12 gauge, 2-3/4" chambers, 20" brl., dbl. triggers, hardwood stock). **$329.00**
Price: IZH43 Bounty Hunter (20 gauge, 3" chambers, 20" bbl., dbl. triggers, walnut stock) **$359.00**

E.M.F. HARTFORD MODEL COWBOY SHOTGUN

Gauge: 12. **Barrel:** 20". **Weight:** NA. **Length:** NA. **Stock:** Checkered walnut. **Sights:** Center bead. **Features:** Exposed hammers; color case-hardened receiver; blued barrel. Introduced 2001. Imported from Spain by E.M.F. Co. Inc.

Price: **$625.00**

FABARM CLASSIC LION DOUBLE SHOTGUNS

Gauge: 12, 3" chambers. **Barrel:** 26", 28", 30" (Cyl., Imp. Cyl., Mod., Imp. Mod., Full choke tubes). **Weight:** 7.2 lbs. **Length:** 44.5"-48.5. **Stock:** English-style or pistol grip oil-finished European walnut. **Features:** Boxlock action with double triggers; automatic ejectors; automatic safety. Introduced 1998. Imported from Italy by Heckler & Koch, Inc.

Price: Grade I **$1,499.00**
Price: Grade II **$2,099.00**
Price: Elite (color case-hardened type finish, 44.5") **$1,689.00**

A.H. Fox DE Grade

Garbi Model 100

Bill Hanus Birdgun

FOX, A.H., SIDE-BY-SIDE SHOTGUNS

Gauge: 16, 20, 28, .410. **Barrel:** Length and chokes to customer specifications. Rust-blued Chromox or Krupp steel. **Weight:** 5-1/2 to 6-3/4 lbs. **Stock:** Dimensions to customer specifications. Hand-checkered Turkish Circassian walnut with hand-rubbed oil finish. Straight, semi or full pistol grip; splinter, Schnabel or beavertail forend; traditional pad, hard rubber buttplate or skeleton butt. **Features:** Boxlock action with automatic ejectors; double or Fox single selective trigger. Scalloped, rebated and color case-hardened receiver; hand finished and hand-engraved. Grades differ in engraving, inlays, grade of wood, amount of hand finishing. Introduced 1993. Made in U.S. by Connecticut Shotgun Mfg.

Price: CE Grade **$11,000.00**
Price: XE Grade **$12,500.00**
Price: DE Grade **$15,000.00**
Price: FE Grade **$20,000.00**
Price: Exhibition Grade **$30,000.00**
Price: 28/.410 CE Grade **$12,500.00**
Price: 28/.410 XE Grade **$14,000.00**
Price: 28/.410 DE Grade **$16,500.00**
Price: 28/.410 FE Grade **$21,500.00**
Price: 28/.410 Exhibition Grade **$30,000.00**
Price: 28 or .410-bore **$1,500.00**

GARBI MODEL 100 DOUBLE SHOTGUN

Gauge: 12, 16, 20, 28. **Barrel:** 26", 28", choked to customer specs. **Weight:** 5-1/2 to 7-1/2 lbs. **Stock:** 14-1/2"x2-1/4"x1-1/2". European walnut. Straight grip, checkered butt, classic forend. **Features:** Sidelock action, automatic ejectors, double triggers standard. Color case-hardened action, coin finish optional. Single trigger; beavertail forend, etc. optional. Five additional models available. Imported from Spain by Wm. Larkin Moore.

Price: From **$4,850.00**

Garbi Model 101 Side-by-Side Shotgun

Similar to the Garbi Model 100 except hand engraved with scroll engraving; select walnut stock; better overall quality than the Model 100. Imported from Spain by Wm. Larkin Moore.

Price: From **$6,250.00**

Garbi Model 103 A & B Side-by-Side Shotguns

Similar to the Garbi Model 100 except has Purdey-type fine scroll and rosette engraving. Better overall quality than the Model 101. Model 103B has nickel-chrome steel barrels, H&H-type easy opening mechanism; other mechanical details remain the same. Imported from Spain by Wm. Larkin Moore.

Price: Model 103A. From **$8,000.00**
Price: Model 103B. From **$11,800.00**

Garbi Model 200 Side-by-Side Shotgun

Similar to the Garbi Model 100 except has heavy-duty locks, magnum proofed. Very fine Continental-style floral and scroll engraving, well figured walnut stock. Other mechanical features remain the same. Imported from Spain by Wm. Larkin Moore.

Price: **$11,200.00**

HANUS BIRDGUN SHOTGUN

Gauge: 16, 20, 28 ga. **Barrel:** 27", 20 and 28 ga.; 28", 16 ga. (skeet 1 & skeet 2). **Weight:** 5 lbs., 4 oz. to 6 lbs., 4 oz. **Stock:** 14-3/8"x1-1/2"x2-3/8", with 1/4" cast-off. Select walnut. **Features:** Boxlock action with ejectors; splinter forend, straight English grip; checkered butt; English leather-covered handguard and AyA snap caps included. Made by AyA. Introduced 1998. Imported from Spain by Bill Hanus Birdguns.

Price: **$2,795.00**

ITHACA CLASSIC DOUBLES SKEET GRADE SxS SHOTGUN

Gauge: 20, 28, 2-3/4" chambers, .410, 3". **Barrel:** 26", 28", 30", fixed chokes. **Weight:** 5 lbs., 14 oz. (20 gauge). **Stock:** 14-1/2"x2-1/4"x1-3/8". High-grade American black walnut, hand-rubbed oil finish; splinter or beavertail forend, straight or pistol grip. **Features:** Double triggers, ejectors; color case-hardened, engraved action body with matted top surfaces. Introduced 1999. Made in U.S. by Ithaca Classic Doubles.

Price: From **$5,999.00**

ITHACA CLASSIC DOUBLES GRADE 4E CLASSIC SXS SHOTGUN

Gauge: 10, 12, 16, 20, 28, .410 bore, 2-3/4" and 3" chambers. **Barrels:** 26", 28", 30". **Weight:** 5 lbs., 5 oz. to 6 lbs., 6 oz. **Features:** Gold-plated triggers, jewelled barrel flats and hand-turned locks. Feather crotch and flame-grained black walnut hand-checkered 28 lpi with fleur-de-lis pattern. Action body engraved with three game scenes and bank note scroll, color case-hardened. Introduced 1999. Made in U.S.A. by Ithaca Classic Doubles.

Price: From **$7,500.00**

ITHACA CLASSIC DOUBLES GRADE 5E SXS SHOTGUN

Gauge: 10, 12, 16, 20, 28, .410 bore, 2-3/4" and 3" chambers. **Barrels:** 26", 28", 30". **Weight:** 5 lbs., 5 oz. to 6 lbs., 6 oz. **Stock:** High-grade Turkish and American walnut and are hand-checkered. **Features:** Completely handmade, based on the early Ithaca engraving patterns of master engraver William McGraw. The hand engraving is at 90% coverage in deep chiseled floral scroll with game scenes in 24kt gold inlays. Available in 12, 16, 20, 28 gauges and .410 bore including two-barrel combination sets in 16/20 ga. and 28/.410 bore. Introduced 2003. Made in U.S.A. by Ithaca Classic Doubles.

Price: From **$8,500.00**

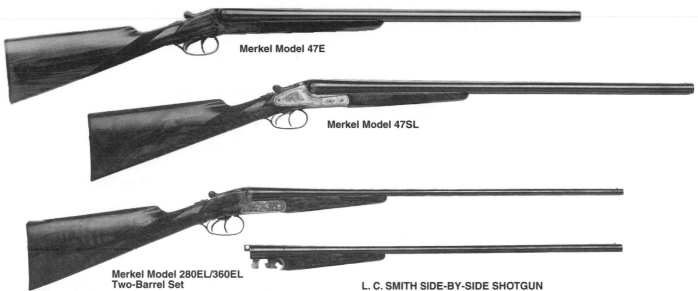

Merkel Model 47E

Merkel Model 47SL

Merkel Model 280EL/360EL
Two-Barrel Set

ITHACA CLASSIC DOUBLES GRADE 6E SIDE-BY-SIDE SHOTGUN
Gauge: 10, 12, 16, 20, 28, .410 bore, 2-3/4" and 3" chambers. **Barrels:** 26", 28", 30". **Weight:** 5 lbs., 5 oz. to 6 lbs., 6 oz. **Stock:** Handmade of best quality American, Turkish or English walnut with hand checkering. **Features:** Features hand engraving of fine English scroll coupled with game scenes and 24kt gold inlays. All metal work is finished in traditional bone and charcoal color case-hardening and deep rust blue. Available in 12, 16, 20, 28 gauges and .410 bore. Introduced 2003. Made in U.S.A. by Ithaca Classic Doubles.
Price: From **$10,000.00**

ITHACA CLASSIC DOUBLES GRADE 7E CLASSIC SXS SHOTGUN
Gauge: 10, 12, 16, 20, 28, .410 bore, 2-3/4" and 3" chambers. **Barrels:** 26", 28", 30". **Weight:** 5 lbs., 5 oz. to 6 lbs., 6 oz. **Stock:** Exhibition grade American black walnut stock and forend with eight-panel fleur-de-lis borders. **Features:** Engraved with banknote scroll and flat 24k gold game scenes: gold setter and gold pointer on opposite action sides, American bald eagle inlaid on bottom plate. Hand polished, jewelled ejectors and locks. Introduced 1999. Made in U.S.A. by Ithaca Classic Doubles.
Price: From **$11,000.00**

ITHACA CLASSIC DOUBLES SOUSA GRADE SIDE-BY-SIDE SHOTGUN
Gauge: 10, 12, 16, 20, 28, .410 bore, 3" chambers. **Barrels:** 26", 28", 30". **Weight:** 5 lbs., 5 oz. to 6 lbs., 6 oz. **Stock:** American black walnut, hand-carved and checkered. **Features:** Presentation grade hand-engraving with 24-karat gold inlays; tuned action and hand-applied finishes. Made in U.S.A. by Ithaca Classic Doubles.
Price: From **$18,000.00**

KIMBER VALIER GRADE I and II SHOTGUN
Gauge: 20, 3" chambers. **Barrels:** 26" or 28", IC and M. **Weight:** 6 lbs. 8 oz. **Stock:** Turkish walnut, English style. **Features:** Sidelock design, double triggers, 50-percent engraving; 24 lpi checkering; auto-ejectors (extractors only on Grade I). Color case-hardened sidelocks, rust blue barrels. Imported from Turkey by Kimber Mfg., Inc.
Price: Grade I **$3,879.00**
Price: Grade II **$4,480.00**

LEBEAU — COURALLY BOXLOCK SIDE-BY-SIDE SHOTGUN
Gauge: 12, 16, 20, 28, .410-bore. **Barrel:** 25" to 32". **Weight:** To customer specifications. **Stock:** French walnut. **Features:** Anson & Deely-type action with automatic ejectors; single or double triggers. Custom gun built to customer specifications. Imported from Belgium by Wm. Larkin Moore.
Price: From **$25,500.00**

L. C. SMITH SIDE-BY-SIDE SHOTGUN
Gauge: 12, 20. **Barrel:** 26", 28". **Weight:** 6 or 6-1/4 lbs. **Stock:** Checkered walnut w/recoil pad. **Features:** 3" chambers, single trigger, selective automatic ejectors; solid rib, bead front sight. Imported from Italy by Marlin. Introduced 2005.
Price: **$1,884.00**

LEBEAU-COURALLY SIDELOCK SIDE-BY-SIDE SHOTGUN
Gauge: 12, 16, 20, 28, .410-bore. **Barrel:** 25" to 32". **Weight:** To customer specifications. **Stock:** Fancy French walnut. **Features:** Holland & Holland-type action with automatic ejectors; single or double triggers. Custom gun built to customer specifications. Imported from Belgium by Wm. Larkin Moore.
Price: From **$56,000.00**

MERKEL MODEL 47E, 147E SIDE-BY-SIDE SHOTGUNS
Gauge: 12, 3" chambers, 16, 2-3/4" chambers, 20, 3" chambers. **Barrel:** 12, 16 ga.-28"; 20 ga.-26-3/4" (Imp. Cyl. & Mod., Mod. & Full). **Weight:** About 6-3/4 lbs. (12 ga.). **Stock:** Oil-finished walnut; straight English or pistol grip. **Features:** Anson & Deeley-type boxlock action with single selective or double triggers, automatic safety, cocking indicators. Color case-hardened receiver with standard arabesque engraving. Imported from Germany by GSI.
Price: Model 47E (H&H ejectors) **$3,295.00**
Price: Model 147E (as above with ejectors) **$3,995.00**

Merkel Model 47SL, 147SL Side-by-Side Shotguns
Similar to Model 47E except H&H style sidelock action with cocking indicators, ejectors. Silver-grayed receiver and sideplates have arabesque engraving, engraved border and screws (Model 47S), or fine hunting scene engraving (Model 147S). Imported from Germany by GSI.
Price: Model 47SL **$5,995.00**
Price: Model 147SL **$7,995.00**
Price: Model 247SL (English-style engraving, large scrolls) **$7,995.00**
Price: Model 447SL (English-style engraving, small scrolls) **$9,995.00**

Merkel Model 280EL, 360EL Shotguns
Similar to Model 47E except smaller frame. Greener cross bolt with double under-barrel locking lugs, fine engraved hunting scenes on silver-grayed receiver, luxury-grade wood, Anson and Deely box-lock action. H&H ejectors, single-selective or double triggers. Introduced 2000. From Merkel.
Price: Model 280EL (28 gauge, 28" barrel, Imp. Cyl. and
Mod. chokes) **$5,795.00**
Price: Model 360EL (.410, 28" barrel, Mod. and
Full chokes) **$5,795.00**
Price: Model 280/360EL two-barrel set (28 and .410 gauge
as above) **$8,295.00**

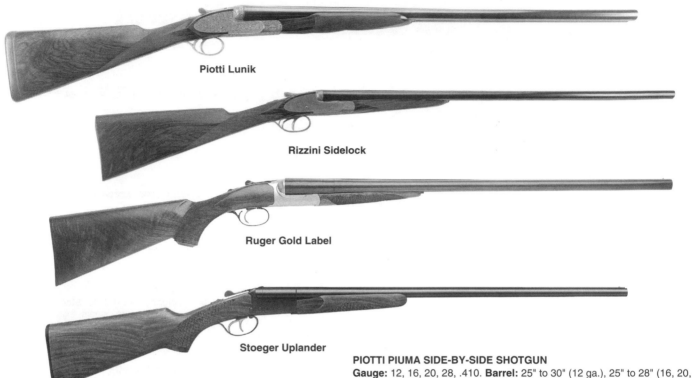

Piotti Lunik

Rizzini Sidelock

Ruger Gold Label

Stoeger Uplander

Merkel Model 280SL and 360SL Shotguns

Similar to Model 280EL and 360EL except has sidelock action, double triggers, English-style arabesque engraving. Introduced 2000. From Merkel.

Price: Model 280SL (28 gauge, 28" barrel, Imp. Cyl. and
Mod. chokes) **$8,495.00**
Price: Model 360SL (.410, 28" barrel, Mod. and
Full chokes) **$8,495.00**
Price: Model 280/360SL two-barrel set **$11,995.00**

PIOTTI KING NO. 1 SIDE-BY-SIDE SHOTGUN

Gauge: 12, 16, 20, 28, .410. **Barrel:** 25" to 30" (12 ga.), 25" to 28" (16, 20, 28, .410). To customer specs. Chokes as specified. **Weight:** 6-1/2 lbs. to 8 lbs. (12 ga. to customer specs.). **Stock:** Dimensions to customer specs. Finely figured walnut; straight grip with checkered butt with classic splinter forend and hand-rubbed oil finish standard. Pistol grip, beavertail forend. **Features:** Holland & Holland pattern sidelock action, automatic ejectors. Double trigger; non-selective single trigger optional. Coin finish standard; color case-hardened optional. Top rib; level, file-cut; concave, ventilated optional. Very fine, full coverage scroll engraving with small floral bouquets. Imported from Italy by Wm. Larkin Moore.
Price: From **$29,600.00**

Piotti King Extra Side-by-Side Shotgun

Similar to the Piotti King No. 1 except with upgraded engraving. Choice of any type of engraving, including bulino game scene engraving and game scene engraving with gold inlays. Engraved and signed by a master engraver. Other mechanical specifications remain the same. Imported from Italy by Wm. Larkin Moore.
Price: From **$35,000.00**

Piotti Lunik Side-by-Side Shotgun

Similar to the Piotti King No. 1 in overall quality. Has Renaissance-style large scroll engraving in relief. Best quality Holland & Holland-pattern sidelock ejector double with chopper lump (demi-bloc) barrels. Other mechanical specifications remain the same. Imported from Italy by Wm. Larkin Moore.
Price: From **$30,900.00**

PIOTTI PIUMA SIDE-BY-SIDE SHOTGUN

Gauge: 12, 16, 20, 28, .410. **Barrel:** 25" to 30" (12 ga.), 25" to 28" (16, 20, 28, .410). **Weight:** 5-1/2 to 6-1/4 lbs. (20 ga.). **Stock:** Dimensions to customer specs. Straight grip stock with walnut checkered butt, classic splinter forend, hand-rubbed oil finish are standard; pistol grip, beavertail forend, satin luster finish optional. **Features:** Anson & Deeley boxlock ejector double with chopper lump barrels. Level, file-cut rib, light scroll and rosette engraving, scalloped frame. Double triggers; single non-selective optional. Coin finish standard, color case-hardened optional. Imported from Italy by Wm. Larkin Moore.
Price: From **$14,800.00**

RIZZINI SIDELOCK SIDE-BY-SIDE SHOTGUN

Gauge: 12, 16, 20, 28, .410. **Barrel:** 25" to 30" (12, 16, 20 ga.), 25" to 28" (28, .410). To customer specs. Chokes as specified. **Weight:** 6-1/2 lbs. to 8 lbs. (12 ga. to customer specs). **Stock:** Dimensions to customer specs. Finely figured walnut; straight grip with checkered butt with classic splinter forend and hand-rubbed oil finish standard. Pistol grip, beavertail forend. **Features:** Sidelock action, auto ejectors. Double triggers or non-selective single trigger standard. Coin finish standard. Imported from Italy by Wm. Larkin Moore.
Price: 12, 20 ga. From **$66,900.00**
Price: 28, .410 bore. From **$75,500.00**

RUGER GOLD LABEL SIDE-BY-SIDE SHOTGUN

Gauge: 12, 3" chambers. **Barrel:** 28" with skeet tubes. **Weight:** 6-1/2 lbs. **Length:** 45". **Stock:** American walnut straight or pistol grip. **Sights:** Gold bead front, full length rib, serrated top. **Features:** Spring-assisted break-open, SS trigger, auto eject. Five interchangeable screw-in choke tubes, combination safety/barrel selector with auto safety reset.
Price: **$2,000.00**

STOEGER UPLANDER SIDE-BY-SIDE SHOTGUNS

Gauge: 16, 28, 2-3/4 chambers. 12, 20, .410, 3" chambers. **Barrel:** 26", 28". **Weight:** 7.3 lbs. **Sights:** Brass bead. **Features:** Double trigger, IC & M fixed choke tubes with gun.
Price: With fixed chokes **$335.00**
Price: With screw-in chokes) **$350.00**
Price: With English stock .... **$335.00 to $350.00**
Price: Upland Special **$375.00**
Price: Upland Supreme with SST, red bar sights **$445.00**
Price: Upland Short Stock (Youth) **$335.00**

Stoeger Silverado Coach

Traditions Uplander V

**Tristar Rota
Model 411**

STOEGER COACH GUN SIDE-BY-SIDE SHOTGUNS

Gauge: 12, 20, .410, 2-3/4", 3" chambers. **Barrel:** 20". **Weight:** 6-1/2 lbs. **Stock:** Brown hardwood, classic beavertail forend. **Sights:** Brass bead. **Features:** IC & M fixed chokes, tang auto safety, auto extractors, black plastic buttplate. 12 ga. and 20 ga. also with English style stock.

Price:	$320.00
Price: Nickel	$375.00
Price: Silverado	$375.00
Price: With English stock	$375.00

TRADITIONS ELITE SERIES SIDE-BY-SIDE SHOTGUNS

Gauge: 12, 3"; 20, 3"; 28, 2-3/4"; .410, 3". **Barrel:** 26". **Weight:** 5 lbs., 12 oz. to 6-1/2 lbs. **Length:** 43" overall. **Stock:** Walnut. **Features:** Chrome-lined barrels; fixed chokes (Elite Field III ST, Field I DT and Field I ST) or choke tubes (Elite Hunter ST); extractors (Hunter ST and Field I models) or automatic ejectors (Field III ST); top tang safety. Imported from Fausti of Italy by Traditions.

Price: Elite Field I DT — 12, 20, 28 ga. or .410; IC and Mod. fixed chokes (F and F on .410); double triggers . . . . **$789.00 to $969.00**
Price: Elite Field I ST — 12, 20, 28 ga. or .410; same as DT but with single trigger . . . . **$969.00 to $1,169.00**
Price: Elite Field III ST — 28 ga. or .410; gold-engraved receiver; high-grade walnut stock **$2,099.00**
Price: Elite Hunter ST — 12 or 20 ga.; blued receiver; IC and Mod. choke tubes **$999.00**

TRADITIONS UPLANDER SERIES SIDE-BY-SIDE SHOTGUNS

Gauge: 12, 3"; 20, 3". **Barrel:** 26", 28". **Weight:** 6-1/4 lbs. to 6-1/2 lbs. **Length:** 43" to 45" overall. **Stock:** Walnut. **Features:** Barrels threaded for choke tubes (Improved Cylinder, Modified and Full); top tang safety, extended trigger guard. Engraved silver receiver with side plates and lavish gold inlays. Imported from Fausti of Italy by Traditions.

Price: Uplander III Silver 12, 20 ga.	$2,699.00
Price: Uplander V Silver 12, 20 ga.	$3,199.00

TRISTAR ROTA MODEL 411 SIDE-BY-SIDE SHOTGUN

Gauge: 12, 16, 20, .410, 3" chambers; 28, 2-3/4". **Barrel:** 12 ga., 26", 28"; 16, 20, 28 ga., .410-bore, 26"; 12 and 20 ga. have three choke tubes, 16, 28 (Imp. Cyl. & Mod.), .410 (Mod. & Full) fixed chokes. **Weight:** 6-1/2 to 7-1/4 lbs. **Stock:** 14-3/8" l.o.p. Standard walnut with pistol grip, splinter-style forend; hand checkered. **Features:** Engraved, color case-hardened boxlock action; double triggers, extractors; solid barrel rib. Introduced 1998. Imported from Italy by Tristar Sporting Arms, Ltd.

Price: **$849.00**

Tristar Rota Model 411D Side-by-Side Shotgun

Similar to Model 411 except automatic ejectors, straight English style stock, single trigger. Solid barrel rib with matted surface; chrome bores; color case-hardened frame; splinter forend. Introduced 1999. Imported from Italy by Tristar Sporting Arms, Ltd.

Price: **$1,110.00**

Tristar Rota Model 411R Coach Gun Side-by-Side Shotgun

Similar to Model 411 except in 12 or 20 gauge only with 20" barrels and fixed chokes (Cyl. & Cyl.). Double triggers, extractors, choke tubes. Introduced 1999. Imported from Italy by Tristar Sporting Arms, Ltd.

Price: **$745.00**

Tristar Rota Model 411F Side-by-Side Shotgun

Similar to Model 411 except silver, engraved receiver, ejectors, IC, M and F choke tubes, English-style stock, single gold trigger, cut checkering. Imported from Italy by Tristar Sporting Arms Ltd.

Price: **$1,608.00**

TRISTAR DERBY CLASSIC SIDE-BY-SIDE SHOTGUN

Gauge: 12. **Barrel:** 28" Mod. & Full fixed chokes. **Features:** Sidelock action, engraved, double trigger, auto ejectors, English straight stock. Made in Europe for Tristar Sporting Arms Ltd.

Price: **$1,059.00**

SHOTGUNS — Bolt Actions & Single Shot

Variety of designs for utility and sporting purposes, as well as for competitive shooting.

Browning BT-99 Trap

EAA Baikal IZH18

EAA Baikal IZH18Max

**H&R Model 928
Ultra Slug Hunter Deluxe**

BERETTA DT10 TRIDENT TRAP TOP SINGLE SHOTGUN
Gauge: 12, 3" chamber. **Barrel:** 34"; five Optima Choke tubes (Full, Full, Imp. Modified, Mod. and Imp. Cyl.). **Weight:** 8.8 lbs. **Stock:** High-grade walnut; adjustable. **Features:** Detachable, adjustable trigger group; Optima Bore for improved shot pattern and reduced recoil; slim Optima Choke tubes; raised and thickened receiver for long life. Introduced 2000. Imported from Italy by Beretta USA.
Price: **$6,995.00**

BRNO ZBK 100 SINGLE BARREL SHOTGUN
Gauge: 12 or 20. **Barrel:** 27.5". **Weight:** 5.5 lbs. **Length:** 44" overall. **Stock:** Beech. **Features:** Polished blue finish; sling swivels. Announced 1998. Imported from the Czech Republic by Euro-Imports.
Price: **$185.00**

BROWNING BT-99 TRAP SHOTGUNS
Gauge: 12, 2-3/4" chamber. **Barrel:** 32" or 34"; Invector choke system (full choke tube only included); High Post Rib; back-bored. **Weight:** 8 lbs., 10 oz. (34" bbl.). **Length:** 50-1/2" overall (34" bbl.). **Stock:** Conventional or adjustable comb. **Features:** Reintroduction of the BT-99 Trap Shotgun. Full beavertail forearm; checkered walnut stock; ejector; rubber butt pad. Reintroduced 2001. Imported by Browning.
Price: Conventional stock, 32" or 34" barrel **$1,290.00**
Price: Adj.-comb stock, 32" or 34" barrel **$1,558.00**
Price: Micro (for small-framed shooters) **$1,290.00**

BROWNING GOLDEN CLAYS SHOTGUN
Gauge: 12, 3" chamber. **Barrel:** 32", 34" with Full, Improved Modified, Modified tubes. **Weight:** 8 lbs. 14 oz. to 9 lbs. **Length:** 49" to 51" overall. **Stock:** Adjustable comb; walnut with high gloss finish; cut checkering. GraCoil recoil reduction system. Imported from Japan by Browning.
Price: 34" bbl. **$3,407.00**
Price: 32" bbl. **$3,407.00**

CHIPMUNK 410 YOUTH SHOTGUN
Gauge: .410. **Barrel:** 18-1/4" tapered, blue. **Weight:** 3.25 lbs. **Length:** 33". **Stock:** Walnut. **Features:** Manually cocking single shot bolt, blued receiver.
Price: **$225.95**

EAA BAIKAL IZH18 SINGLE BARREL SHOTGUN
Gauge: 12 (2-3/4" and 3" chambers), 20 (2-3/4" and 3"), 16 (2-3/4"), .410 (3"). **Barrel:** 26-1/2", 28-1/2"; Modified or Full choke (12 and 20 gauge); Full only (16 gauge), Improved cylinder (20 gauge) and Full or Improved Modified (.410). **Stock:** Walnut-stained hardwood; rubber recoil pad. **Features:** Hammer-forged steel barrel; machined receiver; cross-block safety; cocking lever with external cocking indicator; optional automatic ejector, screw-in chokes and rifle barrel. Imported by European American Armory.
Price: IZH18 (12, 16, 20 or .410) **$109.00**
Price: IZH18 (20 gauge w/Imp. Cyl. or .410 w/Imp. Mod.) **$109.00**

EAA BAIKAL IZH18MAX SINGLE BARREL SHOTGUNS
Gauge: 12, 3"; 20, 3"; 410, 3". **Barrel:** 24" (.410), 26" (.410 or 20 ga.) or 28" (12 ga.). **Weight:** 6.4 to 6.6 lbs. **Stock:** Walnut. **Features:** Polished nickel receiver; vent rib; I.C., Mod. and Full choke tubes; titanium-coated trigger; internal hammer; selectable ejector/extractor; rubber butt pad; de-cocking system. Imported by European American Armory.
Price: (12 or 20 ga., choke tubes) **$229.00**
Price: (.410, Full choke only) **$239.00**
Price: Sporting, 12 ga., ported, Monte Carlo stock **$219.00**

HARRINGTON & RICHARDSON SB2-980 ULTRA SLUG SHOTGUN
Gauge: 12, 20, 3" chamber. **Barrel:** 22" (20 ga. Youth) 24", fully rifled. **Weight:** 9 lbs. **Length:** NA. **Stock:** Walnut-stained hardwood. **Sights:** None furnished; comes with scope mount. **Features:** Uses the H&R 10 gauge action with heavy-wall barrel. Monte Carlo stock has sling swivels; comes with black nylon sling. Introduced 1995. Made in U.S. by H&R 1871, LLC.
Price: **$259.00**

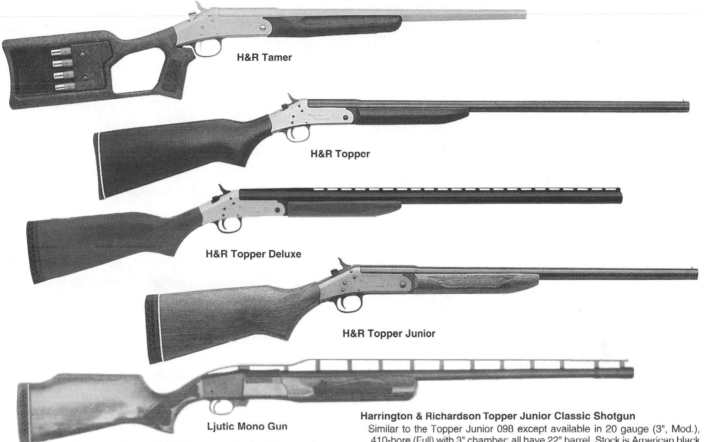

H&R Tamer

H&R Topper

H&R Topper Deluxe

H&R Topper Junior

Ljutic Mono Gun

Harrington & Richardson Model 928 Ultra Slug Hunter Deluxe Shotgun

Similar to the SB2-980 Ultra Slug except uses 12 gauge action and 12 gauge barrel blank bored to 20 gauge, and then fully rifled with 1:28" twist. Has hand-checkered camo laminate Monte Carlo stock and forend. Comes with Weaver-style scope base, offset hammer extension, ventilated recoil pad, sling swivels and nylon sling. Introduced 1997. Made in U.S. by H&R 1871 LLC.

Price: **$315.00**

HARRINGTON & RICHARDSON TAMER SHOTGUN

Gauge: .410, 3" chamber. **Barrel:** 20" (Full). **Weight:** 5-6 lbs. **Length:** 33" overall. **Stock:** Thumbhole grip of high density black polymer. **Features:** Uses H&R Topper action with matte electroless nickel finish. Stock holds four spare shotshells. Introduced 1994. From H&R 1871, LLC.

Price: **$164.00**

HARRINGTON & RICHARDSON TOPPER MODEL 098

Gauge: 12, 16, 20, 28 (2-3/4"), .410, 3" chamber. **Barrel:** 12 ga.-28" (Mod.); 16 ga.-28" (Full.); 20 ga.-26" (Mod.); 28 ga.-26" (Mod.); .410 bore-26" (Full). **Weight:** 5-6 lbs. **Stock:** Black-finish hardwood with full pistol grip; semi-beavertail forend. **Sights:** Gold bead front. **Features:** Break-open action with side-lever release, automatic ejector. Satin nickel frame, blued barrel. Reintroduced 1992. From H&R 1871, LLC.

Price: **$145.00**
Price: Topper Junior 098 (as above except 22" barrel, 20 ga. (Mod.), .410-bore (Full), 12-1/2" length of pull) **$152.00**

Harrington & Richardson Topper Deluxe Model 098

Similar to the standard Topper 098 except 12 gauge only with 3-1/2" chamber, 28" barrel with choke tube (comes with Mod. tube, others optional). Satin nickel frame, blued barrel, black-finished wood. Introduced 1992. From H&R 1871, LLC.

Price: **$169.00**

Harrington & Richardson Topper Junior Classic Shotgun

Similar to the Topper Junior 098 except available in 20 gauge (3", Mod.), .410-bore (Full) with 3" chamber; all have 22" barrel. Stock is American black walnut with cut-checkered pistol grip and forend. Ventilated rubber recoil pad. Blued barrel, blued frame. Introduced 1992. From H&R 1871, LLC.

Price: **$184.00**

ITHACA CLASSIC DOUBLES KNICKERBOCKER TRAP GUN

A reissue of the famous Ithaca Knickerbocker trap gun. Custom only. Introduced 2003. Made in U.S.A. by Ithaca Classic Doubles.

Price: From **$9,000.00**

KRIEGHOFF K-80 SINGLE BARREL TRAP GUN

Gauge: 12, 2-3/4" chamber. **Barrel:** 32" or 34" Unsingle. Fixed Full or choke tubes. **Weight:** About 8-3/4 lbs. **Stock:** Four stock dimensions or adjustable stock available. All hand-checkered European walnut. **Features:** Satin nickel finish. Selective mechanical trigger adjustable for finger position. Tapered step vent rib. Adjustable point of impact.

Price: Standard grade Full Unsingle, from **$9,675.00**

KRIEGHOFF KX-5 TRAP GUN

Gauge: 12, 2-3/4" chamber. **Barrel:** 32", 34"; choke tubes. **Weight:** About 8-1/2 lbs. **Stock:** Factory adjustable stock. European walnut. **Features:** Ventilated tapered step rib. Adjustable position trigger, optional release trigger. Fully adjustable rib. Satin gray electroless nickel receiver. Fitted aluminum case. Imported from Germany by Krieghoff International, Inc.

Price: **$5,195.00**

LJUTIC MONO GUN SINGLE BARREL SHOTGUN

Gauge: 12 only. **Barrel:** 34", choked to customer specs; hollow-milled rib, 35-1/2" sight plane. **Weight:** Approx. 9 lbs. **Stock:** To customer specs. Oil finish, hand checkered. **Features:** Custom gun. Pull or release trigger; removable trigger guard contains trigger and hammer mechanism; Ljutic pushbutton opener on front of trigger guard. From Ljutic Industries.

Price: Std., med. or Olympic rib, custom bbls., fixed choke. **$6,995.00**
Price: As above with screw-in choke barrel **$7,395.00**
Price: Stainless steel mono gun **$7,995.00**

Mossberg SSi One

New England Firearms Camo Turkey

New England Firearms Tracker II

New England Firearms Special Purpose

New England Firearms Survivor

Ljutic LTX Pro 3 Deluxe Mono Gun

Deluxe, lightweight version of the Mono gun with high quality wood, upgrade checkering, special rib height, screw-in chokes, ported and cased.

Price: **$8,995.00**
Price: Stainless steel model **$9,995.00**

MOSSBERG SSi-ONE 12 GAUGE SLUG SHOTGUN

Gauge: 12, 3" chamber. **Barrel:** 24", fully rifled. **Weight:** 8 lbs. **Length:** 40" overall. **Stock:** Walnut, fluted and cut checkered; sling-swivel studs; drilled and tapped for scope base. **Sights:** None (scope base supplied). **Features:** Frame accepts interchangeable rifle barrels (see Mossberg SSi-One rifle listing); lever-opening, break-action design; ambidextrous, top-tang safety; internal eject/extract selector. Introduced 2000. From Mossberg.

Price: **$480.00**

Mossberg SSi-One Turkey Shotgun

Similar to SSi-One 12 gauge slug shotgun, but chambered for 12 ga., 3-1/2" loads. Includes Accu-Mag Turkey Tube. Introduced 2001. From Mossberg.

Price: **$459.00**

NEW ENGLAND FIREARMS CAMO TURKEY SHOTGUNS

Gauge: 10, 3-1/2"; 12, 20, 3" chamber. **Barrel:** 24"; extra-full, screw-in choke tube (10 ga.); fixed full choke (12, 20). **Weight:** NA. **Stock:** American hardwood, green and black camouflage finish with sling swivels and ventilated recoil pad. **Sights:** Bead front. **Features:** Matte metal finish; stock counterweight to reduce recoil; patented transfer bar system for hammer-down safety; includes camo sling and trigger lock. Accepts

other factory-fitted barrels. Introduced 2000. From New England Firearms.
Price: . . . . 10 ga. **$278.00**; 12 ga. **$189.00**
Price: 20 ga. Youth model (22" bbl.) **$189.00**

NEW ENGLAND FIREARMS TRACKER II SLUG GUN

Gauge: 12, 20, 3" chamber. **Barrel:** 24" (Cyl.), rifle bore. **Weight:** 5-1/4 lbs. **Length:** 40" overall. **Stock:** Walnut-finished hardwood with full pistol grip, recoil pad. **Sights:** Blade front, fully adjustable rifle-type rear. **Features:** Break-open action with side-lever release; blued barrel, color case-hardened frame. Introduced 1992. From New England Firearms.

Price: Tracker II **$187.00**

NEW ENGLAND FIREARMS SPECIAL PURPOSE SHOTGUNS

Gauge: 10, 3-1/2" chamber. **Barrel:** 28" (Full), 32" (Mod.). **Weight:** 9.5 lbs. **Length:** 44" overall (28" barrel). **Stock:** American hardwood with walnut or matte camo finish; ventilated rubber recoil pad. **Sights:** Bead front. **Features:** Break-open action with side-lever release; ejector. Matte finish on metal. Introduced 1992. From New England Firearms.

Price: Walnut-finish wood sling and swivels **$215.00**
Price: Camo finish, sling and swivels **$278.00**
Price: Camo finish, 32", sling and swivels **$272.00**
Price: Black matte finish, 24", turkey full choke tube,
sling and swivels **$251.00**

NEW ENGLAND FIREARMS SURVIVOR SHOTGUN

Gauge: .410/45 Colt, 3" chamber. **Barrel:** 22" (Mod.); 20" (.410/45 Colt, rifled barrel, choke tube). **Weight:** 6 lbs. **Length:** 36" overall. **Stock:** Black polymer with thumbhole/pistol grip, sling swivels; beavertail forend. **Sights:** Bead front. **Features:** Buttplate removes to expose storage for extra ammunition; forend also holds extra ammunition. Black or nickel finish. Introduced 1993. From New England Firearms.

Price: .410/45 Colt, black **$203.00**
Price: .410/45 Colt, nickel **$221.00**

SHOTGUNS — Bolt Actions & Single Shot

New England Firearms Standard Pardner

Rossi Single-Shot

Rossi Matched Pair

Savage 210F Slug Warrior

Stoeger Single-Shot

NEW ENGLAND FIREARMS STANDARD PARDNER SHOTGUN
Gauge: 12, 20, .410, 3" chamber; 16, 28, 2-3/4" chamber. **Barrel:** 12 ga. 28" (Full, Mod.), 32" (Full); 16 ga. 28" (Full), 32" (Full); 20 ga. 26" (Full, Mod.); 28 ga. 26" (Mod.); .410-bore 26" (Full). **Weight:** 5-6 lbs. **Length:** 43" overall (28" barrel). **Stock:** Walnut-finished hardwood with full pistol grip. **Sights:** Bead front. **Features:** Transfer bar ignition; break open action with side-lever release. Introduced 1987. From New England Firearms.
Price: $132.00
Price: Youth model (12, 20, 28 ga., .410, 22" barrel, recoil pad) . . . $141.00

ROSSI SINGLE-SHOT SHOTGUN
Gauge: 12, 20, 2-3/4" chamber; .410, 3" chamber. **Barrel:** 28" full, 22" Youth. **Weight:** 5 lbs. **Stock:** Stained hardwood. **Sights:** Bead. **Features:** Break-open, positive ejection, internal transfer bar, trigger block.
Price: $101.00

ROSSI MATCHED PAIR SINGLE-SHOT SHOTGUN/RIFLE
Gauge: .410, 20 or 12. **Barrel:** 22" (18.5" Youth), 28" (23" full). **Weight:** 4-6 lbs. **Stock:** Hardwood (brown or black finish). **Sights:** Bead front.

Features: Break-open internal transfer bar manual external safety; blued or stainless steel finish; sling-swivel studs; Includes matched 22 LR or 22 mag. barrel with fully adjustable front and rear sight. Trigger block system. Introduced 2001. Imported by BrazTech/Taurus.
Price: Blue $139.95
Price: Stainless steel $169.95

SAVAGE MODEL 210F SLUG WARRIOR SHOTGUN
Gauge: 12, 3" chamber; 2-shot magazine. **Barrel:** 24" 1:35" rifling twist. **Weight:** 7-1/2 lbs. **Length:** 43.5" overall. **Stock:** Glass-filled polymer with positive checkering. **Features:** Based on the Savage Model 110 action; 60-degree bolt lift; controlled round feed; comes with scope mount. Introduced 1996. Made in U.S. by Savage Arms.
Price: $475.00
Price: (Camo) $513.00

STOEGER SINGLE-SHOT SHOTGUN
Gauge: 12, 20, .410, 2-3/4", 3" chambers. **Barrel:** 26", 28". **Weight:** 5.4 lbs. **Length:** 40-1/2" to 42-1/2" overall. **Sights:** Brass bead. **Features:** .410, Full fixed choke tubes, screw-in. .410 12 ga. hardwood pistol-grip stock and forend. 20 ga. 26" bbl., hardwood forend.
Price: Blue; Youth $109.00
Price: Youth with English stock $119.00

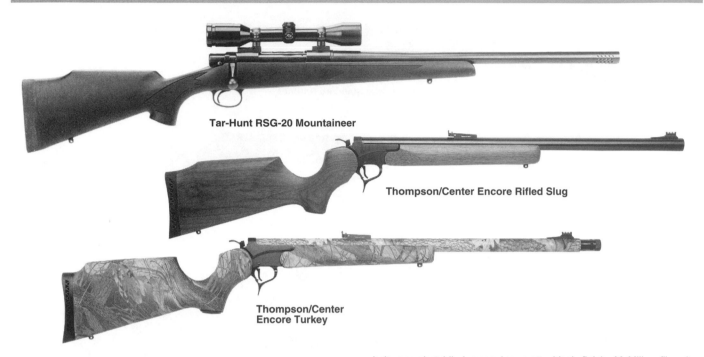

Tar-Hunt RSG-20 Mountaineer

Thompson/Center Encore Rifled Slug

Thompson/Center Encore Turkey

TAR-HUNT RSG-12 PROFESSIONAL RIFLED SLUG GUN

Gauge: 12, 2-3/4" or 3" chamber, 1-shot magazine. **Barrel:** 23", fully rifled with muzzle brake. **Weight:** 7-3/4 lbs. **Length:** 41-1/2" overall. **Stock:** Matte black McMillan fiberglass with Pachmayr Decelerator pad. **Sights:** None furnished; comes with Leupold windage or Weaver bases. **Features:** Uses rifle-style action with two locking lugs; two-position safety; Shaw barrel; single-stage, trigger; muzzle brake. Many options available. Right- and left-hand models at same prices. Introduced 1991. Made in U.S. by Tar-Hunt Custom Rifles, Inc.
Price: 12 ga. Professional model, right- or left-hand; **$2,750.00**

Tar-Hunt RSG-16 Elite Shotgun
Similar to RSG-12 Professional except 16 gauge; right- or left-hand versions.
Price: **$2,750.00**

Tar-Hunt RSG-20 Mountaineer Slug Gun
Similar to the RSG-12 Professional except chambered for 20 gauge (2-3/4" and 3" shells); 23" Shaw rifled barrel, with muzzle brake; two-lug bolt; one-shot blind magazine; matte black finish; McMillan fiberglass stock with Pachmayr Decelerator pad; receiver drilled and tapped for Rem. 700 bases. Right- or left-hand versions. Weighs 6-1/2 lbs. Introduced 1997. Made in U.S. by Tar-Hunt Custom Rifles, Inc.
Price: **$2,750.00**

THOMPSON/CENTER ENCORE RIFLED SLUG GUN

Gauge: 20, 3" chamber. **Barrel:** 26", fully rifled. **Weight:** About 7 lbs. **Length:** 40-1/2" overall. **Stock:** Walnut with walnut forearm. **Sights:** Steel; click-adjustable rear and ramp-style front, both with fiber optics. **Features:** Encore system features a variety of rifle, shotgun and muzzle-loading rifle barrels interchangeable with the same frame. Break-open design operates by pulling up and back on trigger guard spur. Composite stock and forearm available. Introduced 2000.
Price: **$684.00**

THOMPSON/CENTER ENCORE TURKEY GUN

Gauge: 12 ga. **Barrel:** 24". **Features:** All-camo finish, high definition Realtree Hardwoods HD camo.
Price: **$763.00**

CONSULT

SHOOTER'S MARKETPLACE

Page 243, This Issue

Designs for utility, suitable for and adaptable to competitions and other sporting purposes.

Benelli M3 Convertible

Fabarm Tactical

Fabarm FP6

Mossberg Model 500 Persuader

BENELLI M3 CONVERTIBLE SHOTGUN

Gauge: 12, 2-3/4", 3" chambers, 5-shot magazine. **Barrel:** 19-3/4" (Cyl.). **Weight:** 7 lbs., 4oz. **Length:** 41" overall. **Stock:** High-impact polymer with sling loop in side of butt; rubberized pistol grip on stock. **Sights:** Open rifle, fully adjustable. Ghost ring and rifle type. **Features:** Combination pump/auto action. Alloy receiver with inertia recoil rotating locking lug bolt; matte finish; automatic shell release lever. Introduced 1989. Imported by Benelli USA. Price with pistol grip, open rifle sights.

Price: With standard stock, open rifle sights $1,235.00
Price: With ghost ring sight system, standard stock $1,185.00
Price: With ghost ring sights, pistol grip stock $1,165.00

BENELLI M2 TACTICAL SHOTGUN

Gauge: 12, 2-3/4", 3" chambers, 5-shot magazine. **Barrel:** 18.5" IC, M, F choke tubes. **Weight:** 6.7 lbs. **Length:** 39.75" overall. **Stock:** Black polymer. **Sights:** Rifle type with ghost ring system, tritium night sights optional. **Features:** Semi-auto intertia recoil action. Cross-bolt safety; bolt release button; matte-finish metal. Introduced 1993. Imported from Italy by Benelli USA.

Price: With rifle sights, standard stock $1,000.00
Price: With ghost ring rifle sights, standard stock $1,065.00
Price: With ghost ring sights, pistol grip stock $1,065.00
Price: With rifle sights, pistol grip stock $1,000.00
Price: ComforTech stock, rifle sights $1,135.00
Price: Comfortech Stock, Ghost-Ring $1,185.00

Benelli M2 Practical Shotgun

Similar to M2 Tactical shotgun, Picatinny receiver rail for scope mounting, nine-round magazine, 26" compensated barrel and ghost ring sights. Designed for IPSC competition.
Price: $1,335.00

CROSSFIRE SHOTGUN/RIFLE

Gauge/Caliber: 12, 2-3/4" Chamber: 4-shot/223 Rem. (5-shot). **Barrel:** 20" (shotgun), 18" (rifle). **Weight:** About 8.6 lbs. **Length:** 40" overall. **Stock:** Composite. **Sights:** Meprolight night sights. Integral Weaver-style scope rail. **Features:** Combination pump-action shotgun, rifle; single selector, single trigger; dual action bars for both upper and lower actions; ambidextrous selector and safety. Introduced 1997. Made in U.S. From Hesco.

Price: About $1,895.00
Price: With camo finish $1,995.00

FABARM TACTICAL SEMI-AUTOMATIC SHOTGUN

Gauge: 12, 3" chamber. **Barrel:** 20". **Weight:** 6.6 lbs. **Length:** 41.2" overall. **Stock:** Polymer or folding. **Sights:** Ghost ring (tritium night sights optional). **Features:** Gas operated; matte receiver; twin forged action bars; over-sized bolt handle and safety button; Picatinny rail; includes cylinder bore choke tube. New features include polymer pistol grip stock. Introduced 2001. Imported from Italy by Heckler & Koch Inc.
Price: $999.00

FABARM FP6 PUMP SHOTGUN

Gauge: 12, 3" chamber. **Barrel:** 20" (Cyl.); accepts choke tubes. **Weight:** 6.6 lbs. **Length:** 41.25" overall. **Stock:** Black polymer with textured grip, grooved slide handle. **Sights:** Blade front. **Features:** Twin action bars; anodized finish; free carrier for smooth reloading. Introduced 1998. New features include ghost-ring sighting system, low profile Picatinny rail, and pistol grip stock. Imported from Italy by Heckler & Koch, Inc.

Price: (Carbon fiber finish) $499.00
Price: With flip-up front sight, Picatinny rail with rear sight, oversize safety button $499.00

MOSSBERG MODEL 500 PERSUADER SECURITY SHOTGUNS

Gauge: 12, 20, .410, 3" chamber. **Barrel:** 18-1/2", 20" (Cyl.). **Weight:** 7 lbs. **Stock:** Walnut-finished hardwood or black synthetic. **Sights:** Metal bead front. **Features:** Available in 6- or 8-shot models. Top-mounted safety, double action slide bars, swivel studs, rubber recoil pad. Blue, Parkerized, Marinecote finishes. Mossberg Cablelock included. From Mossberg.

Price: 12 ga., 18-1/2", blue, wood or synthetic stock, 6-shot $353.00
Price: Cruiser, 12 ga., 18-1/2", blue, pistol grip, heat shield $357.00
Price: As above, 20 ga. or .410 bore $345.00

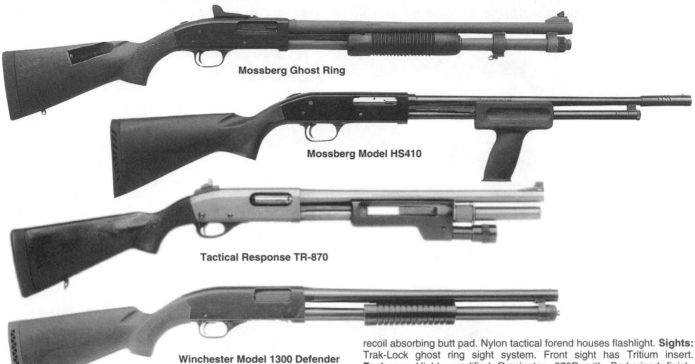

Mossberg Ghost Ring

Mossberg Model HS410

Tactical Response TR-870

Winchester Model 1300 Defender

Mossberg Model 500, 590 Mariner Pump Shotgun

Similar to the Model 500 or 590 Persuader except all metal parts finished with Marinecote metal finish to resist rust and corrosion. Synthetic field stock; pistol grip kit included. Mossberg Cablelock included.
Price: 6-shot, 18-1/2" barrel $497.00
Price: 9-shot, 20" barrel $513.00

Mossberg Model 500, 590 Ghost-Ring Shotgun

Similar to the Model 500 Persuader except has adjustable blade front, adjustable Ghost-Ring rear sight with protective "ears." Model 500 has 18.5" (Cyl.) barrel, 6-shot capacity; Model 590 has 20" (Cyl.) barrel, 9-shot capacity. Both have synthetic field stock. Mossberg Cablelock included. Introduced 1990. From Mossberg.
Price: 500 Parkerized $468.00
Price: 590 Parkerized $543.00
Price: 590 Parkerized Speedfeed stock $586.00

Mossberg Model HS410 Shotgun

Similar to the Model 500 Persuader pump except chambered for 20 gauge or .410 with 3" chamber; has pistol grip forend, thick recoil pad, muzzle brake and has special spreader choke on the 18.5" barrel. Overall length is 37.5", weight is 6.25 lbs. Blue finish; synthetic field stock. Mossberg Cablelock and video included. Introduced 1990.
Price: HS 410 . . . . $355.00

MOSSBERG MODEL 590 SHOTGUN

Gauge: 12, 3" chamber. **Barrel:** 20" (Cyl.). **Weight:** 7-1/4 lbs. **Stock:** Synthetic field or Speedfeed. **Sights:** Metal bead front. **Features:** Top-mounted safety, double slide action bars. Comes with heat shield, bayonet lug, swivel studs, rubber recoil pad. Blue, Parkerized or Marinecote finish. Mossberg Cablelock included. From Mossberg.
Price: Blue, synthetic stock $417.00
Price: Parkerized, synthetic stock $476.00
Price: Parkerized, Speedfeed stock $519.00

TACTICAL RESPONSE TR-870 STANDARD MODEL SHOTGUNS

Gauge: 12, 3" chamber, 7-shot magazine. **Barrel:** 18" (Cyl.). **Weight:** 9 lbs. **Length:** 38" overall. **Stock:** Fiberglass-filled polypropolene with non-snag recoil absorbing butt pad. Nylon tactical forend houses flashlight. **Sights:** Trak-Lock ghost ring sight system. Front sight has Tritium insert. **Features:** Highly modified Remington 870P with Parkerized finish. Comes with nylon three-way adjustable sling, high visibility non-binding follower, high performance magazine spring, Jumbo Head safety, and Side Saddle extended 6-shot shell carrier on left side of receiver. Introduced 1991. From Scattergun Technologies, Inc.
Price: Standard model $815.00
Price: FBI model $770.00
Price: Patrol model $595.00
Price: Border Patrol model $605.00
Price: K-9 model (Rem. 11-87 action) $995.00
Price: Urban Sniper, Rem. 11-87 action $1,290.00
Price: Louis Awerbuck model $705.00
Price: Practical Turkey model $725.00
Price: Expert model $1,350.00
Price: Professional model $815.00
Price: Entry model $840.00
Price: Compact model $635.00
Price: SWAT model $1,195.00

WINCHESTER MODEL 1300 DEFENDER PUMP GUN SHOTGUNS

Gauge: 12, 20, 3" chamber, 5- or 8-shot capacity. **Barrel:** 18" (Cyl.). **Weight:** 6-3/4 lbs. **Length:** 38-5/8" overall. **Stock:** Walnut-finished hardwood stock and ribbed forend, synthetic or pistol grip. **Sights:** Metal bead front or TruGlo® fiber-optic. **Features:** Cross-bolt safety, front-locking rotary bolt, twin action slide bars. Black rubber butt pad. From U.S. Repeating Arms Co.
Price: Practical Defender $392.00
Price: 8-Shot Pistol Grip (pistol grip synthetic stock) $354.00

Winchester Model 1300 Coastal Pump Gun Shotgun

Same as the Defender 8-Shot except has bright chrome finish, nickel-plated barrel, bead front sight. Phosphate coated receiver for corrosion resistance.
Price: $575.00

Winchester Model 1300 Camp Defender® Shotgun

Same as the Defender 8-Shot except has hardwood stock and forearm, fully adjustable open sights and 22" barrel with WinChoke® choke tube system (cylinder choke tube included). Weighs 6-7/8 lbs. Introduced 2001. From U.S. Repeating Arms Co.
Price: Camp Defender® $392.00

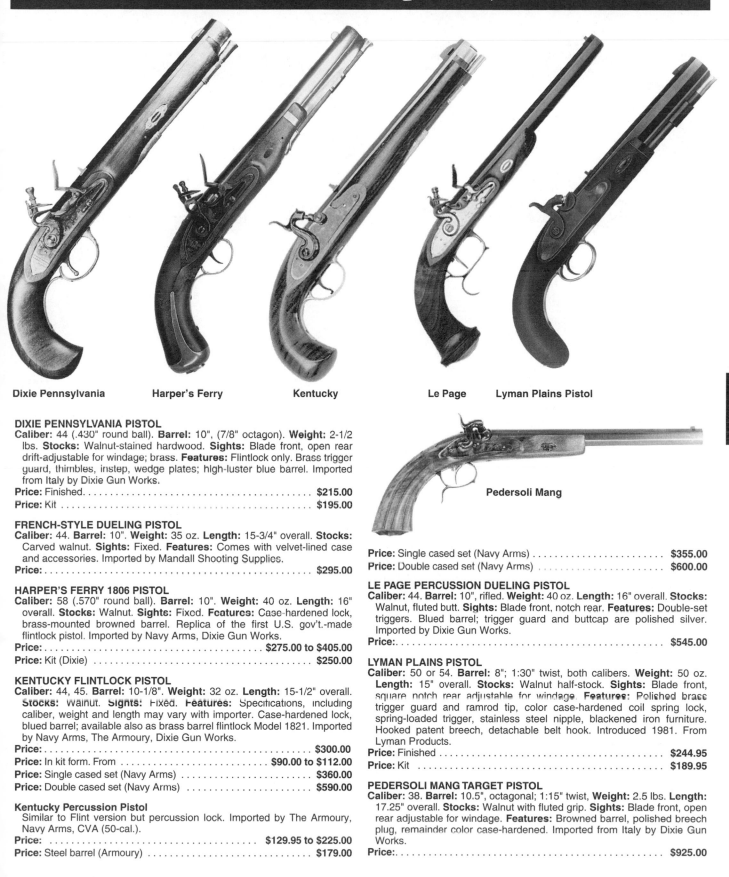

Dixie Pennsylvania   **Harper's Ferry**   **Kentucky**   **Le Page**   **Lyman Plains Pistol**

Pedersoli Mang

DIXIE PENNSYLVANIA PISTOL
Caliber: 44 (.430" round ball). **Barrel:** 10", (7/8" octagon). **Weight:** 2-1/2 lbs. **Stocks:** Walnut-stained hardwood. **Sights:** Blade front, open rear drift-adjustable for windage; brass. **Features:** Flintlock only. Brass trigger guard, thimbles, instep, wedge plates; high-luster blue barrel. Imported from Italy by Dixie Gun Works.
Price: Finished. **$215.00**
Price: Kit **$195.00**

FRENCH-STYLE DUELING PISTOL
Caliber: 44. **Barrel:** 10". **Weight:** 35 oz. **Length:** 15-3/4" overall. **Stocks:** Carved walnut. **Sights:** Fixed. **Features:** Comes with velvet-lined case and accessories. Imported by Mandall Shooting Supplies.
Price: **$295.00**

HARPER'S FERRY 1806 PISTOL
Caliber: 58 (.570" round ball). **Barrel:** 10". **Weight:** 40 oz. **Length:** 16" overall. **Stocks:** Walnut. **Sights:** Fixed. **Features:** Case-hardened lock, brass-mounted browned barrel. Replica of the first U.S. gov't.-made flintlock pistol. Imported by Navy Arms, Dixie Gun Works.
Price: . . . . **$275.00 to $405.00**
Price: Kit (Dixie) **$250.00**

KENTUCKY FLINTLOCK PISTOL
Caliber: 44, 45. **Barrel:** 10-1/8". **Weight:** 32 oz. **Length:** 15-1/2" overall. **Stocks:** Walnut. **Sights:** Fixed. **Features:** Specifications, including caliber, weight and length may vary with importer. Case-hardened lock, blued barrel; available also as brass barrel flintlock Model 1821. Imported by Navy Arms, The Armoury, Dixie Gun Works.
Price: **$300.00**
Price: In kit form. From . . . . **$90.00 to $112.00**
Price: Single cased set (Navy Arms) **$360.00**
Price: Double cased set (Navy Arms) **$590.00**

Kentucky Percussion Pistol
Similar to Flint version but percussion lock. Imported by The Armoury, Navy Arms, CVA (50-cal.).
Price: . . . . **$129.95 to $225.00**
Price: Steel barrel (Armoury) **$179.00**

Price: Single cased set (Navy Arms) **$355.00**
Price: Double cased set (Navy Arms) **$600.00**

LE PAGE PERCUSSION DUELING PISTOL
Caliber: 44. **Barrel:** 10", rifled. **Weight:** 40 oz. **Length:** 16" overall. **Stocks:** Walnut, fluted butt. **Sights:** Blade front, notch rear. **Features:** Double-set triggers. Blued barrel; trigger guard and buttcap are polished silver. Imported by Dixie Gun Works.
Price: **$545.00**

LYMAN PLAINS PISTOL
Caliber: 50 or 54. **Barrel:** 8"; 1:30" twist, both calibers. **Weight:** 50 oz. **Length:** 15" overall. **Stocks:** Walnut half-stock. **Sights:** Blade front, square notch rear adjustable for windage. **Features:** Polished brass trigger guard and ramrod tip, color case-hardened coil spring lock, spring-loaded trigger, stainless steel nipple, blackened iron furniture. Hooked patent breech, detachable belt hook. Introduced 1981. From Lyman Products.
Price: Finished **$244.95**
Price: Kit **$189.95**

PEDERSOLI MANG TARGET PISTOL
Caliber: 38. **Barrel:** 10.5", octagonal; 1:15" twist. **Weight:** 2.5 lbs. **Length:** 17.25" overall. **Stocks:** Walnut with fluted grip. **Sights:** Blade front, open rear adjustable for windage. **Features:** Browned barrel, polished breech plug, remainder color case-hardened. Imported from Italy by Dixie Gun Works.
Price: **$925.00**

BLACKPOWDER PISTOLS — Single Shot, Flint & Percussion

Queen Anne

Traditions Pioneer

Traditions William Parker

Traditions Buckhunter Pro

QUEEN ANNE FLINTLOCK PISTOL
Caliber: 50 (.490" round ball). **Barrel:** 7-1/2", smoothbore. **Stocks:** Walnut. **Sights:** None. **Features:** Browned steel barrel, fluted brass trigger guard, brass mask on butt. Lockplate left in the white. Made by Pedersoli in Italy. Introduced 1983. Imported by Dixie Gun Works.
Price: $275.00
Price: Kit $195.00

TRADITIONS BUCKHUNTER PRO IN-LINE PISTOL
Caliber: 50. **Barrel:** 9-1/2", round. **Weight:** 48 oz. **Length:** 14" overall. **Stocks:** Smooth walnut or black epoxy-coated hardwood grip and forend. **Sights:** Beaded blade front, folding adjustable rear. **Features:** Thumb safety; removable stainless steel breech plug; adjustable trigger, barrel drilled and tapped for scope mounting. From Traditions.
Price: With walnut grip. $229.00
Price: Nickel with black grip $239.00
Price: With walnut grip and 12-1/2" barrel $239.00
Price: Nickel with black grip, muzzle brake and 14-3/4"
fluted barrel $289.00
Price: 45 cal. nickel w/bl. grip,
muzzle brake and 14-3/4" fluted bbl. $289.00

TRADITIONS KENTUCKY PISTOL
Caliber: 50. **Barrel:** 10"; octagon with 7/8" flats; 1:20" twist. **Weight:** 40 oz. **Length:** 15" overall. **Stocks:** Stained beech. **Sights:** Blade front, fixed rear. **Features:** Bird's-head grip; brass thimbles; color case-hardened lock. Percussion only. Introduced 1995. From Traditions.
Price: Finished. $139.00
Price: Kit $109.00

TRADITIONS PIONEER PISTOL
Caliber: 45. **Barrel:** 9-5/8"; 13/16" flats, 1:16" twist. **Weight:** 31 oz. **Length:** 15" overall. **Stocks:** Beech. **Sights:** Blade front, fixed rear. **Features:** V-type mainspring. Single trigger. German silver furniture, blackened hardware. From Traditions.
Price: $139.00
Price: Kit $119.00

TRADITIONS TRAPPER PISTOL
Caliber: 50. **Barrel:** 9-3/4"; 7/8" flats; 1:20" twist. **Weight:** 2-3/4 lbs. **Length:** 16" overall. **Stocks:** Beech. **Sights:** Blade front, adjustable rear.

Features: Double-set triggers; brass buttcap, trigger guard, wedge plate, forend tip, thimble. From Traditions.
Price: Percussion $189.00
Price: Flintlock $209.00
Price: Kit $149.00

TRADITIONS VEST-POCKET DERRINGER
Caliber: 31. **Barrel:** 2-1/4"; brass. **Weight:** 8 oz. **Length:** 4-3/4" overall. **Stocks:** Simulated ivory. **Sights:** Bead front. **Features:** Replica of riverboat gamblers' derringer; authentic spur trigger. From Traditions.
Price: $109.00

TRADITIONS WILLIAM PARKER PISTOL
Caliber: 50. **Barrel:** 10-3/8"; 15/16" flats; polished steel. **Weight:** 37 oz. **Length:** 17-1/2" overall. **Stocks:** Walnut with checkered grip. **Sights:** Brass blade front, fixed rear. **Features:** Replica dueling pistol with 1:20" twist, hooked breech. Brass wedge plate, trigger guard, cap guard; separate ramrod. Double-set triggers. Polished steel barrel, lock. Imported by Traditions.
Price: $269.00

BLACKPOWDER REVOLVERS

Army 1860

Baby Dragoon 1848

Dixie Wyatt Earp

Le Mat Revolver

Navy Arms 1836 Paterson

ARMY 1860 PERCUSSION REVOLVER
Caliber: 44, 6-shot. **Barrel:** 8". **Weight:** 40 oz. **Length:** 13-5/8" overall. **Stocks:** Walnut. **Sights:** Fixed. **Features:** Engraved Navy scene on cylinder; brass trigger guard; case-hardened frame, loading lever and hammer. Some importers supply pistol cut for detachable shoulder stock, have accessory stock available. Imported by Cabela's (1860 Lawman), E.M.F., Navy Arms, The Armoury, Cimarron, Dixie Gun Works (half-fluted cylinder, not roll engraved), Euroarms of America (brass or steel model), Armsport, Traditions (brass or steel), Uberti U.S.A. Inc., United States Patent Fire-Arms.
Price: About **$195.00**
Price: Hartford model, steel frame, German silver trim,
cartouches (E.M.F.) **$215.00**
Price: Single cased set (Navy Arms) **$300.00**
Price: Double cased set (Navy Arms) **$490.00**
Price: 1861 Navy: Same as Army except 36-cal., 7-1/2" bbl.,
weighs 41 oz., cut for shoulder stock; round cylinder
(fluted available), from Cabela's, CVA (brass frame, 44 cal.),
United States Patent Fire-Arms . . . . **$99.95 to $385.00**
Price: Steel frame kit (E.M.F., Euroarms) . . . . **$125.00 to $216.25**
Price: Colt Army Police, fluted cyl., 5-1/2", 36-cal. (Cabela's) **$124.95**
Price: With nickeled frame, barrel and backstrap, gold-tone fluted cylinder,
trigger and hammer, simulated ivory grips (Traditions) **$199.00**

BABY DRAGOON 1848, 1849 POCKET, WELLS FARGO
Caliber: 31. **Barrel:** 3", 4", 5", 6"; seven-groove; RH twist. **Weight:** About 21 oz. **Stocks:** Varnished walnut. **Sights:** Brass pin front, hammer notch rear. **Features:** No loading lever on Baby Dragoon or Wells Fargo models. Unfluted cylinder with stagecoach holdup scene; cupped cylinder pin; no grease grooves; one safety pin on cylinder and slot in hammer face; straight (flat) mainspring. From Armsport, Cimarron F.A. Co., Dixie Gun Works, Uberti U.S.A. Inc.
Price: 6" barrel, with loading lever (Dixie Gun Works) **$275.00**
Price: 4" (Uberti USA Inc.) **$335.00**

CABELA'S 1860 ARMY SNUBNOSE REVOLVER
Caliber: 44. **Barrel:** 3". **Weight:** 2 lbs., 3 oz. **Length:** 9" overall. **Grips:** Hardwood. **Sights:** Blade front, hammer notch near. **Features:** Shortened barrels without loading lever. Brass loading tool included.
Price: Revolver only **$169.99**
Price: With starter kit **$219.99**

CABELA'S 1862 POLICE SNUBNOSE REVOLVER
Caliber: 36. **Barrel:** 3". **Weight:** 2 lbs., 3 oz. **Length:** 8.5" overall. **Grips:** Hardwood. **Sights:** Blade front, hammer notch rear. **Features:** Shortened barrel, removed loading lever. Separate brass loading tool included.
Price: . . . . **$159.99** (revolver only); **$209.99** (with starter kit).

DIXIE WYATT EARP REVOLVER
Caliber: 44. **Barrel:** 12", octagon. **Weight:** 46 oz. **Length:** 18" overall. **Stocks:** Two-piece walnut. **Sights:** Fixed. **Features:** Highly polished brass frame, backstrap and trigger guard; blued barrel and cylinder; case-hardened hammer, trigger and loading lever. Navy-size shoulder stock ($45) requires minor fitting. From Dixie Gun Works.
Price: **$160.00**

LE MAT REVOLVER
Caliber: 44/65. **Barrel:** 6-3/4" (revolver); 4-7/8" (single shot). **Weight:** 3 lbs., 7 oz. **Stocks:** Hand-checkered walnut. **Sights:** Post front, hammer notch rear. **Features:** Exact reproduction with all-steel construction; 44-cal. 9-shot cylinder, 65-cal. single barrel; color case-hardened hammer with selector; spur trigger guard; ring at butt; lever-type barrel release. From Navy Arms.
Price: Cavalry model (lanyard ring, spur trigger guard) **$595.00**
Price: Army model (round trigger guard, pin-type barrel release) . **$595.00**
Price: Naval-style (thumb selector on hammer) **$595.00**

NAVY ARMS NEW MODEL POCKET REVOLVER
Caliber: 31, 5-shot. **Barrel:** 3-1/2", octagon. **Weight:** 15 oz. **Length:** 7-3/4". **Stocks:** Two-piece walnut. **Sights:** Fixed. **Features:** Replica of the Remington New Model Pocket. Available with polished brass frame or nickel-plated finish. Introduced 2000. Imported by Navy Arms.
Price: **$300.00**

NAVY ARMS 1836 PATERSON REVOLVER
Caliber: 36. **Barrel:** 9". **Weight:** 2 lbs., 11 oz. **Length:** NA. **Stocks:** Walnut. **Sights:** NA. **Features:** Hidden trigger, blued barrel, replica of 5-shooter, roll-engraved with stagecoach holdup scene.
Price: . . . . **$340.00 to $499.00**

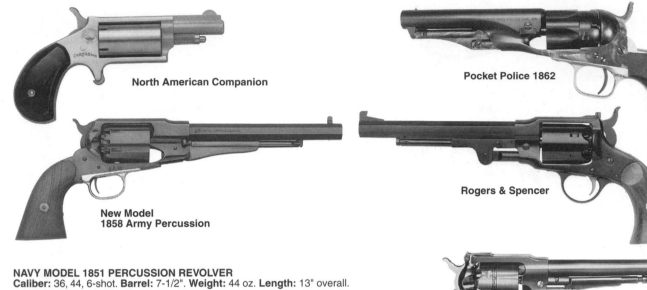

North American Companion

Pocket Police 1862

**New Model
1858 Army Percussion**

Rogers & Spencer

Ruger Old Army

NAVY MODEL 1851 PERCUSSION REVOLVER
Caliber: 36, 44, 6-shot. **Barrel:** 7-1/2". **Weight:** 44 oz. **Length:** 13" overall.
Stocks: Walnut finish. **Sights:** Post front, hammer notch rear. **Features:**
Brass backstrap and trigger guard; some have 1st Model squareback
trigger guard, engraved cylinder with navy battle scene; case-hardened
frame, hammer, loading lever. Imported by The Armoury, Cabela's,
Cimarron F.A. Co., Navy Arms, E.M.F., Dixie Gun Works, Euroarms of
America, Armsport, CVA (44-cal. only), Traditions (44 only), Uberti U.S.A.
Inc., United States Patent Fire-Arms.
Price: Brass frame . . . . $99.95 to $385.00
Price: Steel frame . . . . $130.00 to $285.00
Price: Kit form . . . . $110.00 to $123.95
Price: Engraved model (Dixie Gun Works) $182.50
Price: Single cased set, steel frame (Navy Arms) $280.00
Price: Double cased set, steel frame (Navy Arms) $455.00
Price: Confederate Navy (Cabela's) $89.99
Price: Hartford model, steel frame, German silver trim,
cartouche (E.M.F.) $190.00

NEW MODEL 1858 ARMY PERCUSSION REVOLVER
Caliber: 36 or 44, 6-shot. **Barrel:** 6-1/2" or 8". **Weight:** 38 oz. **Length:**
13-1/2" overall. **Stocks:** Walnut. **Sights:** Blade front, groove-in-frame
rear. **Features:** Replica of Remington Model 1858. Also available from
some importers as Army Model Belt Revolver in 36-cal., a shortened and
lightened version of the 44. Target Model (Uberti U.S.A. Inc., Navy Arms)
has fully adjustable target rear sight, target front, 36 or 44. Imported by
Cabela's, Cimarron F.A. Co., CVA (as 1858 Army, brass frame, 44 only),
Dixie Gun Works, Navy Arms, The Armoury, E.M.F., Euroarms of America
(engraved, stainless and plain), Armsport, Traditions (44 only), Uberti
U.S.A. Inc.
Price: Steel frame, about. . . . . $99.95 to $280.00
Price: Steel frame kit (Euroarms, Navy Arms) . . . . . . $115.95 to $150.00
Price: Single cased set (Navy Arms) $290.00
Price: Double cased set (Navy Arms) $480.00
Price: Stainless steel Model 1858 (Euroarms, Uberti U.S.A. Inc., Cabela's,
Navy Arms, Armsport, Traditions) . . . . $169.95 to $380.00
Price: Target Model, adjustable rear sight (Cabela's, Euroarms, Uberti
U.S.A. Inc., Stone Mountain Arms) . . . . $95.95 to $399.00
Price: Brass frame (CVA, Cabela's, Traditions, Navy
Arms) . . . . $79.95 to $159.95
Price: As above, kit (Dixie Gun Works, Navy Arms) . . . $145.00 to $188.95
Price: Buffalo model, 44-cal. (Cabela's) $119.99
Price: Hartford model, steel frame, German silver trim,
cartouche (E.M.F.) $215.00

NORTH AMERICAN COMPANION PERCUSSION REVOLVER
Caliber: 22. **Barrel:** 1-1/8". **Weight:** 5.1 oz. **Length:** 4-1/2" overall. **Stocks:**
Laminated wood. **Sights:** Blade front, notch fixed rear. **Features:** All

stainless steel construction. Uses standard #11 percussion caps. Comes
with bullets, powder measure, bullet seater, leather clip holster, gun rag.
Long Rifle or Magnum frame size. Introduced 1996. Made in U.S. by North
American Arms.
Price: Long Rifle frame. $156.00

North American Magnum Companion Percussion Revolver
Similar to the Companion except has larger frame. Weighs 7.2 oz., has 1-
5/8" barrel, measures 5-7/16" overall. Comes with bullets, powder
measure, bullet seater, leather clip holster, gun rag. Introduced 1996.
Made in U.S. by North American Arms.
Price: $215.00

POCKET POLICE 1862 PERCUSSION REVOLVER
Caliber: 36, 5-shot. **Barrel:** 4-1/2", 5-1/2", 6-1/2", 7-1/2". **Weight:** 26 oz.
Length: 12" overall (6-1/2" bbl.). **Stocks:** Walnut. **Sights:** Fixed.
Features: Round tapered barrel; half-fluted and rebated cylinder; case-
hardened frame, loading lever and hammer; silver or brass trigger guard
and backstrap. Imported by Dixie Gun Works, Navy Arms (5-1/2" only),
Uberti U.S.A. Inc. (5-1/2", 6-1/2" only), United States Patent Fire-Arms
and Cimarron F.A. Co.
Price: About . . . . $139.95 to $335.00
Price: Single cased set with accessories (Navy Arms) $365.00
Price: Hartford model, steel frame, German silver trim,
cartouche (E.M.F.) $215.00

ROGERS & SPENCER PERCUSSION REVOLVER
Caliber: 44. **Barrel:** 7-1/2". **Weight:** 47 oz. **Length:** 13-3/4" overall.
Stocks: Walnut. **Sights:** Cone front, integral groove in frame for rear.
Features: Accurate reproduction of a Civil War design. Solid frame; extra
large nipple cut-out on rear of cylinder; loading lever and cylinder easily
removed for cleaning. From Dixie Gun Works, Euroarms of America
(standard blue, engraved, burnished, target models), Navy Arms.
Price: . . . . $160.00 to $299.95
Price: Nickel-plated $215.00
Price: Engraved (Euroarms) $287.00
Price: Kit version . . . . $245.00 to $252.00
Price: Target version (Euroarms) . . . . $239.00 to $270.00
Price: Burnished London Gray (Euroarms) . . . . $245.00 to $270.00

Spiller & Burr

3rd U.S. Model Dragoon

Texas Paterson

Walker

RUGER OLD ARMY PERCUSSION REVOLVER

Caliber: 45, 6-shot. Uses .457" dia. lead bullets or 454 conical. **Barrel:** 5-1/2", 7-1/2" (6-groove; 1:16" twist). **Weight:** 2-7/8 lbs. **Length:** 11-1/2" and 13-1/2" overall. **Stocks:** Rosewood, simulated ivory. **Sights:** Ramp front, rear adjustable for windage and elevation; or fixed (groove). **Features:** Stainless steel; standard size nipples, chrome-moly steel cylinder and frame, same lockwork as original Super Blackhawk. Also stainless steel. Includes hard case and lock. Made in USA. From Sturm, Ruger & Co.

Price: Blued steel, fixed sight (Model BP-5F) **$541.00**
Price: Stainless steel, fixed sight (Model KBP-5F-I) **$623.00**
Price: Stainless steel (Model KBP-7) **$577.00**
Price: Stainless steel, fixed sight (KBP-7F) **$577.00**

SHERIFF MODEL 1851 PERCUSSION REVOLVER

Caliber: 36, 44, 6-shot. **Barrel:** 5". **Weight:** 40 oz. **Length:** 10-1/2" overall. **Stocks:** Walnut. **Sights:** Fixed. **Features:** Brass backstrap and trigger guard; engraved navy scene; case-hardened frame, hammer, loading lever. Imported by E.M.F.

Price: Steel frame **$169.95**
Price: Brass frame **$140.00**

SPILLER & BURR REVOLVER

Caliber: 36 (.375" round ball). **Barrel:** 7", octagon. **Weight:** 2-1/2 lbs. **Length:** 12-1/2" overall. **Stocks:** Two-piece walnut. **Sights:** Fixed. **Features:** Reproduction of the C.S.A. revolver. Brass frame and trigger guard. Also available as a kit. From Dixie Gun Works, Navy Arms.

Price: **$150.00**
Price: Kit form (Dixie) **$125.00**
Price: Single cased set (Navy Arms) **$270.00**
Price: Double cased set (Navy Arms) **$430.00**

TEXAS PATERSON 1836 REVOLVER

Caliber: 36 (.375" round ball). **Barrel:** 7-1/2". **Weight:** 42 oz. **Stocks:** One-piece walnut. **Sights:** Fixed. **Features:** Copy of Sam Colt's first commercially-made revolving pistol. Comes with loading tool. From Cimarron F.A. Co., Dixie Gun Works, Navy Arms, Uberti U.S.A. Inc.

Price: About **$495.00**
Price: With loading lever (Uberti U.S.A. Inc.) **$450.00**
Price: Engraved (Navy Arms) **$485.00**

UBERTI 1861 NAVY PERCUSSION REVOLVER

Caliber: 36. **Barrel:** 7-1/2", round. **Weight:** 40-1/2 oz. **Stocks:** One-piece oiled American walnut. **Sights:** Brass pin front, hammer notch rear. **Features:** Rounded trigger guard, German silver blade front sight, "creeping" loading lever. Available with fluted or round cylinder. Imported by Uberti U.S.A. Inc.

Price: Steel backstrap, trigger guard, cut for stock **$265.00**

1ST U.S. MODEL DRAGOON

Caliber: 44. **Barrel:** 7-1/2", part round, part octagon. **Weight:** 64 oz. **Stocks:** One-piece walnut. **Sights:** German silver blade front, hammer notch rear. **Features:** First model has oval bolt cuts in cylinder, square-back flared trigger guard, V-type mainspring, short trigger. Ranger and Indian scene roll-engraved on cylinder. Color case-hardened frame, loading lever, plunger and hammer; blue barrel, cylinder, trigger and wedge. Available with old-time charcoal blue or standard blue-black finish. Polished brass backstrap and trigger guard. From Cimarron F.A. Co., Dixie Gun Works, Uberti U.S.A. Inc., Navy Arms.

Price: . . . . **$295.00 to $435.00**

2nd U.S. Model Dragoon Revolver

Similar to the 1st Model except distinguished by rectangular bolt cuts in the cylinder. From Cimarron F.A. Co., Uberti U.S.A. Inc., United States Patent Fire-Arms, Navy Arms, Dixie Gunworks.

Price: . . . . **$295.00 to $435.00**

3rd U.S. Model Dragoon Revolver

Similar to the 2nd Model except for oval trigger guard, long trigger, modifications to the loading lever and latch. Imported by Cimarron F.A. Co., Uberti U.S.A. Inc., United States Patent Fire-Arms, Dixie Gunworks.

Price: Military model (frame cut for shoulder stock,
steel backstrap . . . . **$295.00 to $435.00**
Price: Civilian (brass backstrap, trigger guard) . . . . . . **$295.00 to $325.00**

1861 NAVY PERCUSSION REVOLVER

Caliber: 36, 6-shot. **Barrel:** 7-1/2", 7-groove, round. **Weight:** 2 lbs., 6 oz. **Length:** 13". **Stocks:** One-piece walnut. **Sights:** German silver blade front sight. **Features:** Rounded trigger guard, "creeping" loading lever, fluted or round cylinder, steel backstrap, trigger guard, cut for stock. Imported by Cimarron F.A. Co., Uberti U.S.A. Inc., Dixie Gunworks.

Price: . . . . **$255.00 to $300.00**

1862 POCKET NAVY PERCUSSION REVOLVER

Caliber: 36, 5-shot. **Barrel:** 5-1/2", 6-1/2", octagonal, 7-groove, LH twist. **Weight:** 27 oz. (5-1/2" barrel). **Length:** 10-1/2" overall (5-1/2" bbl.). **Stocks:** One-piece varnished walnut. **Sights:** Brass pin front, hammer notch rear. **Features:** Rebated cylinder, hinged loading lever, brass or silver-plated backstrap and trigger guard, color-cased frame, hammer, loading lever, plunger and latch, rest blued. Has original-type markings. From Cimarron F.A. Co., Uberti U.S.A. Inc., Dixie Gunworks.

Price: With brass backstrap, trigger guard . . . . **$260.00 to $310.00**

WALKER 1847 PERCUSSION REVOLVER

Caliber: 44, 6-shot. **Barrel:** 9". **Weight:** 84 oz. **Length:** 15-1/2" overall. **Stocks:** Walnut. **Sights:** Fixed. **Features:** Case-hardened frame, loading lever and hammer; iron backstrap; brass trigger guard; engraved cylinder. Imported by Cabela's, Cimarron F.A. Co., Navy Arms, Dixie Gun Works, Uberti U.S.A. Inc., E.M.F., Cimarron, Traditions, United States Patent Fire-Arms.

Price: About . . . . **$225.00 to $445.00**
Price: Single cased set (Navy Arms) **$405.00**
Price: Deluxe Walker with French fitted case (Navy Arms) **$540.00**
Price: Hartford model, steel frame, German silver trim,
cartouche (E.M.F.) **$295.00**

BLACKPOWDER MUSKETS & RIFLES

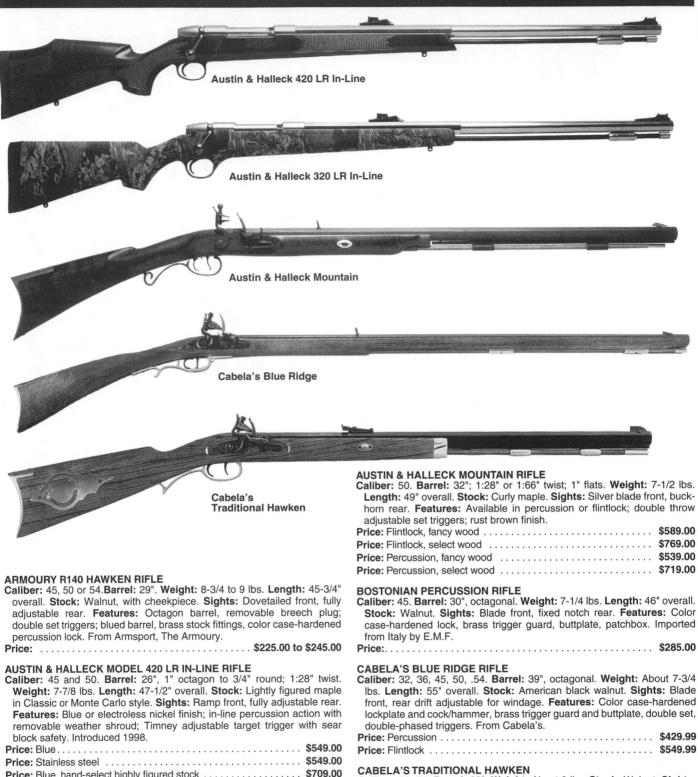

Austin & Halleck 420 LR In-Line

Austin & Halleck 320 LR In-Line

Austin & Halleck Mountain

Cabela's Blue Ridge

Cabela's Traditional Hawken

AUSTIN & HALLECK MOUNTAIN RIFLE
Caliber: 50. **Barrel:** 32"; 1:28" or 1:66" twist; 1" flats. **Weight:** 7-1/2 lbs. **Length:** 49" overall. **Stock:** Curly maple. **Sights:** Silver blade front, buckhorn rear. **Features:** Available in percussion or flintlock; double throw adjustable set triggers; rust brown finish.
Price: Flintlock, fancy wood **$589.00**
Price: Flintlock, select wood **$769.00**
Price: Percussion, fancy wood **$539.00**
Price: Percussion, select wood **$719.00**

BOSTONIAN PERCUSSION RIFLE
Caliber: 45. **Barrel:** 30", octagonal. **Weight:** 7-1/4 lbs. **Length:** 46" overall. **Stock:** Walnut. **Sights:** Blade front, fixed notch rear. **Features:** Color case-hardened lock, brass trigger guard, buttplate, patchbox. Imported from Italy by E.M.F.
Price: **$285.00**

CABELA'S BLUE RIDGE RIFLE
Caliber: 32, 36, 45, 50, .54. **Barrel:** 39", octagonal. **Weight:** About 7-3/4 lbs. **Length:** 55" overall. **Stock:** American black walnut. **Sights:** Blade front, rear drift adjustable for windage. **Features:** Color case-hardened lockplate and cock/hammer, brass trigger guard and buttplate, double set, double-phased triggers. From Cabela's.
Price: Percussion **$429.99**
Price: Flintlock **$549.99**

CABELA'S TRADITIONAL HAWKEN
Caliber: 50, 54. **Barrel:** 29". **Weight:** About 9 lbs. **Stock:** Walnut. **Sights:** Blade front, open adjustable rear. **Features:** Flintlock or percussion. Adjustable double-set triggers. Polished brass furniture, color case-hardened lock. Imported by Cabela's.
Price: Percussion, right-hand **$269.99**
Price: Percussion, left-hand **$269.99**
Price: Flintlock, right-hand **$299.99**

ARMOURY R140 HAWKEN RIFLE
Caliber: 45, 50 or 54. **Barrel:** 29". **Weight:** 8-3/4 to 9 lbs. **Length:** 45-3/4" overall. **Stock:** Walnut, with cheekpiece. **Sights:** Dovetailed front, fully adjustable rear. **Features:** Octagon barrel, removable breech plug; double set triggers; blued barrel, brass stock fittings, color case-hardened percussion lock. From Armsport, The Armoury.
Price: . . . . $225.00 to $245.00

AUSTIN & HALLECK MODEL 420 LR IN-LINE RIFLE
Caliber: 45 and 50. **Barrel:** 26", 1" octagon to 3/4" round; 1:28" twist. **Weight:** 7-7/8 lbs. **Length:** 47-1/2" overall. **Stock:** Lightly figured maple in Classic or Monte Carlo style. **Sights:** Ramp front, fully adjustable rear. **Features:** Blue or electroless nickel finish; in-line percussion action with removable weather shroud; Timney adjustable target trigger with sear block safety. Introduced 1998.
Price: Blue **$549.00**
Price: Stainless steel **$549.00**
Price: Blue, hand-select highly figured stock **$709.00**
Price: Stainless steel, select stock **$739.00**

Austin & Halleck Model 320 LR In-Line Rifle
Similar to the Model 420 LR (45 and 50 calibers) except has black resin synthetic stock with checkered grip and forend. Introduced 1998.
Price: Blue **$419.00**
Price: Stainless steel **$449.00**

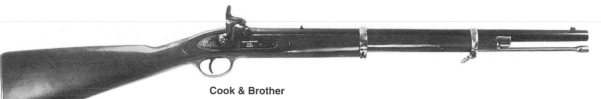

Cook & Brother

Cabela's Sporterized Hawken Hunter Rifle
Similar to the Traditional Hawken except has more modern stock style with rubber recoil pad, blued furniture, sling swivels. Percussion only, in 50- or 54-caliber.
Price: Carbine or rifle, right-hand $329.99

CABELA'S KODIAK EXPRESS DOUBLE RIFLE
Caliber: 50, 54, 58, 72. **Barrel:** Length NA; 1:48" twist. **Weight:** 9.3 lbs. **Length:** 45-1/4" overall. **Stock:** European walnut, oil finish. **Sights:** Fully adjustable double folding-leaf rear, ramp front. **Features:** Percussion. Barrels regulated to point of aim at 75 yards; polished and engraved lock, top tang and trigger guard. From Cabela's.
Price: 50, 54, 58 calibers. $769.99
Price: 72 caliber $799.99

COOK & BROTHER CONFEDERATE CARBINE
Caliber: 58. **Barrel:** 24". **Weight:** 7-1/2 lbs. **Length:** 40-1/2" overall. **Stock:** Select walnut. **Features:** Re-creation of the 1861 New Orleans made artillery carbine. Color case-hardened lock, browned barrel. Buttplate, trigger guard, barrel bands, sling swivels and nosecap of polished brass. From Euroarms of America.
Price: $513.00
Price: Cook & Brother rifle (33" barrel) $552.00

CVA BOBCAT RIFLE
Caliber: 50 percussion. **Barrel:** 26"; 1:48" twist, octagonal. **Weight:** 6 lbs. **Length:** 42" overall. **Stock:** Dura-Grip synthetic or wood. **Sights:** Blade front, open rear. **Features:** Oversize trigger guard; wood ramrod; matte black finish. From CVA.
Price: (Wood stock) $99.95
Price: (Black synthetic stock) $69.95

CVA MOUNTAIN RIFLE
Caliber: 50. **Barrel:** 32"; 1:48" rifling. **Weight:** 8-1/2 lbs. **Length:** NA. **Sights:** Blade front, buckhorn rear. **Features:** Browned steel furniture, patchbox. Made in U.S. From CVA.
Price: $259.95

CVA ST. LOUIS HAWKEN RIFLE
Caliber: 50, 54. **Barrel:** 28", octagon; 15/16" across flats; 1:48" twist. **Weight:** 8 lbs. **Length:** 44" overall. **Stock:** Select hardwood. **Sights:** Beaded blade front, fully adjustable open rear. **Features:** Fully adjustable double-set triggers; synthetic ramrod (kits have wood); brass patchbox, wedge plates, nosecap, thimbles, trigger guard and buttplate; blued barrel; color case-hardened, engraved lockplate. V-type mainspring. Button breech. Introduced 1981. From CVA.
Price: St. Louis Hawken, finished (50-, 54-cal.) $229.95

CVA FIREBOLT MUSKETMAG BOLT-ACTION IN-LINE RIFLES
Caliber: 45 or 50. **Barrel:** 26". **Weight:** 7 lbs. **Length:** 44". **Stock:** Rubber-coated black or Mossy Oak® Break-Up™ camo synthetic. **Sights:** CVA Illuminator Fiber-Optic Sight System. **Features:** Bolt-action, inline ignition system handles up to 150 grains blackpowder or Pyrodex; nickel or matte blue barrel; removable breech plug; trigger-block safety. Three-way ignition system. From CVA.
Price: FiberGrip/nickel, 50 cal. $294.95
Price: Break-Up™/nickel, 50 cal. $259.95
Price: FiberGrip/nickel, 45 cal. $294.95
Price: Break-Up™/nickel, 45 cal. $259.95
Price: FiberGrip/blue, 50 cal. $199.95
Price: Break-Up™/blue, 50 cal. $239.95

Price: FiberGrip/blue, 45 cal. $199.95
Price: Break-Up™/blue, 45 cal. $239.95

CVA Hunterbolt 209 Magnum Rifle
Similar to the Firebolt except has 26" barrel and black or Mossy Oak® Break-Up™ synthetic stock. Three-way ignition system. Weighs 6 lbs. From CVA.
Price: 45 or 50 cal. . . . . $179.95 to $234.95

CVA OPTIMA PRO 209 BREAK-ACTION RIFLE
Caliber: 45, 50. **Barrel:** 29" fluted, blue or nickel. **Weight:** 8.8 lbs. **Stock:** Ambidextrous Mossy Oak® Camo or black FiberGrip. **Sights:** Adj. fiber-optic. **Features:** Break-action, stainless No. 209 breech plug, aluminum loading rod, cocking spur, lifetime warranty.
Price: Mossy Oak® Camo $399.95
Price: Camo, nickel bbl. $379.95
Price: Mossy Oak® Camo/blued $349.95
Price: Black/nickel $329.95
Price: Black/blued $299.95
Price: Blued fluted bbl. $99.95
Price: Nickel fluted bbl. $115.95

CVA Optima 209 Magnum Break-Action Rifle
Similar to Optima Pro but with 26" bbl., nickel or blue finish.
Price: Mossy Oak® Camo/nickel $299.95
Price: Mossy Oak® Camo/blue $279.95
Price: Black/nickel $254.95
Price: Black/blued $224.95

CVA Optima Elite
Similar to Optima Pro but chambered for 45, 50 black powder plus 243, 270, 30-06 centerfire cartridges.
Price: Hardwoods Green HD/blue $415.00
Price: Black Fleck/blue $355.00

CVA BUCKHORN 209 MAGNUM
Caliber: 50. **Barrel:** 24". **Weight:** 6.3 lbs. **Sights:** Illuminator fiber-optic. **Features:** Grip-dot stock, thumb-actuated safety; drilled and tapped for scope mounts.
Price: Black stock, blue barrel $145.00

CVA KODIAK MAGNUM RIFLE
Caliber: 45, 50. No. 209 primer ignition. **Barrel:** 28"; 1:28" twist. **Stock:** Ambidextrous black or Mossy Oak® camo. **Sights:** Fiber-optic. **Features:** Blue or nickel finish, recoil pad, lifetime warranty. From CVA.
Price: Mossy Oak® camo; nickel barrel $355.00
Price: Mossy Oak® camo; blued barrel $333.00
Price: Black stock; nickel barrel $307.00
Price: Black stock; blued barrel $275.00

DIXIE EARLY AMERICAN JAEGER RIFLE
Caliber: 54. **Barrel:** 27-1/2" octagonal; 1:24" twist. **Weight:** 8-1/4 lbs. **Length:** 43-1/2" overall. **Stock:** American walnut; sliding wooden patchbox on butt. **Sights:** Notch rear, blade front. **Features:** Flintlock or percussion. Browned steel furniture. Imported from Italy by Dixie Gun Works.
Price: Flintlock or percussion $795.00

DIXIE DELUXE CUB RIFLE
Caliber: 40. **Barrel:** 28". **Weight:** 6-1/2 lbs. **Stock:** Walnut. **Sights:** Fixed. **Features:** Short rifle for small game and beginning shooters. Brass patchbox and furniture. Flint or percussion. From Dixie Gun Works.
Price: Finished $450.00
Price: Kit $390.00
Price: Super Cub (50-caliber) $485.00

BLACKPOWDER MUSKETS & RIFLES

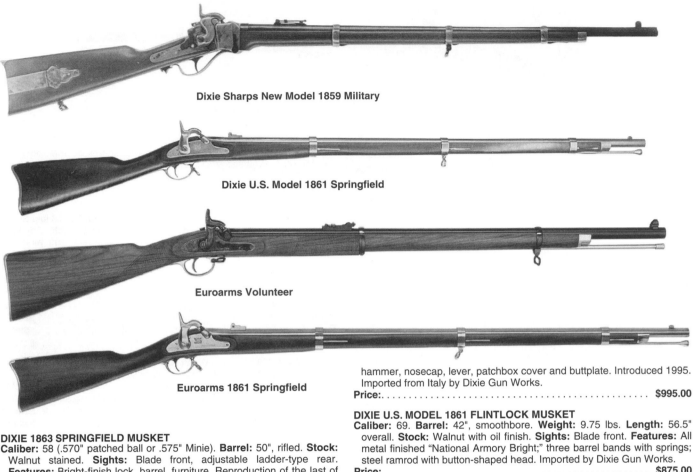

Dixie Sharps New Model 1859 Military

Dixie U.S. Model 1861 Springfield

Euroarms Volunteer

Euroarms 1861 Springfield

DIXIE 1863 SPRINGFIELD MUSKET
Caliber: 58 (.570" patched ball or .575" Minie). **Barrel:** 50", rifled. **Stock:** Walnut stained. **Sights:** Blade front, adjustable ladder-type rear. **Features:** Bright-finish lock, barrel, furniture. Reproduction of the last of the government regulation muzzleloaders. Imported from Japan by Dixie Gun Works.
Price: Finished. $625.00
Price: Kit $550.00

DIXIE INLINE CARBINE
Caliber: 50, 54. **Barrel:** 24"; 1:32" twist. **Weight:** 6.5 lbs. **Length:** 41" overall. **Stock:** Walnut-finished hardwood with Monte Carlo comb. **Sights:** Ramp front with red insert, open fully adjustable rear. **Features:** Sliding bolt fully encloses cap and nipple. Fully adjustable trigger, automatic safety. Aluminum ramrod. Imported from Italy by Dixie Gun Works.
Price: $375.00

DIXIE PEDERSOLI 1857 MAUSER RIFLE
Caliber: 54. **Barrel:** 39-3/8". **Weight:** NA. **Length:** 52" overall. **Stock:** European walnut with oil finish, sling swivels. **Sights:** Fully adjustable rear, lug front. **Features:** Percussion (musket caps). Armory bright finish with color case-hardened lock and barrel tang, engraved lockplate, steel ramrod. Introduced 2000. Imported from Italy by Dixie Gun Works.
Price: $950.00

DIXIE PEDERSOLI 1766 CHARLEVILLE MUSKET
Caliber: 69. **Barrel:** 44-3/4". **Weight:** 10-1/2 lbs. **Length:** 57-1/2" overall. **Stock:** European walnut with oil finish. **Sights:** Fixed rear, lug front. **Features:** Smoothbore flintlock. Armory bright finish with steel furniture and ramrod. Introduced 2000. Imported from Italy by Dixie Gun Works.
Price: $895.00

DIXIE SHARPS NEW MODEL 1859 MILITARY RIFLE
Caliber: 54. **Barrel:** 30", 6-groove; 1:48" twist. **Weight:** 9 lbs. **Length:** 45-1/2" overall. **Stock:** Oiled walnut. **Sights:** Blade front, ladder-style rear. **Features:** Blued barrel, color case-hardened barrel bands, receiver,

hammer, nosecap, lever, patchbox cover and buttplate. Introduced 1995. Imported from Italy by Dixie Gun Works.
Price: $995.00

DIXIE U.S. MODEL 1861 FLINTLOCK MUSKET
Caliber: 69. **Barrel:** 42", smoothbore. **Weight:** 9.75 lbs. **Length:** 56.5" overall. **Stock:** Walnut with oil finish. **Sights:** Blade front. **Features:** All metal finished "National Armory Bright;" three barrel bands with springs; steel ramrod with button-shaped head. Imported by Dixie Gun Works.
Price: $875.00

DIXIE U.S. MODEL 1861 SPRINGFIELD
Caliber: 58. **Barrel:** 40". **Weight:** About 8 lbs. **Length:** 55-13/16" overall. **Stock:** Oil-finished walnut. **Sights:** Blade front, step adjustable rear. **Features:** Exact recreation of original rifle. Sling swivels attached to trigger guard bow and middle barrel band. Lockplate marked "1861" with eagle motif and "U.S. Springfield" in front of hammer; "U.S." stamped on top of buttplate. From Dixie Gun Works.
Price: Kit $550.00

E.M.F. 1863 SHARPS MILITARY CARBINE
Caliber: 54. **Barrel:** 22", round. **Weight:** 8 lbs. **Length:** 39" overall. **Stock:** Oiled walnut. **Sights:** Blade front, military ladder-type rear. **Features:** Color case-hardened lock, rest blued. Imported by E.M.F.
Price: $600.00

EUROARMS VOLUNTEER TARGET RIFLE
Caliber: 451. **Barrel:** 33" (two-band), 36" (three-band). **Weight:** 11 lbs. (two-band). **Length:** 48.75" overall (two-band). **Stock:** European walnut with checkered wrist and forend. **Sights:** Hooded bead front, adjustable rear with interchangeable leaves. **Features:** Alexander Henry-type rifling with 1:20" twist. Color case-hardened hammer and lockplate, brass trigger guard and nosecap, remainder blued. Imported by Euroarms of America, Dixie Gun Works.
Price: Two-band $828.00

EUROARMS 1861 SPRINGFIELD RIFLE
Caliber: 58. **Barrel:** 40". **Weight:** About 10 lbs. **Length:** 55.5" overall. **Stock:** European walnut. **Sights:** Blade front, three-leaf military rear. **Features:** Reproduction of the original three-band rifle. Lockplate marked "1861" with eagle and "U.S. Springfield." White metal. Imported by Euroarms of America.
Price: $579.00

BLACKPOWDER MUSKETS & RIFLES

Gonic Model 93 Thumbhole

Harper's Ferry 1803

J.P. Murray

EUROARMS ZOUAVE RIFLE
Caliber: 58 percussion. **Barrel:** 33". **Overall length:** 49".
Price: $469.00

EUROARMS HARPERS FERRY RIFLE
Caliber: 54 flintlock. **Barrel:** 35". **Overall length:** 50-1/2".
Price: $735.00

EUROARMS RICHMOND RIFLE
Caliber: 58 percussion. **Barrel:** 40". **Overall length:** 49".
Price: $579.00

GONIC MODEL 93 M/L RIFLE
Caliber: 45, 50. **Barrel:** 26"; 1:24" twist. **Weight:** 6-1/2 to 7 lbs. **Length:** 43" overall. **Stock:** American hardwood with black finish **Sights:** Adjustable or aperture rear, hooded post front. **Features:** Adjustable trigger with side safety; unbreakable ramrod; comes with A. Z. scope bases installed. Introduced 1993. Made in U.S. by Gonic Arms, Inc.
Price: Model 93 Standard (blued barrel)................... $720.00
Price: Model 93 Standard (stainless brl., 50 cal. only) $782.00

Gonic Model 93 Deluxe M/L Rifle
Similar to the Model 93 except has classic-style walnut or gray laminated wood stock. Introduced 1998. Made in U.S. by Gonic Arms, Inc.
Price: Blue barrel, sights, scope base, choice of stock........... $902.00
Price: Stainless barrel, sights, scope base, choice of stock
(50 cal. only) $964.00

Gonic Model 93 Mountain Thumbhole M/L Rifles
Similar to the Model 93 except has high-grade walnut or gray laminate stock with extensive hand-checkered panels, Monte Carlo cheekpiece and beavertail forend; integral muzzle brake. Introduced 1998. Made in U.S. by Gonic Arms, Inc.
Price: Blued or stainless $2,700.00

H&R SIDEKICK
Caliber: 50, 209 primer ignition. **Barrel:** 24 or 26 (magnum). **Weight:** 6-1/2 lbs. **Length:** 39-1/4 to 41-1/4. **Stock:** Black matte polymer or hardwood. **Sights:** Adjustable fiber-optic open, tapped for scope mounts. **Features:** Break-action single-shot. Uses No. 209 shotgun primer held in place by special primer carrier. Telescoping brass ramrod. Introduced 2004.
Price: (Wood stock, blued finish, case-hardened frame) .... NA
Price: (Stainless, polymer stock) .... NA

H&R HUNTSMAN
Caliber: 50, 209 primer ignition. **Barrel:** 24". **Weight:** 6-1/2 lbs. **Length:** 40". **Stock:** Black matte polymer or hardwood. **Sights:** Fiber-optic open

sights, tapped for scope mounts. **Features:** Break-open action, transfer-bar safety system, breech plug removable for cleaning. Introduced 2004.
Price: Stainless model .... NA
Price: Blued finish .... NA
Price: Combo model (12 ga., . 50 cal. muzzleloader, .243 Win) .... NA

HARPER'S FERRY 1803 FLINTLOCK RIFLE
Caliber: 54 or 58. **Barrel:** 35". **Weight:** 9 lbs. **Length:** 59-1/2" overall. **Stock:** Walnut with cheekpiece. **Sights:** Brass blade front, fixed steel rear. **Features:** Brass trigger guard, sideplate, buttplate; steel patchbox. Imported by Euroarms of America, Navy Arms (54-cal. only), Cabela's, and Dixie Gun Works.
Price: .... $495.95 to $729.00
Price: 54-cal. (Navy Arms) $625.00
Price: 54-cal. (Cabela's) $599.99
Price: 54-cal. (Dixie Gun Works) $795.00
Price: 54-cal. (Euroarms) $575.00

HAWKEN RIFLE
Caliber: 45, 50, 54 or 58. **Barrel:** 28", blued, 6-groove rifling. **Weight:** 8-3/4 lbs. **Length:** 44" overall. **Stock:** Walnut with cheekpiece. **Sights:** Blade front, fully adjustable rear. **Features:** Coil mainspring, double-set triggers, polished brass furniture. From Armsport and E.M.F.
Price: .... $220.00 to $345.00

J.P. HENRY TRADE RIFLE
Caliber: 54. **Barrel:** 34"; 1" flats. **Weight:** 8-1/2 lbs. **Length:** 45" overall. **Stock:** Premium curly maple. **Sights:** Silver blade front, fixed buckhorn rear. **Features:** Brass buttplate, side plate, trigger guard and nosecap; browned barrel and lock; L&R Large English percussion lock; single trigger. Made in U.S. by J.P. Gunstocks, Inc.
Price: $965.50

J.P. MURRAY 1862-1864 CAVALRY CARBINE
Caliber: 58 (.577" Minie). **Barrel:** 23". **Weight:** 7 lbs., 9 oz. **Length:** 39" overall. **Stock:** Walnut. **Sights:** Blade front, rear drift adjustable for windage. **Features:** Browned barrel, color case-hardened lock, blued swivel and band springs, polished brass buttplate, trigger guard, barrel bands. From Euroarms of America.
Price: $521.00

KENTUCKIAN RIFLE
Caliber: 44. **Barrel:** 35". **Weight:** 7 lbs. (rifle), 5-1/2 lbs. (carbine). **Length:** 51" overall (rifle), 43" (carbine). **Stock:** Walnut stain. **Sights:** Brass blade front, steel V-ramp rear. **Features:** Octagon barrel, case-hardened and engraved lockplates. Brass furniture. Imported by Dixie Gun Works.
Price: Flintlock or Percussion $395.00

Kentucky Flintlock

Knight 50 Caliber DISC In-Line

Knight Master Hunter DISC Extreme

London Armory 1861

KENTUCKY FLINTLOCK RIFLE
Caliber: 44, 45, or 50. **Barrel:** 35". **Weight:** 7 lbs. **Length:** 50" overall. **Stock:** Walnut stained, brass fittings. **Sights:** Fixed. **Features:** Available in carbine model also, 28" bbl. Some variations in detail, finish. Kits also available from some importers. Imported by The Armoury.
Price: About.................................. **$217.95 to $345.00**

Kentucky Percussion Rifle
Similar to Flintlock except percussion lock. Finish and features vary with importer. Imported by The Armoury and CVA.
Price: About... **$259.95**
Price: 45 or 50 cal. (Navy Arms) **$425.00**
Price: Kit, 50 cal. (CVA) **$189.95**

KNIGHT 50 CALIBER DISC IN-LINE RIFLE
Caliber: 50. **Barrel:** 24", 26". **Weight:** 7 lbs., 14 oz. **Length:** 43" overall (24" barrel). **Stock:** Checkered synthetic with palm swell grip, rubber recoil pad, swivel studs; black, Advantage or Mossy Oak® Break-Up camouflage. **Sights:** Bead on ramp front, fully adjustable open rear. **Features:** Bolt-action in-line system uses #209 shotshell primer for ignition; primer is held in plastic drop-in Primer Disc. Available in blued or stainless steel. Made in U.S. by Knight Rifles (Modern Muzzleloading).
Price: .... **$439.95 to $632.45**

Knight Master Hunter II DISC In-Line Rifle
Similar to Knight 50 caliber DISC rifle except features premium, wood laminated two-tone stock, gold-plated trigger and engraved trigger guard, jeweled bolt and fluted, air-gauged Green Mountain 26" barrel. Length 45" overall, weighs 7 lbs., 7 oz. Includes black composite thumbhole stock. Introduced 2000. Made in U.S. by Knight Rifles (Modern Muzzleloading).
Price: **$1,099.95**

KNIGHT MUZZLELOADER DISC EXTREME
Caliber: 45 fluted, 50. **Barrel:** 26". **Stock:** Stainless steel laminate, blued walnut, black composite thumbhole with blued or SS. **Sights:** Fully adjustable metallic. **Features:** New full plastic jacket ignition system.
Price: 50 SS laminate **$703.95**
Price: 45 SS laminate **$769.95**
Price: 50 blue walnut **$626.95**
Price: 45 blue walnut **$703.95**
Price: 50 blue composite **$549.95**
Price: 45 blue composite **$632.45**
Price: 50 SS composite **$632.45**
Price: 45 SS composite **$703.95**

Knight Master Hunter DISC Extreme
Similar to DISC Extreme except fluted barrel, two-tone laminated thumbhole Monte Carlo-style stock, black composite thumbhole field stock included. Jeweled bolt, adjustable premium trigger.
Price: 50 .... **$1,044.95**

KNIGHT AMERICAN KNIGHT M/L RIFLE
Caliber: 50. **Barrel:** 22"; 1:28" twist. **Weight:** 6 lbs. **Length:** 41" overall. **Stock:** Black composite. **Sights:** Bead on ramp front, open fully adjustable rear. **Features:** Double safety system; one-piece removable hammer assembly; drilled and tapped for scope mounting. Introduced 1998. Made in U.S. by Knight Rifles.
Price: blued, black comp **$197.95**
Price: blued, black comp VP **$225.45**

KNIGHT WOLVERINE 209
Caliber: 50. **Barrel:** 22". **Stock:** HD stock with SS barrel, break-up stock blued, black composite thumbhole with stainless steel, standard black composite with blued or SS. **Sights:** Metallic with fiber-optic. **Features:** Double safety system, adjustable match grade trigger, left-hand model available. Full plastic jacket ignition system.
Price: Starting at **$302.45**

KNIGHT REVOLUTION
Caliber: 50, 209 primer ignition. **Barrel:** Stainless, 27". **Weight:** 7 lbs., 14 oz. **Stock:** Walnut, laminated, black composite, Mossy Oak® Break-Up™ or Hardwoods Green finish. **Features:** Blued or stainless finish, adjustable trigger and sights.
Price: .... **NA**

LONDON ARMORY 1861 ENFIELD MUSKETOON
Caliber: 58, Minie ball. **Barrel:** 24", round. **Weight:** 7 to 7-1/2 lbs. **Length:** 40-1/2" overall. **Stock:** Walnut, with sling swivels. **Sights:** Blade front, graduated military-leaf rear. **Features:** Brass trigger guard, nosecap, buttplate; blued barrel, bands, lockplate, swivels. Imported by Euroarms of America, Navy Arms.
Price:. .... **$300.00 to $515.00**
Price: Kit .... **$365.00 to $373.00**

Lyman Trade

Lyman Deerstalker

Lyman Great Plains

Price: 50 or 54 cal., percussion, left-hand, carbine $695.40
Price: 50 or 54 cal., flintlock, left-hand $645.00
Price: 54 cal. flintlock $780.50
Price: 54 cal. percussion $821.80
Price: Stainless steel $959.80

LONDON ARMORY 2-BAND 1858 ENFIELD
Caliber: .577" Minie, .575" round ball. **Barrel:** 33". **Weight:** 10 lbs. **Length:** 49" overall. **Stock:** Walnut. **Sights:** Folding leaf rear adjustable for elevation. **Features:** Blued barrel, color case-hardened lock and hammer, polished brass buttplate, trigger guard, nosecap. From Navy Arms, Euroarms of America, Dixie Gun Works.
Price: . . . . $385.00 to $600.00

LONDON ARMORY 3-BAND 1853 ENFIELD
Caliber: 58 (.577" Minie, .575" round ball, .580" maxi ball). **Barrel:** 39". **Weight:** 9-1/2 lbs. **Length:** 54" overall. **Stock:** European walnut. **Sights:** Inverted "V" front, traditional Enfield folding ladder rear. **Features:** Re-creation of the famed London Armory Company Pattern 1853 Enfield Musket. One-piece walnut stock, brass buttplate, trigger guard and nosecap. Lockplate marked "London Armoury Co." and with a British crown. Blued Baddeley barrel bands. From Dixie Gun Works, Euroarms of America, Navy Arms.
Price: About. . . . . $350.00 to $645.00
Price: Assembled kit (Dixie, Euroarms of America) $495.00

LYMAN TRADE RIFLE
Caliber: 50, 54. **Barrel:** 28" octagon;1:48" twist. **Weight:** 8-3/4 lbs. **Length:** 45" overall. **Stock:** European walnut. **Sights:** Blade front, open rear adjustable for windage or optional fixed sights. **Features:** Fast twist rifling for conical bullets. Polished brass furniture with blue steel parts, stainless steel nipple. Hook breech, single trigger, coil spring percussion lock. Steel barrel rib and ramrod ferrules. Introduced 1980. From Lyman.
Price: 50 cal. percussion $581.80
Price: 50 cal. flintlock $652.80
Price: 54 cal. percussion $581.80
Price: 54 cal. flintlock $652.80

LYMAN DEERSTALKER RIFLE
Caliber: 50, 54. **Barrel:** 24", octagonal; 1:48" rifling. **Weight:** 7-1/2 lbs. **Stock:** Walnut with black rubber buttpad. **Sights:** Lyman #37MA beaded front, fully adjustable fold-down Lyman #16A rear. **Features:** Stock has less drop for quick sighting. All metal parts are blackened, with color case-hardened lock; single trigger. Comes with sling and swivels. Available in flint or percussion. Introduced 1990. From Lyman.
Price: 50 cal. flintlock. $652.80

LYMAN GREAT PLAINS RIFLE
Caliber: 50, 54. **Barrel:** 32"; 1:60" twist. **Weight:** 9 lbs. **Stock:** Walnut. **Sights:** Steel blade front, buckhorn rear adjustable for windage and elevation and fixed notch primitive sight included. **Features:** Blued steel furniture. Stainless steel nipple. Coil spring lock, Hawken-style trigger guard and double-set triggers. Round thimbles recessed and sweated into rib. Steel wedge plates and toe plate. Introduced 1979. From Lyman.
Price: Percussion $469.95
Price: Flintlock $494.95
Price: Percussion kit $359.95
Price: Flintlock kit $384.95
Price: Left-hand percussion $474.95
Price: Left-hand flintlock $499.95

Lyman Great Plains Hunter Model
Similar to Great Plains model except 1:32" twist shallow-groove barrel and comes drilled and tapped for Lyman 57GPR peep sight.
Price:. $959.80

MARKESBERY KM BLACK BEAR M/L RIFLE
Caliber: 36, 45, 50, 54. **Barrel:** 24"; 1:26" twist. **Weight:** 6-1/2 lbs. **Length:** 38-1/2" overall. **Stock:** Two-piece American hardwood, walnut, black laminate, green laminate, black composition, X-Tra or Mossy Oak® Break-Up™ camouflage. **Sights:** Bead front, open fully adjustable rear. **Features:** Interchangeable barrels; exposed hammer; Outer-Line Magnum ignition system uses small rifle primer or standard No. 11 cap and nipple. Blue, black matte, or stainless. Made in U.S. by Markesbery Muzzle Loaders.
Price: American hardwood walnut, blue finish $536.63
Price: American hardwood walnut, stainless $553.09
Price: Black laminate, blue finish $539.67
Price: Black laminate, stainless $556.27
Price: Camouflage stock, blue finish $556.46
Price: Camouflage stock, stainless $573.73
Price: Black composite, blue finish $532.65
Price: Black composite, stainless $549.93
Price: Green laminate, blue finish $539.00
Price: Green laminate, stainless $556.27

Markesbery KM Colorado

Mississippi 1841

Markesbery KM Brown Bear Rifle

Similar to KM Black Bear except one-piece thumbhole stock with Monte Carlo comb. Stock in Crotch Walnut composite, green or black laminate, black composite or X-Tra or Mossy Oak® Break-Up™ camouflage. Made in U.S. by Markesbery Muzzle Loaders, Inc.

Price: Black composite, blue finish $658.83
Price: Crotch Walnut, blue finish $658.83
Price: Camo composite, blue finish $682.64
Price: Walnut wood $662.81
Price: Black wood $662.81
Price: Black laminated wood $662.81
Price: Green laminated wood $662.81
Price: Camo wood $684.69
Price: Black composite, stainless $676.11
Price: Crotch Walnut composite, stainless $676.11
Price: Camo composite, stainless $697.69
Price: Walnut wood, stainless $680.07
Price: Black wood, stainless $680.07
Price: Black laminated wood, stainless $680.07
Price: Green laminate, stainless $680.07
Price: Camo wood, stainless $702.76

Markesbery KM Grizzly Bear Rifle

Similar to KM Black Bear except thumbhole buttstock with Monte Carlo comb. Stock in Crotch Walnut composite, green or black laminate, black composite or X-Tra or Mossy Oak® Break-Up camouflage. Made in U.S. by Markesbery Muzzle Loaders, Inc.

Price: Black composite, blue finish $642.96
Price: Crotch Walnut, blue finish $642.96
Price: Camo composite, blue finish $666.67
Price: Walnut wood $646.93
Price: Black wood $646.93
Price: Black laminate wood $646.93
Price: Green laminate wood $646.93
Price: Camo wood $670.74
Price: Black composite, stainless $660.98
Price: Crotch Walnut composite, stainless $660.98
Price: Black laminate wood, stainless $664.20
Price: Green laminate, stainless $664.20
Price: Camo wood, stainless $685.74
Price: Camo composite, stainless $684.04
Price: Walnut wood, stainless $664.20
Price: Black wood, stainless $664.20

Markesbery KM Polar Bear Rifle

Similar to KM Black Bear except one-piece stock with Monte Carlo comb. Stock in American Hardwood walnut, green or black laminate, black composite, or X-Tra or Mossy Oak® Break-Up™ camouflage. Interchangeable barrel system, Outer-Line ignition system, cross-bolt double safety. Available in 36, 45, 50, 54 caliber. Made in U.S. by Markesbery Muzzle Loaders, Inc.

Price: American Hardwood walnut, blue finish $539.01
Price: Black composite, blue finish $536.63
Price: Black laminate, blue finish $541.17
Price: Green laminate, blue finish $541.17
Price: Camo, blue finish $560.43
Price: American Hardwood walnut, stainless $556.27
Price: Black composite, stainless $556.04
Price: Black laminate, stainless $570.56
Price: Green laminate, stainless $570.56
Price: Camo, stainless $573.94

MARKESBERY KM COLORADO ROCKY MOUNTAIN RIFLE

Caliber: 36, 45, 50, 54. **Barrel:** 24"; 1:26" twist. **Weight:** 6-1/2 lbs. **Length:** 38-1/2" overall. **Stock:** American hardwood walnut, green or black laminate. **Sights:** Firesight bead on ramp front, fully adjustable open rear. **Features:** Replicates Reed/Watson rifle of 1851. Straight grip stock with or without two barrel bands, rubber recoil pad, large-spur hammer. Made in U.S. by Markesbery Muzzle Loaders, Inc.

Price: American hardwood walnut, blue finish $545.92
Price: Black or green laminate, blue finish $548.30
Price: American hardwood walnut, stainless $563.17
Price: Black or green laminate, stainless $566.34

MDM BUCKWACKA IN-LINE RIFLES

Caliber: 45, 50. **Barrel:** 23", 25". **Weight:** 7 to 7-3/4 lbs. **Stock:** Black, walnut, laminated and camouflage finishes. **Sights:** Williams Fire Sight blade front, Williams fully adjustable rear with ghost-ring peep aperture. **Features:** Break-open action; Incinerating Ignition System incorporates 209 shotshell primer directly into breech plug; 50-caliber models handle up to 150 grains of Pyrodex; synthetic ramrod; transfer bar safety; stainless or blued finish. Made in U.S. by Millennium Designed Muzzleloaders Ltd.

Price: 50 cal., blued finish $309.95
Price: 50 cal., stainless $339.95
Price: Camouflage stock .... $359.95 to $389.95

MDM M2K In-Line Rifle

Similar to Buckwacka except adjustable trigger and double-safety mechanism designed to prevent misfires. Made in U.S. by Millennium Designed Muzzleloaders Ltd.

Price: .... $529.00 to $549.00

MISSISSIPPI 1841 PERCUSSION RIFLE

Caliber: 54, 58. **Barrel:** 33". **Weight:** 9-1/2 lbs. **Length:** 48-5/8" overall. **Stock:** One-piece European walnut full stock with satin finish. **Sights:** Brass blade front, fixed steel rear. **Features:** Case-hardened lockplate marked "U.S." surmounted by American eagle. Two barrel bands, sling swivels. Steel ramrod with brass end, browned barrel. From Navy Arms, Dixie Gun Works, E.M.F., Cabela's, Euroarms of America.

Price: About $595.00

Navy Arms 1763 Charleville

Navy Arms Berdan

Navy Arms 1859 Sharps

Navy Arms 1863 C.S. Richmond

Navy Arms Whitworth

NAVY ARMS 1763 CHARLEVILLE
Caliber: 69. **Barrel:** 44-5/8". **Weight:** 8 lbs., 12 oz. **Length:** 59-3/8" overall. **Stock:** Walnut. **Sights:** Brass blade front. **Features:** Replica of French musket used by American troops during the American Revolution. Imported by Navy Arms.
Price: $1,020.00

NAVY ARMS BERDAN 1859 SHARPS RIFLE
Caliber: 54. **Barrel:** 30". **Weight:** 8 lbs., 8 oz. **Length:** 46-3/4" overall. **Stock:** Walnut. **Sights:** Blade front, folding military ladder-type rear. **Features:** Replica of the Union sniper rifle used by Berdan's 1st and 2nd Sharpshooter regiments. Color case-hardened receiver, patchbox, furniture. Double-set triggers. Imported by Navy Arms.
Price: $1,165.00
Price: 1859 Sharps Infantry Rifle (three-band) $1,100.00

NAVY ARMS 1859 SHARPS CAVALRY CARBINE
Caliber: 54. **Barrel:** 22". **Weight:** 7-3/4 lbs. **Length:** 39" overall. **Stock:** Walnut. **Sights:** Blade front, military ladder-type rear. **Features:** Color case-hardened action, blued barrel. Has saddle ring. Introduced 1991. Imported from Navy Arms.
Price: $1,000.00

NAVY ARMS 1861 SPRINGFIELD RIFLE
Caliber: 58. **Barrel:** 40". **Weight:** 10 lbs., 4 oz. **Length:** 56" overall. **Stock:** Walnut. **Sights:** Blade front, military leaf rear. **Features:** Steel barrel, lock and all furniture have polished bright finish. Has 1855-style hammer. Imported by Navy Arms.
Price: $590.00

NAVY ARMS 1863 C.S. RICHMOND RIFLE
Caliber: 58. **Barrel:** 40". **Weight:** 10 lbs. **Length:** NA. **Stocks:** Walnut. **Sights:** Blade front, adjustable rear. **Features:** Copy of three-band rifle musket made at Richmond Armory for the Confederacy. All steel polished bright. Imported by Navy Arms.
Price: $590.00

NAVY ARMS 1863 SPRINGFIELD
Caliber: 58, uses .575 Minie. **Barrel:** 40", rifled. **Weight:** 9-1/2 lbs. **Length:** 56" overall. **Stock:** Walnut. **Sights:** Open rear adjustable for elevation. **Features:** Full-size, three-band musket. Polished bright metal, including lock. From Navy Arms.
Price: Finished rifle $590.00

NAVY ARMS PARKER-HALE VOLUNTEER RIFLE
Caliber: .451. **Barrel:** 32". **Weight:** 9-1/2 lbs. **Length:** 49" overall. **Stock:** Walnut, checkered wrist and forend. **Sights:** Globe front, adjustable ladder-type rear. **Features:** Recreation of the type of gun issued to volunteer regiments during the 1860s. Rigby-pattern rifling, patent breech, detented lock. Stock is glass bedded for accuracy. Imported by Navy Arms.
Price: $905.00

NAVY ARMS PARKER-HALE WHITWORTH MILITARY TARGET RIFLE
Caliber: 45. **Barrel:** 36". **Weight:** 9-1/4 lbs. **Length:** 52-1/2" overall. **Stock:** Walnut. Checkered at wrist and forend. **Sights:** Hooded post front, open step-adjustable rear. **Features:** Faithful reproduction of Whitworth rifle. Trigger has detented lock, capable of fine adjustments without risk of the sear nose catching on the half-cock notch and damaging both parts. Introduced 1978. Imported by Navy Arms.
Price: $930.00

BLACKPOWDER MUSKETS & RIFLES

Navy Arms Smith Carbine

New England Firearms Huntsman

Peifer TS-93

Remington Model 700 ML

NAVY ARMS SMITH CARBINE
Caliber: 50. **Barrel:** 21-1/2". **Weight:** 7-3/4 lbs. **Length:** 39" overall. **Stock:** American walnut. **Sights:** Brass blade front, folding ladder-type rear. **Features:** Replica of breech-loading Civil War carbine. Color case-hardened receiver, rest blued. Cavalry model has saddle ring and bar, Artillery model has sling swivels. Imported by Navy Arms.
Price: Cavalry model **$645.00**
Price: Artillery model **$645.00**

NEW ENGLAND FIREARMS HUNTSMAN
Caliber: 50. **Barrel:** 24". **Weight:** 6-1/2 lbs. **Length:** 40". **Stock:** Walnut-finished American hardwood with pistol grip. **Sights:** Adjustable fiber-optic open sights, tapped for scope base. **Features:** Break-open action, color case-hardened frame, black oxide barrel. Made in U.S.A. by New England Firearms.
Price: **$188.00**

New England Firearms Stainless Huntsman
Similar to Huntsman, but with matte nickel finish receiver and stainless bbl. Introduced 2003. From New England Firearms.
Price: **$81.00**

PACIFIC RIFLE MODEL 1837 ZEPHYR
Caliber: 62. **Barrel:** 30", tapered octagon. **Weight:** 7-3/4 lbs. **Length:** NA. **Stock:** Oil-finished fancy walnut. **Sights:** German silver blade front, semi-buckhorn rear. Options available. **Features:** Improved underhammer action. First production rifle to offer Forsyth rifle, with narrow lands and shallow rifling with 1:14" pitch for high-velocity round balls. Metal finish is slow rust brown with nitre blue accents. Optional sights, finishes and integral muzzle brake available. Introduced 1995. Made in U.S. by Pacific Rifle Co.
Price: From **$995.00**

Pacific Rifle Big Bore African Rifles
Similar to the 1837 Zephyr except in 72-caliber and 8-bore. The 72-caliber is available in standard form with 28" barrel, or as the African with flat buttplate, checkered upgraded wood; weight is 9 lbs. The 8-bore African has dual-cap ignition, 24" barrel, weighs 12 lbs., checkered English

walnut, engraving, gold inlays. Introduced 1998. Made in U.S. by Pacific Rifle Co.
Price: 72-caliber, from **$1,150.00**
Price: 8-bore, from **$2,500.00**

PEIFER MODEL TS-93 RIFLE
Caliber: 45, 50. **Barrel:** 24" Douglas premium; 1:20" twist in 45; 1:28" in 50. **Weight:** 7 lbs. **Length:** 43-1/4" overall. **Stock:** Bell & Carlson solid composite, with recoil pad, swivel studs. **Sights:** Williams bead front on ramp, fully adjustable open rear. Drilled and tapped for Weaver scope mounts with dovetail for rear peep. **Features:** In-line ignition uses #209 shotshell primer; fast lock time; fully enclosed breech; adjustable trigger; automatic safety; removable primer holder. Blue or stainless. Made in U.S. by Peifer Rifle Co. Introduced 1996.
Price: Blue, black stock. **$730.00**
Price: Blue, wood or camouflage composite stock, or stainless with black composite stock **$803.00**
Price: Stainless, wood or camouflage composite stock **$876.00**

PRAIRIE RIVER ARMS PRA BULLPUP RIFLE
Caliber: 50. **Barrel:** 28"; 1:28" twist. **Weight:** 7-1/2 lbs. **Length:** 31-1/2" overall. **Stock:** Hardwood or black all-weather. **Sights:** Blade front, open adjustable rear. **Features:** Bullpup design thumbhole stock. Patented internal percussion ignition system. Left-hand model available. Dovetailed for scope mount. Introduced 1995. Made in U.S. by Prairie River Arms, Ltd.
Price: 4140 alloy barrel, hardwood stock **$199.00**
Price: All Weather stock, alloy barrel **$205.00**

REMINGTON MODEL 700 ML, MLS RIFLES
Caliber: 50, new 45 (MLS Magnum). **Barrel:** 24"; 1:28" twist, 26" (Magnum). **Weight:** 7-3/4 lbs. **Length:** 42" to 44-1/2" overall. **Stock:** Black fiberglass-reinforced synthetic with checkered grip and forend; magnum-style butt-pad. **Sights:** Ramped bead front, open fully adjustable rear. Drilled and tapped for scope mounts. **Features:** Uses the Remington 700 bolt action, stock design, safety and trigger mechanisms; removable stainless steel breech plug, No. 11 nipple; solid aluminum ramrod. Comes with cleaning tools and accessories; 3-way ignition.
Price: ML, blued, 50-caliber only **$415.00**
Price: MLS, stainless, 45 Magnum, 50-caliber **$533.00**
Price: MLS, stainless, Mossy Oak® Break-Up camo stock **$569.00**

C.S. Richmond 1863

Savage 10MLSS-IIXP

Second Model Brown Bess

Thompson/Center Hawken

RICHMOND, C.S., 1863 MUSKET
Caliber: 58. **Barrel:** 40". **Weight:** 11 lbs. **Length:** 56-1/4" overall. **Stock:** European walnut with oil finish. **Sights:** Blade front, adjustable folding leaf rear. **Features:** Reproduction of the three-band Civil War musket. Sling swivels attached to trigger guard and middle barrel band. Lockplate marked "1863" and "C.S. Richmond." All white metal. Brass buttplate and forend cap. Imported by Euroarms of America, Navy Arms, and Dixie Gun Works.
Price: Euroarms **$530.00**
Price: Dixie Gun Works **$675.00**

SAVAGE MODEL 10ML MUZZLELOADER RIFLE SERIES
Caliber: 50. **Barrel:** 24", 1.24 twist, blue or stainless. **Weight:** 7.75 lbs. **Stock:** Black synthetic, Realtree Hardwood JD Camo, brown laminate. **Sights:** Green adjustable rear, Red FiberOptic front. **Features:** XP Models scoped, no sights, designed for smokeless powder, #209 primer ignition. Removeable breech plug and vent liner.
Price: Model 10ML-II. **$531.00**
Price: Model 10ML-II Camo **$569.00**
Price: Model 10MLSS-II Camo **$628.00**
Price: Model 10MLBSS-II **$667.00**
Price: Model 10ML-IIXP **$569.00**
Price: Model 10MLSS-IIXP **$628.00**

SECOND MODEL BROWN BESS MUSKET
Caliber: 75, uses .735" round ball. **Barrel:** 42", smoothbore. **Weight:** 9-1/2 lbs. **Length:** 59" overall. **Stock:** Walnut (Navy); walnut-stained hardwood (Dixie). **Sights:** Fixed. **Features:** Polished barrel and lock with brass trigger guard and buttplate. Bayonet and scabbard available. From Navy Arms, Dixie Gun Works, Cabela's.
Price: Finished. . . . . **$475.00 to $850.00**
Price: Kit (Dixie Gun Works, Navy Arms) . . . . **$575.00 to $625.00**
Price: Carbine (Navy Arms) **$835.00**
Price: Dixie Gun Works **$765.00**

THOMPSON/CENTER FIRE STORM RIFLE
Caliber: 50. **Barrel:** 26"; 1:28" twist. **Weight:** 7 lbs. **Length:** 41-3/4" overall. **Stock:** Black synthetic with rubber recoil pad, swivel studs. **Sights:** Click-adjustable steel rear and ramp-style front, both with fiber-optic inserts. **Features:** Side hammer lock is the first designed for up to three 50-grain Pyrodex pellets; patented Pyrodex Pyramid breech directs ignition fire 360 degrees around base of pellet. Quick Load Accurizor Muzzle System; aluminum ramrod. Flintlock only. Introduced 2000. Made in U.S. by Thompson/Center Arms.
Price: Blue finish, flintlock model with 1:48" twist for round balls, conicals **$436.00**
Price: SST, flintlock **$488.00**

THOMPSON/CENTER ENCORE 209x50 MAGNUM
Caliber: 50. **Barrel:** 26"; interchangeable with centerfire calibers. **Weight:** 7 lbs. **Length:** 40-1/2" overall. **Stock:** American walnut butt and forend, or black composite. **Sights:** TruGlo fiber-optic front and rear. **Features:** Blue or stainless steel. Uses the stock, frame and forend of the Encore centerfire pistol; break-open design using trigger guard spur; stainless steel universal breech plug; uses #209 shotshell primers. Introduced 1998. Made in U.S. by Thompson/Center Arms.
Price: Stainless with camo stock **$772.00**
Price: Blue, walnut stock and forend **$678.00**
Price: Blue, composite stock and forend **$637.00**
Price: Stainless, composite stock and forend **$713.00**
Price: All camo Realtree Hardwoods **$729.00**

THOMPSON/CENTER BLACK DIAMOND RIFLE XR
Caliber: 50. **Barrel:** 26" with QLA; 1:28" twist. **Weight:** 6 lbs., 9 oz. **Length:** 41-1/2" overall. **Stock:** Black Rynite with molded-in checkering and gripcap, or walnut. **Sights:** TruGlo fiber-optic ramp-style front, TruGlo fiber-optic open rear. **Features:** In-line ignition system for musket cap, No. 11 cap, or 209 shotshell primer; removable universal breech plug; stainless steel construction. Selected models available in .45 cal. Made in U.S. by Thompson/Center Arms.
Price: With composite stock, blued **$337.00**
Price: With walnut stock **$412.00**

THOMPSON/CENTER HAWKEN RIFLE
Caliber: 50. **Barrel:** 28" octagon, hooked breech. **Stock:** American walnut. **Sights:** Blade front, rear adjustable for windage and elevation. **Features:** Solid brass furniture, double-set triggers, button rifled barrel, coil-type mainspring. From Thompson/Center Arms.
Price: Percussion model **$590.00**
Price: Flintlock model **$615.00**

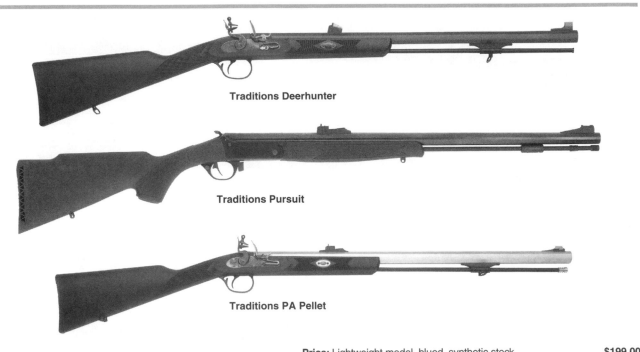

Traditions Deerhunter

Traditions Pursuit

Traditions PA Pellet

TRADITIONS BUCKSKINNER CARBINE
Caliber: 50. **Barrel:** 21"; 15/16" flats, half octagon, half round; 1:20" or 1:66" twist. **Weight:** 6 lbs. **Length:** 37" overall. **Stock:** Beech or black laminated. **Sights:** Beaded blade front, fiber-optic open rear click adjustable for windage and elevation or fiber-optics. **Features:** Uses V-type mainspring, single trigger. Non-glare hardware; sling swivels. From Traditions.
Price: Flintlock **$249.00**
Price: Flintlock, laminated stock **$303.00**

TRADITIONS DEERHUNTER RIFLE SERIES
Caliber: 32, 50 or 54. **Barrel:** 24", octagonal; 15/16" flats; 1:48" or 1:66" twist. **Weight:** 6 lbs. **Length:** 40" overall. **Stock:** Stained hardwood or All-Weather composite with rubber buttpad, sling swivels. **Sights:** Lite Optic blade front, adjustable rear fiber-optics. **Features:** Flint or percussion with color case-hardened lock. Hooked breech, oversized trigger guard, blackened furniture, PVC ramrod. All-Weather has composite stock and C-nickel barrel. Drilled and tapped for scope mounting. Imported by Traditions, Inc.
Price: Percussion, 50; blued barrel; 1:48" twist **$189.00**
Price: Percussion, 54 . . . . **$169.00**
Price: Flintlock, 50 caliber only; 1:48" twist **$179.00**
Price: Flintlock, All-Weather, 50-cal. **$239.00**
Price: Redi-Pak, 50 cal. flintlock **$219.00**
Price: Flintlock, left-handed hardwood, 50 cal. **$209.00**
Price: Percussion, All-Weather, 50 or 54 cal. **$179.00**
Price: Percussion, 32 cal. **$199.00**

Traditions Panther Sidelock Rifle
Similar to Deerhunter rifle, but has blade front and windage-adjustable-only rear sights, black composite stock.
Price: **$129.00**

TRADITIONS PURSUIT BREAK-OPEN MUZZLELOADER
Caliber: 45, 54 and 12 gauge. **Barrel:** 28", tapered, fluted; blued, stainless or Hardwoods Green camo. **Weight:** 8-1/4 lbs. **Length:** 44" overall. **Stock:** Synthetic black or Hardwoods Green. **Sights:** Steel fiber-optic rear, bead front. Introduced 2004 by Traditions, Inc.
Price: Steel, blued, 45 or 50 cal., synthetic stock **$279.00**
Price: Steel, nickel, 45 or 50 cal., synthetic stock **$309.00**
Price: Steel, nickel w/Hardwoods Green stock **$359.00**
Price: Matte blued; 12 ga., synthetic stock **$369.00**
Price: Matte blued; 12 ga. w/Hardwoods Green stock **$439.00**

Price: Lightweight model, blued, synthetic stock **$199.00**
Price: Lightweight model, blued, Mossy Oak®
Break-Up™ Camo stock **$239.00**
Price: Lightweight model, nickel, Mossy Oak®
Break-Up™ Camo stock **$279.00**

TRADITIONS EVOLUTION BOLT-ACTION BLACKPOWDER RIFLE
Caliber: 50 percussion. **Barrel:** 26", fluted with porting. **Sights:** Steel fiber-optic. **Weight:** 7 to 7-1/4 lbs. **Length:** 45" overall. **Features:** Bolt-action, cocking indicator, thumb safety, aluminum ramrod, sling studs. Wide variety of stocks and metal finishes. Introduced 2004 by Traditions, Inc.
Price: Synthetic stock **$279.00**
Price: Walnut X-wood **$349.00**
Price: Brown laminated **$469.00**
Price: Advantage Timber **$369.00**
Price: Synthetic, TruGlo sights **$249.00**
Price: Mossy Oak® Break-up™ **$279.00**
Price: Nickel finish **$309.00**
Price: Beech/nickel, Advantage/nickel, Advantage 54 cal. **$289.00**

TRADITIONS PA PELLET FLINTLOCK
Caliber: 50. **Barrel:** 26", blued, nickel. **Weight:** 7 lbs. **Stock:** Hardwood, synthetic and synthetic break-up. **Sights:** Fiber-optic. **Features:** Removeable breech plug, left-hand model with hardwood stock. 1:48" twist.
Price: Hardwood, blued **$259.00**
Price: Hardwood left, blued **$269.00**

TRADITIONS HAWKEN WOODSMAN RIFLE
Caliber: 50 and 54. **Barrel:** 28"; 15/16" flats. **Weight:** 7 lbs., 11 oz. **Length:** 44-1/2" overall. **Stock:** Walnut-stained hardwood. **Sights:** Beaded blade front, hunting-style open rear adjustable for windage and elevation. **Features:** Percussion only. Brass patchbox and furniture. Double triggers. From Traditions.
Price: 50 or 54 . . . . **$299.00**
Price: 50-cal., left-hand **$279.00**
Price: 50-cal., flintlock **$299.00**

TRADITIONS KENTUCKY RIFLE
Caliber: 50. **Barrel:** 33-1/2"; 7/8" flats; 1:66" twist. **Weight:** 7 lbs. **Length:** 49" overall. **Stock:** Beech; inletted toe plate. **Sights:** Blade front, fixed rear. **Features:** Full-length, two-piece stock; brass furniture; color case-hardened lock. From Traditions.
Price: **$279.00**

Zouave Percussion

TRADITIONS PENNSYLVANIA RIFLE
Caliber: 50. **Barrel:** 40-1/4"; 7/8" flats; 1:66" twist, octagon. **Weight:** 9 lbs. **Length:** 57-1/2" overall. **Stock:** Walnut. **Sights:** Blade front, adjustable rear. **Features:** Brass patchbox and ornamentation. Double-set triggers. From Traditions.
Price: Flintlock $529.00
Price: Percussion $519.00

TRADITIONS SHENANDOAH RIFLE
Caliber: 36, 50. **Barrel:** 33-1/2" octagon; 1:66" twist. **Weight:** 7 lbs., 3 oz. **Length:** 49-1/2" overall. **Stock:** Walnut. **Sights:** Blade front, buckhorn rear. **Features:** V-type mainspring; double-set trigger; solid brass buttplate, patchbox, nosecap, thimbles, trigger guard. Introduced 1996. From Traditions.
Price: Flintlock $419.00
Price: Percussion $399.00
Price: 36 cal. flintlock, 1:48" twist $419.00
Price: 36 cal. percussion, 1:48" twist $449.00

TRADITIONS TENNESSEE RIFLE
Caliber: 50. **Barrel:** 24", octagon; 15/16" flats; 1:66" twist. **Weight:** 6 lbs. **Length:** 40-1/2" overall. **Stock:** Stained beech. **Sights:** Blade front, fixed rear. **Features:** One-piece stock has inletted brass furniture, cheekpiece; double-set trigger; V-type mainspring. Flint or percussion. From Traditions.
Price: Flintlock $339.00
Price: Percussion $329.00

TRADITIONS TRACKER 209 IN-LINE RIFLES
Caliber: 45, 50. **Barrel:** 22" blued or C-nickel finish; 1:28" twist, 50 cal. 1:20" 45 cal. **Weight:** 6 lbs., 4 oz. **Length:** 41" overall. **Stock:** Black, Advantage Timber® composite synthetic. **Sights:** Lite Optic blade front adjustable rear. **Features:** Thumb safety; adjustable trigger; rubber butt pad and sling swivel studs; takes 150 grains of Pyrodex pellets; one-piece breech system takes 209 shotshell primers. Drilled and tapped for scope. From Traditions.
Price: (Black composite or synthetic stock, 22" blued barrel) $129.00
Price: (Black composite or synthetic stock, 22" C-nickel barrel) . . . $139.00
Price: (Advantage Timber® stock, 22" C-nickel barrel) $189.00
Price: (Redi-Pak, black stock and blued barrel, powder flask, capper, ball starter, other accessories) $179.00
Price: (Redi-Pak, synthetic stock and blued barrel, with scope) . . . $229.00

ULTRA LIGHT ARMS MODEL 209 MUZZLELOADER
Caliber: 45 or 50. **Barrel:** 24" button rifled; 1:32" twist. **Weight:** Under 5 lbs. **Stock:** Kevlar/Graphite. **Features:** Recoil pad, sling swivels included. Some color options available. Adj. Timney trigger, positive primer extraction.
Price: $1,100.00

WHITE MODEL 97 WHITETAIL HUNTER RIFLE
Caliber: 45, 50. **Barrel:** 22", 1:20 twist (45 cal.); 1:24 twist (50 cal.). **Weight:** 7.7 lbs. **Length:** 40" overall. **Stock:** Black laminated or black composite. **Sights:** Marble TruGlo fully adjustable, steel rear with white diamond, red bead front with high-visibility inserts. **Features:** In-line ignition with FlashFire one-piece nipple and breech plug that uses standard or magnum No. 11 caps, fully adjustable trigger, double safety system, aluminum ramrod; drilled and tapped for scope. Hard case. Made in U.S.A. by Split Fire Sporting Goods.
Price: Whitetail w/laminated or composite stock $499.95
Price: Adventurer w/26" stainless barrel & thumbhole stock) $699.95
Price: Odyssey w/24" carbon fiber wrapped barrel & thumbhole stock $1,299.95

WHITE MODEL 98 ELITE HUNTER RIFLE
Caliber: 45, 50. **Barrel:** 24", 1:24" twist (50 cal). **Weight:** 8.6 lbs. **Length:** 43-1/2" overall. **Stock:** Black laminate wtih swivel studs. **Sights:** TruGlo fully adjustable, steel rear with white diamond, red bead front with high-visibility inserts. **Features:** In-line ignition with FlashFire one-piece nipple and breech plug that uses standard or magnum No. 11 caps, fully adjustable trigger, double safety system, aluminum ramrod, drilled and tapped for scope, hard gun case. Made in U.S.A. by Split Fire Sporting Goods.
Price: Composite or laminate wood stock $499.95

White Thunderbolt Rifle
Similar to the Elite Hunter but is designed to handle 209 shotgun primers only. Has 26" stainless steel barrel, weighs 9.3 lbs. and is 45-1/2" long. Composite or laminate stock. Made in U.S.A. by Split Fire Sporting Goods.
Price: $599.95

WHITE MODEL 2000 BLACKTAIL HUNTER RIFLE
Caliber: 50. **Barrel:** 22", 1:24" twist (50 cal.). **Weight:** 7.6 lbs. **Length:** 39-7/8" overall. **Stock:** Black laminated with swivel studs with laser engraved deer or elk scene. **Sights:** TruGlo fully adjustable, steel rear with white diamond, red bead front with high-visibility inserts. **Features:** Teflon finished barrel, in-line ignition with FlashFire one-piece nipple and breech plug that uses standard or magnum No. 11 caps, fully adjustable trigger, double safety system, aluminum ramrod, drilled and tapped for scope. Hard gun case. Made in U.S.A. by Split Fire Sporting Goods.
Price: Laminate wood stock, w/laser engraved game scene $599.95

WHITE LIGHTNING II RIFLE
Caliber: 45 and 50 percussion. **Barrel:** 24", 1:32 twist. **Sights:** Adj. rear. **Stock:** Black polymer. **Weight:** 6 lbs. **Features:** In-line, 209 primer ignition system, blued or nickel-plated bbl., adj. trigger, Delrin ramrod, sling studs, recoil pad. Made in U.S.A. by Split Fire Sporting Goods.
Price: $299.95

WHITE ALPHA RIFLE
Caliber: 45, 50 percussion. **Barrel:** 27" tapered, stainless. **Sights:** Marble TruGlo rear, fiber-optic front. **Stock:** Laminated. **Features:** Lever action rotating block, hammerless; adj. trigger, positive safety. All stainless metal, including trigger. Made in U.S.A. by Split Fire Sporting Goods.
Price: $449.95

WINCHESTER APEX SWING-ACTION MAGNUM RIFLE
Caliber: 45, 50. **Barrel:** 28". **Stock:** Mossy Oak® Camo, Black Fleck. **Sights:** Adj. fiber-optic. **Weight:** 7 lbs., 12 oz. **Overall length:** 42". **Features:** Monte Carlo cheekpiece, swing-action design, external hammer.
Price: Mossy Oak®/stainless $489.95
Price: Black Fleck/stainless $449.95
Price: Full Mossy Oak® $469.95
Price: Black Fleck/blued $364.95

WINCHESTER X-150 BOLT-ACTION MAGNUM RIFLE
Caliber: 45, 50. **Barrel:** 26". **Stock:** Hardwoods or Timber HD, Black Fleck, Break-Up™. **Weight:** 8 lbs., 3 oz. **Sights:** Adj. fiber-optic. **Features:** No. 209 shotgun primer ignition, stainless steel bolt, stainless fluted bbl.
Price: Mossy Oak®, Timber, Hardwoods/stainless $349.95
Price: Black Fleck/stainless $299.95
Price: Mossy Oak®, Timber, Hardwoods/blued $279.95
Price: Black Fleck/blued $229.95

ZOUAVE PERCUSSION RIFLE
Caliber: 58, 59. **Barrel:** 32-1/2". **Weight:** 9-1/2 lbs. **Length:** 48-1/2" overall. **Stock:** Walnut finish, brass patchbox and buttplate. **Sights:** Fixed front, rear adjustable for elevation. **Features:** Color case-hardened lockplate, blued barrel. From Navy Arms, Dixie Gun Works, E.M.F., Cabela's, Euroarms of America.
Price: . . . . $415.00 to $515.00

Knight TK2000

CABELA'S BLACKPOWDER SHOTGUNS
Gauge: 10, 12, 20. **Barrel:** 10-ga., 30"; 12-ga., 28-1/2" (Extra-Full, Mod., Imp. Cyl. choke tubes); 20-ga., 27-1/2" (Imp. Cyl. & Mod. fixed chokes). **Weight:** 6-1/2 to 7 lbs. **Length:** 45" overall (28-1/2" barrel). **Stock:** American walnut with checkered grip; 12- and 20-gauge have straight stock, 10-gauge has pistol grip. **Features:** Blued barrels, engraved, color case-hardened locks and hammers, brass ramrod tip. From Cabela's.
Price: 10-gauge $679.99
Price: 12-gauge $579.99
Price: 20-gauge $549.99

DIXIE MAGNUM PERCUSSION SHOTGUN
Gauge: 10, 12, 20. **Barrel:** 30" (Imp. Cyl. & Mod.) in 10-gauge; 28" in 12-gauge. **Weight:** 6-1/4 lbs. **Length:** 45" overall. **Stock:** Hand-checkered walnut, 14" pull. **Features:** Double triggers; light hand engraving; case-hardened locks in 12-gauge, polished steel in 10-gauge; sling swivels. From Dixie Gun Works.
Price: Upland $650.00
Price: 12-ga. kit $445.00
Price: 20-ga. $525.00
Price: 10-ga. $575.00
Price: 10-ga. kit $445.00

KNIGHT TK2000 MUZZLELOADING SHOTGUN (209)
Gauge: 12. **Barrel:** 26", extra-full choke tube. **Weight:** 7 lbs., 9 oz. **Length:** 45" overall. **Stock:** Synthetic black or Advantage Timber HD; recoil pad; swivel studs. **Sights:** Fully adjustable rear, blade front with fiber-optics. **Features:** Receiver drilled and tapped for scope mount; in-line ignition; adjustable trigger; removable breech plug; double safety system; Imp. Cyl. choke tube available. Made in U.S. by Knight Rifles.
Price: . . . . $349.95 to $399.95

KNIGHT VERSATILE TK2002
Gauge: 12. **Stock:** Black composite, blued, Advantage Timber HD finish. Both with sling swivel studs installed. **Sights:** Adjustable metallic TruGlo fiber-optic. **Features:** Full plastic jacket ignition system, screw-on choke tubes, load without removing choke tubes, jug-choked barrel design. Improved cylinder and modified choke tubes available.
Price: . . . . $349.95 to $399.95

NAVY ARMS STEEL SHOT MAGNUM SHOTGUN
Gauge: 10. **Barrel:** 28" (Cyl. & Cyl.). **Weight:** 7 lbs., 9 oz. **Length:** 45-1/2" overall. **Stock:** Walnut, with cheekpiece. **Features:** Designed specifically for steel shot. Engraved, polished locks; sling swivels; blued barrels. Imported by Navy Arms.
Price: $605.00

NAVY ARMS T&T SHOTGUN
Gauge: 12. **Barrel:** 28" (Full & Full). **Weight:** 7-1/2 lbs. **Stock:** Walnut. **Sights:** Bead front. **Features:** Color case-hardened locks, double triggers, blued steel furniture. From Navy Arms.
Price: $580.00

WHITE TOMINATOR SHOTGUN
Caliber: 12. **Barrel:** 25" blue, straight, tapered stainless steel. **Weight:** NA. **Length:** NA. **Stock:** Black laminated or black wood. **Sights:** Drilled and tapped for easy scope mounting. **Features:** Interchangeable choke tubes. Custom vent rib with high visibility front bead. Double safeties. Fully adjustable custom trigger. Recoil pad and sling swivel studs. Made in U.S.A. by Split Fire Sporting Goods.
Price: $349.95

AIRGUNS — Handguns

AIRFORCE TALON SS AIR PISTOL
Caliber: 177, 22. **Barrel:** 12". **Weight:** 5.25 lbs. **Length:** 32.75" overall. **Power:** NA. **Grips:** NA. **Sights:** None, integral mount supplied. **Features:** 400-1000 fps. Fill pressure: 3000 psi. Air tank volume: 490cc.

Price: 22 w/refill clamp, open sights **$559.95**
Price: 177 w/refill clamp, open sights **$559.95**
Price: Gun only (22 or 177) **$459.95**

AirForce Talon Air Pistol
Same as Talon SS but 32.6" long, weights 5.5 lbs.

Price: 22 w/refill clamp, open sights **$539.95**
Price: 177 w/refill clamp, open sights **$539.95**
Price: Gun only **$439.95**

ARS HUNTING MASTER AR6 AIR PISTOL
Caliber: 22 (177 +20 special order). **Barrel:** 12" rifled. **Weight:** 3 lbs. **Length:** 18.25 overall. **Power:** NA. **Grips:** Indonesian walnut with checkered grip. **Sights:** Adjustable rear, blade front. **Features:** 6 shot repeater with rotary magazine, single or double action, receiver grooved for scope, hammer block and trigger block safeties.

Price: . . . . **NA**

BEEMAN P1 MAGNUM AIR PISTOL
Caliber: 177, 5mm, single shot. **Barrel:** 8.4". **Weight:** 2.5 lbs. **Length:** 11" overall. **Power:** Top lever cocking; spring-piston. **Grips:** Checkered walnut. **Sights:** Blade front, square notch rear with click micrometer adjustments for windage and elevation. Grooved for scope mounting. **Features:** Dual power for 177 and 20 cal.: low setting gives 350-400 fps; high setting 500-600 fps. All Colt 45 auto grips fit gun. Dry-firing feature for practice. Optional wood shoulder stock. Imported by Beeman.

Price: 177, 5mm **$440.00**

BEEMAN P3 AIR PISTOL
Caliber: 177 pellet, single shot. **Barrel:** NA. **Weight:** 1.7 lbs. **Length:** 9.6" overall. **Power:** Single-stroke pneumatic; overlever barrel cocking. **Grips:** Reinforced polymer. **Sights:** Adjustable rear, blade front. **Features:** Velocity 410 fps. Polymer frame; automatic safety; two-stage trigger; built-in muzzle brake.

Price: **$180.00**
Price: Combo **$285.00**

BEEMAN/FEINWERKBAU 103 AIR PISTOL
Caliber: 177, single shot. **Barrel:** 10.1", 12-groove rifling. **Weight:** 2.5 lbs. **Length:** 16.5" overall. **Power:** Single-stroke pneumatic, underlever cocking. **Grips:** Stippled walnut with adjustable palm shelf. **Sights:** Blade front, open rear adjustable for windage and elevation. Notch size adjustable for width. Interchangeable front blades. **Features:** Velocity 510 fps. Fully adjustable trigger. Cocking effort 2 lbs. Imported by Beeman.

Price: Right-hand **$1,236.00**
Price: Left-hand **$1,275.00**

BEEMAN/FWB P34 MATCH AIR PISTOL
Caliber: 177, single shot. **Barrel:** 10-5/16", with muzzle brake. **Weight:** 2.4 lbs. **Length:** 16.5" overall. **Power:** Precharged pneumatic. **Grips:** Stippled walnut; adjustable match type. **Sights:** Undercut blade front, fully adjustable match rear. **Features:** Velocity 525 fps; up to 200 shots per CO2 cartridge. Fully adjustable trigger; built-in muzzle brake. Imported from Germany by Beeman.

Price: Right-hand **$1,395.00**
Price: Left-hand **$1,440.00**

BEEMAN HW70A AIR PISTOL
Caliber: 177, single shot. **Barrel:** 6-1/4", rifled. **Weight:** 38 oz. **Length:** 12-3/4" overall. **Power:** Spring, barrel cocking. **Grips:** Plastic, with thumbrest. **Sights:** Hooded post front, square notch rear adjustable for windage and elevation. Comes with scope base. **Features:** Adjustable trigger, 31-lb. cocking effort, 440 fps MV; automatic barrel safety. Imported by Beeman.

Price: **$190.00**

BEEMAN/WEBLEY TEMPEST AIR PISTOL
Caliber: 177, 22, single shot. **Barrel:** 6-7/8". **Weight:** 32 oz. **Length:** 8.9" overall. **Power:** Spring-piston, break barrel. **Grips:** Checkered black plastic with thumbrest. **Sights:** Blade front, adjustable rear. **Features:**

Daisy 662X

Velocity to 500 fps (177), 400 fps (22). Aluminum frame; black epoxy finish; manual safety. Imported from England by Beeman.

Price: **$205.00**

Beeman/Webley Hurricane Air Pistol
Similar to the Tempest except has extended frame in the rear for a click-adjustable rear sight; hooded front sight; comes with scope mount. Imported from England by Beeman.

Price: **$255.00**

BENJAMIN SHERIDAN CO2 PELLET PISTOLS
Caliber: 177, 20, 22, single shot. **Barrel:** 6-3/8", rifled brass. **Weight:** 29 oz. **Length:** 9.8" overall. **Power:** 12-gram CO2 cylinder. **Grips:** Walnut. **Sights:** High ramp front, fully adjustable notched rear. **Features:** Velocity to 500 fps. Turnbolt action with cross-bolt safety. Gives about 40 shots per CO2 cylinder. Black or nickel finish. Made in U.S. by Benjamin Sheridan Co.

Price: Black finish, EB17 (177), EB20 (20) **$190.00**

BENJAMIN SHERIDAN PNEUMATIC PELLET PISTOLS
Caliber: 177, 20, 22, single shot. **Barrel:** 9-3/8", rifled brass. **Weight:** 38 oz. **Length:** 13-1/8" overall. **Power:** Underlever pneumatic, hand pumped. **Grips:** Walnut stocks and pump handle. **Sights:** High ramp front, fully adjustable notch rear. **Features:** Velocity to 525 fps (variable). Bolt action with cross-bolt safety. Choice of black or nickel finish. Made in U.S. by Benjamin Sheridan Co.

Price: Black finish, HB17 (177), HB20 (20) **$190.00**
Price: HB22 (22) **$199.00**

BRNO TAU-7 CO2 MATCH AIR PISTOL
Caliber: 177. **Barrel:** 10.24". **Weight:** 37 oz. **Length:** 15.75" overall. **Power:** 12.5-gram CO2 cartridge. **Grips:** Stippled hardwood with adjustable palm rest. **Sights:** Blade front, open fully adjustable rear. **Features:** Comes with extra seals and counterweight. Blue finish. Imported by Great Lakes Airguns.

Price: **$299.50**

CROSMAN BLACK VENOM AIR PISTOL
Caliber: 177 pellets, BB, 17-shot magazine; darts, single shot. **Barrel:** 4.75" smooth-bore. **Weight:** 16 oz. **Length:** 10.8" overall. **Power:** Spring. **Grips:** NA. **Sights:** Blade front, adjustable rear. **Features:** Velocity to 270 fps (BBs), 250 fps (pellets). Spring-fed magazine; cross-bolt safety. Made in U.S.A. by Crosman Corp.

Price: **$60.00**

CROSMAN MODEL 1377 AIR PISTOL
Caliber: 177, single shot. **Barrel:** 8", rifled steel. **Weight:** 39 oz. **Length:** 13-5/8". **Power:** Hand pumped. **Grips:** NA. **Sights:** Blade front, rear adjustable for windage and elevation. **Features:** Bolt action, molded plastic grip, hand size pump forearm. Cross-bolt safety. From Crosman.

Price: **$60.00**

CROSMAN AUTO AIR II PISTOLS
Caliber: BB, 17-shot magazine; 177 pellet, single shot. **Barrel:** 8-5/8" steel, smooth-bore. **Weight:** 13 oz. **Length:** 10-3/4" overall. **Power:** CO2 Powerlet. **Grips:** NA. **Sights:** Blade front, adjustable rear; highlighted system. **Features:** Velocity to 480 fps (BBs), 430 fps (pellets). Semi-automatic action with BBs, single shot with pellets. Black. From Crosman.

Price: AAIIB **$38.00**
Price: AAIIBRD . . . . **NA**

AIRGUNS — Handguns

EAA MP651K

Gamo PT-80

CROSMAN MODEL 1008 REPEAT AIR PISTOL
Caliber: 177, 8-shot pellet clip. **Barrel:** 4.25", rifled steel. **Weight:** 17 oz. **Length:** 8.625" overall. **Power:** CO2 Powerlet. **Grips:** Checkered black plastic. **Sights:** Post front, adjustable rear. **Features:** Velocity about 430 fps. Break-open barrel for easy loading; single or double semi-automatic action; two 8-shot clips included. Optional carrying case available. From Crosman.
Price: **$60.00**
Price: Model 1008SB (silver and black finish), about **$60.00**

CROSMAN SEMI AUTO AIR PISTOL
Caliber: 177, pellets. **Barrel:** Rifled steel. **Weight:** 40 oz. **Length:** 8.63". **Power:** CO2. **Grips:** NA. **Sights:** Blade front, rear adjustable. **Features:** Velocity up to 430 fps. Synthetic grips, zinc alloy frame. From Crosman.
Price: C40 . . . . **NA**

CROSMAN MAGNUM AIR PISTOLS
Caliber: 177, pellets. **Barrel:** Rifled steel. **Weight:** 27 oz. **Length:** 9.38". **Power:** CO2. **Grips:** NA. **Sights:** Blade front, rear adjustable. **Features:** Single/double action accepts sights and scopes with standard 3/8" dovetail mount. Model 3576W features 6" barrel for increased accuracy. From Crosman.
Price: 3574W. . . . . **NA**
Price: 3576W . . . . **NA**

DAISY/POWERLINE MODEL 15XT AIR PISTOL
Caliber: 177 BB, 15-shot built-in magazine. **Barrel:** NA. **Weight:** NA. **Length:** 7.21". **Power:** CO2. **Grips:** NA. **Sights:** NA. **Features:** Velocity 425 fps. Made in the U.S.A. by Daisy Mfg. Co.
Price: **$36.95**
New! Price: 15XK Shooting Kit **$59.95**

DAISY/POWERLINE 717 PELLET AIR PISTOL
Caliber: 177, single shot. **Barrel:** 9.61". **Weight:** 2.25 lbs. **Length:** 13-1/2" overall. **Grips:** Molded wood-grain plastic with thumbrest. **Sights:** Blade and ramp front, micro-adjustable notched rear. **Features:** Single pump pneumatic pistol. Rifled steel barrel. Cross-bolt trigger block. Muzzle velocity 385 fps. From Daisy Mfg. Co.
Price: **$71.95**

DAISY/POWERLINE 1270 CO2 AIR PISTOL
Caliber: BB, 60-shot magazine. **Barrel:** Smoothbore steel. **Weight:** 17 oz. **Length:** 11.1" overall. **Power:** CO2 pump action. **Grips:** Molded black polymer. **Sights:** Blade on ramp front, adjustable rear. **Features:** Velocity to 420 fps. Cross-bolt trigger block safety; plated finish. Made in U.S. by Daisy Mfg. Co.
Price: **$39.95**

DAISY/POWERLINE MODEL 93 AIR PISTOL
Caliber: BB, 15-shot magazine. **Barrel:** Smoothbore; steel. **Weight:** 1.1 lbs. **Length:** 7.9" overall. **Power:** CO2 powered semi-auto. **Grips:** Molded brown checkered. **Sights:** Blade on ramp front, fixed open rear. **Features:** Velocity to 400 fps. Manual trigger block. Made in U.S.A. by Daisy Mfg. Co.
Price: **$48.95**

Daisy/Powerline 693 Air Pistol
Similar to Model 93 except has velocity to 235 fps.
Price: **$52.95**

DAISY/POWERLINE 622X PELLET PISTOL
Caliber: 22 (5.5mm), 6-shot. **Barrel:** Rifled steel. **Weight:** 1.3 lbs. **Length:** 8.5". **Power:** CO2. **Grips:** Molded black checkered. **Sights:** Fiber-optic front, fixed open rear. **Features:** Velocity 225 fps. Rotary hammer block. Made by Daisy Mfg. Co.
Price: **$69.95**

DAISY/POWERLINE 45 AIR PISTOL
Caliber: BB, 13-shot magazine. **Barrel:** Rifled steel. **Weight:** 1.25 lbs. **Length:** 8.5" overall. **Power:** CO2 powered semi-auto. **Grips:** Molded black checkered. **Sights:** TruGlo fiber-optic front, fixed open rear. **Features:** Velocity to 224 fps. Manual trigger block. Made in U.S.A. by Daisy Mfg. Co.
Price: **$54.95**

Daisy/Powerline 645 Air Pistol
Similar to Model 93 except has distinctive black and nickel finish.
Price: **$59.95**

EAA/BAIKAL IZH-M46 TARGET AIR PISTOL
Caliber: 177, single shot. **Barrel:** 10". **Weight:** 2.4 lbs. **Length:** 16.8" overall. **Power:** Underlever single-stroke pneumatic. **Grips:** Adjustable wooden target. **Sights:** Micrometer fully adjustable rear, blade front. **Features:** Velocity about 420 fps. Hammer-forged, rifled barrel. Imported from Russia by European American Armory.
Price: **$349.00**

GAMO AUTO 45 AIR PISTOL
Caliber: 177, 12-shot. **Barrel:** 4.25". **Weight:** 1.10 lbs. **Length:** 7.50". **Power:** CO2 cartridge, semi-automatic, 410 fps. **Grips:** Plastic. **Sights:** Rear sights adjusts for windage. **Features:** Glock copy; double-action, manual safety. Imported from Spain by Gamo.
Price: **$99.95**

GAMO COMPACT TARGET PISTOL
Caliber: 177, single shot. **Barrel:** 8.26". **Weight:** 1.95 lbs. **Length:** 12.60". **Power:** Spring-piston, 400 fps. **Grips:** Walnut. **Sights:** Micro-adjustable. **Features:** Rifled steel barrel, adjustable match trigger, recoil and vibration-free. Imported from Spain by Gamo.
Price: **$229.95**

GAMO P-23, P-23 LASER PISTOL
Caliber: 177, 12-shot. **Barrel:** 4.25". **Weight:** 1 lb. **Length:** 7.5". **Power:** CO2 cartridge, semi-automatic, 410 fps. **Grips:** Plastic. **Sights:** NA. **Features:** Walther PPK cartridge pistol copy, optional laser sight. Imported from Spain by Gamo.
Price: . . . . **$89.95**, (with laser) **$129.95**

GAMO PT-80, PT-80 LASER PISTOL
Caliber: 177, 8-shot. **Barrel:** 4.25". **Weight:** 1.2 lbs. **Length:** 7.2". **Power:** CO2 cartridge, semi-automatic, 410 fps. **Grips:** Plastic. **Sights:** 3-dot. **Features:** Optional laser sight and walnut grips available. Imported from Spain by Gamo.
Price: . . . . **$108.95,** (with laser) **$129.95**, (with walnut grip) **$119.95**

"GAT" AIR PISTOL
Caliber: 177, single shot. **Barrel:** 7-1/2" cocked, 9-1/2" extended. **Weight:** 22 oz. **Length:** NA. **Power:** Spring-piston. **Grips:** Cast checkered metal. **Sights:** Fixed. **Features:** Shoots pellets, corks or darts. Matte black finish. Imported from England by Stone Enterprises, Inc.
Price: **$24.95**

AIRGUNS — Handguns

HAMMERLI AP40 AIR PISTOL
Caliber: 177. **Barrel:** 10". **Length:** NA. **Power:** NA. **Grips:** Adjustable orthopedic. **Sights:** Fully adjustable micrometer. **Features:** Sleek, light, well balanced and accurate. Imported from Switzerland by Nygord Precision Products.
Price: **$1,195.00**

MARKSMAN 2000 REPEATER AIR PISTOL
Caliber: 177, 18-shot BB repeater. **Barrel:** 2-1/2", smoothbore. **Weight:** 24 oz. **Length:** 8-1/4" overall. **Power:** Spring. **Grips:** NA. **Sights:** NA. **Features:** Velocity to 200 fps. Thumb safety. Uses BBs, darts, bolts or pellets. Repeats with BBs only. From Marksman Products.
Price: **$27.00**

MARKSMAN 2005 LASERHAWK™ SPECIAL EDITION AIR PISTOL
Caliber: 177, 24-shot magazine. **Barrel:** 3.8", smoothbore. **Weight:** 22 oz. **Length:** 10.3" overall. **Power:** Spring-air. **Grips:** Checkered. **Sights:** Fixed fiber-optic front sight. **Features:** Velocity to 300 fps with Hyper-Velocity pellets. Square trigger guard with skeletonized trigger; extended barrel. Shoots BBs, pellets, darts or bolts. Made in the U.S. From Marksman Products.
Price: **$32.00**

MORINI 162E MATCH AIR PISTOLS
Caliber: 177, single shot. **Barrel:** 9.4". **Weight:** 32 oz. **Length:** 16.1" overall. **Power:** Scuba air. **Grips:** Adjustable match type. **Sights:** Interchangeable blade front, fully adjustable match-type rear. **Features:** Power mechanism shuts down when pressure drops to a preset level. Adjustable electronic trigger. Imported from Switzerland by Nygord Precision Products.
Price: **$825.00**
Price: 162 EI **$1,075.00**

MORINI SAM K-11 AIR PISTOL
Caliber: 177. **Barrel:** 10". **Weight:** 38 oz. **Length:** NA. **Grips:** Fully adjustable. **Sights:** Fully adjustable. **Features:** Improved trigger, more angle adjustment on grip. Sophisticated counter balance system. Deluxe aluminum case, two cylinders and manometer. Imported from Switzerland by Nygord Precision Products.
Price: **$975.00**

PARDINI K58 MATCH AIR PISTOLS
Caliber: 177, single shot. **Barrel:** 9". **Weight:** 37.7 oz. **Length:** 15.5" overall. **Power:** Precharged compressed air; single-stroke cocking. **Grips:** Adjustable match type; stippled walnut. **Sights:** Interchangeable post front, fully adjustable match rear. **Features:** Fully adjustable trigger. Short version K-2 available. Imported from Italy by Nygord Precision Products.
Price: **$795.00**
Price: K2S model, precharged air pistol, introduced in 1998 ..... **$945.00**

RWS 9B/9N AIR PISTOLS
Caliber: 177, single shot. **Barrel:** NA. **Weight:** NA. **Length:** NA. **Power:** NA. **Grips:** Plastic with thumbrest. **Sights:** Adjustable. **Features:** Spring-piston powered; 550 fps. Black or nickel finish. Imported from Spain by Dynamit Nobel-RWS.
Price: 9B **$169.00**
Price: 9N **$185.00**

STEYR LP 5CP MATCH AIR PISTOL
Caliber: 177, 5-shot magazine. **Weight:** 40.7 oz. **Length:** 15.2" overall. **Power:** Precharged air cylinder. **Grips:** Adjustable match type. **Sights:** Interchangeable blade front, adjustable matched rear. **Features:** Adjustable sight radius; adjustable trigger. Barrel compensator. One-shot magazine available. Imported from Austria by Nygord Precision Products.
Price: **$1,100.00**

STEYR LP10P MATCH AIR PISTOL
Caliber: 177, single shot. **Barrel:** 9". **Weight:** 38.7 oz. **Length:** 15.3" overall. **Power:** Scuba air. **Grips:** Adjustable Morini match, palm shelf, stippled walnut. **Sights:** Interchangeable blade in 4mm, 4.5mm or 5mm widths, adjustable open rear, interchangeable 3.5mm or 4mm leaves. **Features:** Velocity about 500 fps. Adjustable trigger, adjustable sight radius from 12.4" to 13.2". With compensator. Recoil elimination. Imported from Austria by Nygord Precision Products.
Price: **$1,175.00**

TECH FORCE SS2 OLYMPIC COMPETITION AIR PISTOL
Caliber: 177 pellet, single shot. **Barrel:** 7.4". **Weight:** 2.8 lbs. **Length:** 16.5" overall. **Power:** Spring piston, sidelever. **Grips:** Hardwood. **Sights:** Extended adjustable rear, blade front accepts inserts. **Features:** Velocity 520 fps. Recoilless design; adjustments allow duplication of a firearm's feel. Match-grade, adjustable trigger; includes carrying case. Imported from China by Compasseco, Inc.
Price: **$295.00**

TECH FORCE 35 AIR PISTOL
Caliber: 177 pellet, single shot. **Weight:** 2.86 lbs. **Length:** 14.9" overall. **Power:** Spring-piston, underlever. **Grips:** Hardwood. **Sights:** Micrometer adjustable rear, blade front. **Features:** Velocity 400 fps. Grooved for scope mount; trigger safety. Imported from China by Compasseco, Inc.
Price: **$39.95**

Tech Force 8 Air Pistol
Similar to Tech Force 35 but with break-barrel action, ambidextrous polymer grips.
Price: **$59.95**

Tech Force S2-1 Air Pistol
Similar to Tech Force 8 except basic grips and sights for plinking.
Price: **$29.95**

WALTHER LP300 MATCH PISTOL
Caliber: 177. **Barrel:** 236mm. **Weight:** 1.018g. **Length:** NA. **Power:** NA. **Grips:** NA. **Sights:** Integrated front with three different widths, adjustable rear. **Features:** Adjustable grip and trigger. Imported from Germany by Nygord Precision Products.
Price: **$1,095.00**

CONSULT
SHOOTER'S MARKETPLACE
Page 243, This Issue

Crosman 2289G

AIRFORCE CONDOR RIFLE
Caliber: 177, 22. **Barrel:** 24" rifled. **Weight:** 6.5 lbs. **Length:** 38.75" overall. **Power:** NA. **Grips:** NA. **Sights:** None, integral mount supplied. **Features:** 600-1,300 fps. 3,000 psi fill pressure. Automatic safety. Air tank volume: 490cc.
Price: 22 w/refill clamp and open sights $649.95
Price: 177 w/refill clamp and open sights $599.95
Price: Gun only (22 or 177) $549.95

AIRFORCE TALON AIR RIFLE
Caliber: 177, 22, single-shot. **Barrel:** 18". **Weight:** 5.5 lbs. **Length:** 32.6". **Power:** Precharged pneumatic. **Stock:** NA. **Sights:** Intended for scope use, fiber-optic open sights optional. **Features:** Lothar Walther match barrel, adjustable power levels from 400-1000 FPS, operates on high pressure air from scuba tank or hand pump. Accessories attach to multiple dovetailed mounting rails. Manufactured in the U.S.A. by AirForce Airguns.
Price: $439.95

AIRFORCE TALON SS AIR RIFLE
Caliber: 177, 22, single-shot. **Barrel:** 12". **Weight:** 5.25 lbs. **Length:** 32.75". **Power:** Precharged pneumatic. **Stock:** NA. **Sights:** Intended for scope use, fiber-optic open sights optional. **Features:** Lothar Walther match barrel, adjustable power levels from 400-1000 FPS. Chamber in front of barrel strips away air turbulence, protects muzzle and reduces firing report. Operates on high pressure air from scuba tank or hand pump. Accessories attach to multiple dovetailed mounting rails. Manufactured in the U.S.A. by AirForce Airguns.
Price: $439.95

AIRROW MODEL A-8SRB STEALTH AIR RIFLE
Caliber: 177, 22, 25, 9-shot. **Barrel:** 20"; rifled. **Weight:** 6 lbs. **Length:** 34" overall. **Power:** CO2 or compressed air; variable power. **Stock:** Telescoping CAR-15-type. **Sights:** Variable 3.5-10x scope. **Features:** Velocity 1100 fps in all calibers. Pneumatic air trigger. All aircraft aluminum and stainless steel construction. Mil-spec materials and finishes. From Swivel Machine Works, Inc.
Price: About. $2,299.00

AIRROW MODEL A-8S1P STEALTH AIR RIFLE
Caliber: #2512 16" arrow. **Barrel:** 16". **Weight:** 4.4 lbs. **Length:** 30.1" overall. **Power:** CO2 or compressed air; variable power. **Stock:** Telescoping CAR-15-type. **Sights:** Scope rings only. 7 oz. rechargeable cylinder and valve. **Features:** Velocity to 650 fps with 260-grain arrow. Pneumatic air trigger. Broadhead guard. All aircraft aluminum and stainless steel construction. Mil-spec materials and finishes. A-8S Models perform to 2,000 PSIG above or below water levels. Waterproof case. From Swivel Machine Works, Inc.
Price: $1,699.00

ANSCHUTZ 2002 MATCH AIR RIFLES
Caliber: 177, single shot. **Barrel:** 25.2". **Weight:** 10.4 lbs. **Length:** 44.5" overall. **Stock:** European walnut, blonde hardwood or colored laminated hardwood; stippled grip and forend. Also available with flat-forend walnut stock for benchrest shooting and aluminum. **Sights:** Optional sight set #6834. **Features:** Muzzle velocity 575 fps. Balance, weight match the 1907 ISU smallbore rifle. Uses #5021 match trigger. Recoil and vibration free. Fully adjustable cheekpiece and buttplate; accessory rail under forend. Available in pneumatic and compressed air versions. Imported from Germany by Gunsmithing, Inc., Accuracy International, Champion's Choice.
Price: Right-hand, blonde hardwood stock, with sights $1,275.00
Price: Right-hand, walnut stock $1,275.00
Price: Right-hand, color laminate stock $1,300.00
Price: Right-hand, aluminum stock, butt plate $1,495.00
Price: Left-hand, color laminate stock $1,595.00
Price: Model 2002D-RT Running Target, right-hand, no sights . . $1,248.90
Price: #6834 Sight Set $227.10

ARS HUNTING MASTER AR6 AIR RIFLE
Caliber: 22, 6-shot repeater. **Barrel:** 25-1/2". **Weight:** 7 lbs. **Length:** 41-1/4" overall. **Power:** Precompressed air from 3000 psi diving tank. **Stock:** Indonesian walnut with checkered grip; rubber buttpad. **Sights:** Blade front, adjustable peep rear. **Features:** Velocity over 1000 fps with 32-grain pellet. Receiver grooved for scope mounting. Has 6-shot rotary magazine. Imported by Air Rifle Specialists.
Price: $580.00

ARS/CAREER 707 AIR RIFLE
Caliber: 22, 6-shot repeater. **Barrel:** 23". **Weight:** 7.75 lbs. **Length:** 40.5" overall. **Power:** Precompressed air; variable power. **Stock:** Indonesian walnut with checkered grip, gloss finish. **Sights:** Hooded post front with interchangeable inserts, fully adjustable diopter rear. **Features:** Velocity to 1000 fps. Lever-action with straight-feed magazine; pressure gauge in lower front air reservoir; scope mounting rail included. Imported from the Philippines by Air Rifle Specialists.
Price: $580.00

BEEMAN CROW MAGNUM AIR RIFLE
Caliber: 20, 22, 25, single shot. **Barrel:** 16"; 10-groove rifling. **Weight:** 8.5 lbs. **Length:** 46" overall. **Power:** Gas-spring; adjustable power to 32 foot pounds muzzle energy. Barrel-cocking. **Stock:** Classic-style hardwood; hand checkered. **Sights:** For scope use only; built-in base and 1" rings included. **Features:** Adjustable two-stage trigger. Automatic safety. Available in 22 caliber on special order. Imported by Beeman.
Price: $1,290.00

BEEMAN KODIAK AIR RIFLE
Caliber: 25, single shot. **Barrel:** 17.6". **Weight:** 9 lbs. **Length:** 45.6" overall. **Power:** Spring-piston, barrel cocking. **Stock:** Stained hardwood. **Sights:** Blade front, open fully adjustable rear. **Features:** Velocity to 820 fps. Up to 30 foot pounds muzzle energy. Imported by Beeman.
Price: $670.00

BEEMAN MAKO MKII AIR RIFLE
Caliber: 177, 22 single shot. **Barrel:** 20", with compensator. **Weight:** 5.5 to 7.8 lbs. **Length:** 39" overall. **Power:** Precharged pneumatic. **Stock:** Stained beech; Monte Carlo cheekpiece; checkered grip. **Sights:** None furnished. **Features:** Velocity to 930 fps. Gives over 50 shots per charge. Manual safety; brass trigger blade; vented rubber buttpad. Requires scuba tank for air. Imported from England by Beeman.
Price: $999.00

BEEMAN R1 AIR RIFLE
Caliber: 177, 20 or 22, single shot. **Barrel:** 19.6", 12-groove rifling. **Weight:** 8.5 lbs. **Length:** 45.2" overall. **Power:** Spring-piston, barrel cocking. **Stock:** Walnut-stained beech; cut-checkered pistol grip; Monte Carlo comb and cheekpiece; rubber buttpad. **Sights:** Tunnel front with interchangeable inserts, open rear click-adjustable for windage and elevation. Grooved for scope mounting. **Features:** Velocity 940-1000 fps (177), 860 fps (20), 800 fps (22). Non-drying nylon piston and breech seals. Adjustable metal trigger. Milled steel safety. Right- or left-hand stock. Adjustable cheekpiece and buttplate at extra cost. Custom and Super Laser versions available. Imported by Beeman.
Price: Right-hand $605.00
Price: Left-hand $680.00

BEEMAN R7 AIR RIFLE
Caliber: 177, 20, single shot. **Barrel:** 17". **Weight:** 6.1 lbs. **Length:** 40.2" overall. **Power:** Spring-piston. **Stock:** Stained beech. **Sights:** Hooded front, fully adjustable micrometer click open rear. **Features:** Velocity to 700 fps (177), 620 fps (20). Receiver grooved for scope mounting; double-jointed cocking lever; fully adjustable trigger; checkered grip. Imported by Beeman.
Price: $330.00

BEEMAN R9 AIR RIFLE
Caliber: 177, 20, single shot. **Barrel:** NA. **Weight:** 7.3 lbs. **Length:** 43" overall. **Power:** Spring-piston, barrel cocking. **Stock:** Stained hardwood. **Sights:** Tunnel post front, fully adjustable open rear. **Features:** Velocity to 1000 fps (177), 800 fps (20). Adjustable Rekord trigger; automatic safety; receiver dovetailed for scope mounting. Imported from Germany by Beeman Precision Airguns.
Price: $360.00

Beeman R9 Deluxe Air Rifle
Same as R9 except has extended forend stock, checkered pistol grip, grip cap, carved Monte Carlo cheekpiece. Globe front sight with inserts. Imported by Beeman.
Price: **$440.00**

BEEMAN R11 MKII AIR RIFLE
Caliber: 177, single shot. **Barrel:** 19.6". **Weight:** 8.6 lbs. **Length:** 43.5" overall. **Power:** Spring-piston, barrel cocking. **Stock:** Walnut-stained beech; adjustable buttplate and cheekpiece. **Sights:** None furnished. Has dovetail for scope mounting. **Features:** Velocity 910-940 fps. All-steel barrel sleeve. Imported by Beeman.
Price: **$620.00**

BEEMAN SUPER 12 AIR RIFLE
Caliber: 22, 25, 12-shot magazine. **Barrel:** 19", 12-groove rifling. **Weight:** 7.8 lbs. **Length:** 41.7" overall. **Power:** Precharged pneumatic; external air reservoir. **Stock:** European walnut. **Sights:** None furnished; drilled and tapped for scope mounting; scope mount included. **Features:** Velocity to 850 fps (25-caliber). Adjustable power setting gives 30-70 shots per 400 cc air bottle. Requires scuba tank for air. Imported by Beeman.
Price: **$1,940.00**

BEEMAN RX-2 GAS-SPRING MAGNUM AIR RIFLE
Caliber: 177, 20, 22, 25, single shot. **Barrel:** 19.6", 12-groove rifling. **Weight:** 8.8 lbs. **Power:** Gas-spring piston air; single stroke barrel cocking. **Stock:** Walnut-finished hardwood, hand checkered, with cheekpiece. Adjustable cheekpiece and buttplate. **Sights:** Tunnel front, click-adjustable rear. **Features:** Velocity adjustable to about 1200 fps. Imported by Beeman.
Price: 177, 20, 22 or 25 regular, right-hand **$670.00**

BEEMAN R1 CARBINE
Caliber: 177, 20, 22, 25, single shot. **Barrel:** 16.1". **Weight:** 8.6 lbs. **Length:** 41.7" overall. **Power:** Spring-piston, barrel cocking. **Stock:** Stained beech; Monte Carlo comb and checkpiece; cut checkered pistol grip; rubber buttpad. **Sights:** Tunnel front with interchangeable inserts, open adjustable rear; receiver grooved for scope mounting. **Features:** Velocity up to 1000 fps (177). Non-drying nylon piston and breech seals. Adjustable metal trigger. Machined steel receiver end cap and safety. Right- or left-hand stock. Imported by Beeman.
Price: 177, 20, 22, 25, right-hand . . . . **$605.00;** left-hand **$680.00**

BEEMAN/FEINWERKBAU 603 AIR RIFLE
Caliber: 177, single shot. **Barrel:** 16.6". **Weight:** 10.8 lbs. **Length:** 43" overall. **Power:** Single stroke pneumatic. **Stock:** Special laminated hardwoods and hard rubber for stability. Multi-colored stock also available. **Sights:** Tunnel front with interchangeable inserts, click micrometer match aperture rear. **Features:** Velocity to 570 fps. Recoilless action; double supported barrel; special, short rifled area frees pellet from barrel faster. Fully adjustable match trigger with separately adjustable trigger and trigger slack weight. Trigger and sights blocked when loading latch is open. Imported by Beeman.
Price: Right-hand. **$1,625.00**
Price: Left-hand **$1,775.00**
Price: Junior **$1,500.00**

BEEMAN/FEINWERKBAU 300-S AND 300 JUNIOR MINI-MATCH RIFLE
Caliber: 177, single shot. **Barrel:** 17-1/8". **Weight:** 8.8 lbs. **Length:** 40" overall. **Power:** Spring-piston, single stroke sidelever cocking. **Stock:** Walnut. Stippled grip, adjustable buttplate. Scaled down model for youthful or slightly built shooters. **Sights:** Globe front with interchangeable inserts, micro. adjustable rear. Sights move as a single unit. **Features:** Recoilless, vibration free. Grooved for scope mounts. Steel piston ring. Cocking effort about 9-1/2 lbs. Barrel sleeve optional. Imported by Beeman.
Price: Right-hand . . . . **$1,680.00;** left-hand **$1,825.00**

BEEMAN/FEINWERKBAU P70 AND P70 JUNIOR AIR RIFLE
Caliber: 177, single shot. **Barrel:** 16.6". **Weight:** 10.6 lbs. **Length:** 42.6" overall. **Power:** Precharged pneumatic. **Stock:** Laminated hardwoods and hard rubber for stability. Multi-colored stock also available. **Sights:** Tunnel front with interchangeable inserts, click micrometer match aperture rear. **Features:** Velocity to 570 fps. Recoilless action; double supported barrel; special short rifled area frees pellet from barrel faster. Fully adjustable match trigger with separately adjustable trigger and trigger slack weight. Trigger and sights blocked when loading latch is open. Imported by Beeman.
Price: P70, precharged, right-hand **$1,600.00**
Price: P70, precharged, left-hand **$1,690.00**
Price: P70, precharged, Junior **$1,600.00**
Price: P70, precharged, right-hand, multi **$1,465.00**

BEEMAN/HW 97 AIR RIFLE
Caliber: 177, 20, single shot. **Barrel:** 17.75". **Weight:** 9.2 lbs. **Length:** 44.1" overall. **Power:** Spring-piston, underlever cocking. **Stock:** Walnut-stained beech; rubber buttpad. **Sights:** None. Receiver grooved for scope mounting. **Features:** Velocity 830 fps (177). Fixed barrel with fully opening, direct loading breech. Adjustable trigger. Imported by Beeman Precision Airguns.
Price: Right-hand only **$605.00**

BENJAMIN SHERIDAN PNEUMATIC (PUMP-UP) AIR RIFLE
Caliber: 177 or 22, single shot. **Barrel:** 19-3/8", rifled brass. **Weight:** 5-1/2 lbs. **Length:** 36-1/4" overall. **Power:** Underlever pneumatic, hand pumped. **Stock:** American walnut stock and forend. **Sights:** High ramp front, fully adjustable notched rear. **Features:** Variable velocity to 800 fps. Bolt action with ambidextrous push-pull safety. Black or nickel finish. Made in the U.S. by Benjamin Sheridan Co.
Price: Black finish, Model 397 (177), Model 392 (22) **$224.00**
Price: Nickel finish, Model S397 (177), Model S392 (22) **$245.00**

BRNO TAU-200 AIR RIFLES
Caliber: 177, single shot. **Barrel:** 19", rifled. **Weight:** 7-1/2 lbs. **Length:** 42" overall. **Power:** 6-oz. CO2 cartridge. **Stock:** Wood match style with adjustable comb and buttplate. **Sights:** Globe front with interchangeable inserts, fully adjustable open rear. **Features:** Adjustable trigger. Comes with extra seals, large CO2 bottle, counterweight. Imported by Great Lakes Airguns. Available in Standard Universal, Deluxe Universal, International and Target Sporter versions.
Price: Standard Universal (ambidex. stock with buttstock extender, adj. cheekpiece) **$349.50**
Price: Deluxe Universal (as above but with micro-adj. aperture sight) **$449.50**
Price: International (like Deluxe Universal but with right- or left-hand stock) **$454.50**
Price: Target Sporter (like Std. Universal but with 4x scope, no sights) **$412.50**

BSA MAGNUM GOLDSTAR MAGNUM AIR RIFLE
Caliber: 177, 22, 10-shot repeater. **Barrel:** 17-1/2". **Weight:** 8 lbs., 8 oz. **Length:** 42.5" overall. **Power:** Spring-air, underlever cocking. **Stock:** Oil-finished hardwood; Monte Carlo with cheekpiece, checkered grip; recoil pad. **Sights:** Ramp front, micrometer adjustable rear. Comes with Maxi-Grip scope rail. **Features:** Velocity 950 fps (177), 750 fps (22). Patented 10-shot indexing magazine; Maxi-Grip scope rail protects optics from recoil; automatic anti-beartrap plus manual safety; muzzle brake standard. Imported from U.K. by Precision Sales International, Inc.
Price: **$499.95**

BSA MAGNUM SUPERTEN AIR RIFLE
Caliber: 177, 22 10-shot repeater. **Barrel:** 17-1/2". **Weight:** 7 lbs., 8 oz. **Length:** 37" overall. **Power:** Precharged pneumatic via buddy bottle. **Stock:** Oil-finished hardwood; Monte Carlo with cheekpiece, cut checkered grip; adjustable recoil pad. **Sights:** No sights; intended for scope use. **Features:** Velocity 1000+ fps (177), 1000+ fps (22). Patented 10-shot indexing magazine, bolt-action loading. Left-hand version also available. Imported from U.K. by Precision Sales International, Inc.
Price: **$599.95**

BSA MAGNUM SUPERSTAR™ MK2 MAGNUM AIR RIFLE, CARBINE
Caliber: 177, 22, 25, single shot. **Barrel:** 18-1/2". **Weight:** 8 lbs., 8 oz. **Length:** 43" overall. **Power:** Spring-air, underlever cocking. **Stock:** Oil-finished hardwood; Monte Carlo with cheekpiece, checkered at grip; recoil pad. **Sights:** Ramp front, micrometer adjustable rear. Maxi-Grip scope rail. **Features:** Velocity 950 fps (177), 750 fps (22), 600 fps (25). Patented rotating breech design. Maxi-Grip scope rail protects optics from recoil; automatic anti-beartrap plus manual safety. Imported from U.K. by Precision Sales International, Inc.
Price: Rifle, MKII Carbine (14" barrel, 39-1/2" overall) **$349.95**

Daisy 7840 Buckmaster

BSA MAGNUM SUPERSPORT™ AIR RIFLE, CARBINE
Caliber: 177, 22, 25, single shot. **Barrel:** 18-1/2". **Weight:** 6 lbs., 8 oz. **Length:** 41" overall. **Power:** Spring-air, barrel cocking. **Stock:** Oil-finished hardwood; Monte Carlo with cheekpiece, recoil pad. **Sights:** Ramp front, micrometer adjustable rear. Maxi-Grip scope rail. **Features:** Velocity 950 fps (177), 750 fps (22), 600 fps (25). Patented Maxi-Grip scope rail protects optics from recoil; automatic anti-beartrap plus manual tang safety. Muzzle brake standard. Imported for U.K. by Precision Sales International, Inc.
Price: **$194.95**
Price: Carbine, 14" barrel, muzzle brake **$214.95**

BSA METEOR MK6 AIR RIFLE
Caliber: 177, 22, single shot. **Barrel:** 18-1/2". **Weight:** 6 lbs. **Length:** 41" overall. **Power:** Spring-air, barrel cocking. **Stock:** Oil-finished hardwood. **Sights:** Ramp front, micrometer adjustable rear. **Features:** Velocity 650 fps (177), 500 fps (22). Automatic anti-beartrap; manual tang safety. Receiver grooved for scope mounting. Imported from U.K. by Precision Sales International, Inc.
Price: Rifle **$144.95**
Price: Carbine **$164.95**

CROSMAN MODEL 66 POWERMASTER AIR RIFLES
Caliber: 177 (single shot pellet) or BB, 200-shot reservoir. **Barrel:** 20", rifled steel. **Weight:** 3 lbs. **Length:** 38-1/2" overall. **Power:** Pneumatic; hand-pumped. **Stock:** Wood-grained ABS plastic; checkered pistol grip and forend. **Sights:** Fiber-optic front, fully adjustable open rear. **Features:** Velocity about 645 fps. Bolt action, cross-bolt safety. From Crosman.
Price: Model 66BX **$60.00**
Price: Model 664X (as above, with 4x scope) **$70.00**
Price: Model 664SB (as above with silver and black finish), about .. **$75.00**

CROSMAN REMINGTON GENESIS AIR RIFLE
Caliber: 177 **Power:** Break-action. **Sights:** Fiber-optic front, adj. rear. Dovetailed for scope. **Weight:** 6.5 lbs. **Length:** 43" overall. **Stock:** Synthetic, thumbhole pistol grip. From Crosman.
Price: **$249.99**
Price: W 3-9x40 scope **$279.99**

CROSMAN MODEL 760 PUMPMASTER AIR RIFLES
Caliber: 177 pellets (single shot) or BB (200-shot reservoir). **Barrel:** 19-1/2", rifled steel. **Weight:** 2 lbs., 12 oz. **Length:** 33.5" overall. **Power:** Pneumatic, hand-pump. **Stock:** Walnut-finished ABS plastic stock and forend. **Features:** Velocity to 590 fps (BBs, 10 pumps). Short stroke, power determined by number of strokes. Fiber-optic front sight and adjustable rear sight. Cross-bolt safety. From Crosman.
Price: Model 760B **$40.00**
Price: Model 764SB (silver and black finish), about **$55.00**
Price: Model 760SK .... **NA**
Price: Model 760BRO .... **NA**

CROSMAN MODEL 1077 REPEAT AIR RIFLES
Caliber: 177 pellets, 12-shot clip. **Barrel:** 20.3", rifled steel. **Weight:** 3 lbs., 11 oz. **Length:** 38.8" overall. **Power:** CO2 Powerlet. **Stock:** Textured synthetic or hardwood. **Sights:** Blade front, fully adjustable rear. **Features:** Velocity 590 fps. Removable 12-shot clip. True semi-automatic action. From Crosman.
Price: **$75.00**
Price: 1077W (walnut stock) **$110.00**

CROSMAN 2260 AIR RIFLE
Caliber: 22, single shot. **Barrel:** 24". **Weight:** 4 lbs., 12 oz. **Length:** 39.75" overall. **Power:** CO2 Powerlet. **Stock:** Hardwood. **Sights:** Blade front, adjustable rear open or peep. **Features:** About 600 fps. Made in U.S. by Crosman Corp.
Price: .... **NA**

CROSMAN MODEL 2100 CLASSIC AIR RIFLE
Caliber: 177 pellets (single shot), or BB (200-shot BB reservoir). **Barrel:** 21", rifled. **Weight:** 4 lbs., 13 oz. **Length:** 39-3/4" overall. **Power:** Pump-up, pneumatic. **Stock:** Wood-grained checkered ABS plastic. **Features:** Three pumps give about 450 fps, 10 pumps about 755 fps (BBs). Cross-bolt safety; concealed reservoir holds over 200 BBs. From Crosman.
Price: Model 2100B **$75.00**

CROSMAN MODEL 2200 MAGNUM AIR RIFLE
Caliber: 22, single shot. **Barrel:** 19", rifled steel. **Weight:** 4 lbs., 12 oz. **Length:** 39" overall. **Stock:** Full-size, wood-grained ABS plastic with checkered grip and forend or American walnut. **Sights:** Ramp front, open step-adjustable rear. **Features:** Variable pump power; three pumps give 395 fps, six pumps 530 fps, 10 pumps 595 fps (average). Full-size adult air rifle. Has white line spacers at pistol grip and buttplate. From Crosman.
Price: **$75.00**

DAISY 1938 RED RYDER 60th ANNIVERSARY CLASSIC AIR RIFLE
Caliber: BB, 650-shot repeating action. **Barrel:** Smoothbore steel with shroud. **Weight:** 2.2 lbs. **Length:** 35.4" overall. **Stock:** Walnut stock burned with Red Ryder lariat signature. **Sights:** Post front, adjustable V-slot rear. **Features:** Walnut forend. Saddle ring with leather thong. Lever cocking. Gravity feed. Controlled velocity. From Daisy Mfg. Co.
Price: **$39.00**

DAISY MODEL 840 GRIZZLY AIR RIFLE
Caliber: 177 pellet single shot; or BB 350-shot. **Barrel:** 19", smoothbore, steel. **Weight:** 2.25 lbs. **Length:** 36.8" overall. **Power:** Single pump pneumatic. **Stock:** Molded wood-grain stock and forend. **Sights:** Ramp front, open, adjustable rear. **Features:** Muzzle velocity 320 fps (BB), 300 fps (pellet). Steel buttplate; straight pull bolt action; cross-bolt safety. Forend forms pump lever. From Daisy Mfg. Co.
Price: **$32.95**
Price: 840C Mossy Oak® Break Up™ camo **$49.95**

DAISY MODEL 7840 BUCKMASTER AIR RIFLE
Caliber: 177 pellets, or BB. **Barrel:** Smoothbore steel. **Weight:** 2.25 lbs. **Length:** 36.8" overall. **Power:** Single-pump pneumatic. **Stock:** Molded with checkering and wood-grain. **Sights:** Ramp and blade front, adjustable open rear plus Electronic Point Sight. **Features:** Velocity to 320 fps (BB), 300 fps (pellet). Cross-bolt trigger block safety. From Daisy Mfg. Co.
Price: **$54.95**

DAISY MODEL 105 BUCK AIR RIFLE
Caliber: 177 or BB. **Barrel:** Smoothbore steel. **Weight:** 1.6 lbs. **Length:** 29.8" overall. **Power:** Lever cocking, spring air. **Stock:** Stained solid wood. **Sights:** TruGlo fiber-optic, open fixed rear. **Features:** Velocity to 275. Cross-bolt trigger block safety. From Daisy Mfg. Co.
Price: .... **NA**

Daisy Model 95 Timberwolf Air Rifle
Similar to the 105 Buck except velocity to 325 fps. Weighs 2.4 lbs., overall length 35.2".
Price: **$38.95**

DAISY/POWERLINE 1000 AIR RIFLE
Caliber: 177, single shot. **Barrel:** NA. **Weight:** 6.15 lbs. **Length:** 43" overall. **Power:** Spring-air, barrel cocking. **Stock:** Stained hardwood. **Sights:** Hooded blade front on ramp, adjustable micrometer rear. **Features:** Velocity to 1000 fps. Blued finish; trigger block safety. From Daisy Mfg. Co.
Price: **$208.95**

DAISY/POWERLINE 1170 PELLET RIFLES
Caliber: 177, single shot. **Barrel:** Rifled steel. **Weight:** 5.5 lbs. **Length:** 42.5" overall. **Power:** Spring-air, barrel cocking. **Stock:** Hardwood. **Sights:** Hooded post front, micrometer adjustable open rear. **Features:** Velocity to 800 fps. Monte Carlo comb. From Daisy Mfg. Co.
Price: **$129.95**
Price: Model 131 (velocity to 600 fps) **$117.95**
Price: Model 1150 (black copolymer stock, velocity to 600 fps) **$77.95**

AIRGUNS — Long Guns

DAISY/POWERLINE 856 PUMP-UP AIR RIFLES
Caliber: 177 pellets (single shot) or BB (100-shot reservoir). **Barrel:** Rifled steel with shroud. **Weight:** 2.7 lbs. **Length:** 37.4" overall. **Power:** Pneumatic pump-up. **Stock:** Molded wood-grain with Monte Carlo cheekpiece. **Sights:** Ramp and blade front, open rear adjustable for elevation. **Features:** Velocity from 315 fps (two pumps) to 650 fps (10 pumps). Shoots BBs or pellets. Heavy die-cast metal receiver. Cross-bolt triggerblock safety. From Daisy Mfg. Co.
Price: **$39.95**
Price: 856C **$59.95**

DAISY/POWERLINE 853 AIR RIFLE
Caliber: 177 pellets, single shot. **Barrel:** 20.9"; 12-groove rifling, high-grade solid steel by Lothar Waltherô, precision crowned; bore sized for precision matched pellets. **Weight:** 5.08 lbs. **Length:** 38.9" overall. **Power:** Single-pump pneumatic. **Stock:** Full-length select American hardwood, stained and finished; black buttplate with white spacers. **Sights:** Globe front with four aperture inserts; precision micrometer adjustable rear peep sight mounted on a standard 3/8" dovetailed receiver mount.
Price: **$225.00**

DAISY/POWERLINE EAGLE 7856 PUMP-UP AIR RIFLE
Caliber: 177 (pellets), BB, 100-shot BB magazine. **Barrel:** Rifled steel with shroud. **Weight:** 3.3 lbs. **Length:** 37.4" overall. **Power:** Pneumatic pump-up. **Stock:** Molded wood-grain plastic. **Sights:** Ramp and blade front, adjustable open rear. **Features:** Velocity from 315 fps (two pumps) to 650 fps (10 pumps). Finger grooved forend. Cross-bolt triggerblock safety. From Daisy Mfg. Co.
Price: With 4x scope, about **$49.95**

DAISY/POWERLINE 000 AIR RIFLE
Caliber: 177 pellet or BB, 50-shot BB magazine, single shot for pellets. **Barrel:** Rifled steel. **Weight:** 3.7 lbs. **Length:** 37.6" overall. **Power:** Multi-pump pneumatic. **Stock:** Molded wood grain; Monte Carlo comb. **Sights:** Hooded front, adjustable rear. **Features:** Velocity to 685 fps. (BB). Variable power (velocity, range) increase with pump strokes; resin receiver with dovetailed scope mount. Made in U.S.A. by Daisy Mfg. Co.
Price: **$50.95**

DAISY/YOUTHLINE MODEL 105 AIR RIFLE
Caliber: BB, 400-shot magazine. **Barrel:** 13-1/2". **Weight:** 1.6 lbs. **Length:** 29.8" overall. **Power:** Spring. **Stock:** Molded wood-grain. **Sights:** Blade on ramp front, fixed rear. **Features:** Velocity to 275 fps. Blue finish. Cross-bolt trigger block safety. Made in U.S. by Daisy Mfg. Co.
Price: **$28.95**

DAISY/YOUTHLINE MODEL 95 AIR RIFLE
Caliber: BB, 700-shot magazine. **Barrel:** 18". **Weight:** 2.4 lbs. **Length:** 35.2" overall. **Power:** Spring. **Stock:** Stained hardwood. **Sights:** Blade on ramp front, open adjustable rear. **Features:** Velocity to 325 fps. Cross-bolt trigger block safety. Made in U.S. by Daisy Mfg. Co.
Price: **$30.95**

EAA/BAIKAL MP-512 AIR RIFLES
Caliber: 177, single shot. **Barrel:** 17.7". **Weight:** 6.2 lbs. **Length:** 41.3" overall. **Power:** Spring-piston, single stroke. **Stock:** Black synthetic. **Sights:** Adjustable rear, hooded front. **Features:** Velocity 490 fps. Hammer-forged, rifled barrel; automatic safety; scope mount rail. Imported from Russia by European American Armory.
Price: 177 caliber. **$49.00**
Price: 512M (590 fps) **$65.00**

EAA/BAIKAL IZH-61 AIR RIFLE
Caliber: 177 pellet, 5-shot magazine. **Barrel:** 17.8". **Weight:** 6.4 lbs. **Length:** 31" overall. **Power:** Spring-piston, side-cocking lever. **Stock:** Black plastic. **Sights:** Adjustable rear, fully hooded front. **Features:** Velocity 490 fps. Futuristic design with adjustable stock. Imported from Russia by European American Armory.
Price: **$99.00**

EAA/BAIKAL IZHMP-532 AIR RIFLE
Caliber: 177 pellet, single shot. **Barrel:** 15.8". **Weight:** 9.3 lbs. **Length:** 46.1" overall. **Power:** Single-stroke pneumatic. **Stock:** One- or two-piece competition-style stock with adjustable buttpad, pistol grip. **Sights:** Fully adjustable rear, hooded front. **Features:** Velocity 460 fps. Five-way adjustable trigger. Imported from Russia by European American Armory.
Price: **$599.00**

GAMO DELTA AIR RIFLE
Caliber: 177. **Barrel:** 15.7". **Weight:** 4.2 lbs. **Length:** 37.8". **Power:** Single-stroke pneumatic, 525 fps. **Stock:** Synthetic. **Sights:** TruGlo fiber-optic.
Price: **$89.95**

GAMO YOUNG HUNTER AIR RIFLE
Caliber: 177. **Barrel:** 17.7". **Weight:** 5.5 lbs. **Length:** 41". **Power:** Single-stroke pneumatic, 640 fps. **Stock:** Wood. **Sights:** TruGlo fiber-optic adjustable. **Features:** Rifled steel barrel, hooded front sight, grooved receiver for scope. Imported from Spain by Gamo.
Price: **$129.95**
Price: Combo packed with BSA 4x32 scope and rings **$169.95**

GAMO SPORTER AIR RIFLE
Caliber: 177. **Barrel:** NA. **Weight:** 5.5 lbs. **Length:** 42.5". **Power:** Single-stroke pneumatic, 760 fps. **Stock:** Wood. **Sights:** Adjustable TruGlo fiber-optic. **Features:** Intended to bridge the gap between Gamo's Young Hunter model and the adult-sized Hunter 440. Imported from Spain by Gamo.
Price: **$159.95**

GAMO HUNTER 440 AIR RIFLES
Caliber: 177, 22. **Barrel:** NA. **Weight:** 6.6 lbs. **Length:** 43.3". **Power:** Single-stroke pneumatifc, 1,000 fps (177), 750 fps (22). **Stock:** Wood. **Sights:** Adjustable TruGlo fiber-optic. **Features:** Adjustable two-stage trigger, rifled barrel, raised scope ramp on receiver. Realtree camo model available.
Price: **$229.95**
Price: Hunter 440 Combo with BSA 4x32mm scope **$259.95**

HAMMERLI AR 50 AIR RIFLE
Caliber: 177. **Barrel:** 19.8". **Weight:** 10 lbs. **Length:** 43.2" overall. **Power:** Compressed air. **Stock:** Anatomically-shaped universal and right-hand; match style; multi-colored laminated wood. **Sights:** Interchangeable element tunnel front, adjustable Hammerli peep rear. **Features:** Vibration-free firing release; adjustable match trigger and trigger stop; stainless air tank, built-in pressure gauge. Gives 270 shots per filling. Imported from Switzerland by SIGARMS, Inc.
Price: **$1,653.00**

HAMMERLI MODEL 450 MATCH AIR RIFLE
Caliber: 177, single shot. **Barrel:** 19.5". **Weight:** 9.8 lbs. **Length:** 43.3" overall. **Power:** Pneumatic. **Stock:** Match style with stippled grip, rubber buttpad. Beech or walnut. **Sights:** Match tunnel front, Hammerli diopter rear. **Features:** Velocity about 560 fps. Removable sights; forend sling rail; adjustable trigger; adjustable comb. Imported from Switzerland by SIGARMS, Inc.
Price: Beech stock **$1,355.00**
Price: Walnut stock **$1,395.00**

MARKSMAN BB BUDDY AIR RIFLE
Caliber: 177, 20-shot magazine. **Barrel:** 10.5" smoothbore. **Weight:** 1.6 lbs. **Length:** 33" overall. **Power:** Spring-air. **Stock:** Molded composition. **Sights:** Blade on ramp front, adjustable V-slot rear. **Features:** Velocity 275 fps. Positive feed; automatic safety. Youth-sized lightweight design. Made in U.S. From Marksman Products.
Price: **$27.95**

MARKSMAN 2015 LASERHAWK™ BB REPEATER AIR RIFLE
Caliber: 177 BB, 20-shot magazine. **Barrel:** 10.5" smoothbore. **Weight:** 1.6 lbs. **Length:** Adjustable to 33", 34" or 35" overall. **Power:** Spring-air. **Stock:** Molded composition. **Sights:** Fixed fiber-optic front sight, adjustable elevation V-slot rear. **Features:** Velocity about 275 fps. Positive feed; automatic safety. Adjustable stock. Made in the U.S. From Marksman Products.
Price: **$33.00**

RWS/DIANA MODEL 24 AIR RIFLES
Caliber: 177, 22, single shot. **Barrel:** 17", rifled. **Weight:** 6 lbs. **Length:** 42" overall. **Power:** Spring-air, barrel cocking. **Stock:** Beech. **Sights:** Hooded front, adjustable rear. **Features:** Velocity of 700 fps (177). Easy cocking effort; blue finish. Imported from Germany by Dynamit Nobel-RWS, Inc.
Price: 24, 24C **$215.00**

RWS/Diana Model 34 Air Rifles
Similar to the Model 24 except has 19" barrel, weighs 7.5 lbs. Gives velocity of 1000 fps (177), 800 fps (22). Adjustable trigger, synthetic seals. Comes with scope rail.
Price: 177 or 22 . . . . **$290.00**
Price: Model 34N (nickel-plated metal, black epoxy-coated
wood stock) **$350.00**
Price: Model 34BC (matte black metal, black stock, 4x32 scope,
mounts) **$510.00**

RWS/DIANA MODEL 36 AIR RIFLES
Caliber: 177, 22, single shot. **Barrel:** 19", rifled. **Weight:** 8 lbs. **Length:** 45" overall. **Power:** Spring-air, barrel cocking. **Stock:** Beech. **Sights:** Hooded front (interchangeable inserts available), adjustable rear. **Features:** Velocity of 1000 fps (177-cal.). Comes with scope mount; two-stage adjustable trigger. Imported from Germany by Dynamit Nobel-RWS, Inc.
Price: 36, 36C **$435.00**

RWS/DIANA MODEL 52 AIR RIFLES
Caliber: 177, 22, 25, single shot. **Barrel:** 17", rifled. **Weight:** 8-1/2 lbs. **Length:** 43" overall. **Power:** Spring-air, sidelever cocking. **Stock:** Beech, with Monte Carlo, cheekpiece, checkered grip and forend. **Sights:** Ramp front, adjustable rear. **Features:** Velocity of 1100 fps (177). Blue finish. Solid rubber buttpad. Imported from Germany by Dynamit Nobel-RWS, Inc.
Price: 177, 22 . . . . **$565.00**
Price: 25 . . . . **$605.00**
Price: Model 52 Deluxe (177) **$810.00**
Price: Model 48B (as above except matte black metal, black stock)
. . . . **$535.00**
Price: Model 48 (same as Model 52 except no Monte Carlo
cheekpiece or checkering) **$520.00**

RWS/DIANA MODEL 45 AIR RIFLE
Caliber: 177, single shot. **Weight:** 8 lbs. **Length:** 45" overall. **Power:** Spring-air, barrel cocking. **Stock:** Walnut-finished hardwood with rubber recoil pad. **Sights:** Globe front with interchangeable inserts, micro. click open rear with four-way blade. **Features:** Velocity of 820 fps. Dovetailed base for either micrometer peep sight or scope mounting. Automatic safety. Imported from Germany by Dynamit Nobel-RWS, Inc.
Price: **$350.00**

RWS/DIANA MODEL 46 AIR RIFLES
Caliber: 177, 22, single shot. **Barrel:** 18". **Weight:** 8.2 lbs. **Length:** 45" overall. **Stock:** Hardwood; Monte Carlo. **Sights:** Blade front, adjustable rear. **Features:** Underlever cocking spring-air (950 fps in 177, 780 fps in 22); extended scope rail, automatic safety, rubber buttpad, adjustable trigger. Imported from Germany by Dynamit Nobel-RWS, Inc.
Price: **$470.00**
Price: Model 46E (as above except matte black metal, black stock)
. . . . **$430.00**

RWS/DIANA MODEL 54 AIR RIFLE
Caliber: 177, 22, single shot. **Barrel:** 17". **Weight:** 9 lbs. **Length:** 43" overall. **Power:** Spring-air, sidelever cocking. **Stock:** Walnut with Monte Carlo cheekpiece, checkered grip and forend. **Sights:** Ramp front, fully adjustable rear. **Features:** Velocity to 1000 fps (177), 900 fps (22). Totally recoilless system; floating action absorbs recoil. Imported from Germany by Dynamit Nobel-RWS, Inc.
Price: **$785.00**

RWS/DIANA MODEL 92/93/94 AIR RIFLES
Caliber: 177, 22, single shot. **Barrel:** NA. **Weight:** NA. **Length:** NA. **Stock:** Beechwood; Monte Carlo. **Sights:** Hooded front, fully adjustable rear.

Features: Break-barrel, spring-air; receiver grooved for scope; adjustable trigger; lifetime warranty. Imported from Spain by Dynamit Nobel-RWS, Inc.
Price: Model 92 (auto safety, 700 fps in 177) . . . . **NA**
Price: Model 93 (manual safety, 850 fps in 177) . . . . **NA**
Price: Model 94 (auto safety, 1,000 fps in 177) . . . . **NA**

RWS/DIANA MODEL 350 MAGNUM AIR RIFLE
Caliber: 177, 22, single shot. **Barrel:** 19-1/2". **Weight:** 8 lbs. **Length:** 48". **Stock:** Beechwood; Monte Carlo. **Sights:** Hooded front, fully adjustable rear. **Features:** Break-barrel, spring-air; 1,250 fps. Imported from Germany by Dynamit Nobel-RWS, Inc.
Price: . . . . **NA**

TECH FORCE BS4 OLYMPIC COMPETITION AIR RIFLE
Caliber: 177 pellet, single shot. **Barrel:** NA. **Weight:** 10.8 lbs. **Length:** 43.3" overall. **Power:** Spring piston, sidelever action. **Stock:** Wood with semi-pistol grip, adjustable buttplate. **Sights:** Micro-adjustable competition rear, hooded front. **Features:** Velocity 640 fps. Recoilless action; adjustable trigger. Includes carrying case. Imported from China by Compasseco, Inc.
Price: **$595.00**
Price: Optional diopter rear sight **$79.95**

TECH FORCE 6 AIR RIFLE
Caliber: 177 pellet, single shot. **Barrel:** 14". **Weight:** 6 lbs. **Length:** 35.5" overall. **Power:** Spring-piston, sidelever action. **Stock:** Paratrooper-style folding, full pistol grip. **Sights:** Adjustable rear, hooded front. **Features:** Velocity 800 fps. All-metal construction; grooved for scope mounting. Imported from China by Compasseco, Inc.
Price: **$69.95**

Tech Force 51 Air Rifle
Similar to Tech Force 6, but with break-barrel cocking mechanism and folding stock fitted with recoil pad. Overall length, 36". Weighs 6 lbs. From Compasseco, Inc.
Price: **$69.95**

TECH FORCE 25 AIR RIFLE
Caliber: 177, 22 pellet; single shot. **Barrel:** NA. **Weight:** 7.5 lbs. **Length:** 46.2" overall. **Power:** Spring piston, break-action barrel. **Stock:** Oil-finished wood; Monte Carlo stock with recoil pad. **Sights:** Adjustable rear, hooded front with insert. **Features:** Velocity 1,000 fps (177); grooved receiver and scope stop for scope mounting; adjustable trigger; trigger safety. Imported from China by Compasseco, Inc.
Price: 177 or 22 caliber **$125.00**
Price: Includes rifle and Tech Force 96 red dot point sight **$164.95**

TECH FORCE 36 AIR RIFLE
Caliber: 177 pellet, single shot. **Barrel:** NA. **Weight:** 7.4 lbs. **Length:** 43" overall. **Power:** Spring piston, underlever cocking. **Stock:** Monte Carlo hardwood stock; recoil pad. **Sights:** Adjustable rear, hooded front. **Features:** Velocity 900 fps; grooved receiver and scope stop for scope mounting; auto-reset safety. Imported from China by Compasseco, Inc.
Price: **$89.95**

WHISCOMBE JW SERIES AIR RIFLES
Caliber: 177, 20, 22, 25, single shot. **Barrel:** 15", Lothar Walther. Polygonal rifling. **Weight:** 9 lbs., 8 oz. **Length:** 39" overall. **Power:** Dual spring-piston, multi-stroke; underlever cocking. **Stock:** Walnut with adjustable buttplate and cheekpiece. **Sights:** None furnished; grooved scope rail. **Features:** Velocity 660-1000 (JW80) fps (22-caliber, fixed barrel) depending upon model. Interchangeable barrels; automatic safety; muzzle weight; semi-floating action; twin opposed pistons with counter-wound springs; adjustable trigger. All models include Harmonic Optimization Tunable System. Imported from England by Pelaire Products.
Price: JW50, MKII fixed barrel only **$2,085.00**
Price: JW65, MKII **$2,085.00**
Price: JW80, MKII **$2,195.00**

CH4D Heavyduty Champion

Frame: Cast iron
Frame Type: O-frame
Die Thread: 7/8-14 or 1-14
Avg. Rounds Per Hour: NA
Ram Stroke: 3-1/4"
Weight: 26 lbs.
Features: 1.185" diameter ram with 16 square inches of bearing surface; ram drilled to allow passage of spent primers; solid steel handle; toggle that slightly breaks over the top dead center. Includes universal primer arm with large and small punches. From CH Tool & Die/4D Custom Die.
Price: **$261.98**

CH4D No. 444 4-Station "H" Press

Frame: Aluminum alloy
Frame Type: H-frame
Die Thread: 7/8-14
Avg. Rounds Per Hour: 200
Ram Stroke: 3-3/4"
Weight: 21 lbs.
Features: Two 7/8" solid steel shaft "H" supports; platen rides on permanently lubed bronze bushings; loads smallest pistol to largest magnum rifle cases and has strength to full-length resize. Includes four rams, large and small primer arm and primer catcher. From CH Tool & Die/4D Custom Die, Co.
Price: **$235.46**

CH4D No. 444-X Pistol Champ

Frame: Aluminum alloy
Frame Type: H-frame
Die Thread: 7/8-14
Avg. Rounds Per Hour: 200
Ram Stroke: 3-3/4"
Weight: 12 lbs.
Features: Tungsten carbide sizing die; Speed Seater seating die with tapered entrance to automatically align bullet on case mouth; automatic primer feed for large or small primers; push-button powder measure with easily changed bushings for 215 powder/load combinations; taper crimp die. Conversion kit for caliber changeover available. From CH Tool & Die/4D Custom Die, Co.
Price: . . . . **$292.00 to $316.50**

CORBIN CSP-2 Mega Mite

Frame: NA
Frame Type: NA
Die Thread: NA
Avg. Rounds Per Hour: NA
Ram Stroke: NA
Weight: 80 lbs.
Features: Handles 50 BMG and 20mm, smaller calibers wtih standard reloading adapter kit included. Die adapters for all threads available. Side-roller handle or extra long power handle, left- or right-hand operation. Ram is bearing guided. Uses standard Corbin-H swaging, drawing and jacket-making dies. Cold-forms lead bullets up to 12 gauge. Optional floor stand available.
Price: **$750.00**

CORBIN CSP-2 Hydro Mite Hyrdraulic Drawing/Swaging Press

Frame: NA
Frame Type: NA
Die Thread: 7/8-14
Avg. Rounds Per Hour: NA
Ram Stroke: NA
Weight: 100 lbs. with power unit
Features: Reloads standard calibers, swages bullets up to 458 caliber, draws jackets and extrudes small diameter lead wire. Optional speed and thrust control unit available. Uses Corbin-S swaging and drawing dies. Comes with T-slot ram adaptor for standard shell holders. Make free 22 and 6mm jackets from fired 22 cases using optional Corbin kit.
Price: **$2,995.00**

CORBIN CSP-1 S-Press Benchrest Reloading/Swaging Tool

Frame: NA
Frame Type: NA
Die Thread: NA
Avg. Rounds Per Hour: NA
Ram Stroke: NA
Weight: 22 lbs.
Features: Handles standard calibers and swages bullets up to 458 caliber. Hand built. All moving parts run in bearings. Industrial hard-chromed ram, left- or right-hand operation. Quick stroke change doubles power for bullet swaging. Roller bearing links, expanded neoprene foam grip. Comes with reloading adapter kit for standard T-slot shell holders.
Price: **$329.00**

FORSTER Co-Ax Press B-2

Frame: Cast iron
Frame Type: Modified O-frame
Die Thread: 7/8-14
Avg. Rounds Per Hour: 120
Ram Stroke: 4"
Weight: 18 lbs.
Features: Snap in/snap out die change; spent primer catcher with drop tube threaded into carrier below shellholder; automatic, handle-activated, cammed shellholder with opposing spring-loaded jaws to contact extractor groove; floating guide rods for alignment and reduced friction; no torque on the head due to design of linkage and pivots; shellholder jaws that float with die permitting case to center in the die; right- or left-hand operation; priming device for seating to factory specifications. "S" shellholder jaws included. From Forster Products.
Price: **$336.30**
Price: Extra LS shellholder jaws **$29.00**

CH4D No. 444

CH4D 444-X Pistol Champ

Forster Co-Ax

Corbin CSP-2

METALLIC CARTRIDGE PRESSES

Hollywood Senior Turret

Lee Hand Press

Hornady Lock-N-Load Classic

Lee Reloader

Lee Challenger

HOLLYWOOD Senior Press

Frame: Ductile iron
Frame Type: O-frame
Die Thread: 7/8-14
Avg. Rounds Per Hour: 50-100
Ram Stroke: 6-1/2"
Weight: 50 lbs.
Features: Leverage and bearing surfaces ample for reloading cartridges or swaging bullets. Precision ground one-piece 2-1/2" pillar with base; operating handle of 3/4" steel and 15" long; 5/8" steel tie-down rod for added strength when swaging; heavy steel toggle and camming arms held by 1/2" steel pins in reamed holes. The 1-1/2" steel die bushing takes standard threaded dies; removed, it allows use of Hollywood shotshell dies. From Hollywood Engineering.
Price: **$600.00**

HOLLYWOOD Senior Turret Press

Frame: Ductile iron
Frame Type: H-frame
Die Thread: 7/8-14
Avg. Rounds Per Hour: 50-100
Ram Stroke: 6-1/2"
Weight: 50 lbs.
Features: Same features as Senior press except has three-position turret head; holes in turret may be tapped 1-1/2" or 7/8" or four of each. Height 15". Comes complete with one turret indexing handle; one operating handle and three turret indexing handles; one 5/8" tie down bar for swaging. From Hollywood Engineering.
Price: **$700.00**

HORNADY Lock-N-Load Classic

Frame: Die cast heat-treated aluminum alloy
Frame Type: O-frame
Die Thread: 7/8-14
Avg. Rounds Per Hour: NA
Ram Stroke: 3-5/8"
Weight: 14 lbs.
Features: Features Lock-N-Load bushing system that allows instant die changeovers. Solid steel linkage arms that rotate on steel pins; 30° angled frame design for improved visibility and accessibility; primer arm automatically moves in and out of ram for primer pickup and solid seating; two primer arms for large and small primers; long offset handle for increased leverage and unobstructed reloading; lifetime warranty. Comes as a package with primer catcher, PPS automatic primer feed and three Lock-N-Load die bushings. Dies and shellholder available separately or as a kit with primer catcher, positive priming system, automatic primer feed, three die bushings and reloading accessories. From Hornady Mfg. Co.
Price: Press and Three Die Bushings **$99.95**
Price: Classic Reloading Kit **$259.95**

LEE Hand Press

Frame: ASTM 380 aluminum
Frame Type: NA
Die Thread: 7/8-14
Avg. Rounds Per Hour: 100
Ram Stroke: 3-1/4"
Weight: 1 lb., 8 oz.
Features: Small and lightweight for portability; compound linkage for handling up to 375 H&H and case forming. Dies and shellholder not included. From Lee Precision, Inc.
Price: **$26.98**

LEE Challenger Press

Frame: ASTM 380 aluminum
Frame Type: O-frame
Die Thread: 7/8-14
Avg. Rounds Per Hour: 100
Ram Stroke: 3-1/2"
Weight: 4 lbs., 1 oz.
Features: Larger than average opening with 30° offset for maximum hand clearance; steel connecting pins; spent primer catcher; handle adjustable for start and stop positions; handle repositions for left- or right-hand use; shortened handle travel to prevent springing the frame from alignment. Dies and shellholders not included. From Lee Precision, Inc.
Price: **$47.00**

LEE Classic Cast

Features: Cast iron, O-type. Adjustable handle moves from right to left, start and stop position is adjustable. Large 1-1/8" diameter hollow ram catches primers for disposal. Automatic primer arm with bottom of stroke priming. Two assembled primer arms included. From Lee Precision, Inc.
Price: **$99.00**

LEE Reloader Press

Frame: ASTM 380 aluminum
Frame Type: C-frame
Die Thread: 7/8-14
Avg. Rounds Per Hour: 100
Ram Stroke: 3"
Weight: 1 lb., 12 oz.
Features: Balanced lever to prevent pinching fingers; unlimited hand clearance; left- or right-hand use. Dies and shellholders not included. From Lee Precision, Inc.
Price: **$26.98**

METALLIC CARTRIDGE PRESSES

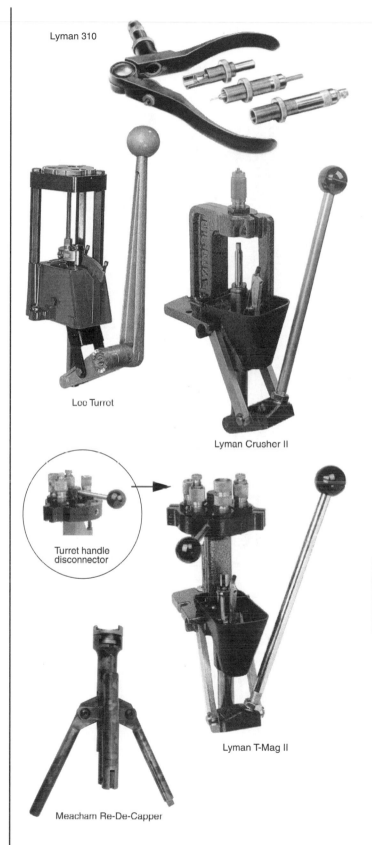

Lyman 310

Lee Turret

Lyman Crusher II

Turret handle disconnector

Lyman T-Mag II

Meacham Re-De-Capper

LEE Turret Press

Frame: ASTM 380 aluminum
Frame Type: O-frame
Die Thread: 7/8-14
Avg. Rounds Per Hour: 300
Ram Stroke: 3"
Weight: 7 lbs., 2 oz.
Features: Replaceable turret lifts out by rotating 30°; T-primer arm reverses for large or small primers; built-in primer catcher; adjustable handle for right- or left-hand use or changing angle of down stroke; accessory mounting hole for Lee Auto-Disk powder measure. Optional Auto-Index rotates die turret to next station for semi-progressive use. Safety override prevents overstressing should turret not turn. From Lee Precision, Inc.
Price: **$69.98**
Price: With Auto-Index **$83.98**
Price: Four-Hole Turret with Auto-Index **$85.98**

LYMAN 310 Tool

Frame: Stainless steel
Frame Type: NA
Die Thread: .609-30
Avg. Rounds Per Hour: NA
Ram Stroke: NA
Weight: 10 oz.
Features: Compact, portable reloading tool for pistol or rifle cartridges. Adaptor allows loading rimmed or rimless cases. Dies set includes neck resizing/decapping die; primer seating chamber; neck expanding die; bullet seating die; and case head adapter. From Lyman Products Corp.
Price: Dies **$45.00**
Price: Handles **$47.50**
Price: Carrying pouch **$9.95**

LYMAN AccuPress

Frame: Die cast
Frame Type: C-frame
Die Thread: 7/8-14
Avg. Rounds Per Hour: 75
Ram Stroke: 3.4"
Weight: 4 lbs.
Features: Reversible, contoured handle for bench mount or hand-held use; for rifle or pistol; compound leverage; Delta frame design. Accepts all standard powder measures. From Lyman Products Corp.
Price: **$34.95**

LYMAN Crusher II

Frame: Cast iron
Frame Type: O-frame
Die Thread: 7/8-14
Avg. Rounds Per Hour: 75
Ram Stroke: 3-7/8"
Weight: 19 lbs.
Features: Reloads both pistol and rifle cartridges; 1" diameter ram; 4-1/2" press opening for loading magnum cartridges; direct torque design; right- or left-hand use. New base design with 14 square inches of flat mounting surface with three bolt holes. Comes with priming arm and primer catcher. Dies and shellholders not included. From Lyman Products Corp.
Price: **$116.50**

LYMAN T-Mag II

Frame: Cast iron with silver metalflake powder finish
Frame Type: Turret
Die Thread: 7/8-14
Avg. Rounds Per Hour: 125
Ram Stroke: 3-13/16"
Weight: 18 lbs.
Features: Re-engineered and upgraded with new turret system for ease of indexing and tool-free turret removal for caliber changeover; new flat machined base for bench mounting; new nickel-plated non-rust handle and links; and new silver hammertone powder coat finish for durability. Right- or left-hand operation; handles all rifle or pistol dies. Comes with priming arm and primer catcher. Dies and shellholders not included. From Lyman Products Corp.
Price: **$164.95**
Price: Extra turret **$37.50**

MEACHAM Anywhere Portable Reloading Press

Frame: Anodized 6061 T6 aircraft aluminum
Frame Type: Cylindrical
Die Thread: 7/8-14
Avg. Rounds Per Hour: NA
Ram Stroke: 2.7"
Weight: 2 lbs. (hand held); 5 lbs. (with docking kit)
Features: A lightweight portable press that can be used hand-held, or with a docking kit, can be clamped to a table top up to 9.75" thick. Docking kit includes a threaded powder measure mount and holder for the other die. Designed for neck sizing and bullet seating of short action cartridges, it can be used for long action cartridges with the addition of an Easy Seater straight line seating die. Dies not included.
Price: **$99.95**
Price: (with docking kit) **$144.95**
Price: Easy Seater **$114.95**
Price: Re-De-Capper . . . . **NA**

METALLIC CARTRIDGE PRESSES

Ponsness/Warren
Metal-Matic P-200

RCBS Partner

RCBS
AmmoMaster
Single

RCBS
Rock
Chucker
Supreme

RCBS Reloader
Special-5

PONSNESS/WARREN Metal-Matic P-200

Frame: Die cast aluminum
Frame Type: Unconventional
Die Thread: 7/8-14
Avg. Rounds Per Hour: 200+
Weight: 18 lbs.
Features: Designed for straight-wall cartridges; die head with 10 tapped holes for holding dies and accessories for two calibers at one time; removable spent primer box; pivoting arm moves case from station to station. Comes with large and small primer tool. Optional accessories include primer feed, extra die head, primer speed feeder, powder measure extension and dust cover. Dies, powder measure and shellholder not included. From Ponsness/Warren.

Price: **$215.00**
Price: Extra die head **$44.95**
Price: Powder measure extension **$29.95**
Price: Primer feed **$44.95**
Price: Primer speed feed **$14.50**
Price: Dust cover **$21.95**

RCBS Partner

Frame: Aluminum
Frame Type: O-frame
Die Thread: 7/8-14
Avg. Rounds Per Hour: 50-60
Ram Stroke: 3-5/8"
Weight: 5 lbs.
Features: Designed for the beginning reloader. Comes with primer arm equipped with interchangeable primer plugs and sleeves for seating large and small primers. Shellholder and dies not included. Available in kit form (see Metallic Presses-Accessories). From RCBS.

Price: **$69.95**

RCBS AmmoMaster Single

Frame: Aluminum base; cast iron top plate connected by three steel posts.
Frame Type: NA
Die Thread: 1-1/4"-12 bushing; 7/8-14 threads
Avg. Rounds Per Hour: 50-60
Ram Stroke: 5-1/4"
Weight: 19 lbs.
Features: Single-stage press convertible to progressive. Will form cases or swage bullets. Case detection system to disengage powder measure when no case is present in powder charging station; five-station shellplate; Uniflow Powder measure with clear powder measure adaptor to make bridged powders visible and correctable. 50-cal. conversion kit allows reloading 50 BMG. Kit includes top plate to accommodate either 1-3/8" x 12 or 1-1/2" x 12 reloading dies. Piggyback die plate for quick caliber change-overs available. Reloading dies not included. From RCBS.

Price: **$229.95**
Price: 50 conversion kit **$109.95**
Price: Piggyback/AmmoMaster die plate **$23.95**
Price: Piggyback/AmmoMaster shellplate **$31.95**
Price: Press cover **$13.95**

RCBS Reloader Special-5

Frame: Aluminum
Frame Type: 30° offset O-frame
Die Thread: 1-1/4"-12 bushing; 7/8-14 threads
Avg. Rounds Per Hour: 50-60
Ram Stroke: 3-1/16"
Weight: 7.5 lbs.
Features: Single-stage press convertible to progressive with RCBS Piggyback II. Primes cases during resizing operation. Will accept RCBS shotshell dies. From RCBS.

Price: **$123.95**

RCBS Rock Chucker Supreme

Frame: Cast iron
Frame Type: O-frame
Die Thread: 1-1/4"-12 bushing; 7/8-14 threads
Avg. Rounds Per Hour: 50-60
Ram Stroke: 3-1/16"
Weight: 17 lbs.
Features: Redesigned to allow loading of longer cartridge cases. Made for heavy-duty reloading, case forming and bullet swaging. Provides 4" of ram-bearing surface to support 1" ram and ensure alignment; ductile iron toggle blocks; hardened steel pins. Comes standard with Universal Primer Arm and primer catcher. Can be converted from single-stage to progressive with Piggyback II conversion unit. From RCBS.

Price: **$155.95**

METALLIC CARTRIDGE PRESSES

REDDING T-7 Turret Press

Frame: Cast iron
Frame Type: Turret
Die Thread: 7/8-14
Avg. Rounds Per Hour: NA
Ram Stroke: 3.4"
Weight: 23 lbs., 2 oz.
Features: Strength to reload pistol and magnum rifle, case form and bullet swage; linkage pins heat-treated, precision ground and in double shear; hollow ram to collect spent primers; removable turret head for caliber changes; progressive linkage for increased power as ram nears die; rear turret support for stability and precise alignment; 7-station turret head; priming arm for both large and small primers. Also available in kit form with shellholder and one die set. From Redding Reloading Equipment.
Price: **$336.00**
Price: Kit **$382.00**

REDDING Boss

Frame: Cast iron
Frame Type: O-frame
Die Thread: 7/8-14
Avg. Rounds Per Hour: NA
Ram Stroke: 3.4"
Weight: 11 lbs., 8 oz.
Features: 36° frame offset for visibility and accessibility; primer arm positioned at bottom ram travel; positive ram travel stop machined to hit exactly top-dead-center. Also available in kit form with shellholder and set of Redding A dies. From Redding Reloading Equipment.
Price: **$156.00**
Price: Kit **$204.00**
Price: Big Boss Press (heavier frame,
longer stroke for mag. cartridges) .... **$178.50 to $223.50**

REDDING Ultramag

Frame: Cast iron
Frame Type: Non-conventional
Die Thread: 7/8-14
Avg. Rounds Per Hour: NA
Ram Stroke: 4-1/8"
Weight: 23 lbs., 6 oz.
Features: Unique compound leverage system connected to top of press for tons of ram pressure; large 4-3/4" frame opening for loading outsized cartridges; hollow ram for spent primers. Kit available with shellholder and one set Redding A dies. From Redding Reloading Equipment.
Price: **$351.00**
Price: Kit **$396.00**

ROCK CRUSHER Press

Frame: Cast iron
Frame Type: O-frame
Die Thread: 2-3/4"-12 with bushing
reduced to 1-1/2"-12
Avg. Rounds Per Hour: 50
Ram Stroke: 6"
Weight: 67 lbs.
Features: Designed to load and form ammunition from 50 BMG up to 23x115 Soviet. Frame opening of 8-1/2" x 3-1/2"; 1-1/2" x 12"; bushing can be removed and bushings of any size substituted; ram pressure can exceed 10,000 lbs. with normal body weight; 40mm diameter ram. Angle block for bench mounting and reduction bushing for RCBS dies available. Accessories for Rock Crusher include powder measure, dies, shellholder, bullet puller, priming tool, case gauge and others. From The Old Western Scrounger.
Price: **$795.00**
Price: Angle block **$57.95**
Price: Reduction bushing **$21.00**
Price: Shellholder **$47.25**
Price: Priming tool, 50 BMG, 20 Lahti **$65.10**

Progressive Presses

CORBIN Benchrest S-Press

Frame: All steel
Frame Type: O-Frame
Die Thread: 7/8-14 and
T-slot adapter
Avg. Rounds Per Hour: NA
Ram Stroke: 4"
Weight: 22 lbs.
Features: Roller bearing linkage, removeable head, right- or left-hand mount.
Price: **$298.00**

DILLON RL 550B

Frame: Aluminum alloy
Frame Type: NA
Die Thread: 7/8-14
Avg. Rounds Per Hour: 500-600
Ram Stroke: 3-7/8"
Weight: 25 lbs.
Features: Four stations; removable tool head to hold dies in alignment and allow caliber changes without die adjustment; auto priming system that emits audible warning when primer tube is low; a 100-primer capacity magazine contained in DOM steel tube for protection; new auto powder measure system with simple mechanical connection between measure and loading platform for positive powder bar return; a separate station for crimping with star-indexing system; 220 ejected-round capacity bin; 3/4-lb. capacity powder measure.

Height above bench, 35"; requires 3/4" bench overhang. Will reload 120 different rifle and pistol calibers. Comes with one caliber conversion kit. Dies not included. From Dillon Precision Products, Inc.
Price: **$349.95**

DILLON Super 1050

Frame: Ductile iron
Frame Type: Platform type
Die Thread: 7/8-14
Avg. Rounds Per Hour: 1000-1200
Ram Stroke: 2-5/16"
Weight: 62 lbs.
Features: Eight stations; auto case feed; primer pocket swager for military cartridge cases; auto indexing; removable tool head; auto prime system with 100-primer capacity; low primer supply alarm; positive powder bar return; auto powder measure; 515 ejected round bin capacity; 500-600 case feed capacity; 3/4-lb. capacity powder measure. Has lengthened frame and short-stroke crank to accommodate long calibers. Loads all pistol rounds as well as 30 M1 Carbine, 223, and 7.62x39 rifle rounds. Height above the bench, 43". Dies not included. From Dillon Precision Products, Inc.
Price: **$1,449.95**

DILLON Square Deal B

Frame: Zinc alloy
Frame Type: NA
Die Thread: None
(unique Dillon design)
Avg. Rounds Per Hour: 400-500
Ram Stroke: 2-5/16"
Weight: 17 lbs.
Features: Four stations; auto indexing; removable tool head; auto prime system with 100-primer capacity; low primer supply alarm; auto powder measure; positive powder bar return; 170 ejected round capacity bin; 3/4-lb. capacity powder measure. Height above the bench, 34". Comes complete with factory adjusted carbide die set. From Dillon Precision Products, Inc.
Price: **$289.95**

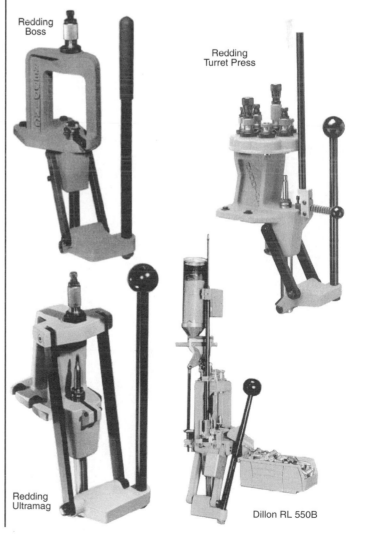

Redding
Boss

Redding
Turret Press

Redding
Ultramag

Dillon RL 550B

METALLIC CARTRIDGE PRESSES

DILLON XL 650

Frame: Aluminum alloy
Frame Type: NA
Die Thread: 7/8-14

Avg. Rounds Per Hour: 800-1000
Ram Stroke: 4-9/16"
Weight: 46 lbs.

Features: Five stations; auto indexing; auto case feed; removable tool head; auto prime system with 100-primer capacity; low primer supply alarm; auto powder measure; positive powder bar return; 220 ejected round capacity bin; 3/4-lb. capacity powder measure. 500-600 case feed capacity with optional auto case feed. Loads all pistol/rifle calibers less than 3-1/2" in length. Height above the bench, 44"; 3/4" bench overhang required. From Dillon Precision Products, Inc.
Price: Less dies **$459.95**

HORNADY Lock-N-Load AP

Frame: Die cast heat-treated aluminum alloy
Frame Type: O-frame
Die Thread: 7/8-14

Avg. Rounds Per Hour: NA
Ram Stroke: 3-3/4"
Weight: 26 lbs.

Features: Features Lock-N-Load bushing system that allows instant die changeovers; five-station die platform with option of seating and crimping separately or adding taper-crimp die; auto prime with large and small primer tubes with 100-primer capacity and protective housing; brass kicker to eject loaded rounds into 80-round capacity cartridge catcher; offset operating handle for leverage and unobstructed operation; 2" diameter ram driven by heavy-duty cast linkage arms rotating on steel pins. Comes with five Lock-N-Load die bushings, shellplate, deluxe powder measure, auto powder drop, and

auto primer feed and shut-off, brass kicker and primer catcher. Lifetime warranty. From Hornady Mfg. Co.
Price: **$367.65**

LEE Load-Master

Frame: ASTM 380 aluminum
Frame Type: O-frame
Die Thread: 7/8-14

Avg. Rounds Per Hour: 600
Ram Stroke: 3-1/4"
Weight: 8 lbs., 4 oz.

Features: Available in kit form only. A 1-3/4" diameter hard chrome ram for han-dling largest magnum cases; loads rifle or pistol rounds; five station press to fac-tory crimp and post size; auto indexing with wedge lock mechanism to hold one ton; auto priming; removable turrets; four-tube case feeder with optional case collator and bullet feeder (late 1995); loaded round ejector with chute to optional loaded round catcher; quick change shellplate; primer catcher. Dies and shell-holder for one caliber included. From Lee Precision, Inc.
Price: Rifle **$320.00**
Price: Pistol **$330.00**
Price: Extra turret **$14.98**
Price: Adjustable charge bar **$9.98**

LEE Pro 1000

Frame: ASTM 380 aluminum and steel
Frame Type: O-frame
Die Thread: 7/8-14

Avg. Rounds Per Hour: 600
Ram Stroke: 3-1/4"
Weight: 8 lbs., 7 oz.

Features: Optional transparent large/small case feeder; deluxe auto-disk case-activated powder measure; case sensor for primer feed. Comes complete with carbide die set (steel dies for rifle) for one caliber. Optional accessories include: case feeder for large/small pistol cases or rifle cases; shell plate carrier with auto prime, case ejector, auto-index and spare parts; case collator for case feeder. From Lee Precision, Inc.
Price: **$199.98**

PONSNESS/WARREN Metallic II

Frame: Die cast aluminum
Frame Type: H-frame
Die Thread: 7/8-14

Avg. Rounds Per Hour: 150+
Ram Stroke: NA
Weight: 32 lbs.

Features: Die head with five tapped 7/8-14 holes for dies, powder measure or other accessories; pivoting die arm moves case from station to station; depriming tube for removal of spent primers; auto primer feed; interchangeable die head. Optional accessories include additional die heads, powder measure extension tube to accommodate any standard powder measure, primer speed feeder to feed press primer tube without disassembly. Comes with small and large primer seating tools. Dies, powder measure and shellholder not included. From Ponsness/Warren.
Price: **$375.00**
Price: Extra die head **$56.95**
Price: Primer speed feeder **$14.50**
Price: Powder measure extension **$29.95**
Price: Dust cover **$27.95**

RCBS Pro 2000™

Frame: Cast iron
Frame Type: H-Frame
Die Thread: 7/8-14

Avg. Rounds Per Hour: 500-600
Ram Stroke: NA
Weight: NA

Features: Five-station manual indexing; full-length sizing; removable die plate; fast caliber conversion. Uses APS Priming System. From RCBS.
Price: **$42.95**

RCBS Turret Press

Frame: Cast iron
Frame Type: NA
Die Thread: 7/8-14

Avg. Rounds Per Hour: 50 to 200
Ram Stroke: NA
Weight: NA

Features: Six-station turret head; positive alignment; on-press priming.
Price: **$214.95**

STAR Universal Pistol Press

Frame: Cast iron w/aluminum base
Frame Type: Unconventional
Die Thread: 11/16-24 or 7/8-14

Avg. Rounds Per Hour: 300
Ram Stroke: NA
Weight: 27 lbs.

Features: Four or five-station press depending on need to taper crimp; handles all popular handgun calibers from 32 Long to 45 Colt. Comes completely assembled and adjusted with carbide dies (except 30 Carbine) and shellholder to load one caliber. Prices slightly higher for 9mm and 30 Carbine. From Star Machine Works.
Price: With taper crimp **$1,055.00**
Price: Without taper crimp **$1,025.00**
Price: Extra tool head, taper crimp **$425.00**
Price: Extra tool head, w/o taper crimp **$395.00**

Lee Load-Master

RCBS Turret

Fully-automated
Star Universal

DILLON SL 900

Press Type: Progressive
Avg. Rounds Per Hour: 700-900
Weight: 51 lbs.
Features: 12-ga. only; factory adjusted to load AA hulls; extra large 25-pound capacity shot hopper; fully-adjustable case-activated shot system; hardened steel starter crimp die; dual-action final crimp and taper die; tilt-out wad guide; auto prime; auto index; strong mount machine stand. From Dillon Precision Products.
 Price: **$844.90**

HOLLYWOOD Automatic Shotshell Press

Press Type: Progressive
Avg. Rounds Per Hour: 1,800
Weight: 100 lbs.
Features: Ductile iron frame; fully automated press with shell pickup and ejector; comes completely set up for one gauge; one starter crimp; one finish crimp; wad guide for plastic wads; decap and powder dispenser unit; one wrench for inside die lock screw; one medium and one large spanner wrench for spanner nuts; one shellholder; powder and shot measures. Available for 10, 12, 20, 28 or 410. From Hollywood Engineering.
 Price: **$3,600.00**

HOLLYWOOD Senior Turret Press

Press Type: Turret
Avg. Rounds Per Hour: 200
Weight: 50 lbs.
Features: Multi-stage press constructed of ductile iron comes completely equipped to reload one gauge; one starter crimp; one finish crimp; wad guide for plastic wads; decap and powder dispenser unit; one wrench for inside die lock screw; one medium and one large spanner wrench for spanner nuts; one shellholder; powder and shot measures. Available for 10, 12, 16, 20, 28 or 410. From Hollywood Engineering.
 Price: Press only **$700.00**
 Price: Dies **$195.00**

HORNADY 366 Auto

Press Type: Progressive
Avg. Rounds Per Hour: NA
Weight: 25 lbs.
Features: Heavy-duty die cast and machined steel body and components; auto primer feed system; large capacity shot and powder tubes; adjustable for right- or left-hand use; automatic charge bar with shutoff; swing-out wad guide; primer catcher at base of press; interchangeable shot and powder bushings; life-time warranty. Available for 12, 20, 28 2-3/4" and 410 2-1/2". From Hornady Mfg. Co.
 Price: **$434.95**
 Price: Die set, 12, 20, 28 . . . . **$196.86**
 Price: Magnum conversion dies, 12, 20 . . . . **$43.25**

LEE Load-All II

Press Type: Single stage
Avg. Rounds Per Hour: 100
Weight: 3 lbs. 3 oz.
Features: Loads steel or lead shot; built-in primer catcher at base with door in front for emptying; recesses at each station for shell positioning; optional primer feed. Comes with safety charge bar with 24 shot and powder bushings. Available for 12-, 16- or 20-gauge. From Lee Precision, Inc.
 Price: **$49.98**

MEC 600 Jr. Mark V

Press Type: Single stage
Avg. Rounds Per Hour: 200
Weight: 10 lbs.
Features: Spindex crimp starter for shell alignment during crimping; a cam-action crimp die; Pro-Check to keep charge bar properly positioned; adjustable for three shells. Available in 10, 12, 16, 20, 28 gauges and 410 bore. Die set not included. From Mayville Engineering Company, Inc.
 Price: **$120.50**
 Price: Die set **$61.16**

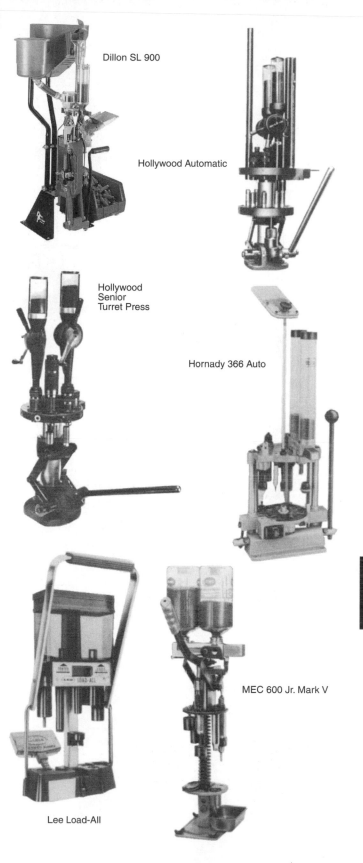

Dillon SL 900

Hollywood Automatic

Hollywood Senior Turret Press

Hornady 366 Auto

MEC 600 Jr. Mark V

Lee Load-All

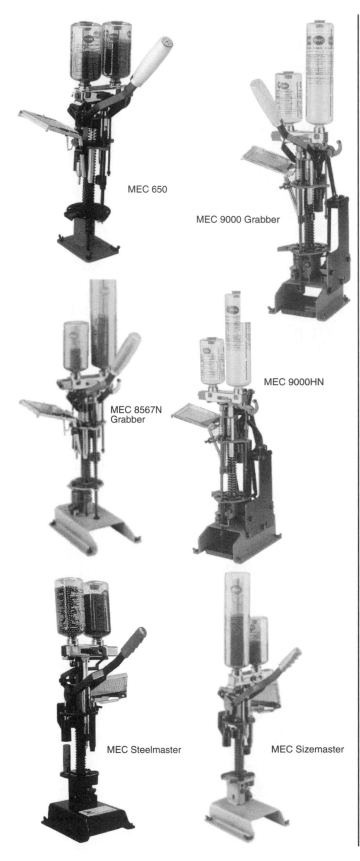

MEC 650

MEC 9000 Grabber

MEC 9000HN

MEC 8567N Grabber

MEC Steelmaster

MEC Sizemaster

MEC 650N

Press Type: Progressive
Avg. Rounds Per Hour: 400
Weight: 19 lbs.
Features: Six-station press; does not resize except as separate operation; auto primer feed standard; three crimping stations for starting, closing and tapering crimp. Die sets not available. Available in 12, 16, 20, 28 and 410. From Mayville Engineering Company, Inc.
Price: **$240.00**

MEC 8567N Grabber

Press Type: Progressive
Avg. Rounds Per Hour: 400
Weight: 22 lbs.
Features: Six-station press; auto primer feed; auto-cycle charging; three-stage crimp; power ring resizer returns base to factory specs; resizes high and low base shells; optional kits to reload three shells and steel shot. Available in 12, 16, 20, 28 gauge and 410 bore. From Mayville Engineering Company, Inc.
Price: **$338.05**
Price: 3" kit, 12-ga. **$70.70**
Price: 3" kit, 20-ga. **$40.40**
Price: Steel shot kit **$35.35**

MEC 9000GN

Press Type: Progressive
Avg. Rounds Per Hour: 400
Weight: 26 lbs.
Features: All same features as the MEC Grabber but with auto-indexing and auto-eject. Finished shells automatically ejected from shell carrier to drop chute for boxing. Available in 12, 16, 20, 28 and 410. From Mayville Engineering Company, Inc.
Price: **$407.70**

MEC 9000HN

Press Type: Progressive
Avg. Rounds Per Hour: 400
Weight: 30 lbs.
Features: Same features as 9000GN with addition of foot pedal-operated hydraulic system for complete automation. Operates on standard 110V household current. Comes with bushing-type charge bar and three bushings. Available in 12, 16, 20, 28 gauge and 410 bore. From Mayville Engineering Company, Inc.
Price: **$958.00**

MEC 8120 Sizemaster

Press Type: Single stage
Avg. Rounds Per Hour: 150
Weight: 20 lbs.
Features: Power ring eight-fingered collet resizer returns base to factory specs; handles brass or steel, high or low base heads; auto primer feed; adjustable for three shells. Available in 10, 12, 16, 20, 28 gauges and 410 bore. From Mayville Engineering Company, Inc.
Price: **$196.79**
Price: Die set, 12, 16, 20, 28, 410 . . . . **$72.11**
Price: Die set, 10-ga. **$88.59**

MEC Steelmaster

Press Type: Single stage
Avg. Rounds Per Hour: 150
Weight: 20 lbs.
Features: Same features as Sizemaster except can load steel shot. Press is available for 3-1/2" 10-ga. and 12-ga. 2-3/4", 3" or 3-1/2". For loading lead shot, die sets available in 10, 12, 16, 20, 28 and 410. From Mayville Engineering Company, Inc.
Price: **$196.79**
Price: 12 ga. 3-1/2" **$220.41**

SHOTSHELL RELOADING PRESSES

PONSNESS/WARREN Du-O-Matic 375C

Press Type: Progressive
Avg. Rounds Per Hour: NA
Weight: 31 lbs.
Features: Steel or lead shot reloader; large shot and powder reservoirs; bushing access plug for dropping in shot buffer or buckshot; positive lock charging ring to prevent accidental flow of powder; double-post construction for greater leverage; removable spent primer box; spring-loaded ball check for centering size die at each station; tip-out wad guide; two-gauge capacity tool head. Available in 10 (extra charge), 12, 16, 20, 28 and 410 with case lengths of 2-1/2", 2-3/4", 3" and 3-1/2". From Ponsness/ Warren.

Price: 12-, 20-, and 28-ga., 2-3/4" and 410, 2-1/2"	$289.00
Price: 12-ga. 3-1/2"; 3" 12, 20, 410	$305.00
Price: 12, 20 2-3/4"	$383.95
Price: 10-ga. press	$315.00

Ponsness/Warren
Hydro-Multispeed

PONSNESS/WARREN Hydro-Multispeed

Hydraulic system developed for Ponsness/Warren L/S-1000. Usable for the 950, 900 and 800 series presses. Three reloading speed settings operated with variable foot pedal control. Features stop/reverse at any station; automatic shutdown with pedal control release; fully adjustable hydraulic cylinder rod to prevent racking or bending of machine; quick disconnect hoses for ease of installation. Preassembled with step-by-step instructions. From Ponsness/Warren.

Price:	$879.00
Price: Cylinder kit	$399.95

PONSNESS/WARREN L/S-1000

Frame: Die cast aluminum
Avg. Rounds Per Hour: NA
Weight: 55 lbs.
Features: Fully progressive press to reload steel, bismuth or lead shot. Equipped with new Uni-Drop shot measuring and dispensing system which allows the use of all makes of shot in any size. Shells automatically resized and deprimed with new Auto-Size and De-Primer system. Loaded rounds drop out of shellholders when completed. Each shell pre-crimped and final crimped with Tru-Crimp system. Available in 10-gauge 3-1/2" or 12-gauge 2-3/4" and 3". 12-gauge 3-1/2" conversion kit also available. 20-gauge 2-3/4" and 3" special order only. From Ponsness/Warren.

Price: 12 ga.	$849.00
Price: 10 ga.	$895.00
Price: Conversion kit	$199.00

Ponsness/Warren
Du-O-Matic 375C

Ponsness/Warren
Size-O-Matic
900 Elite

PONSNESS/WARREN Size-O-Matic 900 Elite

Press Type: Progressive
Avg. Rounds Per Hour: 500-800
Weight: 49 lbs.
Features: Progressive eight-station press; frame of die-cast aluminum; center post design index system ensures positive indexing; timing factory set, drilled and pinned. Automatic features include index, deprime, reprime, powder and shot drop, crimp start, tapered final crimp, finished shell ejection. Available in 12, 20, 28 and 410. 16-ga. special order. Kit includes new shellholders, seating port, resize/primer knockout assembly, new crimp assembly. From Ponsness/Warren.

Price:	$749.00
Price: Conversion tooling, 12, 20, 28, 410	$189.00

PONSNESS/WARREN Platinum 2000

Press Type: Progressive
Avg. Rounds Per Hour: 500-800
Weight: 52 lbs.
Features: Progressive eight-station press, similar to 900 and 950 except has die removal system that allows removal of any die component during reloading cycle. Comes standard with 25-lb. shot tube, 19" powder tube, brass adjustable priming feed allows adjustment of primer seating depth. From Ponsness/Warren.

Price:	$889.00

RCBS The Grand

Press Type: Progressive
Avg. Rounds Per Hour: NA
Weight: NA
Features: Constructed from a high-grade aluminum casting, allows complete resizing of high and low base hulls. Available for 12 and 20 gauge.

Price:	$688.95

Ponsness/Warren
Platinum 2000

RCBS The Grand

Maker and Model	Magn.	Field at 100 Yds. (feet)	Eye Relief (in.)	Length (in.)	Tube Dia. (in.)	W & E Adjustments	Weight (ozs.)	Price	Other Data
ADCO									
Magnum 50 mm[5]	0			4.1	45 mm	Int.	6.8	$269.00	[1]Multi-Color Dot system changes from red to green. [2]For airguns,
MIRAGE Ranger 1"	0			5.2	1	Int.	3.9	159.00	paint ball, rimfires. Uses common lithium water battery. [3]Comes with
MIRAGE Ranger 30mm	0			5.5	30mm	Int.	5	159.00	standard dovetail mount. [4].75" dovetail mount; poly body; adj. inten-
MIRAGE Competitor	0			5.5	30mm	Int.	5.5	229.00	sity diode. [5]10 MOA dot; black or nickel. [6]Square format; with mount
IMP Sight[2]	0			4.5		Int.	1.3	17.95	battery. From ADCO Sales.
Square Shooter 2[3]	0			5		Int.	5	99.00	
MIRAGE Eclipse[1]	0			5.5	30mm	Int.	5.5	229.00	
Champ Red Dot	0			4.5		Int.	2	33.95	
Vantage 1"	0			3.9	1	Int.	3.9	129.00	
Vantage 30mm	0			4.2	30mm	Int.	4.9	159.00	
Vision 2000[6]	0	60		4.7		Int.	6.2	79.00	
e-dot ESB[1]	0			4.12	1	Int.	3.7	139.00	
e-dot E1B	0			4.12	1	Int.	3.7	99.00	
e-dot ECB	0			3.8	30mm	Int.	6.4	99.00	
e-dot E30B	0			4.3	30mm	Int.	4.6	99.00	
AIMPOINT									
Comp	0			4.6	30mm	Int.	4.3	331.00	Illuminates red dot in field of view. Noparallax (dot does not need to
Comp M[4]	0			5	30mm	Int.	6.1	409.00	be centered). Unlimited field of view and eye relief. On/off, adj. inten-
Series 5000[3]	0			6	30mm	Int.	6	297.00	sity. Dot covers 3" @100 yds. [1]Comes with 30mm rings, battery, lense
Series 3000 Universal[2]	0			6.25	1	Int.	6	232.00	cloth. [2] Requires 1" rings. Black finish. AP Comp avail. in black, blue,
Series 5000/2x[1]	2			7	30mm	Int.	9	388.00	SS, camo. [3]Black finish (AP 5000-B); avail. with regular 3-min. or 10-min. Mag Dot as B2 or S2. [4]Band pass reflection coating for compat-ibility with night vision equipment; U.S. Army contract model; with anti-reflex coated lenses (Comp ML), **$359.00**. From Aimpoint U.S.A.
APEX									
Model 4030		3-9x		40/14	42mm	Int.		250.00	
Model 4035		3.5-10x		28/10	50mm	Int.		285.00	
Model 4040		4-16x		23.6/6.2	50mm	Int.		300.00	
Model 4045		6-24x		15/4	50mm	Int.		310.00	
ARMSON O.E.G.									
Standard	0			5.125	1	Int.	4.3	202.00	Shown red dot aiming point. No batteries needed. Standard model
22 DOS[1]	0			3.75		Int.	3	127.00	fits 1" ring mounts (not incl.). Other O.E.G. models for shotguns and
22 Day/Night	0			3.75		Int.	3	169.00	rifles can be special ordered. [1]Daylight Only Sight with .375" dovetail
M16/AR-15	0			5.125		Int.	5.5	226.00	mount for 22s. Does not contain tritium. From Trijicon, Inc.
ARTEMIS 2000									
4x32	4	34.4	3.15	10.7	1	Int.	17.5	215.00	Click-stop windage and elevation adjustments; constantly centered
6x42	6	23	3.15	13.7	1	Int.	17.5	317.00	reticle; rubber eyepiece ring; nitrogen filled. Imported from the Czech
7x50	7	18.7	3.15	13.9	1	Int.	17.5	329.00	Republic by CZ-USA.
1.5-6x42	1.5-6	40-12.8	2.95	12.4	30mm	Int.	19.4	522.00	
2-8x42	2-8	31-9.5	2.95	13.1	30mm	Int.	21.1	525.00	
3-9x42	3-9	24.6-8.5	2.95	12.4	30mm	Int.	19.4	466.00	
3-12x50	3-12	20.6-6.2	2.95	14	30mm	Int.	22.9	574.00	
BEC									
EuroLux									
EL2510x56	2.5-10	39.4-11.5	3.25-2	15.1	30mm	Int.	25.4	249.90	Black matte finish. Multi-coated lenses; 1/4-MOA click adjustments
EL39x42	3-9	34.1-13.2	3.5-3	12.3	30mm	Int.	17.7	99.80	(1/2- MOA on EL4x25, AR4x22WA); fog and water-proof. [1]For AR-
EL28x36	2-8	44.9-11.5	3.8-3	12.2	30mm	Int.	15.9	149.50	15; bullet drop compensator; q.d. mount. [2]Rubber armored. Imported
ELA39x40RB[2]	3-9	39-13	3	12.7	30mm	Int.	14.3	95.95	by BEC Inc. Partial listing shown. Contact BEC for complete details.
EL6x42	6	21	3	12.6	30mm	Int.	14.8	69.00	[3]All Goldlabel scopes feature lighted reticles and finger-adjustable
EL4x42	4	29	3	12.6	30mm	Int.	14.8	59.60	windage and elevation adjustments. [4]Bullet-drop compensator sys-
EL4x36	4	29	3	12	30mm	Int.	14	49.90	tem for Mini-14 and AR-15 rifles.
EL4x25	4	26	3	7	30mm	Int.	7.6	37.00	
AR4x22WA[1]	4	24	3	7	34mm	Int.	13.6	109.97	
Goldlabel[3]									
GLI 624x50	6-24	16-4	3.5-3	15.3	1	Int.	22.5	139.00	
GLI 416x50	4-16	25-6	3.5-3	13.5	1	Int.	21.8	135.00	
GLI 39x40R[2]	3-9	39-13	3.5-3	12.7	28mm	Int.	18.5	99.00	
GLC 5x42BD[4]	5	24	3.5	8.7	1	Int.	16.5	79.00	
BEEMAN									
Rifle Scopes									
5045[1]	4-12	26.9-9	3	13.2	1	Int.	15	275.00	All scopes have 5 point reticle, all glass fully-coated lenses. [1]Parallel
5046[1]	6-24	18-4.5	3	16.9	1	Int.	20.2	395.00	adjustable. [2]Reticle lighted by ambient light. [3]Available with lighted
5050[1]	4	26	3.5	11.7	1	Int.	11	80.00	Electro-Dot reticle. Imported by Beeman.
5055[1]	3-9	38-13	3.5	10.75	1	Int.	11.2	90.00	
5060[1]	4-12	30-10	3	12.5	1	Int.	16.2	210.00	
5065[1]	6-18	17-6	3	14.7	1	Int.	17.3	265.00	
5066RL[2]	2-7	58-15	3	11.4	1	Int.	17	380.00	
5047L[2]	4	25	3.5	7	1	Int.	13.7	NA	
Pistol Scopes									
5021	2	19	10-24	9.1	1	Int.	7.4	85.50	
5020	1.5	14	11-16	8.3	.75	Int.	3.6	NA	
BROWNING									
882732M	2-7	42.5-12.1	3.7	11.6	1	Int.	11.7	335.95	
883940M	3-9	32-11	3.4	12.4	1	Int.	13.1	351.95	
883950M	3-9	30-10	3.4	15.7	1	Int.	18.9	419.95	
88412M	4-12	26.8-8.8	3.4	13.4	1	Int.	18.3	449.95	
885154M	5-15	20.9-7	3.4	14.4	1	Int.	19.1	489.95	
888244M	8-24	12-4	3.4	14.2	1	Int.	19.6	589.95	
BSA									
Catseye[1]									
CE1545x32	1.5-4.5	78-23	4	11.25	1	Int.	12	91.95	[1]Waterproof, fogproof; multi-coated lenses; finger-adjustable knobs.
CE310x44	3-10	39-12	3.25	12.75	1	Int.	16	151.95	[2]Waterproof, fogproof; matte black finish. [3]With 4" sunshade; target
CE3510x50	3.5-10	30-10.5	3.25	13.25	1	Int.	17.25	171.95	knobs; 1/8-MOA click adjustments. [4]Adjustable for parallax; with sun
CE416x50	4-16	25-6	3	15.25	1	Int.	22	191.95	shades; target knobs, 1/8-MOA adjustments. Imported by BSA.
CE624x50	6-24	16-3	3	16	1	Int.	23	222.95	[5]Illuminated reticle model; also available in 3-10x, 3.5-10x, and 3-9x.
CE1545x32IR	1.5-4.5	78-23	5	11.25	1	Int.	12	121.95	[6]Red dot sights also available in 42mm and 50mm versions. [7]Includes Universal Bow Mount. [8]Five other models offered. From BSA.

Maker and Model	Magn.	Field at 100 Yds. (feet)	Eye Relief (in.)	Length (in.)	Tube Dia. (in.)	W & E Adjustments	Weight (ozs.)	Price	Other Data
BSA *(cont.)*									
Deer Hunter[2]									
DH25x20	2.5	72	6	7.5	1	Int.	7.5	59.95	
DH4x32	4	32	3	12	1	Int.	12.5	49.95	
DH39x32	3-9	39-13	3	12	1	Int.	11	69.95	
DH39x40	3-9	39-13	3	13	1	Int.	12.1	89.95	
DH39x50	3-9	41-15	3	12.75	1	Int.	13	109.95	
DH2510x44	2.5-10	42-12	3	13	1	Int.	12.5	99.95	
DH1545x32	1.5-4.5	78-23	5	11.25	1	Int.	12	79.95	
Contender[3]									
CT24x40TS	24	6	3	15	1	Int.	18	129.95	
CT36x40TS	36	3	3	15.25	1	Int.	19	139.95	
CT312x40TS	3-12	28-7	3	13	1	Int.	17.5	129.95	
CT416x40TS	4-16	21-5	3	13.5	1	Int.	18	131.95	
CT624x40TS	6-24	16-4	3	15.5	1	Int.	20	149.95	
CT832x40TS	8-32	11-3	3	15.5	1	Int.	20	171.95	
CT312x50TS	3-12	28-7	3	13.75	1	Int.	21	131.95	
CT416x50TS	4-16	21-5	3	15.25	1	Int.	22	151.95	
CT624x50TS	6-24	16-4	3	16	1	Int.	23	171.95	
CT832x50TS	8-32	11-3	3	16.5	1	Int.	24	191.95	
Pistol									
P52x20	?	NA	NA	NA	NA	Int	NA	89.95	
Platinum[4]									
PT24x44TS	24	4.5	3	16.25	1	Int.	17.9	189.55	
PT36x44TS	36	3	3	14.9	1	Int.	17.9	199.95	
PT624x44TS	6-24	15-4.5	3	15.25	1	Int.	18.5	221.95	
PT832x44TS	8-32	11-3.5	3	17.25	1	Int.	19.5	229.95	
.22 Special									
S39x32WR	3-9	37.7-14.1	3	12	1	Int.	12.3	89.95	
S4x32WR	4	26	3	10.75	1	Int.	9	39.95-44.95	
Air Rifle									
AR4x32	4	33	3	13	1	Int.	14	69.95	
AR27x32	2-7	48	3	12.25	1	Int.	14	79.95	
AR312x44	3-12	36	3	12.25	1	Int.	15	109.95	
Red Dot									
RD30[6]	0			3.8	30mm	Int.	5	59.95	
PB30[6]	0			3.8	30mm	Int.	4.5	79.95	
Bow30[7]	0			NA	30mm	Int.	5	89.95	
Big Cat									
BigCat[8]	3.5-10	30-11	5	9.7	1	Int.	16.8	219.95	
BURRIS									
Mr. T Black Diamond Titanium									
2.5-10x50A	2.5-10	4.25-4.75		13.6			29	1,518.00	
4-16x50	4-16	27-7.5	3.3-3.8	13.6	30mm	Int.	27	1,594.00	
Black Diamond									
3-12x50[3,4,6]	3.2-11.9	34-12	3.5-4	13.8	30mm	Int.	25	974.00	
6-24x50	6-24	18-6	3.5-4	16.2	30mm	Int.	25	1,046.00	
Fullfield II									
2.5x9	2.5	55	3.5-3.75	10.25	1	Int.	9	307.00	
1.75-5x[1,2,9,10]	1.7-4.6	66-25	3.5-3.75	10.875	1	Int.	13	400.00	
3-9x40[1,2,3,10]	3.3-8.7	38-15	3.5-3.75	12.625	1	Int.	15	336.00	
3-9x50	3-9	35-15	3.5-3.75	13	1	Int.	18	481.00	
3.5-10x50mm[3,5,10]	3.7-9.7	29.5-11	3.5-3.75	14	1	Int.	19	542.00	
4.5-14x[1,4,8,11]	4.4-11.8	27-10	3.5-3.75	15	1	Int.	18	585.00	
6.5-20x[1,3,4,6,7,8]	6.5-17.6	16.7	3.5-3.75	15.8	1	Int.	18.5	656.00	
Compact Scopes									
1x XER[3]	1	51	4.5-20	8.8	1	Int.	7.9	320.00	
4x[4,5]	3.6	24	3.75-5	8.25	1	Int.	7.8	397.00	
6x[1,4]	5.5	17	3.75-5	9	1	Int.	8.2	397.00	
6x HBR[1,5,8]	6	13	4.5	11.25	1	Int.	13	415.00	
1-4x XER[3]	1-3.8	53-15	4.25-30	8.8	1	Int.	10.3	467.00	
3-9x[4,5]	3.6-8.8	25-11	3.75-5	12.625	1	Int.	11.5	442.00	
4-12x[1,4,6]	4.5-11.6	19-8	3.75-4	15	1	Int.	15	534.00	
Signature Series									
1.5-6x[2,3,5,9,10]	1.7-5.8	70-20	3.5-4	10.8	1	Int.	13	601.00	
8x3[2,5,11]	2.1-7.7	53-17	3.5-4	11.75	1	Int.	14	840.00	
3-10x[3,5,10,13]	3.3-8.8	36-14	3.5-4	12.875	1	Int.	15.5	665.00	
3-12x[3,10]	3.3-11.7	34-9	3.5-4	14.25	1	Int.	21	701.00	
4-16x[1,3,5,6,8,10]	4.3-15.7	33-9	3.5-4	15.4	1	Int.	23.7	760.00	
6-24x[1,3,5,6,8,10,13]	6.6-23.8	17-6	3.5-4	16	1	Int.	22.7	787.00	
8-32x[8,10,12]	8.6-31.4	13-3.8	3.5-4	17	1	Int.	24	840.00	
Speeddot 135[14]									
Red Dot	1			1.06	06mm	Int.	6	201.00	
Handgun									
1.50-4x LER[1,5,10]	1.6-3	16-11	11-25	10.25	1	Int.	11	411.00	
2-7x LER[3,4,5,10]	2-6.5	21-7	7-27	9.5	1	Int.	12.6	458.00	
2x LER[4,5,6]	1.7	21	10-24	8.75	1	Int.	6.8	286.00	
4x LER[1,4,5,6,10]	3.7	11	10-22	9.625	1	Int.	9	338.00	
3x12x LER[1,4,6]	9.5	4	8-12	13.5	1	Int.	14	558.00	
Scout Scope									
1xXER[3,9]	1.5	32	4-24	9	1	Int.	7.0	320.00	
2.75x[3,9]	2.7	15	7-14	9.375	1	Int.	7.0	356.00	
BUSHNELL (Bausch & Lomb Elite rifle scopes sold under Bushnell brand)									
Elite 4200 RainGuard									
42-6244M[1]	6-24	18-6	3	16.9	1	Int.	20.2	639.95	
42-2104G[2]	2.5-10	41.5-10.8	3	13.5	1	Int.	16	563.95	
42-2151M[6,9]	2.5-10	40.3-10.8	3.3	14.3	1	Int.	18	699.95	
42 1636M[3]	1.5-6	61.8-16.1	3	12.8	1	Int.	15.4	533.95	
42-4164M[5,6]	4-16	26-7	3.5	18.6	1	Int.	18.6	565.95	
42-4165M[5]	4-16	26-7	3	15.6	1	Int.	22	731.95	
42-8324M	8-32	14-3.75	3.3	18	1	Int.	22	703.95	

Available in Carbon Black, Titanium Gray and Autumn Gold finishes. **Black Diamond & Fullfield:** All scopes avail. with Plex reticle. Steel-on-steel click adjustments. [2]Post crosshair reticle extra. [3]Matte satin finish. [4]Available with parallax adjustment (standard on 10x, 12x, 6-12x, 6-18x, 6x HBR and 3-12x Signature). [5]Silver matte finish extra. [6]Target knobs extra, standard on silhouette models. LER and XER with P.A., 8x HBR. [7]Sunshade avail. [8]Avail. with Fine Plex reticle. [9]Available with Heavy Plex reticle. [10]Available with Posi-Lock. [11]Available with Peep Plex reticle. [12]Also avail. for rimfires, airguns. [13]Selected models available with camo finish.
Signature Series: LER=Long Eye Relief; IER=Intermediate Eye Relief; XER=Extra Eye Relief.
Speeddot 135: [14]Waterproof, fogproof, coated lenses, 11 brightness set tings; 3-MOA or 11-MOA dot size; includes Weaver-style rings and battery. **Partial listing shown.** Contact Burris for complete details.

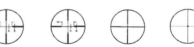

Plex | Fine Plex | Peep Plex | Target Dot

Heavy Plex & Electro-Dot Plex | Ballistic Mil-Dot | Mil-Dot

(Bushnell) [1]Wide Angle. [2]Also silver finish. [3]Also silver finish. [4]Matte finish. [5]Also silver finish. [6]Adj. obj. [8]Variable intensity; Circle-X reticle. [9]Blackpowder scope; extended eye relief, Circle-X reticle. [10]50mm objective. [11]With Circle-X reticle, matte finish. [12]Matte finish, adjustable objective.

SCOPES / Hunting, Target & Varmint

Maker and Model	Magn.	Field at 100 Yds. (feet)	Eye Relief (in.)	Length (in.)	Tube Dia. (in.)	W & E Adjustments	Weight (ozs.)	Price	Other Data
BUSHNELL *(cont.)*									(Bushnell Elite)
Elite 3200 RainGuard									[1]Adj. objective, sunshade; with 1/4-MOA dot or Mil Dot reticle. [2]Also
32-5155M	5-15	21-7	3	15.9	1	Int.	19	463.95	in matte and silver finish. [3]Only in matte finish. [4]Also in matte and
32-4124A[1]	4-12	26.9-9	3	13.2	1	Int.	15	411.95	silver finish. [5]Adjustable objective. [6]50mm objective; also in matte
32-1040M	10	11	3.5	11.7	1	Int.	15.5	279.95	finish. [7]Also in silver finish. [8]40mm. [9]Ill. dot reticle. **Partial listings**
32-3940G[4]	3-9	33.8-11.5	3	12.6	1	Int.	13	279.95	**shown. Contact Bushnell Performance Optics for details.**
32-2732M	2-7	44.6-12.7	3	11.6	1	Int.	12	265.95	
32-39544G[6]	3-9	31.5-10.5	3	15.7	1	Int.	19	335.95	
32-3955E	3-9	31.5-10.5	3	15.6	30mm	Int.	22	561.95	A reticle is the crosshair or pattern placed in the eyepiece
Elite 3200 Handgun RainGuard									of the scope which establishes the gun's position on the target.
32-2632M[7]	2-6	10-4	20	9	1	Int.	10	389.95	
32-2636[10]	2-6	10-4	20	9	1	Int.	10	431.95	
Holosight									
.51-0021	1x	Unlimited	6"/10'	4.1	NA	Int.	6.4	389.95	
.53-0021	1x	Unlimited	Unlimited	6	NA	Int.	12	299.95	
.53-0029	1x	Unlimited	Unlimited	6	NA	Int.	12	299.95	
Legend									
.75-2732M	2-7	56-16	3.5	11.6	1	Int.	11.6	187.95	
.75-3940M	3-9	36-13	3.5	13.1	1	Int.	14.6	207.95	
.75-3950M	3-9	36-13	3.5	13.1	1	Int.	16	227.95	
.75-4124M	4-12	30.9-10.1	3.5	14.4	1	Int.	17.3	265.95	
.75-5154M	5-15	23.8	3.5	14.6	1	Int.	17.7	277.95	
Trophy									
73-0134	1	68	Unlimited	5.5	1	Int.	6	119.95	
73-1500[1]	1.75-5	68-23	3.5	10.8	1	Int.	12.3	155.95	
73-4124[1]	4-12	32-11	3	12.5	1	Int.	16.1	263.95	
73-3940[2]	3-9	42-14	3	11.7	1	Int.	13.2	139.95	
73-6184[7]	6-18	17.3-6	3	14.8	1	Int.	17.9	331.95	
Turkey & Brush									
73-1421[11]	1.75-4	73-30	3.5	10.8	32mm	Int.	10.9	149.95	
HOLOsight Model[8]	1			6		Int.	8.7	389.95	
Trophy Handgun									
73-2632[3]	2-6	21-7	9-26	9.1	1	Int.	10.9	251.95	
Banner									
71-1545	1.5-4.5	67-23	3.5	10.5	1	Int.	10.5	101.95	
71-3944[9]	3-9	36-13	4	11.5	1	Int.	12.5	109.95	
71-3950[10]	3-9	26-10	3	16	1	Int.	19	163.95	
71-4124[7]	4-12	29-11	3	12	1	Int.	15	138.95	
71-6185[10]	6-18	17-6	3	16	1	Int.	18	209.95	
Sportsman									
72-0038	3-9	37-14	3.5	12	1	Int.	6	69.95	
72-0039	3-9	38-13	3.5	10.75	1	Int.	11.2	101.95	
72-0412[7]	4-12	27-9	3.2	13.1	1	Int.	14.6	123.95	
72-1393[6]	3-9	35-12	3.5	11.75	1	Int.	10	59.95	
72-1545	1.5-4.5	69-24	3	10.7	1	Int.	8.6	75.95	
72-1548[11]	1.5-4.5	71-25	3.5	10.4	1	Int.	11.8	95.95	
72-1403	4	29	4	11.75	1	Int.	9.2	49.95	
72-3940M	3-9	42-14	3	12.7	1	Int.	12.5	83.95	
22 Rimfire									
76-2239	3-9	40-13	3	11.75	1	Int.	11.2	53.95	
76-2243	4	30	3	11.5	1	Int.	10	45.95	
EUROPTIK SUPREME									
4x36K	4	39	3.5	11.6	26mm	Int.	14	795.00	[1]Military scope with adjustable parallax. Fixed powers have 26mm
6x42K	6	21	3.5	13	26mm	Int.	15	875.00	tubes, variables have 30mm tubes. Some models avail. with steel
8x56K	8	18	3.5	14.4	26mm	Int.	20	925.00	tubes. All lenses multi-coated. Dust and water tight. From Europtik.
1.5-6x42K	1.5-6	61.7-23	3.5	12.6	30mm	Int.	17	1,095.00	
2-8x42K	2-8	52-17	3.5	13.3	30mm	Int.	17	1,150.00	
2.5-10x56K	2.5-10	40-13.6	3.5	15	30mm	Int.	21	1,295.00	
3-12x56 Super	3-12	10.8-34.7	3.5-2.5	15.2	30mm	Int.	24	1,495.00	
4-16x56 Super	4-16	9.8-3.9	3.1	18	30mm	Int.	26	1,575.00	
3-9x40 Micro	3-9	3.2-12.1	2.7	13	1	Int.	14	1,450.00	
2.5-10x46 Micro	2.5-10	13.7-33.4	2.7	14	30mm	Int.	20	1,395.00	
4-16x56 EDP[1]	4-16	22.3-7.5	3.1	18	30mm	Int.	29	1,995.00	
7-12x50 Target	7-12	8.8-5.5	3.5	15	30mm	Int.	21	1,495.00	
JAEGER									
ST-10		10, 17	Varies	13	30mm, 35mm		34	895.00	All scopes available w/standard and extra-long eye relief eyepiece.
SN-1 Long Range		17, 22, 42	12.35 (10x)	Varies	30mm, 35mm, 40mm		36	2,395.00	Variable power military and police tactical scope systems are also available. Offers scope rings and bases. By U.S.O. Jaeger.
SN6 2d Perimeter		10, 17, 22	12.35 (10x)	Varies	30mm, 35mm, 40mm		34	1,295.00	
SN-9 Extreme Range		22, 42	6.2 (22x)	Varies			62.4	2,600.00	
SN-12 CQB		3, 4	38 (3x)	7.5	1		34	865.00	
USMC 10x Sniper		10	10.36	12.5	1		34	2,500.00	
USMC M40A3		10	10.36	12.5	1		34	NA	
JH-4 Safari		1-4	119-34	9.25	30mm		31	1,195.00	
JH-3 Denali		1.8-10x	48.7-12.35	13	30mm		32	1,695.00	
JH-3 Serengeti		3.2-17x		14.5	30mm		33	1,895.00	
JH-T-PAL Chucker		3.8-22x	30-6.2	17.5	30mm		34	1,995.00	
KAHLES									
C-1 Series									Aluminum tube. Multi-coated, waterproof. [1]Also available with illumi-
C1-4	1-1.4	108-31.8	3.55	10.83	30mm	Int.	14.6	943.33	nated reticle. Imported from Austria by Swarovski Optik.
C5-6x42	1.5-6	72-21.3	3.55	12.01	30mm	Int.	16.4	1,043.33	
C2.5-10	2.5-10	43.5-12.9	3.55	12.8	30mm	Int.	17.3	1,187.76	
C3-12	3-12	37.5-10.8	3.55	13.98	30mm	Int.	19.4	1,332.22	
American Hunter Riflescopes									
2-7x36	2-7	48-27.3	3.35	11.06	1	Int.	12.2	621.11	
3-9	3-9	39-14.5	3.35	12.09	1	Int.	13.1	732.22	
3.5-10	3.5-10	33.6-11.7	3.35	12.76	30mm	Int.	14.5	843.33	

MULTI-X

CIRCLE-X

MIL DOT

3-2-1 LOW-LIGHT

1/4 M.O.A.

EUROPEAN

Maker and Model	Magn.	Field at 100 Yds. (feet)	Eye Relief (in.)	Length (in.)	Tube Dia. (in.)	W & E Adjustments	Weight (ozs.)	Price	Other Data
KAHLES *(cont.)*									
Compact Fixed Power									
4x36	4	34.5	3.15	11.22	1	Int.	12.7	665.56	
6x42	6	23.4	3.15	12.4	1	Int.	14.5	854.44	
Compact 30mm Riflescopesw/Illuminated Reticle									
CSX 1-4	1.1-4	110.94-31.78	3.55	11.04	30mm	Int.	15.4	1,476.00	
CSX 2.5-10	1.5-6	74.96-21.29	3.55	12.2	30mm	Int.	17.15	1,665.55	
CSX 2.5-10	2.5-10	43.5-12.9	3.55	12.8	30mm	Int.	18.3	1,743.00	
Compact 30mm Riflescopes, Illumited									
CB 1.5-6	1.5-6	72-21.3	3.55	12.01	30mm	Int.	16.4	1,498.89	
CB 2.5-10	2.5-10'	43.5-12.9	3.55	12.8	30mm	Int.	17.3	965.55	
CB 3-12	3-12	37.5-10.8	3.55	13.98	30mm	Int.	19.4	1,743.33	
CL 1" Riflescopes									
CL3-9x42	3-9	39-15	3.60	12.09	1	Int.	14.46	887.78	
CL3-10	3-10	34-12	3.60	12.59	1	Int.	16.4	965.55	
CL4-12	4-12	29-10	3.60	12.59	1	Int.	18.34	998.89	
CL 1" Riflescopes with Multizer									
CL3-9x42	3-9	39-15	3.60	12.09	1	Int.	14.99	1,076.67	
CL3-10x50	3-10	34-12	3.60	12.59	1	Int.	16.93	1,110.00	
CL4-12x52	4-12	29-10	3.60	12.59	1	Int.	18.87	1,176.67	
LEATHERWOOD									
Uni-Dial*									*Elevation adjustment is 1/8" and windage adjustment is 1/4". All air-glass surfaces are fully multi-coated to maximize light transmission.
U3510x50 3.5-10	50	36.7-12.8	3.25	13.11			18.7	299.00	
U412-50 4-12	50	30.6-10.2	3.25	14.53			22.1	339.00	
U618-50 6-18	50	20.4-7.5	3.25	15.35			22	367.50	
U6520x50 6.5-20	50	18.8-6.3	3.25	15.43			23.5	375.00	
U3501x50MD 3.5-10	50	36.7-12.8	3.25	13.11			18.7	437.50	
Distinguished									
D3510x50 3.5-10	50	36.7-12.8	3.25	13.11			17.2	199.00	
D412x50 4-12	50	30.6-10.2	3.25	14.53			20.6	239.00	
D618x5- 6-18	50	20.4-7.5	3.25	15.35			21.5	267.00	
D6520x50 6.5-20	50	18.8-6.3	3.35	15.43			22	275.00	
D3510x50MD 3.5-10	50	36.7-12.8	3.25	13.11			17.2	337.00	
Expert									
E412x44 4-12	44	30.6-10.7	3.25	14.53			19.7	149.00	
E618x44 6-18	44	20.4-6.8	3.25	15.35			20.2	159.00	
E6520x44 6.5-20	44	18.8-6.28	3.25	15.43			21.2	169.00	
E6520x44MD 4-12	44	30.6-10.7	3.25	14.53			19.7	223.50	
Sharpshooter									
S39x40 3-9	40	41-15	3.25	13			13.5	95.00	
S39x40IN 3-9	40	39-13	3.25	12.75			14	105.00	
S39x50 3-9	50	41-13	3.25	12.75			14.5	112.00	
S3510x50 3.5-10	50	36.7-12.8	3.25	13.11			16.2	119.00	
S310x44 3-10	44	40.8-12.8	3.25	13.11			15.2	107.00	
S55-16x44 5.5-16	44	21.9-7.5	3.25	14.41			19.9	149.00	
S6520x44 6.5-20	44	18.8-6.28	3.25	15.43			21.7	145.00	
Long Eye Relief									
LER2732 2-7	32	18.88-0.28	11.2-0.7	11.08			11.57	185.00	
Double-Duce Rimfire									
RF4x32 4	02	00	2	12			11	49.50	
RF39x32 3-9	32	38.5-13	3	12.5			12	69.50	
LEICA									
Ultravid 1.75-6x32	1.75-6	47-18	4.8-3.7	11.25	30mm	Int.	14	749.00	Aluminum tube with hard anodized matte black finish with titanium accents; finger-adjustable windage and elevation with 1/4-MOA clicks. Made in U.S. From Leica.
Ultravid 3.5-10x42	3.5-10	29.5-10.7	4.6-3.6	12.62	30mm	Int.	16	849.00	
Ultravid 4.5-14x42	4.5-14	20.5-7.4	5-3.7	12.28	30mm	Int.	18	949.00	

Leicaplex Standard   Leica Dot   Standard Dot   Crosshair   Euro   Post & Plex

Maker and Model	Magn.	Field at 100 Yds. (feet)	Eye Relief (in.)	Length (in.)	Tube Dia. (in.)	W & E Adjustments	Weight (ozs.)	Price	Other Data
LEUPOLD									
M8-3.5x10	3.2-9.5	29.9	4.7	13.5	30mm	Int.	19.5	1,124.99	Constantly centered reticles, choice of Duplex, tapered CPC, Leupold Dot, Crosshair and Dot. CPC and Dot reticles extra. [1]2x and 4x scopes have from 12"-24" of eye relief and are suitable for handguns, top ejection arms and muzzleloaders. [2]3x9 Compact, 6x Compact, 12x, 3x9, and 6.5x20 come with adjustable objective. Sunshade available for all adjustable objective scopes, **$23.20–$41.10**. [3]Long Range scopes have side focus parallax adjustment, additional windage and elevation travel. Partial listing shown. **Contact Leupold for complete details.**
M8-2.7-28	2.66	41	3.8	9.9	1	Int.	8.2	299.99	
M8-4X Compact RF	3.6	25.5	4.5	9.2	1	Int.	7.5	289.99	
Vari-X 2-7x	2.5-6.5	41.7-17.3	4.2	10.8	1	Int.	10	299.99	
Vari-X 3-9x	3.3-8.5	32-13.1	4.2	12.2	1	Int.	12	314.99	
M8-4X	4	24	4	10.5	1	Int.	9.3	249.99	
M8-6x36mm	5.9	17.7	4.3	11.3	1	Int.	10	469.99	
M8-6x42mm	6	17	4.5	11.9	1	Int.	11.3	424.99	
M8-12x40	11.6	9.1	4.2	13	1	Int.	13.5	474.99	
Vari-X 3-9x	3.5-8.6	32.9-13.1	4.2	12.2	1	Int.	12	454.99	
Vari-X-III 1.5-5x20	1.5-4.5	65-17	4.4-3.6	9.4	1	Int.	9.7	499.99	
Vari-X-III 1.75-6x32	1.9-5.6	51	4.4-3.2	11.4	1	Int.	11.6	499.99	
Vari-X-III 2.5x8	2.6-7.8	37-13.5	4.4-3.5	11.4	1	Int.	11.6	499.99	
Vari-X-III 3.5-10x40	3.9-9.6	29.7-11	4.4-3.5	12.6	1	Int.	13	549.99	
Vari-X-III 3.5-10x50	3.3-9.5	29.8-11	4.4-3.5	12.2	1	Int.	15.1	624.99	
Vari-X-III 4.5-14x40	4.8-14.2	19.9	4.4-3.6	12.6	1	Int.	13.2	699.99	
*Vari-X-III 4.5-14x50	4.9-14.4	19.1	4.4-3.6	12.6	1	Int.	16	789.99	
Vari-X-III 4.5-14x50 LRT[4]	4.9-14.3	19-6	5-3.7	12.1	30mm	Int.	17.5	999.00	
Vari-X-III 6.5-20 A.O.	6.5-19.2	14.3-5.6	5-3.6	14.3	1	Int.	16	749.99	
Vari-X III 6.5-20xLRT	6.5-19.2	14.3-5.5	4.4	14.2	1	Int.	21	974.99	
Vari-X III 8.5-25x40 LRT	8.3-24.3	11.3-4.3	5.2	14.3	1	Int.	21	1,039.99	
Vari-X III 8.5-25x 50 LRT[4]	8.3-24.3	11.3-4.3	5.2-7	14.4	30mm	Int.	21	1,149.99	
Mark 4 M1-10x40	10	11.1	3.6	13.125	30mm	Int.	21	1,124.99	
Mark 4 M1-16x40	16	6.6	4.1	12.875	30mm	Int.	22	1,509.99	
Mark 4 M3-10x40LRT	10	13.1	3.4	13.125	30mm	Int.	21	939.99	
Mark 4 6.5x20[2]	6.5-19.5	14.3-5.5	5.5-3.8	11.2	30mm	Int.	16	1,198.99	

Duplex   CPC   Post & Duplex

Leupold Dot   Dot

Maker and Model	Magn.	Field at 100 Yds. (feet)	Eye Relief (in.)	Length (in.)	Tube Dia. (in.)	W & E Adjustments	Weight (ozs.)	Price	Other Data
LEUPOLD *(cont.)*									
LPS 1.5-6x42	1.5-6	58.7-15.7	4	11.2	30mm	Int.	16	1,198.99	
LPS 2.5-10x45	2.6-9.8	37.2	4.5-3.8		1	Int.	17.2	1,119.99	
LPS 3.5-14x52	3.5-14	28-7.2	4	13.1	30mm	Int.	22	1,249.99	
Rimfire									
Vari-X 2-7x RF Special	3.6	25.5	4.5	9.2	1	Int.	7.5	299.99	
Shotgun									
M8 2.5x20	2.3	39.5	4.9	8.4	1	Int.	6	249.99	
LYMAN									
Super TargetSpot[1]	10, 12, 15, 20, 25, 30	5.5	2	24.3	.75	Int.	27.5	685.00	Made under license from Lyman to Lyman's orig. specs. Blue steel. Threepoint suspension rear mount with .25-min. click adj. Data listed for 20x model. [1]Price appx. Made in U.S. by Parsons Optical Mfg. Co.
McMILLAN									
Vision Master 2.5-10x	2.5-10	14.2-4.4	4.3-3.3	13.3	30mm	Int.	17	1,250.00	42mm obj. lens; .25-MOA clicks; nitrogen filled, fogproof, waterproof;
Vision Master Model 1[1]	2.5-10	14.2-4.4	4.3-3.3	13.3	30mm	Int.	17	1,250.00	etched duplex-type reticle. [1]Tactical Scope with external adj. knobs, military reticle; 60+ min. adj.
MEOPTA									
Artemis									
4x32A[1]	4	34	3.15	11	1	Int.	14.7	194.00	Steel tubes are waterproof, dustproof, and shockproof; nitrogen filled.
6x42A[1]	6	23	3.15	13.6	1	Int.	18.2	267.00	Anti-reflective coatings, protective rubber eye piece, clear caps.
7x50A[1]	7	18	3.15	14.1	1	Int.	19	278.00	Made in Czech Replublic by Meopta. [1]Range finder reticles available. Partial listing shown.
MEPROLIGHT									
Meprolight Reflex Sights 14-21 5.5 MOA 1x30[1]	1			4.4	30mm	Int.	5.2	335.00	[1]Also available with 4.2 MOA dot. Uses tritium and fiber-optics, no batteries required. From Hesco, Inc.
MILLETT									
Buck 3-9x44	3-9	38-14	3.25-4	13	1	Int.	16.2	238.00	[1]3-MOA dot. .25-MOA dot. 33-, 5-, 8-, 10-MOA dots. 410-MOA dot.
Buck 3.5-10x50	3.5-10	NA	NA	NA	1	NA	NA	258.00	All have click adjustments; waterproof, shockproof; 11 dot intensity
Buck 3-12x44 A/O	3-12	NA	NA	NA	1	NA	NA	258.00	settings. All avail. in matte/black or silver finish. From Millett Sights.
Buck 4-16x44 A/O	4-16	NA	NA	NA	1	NA	NA	270.00	
Buck Varmint 4-16x56	4-16	NA	NA	NA	30mm	NA	NA	318.00	
Buck Varmint 6-25x56	6-25	NA	NA	NA	30mm	NA	NA	338.00	
Buck Varmint 6-25x56	6-25	NA	NA	NA	30mm	NA	NA	370.00	
Buck Lightning 1.5-6x44	1.5-6	NA	NA	NA	1	NA	NA	270.00	
Buck Lightning 3-9x44	3-9	NA	NA	NA	1	NA	NA	270.00	
Buck Silver 3-9x40	3-9	NA	NA	NA	1	NA	NA	129.95	
Buck Silver 4-12x40 A/O	4-12	NA	NA	NA	1	NA	NA	172.00	
Buck Silver 6-18x40 A/O	6-18	NA	NA	NA	1	NA	NA	172.00	
Buck Silver Compact 2x20	2	NA	NA	NA	1	NA	NA	99.50	
Buck Silver Compact 4x32	4	NA	NA	NA	1	NA	NA	105.00	
Buck Silver Compact 1.5-4x32	1.5-4	NA	NA	NA	1	NA	NA	136.00	
SP-1 Compact[1] Red Dot	1	36.65		4.1	1	Int.	3.2	147.45	
SP-2 Compact[2] Red Dot	1	58		4.5	30mm	Int.	4.3	147.45	
MultiDot SP[3]	1	50		4.8	30mm	Int.	5.3	179.45	
30mm Wide View[4]	1	60		5.5	30mm	Int.	5	179.45	
MIRADOR									
RXW 4x40[1]	4	37	3.8	12.4	1	Int.	12	179.95	[1]Wide angle scope. Multi-coated objective lens. Nitrogen filled; water-
RXW 1.5-5x20[1]	1.5-5	46-17.4	4.3	11.1	1	Int.	10	188.95	proof; shockproof. From Mirador Optical Corp.
RXW 3-9x40	3-9	43-14.5	3.1	12.9	1	Int.	13.4	251.95	
NIGHTFORCE									
3.5-15x50	3.5-15	27.6-9.7.3		14.7	30mm		30	1,278.90	Lighted reticles with eleven intensity levels. Most scopes have choice
3.5-15x56	3.5-15	27.6-7	3	14.8	30mm	Int.	31	1,309.77	of reticles. From Lightforce U.S.A.
5.5-22x56	5.5-22	17.5-4.47		15	30mm	Int.	31	1,385.90	
5.5-22x56	5.5-22	17.5-4.7		15.2	30mm	Int.	32	1,300.18	
8-32x56	8-32	12.1-3.1		15.9	30mm	Int.	34	1,519.25	
12-42x56	12-42	8.2-2.4		16.1	30mm	Int.	34	1,648.24	
3.5-15x36	3.5-15	24.5-6.9		15.8	30mm	Int.	32	1,000.83	
8-32x56	8-32	9.4-3.1	3	16.6	30mm	Int.	36	997.90	
12-42x56	12-42	6.7-2.3	3	17	30mm	Int.	36	1,053.64	
NIKON									
Buckmasters									
4x40	4	30.4	3.3	12.7	1	Int.	11.8	159.95	Super multi-coated lenses and blackening of all internal metal parts
3-9x40[4]	3.3-8.6	33.8-11.3	3.5-3.4	12.7	1	Int.	13.4	209.95	for maximum light gathering capability; positive .25-MOA; fogproof;
3-9x50	3.3-8.6	33.8-11.3	3.5-3.4	12.9	1	Int.	18.2	299.95	waterproof; shockproof; luster and matte finish. [1]Also available in
4-12x50	4-12	24.3-8.0	3.7	13.9	1	Int.	20.6	349.95	matte silver finish. [2]Available in silver matte finish. [3]Available with
Monarch UCC									TurkeyPro or Nikoplex reticle. [4]Silver Shadow finish; black matte
4x40[2]	4	26.7	3.5	11.7	1	Int.	11.7	229.95	$296.95. Partial listing shown. From Nikon, Inc.
1.5-4.5x20[3]	1.5-4.5	67.8-22.5	3.7-3.2	10.1	1	Int.	9.5	239.95	
2-7x32	2-7	46.7-13.7	3.9-3.3	11.3	1	Int.	11.3	269.95	
3-9x40[1]	3-9	33.8-11.3	3.6-3.2	12.5	1	Int.	12.5	299.95	
3.5-10x50	3.5-10	25.5-8.9	3.9-3.8	13.7	1	Int.	15.5	439.95	
4-12x40 A.O.	4-12	25.7-8.6	3.6-3.2	14	1	Int.	16.6	369.95	
6.5-20x44	6.5-19.4	16.2-5.4	3.5-3.1	14.8	1	Int.	19.6	469.95	
2x20 EER	2	22	26.4	8.1	1	Int.	6.3	169.95	
NORINCO									
N2520	2.5	44.1	4		1	Int.		52.28	Partial listing shown. Some with Ruby Lens coating, blue/black and
N420	4	29.3	3.7		1	Int.		52.70	matte finish. Imported by Nic Max, Inc.
N640	6	20	3.1		1	Int.		67.88	
N154520	1.5-4.5	63.9-23.6	4.1-3.2		1	Int.		80.14	
N251042	2.5-10	27-11			1	Int.		206.60	
N3956	3-9	35.1-6.3	3.7-2.6		1	Int.		231.88	
N31256	3-12	26-10	3.5-2.8		1	Int.		290.92	
NC2836M	2-8	50.8-14.8	3.6-2.7		1	Int.		255.60	

Maker and Model	Magn.	Field at 100 Yds. (feet)	Eye Relief (in.)	Length (in.)	Tube Dia. (in.)	W & E Adjustments	Weight (ozs.)	Price	Other Data
PARSONS									
Parsons Long Scope	6	10	2	28-34+	.75	Ext.	13	475.00-525.00	Adj. for parallax, focus. Micrometer rear mount with .25-min. click adjustments. Price is approximate. Made in U.S. by Parsons Optical Mfg. Co.
PENTAX									
Lightseeker 1.75-6x[1]	1.75-6	71-20	3.5-4	10.8	1	Int.	13	546.00	[1]Glossy finish; Matte finish, Heavy Plex or Penta-Plex, **$546.00**. [2]Glossy finish; Matte finish, **$594.00**. [3]Glossy finish; Matte finish **$628.00**; Heavy Plex, add **$20.00**. [4]Matte finish; Mil-Dot, **$798.00**. [5]Glossy finish; Matte finish, **$652.00**; Heavy Plex, add **$10.00**. [6]Glossy finish; Matte finish, **$816.00**; with Heavy Plex, **$830.00**; with Mil-Dot, **$978.00**. [7]Matte finish; with Mil-Dot, **$1,018.00**. [8]Matte finish, with Mil-Dot, **$1098.00**. [9]Lightseeker II, Matte finish, **$844.00**. [10]Lightseeker II, Glossy finish, **$636.00**. [11]Lightseeker II, Matte finish, **$660.00**. [12]Lightseeker II, Matte finish, **$878.00**. [13]Matte finish; Advantage finish, Break-up Mossy Oak finish, Treestand Mossy Oak finish, **$364.00**. From Pentax Corp.
Lightseeker 2-8x[2]	2-8	53-17	3.5-4	11.7	1	Int.	14	594.00	
Lightseeker 3-9x[3,4,10,11]	3-9	36-14	3.5-4	12.7	1	Int.	15	594.00	
Lightseeker 3.5-10x[5]	3.5-10	29.5-11	3.5-4	14	1	Int.	19.5	630.00	
Lightseeker 4-16x[6,9]	4-16	33-9	3.5-4	15.4	1	Int.	22.7	888.00	
Lightseeker 6-24x[7,12]	6-24	18.5-5	3.5-4	16	1	Int.	23.7	1,028.00	
Lightseeker 8.5-32x[8]	8.5-32	13-3.8	3.5-4	17.2	1	Int.	24	968.00	
Shotgun									
Lightseeker 2.5x1[3]	2.5	55	3.5-4	10	1	Int.	9	398.00	
Lightseeker Zero-X SG Plus	0	51	4.5-15	8.9	1	Int.	7.9	372.00	
Lightseeker Zero-X/V Still-Target	0-4	53.8-15	3.5-7	8.9	1	Int.	10.3	476.00	
Lightseeker Zero X/V	0-4	53.8-15	3.5-7	8.9	1	Int.	10.3	454.00	

Pentax Reticles

Heavy Plex	Fine Plex	Penta-Plex	Deepwoods Plex	Comp-Plex	Mil-dot

Maker and Model	Magn.	Field at 100 Yds. (feet)	Eye Relief (in.)	Length (in.)	Tube Dia. (in.)	W & E Adjustments	Weight (ozs.)	Price	Other Data
RWS									
300	4	36	3.5	11.75	1	Int.	13.2	170.00	
450	3-9	43-14	3.5	12	1	Int.	14.3	215.00	
SCHMIDT & BENDER									
Fixed									
4x36	4	30	3.25	11	1	Int.	14	859.00	All scopes have 30-yr. warranty, click adjustments, centered reticles, rotation indicators. [1]Glass reticle; aluminum. Available in aluminum with mounting rail. [2]Aluminum only. [3]Aluminum tube. Choice of two bullet drop compensators, choice of two sunshades, two range finding reticles. From Schmidt & Bender, Inc. [4]Parallax adjustment in third turret; extremely fine crosshairs. [5]Available with illuminated reticle that glows red; third turret houses on/off switch, dimmer and battery. [6]4-16x50/Long Range. [7]Also with Long Eye Relief. From Schmidt & Bender, Inc. Available with illuminated crosshairs and parallax adjustment.
6x42	6	21	3.25	13	1	Int.	17	999.00	
8x56	8	16.5	3.25	14	1	Int.	22	1,099.00	
10x42	10	10.5	3.25	13	1	Int.	18	999.00	
Variables									
1.25-4x20[5]	1.25-4	96-16	3.75	10	30mm	Int.	15.5	1,199.00	
1.5-6x42[1,5]	1.5-6	60-19.5	3.70	12	30mm	Int.	19.7	1,299.00	
2.5-10x56[1,5]	2.5-10	37.5-12	3.90	14	30mm	Int.	24.6	1,479.00	
3-12x42[2]	3-12	34.5-11.5	3.90	13.5	30mm	Int.	19	1,479.00	
3-12x50[1,5]	3-12	33.3-12.6	3.90	13.5	30mm	Int.	22.9	1,499.00	
4-16x50 Varmint[4,6]	4-16	22.5-7.5	3.90	14	30mm	Int.	26	1,799.00	
Police/Marksman II									
3-12x50[7]	3-12	33.3-12.6	3.74	13.9	34mm	Int.	18.5	2,799.00	
SCHMIDT & BENDER ZENITH SERIES									
3-12x50	3-12	33.3-11.4	3.70	13.71	NA	NA	23.4	1,599.00-1,795.00	
2.5-10x56	2.5-10	30.6-12	3.70	14.81	NA	NA	24	1,490.00-1,795.00	

No 1 (fixed)	No. 1 variable	No. 2	No. 3	No. 4	No. 6	No. 7	No. 8	No. 8 Dot	No. 9

Maker and Model	Magn.	Field at 100 Yds. (feet)	Eye Relief (in.)	Length (in.)	Tube Dia. (in.)	W & E Adjustments	Weight (ozs.)	Price	Other Data
SIGHTRON									
Variables									
SII 1.56x42	1.5-6	50-15	3.8-4	11.69	1	Int.	15.35	372.25	[1]Adjustable objective. [2]3MOA dot; also with 5 or 10 MOA dot. [3]Variable 3, 5, 10 MOA dot; black finish; also stainless. [4]Satin black; also stainless. Electronic Red Dot scopes come with ring mount, front and rear extension tubes, polarizing filter, battery, haze filter caps, wrench. Rifle, pistol, shotgun scopes have aluminum tubes. Exac Trak adjustments. Lifetime warranty. From Sightron, Inc. 53" sun shade. [6]Mil-Dot or Plex reticle. [7]Dot or Plex reticle. [8]Double Diamond reticle.
SII 2.58x42	2.5-8	36-12	3.6-4.2	11.89	1	Int.	12.82	338.40	
SII 39x42[4,6,7]	3-9	34-12	3.0-4.2	12.00	1	Int.	13.22	356.22	
SII 312x12[6]	3-12	32-9	3.6-4.2	11.89	1	Int.	12.99	421.55	
SII 3.510x42	3.5-10	32-11	3.6	11.89	1	Int.	13.16	421.01	
SII 4.514x42[1]	4.5-14	22-7.9	3.6	13.88	1	Int.	16.07	481.14	
Target									
SII 24x44	24	4.1	4.33	13.30	1	Int.	15.87	441.82	
SII 416x42[1,4,5,6,7]	4-16	26-7	3.6	13.62	1	Int.	16	481.11	
SII 624-42[1,4,5,7]	6-24	16-5	3.6	14.6	1	Int.	18.7	562.96	
Compact									
SII 4x32	4	25	4.5	9.69	1	Int.	9.34	266.86	
SII2.5-10x32	2.5-10	41-10.5	3.75-3.5	10.9	1	Int.	10.39	338.40	
Shotgun									
SII 2.5x20SG	2.5	41	4.3	10.28	1	Int.	8.46	266.88	
Pistol									
SII 1x28P[4]	1	30	9-24	9.49	1	Int.	8.46	314.79	
SII 2x28P[4]	2	16-10	9-24	9.49	1	Int.	8.28	314.79	
SIMMONS									
22 Mag.									
801022	4	29.5	3	11.75			11	49.99	[1]Matte; also polished finish. [2]Silver; also black matte or polished. [3]Black matte finish. [4]Granite finish. [5]Camouflage. [6]Black polish. [7]With ring mounts. [8]Silver; black polish avail. [10]50mm obj.; black matte. [11]Black or silver matte. [12]75-yd. parallax; black or silver matte. [13]TV view. [14]Adj. obj. [15]Silver matte. [16]Adj. objective; 4" sunshade; black matte. [17]Octagon body; rings included; black matte or silver finish. [18]Black matte finish; also available in silver. [19]Smart reticle. [20]Target turrets. [21]With dovetail rings. [23]With 3V lithium battery, extension tube, polarizing filter, Weaver rings. **Only selected models shown.** Contact Simmons Outdoor Corp. for complete details.
801031	4	23.5	5	7.25			8.25	49.99	
801037	3-9	29.5	3.3	11.5			10	59.99	
AETEC									
21008	2.8-10	44-14	5	11.9	1	Int.	15.5	189.99	
2104[16]	3.8-12	33-11	4	13.5	1	Int.	20	199.99	
44Mag									
M-1044[3]	3-10	34-10.5	3	12.75	1	Int.	15.5	149.99	
M-1045[3]	4-12	29.5-9.5	3	13.2	1	Int.	18.25	169.99	
M-1047[3]	6.5-20	14-.5	2.6-3.4	12.8	1	Int.	19.5	199.99	
1048[3,20] (3)	6.5-20	16-5.5	2.6-3.4	14.5	1	Int.	20	219.99	
M-1050DM[3,19]	3.8-12	26-9	3	13.08	1	Int.	16.75	189.99	

Maker and Model	Magn.	Field at 100 Yds. (feet)	Eye Relief (in.)	Length (in.)	Tube Dia. (in.)	W & E Adjustments	Weight (ozs.)	Price	Other Data
SIMMONS *(cont.)*									
8-Point									
4-12x40mmAO[3]	4-12	29-10	3-2 7/8	13.5	1	Int.	15.75	99.99	
4x32mm[3]	4	28.75	3	11.625	1	Int.	14.25	34.99	
3-9x32mm[3]	3-9	37.5-13	3-2 7/8	11.875	1	Int.	11.5	39.99	
3-9x40mm[18]	3-9	37-13	3-2 7/8	12.25	1	Int.	12.25	49.99-79.99	
3-9x50mm[3]	3-9	32-11.75	3-2 7/8	13	1	Int.	15.25	79.99	
Prohunter									
7700	2-7	53-16.25	3	11.5	1	Int.	12.5	79.99	
7710[2]	3-9	36-13	3	12.6	1	Int.	13.5	89.99	
7716	4-12	26-9	3	12.6	1	Int.	16.75	129.99	
7721	6-18	18.5-6	3	13.75	1	Int.	16	144.99	
7740[3]	6	21.75	3	12.5	1	Int.	12	99.99	
Prohunter Handgun									
7732[18]	2	22	9-17	8.75	1	Int.	7	109.99	
7738[18]	4	15	11.8- 17.6	8.5	1	Int.	8	129.99	
82200[9]	2-6							159.99	
Whitetail Classic									
WTC 11[4]	1.5-5	75-23	3.4-3.2	9.3	1	Int.	9.7	184.99	
WTC 12[4]	2.5-8	45-14	3.2-3	11.3	1	Int.	13	199.99	
WTC 13[4]	3.5-10	30-10.5	3.2-3	12.4	1	Int.	13.5	209.99	
WTC 15[4]	3.5-10	29.5-11.5	3.2	12.75	1	Int.	13.5	289.99	
WTC 45[4]	4.5-14	22.5-8.6	3.2	13.2	1	Int.	14	265.99	
Whitetail Expedition									
1.5-6x32mm[3]	1.5-6	72-19	3	11.16	1	Int.	15	259.99	
3-9x42mm[3]	3-9	40-13.5	3	13.2	1	Int.	17.5	269.99	
4-12x42mm[3]	4-12	29-9.6	3	13.46	1	Int.	21.25	299.99	
6-18x42mm[3]	6-18	18.3-6.5	3	15.35	1	Int.	22.5	319.99	
Pro50									
8800[10]	4-12	27-9	3.5	13.2	1	Int.	18.25	179.99	
8810[10]	6-18	17-5.8	3.6	13.2	1	Int.	18.25	174.99	
808825	3.5-10	32-8.75	3.5	3.25	1	Int.	14.5	179.99	
808830	2.5-10	39-12.2	2.75	12.75	1	Int.	15.9	179.99	
Shotgun									
2100[4]	4	16	5.5	8.8	1	Int.	9.1	84.99	
2100[5]	2.5	24	6	7.4	1	Int.	7	59.99	
7789D	2	31	5.5	8.8	1	Int.	8.75	99.99	
7790D	4	17	5.5	8.5	1	Int.	8.75	114.99	
7791D	1.5-5	76-23.5	3.4	9.5	1	Int.	10.75	138.99	
Blackpowder									
BP0420M17	4	19.5	4	7.5	1	Int.	8.3	59.99	
BP2732M12	2-7	57.7-16.6	3	11.6	1	Int.	12.4	129.99	
Red Dot									
5100421	1			4.8	30mm	Int.	4.7	44.99	
5111222	1			5.25	42mm	Int.	6	49.99	
Pro Air Gun									
21608 A.O.	4	25	3.5	12	1	Int.	11.3	99.99	
21613 A.O.	4-12	25-9	3.1-2.9	13.1	1	Int.	15.8	179.99	
21619 A.O.	6-18	18-7	2.9-2.7	13.8	1	Int.	18.2	189.99	
SPRINGFIELD ARMORY									
	6		3.5	13	1	Int.	14.7	379.00	
4-14x70 Tactical Government Model[2]	4-14		3.5	14.25	1	Int.	15.8	395.00	
4-14x56 1st Gen. Government Model[3]	4-14		3.5	14.75	30mm	Int.	23	480.00	
10x56 Mil-Dot Government Model[4]	10		3.5	14.75	30mm	Int.	28	672.00	
6-20x56 Mil-Dot Government Model	6-20		3.5	18.25	30mm	Int.	33	899.00	
SWAROVSKI OPTIK									
PH Series									
1.25-4x24[1]	1.25-4	98.4-31.2	3.15	10.63	30mm	Int.	16.2	1,333.23	
1.5-6x42[1]	1.5-6	65.4-21	3.15	12.99	30mm	Int.	20.8	1,483.34	
2.5-10x42[1,2]	2.5-10	39.6-12.6	3.15	13.23	30mm	Int.	19.8	1,705.56	
3-12x50[1]	3-12	33-10.5	3.15	14.33	30mm	Int.	22.4	1,727.78	
4-16x50	4-16	30-8.5	3.15	14.22	30mm	Int.	22.3	1,754.44	
6-24x50	6-24	18.6-5.4	3.15	15.4	30mm	Int.	23.6	1,976.67	
AV Series									
3-9x36	3-9	39-13.5	3.35	11.8	1	Int.	11.7	854.44	
3-10x42AV[4]	3-10	33-11.7	3.35	12.44	1	Int.	12.7	943.33	
4-12x50AV[4]	4-12	29.1-9.9	3.35	13.5	1	Int.	13.9	987.78	
6-18x50	6-18	17.4-6.6	3.5	14.84	1	Int.	20.3	1,065.56	
SWIFT									
600 4x15	4	17	2.8	10.6	.75	Int.	3.5	15.00	
601 3-7x20	3-7	25-12	3-2.9	11	.75	Int.	5.6	35.00	
650 4x32	4	26	4	12	1	Int.	9.1	75.00	
653 4x40WA[1]	4	35	4	12.2	1	Int.	12.6	125.00	
654 3-9x32	3-9	35-12	3.4-2.9	12	1	Int.	9.8	125.00	
656 3-9x40WA[1]	3-9	40-14	3.4-2.8	12.6	1	Int.	12.3	140.00	
657 6x40	6	28	4	12.6	1	Int.	10.4	125.00	
658 2-7x40WA[3]	2-7	55-18	3.3-3	11.6	1	Int.	12.5	160.00	
659 3.5-10x44WA	3.5-10	34-12	3-2.8	12.8	1	Int.	13.5	230.00	
665 1.5-4.5x21	1.5-4.5	69-24.5	3.5-3	10.9	1	Int.	9.6	125.00	
665M 1.5-4.5x21	1.5-4.5	69-24.5	3.5-3	10.9	1	Int.	9.6	125.00	
666M Shotgun 1x20	1	113	3.2	7.5	1	Int.	9.6	130.00	
667 Fire-Fly[2]	1	40		5.4	30mm	Int.	5	220.00	
668M 4x32	4	25	4	10	1	Int.	8.9	120.00	

Reticle illustrations (Simmons): Truplex™ Smart ProDiamond® Crossbow

Reticle illustrations (Swarovski): TDS No. 4 No. 4A No. 7A Plex No. 24

[1]Range finding reticle with automatic bullet drop compensator for 308 match ammo to 700 yds. [2]Range finding reticle with automatic bullet drop compensator for 223 match ammo to 700 yds. [3]Also avail. as 2nd Gen. with target knobs and adj. obj., **$549.00**; as 3rd Gen. with illuminated reticle, **$749.00**; as Mil-Dot model with illuminated Target Tracking reticle, target knobs, adj. obj., **$698.00**. [4]Unlimited range finding, target knobs, adj. obj., illuminated Target Tracking green reticle. All scopes have matte black finish, internal bubble level, 1/4-MOA clicks. From Springfield, Inc.

All Swift scopes, with the exception of the 4x15, have Quadraplex reticles and are fogproof and waterproof. The 4x15 has crosshair reticle and is non-waterproof. [1]Available in regular matte black or silver finish. [2]Comes with ring mounts, wrench, lens caps, extension tubes, filter, battery. [3]Regular and matte black finish. [4]Speed Focus scopes. Partial listing shown. From Swift Instruments.

Maker and Model	Magn.	Field at 100 Yds. (feet)	Eye Relief (in.)	Length (in.)	Tube Dia. (in.)	W & E Adjustments	Weight (ozs.)	Price	Other Data
SWIFT *(cont.)*									
669M 6-18x44	6-18	18-6.5	2.8	14.5	1	Int.	17.6	220.00	
680M	3.9	43-14	4	18	40mm	Int.	17.5	399.95	
681M	1.5-6	56-13	4	11.8	40mm	Int.	17.5	399.95	
682M	4-12	33-11	4	15.4	50mm	Int.	21.7	499.95	
683M	2-7	55-17	3.3	11.6	32mm	Int.	10.6	499.95	
Premier Rifle Scopes									
648M[1] 1.5-4.5	32	71-25	3.05-3.27	10.41		Int.	12.7	179.95	
649R 4-12	50	29.5-9.5	3.3-3	13.8	1	Int.	15.8	245.00	
658M 2-7	40	55-18	3.3-3	11.6	1	Int.	12.5	175.00	
659S 3.5-10	44	34-12	3-2.8	12.8	1	Int.	13.5	215.00	
669M 6-18	44	18-6.5	2.8	14.5	1	Int.	17.6	230.00	
671M 3-9	50	35-25	3.24-3.12	15.5	1	Int.	18.2	250.00	
672M 6-18	50	19-6.7	3.25-3	15.8	1	Int.	20.9	260.00	
674M 3-9	40	40-14.2	3.6-2.9	12	1	Int.	13.1	170.00	
676S 4-12	40	29.3-10.5	3.15-2.9	12.4	1	Int.	15.4	180.00	
677M 6-24	50	18-5	3.1-3.2	15.9	1	Int.	20.8	280.00	
678M 8-32	50	13-3.5	3.13-2.94	16.9	1	Int.	21.5	290.00	
685M[3] 3-9	40	39-13.5	3.7-2.8	12.4	1	Int.	20.5	189.95	
686M[3] 6.5-20	44	19-6.5	2.7	15.6	1	Int.	23.6	249.95	
687M[2] 4.5-14	44	25.5-8.5	3.2	14.1	1	Int.	21.5	220.00	
688M[2] 6-18	44	19.597	2.8	15.4	1	Int.	22.6	240.00	
Standard Rifle Scopes									
587[5] 4	32	25	3.1	11.7	1	Int.	13	50.00	
653M 4	40	35	4	12.2	1	Int.	12.0	128.00	
654M 3-9	32	35-12	3.4-2.9	12	1	Int.	9.8	125.00	
656 3-9	40	40-14	3.4-2.8	12.6	1	Int.	12.3	140.00	
657M 6	40	28	4	12.6	1	Int.	10.4	125.00	
660M[4] 2-6	32	14-4.5	20-12.6	5.5	1	Int.	10.6	241.80	
661M[4] 4	32	6.6	13.8	9.4	1	Int.	9.9	130.00	
663S[4] 4	32	9.8	7.3	7.2	1	Int.	8.5	130.00	
665M 1.5-4.5	21	69-24.5	3.5-3	10.8	1	Int.	9.6	125.00	
668M 4	32	25	4	10	1	Int.	8.9	120.00	
TASCO									
Titan									
DWCP3510	50	30-10.5	3.75	13	1	Int.	17.1	191.95	
DWCP39X	44	39-14	305	12.75	1	Int.	16.5	173.95	
T156X	42N	59-20	3.5	12	1	Int.	16.4	293.95	
T312X52N	3-12	27-10	4.5	14	1	Int.	20.7	335.95	
T312X52N4A	3-12	27-10	4.5	14	1	Int.	20.7	335.95	
T39X42N	3-9	37-13	3.5	12.5	1	Int.	16	201.95	
Target & Varmint									
VAR211042M	1.5-10	35.9	3	14	1	Int.	19.1	89.95	
MAG624X40	6-24	17-4	3	16	1	Int.	19.1	113.95	
VAR624X42M	6-24	13-3.7	7	16	1	Int.	19.6	113.95	
TG624X44DS	15-4.5	15-4.5	3	16.5	1	Int.	19.6	199.95	
TG104040DS	10-40	11-2.5	3.25	15.5	1	Int.	25.5	211.95	
TG832X44DS	8-32	11-3.5	3.25	17	1	Int.	20	219.95	
WL39x401K	3-9	41-14	3.5	12.75	1	Int.	13	83.95	
World Class									
BA1545X32	1.5-4.5	77-23	4	11.25	1	Int.	12	59.95	
DWC28x32	2-8	50-17	4	10.5	1	Int.	12.5	69.96	
DWC39X40N	3-9	41-15	3.5	12.75	1	Int.	13	73.95	
WA39X40N	3-9	41-15	3.5	12.75	1	Int.	13	73.95	
WA39X40STN	3-9	41-15	3.5	12.75	1	Int.	13	73.95	
DWC39X50N	3-9	41-13	3	12.5	1	Int.	15.8	87.95	
DWC39X40M	3-9	41-15	3.5	12.75	1	Int.	13	73.95	
MAG321X40	3-12	26.5-7.3	3	14	1	Int.	18	95.95	
DWC416X40	4-16	22.5-5-9	3.7	14	1	Int.	16	103.95	
DWC416X50	4-16	28-7	3	16	1	Int.	20.5	123.95	
ProPoint									
PDP2	1	40	Un.	5	1	Int.	5.5	117.95	
PDP3CMP	1	68	Un.	4.75	1	Int.	5.4	167.06	
PDP3	1	52	Un.	5	1	Int.	5.5	137.95	
PD3ST1	1	52	Un.	5	1	Int.	5.5	143.95	
PDPRGD	1	60	Un.	5.4	1	Int.	5.7	91.95	
Golden Antler									
DMGA39X32T	3-9	39-13	3	13.5	1	Int.	12.2	49.95	
DMGA4X32T	4	32	3	13.25	1	Int.	11	37.95	
GA3940	3-9	41-15	3	12.75	1	Int.	13	57.95	
GA2532CB	2.5	43	3.2	11.4	1	Int.	10.1	43.95	
GA3932AGD	3-9	39	3	13.25	1	Int.	12	43.95	
Pronghorn									
PH39X40D	3-9	39-13	3	13	1	Int.	12.1	47.95	
PH39X32S	3-9	39-13	3	12	1	Int.	11	41.95	
PH4X32D	4	32	3	12	1	Int.	11	32.95	
PH2533	2.5	43	3.2	11.4	1	Int.	10.1	32.95	
PH3950D	3-9	33	3.3	13	1	Int.	14.8	57.95	
.22 Riflescopes									
MAG39X32D	3-9	17.75-6	3	12.75	1	Int.	11.3	55.95	
MAG4X32SD	4	13.5	3	12.75	1	Int.	12.1	43.95	
MAG4X32STD	4	13.5	3	12.75	1	Int.	21.1	43.95	
Rimfire									
EZ01D	1	35	Un.	4.75	1	Int.	2.5	17.95	
RF37X20D	3-7	24	2.5	11.5	1	Int.	5.7	23.95	
RF4X15D	4	20.5	2.5	11	1	Int.	3.8	7.95	
RF4X20WAD	4	23	2.5	10.5	1	Int.	3.8	9.95	
Red Dot									
BKR30	1	57	Un.	3.75	1	Int.	6	45.95	
BKR3022* (22 rimfire)	1	57	Un.	3.75	1	Int.	6	45.95	
BKR42	1	62	Un.	3.75	1	Int.	6.7	57.95	

SCOPES / Hunting, Target & Varmint

Maker and Model	Magn.	Field at 100 Yds. (feet)	Eye Relief (in.)	Length (in.)	Tube Dia. (in.)	W & E Adjustments	Weight (ozs.)	Price	Other Data
THOMPSON/CENTER RECOIL PROOF SERIES									
Pistol Scopes									
8315[2]	2.5-7	15-5	8-21, 8-11	9.25	1	Int.	9.2	364.00	[1]Black finish; silver optional. [2]Black; lighted reticle. From Thompson/Center Arms.
8326[4]	2.5-7	15-5	8-21, 8-11	9.25	1	Int.	10.5	432.00	
Muzzleloader Scopes									
8658	1	60	3.8	9.125	1	Int.	10.2	146.00	
8662	4	16	3	8.8	1	Int.	9.1	141.00	
TRIJICON									
ReflexII 1x24	1		4.25			Int.	4.2	425.00	[1]Advanced Combat Optical Gunsight for AR-15, M16, with integral mount. Other mounts available. All models feature tritium and fiber optics dual-lighting system that requires no batteries. From Trijicon, Inc.
TA44 1.5x16[1]	1.5	39	2.4	5.34		Int.	5.31	895.00	
TA45 1.5x24[1]	1.5	25.6	3.6	5.76		Int.	5.92	950.00	
TA47 2x20[1]	2	33.1	2.1	5.3		Int.	5.82	950.00	
TA50 3x24[1]	3	29.5	1.4	5		Int.	5.89	950.00	
TA11 3.5x35[1]	3.5	25.6	2.4	8		Int.	14	1,295.00	
TA01 4x32[1]	4	36.8	1.5	5.8		Int.	9.9	950.00	
Variable AccuPoint									
3-9x40	3-9	33.8-11.3	3.6-3.2	12.2	1	Int.	12.8	720.00	
1.25-4x24	1.25-4	61.6-20.5	4.8-3.4	10.2	1	Int.	11.4	700.00	
ULTRA DOT									
Micro-Dot Scopes[1]									
1.5-4.5x20 Rifle	1.5-4.5	80-26	3	9.8	1	Int.	10.5	297.00	[1]Brightness-adjustable fiber optic red dot reticle. Waterproof, nitrogen-filled one-piece tube. Tinted see-through lens covers and battery included. [2]Parallax adjustable. [3]Ultra Dot sights include rings, battery, polarized filter, and 5-year warranty. All models available in black or satin finish. [4]Illuminated red dot has eleven brightness settings. Shock-proof aluminum tube. From Ultra Dot Distribution.
2-7x32	2-7	54-18	3	11	1	Int.	12.1	308.00	
3-9x40	3-9	40-14	3	12.2	1	Int.	13.3	327.00	
4x-12x56[2]	4-12	30-10	3	14.3	1	Int.	18.3	417.00	
Ultra-Dot Sights[3]									
Ultra-Dot 25[4]	1			5.1	1	Int.	3.9	159.00	
Ultra-Dot 30[4]	1			5.1	30mm	Int.	4	179.00	
UNERTL									
1" Target	6, 8, 10	16-10	2	21.5	.75	Ext.	21	675.00	[1]Dural .25-MOA click mounts. Hard coated lenses. Non-rotating objective lens focusing. [2].25-MOA click mounts. [3]With target mounts. [4]With calibrated head. [5]Same as 1" Target but without objective lens focusing. [6]With new Posa mounts. [7]Range focus unit near rear of tube. Price is with Posa or standard mounts. Magnum clamp. From Unertl.
10X	10	10.3	3	12.5	1	Ext.	35	2,500.00	
1.25" Target[1]	8, 10, 12, 14	12-16	2	25	.75	Ext.	21	715.00	
1.5" Target	10, 12, 14, 16, 18, 20	11.5-3.2	2.25	25.5	.75	Ext.	31	753.50	
2" Target[2]	10, 12, 14, 16, 18, 24, 30, 32, 36	8	2.25	26.25	1	Ext.	44	918.50	
Varmint, 1.25"[3] 3" Ultra Varmint, 2"[4]	15	12.6-7	2.25	24	1	Ext.	34	918.50	
Small Game[5]	3, 4, 6	25-17	2.25	18	.75	Ext.	16	550.00	
Programmer 200[7]	10, 12, 14, 16, 18, 20, 24, 30, 36	11.3-4		26.5	1	Ext.	45	1,290.00	
B8									
Tube Sight				17		Ext.		420.00	
U.S. OPTICS									
SN-1/TAR Fixed Power System									
16.2x	15	8.6	4.3	16.5	30mm	Int.	27	1,700.00	Prices shown are estimates; scopes built to order; choice of reticles; choice of front or rear focal plane; extra-heavy MIL-SPEC construction; extra-long turrets; individual W&E rebound springs; up to 100mm dia. objectives; up to 50mm tubes; all lenses multi-coated. Other magnifications available. [1]Modular components allow a variety of fixed or variable magnifications, night vision, etc. Made in U.S. by U.S. Optics.
22.4x	20	5.8	3.8	18	30mm	Int.	29	1,800.00	
26x	24	5	3.4	18	30mm	Int.	31	1,900.00	
31x	30	4.6	3.5	18	30mm	Int.	32	2,100.00	
37x	36	4	3.6	18	30mm	Int.	32	2,300.00	
48x	50	3	3.8	18	30mm	Int.	32	2,500.00	
Variables									
SN-2	4-22	26.8-5.8	5.4-3.8	18	30mm	Int.	24	1,762.00	
SN-3	1.6-8		4.4-4.8	18.4	30mm	Int.	36	1,435.00	
SN-4	1-4	116-31.2	4.6-4.9	18	30mm	Int.	35	1,065.00	
Fixed Power									
SN-6	8, 10, 17, 22	14-8.5	3.8-4.8	9.2	30mm	Int.	18	1,195.00	
SN-8 Modular[1]	4, 10, 20, 40	32	3.3	7.5	30mm	Int.	11.1	890.00-4,000.00	
WEAVER									
Riflescopes									
K2.5[1]	2.5	35	3.7	9.5	1	Int.	7.3	132.86	[1]Gloss black. [2]Matte black. [3]Silver. [4]Satin. [5]Silver and black (slightly higher in price). [6]Field of view measured at 18" eye relief. .25 MOA click adjustments, except T-Series which vary from .125 to .25 clicks. One-piece tubes with multi-coated lenses. All scopes are shock-proof, waterproof, and fogproof. Dual-X reticle available in all except V24 which has a fine X-hair and dot; T-Series in which certain models are available in fine X-hair and dots; Qwik-Point red dot scopes which are available in fixed 4 or 12 MOA, or variable 4-8-12 MOA. V16 also available with fine X-hair, dot or Dual-X reticle. T-Series scopes have Micro-Trac® adjustments. From Weaver Products.
K4[1,2]	3.7	26.5	3.3	11.3	1	Int.	10	149.99	
K6[1]	5.7	18.5	3.3	11.4	1	Int.	10	154.99	
KT15[1]	14.6	7.5	3.2	12.9	1	Int.	14.7	281.43	
V3[1,2]	1.1-2.8	88-32	3.9-3.7	9.2	1	Int.	8.5	189.99	
V9[1,2]	2.8-8.7	33-11	3.5-3.4	12.1	1	Int.	11.1	249.99-299.99	
V9x50[1,2]	3-9	29.4-9.9	3.6-3	13.1	1	Int.	14.5	239.99	
V10[1-3]	2.2-9.6	38.5-9.5	3.4-3.3	12.2	1	Int.	11.2	259.99-269.99	
V10-50[1-3]	2.3-9.7	40.2-9.2	2.9-2.8	13.75	1	Int.	15.2	279.99	
V16 MDX[2,3]	3.8-15.5	26.8-6.8	3.1	13.9	1	Int.	16.5	329.99	
V16 MFC[2,3]	3.8-15.5	26.8-6.8	3.1	13.9	1	Int.	16.5	329.99	
V16 MDT[2,3]	3.8-15.5	26.8-6.8	3.1	13.9	1	Int.	16.5	329.99	
V24 Varmint[2]	6-24	15.3-4	3.15	14.3	1	Int.	17.5	379.99-399.99	
Handgun									
H2[1-3]	2	21	4-29	8.5	1	Int.	6.7	161.43	
H4[1-3]	4	18	11.5-18	8.5	1	Int.	6.7	175.00	
VH4[1-3]	1.5-4	13.6-5.8	11-17	8.6	1	Int.	8.1	215.71	
VH8[1-3]	2.5-8	8.5-3.7	12.16	9.3	1	Int.	8.3	228.57	
Rimfire									
RV7[2]	2.5-7	37-13	3.7-3.3	10.75	1	Int.	10.7	148.57	
Grand Slam									
6-20x40mm Varminter Reticle[2]	6-20X	16.5-5.25	2.75-3	14.48	1	Int.	17.75	419.99	

SCOPES / Hunting, Target & Varmint

Maker and Model	Magn.	Field at 100 Yds. (feet)	Eye Relief (in.)	Length (in.)	Tube Dia. (in.)	W & E Adjustments	Weight (ozs.)	Price	Other Data
WEAVER *(cont.)*									
6-20x40mm Fine Crosshairs w/Dot[2]	6-20X	16.5-5.25	2.75-3	14.48	1	Int.	17.75	419.99	
1.5-5x32mm[2]	1.5-5X	71-21	3.25	10.5	1	Int.	10.5	349.99	
4.75x40mm[2]	4.75X	14.75	3.25	11	1	Int.	10.75	299.99	
3-10x40mm[2]	3-10X	35-11.33	3.5-3	12.08	1	Int.	12.08	329.99	
3.5-10x50mm[2]	3.5-10X	30.5-10.8	3.5-3	12.96	1	Int.	16.25	389.99	
4.5-14x40mm	4.5-14X	22.5-10.5	3.5-3	14.48	1	Int.	17.5	399.99	
T-Series									
T-64	614	14	3.58	12.75	1	Int.	14.9	424.95	
T-36[3-4]	36	3	3	15.1	1	Int.	16.7	489.99	
ZEISS									
ZM/Z									
6x42MC	6	22.9	3.2	12.7	1	Int.	13.4	749.00	[1]Also avail. with illuminated reticle. [2]Illuminated Vari-point reticle.
8x56MC	8	18	3.2	13.8	1	Int.	17.6	829.00	Black matte finish. All scopes have .25-min. click-stop adjustments.
1.25-4x24MC	1.25-4	105-33	3.2	11.46	30mm	Int.	17.3	779.00	Choice of Z-Plex or fine crosshair reticles. Rubber armored objective
1.5-6x42MC	1.5-6	65.5-22.9	3.2	12.4	30mm	Int.	18.5	899.00	bell, rubber eyepiece ring. Lenses have T-Star coating for highest
2.5-10x48MC[1]	2.5-10	33-11.7	3.2	14.5	30mm	Int.	24	1,029.00	light transmission. VM/V scopes avail. with rail mount. Partial listing
3-12x56MC[1]	3-12	27.6-9.9	3.2	15.3	30mm	Int.	25.8	1,099.00	shown. From Carl Zeiss Optical, Inc.
Conquest									
3-9x40MC[3]	3-9	37.5	3.34	12.30	1	Int.	17.28	499.99	[1]Stainless [2]Turkey reticle. [3]Black matte finish. All scopes have .25-
3-9x40MC[1]	3-9	37.5	3.34	12.36	1	Int.	17.28	529.99	min. click-stop adjustments. Choice of Z-Plex, Turkey or fine
3-9x40S[3]	3-9	37.5	3.34	12.36	1	Int.	17.28	499.99	crosshair reticles. Coated lenses for highest light transmisison. Partial
3-9x40S[2,3]	3-9	37.5	3.34	12.36	1	Int	17.28	529.99	listing shown. From Carl Zeiss Optical, Inc.
3-12x56MC[3]	2.5-10	27.6	3.2	15.3	30mm	Int.	25.8	1,049.00	
3-12x56MC[1]	3-12	27.6	3.2	15.3	30mm	Int.	25.8	1,079.00	
VM/V									
1.1-4x24 VariPoint T[2]	1.1-4	120-34	3.5	11.8	30mm	Int.	15.8	1,699.00	
1.5-6x42T*	1.5-6	65.5-22.9	3.2	12.4	30mm	Int.	18.5	1,299.00	
2.5-10x50T*[1]	2.5-10	47.1-13	3.5	12.5	30mm	Int.	16.25	1,499.00	
3-12x56T*	3-12	37.5-10.5	3.5	13.5	30mm	Int.	19.5	1,499.00	
3-9x42T*	3-9	42-15	3.74	13.3	1	Int.	15.3	1,999.00	
5-15x42T*	5-15	25.7-8.5	3.74	13.3	1	Int.	15.4	1,399.00	

Hunting scopes in general are furnished with a choice of reticlecrosshairs, post with crosshairs, tapered or blunt post, or dot crosshairs, etc.
The great majority of target and varmint scopes have medium or fine crosshairs but post or dot reticles may be ordered.
W=windage; E=Elevation; MOA=Minute of Angle or 1" (approx.) at 100 yards.

LASER SIGHTS

Lasergrips LG-206

Alpec Mini Shot

Laser Devices ULS 2001 with TLS 8R light

Maker and Model	Wave length (nm)	Beam Color	Lens	Operating Temp. (degrees F.)	Weight (ozs.)	Price	Other Data
ALPEC							[1]Range 1000 yards. [2]Range 300 yards. Mini Shot II range 500 yards, output 650mm, **$129.95**. [3]Range 300 yards; Laser Shot II 500 yards; Super Laser Shot 1000 yards.
Power Shot[1]	635	Red	Glass	NA	2.5	$199.95	Black or stainless finish aluminum; removable pressure or push-button switch.
Mini Shot[2]	670	Red	Glass	NA	2.5	$99.95	Mounts for most handguns, many rifles and shotguns. From Alpec Team, Inc.
Laser Shot[3]	670	Red	Glass	NA	3.0	$99.95	
BEAMSHOT							[1]Black or silver finish; adj. for windage and elevation; 300-yd. range; also M1000/S (500-yd. range), M1000/u (800-yd.). [2]Black finish; 300-, 500-, 800-yd. models. All come with removable touch pad switch, 5" cable. Mounts to fit virtually any firearm. From Quarton USA Co.
1000[1]	670	Red	Glass	NA	3.8	NA	
3000[2]	635/670	Red	Glass	NA	2.0	NA	
1001/u	635	Red	Glass	NA	3.8	NA	
780	780	Red	Glass	NA	3.8	NA	
BSA							[1]Comes with mounts for 22/air rifle and Weaver-style bases.
LS650[1]	N/A	Red	NA	NA	NA	$49.95	
LASERAIM							[1]Red dot/laser combo; 300-yd. range: LA3xHD Hotdot has 500-yd. range **$249.00**; 4 MOA dot size, laser gives 2" dot size at 100 yds. 230mm obj. lens; [4]MOA dot at 100 yds: fits Weaver base. 3300-yd range; 2" dot at 100 yds.; rechargeable Nicad
LA10 Hotdot[4]				NA	NA	$199.00	battery 41.5-mile range; 1" dot at 100 yds.; 20+ hrs. batt. life. [5]1.5-mile range; 1"
Lasers							at 100 yds; rechargeable Nicad battery (comes with in-field charger); [6]Black or satin finish. With mount, **$169.00**. [7]Laser projects 2" dot at 100 yds.: with rotary switch; with Hotdot **$237.00**; with Hotdot touch switch **$357.00**. [8]For Glock 17-27; G1 Hotdot
MA-35RB Mini Aimer[7]				NA	1.0	$129.00	**$299.00**; price installed. [10]Fits std. Weaver base, no rings required; 6-MOA dot;
G1 Laser[8]				NA	2.0	$229.00	seven brightness settings. All have W&E adj.; black or satin silver finish. From Laser-aim Technologies, Inc.
LASER DEVICES							[1]For S&W P99 semi-auto pistols; also BA-2, 5 oz., **$339.00**. [2]For revolvers. [3]For HK, Walther P99. [4]For semi-autos. [5]For rifles; also FA-4/ULS, 2.5 oz., **$325.00**. [6]For
BA-1[1]	632	Red	Glass	NA	2.4	$372.00	HK sub guns. [7]For military rifles. [8]For shotguns. [9]For SIG-Pro pistol. [10]Universal,
BA-3[3]	632	Red	Glass	NA	3.3	$332.50	semi-autos. [11]For AR-15 variants. All avail. with Magnum Power Point (650nM) or
BA-5[3]	632	Red	Glass	NA	3.2	$372.00	daytime-visible Super Power Point (632nM) diode. Infrared diodes avail. for law
Duty-Grade[4]	632	Red	Glass	NA	3.5	$372.00	enforcement. From Laser Devices, Inc.
FA-4[5]	632	Red	Glass	NA	2.6	$358.00	
LasTac[1]	632	Red	Glass	NA	5.5	$298.00 to 477.00	
MP-5[6]	632	Red	Glass	NA	2.2	$495.00	
MR-2[7]	632	Red	Glass	NA	6.3	$485.00	
SA-2[8]	632	Red	Glass	NA	3.0	$360.00	
SIG-Pro[9]	632	Red	Glass	NA	2.6	$372.00	
ULS-2001[10]	632	Red	Glass	NA	4.5	$210.95	
Universal AR-2A	632	Red	Glass	NA	4.5	$445.00	
LASERGRIPS							Replaces existing grips with built-in laser high in the right grip panel. Integrated pressure sensitive pad in grip activates the laser. Also has master on/off switch.
LG-201[1]	633	Red-Orange	Glass	NA		$299.00	[1]For Colt 1911/Commander. [2]For all Glock models. Option on/off switch. Requires
LG-206[3]	633	Red-Orange	Glass	NA		$229.00	factory installation. [3]For S&W K, L, N frames, round or square butt (LG-207); [4]For
LG-085[4]	633	Red-Orange	Glass	NA		$229.00	Taurus small-frame revolvers. [5]For Ruger SP-101. [6]For SIG Sauer P226. From
LG-101[5]	633	Red-Orange	Glass	NA		$229.00	Crimson Trace Corp. [7]For Beretta 92/96. [8]For Ruger MK II. [9]For S&W J-frame. [10]For
LG-226[6]	633	Red-Orange	Glass	NA		$229.00	Sig Sauer P228/229. [11]For Colt 1911 full size, wraparound. [12]For Beretta 92/96,
GLS-630[2]	633	Red-Orange	Glass	NA		$595.00	wraparound. [13]For Colt 1911 compact, wraparound. [14]For S&W J-frame, rubber.
LG-202[7]	633	Red-Orange	Glass	NA		$299.00	
LG-203[8]	633	Red-Orange	Glass	NA		$299.00	
LG-205[9]	633	Red-Orange	Glass	NA		$299.00	
LG-229[10]	633	Red-Orange	Glass	NA		$299.00	
LG-301[11]	633	Red-Orange	Glass	NA		$329.00	
LG-302[12]	633	Red-Orange	Glass	NA		$329.00	
LG-304[13]	633	Red-Orange	Glass	NA		$329.00	
LG-305[14]	633	Red-Orange	Glass	NA		$299.00	
LASERLYTE							[1]Dot/circle or dot/crosshair projection; black or stainless. [2]Also 635/645mm model. From Tac Star Laserlyte. in grip activates the laser. Also has master on/off switch.
LLX-0006-140/090[1]	635/645	Red		NA	1.4	$159.95	
WPL-0004-140/090[2]	670	Red		NA	1.2	$109.95	
TPL-0004-140/090[2]	670	Red		NA	1.2	$109.95	
T7S-0004-140[2]	670	Red		NA	0.8	$109.95	
LASERMAX							Replaces the recoil spring guide rod; includes a customized takedown lever that serves as the laser's insta in grip activates the laser. Also has master on/off switch.
LMS-1000 Internal Guide Rod	635	Red-Orange	Glass	40-120	.25	$389.00	[1]For Colt 1911/Commant on/off switch. For Glock, Smith & Wesson, SIGARMS, Beretta, Colt, Kimber, Springfield Gov't. Model 1911, Heckler & Koch and select Taurus models. Installs in most pistols without gunsmithing. Battery life 1/2-hour to 2 hours in continuous use. From Laser Max.

Maker, Model, Type	Adjust.	Scopes	Price
ADCO			
Std. Black or nickel		1"	$13.95
Std. Black or nickel		30mm	$13.95
Rings Black or nickel		30mm with 3/8" grv.	$13.95
Rings Black or nickel		1" raised 3/8" grv.	$13.95
AIMTECH			
AMT Auto Mag II .22 Mag.	No	Weaver rail	$56.99
Astra .44 Mag Revolver	No	Weaver rail	$63.25
Beretta/Taurus 92/99	No	Weaver rail	$63.25
Browning Buckmark/Challenger II	No	Weaver rail	$56.99
Browning Hi-Power	No	Weaver rail	$63.25
Glock 17, 17L, 19, 23, 24 etc. no rail	No	Weaver rail	$63.25
Glock 20, 21 no rail	No	Weaver rail	$63.25
Glock 9mm and .40 with access. rail	No	Weaver rail	$74.95
Govt. 45 Auto/.38 Super	No	Weaver rail	$63.25
Hi-Standard (Mitchell version) 107	No	Weaver rail	$63.25
H&K USP 9mm/40 rail mount	No	Weaver rail	$74.95
Rossi 85/851/951 Revolvers	No	Weaver rail	$63.25
Ruger Mk I, Mk II	No	Weaver rail	$49.95
Ruger P85/P89	No	Weaver rail	$63.25
S&W K, L, N frames	No	Weaver rail	$63.25
S&W K, L, N with tapped top strap*	No	Weaver rail	$69.95
S&W Model 41 Target 22	No	Weaver rail	$63.25
S&W Model 52 Target 38	No	Weaver rail	$63.25
S&W Model 99 Walther frame rail mount	No	Weaver rail	$74.95
S&W 2nd Gen. 59/459/659 etc.	No	Weaver rail	$56.99
S&W 3rd Gen. full size 5906 etc.	No	Weaver rail	$69.95
S&W 422, 622, 2206	No	Weaver rail	$56.99
S&W 645/745	No	Weaver rail	$56.99
S&W Sigma	No	Weaver rail	$64.95
Taurus PT908	No	Weaver rail	$63.25
Taurus 44 6.5" bbl.	No	Weaver rail	$69.95
Walther 99	No	Weaver rail	$74.95
Shotguns			
Benelli M-1 Super 90	No	Weaver rail	$44.95
Benelli Montefeltro	No	Weaver rail	$44.95
Benelli Nova	No	Weaver rail	$69.95
Benelli Super Black Eagle	No	Weaver rail	$49.95
Browning A-5 12-ga.	No	Weaver rail	$40.95
Browning BPS 12-ga.	No	Weaver rail	$40.95
Browning Gold Hunter 12-ga.	No	Weaver rail	$44.95
Browning Gold Hunter 20-ga.	No	Weaver rail	$49.95
Browning Gold Hunter 10-ga.	No	Weaver rail	$49.95
Beretta 303 12-ga.	No	Weaver rail	$44.95
Beretta 390 12-ga.	No	Weaver rail	$44.95
Beretta Pintail	No	Weaver rail	$44.95
H&K Fabarms Gold/Silver Lion	No	Weaver rail	$49.95
Ithaca 37/87 12-ga.	No	Weaver rail	$40.95
Ithaca 37/87 20-ga.	No	Weaver rail	$40.95
Mossberg 500/Maverick 12-ga.	No	Weaver rail	$40.95
Mossberg 500/Maverick 20-ga.	No	Weaver rail	$40.95
Mossberg 835 3.5" Ulti-Mag	No	Weaver rail	$40.95
Mossberg 5500/9200	No	Weaver rail	$40.95
Remington 1100/1187 12-ga.	No	Weaver rail	$42.80
Remington 1100/1187 12-ga. LH	No	Weaver rail	$42.80
Remington 1100/1187 20-ga.	No	Weaver rail	$40.95
Remington 1100/1187 20-ga. LH	No	Weaver rail	$40.95
Remington 870 12-ga.	No	Weaver rail	$40.95
Remington 870 12-ga. LH	No	Weaver rail	$40.95
Remington 870 20-ga.	No	Weaver rail	$42.80
Remington 870 20-ga. LH	No	Weaver rail	$42.80
Remington 870 Express Magnum	No	Weaver rail	$40.95
Remington SP-10 10-ga.	No	Weaver rail	$49.95
Winchester 1300 12-ga.	No	Weaver rail	$40.95
Winchester 1400 12-ga.	No	Weaver rail	$40.95
Winchester Super X2	No	Weaver rail	$44.95
"Rib Rider" Ultra Low Profile Mounts Non See-Through 2-piece rib attached			
Mossberg 500/835/9200	No	Weaver rail	$29.95
Remington 1100/1187/870	No	Weaver rail	$29.95
Winchester 1300	No	Weaver rail	$29.95
1-Piece Rib Rider Low Rider Mounts			
Mossberg 500/835/9200	No	Weaver rail	$29.95
Remington 1100/1187/870	No	Weaver rail	$29.95
Winchester 1300	No	Weaver rail	$29.95
2-Piece Rib Rider See-Through			
Mossberg 500/835/9200	No	Weaver rail	$29.95
Remington 1100/1187/870	No	Weaver rail	$29.95
Winchester 1300	No	Weaver rail	$29.95

Maker, Model, Type	Adjust.	Scopes	Price
AIMTECH (cont.)			
1-Piece Rib Rider See-Through			
Mossberg 500/835/9200	No	Weaver rail	$29.95
Remington 1100/1187/870	No	Weaver rail	$29.95
Winchester 1300	No	Weaver rail	$29.95
Rifles			
AR-15/M16	No	Weaver rail	$21.95
Browning A-Bolt	No	Weaver rail	$21.95
Browning BAR	No	Weaver rail	$21.95
Browning BLR	No	Weaver rail	$21.95
CVA Apollo	No	Weaver rail	$21.95
Marlin 336	No	Weaver rail	$21.95
Mauser Mark X	No	Weaver rail	$21.95
Modern Muzzleloading	No	Weaver rail	$21.95
Remington 700 Short Action	No	Weaver rail	$21.95
Remington 700 Long Action	No	Weaver rail	$21.95
Remington 7400/7600	No	Weaver rail	$21.95
Ruger 10/22	No	Weaver rail	$21.95
Ruger Mini 14 Scout Rail**	No	Weaver rail	$89.50
Savage 110, 111, 113, 114, 115, 116	No	Weaver rail	$21.95
Thompson Center Thunderhawk	No	Weaver rail	$21.95
Traditions Buckhunter	No	Weaver rail	$21.95
White W Series	No	Weaver rail	$21.95
White G Series	No	Weaver rail	$21.95
White WG Series	No	Weaver rail	$21.95
Winchester Model 70	No	Weaver rail	$21.95
Winchester 94 AE	No	Weaver rail	$21.95

All mounts no-gunsmithing, iron sight usable. Rifle mounts are solid see-through bases. All mounts accommodate standard Weaver-style rings of all makers. From Aimtech division, L&S Technologies, Inc. *3-blade sight mount combination. **Replacement handguard and mounting rail.

Maker, Model, Type	Adjust.	Scopes	Price
A.R.M.S.			
M16A1, A2, AR-15	No	Weaver rail	$59.95
Multibase	No	Weaver rail	$59.95
#19 ACOG Throw Lever Mt.	No	Weaver rail	$150.00
#19 Weaver/STANAG Throw Lever Rail	No	Weaver rail	$140.00
STANAG Rings	No	30mm	$75.00
Throw Lever Rings	No	Weaver rail	$99.00
Ring Inserts	No	1", 30mm	$29.00
#22M68 Aimpoint Comp Ring Throw Lever	No		$99.00
#38 Std. Swan Sleeve[1]	No		$180.00
#39 A2 Plus Mod. Mt.	No	#39T rail	$125.00

[1]Avail. in three lengths. From A.R.M.S., Inc.

Maker, Model, Type	Adjust.	Scopes	Price
ARMSON			
AR-15[1]	No	1"	$45.00
Mini-14[2]	No	1"	$66.00
H&K[3]	No	1"	$82.00

[1]Fastens with one nut. [2]Models 181, 182, 183, 184, etc. [3]Claw mount. From Trijicon, Inc.

Maker, Model, Type	Adjust.	Scopes	Price
AO			
AO/Lever Scout Scope	No	Weaver rail	$50.00

No gunsmithing required for lever-action rifles with 8" Weaver-style rails; surrounds barrel shank; 6" long, low profile. AO Sight Systems Inc.

Maker, Model, Type	Adjust.	Scopes	Price
B-SQUARE			
Pistols (centerfire)			
Beretta 92, 96/Taurus 99	No	Weaver rail	$69.95
Colt M1911	E only	Weaver rail	$69.95
Desert Eagle	No	Weaver rail	$69.95
Glock	No	Weaver rail	$69.95
H&K USP, 9mm and 40 S&W	No	Weaver rail	$69.95
Ruger P85/89	E only	Weaver rail	$69.95
SIG Sauer P226	E only	Weaver rail	$69.95
Pistols (rimfire)			
Browning Buck Mark	No	Weaver rail	$32.95
Colt 22	No	Weaver rail	$49.95
Ruger Mk I/II, bull or taper	No	Weaver rail	$32.95-49.95
Smith & Wesson 41, 2206	No	Weaver rail	$36.95-49.95
Revolvers			
Colt Anaconda/Python	No	Weaver rail	$35.95-74.95
Ruger Single-Six	No	Weaver rail	$64.95
Ruger GP-100	No	Weaver rail	$64.95
Ruger Blackhawk, Super	No	Weaver rail	$64.95
Ruger Redhawk, Super	No	Weaver rail	$64.95

SCOPE RINGS & BASES

Maker, Model, Type	Adjust.	Scopes	Price
B-SQUARE (cont.)			
Smith & Wesson K, L, N	No	Weaver rail	$36.95-74.95
Taurus 66, 669, 607, 608	No	Weaver rail	$64.95
Rifles (sporting)			
Browning BAR, A-Bolt	No	Weaver rail	$45.90
Marlin MR7	No	Weaver rail	$45.90
Mauser 98 Large Ring	No	Weaver rail	$45.90
Mauser 91/93/95/96 Small Ring	No	Weaver rail	$45.90
Remington 700, 740, 742, 760	No	Weaver rail	$45.90
Remington 7400, 7600	No	Weaver rail	$45.90
Remington Seven	No	Weaver rail	$45.90
Rossi 62, 59 and 92	No	Weaver rail	$44.95
Ruger Mini-14	W&E	Weaver rail	$66.95
Ruger 96/22	No	Weaver rail	$45.90
Ruger M77 (short and long)	No	Weaver rail	$62.95
Ruger 10/22 (reg. and See-Thru)	No	Weaver rail	$45.90
Savage 110-116, 10-16	No	Weaver rail	$45.90
Modern Military (rings incl.)			
AK-47/MAC 90	No	Weaver rail	$49.95
Colt AR-15	No	Weaver rail	$66.95-81.95
FN/FAL/LAR (See-Thru rings)	No	Weaver rail	$81.95
Classic Military (rings incl.)			
FN 49	No	Weaver rail	$72.95
Hakim	No	Weaver rail	$72.95
Mauser 38, 94, 96, 98	E only	Weaver rail	$72.95
Mosin-Nagant (all)	E only	Weaver rail	$72.95
Air Rifles			
RWS, Diana, BSA, Gamo	W&E	11mm rail	$49.95-59.95
Weihrauch, Anschutz, Beeman, Webley	W&E	11mm rail	$59.95-69.95
Shotguns/Slug Guns			
Benelli Super 90 (See-Thru)	No	Weaver rail	$53.95
Browning BPS, A-5 9 (See-Thru)	No	Weaver rail	$53.95
Browning Gold 10/12/20-ga. (See- Thru)	No	Weaver rail	$53.95
Ithaca 37, 87	No	Weaver rail	$53.95
Mossberg 500/Mav. 88	No	Weaver rail	$53.95
Mossberg 835/Mav. 91	No	Weaver rail	$53.95
Remington 870/1100/11-87	No	Weaver rail	$53.95
Remington SP10	No	Weaver rail	$53.95
Winchester 1200-1500	No	Weaver rail	$53.95

Prices shown for anodized black finish; add $10 for stainless finish. Partial listing of mounts shown here. Contact B-Square for complete listing and details.

Maker, Model, Type	Adjust.	Scopes	Price
BEEMAN			
Two-Piece, Med.	No	1"	$31.50
Deluxe Two-Piece, High	No	1"	$33.00
Deluxe Two-Piece	No	30mm	$41.00
Deluxe One-Piece	No	1"	$50.00
Dampa Mount	No	1"	$120.00

All grooved receivers and scope bases on all known air rifles and 22-cal. rimfire rifles (1/2" to 5/8" 6mm to 15mm).

Maker, Model, Type	Adjust.	Scopes	Price
BOCK			
Swing ALK[1]	W&E	1", 26mm, 30mm	$349.00
Safari KEMEL[2]	W&E	1", 26mm, 30mm	$149.00
Claw KEMKA[3]	W&E	1", 26mm, 30mm	$224.00
ProHunter Fixed[4]	No	1", 26mm, 30mm	$95.00

[1]Q.D.: pivots right for removal. For Steyr-Mannlicher, Win. 70, Mauser 98, Dakota, Sako, Sauer 80, 90. Magnum has extra-wide rings, same price. [2]Heavy-duty claw-type reversible for front or rear removal. For Steyr-Mannlicher rifles. [3]True claw mount for bolt-action rifles. Also in extended model. For Steyr-Mannlicher, Win. 70, Rem. 700. Also avail. as Gunsmith Bases, not drilled or contoured same price. [4]Extra-wide rings. Imported from Germany by GSI, Inc.

Maker, Model, Type	Adjust.	Scopes	Price
BSA			
AA Airguns	Yes	Super Ten, 240 Magnum, Maxi gripped scope rail equipped air rifles	$59.99 (adj). $29.99 (fixed)

Maker, Model, Type	Adjust.	Scopes	Price
BURRIS			
Supreme (SU) One-Piece (T)[1]	W only	1" split rings, 3 heights	1-piece base - $23.00-27.00
Trumount (TU) Two-Piece (T)	W only	1" split rings, 3 heights	2-piece base - $21.00-30.00
Trumount (TU) Two-Piece Ext.	W only	1" split rings	$26.00
Browning 22-cal. Auto Mount[2]	No	1" split rings	$20.00
1" 22-cal. Ring Mounts[3]	No	1" split rings	$24.00-41.00
L.E.R. (LU) Mount Bases[4]	W only	1" split rings	$24.00-52.00
L.E.R. No Drill-No Tap Bases[4,7,8]	W only	1" split rings	$48.00-52.00
Extension Rings[5]	No	1" scopes	$28.00-46.00

Maker, Model, Type	Adjust.	Scopes	Price
BURRIS (cont.)			
Ruger Ring Mount[6,9]	W only	1" split rings	$50.00-68.00
Std. 1" Rings[9]		Low, medium, high heights	$29.00-43.00
Zee Rings[9]		Fit Weaver bases; medium and high heights	$29.00-44.00
Signature Rings	No	30mm split rings	$68.00
Rimfire/Airgun Rings	W only	1" split rings, med. & high	$24.00-41.00
Double Dovetail (DD) Bases	No	30mm Signature	$23.00-26.00

[1]Most popular rifles. Universal rings, mounts fit Burris, Universal, Redfield, Leupold and Browning bases. Comparable prices. [2]Browning Standard 22 Auto rifle. [3]Grooved receivers. [4]Universal dovetail; accepts Burris, Universal, Redfield, Leupold rings. For Dan Wesson, S&W, Virginian, Ruger Blackhawk, Win. 94. [5]Medium standard front, extension rear, per pair. Low standard front, extension rear per pair. [6]Compact scopes, scopes with 2" bell for M77R. [7]Selected rings and bases available with matte Safari or silver finish. [8]For S&W K, L, N frames, Colt Python, Dan Wesson with 6" or longer barrels. [9]Also in 30mm.

Maker, Model, Type	Adjust.	Scopes	Price
CATCO			
Enfield Drop-In	No	1"	$39.95

Uses Weaver-style rings (not incl.). No gunsmithing required. See-Thru design. From CATCO.

Maker, Model, Type	Adjust.	Scopes	Price
CLEAR VIEW			
Universal Rings, Mod. 101[1]	No	1" split rings	$21.95
Standard Model[2]	No	1" split rings	$21.95
Broad View[3]	No	1"	$21.95
22 Model[4]	No	3/4", 7/8", 1"	$13.95
SM-94 Winchester[5]	No	1" split rings	$23.95
94 EJ[6]	No	1" split rings	$21.95

[1]Most rifles by using Weaver-type base; allows use of iron sights. [2]Most popular rifles; allows use of iron sights. [3]Most popular rifles; low profile, wide field of view. [4]22 rifles with grooved receiver. [5]Side mount. [6]For Win. A.E. From Clear View Mfg.

Maker, Model, Type	Adjust.	Scopes	Price
CONETROL			
Huntur[1] (base & rings)	W only	1", split rings, 3 heights	$99.96
Gunnur[2] (base & rings)	W only	1", split rings, 3 heights	$119.88
Custum[3] (base & rings)	W only	1", split rings, 3 heights	$149.88
One-Piece Side Mount Base[4]	W only		
DapTar Bases[5]	W only		
Pistol Bases, 2- or 3-ring[6]	W only		
Fluted Bases[7]	W only		$149.88
Metric Rings[8]	W only	26mm, 26.5mm, 30mm	$99.96-149.88

[1]All popular rifles, including metric-drilled foreign guns. Price shown for base, two rings. Matte finish. [2]Gunnur grade has mirror-finished rings to match scopes. Satin-finish base to match guns. Price shown for base, two rings. [3]Custom grade has mirror-finished rings and mirror-finished, streamlined base. Price shown for base, two rings. [4]Win. 94, Krag, older split-bridge Mannlicher-Schoenauer, Mini-14, etc. Prices same as above. [5]For all popular guns with integral mounting provision, including Sako, BSA Ithacagun, Ruger, Tikka, H&K, BRNO and many others. Also for grooved-receiver rimfires and air rifles. Prices same as above. [6]For XP-100, T/C Contender, Colt SAA, Ruger Blackhawk, S&W and others. [7]Sculptured two-piece bases as found on fine custom rifles. Price shown is for base alone. Also available unfinished $99.96, or finished but unblued $119.88. [8]26mm, 26.5mm, and 30mm rings made in projectionless style, in three heights. Three-ring mount for T/C Contender and other pistols in Conetrol's three grades. Any Conetrol mount available in stainless steel add 50 percent. Adjust-Quik-Detach (AQD) mounting is now available from Conetrol. Jam screws return the horizontal-split rings to zero. Adjustable for windage. AQD bases $89.94. AQD rings $99.96. (Total cost of complete setup, rings and two-piece base, is $179.88).

Maker, Model, Type	Adjust.	Scopes	Price
CUSTOM QUALITY			
Custom See-Thru	No	Up to 44mm	$29.95
Dovetail 101-1 See-Thru	No	1"	$29.95
Removable Rings	No	1"	$29.95
Solid Dovetail	No	1", 30mm vertically split	$29.95
Dovetail 22 See-Thru	No	1"	$29.95

Mounts for many popular rifles. From Custom Quality Products, Inc.

Maker, Model, Type	Adjust.	Scopes	Price
EAW			
Quick-Loc Mount	W&E	1", 26mm	$315.00
	W&E	30mm	$325.00
Magnum Fixed Mount	W&E	1", 26mm	$270.00
	W&E	30mm	$285.00

Fit most popular rifles. Available in 4 heights, 4 extensions. Reliable return to zero. Stress-free mounting. Imported by New England Custom Gun Svc.

Maker, Model, Type	Adjust.	Scopes	Price
EXCEL INDUSTRIES, INC.			
Titanium Weaver-Style Rings	No	1" and 30mm, low and high	$179.00
Steel Weaver-Style Rings	No	1" and 30mm, low and high	$149.00
Flashlight Mounts - Titanium and Steel	No	1" and 30mm, low and high	$89.50/75.00

SCOPE RINGS & BASES

Maker, Model, Type	Adjust.	Scopes	Price
GENTRY			
Feather-Light Rings and Bases	No	1", 30mm	$90.00-125.00

Bases for Rem. Seven, 700, Mauser 98, Browning A-Bolt, Weatherby Mk. V, Win. 70, HVA, Dakota. Two-piece base for Rem. Seven, chrome-moly or stainless. Rings in matte, regular blue, or stainless gray; four heights. From David Gentry.

Maker, Model, Type	Adjust.	Scopes	Price
GRIFFIN & HOWE			
Topmount[1]	No	1", 30mm	$625.00
Sidemount[2]	No	1", 30mm	$255.00
Garand Mount[3]	No	1"	$255.00

[1]Quick-detachable, double-lever mount with 1" rings, installed; with 30mm rings $875.00. [2]Quick-detachable, double-lever mount with 1" rings; with 30mm rings $375.00; installed, 1" rings. $405.00; installed, 30mm rings $525.00. [3]Price installed, with 1" rings $405.00. From Griffin & Howe.

Maker, Model, Type	Adjust.	Scopes	Price
G. G. & G.			
Remington 700 Rail	No	Weaver base	$135.00
Sniper Grade Rings	No	30mm	$159.95
M16/AR15 F.I.R.E. Std.[1]	No	Weaver rail	$75.00
M16/AR15 F.I.R.E. Scout	No	Weaver rail	$82.95
Aimpoint Standard Ring	No		$164.95
Aimpoint Cantilever Ring	No	Weaver rail	$212.00

[1]For M16/A3, AR15 flat top receivers; also in extended length. [2]For Aimpoint 5000 and Comp; quick detachable; spare battery compartment. [3]Low profile; quick release. From G. G. & G.

Maker, Model, Type	Adjust.	Scopes	Price
IRONSIGHTER			
Ironsighter See-Through Mounts[1]	No	1" split rings	$29.40-64.20
Ironsighter S-9[4]	No	1" split rings	$45.28
Ironsighter AR-15/M-16[8]	No	1", 30mm	$70.10
Ironsighter 22-Cal.Rimfire[2]	No	1"	$18.45
Model #570[9]	No	1" split rings	$29.40
Model #573[9]	No	30mm split rings	$45.28
Model #727[3]	No	.875" split rings	$18.45
Blackpowder Mount[7]	No		$34.20-78.25

[1]Most popular rifles. Rings have oval holes to permit use of iron sights. [2]For 1" dia. scopes. [3]For .875 dia. scopes. [4]For 1" dia. extended eye relief scopes. [7]Fits most popular blackpowder rifles; two-piece (CVA, Knight, Marlin and Austin & Halleck) and one-piece integral (T/C). [8]Model 716 with 1" #540 rings; fits Weaver-style bases. Some models in stainless finish. [9]New detachable Weaver-style rings fit all Weaver-style bases. **Price: $26.95.** From Ironsighter Co.

Maker, Model, Type	Adjust.	Scopes	Price
K MOUNT By KENPATABLE			
Shotgun Mount	No	1", laser or red dot device	$49.95
SKS[1]	No	1"	$39.95

Wrap-around design; no gunsmithing required. Models for Browning BPS, A-5 12-ga., Sweet 16, 20, Rem. 870/1100 (LTW, and L.H.), S&W 916, Mossberg 500, Ithaca 37 & 51 12-ga., S&W 1000/3000, Win. 1400. [1]Requires simple modification to gun. From KenPatable Ent.

Maker, Model, Type	Adjust.	Scopes	Price
KRIS MOUNTS			
Side-Saddle[1]	No	1", 26mm split rings	$12.98
Two-Piece (T)[2]	No	1", 26mm split rings	$8.98
One Piece (T)[3]	No	1", 26mm split rings	$12.98

[1]One-piece mount for Win. 94. [2]Most popular rifles and Ruger. [3]Blackhawk revolver. Mounts have oval hole to permit use of iron sights.

Maker, Model, Type	Adjust.	Scopes	Price
KWIK-SITE			
Adapter	No	1"	$27.95-57.95
KS-W2[2]	No	1"	$21.95
KS-W94[3]	No	1"	$42.95
KS-WEV (Weaver-style rings)	No	1"	$19.95
KS-WEV-HIGH	No	1"	$19.95
KS-T22 1"[4]	No	1"	$17.95
KS-FL Flashlite[5]	No	Mini or C cell flash light	$37.95
KS-T88[6]	No	1"	$21.95
KS-T89	No	30mm	$21.95
KSN 22 See-Thru	No	1", 7/8"	$17.95
KSN-T22	No	1", 7/8"	$17.95
KSN-M-16 See-Thru (for M16 + AR-15)	No	1"	$49.95
KS-202[1]	No	1"	$27.97
KS-203	No	30mm	$42.95
KSBP[7]	No	Integral	$76.95
KSB Base Set	No		$5.95
Combo Bases & Rings	No	1"	$21.95

Bases interchangeable with Weaver bases. [1]Most rifles. Allows use of iron sights. [2]22-cal rifles with grooved receivers. Allows use of iron sights. [3]Model 94, 94 Big Bore. No drilling or tapping. Also in adjustable model $57.95. [4]Non-See-Thru model for grooved receivers. [5]Allows C-cell or Mini Mag Lites to be mounted atop See-Thru mounts. [6]Fits any Redfield, Tasco, Weaver or Universal-style Kwik-Site dovetail base. [7]Blackpowder mount with integral rings and sights. [8]Shotgun side mount. Bright blue, black matte or satin finish. Standard, high heights.

Maker, Model, Type	Adjust.	Scopes	Price
LASER AIM	No	Laser Aim	$19.99-69.00

Mounts Laser Aim above or below barrel. Available for most popular hand guns, rifles, shotguns, including militaries. From Laser Aim Technologies, Inc.

Maker, Model, Type	Adjust.	Scopes	Price
LEUPOLD			
STD Bases[1]	W only	One- or two-piece bases	$25.40
STD Rings[2]		1" super low, low, medium, high	$33.60
DD RBH Handgun Mounts[2]	No		$34.00
Dual Dovetail Bases[3]	No		$25.40
Dual Dovetail Rings[8]		1", low, med, high	$33.60
Ring Mounts[4,5,6]	No	7/8", 1"	$102.80
22 Rimfire[8]	No	7/8", 1"	$73.60
Gunmaker Base[7]	W only	1"	$73.60
Quick Release Rings		1", low, med., high	$43.00-81.00
Quick Release Bases[9]	No	1", one- or two- piece	$73.60

[1]Base and two rings; Casull, Ruger, S&W, T/C; add $5.00 for silver finish. [2]Rem. 700, Win. 70-type actions. For Ruger No. 1, 77, 77/22; interchangeable with Ruger units. For dovetailed rimfire rifles. Sako; high, medium, low. [7]Must be drilled, tapped for each action. [8]13mm dovetail receiver. [9]BSA Monarch, Rem. 40x, 700, 721, 725, Ruger M77, S&W 1500, Weatherby Mark V, Vanguard, Win. M70.

Maker, Model, Type	Adjust.	Scopes	Price
MARLIN			
One-Piece QD (T)	No	1" split rings	$10.10

Most Marlin lever actions.

Maker, Model, Type	Adjust.	Scopes	Price
MILLETT			
Black Onyx Smooth		1", low, medium, high	$32.71
Chaparral Engraved		engraved	$50.87
One-Piece Bases[6]	Yes	1"	$26.41
Universal Two-Piece Bases			
700 Series	W only	Two-piece bases	$26.41
FN Series	W only	Two-piece bases	$26.41
70 Series[1]	W only	1", two-piece bases	$26.41
Angle-Loc Rings[2]	W only	1", low, medium, high	$35.49
Ruger 77 Rings[3]		1"	$38.14
Shotgun Rings[4]		1"	$32.55
Handgun Bases, Rings[5]		1"	$36.07-80.38
30mm Rings[7]		30mm	$20.95-41.63
Extension Rings[8]		1"	$40.43-56.44
See-Thru Mounts[9]	No	1"	$29.35-31.45
Shotgun Mounts[10]	No	1"	$52.45
Timber Mount	No	1"	$81.90

BRNO, Rem. 40x, 700, 722, 725, 7400 Ruger 77 (round top), Marlin, Weatherby, FN Mauser, FN Brownings, Colt 57, Interarms Mark X, Parker-Hale, Savage 110, Sako (round receiver), many others. [1]Fits Win. M70 70XTR, 670, Browning BBR, BAR, BLR, A-Bolt, Rem. 7400/7600, Four, Six, Marlin 336, Win. 94 A. E., Sav. 110. [2]To fit Weaver-type bases. [3]Engraved. Smooth $34.60. [4]For Rem. 870, 1100; smooth. [5]Two- and three-ring sets for Colt Python, Trooper, Diamondback, Peacekeeper, Dan Wesson, Ruger Redhawk, Super Redhawk. [6]Turn-in bases and Weaver-style for most popular rifles and T/C Contender, XP-100 pistols. [7]Both Weaver and turn-in styles; three heights. [8]Mod. or high; ext. front std. rear, ext. rear std. front, ext. front ext. rear; $40.90 for double extension. [9]Many popular rifles, Knight MK-85, T/C Hawken, Renegade, Mossberg 500 Slugster, 835 slug. [10]Rem. 879/1100, Win. 1200, 1300/1400, 1500, Mossberg 500. Some models available in nickel at extra cost. New Angle-Loc two-piece bases fit all Weaver-style rings. In smooth, matte and nickel finishes, they are available for Browning A-Bolt, Browning BAR/BLR, Interarms MK X, FN, Mauser 98, CVA rifles with octagon barrels, CVA rifles with round receiver, Knight MK 85, Knight Wolverine, Remington 700, Sauer SHR 970, Savage 110, Winchester 70 $24.95 to $28.95. From Millett Sights.

Maker, Model, Type	Adjust.	Scopes	Price
MMC			
AK[1]	No		$39.95
FN FAL/LAR[2]	No		$59.95

[1]Fits all AK derivative receivers; Weaver-style base; low-profile scope position. [2]Fits all FAL versions; Weaver-style base. From MMC.

Maker, Model, Type	Adjust.	Scopes	Price
REDFIELD			
JR-SR (T)1. One/two-piece bases.	W only	3/4", 1", 26mm, 30mm	JR: $15.99-46.99 SR:15.99-33.49
Ring (T)[2]	No	3/4" and 1"	$27.95-29.95
Widefield See-Thru Mounts	No	1"	$15.95
Ruger Rings[4]	No	1", med., high	$30.49-36.49
Ruger 30mm[5]	No	1"	$37.99-40.99

[1]Low, med. & high, split rings. Reversible extension front rings for 1". Two-piece bases for Sako. Colt Sauer bases $39.95. Med. Top Access JR rings nickel-plated $28.95. SR two-piece ABN mount nickel-plated $22.95. [2]Split rings for grooved 22s; 30mm, black matte $42.95. [3]Used with MP scopes for S&W K, L or N frame, XP-100, T/C Contender, Ruger receivers. [4]For Ruger Model 77 rifles, medium and high; medium only for M77/22. [5]For Model 77. Also in matte finish $45.95. [6]Aluminum 22 groove mount $14.95, base and medium rings $18.95. Scout mounts available for Mosin Nagant, Schmidt Rubin K-31, 98K Mauser, Husqvarna Mauser, Persian Mauser, Turkish Mauser.

SCOPE RINGS & BASES

Maker, Model, Type	Adjust.	Scopes	Price
S&K			
Insta-Mount (T) Bases and Rings[1]	W only	Uses S&K rings only	$47.00-117.00
Conventional Rings and Bases[2]	W only	1" split rings	From $65.00
Sculptured Bases, Rings[2]	W only	1", 26mm, 30mm	From $65.00
Smooth Contoured Rings[3]	Yes	1", 26mm, 30mm	$90.00-120.00

[1]1903, A3, M1 Carbine, Lee Enfield #1. MkIII, #4, #5, M1917, M98 Mauser, AR-15, AR-180, M-14, M-1, Ger. K-43, Mini-14, M1-A, Krag, AKM, Win. 94, SKS Type 56, Daewoo, H&K. [2]Most popular rifles already drilled and tapped and Sako, Tikka dovetails. [3]No projections; weigh 1/2-oz. each; matte or gloss finish. Horizontally and vertically split rings, matte or high gloss.

Maker, Model, Type	Adjust.	Scopes	Price
SAKO			
QD Dovetail	W only	1"	$70.00-155.00

Sako, or any rifle using Sako action, 3 heights available. Stoeger, importer.

Maker, Model, Type	Adjust.	Scopes	Price
SPRINGFIELD, INC.			
M1A Third Generation	No	1" or 30mm	$123.00
M1A Standard	No	1" or 30mm	$77.00
M6 Scout Mount	No		$29.00

Weaver-style bases. From Springfield, Inc.

Maker, Model, Type	Adjust.	Scopes	Price
TALBOT			
QD Bases	No		$180.00-190.00
Rings	No	1", 30mm	$50.00-70.00

Blue or stainless steel; standard or extended bases; rings in three heights. For most popular rifles. From Talbot QD Mounts.

Maker, Model, Type	Adjust.	Scopes	Price
TASCO			
Centerfire rings	Integral	1", 30mm, matte black	$5.95
High centerfire rings	Special high	1", matte black aluminum	$5.95
.22/airgun rings	Yes	1", matte black aluminum	$5.95
.22/airgun "Quick Peep" rings	Yes	1", matte black aluminum	$5.95

Maker, Model, Type	Adjust.	Scopes	Price
THOMPSON/CENTER			
Duo-Ring Mount[1]	No	1"	$78.00
Weaver-Style Bases	No		$14.00-28.50
Weaver-Style Rings[2]	No	1"	$36.00

[1]Attaches directly to T/C Contender bbl., no drilling/tapping; also for T/C M/L rifles, needs base adapter; blue or stainless. [2]Medium and high; blue or silver finish. From Thompson/Center.

Maker, Model, Type	Adjust.	Scopes	Price
UNERTL			
1/4 Click[1]	Yes	3/4", 1" target scopes	Per set $285.00

[1]Unertl target or varmint scopes. Posa or standard mounts, less bases. From Unertl.

Maker, Model, Type	Adjust.	Scopes	Price
WARNE			
Premier Series (all steel)			
T.P.A. (Permanently Attached)	No	1", 4 heights 30mm, 2 heights	$87.75-98.55
Premier Series Rings fit Premier Series Bases			
Premier Series (all-steel Q.D. rings)			
Premier Series (all steel) Quick detachable lever	No	1", 4 heights 26mm, 2 heights 30mm, 3 heights	$129.95-131.25 $142.00
BRNO 19mm	No	1", 3 heights 30mm, 2 heights	$125.00-136.70
BRNO 16mm	No	1", 2 heights	$125.00
Ruger	No	1", 4 heights 30mm, 3 heights	$125.00-136.70
Ruger M77	No	1", 3 heights 30mm, 2 heights	$125.00-136.70
Sako Medium & Long Action	No	1", 4 heights 30mm, 3 heights	$125.00-136.70
Sako Short Action	No	1", 3 heights	$125.00
All-Steel One-Piece Base, ea.			$38.50
All-Steel Two-Piece Base, ea.			$14.00
Maxima Series (fits all Weaver-style bases)			
Permanently Attached[1]	No	1", 3 heights 30mm, 3 heights	$25.50 $36.00
Adjustable Double Lever[2]	No	1", 3 heights 30mm, 3 heights	$72.60 $80.75
Thumb Knob	No	1", 3 heights 30mm, 3 heights	$59.95 $68.25
Stainless-Steel Two-Piece Base, ea.			$15.25

Vertically split rings with dovetail clamp, precise return to zero. Fit most popular rifles, handguns. Regular blue, matte blue, silver finish. [1]All-Steel, non-Q.D. rings. [2]All-steel, Q.D. rings. From Warne Mfg. Co.

Maker, Model, Type	Adjust.	Scopes	Price
WEAVER			
Top Mount	No	7/8", 1", 30mm, 33mm	$24.95-38.95
Side Mount	No	1", 1" long	$14.95-34.95
Tip-Off Rings	No	7/8", 1"	$24.95-32.95
Pivot Mounts	No	1"	$38.95
Complete Mount Systems			
Pistol	No	1"	$75.00-105.00
Rifle	No	1"	$32.95
SKS Mount System	No	1"	$49.95
Pro-View (no base required)	No	1"	$13.95-15.95
Converta-Mount, 12-ga. (Rem. 870, Moss. 500)	No	1", 30mm	$74.95
See-Thru Mounts			
Detachable	No	1"	$27.00-32.00
System (no base required)	No	1"	$15.00-35.00
Tip-Off	No	1"	$15.00

Nearly all modern rifles, pistols, and shotguns. Detachable rings in standard, See-Thru, and extension styles, in Low, Medium, High or X-High heights; gloss (blued), silver and matte finishes to match scopes. Extension rings are only available in 1" High style and See-Thru X-tensions only in gloss finish. Tip-Off rings only for 3/8" grooved receivers or 3/8" grooved adaptor bases; no base required. See-Thru & Pro-View mounts for most modern big bore rifles, some in silver. No Drill & Tap Pistol systems in gloss or silver for Colt Python, Trooper, 357, Officer's Model, Ruger Single-Six, Security-Six (gloss finish only), Blackhawk, Super Blackhawk, Blackhawk SRM 357, Redhawk, Mini-14 Series (not Ranch), Ruger 22 Auto Pistols, Mark II, Smith & Wesson I- and current K-frames with adj. rear sights. Converta-Mount Systems in Standard and See-Under for Mossberg 500 (12- and 20-ga.), Remington 870, 11-87 (12- and 20- ga. lightweight), Winchester 1200, 1300, 1400, 1500. Converta-Brackets, bases, rings also available for Beretta A303 and A390, Browning A-5, BPS Pump, Ithaca 37, 87. From Weaver.

Maker, Model, Type	Adjust.	Scopes	Price
WEIGAND			
Browning Buck Mark[1]	No		$29.95
Integra Mounts[2]	No		$39.95-69.00
S&W Revolver[3]	No		$29.95
Ruger 10/22[4]	No		$14.95-39.95
Ruger Revolver[5]	No		$29.95
Taurus Revolver[4]	No		$29.95-65.00
Lightweight Rings	No	1", 30mm	$29.95-39.95
1911			
SM3[6]	No	Weaver rail	$99.95
APCMNT[7]	No		$69.95

[1]No gunsmithing. [2]S&W K, L, N frames, Taurus vent rib models, Colt Anaconda/Python, Ruger Redhawk, Ruger 10/22. [3]K, L, N frames. [4]Three models. [5]Redhawk, Blackhawk, GP-100. [6]3rd Gen., drill and tap, without slots $59.95. [7]For Aimpoint Comp. Red Dot scope, silver only. From Weigand Combat Handguns, Inc.

Maker, Model, Type	Adjust.	Scopes	Price
WIDEVIEW			
Premium 94 Angle Eject and side mount	No	1"	$22.44
Premium See-Thru	No	1"	$22.44
22 Premium See-Thru	No	3/4", 1"	$16.47
Universal Ring Angle Cut	No	1"	$31.28
Universal Ring Straight Cut	No	1"	$18.70
Solid Mounts			
Lo Ring Solid[1]	No	1"	$22.44
Hi Ring Solid[1]	No	1"	$18.14
SR Rings		1", 30mm	$16.32
22 Grooved Receiver	No	1"	$16.32
Blackpowder Mounts[2]	No	1"	$22.44
High, extra-high ring mounts with base	No	up to 60mm	$30.16
AR15 and M16	No		$32.92

[1]For Weaver-type base. Models for many popular rifles. Low ring, high ring and grooved receiver types. [2]No drilling, tapping, for T/C Renegade, Hawken, CVA, Knight Traditions guns. From Wideview Scope Mount Corp.

Maker, Model, Type	Adjust.	Scopes	Price
WILLIAMS			
Side Mount with HCO Rings[1]	No	1", split or extension rings	$74.35
Side Mount, Offset Rings[2]	No	Same	$61.45
Sight-Thru Mounts[3]	No	1", 7/8" sleeves	$19.50
Streamline Mounts	No	1" (bases form rings)	$26.50

[1]Most rifles, Br. S.M.L.E. (round rec.) $14.41 extra. [2]Most rifles including Win. 94 Big Bore. [3]Many modern rifles, including CVA Apollo, others with 1" octagon barrels.

Maker, Model, Type	Adjust.	Scopes	Price
YORK			
M-1 Garand	Yes	1"	$39.95

Centers scope over the action. No drilling, tapping or gunsmithing. Uses standard dovetail rings. From York M-1 Conversions.

NOTES

(S) Side Mount; (T) Top Mount; 22mm=.866"; 25.4mm=1.024"; 26.5mm=1.045"; 30mm=1.81".

METALLIC SIGHTS

Sporting Leaf and Open Sights

AUTOMATIC DRILLING REAR SIGHT Most German and Austrian drillings have this kind of rear sight. When rifle barrel is selected, the rear sight automatically comes to the upright position. Base length 2.165", width .472", folding leaf height .315". From New England Custom Gun Service.
Price: **$85.00**

CLASSIC MARBLE/WILLIAMS-STYLE FULLY ADJUSTABLE REAR SPORTING SIGHTS Screw-on attachment. Dovetailed graduated windage and elevation adjustment. Elevation and windage lock with set screws. Available in steel or lightweight alloy construction. From Sarco, Inc.
Price: **$13.50**

ERA MASTERPIECE ADJUSTABLE REAR SIGHTS Precision-machined, all-steel, polished and blued. Attaches with 8-36 socket-head screw. Use small screwdriver to adjust windage and elevation. Available for various barrel widths. From New England Custom Gun Service.
Price: **$95.00**

ERA CLASSIC ADJUSTABLE REAR SIGHT Similar to the Masterpiece unit except windage is adjusted by pushing sight sideways, then locking with a reliable clamp. Precision machined all-steel construction, polished, with 6-48 fastening screw and Allen wrench. Shallow "V" and "U" notch. Length 2.170", width .550". From New England Custom Gun Service.
Price: **$79.00**

ERA EXPRESS SIGHTS A wide variety of open sights and bases for custom installation. Partial listing shown. From New England Custom Gun Service.
Price: One-leaf express **$79.00**
Price: Two-leaf express **$89.00**
Price: Three-leaf express **$99.00**
Price: Bases for above .... **$40.00 to $53.00**
Price: Standing rear sight, straight **$19.00**
Price: Base for above **$30.00**

ERA CLASSIC EXPRESS SIGHTS Standing or folding leaf sights are securely locked to the base with the ERA Magnum Clamp, but can be loosened for sighting in. Base can be attached with two socket-head cap screws or soldered. Finished and blued. Barrel diameters from .600" to .930". From New England Custom Gun Service.
Price: One-leaf express **$125.00**
Price: Two-leaf express **$135.00**
Price: Three-leaf express **$145.00**

ERA MASTERPIECE REAR SIGHT Adjustable for windage and elevation, and adjusted and locked with a small screwdriver. Comes with 8-36 socket-head cap screw and wrench. Barrel diameters from .600" to .930".
Price: **$95.00**

G.G. & G. SAME PLANE APERTURE M-16/AR-15 A2-style dual aperture rear sight with both large and small apertures centered on the same plane.
Price: **$45.00**

LYMAN No. 16 Middle sight for barrel dovetail slot mounting. Folds flat when scope or peep sight is used. Sight notch plate adjustable for elevation. White triangle for quick aiming. Designed to fit 3/8" dovetail slots. Three heights: A-.400" to .500", B-.345" to .445", C-.500" to .600". A slot blank designed to fill dovetail notch when sight is removed is available
Price: **$5.00**
Price: **$13.25**

MARBLE FALSE BASE #76, #77, #78 New screw-on base for most rifles replaces factory base. 3/8" dovetail slot permits installation of any folding rear sight. Can be had in sweat-on models also.
Price: **$8.00**

MARBLE FOLDING LEAF Flattop or semi-buckhorn style. Folds down when scope or peep sights are used. Reversible plate gives choice of "U" or "V" notch. Adjustable for elevation.
Price: **$16.00**
Price: Also available with both windage and elevation adjustment. **$18.00**

MARBLE SPORTING REAR With white enamel diamond, gives choice of two "U" and two "V" notches of different sizes. Adjustment in height by means of double step elevator and sliding notch piece. For all rifles; screw or dovetail installation.
Price: .... **$16.00 to $17.00**

MARBLE #20 UNIVERSAL New screw or sweat-on base. Both have .100" elevation adjustment. In five base sizes. Three styles of U-notch, square notch, peep. Adjustable for windage and elevation.
Price: Screw-on **$23.00**
Price: Sweat-on **$21.00**

MILLETT SPORTING & BLACKPOWDER RIFLE Open click adjustable rear fits 3/8" dovetail cut in barrel. Choice of white outline, target black or open express V rear blades. Also available is a replacement screw-on sight with express V, .562" hole centers. Dovetail fronts in white or blaze orange in seven heights (.157"-.540").
Price: Dovetail or screw-on rear **$58.38**
Price: Front sight **$12.96**

MILLETT SCOPE-SITE Open, adjustable or fixed rear sights dovetail into a base integral with the top scope-mounting ring. Blaze orange front ramp sight is integral with the front ring half. Rear sights have white outline aperture. Provides fast, short-radius, Patridge-type open sights on the top of the scope. Can be used with all Millett rings, Weaver-style bases, Ruger 77 (also fits Redhawk), Ruger Ranch Rifle, No. 1, No. 3, Rem. 870, 1100; Burris, Leupold and Redfield bases.
Price: Scope-Site top only, windage only **$31.15**
Price: As above, fully adjustable **$66.10**
Price: Scope-Site Hi-Turret, fully adjustable, low, medium, high. **$66.10**

RUGER WINDAGE ADJUSTABLE FOLDING REAR SIGHT Fits all Ruger rifles produced with standard folding rear sights. Available in low (.480"), medium (.503") and high (.638") heights. From Sturm, Ruger & Co., Inc.
Price: **$19.80**

TRIJICON 3-DOT NIGHT SIGHTS Self-luminous and machined from steel. Available for the M16/AR-15, H&K rifles. Front and rear sets and front only.
Price: .... **$60.00 to $84.00**

WHITWORTH-STYLE ENGLISH 3 LEAF EXPRESS SIGHTS Folding leafs marked in 100, 200 and 300 yard increments. Slide assembly is dovetailed in base. Available in four different styles: 3 folding leaves, flat bottom; 1 fixed, 2 folding leaves, flat bottom; 3 folding leaves, round bottom; 1 fixed, 2 folding leaves, round bottom. Available from Sarco, Inc.
Price: **$49.95**

WICHITA MULTI RANGE SIGHT SYSTEM Designed for silhouette shooting. System allows you to adjust the rear sight to four repeatable range settings, once it is pre-set. Sight clicks to any of the settings by turning a serrated wheel. Front sight is adjustable for weather and light conditions with one adjustment. Specify gun when ordering.
Price: Rear sight **$125.00**
Price: Front sight **$95.00**

WILLIAMS DOVETAIL OPEN SIGHT (WDOS) Open rear sight with windage and elevation adjustment. Furnished "U" notch or choice of blades. Slips into dovetail and locks with gib lock. Heights from .281" to .531".
Price: With blade **$19.50**
Price: Less blade **$12.45**
Price: Rear sight blades, each **$7.05**

WILLIAMS GUIDE OPEN SIGHT (WGOS) Open rear sight with windage and elevation adjustment. Bases to fit most military and commercial barrels. Choice of square "U" or "V" notch blade, 3/16", 1/4", 5/16", or 3/8" high.
Price: Less blade **$19.50**
Price: Extra blades, each **$7.05**

WILLIAMS WGOS OCTAGON Open rear sight for 1" octagonal barrels. Installs with two 6-48 screws and uses same hole spacing as most T/C muzzleloading rifles. Four heights, choice of square, U, V, or B blade.
Price: **$26.95**

WILLIAMS WSKS, WAK47 Replaces original military-type rear sight. Adjustable for windage and elevation. No drilling or tapping. Peep aperture or open. For SKS carbines, AK-47-style rifles.
Price: Aperture **$25.95**
Price: Open **$24.95**

WILLIAMS WM-96 Fits Mauser 96-type military rifles. Replaces original rear sight with open blade or aperture. Fully adjustable for windage and elevation. No drilling or tapping.
Price: Aperture **$25.95**
Price: Open **$24.95**

WILLIAMS FIRE RIFLE SETS Replacement front and rear fiber-optic sights. Red bead front, two green elements in the fully-adjustable rear. Made of CNC-machined metal.
Price: For Ruger 10/22 .... **$24.95**
Price: For most Marlin and Win. (3/8" dovetail) **$35.95**
Price: For Remington (newer-style sight base) **$23.95**

Aperture and Micrometer Receiver Sights

A2 REAR SIGHT KIT Featuring an exclusive numbered windage knob. For .223 AR-style rifles. From ArmaLite, Inc.
Price: **$55.00**

AO GHOST RING HUNTING SIGHT Fully adjustable for windage and elevation. Available for most rifles, including blackpowder guns. Minimum gunsmithing required for most installations; matches most mounting holes. From AO Sight Systems, Inc.
Price: **$90.00**

AO AR-15/M-16 APERTURE Drop-in replacement of factory sights. Both apertures are on the same plane. Large ghost ring has .230" inside diameter; small ghost ring has .100" inside diameter. From AO Sight Systems, Inc.
Price: **$30.00**

AO BACKUP GHOST RING SIGHTS Mounts to scope base and retains zero when reinstalled in the field. Affords same elevation/windage adjustability as AO hunting ghost rings. Included are both .191" and .230" apertures and test posts. Available for Ruger, Dakota, Remington 700 and other rifles. From AO Sight Systems, Inc.
Price: **$65.00**

AO TACTICAL SIGHTS For HK UMP/USC/G36/SL8/M P5. The Big Dot tritium or standard dot tritium is mated with a large .300" diameter rear ghost ring. The "same plane" rear aperture flips from the .300" to a .230" diameter ghost ring. From AO Sight Systems, Inc.
Price: .... **$90.00 to $120.00**

AO Ghost Ring

BEEMAN/FEINWERKBAU 5454 MATCH APERTURE SIGHT Small size, new-design sight uses constant-pressure flat springs to eliminate point of impact shifts.
Price: **$350.00**

METALLIC SIGHTS

BEEMAN SPORT APERTURE SIGHT Positive click micrometer adjustments. Standard units with flush surface screwdriver adjustments. Deluxe version has target knobs. For air rifles with grooved receivers.
Price: Standard **$40.00**
Price: Deluxe. **$50.00**

BUSHMASTER COMPETITION A2 REAR SIGHT ASSEMBLY Elevation and windage mechanism feature either 1/2- or 1/4-minute of adjustment. Long distance aperture allows screw-in installation of any of four interchangeable micro-apertures.
Price: 1/2 M.O.A **$109.95**
Price: 1/4 M.O.A **$114.95**

DPMS NATIONAL MATCH Replaces the standard A2 rear sight on M16/AR-15 rifles. Has 1/4-minute windage and 1/2-minute elevation adjustments. Includes both a .052" and .200" diameter aperture.
Price: **$92.99**

ENFIELD No. 4 TARGET/MATCH SIGHT Originally manufactured by Parker-Hale, has adjustments up to 1,300 meters. Micrometer click adjustments for windage. Adjustable aperture disc has six different openings from .030" to .053". From Sarco, Inc.
Price: **$49.95**

EAW RECEIVER SIGHT A fully adjustable aperture sight that locks securely into the EAW quick-detachable scope mount rear base. Made by New England Custom Gun Service.
Price: **$80.00**

ERA SEE-THRU Contains fiber-optic center dot. Fits standard 3/8" American dovetails. Locks in place with set screw. Ideal for use on moving targets. Width 19.5mm. Available in low (.346"), medium (.425") and high (.504") models. From New England Custom Gun Service.
Price: **$40.00**

G. G.& G. MAD IRIS Multiple Aperture Device is a four-sight, rotating aperture disk with small and large apertures on the same plane. Mounts on M-16/AR-15 flattop receiver. Fully adjustable.
Price: **$141.95**
Price: A2 IRIS, two apertures, full windage adjustments **$124.95**

KNIGHT'S ARMAMENT 600 METER FOLDING REAR SIGHT Click adjustable from 200 to 600 meters with clearly visible range markings. Intermediate clicks allows for precise zero at known ranges. Allows use of optical scopes by folding down. Mounts on rear of upper receiver rail on SR-25 and similar rifles. From Knight's Armament Co.
Price: **$181.00**

KNIGHT'S ARMAMENT FOLDING 300M SIGHT Mounts on flat-top upper receivers on SR-25 and similar rifles. May be used as a back-up iron sight for a scoped rifle/carbine or a primary sight. Peep insert may be removed to expose the 5mm diameter ghost ring aperture. From Knight's Armament Co.
Price: **$144.00**

LYMAN NO. 2 TANG SIGHT Designed for the Winchester Model 94. Has high index marks on aperture post; comes with both .093" quick sighting aperture, .040" large disk aperture, and replacement mounting screws.
Price: **$76.00**
Price: For Marlin lever actions. **$76.00**

LYMAN NO. 57 1/4-minute clicks. Stayset knobs. Quick-release slide, adjustable zero scales. Made for almost all modern rifles.
Price: **$67.50**
Price: No. 57SME, 57SMET (for White Systems Model 91 and Whitetail rifles) . **$62.50**

Lyman No. 57

LYMAN 57GPR Designed especially for the Lyman Great Plains Rifle. Mounts directly onto the tang of the rifle and has 1/4-minute micrometer click adjustments.
Price: **$62.50**

LYMAN NO. 66 Fits close to the rear of flat-sided receivers, furnished with Stayset knobs. Quick-release slide, 1/4-min. adjustments. For most lever or slide action or flat-sided automatic rifles.
Price: **$67.50**
Price: No. 66MK (for all current versions of the Knight MK-85 in-line rifle with flat-sided receiver) **$67.50**
Price: No. 66 SKS fits Russian and Chinese SKS rifles; large and small apertures **$67.50**
Price: No. 66 WB for Model 1886 Winchester lever actions **$67.50**

LYMAN NO. 66U Lightweight, designed for most modern shotguns with a flat-sided, round-top receiver. 1/4-minute clicks. Requires drilling, tapping. Not for Browning A-5, Rem. M11.
Price: **$71.50**

LYMAN 90MJT RECEIVER SIGHT Mounts on standard Lyman and Williams FP bases. Has 1/4-minute audible micrometer click adjustments, target knobs with direction indicators. Adjustable zero scales, quick-release slide. Large 7/8" diameter aperture disk.
Price: Right- or left-hand **$74.95**

LYMAN RECEIVER SIGHT Audible-click adjustments for windage and elevation, coin-slotted "stayset" knobs and two interchangeable apertures. For Mauser, Springfield, Sako, T/C Hawken, Rem. 700, Win. 70, Savage 110, SKS, Win. 94, Marlin 336 and 1894.
Price: **$53.99**

LYMAN 1886 #2 TANG SIGHT Fits the Winchester 1886 lever action rifle and replicas thereof not containing a tang safety. Has height index marks on the aperture post and an .800" maximum elevation adjustment. Included is a .093" x 1/2" quick-sighting aperture and .040 x 5/8" target disk.
Price: **$76.00**

MARBLE PEEP TANG SIGHT All-steel construction. Micrometer-like click adjustments for windage and elevation. For most popular old and new lever-action rifles.
Price: **$125.00**

MILLETT PEEP RIFLE SIGHTS Fully adjustable, heat-treated nickel steel peep aperture receiver sight for the Mini-14. Has fine windage and elevation adjustments; replaces original.
Price: Rear sight, Mini-14. . . . . **$51.45**
Price: Front sight, Mini-14 . . . . **$19.69**
Price: Front and rear combo with hood **$67.20**

NATIONAL MATCH REAR SIGHT KIT For AR-15 style rifles. From Armalite, Inc.
Price: 1/2 W, 1/2 E **$80.00**
Price: 1/4 W, 1/2 E **$80.00**

NECG PEEP SIGHT FOR WEAVER SCOPE MOUNT BASES Attaches to Weaver scope mount base. Windage adjusts with included Allen wrenches, elevation with a small screwdriver. Furnished with two apertures (.093" and .125" diameter hole) and two interchangeable elevation slides for high or low sight line. From New England Custom Gun Service.
Price: **$85.00**

NECG RUGER PEEP SIGHT Made for Ruger M-77 and No. 1 rifles, it is furnished with .093" and .125" opening apertures. Can be installed on a standard Ruger rear mount base or quarter rib. Tightening the aperture disk will lock the elevation setting in place. From New England Custom Gun Service.
Price: **$85.00**

T/C HUNTING STYLE TANG PEEP SIGHT Compact, all steel construction, with locking windage and elevation adjustments. For use with "bead style" and fiber-optic front sights. Models available to fit all traditional T/C muzzleloading rifles. From Thompson/Center Arms.
Price: **$60.00**

WILLIAMS APERTURE SIGHT Made to fit SKS rifles.
Price: **$25.95**

WILLIAMS FIRE SIGHT PEEP SETS Combines the Fire Sight front bead with Williams fully adjustable metallic peep rear.
Price: For SKS **$39.95**
Price: For Ruger 10/22. . . . . **$47.95**
Price: For Marlin or Winchester lever actions **$80.95**

WILLIAMS FP Internal click adjustments. Positive locks. For virtually all rifles, T/C Contender, Heckler & Koch HK-91, Ruger Mini-14, plus Win., Rem., and Ithaca shotguns.
Price: From. **$69.95**
Price: With target knobs. **$81.50**
Price: FP-GR (for dovetail-grooved receivers, .22s and air guns). **$69.95**
Price: FP-94BBSE (for Win. 94 Big Bore A.E.; uses top rear scope mount holes) **$69.95**

WILLIAMS TARGET FP Similar to the FP series but developed for most bolt-action rimfire rifles. Target FP High adjustable from 1.250" to 1.750" above centerline of bore; Target FP Low adjustable from .750" to 1.250". Attaching bases for Rem. 540X, 541-S, 580, 581, 582 (#540); Rem. 510, 511, 512, 513-T, 521-T (#510); Win. 75 (#75); Savage-Anschutz 64 and Mark 12 (#64). Some rifles require drilling, tapping.
Price: High or Low **$77.95**
Price: Base only. **$19.75**
Price: Mount holes **$59.95**

WILLIAMS 5-D SIGHT Low cost sight for shotguns, 22s and the more popular big game rifles. Adjustment for windage and elevation. Fits most guns without drilling and tapping. Also for British SMLE, Winchester M94 Side Eject.
Price: From. **$37.95**
Price: With shotgun aperture **$37.95**

WILLIAMS 5D RECEIVER SIGHT Alloy construction and similar design to the FP model except designed to fit Win. 94, Marlin 336, Marlin 1895, Mauser 98.
Price: **$37.95**

WILLIAMS GUIDE (WGRS) Receiver sight for 30 M1 Carbine, M1903A3 Springfield, Savage 24s, Savage-Anschutz and Weatherby XXII. Utilizes military dovetail; no drilling. Double-dovetail windage adjustment, sliding dovetail adjustment for elevation.
Price: . . . . **$35.95 to $47.95**

Vernier Tang Sights

BALLARD TANG SIGHTS Available in variety of models including short & long staff hunter, Pacific & Montana, custom units allowing windage & elevation adjustments. Uses 8x40 base screws with screw spacing of 1.120". From Axtell Rifle Co.
Price: . . . . **$175.00 to $325.00**

LYMAN TANG SIGHT Made for Win. 94, 1886, Marlin 30, 336 and 1895.
Price: . . . . **$59.99 to $64.99**

MARLIN TANG SIGHTS Available in short and long staff hunter models using 8x40 base screws and screw spacing of 1.120". From Axtell Rifle Co.
Price: . . . . **$170.00 to $180.00**

PEDERSOLI CREEDMORE Adjustable for windage and elevation, fits Traditions by Pedersoli rifles and other brands. From Dixie Gun Works.
Price: **$110.00**

REMINGTON TANG SIGHTS Available in short-range hunter and vernier, mid- and long-range vernier and custom models with windage and elevation adjustments. Uses 10x28 base screws, with screw spacing of 1.940". Eye disk has .052" hole with 10x40 thread. From Axtell Rifle Co.
Price: . . . . **$175.00 to $325.00**

METALLIC SIGHTS

SHARPS TANG SIGHTS Reproduction tang sights as manufactured for various Sharps rifles through 1859-1878. Wide variety of models available including standard issue sporting peep, Hartford transition mid and long range, and custom express sights. From Axtell Rifle Co.
Price: . . . . $150.00 to $340.00

STEVENS CUSTOM Available in thin base short and long staff hunter, mid and long range sporting vernier, custom mid and long range (custom models allow windage and elevation adjustments) models. Uses 5x40 base screws with screw spacing of 1.485". From Axtell Rifle Co.
Price: . . . . $170.00 to $325.00

TAURUS TANG SIGHT Made of blue steel, available for Taurus Models 62, 72, 172, 63, 73 and 173. Folds down, aperture disk sight, height index marks on aperture post.
Price: $77.00

WINCHESTER & BROWNING TANG SIGHTS Available in variety of models, including thin and thick base short and long staff hunter, mid and long range sporting vernier and custom units. Screw spacing of 2.180" on all models. From Axtell Rifle Co.
Price: . . . . $170.00 to $325.00

Globe Target Front Sights

AXTELL CUSTOM GLOBE Designed similar to the original Winchester #35 sight, it contains five inserts. Also available with spirit level. From Axtell Rifle Co.
Price: . . . . $125.00 to $175.00

BALLARD FRONT SIGHTS Available in windgauge with spirit level, globe with clip, and globe with spirit level (all with five inserts) and beach combination with gold-plated rocker models. Dovetail of .375" for all. From Axtell Rifle Co.
Price: . . . . $125.00 to $240.00

LYMAN 20 MJT TARGET FRONT Has 7/8" diameter, one-piece steel globe with 3/8" dovetail base. Height is .700" from bottom of dovetail to center of aperture; height on 20 LJT is .750". Comes with seven Anschutz-size steel inserts: two posts and five apertures .126" through .177".
Price: 20 MJT or 20 LJT $33.75

Lyman No. 17A Target

LYMAN No. 17A TARGET Includes seven interchangeable inserts: four apertures, one transparent amber and two posts .50" and .100" in width.
Price: $28.25
Price: Insert set $13.25

LYMAN 17AEU Similar to the Lyman 17A except has a special dovetail design to mount easily onto European muzzleloaders such as CVA, Traditions and Investarm. All steel, comes with eight inserts.
Price: $26.00

LYMAN No. 93 MATCH Has 7/8" diameter, fits any rifle with a standard dovetail mounting block. Comes with seven target inserts and accepts most Anschutz accessories. Hooked locking bolt and nut allows quick removal, installation. Base available in .860" (European) and .562" (American) hole spacing.
Price: $45.00

MAYNARD FRONT SIGHTS Custom globe with five inserts and clip. Also available with spirit level bracket and windgauge styles. From Axtell Rifle Co.
Price: . . . . $125.00 to $240.00

PEDERSOLI GLOBE A tunnel front sight with 12 interchangeable inserts for high precision target shooting. Fits Traditions by Pedersoli and other rifles.
Price: $69.95

REMINGTON FRONT SIGHTS Available in windgauge with spirit level, custom globe with clip and custom globe with spirit level (all with five inserts) and beach combination with gold-plated rocker models. Dovetail .460". From Axtell Rifle Co.
Price: . . . . $125.00 to $250.00

SHARPS FRONT SIGHTS Original-style globe with non-moveable post and pinhead. Also available with windgauge and spirit level. From Axtell Rifle Co.
Price: . . . . $100.00 to $265.00

WILLIAMS TARGET GLOBE FRONT Adapts to many rifles. Mounts to the base with a knurled locking screw. Height is .545" from center, not including base. Comes with inserts.
Price: $47.95
Price: Dovetail base (low) .220" $18.95
Price: Dovetail base (high) .465" $18.95
Price: Screw-on base, .300" height, .300" radius $16.95
Price: Screw-on base, .450" height, .350" radius $16.95
Price: Screw-on base, .215" height, .400" radius $16.95

WINCHESTER & BROWNING FRONT SIGHTS Available in windgauge with spirit level, globe with clip, globe with spirit level (all with five inserts) and beach combination with gold-plated rocker models. From Axtell Rifle Co.
Price: . . . . $125.00 to $240.00

Front Sights

AO TACTICAL SIGHTS Three types of drop-in replacement front posts—round top or square top night sight posts in standard and Big Dot sizes, or white stripe posts in .080 and .100 widths. For AR15 and M16 rifles. From AO Sight Systems, Inc.
Price: . . . . $30.00 to $90.00

AO RIFLE TEST POSTS Allows easy establishment of correct front post height. Provides dovetail post with .050" segments to allow shooter to "shoot-n-snip", watching point-of-impact walk into point of aim. Available for 3/8" standard dovetail, Ruger-style or Mauser. From AO Sight Systems, Inc.
Price: $5.00

AR-10 DETACHABLE FRONT SIGHT Allows use of the iron rear sight, but are removable for use of telescopic sights with no obstruction to the sight line. For AR-style rifles. From ArmaLite, Inc.
Price: . . . . $50.00 to $70.00

BUSHMASTER FLIP-UP FRONT SIGHT Made for V Match AR-style rifles, this sight unit slips over milled front sight bases and clamps around barrel. Locks with the push of a button. For use with flip-up style rear sights or the A3 removable carry handle. From Bushmaster Firearms.
Price: $99.95

BUSHMASTER A2 COMPETITION FRONT SIGHT POST Surface ground on three sides for optimum visual clarity. Available in two widths: .052"; and .062". From Bushmaster Firearms.
Price: $12.95

CLASSIC STREAMLINED FRONT SPORTER RAMP SIGHT Comes with blade and sight cover. Serrated and contoured ramp. Screw-on attachment. Slide-on sight cover is easily detachable. Gold bead. From Sarco, Inc.
Price: $13.50

ERA BEADS FOR RUGER RIFLES White bead and fiber-optic front sights that replace the standard sights on M-77 and No. 1 Ruger rifles. Using 3/32" beads, they are available in heights of .330", .350", .375", .415" and .435". From New England Custom Gun Service.
Price: . . . . $22.00 to $33.00

ERA FRONT SIGHTS European-type front sights inserted from the front. Various heights available. From New England Custom Gun Service.
Price: 5/64" silver bead $18.00
Price: 3/32" silver bead $20.00
Price: Sourdough bead $20.50
Price: Fiber-optic $35.00
Price: Folding night sight with ivory bead $49.50

Knight's Armament

KNIGHT'S ARMAMENT FRONT STANDING/FOLDING SIGHT Mounts to the SR-25 rifle barrel gas block's MilStd top rail. Available in folding sight model. From Knight's Armament Co.
Price: . . . . $145.00 to $175.00

KNIGHT'S ARMAMENT CARRYING HANDLE SIGHT Rear sight and carry handle for the SR-25 rifle. Has fixed range and adjustable windage. From Knight's Armament Co.
Price: $181.15

KNIGHT'S ARMAMENT MK II FOLDING FRONT SIGHT For the SR-25 rifle. Requires modified handguard. From Knight's Armament Co.
Price: $175.00

KNIGHT'S ARMAMENT FOR FREE-FLOATING RAS Mounts to free-floating SR-25 and SR-15 RAS (rail adapter system) rifle forends. Adjustable for elevation. Made of aluminum. From Knight's Armament Co.
Price: $155.25

KNS PRECISION SYSTEMS SIGHT Screws into front base. Hooded for light consistency; precision machined with fine wire crosshairs measuring .010" thick. Aperture measures .240" diameter. Standard and duplex reticles. Available for AK-47, MAK-90, AR-15, M16, FN-FAL, H&K 91, 93, 94, MP5, SP89, L1A1, M1 Garand.
Price: $25.99

METALLIC SIGHTS

LYMAN AR-15 FIRE SIGHTS Front metallic sight, fully adjustable for elevation, no gunsmithing required.
Price: **$41.95**

LYMAN HUNTING SIGHTS Made with gold or white beads 1/16" to 3/32" wide and in varying heights for most military and commercial rifles. Dovetail bases.
Price: **$8.95**

MARBLE STANDARD Ivory, red, or gold bead. For all American-made rifles, 1/16" wide bead with semi-flat face that does not reflect light. Specify type of rifle when ordering.
Price: **$10.00**

MARBLE CONTOURED Has 3/8" dovetail base, .090" deep, 5/8" long. Uses standard 1/16" or 3/32" bead, ivory, red, or gold. Specify rifle type when ordering.
Price: **$11.50**

NATIONAL MATCH FRONT SIGHT POST Has .050" blade. For AR-style rifle. From ArmaLite, Inc.
Price: **$12.00**

T/C FIBER-OPTIC FRONT MUZZLELOADER SIGHT Ramp-style steel with fiber-optic bead for all traditional cap locks, both octagonal and round barrels with dovetail, and most T/C rifles. From Thompson/Center Arms.
Price: . . . . **$16.95 to $36.00**

TRIJICON NIGHT SIGHT Self-luminous tritium gas-filled front sight for the M16/AR-15 series.
Price: **$60.00**

WILLIAMS STREAMLINED HOODLESS RAMP Available in 3/16", 5/16", 3/8", and 7/16" models.
Price: Less blade **$15.49**

WILLAMS SHORTY RAMPS Available in 1/8", 3/16", 9/32" and 3/8" models.
Price: Less blade **$15.49**

WILLIAMS GOLD BEAD Available in .312", .343", and .406" high models all with 3/32" bead.
Price: **$8.49**

WILLIAMS RISER BLOCKS For adding .250" height to front sights when using a receiver sight. Two widths available: .250" for Williams Streamlined Ramp or .340" on all standard ramps having this base width. Uses standard 3/8" dovetail.
Price: **$5.46**

WILLIAMS AR-15 FIRESIGHT Fiber-optic unit attaches to any standard AR-15-style front sight assembly. Machined from aircraft-strength aluminum. Adjustable for elevation. Green-colored light-gathering fiber-optics. From Williams Gun Sight Co.
Price: . . . . **NA**

XS AR-15/M-16 FRONT SIGHTS Drop-in replacement sight post. Double faced so it can be rotated 180° for 2.5 MOA elevation adjustment. Available in .080" width with .030" white stripe, or .100" with .040" stripe. From XS Sight Systems.
Price: **$30.00**
Price: Tritium Dot Express **$60.00**

Ramp Sights

ERA MASTERPIECE Banded ramps, 21 sizes, hand-detachable beads and hood, beads inserted from the front. Various heights available. From New England Custom Gun Service.
Price: Banded ramp **$69.00**
Price: Hood **$18.00**
Price: 1/16" silver bead **$18.00**
Price: 3/32" silver bead **$20.00**
Price: Sourdough bead **$20.00**
Price: Fiber-optic **$35.00**
Price: Folding night sight with ivory bead **$49.00**

HOLLAND & HOLLAND-STYLE FRONT SIGHT RAMPS Banded and screw-on models in the Holland & Holland-style night sight. Flips forward to expose a .0781" silver bead. Flips back for use of the .150" diameter ivory bead for poor light or close-up hunting. Band thickness .040", overall length 3.350", band length 1.180". From New England Custom Gun Service.
Price: . . . . **$100.00 to $115.00**

LYMAN NO. 18 SCREW-ON RAMP Used with 8-40 screws but may also be brazed on. Heights from .10" to .350". Ramp without sight.
Price: **$13.75**

MARBLE FRONT RAMPS Available in polished or dull matte finish or serrated style. Standard 3/8 x .090" dovetail slot. Made for MR-width (.340") front sights. Can be used as screw-on or sweat-on. Heights: .100", .150", .300".
Price: Polished or matte **$14.00**
Price: Serrated **$10.00**

NECG UNIVERSAL FRONT SIGHTS Available in five ramp heights and three front sight heights. Sights can be adjusted up or down .030" with an Allen wrench. Slips into place and then locks into position with a set screw. Six different front sight shapes are offered, including extra large and fiber-optic. All hoods except the extra low ramp slide on from the rear and click in place. Extra low ramp has spring-loaded balls to lock hood. Choose from three hood sizes. From New England Custom Gun Service.
Price: **$25.00**

T/C FIBER-OPTIC MUZZLELOADER SIGHT Click adjustable for windage and elevation. Steel construction fitted with Tru-Glo™ fiber-optics. Models available for most T/C muzzleloading rifles. Fits others with 1" and 15/16" octagon barrels with a hole spacing of .836" between screws. From Thompson/Center Arms.
Price: **$38.25**

WILLIAMS SHORTY RAMP Companion to "Streamlined" ramp, about 1/2" shorter. Screw-on or sweat-on. It is furnished in 1/8", 3/16", 9/32", and 3/8" heights without hood only. Also for shotguns.
Price: **$19.95**
Price: With dovetail lock **$20.95**

WILLIAMS STREAMLINED RAMP Available in screw-on or sweat-on models. Furnished in 9/16", 7/16", 3/8", 5/16", 3/16" heights.
Price: **$23.95**
Price: Sight hood **$6.10**

WILLIAMS STREAMLINED FRONT SIGHTS Narrow (.250" width) for Williams Streamlined ramps and others with 1/4" top width; medium (.340" width) for all standard factory ramps. Available with white, gold or fluorescent beads, 1/16" or 3/32".
Price: . . . . **$10.50 to $10.95**

Handgun Sights

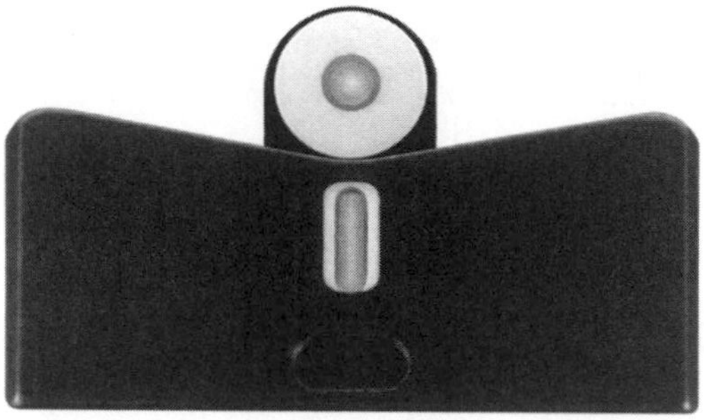

AO Express

AO EXPRESS SIGHTS Low-profile, snag-free express-type sights. Shallow V rear with white vertical line, white dot front. All-steel, matte black finish. Rear is available in different heights. Made for most pistols, many with double set-screws. From AO Sight Systems, Inc.
Price: Standard Set, front and rear **$60.00**
Price: Big Dot Set, front and rear **$60.00**
Price: Tritium Set, Standard or Big Dot **$90.00**
Price: 24/7 Pro Express, Std. or Big Dot tritium **$120.00**

BO-MAR DELUXE BMCS Gives 3/8" windage and elevation adjustment at 50 yards on Colt Gov't 45; sight radius under 7". For GM and Commander models only. Uses existing dovetail slot. Has shield-type rear blade.
Price: **$65.95**
Price: BMCS-2 (for GM and 9mm) **$68.95**
Price: Flat bottom **$65.95**
Price: BMGC (for Colt Gold Cup), angled serrated blade, rear **$68.95**
Price: BMGC front sight **$12.95**
Price: BMCZ-75 (for CZ-75,TZ-75, P-9 and most clones). Works with factory front **$68.95**

BO-MAR FRONT SIGHTS Dovetail-style for S&W 4506, 4516, 1076; undercut-style (.250", .280", 5/16" high); Fast Draw-style (.210", .250", .230" high).
Price: **$12.95**

BO-MAR BMU XP-100/T/C CONTENDER No gunsmithing required; has .080" notch.
Price: **$77.00**

BO-MAR BMML For muzzleloaders; has .062" notch, flat bottom.
Price: **$65.95**
Price: With 3/8" dovetail **$65.95**

BO-MAR RUGER "P" ADJUSTABLE SIGHT Replaces factory front and rear sights.
Price: Rear sight **$65.95**
Price: Front sight **$12.00**

BO-MAR BMR Fully adjustable rear sight for Ruger MKI, MKII Bull barrel autos.
Price: Rear **$65.95**
Price: Undercut front sight **$12.00**

BO-MAR GLOCK Fully adjustable, all-steel replacement sights. Sight fits factory dovetail. Longer sight radius. Uses Novak Glock .275" high, .135" wide front, or similar.
Price: Rear sight **$68.95**
Price: Front sight **$20.95**

BO-MAR LOW PROFILE RIB & ACCURACY TUNER Streamlined rib with front and rear sights; 7-1/8" sight radius. Brings sight line closer to the bore than standard or extended sight and ramp. Weight 5 oz. Made for Colt Gov't 45, Super 38, and Gold Cup 45 and 38.
Price: **$140.00**

BO-MAR COMBAT RIB For S&W Model 19 revolver with 4" barrel. Sight radius 5-3/4", weight 5-1/2 oz.
Price: **$127.00**

BO-MAR WINGED RIB For S&W 4" and 6" length barrels: K-38, M10, HB 14 and 19. Weight for the 6" model is about 7-1/4 oz.
Price: **$140.00**

BO-MAR COVER-UP RIB Adjustable rear sight, winged front guards. Fits right over revolver's original front sight. For S&W 4" M-10HB, M-13, M-58, M-64 & 65, Ruger 4" models SDA-34, SDA-84, SS-34, SS-84, GF-34, GF-84.
Price: **$130.00**

CHIP MCCORMICK "DROP-IN" A low mount sight that fits any 1911-style slide with a standard military-type dovetail sight cut (60 x .290"). Dovetail front sights also available. From Chip McCormick Corp.
Price: **$47.95**

METALLIC SIGHTS

CHIP MCCORMICK FIXED SIGHTS Same sight picture (.110" rear - .110" front) that's become the standard for pro combat shooters. Low mount design with rounded edges. For 1911-style pistols. May require slide machining for installation. From Chip McCormick Corp.
Price: ... **$24.95**

C-MORE SIGHTS Replacement front sight blades offered in two types and five styles. Made of DuPont Acetal, they come in a set of five high-contrast colors: blue, green, pink, red and yellow. Easy to install. Patridge-style for Colt Python (all barrels), Ruger Super Blackhawk (7-1/2"), Ruger Blackhawk (4-5/8"); ramp-style for Python (all barrels), Blackhawk (4-5/8"), Super Blackhawk (7-1/2" and 10-1/2"). From C-More Systems.
Price: Per set ... **$19.95**

G.G. & G. GHOST RINGS Replaces the factory rear sight without gunsmithing. Black phosphate finish. Available for Colt M1911 and Commander, Beretta M92F, Glock, S&W, SIG Sauer.
Price: ... **$65.00**

Heinie Slant Pro

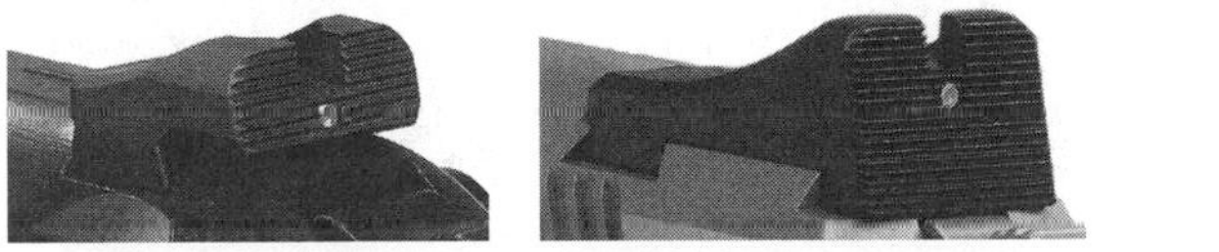

HEINIE SLANT PRO Made with a slight forward slant, the unique design of these rear sights is snag-free for unimpeded draw from concealment. The combination of the slant and the rear serrations virtually eliminates glare. Made for most popular handguns. From Heinie Specialty Products.
Price: ... **$50.35 to $122.80**

HEINIE STRAIGHT EIGHT SIGHTS Consists of one tritium dot in the front sight and a slightly smaller tritium dot in the rear sight. When aligned correctly, an elongated 'eight' is created. The tritium dots are green in color. Designed with the belief that the human eye can correct vertical alignment faster than horizontal. Available for most popular handguns. From Heinie Specialty Products.
Price: ... **$104.95 to $122.80**

HEINIE CROSS DOVETAIL FRONT SIGHTS Made in a variety of heights, the standard dovetail is 60° x .305" x .062" with a .002 taper. From Heinie Specialty Products.
Price: ... **$20.95 to $47.20**

JP GHOST RING Replacement bead front, ghost ring rear for Glock and M1911 pistols. From JP Enterprises.
Price: ... **$79.95**
Price: Bo-Mar replacement leaf with JP dovetail front bead ... **$99.95**

LES BAER CUSTOM ADJUSTABLE LOW MOUNT REAR SIGHT Considered one of the top adjustable sights in the world for target shooting with 1911-style pistols. Available with tritium inserts. From Les Baer Custom.
Price: ... **$19.00** (standard); **$99.00** (tritium)

LES BAER DELUXE FIXED COMBAT SIGHT A tactical-style sight with a very low profile. Incorporates a no-snag design and has serrations on sides. For 1911-style pistols. Available with tritium inserts for night shooting. From Les Baer Custom.
Price: ... **$26.00** (standard); **$67.00** (with tritium)

LES BAER DOVETAIL FRONT SIGHT Blank dovetail sight machined from bar stock. Can be contoured to many different configurations to meet user's needs. Available with tritium insert. From Les Baer Custom.
Price: ... **$17.00** (standard); **$47.00** (with tritium insert)

LES BAER FIBER-OPTIC FRONT SIGHT Dovetail .330 x 65°, .125" wide post, .185" high, .060" diameter. Red and green fiber-optic. From Les Baer Custom.
Price: ... **$24.00**

LES BAER PPC-STYLE ADJUSTABLE REAR SIGHT Made for use with custom built 1911-style pistols, allows the user to preset three elevation adjustments for PPC-style shooting. Milling required for installation. Made from 4140 steel. From Les Baer Custom.
Price: ... **$120.00**

LES BAER DOVETAIL FRONT SIGHT WITH TRITIUM INSERT This fully contoured and finished front sight comes ready for gunsmith installation. From Les Baer Custom.
Price: ... **$47.00**

MMC TACTICAL ADJUSTABLE SIGHTS Low-profile, snag-free design, 22 click positions for elevation, drift adjustable for windage. Machined from 4140 steel and heat treated to 40 RC. Tritium and non-tritium, 10 different configurations and colors. Three different finishes. For 1911s, all Glock, HK USP, S&W, Browning Hi-Power.
Price: Sight set, tritium ... **$139.00**
Price: Sight set, white outline or white dot ... **$124.00**
Price: Sight set, black ... **$124.00**

MEPROLIGHT TRITIUM NIGHT SIGHTS Replacement sight assemblies for low-light conditions. Available for pistols (fixed and adj.), rifles, shotguns, 12-year warranty for useable illumination, while non-TRU-DOT have a 5-year warranty. Distributed in American by Kimber.
Price: Kahr K9, K40, fixed, TRU-DOT ... **$105.00**
Price: Ruger Mini-14R sights (front only) ... **$55.00**
Price: SIG Sauer P220, P225, P226, P228, TRU-DOT ... **$105.00**
Price: S&W autos, fixed or adjustable, TRU-DOT ... **$105.00**
Price: Walther P-99, fixed, TRU-DOT ... **$105.00**
Price: Shotgun bead ... **$34.00**
Price: Beretta M92, Cougar, Brigadier, fixed, TRU-DOT ... **$105.00**
Price: Browning Hi-Power, adjustable, TRU-DOT ... **$105.00**
Price: Colt M1911 Govt., adjustable, TRU-DOT ... **$105.00**

MILLETT SERIES 100 REAR SIGHTS All-steel highly visible, click adjustable. Blades in white outline, target black, silhouette, 3-dot. Fit most popular revolvers and autos.
Price: ... **$51.77 to $84.00**

MILLETT BAR-DOT-BAR TRITIUM NIGHT SIGHTS Replacement front and rear combos fit most automatics. Horizontal tritium bars on rear, dot front sight.
Price: ... **$152.25**

MILLETT BAR/DOT Made with orange or white bar or dot for increased visibility. Available for Beretta 84, 85, 92S, 92SB, Browning, Colt Python & Trooper, Ruger GP 100, P85, Redhawk, Security Six.
Price: ... **$14.99 to $24.99**

MILLETT 3-DOT SYSTEM SIGHTS The 3-Dot System sights use a single white dot on the front blade and two dots flanking the rear notch. Fronts available in Dual-Crimp and Wide Stake-On styles, as well as special applications. Adjustable rear sight available for most popular auto pistols and revolvers including Browning Hi-Power, Colt 1911 Government and Ruger P85.
Price: Front, from ... **$16.80**
Price: Adjustable rear ... **$55.60**

MILLETT REVOLVER FRONT SIGHTS All-steel replacement front sights with either white or orange bar. Easy to install. For Ruger GP-100, Redhawk, Security-Six, Police-Six, Speed-Six, Colt Trooper, Diamondback, King Cobra, Peacemaker, Python, Dan Wesson 22 and 15-2.
Price: ... **$13.60 to $16.00**

MILLETT DUAL-CRIMP FRONT SIGHT Replacement front sight for automatic pistols. Dual-Crimp uses an all-steel two-point hollow rivet system. Available in eight heights and four styles. Has a skirted base that covers the front sight pad. Easily installed with the Millett Installation Tool Set. Available in blaze orange bar, white bar, serrated ramp, plain post. Available in heights of .185", .200", .225", .275", .312", .340" and .410".
Price: ... **$16.80**

MILLETT STAKE-ON FRONT SIGHT Replacement front sight for automatic pistols. Stake-On sights have skirted base that covers the front sight pad. Easily installed with the Millet Installation Tool Set. Available in seven heights and four styles: blaze orange bar, white bar, serrated ramp, plain post. Available for Glock 17L and 24, others.
Price: ... **$16.80**

MILLETT ADJUSTABLE TARGET Positive light-deflection serration and slant to eliminate glare and sharp edge sight notch. Audible "click" adjustments. For AMT Hardballer, Beretta 84, 85, 92S, 92SB, Browning Hi-Power, Colt 1911 Government and Gold Cup, Colt revolvers, Dan Wesson 15, 41, 44, Ruger revolvers, Glock 17, 17L, 19, 20, 21, 22, 23.
Price: ... **$44.99**

MILLETT ADJUSTABLE WHITE OUTLINE Similar to the Target sight, except has a white outline on the blade to increase visibility. Available for the same handguns as the Target model, plus BRNO CZ-75/TZ-75/TA-90 without pin on front sight, and Ruger P85.
Price: ... **$44.99 to $49.99**

OMEGA OUTLINE SIGHT BLADES Replacement rear sight blades for Colt and Ruger single action guns and the Interarms Virginian Dragoon. Standard Outline available in gold or white notch outline on blue metal. From Omega Sales, Inc.
Price: ... **$10.00**

OMEGA MAVERICK SIGHT BLADES Replacement "peep-sight" blades for Colt, Ruger SAs, Virginian Dragoon. Three models available: No. 1, plain; No. 2, single bar; No. 3, double bar rangefinder. From Omega Sales, Inc.
Price: Each ... **$10.00**

ONE RAGGED HOLE Replacement rear sight ghost ring sight for Ruger handguns. Fits Blackhawks, Redhawks, Super Blackhawks, GP series and Mk II target pistols with adjustable sights. From One Ragged Hole, Tallahassee, Florida.
Price: ... **NA**

PACHMAYR ACCU-SET Low-profile, fully adjustable rear sight to be used with existing front sight. Available with target, white outline or 3-dot blade. Blue finish. Uses factory dovetail and locking screw. For Browning, Colt, Glock, SIG Sauer, S&W and Ruger autos. From Pachmayr.
Price: ... **$59.98**

P-T TRITIUM NIGHT SIGHTS Self-luminous tritium sights for most popular handguns, Colt AR-15, H&K rifles and shotguns. Replacement handgun sight sets available in 3-dot-style (green/green, green/yellow, green/orange) with bold outlines around inserts; Bar-Dot available in green/green with or without white outline rear sight. Functional life exceeds 15 years. From Innovative Weaponry, Inc.
Price: Handgun sight sets ... **$89.00**
Price: Rifle sight sets ... **$89.00**
Price: Rifle, front only ... **$45.00**
Price: Shotgun, front only ... **$45.00**

T/C ENCORE FIBER-OPTIC SIGHT SETS Click adjustable, steel rear sight and ramp-style front sight, both fitted with Tru-Glo™ fiber-optics. Specifically-designed for the T/C Encore pistol series. From Thompson/Center Arms.
Price: ... **$49.35**

T/C ENCORE TARGET REAR SIGHT Precision, steel construction with click adjustments (via knurled knobs) for windage and elevation. Models available with low, medium and high blades. From Thompson/Center Arms.
Price: ... **$54.00**

METALLIC SIGHTS

TRIJICON NIGHT SIGHTS Three-dot night sight system uses tritium lamps in the front and rear sights. Tritium "lamps" are mounted in silicone rubber inside a metal cylinder. A polished crystal sapphire provides protection and clarity. Inlaid white outlines provide 3-dot aiming in daylight also. Available for most popular handguns including Glock 17, 19, 20, 21, 23, 24, 25, 26, 29, 30, H&K USP, Ruger P94, SIG P220, P225, 226, Colt 1911. Front and rear sets available. From Trijicon, Inc.
Price: . . . . . **$80.00 to $299.00**

TRIJICON 3-DOT Self-luminous front iron night sight for the Ruger SP101.
Price: **$50.00**

WICHITA SERIES 70/80 SIGHT Provides click windage and elevation adjustments with precise repeatability of settings. Sight blade is grooved and angled back at the top to reduce glare. Available in Low Mount Combat or Low Mount Target-styles for Colt 45s and their copies, S&W 645, Hi-Power, CZ 75 and others.
Price: Rear sight, target or combat **$75.00**
Price: Front sight, Patridge or ramp **$18.00**

WICHITA GRAND MASTER DELUXE RIBS Ventilated rib has wings machined into it for better sight acquisition and is relieved for Mag-Na-Porting. Milled to accept Weaver see-through-style rings. Made of stainless; front and rear sights blued. Has Wichita Multi-Range rear sight system, adjustable front sight. Made for revolvers with 6" barrel.
Price: Model 301S, 301B (adj. sight K frames with custom bbl. of 1" to 1.032" dia. L and N frame with 1.062" to 1.100" dia. bbl.) **$225.00**
Price: Model 303S, 303B (adj. sight K, L, N frames with factory barrel) **$225.00**

WICHITA MULTI-RANGE QUICK CHANGE SIGHTING SYSTEM Multi-range rear sight can be pre-set to four positive repeatable range settings. Adjustable front sight allows compensation for changing lighting and weather conditions with just one front sight adjustment. Front sight comes with Lyman 17A Globe and set of apertures.
Price: Rear sight **$125.00**
Price: Front, sight **$95.00**

WILLIAMS FIRE SIGHT SETS Red fiber-optic metallic sight replaces the original. Rear sight has two green fiber-optic elements. Made of CNC-machined aluminum. Fits all Glocks, Ruger P-Series (except P-85), S&W 910, Colt Gov't. Model Series 80, Ruger GP 100 and Redhawk, and SIG Sauer (front only).
Price: Front and rear set **$45.95**
Price: SIG Sauer front **$22.95**
Price: Browning BuckMark sight set **$45.95**
Price: Taurus PT111, PT140, PT145, PT1232, PT138 . . . . . **$45.95**
Price: Ruger P Series, Glock, S&W 910, Colt Gov't. Series 80, Springfield XD **$44.95**

WILSON ADJUSTABLE REAR SIGHTS Machined from steel, the click adjustment design requires simple cuts and no dovetails for installation. Available in several configurations: matte black standard blade with .128" notch; with .110" notch; with tritium dots and .128" square or "U" shaped notch; and Combat Pyramid. From Wilson Combat.
Price: . . . . . **$24.95 to $69.95**

WILSON NITE-EYES SIGHTS Low-profile, snag-free design with green and yellow tritium inserts. For 1911-style pistols. From Wilson Combat.
Price: **$119.95**

WILSON TACTICAL COMBAT SIGHTS Low-profile and snag-free in design, the sight employs the Combat Pyramid shape. For many 1911-style pistols and some Glock models. From Wilson Combat.
Price: **$139.95**

Shotgun Sights

AO SHOTGUN SIGHTS 24/7 Pro Express sights fit Remington rifle sighted barrels. Front sight dovetails into existing ramp, rear installs on Remington rear ramp. Available in Big Dot tritium or Standard Dot tritium. Three other styles (for pedestal base, beaded, and ribbed barrels) provide a Big Dot tritium front that epoxies over the existing bead front sight. From AO Sight Systems, Inc.
Price: 24/7 tritium Sets . . . . . **$90.00 to $120.00**
Price: Big Dot tritium (front only) **$60.00**

ACCURA-SITE For shooting shotgun slugs. Three models to fit most shotguns: "A" for vent rib barrels, "B" for solid ribs, "C" for plain barrels. Rear sight has windage and elevation provisions. Easily removed and replaced. Includes front and rear sights. From All's, The Jim Tembeils Co.
Price: . . . . . **$27.95 to $34.95**

FIRE FLY EM-109 SL SHOTGUN SIGHT Made of aircraft-grade aluminum, this 1/4-oz. "channel" sight has a thick, sturdy hollowed post between the side rails to give a Patridge sight picture. All shooting is done with both eyes open, allowing the shooter to concentrate on the target, not the sights. The hole in the sight post gives reduced-light shooting capability and allows for fast, precise aiming. For sport or combat shooting. Model EM-109 fits all vent rib and double barrel shotguns and muzzleloaders with octagon barrel. Model MOC-110 fits all plain barrel shotguns without screw-in chokes. From JAS, Inc.
Price: **$35.00**

LYMAN Three sights of oversized ivory beads. No. 10 Front (press fit) for double barrel or ribbed single barrel guns **$4.50**; No. 10D Front (screw fit) for non-ribbed single barrel guns (comes with wrench) **$5.50**; No. 11 Middle (press fit) for double and ribbed single barrel guns.
Price: **$4.75**

MMC M&P COMBAT SHOTGUN SIGHT SET A durable, protected ghost ring aperture, combat sight made of steel. Fully adjustable for windage and elevation.
Price: M&P Sight Set (front and rear) **$73.45**
Price: As above, installed **$83.95**

MMC TACTICAL GHOST RING SIGHT Click adjustable for elevation with 30 MOA total adjustment in 3 MOA increments. Click windage adjustment. Machined from 4140 steel, heat-treated to 40 RC. Front sight available in banded tactical or serrated ramp. Front and rear sights available with or without tritium. Available in three different finishes.
Price: Rear Ghost Ring with tritium **$119.95**
Price: Rear Ghost Ring without tritium **$99.95**
Price: Front Banded Tactical with tritium **$59.95**
Price: Front Banded Tactical without tritium **$39.95**
Price: Front serrated ramp **$24.95**

MARBLE SHOTGUN BEAD SIGHTS No. 214-Ivory front bead, 11/64", tapered shank **$4.40**; No. 223-Ivory rear bead, .080", tapered shank **$4.40**; No. 217-Ivory front bead, 11/64", threaded shank **$4.75**; No. 223-T-Ivory rear bead, .080, threaded shank **$5.95**. Reamers, taps and wrenches available from Marble Arms.

MEPROLIGHT Ghost ring sight set for Benelli tactical shotguns. From Meprolight, Inc.
Price: **$100.00**

MILLETT SHURSHOT SHOTGUN SIGHT A sight system for shotguns with ventilated rib. Rear sight attaches to the rib, front sight replaces the front bead. Front has an orange face, rear has two orange bars. For 870, 1100 or other models.
Price: Rear, fixed **$13.81**
Price: Adjustable front and rear set **$32.55**
Price: Front **$13.60**

NECG IVORY SHOTGUN BEAD Genuine ivory shotgun beads with 6-48 thread. Available in heights of .157" and .197". From New England Custom Gun Service.
Price: **$12.00**

POLY-CHOKE Replacement front shotgun sights in four styles: Xpert, Poly Bead, Xpert Mid Rib sights, and Bev-L-Block. Xpert Front available in 3x56, 6x48 thread, 3/32" or 5/32" shank length, gold, ivory **$4.70**; Sun Spot orange bead **$5.95**; Poly Bead is standard replacement 1/8" bead, 6x48 **$2.95**; Xpert Mid Rib in tapered carrier (ivory only) **$5.95**, or 3x56 threaded shank (gold only) **$2.95**; Hi and Lo Blok sights with 6x48 thread, gold or ivory **$5.25**. From Marble Arms.

SLUG SIGHTS Made of non-marring black nylon, front and rear sights stretch over and lock onto barrel. Sights are low profile with blaze orange front blade. Adjustable for windage and elevation. For plain-barrel (non-ribbed) guns in 12-, 16- and 20-gauge, and for shotguns with 5/16" and 3/8" ventilated ribs. From Innovision Ent.
Price: **$11.95**

TRIJICON 3-DOT NIGHT SIGHTS Self-luminous and machined from steel. Available for Remington 870, 1100, 1187.
Price: . . . . . **$75.00 to $175.00**

WILLIAMS GUIDE BEAD SIGHT Fits all shotguns, 1/8" ivory, red or gold bead. Screws into existing sight hole. Various thread sizes and shank lengths.
Price: **$8.50**

WILLIAMS UNIVERSAL SLUGGER Shotgun fire sight set. Fiber-optic, front and rear metallic sights attach to most vent ribs. Adjustable for windage and elevation. No gunsmithing required.
Price: **$39.95**

WILLIAMS FIRE SIGHTS Fiber-optic light gathering front sights in red or yellow, glow with natural light. Fit 1/4", 5/16" or 3/8" vent ribs, most popular shotguns.
Price: **$13.95**

Sight Attachments

MERIT ADJUSTABLE APERTURES Eleven clicks give 12 different apertures. No. 3 Disc and Master, primarily target types, 0.22" to .125"; No. 4, 1/2" dia. hunting type, .025" to .155". Available for all popular sights. The Master, with flexible rubber light shield, is particularly adapted to extension, scope height, and tang sights. All models have internal click springs; are hand fitted to minimum tolerance.
Price: No. 3 Master Disk **$66.00**
Price: No. 3 Target Disc (Plain Face) **$56.00**
Price: No. 4 Hunting Disc **$48.00**

MERIT LENS DISC Similar to Merit Iris Shutter (Model 3 or Master) but incorporates provision for mounting prescription lens integrally. Lens may be obtained locally from your optician. Sight disc is 7/16" wide (Model 3), or 3/4" wide (Master).
Price: No. 3 Target Lens Disk **$68.00**
Price: No. 3 Master Lens Disk **$78.00**

MERIT OPTICAL ATTACHMENT For iron sight shooting with handgun or rifle. Instantly attached by rubber suction cup to prescription or shooting glasses. Swings aside. Aperture adjustable from .020" to .156".
Price: **$65.00**

WILLIAMS APERTURES Standard thread, fits most sights. Regular series 3/8" to 1/2" O.D., .050" to .125" hole. "Twilight" series has white reflector ring.
Price: Regular series **$4.97**
Price: Twilight series **$6.79**
Price: Wide open 5/16" aperture for shotguns, fits 5-D or Foolproof sights (specify model) **$8.77**

SPOTTING SCOPES

Bushnell Collapsible Spotting Scope

ALPEN MODEL 711 20x50 mini-scope, 20x, 50mm eyepiece, field of view at 1,000 yds. 147 ft., multi-coated lens, weighs 10 oz., waterproof.
Price: $60.97

ALPEN MODEL 722 12-36x compact, 50mm eyepiece, field of view at 115/59, multi-coated lens, weighs 27 oz., waterproof.
Price: $124.20

ALPEN MODEL 725 and 728 Compact 15-45x60, 60mm obj., center focus, multi-coated lens, field of view at 115/59, weighs 27 oz., waterproof.
Price: .... $151.62 and $154.85

ALPEN MODEL 730 15-30x50, 60mm obs., field of view at 136-99, multi-coated lens, weighs 28 oz., waterproof.
Price: $116.14

ALPEN MODEL 788 20-60x80, 80mm obj., field of view at 93/47, multi-coated lens, weighs 64 oz., waterproof.
Price: $385.51

BROWNING 15-45x zoom, 65mm objective lens. Weighs 48 oz. Waterproof, fogproof. Tripod, soft and hard cases included.
Price: $559.95

BUSHNELL DISCOVERER, 15x to 60x zoom, 60mm objective. Constant focus throughout range. Field of view at 1,000 yds. 38 ft. (60x), 150 ft. (15x). Comes with lens caps. Length: 17-1/2"; weighs 48.5 oz.
Price: $342.95

BUSHNELL ELITE 15x to 45x zoom, 60mm objective. Field of view at 1,000 yds., 125-65 ft. Length: 12.2"; weighs 26.5 oz. Waterproof, armored. Tripod mount. Comes with black case.
Price: $586.95

BUSHNELL ELITE ZOOM 20x-60x, 70mm objective. Roof prism. Field of view at 1,000 yds. 90-50 ft. Length: 16"; weighs 40 oz. Waterproof, armored. Tripod mount. Comes with black case.
Price: $806.95

BUSHNELL 80MM ELITE 20x-60x zoom, 80mm objective. Field of view at 1,000 yds. 98-50 ft. (zoom). Weighs 51 oz. (20x), 54 oz. (zoom); length: 17". Interchangeable bayonet-style eyepieces. Built-in peep sight.
Price: With EDPrime Glass $1,173.95

BUSHNELL TROPHY 65mm objective, 20x-60x zoom. Field of view at 1,000 yds. 90 ft. (20x), 45 ft. (60x). Length: 12.7"; weighs 20 oz. Black rubber armored, waterproof. Case included.
Price: $297.95

BUSHNELL COMPACT TROPHY 50mm objective, 20x-50x zoom. Field of view at 1,000 yds. 92 ft. (20x), 52 ft. (50x). Length: 12.2"; weighs 17 oz. Black rubber armored, waterproof. Case included.
Price: $257.95

BUSHNELL COMPACT SENTRY 12-36 zoom, 50mm objective. Field of view at 1,000 yds. 140-46 ft. Length: 8.7"; weighs 21.5 oz. Black rubber armored. Comes with hard-side and soft-side carry cases. Waterproof.
Price: $199.95

BUSHNELL SPACEMASTER 20x-45x zoom. Long eye relief. Rubber armored, prismatic. 60mm objective. Field of view at 1,000 yds. 90-58 ft. Minimum focus 20 ft. Length: 12.7"; weighs 43 oz.
Price: With tripod, carrying case and 20x-45x LER eyepiece. $491.95

BUSHNELL SPACEMASTER COLLAPSIBLE 15-45x zoom, 50mm objective lens. Field of view at 1,000 yds., 113 ft. (15x), 52 ft. (45x). Length: 8". Weighs 22.8 oz. Comes with tripod, window mount and case.
Price: $209.95

BUSHNELL SPORTVIEW 15x-45x zoom, 50mm objective. Field of view at 1,000 yds. 103 ft. (15x), 35 ft. (45x). Length: 17.4"; weighs 34.4 oz.
Price: With tripod and carrying case $91.95

CELESTRON MINI 50MM ZOOM Offset 45° or straight body. Comes with 12x36x eyepiece. 50mm obj. Field of view at 1,000 yds. 160 (or 82), waterproof. Length: 8.5"; weighs 1.4 lbs.
Price: .... NA

CELESTRON ULTIMA SERIES Offset 45° or straight body. 18x55, 20-60 zoom or 22-60 zoom. Aperture: 65mm, 80mm or 100mm, field of view at 1,000 yds., 89' at 18x, 38' at 55x, 105' at 20x, 95' at 22x, 53' at 66x. Length: 13", 16" or 19". Weighs 2.3 to 4.5 lbs.
Price: Body... NA

HERMES 1 70mm objective, 16x, 25x, 40x. Field of view at 1,000 meters 160 ft. (16x), 75 ft. (40x). Length: 12.2"; weighs 33 oz. From CZ-USA.
Price: Body... $359.00
Price: 25x eyepiece $86.00
Price: 40x eyepiece $128.00

KOWA TS-500 SERIES Offset 45° or straight body. Comes with 20-40x zoom eyepiece or 20x fixed eyepiece. 50mm obj. Field of view at 1,000 yds.: 171 ft. (20x fixed), 132-74 ft. (20-40x zoom). Length: 8.9-10.4", weighs 13.4-14.8 oz.
Price: TS-501 (offset 45° body w/20x fixed eyepiece) $258.00
Price: TS-502 (straight body w/20x fixed eyepiece) $231.00
Price: TS-501Z (offset 45° body w/20-40x zoom eyepiece) $321.00
Price: TS-502Z (straight body w/20-40x zoom eyepiece) $290.00

KOWA TS-660 SERIES Offset 45° or straight body. Fully waterproof. Available with ED lens. Sunshade and rotating tripod mount. 66mm obj. Field of view at 1,000 yds.: 177 ft. (20xW), 154 ft. (27xW), 131 ft. (30xW), 102 ft. (25x), 92 ft. (25xLER), 108-79 ft. (20-40x multi-coated zoom), 98-62 ft. (20-60x high grade zoom). Length: 12.3"; weighs 34.9-36.7 oz.
Price: TSN-662 body (straight) $610.00
Price: TSN-663 body (45 offset, ED lens) $1,070.00
Price: TSN-664 body (straight, ED lens) $1,010.00
Price: TSE-Z6 (20-40x multi-coatedzoom eyepiece) $378.00
Price: TSE-17HB (25x long eye relief eyepiece) $240.00
Price: TSE-14W (30x wide angle high-grade eyepiece) $288.00
Price: TSE-21WB (20x wide-angle eyepiece) $230.00
Price: TSE-15 WM (27x wide-angle eyepiece) $182.00
Price: TSE-16 PM (25x eyepiece) $108.00
Price: TSN-DA1 digital photo adapter $105.00
Price: DA1 adapter rings $43.00
Price: TSN-PA2 (800mm photo adapter)...................... $269.00
Price: TSN-PA4 (1200mm photo adapter) $330.00
Price: Camera mounts (for use with photo adapter) $30.00
Price Eyepieces for TSN 77mm series,
TSN-660 series, 661 body (45° offset) $660.00

KOWA TSN-660 SERIES Offset 45° or straight body. Fully waterproof. Available with fluorite lens. Sunshade and rotating tripod mount. 66mm obj., field of view at 1,000 yds: 177 ft. (20x), 154 ft. (27xW), 131 ft. (30xW), 102 ft. (25x), 92 ft. (25xLER), 62 ft. (40x), 108-79 ft. (20-40x Multi-Coated Zoom), 102-56 ft. (20-60x zoom), 98-62 ft. (20-60x High Grade Zoom). Length: 12.3"; weighs 34.9-36.7 oz. Note: Eyepieces for TSN 77mm Series, TSN-660 Series, and TSN610 Series are interchangeable.
Price: TSN-661 body (45° offset) $660.00
Price: TSN-662 body (straight) $610.00
Price: TSN-663 body (45° offset, fluorite lens) $1,070.00
Price: TSN-664 body (straight, fluorite lens) $1,010.00
Price: TSE-Z4 (20-60x high-grade zoom eyepiece) $378.00
Price: TSE-Z6 (20-40x multi-coated zoom eyepiece) $250.00
Price: TSE-17HB (25x long eye relief eyepiece) $240.00
Price: TSE-14W (30x wide angle eyepiece) $288.00
Price: TSE-21WB (20x wide angle eyepiece) $230.00
Price: TSE-15PM (27x wide angle eyepiece) $182.00
Price: TSE-10PM (40x eyepiece)............................ $108.00
Price: TSE-16PM (25x eyepiece) $105.00
Price: TSN-DA1 (digital photo adapter) $105.00
Price: Adapter rings for DA1 .... $43.00
Price: TSN-PA2 (800mm photo adapter)...................... $269.00
Price: TSN-PA4 (1200mm photo adapter) $330.00
Price: Camera mounts (for use with photo adapter) $30.00

KOWA TSN-820M SERIES Offset 45° or straight body. Fully waterproof. Available with fluorite lens. Sunshade and rotating tripod mount. 82mm obj., field of view at 1,000 yds: 75 ft. (27xLER, 50xW), 126 ft. (32xW), 115-58 ft. (20-60xZoom). Length: 15"; weighs 49.4-52.2 oz.
Price: TSN-821M body (45° offset) $850.00
Price: TSN-822M body (straight) $770.00
Price: TSN-823M body (45° offset, fluorite lens) $1,850.00
Price: TSN-824M body (straight, fluorite lens) $1,730.00
Price: TSE-Z7 (20-60x zoom eyepiece) $433.00
Price: TSE-9W (50x wide angle eyepiece) $345.00
Price: TSE-14WB (32x wide angle eyepiece) $366.00
Price: TSE-17HC (27x long eye relief eyepiece) $248.00
Price: TSN-DA1 (digital photo adapter) $105.00
Price: Adapter rings for DA1 .... $43.00
Price: TSN-PA2C (850mm photo adapter) $300.00
Price: Camera mounts (for use with photo adapter) $30.00

LEUPOLD 10-20x40mm COMPACT 40mm objective, 10-20x. Field of view at 100 yds. 19.9-13.6 ft.; eye relief 18.5mm (10x). Overall length: 7.5", weighs 15.8 oz. Rubber armored.
Price: $439.95

LEUPOLD 55-30x50 COMPACT 50mm objective, 15-30x. Field of view at 100 yds. 13.6 ft.; eye relief 17.5mm; Overall length: 11"; weighs 1.5 oz.
Price: $564.99

LEUPOLD Wind River Sequoia 15-30x60mm, 60mm objective, 15-30x. Field of view at 100 yds.: 13.1 ft.; eye relief 16.5mm. Overall length: 13". Weighs 35.1 oz.
Price: $294.99

SPOTTING SCOPES

LEUPOLD Wind River Sequoia 15-45x60mm Angled. Armored, 15-45x. Field of view at 100 yds.: 13.1-6.3 ft.; eye relief: 16.5-13.0. Overall length: 12.5". Weighs 35.1 oz.
Price: **$309.99**

LEUPOLD Golden Ring 12-40x60mm; 12.7x38.1x. Field of view at 100 yds.: 16.8-5.2 ft.; eye relief: 30.0; Overall length: 12.4". Weighs 37.0 oz.
Price: **$1,124.99**

LEUPOLD Golden Ring 15-30x50mm Compact Armored; 15.2-30.4x; field of view at 100 yds.: 13.6-8.9 ft.; eye relief: 17.5-17.1; overall length: 11.0". Weighs 21.5 oz.
Price: **$564.99**

MIRADOR TTB SERIES Draw tube armored spotting scopes. Available with 75mm or 80mm objective. Zoom model (28x-62x, 80mm) is 11-7/8" (closed), weighs 50 oz. Field of view at 1,000 yds. 70-42 ft. Comes with lens covers.
Price: 28-62x80mm **$1,133.95**
Price: 32x80mm **$971.95**
Price: 26-58x75mm **$989.95**
Price: 30x75mm **$827.95**

MIRADOR SSD SPOTTING SCOPES 60mm objective, 15x, 20x, 22x, 25x, 40x, 60x, 20-60x; field of view at 1,000 yds. 37 ft.; length: 10 1/4"; weighs 33 oz.
Price: 25x **$575.95**
Price: 22x Wide Angle **$593.95**
Price: 20-60x Zoom **$746.95**
Price: As above, with tripod, case **$944.95**

MIRADOR SIA SPOTTING SCOPES Similar to the SSD scopes except with 45° eyepiece. Length: 12-1/4"; weighs 39 oz.
Price: 25x **$809.95**
Price: 22x Wide Angle **$827.95**
Price: 20-60x Zoom **$980.95**

MIRADOR SSR SPOTTING SCOPES 50mm or 60mm objective. Similar to SSD except rubber armored in black or camouflage. Length: 11-1/8"; weighs 31 oz.
Price: Black, 20x **$521.95**
Price: Black, 18x Wide Angle **$539.95**
Price: Black, 16-48x Zoom **$692.95**
Price: Black, 20x, 60mm, EER **$692.95**
Price: Black, 22x Wide Angle, 60mm **$701.95**
Price: Black, 20-60x Zoom **$854.95**

MIRADOR SSF FIELD SCOPES Fixed or variable power, choice of 50mm, 60mm, 75mm objective lens. Length: 9-3/4"; weighs 20 oz. (15-32x50).
Price: 20x50mm **$359.95**
Price: 25x60mm **$440.95**
Price: 30x75mm **$584.95**
Price: 15-32x50mm Zoom **$548.95**
Price: 18-40x60mm Zoom **$629.95**
Price: 22-47x75mm Zoom **$773.95**

MIRADOR SRA MULTI ANGLE SCOPES Similar to SSF Series except eyepiece head rotates for viewing from any angle.
Price: 20x50mm **$503.95**
Price: 25x60mm **$647.95**
Price: 30x75mm **$764.95**
Price: 15-32x50mm Zoom **$692.95**
Price: 18-40x60mm Zoom **$836.95**
Price: 22-47x75mm Zoom **$953.95**

MIRADOR SIB FIELD SCOPES Short-tube, 45° scopes with porro prism design. 50mm and 60mm objective. Length: 10 1/4"; weighs 18.5 oz. (15-32x50mm); field of view at 1,000 yds. 129-81 ft.
Price: 20x50mm **$386.95**
Price: 25x60mm **$449.95**
Price: 15-32x50mm Zoom **$575.95**
Price: 18-40x60mm Zoom **$638.95**

NIKON FIELDSCOPES 60mm and 78mm lens. Field of view at 1,000 yds. 105 ft. (60mm, 20x), 126 ft. (78mm, 25x). Length: 12.8" (straight 60mm), 12.6" (straight 78mm); weighs 34.5 to 47.5 oz. Eyepieces available separately.
Price: 60mm straight body **$499.99**
Price: 60mm angled body **$519.99**
Price: 60mm straight ED body **$779.99**
Price: 60mm angled ED body **$849.99**
Price: 78mm straight ED body **$899.99**
Price: 78mm angled ED body **$999.99**
Price: Eyepieces (15x to 60x) . . . . **$146.95 to $324.95**
Price: 20-45x eyepiece (25-56x for 78mm) **$320.55**

NIKON 60mm objective, 20x fixed power or 15-45x zoom. Field of view at 1,000 yds. 145 ft. (20x). Gray rubber armored. Straight or angled eyepiece. Weighs 44.2 oz., length: 12.1" (20x).
Price: 20x60 fixed (with eyepiece) **$290.95**
Price: 15-45x zoom (with case, tripod, eyepiece) **$578.95**

PENTAX PF-80ED 80mm objective lens available in 18x, 24x, 36x, 48x, 72x and 20-60x. Length: 15.6", weighs 11.9 to 19.2 oz.
Price: **$1,320.00**

SIGHTRON SII 2050X63 63mm objective lens, 20x-50x zoom. Field of view at 1,000 yds 91.9 ft. (20x), 52.5 ft. (50x). Length: 14"; weighs 30.8 oz. Black rubber finish. Also available with 80mm objective lens.
Price: 63mm or 80mm **$339.95**

SIMMONS 1280 50mm objective, 15-45x zoom. Black matte finish. Ocular focus. Peep finder sight. Waterproof. Field of view at 95-51 ft. 1,000 yds. Weights 33.5 oz., length: 12".
Price: With tripod **$189.99**

SIMMONS 1281 60mm objective, 20-60x zoom. Black matte finish. Ocular focus. Peep finder sight. Waterproof. Field of view at 78-43 ft. 1,000 yds. Weighs 34.5 oz. Length: 12".
Price: With tripod **$209.99**

SIMMONS 77206 PROHUNTER 50mm objectives, 25x fixed power. Field of view at 1,000 yds. 113 ft.; length: 10.25"; weighs 33.25 oz. Black rubber armored.
Price: With tripod case **$160.60**

SIMMONS 41200 REDLINE 50mm objective, 15x-45x zoom. Field of view at 1,000 yds. 104-41 ft.; length: 16.75"; weighs 32.75 oz.
Price: With hard case and tripod **$74.99**
Price: 20-60x, 60mm objective **$99.99**

SWAROVSKI ATS-STS 65mm or 80mm objective, 20-60x zoom, or fixed 20x, 30x 45x eyepieces. Field of view at 1,000 yds. 180 ft. (20xSW), 126 ft. (30xSW), 84 ft. (45xSW), 108-60 ft. (20-60xS) for zoom. Length: 13.98" (ATS/STS 80), 12.8" (ATS/STS 65); weighs 45.93 oz. (ATS 80), 47.70 oz. (ATS 80HD), 45.23 oz. (STS 80), 46.9 oz. (STS 80 HD), 38.3 oz. (ATS 65), 39.9 oz. (ATS 65HD) 38.1 oz. (STS 65), 39.2 oz. (STS 65 HD).
Price: ATS 65 (angled eyepiece) **$1,154.44**
Price: STS 65 (straight eyepiece) **$1,154.44**
Price: ATS-80 . . . . **$1,410.00**
Price: ATS-80 (HD) **$1,898.89**
Price: 20xSW **$332.00**
Price: 30xSW **$332.00**
Price: 45xSW **$398.89**

SWIFT LYNX M836 15x-45x zoom, 60mm objective. Weighs 7 lbs., length: 14". Has 45° eyepiece, sunshade.
Price: **$315.00**

SWIFT NIGHTHAWK M849U 80mm objective, 20x-60x zoom, or fixed 19, 25x, 31x, 50x, 75x eyepieces. Has rubber armored body, 1.8x optical finder, retractable lens hood, 45° eyepiece. Field of view at 1,000 yds. 60 ft. (28x), 41 ft. (75x). Length: 13.4 oz.; weighs 39 oz.
Price: Body only **$870.00**
Price: 20-68x eyepiece **$370.00**
Price: Fixed eyepieces . . . . **$130.00 to $240.00**
Price: Model 849 (straight) body **$795.00**

SWIFT LYNX 60mm objective, 15-45x zoom, 45° inclined roof prism, magenta coated on all air-to-glass surfaces, rubber armored body, length: 14", weighs 30 oz. Equipped with sun shade, threaded dust covers and low level tripod.
Price: complete **$330.00**

SWIFT TELEMASTER M841 60mm objective. 15x to 60x variable power. Field of view at 1,000 yds. 160 feet (15x) to 40 feet (60x). Weighs 3.25 lbs.; length: 18" overall.
Price: **$399.50**

SWIFT PANTHER M844 15x-45x zoom or 22x WA, 15x, 20x, 40x. 60mm objective. Field of view at 1,000 yds. 141 ft. (15x), 68 ft. (40x), 95-58 ft. (20x-45x).
Price: Body only **$380.00**
Price: 15x-45x zoom eyepiece **$120.00**
Price: 20x-45x zoom (long eye relief) eyepiece **$140.00**
Price: 15x, 40x eyepiece **$65.00**
Price: 22x WA eyepiece **$80.00**

SWIFT M700T 12x-36x, 50mm objective. Field of view at 100 yds. 16 ft. (12x), 9 ft. (36x). Length: 14"; weighs 3.22 lbs. (with tripod).
Price: **$30.00**

TASCO 15-45x zoom, 50mm objective lens, 20x-60x zoom. Field of view at 100 yds. 19 ft. (15x) Length: 16". Weighs 19 oz. Matte black finish.
Price: **$67.95**

TASCO 20-60x zoom, 60mm objective, 12-36x zoom. Field of view at 100 yds. 12 ft. (20x). Length: 20". Weighs 50 oz. Black finish.
Price: **$95.95**

TASCO 18-36x zoom 50mm objective. Field of view at 100 yds. 12 ft. (18x). Length: 14.5". Weighs 31 oz. Camo or black rubber armor. Includes carrying case.
Price: **$131.95**

UNERTL "FORTY-FIVE" 54mm objective. 20x (single fixed power). Field of view at 100 yds. 10',10"; eye relief 1"; focusing range infinity to 33 ft. Weighs about 32 oz.; overall length: 15-3/4". With lens covers.
Price: With mono-layer magnesium coating **$810.00**

UNERTL STRAIGHT PRISMATIC 24x63. 63.5mm objective, 24x. Field of view at 100 yds., 7 ft. Relative brightness, 6.96. Eye relief 1/2". Weighs 40 oz.; length: closed 19". Push-pull and screw-focus eyepiece. 16x and 32x eyepieces **$125.00 each.**
Price: **$786.00**

UNERTL 20x STRAIGHT PRISMATIC 54mm objective, 20x. Field of view at 100 yds. 8.5 ft. Relative brightness 6.1. Eye relief 1/2". Weighs 36 oz.; length: closed 13-1/2". Complete with lens covers.
Price: **$695.00**

UNERTL TEAM SCOPE 100mm objective. 15x, 24x, 32x eyepieces. Field of view at 100 yds. 13 to 7.5 ft. Relative brightness, 39.06 to 9.79. Eye relief 2" to 1-1/2". Weighs 13 lbs.; length: 29-7/8" overall. Metal tripod, yoke and wood carrying case furnished (total weighs 80 lbs.).
Price: **$3,624.50**

WEAVER 20x50 50mm objective. Field of view 124 ft. at 100 yds. Eye relief .85"; weighs 21 oz.; overall length: 10". Waterproof, armored.
Price: **$249.99**

WEAVER 15-40x60 ZOOM 60mm objective. 15x-40x zoom. Field of view at 100 yds. 119 ft. (15x), 66 ft. (60x). Overall length: 12.5", weighs 26 oz. Waterproof, armored.
Price: **$399.99**

CHOKES AND BRAKES

Briley Screw-In Chokes

Installation of these choke tubes requires that all traces of the original choking be removed, the barrel threaded internally with square threads and then the tubes are custom fitted to the specific barrel diameter. The tubes are thin and, therefore, made of stainless steel. Cost of installation for single-barrel guns (pumps, autos), lead shot, 12-gauge, **$149.00**, 20-gauge **$159.00**; steel shot **$179.00** and **$189.00**, all with three chokes; un-single target guns run **$219.00**; over/unders and side-by-sides, lead shot, 12-gauge, **$369.00**, 20-gauge **$389.00**; steel shot **$469.00** and **$489.00**, all with five chokes. For 10-gauge auto or pump with two steel shot chokes, **$189.00**; over/unders, side-by-sides with three steel shot chokes, **$349.00**. For 16-gauge auto or pump, three lead shot chokes, **$179.00**; over/unders, side-by-sides with five lead shot chokes, **$449.00**. The 28 and 410-bore run **$179.00** for autos and pumps with three lead shot chokes, **$449.00** for over/unders and side-by-sides with five lead shot chokes.

Carlson's Choke Tubes

Manufactures choke tubes for Beretta, Benelli, Remington, Winchester, Browning Invector and Invector Plus, TruChokes, FranChokes, American Arms, Ruger and more. All choke tubes are manufactured from corrosion resistant stainless steel. Most tubes are compatible with lead, steel, Hevi-shot, etc. Available in flush mount, extended sporting clay and extended turkey designs, ported and non-ported. Also offers sights, rifled choke tubes and other accessories for most shotgun models. Prices range from **$18.95** to **$36.95**.

Cutts Compensator

The Cutts Compensator is one of the oldest variable choke devices available. Manufactured by Lyman Gunsight Corporation, it is available with a steel body. A series of vents allows gas to escape upward and downward. For the 12-ga. Comp body, six fixed-choke tubes are available: the Spreader–popular with skeet shooters; Improved Cylinder; Modified; Full; Superfull, and Magnum Full. Full, Modified and Spreader tubes are available for 12 or 20. Cutts Compensator, complete with wrench, adaptor and any single tube **$87.50**. All single choke tubes **$26.00** each. No factory installation available.

Dayson Automatic Brake System

This system fits most single barrel shotguns threaded for choke tubes, and cuts away 30 grooves on the exterior of a standard one-piece wad as it exits the muzzle. This slows the wad, allowing shot and wad to separate faster, reducing shot distortion and tightening patterns. The A.B.S. choke tube is claimed to reduce recoil by about 25 percent, and with the muzzle brake up to 60 percent. Ventilated choke tubes available from .685" to .725", in .005" increments. Model I ventilated choke tube for use with A.B.S. muzzle brake, **$49.95**; for use without muzzle brake, **$52.95**; A.B.S. muzzle brake, from **$69.95**. Contact Dayson Arms for more data.

Gentry Quiet Muzzle Brake

Developed by gunmaker David Gentry, the "Quiet Muzzle Brake" is said to reduce recoil by up to 85 percent with no loss of accuracy or velocity. There is no increase in noise level because the noise and gases are directed away from the shooter. The barrel is threaded for installation and the unit is blued to match the barrel finish. Price, installed, is **$150.00**. Add **$15.00** for stainless steel, **$45.00** for knurled cap to protect threads. Shipping extra.

JP Muzzle Brake

JP Muzzle Brake

Designed for single shot handguns, AR-15, Ruger Mini-14, Ruger Mini Thirty and other sporting rifles, the JP muzzle brake redirects high pressure gases against a large frontal surface which applies forward thrust to the gun. All gases are directed up, rearward and to the sides. Priced at **$79.95** (AR-15 or sporting rifles), **$89.95** (bull barrel and SKS, AK models), **$89.95** (Ruger Minis), dual chamber model **$79.95**. From JP Enterprises, Inc.

KDF Slim Line Muzzle Brake

This threaded muzzle brake has 30 pressure ports that direct combustion gases in all directions to reduce felt recoil up to a claimed 80 percent without affecting accuracy or ballistics. Reduces felt recoil of a 30-06 to that of a 243. Price, installed, is **$199.00**. From KDF, Inc.

KDF Kick Arrestor

This mercury-filled, inertia-type recoil reducer is installed in the butt of a wood or synthetic stock (rifle or shotgun) to reduce recoil up to 20 percent. Adds 16 oz. to the weight of the gun Measures 6.25; L x .75" in diameter. Price, installed, is **$165.00**. From KDF, Inc.

Laseraim

Simple, no-gunsmithing compensator reduces felt recoil and muzzle flip by up to 30 percent. Machined from single piece of stainless steel (Beretta/Taurus model made of aircraft aluminum). In black and polished finish. For Colt Government/Commander and Beretta/Taurus full-size pistols. Weighs 1 ounce. **$49.00**. From Laseraim Arms Inc.

Mag-Na-Port

Electrical Discharge Machining works on any firearm except those having non-conductive shrouded barrels. EDM is a metal erosion technique using carbon electrodes that control the area to be processed. The Mag-Na-Port venting process utilizes small trapezoidal openings to direct powder gases upward and outward to reduce recoil. No effect is had on bluing or nickeling outside the Mag-Na-Port area so no refinishing is needed. Rifle-style porting on single shot or large caliber handguns with barrels 7-1/2" or longer is **$115.00**; Dual Trapezoidal porting on most handguns with minimum barrel length of 3", **$115.00**; standard revolver porting, **$88.50**; Scandium/titanium-sleeved barrels **$139.50** (2 ports) or **$195.00** (4 ports); porting through the slide and barrel for semi-autos, **$129.50**; traditional rifle porting, **$135.00**. Prices do not include shipping, handling and insurance. From Mag-Na-Port International.

Mag-Na-Brake

A screw-on brake under 2" long with progressive integrated exhaust chambers to neutralize expanding gases. Gases dissipate with an opposite twist to prevent the brake from unscrewing, and with a 5° forward angle to minimize sound pressure level. Available in blue, satin blue, bright or satin stainless. Standard and Light Contour installation cost **$195.00** for bolt-action rifles, many single action and single shot handguns. A knurled thread protector supplied at extra cost. Also available in Varmint-style with exhaust chambers covering 220° for prone-position shooters. From Mag-Na-Port International.

Poly-Choke

Marble Arms Corp., manufacturer of the Poly-Choke adjustable shotgun choke, now offers two models in 12-, 16-, 20-, and 28-gauge–the ventilated and standard-style chokes. Each provides nine choke settings including Xtra-Full and Slug. The ventilated model reduces 20 percent of a shotgun's recoil, the company claims, and is priced at **$135.00**. The standard model is **$125.00**. Postage not included. Contact Marble Arms for more data.

Pro-port

A compound ellipsoid muzzle venting process similar to Mag-Na-Porting, only exclusively applied to shotguns. Like Mag-Na-Porting, this system reduces felt recoil, muzzle jump, and shooter fatigue. Pro-Port is a patented process and installation is available in both the U.S. and Canada. Cost for the Pro-Port process is **$139.00** for over/unders (both barrels); **$110.00** for only the top or bottom barrel; and **$88.50** for single-barrel shotguns. Optional pigeon porting costs **$25.00** extra per barrel. Prices do not include shipping and handling. From Pro-port Ltd.

Que Industries Adjustable Muzzle Brake

The Que Brake allows for fine-tuning of a rifle's accuracy by rotating the brake to one of 100 indexed stops. Mounts in minutes without barrel modification with heat-activated tensioning ring. The slotted exhaust ports reduce recoil by venting gases sideways, away from rifle. **$189.50**. From Que Industries.

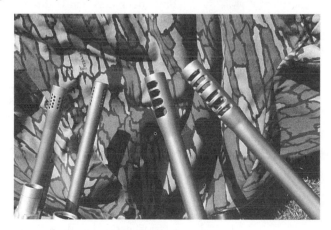

SSK Arrestor muzzle brakes

SSK Arrestor Brake

This is a true muzzle brake with an expansion chamber. It takes up about 1" of barrel and reduces velocity accordingly. Some Arrestors are added to a barrel, increasing its length. Said to reduce the felt recoil of a 458 to that approaching a 30-06. Can be set up to give zero muzzle rise in any caliber, and can be added to most guns. For handgun or rifle. Prices start at **$95.00**. Contact SSK Industries for full data.

THE 2006 Gun Digest WEB DIRECTORY

by Holt Bodinson

How old is the World Wide Web that is the basis of so much firearms e-commerce? Hard as it might be to believe, the World Wide Web did not debut until 1991—a mere 14 years ago.

This past year was significant because the person who created the World Wide Web, who never claimed a penny or royalty for his creation, was knighted. Tim Berners-Lee, a 25-year-old graduate of Oxford at the time, had a vision. "Suppose," he wrote, "all the information stored on computers everywhere was linked. Suppose I could program my computer to create a space in which every computer...on the planet would be available to me and to anyone else."

Sir Berners-Lee went on to do it, giving us the coding system HTML (HyperTextMarkup Language), the Web page address system or URL (Univeral Resource Locator), a set of rules or HTTP (HyperText Transfer Protocol) to link documents across the Internet, and the first rudimentary Web browser, permitting users to view other users' files.

And look where we are 14 years later!

The firearms industry has done a remarkably good job of adapting to e-commerce. More and more firearm related businesses are striking out and creating their own discrete web pages, and it's never been easier with the inexpensive software programs now available.

Firearm auction sites like Auction Arms or Gun Broker have brought together collectors from around the world. But beware! If you are buying a firearm over the Internet, insist on a 3-day inspection privilege. Speaking from personal experience, "a bright and shiny bore" often arrives as a "bright, shiny, and pitted bore!"

The Gun Digest Web Directory is in its seventh year of publication.

The Internet is proving to be a dynamic environment and since our last edition, there have been numerous changes. Companies have consolidated and adopted a new owner's web site address. New companies have appeared and old companies have disappeared. Search engines are now more powerful than ever and seem to root out even the most obscure reference to a product name or manufacturer.

The following index of current web addresses is offered to our readers as a convenient jumping-off point. Half the fun is just exploring what's out there. Considering that most of the web pages have hot links to other firearm-related web pages, the Internet trail just goes on-and-on once you've taken the initial step to go online.

Here are a few pointers:

If the web site you desire is not listed, try using the full name of the company or product, typed without spaces, between www.-and-.com, for example, www.krause.com. Probably 95 percent of current Web sites are based on this simple, self-explanatory format.

Try a variety of search engines like Microsoft Internet Explorer, Metacrawler, GoTo.com, Yahoo, HotBot, AltaVista, Lycos, Excite, InfoSeek, Looksmart, Google, and WebCrawler while using key words such as gun, firearm, rifle, pistol, blackpowder, shooting, hunting– frankly, any word that relates to the sport. Each search engine seems to comb through the World Wide Web in a different fashion and produces different results. We find Google to be among the best. Accessing the various search engines is simple. Just type www.google.com for example, and you're on your way.

Welcome to the digital world of firearms. Enjoy our Directory!

WEB DIRECTORY

Ammunition and Components

3-D Ammunition www.3dammo.com
Accurate Arms Co. Inc www.accuratepowder.com
ADCO/Nobel Sport Powder www.adcosales.com
Aguila Ammunition www.aguilaammo.com
Alliant Powder www.alliantpowder.com
American Ammunition www.a-merc.com
American Pioneer Powder www.americanpioneerpowder.com
Ammo Depot www.ammodepot.com
Arizona Ammunition, Inc. www.arizonaammunition.com
A-Zoom Ammo www.a-zoom.com
Ballistic Products, Inc. www.ballisticproducts.com
Barnaul Cartridge Plant www.ab.ru/~stanok
Barnes Bullets www.barnesbullets.com
Baschieri & Pellagri www.baschieri-pellagri.com
Beartooth Bullets www.beartoothbullets.com
Bell Brass www.bellbrass.com
Berger Bullets, Ltd. www.bergerbullets.com
Berry's Mfg., Inc. www.berrysmfg.com
Big Bore Bullets of Alaska www.awloo.com/bbb/index.htm
Big Bore Express www.powerbeltbullets.com
Bismuth Cartridge Co. www.bismuth-notox.com
Black Dawge Cartridge www.blackdawgecartridge.com
Black Hills Ammunition, Inc. www.black-hills.com
Brenneke of America Ltd. www.brennekeusa.com
Buffalo Arms www.buffaloarms.com
Calhoon, James, Bullets www.jamescalhoon.com
Cartuchos Saga www.saga.es
Cast Performance Bullet www.castperformance.com
CCI www.cci-ammunition.com
Century Arms www.centuryarms.com
Cheaper Than Dirt www.cheaperthandirt.com
Cheddite France www.cheddite.com
Claybuster Wads www.claybusterwads.com
Clean Shot Powder www.cleanshot.com
Cole Distributing www.cole-distributing.com
Combined Tactical Systems www.less-lethal.com
Cor-Bon/Glaser www.cor-bon.com
Cowboy Bullets www.cowboybullets.com
Denver Bullet Co. denbullets@aol.com
Dillon Precision www.dillonprecision.com
Dionisi Cartridge www.dionisi.com
DKT, Inc. www.dktinc.com
Down Range Mfg. www.downrangemfg.com
Dynamit Nobel RWS Inc. www.dnrws.com
Elephant/Swiss Black Powder www.elephantblackpowder.com
Eley Ammunition www.remington.com
Eley Hawk Ltd. www.eleyhawk.com
Eley Limited www.eley.co.uk
Estate Cartridge www.estatecartridge.com
Extreme Shock Munitions www.extremeshockusa.com
Federal Cartridge Co. www.federalpremium.com
Fiocchi of America www.fiocchiusa.com
Fowler Bullets www.benchrest.com/fowler
Garrett Cartridges www.garrettcartridges.com
Gentner Bullets www.benchrest.com/gentner/
Glaser Safety Slug, Inc. www.corbon.com
GOEX Inc. www.goexpowder.com
Graf & Sons www.grafs.com
Hawk Bullets www.hawkbullets.com
Hevi.Shot www.hevishot.com
Hi-Tech Ammunition www.iidbs.com/hitech
Hodgdon Powder www.hodgdon.com
Hornady www.hornady.com
Hull Cartridge www.hullcartridge.com
Huntington Reloading Products www.huntingtons.com
Impact Bullets www.impactbullets.com
IMR Smokeless Powders www.imrpowder.com
International Cartridge Corp www.internationalcartridgecorp.com
Israel Military Industries www.imisammo.co.il
ITD Enterprise www.itdenterprising.com
Kent Cartridge America www.kentgamebore.com
Knight Bullets www.benchrest.com/knight/
Kynoch Ammunition www.kynochammunition.com
Lapua www.lapua.com
Lawrence Brand Shot www.metalico.com
Lazzeroni Arms Co. www.lazzeroni.com
Leadheads Bullets www.proshootpro.com
Liberty Shooting Supplies www.libertyshootingsupplies.com
Lightfield Ammunition Corp www.lightfieldslugs.com
Lomont Precision Bullets www.klomont.com/kent
Lost River Ballistic Technologies, Inc. www.lostriverballistic.com
Lyman www.lymanproducts.com
Magnus Bullets www.magnusbullets.com
MagSafe Ammunition www.realpages.com/magsafeammo
Magtech www.magtechammunition.com
Mast Technology www.bellammo.com
Masterclass Bullet Co. www.mastercast.com

Meister Bullets www.meisterbullets.com
Midway U.S.A. www.midwayusa.com
Miltex, Inc. www.miltexusa.com
Mitchell Mfg. Co. www.mitchellsales.com
MK Ballistic Systems www.mkballistics.com
Mullins Ammunition www.mullinsammunition.com
National Bullet Co. www.nationalbullet.com
Nobel Sport www.adcosales.com
Nobel Sport www.snpe.com
Norma www.norma.cc
North Fork Technologies www.northforkbullets.com
Nosler Bullets, Inc. www.nosler.com
Old Western Scrounger www.ows-ammunition.com
Oregon Trail/Trueshot Bullets www.trueshotbullets.com
Pattern Control www.patterncontrol.com
PMC-Eldorado Cartridge www.pmcammo.com
Polywad www.polywad.com
PowerBelt Bullets www.powerbeltbullets.com
Precision Ammunition www.precisionammo.com
Precision Reloading www.precisionreloading.com
Pro Load Ammunition www.proload.com
Rainier Ballistics www.rainierballistics.com
Ram Shot Powder www.ramshot.com
Reloading Specialties Inc. www.reloadingspecialties.com
Remington www.remington.com
Roc Imports (GPA bullets) www.roc-import.com
Rocky Mountain Cartridge www.rockymountaincartridge.com
RWS www.dnrws.com
Schuetzen Powder www.schuetzenpowder.com
Sellier & Bellot U.S.A. inc. www.sb-usa.com
Shilen www.shilen.com
Sierra www.sierrabullets.com
Speer Bullets www.speer-bullets.com
Sporting Supplies Int'l Inc. www.ssiintl.com
Starline www.starlinebrass.com
Swift Bullets Co. www.swiftbullet.com
Top Brass www.top-brass.com
Triton Cartridge www.a-merc.com
Trueshot Bullets www.trueshotbullets.com
Tru-Tracer www.trutracer.com
Ultramax Ammunition www.ultramaxammunition.com
Vihtavuori Lapua www.vihtavuori-lapua.com
West Coast Bullets www.westcoastbullet.com
Western Powders Inc. www.westernpowders.com
Widener's Reloading & Shooters Supply www.wideners.com
Winchester Ammunition www.winchester.com
Wolf Ammunition www.wolfammo.com
Woodleigh Bullets www.woodleighbullets.com.au
Zanders Sporting Goods www.gzanders.com

Cases, Safes, Gun Locks, and Cabinets

Ace Case Co. www.acecase.com
AG English Sales Co. www.agenglish.com
All Americas' Outdoors www.innernet.net/gunsafe
Alpine Cases www.alpinecases.com
Aluma Sport by Dee Zee www.deezee.com
American Security Products www.amsecusa.com
Americase www.americase.com
Avery Outdoors, Inc. www.averyoutdoors.com
Bear Track Cases www.beartrackcases.com
Boyt Harness Co. www.boytharness.com
Bulldog Gun Safe Co. www.gardall.com
Cannon Safe Co. www.cannonsafe.com
CCL Security Products www.cclsecurity.com
Concept Development Corp. www.saf-t-blok.com
Doskocil Mfg. Co. www.doskocilmfg.com
Fort Knox Safes www.ftknox.com
Franzen Security Products www.securecase.com
Frontier Safe Co. www.frontiersafe.com
Granite Security Products www.granitesafe.com
Gunlocker Phoenix U.S.A. Inc. www.gunlocker.com
GunVault www.gunvault.com
Hakuba U.S.A. Inc. www.hakubausa.com
Heritage Safe Co. www.heritagesafecompany.com
Hide-A-Gun www.hide-a-gun.com
Homak Safes www.homak.com
Hunter Company www.huntercompany.com
Kalispel Case Line www.kalispelcaseline.com
Knouff & Knouff, Inc. www.kkair.com
Knoxx Industries www.knoxx.com
Kolpin Mfg. Co. www.kolpin.com
Liberty Safe & Security www.libertysafe.com
New Innovative Products www.starlightcases.com
Noble Security Systems Inc. www.noble.co.il
Phoenix U.S.A. Inc. www.gunlocker.com
Plano Molding Co. www.planomolding.com
Rhino Gun Cases www.rhinoguns.com
Rhino Safe www.rhinosafe.com

Safe Tech, Inc. www.safrgun.com
Saf-T-Hammer www.saf-t-hammer.com
Saf-T-Lok Corp. www.saf-t-lok.com
San Angelo All-Aluminum Products Inc. sasptuld@x.netcom.com
Securecase www.securecase.com
Shot Lock Corp. www.shotlock.com
Smart Lock Technology Inc. www.smartlock.com
Sportsmans Steel Safe Co. www.sportsmansteelsafes.com
Stack-On Products Co. www.stack-on.com
Sun Welding www.sunwelding.com
T.Z. Case Int'l. www.tzcase.com
Versatile Rack Co. www.versatilegunrack.com
V-Line Industries www.vlineind.com
Winchester Safes www.fireking.com
Ziegel Engineering www.ziegeleng.com
Zonetti Armor www.zonettiarmor.com

Choke Devices, Recoil Reducers, and Accuracy Devices

100 Straight Products www.100straight.com
Answer Products Co. www.answerrifles.com
Briley Mfg www.briley.com
Carlson's www.choketube.com
Colonial Arms www.colonialarms.com
Comp-N-Choke www.comp-n-choke.com
Hastings www.hastingsbarrels.com
Kick's Industries www.kicks-ind.com
Mag-Na-Port Int'l Inc. www.magnaport.com
Sims Vibration Laboratory www.limbsaver.com
Teague Precision Chokes www.teague.ca
Truglo www.truglo.com

Chronographs and Ballistic Software

Barnes Ballistic Program www.barnesbullets.com
Ballisticard Systems www.ballisticards.com
Competition Electronics www.competitionelectronics.com
Competitive Edge Dynamics www.cedhk.com
Hodgdon Shotshell Program www.hodgdon.com
Lee Shooter Program www.leeprecision.com
Load From A Disk www.loadammo.com
Oehler Research Inc. www.oehler-research.com
PACT www.pact.com
ProChrony www.competitionelectronics.com
Quickload www.neconos.com
RCBS Load www.rcbs.com
Shooting Chrony Inc www.shootingchrony.com
Sierra Infinity Ballistics Program www.sierrabullets.com

Cleaning Products

Accupro www.accupro.com
Ballistol U.S.A. www.ballistol.com
Birchwood Casey www.birchwoodcasey.com
Blue Wonder www.bluewonder.com
Bore Tech www.boretech.com
Break-Free, Inc. www.break-free.com
Bruno Shooters Supply www.brunoshooters.com
Butch's Bore Shine www.lymanproducts.com
C.J. Weapons Accessories www.cjweapons,com
Clenzoil www.clenzoil.com
Corrosion Technologies www.corrosionx.com
Dewey Mfg. www.deweyrods.com
Eezox Inc. www.xmission.com
G 96 www.g96.com
Hollands Shooters Supply www.hollandgun.com
Hoppes www.hoppes.com
Hydrosorbent Products www.dehumidify.com
Inhibitor VCI Products www.theinhibitor.com
Iosso Products www.iosso.com
KG Industries www.kgcoatings.com
Kleen-Bore Inc. www.kleen-bore.com
L&R Mfg. www.lrultrasonics.com
Lyman www.lymanproducts.com
Mil-Comm Products www.mil-comm.com
Militec-1 www.militec-1.com
Mpro7 Gun Care www.mp7.com
Otis Technology, Inc. www.otisgun.com
Outers www.outers-guncare.com
Ox-Yoke Originals Inc. www.oxyoke.com
Parker-Hale Ltd. www.parker-hale.com
Prolix Lubricant www.prolixlubricant.com
ProShot Products www.proshotproducts.com
ProTec Lubricants www.proteclubricants.com
Rusteprufe Labs www.rusteprufe.com
Sagebrush Products www.sagebrushproducts.com
Sentry Solutions Ltd. www.sentrysolutions.com
Shooters Choice Gun Care www.shooters-choice.com
Silencio www.silencio.com
Slip 2000 www.slip2000.com

Stony Point Products www.stoneypoint.com
Tetra Gun www.tetraproducts.com
The TM Solution thetmsolution@comsast.net
World's Fastest Gun Bore Cleaner www.michaels-oregon.com

Firearm Manufacturers and Importers

AAR, Inc. www.iar-arms.com
Accuracy Int'l North America www.accuracyinternational.org
Accuracy Rifle Systems www.mini-14.net
Ace Custom 45's www.acecustom45.com
Advanced Weapons Technology www.AWT-Zastava.com
AIM www.aimsurplus.com
AirForce Airguns www.airforceairguns.com
Airguns of Arizona www.airgunsofarizona.com
Airgun Express www.airgunexpress.com
Alchemy Arms www.alchemyltd.com
Alexander Arms www.alexanderarms.com
American Derringer Corp. www.amderringer.com
American Spirit Arms Corp. www.gunkits.com
American Western Arms www.awaguns.com
Anics Corp. www.anics.com
Answer Products Co. www.answerrifles.com
AR-7 Industries, LLC www.ar-7.com
Ares Defense Systems www.aresdefense.com
Armalite www.armalite.com
Armi Sport www.armisport.com
Armory U.S.A. www.globaltraders.com
Armsco www.armsco.net
Armscorp U.S.A. Inc. www.armscorpusa.com
Arnold Arms www.arnoldarms.com
Arsenal Inc. www.arsenalinc.com
Arthur Brown Co. www.eabco.com
Austin & Halleck www.austinhalleck.com
Autauga Arms, Inc. www.autaugaarms.com
Auto-Ordnance Corp. www.tommygun.com
AWA Int'l www.awaguns.com
Axtell Rifle Co. www.riflesmith.com
Aya www.aya-fineguns.com
Baikal www.baikalinc.ru/eng/
Ballard Rifles, LLC www.ballardrifles.com
Barrett Firearms Mfg. www.barrettrifles.com
Beeman Precision Airguns www.beeman.com
Benelli U.S.A. Corp. www.belliusa.com
Benjamin Sheridan www.crosman.com
Beretta U.S.A. Corp. www.berettausa.com
Bernardelli www.bernardelli.com
Bersa www.bersa-llama.com
Bill Hanus Birdguns www.billhanusbirdguns.com
Bleiker www.bleiker.ch
Bluegrass Armory www.bluegrassarmory.com
Bond Arms www.bondarms.com
Borden's Rifles, Inc. www.bordensrifles.com
Boss & Co. www.bossguns.co.uk
Bowen Classic Arms www.bowenclassicarms.com
Briley Mfg www.briley.com
BRNO Arms www.zbrojovka.com
Brown, David McKay www.mckaybrown.com
Brown, Ed Products www.brownprecision.com
Browning www.browning.com
BSA Guns www.bsaguns.com
BUL Ltd. www.bultransmark.com
Bushmaster Firearms/Quality Parts www.bushmaster.com
BWE Firearms www.bwefirearms.com
Cape Outfitters www.doublegun.com
Carbon 15 www.professional-ordnance.com
Caspian Arms, Ltd. www.caspianarmsltd.8m.com
Casull Arms Corp. www.casullarms.com
CDNN Investments, Inc. www.cdninvestments.com
Century Arms www.centuryarms.com
Chadick's Ltd. www.chadicks-ltd.com
Champlin Firearms www.champlinarms.com
Chapuis Arms www.doubleguns.com/chapuis.htm
Charles Daly www.charlesdaly.com
Charter 2000, Inc. www.charterfirearms.com
Christensen Arms www.christensenarms.com
Cimarron Firearms Co. www.cimarron-firearms.com
Clark Custom Guns www.clarkcustomguns.com
Cobra Enterprises www.cobrapistols.com
Cogswell & Harrison www.cogswell.co.uk/home.htm
Colt's Mfg Co. www.colt.com
Compasseco, Inc. www.compasseco.com
Connecticut Valley Arms www.cva.com
Cooper Firearms www.cooperfirearms.com
Corner Shot www.cornershot.com
Crosman www.crosman.com
Crossfire, L.L.C. www.crossfirelle.com
C.Sharp Arms Co. www.csharparms.com
CZ U.S.A. www.cz-usa.com

WEB DIRECTORY

Daisy Mfg Co. www.daisy.com
Dakota Arms Inc. www.dakotaarms.com
Dan Wesson Firearms www.danwessonfirearms.com
Davis Industries www.davisindguns.com
Detonics U.S.A. www.detonicsusa.com
Dixie Gun Works www.dixiegunworks.com
Dlask Arms Corp. www.dlask.com
D.P.M.S., Inc. www.dpmsinc.com
D.S.A., Inc. www.dsarms.com
Dumoulin www.dumoulin-herstal.com
Dynamit Noble www.dnrws.com
Eagle Imports, Inc. www.bersa-llama.com
EDM Arms www.edmarms.com
E.M.F. Co. www.emf-company.com
Enterprise Arms www.enterprise.com
European American Armory Corp. www.eaacorp.com
Evans, William www.williamevans.com
Fabarm www.fabarm.com
FAC-Guns-N-Stuff www.gunsnstuff.com
Falcon Pneumatic Systems www.falcon-airguns.com
Fausti Stefano www.faustistefanoarms.com
Firestorm www.firestorm-sgs.com
Flodman Guns www.flodman.com
FN Herstal www.fnherstal.com
FNH U.S.A. www.fnhusa.com
Franchi www.franchiusa.com
Freedom Arms www.freedomarms.com
Galazan www.connecticutshotgun.com
Gambo Renato www.renatogamba.it
Gamo www.gamo.com
Gary Reeder Custom Guns www.reeder-customguns.com
Gazelle Arms www.gazellearms.com
Gibbs Rifle Company www.gibbsrifle.com
Glock www.glock.com
Griffin & Howe www.griffinhowe.com
Grizzly Big Boar Rifle www.largrizzly.com
GSI Inc. www.gsifirearms.com
Guerini www.gueriniusa.com
Hammerli www.hammerli.com
Hatsan Arms Co. www.hatsan.com.tr
Heckler and Koch www.hk-usa.com
Henry Repeating Arms Co. www.henryrepeating.com
Heritage Mfg. www.heritagemfg.com
Heym www.heym-waffenfabrik.de
High Standard Mfg. www.highstandard.com
Hi-Point Firearms www.hi-pointfirearms.com
Holland & Holland www.hollandandholland.com
H&R Firearms www.marlinfirearms.com
H-S Precision www.hsprecision.com
Hunters Lodge Corp. www.hunterslodge.com
IAR Inc. www.iar-arms.com
Imperial Miniature Armory www.1800miniature.com
Interarms www.interarms.com
International Military Antiques, Inc. www.ima-usa.com
Inter Ordnance www.interordnance.com
Intrac Arms International LLC www.hsarms.com
Israel Arms www.israelarms.com
Ithaca Gun Co. www.ithacagun.com
Izhevsky Mekhanichesky Zavod www.baikalinc.ru
Jarrett Rifles, Inc. www.jarrettrifles.com
J&G Sales, Ltd. www.jgsales.com
Johannsen Express Rifle www.johannsen-jagd.de
JP Enterprises, Inc. www.jprifles.com
Kahr Arms/Auto-Ordnance www.kahr.com
K.B.I. www.kbi-inc.com
Kel-Tec CNC Ind., Inc. www.kel-tec.com
Kifaru www.kifaru.net
Kimber www.kimberamerica.com
Knight's Armament Co. www.knightsarmament.com
Knight Rifles www.knightrifles.com
Korth www.korthwaffen.de
Krieghoff GmbH www.krieghoff.de
KY Imports, Inc. www.kyimports.com
Krieghoff Int'l www.krieghoff.com
L.A.R Mfg www.largrizzly.com
Lazzeroni Arms Co. www.lazzeroni.com
Legacy Sports International www.legacysports.com
Les Baer Custom, Inc. www.lesbaer.com
Linebaugh Custom Sixguns www.sixgunner.com/linebaugh
Ljutic www.ljuticgun.com
Llama www.bersa-llama.com
Lone Star Rifle Co. www.lonestarrifle.com
Magnum Research www.magnumresearch.com
Markesbery Muzzleloaders www.markesbery.com
Marksman Products www.marksman.com
Marlin www.marlinfirearms.com
Mauser www.mauserwaffen.de
McMillan Bros Rifle Co. www.mcfamily.com

Meacham Rifles www.meachamrifles.com
Merkel www.hk-usa.com
Miller Arms www.millerarms.com
Miltech www.miltecharms.com
Miltex, Inc. www.miltexusa.com
Mitchell's Mausers www.mitchellsales.com
MK Ballistic Systems www.mkballistics.com
M-Mag www.mmag.com
Montana Rifle Co. www.montanarifleman.com
Navy Arms www.navyarms.com
Nesika www.nesika.com
New England Arms Corp. www.newenglandarms.com
New England Custom Gun Svc, Ltd. www.newenglandcustomgun.com
New England Firearms www.hr1871.com
New Ultra Light Arms www.newultralight.com
North American Arms www.northamericanarms.com
Nosler Bullets, Inc. www.nosler.com
Nowlin Mfg. Inc. www.nowlinguns.com
O.F. Mossberg & Sons www.mossberg.com
Ohio Ordnance Works www.ohioordnanceworks.com
Olympic Arms www.olyarms.com
Panther Arms www.dpmsinc.com
Para-Ordnance www.paraord.com
Pedersoli Davide & Co. www.davide-pedersoli.com
Perazzi www.perazzi.com
Power Custom www.powercustom.com
Purdey & Sons www.purdey.com
Remington www.remington.com
Republic Arms Inc. www.republicarmsinc.com
Rigby www.johnrigbyandco.com
Rizzini Di Rizzini www.rizzini.it
Robar Companies, Inc. www.robarguns.com
Robinson Armament Co. www.robarm.com
Rock River Arms, Inc. www.rockriverarms.com
Rogue Rifle Co. Inc. www.chipmunkrifle.com
Rohrbaugh Firearms www.rohrbaughfirearms.com
Rossi Arms www.rossiusa.com
RPM www.rpmxlpistols.com
RWS www.dnrws.com
Sabatti SPA www.sabatti.com
Saco Defense www.sacoinc.com
Safari Arms www.olyarms.com
Sako www.berettausa.com
Samco Global Arms Inc. www.samcoglobal.com
Sarco Inc. www.sarcoinc.com
Savage Arms Inc. www.savagearms.com
Scattergun Technologies Inc. www.wilsoncombat.com
Searcy Enterprises www.searcyent.com
Shiloh Sharps www.shilohrifle.com
SIG Arms, Inc. www.sigarms.com
Simpson Ltd. www.simpsonltd.com
SKB Shotguns www.skbshotguns.com
Smith & Wesson www.smith-wesson.com
SOG International, Inc. soginc@go-concepts.com
Sphinx System www.sphinxarms.com
Springfield Armory www.springfield-armory.com
SSK Industries www.sskindustries.com
Steyr Mannlicher www.steyr-mannlicher.com
Strayer-Voigt Inc. www.sviguns.com
Sturm, Ruger & Company www.ruger-firearms.com
Tactical Solutions www.tacticalsol.com
Tar-Hunt Slug Guns, Inc. www.tar-hunt.com
Taser Int'l www.taser.com
Taurus www.taurususa.com
Taylor's & Co., Inc. www.taylorsfirearms.com
Tennessee Guns www.tennesseeguns.com
The 1877 Sharps Co. www.1877sharps.com
Thompson Center Arms www.tcarms.com
Tikka www.berettausa.com
TNW, Inc. tncorp@aol.com
Traditions www.traditionsfirearms.com
Uberti www.ubertireplicas.com
U.S. Firearms Mfg. Co. www.usfirearms.com
U.S. Repeating Arms Co. www.winchester-guns.com
Ultra Light Arms www.newultralight.com
Valkyrie Arms www.valkyriearms.com
Vektor Arms www.vektorarms.com
Volquartsen Custom Ltd. www.volquartsen.com
Vulcan Armament www.vulcanarmament.com
Walther U.S.A. www.waltheramerica.com
Weatherby www.weatherby.com
Webley and Scott Ltd. www.webley.co.uk
Westley Richards www.westleyrichards.com
Widley www.widleyguns.com
Wild West Guns www.wildwestguns.com
William Larkin Moore & Co. www.doublegun.com
Wilson Combat www.wilsoncombat.com
Winchester Firearms www.winchester-guns.com

WEB DIRECTORY

Gun Parts, Barrels, After-Market Accessories

300 Below www.300below.com
Accuracy International of North America www.accuracyinternational.org
Accuracy Speaks, Inc. www.accuracyspeaks.com
Advanced Barrel Systems www.carbonbarrels.com
Advantage Arms www.advantagearms.com
AK-U.S.A. www.ak-103.com
American Spirit Arms Corp. www.gunkits.com
AMT Gun Parts www.amt-gunparts.com
Badger Barrels, Inc. www.badgerbarrels.com
Bar-Sto Precision Machine www.barsto.com
Battenfeld Technologies www.battenfeldtechnologies.com
Belt Mountain Enterprises www.beltmountain.com
Brownells www.brownells.com
B-Square www.b-square.com
Buffer Technologies www.buffertech.com
Bullberry Barrel Works www.bullberry.com
Bushmaster Firearms/Quality Parts www.bushmaster.com
Butler Creek Corp www.butler-creek.com
Cape Outfitters Inc. www.capeoutfitters.com
Caspian Arms Ltd. www.caspianarms.com
Cheaper Than Dirt www.cheaperthandirt.com
Chesnut Ridge www.chestnutridge.com/
Chip McCormick Corp www.chipmccormickcorp.com
Choate Machine & Tool Co. www.riflestock.com
Cierner, Jonathan Arthur www.22lrconversions.com
CJ Weapons Accessories www.cjweapons.com
Clerke International Arms (Bo Clerke) www.clerkebarrels.com
Colonial Arms www.colonialarms.com
Comp-N-Choke www.comp-n-choke.com
Cylinder & Slide Shop www.cylinder-slide.com
Digi-Twist www.fmtcorp.com
Dixie Gun Works www.dixiegun.com
Douglas Barrels www.benchrest.com/douglas/
DPMS www.dpmsinc.com
D.S.Arms, Inc. www.dsarms.com
eBay www.ebay.com
Ed Brown Products www.edbrown.com
EFK Marketing/Fire Dragon Pistol Accessories www.flmfire.com
E.R. Shaw www.ershawbarrels.com
Federal Arms www.fedarms.com
Forrest Inc. www.gunmags.com
Fulton Armory www.fulton-armory.com
Galazan www.connecticutshotgun.com
Gemtech www.gem-tech.com
Gentry, David www.gentrycustom.com
GG&G www.gggaz.com
Green Mountain Rifle Barrels www.gmriflebarrel.com
Gun Parts Corp. www.e-gunparts.com
Harris Engineering www.harrisbipods.com
Hart Rifle Barrels www.hartbarrels.com
Hastings Barrels www.hastingsbarrels.com
Heinie Specialty Products www.heinie.com
Holland Shooters Supply www.hollandgun.com
100 Straight Products www.100straight.com
I.M.A. www.ima-U.S.A..com
Jarvis, Inc. www.jarvis-custom.com
J&T Distributing www.jtdistributing.com
John's Guns www.johnsguns.com
John Masen Co. www.johnmasen.com
Jonathan Arthur Ciener, Inc. www.22lrconversions.com
JP Enterprises www.jpar15.com
Keng's Firearms Specialities www.versapod.com
KG Industries www.kgcoatings.com
Kick Eez www.kickeez.com
Kidd Triggers www.coolguyguns.com
King's Gunworks www.kingsgunworks.com
Knoxx Industries www.knoxx.com
Krieger Barrels www.kriegerbarrels.com
K-VAR Corp. www.k-var.com
Les Baer Custom, Inc. www.lesbaer.com
Lilja Barrels www.riflebarrels.com
Lone Star Rifle Co. www.lonestarrifles.com
Lone Wolf Dist. www.lonewolfdist.com
Lothar Walther Precision Tools Inc. www.lothar-walther.de
M&A Parts, Inc. www.m-aparts.com
MAB Barrels www.mab.com.au
Majestic Arms www.majesticarms.com
Marvel Products, Inc. www.marvelprod.com
MEC-GAR SrL www.mec-gar.com
Mesa Tactical www.mesatactical.com
Michaels of Oregon Co. www.michaels-oregon.com
North Mfg. Co. www.rifle-barrels.com
Numrich Gun Parts Corp. www.e-gunparts.com
Pachmayr www.pachmayr.com
Pac-Nor Barrels www.pac-nor.com
Para Ordinance Pro Shop www.ltms.com
Point Tech Inc. pointec@ibm.net

Promag Industries www.promagindustries.com
Power Custom, Inc. www.powercustom.com
Red Star Arms www.redstararms.com
Rocky Mountain Arms www.rockymountainarms.com
Royal Arms Int'l www.royalarms.com
R.W. Hart www.rwhart.com
Sarco Inc. www.sarcoinc.com
Scattergun Technologies Inc. www.wilsoncombat.com
Schuemann Barrels www.schuemann.com
Seminole Gunworks Chamber Mates www.chambermates.com
Shilen www.shilen.com
Sims Vibration Laboratory www.limbsaver.com
Smith & Alexander Inc. www.smithandalexander.com
Speed Shooters Int'l www.shooternet.com/ssi
Sprinco U.S.A. Inc. sprinco@primenet.com
STI Int'l www.stiguns.com
S&S Firearms www.ssfirearms.com
SSK Industries www.sskindustries.com
Sunny Hill Enterprises www.sunny-hill.com
Tactical Innovations www.tacticalinc.com
Tapco www.tapco.com
Trapdoors Galore www.trapdoors.com
Triple K Manufacturing Co. Inc. www.triplek.com
U.S.A. Magazines Inc. www.usa-magazines.com
Verney-Carron SA www.verney-carron.com
Volquartsen Custom Ltd. www.volquartsen.com
W.C. Wolff Co. www.gunsprings.com
Waller & Son www.wallerandson.com
Weigand Combat Handguns www.weigandcombat.com
Western Gun Parts www.westerngunparts.com
Wilson Arms www.wilsonarms.com
Wilson Combat www.wilsoncombat.com
Wisner's Inc. www.gunpartsspecialist.com
Z-M Weapons www.zmweapons.com/home.htm

Gunsmithing Supplies and Instruction

American Gunsmithing Institute www.americangunsmith.com
Battenfeld Technologies www.battenfeldtechnologies.com
Brownells, Inc. www.brownells.com
B-Square Co. www.b-square.com
Clymer Mfg. Co. www.clymertool.com
Craftguard Metal Finishing crftgrd@aol.com
Dem-Bart www.dembartco.com
Doug Turnbull Restoration www.turnbullrestoration.com
Du-Lite Corp. www.dulite.com
Dvorak Instruments www.dvorakinstruments.com
Gradiant Lens Corp. www.gradientlens.com
Gunline Tools www.gunline.com
JGS Precision Tool Mfg. LLC www.jgstools.com
Mag-Na-Port International www.magnaport.com
Manson Precision Reamers www.mansonreamers.com
Midway www.midwayusa.com
Murray State College www.mscok.edu
Olympus America Inc. www.olympus.com
Pacific Tool & Gauge www.pacifictoolandgauge.com
Trinidad State Junior College www.trinidadstate.edu

Handgun Grips

Ajax Custom Grips, Inc. www.ajaxgrips.com
Altamont Co. www.altamontco.com
Badger Grips www.pistolgrips.com
Barami Corp. www.hipgrip.com
Blu Magnum Grips www.blumagnum.com
Buffalo Brothers www.buffalobrothers.com
Crimson Trace Corp. www.crimsontrace.com
Eagle Grips www.eaglegrips.com
Falcon Industries www.ergogrips.net
Hogue Grips www.getgrip.com
Kirk Ratajesak www.kgratajesak.com
Lett Custom Grips www.lettgrips.com
N.C. Ordnance www.gungrip.com
Nill-Grips U.S.A. www.nill-grips.com
Pachmayr www.pachmayr.com
Pearce Grips www.pearcegrip.com
Trausch Grips Int.Co. www.trausch.com
Tyler-T Grips www.t-grips.com
Uncle Mike's: www.uncle-mikes.com

Holsters and Leather Products

Akah www.akah.de
Aker Leather Products www.akerleather.com
Alessi Distributor R&F Inc. www.alessiholsters.com
Alfonso's of Hollywood www.alfonsogunleather.com
Armor Holdings www.holsters.com
Bagmaster www.bagmaster.com
Bianchi International www.bianchi-intl.com
Blackhills Leather www.blackhillsleather.com

BodyHugger Holsters www.nikolais.com
Boyt Harness Co. www.boytharness.com
Brigade Gun Leather www.brigadegunleather.com
Chimere www.chimere.com
Classic Old West Styles www.cows.com
Conceal It www.conceal-it.com
Concealment Shop Inc. www.theconcealmentshop.com
Coronado Leather Co. www.coronadoleather.com
Creedmoor Sports, Inc. www.creedmoorsports.com
Custom Leather Wear www.customleatherwear.com
Defense Security Products www.thunderwear.com
Dennis Yoder www.yodercustomleather.com
DeSantis Holster www.desantisholster.com
Dillon Precision www.dillonprecision.com
Don Hume Leathergoods, Inc. www.donhume.com
Ernie Hill International www.erniehill.com
Fist www.fist-inc.com
Fobus U.S.A. www.fobusholster.com
Front Line Ltd. frontline@internet-zahav.net
Galco www.usgalco.com
Gilmore's Sports Concepts www.gilmoresports.com
Gould & Goodrich www.goulduse.com
Gunmate Products www.gun-mate.com
Hellweg Ltd. www.hellwegltd.com
Hide-A-Gun www.hide-a-gun.com
Holsters.Com www.holsters.com
Horseshoe Leather Products www.horseshoe.co.uk
Hunter Co. www.huntercompany.com
Kirkpatrick Leather Company www.kirkpatrickleather.com
KNJ www.knjmfg.com
Kramer Leather www.kramerleather.com
Law Concealment Systems www.handgunconcealment.com
Levy's Leathers Ltd. www.levysleathers.com
Michaels of Oregon Co. www.michaels-oregon.com
Milt Sparks Leather www.miltsparks.com
Mitch Rosen Extraordinary Gunleather www.mitchrosen.com
Old World Leather www.gun-mate.com
Pacific Canvas & Leather Co. paccanadleather@directway.com
Pager Pal www.pagerpal.com
Phalanx Corp. www.smartholster.com
PWL www.pwlusa.com
Rumanya Inc. www.rumanya.com
S.A. Gunleather www.elpasoleather.com
Safariland Ltd. Inc. www.safariland.com
Shooting Systems Group Inc. www.shootingsystems.com
Strictly Anything Inc. www.strictlyanything.com
Strong Holster Co. www.strong-holster.com
The Belt Co. www.conceal-it.com
The Leather Factory Inc. lflandry@flash.net
The Outdoor Connection www.outdoorconnection.com
Top-Line U.S.A. inc. www.toplineusa.com
Triple K Manufacturing Co. www.triplek.com
Wilson Combat www.wilsoncombat.com

Miscellaneous Shooting Products

10X Products Group www.10Xwear.com
Aero Peltor www.aearo.com
American Body Armor www.americanbodyarmor.com
Armor Holdings Products www.armorholdings.com
Battenfeld Technologies www.battenfeldtechnologies.com
Beamhit www.beamhit.com
Beartooth www.beartoothproducts.com
Bodyguard by S&W www.yourbodyguard.com
Burnham Brothers www.burnhambrothers.com
Collectors Armory www.collectorsarmory.com
Dalloz Safety www.cdalloz.com
Deben Group Industries Inc. www.deben.com
Decot Hy-Wyd Sport Glasses www.sportyglasses.com
E.A.R., Inc. www.earinc.com
First Choice Armor www.firstchoicearmor.com
Gunstands www.gunstands.com
Howard Leight Hearing Protectors www.howardleight.com
Hunters Specialities www.hunterspec.com
Johnny Stewart Wildlife Calls www.hunterspec.com
Merit Corporation www.meritcorporation.com
Michaels of Oregon www.michaels-oregon.com
MPI Outdoors www.mpioutdoors.com
MTM Case-Gard www.mtmcase-gard.com
North Safety Products www.northsafety-brea.com
Plano Molding www.planomolding.com
Pro-Ears www.pro-ears.com
Second Chance Body Armor Inc. www.secondchance.com
Silencio www.silencio.com
Smart Lock Technologies www.smartlock.com
Surefire www.surefire.com
Taser Int'l www.taser.com
Walker's Game Ear Inc. www.walkersgameear.com

Muzzleloading Firearms and Products

American Pioneer Powder www.americanpioneerpowder.com
Austin & Halleck, Inc. www.austinhalleck.com
Black Powder Products www.bpiguns.com
CVA www.cva.com
Davis, Vernon C. & Co. www.mygunroom/vcdavis&co/
Dixie Gun Works, Inc. www.dixiegun.com
Elephant/Swiss Black Powder www.elephantblackpowder.com
Goex Black Powder www.goexpowder.com
Jedediah Starr Trading Co. www.jedediah-starr.com
Jim Chambers Flintlocks www.flintlocks.com
Kahnke Gunworks www.powderandbow.com/kahnke/
Knight Rifles www.knightrifles.com
Log Cabin Shop www.logcabinshop.com
Lyman www.lymanproducts.com
Millennium Designed Muzzleloaders www.mdm-muzzleloaders.com
Mountain State Muzzleloading www.mtnstatemuzzleloading.com
MSM, Inc. www.msmfg.com
Muzzleload Magnum Products www.mmpsabots.com
Muzzleloading Technologies, Inc. www.mtimuzzleloading.com
Navy Arms www.navyarms.com
October Country Muzzleloading www.oct-country.com
Ox-Yoke Originals Inc. www.oxyoke.com
Palmetto Arms www.palmetto.it
Rightnour Mfg. Co. Inc. www.rmcsports.com
The Rifle Shop trshoppe@aol.com
Thompson Center Arms www.tcarms.com
Traditions Performance Muzzleloading www.traditionsfirearms.com

Publications, Videos, and CDs

A&J Arms Booksellers www.ajarmsbooksellers.com
Airgun Letter www.airgunletter.com
American Firearms Industry www.amfire.com
American Handgunner www.americanhandgunner.com
American Hunter www.nrapublications.org
American Rifleman www.nrapublications.org
American Shooting Magazine www.americanshooting.com
Blacksmith sales@blacksmithcorp.com
Blackpowder Hunting www.blackpowderhunting.org
Black Powder Cartridge News www.blackpowderspg.com
Black Powder Journal www.blackpowderjournal.com
Blue Book Publications www.bluebookinc.com
Combat Handguns www.combathandguns.com
Countrywide Press www.countrysport.com
DBI Books/Krause Publications www.krause.com
Delta Force www.infogo.com/delta
Gun List www.gunlist.com
Gun Video www.gunvideo.com
GUNO Magazine www.gunsmagazine.com
Guns & Ammo www.gunsandammomag.com
Gunweb Magazine WWW Links www.imags.com
Gun Week www.gunweek.com
Gun World www.gunworld.com
Harris Publications www.harrispublications.com
Heritage Gun Books www.gunbooks.com
Krause Publications www.krause.com
Law and Order www.hendonpub.com
Moose Lake Publishing MooselakeP@aol.com
Munden Enterprises Inc. www.bob-munden.com
Outdoor Videos www.outdoorvideos.com
Precision Shooting www.precisionshooting.com
Ray Riling Arms Books www.rayrilingarmsbooks.com
Rifle and Handloader Magazines www.riflemagazine.com
Safari Press Inc. www.safaripress.com
Shoot! Magazine www.shootmagazine.com
Shooters News www.shootersnews.com
Shooting Illustrated www.nrapublications.org
Shooting Industry www.shootingindustry.com
Shooting Sports Retailer www.shootingsportsretailer.com
Shooting Sports U.S.A. www.nrapublications.org
Shotgun News www.shotgunnews.com
Shotgun Report www.shotgunreport.com
Shotgun Sports Magazine www.shotgun-sports.com
Small Arms Review www.smallarmsreview.com
Small Caliber News www.smallcaliber.com
Sporting Clays Web Edition www.sportingclays.net
Sports Afield www.sportsafield.comm
Sports Trend www.sportstrend.com
Sportsmen on Film www.sportsmenonfilm.com
The Gun Journal www.shooters.com
The Shootin Iron www.off-road.com/4x4web/si/si.html
The Single Shot Exchange Magazine singleshot@earthlink.net
The Sixgunner www.sskindustries.com
Voyageur Press www.voyageurpress.com
VSP Publications www.gunbooks.com
Vulcan Outdoors Inc. www.vulcanpub.com

Reloading Tools and Supplies

Ballisti-Cast Mfg. www.ballisti-cast.com
Battenfeld Technologies www.battenfeldtechnologies.com
Bruno Shooters Supply www.brunoshooters.com
CH/4D Custom Die www.ch4d.com
Colorado Shooters Supply www.hochmoulds.com
Corbin Mfg & Supply Co. www.corbins.com
Dillon Precision www.dillonprecision.com
Forster Precision Products www.forsterproducts.com
Hanned Line www.hanned.com
Harrell's Precision www.harrellsprec.com
Holland's Shooting Supplies www.hollandgun.com
Hornady www.hornady.com
Huntington Reloading Products www.huntingtons.com
J & J Products Co. www.jandjproducts.com
Lead Bullet Technology LBTisaccuracy@lmbris.net
Lee Precision, Inc. www.leeprecision.com
Littleton Shotmaker www.leadshotmaker.com
Load Data www.loaddata.com
Lyman www.lymanproducts.com
Magma Engineering www.magmaengr.com
Mayville Engineering Co. (MEC) www.mecreloaders.com
Midway www.midwayusa.com
Moly-Bore www.molybore.com
MTM Case-Guard www.mtmcase-guard.com
NECO www.neconos.com
NEI www.neihandtools.com
Neil Jones Custom Products www.neiljones.com
Ponsness/Warren www.reloaders.com
Ranger Products www.pages.prodigy.com/rangerproducts.home.htm
Rapine Bullet Mold Mfg Co. www.customloads.com/rapine.html
RCBS www.rcbs.com
Redding Reloading Equipment www.redding-reloading.com
Russ Haydon's Shooting Supplies www.shooters-supply.com
Sinclair Int'l Inc. www.sinclairintl.com
Stoney Point Products Inc www.stoneypoint.com
Thompson Bullet Lube Co. www.thompsonbulletlube.com
Vickerman Seating Die www.castingstuff.com
Wilson(L.E. Wilson) www.lewilson.com

Rests— Bench, Portable, Attachable

Battenfeld Technolgies www.battenfeldtechnologies.com
Bench Master www.bench-master.com
B-Square www.b-square.com
Bullshooter www.bullshooterssightingin.com
Desert Mountain Mfg. www.bench-master.com
Harris Engineering Inc. www.harrisbipods.com
Kramer Designs www.snipepod.com
L Thomas Rifle Support www.ltsupport.com
Level-Lok www.levellok.com
Midway www.midwayusa.com
Predator Sniper Styx www.predatorsniperstyx.com
Ransom International www.ransom-intl.com
R.W. Hart www.rwhart.com
Sinclair Intl, Inc. www.sinclairintl.com
Stoney Point Products www.stoneypoint.com
Target Shooting www.targetshooting.com
Varmint Masters www.varmintmasters.com
Versa-Pod www.versa-pod.com

Scopes, Sights, Mounts and Accessories

Accusight www.accusight.com
ADCO www.shooters.com/adco/index/htm
Adirondack Opitcs www.adkoptics.com
Aimpoint www.aimpoint.com
Aim Shot, Inc. www.miniosprey.com
Aimtech Mount Systems www.aimtech-mounts.com
Alpec Team, Inc. www.alpec.com
Alpen Outdoor Corp. www.alpenoutdoor.com
American Technologies Network, Corp. www.atncorp.com
AmeriGlo, LLC www.ameriglo.net
AO Sight Systems Inc. www.aosights.com
Ashley Outdoors, Inc. www.ashleyoutdoors.com
ATN www.atncorp.com
Badger Ordnance www.badgerordnance.com
Beamshot-Quarton www.beamshot.com
BSA Optics www.bsaoptics.com
B-Square Company, Inc. www.b-square.com
Burris www.burrisoptics.com
Bushnell Performance Optics www.bushnell.com
Carl Zeiss Optical Inc. www.zeiss.com
Carson Optical www.carson-optical.com
C-More Systems www.cmore.com
Conetrol Scope Mounts www.conetrol.com
Crimson Trace Corp. www.crimsontrace.com
Crossfire L.L.C. www.amfire.com/hesco/html
DCG Supply Inc. www.dcgsupply.com

D&L Sports www.dlsports.com
EasyHit, Inc. www.easyhit.com
EAW www.eaw.de
Elcan Optical Technologies www.armament.com, www.elcan.com
Electro-Optics Technologies www.eotechmdc.com/holosight
Europtik Ltd. www.europtik.com
Fujinon, Inc. www.fujinon.com
Gilmore Sports www.gilmoresports.com
Hakko Co. Ltd. www.hakko-japan.co.jp
Hesco www.hescosights.com
Hitek Industries www.nightsight.com
HIVIZ www.hivizsights.com
Horus Vision www.horusvision.com
Hunter Co. www.huntercompany.com
Innovative Weaponry, Inc. www.ptnightsights.com
Ironsighter Co. www.ironsighter.com
ITT Night Vision www.ittnightvision.com
Kahles www.kahlesoptik.com
Kowa Optimed Inc. www.kowascope.com
Kwik-Site Co. www.kwiksitecorp.com
Laser Bore Sight www.laserboresight.com
Laser Devices Inc. www.laserdevices.com
Lasergrips www.crimsontrace.com
LaserLyte www.laserlytesights.com
LaserMax Inc. www.lasermaxinc.com
Laser Products www.surefire.com
Leapers, Inc. www.leapers.com
Leatherwood www.leatherwoodoptics.com
Leica Camera Inc. www.leica-camera.com/usa
Leupold www.leupold.com
LightForce/NightForce U.S.A. www.nightforcescopes.com
Lyman www.lymanproducts.com
Lynx www.b-square.com
Marble's Outdoors www.marblesoutdoors.com
MDS, Inc. www.mdsincorporated.com
Meopta www.meopta.com
Meprolight www.kimberamerica.com
Micro Sight Co. www.microsight.com
Millett www.millettsights.com
Miniature Machine Corp. www.mmcsight.com
Montana Vintage Arms www.montanavintagearms.com
Mounting Solutions Plus www.mountsplus.com
NAIT www.nait.com
Newcon International Ltd. newconsales@newcon-optik.com
Night Force Optics www.nightforcescopes.com
Night Owl Optics www.nightowloptics.com
Nikon Inc. www.nikonusa.com
North American Integrated Technologies www.nait.com
O.K. Weber, Inc. www.okweber.com
Optolyth-Optic www.optolyth.de
Pentax Corp. www.pentaxlightseeker.com
Premier Reticle www.premierreticles.com
Redfield www.redfieldoptics.com
R&R Int'l Trade www.nightoptic.com
Schmidt & Bender www.schmidt-bender.com
Scopecoat www.scopecoat.com
Scopelevel www.scopelevel.com
Segway Industries www.segway-industries.com
Shepherd Scope Ltd. www.shepherdscopes.com
Sightron www.sightron.com
Simmons www.simmonsoptics.com
S&K www.scopemounts.com
Springfield Armory www.springfield-armory.com
Sure-Fire www.surefire.com
Swarovski/Kahles www.swarovskioptik.com
Swift Optics www.swiftoptics.com
Talley Mfg. Co. www.talleyrings.com
Tasco www.tascosales.com
Trijicon Inc. www.trijicon.com
Truglo Inc. www.truglo.com
UltraDot www.ultradotusa.com
Unertl Optical Co. www.unertlopics.com
US Night Vision www.usnightvision.com
U.S. Optics Technologies Inc. www.usoptics.com
Valdada-IOR Optics www.valdada.com
Warne www.warnescopemounts.com
Weaver Scopes www.weaveroptics.com
Wilcox Industries Corp www.wilcoxind.com
Williams Gun Sight Co. www.williamsgunsight.com
Zeiss www.zeiss.com

Shooting Organizations, Schools and Ranges

Amateur Trapshooting Assoc. www.shootata.com
American Custom Gunmakers Guild www.acgg.org
American Gunsmithing Institute www.americangunsmith.com
American Pistolsmiths Guild www.americanpistol.com
American Shooting Sports Council www.assc.com
American Single Shot Rifle Assoc. www.assra.com

WEB DIRECTORY

Antique Shooting Tool Collector's Assoc. www.oldshootingtools.org
Assoc. of Firearm & Tool Mark Examiners www.afte.org
BATF www.atf.ustreas.gov
Blackwater Lodge and Training Center www.blackwaterlodge.com
Boone and Crockett Club www.boone-crockett.org
Buckmasters, Ltd. www.buckmasters.com
Cast Bullet Assoc. www.castbulletassoc.org
Citizens Committee for the Right to Keep & Bear Arms www.ccrkba.org
Civilian Marksmanship Program www.odcmp.com
Colorado School of Trades www.gunsmith-school.com
Ducks Unlimited www.ducks.org
Fifty Caliber Shooters Assoc. www.fcsa.org
Firearms Coalition www.nealknox.com
Front Sight Firearms Training Institute www.frontsight.com
German Gun Collectors Assoc. www.germanguns.com
Gun Clubs www.associatedgunclubs.org
Gun Owners' Action League www.goal.org
Gun Owners of America www.gunowners.org
Gun Trade Asssoc. Ltd. www.brucepub.com/gta
Gunsite Training Center,Inc. www.gunsite.com
Handgun Hunters International www.sskindustries.com
Hunting and Shooting Sports Heritage Fund www.hsshf.org
International Defense Pistol Assoc. www.idpa.org
International Handgun Metallic Silhouette Assoc. www.ihmsa.org
International Hunter Education Assoc. www.ihea.com
International Single Shot Assoc. www.issa-schuetzen.org
Jews for the Preservation of Firearms Ownership www.jpfo.org
Mule Deer Foundation www.muledeer.org
Muzzle Loaders Assoc. of Great Britain www.mlagb.com
National 4-H Shooting Sports www.4-hshootingsports.org
National Benchrest Shooters Assoc. www.benchrest.com
National Muzzle Loading Rifle Assoc. www.nmlra.org
National Reloading Manufacturers Assoc www.reload-nrma.com
National Rifle Assoc. www.nra.org
National Rifle Assoc. ILA www.nraila.org
National Shooting Sports Foundation www.nssf.org
National Skeet Shooters Association www.nssa-nsca.com
National Sporting Clays Assoc. www.nssa-nsca.com
National Wild Turkey Federation www.nwtf.com
NICS/FBI www.fbi.gov
North American Hunting Club www.huntingclub.com
Order of Edwardian Gunners (Vintagers) www.vintagers.org
Pennsylvania Gunsmith School www.pagunsmith.com
Quail Unlimited www.qu.org
Right To Keep and Bear Arms www.rkba.org
Rocky Mountain Elk Foundation www.rmef.org
SAAMI www.saami.org
Safari Club International www.scifirstforhunters.org
Second Amendment Foundation www.saf.org
Second Amendment Sisters www.2asisters.org
Shooting Ranges Int'l www.shootingranges.com
Single Action Shooting Society www.sassnet.com
Students for Second Amendment www.sf2a.org
S&W Academy and Nat'l Firearms Trng. Center www.sw-academy.com
Tactical Defense Institute www.tdiohio.com
Ted Nugent United Sportsmen of America www.tnugent.com
Thunder Ranch www.thunderranchinc.com
Trapshooters Homepage www.trapshooters.com
Trinidad State Junior College www.trinidadstate.edu
U.S. Int'l Clay Target Assoc. www.usicta.com
United States Fish and Wildlife Service www.fws.gov
U.S. Practical Shooting Assoc. www.uspsa.org
U.S.A. Shooting www.U.S.A.shootng.com
Varmint Hunters Assoc. www.varminthunter.org
U.S. Sportsmen's Alliance www.ussportsmen.org
Women Hunters www.womanhunters.com
Women's Shooting Sports Foundation www.wssf.org

Stocks

Advanced Technology www.atigunstocks.com
Battenfeld Technologies www.battenfeldtechnologies.com
Bell & Carlson, Inc. www.bellandcarlson.com
Boyd's Gunstock Industries, Inc. www.boydgunstocks.com
Butler Creek Corp www.butler-creek.com
Calico Hardwoods, Inc. www.calicohardwoods.com
Choate Machine www.riflestock.com
Elk Ridge Stocks www.reamerrentals.com/elk_ridge.htm
Fajen www.battenfeldtechnologies.com
Great American Gunstocks www.gunstocks.com
Herrett's Stocks www.herrettstocks.com
High Tech Specialties www.bansnersrifle.com/hightech
Holland's Shooting Supplies www.hollandgun.com
Knoxx Industries www.knoxx.com
Lone Wolf www.lonewolfriflestocks.com
McMillan Fiberglass Stocks www.mcmfamily.com
MPI Stocks www.mpistocks.com
Precision Gun Works www.precisiongunstocks.com
Ram-Line www.outers-guncare.com

Rimrock Rifle Stock www.rimrockstocks.com
Royal Arms Gunstocks www.imt.net/~royalarms
S&K Industries www.sandkgunstocks.com
Speedfeed, Inc. www.speedfeedinc.com
Tiger-Hunt Curly Maple Gunstocks www.gunstockwood.com
Wenig Custom Gunstocks Inc. www.wenig.com

Targets and Range Equipment

Action Target Co. www.actiontarget.com
Advanced Interactive Systems www.ais-sim.com
Birchwood Casey www.birchwoodcasey.com
Caswell Meggitt Defense Systems www.mds-caswell.com
Champion Traps & Targets www.championtarget.com
Just Shoot Me Products www.ballistictec.com
Laser Shot www.lasershot.com
MTM Products www.mtmcase-gard.com
Natiional Target Co. www.nationaltarget.com
Newbold Target Systems www.newboldtargets.com
Porta Target,Inc. www.portatarget.com
Range Management Services Inc. www.casewellintl.com
Range Systems www.shootingrangeproducts.com
Reactive Target Systems Inc. chrts@primenet.com
ShatterBlast Targets www.daisy.com
Super Trap Bullet Containment Systems www.supertrap.com
Thompson Target Technology www.thompsontarget.com
Tombstone Tactical Targets www.tttargets.com
Visible Impact Targets www.crosman.com
White Flyer www.whiteflyer.com

Trap and Skeet Shooting Equipment and Accessories

Auto-Sporter Industries www.auto-sporter.com
10X Products Group www.10Xwear.com
Claymaster Traps www.claymaster.com
Do-All Traps, Inc. www.do-alltraps.com
Laporte U.S.A. www.laporte-shooting.com
Outers www.blount.com
Trius Products Inc. www.triustraps.com
White Flyer www.whiteflyer.com

Triggers

Brownells www.brownells.com
Chip McCormick Corp. www.chipmccormickcorp.com
Huber Concepts www.huberconcepts.com
Kidd Triggers. www.coolguyguns.com
Shilen www.shilen.com
Timney Triggers www.timneytrigger.com

Major Shooting Web Sites and Links

24 Hour Campfire www.24hourcampfire.com
Alphabetic Index of Links www.gunsgunsguns.com
Auction Arms www.auctionarms.com
Benchrest Central www.benchrest.com
Bullseye Pistol www.bullseyepistol.com
Firearms History www.researchpress.co.uk/firearms
Firearm News www.firearmnews.com
Gun Broker Auctions www.gunbroker.com
Gun Index www.gunindex.com
Gun Industry www.gunindustry.com
Gun Blast www.gunblast.com
Gun Boards www.gunboards.com
Gun Broker www.gunbroker.com
Gun Law www.gunlaw.com
Gun Manuals www.gunmanuals.ch/manuals.htm
Gun Nuts Firearm Schematics www.gunuts.com
Guns For Sale www.gunsamerica.com
Guns Unified Nationally Endorsing Dignity www.guned.com
Gun Shop Finder www.gunshopfinder.com
Hunting Information(NSSF) www.huntinfo.org
Hunting Net www.hunting.net
Hunting Network www.huntingnetwork.com
Keep and Bear Arms www.keepandbeararms.com
Leverguns www.leverguns.com
Outdoor Yellow Pages www.outdoorsyp.com
Real Guns www.realguns.com
Rec.Guns www.recguns.com
Shooter's Online Services www.shooters.com
Shotgun Sports Resource Guide www.shotgunsports.com
Sixgunner www.sixgunner.com
Sportsman's Web www.sportsmansweb.com
Surplus Rifles www.surplusrifle.com

PERIODICAL PUBLICATIONS

AAFTA News (M)
5911 Cherokee Ave., Tampa, FL 33604. Official newsletter of the American Airgun Field Target Assn.

The Accurate Rifle
Precisions Shooting, Inc., 222 Mckee Street, Manchester CT 06040. $37 yr. Dedicated to the rifle accuracy enthusiast.

Action Pursuit Games Magazine (M)
CFW Enterprises, Inc., 4201 W. Vanowen Pl., Burbank, CA 91505 818-845-2656. $4.99 single copy U.S., $5.50 Canada. Editor: Dan Reeves. World's leading magazine of paintball sports.

Air Gunner Magazine
4 The Courtyard, Denmark St., Wokingham, Berkshire RG11 2AZ, England/011-44-734-771677. $U.S. $44 for 1 yr. Leading monthly airgun magazine in U.K.

Airgun Ads
Box 33, Hamilton, MT 59840/406-363-3805; Fax: 406-363-4117. $35 1 yr. (for first mailing; $20 for second mailing; $35 for Canada and foreign orders.) Monthly tabloid with extensive For Sale and Wanted airgun listings.

The Airgun Letter
Gapp, Inc., 4614 Woodland Rd., Ellicott City, MD 21042-6329/410-730-5496; Fax: 410-730-9544; e-mail: staff@airgnltr.net; http://www.airgunletter.com. $21 U.S., $24 Canada, $27 Mexico and $33 other foreign orders, 1 yr. Monthly newsletter for airgun users and collectors.

Airgun World
4 The Courtyard, Denmark St., Wokingham, Berkshire RG40 2AZ, England/011-44-734-771677. Call for subscription rates. Oldest monthly airgun magazine in the U.K., now a sister publication to *Air Gunner*.

Alaska Magazine
Morris Communications, 735 Broad Street, Augusta, GA 30901/706-722-6060. Hunting, Fishing and Life on the Last Frontier articles of Alaska and western Canada.

American Firearms Industry
Nat'l. Assn. of Federally Licensed Firearms Dealers, 2455 E. Sunrise Blvd., Suite 916, Ft. Lauderdale, FL 33304. $35.00 yr. For firearms retailers, distributors and manufacturers.

American Guardian
NRA, 11250 Waples Mill Rd., Fairfax, VA 22030. Publications division. $15.00 1 yr. Magazine features personal protection; home-self-defense; family recreation shooting; women's issues; etc.

American Gunsmith
Belvoir Publications, Inc., 75 Holly Hill Lane, Greenwich, CT 06836-2626/203-661-6111. $49.00 (12 issues). Technical journal of firearms repair and maintenance.

American Handgunner*
Publisher's Development Corp., 591 Camino de la Reina, Suite 200, San Diego, CA 92108/800-537-3006 $16.95 yr. Articles for handgun enthusiasts, competitors, police and hunters.

American Hunter (M)
National Rifle Assn., 11250 Waples Mill Rd., Fairfax, VA 22030 (Same address for both.) Publications Div. $35.00 yr. Wide scope of hunting articles.

American Rifleman (M)
National Rifle Assn., 11250 Waples Mill Rd., Fairfax, VA 22030 (Same address for both). Publications Div. $35.00 yr. Firearms articles of all kinds.

American Survival Guide
McMullen Angus Publishing, Inc., 774 S. Placentia Ave., Placentia, CA 92670-6846. 12 issues $19.95/714-572-2255; FAX: 714-572-1864.

Armes & Tir*
c/o FABECO, 38, rue de Trévise 75009 Paris, France. Articles for hunters, collectors, and shooters. French text.

Arms Collecting (Q)
Museum Restoration Service, P.O. Box 70, Alexandria Bay, NY 13607-0070. $22.00 yr.; $62.00 3 yrs.; $112.00 5 yrs.
Australian Shooter *(formerly Australian Shooters Journal)*
Sporting Shooters' Assn. of Australia, Inc., P.O. Box 2066, Kent Town SA 5071, Australia. $60.00 yr. locally; $65.00 yr. overseas surface mail. Hunting and shooting articles.

The Backwoodsman Magazine
P.O. Box 627, Westcliffe, CO 81252. $16.00 for 6 issues per yr.; $30.00 for 2 yrs.; sample copy $2.75. Subjects include muzzle-loading, woodslore, primitive survival, trapping, homesteading, blackpowder cartridge guns, 19th century how-to.

Black Powder Cartridge News (Q)
SPG, Inc., P.O. Box 761, Livingston, MT 59047/Phone/Fax: 406-222-8416. $17 yr. (4 issues) ($6 extra 1st class mailing). For the blackpowder cartridge enthusiast.

Blackpowder Hunting (M)
Intl. Blackpowder Hunting Assn., P.O. Box 1180Z, Glenrock, WY 82637/307-436-9817. $20.00 1 yr., $36.00 2 yrs. How-to and where-to features by experts on hunting; shooting; ballistics; traditional and modern blackpowder rifles, shotguns, pistols and cartridges.

Black Powder Times
P.O. Box 234, Lake Stevens, WA 98258. $20.00 yr.; add $5 per year for Canada, $10 per year other foreign. Tabloid newspaper for blackpowder activities; test reports.

Blade Magazine
Krause Publications, 700 East State St., Iola, WI 54990-0001. $25.98 for 12 issues. Foreign price (including Canada-Mexico) $50.00. A magazine for all enthusiasts of handmade, factory and antique knives.

Caliber
GFI-Verlag, Theodor-Heuss Ring 62, 50668 Koln, Germany. For hunters, target shooters and reloaders.

The Caller (Q) (M)
National Wild Turkey Federation, P.O. Box 530, Edgefield, SC 29824. Tabloid newspaper for members; 4 issues per yr. (membership fee $25.00)

Cartridge Journal (M)
Robert Mellichamp, 907 Shirkmere, Houston, TX 77008/713-869-0558. Dues $12 for U.S. and Canadian members (includes the newsletter); 6 issues.

The Cast Bullet*(M)
Official journal of The Cast Bullet Assn. Director of Membership, 203 E. 2nd St., Muscatine, IA 52761. Annual membership dues $14, includes 6 issues.

Cibles
14, rue du Patronage-Laique, BP 2057, 52902 Chaumont, cedex 9, France. French-language arms magazine also carries a small amount of arms-related and historical content. 12 issues per year. Tel/03-25-03-87-47/Email cibeles@graphycom.com; Website: www.graphycom.com

COLTELLI, che Passione (Q)
Casella postale N.519, 20101 Milano, Italy/Fax:02-48402857. $15 1 yr., $27 2 yrs. Covers all types of knives—collecting, combat, historical. Italian text.

Combat Handguns*
Harris Publications, Inc., 1115 Broadway, New York, NY 10010.

Deer & Deer Hunting Magazine
Krause Publications, 700 E. State St., Iola, WI 54990-0001. $19.95 yr. (9 issues). For the serious deer hunter. Website: www.krause.com

The Derringer Peanut (M)
The National Association of Derringer Collectors, P.O. Box 20572, San Jose, CA 95160. A newsletter dedicated to developing the best derringer information. Write for details.

Deutsches Waffen Journal
Journal-Verlag Schwend GmbH, Postfach 100340, D-74503 Schwäbisch Hall, Germany/0791-404-500; FAX:0791-404-505 and 404-424. DM102 p. yr. (interior); DM125.30 (abroad), postage included. Antique and modern arms and equipment. German text.

Double Gun Journal
P.O. Box 550, East Jordan, MI 49727/800-447-1658. $35 for 4 issues.

Ducks Unlimited, Inc. (M)
1 Waterfowl Way, Memphis, TN 38120

The Engraver (M) (Q)
P.O. Box 4365, Estes Park, CO 80517/970-586-2388; Fax: 970-586-0394. Mike Dubber, editor. The journal of firearms engraving.

The Field
King's Reach Tower, Stamford St., London SE1 9LS England. £36.40 U.K. 1 yr.; 49.90 (overseas, surface mail) yr.; £82.00 (overseas, air mail) yr. Hunting and shooting articles, and all country sports.

Field & Stream
Time4 Media, Two Park Ave., New York, NY 10016/212-779-5000. 12 issues/$19.97. Monthly shooting column. Articles on hunting and fishing.

Field Tests
Belvoir Publications, Inc., 75 Holly Hill Lane; P.O. Box 2626, Greenwich, CT 06836-2626/203-661-6111; 800-829-3361 (subscription line). U.S. & Canada $29 1 yr., $58 2 yrs.; all other countries $45 1 yr., $90 2 yrs. (air).

Fur-Fish-Game
A.R. Harding Pub. Co., 2878 E. Main St., Columbus, OH 43209. $15.95 yr. Practical guidance regarding trapping, fishing and hunting.

The Gottlieb-Tartaro Report
Second Amendment Foundation, James Madison Bldg., 12500 NE 10th Pl., Bellevue, WA 98005/206-454-7012;Fax:206-451-3959. $30 for 12 issues. An insiders guide for gun owners.

Gray's Sporting Journal
Gray's Sporting Journal, P.O. Box 1207, Augusta, GA 30903. $36.95 per yr. for 6 issues. Hunting and fishing journals. Expeditions and Guides Book (Annual Travel Guide).

Gun List†
700 E. State St., Iola, WI 54990. $37.98 yr. (26 issues); $66.98 2 yrs. (52 issues). Indexed market publication for firearms collectors and active shooters; guns, supplies and services. Website: www.krause.com

Gun News Digest (Q)
Second Amendment Fdn., P.O. Box 488, Station C, Buffalo, NY 14209/716-885-6408; Fax:716-884-4471. $10 U.S.; $20 foreign.

The Gun Report
World Wide Gun Report, Inc., Box 38, Aledo, IL 61231-0038. $33.00 yr. For the antique and collectable gun dealer and collector.

Gunmaker (M) (Q)
ACGG, P.O. Box 812, Burlington, IA 52601-0812. The journal of custom gunmaking.

The Gunrunner
Div. of Kexco Publ. Co. Ltd., Box 565G, Lethbridge, Alb., Canada T1J 3Z4. $23.00 yr., sample $2.00. Monthly newspaper, listing everything from antiques to artillery.

Gun Show Calendar (Q)
700 E. State St., Iola, WI 54990. $14.95 yr. (4 issues). Gun shows listed; chronologically and by state. Website: www.krause.com

Gun Tests
11 Commerce Blvd., Palm Coast, FL 32142. The consumer resource for the serious shooter. Write for information.

Gun Trade News
Bruce Publishing Ltd., P.O. Box 82, Wantage, Ozon OX12 7A8, England/44-1-235-771770; Fax: 44-1-235-771848. Britain's only "trade only" magazine exclusive to the gun trade.

Gun Week†
Second Amendment Foundation, P.O. Box 488, Station C, Buffalo, NY 14209. $35.00 yr. U.S. and possessions; $45.00 yr. other countries. Tabloid paper on guns, hunting, shooting and collecting (36 issues).

Gun World
Y-Visionary Publishing, LP 265 South Anita Drive, Ste. 120, Orange, CA 92868. $21.97 yr.; $34.97 2 yrs. For the hunting, reloading and shooting enthusiast.

Guns & Ammo
Primedia, 6420 Wilshire Blvd., Los Angeles, CA 90048/213-782-2780. $23.94 yr. Guns, shooting, and technical articles.

Guns
Publishers Development Corporation, P.O. Box 85201, San Diego, CA 92138/800-537-3006. $19.95 yr. In-depth articles on a wide range of guns, shooting equipment and related accessories for gun collectors, hunters and shooters.

Guns Review
Ravenhill Publishing Co. Ltd., Box 35, Standard House, Bonhill St., London EC 2A 4DA, England. £20.00 sterling (approx. U.S. $38 USA & Canada) yr. For collectors and shooters.

H.A.C.S. Newsletter (M)
Harry Moon, Pres., P.O. Box 50117, South Slope RPO, Burnaby BC, V5J 5G3, Canada/604-438-0950; Fax:604-277-3646. $25 p. yr. U.S. and Canada. Official newsletter of The Historical Arms Collectors of B.C. (Canada).

Handgunner*
Richard A.J. Munday, Seychelles house, Brightlingsen, Essex CO7 ONN, England/012063-305201. £18.00 (sterling).

Handguns*
Primedia, 6420 Wilshire Blvd., Los Angeles, CA 90048/323-782-2868. For the handgunning and shooting enthusiast.

Handloader*
Wolfe Publishing Co., 2626 Stearman Road, Ste. A, Prescott, AZ 86301/520-445-7810;Fax:520-778-5124. $22.00 yr. The journal of ammunition reloading.

INSIGHTS*
NRA, 11250 Waples Mill Rd., Fairfax, VA 22030. Editor, John E. Robbins. $15.00 yr., which includes NRA junior membership; $10.00 for adult subscriptions (12 issues). Plenty of details for the young hunter and target shooter; emphasizes gun safety, marksmanship training, hunting skills.

International Arms & Militaria Collector (Q)
Arms & Militaria Press, P.O. Box 80, Labrador, Qld. 4215, Australia. A$39.50 yr. (U.S. & Canada), 2 yrs. A$77.50; A$37.50 (others), 1 yr., 2 yrs. $73.50 all air express mail; surface mail is less. Editor: Ian D. Skennerton.

International Shooting Sport*/UIT Journal
International Shooting Union (UIT), Bavariaring 21, D-80336 Munich, Germany. Europe: (Deutsche Mark) DM44.00 yr., 2 yrs. DM83.00; outside Europe: DM50.00 yr., 2 yrs. DM95.00 (air mail postage included.) For international sport shooting.

Internationales Waffen-Magazin
Habegger-Verlag Zürich, Postfach 9230, CH-8036 Zürich, Switzerland. SF 105.00 (approx. U.S. $73.00) surface mail for 10 issues. Modern and antique arms, self-defense. German text; English summary of contents.

The Journal of the Arms & Armour Society (M)
A. Dove, P.O. Box 10232, London, SW19 2ZD England. £15.00 surface mail; £20.00 airmail sterling only yr. Articles for the historian and collector.

Journal of the Historical Breechloading Smallarms Assn.
Published annually. P.O. Box 12778, London, SE1 6XB, England. $21.00 yr. Articles for the collector plus mailings of short articles on specific arms, reprints, newsletters, etc.

Knife World
Knife World Publications, P.O. Box 3395, Knoxville, TN 37927. $15.00 yr.; $25.00 2 yrs. Published monthly for knife enthusiasts and collectors. Articles on custom and factory knives; other knife-related interests, monthly column on knife identification, military knives.

Man At Arms*
P.O. Box 460, Lincoln, RI 02865. $27.00 yr., $52.00 2 yrs. plus $8.00 for foreign subscribers. The N.R.A. magazine of arms collecting-investing, with excellent articles for the collector of antique arms and militaria.

The Mannlicher Collector (Q)(M)
Mannlicher Collectors Assn., Inc., P.O. Box 7144, Salem Oregon 97303. $20/ yr. subscription included in membership.

MAGNUM
Rua Madre Rita Amada de Jesus, 182 , Granja Julieta, Sao Paulo – SP – 04721-050 Brazil. No details.

---

*Published bi-monthly
† Published weekly
‡Published three times per month. All others are published monthly.

M=Membership requirements; write for details.
Q=Published Quarterly.

PERIODICAL PUBLICATIONS

MAN/MAGNUM
S.A. Man (Pty) Ltd., P.O. Box 35204, Northway, Durban 4065, Republic of South Africa. SA Rand 200.00 for 12 issues. Africa's only publication on hunting, shooting, firearms, bushcraft, knives, etc.

The Marlin Collector (M)
R.W. Paterson, 407 Lincoln Bldg., 44 Main St., Champaign, IL 61820.

Muzzle Blasts (M)
National Muzzle Loading Rifle Assn., P.O. Box 67, Friendship, IN 47021/812-667-5131. $35.00 yr. annual membership. For the blackpowder shooter.

Muzzleloader Magazine*
Scurlock Publishing Co., Inc., Dept. Gun, Route 5, Box 347-M, Texarkana, TX 75501. $18.00 U.S.; $22.50 U.S./yr. for foreign subscribers. The publication for blackpowder shooters.

National Defense (M)*
American Defense Preparedness Assn., Two Colonial Place, Suite 400, 2101 Wilson Blvd., Arlington, VA 22201-3061/703-522-1820; FAX: 703-522-1885. $35.00 yr. Articles on both military and civil defense field, including weapons, materials technology, management.

National Knife Magazine (M)
Natl. Knife Coll. Assn., 7201 Shallowford Rd., P.O. Box 21070, Chattanooga, TN 37424-0070. Membership $35 yr.; $65.00 International yr.

National Rifle Assn. Journal (British) (Q)
Natl. Rifle Assn. (BR.), Bisley Camp, Brookwood, Woking, Surrey, England. GU24, OPB. £24.00 Sterling including postage.

National Wildlife*
Natl. Wildlife Fed., 1400 16th St. NW, Washington, DC 20036, $16.00 yr. (6 issues); *International Wildlife,* 6 issues, $16.00 yr. Both, $22.00 yr., includes all membership benefits. Write attn.: Membership Services Dept., for more information.

New Zealand GUNS*
Waitekauri Publishing, P.O. 45, Waikino 3060, New Zealand. $NZ90.00 (6 issues) yr. Covers the hunting and firearms scene in New Zealand.

New Zealand Wildlife (Q)
New Zealand Deerstalkers Assoc., Inc., P.O. Box 6514, Wellington, N.Z. $30.00 (N.Z.). Hunting, shooting and firearms/game research articles.

North American Hunter* (M)
P.O. Box 3401, Minnetonka, MN 55343/612-936-9333; e-mail: huntingclub@pclink.com. $18.00 yr. (7 issues). Articles on all types of North American hunting.

Outdoor Life
Time4 Media, Two Park Ave., New York, NY 10016. $14.97/10 issues. Extensive coverage of hunting and shooting. Shooting column by Jim Carmichel.

La Passion des Courteaux (Q)
Phenix Editions, 25 rue Madomoiselle, 75015 Paris, France. French text.

Paintball Games International Magazine
Aceville Publications, Castle House, 97 High St., Colchester, Essex, England CO1 1TH/011 [illegible]. Write for subscription rates. Leading magazine in the U.K. covering competitive paintball activities.

Paintball News
PBN Publishing, P.O. Box 1608, 24 Henniker St., Hillsboro, NH 03244/603-464-6080. $35 U.S. 1 yr. Bi-weekly. Newspaper covering the sport of paintball, new product reviews and industry features.

Paintball Sports (Q)
Paintball Publications, Inc., 540 Main St., Mount Kisco, NY 10549/941-241-7400. $24.75 U.S. 1 yr., $32.75 foreign. Covering the competitive paintball scene.

Performance Shooter
Belvoir Publications, Inc., 75 Holly Hill Lane, Greenwich, CT 06836-2626/203-661-6111. $45.00 yr. (12 issues). Techniques and technology for improved rifle and pistol accuracy.

Petersen's HUNTING Magazine
Primedia, 6420 Wilshire Blvd., Los Angeles, CA 90048. $19.94 yr.; Canada $29.34 yr.; foreign countries $29.94 yr. Hunting articles for all game; test reports.

P.I. Magazine
America's Private Investigation Journal, 755 Bronx Dr., Toledo, OH 43609. Chuck Klein, firearms editor with column about handguns.

Pirsch
BLV Verlagsgesellschaft GmbH, Postfach 400320, 80703 Munich, Germany/089-12704-0;Fax:089-12705-354. German text.

Point Blank
Citizens Committee for the Right to Keep and Bear Arms (sent to contributors), Liberty Park, 12500 NE 10th Pl., Bellevue, WA 98005

POINTBLANK (M)
Natl. Firearms Assn., Box 4384 Stn. C, Calgary, AB T2T 5N2, Canada. Official publication of the NFA.

The Police Marksman*
6000 E. Shirley Lane, Montgomery, AL 36117. $17.95 yr. For law enforcement personnel.

Police Times (M)
3801 Biscayne Blvd., Miami, FL 33137/305 573-0070.

Popular Mechanics
Hearst Corp., 224 W. 57th St., New York, NY 10019. Firearms, camping, outdoor oriented articles.

Precision Shooting
Precision Shooting, Inc., 222 McKee St., Manchester, CT 06040. $37.00 yr. U.S. Journal of the International Benchrest Shooters, and target shooting in general. Also considerable coverage of varmint shooting, as well as big bore, small bore, schuetzen, lead bullet, wildcats and precision reloading.

Rifle*
Wolfe Publishing Co., 2626 Stearman Road, Ste. A, Prescott, AZ 86301/520-445-7810; Fax: 520-778-5124. $19.00 yr. The sporting firearms journal.

Rifle's Hunting Annual
Wolfe Publishing Co., 2626 Stearman Road, Ste. A, Prescott, AZ 86301/520-445-7810; Fax: 520-778-5124. $4.99 Annual. Dedicated to the finest pursuit of the hunt.

Rod & Rifle Magazine
Lithographic Serv. Ltd., P.O. Box 38-138, Wellington, New Zealand. $50.00 yr. (6 issues). Hunting, shooting and fishing articles.

Safari* (M)
Safari Magazine, 4800 W. Gates Pass Rd., Tucson, AZ 85745/602-620-1220. $55.00 (6 times). The journal of big game hunting, published by Safari Club International. Also publish *Safari Times*, a monthly newspaper, included in price of $55.00 national membership.

Second Amendment Reporter
Second Amendment Foundation, James Madison Bldg., 12500 NE 10th Pl., Bellevue, WA 98005. $15.00 yr. (non-contributors).

Shoot! Magazine*
Shoot! Magazine Corp., 1770 West State Stret PMB 340, Boise ID 83702/208-368-9920; Fax: 208-338-8428. Website: www.shootmagazine.com; $32.95 (6 times/yr.). Articles of interest to the cowboy action shooter, or others interested the Western-era firearms and ammunition.

Shooter's News
23146 Lorain Rd., Box 349, North Olmsted, OH 44070/216-979-5258;Fax:216-979-5259. $29 U.S. 1 yr., $54 2 yrs.; $52 foreign surface. A journal dedicated to precision riflery.

Shooting Industry
Publisher's Dev. Corp., 591 Camino de la Reina, Suite 200, San Diego, CA 92108. $50.00 yr. To the trade. $25.00.

Shooting Sports USA
National Rifle Assn. of America, 11250 Waples Mill Road, Fairfax, VA 22030. Annual subscriptions for NRA members are $5 for classified shooters and $10 for non-classified shooters. Non-NRA member subscriptions are $15. Covering events, techniques and personalities in competitive shooting.

Shooting Sportsman*
P.O. Box 11282, Des Moines, IA 50340/800-666-4955 (for subscriptions). Editorial: P.O. Box 1357, Camden, ME 04843. $19.95 for six issues. The magazine of wingshooting and fine guns.

The Shooting Times & Country Magazine (England)†
IPC Magazines Ltd., King's Reach Tower, Stamford St, 1 London SE1 9LS, England/0171-261-6180;Fax:0171-261-7179. £65 (approx. $98.00) yr.; £79 yr. overseas (52 issues). Game shooting, wild fowling, hunting, game fishing and firearms articles. Britain's best selling field sports magazine.

Shooting Times
Primedia, 2 News Plaza, P.O. Box 1790, Peoria, IL 61656/309-682-6626. $16.97 yr. Guns, shooting, reloading; articles on every gun activity.

The Shotgun News‡
Primedia, 2 News Plaza, P.O. Box 1790, Peoria, IL 61656/800-495-8362. 36 issues/ yr. @ $28.95; 12 issues/yr. @ $19.95. foreign subscription call for rates. Sample copy $4.00. Gun ads of all kinds.

SHOT Business
National Shooting Sports Foundation, Flintlock Ridge Office Center, 11 Mile Hill Rd., Newtown, CT 06470-2359/203-426-1320; FAX: 203-426-1087. For the shooting, hunting and outdoor trade retailer.

Shotgun Sports
P.O. Box 6810, Auburn, CA 95604/916-889-2220; FAX:916-889-9106. $31.00 yr. Trapshooting how-to's, shotshell reloading, shotgun patterning, shotgun tests and evaluations, Sporting Clays action, waterfowl/upland hunting. Call 1-800-676-8920 for a free sample copy.

The Single Shot Exhange Magazine
PO box 1055, York SC 29745/803 [illegible] phone/fax. $31.50/yr., monthly. Articles of interest to the blackpowder cartridge shooter and antique arms collector.

Single Shot Rifle Journal* (M)
Editor John Campbell, PO Box 595, Bloomfield Hills, MI 48303/248-458-8415. Email: jcampbel@dmbb.com Annual dues $35 for 6 issues. Journal of the American Single Shot Rifle Assn.

The Sixgunner (M)
Handgun Hunters International, P.O. Box 357, MAG, Bloomingdale, OH 43910

The Skeet Shooting Review
National Skeet Shooting Assn., 5931 Roft Rd., San Antonio, TX 78253. $20.00 yr. (Assn. membership includes mag.) Competition results, personality profiles of top Skeet shooters, how-to articles, technical, reloading information.

Soldier of Fortune
Subscription Dept., P.O. Box 348, Mt. Morris, IL 61054. $29.95 yr.; $39.95 Canada; $50.95 foreign.
Sporting Classics

Sporting Classics, Inc.
PO Box 23707, Columbia, SC 29223/1-800-849-1004. 1 yr./6 issues/$23.95; 2 yrs./12 issues/$38.95; 3 yrs./18 issues/$47.95. Firearms & outdoor articles and columns.

Sporting Clays Magazine
Patch Communications, 5211 South Washington Ave., Titusville, FL 32780/407-268-5010; FAX: 407-267-7216. $29.95 yr. (12 issues). Official publication of the National Sporting Clays Association.

Sporting Goods Business
Miller Freeman, Inc., One Penn Plaza, 10th Fl., New York, NY 10119-0004. Trade journal.

Sporting Goods Dealer
Two Park Ave., New York, NY 10016. $100.00 yr. Sporting goods trade journal.

Sporting Gun
Bretton Court, Bretton, Peterborough PE3 8DZ, England. £27.00 (approx. U.S. $36.00), airmail £35.50 yr. For the game and clay enthusiasts.

Sports Afield
15621 Chemical Lane, Huntington Beach CA 92648. U.S./800-234-3537. International/714-894-9080. Nine issues for $29.97. Website: www.sportsafield.com. America's oldest outdoor publication is now devoted to high-end sporting pursuits, especially in North America and Africa.

The Squirrel Hunter
P.O. Box 368, Chireno, TX 75937. $14.00 yr. Articles about squirrel hunting.

Stott's Creek Calendar
Stott's Creek Printers, 2526 S 475 W, Morgantown, IN 46160/317-878-5489. 1 yr (3 issues) $11.50; 2 yrs. (6 issues) $20.00. Lists all gun shows everywhere in convenient calendar form; call for information.

Super Outdoors
2695 Aiken Road, Shelbyville, KY 40065/502-722-9463; 800-404-6064; Fax: 502-722-8093. Mark Edwards, publisher. Contact for details.

TACARMI
Via E. De Amicis, 25; 20123 Milano, Italy. $100.00 yr. approx. Antique and modern guns. (Italian text.)

Territorial Dispatch—1800s Historical Publication (M)
National Assn. of Buckskinners, 4701 Marion St., Suite 324, Livestock Exchange Bldg., Denver, CO 80216. Michael A. Nester & Barbara Wyckoff, editors. 303-297-9671.

Trap & Field
1000 Waterway Blvd., Indianapolis, IN 46202. $25.00 yr. Official publ. Amateur Trapshooting Assn. Scores, averages, trapshooting articles.

Turkey Call* (M)
Natl. Wild Turkey Federation, Inc., P.O. Box 530, Edgefield, SC 29824. $25.00 with membership (6 issues per yr.)

Turkey & Turkey Hunting*
Krause Publications, 700 E. State St., Iola, WI 54990-0001. $13.95 (6 issue p. yr.). Magazine with leading-edge articles on all aspects of wild turkey behavior, biology and the successful ways to hunt better with that info. Learn the proper techniques to calling, the right equipment, and more.

The U.S. Handgunner* (M)
U.S. Revolver Assn., 40 Larchmont Ave., Taunton, MA 02780. $10.00 yr. General handgun and competition articles. Bi-monthly sent to members.

U.S. Airgun Magazine
P.O. Box 2021, Benton, AR 72018/800-247-4867; Fax: 501-316-8549. 10 issues a yr. Cover the sport from hunting, 10-meter, field target and collecting. Write for details.

The Varmint Hunter Magazine (Q)
The Varmint Hunters Assn., Box 759, Pierre, SD 57501/800-528-4868. $24.00 yr.

Waffenmarkt-Intern
GFI-Verlag, Theodor-Heuss Ring 62, 50668 K"ln, Germany. Only for gunsmiths, licensed firearms dealers and their suppliers in Germany, Austria and Switzerland.

Wild Sheep (M) (Q)
Foundation for North American Wild Sheep, 720 Allen Ave., Cody, WY 82414. Website: http://iigi.com/os/non/fnaws/fnaws.htm; e-mail: fnaws@wyoming.com. Official journal of the foundation.

Wisconsin Outdoor Journal
Krause Publications, 700 E. State St., Iola, WI 54990-0001. $17.97 yr. (8 issues). For Wisconsin's avid hunters and fishermen, with features from all over that state with regional reports, legislative updates, etc. Website: www.krause.com

Women & Guns
P.O. Box 488, Sta. C, Buffalo, NY 14209. $24.00 yr. U.S.; $72.00 foreign (12 issues). Only magazine edited by and for women gun owners.

World War II*
Cowles History Group, 741 Miller Dr. SE, Suite D-2, Leesburg, VA 20175-8920. Annual subscriptions $19.95 U.S.; $25.95 Canada; 43.95 foreign. The title says it—WWII; good articles, ads, etc.

---

*Published bi-monthly
† Published weekly
‡Published three times per month. All others are published monthly

M=Membership requirements; write for details.
Q=Published Quarterly.

THE ARMS LIBRARY

FOR COLLECTOR ◆ HUNTER ◆ SHOOTER ◆ OUTDOORSMAN

IMPORTANT NOTICE TO BOOK BUYERS

Books listed here may be bought from **Ray Riling Arms Books Co.,** 6844 Gorsten St., Philadelphia, PA 19119, Phone 215-438-2456; FAX: 215-438-5395. E-mail: sales@rayrilingarmsbooks.com. Larry Riling is the researcher and compiler of "The Arms Library" and a seller of gun books for over 32 years. The Riling stock includes books classic and modern, many hard-to-find items, and many not obtainable elsewhere. These pages list a portion of the current stock. They offer prompt, complete service, with delayed shipments occurring only on out-of-print or out-of-stock books.

Visit our Web site at **www.rayrilingarmsbooks.com** and order all of your favorite titles online from our secure site.

NOTICE FOR ALL CUSTOMERS: Remittance in U.S. funds must accompany all orders. For your convenience we accept VISA, MasterCard, Discover & American Express. For shipments in the U.S., add $7.00 for the 1st book and $2.00 for each additional book for postage and insurance. Min-

imum order $10.00. International Orders add $13.00 for the 1st book and $5.00 for each additional book. All International orders are shipped at the buyer's risk unless an additional $5 for insurance is included. USPS does not offer insurance to all countries unless shipped Air-Mail. Please e-mail or call for pricing.

Payments in excess of order or for "Backorders" are credited or fully refunded at request. Books "As-Ordered" are not returnable except by permission and a handling charge on these of 10% or $2.00 per book, whichever is greater, is deducted from refund or credit. Only Pennsylvania customers must include current sales tax.

A full variety of arms books also available from **Rutgers Book Center**, 127 Raritan Ave., Highland Park, NJ 08904/908-545-4344; FAX: 908-545-6686 or **I.D.S.A. Books**, 1324 Stratford Drive, Piqua, OH 45356/937-773-4203; FAX: 937-778-1922.

BALLISTICS AND HANDLOADING

ABC's of Reloading, 7th Edition, by Bill Chevalier, Iola, WI, Krause Publications, 2005. 288 pp., illustrated with 550 b&w photos. Softcover. NEW. $21.95
Accurate Arms Loading Guide Number 2, by Accurate Arms, McEwen, TN, Accurate Arms Company, Inc., 2000. Paper covers. $22.95
  Includes new data on smokeless powders XMR4064 and XMP5744 as well as a special section on cowboy action shooting. The new manual includes 50 new pages of data. An appendix includes nominal rotor charge weights, bullet diameters.
The American Cartridge, by Charles Suydam, Borden Publishing Co. Alhambra, CA, 1986. 184 pp., illus. Softcover $24.95
  An illustrated study of the rimfire cartridge in the United States.
Ammo and Ballistics II, by Robert W. Forker, Safari Press, Inc., Huntington Beach, CA, 2002. 298 pp., illus. Paper covers. $19.95
  Ballistic data on 125 calibers and 1,400 loads out to 500 yards.
Barnes Bullets Reloading Manual Number 3, Orem, Barnes, 2001. 786 pp. Hardcover. NEW. $29.95
Barnes Reloading Manual #3, Barnes Bullets, American Fork, UT, 2003. 668 pp., illus. $29.95
  Features data and trajectories on the new weight X, XBT and Solids in calibers from .22 to .50 BMG.
Blackpowder Loading Manual, 3rd Edition, by Sam Fadala, DBI Books, a division of Krause Publications, Iola, WI, 1995. 368 pp., illus. Paper covers. $20.95
  Revised and expanded edition of this landmark blackpowder loading book. Covers hundreds of loads for most of the popular blackpowder rifles, handguns and shotguns.
Black Powder, Pig Lead and Steel Silhouettes, by Paul A. Matthews, Prescott, AZ, Wolfe Publishing, 2002. 132 pp., illustrated with b&w photographs and detailed drawings and diagrams. Softcover. NEW. $16.95
Cartridges of the World, 10th Edition; Revised and Expanded by Frank C. Barnes, Iola, WI, Krause Publications, 2003. 526 pp., 450 b&w photos. Softcover. NEW. $24.95
Cartridge Reloading Tools of the Past, by R.H. Chamberlain, and Tom Quigley, Castle Rock, WA, 1998. 167 pp., illus. Paper covers. $25.00
  A detailed treatment of the extensive Winchester and Ideal line of handloading tools and bullet molds, plus Remington, Marlin, Ballard, Browning, Maynard, and many others.
Cast Bullets for the Black Powder Rifle, by Paul A. Matthews, Wolfe Publishing Co., Prescott, AZ, 1996. 133 pp., illus. Paper covers. $22.50
  The tools and techniques used to make your cast bullet shooting a success.
Complete Blackpowder Handbook, 4th Edition, by Sam Fadala, DBI Books, a division of Krause Publications, Iola, WI, 2001. 400 pp., illus. Paper covers. $22.95
  Expanded and completely rewritten edition of the definitive book on the subject of blackpowder.
Complete Reloading Manual, One Book / One Caliber, CA, Load Books USA, 2000. $7.95 each
  Contains unabridged information from U.S. bullet and powder makers. With thousands of proven and tested loads, plus dozens of various bullet designs and different powders. Spiral bound. Available in all calibers.
Designing and Forming Custom Cartridges for Rifles and Handguns, by Ken Howell. Precision Shooting, Manchester, CT. 2002. 600 pp., illus. $59.95
  The classic work in its field, out of print for the last few years and virtually unobtainable on the used book market, now returns in an exact reprint of the original. Full size (8-1/2" x 11"), hardcovers. Dozens of cartridge drawings never published anywhere before–dozens you've never heard of (guaranteed!). Precisely drawn to the dimensions specified by the men who designed them, the factories that made them, and the authorities that set the standards. All drawn to the same format and scale (1.5x) for most, how to form them from brass. Other practical information included.
Early Gunpowder Artillery 1300-1600 by John Norris, London, The Crowood Press, 2003. 1st edition. 141 pp., with 160 b&w photos. Hardcover. New in new dust jacket. $34.95
Early Loading Tools & Bullet Molds, Pioneer Press, 1988. 88 pp., illus. Softcover. $7.50

German 7.9mm Military Ammunition 1888-1945, by Daniel Kent, Ann Arbor, MI, Kent, 1990. 153 pp., plus appendix. illus., b&w photos. $35.00
Handbook for Shooters and Reloaders, by P.O. Ackley, Salt Lake City, UT, 1998, (Vol. I), 567 pp., illus. Includes a separate exterior ballistics chart. $24.95; (Vol. II), a new printing with specific new material. 495 pp., illus. $20.95
Handgun Stopping Power; The Definitive Study, by Marshall & Sandow. Boulder, CO, Paladin Press, 1992. 240 pp. $45.00
  Offers accurate predictions of the stopping power of specific loads in calibers from 380 Auto to 45 ACP, as well as such specialty rounds as the Glaser Safety Slug, Federal Hydra-Shok, MagSafe, etc. This is the definitive methodology for predicting the stopping power of handgun loads, the first to take into account what really happens when a bullet meets a man.
Handloader's Digest: 18th Edition edited by Ken Ramage, Iola, WI, Krause Publications, 2003. 300 b&w photos, 256 pp. Softcover. NEW. $19.95
Handloader's Manual of Cartridge Conversions, 2nd Revised Edition by John J., Donnelly, Stoeger Publishing Co., So. Hackensack, NJ, 2002. Unpaginated. $39.95
  From 14 Jones to 70-150 Winchester in English and American cartridges, and from 4.85 U.K. to 15.2x28R Gevelot in metric cartridges. Over 900 cartridges described in detail.
Hatcher's Notebook, by S. Julian Hatcher, Stackpole Books, Harrisburg, PA, 1992. 488 pp., illus. $39.95
  A reference work for shooters, gunsmiths, ballisticians, historians, hunters and collectors.
Headstamped Cartridges and Their Variations; Volume 2 by Daniel L. Shuey, W.R.A. Co., Rockford, IL, WCF Publications, 2003. 351 pp. illustrated with b&w photos. Hardcover. NEW. $55.00
History & Development of Small Arms Ammunition, Volume 1, Second Edition–With A Value Guide, Martial Long Arms, Flintlock through Rimfire, by George A. Hoyem, Missoula, MI, Armory Publications, 2005. Hardcover. New in new dust jacket. $60.00
Hornady Handbook of Cartridge Reloading, 6th Edition, Vol. I and II, edited by Larry Steadman, Hornady Mfg. Co., Grand Island, NE, 2003., illus. $49.95
  Two volumes; Volume 1, 773 pp.; Volume 2, 717 pp. New edition of this famous reloading handbook covers rifle and handgun reloading data and ballistic tables. Latest loads, ballistic information, etc.
How-To's for the Black Powder Cartridge Rifle Shooter, by Paul A. Matthews, Wolfe Publishing Co., Prescott, AZ, 1995. 45 pp. Paper covers. $22.50
  Covers lube recipes, good bore cleaners and over-powder wads. Tips include compressing powder charges, combating wind resistance, improving ignition and much more.
The Hunter's Guide to Accurate Shooting, by Wayne van Zwoll, Guilford, CT, Lyons Press, 2002. 1st edition. 288 pp. Hardcover. New in new dust jacket. $29.95
The Illustrated Reference of Cartridge Dimensions, edited by Dave Scovill, Wolfe Publishing Co., Prescott, AZ, 1994. 343 pp., illus. Paper covers. $19.00
  A comprehensive volume with over 300 cartridges. Standard and metric dimensions have been taken from SAAMI drawings and/or fired cartridges.
Loading the Black Powder Rifle Cartridge, by Paul A. Matthews, Wolfe Publishing Co., Prescott, AZ, 1993. 121 pp., illus. Paper covers. $22.50
  Author Matthews brings the blackpowder cartridge shooter valuable information on the basics, including cartridge care, lubes and moulds, powder charges and developing and testing loads in his usual authoritative style.
Lyman 48th Reloading Handbook, No. 48. Connecticut, Lan Publishing Corporation, 2003. 48th edition. 480 pp. Softcover. NEW. $26.95
Lyman Cast Bullet Handbook, 3rd Edition, edited by C. Kenneth Ramage, Lyman Publications, Middlefield, CT, 1980. 416 pp., illus. Paper covers. $19.95
  Information on more than 5000 tested cast bullet loads and 19 pages of trajectory and wind drift tables for cast bullets.
Lyman Black Powder Handbook, 2nd Edition, edited by Sam Fadala, Lyman Products for Shooters, Middlefield, CT, 2000. 239 pp., illus. Paper covers. $19.95
  Comprehensive load information for the modern blackpowder shooter.
Lyman Shotshell Handbook, 4th Edition, edited by Edward A. Matunas, Lyman Products Co., Middlefield, CT, 1996. 330 pp., illus. Paper covers. $24.95
  Has 9,000 loads, including slugs and buckshot, plus feature articles and a full color I.D. section. Superb reference text.

ARMS LIBRARY

Make It Accurate - Get the Maximum Performance from Your Hunting Rifle, by Craig Boddington, Long Beach, CA, Safari Press, 1999. Hardcover. New in new dust jacket. $24.95

Metallic Cartridge Conversions: The History of the Guns and Modern Reproductions, by Dennis Adler, Foreword by R. L. Wilson, lola, WI, Krause Publications, 2003. 1st edition. 208 pp. 250 color photos. Hardcover. New in new dust jacket. $39.95

Modern Exterior Ballistics, by Robert L. McCoy, Schiffer Publishing Co., Atglen, PA, 1999. 128 pp. $95.00

Advanced students of exterior ballistics and flight dynamics will find this comprehensive textbook on the subject a useful addition to their libraries.

Modern Reloading 2nd Edition, by Richard Lee, Inland Press, 2003. 623 pp., illus. $29.95

The how-to's of rifle, pistol and shotgun reloading plus load data for rifle and pistol calibers.

Modern Reloading Manual, 2nd Edition by Richard Lee, privately printed, 2003. 510 pp., illus. Hardcover. NEW. $24.95

Mr. Single Shot's Cartridge Handbook, by Frank de Haas, Mark de Haas, Orange City, IA, 1996. 116 pp., illus. Paper covers. $21.50

This book covers most of the cartridges, both commercial and wildcat, that the author has known and used.

Nosler Reloading Manual #5, edited by Gail Root, Nosler Bullets, Inc., Bend, OR, 2002. 516 pp., illus. $29.99

Combines information on their ballistic tip, partition and handgun bullets with traditional powders and new powders never before used, plus trajectory information from 100 to 500 yards.

The Paper Jacket, by Paul Matthews, Wolfe Publishing Co., Prescott, AZ, 1991. Paper covers. $14.50

Up-to-date and accurate information about paper-patched bullets.

Reloading for Shotgunners, 4th Edition, by Kurt D. Fackler, and M.L. McPherson, DBI Books, a division of Krause Publications, Iola, WI, 1997. 320 pp., illus. Paper covers. $19.95

Expanded reloading tables with over 11,000 loads. Bushing charts for every major press and component maker. All new presentation on all aspects of shotshell reloading by two of the top experts in the field.

Reloading Tools, Sights and Telescopes for S/S Rifles, by Gerald O. Kelver, Brighton, CO, 1982. 163 pp., illus. Softcover. $15.00

A listing of most of the famous makers of reloading tools, sights and telescopes with a brief description of the products they manufactured.

The Rimfire Cartridge in the United States and Canada, Illustrated History of Rimfire Cartridges, Manufacturers, and the Products Made from 1857-1984, by John L. Barber, Thomas Publications, Gettysburg, PA 2000. 1st edition. Profusely illus. 221 pp. $50.00

The author has written an encyclopedia of rimfire cartridges from the 22 to the massive 1.00 in. Gatling. Fourteen chapters, six appendices and an excellent bibliography.

Round Ball to Rimfire: A History of Civil War Small Arms Ammunition, Vol. 3, by Dean S. Thomas, Gettysburg, PA, Thomas Publications, 2003. 488 pp. Hardcover. NEW. $49.95

Federal pistols, revolvers and miscellaneous essays.

Shotshells & Ballistics, Safari Press, 2002. 275 pp., photos. Softcover, $19.95

Accentuated with photos from the field and the range, this is a reference book unlike any other.

Sierra Reloading Manual, 5th Edition: Rifle and Handgun Manual of Reloading Data. Sedalia, MO, Sierra Bullets, 2003. Hardcover. NEW. $39.95

Sixgun Cartridges and Loads, by Elmer Keith, The Gun Room Press, Highland Park, NJ, 1986. 151 pp., illus. $24.95

A manual covering the selection, uses and loading of the most suitable and popular revolver cartridges. Originally published in 1936. Reprint.

Speer Reloading Manual No. 13, edited by members of the Speer research staff, Omark Industries, Lewiston, ID, 1999. 621 pp., illus. $24.95

With 13 new sections containing the latest technical information and reloading trends for both novice and expert in this latest edition. More than 9,300 loads are listed, including new propellant powders from Accurate Arms, Alliant, Hodgdon and Vihtavuori.

Stopping Power: A Practical Analysis of the Latest Handgun Ammunition, by Marshall & Sanow, Boulder, CO, Paladin Press, 2002. 1st edition. 600+ photos, 360 pp. Softcover. $49.95

If you want to know how handgun ammunition will work against human targets in the future, you must look at how similar ammo has worked against human targets in the past. Stopping Power bases its conclusions on real world facts from real-world gunfights. It provides the latest street results of actual police and civilian shootings in all of the major handgun calibers, from 22 LR to 45 ACP, plus more than 30 chapters of vital interest to all gun owners. The only thing worse than being involved in a gunfight is losing one. The info in this book will help you choose the right bullets for your gun so you don't lose.

Street Stoppers, The Latest Handgun Stopping Power Street Results, by Marshall & Lanow, Boulder, CO, Paladin Press, 1996. 374 pp., illus. Softcover. $42.95

Street Stoppers is the long-awaited sequel to Handgun Stopping Power. It provides the latest results of real-life shootings in all of the major handgun calibers, plus more than 25 thought-provoking chapters that are vital to anyone interested in firearms, wound ballistics, and combat shooting. This book also covers the street results of the hottest new caliber to hit the shooting world in years, the 40 Smith & Wesson. Updated street results of the latest exotic ammunition including Remington Golden Saber and CCI-Speer Gold Dot, plus the venerable offerings from MagSafe, Glaser, Cor-Bon and others. A fascinating look at the development of Hydra-Shok ammunition is included.

Understanding Ballistics, Revised 2nd Edition by Robert A. Rinker, Mulberry House Publishing Co., Corydon, IN, 2000. 430 pp., illus. Paper covers. New, revised and expanded. $24.95

Explains basic to advanced firearm ballistics in understandable terms.

Why Not Load Your Own?, by Col. T. Whelen, Gun Room Press, Highland Park, NJ 1996, 4th ed., rev. 237 pp., illus. $20.00

A basic reference on handloading, describing each step, materials and equipment. Includes loads for popular cartridges.

Wildcat Cartridges Volumes 1 & 2 Combination, by the editors of *Handloaders* magazine, Wolfe Publishing Co., Prescott, AZ, 1997. 350 pp., illus. Paper covers. $39.95

A profile of the most popular information on wildcat cartridges that appeared in the *Handloaders* magazine.

COLLECTORS

The 1 October 1934 SS Dienstalterliste, by the Ulric of England Research Unit San Jose, CA, R. James Bender Publishing, 1994. Reprint softcover. NEW. $29.95

The 10. Panzer Division: In Action in the East, West and North Africa 1939-1943, by Jean Resta and N. Moller, Canada, J.J. Fedorowicz Publishing Inc., 2003. 1st edition. Hardcover. NEW. $89.95

18th Century Weapons of the Royal Welsh Fuziliers from Flixton Hall, by Erik Goldstein, Thomas Publications, Gettysburg, PA, 2002. 1st edition. 126 pp., illustrated with b&w photos. Softcover. $19.95

The .45-70 Springfield Book I, by Albert Frasca and Robert Hill, Frasca Publishing, 2000. Memorial edition. Hardback with gold embossed cover and spine. $95.00

The Memorial edition reprint of the 45-70 Springfield was done to honor Robert H. Hill who was an outstanding Springfield collector, historian, researcher, and gunsmith. Only 1,000 of these highly regarded books were printed, using the same binding and cover material as the original 1980 edition. The book is considered the bible for 45-70 Springfield Trapdoor collectors.

The .45-70 Springfield Book II 1865-1893, by Albert Frasca, Frasca Publishing, Springfield, Ohio 1997 Hardback with gold embossed cover and spine. 400+ pp. and 400+ photographs which cover ALL the trapdoor Springfield models. Hardback with gold embossed cover and spine. $85.00

A MUST for the trapdoor collector!

The .45-70 Springfield, by Joe Poyer and Craig Riesch, North Cape Publications, Tustin, CA, 1996. 150 pp., illus. Paper covers. $16.95

A revised and expanded second edition of a best-selling reference work organized by serial number and date of production to aid the collector in identifying popular "Trapdoor" rifles and carbines.

'51 Colt Navies, by Nathan L. Swayze, The Gun Room Press, Highland Park, NJ, 1993. 243 pp., illus. $59.95

The Model 1851 Colt Navy, its variations and markings.

The 1862 U.S. Cavalry Tactics, by Philip St. George Cooke, Mechanicsburg, PA, Stackpole Books, 2004. 416 pp. Hardcover. New in new dust jacket. $19.89

A Collector's Guide to the '03 Springfield, by Bruce N. Canfield, Andrew Mowbray Inc., Lincoln, RI, 1989. 160 pp., illus. Paper covers. $24.00

A comprehensive guide follows the '03 through its unparalleled tenure of service. Covers all of the interesting variations, modifications and accessories of this highly collectible military rifle.

A Collector's Guide to United States Combat Shotguns, by Bruce N. Canfield, Andrew Mowbray Inc., Lincoln, RI, 1992. 184 pp., illus. Paper covers. $24.00

This book provides full coverage of combat shotguns, from the earliest examples right up to the Gulf War and beyond.

A Collector's Guide to Winchester in the Service, by Bruce N. Canfield, Andrew Mowbray, Inc., Lincoln, RI, 1991. 192 pp., illus. Paper covers. $24.00

The firearms produced by Winchester for the national defense. From Hotchkiss to the M14, each firearm is examined and illustrated.

A Concise Guide to the Artillery at Gettysburg, by Gregory Coco, Thomas Publications, Gettysburg, PA, 1998. 96 pp., illus. Paper covers. $10.00

Coco's 10 book on Gettysburg is a beginner's guide to artillery and its use at the battle. It covers the artillery batteries describing the types of cannons, shells, fuses, etc. using interesting narrative and human interest stories.

A Glossary of the Construction, Decoration and Use of Arms and Armor in All Countries and in All Times, by George Cameron Stone, Dover Publishing, New York 1999. Softcover. $39.95

An exhaustive study of arms and armor in all countries through recorded history - from the Stone Age up to WWII. With over 4,500 b&w illustrations, this Dover edition is an unabridged republication of the work originally published in 1934 by the Southworth Press, Portland, MA. A new Introduction has been specially prepared for this edition.

A Guide to American Trade Catalogs 1744-1900, by Lawrence B. Romaine, Dover Publications, New York, NY. 422 pp., illus. Paper covers. $12.95

A Guide to Ballard Breechloaders, by George J. Layman, Pioneer Press, Union City, TN, 1997. 261 pp., illus. Paper covers. $19.95

Documents the saga of this fine rifle from the first models made by Ball & Williams of Worchester, to its production by the Marlin Firearms Co., to the cessation of 19th century manufacture in 1891, and finally to the modern reproductions made in the 1990s.

A Guide to the Maynard Breechloader, by George J. Layman, George J. Layman, Ayer, MA, 1993. 125 pp., illus. Paper covers. $11.95

The first book dedicated entirely to the Maynard family of breech-loading firearms. Coverage of the arms is given from the 1850s through the 1880s.

A Guide to U. S. Army Dress Helmets 1872-1904, by Kasal and Moore, North Cape Publications, 2000. 88 pp., illus. Paper covers. $15.95

This thorough study provides a complete description of the Model 1872 and 1881 dress helmets worn by the U.S. Army.

A Study of Remington's Smoot Patent and Number Four Revolvers, by Parker Harry, Parker Ora Lee, and Joan Reisch, Foreword by Roy M. Marcot, Santa Ana, CA, Armslore Press, Graphic Publishers, 2003. 1st edition. 120 pp., profusely illus., plus 8-page color section. Softcover. $17.95

A detailed, pictorial essay on Remington's early metallic cartridge-era pocket revolvers: their design, development, patents, models, identification and variations. Includes the biography of arms inventor Wm. S. Smoot, for the first time ever!, as well as a mini-history of the Remington Arms Company.

Accoutrements of the United States Infantry, Riflemen, and Dragoons 1834-1839, by R.T. Huntington, Historical Arms Series No. 20. Canada, Museum Restoration. 58 pp. illus. Softcover. $8.95

Although the 1841 edition of the U.S. Ordnance Manual provides ample information on the equipment that was in use during the 1840s, it is evident that the patterns of equipment that it describes were not introduced until 1838 or 1839. This guide is intended to fill this gap in our knowledge by providing an overview of what we now know about the accoutrements that were issued to the regular infantryman, rifleman, and dragoon, in the 1830s with excursions into earlier and later years.

Ackermann Military Prints: Uniforms of the British and Indian Armies 1840-1855, by William Y. Carman with Robert W. Kenny Jr., Schiffer Publications, Atglen, PA, 2002. 1st edition. 176 pp., with over 160 color images. $69.95

ARMS LIBRARY

Afrikakorps: Rommel's Tropical Army in Original Color, by Bernd Peitz, Gary Wilkins. Atglen, PA, Schiffer Publications, 2004. 1st edition. 192 pp., with over 200 color and b&w photographs. Hardcover. New in new dust jacket. $59.95

Air Guns, by Eldon G. Wolff, Duckett's Publishing Co., Tempe, AZ, 1997. 204 pp., illus. Paper covers. $35.00

Historical reference covering many makers, European and American guns, canes and more.

All About Southerners, including a detailed look at the characteristics and design of the "Best Little Pistol in the World," by Lionel J. Bogut, Sun City, CA, White Star, Inc., 2002. A limited edition of 1,000 copies. Signed and numbered. 114 pp., including bibliography, and plenty of b&w photographs and detailed drawings. Hardcover. $29.95

Allgemeine-SS The Commands, Units and Leaders of the General SS, by Mark C. Yerger, Atglen, PA, Schiffer Publications, 1997. 1st edition. Hardcover. New in new dust jacket. $49.95

Allied and Enemy Aircraft: May 1918; Not to be Taken from the Front Lines, Historical Arms Series No. 27. Canada, Museum Restoration. Softcover. $8.95

The basis for this title is a very rare identification manual published by the French government in 1918 that illustrated 60 aircraft with three or more views: French, English American, German, Italian, and Belgian, which might have been seen over the trenches of France. Each is described in a text translated from the original French. This is probably the most complete collection of illustrations of WWI aircraft that has survived.

American Beauty; The Prewar Colt National Match Government Model Pistol, by Timothy J. Mullin, Collector Grade Publications, Cobourg, Ontario, Canada. 72 pp., illus. $34.95

Includes over 150 serial numbers, and 20 spectacular color photos of factory engraved guns and other authenticated upgrades, including rare "double-carved" ivory grips.

American Civil War Artillery 1861-65: Field Artillery, by Philip Oxford Katcher, United Kingdom, Osprey Publishing, 2001. 1st edition. 48 pp. Softcover. $14.95

Perhaps the most influential arm of either army in the prosecution of the American Civil War, the artillery of both sides grew to be highly professional organizations. This book covers all the major artillery pieces employed, including the Napoleon, Parrott Rifle and Mountain Howitzer.

American Military and Naval Belts, 1812-1902, by R. Stephen Dorsey, Eugene, OR, Collectors Library, 2002. 1st edition. Hardcover. $80.00

With introduction by Norm Flayderman, this massive work is the NEW key reference on sword belts, waist belts, sabre belts, shoulder belts and cartridge belts (looped and non-looped). At over 460 pp., this 8-1/2" x 11" book offers over 840 photos (primarily in color) and original period drawings. In addition, this work offers the first, comprehensive research on the Anson Mills woven cartridge belts: the man, the company and its personalities, the belt-related patents and the government contracts from 1880 through 1902. This book is a "must" for all accoutrements collectors, military historians and museums.

American Military Belt Plates, by Michael J. O'Donnell and J. Duncan Campbell. Alexandria, VA, O'Donnell Publishing, 2000. 2nd edition. 614 pp., illus. Hardcover $49.00

At last available and well worth the wait! This massive study encompasses all the known plates from the Revolutionary War through the Spanish-American conflict. A sweeping, handsomely presented study that covers 1776 through 1910. Over 1,025 specimens are illustrated front and back along with many images of soldiers wearing various plates.

American Military Headgear Insignia, by Michael J. O'Donnell and J. Duncan, Campbell, Alexandria, VA, O'Donnell Publishing, 2004. 1st edition. 311 pp., 703 photo figures, 4 sketches. Hardcover. New in new dust jacket. $89.95

The American Military Saddle, 1776-1945, by R. Stephen Dorsey and Kenneth L. McPheeters, Collector's Library, Eugene, OR, 1999. 400 pp., illus. $67.00

The most complete coverage of the subject ever written on the American Military Saddle. Nearly 1,000 actual photos and official drawings, from the major public and private collections in the U.S. and Great Britain.

American Police Collectibles; Dark Lanterns and Other Curious Devices, by Matthew G. Forte, Turn of the Century Publishers, Upper Montclair, NJ, 1999. 248 pp., illus. $24.95

For collectors of police memorabilia (handcuffs, police dark lanterns, mechanical and chain nippers, rattles, billy clubs and nightsticks) and police historians.

An Introduction to the Civil War Small Arms, by Earl J. Coates and Dean S. Thomas, Thomas Publishing Co., Gettysburg, PA, 1990. 96 pp., illus. Paper covers. $10.00

The small arms carried by the individual soldier during the Civil War.

Arming the Glorious Cause; Weapons of the Second War for Independence, by James B. Whisker, Daniel D. Hartzler and Larry W. Tantz, Old Bedford Village Press, Bedford, PA., 1998. 175 pp., illus. $45.00

A photographic study of Confederate weapons.

Arms & Accoutrements of the Mounted Police 1873-1973, by Roger F. Phillips, and Donald J. Klancher, Museum Restoration Service, Ont., Canada, 1982. 224 pp., illus. $49.95

A definitive history of the revolvers, rifles, machine guns, cannons, ammunition, swords, etc. used by the NWMP, the RNWMP and the RCMP during the first 100 years of the Force.

Arms and Armor in Colonial America 1526-1783, by Harold Peterson, Dover Publishing, New York, 2000. 350 pp. with over 300 illustrations, index, bibliography and appendix. Softcover. $34.95

Over 200 years of firearms, ammunition, equipment and edged weapons.

Arms and Armor in the Art Institute of Chicago, by Waltler J. Karcheski, Bulfinch, New York 1999. 128 pp., 103 color photos, 12 b&w illustrations. $50.00

The George F. Harding Collection of arms and armor is the most visited installation at the Art Institute of Chicago–a testament to the enduring appeal of swords, muskets and the other paraphernalia of medieval and early modern war. Organized both chronologically and by type of weapon, this book captures the best of this astonishing collection in 115 striking photographs - most in color–accompanied by illuminating text. Here are intricately filigreed breastplates and ivory-handled crossbows, samurai katana and Toledo-steel scimitars, elaborately decorated maces and beautifully carved flintlocks–a treat for anyone who has ever been beguiled by arms, armor and the age of chivalry.

Arms Makers of Maryland, by Daniel D. Hartzler, George Shumway, York, PA, 1975. 200 pp., illus. $50.00

A thorough study of the gunsmiths of Maryland who worked during the late 18th and early 19th centuries.

Arms Makers of Western Pennsylvania, by James B. Whisker, Old Bedford Village Press. 1st edition. Deluxe hardbound edition, 176 pp., $50.00

Printed on fine coated paper with many large photographs and detailed text describing the period, lives, tools, and artistry of the Arms Makers of Western Pennsylvania.

Arsenal of Freedom: The Springfield Armory 1890-1948, by Lt. Col. William Brophy, Andrew Mowbray, Inc., Lincoln, RI,1997. 20 pgs. of photos. 400 pp. As new, Softcover. $29.95

A year-by-year account drawn from offical records. Packed with reports, charts, tables and line drawings.

The Art of Gun Engraving, by Claude Gaier and Pietro Sabatti, Knickerbocker Press, N.Y., 1999. 160 pp., illus. $34.95

The richness and detail lavished on early firearms represents a craftmanship nearly vanished. Beginning with crossbows, hunting scenes, portraits, or mythological themes are intricately depicted within a few square inches of etched metal. The full-color photos contained herein recaptures this lost art with exquisite detail.

Astra Automatic Pistols, by Leonardo M. Antaris, FIRAC Publishing Co., Sterling, CO, 1989. 248 pp., illus. $55.00

Charts, tables, serial ranges, etc. The definitive work on Astra pistols.

Austrian & German Guns and Rifles (Fucili Da Caccia Austriaci E Tedeschi), by Marco E. Nobili, Italy, Il Volo Srl, 2000. 1st printing. 304 pp., illustrated with b&w photographs, plus 16 full color plates. Text in Italian and English. Hardcover. New in very good dust jacket. $189.95

Ballard: The Great American Single Shot Rifle, by John T. Dutcher. Denver, CO, privately printed, 2002. 1st edition. 380 pp., illustrated with b&w photos, with 8-page color insert. Hardcover. New in new dust jacket. $79.95

Basic Documents on U.S. Martial Arms, commentary by Col. B.R. Lewis, reissue by Ray Riling, Phila., PA, 1956 and 1960. Rifle Musket Model 1855. Each $10.00

The first issue rifle of musket caliber, a muzzleloader equipped with the Maynard Primer, 32 pp. Rifle Musket Model 1863. The typical Union muzzleloader of the Civil War, 26 pp. Breech-Loading Rifle Musket Model 1866. The first of our 50-caliber breechloading rifles, 12 pp. Remington Navy Rifle Model 1870. A commercial type breech-loader made at Springfield, 16 pp. Lee Straight Pull Navy Rifle Model 1895. A magazine cartridge arm of 6mm caliber, 23 pp. Breech-Loading Arms (five models) 27 pp. Ward-Burton Rifle Musket 1871, 16 pp.

Battle Colors: Insignia and Aircraft Markings of the Eighth Air Force in World War II, by Robert A. Watkins, Atglen, PA, Schiffer Publications, 2004. 1st edition. Softcover. $45.00

Battle Weapons of the American Revolution, by George C. Neuman, Scurlock Publishing Co., Texarkana, TX, 2001. 400 pp. Illus. Softcovers. $44.95

The most extensive photographic collection of Revolutionary War weapons ever in one volume. More than 1,600 photos of over 500 muskets, rifles, swords, bayonets, knives and other arms used by both sides in America's War for Independence.

The Bedford County Rifle and Its Makers, by Calvin Hetrick, Introduction by George Shumway, George Shumway Pub., 1975. 40 pp. illus. Softcover. $10.00

The author's study of the graceful and distinctive muzzle-loading rifles made in Bedford County, Pennsylvania, stands as a milestone on the long path to the understanding of America's longrifles.

The Belgian Rattlesnake; The Lewis Automatic Machine Gun, by William M. Easterly, Collector Grade Publications, Cobourg, Ontario, Canada, 1998. 584 pp., illus. $79.95

The most complete account ever published on the life and times of Colonel Isaac Newton Lewis and his crowning invention, the Lewis Automatic machine gun.

Beretta Automatic Pistols, by J.B. Wood, Stackpole Books, Harrisburg, PA, 1985. 192 pp., illus. $26.95

Only English-language book devoted to the Beretta line. Includes all important models.

Best of Holland & Holland, England's Premier Gunmaker, by Michael McIntosh and Jan G. Roosenburg. Safari Press, Inc., Long Beach, CA, 2002. 1st edition. 298 pp. Profuse color illustrations. $69.95

Holland & Holland has had a long history of not only building London's "best" guns but also providing superior guns–the ultimate gun in finish, engraving, and embellishment. From the days of old in which a maharaja would order 100 fancifully engraved H&H shotguns for his guests to use at his duck shoot, to the recent elaborately decorated sets depicting the Apollo 11 moon landing or the history of the British Empire, all of these guns represent the zenith in the art and craft of gunmaking and engraving. These and other H&H guns in the series named "Products of Excellence" are a cut above the ordinary H&H gun and hark back to a time when the British Empire ruled over one-third of the globe–a time when rulers, royalty, and the rich worldwide came to H&H for a gun that would elevate them above the crowd. In this book, master gunwriter and acknowledged English gun expert Michael McIntosh and former H&H director Jan Roosenburg show us in words and pictures the finest products ever produced by H&H and, many would argue, by any gun company on earth. From a dainty and elegant 410 shotgun with gold relief engraving of scenes from Greek and Roman antiquity, to the massive 700 Nitro Express double rifle, some of the most expensive and opulent guns ever produced on earth parade through these pages. An overview of the Products of Excellence series is given as well as a description and history of these special H&H guns. Never before have so many superlative guns from H&H–or any other maker for that manner–been displayed in one book. Many photos shown are firearms from private collections which cannot be seen publicly anywhere except in this book. In addition, many interesting details and a general history of H&H are provided.

The Big Guns, Civil War Siege, Seacoast, and Naval Cannon, by Edwin Olmstead, Wayne E. Stark, and Spencer C. Tucker, Museum Restoration Service, Bloomfield, Ontario, Canada, 1997. 360 pp., illus. $80.00

This book is designed to identify and record the heavy guns available to both sides by the end of the Civil War.

Blue Book of Air Guns, 4th Edition, edited by S.P. Fjestad, Blue Book Publications, Inc. Minneapolis, MN 2005. $24.95

This new edition simply contains more airgun values and information than any other single publication.

Blue Book of Gun Values, 26th Edition, edited by S.P. Fjestad, Blue Book Publications, Inc. Minneapolis, MN 2005. $39.95

This new edition simply contains more firearm values and information than any other single publication. Expanded to over 1,600 pages featuring over 100,000 firearms prices, the new Blue Book of Gun Values also contains over 3/4-million words of text–no other book is even close! Most of the information contained in this publication is simply not available anywhere else, for any price!

ARMS LIBRARY

Blue Book of Modern Black Powder Values, 4th Edtion by Dennis Adler, Blue Book Publications, Inc. Minneapolis, MN 2005. 271 pp., illus. 41 color photos. Softcover. $24.95

This new title contains more up-to-date blackpowder values and related information than any other single publication. This new book will keep you up-to-date on modern blackpowder models and prices, including most makes and models introduced this year!

The Blunderbuss 1500-1900, by James D. Forman, Historical Arms Series No. 32. Canada, Museum Restoration, 1994. 40 pp., illus. Softcover. $8.95

An excellent and authoritative booklet giving tons of information on the Blunderbuss, a very neglected subject.

Boarders Away Volume I: With Steel-Edged Weapons & Polearms, by William Gilkerson, Andrew Mowbray, Inc. Publishers, Lincoln, RI, 1993. 331 pp. $48.00

Contains the essential 24-page chapter "War at Sea" which sets the historical and practical context for the arms discussed. Includes chapters on Early Naval Weapons, Boarding Axes, Cutlasses, Officers Fighting Swords and Dirks, and weapons at hand of Random Mayhem.

Boarders Away, Volume II: Firearms of the Age of Fighting Sail, by William Gilkerson, Andrew Mowbray, Inc. Publishers, Lincoln, RI, 1993. 331 pp., illus. $65.00

Covers the pistols, muskets, combustibles and small cannons used aboard American and European fighting ships, 1626-1826.

Boston's Gun Bible, by Boston T. Party, Ignacio, CO, Javelin Press, August 2000. Expanded edition. Softcover. $28.00

This mammoth guide for gun owners everywhere is a completely updated and expanded edition (more than 500 new pages!) of Boston T. Party's classic Boston on Guns and Courage. Boston gives new advice on which shoulder weapons and handguns to buy and why, before exploring such topics as why you should consider not getting a concealed carry permit, what guns and gear will likely be outlawed next, how to spend within your budget, why you should go to a quality defensive shooting academy now, which guns and gadgets are inferior and why, how to stay off illegal government gun registration lists, how to spot an undercover agent trying to entrap law-abiding gun owners and much more.

The Bren Gun Saga, by Thomas B. Dugelby, Collector Grade Publications, Cobourg, Ontario, Canada, 1999, revised and expanded edition. 406 pp., illus. $65.95

A modern, definitive book on the Bren in this revised expanded edition, which in terms of numbers of pages and illustrations is nearly twice the size of the original.

British Board of Ordnance Small Arms Contractors 1689-1840, by De Witt Bailey, Rhyl, England, W. S. Curtis, 2000. 150 pp. $18.00

Thirty years of research in the Archives of the Ordnance Board in London has identified more than 600 of these suppliers. The names of many can be found marking the regulation firearms of the period. In the study, the contractors are identified both alphabetically and under a combination of their date period together with their specialist trade.

The British Enfield Rifles, Volume 1, The SMLE MK I and MK III Rifles, by Charles R. Stratton, North Cape Pub., Tustin, CA, 1997. 150 pp., illus. Paper covers. $16.95

A systematic and thorough examination on a part-by-part basis of the famous British battle rifle that endured for nearly 70 years as the British Army's number one battle rifle.

The British Enfield Rifles, Volume 2, No. 4 and No. 5 Rifles, by Charles R. Stratton, North Cape Publications, Tustin, CA, 1999. 150 pp., illus. Paper covers. $16.95

The historical background for the development of both rifles describing each variation and an explanation of all the marks, numbers and codes found on most parts.

The British Enfield Rifles, Volume 4, The Pattern 1914 and U. S. Model 1917 Rifles, by Charles R. Stratton, North Cape Publications, Tustin, CA, 2000. Paper covers. $16.95

One of the least known American and British collectible military rifles is analyzed on a part by part basis. All markings and codes, refurbishment procedures and WWII upgrade are included as are the various sniper rifle versions.

The British Falling Block Breechloading Rifle from 1865, by Jonathan Kirton, Tom Rowe Books, Maynardsville, TN, 2nd edition, 1997. 380 pp., illus. $70.00

Expanded edition of a comprehensive work on the British falling block rifle.

British Gun Engraving, by Douglas Tate, Safari Press, Inc., Huntington Beach, CA, 1999. 240 pp., illus. Limited, signed and numbered edition, in a slipcase. $80.00

A historic and photographic record of the last two centuries.

British Gunmakers: Volume One – London, by Nigel Brown, London, Quiller, 2004. 1st edition 280 pp., 33 colour, 43 b&w photographs, line drawings. Hardcover. NEW. $99.95

British Military Flintlock Rifles 1740-1840, With a Remarkable Wealth of Data about the Riflemen and Regiments that Carried These Weapons, by De Witt Bailey, Andrew Mowbray, Inc. Lincoln, RI, 2002. 1st edition. 264 pp. with over 320 photographs. Hardcover. $47.95

Pattern 1776 Rifles, the Ferguson Breechloader, the famous Baker Rifle, rifles of the Hessians and other German Mercenaries, American Loyalist rifles, rifles given to Indians, Cavalry rifles and rifled carbines, bayonets, accoutrements, ammunition and more.

British Service Rifles and Carbines 1888-1900, by Alan M. Petrillo, Excaliber Publications, Latham, NY, 1994. 72 pp., illus. Paper covers. $11.95

A complete review of the Lee-Metford and Lee-Enfield rifles and carbines.

British Single Shot Rifles, Volume 1, Alexander Henry, by Wal Winfer, Tom Rowe, Maynardsville, TN, 1998, 200 pp., illus. $50.00

Detailed study of the single shot rifles made by Henry. Illustrated with hundreds of photographs and drawings.

British Single Shot Rifles Volume 2, George Gibbs, by Wal Winfer, Tom Rowe, Maynardsville, TN, 1998. 177 pp., illus. $50.00

Detailed study of the Farquharson as made by Gibbs. Hundreds of photos.

British Single Shot Rifles, Volume 3, Jeffery, by Wal Winfer, Rowe Publications, Rochester, N.Y., 1999. 260 pp., illus. $60.00

The Farquharsen as made by Jeffery and his competitors, Holland & Holland, Bland, Westley, Manton. Large section on the development of nitro cartridges including the 600.

British Single Shot Rifles, Vol. 4; Westley Richards, by Wal Winfer, Rowe Publications, Rochester, N.Y., 2000. 265 pp., illus., photos. $60.00

In this 4th volume, Winfer covers a detailed study of the Westley Richards single shot rifles, including Monkey Tails, Improved Martini, 1872,1873, 1878,1881, 1897 Falling Blocks. He also covers Westley Richards cartridges, history and reloading information.

British Sporting Guns & Rifles, compiled by George Hoyem, Armory Publications, Coeur d'Alene, ID, 1997. 1024 pp., illus. Two volumes. $250.00

Eighteen old sporting firearms trade catalogs and a rare book reproduced with their color covers in a limited, signed and numbered edition.

Broad Arrow: British & Empire Factory Production, Proof, Inspection, Armourers, Unit & Issue Markings, by Ian Skennerton. Australia, Arms & Militaria Press, 2001. 140 pp., circa 80 illus. Stiff paper covers. $29.95

Thousands of service markings are illustrated and their applications described. Invaluable reference on units, also ideal for medal collectors.

Browning Dates of Manufacture, compiled by George Madis, Art and Reference House, Brownsboro, TX, 1989. 48 pp. $7.50

Gives the date codes and product codes for all models from 1824 to the present.

Browning–Sporting Arms of Distinction 1903-1992, by Matt Eastman, Long Beach, CA, Safari Press, 2004. 428 pp., profuse illus. Hardcover. New in new dust jacket. $50.00

Browning Sporting Firearms: Dates of Manufacture, by D. R. Morse. Phoenix, AZ, Firing Pin Enterprizes, 2003. 37 pp. Softcover. New. $6.95

Covers their pistols, revolvers, rifles, shotguns and commemoratives, plus, models and serial numbers.

Bullard Firearms, by G. Scott Jamieson, Schiffer Publications, Atglen, PA 2002. 1st edition. 400 pp., with over 1100 color and b&w photographs, charts, diagrams. Hardcover. $100.00

Bullard Firearms is the story of a mechanical genius whose rifles and cartridges were the equal of any made in America in the 1880s, yet little of substance had been written about James H. Bullard or his arms prior to 1988 when the first edition, called Bullard Arms, was published. This greatly expanded volume, with over 1,000 b&w and 150 color plates, most not previously published, answers many of the questions posed in the first edition. The final chapter outlines, in chart form, almost 500 Bullard rifles by serial number, caliber and type. Quick and easy to use, this book is a real benefit for collectors and dealers alike.

Burning Powder, compiled by Major D.B. Wesson, Wolfe Publishing Company, Prescott, AZ, 1992. 110 pp. Soft cover. $10.95

A rare booklet from 1932 for Smith & Wesson collectors.

The Burnside Breech Loading Carbines, by Edward A. Hull, Andrew Mowbray, Inc., Lincoln, RI, 1986. 95 pp., illus. $16.00

No. 1 in the "Man at Arms Monograph Series." A model-by-model historical/technical examination of one of the most widely used cavalry weapons of the American Civil War based upon important and previously unpublished research.

C.S. Armory Richmond: History of the Confederate States Armory, Richmond, VA and the Stock Shop at the C.S. Armory, Macon, GA., by Paul Davies, privately printed, 2000. 368 pp., illustrated with b&w photos. Hardcover. $75.00

The American Society of Arms Collectors is pleased to recommend C.S. Armory Richmond as a useful and valuable reference for collectors and scholars in the field of antique firearms. Gives fantastic explanations of machinery, stocks, barrels, and every facet of the production process during the timeframe covered in this book.

Cacciare A Palla: Uso E Tecnologia Dell'arma Rigata, by Marco E. Nobili, Italy, Il Volo Srl, 1994. 4th Edition - 1st printing. 397 pp., illustrated with b&w photographs. Hardcover. New in new dust jacket. $75.00

The Call of Duty; Military Awards and Decorations of the United States of America, by John E. Strandberg, LTC and Roger James Bender, San Jose, CA, R. James Bender Publishing, 2005. (New expanded edition). 559 pp. illustrated with 1,293 photos (most in color). Hardcover. NEW. $67.95

Camouflage Uniforms of European and NATO Armies; 1945 to the Present, by J. F. Borsarello, Atglen, PA, Schiffer Publications. Over 290 color and b&w photographs, 120 pp. Softcover. $29.95

This full-color book covers nearly all of the NATO, and other European armies' camouflaged uniforms, and not only shows and explains the many patterns, but also their efficacy of design. Described and illustrated are the variety of materials tested in over 40 different armies, and includes the history of obsolete trial tests from 1945 to the present time. This book provides a superb reference for the historian, reenactor, designer, and modeler.

Camouflage Uniforms of the Waffen SS A Photographic Reference, by Michael Beaver, Schiffer Publishing, Atglen, PA. Over 1,000 color and b&w photographs and illustrations, 296 pp. $69.95

Finally a book that unveils the shroud of mystery surrounding Waffen-SS camouflage clothing. Illustrated here, both in full color and in contemporary b&w photographs, this unparalleled look at Waffen-SS combat troops and their camouflage clothing will benefit both the historian and collector.

Canadian Colts for the Boer War, by Col. Robert D. Whittington III. Hooks, TX, Brownlee Books, 2003. A limited edition of 1,000 copies. Numbered. 5 pp. Paper covers. New. $15.00

A study of Colt Revolvers issued to the First and Second Canadian Contingents Special Service Force.

Canadian Colts for the Boer War, Part 2, Col. Robert D. by Whittington III, Hooks, TX, Brownlee Books, 2005. A limited edition of 1,000 copies. Numbered. 5 pp. Paper covers, NEW. $5.00

Canadian Gunsmiths from 1608: A Checklist of Tradesmen, by John Belton, Historical Arms Series No. 29. Canada, Museum Restoration, 1992. 40 pp., 17 illustrations. Softcover. $8.95

This checklist is a greatly expanded version of HAS No. 14, listing the names, occupation, location, and dates of more than 1,500 men and women who worked as gunmakers, gunsmiths, armorers, gun merchants, gun patent holders, and a few other gun related trades. A collection of contemporary gunsmiths' letterhead have been provided to add color and depth to the study.

Canadian Militaria Directory & Sourcebook Second Edition, by Clive M. Law, Ont. Canada, Service Publications, 1998. pp. 90. Softcover. NEW. $14.95

Cap Guns, by James Dundas, Schiffer Publishing, Atglen, PA, 1996. 160 pp., illus. Paper covers. $29.95

Over 600 full-color photos of cap guns and gun accessories with a current value guide.

Carbines of the Civil War, by John D. McAulay, Pioneer Press, Union City, TN, 1981. 123 pp., illus. Paper covers. $12.95

A guide for the student and collector of the colorful arms used by the Federal cavalry.

Carbines of the U.S. Cavalry 1861-1905, by John D. McAulay, Andrew Mowbray Publishers, Lincoln, RI, 1996. $35.00

Covers the crucial use of carbines from the beginning of the Civil War to the end of the cavalry carbine era in 1905.

ARMS LIBRARY

Cartridge Carbines of the British Army, by Alan M. Petrillo, Excalibur Publications, Latham, NY, 1998. 72 pp., illus. Paper covers. $11.95

Begins with the Snider-Enfield which was the first regulation cartridge carbine introduced in 1866 and ends with the 303 caliber No.5, Mark 1 Enfield.

Cartridge Reloading Tools of the Past, by R.H. Chamberlain and Tom Quigley, Castle Rock, WA, 1998. 167 pp., illus. Paper covers. $25.00

A detailed treatment of the extensive Winchester and Ideal lines of handloading tools and bulletmolds plus Remington, Marlin, Ballard, Browning and many others.

Cartridges for Collectors, by Fred Datig, Pioneer Press, Union City, TN, 1999. Three volumes of 176 pp. each. Vol. 1 (Centerfire); Vol. 2 (Rimfire and Misc.) types. Volume 1, softcover only, $19.95. Volumes 2 and 3, hardcover. $19.95

Vol. 3 (Additional Rimfire, Centerfire, and Plastic.). All illustrations are shown in full-scale drawings.

Civil War Arms Makers and Their Contracts, edited by Stuart C. Mowbray and Jennifer Heroux, Andrew Mowbray Publishing, Lincoln, RI, 1998. 595 pp. $39.50

A facsimile reprint of the Report by the Commissioner of Ordnance and Ordnance Stores, 1862.

Civil War Arms Purchases and Deliveries, edited by Stuart C. Mowbray, Andrew Mowbray Publishing, Lincoln, RI, 1998. 300pp., illus. $39.50

A facsimile reprint of the master list of Civil War weapons purchases and deliveries including Small Arms, Cannon, Ordnance and Projectiles.

Civil War Battles of the Western Theatre, by Walter Crutcher (Foreword), Bryan S. Bush. Paducah, KY, Turner Publishing, 2000. 204 pp. Hardcover. New in new dust jacket. $39.89

Civil War Breech Loading Rifles, by John D. McAulay, Andrew Mowbray, Inc., Lincoln, RI, 1991. 144 pp., illus. Paper covers. $15.00

All the major breech-loading rifles of the Civil War and most, if not all, of the obscure types are detailed, illustrated and set in their historical context.

Civil War Cartridge Boxes of the Union Infantryman, by Paul Johnson, Andrew Mowbray, Inc., Lincoln, RI, 1998. 352 pp., illus. $45.00

There were four patterns of infantry cartridge boxes used by Union forces during the Civil War. The author describes the development and subsequent pattern changes to these cartridge boxes.

Civil War Collector's Price Guide; Expanded Millennium Edition, by North South Trader, Orange, VA, Publisher's Press, 2000. 9th edition. 260 pps., illus. Softcover. $29.95

All updated prices, scores of new listings, and hundreds of new pictures! It's the one reference work no collector should be without. An absolute must.

Civil War Collector's Price Guide; 30th Anniversary 10th Edition, Orange, VA, Publisher's Press, 2003. All 260 pps., illus. Softcover. NEW. $34.95

Civil War Commanders, by Dean Thomas, Thomas Publications, Gettysburg, PA. 1998. 72 pp., illus., photos. Paper covers. $9.95

138 photographs and capsule biographies of Union and Confederate officers. A convenient personalities reference guide.

Civil War Guns, by William B. Edwards, Thomas Publications, Gettysburg, PA, 1997. 444 pp., illus. $40.00

The complete story of Federal and Confederate small arms; design, manufacture, identifications, procurement issue, employment, effectiveness, and postwar disposal by the recognized expert.

Civil War Heavy Explosive Ordnance: A Guide to Large Artillery Projectiles, Torpedoes, and Mines, by Jack Bell, Denton, TX, University of North Texas Press, 2003. 1,016 b&w photos. 537 pp. Hardcover. New in new dust jacket. $50.00

Civil War Infantryman: In Camp, on the March, and in Battle, by Dean Thomas, Thomas Publications, Gettysburg, PA. 1998. 72 pp., illus. Softcovers. $12.95

Uses first-hand accounts to shed some light on the "common soldier" of the Civil War from enlistment to muster-out, including camp, marching, rations, equipment, fighting, and more.

Civil War Pistols, by John D. McAulay, Andrew Mowbray Inc., Lincoln, RI, 1992. 166 pp., illus. $38.50

A survey of the handguns used during the American Civil War.

Civil War Relic Hunting A to Z, by Robert Buttafuso, Sheridan Books, 2000. 1st edition. illus., 91 pp., b&w illustrations. Softcover. NEW. $21.95

Civil War Sharps Carbines and Rifles, by Earl J. Coates and John D. McAulay, Thomas Publications, Gettysburg, PA, 1996. 108 pp., illus. Paper covers. $12.95

Traces the history and development of the firearms including short histories of specific serial numbers and the soldiers who received them.

Civil War Small Arms of the U.S. Navy and Marine Corps, by John D. McAulay, Mowbray Publishing, Lincoln, RI, 1999. 186 pp., illus. $39.00

The first reliable and comprehensive guide to the firearms and edged weapons of the Civil War Navy and Marine Corps.

Col. Burton's Spiller & Burr Revolver, by Matthew W. Norman, Mercer University Press, Macon, GA, 1997. 152 pp., illus. $22.95

A remarkable archival research project on the arm together with a comprehensive story of the establishment and running of the factory.

Collecting Military Headgear; A Guide to 5000 Years of Helmet History, by Robert Atglen Attard, PA, Schiffer Publications, 2004. 1st edition. Hardcover. New in new dust jacket. $69.95

Collecting Third Reich Recordings, by Stuart McKenzie, San Jose, CA, R. James Bender Publishing, 2001. 1st edition. Softcover. NEW. $29.95

Collector's Illustrated Encyclopedia of the American Revolution, by George C. Neumann and Frank J. Kravic, Rebel Publishing Co., Inc., Texarkana, TX, 1989. 286 pp., illus. $42.95

A showcase of more than 2,300 artifacts made, worn, and used by those who fought in the War for Independence.

Colonel Thomas Claiborne Jr. and the Colt Whitneyville-Walker Pistol, by Col. Robert D. Whittington III, Hooks, TX, Brownlee Books, 2005. A limited edition of 1,000 copies. Numbered. 8 pp. Paper covers, NEW. $7.50

Colonels in Blue: Union Army Colonels of the Civil War, by Roger Hunt, New York, Atglen, PA, Schiffer Publications, 2003. 1st edition. 288 pp., with over 640 b&w photographs. Hardcover. New in new dust jacket. $59.95

Colonial Frontier Guns, by T.M. Hamilton, Pioneer Press, Union City, TN, 1988. 176 pp., illus. Paper covers. $17.50

A complete study of early flint muskets of this country.

The Colt 1909 Military Revolvers; The 1904 Thompson-Lagarde Report, and General John J. Pershing, by Col. Robert D. Whittington III, Hooks, TX, Brownlee Books, 2005. A limited edition of 1,000 copies. Numbered. 10 pp. Paper covers. NEW. $10.00

Colt and Its Collectors Exhibition Catalog for Colt: The Legacy of A Legend, Buffalo Bill Historical Center, Cody, Wyoming. Colt Collectors Association, 2003. 1st edition. Hardcover. New in new dust jacket. $125.00

Colt and Its Collectors accompanies the upcoming special exhibition, Colt: The Legacy of a Legend, opening at the Buffalo Bill Historical Center in May 2003. Numerous essays, over 750 color photographs by Paul Goodwin.

The Colt Armory, by Ellsworth Grant, Man-at-Arms Bookshelf, Lincoln, RI, 1996. 232 pp., illus. $35.00

A history of Colt's Manufacturing Company.

The Colt Engraving Book, Volumes I & II, by R. L. Wilson. Privately printed, 2001. Each volume is appx. 500 pp., with 650 illustrations, most in color. $390.00

This third edition from the original texts of 1974 and 1982 has been fine-tuned and dramatically expanded, and is by far the most illuminating and complete. With over 1,200 illustrations, more than 2/3 of which are in color, this book joins the author's The Book of Colt Firearms, and Fine Colts as companion volumes. Approximately 1,000 pages in two volumes, each signed by the author, serial numbered, and strictly limited to 3000 copies. Volume I covers from the Paterson and pre-Paterson period through c.1921 (end of the Helfricht period). Volume II commences with Kornbrath, and Glahn, and covers Colt embellished arms from c.1919 through 2000.

The Colt Model 1905 Automatic Pistol, by John Potocki, Andrew Mowbray Publishing, Lincoln, RI, 1998. 191 pp., illus. $28.00

Covers all aspects of the Colt Model 1905 Automatic Pistol, from its invention by the legendary John Browning to its numerous production variations.

Colt Peacemaker British Model, by Keith Cochran, Cochran Publishing Co., Rapid City, SD, 1989. 160 pp., illus. $35.00

Covers those revolvers Colt squeezed in while completing a large order of revolvers for the U.S. Cavalry in early 1874, to those magnificent cased target revolvers used in the pistol competitions at Bisley Commons in the 1890s.

Colt Peacemaker Encyclopedia, by Keith Cochran, Cochran Publishing Co., Rapid City, SD, 1986. 434 pp., illus. $60.00

A must-have book for the Peacemaker collector.

Colt Peacemaker Encyclopedia, Volume 2, by Keith Cochran, Cochran Publishing Co., SD, 1992. 416 pp., illus. $60.00

Included in this volume are extensive notes on engraved, inscribed, historical and noted revolvers, as well as those revolvers used by outlaws, lawmen, movie and television stars.

Colt Pistols, Texas, and the U.S. Army 1847-1861, by Col. Robert D. Whittington III, Hooks, TX, Brownlee Books, 2005. A limited edition of 1,000 copies. Numbered. 8 pp. Paper covers, NEW. $7.50

Colt Presentations: From the Factory Ledgers 1856-1869, by Herbert G. Houze. Lincoln, RI, Andrew Mowbray, Inc., 2003. 112 pp., 45 b&w photos. Softcover. $21.95

Samuel Colt was a generous man. He also used gifts to influence government decision makers. But after Congress investigated him in 1854, Colt needed to hide the gifts from prying eyes, which makes it very difficult for today's collectors to document the many revolvers presented by Colt and the factory. Using the original account journals of the Colt's Patent Fire Arms Manufacturing Co., renowned arms authority Herbert G. Houze finally gives us the full details behind hundreds of the most exciting Colts ever made.

Colt Revolvers and the Tower of London, by Joseph G. Rosa, Royal Armouries of the Tower of London, London, England, 1988. 72 pp., illus. Softcover. $15.00

Details the story of Colt in London through the early cartridge period.

Colt Single Action Army Revolver Study: New Discoveries, by Kenneth Moore, Lincoln, RI, Andrew Mowbray, Inc., 2003. 1st edition. 200 pp., with 77 photos and illustrations. Hardcover. New. $49.95

25 years after co-authoring the classic Study of the Colt Single Action Army Revolver, Ken fills in the gaps and sets the record straight. Decades in the making, this impressive new study brings us entirely up to date, including all the new research that the author has painstakingly gathered over the years. The serial number data alone will astound you. Includes, ejector models, special section on low serial numbers, U.S. Army testing data, new details about militia S.A.A.'s plus a true wealth of cartridge info.

Colt Single Action Army Revolvers: The Legend, the Romance and the Rivals, by "Doc" O'Meara, Krause Publications, Iola, WI, 2000. 160 pp., illustrated with 250 photos in b&w and a 16-page color section. $22.95

Production figures, serial numbers by year, and rarities.

Colt Single Action Army Revolvers and Alterations, by C. Kenneth Moore, Mowbray Publishers, Lincoln, RI, 1999. 112 pp., illus. $35.00

A comprehensive history of the revolvers that collectors call "Artillery Models." These are the most historical of all S.A.A. Colts, and this new book covers all the details.

Colt Single Action Army Revolvers and the London Agency, by C. Kenneth Moore, Andrew Mowbray Publishers, Lincoln, RI, 1990. 144 pp., illus. $35.00

Drawing on vast documentary sources, this work chronicles the relationship between the London Agency and the Hartford home office.

Colt Sporting Firearms: Dates of Manufacture, by D.R. Morse, Phoenix, AZ, Firing Pin Enterprizes, 2003. 82 pp. Softcover. New. $6.95

Covers their pistols, revolvers, rifles, shotguns and commemoratives, plus models and serial numbers.

The Colt U.S. General Officers' Pistols, by Horace Greeley IV, Andrew Mowbray Inc., Lincoln, RI, 1990. 199 pp., illus. $38.00

These unique weapons, issued as a badge of rank to General Officers in the U.S. Army from WWII onward, remain highly personal artifacts of the military leaders who carried them. Includes serial numbers and dates of issue.

Colts from the William M. Locke Collection, by Frank Sellers, Andrew Mowbray Publishers, Lincoln, RI, 1996. 192 pp., illus. $55.00

This important book illustrates all of the famous Locke Colts, with captions by arms authority Frank Sellers.

Colt's Dates of Manufacture 1837-1978, by R.L. Wilson, published by Maurie Albert, Coburg, Australia; N.A. distributor Madis Books, TX, 1997. 61 pp. $7.50

An invaluable pocket guide to the dates of manufacture of Colt firearms up to 1978.

Colt's Pocket '49: Its Evolution Including the Baby Dragoon and Wells Fargo, by Robert Jordan and Darrow Watt, privately printed, Loma Mar, CA 2000. 304 pp., with 984 color photos, illus. Beautifully bound in a deep blue leather-like case. $125.00

Detailed information on all models and covers engaving, cases, accoutrements, holsters, fakes, and much more. Included is a summary booklet containing information such as serial numbers, production ranges and identifing photos. This book is a masterpiece on its subject.

Colt's SAA Post War Models, by George Garton, The Gun Room Press, Highland Park, NJ, 1995. 166 pp., illus. $39.95

Complete facts on the post-war Single Action Army revolvers. Information on calibers, production numbers and variations taken from factory records.

Combat Helmets of the Third Reich: A Study in Photographs, by Thomas Kibler, Pottsboro, TX, Reddick Enterprises, 2003. 1st edition. 96 pp., illustrated in full color. Pictorial softcover. NEW. $19.95

The Combat Perspective The Thinking Man's Guide to Self-Defense, by Gabriel Suarez, Boulder, CO, Paladin Press, 2003. 1st edition. 112 pp. Softcover. NEW. $15.00

Complete Guide to all United States Military Medals 1939 to Present, by Colonel Frank C. Foster, Medals of America Press, Fountain Inn, SC, 2000. 121 pp., illus., photos. $29.95

Complete criteria for every Army, Navy, Marine, Air Force, Coast Guard, and Merchant Marine award since 1939. All decorations, service medals, and ribbons shown in full color and accompanied by dates and campaigns, as well as detailed descriptions on proper wear and display.

Complete Guide to the M1 Garand and the M1 Carbine, by Bruce N. Canfield, 2nd printing, Andrew Mowbray Inc., Lincoln, RI, 1999. 296 pp., illus. $39.50

Expanded and updated coverage of both the M1 Garand and the M1 Carbine, with more than twice as much information as the author's previous book on this topic.

The Complete Guide to U.S. Infantry Weapons of the First War, by Bruce Canfield, Andrew Mowbray, Publisher, Lincoln, RI, 2000. 304 pp., illus. $39.95

The definitive study of the U.S. Infantry weapons used in WWI.

The Complete Guide to U.S. Infantry Weapons of World War Two, by Bruce Canfield, Andrew Mowbray, Publisher, Lincoln, RI, 1995. 303 pp., illus. $39.95

A definitive work on the weapons used by the United States Armed Forces in WWII.

Confederate Belt Buckles & Plates by Steve E. Mullinax, O'Donnell Publishing, Alexandria, VA, 1999. Expanded edition. 247 pp., illus. Hardcover. $34.00

Hundreds of crisp photographs augment this classic study of Confederate accoutrement plates.

Confederate Carbines & Musketoons Cavalry Small Arms Manufactured in and for the Southern Confederacy 1861-1865. by John M. Murphy, Santa Ana, CA, privately printed, 2002. Reprint. Hardcover. New in new dust jacket. $79.95

Confederate Rifles & Muskets: Infantry Small Arms Manufactured in the Southern Confederacy 1861-1865, by John M. Murphy. Santa Ana, CA, privately printed, 1996. Reprint. 768 pp., 8 pp. color plates, profusely illustrated. Hardcover. $119.95

The first in-depth and academic analysis and discussion of the "long" longarms produced in the South by and for the Confederacy during the American Civil War. The collection of Dr. Murphy is doubtless the largest and finest grouping of Confederate longarms in private hands today.

Confederate Saddles & Horse Equipment, by Ken R. Knopp, Orange, VA, Publisher's Press, 2002. 194 pps., illus. Hardcover. $39.95

Confederate Saddles & Horse Equipment is a pioneer work on the subject. After 10 years of research Ken Knopp has compiled a thorough and fascinating study of the little-known field of Confederate saddlery and equipment. His analysis of ordnance operations coupled with his visual presentation of surviving examples offers an indispensable source for collectors and historians.

Cooey Firearms, Made in Canada 1919-1979, by John A. Belton, Museum Restoration, Canada, 1998. 36pp., with 46 illus. Paper covers. $8.95

More than 6 million rifles and at least 67 models were made by this small Canadian riflemaker. They have been identified from the first 'Cooey Canuck' through the last variations made by the 'Winchester-Cooey'. Each is descibed and most are illustrated in this first book on the Cooey.

Cougar Attacks: Encounters of the Worst Kind, by Kathy Etling, New York, Lyons Press, 2004. 1st edition. Softcover. NEW. $14.95

Cowboy and Gunfighter Collectible, by Bill Mackin, Mountain Press Publishing Co., Missoula, MT, 1995. 178 pp., illus. Paper covers. $25.00

A photographic encyclopedia with price guide and makers' index.

Cowboy Collectibles and Western Memorabilia, by Bob Bell and Edward Vebell, Schiffer Publishing, Atglen, PA, 1992. 160 pp., illus. Paper covers. $29.95

The exciting era of the cowboy and the wild west collectibles including rifles, pistols, gun rigs, etc.

Cowboy Culture: The Last Frontier of American Antiques, by Michael Friedman, Schiffer Publishing, Ltd., West Chester, PA, 2002. 300 pp., illus. $89.95

Covers the artful aspects of the old west, the antiques and collectibles. Illustrated with clear color plates of over 1,000 items such as spurs, boots, guns, saddles, etc.

Cowboys and the Trappings of the Old West, by William Manns and Elizabeth Clair Flood, Zon International Publishing Co., Santa Fe, NM, 1997, 1st edition. 224 pp., illus. $45.00

A pictorial celebration of the cowboy dress and trappings.

Custer & His Wolverines: The Michigan Cavalry Brigade, 1861-1865, by Edward G. Longacre, Cambridge, MA, Da Capo Press, 2004. 2nd edition, 24 b&w photos, 5 maps; 6" x 9", 352 pp. Softcover. NEW. $18.00

Custom Firearms Engraving, by Tom Turpin, Krause Publications, Iola, WI, 1999. 208 pp., illus. $49.95

Over 200 four-color photos with more than 75 master engravers profiled. Engravers directory with addresses in the U.S. and abroad.

Daisy Air Rifles & BB Guns: The First 100 Years, by Neal Punchard. St. Paul, MN, Motorbooks, 2002. 1st edition. 10" x 10", 156 pp., 300 color. Hardcover. $29.95

Flash back to the days of your youth and recall fond memories of your Daisy. Daisy Air Rifles and BB Guns looks back fondly on the first 100 years of Daisy BB rifles and pistols, toy and cork guns, accessories, packaging, period advertising and literature.

The Decorations, Medals, Ribbons, Badges and Insignia of the United States Army; World War II to Present, by Col. Frank C. Foster, Medals of America Press, Fountain Inn, SC. 2001. 145 pp., illus. $29.95

The most complete guide to United States Army medals, ribbons, rank, insignia and patches from WWII to the present day. Each medal and insignia shown in full color. Includes listing of respective criteria and campaigns.

The Decorations, Medals, Ribbons, Badges and Insignia of the United States Navy; World War II to Present, by James G. Thompson, Medals of America Press, Fountain Inn, SC. 2000. 123 pp., illus. $29.95

The most complete guide to United States Army medals, ribbons, rank, insignia and patches from WWII to the present day. Each medal and insignia shown in full color. Includes listing of respective criteria and campaigns.

Defending the Dominion, Canadian Military Rifles, 1855-1955, by David Edgecombe. Service Publications, Ont., Canada, 2003. 168 pp., with 60+ illustrations. Hardcover. $39.95

This book contains much new information on the Canadian acquisition, use and disposal of military rifles during the most significant century in the development of small arms. In addition to the venerable Martini-Henry, there are chapters on the Winchester, Snider, Starr, Spencer, Peabody, Enfield rifles and others.

The Derringer in America, Volume 1, The Percussion Period, by R.L. Wilson and L.D. Eberhart, Andrew Mowbray Inc., Lincoln, RI, 1985. 271 pp., illus. $48.00

A long awaited book on the American percussion derringer.

The Derringer in America, Volume 2, the Cartridge Period, by L.D. Eberhart and R.L. Wilson, Andrew Mowbray Inc., Publishers, Lincoln, RI, 1993. 284 pp., illus. $65.00

Comprehensive coverage of cartridge derringers organized alphabetically by maker. Includes all types of derringers known by the authors to have been offered in the American market.

The Devil's Paintbrush: Sir Hiram Maxim's Gun, by Dolf Goldsmith, 3rd Edition, expanded and revised, Collector Grade Publications, Toronto, Canada, 2002. 384 pp., illus. $79.95

The classic work on the world's first true automatic machine gun.

Die Wehrmacht, Volume One, by Uwe Feist, Ryton Publications, Bellingham, WA, 2000. Large format (8-3/4" x 11-1/2") hardbound book with over 250 b&w photos and 240 color prints, all on high quality coated paper. Hardcover. $65.00

This is a great reference book, the first in a new series dedicated to the weapons, uniforms and equipment of the German Wehrmacht in WWII. Includes color photos of each weapon, plus hundreds of wartime photos.

Dr. Josephus Requa Civil War Dentist and the Billinghurst-Requa Volley Gun, by John M. Hyson Jr., and Margaret Requa DeFrancisco, Museum Restoration Service, Bloomfield, Ont., Canada, 1999. 36 pp., illus. Paper covers. $8.95

The story of the inventor of the first practical rapid-fire gun to be used during the American Civil War.

The Dutch Luger (Parabellum) A Complete History, by Bas J. Martens and Guus de Vries, Ironside International Publishers, Inc., Alexandria, VA, 1995. 268 pp., illus. $49.95

The history of the Luger in the Netherlands. An extensive description of the Dutch pistol and trials and the different models of the Luger in the Dutch service.

E. F.Lli Piotti Italian Fine Gun Maker, by Marco Nobili, Italy, Il Volo Srl, 2000. 1st printing. 221 pp., illustrated with b&w photographs, plus 22 full color plates. Text in Italian and English. Hardcover. New in new dust jacket. $189.95

E.C. Prudhomme's Gun Engraving Review, by E. C. Prudhomme, R&R Books, Livonia, NY, 1994. 164 pp., illus. $60.00

As a source for engravers and collectors, this book is an indispensable guide to styles and techniques of the world's foremost engravers.

The Eagle on U.S. Firearms, by John W. Jordan, Pioneer Press, Union City, TN, 1992. 140 pp., illus. Paper covers. $17.50

Stylized eagles have been stamped on government owned or manufactured firearms in the U.S. since the beginning of our country. This book lists and illustrates these various eagles in an informative and refreshing manner.

Early Gunpowder Artillery 1300-1600, by John Norris, London, The Crowood Press, 2003. 1st edition. 141 pp., with 160 b&w photos. Hardcover. $34.95

In the 300-year time span covered by this book, gunpowder artillery was developed from a novelty to a serious weapon of war. By 1600 the cannon was to be found in large numbers on the battlefield, on board ship and on defensive positions on buildings and city walls. Illustrated with contemporary and modern photographs of surviving and recreated weapons, Early Gunpowder Artillery 1300-1600 sheds light on these earliest ancestors of the modern cannon and field gun.

Emblems of Honor; Patches and Insignia of the U.S. Army from the Great War to the Early Cold War Vol. Iv Armor - Cavalry - Tank Destroyer, by Kurt Keller, Constabulary, PA, privately printed, 2005. 1st edition, signed. 232 pp., with over 600 color photos. Hardcover. New in new dust jacket. $59.95

The Emma Gees, by Capt. Herbert W. McBride, Mt. Ida, AR, Lancer Publishing, 2003. 224 pp., b&w photos. Softcover. NEW. $19.95

Encyclopedia of Rifles & Handguns; A Comprehensive Guide to Firearms, edited by Sean Connolly, Chartwell Books, Inc., Edison, NJ., 1996. 160 pp., illus. $26.00

Encyclopedia of United States Army Insignia and Uniforms, by William Emerson, OK, University of Oklahoma Press, 1996. Hardcover. NEW. $134.95

Enemies Foreign and Domestic, by Matthew Bracken, San Diego, CA, Steelcutter Publishing, 2003. Softcover. NEW. $19.89

Eprouvettes: A Comprehensive Study of Early Devices for the Testing of Gunpowder, by R.T.W. Kempers, Royal Armouries Museum, Leeds, England, 1999. 352 pp., illustrated with 240 b&w and 28 color plates. $125.00

Equipment of the WWII Tommy, by David Gordon, Missoula, MT, Pictorial Histories Publishing, 2004. 1st edition. Softcover. NEW. $24.95

Fifteen Years in the Hawken Lode, by John D. Baird, The Gun Room Press, Highland Park, NJ, 1976. 120 pp., illus. $24.95

A collection of thoughts and observations gained from many years of intensive study of the guns from the shop of the Hawken brothers.

Fighting Colors: The Creation of Military Aircraft Nose Art, by Gary Velasco, Paducah, KY, Turner Publishing, 2005. 1st edition. Hardcover. New in new dust jacket. $57.95

Fighting Iron, by Art Gogan, Andrew Mowbray, Inc., Lincoln, R.I., 2002. 176 pp., illus. $28.00

It doesn't matter whether you collect guns, swords, bayonets or accoutrement–sooner or later you realize that it all comes down to the metal. If you don't understand the metal, you don't understand your collection.

ARMS LIBRARY

Fine Colts, The Dr. Joseph A. Murphy Collection, by R.L. Wilson, Sheffield Marketing Associates, Inc., Doylestown, PA, 1999. 258 pp., illus. Limited edition signed and numbered. $99.00
This lavish work covers exquisite, deluxe and rare Colt arms from Paterson and other percussion revolvers to the cartridge period and up through modern times.

Firearm Suppressor Patents; Volume 1: United States Patents, by N.R. Parker, Foreword by Alan C. Paulson, Boulder, CO, Paladin Press, 2004. 392 pp., illus. Softcover. NEW. $45.00

Firearms, by Derek Avery, Desert Publications, El Dorado, AR, 1999. 95 pp., illus. $9.95
The firearms included in this book are by necessity only a selection, but nevertheless one that represents the best and most famous weapons seen since the WWII.

Firearms and Tackle Memorabilia, by John Delph, Schiffer Publishing, Ltd., West Chester, PA, 1991. 124 pp., illus. $39.95
A collector's guide to signs and posters, calendars, trade cards, boxes, envelopes, and other highly sought after memorabilia. With a value guide.

Firearms from Europe, 2nd Edition, by David Noe, Larry W. Yantz, Dr. James B. Whisker, Rowe Publications, Rochester, N.Y., 2002. 192 pp., illus. $45.00
A history and description of firearms imported during the American Civil War by the United States of America and the Confederate States of America.

Firearms of the American West 1803-1865, Volume 1, by Louis A. Garavaglia and Charles Worman, University of Colorado Press, Niwot, CO, 1998. 402 pp., illus. $79.95
Traces the development and uses of firearms on the frontier during this period.

Firearms of the American West 1866-1894, Volume 2, by Louis A. Garavaglia and Charles G. Worman, University of Colorado Press, Niwot, CO, 1998. 416 pp., illus. $79.95
A monumental work that offers both technical information on all of the important firearms used in the West during this period and a highly entertaining history of how they were used, who used them, and why.

Firepower from Abroad, by Wiley Sword, Andrew Mowbray Publishing, Lincoln, R.I., 2000. 120 pp., illus. $23.00
The Confederate Enfield and the LeMat revolver and how they reached the Confederate market.

Flayderman's Guide to Antique American Firearms and Their Values, 8th Edition, edited by Norm Flayderman, Krause Publications, Iola, WI, 2001. 692 pp., illus. Paper covers. $34.95
A completely updated and new edition with more than 3,600 models and variants extensively described with all marks and specifications necessary for quick identification.

The FN-FAL Rifle, et al, by Duncan Long, Paladin Press, Boulder, CO, 1999. 144 pp., illus. Paper covers. $18.95
Detailed descriptions of the basic models produced by Fabrique Nationale and the myriad variants that evolved as a result of the firearms' universal acceptance.

Freund & Bro. Pioneer Gunmakers to the West, by F.J. Pablo Balentine, Graphic Publishers, Newport Beach, CA, 1997. 380 pp., illus. $69.95
The story of Frank W. and George Freund, skilled German gunsmiths who plied their trade on the Western American frontier during the final three decades of the nineteenth century.

The Fusil de Tulole in New France, 1691-1741, by Russel Bouchard, Museum Restorations Service, Bloomfield, Ontario, Canada, 1997. 36 pp., illus. Paper covers. $8.95
The development of the company and the identification of their arms.

The Gas Trap Garand, by Billy Pyle, Collector Grade Publications, Cobourg, Ontario, Canada, 1999 316 pp., illus. $59.95
The in-depth story of the rarest Garands of them all, the initial 80 Model Shop rifles made under the personal supervision of John Garand himself in 1934 and 1935, and the first 50,000 plus production "gas trap" M1's manufactured at Springfield Armory between August, 1937 and August, 1940.

George Schreyer, Sr. and Jr., Gunmakers of Hanover, Pennsylvania, by George Shumway, George Shumway Publishers, York, PA, 1990. 160pp., illus. $50.00
This monograph is a detailed photographic study of almost all known surviving longrifles and smoothbore guns made by highly regarded gunsmiths George Schreyer, Sr. and George Schreyer Jr.

The German Assault Rifle 1935-1945, by Peter R. Senich, Paladin Press, Boulder, CO, 1987. 328 pp., illus. $60.00
A complete review of machine carbines, machine pistols and assault rifles employed by Hitler's Wehrmacht during WWII.

German Belt Buckles 1845-1945: Buckles of the Enlisted Soldiers, by Peter Nash Atglen, PA, Schiffer Publications, 2003. 1st edition. Hardcover. New in new dust jacket. $59.95

German Camouflaged Helmets of the Second World War; Volume 1: Painted and Textured Camouflage, by Branislav Atglen Radovic, PA, Schiffer Publications, 2004. 1st edition. Hardcover. New in new dust jacket. $79.95

German Camouflaged Helmets of the Second World War; Volume 2: Wire, Netting, Covers, Straps, Interiors, Miscellaneous, by Branislav Atglen Radovic, PA, Schiffer Publications, 2004. 1st edition. Hardcover. New in new dust jacket. $79.95

German Cross in Gold - Holders of the SS and Police, by Mark Yerger, San Jose, CA, Bender Publishing, 2004. 1st edition. 432 pp., 295 photos and illustrations, deluxe binding. Hardcover. NEW. $44.95

The German K98k Rifle, 1934-1945: The Backbone of the Wehrmacht, by Richard D. Law, Collector Grade Publications, Toronto, Canada, 1993. 336 pp., illus. $69.95
The most comprehensive study ever published on the 14,000,000 bolt-action K98k rifles produced in Germany between 1934 and 1945.

German Machine Guns, by Daniel D. Musgrave, revised edition, Ironside International Publishers, Inc. Alexandria, VA, 1992. 586 pp., 650 illus. $49.95
The most definitive book ever written on German machine guns. Covers the introduction and development of machine guns in Germany from 1899 to the rearmament period after WWII.

German Military Abbreviations, by Military Intelligence Service, Canada, Service Publications. 268 pp. Stiff paper covers. NEW. $16.95

German Military Rifles and Machine Pistols, 1871-1945, by Hans Dieter Gotz, Schiffer Publishing Co., West Chester, PA, 1990. 245 pp., illus. $35.00
This book portrays, in words and pictures, the development of the modern German weapons and their ammunition, including the scarcely known experimental types.

German Paratroops: Uniforms, Insignia & Equipment of the Fallschirmjager in World War II, by Robert Atglen Kurtz, PA, Schiffer Publications, 2003. 1st edition. Hardcover. New in new dust jacket. $59.95

German Print Advertising 1933-1945, by Ray and Josephine Cowdery, self published, 2004. 1st Am. edition. Hardcover. 176 pp. NEW. $45.00

German Tanks of World War II in Color, by Michael Green; Thomas Anderson; Frank Schultz, St. Paul, MN, MBI Publishing Company, 2000. 1st edition. Softcover. NEW. $14.95

Gods and Generals Photographic Companion, by Rob Gibson and Dennis Frye. Gettysburg, PA, Thomas Publications, 2003. 1st edition. 88 pp. Softcover. NEW. $19.95

Gold Dust & Gunsmoke, by John Boessenecker, New York, John Wiley & Sons, 2000. 370 pp. Softcover. NEW. $10.00

Government Issue: U.S. Army European Theater of Operations Collector Guide, by Henry-Paul Enjames, Philippe Charbonnier, France, Histoire & Collections, 2004. Hardcover, NEW. $49.89

The Government Models, by William H.D. Goddard, Andrew Mowbray Publishing, Lincoln, RI, 1998. 296 pp., illus. $58.50
The most authoritative source on the development of the Colt model of 1911.

Grasshoppers and Butterflies, by Adrian B. Caruana, Museum Restoration Service, Alexandria Bay, N.Y., 1999. 32 pp., illus. Paper covers. $8.95
No.39 in the Historical Arms Series. The light 3 pounders of Pattison and Townsend.

The Greener Story, by Graham Greener, Quiller Press, London, England, 2000. 256 pp., illustrated with 32 pp. of color photos. $69.95
W.W. Greener, his family history, inventions, guns, patents, and more.

The Greenhill Dictionary of Guns and Gunmakers: From Colt's First Patent to the Present Day, 1836-2001, by John Walter, Greenhill Publishing, 2001, 1st edition, 576 pp., illustrated with 200 photos, 190 trademarks and 40 line drawings, Hardcover. $59.95
Covers military small arms, sporting guns and rifles, air and gas guns, designers, inventors, patentees, trademarks, brand names and monograms.

Grenade - British and Commonwealth Hand and Rifle Grenades, by Rick Landers, Norman Bonney and Gary Oakley. Australia, privately printed, 2001. 1st edition. 294 pp., illustrated with b&w photos drawings. Hardcover. New in new dust jacket. $69.95
Covers from Type No.1 to No. 95 includes dischargers, fuzes, markings, equipment.

The Gun and Its Development, by W.W. Greener, New York, Lyons Press, 2002. 9th Edition. Rewritten, and with many additional illustrations. 804 pp. plus advertising section. Contains over 700 illustrations plus many tables. Softcover. $19.95
A famed book of great value, truly encyclopedic in scope and sought after by firearms collectors.

Gun Powder Cans & Kegs, by Ted and David Bacyk and Tom Rowe, Rowe Publications, Rochester, NY, 1999. 150 pp., illus. $65.00
The first book devoted to powder tins and kegs. All cans and kegs in full color. With a price guide and rarity scale.

Gun Tools, Their History and Identification by James B. Shaffer, Lee A. Rutledge and R. Stephen Dorsey, Collector's Library, Eugene, OR, 1992. 375 pp., illus. $30.00
Written history of foreign and domestic gun tools from the flintlock period to WWII.

Gun Tools, Their History and Identifications, Volume 2, by Stephen Dorsey and James B. Shaffer, Collectors' Library, Eugene, OR, 1997. 396 pp., illus. Paper covers. $30.00
Gun tools from the Royal Armouries Museum in England, Pattern Room, Royal Ordnance Reference Collection in Nottingham and from major private collections.

Gunmakers of London 1350-1850 with Supplement, by Howard L. Blackmore, Museum Restoration Service, Alexandria Bay, NY, 1999. 222 pp., illus. Two volumes. Slipcased. $135.00
A listing of all the known workmen of gun making in the first 500 years, plus a history of the guilds, cutlers, armourers, founders, blacksmiths, etc. 260 gunmarks are illustrated. Supplement is 156 pages, and begins with an introductory chapter on "foreign" gunmakers followed by records of all the new information found about previously unidentified armourers, gunmakers and gunsmiths.

The Guns of Dagenham: Lanchester, Patchett, Sterling, by Peter Laidler and David Howroyd, Collector Grade Publications, Inc., Cobourg, Ont., Canada, 1995. 310 pp., illus. $39.95
An in-depth history of the small arms made by the Sterling Company of Dagenham, Essex, England, from 1940 until Sterling was purchased by British Aerospace in 1989 and closed.

The Guns of Remington: Historic Firearms Spanning Two Centuries, compiled by Howard M. Madaus, Biplane Productions, Publisher, in cooperation with Buffalo Bill Historical Center, Cody, WY, 1998. 352 pp., illustrated with over 800 color photos. $79.95
A complete catalog of the firearms in the exhibition, "It Never Failed Me: The Arms & Art of Remington Arms Company" at the Buffalo Bill Historical Center, Cody, Wyoming.

Guns of the Western Indian War, by R. Stephen Dorsey, Collector's Library, Eugene, OR, 1997. 220 pp., illus. Paper covers. $30.00
The full story of the guns and ammunition that made western history in the turbulent period of 1865-1890.

The Guns that Won the West: Firearms of the American Frontier, 1865-1898, by John Walter, Stackpole Books, Inc., Mechanicsburg, PA., 1999. 256 pp., illus. $34.95
Here is the story of the wide range of firearms from pistols to rifles used by plainsmen and settlers, gamblers, native Americans and the U.S. Army.

Gunsmiths of Illinois, by Curtis L. Johnson, George Shumway Publishers, York, PA, 1995. 160 pp., illus. $50.00
Genealogical information is provided for nearly 1,000 gunsmiths. Contains hundreds of illustrations of rifles and other guns, of handmade origin, from Illinois.

The Gunsmiths of Manhattan, 1625-1900: A Checklist of Tradesmen, by Michael H. Lewis, Museum Restoration Service, Bloomfield, Ont., Canada, 1991. 40 pp., illus. Paper covers. $8.95
This listing of more than 700 men in the arms trade in New York City prior to about the end of the 19th century will provide a guide for identification and further research.

Gunsmiths of Maryland, by Daniel D. Hartzler and James B. Whisker, Old Bedford Village Press, Bedford, PA, 1998. 208 pp., illus. $45.00
Covers firelock Colonial period through the breech-loading patent models. Featuring longrifles.

ARMS LIBRARY

Gunsmiths of the Carolinas 1660-1870, by Daniel D. Hartzler and James B. Whisker, Old Bedford Village Press, Bedford, PA, 1998. 176 pp., illus. $40.00
This deluxe hard bound edition is printed on fine coated paper, with about 90 pages of large photographs of fine longrifles from the Carolinas, and about 90 pages of detailed research on the gunsmiths who created the highly prized and highly collectable longrifles.

Gunsmiths of Virginia, by Daniel D. Hartzler and James B. Whisker, Old Bedford Village Press, Bedford, PA, 1992. 206 pp., illus. $40.00
A photographic study of American longrifles.

Gunsmiths of West Virginia, by Daniel D. Hartzler and James B. Whisker, Old Bedford Village Press, Bedford, PA, 1998. 176 pp., illus. $40.00
A photographic study of American longrifles.

Gunsmiths of York County, Pennsylvania, by Daniel D. Hartzler and James B. Whisker, Old Bedford Village Press, Bedford, PA, 1998. 160 pp., illus. $40.00
Photographs and research notes on the longrifles and gunsmiths of York County, Pennsylvania.

Harrington & Richardson Sporting Firearms: Dates of Manufacture 1871-1991, by D.R. Morse. Phoenix, AZ, Firing Pin Enterprizes, 2003. 14 pp. Softcover. NEW. $6.95
Covers their pistols, revolvers, rifles, shotguns and commemoratives, plus models.

The Hawken Rifle: Its Place in History, by Charles E. Hanson Jr., The Fur Press, Chadron, NE, 1979. 104 pp., illus. Paper covers. $15.00
A definitive work on this famous rifle.

Hi-Standard Sporting Firearms: Dates of Manufacture, by D.R. Morse. 1926-1992. Phoenix, AZ, Firing Pin Enterprizes, 2003. 22 pp. Softcover. New. $6.95
Covers their pistols, revolvers, rifles, shotguns and commemoratives, plus models and serial numbers.

High Standard: A Collector's Guide to the Hamden & Hartford Target Pistols, by Tom Dance, Andrew Mowbray, Inc., Lincoln, RI, 1991. 192 pp., illus. Paper covers. $24.00
From Citation to Supermatic, all of the production models and specials made from 1951 to 1984 are covered according to model number or series.

Historical Hartford Hardware, by William W. Dalrymple, Colt Collector Press, Rapid City, SD, 1976. 42 pp., illus. Paper covers. $10.00
Historically associated Colt revolvers.

The History of Colt Firearms, by Dean Boorman, Lyons Press, New York, NY, 2001. 144 pp., illus. $29.95
Discover the fascinating story of the world's most famous revolver, complete with more than 150 stunning full-color photographs.

History of Modern U.S. Military Small Arms Ammunition, Volume 1, 1880-1939, revised by F.W. Hackley, W.H. Woodin and E.L. Scranton, Thomas Publications, Gettysburg, PA, 1998. 328 pp., illus. $49.95
This revised edition incorporates all publicly available information concerning military small arms ammunition for the period 1880 through 1939 in a single volume.

History of Modern U.S. Military Small Arms Ammunition, Volume 2, 1940-1945, by F.W. Hackley, W.H. Woodin and E.L. Scranton, Gun Room Press, Highland Park, NJ. 300+ pp., illus. $39.95
Based on decades of original research conducted at the National Archives, numerous military, public and private museums and libraries, as well as individual collections, this edition incorporates all publicly available information concerning military small arms ammunition for the period 1940 through 1945.

The History of Smith & Wesson Firearms, by Dean Boorman, Lyons Press, New York, NY, 2002. 44 pp., illustrated in full color. Hardcover. New in new dust jacket. $29.95
The definitive guide to one of the world's best-known firearms makers. Takes the story through the years of the Military and Police 38 and of the Magnum cartridge, to today's wide range of products for law-enforcement customers.

The History of Winchester Rifles, by Dean Boorman, Lyons Press, New York, NY, 2001. 144 pp., illus. 150 full-color photos. $29.95
A captivating and wonderfully photographed history of one of the most legendary names in gun lore.

Honour Bound: The Chauchat Machine Rifle, by Gerard Demaison and Yves Buffetaut, Collector Grade Publications, Inc., Cobourg, Ont., Canada, 1995. $39.95
The story of the CSRG (Chauchat) machine rifle, the most manufactured automatic weapon of WWI.

Hunting Weapons from the Middle Ages to the Twentieth Century, by Howard L. Blackmore, Dover Publications, Meneola, NY, 2000. 480 pp., illus. Paper covers. $16.95
Dealing mainly with the different classes of weapons used in sport–swords, spears, crossbows, guns, and rifles–from the Middle Ages until the present day.

Identification Handbook of British Grenades 1900-1960 (Numerical Series), by Rick Landers, Norman Bonney and Gary Oakley. Australia. Privately printed, 2001. 1st edition. 48 pp., illustrated with b&w photos and drawings. Softcover. New. $10.95
Description, illustration and identification details of all British grenades in the numerical series.

Illustrations of United States Military Arms 1776-1903 and Their Inspector's Marks, compiled by Turner Kirkland, Pioneer Press, Union City, TN, 1988. 37 pp., illus. Paper covers. $7.00
Reprinted from the 1949 Bannerman catalog. Valuable information for both the advanced and beginning collector.

Imperial German Military Officers' Helmets and Headdress 1871-1918, by Thomas N.G. Stubbs, Atglen, PA, Schiffer Publications, 2003. 1st edition. Hardcover. New in new dust jacket. $79.95

Imperial Japanese Grenade Rifles and Launchers, by Gregory A. Babich and Thomas A. Keep Lemont, PA, Dutch Harlow Publishing, 2004. 1st edition. Hardcover. New in new dust jacket. $75.00

Indian War Cartridge Pouches, Boxes and Carbine Boots, by R. Stephen Dorsey, Collector's Library, Eugene, OR, 1993. 156 pp., illus. Paper covers. $20.00
The key reference work to the cartridge pouches, boxes, carbine sockets and boots of the Indian War period 1865-1890.

International Armament, with History, Data, Technical Information and Photographs of Over 800 Weapons, 2nd edition, new printing, by George B. Johnson, Alexandria, VA, Ironside International, 2002. Hardcover. New in new dust jacket. $59.95
The development and progression of modern military small arms. All significant weapons have been included and examined in depth. Over 800 photographs and illustrations with both historical and technical data. Two volumes are now bound into one book.

Islamic Weapons Maghrib to Mohul, by Anthony C. Tirri, Canada, John Denner, 2003. 1st edition. 483 pp. Hardcover. New in new dust jacket. $149.95

Ithaca Iver Johnson Sporting Firearms: Dates of Manufacture, by D.R. Morse, Phoenix, AZ, Firing Pin Enterprizes, 2003. Softcover. NEW. $6.95

J. P. Sauer & Sohn, Sauer "Dein Waffenkamerad" Volume 2, by Cate & Krause, Walsworth Publishing, Chattanooga, TN, 2000. 440 pp., illus. $69.95
A historical study of Sauer automatic pistols. This new volume includes a great deal of new knowledge that has surfaced about the J.P. Sauer firm. You will find new photos, documentation, serial number ranges and historial facts which will expand the knowledge and interest in the oldest and best of the German firearms companies.

Jaeger Rifles, Collected Articles Published in Muzzle Blasts, by George Shumway, York PA, 2003. Reprint. 108 pp., illus. Stiff paper covers. New. $30.00
Thirty-six articles previously published in Muzzle Blasts are reproduced here.

Japanese Rifles of World War Two, by Duncan O. McCollum, Excalibur Publications, Latham, NY, 1996. 64 pp., illus. Paper covers. $18.95
A sweeping view of the rifles and carbines that made up Japan's arsenal during the conflict.

Kalashnikov "Machine Pistols, Assault Rifles, and Machine Guns, 1945 to the Present", by John Walter, Stackpole Books, Mechanicsburg, PA 1999, hardcover, photos, illus., 146 pp. $22.95
This exhaustive work published by Greenhill Military Manuals features a gun-by-gun directory of Kalashnikov variants. Technical specifications and illustrations are provided throughout, along with details of sights, bayonets, markings and ammunition. A must for the serious collector and historian.

The Kentucky Pistol, by Roy Chandler and James Whisker, Old Bedford Village Press, Bedford, PA, 1997. 225 pp., illus. $60.00
A photographic study of Kentucky pistols from famous collections.

The Kentucky Rifle, by Captain John G.W. Dillin, George Shumway Publisher, York, PA, 1993. 221 pp., illus. $50.00
This well-known book was the first attempt to tell the story of the American longrifle. This edition retains the original text and illustrations with supplemental footnotes provided by Dr. George Shumway.

Know Your Broomhandle Mausers, by R.J. Berger, Blacksmith Corp., Southport, CT, 1996. 96 pp., illus. Paper covers. $14.95
An interesting story on the big Mauser pistol and its variations.

Law Enforcement Memorabilia Price and Identification Guide, by Monty McCord, DBI Books, a division of Krause Publications, Inc. Iola, WI, 1999. 208 pp., illus. Paper covers. $19.95

Lebeau and Courally Guns & Rifles Maker Since 1865, by Marco E. Nobili, Italy, Il Volo Srl, 1997. 1st printing. 176 pp., illustrated with b&w photographs, plus 16 full-color plates. Text in Italian and English. Hardcover. New in new dust jacket. $189.95

Legendary Sporting Guns, by Eric Joly, Abbeville Press, New York, N.Y., 1999. 228 pp., illus. $65.00
A survey of hunting through the ages and relates how many different types of firearms were created and refined for use afield.

Legends and Reality of the AK, by Val Shilin and Charlie Cutshaw, Paladen Press, Boulder, CO, 2000. 192 pp., illus. Paper covers. $35.00
A behind-the-scenes look at history, design and impact of the Kalashnikov family of weapons.

The Light 6-Pounder Battalion Gun of 1776, by Adrian Caruana, Museum Restoration Service, Bloomfield, Ontario, Canada, 2001. 76 pp., illus. Paper covers. $8.95

The London Gun Trade, 1850-1920, by Joyce E. Gooding, Museum Restoration Service, Bloomfield, Ontario, Canada, 2001. 48 pp., illus. Paper covers. $8.95
Names, dates and locations of London gunmakers working between 1850 and 1920 are listed. Compiled from the original Kelly's post office directories of the City of London.

The London Gunmakers and the English Duelling Pistol, 1770-1830, by Keith R. Dill, Museum Restoration Service, Bloomfield, Ontario, Canada, 1997. 36 pp., illus. Paper covers. $8.95
Ten gunmakers made London one of the major gunmaking centers of the world. This book examines how the design and construction of their pistols contributed to that reputation and how these characteristics may be used to date flintlock arms.

Longrifles of Pennsylvania, Volume 1, Jefferson, Clarion & Elk Counties, by Russel H. Harringer, George Shumway Publisher, York, PA, 1984. 200 pp., illus. $50.00
First in series that will treat in great detail the longrifles and gunsmiths of Pennsylvania.

The Luger Handbook, by Aarron Davis, Krause Publications, Iola, WI, 1997. 112 pp., illus. Paper covers. $9.95
Quick reference to classify Luger models and variations with complete details including proofmarks.

The Luger Story, by John Walter, Stackpole Books, Mechanicsburg, PA, 2001. 256 pp., illus. Paper covers $19.95
The standard history of the world's most famous handgun.

Lugers at Random, by Charles Kenyon Jr., Handgun Press, Glenview, IL, 1990. 420 pp., illus. $59.95
A new printing of this classic, comprehensive reference for all Luger collectors.

The M 1 Carbine: A Revolution in Gun Stocking, by Grafton H. Cook II and Barbara W. Cook, Lincoln, RI, Andrew Mowbray, Inc., 2002. 1st edition. 208 pp., heavily illustrated with 157 rare photographs of the guns and the men and women who made them. Softcover. $29.95
Shows you, step by step, how M1 carbine stocks were made, right through to assembly with the hardware. Learn about M1 Carbine development, and how the contracting and production process actually worked. Also contains lots of detailed information about other military weapons, like the M1A1, the M1 Garand, the M14 and much, much more.

M1 Carbine: Design, Development, and Production, by Larry Ruth, Gun Room Press, Highland Park, NJ, 1987. 291 pp., illus. Paper $19.95
The origin, development, manufacture and use of this famous carbine of WWII.

The M1 Carbine Owner's Guide, by Larry Ruth and Scott A. Duff, Scott A. Duff Publications, Export, PA, 1997. 126 pp., illus. Paper covers. $21.95
This book answers the questions M1 owners most often ask concerning maintenance activities not encounted by military users.

The M1 Garand: Owner's Guide, by Scott A. Duff, Scott A. Duff Publications, Export, PA, 1998. 132 pp., illus. Paper covers. $21.95
This book answers the questions M1 owners most often ask concerning maintenance activities not encounted by military users.

ARMS LIBRARY

The M1 Garand: Post World War, by Scott A. Duff, Scott A. Duff Publications, Export, PA, 1990. 139 pp., illus. Softcover. $21.95

A detailed account of the activities at Springfield Armory through this period. International Harvester, H&R, Korean War production and quantities delivered. Serial numbers.

The M1 Garand: World War II, by Scott A. Duff, Scott A. Duff Publications, Export, PA, 2001. 210 pp., illus. Paper covers. $34.95

The most comprehensive study available to the collector and historian on the M1 Garand of WWII.

The M1 Garand 1936 to 1957, by Joe Poyer and Craig Riesch, North Cape Publications, Tustin, CA, 1996. 216 pp., illus. Paper covers. $19.95

Describes the entire range of M1 Garand production in text and quick-scan charts.

The M1 Garand Serial Numbers and Data Sheets, by Scott A. Duff, Scott A. Duff Publications, Export, PA, 1995. 101 pp., illus. Paper covers. $11.95

Provides the reader with serial numbers related to dates of manufacture and a large sampling of data sheets to aid in identification or restoration.

Machine Guns, by Ian V. Hogg, Iola, WI, Krause Publications, 2002. 1st edition. 336 pp., illustrated with b&w photos with a 16-page color section. Softcover. $29.95

A detailed history of the rapid-fire gun, 14th Century to present. Covers the development, history and specifications.

Made in the C.S.A.: Saddle Makers of the Confederacy, by Ken R. Knopp, Hattiesburg, MS, privately printed, 2003. 1st edition signed. 205 pp., illus., signed by the author. Softcover. NEW. $30.00

Maine Made Guns and Their Makers, by Dwight B. Demeritt Jr., Maine State Museum, Augusta, ME, 1998. 209 pp., illus. $55.00

An authoritative, biographical study of Maine gunsmiths.

Marlin Firearms: A History of the Guns and the Company That Made Them, by Lt. Col. William S. Brophy, USAR, Ret., Stackpole Books, Harrisburg, PA, 1989. 672 pp., illus. $80.00

The definitive book on the Marlin Firearms Co. and their products.

Martini-Henry .450 Rifles & Carbines, by Dennis Lewis, Excalibur Publications, Latham, NY, 1996. 72 pp., illus. Paper covers. $11.95

The stories of the rifles and carbines that were the mainstay of the British soldier through the Victorian wars.

Mauser Bolt Rifles, by Ludwig Olson, F. Brownell & Son, Inc., Montezuma, IA, 1999. 364 pp., illus. $64.95

The most complete, detailed, authoritative and comprehensive work ever done on Mauser bolt rifles. Completely revised deluxe 3rd edition.

Mauser Military Rifle Markings, by Terence W. Lapin, Arlington, VA, Hyrax Publishers, LLC, 2001. 167 pp., illus. 2nd edition. Revised and expanded. Softcover. $22.95

A general guide to reading and understanding the often mystifying markings found on military Mauser rifles. Includes German Regimental markings as well as German police markings and WWII German Mauser subcontractor codes. A handy reference to take to gun shows.

Mauser Military Rifles of the World, 3rd Edition, by Robert Ball, Krause Publications, Iola, WI, 2003. 304 pp., illustrated with 1,000 b&w photos and a 48-page color section. $44.95

This 3rd edition brings more than 100 new photos of these historic rifles and the wars in which they were carried.

Mauser Smallbores Sporting, Target and Training Rifles, by Jon Speed, Collector Grade Publications, Cobourg, Ontario, Canada 1998. 349 pp., illus. $67.50

A history of all the smallbore sporting, target and training rifles produced by the legendary Mauser-Werke of Obendorf Am Neckar.

Metallic Cartridge Conversions: The History of the Guns and Modern Reproductions, by Dennis Adler, Foreword by R. L. Wilson. Krause Publications, 2003. 208 pp., 250 color photos. Hardcover. $39.95

Collectors and enthusiasts will track the history of the original conversions of the 1800s through historic text and both new and archival photographs. All current modern reproductions are represented with photos, technical details, and performance test results. In-depth coverage of the original revolvers includes models from Colt, Remington, Smith & Wesson, Rollin White, Richards, and Richards-Mason. Modern guns from American Western Arms, Navy Arms, and Cimarron F.A. Co. are highlighted. Color section highlights engraved and presentation models.

Military Holsters of World War II, by Eugene J. Bender, Rowe Publications, Rochester, NY, 1998. 200 pp., illus. $45.00

A revised edition with a new price guide of the most definitive book on this subject.

The Military Remington Rolling Block Rifle, by George Layman, Pioneer Press, TN, 1998. 146 pp., illus. Paper covers. $24.95

A standard reference for those with an interest in the Remington rolling block family of firearms.

Military Rifles of Japan, 5th Edition, by F.L. Honeycutt, Julin Books, Lake Park, FL, 1999. 208 pp., illus. $42.00

A new revised and updated edition. Includes the early Murata-period markings, etc.

Military Small Arms Data Book, by Ian V. Hogg, Stackpole Books, Mechanicsburg, PA, 1999. 336 pp., illus. $44.95

Data on more than 1,500 weapons. Covers a vast range of weapons from pistols to anti-tank rifles. Essential data, 1870-2000, in one volume.

Modern Gun Identification & Value Guide, 13th Edition, by Russell and Steve Quertermous, Collector Books, Paducah, KY, 1998. 504 pp., illus. Paper covers. $14.95

Features current values for over 2,500 models of rifles, shotguns and handguns, with over 1,800 illustrations.

More Single Shot Rifles, by James C. Grant, Gun Room Press, Highland Park, NJ, 1976. 324 pp., illus. $35.00

Details the guns made by Frank Wesson, Milt Farrow, Holden, Borchardt, Stevens, Remington, Winchester, Ballard and Peabody-Martini.

Mortimer, the Gunmakers, 1753-1923, by H. Lee Munson, Andrew Mowbray Inc., Lincoln, RI, 1992. 320 pp., illus. $65.00

Seen through a single, dominant, English gunmaking dynasty, this fascinating study provides a window into the classical era of firearms artistry.

The Mosin-Nagant Rifle, by Terence W. Lapin, North Cape Publications, Tustin, CA, 1998. 30 pp., illus. Paper covers. $19.95

The first ever complete book on the Mosin-Nagant rifle written in English. Covers every variation.

Mossberg Sporting Firearms: Dates of Manufacture, by D.R. Morse, Phoenix, AZ, Firing Pin Enterprizes, 2003. Softcover. NEW. $6.95

Covers their pistols, revolvers, rifles, shotguns and commemoratives, plus models and serial numbers.

The MP38, 40, 40/1 & 41 Submachine Gun, by de Vries & Martens. Propaganda Photo Series, Volume II. Alexandria, VA, Ironside International, 2001. 1st edition. 150 pp., illustrated with 200 high quality b&w photos. Hardcover. $34.95

Covers all essential information on history and development, ammunition and accessories, codes and markings, and contains photos of nearly every model and accessory. Includes a unique selection of original German WWII propaganda photos, most never published before.

The Navy Luger, by Joachim Gortz and John Walter, Handgun Press, Glenview, IL, 1988. 128 pp., illus. $24.95

The 9mm Pistole 1904 and the Imperial German Navy. A concise illustrated history.

The New World of Russian Small Arms and Ammunition, by Charlie Cutshaw, Paladin Press, Boulder, CO, 1998. 160 pp., illus. $42.95

Detailed descriptions, specifications and first-class illustrations of the AN-94, PSS silent pistol, Bizon SMG, Saifa-12 tactical shotgun, the GP-25 grenade launcher and more cutting edge Russian weapons.

The Number 5 Jungle Carbine, by Alan M. Petrillo, Excalibur Publications, Latham, NY, 1994. 32 pp., illus. Paper covers. $7.95

A comprehensive treatment of the rifle that collectors have come to call the "Jungle Carbine"–the Lee-Enfield Number 5, Mark 1.

Observations on Colt's Second Contract, November 2, 1847, by G. Maxwell Longfield and David T. Basnett, Museum Restoration Service, Bloomfield, Ontario, Canada, 1997. 36 pp., illus. Paper covers. $6.95

This study traces the history and the construction of the Second Model Colt Dragoon supplied in 1848 to the U.S. Cavalry.

The Official Soviet SVD Manual, by Major James F. Gebhardt (Ret.), Paladin Press, Boulder, CO, 1999. 112 pp., illus. Paper covers. $22.00

Operating instructions for the 7.62mm Dragunov, the first Russian rifle developed from scratch specifically for sniping.

Old Gunsights: A Collector's Guide, 1850 to 2000, by Nicholas Stroebel, Krause Publications, Iola, WI, 1998. 320 pp., illus. Paper covers. $29.95

An in-depth and comprehensive examination of old gunsights and the rifles on which they were used to get accurate feel for prices in this expanding market.

Orders, Decorations and Badges of the Socialist Republic of Vietnam and the National Front for the Liberation of South Vietnam, by Edward J. Emering, Schiffer Publications, Atglen, PA. 2000. 96 pages, 190 color and b&w photographs, line drawings. $24.95

The Orders and Decorations of the "enemy" during the Vietnam War have remained shrouded in mystery for many years. References to them are scarce and interrogations of captives during the war often led to the proliferation of misinformation concerning them. Includes value guide.

Ordnance Tools, Accessories & Appendages of the M1 Rifle, by Billy Pyle. Houston, TX, privately printed, 2002. 2nd edition. 206 pp., illustrated with b&w photos. Softcover $40.00

The P-08 Parabellum Luger Automatic Pistol, edited by J. David McFarland, Desert Publications, Cornville, AZ, 1982. 20 pp., illus. Paper covers. $11.95

Covers every facet of the Luger, plus a listing of all known Luger models.

Packing Iron, by Richard C. Rattenbury, Zon International Publishing, Millwood, NY, 1993. 216 pp., illus. $45.00

The best book yet produced on pistol holsters and rifle scabbards. Over 300 variations of holster and scabbards are illustrated in large, clear plates.

Painted Steel, Steel Pots Volume 2, by Chris Armold, Bender Publishing, San Jose, CA, 2001. 384 pp. - 1,053 photos, hundreds in color. $57.95

From the author of "Steel Pots: The History of America's Steel Combat Helmets" comes "Painted Steel: Steel Pots, Vol. II." This companion volume features detailed chapters on painted and unit marked helmets of WWI and WWII, plus a variety of divisional, regimental and subordinate markings. Special full-color plates detail subordinate unit markings such as the tactical markings used by the U.S. 2nd Division in WWI.

Pattern Dates for British Ordnance Small Arms, 1718-1783, by DeWitt Bailey, Thomas Publications, Gettysburg, PA, 1997. 116 pp., illus. Paper covers. $20.00

The weapons discussed in this work are those carried by troops sent to North America between 1737 and 1783, or shipped to them as replacement arms while in America.

Percussion Ammunition Packets 1845-1888 Union, Confederate & European, by John J. Malloy, Dean S. Thomas and Terry A. White with Foreward by Norm Flayderman. Gettysburg, PA, Thomas Publications, 2003. 1st edition. 134 pp., illustrated with color photos. Hardcover. New. $75.00

Finally a means to recognize the untold variety of labeled types of ammunition box labels.

Peters & King, by Thomas D. Schiffer. Krause Publications, Iola, WI 2002. 1st edition. 256 pp., 200+ b&w photos with a 32-page color section. Hardcover. $44.95

Discover the history behind Peters Cartridge and King Powder and see how they shaped the arms industry into what it is today and why their products fetch hundreds, even thousands of dollars at auctions. Current values are provided for their highly collectible product packaging and promotional advertising premiums such as powder kegs, tins, cartridge boxes, and calendars.

The Pitman Notes on U.S. Martial Small Arms and Ammunition, 1776-1933, Volume 2, Revolvers and Automatic Pistols, by Brig. Gen. John Pitman, Thomas Publications, Gettysburg, PA, 1990. 192 pp., illus. $29.95

A most important primary source of information on United States military small arms and ammunition.

Plates and Buckles of the American Military 1795-1874, by Sydney C. Kerksis, Orange, VA, Publisher's Press, 1998. 5th edition. 568 pp., illustrated with hundreds of b&w photos. Hardcover. $39.00

The single most comprehensive reference for U.S. and Confederate plates.

The Presentation and Commercial Colt Walker Pistols, by Col. Robert D. Whittington III, Hooks, TX, Brownlee Books, 2003. A limited edition of 1,000 copies. Numbered. 21 pp. Paper covers. New. $15.00

A study of events at the Whitneyville Armoury and Samuel Colt's Hartford Factory from 1 June 1847 to 29 November 1848.

Production Statistics U.S. Arms Makers From Armalite to Winchester, by Phoenix, AZ, Firing Pin Enterprizes, 1997. 262 pp. Softcover. NEW. $19.95

ARMS LIBRARY

Proud Promise: French Autoloading Rifles, 1898-1979, by Jean Huon, Collector Grade Publications, Inc., Cobourg, Ont., Canada, 1995. 216 pp., illus. $39.95
The author has finally set the record straight about the importance of French contributions to modern arms design.

Purdey Gun and Rifle Makers: The Definitive History, by Donald Dallas, Quiller Press, London, 2000. 245 pp., illus. Color throughout. A limited edition of 3,000 copies. Signed and numbered. With a PURDEY book plate. $99.95

The Queen Anne Pistol, 1660-1780: A History of the Turn-Off Pistol, by John W. Burgoyne, Bloomfield, Ont., Canada, Museum Restoration Service, 2002. 1st edition - Historical Arms New Series No. 1. 120 pp., a detailed, fast moving, thoroughly researched text and almost 200 cross-referenced illustrations. Pictorial hardcover. $35.00
This distinctive breech-loading arm was developed in the middle years of the 17th century but found popularity during the reign of the monarch (1702-1714), by whose name it is known.

Red Shines The Sun: A Pictorial History of the Fallschirm-Infantrie, by Eric Queen. San Jose, CA, R. James Bender Publishing, 2003. 1st edition. Hardcover. $69.95
A culmination of 12 years of research, this reference work traces the history of the Army paratroopers of the Fallschirm-Infanterie from their origins in 1937, to the expansion to battalion strength in 1938, then on through operations at Wola Gulowska (Poland), and Moerdijk (Holland). This 240-page comprehensive look at their history is supported by 600 images, many of which are in full color, and nearly 90% are previously unpublished.

Reloading Tools, Sights and Telescopes for Single Shot Rifles, by Gerald O. Kelver, Brighton, CO, 1982. 163 pp., illus. Paper covers. $13.95
A listing of most of the famous makers of reloading tools, sights and telescopes with a brief description of the products they manufactured.

The Remington-Lee Rifle, by Eugene F. Myszkowski, Excalibur Publications, Latham, NY, 1995. 100 pp., illus. Paper covers. $22.50
Features detailed descriptions, including serial number ranges, of each model from the first Lee magazine rifle produced for the U.S. Navy to the last Remington-Lee small bore shipped to the Cuban Rural Guard.

Remington 'America's Oldest Gunmaker', The Official Authorized History of the Remington Arms Company, by Roy Marcot. Madison, NC, Remington Arms Company, 1999. 1st edition. 312 pp., with 167 b&w illustrations, plus 291 color plates. $79.95
This is without a doubt the finest history of that firm ever to have been compiled. Based on firsthand research in the Remington company archives, it is extremely well written.

Remington Sporting Firearms: Dates of Manufacture, by D.R. Morse, Phoenix, AZ, Firing Pin Enterprizes, 2003. 43 pp. Softcover. New. $6.95
Covers their pistols, revolvers, rifles, shotguns and commemoratives, plus models and serial numbers.

Remington's Vest Pocket Pistols, by Robert E. Hatfield, Lincoln, RI, Andrew Mowbray, Inc., 2002. 117 pp. Hardcover. $29.95
While Remington Vest Pocket pistols have always been popular with collectors, very little solid information has been available about them. Inside you will find 100+ photographs, serial number data, exploded views of all four Remington Vest Pocket pistol sizes, component parts lists and a guide to disassembly and reassembly. Also includes a discussion of Vest Pocket Wire-Stocked Buggy/Bicycle rifles, plus the documented serial number story.

Revolvers of the British Services 1854-1954, by W.H.J. Chamberlain and A.W.F. Taylerson, Museum Restoration Service, Ottawa, Canada, 1989. 80 pp., illus. $27.50
Covers the types issued among many of the United Kingdom's naval, land or air services.

Rifles of the U.S. Army 1861-1906, by John D. McAulay, Andrew Mowbray, Inc., Lincoln, RI, 2003. 1st edition. Over 40 rifles covered, 278 pp., illus. Hardcover. New. $47.95
There have been several excellent books written about the manufacture of rifles for the U.S. Army from the time of the Civil War to the early 20th century. However, few of these books have focused upon what happened to these rifles after they were issued. This exciting new book by renowned authority John McAulay fills this gap. It gives the reader detailed coverage of the issue and actual field service of America's fighting rifles, both in peacetime and in war, including their military service with the infantry, artillery, cavalry and engineers.
One feature that all readers will value is the impressive number of historical photos, taken during the Civil War, the Mexican War, the Indian Wars, the Spanish-American War, the Philippine Insurrection and more, showing these rifles in the hands of the men who fought with them. Procurement information, issue details and historical background.

Rifles of the World, by Oliver Achard, Chartwell Books, Inc., Edison, NJ, 141 pp., illus. $24.95
A unique insight into the world of long guns, not just rifles, but also shotguns, carbines and all the usual multi-barreled guns that once were so popular with European hunters, especially in Germany and Austria.

Round Ball to Rimfire: A History of Civil War Small Arms Ammunition, Vol. 1, by Dean Thomas, Thomas Publications, Gettysburg, PA, 1997. 144 pp., illus. $40.00
The first of a two-volume set of the most complete history and guide for all small arms ammunition used in the Civil War. The information includes data from research and development to the arsenals that created it.

Round Ball to Rimfire: A History of Civil War Small Arms Ammunition, Vol. 2, by Dean Thomas, Thomas Publications, Gettysburg, PA 2002. 528 pp. Hardcover. $49.95
Completely discusses the ammunition for Federal breechloading carbines and rifles. The seven chapters with 18 appendices detailing the story of the 27 or so different kinds of breechloaders actually purchased or ordered by the Ordnance Department during the Civil War. The book is conveniently divided by the type of priming–external or internal–and then alphabetically by maker or supplier. A wealth of new information and research has proven that these weapons either functioned properly or were inadequate relative to the design and ingenuity of the proprietary cartridges.

Round Ball to Rimfire: A History of Civil War Small Arms Ammunition, Vol. 3, by Dean Thomas, Thomas Publications, Gettysburg, PA, 2003. 488 pp., illus. $49.95
Completely discusses the ammunition for Federal pistols and revolvers. The seven chapters with 18 appendices detailing the story of the 27 or so different kinds of breechloaders actually purchased or ordered by the Ordnance Department during the Civil War. A wealth of new information and research has proven that these weapons either functioned properly or were inadequate relative to the design and ingenuity of the proprietary cartridges.

Ruger and his Guns, by R.L. Wilson, Simon & Schuster, New York, NY, 1996. 358 pp., illus. $65.00
A history of the man, the company and their firearms.

Russell M. Catron and His Pistols, by Warren H. Buxton, Ucross Books, Los Alamos, NM, 1998. 224 pp., illus. Paper covers. $49.50
An unknown American firearms inventor and manufacturer of the mid-twentieth century. Military, commerical, ammunition.

The SAFN-49 and the FAL, by Joe Poyer and Dr. Richard Feirman, North Cape Publications, Tustin, CA, 1998. 160 pp., illus. Paper covers. $14.95
The first complete overview of the SAFN-49 battle rifle, from its pre-WWII beginnings to its military service in countries as diverse as the Belgian Congo and Argentina. The FAL was a "light" version of the SAFN-49 and it became the Free World's most adopted battle rifle.

Savage Sporting Firearms: Dates of Manufacture 1907-1997, by D.R. Morse. Phoenix, AZ, Firing Pin Enterprizes, 2003. 22 pp. Softcover. New. $6.95
Covers their pistols, revolvers, rifles, shotguns and commemoratives, plus models and serial numbers.

Scale Model Firearms, by Joseph D. Kramer. Pittsburgh, PA, privately printed, 1999. 1st edition. 136 pp., oversize, many color photos, index. Softcover. New. $35.00
Each of the models, which are nearly all in one-half scale, require a year or more to complete and in most cases only one example was made. Mr. R. E. Hutchen's uncompromising devotion to the production of these models, is a tribute to a man who is known internationally to be the finest maker of model firearms in the world.

Scottish Firearms, by Claude Blair and Robert Woosnam-Savage, Museum Restoration Service, Bloomfield, Ont., Canada, 1995. 52 pp., illus. Paper covers. $8.95
This revision of the first book devoted entirely to Scottish firearms is supplemented by a register of surviving Scottish long guns.

Sharps Firearms, by Frank Seller, Denver, CO, 1998. 358 pp., illus. $59.95
Traces the development of Sharps firearms with full range of guns made including all martial variations.

Silk and Steel: Women at Arms, by R. L. Wilson, New York, Random House, 2003. 1st edition. 300+ Striking four-color images; 8-1/2" x 11", 320 pgs. Hardcover. New in new dust jacket. (9775). $65.00
Beginning with Artemis and Diana, goddesses of hunting, evolving through modern times, here is the first comprehensive presentation on the subject of women and firearms. No object has had a greater impact on world history over the past 650 years than the firearm, and a surprising number of women have been keen on the subject, as shooters, hunters, collectors, engravers, and even gunmakers.

The SKS Carbine, by Steve Kehaya and Joe Poyer, North Cape Publications, Tustin, CA, 1997. 150 pp., illus. Paper covers. $16.95
The first comprehensive examination of a major historical firearm used through the Vietnam conflict to the diamond fields of Angola.

The SKS Type 45 Carbines, by Duncan Long, Desert Publications, El Dorado, AZ, 1992. 110 pp., illus. Paper covers. $19.95
Covers the history and practical aspects of operating, maintaining and modifying this abundantly available rifle.

Slave Badges and the Slave-Hire System in Charleston, South Carolina, 1783-1865, by Harlan Greene, Harry S. Hutchins Jr., Brian E. Hutchins. Jefferson, NC, McFarland & Company, 2004. 152 pp. Hardcover, NEW. $35.00

Smith & Wesson 1857-1945, by Robert J. Neal and Roy G. Jinks, R&R Books, Livonia, NY, 1996. 434 pp., illus. $50.00
The bible for all existing and aspiring Smith & Wesson collectors.

Smith & Wesson Sporting Firearms: Dates of Manufacture, by D.R. Morse, Phoenix, AZ, Firing Pin Enterprizes, 2003. 76 pp. Softcover. NEW. $6.95
Covers their pistols, revolvers, rifles, shotguns and commemoratives, plus models and serial numbers.

Sniper Variations of the German K98k Rifle, by Richard D. Law, Collector Grade Publications, Ontario, Canada, 1997. 240 pp., illus. $47.50
Volume 2 of "Backbone of the Wehrmacht" the author's in-depth study of the German K98k rifle. This volume concentrates on the telescopic-sighted rifle of choice for most German snipers during WWII.

Southern Derringers of the Mississippi Valley, by Turner Kirkland, Pioneer Press, Tenn., 1971. 80 pp., illus., paper covers. $4.00
A guide for the collector and a much-needed study.

Soviet Russian Postwar Military Pistols and Cartridges, by Fred A. Datig, Handgun Press, Glenview, IL, 1988. 152 pp., illus. $29.95
Thoroughly researched, this definitive sourcebook covers the development and adoption of the Makarov, Stechkin and the new PSM pistols. Also included in this source book is coverage on Russian clandestine weapons and pistol cartridges.

Soviet Russian Tokarev "TT" Pistols and Cartridges 1929-1953, by Fred Datig, Graphic Publishers, Santa Ana, CA, 1993. 168 pp., illus. $39.95
Details of rare arms and their accessories are shown in hundreds of photos. It also contains a complete bibliography and index.

Spencer Repeating Firearms, by Roy M. Marcot, New York, Rowe Publications, 2002. 316 pp.; numerous b&w photos and illustrations. Hardcover. $65.00

Sporting Collectibles, by Jim and Vivian Karsnitz, Schiffer Publishing Ltd., West Chester, PA, 1992. 160 pp., illus. Paper covers. $[illegible]
The fascinating world of hunting related collectibles presented in an informative text.

The Springfield 1903 Rifles, by Lt. Col. William S. Brophy, USAR, Ret., Stackpole Books Inc., Harrisburg, PA, 1985. 608 pp., illus. $75.00
The illustrated, documented story of the design, development, and production of all the models, appendages, and accessories.

Springfield Model 1903 Service Rifle Production and Alteration, 1905-1910, by C.S. Ferris and John Beard, Arvada, CO, 1995. 66 pp., illus. Paper covers. $12.50
A highly recommended work for any serious student of the Springfield Model 1903 rifle.

Springfield Shoulder Arms 1795-1865, by Claud E. Fuller, S. & S. Firearms, Glendale, NY, 1996. 76 pp., illus. Paper covers. $14.95
Exact reprint of the scarce 1930 edition of one of the most definitive works on Springfield flintlock and percussion muskets ever published.

SS Headgear, by Kit Wilson. Johnson Reference Books, Fredericksburg, VA. 72 pp., 15 full-color plates and over 70 b&w photos. $16.50
An excellent source of information concerning all types of SS headgear, to include Allgemeine-SS, Waffen-SS, visor caps, helmets, overseas caps, M-43's and miscellaneous headgear. Also includes a guide on the availability and current values of SS headgear. This guide was compiled from auction catalogs, dealer price lists, and input from advanced collectors in the field.

ARMS LIBRARY

SS Helmets: A Collector's Guide, Vol 1, by Kelly Hicks, Johnson Reference Books, Fredericksburg, VA. 96 pp., illus. $17.50

Deals only with SS helmets and features some very nice color close-up shots of the different SS decals used. Over 85 photographs, 27 in color. The author has documented most of the known types of SS helmets, and describes in detail all of the vital things to look for in determining the originality, style type, and finish.

SS Helmets: A Collector's Guide, Vol 2, by Kelly Hicks. Johnson Reference Books, Fredericksburg, VA. 2000. 128 pp. 107 full-color photos, 14 period photos. $25.00

Volume II contains dozen of highly detailed, full-color photos of rare and original SS and Field Police helmets, featuring both sides as well as interior view. The outstanding decal section offers detailed close-ups of original SS and Police decals, and in conjunction with Volume I, completes the documentation of virtually all types of original decal variations used between 1934 and 1945.

SS Steel; Parade and Combat Helmets of Germany's Third Reich Elite, by Kelly Hicks, San Jose, CA, Bender Publishing, 2004. 1st edition. 241 pp., 400 photos and illustrations in color, deluxe binding. Hardcover. NEW. $44.95

SS Uniforms, Insignia and Accoutrements, by A. Hayes. Schiffer Publications, Atglen, PA. 1996. 248 pp., with over 800 color and b&w photographs. $69.95

This new work explores in detailed color the complex subject of Allgemeine and Waffen-SS uniforms, insignia, and accoutrements. Hundreds of authentic items are extensively photographed in close-up to enable the reader to examine and study.

Standard Catalog of Firearms, 15th Edition, by Ned Schwing, Krause Publications, Iola, WI, 2005. 1504 pp., illus. 7,000 b&w photos plus a 16-page color section. Paper covers. $34.95

This is the largest, most comprehensive and best-selling firearm book of all time! And this year's edition is a blockbuster for both shooters and firearm collectors. More than 14,000 firearms are listed and priced in up to six grades of condition. That's almost 100,000 prices! Gun enthusiasts will love the new full-color section of photos highlighting the finest firearms sold at auction this past year.

Steel Pots: The History of America's Steel Combat Helmets, by Chris Armold. Bender Publishing, San Jose, CA, 2000. $47.95

Packed with hundreds of color photographs, detailed specification diagrams and supported with meticulously researched data, this book takes the reader on a fascinating visual journey covering 80 years of American helmet design and development.

Sturm Ruger Sporting Firearms: Dates of Manufacture, by D.R. Morse, Phoenix, AZ, Firing Pin Enterprizes, 2003. 22 pp. Softcover, NEW. $6.95

Covers their pistols, revolvers, rifles, shotguns and commemoratives, plus models and serial numbers.

The Sumptuous Flaske, by Herbert G. Houze, Andrew Mowbray, Inc., Lincoln, RI, 1989. 158 pp., illus. Softcover. $35.00

Catalog of a recent show at the Buffalo Bill Historical Center bringing together some of the finest European and American powder flasks of the 16th to 19th centuries.

The Swedish Mauser Rifles, by Steve Kehaya and Joe Poyer, North Cape Publications, Tustin, CA, 1999. 267 pp., illus. Paper covers. $19.95

Every known variation of the Swedish Mauser carbine and rifle is described, all match and target rifles and all sniper versions. Includes serial number and production data.

System Lefaucheaux: Continuing the Study of Pinfire Cartridge Arms Including Their Role in the American Civil War, by Chris C. Curtis, Foreword by Norm Flayderman, Armslore Press, 2002. 1st edition. 312 pp., heavily illustrated with b&w photos. Hardcover. New in new dust jacket. $44.95

Thompson: The American Legend, by Tracie L. Hill, Collector Grade Publications, Ontario, Canada, 1996. 584 pp., illus. $85.00

The story of the first American submachine gun. All models are featured and discussed.

Thoughts on the Kentucky Rifle in its Golden Age, by Joe K. Kindig, III. York, PA, George Shumway Publisher, 2002. Annotated second edition. 561 pp.; Illustrated. This scarce title, long out of print, is once again available. Hardcover. $85.00

The definitive book on the Kentucky Rifle, illustrating 266 of these guns in 856 detailed photographs.

Tin Lids–Canadian Combat Helmets, #2 in "Up Close" Series, by Roger V. Lucy, Ottawa, Ontario, Service Publications, 2000. 2nd edition. 48 pp. Softcover. NEW. $17.95

Toys That Shoot and Other Neat Stuff, by James Dundas, Schiffer Books, Atglen, PA, 1999. 112 pp., illus. Paper covers. $24.95

Shooting toys from the twentieth century, especially 1920s to 1960s, in over 420 color photographs of BB guns, cap shooters, marble shooters, squirt guns and more. Complete with a price guide.

Trade Guns of the Hudson's Bay Company 1670-1970, Historical Arms New Series No. 2. by S. James Gooding, Bloomfield, Ont. Canada, Museum Restoration Service, 2003. 1st edition. 158 pp., thoroughly researched text. Includes bibliographical references. Pictorial hardcover. NEW. $35.00

The Trapdoor Springfield, by M.D. Waite and B.D. Ernst, The Gun Room Press, Highland Park, NJ, 1983. 250 pp., illus. $39.95

The first comprehensive book on the famous standard military rifle of the 1873-92 period.

Treasures of the Moscow Kremlin: Arsenal of the Russian Tsars, A Royal Armories and the Moscow Kremlin exhibition, HM Tower of London 13, June 1998 to 11 September, 1998. BAS Printers, Over Wallop, Hampshire, England. xxii plus 192 pp. over 180 color illustrations. Text in English and Russian. $65.00

For this exhibition catalog, each of the 94 objects on display are photographed and described in detail to provide the most informative record of this important exhibition.

U.S. Army Headgear 1812-1872, by John P. Langellier and C. Paul Loane. Atglen, PA, Schiffer Publications, 2002. 167 pp., with over 350 color and b&w photos. Hardcover. $69.95

This profusely illustrated volume represents more than three decades of research in public and private collections by military historian John P. Langellier and Civil War authority C. Paul Loane.

U.S. Army Rangers & Special Forces of World War II Their War in Photographs, by Robert Todd Ross, Atglen, PA, Schiffer Publications, 2002. 216 pp., over 250 b&w and color photographs. Hardcover. $59.95

Never before has such an expansive view of WWII elite forces been offered in one volume. An extensive search of public and private archives unearthed an astonishing number of rare and never before seen images, including color. Most notable are the nearly 20 exemplary photographs of Lieutenant Colonel William O. Darby's Ranger Force in Italy, taken by Robert Capa, considered by many to be the greatest combat photographer of all time.

U.S. Handguns of World War II: The Secondary Pistols and Revolvers, by Charles W. Pate, Andrew Mowbray, Inc., Lincoln, RI, 1998. 515 pp., illus. $39.00

This indispensable new book covers all of the American military handguns of WWII except for the M1911A1 Colt automatic.

U.S. Martial Single Shot Pistols, by Daniel D. Hartzler and James B. Whisker, Old Bedford Village Press, Bedford, PA, 1998. 128 pp., illus. $45.00

A photographic chronicle of military and semi-martial pistols supplied to the U.S. Government and the several States.

U.S. Military Arms Dates of Manufacture from 1795, by George Madis, Dallas, TX, 1995. 64 pp. Softcover. $9.95

Lists all U.S. military arms of collector interest alphabetically, covering about 250 models.

U.S. M1 Carbines: Wartime Production, by Craig Riesch, North Cape Publications, Tustin, CA, 1994. 72 pp., illus. Paper covers. $16.95

Presents only verifiable and accurate information. Each part of the M1 Carbine is discussed fully in its own section; including markings and finishes.

U.S. Naval Handguns, 1808-1911, by Fredrick R. Winter, Andrew Mowbray Publishers, Lincoln, RI, 1990. 128 pp., illus. $26.00

The story of U.S. Naval handguns spans an entire century–included are sections on each of the important naval handguns within the period.

U.S. Silent Service - Dolphins & Combat Insignia 1924-1945, by David Jones. Bender Publishing, San Jose, CA, 2001. 224 pp., 532 photos (most in full color). $39.95

After eight years of extensive research, the publication of this book is a submarine buff and collector's dream come true. This beautiful full-color book chronicles, with period letters and sketches, the developmental history of U.S. submarine insignia prior to 1945. It also contains many rare and never before published photographs, plus interviews with WWII submarine veterans, from enlisted men to famous skippers. All known contractors are covered plus embroidered versions, mess dress variations, the Roll of Honor, submarine combat insignia, battleflags, launch memorabilia and related submarine collectibles (postal covers, match book covers, jewelry, posters, advertising art, postcards, etc.).

Uniform and Dress Army and Navy of the Confederate States of America (Official Regulations), by Confederate States of America., Ray Riling Arms Books, Philadelphia, PA, 1960. $20.00

A portfolio containing a complete set of nine color plates especially prepared for framing, reproduced in exactly 200 sets from the very rare Richmond, VA., 1861 regulations.

Uniforms & Equipment of the Austro-Hungarian Army in World War One, by Spencer A. Coil, Atglen, PA, Schiffer Publications, 2003. 1st edition. 352 pp., with over 550 b&w and color photographs. Hardcover. New in new dust jacket. $69.95

Uniforms and Insignia of the Cossacks in the German Wehrmacht in World War II, by Peter Schuster and Harald Tiede, Atglen, PA, Schiffer Publications, 2003. 1st edition. 160 pp., illustrated with over 420 b&w and color photographs. Hardcover. New in new dust jacket. $49.95

Uniforms & Equipment of the Imperial German Army 1900-1918: A Study in Period Photographs, by Charles Woolley, Schiffer Publications, Atglen, PA, 2000. 375 pp., over 500 b&w photographs and 50 color drawings. Fully illustrated. $69.95

Features formal studio portraits of pre-war dress and wartime uniforms of all arms. Also contains photo postal cards taken in the field of Infantry, Pionier, Telegraph-Signal, Landsturm, and Mountain Troops, vehicles, artillery, musicians, the Bavarian Leib Regiment, specialized uniforms and insignia, small arms close-ups, unmotorized transport, group shots and Balloon troops and includes a 60-page full-color uniform section reproduced from rare 1914 plates.

Uniforms of the Third Reich: A Study in Photographs, by Maguire Hayes, Schiffer Publications, Atglen, PA, 1997. 200 pp., with over 400 color photographs. $69.95

This new book takes a close look at a variety of authentic WWII era German uniforms including examples from the Army, Luftwaffe, Kriegsmarine, Waffen-SS, Allgemeine-SS, Hitler youth and political leaders. The pieces are shown in large full frame front and rear shots, and in painstaking detail to show tailors' tags, buttons, insignia detail etc. and allow the reader to see what the genuine article looks like. Various accoutrements worn with the uniforms are also included to aid the collector.

Uniforms of the United States Army, 1774-1889, by Henry Alexander Ogden, Dover Publishing, Mineola, NY. 1998. 48 pp. of text plus 44 color plates. Softcover. $9.95

A republication of the work published by the quarter-master general, United States army in 1890. A striking collection of lithographs and a marvelous archive of military, social, and costume history portraying the gamut of U.S. Army uniforms from fatigues to full dress, between 1774 and 1889.

Uniforms of the Waffen-SS; Black Service Uniform - LAH Guard Uniform - SS Earth-Grey Service Uniform - Model 1936 Field Service Uniform - 1939-1940 - 1941 Volume 1, by Michael D. Beaver, Schiffer Publications, Atglen, PA, 2002. 272 pp., with 500 color, and b&w photos. $79.95

This spectacular work is a heavily documented record of all major clothing articles of the Waffen-SS. Hundreds of unpublished photographs were used in production. Original and extremely rare SS uniforms of various types are carefully photographed and presented here. Among the subjects covered in this multi volume series are field-service uniforms, sports, drill, dress, armored personnel, tropical, and much more. This book is indispensable and an absolute must-have for any serious historian of WWII German uniforms.

Uniforms of the Waffen-SS; Sports and Drill Uniforms - Black Panzer Uniform - Camouflage - Concentration Camp Personnel-SD-SS Female Auxiliaries, Volume 3, by Michael D. Beaver, Schiffer Publications, Atglen, PA, 2002. 272 pp., with 500 color, and b&w photos. $79.95

Uniforms of the Waffen-SS; 1942-1943 - 1944-1945 - Ski Uniforms - Overcoats - White Service Uniforms - Tropical Clothing, Volume 2, by Michael D. Beaver, Schiffer Publications, Atglen, PA, 2002. 272 pp., with 500 color, and b&w photos. $79.95

Uniforms, Organization, and History of the German Police, Volume I, by John R. Angolia and Hugh Page Taylor, San Jose, CA, R. James Bender Publishing, 2004. 704 pp. illustrated with b&w and color photos. Hardcover. NEW. $59.95

Uniforms, Organization, and History of the NSKK/NSFK, by John R. Angolia and David Littlejohn, Bender Publishing, San Jose, CA, 2000. $44.95

This work is part of the on-going study of political organizations that formed the structure of the Hitler hierarchy, and is authored by two of the most prominent authorities on the subject of uniforms and insignia of the Third Reich. This comprehensive book covers details on the NSKK and NSFK such as history, organization, uniforms, insignia, special insignia, flags and standards, gorgets, daggers, awards, "day badges," and much more!

ARMS LIBRARY

United States Martial Flintlocks, by Robert M. Reilly, Mowbray Publishing Co., Lincoln, RI, 1997. 264 pp., illus. $40.00
A comprehensive history of American flintlock longarms and handguns (mostly military) c. 1775 to c. 1840.

Variations of Colt's New Model Police and Pocket Breech Loading Pistols, by John D. Breslin, William Q. Pirie and David E. Price, Lincoln, RI, Andrew Mowbray Publishers, 2002. 1st edition. 158 pp., heavily illustrated with over 160 photographs and superb technical detailed drawings and diagrams. Pictorial hardcover. $37.95
A type-by-type guide to what collectors call small frame conversions.

Vietnam Order of Battle, by Shelby L. Stanton, William C. Westmoreland. Mechanicsburg, PA, Stackpole Books, 2003. 1st edition. 416 pp., 32 in full color, 101 pp. halftones. Hardcover. New in new dust jacket. $69.95

Visor Hats of the United States Armed Forces 1930-1950, by Joe Tonelli, Atglen, PA, Schiffer Publications, 2003. 1st edition. Hardcover. New in new dust jacket. $79.95

The W.F. Cody Buffalo Bill Collector's Guide with Values, by James W. Wojtowicz, Collector Books, Paducah, KY, 1998. 271 pp., illus. $24.95
A profusion of colorful collectibles including lithographs, programs, photographs, books, medals, sheet music, guns, etc. and today's values.

The Walker's Walkers Controversy is Solved, by Col. Robert D. Whittington III, Hooks, TX, Brownlee Books, 2003. A limited edition of 1,000 copies. Numbered. 17 pp. Paper covers. New. $15.00
The truth about serial numbers on the Colt Whitneyville-Walker pistols presented to Captain Samuel Hamilton Walker by Sam Colt and J. B. Colt on July 28th, 1847.

Walther: A German Legend, by Manfred Kersten, Safari Press, Inc., Huntington Beach, CA, 2000. 400 pp., illus. $85.00
This comprehensive book covers, in rich detail, all aspects of the company and its guns, including an illustrious and rich history, the WWII years, all the pistols (models 1 through 9), the P-38, P-88, the long guns, 22 rifles, centerfires, Wehrmacht guns, and even a gun that could shoot around a corner.

The Walther Handgun Story: A Collector's and Shooter's Guide, by Gene Gangarosa, Steiger Publications, 1999. 300 pp., illus. Paper covers. $21.95
Covers the entire history of the Walther empire. Illustrated with over 250 photos.

Walther Models PP & PPK, 1929-1945 – Volume 1, by James L. Rankin, Coral Gables, FL, 1974. 142 pp., illus. $40.00
Complete coverage on the subject as to finish, proofmarks and Nazi Party inscriptions.

Walther P-38 Pistol, by Maj. George Nonte, Desert Publications, Cornville, AZ, 1982. 100 pp., illus. Paper covers. $12.95
Complete volume on one of the most famous handguns to come out of WWII. All models covered.

Walther Pistols: Models 1 Through P99, Factory Variations and Copies, by Dieter H. Marschall, Ucross Books, Los Alamos, NM. 2000. 140 pp., with 140 b&w illustrations, index. Paper covers. $19.95
This is the English translation, revised and updated, of the highly successful and widely acclaimed German language edition. This book provides the collector with a reference guide and overview of the entire line of the Walther military, police, and self-defense pistols from the very first to the very latest. Models 1-9, PP, PPK, MP, AP, HP, P.38, P1, P4, P38K, P5, P88, P99 and the Manurhin models. Variations, where issued, serial ranges, calibers, marks, proofs, logos, and design aspects in an astonishing quantity and variety are crammed into this very well researched and highly regarded work.

Walther Volume II, Engraved, Presentation and Standard Models, by James L. Rankin, J.L. Rankin, Coral Gables, FL, 1977. 112 pp., illus. $40.00
The new Walther book on embellished versions and standard models. Has 88 photographs, including many color plates.

Walther, Volume III, 1908-1980, by James L. Rankin, Coral Gables, FL, 1981. 226 pp., illus. $40.00
Covers all models of Walther handguns from 1908 to date, includes holsters, grips and magazines.

Warman's Civil War Collectibles (Encyclopedia of Antiques and Collectibles), Iola, WI, Krause Publications, 2003. 1st edition. This new volume is a huge 518 pp. full of information on Civil War memorabilia that you'll thrill to, as there are more than 1,000 images plus over 3,000 price listings! Softcover. NEW. $16.95

Winchester an American Legend, by R.L. Wilson, New York, Book Sales, 2004. Reprint. Hardcover. New in new dust jacket. $39.95

Winchester Bolt Action Military & Sporting Rifles 1877 to 1937, by Herbert G. Houze, Andrew Mowbray Publishing, Lincoln, RI, 1998. 295 pp., illus. $45.00
Winchester was the first American arms maker to commercially manufacture a bolt action repeating rifle, and this book tells the exciting story of these Winchester bolt actions.

The Winchester Book, by George Madis, David Madis Gun Book Distributor, Dallas, TX, 2000. 650 pp., illus. $54.50
A new, revised 25th anniversary edition of this classic book on Winchester firearms. Complete serial ranges have been added.

Winchester Commemoratives, by Tom Trolard, Coos Bay, OR, Commemorative Investments Press Library, 2003. 2nd printing - Limited to 1,500 copies. Signed by the author. Hardcover. New in new dust jacket. $109.95

Winchester Dates of Manufacture 1849-1984, by George Madis, Art & Reference House, Brownsboro, TX, 1984. 59 pp. $9.50
A most useful work, compiled from records of the Winchester factory.

Winchester Engraving, by R.L. Wilson, Beinfeld Books, Springs, CA, 1989. 500 pp., illus. $135.00
A classic reference work of value to all arms collectors.

The Winchester Handbook, by George Madis, Art & Reference House, Lancaster, TX, 1982. 287 pp., illus. $26.95
The complete line of Winchester guns, with dates of manufacture, serial numbers, etc.

Winchester Lever Action Repeating Firearms, Vol. 1, The Models of 1866, 1873 and 1876, by Arthur Pirkle, North Cape Publications, Tustin, CA, 1995. 112 pp., illus. Paper covers. $19.95
Complete, part-by-part description, including dimensions, finishes, markings and variations throughout the production run of these fine, collectible guns.

Winchester Lever Action Repeating Rifles, Vol. 2, The Models of 1886 and 1892, by Arthur Pirkle, North Cape Publications, Tustin, CA, 1996. 150 pp., illus. Paper covers. $19.95
Describes each model on a part-by-part basis by serial number range complete with finishes, markings and changes.

Winchester Lever Action Repeating Rifles, Vol. 3, The Model of 1894, by Arthur Pirkle, North Cape Publications, Tustin, CA, 1998. 150 pp., illus. Paper covers. $19.95
The first book ever to provide a detailed description of the Model 1894 rifle and carbine.

The Winchester Lever Legacy, by Clyde "Snooky" Williamson, Buffalo Press, Zachary, LA, 1988. 664 pp., illus. $75.00
A book on reloading for the different calibers of the Winchester lever action rifle.

The Winchester Model 1876 "Centennial" Rifle, by Herbert G. Houze. Lincoln, RI, Andrew Mowbray, Inc., 2001. Illustrated with over 180 b&w photographs. 192 pp. Hardcover. $45.00
The first authoritative study of the Winchester Model 1876 written using the company's own records. This book dispels the myth that the Model 1876 was merely a larger version of the Winchester company's famous Model 1873 and instead traces its true origins to designs developed immediately after the American Civil War. The specifics of the model–such as the numbers made in its standard calibers, barrel lengths, finishes and special order features–are fully listed here for the first time. For Winchester collectors, and those interested in the mechanics of the 19th-century arms industry, this book provides a wealth of previously unpublished information.

Winchester Pocket Guide: Identification & Pricing for 50 Collectible Rifles and Shotguns, by Ned Schwing, Iola, WI, Krause Publications, 2004. 1st edition. 224 pp., illus. Softcover. NEW. $12.95

Winchester Repeating Arms Company Its History & Development from 1865 to 1981, by Herbert G. Houze, Iola, WI, Krause Publications, 2004. 1st edition. Softcover. NEW. $34.98

The Winchester Single-Shot, Volume 1; A History and Analysis, by John Campbell, Andrew Mowbray, Inc., Lincoln, RI, 1995. 272 pp., illus. $55.00
Covers every important aspect of this highly-collectible firearm.

The Winchester Single-Shot, Volume 2; Old Secrets and New Discoveries, by John Campbell, Andrew Mowbray, Inc., Lincoln, RI, 2000. 280 pp., illus. $55.00
An exciting follow-up to the classic first volume.

Winchester Sporting Firearms: Dates of Manufacture, by D.R. Morse, Phoenix, AZ, Firing Pin Enterprizes, 2003. 45 pp. Softcover. NEW. $6.95
Covers their pistols, revolvers, rifles, shotguns and commemoratives, plus models and serial numbers.

The Winchester-Lee Rifle, by Eugene Myszkowski, Excalibur Publications, Tucson, AZ 2000. 96 pp., illus. Paper covers. $22.95
The development of the Lee Straight Pull, the cartridge and the approval for military use. Covers details of the inventor and memorabilia of Winchester-Lee related material.

World War One Collectors Handbook Volumes 1 and 2, by Paul Schulz, Hayes Otoupalik and Dennis Gordon, Missoula, MT, privately printed, 2002. Two volumes in one edition. 110 pp., loaded with b&w photos. Softcover. NEW. $21.95
Covers, uniforms, insignia, equipment, weapons, souvenirs and miscellaneous. Includes price guide. For all of you Doughboy collectors, this is a must.

World War II German War Booty, A Study in Photographs, by Thomas M. Johnson, Atglen, PA, Schiffer Publications, 2003. 1st edition. 368 pp. Hardcover. New in new dust jacket. $79.95

Worldwide Webley and the Harrington and Richardson Connection, by Stephen Cuthbertson, Ballista Publishing and Distributing Ltd., Gabriola Island, Canada, 1999. 259 pp., illus. $50.00
A masterpiece of scholarship. Over 350 photographs plus 75 original documents, patent drawings, and advertisements accompany the text.

The World's Great Handguns: From 1450 to the Present Day, by Roger Ford, Secaucus, NJ, Chartwell Books, Inc., 1997. 1st edition. 176 pp. Hardcover. New in new dust jacket. $19.95

EDGED WEAPONS

2005 Sporting Knives: Folders, Fixed Blades, Pocket, Military, Gent's Knives, Multi-Tools and Swords, Comprehensive Coverage of Commercial Sporting Knives, by Joe Kertzman, Iola, WI, Krause Publications, 2004. 4th edition. $22.99

A Guide to Military Dress Daggers, Volume 1, by Kurt Glemser, Johnson Reference Books, Fredericksburg, VA, 1991. 160 pp., illus. Softcover. $26.50
Very informative guide to dress daggers of foreign countries, to include an excellent chapter on DDR daggers. There is also a section on reproduction Third Reich period daggers. Provides, for the first time, identification of many of the war-time foreign dress daggers.

A Guide to Military Dress Daggers, Volume 2, by Kurt Glemser, Johnson Reference Books, Fredericksburg, VA, 1993. 160 pp., illus. $32.50
As in the first volume, reproduction daggers are covered in depth (Third Reich, East German, Italian, Polish and Hungarian). American Navy dirks are featured for the first time. Bulgarian Youth daggers, Croatian daggers and Imperial German Navy dagger scabbards all have chapters devoted to them. Continues research initiated in Volume I on such subjects as dress daggers, Solingen export daggers, East German daggers and Damascus Smith Max Dinger.

A Guide to Military Dress Daggers, Volume 3, by Kurt Glemser, Johnson Reference Books, Fredericksburg, VA, 1996. 260 pp., illus. $39.50
Includes studies of Swedish daggers, Italian Cadet daggers, Rumanian daggers, Austrian daggers, Dress daggers of the Kingdom of Yugoslavia, Czechoslovakian daggers, Paul Dinger Damastschmied, Swiss Army daggers, Polish daggers (1952-1994), and Hungarian Presentation daggers.

A Guide to Military Dress Daggers, Volume 4, by Kurt Glemser, Johnson Reference Books, Fredericksburg, VA, 2001. 252 pp., illus. $49.50
Several chapters dealing with presentation daggers to include a previously unknown series of East German daggers. Other chapters cover daggers in wear; Czech & Slovak daggers; Turkish daggers; Swiss Army daggers; Solingen Export daggers; miniature daggers, youth knives.

A Photographic Supplement of Confederate Swords, with addendum, by William A. Albaugh III, Broadfoot Publishing, Wilmington, NC. 1999. 205 plus 54 pp. of the addendum, illustrated with b&w photos. $45.00

ARMS LIBRARY

Advertising Cutlery; With Values, by Richard White, Schiffer Publishing, Ltd., Atglen, PA, 176 pp., with over 400 color photos. Softcover. $29.95

Advertising Cutlery is the first-ever publication to deal exclusively with the subject of promotional knives. Containing over 400 detailed color photographs, this book explores over 100 years of advertisements stamped into the sides of knives. In addition to the book's elegant photographic presentation, extensive captions and text give the reader the background information necessary for evaluating collectible advertising knives.

Allied Military Fighting Knives; And the Men Who Made Them Famous, by Robert A. Buerlein, Paladin Press, Boulder, CO, 2001. 185 pp., illustrated with b&w photos. Softcover. $35.00

The American Eagle Pommel Sword: The Early Years 1794-1830, by Andrew Mowbray, Manrat Arms Publications, Lincoln, RI, 1997. 244 pp., illus. $65.00

The standard guide to the most popular style of American sword.

American Knives; The First History and Collector's Guide, by Harold L. Peterson, The Gun Room Press, Highland Park, NJ, 1980. 178 pp., illus. $24.95

A reprint of this 1958 classic. Covers all types of American knives.

American Military Bayonets of the 20th Century, by Gary M. Cunningham, Scott A. Duff Publications, Export, PA, 1997. 116 pp., illus. Paper covers. $21.95

A guide for collectors, including notes on makers, markings, finishes, variations, scabbards, and production data.

American Premium Guide To Knives & Razors; Identification and Value Guide 6th Edition, by Jim Sargent, lola, WI, Krause Publications, 2004. 504 pp. plus 2,500 b&w photos. Softcover. NEW. $24.99

American Primitive Knives 1770-1870, by G.B. Minnes, Museum Restoration Service, Ottawa, Canada, 1983. 112 pp., illus. $24.95

Origins of the knives, outstanding specimens, structural details, etc.

American Socket Bayonets and Scabbards, by Robert M. Reilly, 2nd printing, Andrew Mowbray, Inc., Lincoln, RI, 1998. 208 pp., illus. $45.00

Full coverage of the socket bayonet in America, from Colonial times through the post-Civil War.

The American Sword, 1775-1945, by Harold L. Peterson, Ray Riling Arms Books, Co., Phila., PA, 2001. 286 pp. plus 60 pp. of illus. $49.95

1977 reprint of a survey of swords worn by U.S. uniformed forces, plus the rare "American Silver Mounted Swords, (1700-1815)."

American Swords and Sword Makers, by Richard H. Bezdek, Paladin Press, Boulder, CO, 1994. 648 pp., illus. $79.95

The long-awaited definitive reference volume to American swords, sword makers and sword dealers from Colonial times to the present.

American Swords & Sword Makers Volume 2, by Richard H. Bezdek, Paladin Press, Boulder, CO, 1999. 376 pp., illus. $69.95

More than 400 stunning photographs of rare, unusual and one-of-a-kind swords from the top collections in the country.

American Swords from the Philip Medicus Collection, edited by Stuart C. Mowbray, with photographs and an introduction by Norm Flayderman, Andrew Mowbray Publishers, Lincoln, RI, 1998. 272 pp., with 604 swords illustrated. $55.00

Covers all areas of American sword collecting.

The Ames Sword Company Catalog: An Exact Reprint of the Original 19th Century Military and Fraternal Sword Catalog, by Stuart C. Mowbray, Lincoln, RI, Andrew Mowbray, Inc., 2003. 1st edition. 200 pp., 541 swords illustrated with original prices and descriptions. Pictorial hardcover. $37.50

The level of detail in these original catalog images will surprise you. Dealers who sold Ames swords used this catalog in their stores, and every feature is clearly shown. Reproduced directly from the incredibly rare originals, military, fraternal and more! The key to identifying hundreds of Ames swords! Shows the whole Ames line, including swords from the Civil War and even earlier. Lots of related military items like belts, bayonets, etc.

The Ames Sword Company, 1829-1935, by John D. Hamilton, Andrew Mowbray Publisher, Lincoln, RI, 1995. 255 pp., illus. $45.00

An exhaustively researched and comprehensive history of America's foremost sword manufacturer and arms supplier during the Civil War.

Antique American Switchblades; Identification & Value Guide, by Mark Erickson, lola, WI, Krause Publications, 2004. 1st edition. Softcover. NEW. $19.95

Antlers & Iron II, by Krause Publications, Iola, WI, 1999. 40 pp., illustrated with 100 photos. Paper cover. $12.00

Lays out actual plans so you can build your mountain man folding knife using ordinary hand tools. Step-by-step instructions, with photos, design, antler slotting and springs.

The Art of Throwing Weapons, by James W. Madden, Paladin Press, Boulder, CO, 1993. 102 pp., illus. $14.00

This comprehensive manual covers everything from the history and development of the five most common throwing weapons–spears, knives, tomahawks, shurikens and boomerangs–to their selection or manufacture, grip, distances, throwing motions and advanced combat methods.

Arte of Defence an Introduction to the Use of the Rapier, by William E. Wilson, Union City, CA, Chivalry Bookshelf, 2002. 1st edition. 167 pp., illustrated with over 300 photographs. Softcover $24.95

Axes of War and Power, by James Gamble, Douglas, CA, privately printed, 2002. 1st edition. Softcover. NEW. $19.95

Battle Blades: A Professional's Guide to Combat Fighting Knives, by Greg Walker; Foreword by Al Mar, Paladin Press, Boulder, CO, 1993. 168 pp., illus. $40.95

The author evaluates daggers, Bowies, switchblades and utility blades according to their design, performance, reliability and cost.

The Bayonet in New France, 1665-1760, by Erik Goldstein, Museum Restoration Service, Bloomfield, Ontario, Canada, 1997. 36 pp., illus. Paper covers. $8.95

Traces bayonets from the recently developed plug bayonet, through the regulation socket bayonets, which saw service in North America.

Bayonets from Janzen's Notebook, by Jerry Jansen, Cedar Ridge Publications, Tulsa, OK, 2000. 6th printing. 258 pp., illus. Hardcover. $45.00

This collection of over 1,000 pieces is one of the largest in the U.S.

Bayonets: An Illustrated History, by Martin J. Brayley, lola, WI, Krause Publications, 2004. 1st edition 256 pp., illus. Softcover. NEW. $29.95

Bayonets, Knives & Scabbards; United States Army Weapons Report 1917 Thru 1945, edited by Frank Trzaska, Knife Books, Deptford, NJ, 1999. 80 pp., illus. Paper covers. $15.95

Follows the United States edged weapons from the close of WWI through the end of WWII. Manufacturers involved, dates, numbers produced, problems encountered, and production data.

The Best of U.S. Military Knives, Bayonets & Machetes, by M.H. Cole, edited by Michael W. Silvey. Privately printed, 2002. Hardcover. New in new dust jacket. $59.95

Book of Edged Weapons, Ephrata, Pennsylvania, Science Press Division, 2004. 351 pp. illustrated with b&w photos. Hardcover. NEW. $40.00

The Book of the Sword, by Richard F. Burton, Dover Publications, New York, NY, 1987. 199 pp., illus. Paper covers. $12.95

Traces the sword's origin from its birth as a charged and sharpened stick through diverse stages of development.

Borders Away, Volume 1: With Steel, by William Gilkerson, Andrew Mowbray, Inc., Lincoln, RI, 1991. 184 pp., illus. $48.00

A comprehensive study of naval armament under fighting sail. This first volume covers axes, pikes and fighting blades in use from 1626 to 1826.

Borders Away, Volume 2: Firearms of the Age of Fighting Sail, by William Gilkerson, Andrew Mowbray, Inc., Lincoln, RI, 1999. 331 pp., illus. with 200 photos, 16-color plates. $65.00

Completing a two-volume set, this impressive work covers the pistols, muskets, combustibles, and small cannons once employed aboard American and European fighting ships.

Bowie and Big-Knife Fighting System, by Dwight C. McLemore, Boulder, CO, Paladin Press, 2003. 240 pp., illus. Softcover. NEW. $35.00

The Bowie Knife: Unsheathing an American Legend, by Norm Flayderman, Lincoln, RI, Andrew Mowbray, Inc., 2004. 1st edition. New in new dust jacket. $79.95

Bowie Knives and Bayonets of the Ben Palmer Collection, 2nd Edition, by Ben Palmer, Bill Moran and Jim Phillips. Williamstown, NJ, Phillips Publications, 2002. 224 pp. Illustrated with photos. Hardcover. $49.95

Vastly expanded with more than 300 makers, distributors and dealers added to the makers list; chapter on the Bowie knife photograph with 50 image photo gallery of knife holders from the Mexican War, Civil War, and the West; contains a chapter on Bowie Law; includes several unpublished Bowie documents, including the first account of the Alamo. As things stand, it is a 'must' read for collectors, particularly if you're looking for photos of some knives not often seen, or curious about what Bill Moran might have to say about some of the old Bowie designs.

Bowies, Big Knives, and the Best of Battle Blades, by Bill Bagwell, Paladin Press, Boulder, CO. 2001. 184 pp., illus. Paper covers. $30.00

This book binds the timeless observations and invaluable advice of master bladesmith and blade combat expert Bill Bagwell under one cover for the first time. Here, you'll find all of Bagwell's classic SOF columns, plus all-new material linking his early insights with his latest conclusions.

British & Commonwealth Bayonets, by Ian D. Skennerton and Robert Richardson, I.D.S.A. Books, Piqua, OH, 1986. 404 pp., 1300 illus. $40.00

Civil War Cavalry & Artillery Sabers, 1833-1865, by John H. Thillmann, Andrew Mowbray, Inc. Lincoln, RI, 2002. 1st edition. 500+ pp., over 50 color photographs, 1,373 b&w illustrations, coated paper, dust jacket, premium hardcover binding. Hardcover. $79.95

Clandestine Edged Weapons, by William Windrum, Phillips Publications, Williamstown, NJ, 2001. 74 pp., illustrated with b&w photographs. Pictorial softcover. $9.95

Collecting Indian Knives, 2nd Edition, by Lar Hothem, Krause Publications, Iola, WI, 2000. 176 pp., illus. Paper covers. $19.95

Expanded and updated with new photos and information, this 2nd edition will be a must have for anyone who collects or wants to learn about chipped Indian artifacts in the knife family. With an emphasis on prehistoric times, the book is loaded with photos, values and identification guidelines to help identify blades as to general time-period and, in many cases, help date sites where such artifacts are found. Includes information about different regional materials and basic styles, how knives were made and for what they were probably used.

Collecting the Edged Weapons of Imperial Germany, by Johnson & Wittmann, Johnson Reference Books, Fredericksburg, VA, 1989. 363 pp., illus. $39.50

An in-depth study of the many ornate military, civilian, and government daggers and swords of the Imperial era.

Collector's Guide to Ames U.S. Contract Military Edged Weapons: 1832-1906, by Ron G. Hickox, Pioneer Press, Union City, IN, 1993. 70 pp., illus. Paper covers. $17.50

While this book deals primarily with edged weapons made by the Ames Manufacturing Company, this guide refers to other manufacturers of United States swords.

Collector's Guide to E.C. Simmons Keen Kutter Cutlery Tools, by Jerry and Elaine Heuring, Paducah, KY, Collector Books, 2000. 1st edition. 192 pp. Softcover. NEW. $19.95

Collector's Guide to Switchblade Knives, an Illustrated Historical and Price Reference, by Richard V. Langston, Paladin Press, Boulder, CO. 2001. 224 pp., illus. $49.95

It has been more than 20 years since a major work on switchblades has been published, and never has one showcased as many different types as Rich Langston's new book. The Collector's Guide to Switchblade Knives contains a history of the early cutlery industry in America; a detailed examination of the evolution of switchblades; and a user-friendly, up-to-the-minute, illustrated reference section that helps collectors and novices alike identify all kinds of knives, from museum-quality antiques to Granddad's old folder that's been hidden in the attic for decades.

The Complete Bladesmith: Forging Your Way to Perfection, by Jim Hrisoulas, Paladin Press, Boulder, CO, 1987. 192 pp., illus. $42.95

Novices as well as the experienced bladesmith will benefit from this definitive guide to smithing world-class blades.

The Complete Book of Pocketknife Repair, by Ben Kelly Jr., Krause Publications, Iola, WI, 1995. 130 pp., illus. Paper covers. $10.95

Everything you need to know about repairing knives can be found in this step-by-step guide to knife repair.

Confederate Edged Weapons, by W.A. Albaugh, R&R Books, Lavonia, NY, 1994. 198 pp., illus. $40.00

The master reference to edged weapons of the Confederate forces. Features precise line drawings and an extensive text.

ARMS LIBRARY

The Connoisseur's Book of Japanese Swords, by Kodauska Nagayama, International, Tokyo, Japan, 1997. 348 pp., illus. $75.00
Translated by Kenji Mishina. A comprehensive guide to the appreciation and appraisal of the blades of Japanese swords. The most informative guide to the blades of Japanese swords ever to appear in English.

Counterfeiting Antique Cutlery, by Gerald Witcher, National Brokerage and Sales, Inc., Brentwood, TN. 1997. 512 pp., illustrated with 1,500-2,000 b&w photographs. $24.95

Daggers and Fighting Knives of the Western World: From the Stone Age til 1900, by Harold Peterson, Dover Publishing, Mineola, NY, 2001. 96 pp., plus 32 pp. of matte stock. Over 100 illustrations. Softcover. $9.95
The only full-scale reference book devoted entirely to the subject of fighting knives, flint knives, daggers of all sorts, scramasaxes, hauswehren, dirks and more. 108 plates, bibliography and Index.

The Earliest Commando Knives, by William Windrum. Phillips Publications, Williamstown, NJ. 2001. 74 pp., illus. Softcover. $9.95

Edged Weapon Accouterments of Germany 1800-1945, Kreutz, Hofmann, Johnson, Reddick, Pottsboro, TX, Reddick Enterprises, 2002. 1st edition. Hardcover. NEW. $49.00

Eickhorn Edged Weapons Exports, Vol. 1: Latin America, by A.M. de Quesada Jr. and Ron G. Hicock, Pioneer Press, Union City, TN, 1996. 120 pp., illus. Softcovers. $15.00
This research studies the various Eickhorn edged weapons and accessories manufactured for various countries outside of Germany.

Exploring the Dress Daggers and Swords of the SS, by Thomas T. Wittmann, Johnson Reference Books, Fredericksburg, VA, 2003. 1st edition. 750 pp., illustrated with nearly 1000 photographs, many in color. $150.00
Covers all model SS Service Daggers, Chained SS Officer Daggers, Himmler & Rohm Inscriptions, Damascus presentations, SS Officer Degen, Himmler Birthday Degen, Silver Lionhead Swords, Blade etch study & much more. Profusely illustrated with historically important period in-wear photographs. Most artifacts appearing for the first time in reference.

Exploring the Dress Daggers of the German Army, by Thomas T. Wittmann, Johnson Reference Books, Fredericksburg, VA, 1995. 350 pp., illus. $69.95
The first in-depth analysis of the dress daggers worn by the German Army.

Exploring the Dress Daggers of the German Luftwaffe, by Thomas T. Wittmann, Johnson Reference Books, Fredericksburg, VA, 1998. 350 pp., illus. $79.95
Examines the dress daggers and swords of the German Luftwaffe. The designs covered include the long DLV patterns, the Glider Pilot designs of the NSFK and DLV, 1st and 2nd model Luftwaffe patterns, the Luftwaffe sword and the General Officer Degen. Many are pictured for the first time in color.

Exploring The Dress Daggers of the German Navy, by Thomas T. Wittmann, Johnson Reference Books, Fredericksburg, VA, 2000. 560 pp., illus. $89.95
Explores the dress daggers and swords of the Imperial, Weimar, and Third Reich eras, from 1844-1945. Provides detailed information, as well as many superb b&w and color photographs of individual edged weapons. Many are pictured for the first time in full color.

Fighting Tomahawk: An Illustrated Guide to Using the Tomahawk and Long Knife as Weapons, by Dwight C. McLemore, Boulder, CO, Paladin Press, 2004. 1st edition. 296 pp. Softcover. NEW. $39.95

The First Commando Knives, by Prof. Kelly Yeaton and Col. Rex Applegate, Phillips Publications, Williamstown, NJ, 1996. 115 pp., illus. Paper covers. $12.95
Here is the full story of the Shanghai origins of the world's best known dagger.

George Schrade and His Accomplishments, by George Schrade, privately printed, 2004. 84 pp. Softcover. NEW. $25.00

German Clamshells and Other Bayonets, by G. Walker and R.J. Weinard, Johnson Reference Books, Fredericksburg, VA, 1994. 157 pp., illus. $22.95
Includes unusual bayonets, many of which are shown for the first time. Current market values are listed.

German Etched Dress Bayonets (Extra Seitengewehr) 1933-1945, by Wayne H. Techet. Printed by the author, Las Vegas, NV. 2002. Color section and value guide. 262 pp. Limited edition of 1,300 copies. Signed and numbered. $55.00
Photographs of over 200 obverse and reverse motifs. Rare SS and Panzer patterns pictured for the first time, with an extensive chapter on reproductions and Red Flags.

German Swords and Sword Makers: Edged Weapons Makers from the 14th to the 20th Centuries, by Richard H. Bezdek, Paladin Press, Boulder, CO, 2000. 248 pp., illus. $59.95
This book contains the most information ever published on German swords and edged weapons makers from the Middle Ages to the present.

Greenhill Military Manual: Combat Knives, by Leroy Thompson, London, Greenhill Publishing, 2004. 1st edition. Hardcover. NEW. $24.00

The Halberd and other European Polearms 1300-1650, by George Snook, Museum Restoration Service, Bloomfield, Ontario, Canada, 1998. 40 pp., illus. Paper covers. $8.95
A comprehensive introduction to the history, use, and identification of the staff weapons of Europe.

Highland Swordsmanship: Techniques of the Scottish Swordmasters, edited by Mark Rector. Chivalry Bookshelf, Union City, CA, 2001. 208 pp., Includes more than 100 illustrative photographs. Softcover $29.95
Rector has done a superb job at bringing together two influential yet completely different 18th century fencing manuals from Scotland. Adding new interpretive plates, Mark offers new insights and clear presentations of many useful techniques. With contributions by Paul MacDonald and Paul Wagner, this book promises to be a treat for students of historical fencing, Scottish history and reenactors.

How to Make a Tactical Folder, by Bob Tetzuola, Krause Publications, Iola, WI, 2000. 160 pp., illus. Paper covers. $16.95
Step-by-step instructions and outstanding photography guide the knifemaker from start to finish.

How to Make Folding Knives, by Ron Lake, Frank Centofante and Wayne Clay, Krause Publications, Iola, WI, 1995. 193 pp., illus. Paper covers. $13.95
With step-by-step instructions, learn how to make your own folding knife from three top custom makers.

How to Make Knives, by Richard W. Barney and Robert W. Loveless, Krause Publications, Iola, WI, 1995. 182 pp., illus. Paper covers. $13.95
Complete instructions from two premier knife makers on making high-quality, handmade knives.

How to Make Multi-Blade Folding Knives, by Eugene Shadley & Terry Davis, Krause Publications, Iola, WI, 1997. 192 pp., illus. Paper covers. $19.95
This step-by-step instructional guide teaches knifemakers how to craft these complex folding knives.

KA-BAR: The Next Generation of the Ultimate Fighting Knife, by Greg Walker, Paladin Press, Boulder, CO, 2001. 88 pp., illus. Softcover. $16.00
The KA-BAR fighting/utility knife is the most widely recognized and popular combat knife ever to be produced in the United States. Since its introduction on 23 November 1942, the KA-BAR has performed brilliantly on the battlefields of Europe, the South Pacific, Korea, Southeast Asia, Central America and the Middle East, earning its moniker as the "ultimate fighting knife."

Kalashnikov Bayonets: The Collector's Guide to Bayonets for the AK and its Variations, by Martin D. Ivie, Texas, Diamond Eye Publications, 2002. 1st edition. 220 pp., with over 250 color photos and illustrations. Hardcover. $59.95

Knife and Tomahawk Throwing: The Art of the Experts, by Harry K. McEvoy, Charles E. Tuttle, Rutland, VT, 1989. 150 pp., illus. Softcover. $8.95
The first book to employ side-by-side the fascinating art and science of knives and tomahawks.

The Knife in Homespun America and Related Items: Its Construction and Material, as used by Woodsmen, Farmers, Soldiers, Indians and General Population, by Madison Grant, York, PA, privately printed, 1984. 1st edition. 187 pp., profusely illustrated. $45.00
Shows over 300 examples of knives and related items made and used by woodsmen, farmers, soldiers, Indians and the general frontier population.

Knife Talk, The Art and Science of Knifemaking, by Ed Fowler, Krause Publications, Iola, WI, 1998. 158 pp., illus. Paper covers. $14.95
Valuable how-to advice on knife design and construction plus 20 years of memorable articles from the pages of "*Blade*" Magazine.

Knifemakers of Old San Francisco, by Bernard Levine, 2nd edition, Paladin Press, Boulder, CO, 1998. 150 pp., illus. $39.95
The definitive history of the knives and knife-makers of 19th century San Francisco.

Knives 2005 25th Anniversary Edition, edited by Joe Kertzman, Iola, WI, Krause Publications, 2004. Softcover. NEW. $24.99

Knives of the United States Military - World War II, by Michael W. Silvey, privately printed, Sacramento, CA 1999. 250 pp., illustrated with full color photos. $60.00
240 full-page color plates depicting the knives of WWII displayed against a background of wartime accoutrements and memorabilia. The book focuses on knives and their background.

Knives of the United States Military in Vietnam: 1961-1975, by Michael W. Silvey, privately printed, Sacramento, CA., 139 pp. Hardcover. $45.00
A beautiful color celebration of the most interesting and rarest knives of the Vietnam War, emphasizing SOG knives, Randalls, Gerbers, Eks, and other knives of this era. Shown with these knives are the patches and berets of the elite units who used them.

Les Baionnettes Reglementaires Francises de 1840 a 1918 "The Bayonets; Military Issue 1840-1918", by French Assoc. of Bayonet Collectors, 2000. 77 pp. illus. $24.95
Profusely illustrated. By far the most comprehensive guide to French military bayonets done for this period. Includes hundreds of illustrations. 77 large 8-1/4" x 11-1/2" pages. French text. Color photos are magnificent!

The Master Bladesmith: Advanced Studies in Steel, by Jim Hrisoulas, Paladin Press, Boulder, CO, 1990. 296 pp., illus. $49.95
The author reveals the forging secrets that for centuries have been protected by guilds.

Medieval Swordsmanship, Illustrated Methods and Techniques, by John Clements, Paladin Press, Boulder, CO, 1998. 344 pp., illus. $40.00
The most comprehensive and historically accurate view ever written of the lost fighting arts of Medieval knights.

The Military Knife & Bayonet Book, by Homer Brett, World Photo Press, Japan. 2001. 392 pp., illus. $69.95
Professional studio color photographs with more than 1,000 military knives and knife-bayonets illustrated. Both the U.S. and foreign sections are extensive, and includes standard models, prototypes and experimental models. Many of the knives and bayonets photographed have never been previously illustrated in any other book. The U.S. section also includes the latest developments in military Special Operations designs. Written in Japanese and English.

Military Knives: A Reference Book, by Frank Trzaska (editor), Knife Books, Deptford, NJ, 2001. 255 pp., illus. Softcover. $17.95
A collection of your favorite Military Knife articles from the pages of *Knife World* magazine. 67 articles ranging from the Indian Wars to the present day modern military knives.

Modern Combat Blades, by Duncan Long, Paladin Press, Boulder, CO, 1993. 128 pp., illus. $30.00
Long discusses the pros and cons of bowies, bayonets, commando daggers, kukris, switchblades, butterfly knives, belt-buckle blades and many more.

The Modern Swordsman, by Fred Hutchinson, Paladin Press, Boulder, CO, 1999. 80 pp., illus. Paper covers. $22.00
Realistic training for serious self-defense.

Officer Swords of the German Navy 1806-1945, Claus P. Stefanski & Dirk, Schiffer Publications, Atglen, PA, 2002. 1st edition. 176 pp., with over 250 b&w and color photos. Hardcover. $59.95

Official Price Guide to Collector Knives; 14th Edition, by C. Houston Price, New York, House of Collectibles, 2004. 500 photos, 8 pp. in color. 497 pp. Softcover. NEW. $17.95

Official Scout Blades with Prices, by Ed Holbrook, privately printed, 2004. Softcover. NEW. $25.00

Old German Target Arms: Alte Schiebenwaffen; Volume 1, by Jesse Thompson, C. Ron Dillon, Allen Hallock, Bill Loos, Rochester, NY, Tom Rowe Publications, 2003. 1st edition. Hardcover. New in new dust jacket. $98.00

On Damascus Steel, by Dr. Leo S. Figiel, Atlantis Arts Press, Atlantis, FL, 1991. 145 pp., illus. $65.00
The historic, technical and artistic aspects of Oriental and mechanical Damascus. Persian and Indian sword blades, from 1600-1800, which have never been published, are illustrated.

The Pattern-Welded Blade: Artistry in Iron, by Jim Hrisoulas, Paladin Press, Boulder, CO, 1994. 120 pp., illus. $44.95
Reveals the secrets of this craft–from the welding of the starting billet to the final assembly of the complete blade.

ARMS LIBRARY

Pocket Knives of the United States Military, by Michael W. Silvey, Sacramento, CA, privately printed, 2002. 135 pp. Hardcover. $34.95

This beautiful new full color book is the definitive reference on U.S. military folders. Pocket Knives of the United States Military is organized into the following sections: Introduction, The First Folders, WWI, WWII, and Postwar (which covers knives up through the late 1980s). Essential reading for pocketknife and military knife collectors alike!

The Randall Chronicles, by Pete Hamilton, privately printed, 2002. 160 pp., profusely illustrated in color. Hardcover in dust jacket. $79.95

Randall Fighting Knives In Wartime: WWII, Korea, and Vietnam, by Robert E. Hunt. Sacramento, CA, privately printed, 2002. 1st edition. 192 pp. Hardcover. $44.95

While other books on Randall knives have been published, this new title is the first to focus specifically on Randalls with military ties. There are three main sections, containing more than 80 knives from the WWII, Korea, and Vietnam War periods. Each knife is featured in a high quality, full page, full color photograph, with the opposing page carrying a detailed description of the knife and its history or other related information.

Randall Made Knives, by Robert L. Gaddis, Paladin Press, Boulder, CO, 2000. 292 pp., illus. $59.95

Plots the designs of all 24 of Randall's unique knives. This step-by-step book, seven years in the making, is worth every penny and moment of your time.

Randall Military Models; Fighters, Bowies and Tang Knives, by Robert E. Hunt, Sacramento, CA, privately printed, 2004. 1st edition. Hardcover. New in new dust jacket. $74.95

Remington Knives–Past & Present, by Ron Stewart and Roy Ritchie, Paducah, KY, Collector Books, 2005. 1st edition. 288 pp. Softcover. NEW. $16.95

Renaissance Swordsmanship, by John Clements, Paladin Press, Boulder, CO, 1997. 152 pp., illus. Paper covers. $25.00

The illustrated use of rapiers and cut-and-thrust swords.

Rice's Trowel Bayonet, reprinted by Ray Riling Arms Books Co., Philadelphia, PA, 1968. 8 pp., illus. Paper covers. $3.00

A facsimile reprint of a rare circular originally published by the U.S. government in 1875 for the information of U.S. troops.

The Scottish Dirk, by James D. Forman, Museum Restoration Service, Bloomfield, Ont., Canada, 1991. 60 pp., illus. Paper covers. $8.95

More than 100 dirks are illustrated with a text that sets the dirk and Sgian Dubh in their socio-historic content following design changes through more than 300 years of evolution.

Seitengewehr: History of the German Bayonet, 1919-1945, by George T. Wheeler, Johnson Reference Books, Fredericksburg, VA, 2000. 320 pp., illus. $44.95

Provides complete information on Weimar and Third Reich bayonets, as well as their accompanying knots and frogs. Illustrates re-issued German and foreign bayonets utilized by both the Reichswehr and the Wehrmacht, and details the progression of newly manufactured bayonets produced after Hitler's rise to power. Photos illustrate rarely seen bayonets worn by the Polizei, Reichsbahn, Postschutz, Hitler Jugend, and other civil and political organizations. German modified bayonets from other countries are pictured and described. Book contains an up-to-date price guide including current valuations.

Silver Mounted Swords: The Lattimer Family Collection; Featuring Silver Hilts Through the Golden Age, by Daniel Hartzler, Rowe Publications, New York, 2000. 300 pp., with over 1,000 illustrations and 1,350 photos. Oversize 9" x12". $75.00

The world's largest Silver Hilt collection.

Small Arms Identification Series, No. 6. British Service Sword & Lance Patterns, by Ian Skennerton, I.D.S.A. Books, Piqua, OH, 1994. 48 pp. $12.50

Small Arms Series, No. 2. The British Spike Bayonet, by Ian Skennerton, I.D.S.A. Books, Piqua, OH, 1982. 32 pp., 30 illus. $9.00

Socket Bayonets of the Great Powers, by Robert W. Shuey, Excalibur Publications, Tucson, AZ, 2000 96 pp., illus. Paper covers $22.95

With 175 illustrations, the author brings together, in one place, many of the standard socket arrangements used by some of the " Great Powers." With an illustrated glossary of blade shape and socket design.

The Socket in the British Army 1667-1783, by Erik Goldstein, Andrew Mowbray, Inc., Lincoln, RI, 2001. 136 pp., illus. $23.00

The spectacle of English "redcoats" on the attack, relentlessly descending upon enemy lines with fixed bayonets, is one of the most chilling images from European history and the American Revolution. Drawing upon new information from archaeological digs and archival records, the author explains how to identify each type of bayonet and shows which bayonets were used where and with which guns.

Standard Guide to Razors, 2nd Edition, by Roy Ritchie and Ron Stewart. Paducah, KY, Collector Books, 1999 values. 224 pp. Softcover. NEW. $9.95

Switchblade: The Ace of Blades, Revised and Updated, by Ragnar Benson and edited by Michael D. Janich, Boulder, CO, Paladin Press, 2004. 104 pp. Softcover. NEW. $16.00

Switchblades of Italy, by Tim Zinser, Dan Fuller and Neal Punchard. Paducah, KY, Turner Publishing, 2002. 128 pp. Hardcover. New in new dust jacket. $39.89

Swords and Blades of the American Revolution, by George C. Neumann, Rebel Publishing Co., Inc., Texarkana, TX, 1991. 288 pp., illus. $36.95

The encyclopedia of bladed weapons–swords, bayonets, spontoons, halberds, pikes, knives, daggers, axes–used by both sides, on land and sea, in America's struggle for independence.

Swords and Sabers of the Armory at Springfield, by Burton A. Kellerstedt, New Britain, CT, 1998. 121 pp., illus. Softcover. $29.95

The basic and most important reference for its subject, and one that is unlikely to be surpassed for comprehensiveness and accuracy.

Swords and Sword Makers of England and Scotland, by Richard H. Bezdek, Boulder, CO, Paladin Press, 2003. 1st edition. 424 pp., illus. Hardcover. New in new dust jacket. $69.95

Covers English sword makers from the 14th century and Scottish makers from the 16th century all the way through the renowned Wilkinson Sword Company and other major sword manufacturers of today. The important early English sword- and blade-making communities of Hounslow Heath and Shotley Bridge, and the influential Cutlers Company of London. The book concludes with dozens of beautiful illustrations of hilt designs taken directly from famed sword hilt maker Matthew Boulton's 18th-century pattern book and more than 450 spectacular photographs of English and Scottish swords of every type and era from some of the world's major collections.

Tactical Folding Knife; A Study of the Anatomy and Construction of the Liner-Locked Folder, by Bob Terzuola, Krause Publications, Iola, WI. 2000. 160 pp., 200 b&w photos, illus. Paper covers. $16.00

Step-by-step instructions and outstanding photography guide the knifemaker from start to finish. This book details everything from the basic definition of a tactical folder to the final polishing as the knife is finished.

Tactical Knives, by Dietmar Pohl, lola, WI, Krause Publications, 2003. 1st edition. Softcover. NEW. $24.95

Travels for Daggers, Historic Edged Weaponry, by Eiler R. Cook, Hendersonville, NC, 2004. 1st edition. Hardcover. New in new dust jacket. $50.00

The U.S. M-3 Trench Knife of World War Two, by Vincent J. Coniglio and Robert S. Laden. Matamoras, PA, privately printed, 2003. 2nd printing. Softcover. NEW. $18.00

U.S. Military Knives, Bayonets and Machetes Price Guide, 4th Edition, by Frank Trzaska (editor), Knife Books, Deptford, NJ, 2001. 80 pp., illus. Softcover. $7.95

This volume follows in the tradition of the previous three versions of using major works on the subject as a reference to keep the price low to you.

U.S. Naval Officers; Their Swords and Dirks Featuring the Collection of the United States Naval Academy Museum, by Peter Tuite, Lincoln, RI, Andrew Mowbray, Inc., 2005. 1st edition. 240 pp., illustrated with over 500 color photos. Pictorial hardcover. NEW. $75.00

Wayne Goddard's $50 Knife Shop, by Wayne Goddard, Krause Publications, Iola, WI, 2000. 160 pp., illus. Softcover. $19.95

This book expands on information from Goddard's popular column in *Blade* magazine to show knifemakers of all skill levels how to create helpful gadgets and supply their shop on a shoestring.

The Wittmann German Dagger Price Guide for 2004, by David Hohaus and Thomas Wittmann, Moorestown, NJ, privately printed, 2004. 1st edition. Stiff paper covers. NEW. $11.95

Wonder of Knifemaking, by Wayne Goddard, Krause Publications, Iola, WI. 2000. 160 pp., illustrated with 150 b&w photos and 16-page color section. Softcover. $19.95

Master bladesmith Wayne Goddard draws on his decades of experience to answer questions of knifemakers at all levels. As a columnist for *Blade* magazine, Goddard has been answering real questions from real knifemakers for the past eight years. Now, all the details are compiled in one place as a handy reference for every knifemaker, amateur or professional.

GENERAL

Action Shooting: Cowboy Style, by John Taffin, Krause Publications, Iola, WI, 1999. 320 pp., illus. $39.95

Details on the guns and ammunition. Explanations of the rules used for many events.

Advanced Muzzleloader's Guide, by Toby Bridges, Stoeger Publishing Co., So. Hackensack, NJ, 1985. 256 pp., illus. Paper covers. $14.95

The complete guide to muzzle-loading rifles, pistols and shotguns–flintlock and percussion.

Aids to Musketry for Officers & NCOs, by Capt. B.J. Friend, Excalibur Publications, Latham, NY, 1996. 40 pp., illus. Paper covers. $7.95

A facsimile edition of a pre-WWI British manual filled with useful information for training the common soldier.

Airgun Odyssey, by Steve Hanson, Manchester, CT, Precision Shooting, Inc., 2004. 1st edition. 175 pp. Pictorial softcover. $27.95

America's Great Gunmakers, by Wayne van Zwoll, Stoeger Publishing Co., So. Hackensack, NJ, 1992. 288 pp., illus. Paper covers. $16.95

This book traces in great detail the evolution of guns and ammunition in America and the men who formed the companies that produced them.

American Air Rifles, by James E. House. Krause Publications, Iola, WI, 2002. 1st edition. 208 pp., with 198 b&w photos. Softcover. $22.95

Air rifle ballistics, sights, pellets, games, and hunting caliber recommendations are thoroughly explained to help shooters get the most out of their American air rifles. Evaluation of more than a dozen American-made and American-imported air rifle models.

American and Imported Arms, Ammunition and Shooting Accessories, Catalog No. 18 of the Shooter's Bible, Stoeger, Inc., reprinted by Fayette Arsenal, Fayetteville, NC, 1988. 142 pp., illus. Paper covers. $10.95

A facsimile reprint of the 1932 Stoeger's Shooter's Bible.

The American B.B. Gun: A Collector's Guide, by Arni T. Dunathan. A.S. Barnes and Co., Inc., South Brunswick, 2001. 154 pp., illustrated with nearly 200 photographs, drawings and detailed diagrams. Hardcover. $35.00

Annie Oakley of the Wild West, by Walter Havighurst, New York, Castle Books, 2000. 246 pp. Hardcover. New in new dust jacket. $10.00

Armed and Female, by Paxton Quigley, E.P. Dutton, New York, NY, 2001. 237 pp., illus. Softcover $9.95

The first complete book on one of the hottest subjects in the media today, the arming of the American woman.

Arming the Glorious Cause: Weapons of the Second War for Independence, by James B. Whisker, Daniel D. Hartzler and Larry W. Yantz, R & R Books, Livonia, NY, 1998. 175 pp., illus. $45.00

A photographic study of Confederate weapons.

Armor Battles of the Waffen SS:1943-45, by Will Fey, translated by Henri Henschler Mechanicsburg, PA, Greenhill Books, 2003. 1st edition. 384 pp., 32 b&w photos in a 16-page section, 15 drawings & 4 maps. Softcover. NEW. $19.95

Arms & Armor in the Art Institute of Chicago, by Walter J. Karcheski Jr., Bulfinch Press, Boston, MA, 1995. 128 pp., illus. $35.00

Now, for the first time, the Art Institute of Chicago's arms and armor collection is presented in the visual delight of 103 color illustrations.

Arms for the Nation: Springfield Longarms, edited by David C. Clark, Scott A. Duff, Export, PA, 1994. 73 pp., illus. Paper covers. $9.95

A brief history of the Springfield Armory and the arms made there.

Arrowmaker Frontier Series Volume 1, by Roy Chandler, Jacksonville, NC, Ron Brigade Armory, 2000. 390 pp. Hardcover. New in new dust jacket. $38.95

Arsenal of Freedom, The Springfield Armory, 1890-1948: A Year-by-Year Account Drawn from Official Records, compiled and edited by Lt. Col. William S. Brophy,

ARMS LIBRARY

USAR Ret., Andrew Mowbray, Inc., Lincoln, RI, 1991. 400 pp., illus. Softcover. $29.95

A "must buy" for all students of American military weapons, equipment and accoutrements.

The Art of American Arms Makers Marketing Guns, Ammunition, and Western Adventure During the Golden Age of Illustration, by Richard C., Rattenbury, Oklahoma City, OK, National Cowboy Museum, 2004. 132 pp. of color photos. Softcover. NEW. $29.95

The Art of American Game Calls, by Russell E. Lewis, Paducah, KY, Collector Books, 2005. 1st edition. 176 pp. Pictorial hardcover. NEW. $24.95

The Art of Blacksmithing, by Alex W. Bealer, New York, Book Sales, 1996. Revised edition. 440 pp. Hardcover. New in new dust jacket. $10.00

The Art of Remington Arms, Sporting Classics, 2004, by Tom Davis. 1st edition. Hardcover. NEW. $60.00

Battle of the Bulge: Hitler's Alternate Scenarios, by Peter Tsouras, Mechanicsburg, PA, Stackpole Books, 2004. 1st edition. 256 pp., 24 b&w photos, 10 maps. Hardcover. NEW. $34.95

The Belgian Rattlesnake: The Lewis Automatic Machine Gun, by William M. Easterly, Collector Grade Publications, Inc., Cobourg, Ont. Canada, 1998. 542 pp., illus. $79.95

A social and technical biography of the Lewis automatic machine gun and its inventors.

The Benchrest Shooting Primer, edited by Dave Brennan, Precision Shooting, Inc., Manchester, CT, 2000. 2nd edition. 420 pp., illustrated with b&w photographs, drawings and detailed diagrams. Pictorial softcover. $24.95

The very best articles on shooting and reloading for the most challenging of all the rifle accuracy disciplines…benchrest shooting.

The Big Guns: Civil War Siege, Seacoast, and Naval Cannon, by Edwin Olmstead, Wayne E. Stark and Spencer C. Tucker, Museum Restoration Service, Bloomfield, Ontario, Canada, 1997. 360 pp., illus. $80.00

This book is designed to identify and record the heavy guns available to both sides during the Civil War.

Black Powder, Pig Lead And Steel Silhouettes, by Paul A. Matthews, Wolfe Publishing, Prescott, AZ, 2002. 132 pp., illustrated with b&w photographs and detailed drawings and diagrams. Softcover. $16.95

The Black Rifle Frontier Series Volume 2, by Roy Chandler, Jacksonville, NC, Iron Brigade Armory, 2002. 226 pp. Hardcover. New in new dust jacket. $42.95

In 1760, inexperienced Jack Elan settles in Sherman's Valley, suffers tragedy, is captured by hostiles, escapes, and fights on. This is the "2nd" book in the Frontier Series.

Blue Book of Airguns 4th Edition, by Robert Beeman and John Allen, Minneapolis, MN, Blue Book Publications, Inc., 2004. Softcover. NEW. $17.39

Blue Book of Gun Values, 25th Edition (2004 Edition), by S.P. Fjestad, Minneapolis, MN, Blue Book Publications, Inc., 628 pp., illus. Paper covers. $27.95

Blue Book of Modern Black Powder Values, 4th Edition, by Dennis Adler, John Allen, Minneapolis, MN, Blue Book Publications, Inc., 2004. Softcover. NEW. $18.95

British Small Arms of World War II, by Ian D. Skennerton, Arms & Militaria Press, Australia, 1988. 110 pp., 37 illus. $25.00

Carbine and Shotgun Speed Shooting: How to Hit Hard and Fast in Combat, by Steve Moses. Paladin Press, Boulder, CO. 2002. 96 pp., illus. Softcover $18.00

In this groundbreaking book, he breaks down the mechanics of speed shooting these weapons, from stance and grip to sighting, trigger control and more, presenting them in a concise and easily understood manner.

Cavalry Raids of the Civil War, by Col. Robert W. Black, Mechanicsburg, PA, Stackpole Books, 2004. 1st edition. 288 pp., 30 b&w drawings. Softcover. NEW. $17.95

CO2 Pistols and Rifles, by James E. House, Iola, WI, Krause Publications, 2004. 1st edition 240 pp., with 198 b&w photos. Softcover. NEW. $24.95

The Complete .50-caliber Sniper Course, by Dean Michaelis, Paladin Press, Boulder, CO, 2000. 576 pp., illus., $60.00

The history from German Mauser T-Gewehr of WWI to the Soviet PTRD and beyond. Includes the author's Program of Instruction for Special Operations Hard-Target Interdiction Course.

The Complete Blackpowder Handbook, 4th Edition, by Sam Fadala, DBI Books, a division of Krause Publications, Iola, WI, 2002. 400 pp., illus. Paper covers. $21.95

Expanded and completely rewritten edition of the definitive book on the subject of blackpowder.

The Complete Guide to Game Care and Cookery, 4th Edition, by Sam Fadala, Krause Publications, Iola, WI, 2003. 320 pp., illus. Paper covers. $21.95

Over 500 photos illustrating the care of wild game in the field and at home with a separate recipe section providing over 400 tested recipes.

The Concealed Handgun Manual, 4th Edition, by Chris Bird, San Antonio, TX, Privateer Publications, 2004. 332 pp., illus. Softcover, NEW. $21.95

Cowboys & the Trappings of the Old West, by William Manns & Elizabeth Clair Flood, Santa Fe, NM, ZON International Publishing Company, 1997. 224 pp., 550 colorful photos. Foreword by Roy Rogers. Hardcover. $45.00

Big & beautiful book covering: Hats, boots, spurs, chaps, guns, holsters, saddles and more. It's really a pictorial cele bration of the old time buckaroo. This exceptional book presents all the accoutrements of the cowboy life in a comprehensive tribute to the makers. The history of the craftsmen and the evolution of the gear are lavishly illustrated.

Cowgirls: Women of the Wild West, by Elizabeth Clair Flood and William Maims, edited by Helene Helene, Santa Fe, NM, ZON International Publishing Company, 2000. 1st edition. Hardcover. New in new dust jacket. $45.00

Custom Firearms Engraving, by Tom Turpin, Krause Publications, Iola, WI, 1999. 208 pp., illus. $49.95

Provides a broad and comprehensive look at the world of firearms engraving. The exquisite styles of more than 75 master engravers are shown on beautiful examples of handguns, rifles, shotguns, and other firearms, as well as knives.

Daisy Air Rifles & BB Guns: The First 100 Years, by Neal Punchard, St. Paul, MN, Motorbooks, 2002. 1st edition. Hardcover, 10" x 10", 156 pp., 300 color. Hardcover. NEW. $29.95

Dead On, by Tony Noblitt and Warren Gabrilska, Paladin Press, Boulder, CO, 1998. 176 pp., illus. Paper covers. $22.00

The long-range marksman's guide to extreme accuracy.

Do or Die A Supplementary Manual on Individual Combat, by Lieut. Col. A.J. Drexel Biddle, U.S.M.C.R., Boulder, CO, Paladin Press, 2004. 80 pp., illus. Softcover, NEW. $15.00

Down to Earth: The 507th Parachute Infantry Regiment in Normandy: June 6-july 11 1944, by Martin Morgan ICA, Atglen, PA, Schiffer Publishing, 2004. 1st edition. 304 pp., color and b&w photos. Hardcover. New in new dust jacket. $69.95

Early American Flintlocks, by Daniel D. Hartzler and James B. Whisker, Bedford Valley Press, Bedford, PA 2000. 192 pp., Illustrated. $45.00

Covers early Colonial guns, New England guns, Pennsylvania Guns and Southern guns.

Effective Defense: The Woman, the Plan, the Gun, by Gila Hayes, Onalaska, WA, Police Bookshelf, 2000. 2nd edition. Photos, 264 pp. Softcover. NEW. $16.95

Elmer Keith: The Other Side of a Western Legend, by Gene Brown., Precision Shooting, Inc., Manchester, CT 2002. 1st edition. 168 pp., illustrated with b&w photos. Softcover. $19.95

An updated and expanded edition of his original work, incorporating new tales and information that have come to light in the past six years. Gene Brown was a long time friend of Keith, and today is unquestionably the leading authority on Keith's books.

Encyclopedia of Native American Bows, Arrows and Quivers, by Steve Allely and Jim Hamm, The Lyons Press, N.Y., 1999. 160 pp., illus. $29.95

A landmark book for anyone interested in archery history, or Native Americans.

The Exercise of Armes, by Jacob de Gheyn, Dover Publications, Inc., Mineola, NY, 1999. 144 pp., illus. Paper covers. $14.95

Republications of all 117 engravings from the 1607 classic military manual. A meticulously accurate portrait of uniforms and weapons of the 17th century Netherlands.

Fighting Iron: A Metals Handbook for Arms Collectors, by Art Gogan, Mowbray Publishers, Inc., Lincoln, RI, 2002. 176 pp., illus. $28.00

A guide that is easy to use, explains things in simple English and covers all of the different historical periods that we are interested in.

Fine Art of the West, by Byron B. Price and Christopher Lyon, New York, Abbeville Press, 2004. Hardcover. NEW. $75.00

Firearms Assembly Disassembly; Part 4: Centerfire Rifles (2nd Edition), by J. B. Wood, Iola, WI, Krause Publications, 2004. 2nd edition. 576 pp., 1,750 b&w photos. Softcover. NEW. $24.95

Fireworks: A Gunsight Anthology, by Jeff Cooper, Paladin Press, Boulder, CO, 1998. 192 pp., illus. Paper cover. $27.00

A collection of wild, hilarious, shocking and always meaningful tales from the remarkable life of an American firearms legend.

Fort Robinson, Frontier Series, Volume 4, by Roy Chandler, Jacksonville, NC, Ron Brigade Armory, 2003. 1st edition. 560 pp. Hardcover. New in new dust jacket. $39.95

Frederic Remington: The Color of Night, by Nancy Anderson, Princeton University Press, 2003. 1st edition. 136 color illus, 24 halftones; 10" x 11", 208 pgs. Hardcover, New in new dust jacket. $49.95; UK $52.49

From a Stranger's Doorstep to the Kremlin Gate, by Mikhail Kalashnikov, Ironside International Publishers, Inc., Alexandria, VA, 1999. 460 pp., illus. $34.95

A biography of the most influential rifle designer of the 20th century. His AK-47 assault rifle has become the most widely used (and copied) assault rifle of this century.

The Frontier Rifleman, by H.B. LaCrosse Jr., Pioneer Press, Union City, TN, 1989. 183 pp., illus. Softcover. $17.50

The Frontier rifleman's clothing and equipment during the era of the American Revolution, 1760-1800.

Galloping Thunder: The Stuart Horse Artillery Battalion, by Robert Trout, Mechanicsburg, PA, Stackpole Books, 2002. 1st edition. Hardcover, NEW. $39.95

The Gatling Gun: 19th Century Machine Gun to 21st Century Vulcan, by Joseph Berk, Paladin Press, Boulder, CO, 1991. 136 pp., illus. $34.95

Here is the fascinating on-going story of a truly timeless weapon, from its beginnings during the Civil War to its current role as a state-of-the-art modern combat system.

German Artillery of World War Two, by Ian V. Hogg, Stackpole Books, Mechanicsburg, PA, 1997. 304 pp., illus. $44.95

Complete details of German artillery use in WWII.

Gone Diggin: Memoirs of a Civil War Relic Hunter, by Toby Law, Orange, VA, Publisher's Press, 2002. 1st edition signed. 151 pp., illustrated with b&w photos. $24.95

The true story of one relic hunter's life - The author kept exacting records of every relic hunt and every relic hunter he was with working with.

Grand Old Lady of No Man's Land: The Vickers Machine Gun, by Dolf L. Goldsmith, Collector Grade Publications, Cobourg, Canada, 1994. 600 pp., illus. $79.95

Goldsmith brings his years of experience as a U.S. Army armourer, machine gun collector and shooter to bear on the Vickers, in a book sure to become a classic in its field.

Greenhill Military Manuals; Small Arms: Pistols and Rifles, by Ian Hogg; London, Greenhill Press, 2003. Revised. 160 pp., illus. Hardcover. $24.00

This handy reference guide, by the leading small arms author, provides descriptions, technical specifications and illustrations of 75 of the most important pistols and rifles, including the Heckler & Koch USP/SOCOM pistols, the FN Five-seven 5.7mm pistol, the Heckler & Koch G36 rifle and much more.

Gun Digest 2005, 59th Annual Edition, edited by Ken Ramage, Iola, WI, Krause Publications, 2004. Softcover. NEW. $24.95

This all new 59th edition continues the editorial excellence, quality, content and comprehensive cataloguing that firearms enthusiasts have come to know and expect. The most read gun book in the world for the last half century.

Gun Digest Blackpowder Loading Manual New 4th Edition, by Sam Fadala, Iola, WI, Krause Publications, 2004. 352 pp., illus. Softcover. NEW. $27.95

The Gun Digest Book of Deer Guns, edited by Dan Shideler, Iola, WI, Krause Publications, 2004. 1st edition Softcover, NEW. $14.99

The Gun Digest Book of Guns for Personal Defense Arms & Accessories for Self-Defense, edited by Kevin Michalowski, Iola, WI, Krause Publications, 2004. 1st edition Softcover. NEW. $14.99

Gun Engraving, by C. Austyn, Safari Press Publication, Huntington Beach, CA, 1998. 128 pp., plus 24 pp. of color photos. $50.00

A well-illustrated book on fine English and European gun engravers. Includes a fantastic pictorial section that lists types of engravings and prices.

Gun Notes, Volume 1, by Elmer Keith, Safari Press, Huntington Beach, CA, 2002. 219 pp., illus. Softcover. $24.95

A collection of Elmer Keith's most interesting columns and feature stories that appeared in "Guns & Ammo" magazine from 1961 to the late 1970's.

ARMS LIBRARY

Gun Notes, Volume 2, by Elmer Keith, Safari Press, Huntington Beach, CA, 2002. 292 pp., illus. Softcover. $24.95

Covers articles from Keith's monthly column in "Guns & Ammo" magazine during the period from 1971 through Keith's passing in 1982.

The Gun That Made the Twenties Roar, by Wm. J. Helmer, The Gun Room Press, Highland Park, NJ, 1977. Over 300 pp., illus. $24.95

Historical account of John T. Thompson and his invention, the infamous "Tommy Gun."

Guns & Shooting: A Selected Bibliography, by Ray Riling, Ray Riling Arms Books Co., Phila., PA, 1982. 434 pp., illus. Limited, numbered edition. $75.00

A limited edition of this superb bibliographical work, the only modern listing of books devoted to guns and shooting.

Guns Illustrated 2005: 37th Edition, edited by Ken Ramage, lola, WI, Krause Publications, 2004. Softcover. NEW. $21.95

Highly informative, technical articles on a wide range of shooting topics by some of the top writers in the industry. A catalog section lists more than 3,000 firearms currently manufactured in or imported to the U.S.

The Guns of the Gunfighters: Lawmen, Outlaws & TV Cowboys, by Doc O'Meara, Iola, WI, Krause Publications, 2003. 1st edition. 16-page color section, 225 b&w photos. Hardcover. $34.95

Explores the romance of the Old West, focusing on the guns that the good guys & bad guys, real & fictional characters, carried with them. Profiles of more than 50 gunslingers, half from the Old West and half from Hollywood, include a brief biography of each gunfighter, along with the guns they carried. Fascinating stories about the TV and movie celebrities of the 1950s and 1960s detail their guns and the skill–or lack thereof–they displayed.

Guns, Bullets, and Gunfighters, by Jim Cirillo, Paladin Press, Boulder, CO, 1996. 119 pp., illus. Paper covers. $16.00

Lessons and tales from a modern-day gunfighter.

Gunstock Carving: A Step-by-Step Guide to Engraving Rifles and Shotguns, by Bill Janney, East Pertsburg, PA, Fox Chapel Publishing, October 2002. 89 pp., illustrated in color. Softcover. $19.95

Learn gunstock carving from an expert. Includes step-by-step projects and instructions, patterns, tips and techniques.

Hand-To-Hand Combat: United States Naval Institute, by U.S. Navy Boulder, CO, Paladin Press, 2003. 1st edition. 240 pp. Softcover. $25.00

Now you can own one of the classic publications in the history of U.S. military close-quarters combat training. In 11 photo-heavy chapters, Hand-to-Hand Combat covers training tips; vulnerable targets; the brutal fundamentals of close-in fighting; frontal and rear attacks; prisoner search and control techniques; disarming pistols, rifles, clubs and knives; offensive means of "liquidating an enemy"; and much more. After reading this book (originally published by the United States Naval Institute in 1943), you will see why it has long been sought by collectors and historians of hand-to-hand combat.

Hidden in Plain Sight, "A Practical Guide to Concealed Handgun Carry" (Revised 2nd Edition), by Trey Bloodworth and Mike Raley, Paladin Press, Boulder, CO, 1997, softcover, photos, 176 pp. $20.00

Concerned with how to comfortably, discreetly and safely exercise the privileges granted by a CCW permit? This invaluable guide offers the latest advice on what to look for when choosing a CCW, how to dress for comfortable, effective concealed carry, traditional and more unconventional carry modes, accessory holsters, customized clothing and accessories, accessibility data based on draw-time comparisons and new holsters on the market. Includes 40 new manufacturer listings.

HK Assault Rifle Systems, by Duncan Long, Paladin Press, Boulder, CO, 1995. 110 pp., illus. Paper covers. $27.95

The little known history behind this fascinating family of weapons tracing its beginnings from the ashes of WWII to the present time.

Holsters for Combat and Concealed Carry, by R.K. Campbell, Boulder, CO, Paladin Press, 2004. 1st edition. 144 pp. Softcover. NEW. $22.00

The Hunter's Guide to Accurate Shooting, by Wayne van Zwoll, Guilford, CT, Lyons Press, 2002. 1st edition. 288 pp. Hardcover. $29.95

Firearms expert van Zwoll explains exactly how to shoot the big-game rifle accurately. Taking into consideration every pertinent factor, he shows a step-by-step analysis of shooting and hunting with the big-game rifle.

The Hunting Time: Adventures in Pursuit of North American Big Game: A Forty-Year Chronicle, by John E. Howard, Deforest, WI, Saint Huberts Press, 2002. 1st edition. 537 pp., illustrated with drawings. Hardcover. $29.95

From a novice's first hunt for whitetailed deer in his native Wisconsin, to a seasoned hunter's pursuit of a Boone and Crockett Club record book caribou in the northwest territories, the author carries the reader along on his forty year journey through the big game fields of North America.

Indian Tomahawks and Frontiersmen Belt Axes, by Daniel Hartzler & James Knowles, New Windsor, MD, privately printed, 2002. 4th revised edition. 279 pp., illustrated with photos and drawings. Hardcover. $65.00

This fourth revised edition has over 160 new tomahawks and trade axes added since the first edition, also a list of 205 makers names. There are 15 chapters from the earliest known tomahawks to the present day. Some of the finest tomahawks in the country are shown in this book with 31 color plates. This comprehensive study is invaluable to any collector.

Jack O'Connor Catalogue of Letters, by Ellen Enzler Herring, Agoura, CA, Trophy Room Books, 2002. 1st edition. Hardcover. NEW. $55.00

Jack O'Connor - The Legendary Life of America's Greatest Gunwriter, by R. Anderson, Long Beach, CA, Safari Press, 2002. 1st edition. 240 pp., profuse photos. Hardcover. $29.95

This is the book all hunters in North America have been waiting for–the long-awaited biography on Jack O'Connor! Jack O'Connor was the preeminent North American big-game hunter and gunwriter of the twentieth century, and Robert Anderson's masterfully written new work is a blockbuster filled with fascinating facts and stories about this controversial character. O'Connor's lifelong friend Buck Buckner has contributed two chapters on his experiences with the master of North American hunting.

Joe Rychertinik Reflects on Guns, Hunting, and Days Gone By, by Joe Rychertinik, Precision Shooting, Inc., Manchester, CT, 1999. 281 pp., illus. Thirty articles by a master story-teller. Paper covers. $16.95

Kill or Get Killed, by Col. Rex Applegate, Paladin Press, Boulder, CO, 1996. 400 pp., illus. $49.95

The best and longest-selling book on close combat in history.

The Lost Classics of Jack O'Connor, edited by Jim Casada, Columbia, SC, Live Oak Press, 2004. 1st edition. Hardcover. New in new dust jacket. $35.00

Manual for H&R Reising Submachine Gun and Semi-Auto Rifle, edited by George P. Dillman, Desert Publications, El Dorado, AZ, 1994. 81 pp., illus. Paper covers. $14.95

A reprint of the Harrington & Richardson 1943 factory manual and the rare military manual on the H&R submachine gun and semi-auto rifle.

The Manufacture of Gunflints, by Sydney B.J. Skertchly, facsimile reprint with new introduction by Seymour de Lotbiniere, Museum Restoration Service, Ontario, Canada, 1984. 90 pp., illus. $24.50

Limited edition reprinting of the very scarce London edition of 1879.

Master Tips, by J. Winokur, Potshot Press, Pacific Palisades, CA, 1985. 96 pp., illus. Paper covers. $11.95

Basics of practical shooting.

The Military and Police Sniper, by Mike R. Lau, Precision Shooting, Inc., Manchester, CT, 1998. 352 pp., illus. Paper covers. $44.95

Advanced precision shooting for combat and law enforcement.

Military Rifle & Machine Gun Cartridges, by Jean Huon, Paladin Press, Boulder, CO, 1990. 392 pp., illus. $34.95

Describes the primary types of military cartridges and their principal loadings, as well as their characteristics, origin and use.

Military Small Arms of the 20th Century, 7th Edition, by Ian V. Hogg and John Weeks, DBI Books, a division of Krause Publications, Iola, WI, 2000. 416 pp., illus. Paper covers. Over 800 photographs and illustrations. $24.95

Covers small arms of 46 countries.

Modern Custom Guns, Walnut, Steel, and Uncommon Artistry, by Tom Turpin, Krause Publications, Iola, WI, 1997. 206 pp., illus. $49.95

From exquisite engraving to breathtaking exotic woods, the mystique of today's custom guns is expertly detailed in word and awe-inspiring color photos of rifles, shotguns and handguns.

Modern Gun Values: 12th Edition, edited by Ken Ramage, Krause Publications, Iola, WI, 2003. Softcover. NEW. $21.95

Modern Machine Guns, by John Walter, Stackpole Books, Inc., Mechanicsburg, PA, 2000. 144 pp., with 146 illustrations. $22.95

A compact and authoritative guide to post-war machine-guns. A gun-by-gun directory identifying individual variants and types including detailed evaluations and technical data.

Modern Sporting Guns, by Christopher Austyn, Safari Press, Huntington Beach, CA, 1994. 128 pp., illus. $40.00

A discussion of the "best" English guns; round action, over-and-under, boxlocks, hammer guns, bolt action and double rifles as well as accessories.

The More Complete Cannoneer, by M.C. Switlik, Museum & Collectors Specialties Co., Monroe, MI, 1990. 199 pp., illus. $19.95

Compiled agreeably to the regulations for the U.S. War Department, 1861, and containing current observations on the use of antique cannons.

More Tactical Reality; Why There's No Such Thing as an Advanced Gunfight, by Louis Awerbuck, Boulder, CO, Paladin Press, 2004. 144 pp. Softcover. NEW. $25.00

The MP-40 Machine Gun, Desert Publications, El Dorado, AZ, 1995. 32 pp., illus. Paper covers. $11.95

A reprint of the hard-to-find operating and maintenance manual for one of the most famous machine guns of WWII.

Naval Percussion Locks and Primers, by Lt. J. A. Dahlgren, Museum Restoration Service, Bloomfield, Canada, 1996. 140 pp., illus. $35.00

First published as an Ordnance Memoranda in 1853, this is the finest existing study of percussion locks and primers origin and development.

The Official Soviet AKM Manual, translated by Maj. James F. Gebhardt (Ret.), Paladin Press, Boulder, CO, 1999. 120 pp., illus. Paper covers. $18.00

This official military manual, available in English for the first time, was originally published by the Soviet Ministry of Defence. Covers the history, function, maintenance, assembly and disassembly, etc. of the 7.62mm AKM assault rifle.

The One-Round War: U.S.M.C. Scout-Snipers in Vietnam, by Peter Senich, Paladin Press, Boulder, CO, 1996. 384 pp., illus. Paper covers $59.95

Sniping in Vietnam focusing specifically on the Marine Corps program.

Optics Digest: Scopes, Binoculars, Rangefinders, and Spotting Scopes, by Clair Rees, Long Beach, CA, Safari Press, 2005. 1st edition. 189 pp. Softcover. NEW. $24.95

OSS Special Operations in China, by Col. F. Mills and John W. Brunner, Williamstown, NJ, Phillips Publications, 2003. 1st edition. 550 pp., illustrated with photos. Hardcover. New in new dust jacket. $34.95

Paintball Digest The Complete Guide to Games, Gear, and Tactics, by Richard Sapp, lola, WI, Krause Publications, 2004. 1st edition. 272 pp. Softcover. NEW. $19.99

Paleo-Indian Artifacts: Identification & Value Guide, by Lar Hothem, Paducah, KY, Collector Books, 2005. 1st edition. 379 pp. Pictorial hardcover. NEW. $29.95

Panzer Aces German Tank Commanders of WWII, by Franz Kurowski, translated by David Johnston, Mechanicsburg, PA, Stackpole Books, 2004. 1st edition. 448 pp., 50 b&w photos Softcover. NEW. $19.95

Parker Brothers: Knight of the Trigger, by Ed Muderlak, Davis, IL, Old Reliable Publishing, 2002. 223 pp. $25.00

Knight of the Trigger tells the story of the Old West when Parker's most famous gun saleman traveled the country by rail, competing in the pigeon ring, hunting with the rich and famous, and selling the "Old Reliable" Parker shotgun. The life and times of Captain Arthur William du Bray, Parker Brothers' on-the-road sales agent from 1884 to 1926, is described in a novelized version of his interesting life.

Peril in the Powder Mills: Gunpowder & Its Men, by David McMahon & Anne Kelly Lane, West Conshohocken, PA, privately printed, 2004. 1st edition. 118 pp. Softcover. NEW. $18.95

Powder Horns and their Architecture; And Decoration as Used by the Soldier, Indian, Sailor and Traders of the Era, by Madison Grant, York, PA, privately printed, 1987. 165 pp., profusely illustrated. Hardcover. $45.00

Covers homemade pieces from the late eighteenth and early nineteenth centuries.

Practically Speaking: An Illustrated Guide - The Game, Guns and Gear of the International Defensive Pistol Association, by Walt Rauch, Lafayette Hills, PA, privately printed, 2002. 1st edition. 79 pp., illustrated with drawings and color photos. Softcover. $24.95

The game, guns and gear of the International Defensive Pistol Association with real-world applications.

ARMS LIBRARY

Present Sabers: A Popular History of the U.S. Horse Cavalry, by Allan T. Heninger, Tucson, AZ, Excalibur Publications, 2002. 1st edition. 160 pp., with 148 photographs, 45 illustrations and 4 charts. Softcover. $24.95

An illustrated history of America's involvement with the horse cavalry, from its earliest beginnings during the Revolutionary War through its demise in WWII. The book also contains several appendices, as well as depictions of the regular insignia of all the U.S. Cavalry units.

Principles of Personal Defense, by Jeff Cooper, Paladin Press, Boulder, CO, 1999. 56 pp., illus. Paper covers. $14.00

This revised edition of Jeff Cooper's classic on personal defense offers great new illustrations and a new preface while retaining the theory of individual defense behavior presented in the original book.

The Quotable Hunter, edited by Jay Cassell and Peter Fiduccia, The Lyons Press, N.Y., 1999. 224 pp., illus. $20.00

This collection of more than three hundred memorable quotes from hunters through the ages captures the essence of the sport, with all its joys idiosyncrasies, and challenges.

Renaissance Drill Book, by Jacob de Gheyn, edited by David J. Blackmore, Mechanicsburg, PA, Greenhill Books, 2003. 1st edition. 248 pp., 117 illustrations. Hardcover. $24.95

Jacob de Gheyn's Exercise of Armes was an immense success when first published in 1607. It is a fascinating 17th-century military manual, designed to instruct contemporary soldiers how to handle arms effectively, and correctly, and it makes for a unique glimpse into warfare as waged in the Thirty Years War and the English Civil War. In addition, detailed illustrations show the various movements and postures to be adopted during use of the pike.

A Rifleman Went to War, by H. W. McBride, Lancer Militaria, Mt. Ida, AR, 1987. 398 pp., illus. $29.95

The classic account of practical marksmanship on the battlefields of WWI.

Running Recon, A Photo Journey with SOG Special Ops Along the Ho Chi Minh Trail, by Frank Greco, Boulder, CO, Paladin Press, 2004. 1st edition. Hardcover. $79.95

Running Recon is a combination of military memoir and combat photography book. It reflects both the author's experience in Kontum, Vietnam, from April 1969 to April 1970 as part of the top-secret Studies and Observation Group (SOG) and the collective experience of SOG veterans in general. What sets it apart from other Vietnam books is its wealth of more than 700 photographs, many never before published, from the author's personal collection and those of his fellow SOG veterans.

Sharpshooting for Sport and War, by W.W. Greener, Wolfe Publishing Co., Prescott, AZ, 1995. 192 pp., illus. $30.00

This classic reprint explores the *first* expanding bullet; service rifles; shooting positions, trajectories; recoil; external ballistics; and other valuable information.

Shooting Buffalo Rifles of the Old West, by Mike Venturino, MLV Enterprises, Livingston, MT, 2002. 278 pp., illustrated with b&w photos. Softcover. $30.00

This tome will take you through the history, the usage, the many models, and the actual shooting (and how to's) of the many guns that saw service on the Frontier and are lovingly called "Buffalo Rifles" today. If you love to shoot your Sharps, Ballards, Remingtons, or Springfield "Trapdoors" for hunting or competition, or simply love Old West history, your library WILL NOT be complete without this latest book from Mike Venturino!

Shooting Colt Single Actions, by Mike Venturino, MLV Enterprises, Livingston, MT, 1997. 205 pp., illus. Softcover. $25.00

A complete examination of the Colt Single Action including styles, calibers and generations, b&w photos throughout.

Shooting Lever Guns of the Old West, by Mike Venturino, MLV Enterprises, Livingston, MT, 1999. 300 pp., illus. Softcover. $27.95

Shooting the lever action type repeating rifles of our American West.

Shooting Sixguns of the Old West, by Mike Venturino, MLV Enterprises, Livingston, MT, 1997. 221 pp., illus. Paper covers. $26.50

A comprehensive look at the guns of the early West: Colts, Smith & Wesson and Remingtons, plus blackpowder and reloading specs.

Shooting to Live, by Capt. W.E. Fairbairn and Capt. E.A. Sykes, Paladin Press, Boulder, CO, 1997. 4-1/2" x 7", soft cover, illus., 112 pp. $14.00

Shooting to Live is the product of Fairbairn's and Sykes' practical experience with the handgun. Hundreds of incidents provided the basis for the first true book on life-or-death shootouts with the pistol. Shooting to Live teaches all concepts, considerations and applications of combat pistol craft.

Small Arms of World War II, by Chris Chant, St. Paul, MN, MBI Publishing Company, 2001. 1st edition. 96 pp., single page on each weapon with photograph, description, and a specifications table. Hardcover. New. $13.95

Detailing the design and development of each weapon, this book covers the most important infantry weapons used by both Allied and Axis soldiers between 1939 and 1945. These include both standard infantry bolt-action rifles, such as the German Kar 98 and the British Lee-Enfield, plus the automatic rifles that entered service toward the end of the war, such as the Stg 43. As well as rifles, this book also features submachine guns, machine guns and handguns and a specifications table for each weapon.

Sniper Training, FM 23-10, Reprint of the U.S. Army field manual of August, 1994, Paladin Press, Boulder, CO, 1995. 352 pp., illus. Paper covers. $30.00

The most up-to-date U.S. military sniping information and doctrine.

Song of Blue Moccasin, by Roy Chandler, Jacksonville, NC, Ron Brigade Armory, 2004. 231 pp. Hardcover. New in new dust jacket. $45.00

Special Operations: Weapons and Tactics, by Timothy Mullin, London, Greenhill Press, 2003. 1st edition. 176 pp., with 189 illustrations. $39.95

The tactics and equipment of Special Forces explained in full, Contains 200 images of weaponry and training. This highly illustrated guide covers the full experience of special operations training from every possible angle. There is also considerable information on nonfirearm usage, such as specialized armor and ammunition.

Standard Catalog of Firearms, 15th Edition, by Ned Schwing, Iola, WI, Krause Publications, 2005. 1504 pp., illus. 7,000 b&w photos plus a 16-page color section. Paper covers. $34.95

This is the largest, most comprehensive and best-selling firearm book of all time! And this year's edition is a blockbuster for both shooters and firearm collectors. More than 14,000 firearms are listed and priced in up to six grades of condition. That's almost 100,000 prices! Gun enthusiasts will love the new full-color section of photos highlighting the finest firearms sold at auction this past year.

Standard Catalog of Military Firearms 2nd Edition: The Collector's Price & Reference Guide, by Ned Schwing, Iola, WI, Krause Publications, 2003. 448 pp. Softcover. $22.99

A companion volume to Standard Catalog of Firearms, this revised and expanded second edition comes complete with all the detailed information readers found useful and more. Listings beginning with the early cartridge models of the 1870s to the latest high-tech sniper rifles have been expanded to include more models, variations, historical information, and data, offering more detail for the military firearms collector, shooter, and history buff. Identification of specific firearms is easier with nearly 250 additional photographs. Plus, readers will enjoy "snap shots," small personal articles from experts relating real-life experiences with exclusive models. Revised to include every known military firearm available to the U.S. collector. Special feature articles on focused aspects of collecting and shooting.

Stress Fire, Vol. 1: Stress Fighting for Police, by Massad Ayoob, Police Bookshelf, Concord, NH, 1984. 149 pp., illus. Paper covers. $11.95

Gunfighting for police, advanced tactics and techniques.

Survival Guns, by Mel Tappan, Desert Publications, El Dorado, AZ, 1993. 456 pp., illus. Paper covers. $25.00

Discusses in a frank and forthright manner which handguns, rifles and shotguns to buy for personal defense and securing food, and the ones to avoid.

The Tactical Advantage, by Gabriel Suarez, Paladin Press, Boulder, CO, 1998. 216 pp., illus. Paper covers. $22.00

Learn combat tactics that have been tested in the world's toughest schools.

Tactical Marksman, by Dave M. Lauch, Paladin Press, Boulder, CO, 1996. 165 pp., illus. Paper covers. $35.00

A complete training manual for police and practical shooters.

Tim Murphy Rifleman Frontier Series Volume 3, by Roy Chandler, Jacksonville, NC, Iron Brigade Armory, 2003. 1st edition. 396 pp. Hardcover. $39.95

Tim Murphy may be our young nation's earliest recognized hero. Murphy was seized by Seneca Tribesmen during his infancy. Traded to the Huron, he was renamed and educated by Sir William Johnson, a British colonial officer. Freed during the prisoner exchange of 1764, Murphy discovered his superior ability with a Pennsylvania longrifle. An early volunteer in the Pennsylvania militia, Tim Murphy served valiantly in rifle companies including the justly famed Daniel Morgan's Riflemen. This is Murphy's story.

To Ride, Shoot Straight, and Speak the Truth, by Jeff Cooper, Paladin Press, Boulder, CO, 1997, 5-1/2" x 8-1/2", soft-cover, illus., 384 pp. $32.00

Combat mind-set, proper sighting, tactical residential architecture, nuclear war - these are some of the many subjects explored by Jeff Cooper in this illustrated anthology. The author discusses various arms, fighting skills and the importance of knowing how to defend oneself, and one's honor, in our rapidly changing world.

Trailriders Guide to Cowboy Action Shooting, by James W. Barnard, Pioneer Press, Union City, TN, 1998. 134 pp., plus 91 photos, drawings and charts. Paper covers. $24.95

Covers the complete spectrum of this shooting discipline, from how to dress to authentic leather goods, which guns are legal, calibers, loads and ballistics.

U.S. Marine Corp Rifle and Pistol Marksmanship, 1935, reprinting of a government publication, Lancer Militaria, Mt. Ida, AR, 1991. 99 pp., illus. Paper covers. $11.95

The old corps method of precision shooting.

U.S. Marine Corps Scout/Sniper Training Manual, Lancer Militaria, Mt. Ida, AR, 1989. Softcover. $27.95

Reprint of the original sniper training manual used by the Marksmanship Training Unit of the Marine Corps Development and Education Command in Quantico, Virginia.

U.S. Marine Corps Scout-Sniper, World War II and Korea, by Peter R. Senich, Paladin Press, Boulder, CO, 1994. 236 pp., illus. $44.95

The most thorough and accurate account ever printed on the training, equipment and combat experiences of the U.S. Marine Corps Scout-Snipers.

U.S. Marine Corps Sniping, Lancer Militaria, Mt. Ida, AR, 1989. Irregular pagination. Softcover. $18.95

A reprint of the official Marine Corps FMFM1-3B.

U.S. Marine Uniforms-1912-1940, by Jim Moran, Williamstown, NJ, Phillips Publications, 2001. 174 pp., illustrated with b&w photographs. Hardcover. $49.95

The Ultimate Sniper, by Major John L. Plaster, Paladin Press, Boulder, CO, 1994. 464 pp., illus. Paper covers. $49.95

An advanced training manual for military and police snipers.

Uniforms And Equipment of the Imperial Japanese Army in World War II, by Mike Hewitt, Atglen, PA, Schiffer Publications, 2002. 176 pp., with over 520 color and b&w photos. Hardcover. $59.95

Unrepentant Sinner, by Col. Charles Askins, Paladin Press, Boulder, CO, 2000. 322 pp., illus. $29.95

The autobiography of Colonel Charles Askins.

Vietnam Order of Battle, by Shelby L. Stanton, William C. Westmoreland, Mechanicsburg, PA, Stackpole Books, 2003. 1st edition. 416 pp., 32 in full color, 101 halftones. Hardcover. $69.95

A monumental, encyclopedic work of immense detail concerning U.S. Army and allied forces that fought in the Vietnam War from 1962 through 1973. Extensive lists of units providing a record of every Army unit that served in Vietnam, down to and including separate companies, and also including U.S. Army aviation and riverine units. Shoulder patches and distinctive unit insignia of all divisions and battalions. Extensive maps portraying unit locations at each six-month interval. Photographs and descriptions of all major types of equipment employed in the conflict. Plus much more!

Weapons of Delta Force, by Fred Pushies, St. Paul, MN, MBI Publishing Company, 2002. 1st edition. 128 pgs., 100 b&w and 100 color illustrated. Hardcover. $24.95

America's elite counter-terrorist organization, Delta Force, is a handpicked group of the U.S. Army's finest soldiers. Delta uses some of the most sophisticated weapons in the field today, and all are detailed in this book. Pistols, sniper rifles, special mission aircraft, fast attack vehicles, SCUBA and paratroper gear, and more are presented in this fully illustrated account of our country's heroes and their tools of the trade.

Weapons of the Waffen-SS, by Bruce Quarrie, Sterling Publishing Co., Inc., 1991. 168 pp., illus. $24.95

An in-depth look at the weapons that made Hitler's Waffen-SS the fearsome fighting machine it was.

ARMS LIBRARY

Weatherby: The Man, The Gun, The Legend, by Grits and Tom Gresham, Cane River Publishing Co., Natchitoches, LA, 1992. 290 pp., illus. $24.95
A fascinating look at the life of the man who changed the course of firearms development in America.

The Winchester Era, by David Madis, Art & Reference House, Brownsville, TX, 1984. 100 pp., illus. $19.95
Story of the Winchester company, management, employees, etc.

With British Snipers to the Reich, by Capt. C. Shore, Lander Militaria, Mt. Ida, AR, 1988. 420 pp., illus. $29.95
One of the greatest books ever written on the art of combat sniping.

The World's Machine Pistols and Submachine Guns - Vol. 2a 1964 to 1980, by Nelson & Musgrave, Ironside International, Alexandria, VA, 2000. 673 pp. $59.95
Containing data, history and photographs of over 200 weapons. With a special section covering shoulder stocked automatic pistols, 100 additional photos.

The World's Sniping Rifles, by Ian V. Hogg, Stackpole Books, Mechanicsburg, 1998. 144 pp., illus. $24.00
A detailed manual with descriptions and illustrations of more than 50 high-precision rifles from 14 countries and a complete analysis of sights and systems.

Wyatt Earp: A Biography of the Legend: Volume 1: The Cowtown Years, by Lee A. Silva, Santa Ana, CA, privately printed, 2002. 1st edition signed. Hardcover. New in new dust jacket. $86.95

GUNSMITHING

Accurizing the Factory Rifle, by M.L. McPhereson, Precision Shooting, Inc., Manchester, CT, 1999. 335 pp., illus. Paper covers. $44.95
A long-awaiting book, which bridges the gap between the rudimentary (mounting sling swivels, scope blocks and that general level of accomplishment) and the advanced (precision chambering, barrel fluting, and that general level of accomplishment) books that are currently available today.

The Art of Engraving, by James B. Meek, F. Brownell & Son, Montezuma, IA, 1973. 196 pp., illus. $42.95
A complete, authoritative, imaginative and detailed study in training for gun engraving. The first book of its kind–and a great one.

Checkering and Carving of Gun Stocks, by Monte Kennedy, Stackpole Books, Harrisburg, PA, 1962. 175 pp., illus. $39.95
Revised, enlarged cloth-bound edition of a much sought-after, dependable work.

Firearms Assembly/Disassembly, Part I: Automatic Pistols, 2nd Revised Edition, The Gun Digest Book of, by J.B. Wood, DBI Books, a division of Krause Publications, Iola, WI, 1999. 480 pp., illus. Paper covers. $24.95
Covers 58 popular autoloading pistols plus nearly 200 variants of those models integrated into the text and completely cross-referenced in the index.

Firearms Assembly/Disassembly Part II: Revolvers, Revised Edition, The Gun Digest Book of, by J.B. Wood, DBI Books, a division of Krause Publications, Iola, WI, 1997. 480 pp., illus. Paper covers. $27.95
Covers 49 popular revolvers plus 130 variants. The most comprehensive and professional presentation available to either hobbyist or gunsmith.

Firearms Assembly/Disassembly Part III: Rimfire Rifles, Revised Edition, The Gun Digest Book of, by J. B. Wood, DBI Books, a division of Krause Publications, Iola, WI, 1994. 480 pp., illus. Paper covers. $19.95
Greatly expanded edition covering 65 popular rimfire rifles plus over 100 variants all completely cross-referenced in the index.

Firearms Assembly/Disassembly Part IV: Centerfire Rifles, 3rd Revised Edition, The Gun Digest Book of, by J.B. Wood, Krause Publications, Iola, WI, 2004. 480 pp., illus. Paper covers. $24.95
Covers 54 popular centerfire rifles plus 300 variants. The most comprehensive and professional presentation available to either hobbyist or gunsmith.

Firearms Assembly/Disassembly, Part V: Shotguns, Revised Edition, The Gun Digest Book of, by J.B. Wood, Krause Publications, Iola, WI, 2002. 480 pp., illus. Paper covers. $24.95
Covers 46 popular shotguns plus over 250 variants with step-by-step instructions on how to dismantle and reassemble each. The most comprehensive and professional presentation available to either hobbyist or gunsmith.

Firearms Assembly 3: The NRA Guide to Rifle and Shotguns, NRA Books, Wash., DC, 1980. 264 pp., illus. Paper covers. $14.95
Text and illustrations explaining the takedown of 125 rifles and shotguns, domestic and foreign.

Firearms Assembly 4: The NRA Guide to Pistols and Revolvers, NRA Books, Wash., DC, 1980. 253 pp., illus. Paper covers. $14.95
Text and illustrations explaining the takedown of 124 pistol and revolver models, domestic and foreign.

Firearms Bluing and Browning, by R.H. Angier, Stackpole Books, Harrisburg, PA. 151 pp., illus. $19.95
A world master gunsmith reveals his secrets of building, repairing and renewing a gun, quite literally, lock, stock and barrel. A useful, concise text on chemical coloring methods for the gunsmith and mechanic.

Guns and Gunmaking Tools of Southern Appalachia, by John Rice Irwin, Schiffer Publishing Ltd., 1983. 118 pp., illus. Paper covers. $9.95
The story of the Kentucky rifle.

Gunsmith Kinks, by F.R. (Bob) Brownell, F. Brownell & Son, Montezuma, IA, 1st ed., 1969. 496 pp., well illus. $22.98
A widely useful accumulation of shop kinks, short cuts, techniques and pertinent comments by practicing gunsmiths from all over the world.

Gunsmith Kinks 2, by Bob Brownell, F. Brownell & Son, Publishers, Montezuma, IA, 1983. 496 pp., illus. $22.95
A collection of gunsmithing knowledge, shop kinks, new and old techniques, shortcuts and general know-how straight from those who do them best–the gunsmiths.

Gunsmith Kinks 3, edited by Frank Brownell, Brownells Inc., Montezuma, IA, 1993. 504 pp., illus. $24.95
Tricks, knacks and "kinks" by professional gunsmiths and gun tinkerers. Hundreds of valuable ideas are given in this volume.

Gunsmith Kinks 4, edited by Frank Brownell, Brownells Inc., Montezuma, IA, 2001. 564 pp., illus. $27.75
332 detailed illustrations. 560+ pages with 706 separate subject headings and over 5000 cross-indexed entries. An incredible gold mine of information.

The Gunsmith of Grenville County: Building the American Longrifle, by Peter Alexander, Texarkana, TX, Scurlock Publishing Co., 2002. 400 pp.in, with hundreds of illustrations, and six color photos of original rifles. Stiff paper covers. $45.00
The most extensive how-to book on building longrifles ever published. Takes you through every step of building your own longrifle, from shop set up and tools to engraving, carving and finishing.

Gunsmithing, by Roy F. Dunlap, Stackpole Books, Harrisburg, PA, 1990. 742 pp., illus. $34.95
A manual of firearm design, construction, alteration and remodeling. For amateur and professional gunsmiths and users of modern firearms.

Gunsmithing at Home: Lock, Stock and Barrel, by John Traister, Stoeger Publishing Co., Wayne, NJ, 1997. 320 pp., illus. Paper covers. $19.95
A complete step-by-step fully illustrated guide to the art of gunsmithing.

Gunsmithing Shotguns: The Complete Guide to Care & Repair, by David Henderson, New York, Globe Pequot, 2003. 1st edition. Hardcover. NEW. $24.95

Gunsmithing Tips and Projects, a collection of the best articles from the *Handloader* and *Rifle* magazines, by various authors, Wolfe Publishing Co., Prescott, AZ, 1992. 443 pp., illus. Paper covers. $25.00
Includes such subjects as shop, stocks, actions, tuning, triggers, barrels, customizing, etc.

Gunsmithing: Guns of the Old West: Expanded 2nd Edition, by David Chicoine, Iola, WI, Krause Publications, 2004. 446 pp.in, illus. Softcover. NEW. $29.95

Gunsmithing: Pistols & Revolvers: Expanded 2nd Edition, by Patrick Sweeney, Iola, WI, Krause Publications, 2004. Softcover, NEW. $19.99

Gunsmithing: Rifles, by Patrick Sweeney, Krause Publications, Iola, WI, 1999. 352 pp., illus. Paper covers. $24.95
Tips for lever-action rifles. Building a custom Ruger 10/22. Building a better hunting rifle.

Home Gunsmithing the Colt Single Action Revolvers, by Loren W. Smith, Ray Riling Arms Books, Co., Phila., PA, 2001. 119 pp., illus. $29.95
Affords the Colt Single Action owner detailed, pertinent information on the operating and servicing of this famous and historic handgun.

How to Convert Military Rifles, Williams Gun Sight Co., Davision, MI, new and enlarged seventh edition, 1997. 76 pp., illus. Paper covers. $13.95
This latest edition updated the changes that have occured over the past thirty years. Tips, instructions and illustratons on how to convert popular military rifles as the Enfield, Mauser 96 and SKS just to name a few are presented.

Mauser M98 & M96, by R.A. Walsh, Wolfe Publishing Co., Prescott, AR, 1998. 123 pp., illus. Paper covers. $32.50
How to build your own favorite custom Mauser rifle from two of the best bolt action rifle designs ever produced–the military Mauser Model 1898 and Model 1896 bolt rifles.

Mr. Single Shot's Gunsmithing-Idea-Book, by Frank de Haas, Mark de Haas, Orange City, IA, 1996. 168 pp., illus. Paper covers. $22.50
Offers easy to follow, step-by-step instructions for a wide variety of gunsmithing procedures all reinforced by plenty of photos.

Professional Stockmaking, by D. Wesbrook, Wolfe Publishing Co., Prescott, AZ, 1995. 308 pp., illus. $54.00
A step-by-step how-to with complete photographic support for every detail of the art of working wood into riflestocks.

Recreating the American Longrifle, by William Buchele, et al, George Shumway Publisher, York, Pa, 5th edition, 1999. 175 pp., illus. $40.00
Includes full size plans for building a Kentucky rifle.

The Story of Pope's Barrels, by Ray M. Smith, R&R Books, Livonia, NY, 1993. 203 pp., illus. $39.00
A reissue of a 1960 book whose author knew Pope personally. It will be of special interest to Schuetzen rifle fans, since Pope's greatest days were at the height of the Schuetzen-era before WWI.

Survival Gunsmithing, by J.B. Wood, Desert Publications, Cornville, AZ, 1986. 92 pp., illus. Paper covers. $11.95
A guide to repair and maintenance of the most popular rifles, shotguns and handguns.

The Tactical 1911, by Dave Lauck, Paladin Press, Boulder, CO, 1998. 137 pp., illus. Paper covers. $20.00
Here is the only book you will ever need to teach you how to select, modify, employ and maintain your Colt.

HANDGUNS

.22 Caliber Handguns; A Shooter's Guide, by D.F. Geiger, Lincoln, RI, Andrew Mowbray, Inc., 2003. 1st edition. Softcover. $21.95

The .380 Enfield No. 2 Revolver, by Mark Stamps and Ian Skennerton, I.D.S.A. Books, Piqua, OH, 1993. 124 pp., 80 illus. Paper covers. $19.95

9mm Parabellum; The History & Development of the World's 9mm Pistols & Ammunition, by Klaus-Peter Konig and Martin Hugo, Schiffer Publishing Ltd., Atglen, PA, 1993. 304 pp., illus. $39.95
Detailed history of 9mm weapons from Belguim, Italy, Germany, Israel, France, U.S.A., Czechoslovakia, Hungary, Poland, Brazil, Finland and Spain.

Advanced Master Handgunning, by Charles Stephens, Paladin Press, Boulder, CO, 1994. 72 pp., illus. Paper covers. $14.00
Secrets and surefire techniques for winning handgun competitions.

Advanced Tactical Marksman More High Performance Techniques for Police, Military, and Practical Shooters, by Dave M. Lauck. Paladin Press, Boulder, CO, 2002. 1st edition. 232 pp., photos, illus. Softcover $35.00
Lauck, one of the most respected names in high-performance shooting and gunsmithing, refines and updates his 1st book. Dispensing with overcomplicated mil-dot formulas and minute-of-angle calculations, Lauck shows you how to achieve superior accuracy and figure out angle shots, train for real-world scenarios, choose optics and accessories.

American Beauty: The Prewar Colt National Match Government Model Pistol, by Timothy Mullin, Collector Grade Publications, Canada, 1999. 72 pp., 69 illus. $34.95
69 illustrations, 20 in full color photos of factory engraved guns and other authenticated upgrades, including rare 'double-carved' ivory grips.

ARMS LIBRARY

The Automatic Pistol, by J.B.L. Noel, Foreword by Timothy J. Mullin, Boulder, CO, Paladin Press, 2004. 128 pp., illus. Softcover. NEW. $14.00

The Ayoob Files: The Book, by Massad Ayoob, Police Bookshelf, Concord, NH, 1995. 223 pp., illus. Paper covers. $14.95

The best of Massad Ayoob's acclaimed series in *American Handgunner* magazine.

The Belgian Browning Pistols 1889-1949, by Anthony Vanderlinden, Wet Dog Publications, Geensboro, NC 2001. Limited edition of 2000 copies, signed by the author. 243 pp. plus index. Illustrated with b&w photos. Hardcover. $65.00

Includes the 1899 Compact, 1899 Large, 1900, 1903, Grand Browning, 1910, 1922 Grand Rendement and high power pistols. Also includes a chapter on holsters.

Big Bore Handguns, by John Taffin, Krause Publications, Iola, WI, 2002. 1st edition. 352 pp., 320 b&w photos with a 16-page color section. Hardcover. $39.95

Gives honest reviews and an inside look at shooting, hunting, and competing with the biggest handguns around. Covers handguns from major gunmakers, as well as handgun customizing, accessories, reloading, and cowboy activities. Significant coverage is also given to handgun customizing, accessories, reloading, and popular shooting hobbies including hunting and cowboy activities.

Big Bore Sixguns, by John Taffin, Krause Publications, Iola, WI, 1997. 336 pp., illus. $39.95

The author takes aim on the entire range of big bores from .357 Magnums to .500 Maximums, single actions and cap-and-ball sixguns to custom touches for big bores.

Bill Ruger's .22 Pistol: A Photographic Essay of the Ruger Rimfire Pistol, by Don Findlay, New York, Simon & Schuster, 2000. 2nd printing. Hardcover, NEW. $100.00

The Browning High Power Automatic Pistol (Expanded Edition), by Blake R. Stevens, Collector Grade Publications, Canada, 1996. 310 pp., with 313 illus. $49.95

An in-depth chronicle of seventy years of High Power history, from John M. Browning's original 16-shot prototypes to the present. Profusely illustrated with rare original photos and drawings from the FN Archive to describe virtually every sporting and military version of the High Power. The Expanded Edition contains 30 new pages on the interesting Argentine full-auto High Power, the latest FN 'MK3' and BDA9 pistols, plus FN's revolutionary P90 5.7x28mm Personal Defense Weapon, and more!

Browning Hi-Power Pistols, Desert Publications, Cornville, AZ, 1982. 20 pp., illus. Paper covers. $11.95

Covers all facets of the various military and civilian models of the Browning Hi-Power pistol.

Canadian Military Handguns 1855-1985, by Clive M. Law, Museum Restoration Service, Bloomfield, Ont., Canada, 1994. 130pp., illus. $40.00

A long-awaited and important history for arms historians and pistol collectors.

Collecting U. S. Pistols & Revolvers, 1909-1945, by J. C. Harrison. The Arms Chest, Oklahoma City, OK, 1999. 2nd edition (revised). 185 pp., illus. Spiral bound. $35.00

Valuable and detailed reference book for the collector of U.S. pistols & revolvers. Identifies standard issue original military models of the M1911, M1911A1 and M1917 Cal .45 pistols and revolvers as produced by all manufacturers from 1911 through 1945. Plus .22 Ace models, National Match models, and similar foreign military models produced by Colt or manufactured under Colt license, plus arsenal repair, refinish and lend-lease models.

The Colt .45 Auto Pistol, compiled from U.S. War Dept. Technical Manuals, and reprinted by Desert Publications, Cornville, AZ, 1978. 80 pp., illus. Paper covers. $12.95

Covers every facet of this famous pistol from mechanical training, manual of arms, disassembly, repair and replacement of parts.

Colt Single Action Army Revolver Study: New Discoveries, by Kenneth Moore, Lincoln, RI, Andrew Mowbray, Inc., 2003. 1st edition. Hardcover. NEW. $47.95

The Combat Perspective; The Thinking Man's Guide to Self-Defense, by Gabriel Suarez, Boulder, CO, Paladin Press, 2003. 1st edition. 112 pp. Softcover. $15.00

In The Combat Perspective, Suarez keys in on developing your knowledge about and properly organizing your mental attitude toward combat to improve your odds of winning – not just surviving – such a fight. The principles are as applicable to the bladesman as they are to the rifleman, to the unarmed fighter as they are to the sniper. In this book he examines each in a logical and scientific manner, demonstrating why, when it comes to defending your life, the mental edge is at least as critical to victory as the tactical advantage.

Complete Encyclopedia of Pistols & Revolvers, by A.E. Hartnik, Knickerbocker Press, New York, NY, 2003. 272 pp., illus. $19.95

A comprehensive encyclopedia specially written for collectors and owners of pistols and revolvers.

Concealable Pocket Pistols: How to Choose and Use Small-Caliber Handguns, by Terence McLeod, Paladin Press, 2001. 1st edition. 80 pp. Softcover. $14.00

Small-caliber handguns are often maligned as too puny for serious self-defense, but millions of Americans own and carry these guns and have used them successfully to stop violent assaults. This is the first book ever devoted to eliminating the many misconceptions about the usefulness of these popular guns. Find out what millions of Americans already know about these practical self-defense tools.

The Custom Government Model Pistol, by Layne Simpson, Wolfe Publishing Co., Prescott, AZ, 1994. 639 pp., illus. Paper covers. $26.95

The book about one of the world's greatest firearms and the things pistolsmiths do to make it even greater.

The Custom Revolver, by Hamilton S. Bowen, Foreword by Ross Seyfried. Louisville, TN, privately printed, 2001. 1st edition. New in new dust jacket. $49.95

The Darling Pepperbox: The Story of Samuel Colt's Forgotten Competitors in Bellingham, Mass. and Woonsocket, RI, by Stuart C. Mowbray, Lincoln, RI, Andrew Mowbray, Inc., 2004. 1st edition. 104 pp. Softcover. NEW. $19.95

Developmental Cartridge Handguns of .22 Calibre, as Produced in the United States & Abroad from 1855 to 1875, by John S. Laidacker, Atglen, PA, Schiffer Publications, 2003. Reprint. 597 pp., with over 860 b&w photos, drawings, and charts. Hardcover. $100.00

This book is a reprint edition of the late John Laidacker's personal study of early .22 Cartridge Handguns from 1855-1875. Laidacker's primary aim was to offer a quick reference to the collector, and his commentary on the wide variety of types, variations and makers, as well as detailed photography, make this a superb addition to any firearm library.

Engraved Handguns of .22 Calibre, by John S. Laidacker, Atglen, PA, Schiffer Publications, 2003. 1st edition. 192 pp., with over 400 color and b&w photos. $69.95

The Farnam Method of Defensive Handgunning, by John S. Farnam, Police Bookshelf, 1999. 191 pp., illus. Paper covers. $24.00

A book intended to not only educate the new shooter, but also to serve as a guide and textbook for his and his instructor's training courses.

Fast and Fancy Revolver Shooting, by Ed McGivern, Anniversary Edition, Winchester Press, Piscataway, NJ, 1984. 484 pp., illus. $19.95

A fascinating volume, packed with handgun lore and solid information by the acknowledged dean of revolver shooters.

German Handguns: The Complete Book of the Pistols and Revolvers of Germany, 1869 to the Present, by Ian Hogg, Greenhill Publishing, 2001. 320 pp., 270 illustrations. Hardcover. $49.95

Ian Hogg examines the full range of handguns produced in Germany from such classics as the Luger M1908, Mauser HsC and Walther PPK, to more unusual types such as the Reichsrevolver M1879 and the Dreyse 9mm. He presents the key data (length, weight, muzzle velocity, and range) for each weapon discussed and also gives its date of introduction and service record, evaluates and discusses peculiarities, and examines in detail particular strengths and weaknesses.

Glock: The New Wave in Combat Handguns, by Peter Alan Kasler, Paladin Press, Boulder, CO, 1993. 304 pp., illus. $27.00

Kasler debunks the myths that surround what is the most innovative handgun to be introduced in some time.

Glock's Handguns, by Duncan Long, Desert Publications, El Dorado, AR, 1996. 180 pp., illus. Paper covers. $19.95

An outstanding volume on one of the world's newest and most successful firearms of the century.

Greenhill Military Manual: Combat Handguns, by Leroy Thompson, London, Greenhill Publishing, 2004. 1st edition Hardcover. NEW. $24.00

Gun Digest Book of Combat Handgunnery 5th Edition, Complete Guide to Combat Shooting, by Massad Ayoob, lola, WI, Krause Publications, 2002. Softcover. NEW. $19.95

The Gun Digest Book of the 1911, by Patrick Sweeney, Krause Publications, Iola, WI, 2002. 336 pp., with 700 b&w photos. Softcover. $27.95

Complete guide of all models and variations of the Model 1911. The author also includes repair tips and information on buying a used 1911.

Gun Digest Book of the Glock; A Comprehensive Review, Design, History and Use, Iola, WI, Krause Publications, 2003. 1st edition. 303 pp., with 500 b&w photos. Softcover. 24.95

Examine the rich history and unique elements of the most important and influential firearms design of the past 50 years, the Glock autoloading pistol. This comprehensive review of the revolutionary pistol analyzes the performance of the various models and chamberings and features a complete guide to available accessories and little-known factory options. You'll see why it's the preferred pistol for law enforcement use and personal protection.

Hand Cannons: The World's Most Powerful Handguns, by Duncan Long, Paladin Press, Boulder, CO, 1995. 208 pp., illus. Paper covers. $22.00

Long describes and evaluates each powerful gun according to their features.

Handgun Stopping Power "The Definitive Study," by Evan P. Marshall & Edwin J. Sanow, Paladin Press, Boulder, CO, 1997. 240 pp. photos. Softcover. $45.00

Dramatic first-hand accounts of the results of handgun rounds fired into criminals by cops, storeowners, cabbies and others are the heart and soul of this long-awaited book. This is the definitive methodology for predicting the stopping power of handgun loads, the first to take into account what really happens when a bullet meets a man.

Handguns 2005: 17th Edition, edited by Ken Ramage, lola, WI, Krause Publications, 2004. Softcover. NEW. $24.99

Target shooters, handgun hunters, collectors and those who rely upon handguns for self-defense will want to pack this value-loaded and entertaining volume in their home libraries. Shooters will find the latest pistol and revolver designs and accessories, plus test reports on several models. The handgun becomes an artist's canvas in a showcase of engraving talents. The catalog section–with comprehensive specs on every known handgun in production–includes a new display of semi-custom handguns, plus an expanded, illustrated section on the latest grips, sights, scopes and other aiming devices. Offer easy access to products, services and manufacturers.

Handguns of the Armed Organizations of the Soviet Occupation Zone and German Democratic Republic, by Dieter H. Marschall, Los Alamos, NM, Ucross Books, 2000. Softcover. NEW. $29.95

Translated from German this groundbreaking treatise covers the period from May 1945 through 1996. The organizations that used these pistols are described along with the guns and holsters. Included are the P08, P38, PP, PPK, P1001, PSM, Tokarev, Makarov, (including .22 LR, cutaway, silenced, Suhl marked), Stechlin, plus Hungarian, Romanian and Czech pistols.

Heckler & Koch's Handguns, by Duncan Long, Desert Publications, El Dorado, AR, 1996. 142 pp., illus. Paper covers. $19.95

Traces the history and the evolution of H&K's pistols from the company's beginning at the end of WWII to the present.

Hidden in Plain Sight, by Trey Bloodworth & Mike Raley, Professional Press, Chapel Hill, NC, 1995. Paper covers. $19.95

A practical guide to concealed handgun carry.

High Standard: A Collectors Guide to the Hamden & Hartford Target Pistols, by Tom Dance, Andrew Mowbray, Inc., Lincoln, RI, 1999. 192 pp., heavily illustrated with b&w photographs and technical drawings. $24.00

From Citation to Supermatic, all of the production models and specials made from 1951 to 1984 are covered according to model number or series, making it easy to understand the evolution to this favorite of shooters and collectors.

High Standard Automatic Pistols 1932-1950, by Charles E. Petty, The Gun Room Press, Highland Park, NJ, 1989. 124 pp., illus. $14.95

A definitive source of information for the collector of High Standard arms.

Hi-Standard Pistols and Revolvers, 1951-1984, by James Spacek, Chesire, CT, 1998. 128 pp., illus. Paper covers. $4.95

Technical details, marketing features and instruction/parts manual of every model High Standard pistol and revolver made between 1951 and 1984. Most accurate serial number information available.

ARMS LIBRARY

History of Smith & Wesson Firearms, by Dean Boorman, New York, Lyons Press, 2002. 1st edition. 144 pp., illustrated in full color. Hardcover. $29.95

The definitive guide to one of the world's best-known firearms makers. Takes the story through the years of the Military & Police .38 & of the Magnum cartridge, to today's wide range of products for law-enforcement customers.

How to Become a Master Handgunner: The Mechanics of X-Count Shooting, by Charles Stephens, Paladin Press, Boulder, CO, 1993. 64 pp., illus. Paper covers. $14.00

Offers a simple formula for success to the handgunner who strives to master the technique of shooting accurately.

The Inglis Diamond: The Canadian High Power Pistol, by Clive M. Law, Collector Grade Publications, Canada, 2001. 312 pp., illus. $49.95

This definitive work on Canada's first and indeed only mass produced handgun, in production for a very brief span of time and consequently made in relatively few numbers, the venerable Inglis-made Browning High Power covers the pistol's initial history, the story of Chinese and British adoption, use post-war by Holland, Australia, Greece, Belgium, New Zealand, Peru, Brasil and other countries. All new information on the famous light-weights and the Inglis Diamond variations. Completely researched through official archives in a dozen countries. Many of the bewildering variety of markings have never been satisfactorily explained until now

Japanese Military Cartridge Handguns 1893-1945, A Revised and Expanded Edition of Hand Cannons of Imperial Japan, by Harry L. Derby III and James D. Brown, Atglen, PA, Schiffer Publications, 2003. 1st edition. Hardcover. New in new dust jacket. $79.95

When originally published in 1981, The Hand Cannons of Imperial Japan was heralded as one of the most readable works on firearms ever produced. To arms collectors and scholars, it remains a prized source of information on Japanese handguns, their development, and their history. In this new Revised and Expanded edition, original author Harry Derby has teamed with Jim Brown to provide a thorough update reflecting twenty years of additional research. An appendix on valuation has also been added, using a relative scale that should remain relevant despite inflationary pressures. For the firearms collector, enthusiast, historian or dealer, this is the most complete and up-to-date work on Japanese military handguns ever written.

Know Your 45 Auto Pistols–Models 1911 & A1, by E.J. Hoffschmidt, Blacksmith Corp., Southport, CT, 1974. 58 pp., illus. Paper covers. $14.95

A concise history of the gun with a wide variety of types and copies.

Know Your Ruger Single Actions: The Second Decade 1963-1973, by John C. Dougan, Blacksmith Corp., North Hampton, OH, 1994. 143 pp., illus. Paper covers. $19.95

Know Your Ruger S/A Revolvers 1953-1963 (revised edition), by John C. Dougan. Blacksmith Corp., North Hampton, OH, 2002. 191 pp., illus. Paper covers. $19.95

Know Your Walther P38 Pistols, by E.J. Hoffschmidt, Blacksmith Corp., Southport, CT, 1974. 77 pp., illus. Paper covers. $14.95

Covers the Walther models Armee, M.P., H.P., P.38–history and variations.

Know Your Walther PP & PPK Pistols, by E.J. Hoffschmidt, Blacksmith Corp., Southport, CT, 1975. 87 pp., illus. Paper covers. $14.95

A concise history of the guns with a guide to the variety and types.

La Connaissance du Luger, Tome 1, (The Knowledge of Luger, Volume 1, translated), by Gerard Henrotin, H & L Publishing, Belguim, 1996. b&w and color photos. French text. 144 pp., illus. $45.00

Living with Glocks: The Complete Guide to the New Standard in Combat Handguns, by Robert H. Boatman, Boulder, CO, Paladin Press, 2002. 1st edition. 184 pp., illus. Hardcover. $29.95

In addition to demystifying the enigmatic Glock trigger, Boatman describes and critiques each Glock model in production. Separate chapters on the G36, the enhanced G20 and the full-auto G18 emphasize the job-specific talents of these standout models for those seeking insight on which Glock pistol might best meet their needs. And for those interested in optimizing their Glock's capabilities, this book addresses all the peripherals–holsters, ammo, accessories, silencers, modifications and conversions, training programs and more.

Luger Artiglieria: (The Luger Artillery: From the Prototypes up to the Mauser Commemorative, the History and the Accessories), by Mauro Baudino, Italy, Editoriale Olimpia, 2003. 1st edition. Softcover. NEW. $31.95

The Luger Handbook, by Aarron Davis, Krause Publications, Iola, WI, 1997. 112 pp., illus. Paper covers. $9.95

Now you can identify any of the legendary Luger variations using a simple decision tree. Each model and variation includes pricing information, proof marks and detailed attributes in a handy, user-friendly format. Plus, it's fully indexed. Instantly identify that Luger!

The Luger Story, by John Walter, Stackpole Books, Mechanicsburg, PA, 2001. 256 pp., illus. Paper covers. $19.95

The standard history of the world's most famous handgun.

Lugers at Random (Revised Format Edition), by Charles Kenyon Jr., Handgun Press, Glenview, IL, 2000. 420 pp., illus. $59.95

A new printing of this classic, comprehensive reference for all Luger collectors.

The Mauser Self-Loading Pistol, by Belford & Dunlap, Borden Publishing Co., Alhambra, CA. Over 200 pp., 300 illus., large format. $29.95

The long-awaited book on the "Broom Handles," covering their inception in 1894 to the end of production. Complete and in detail: pocket pistols, Chinese and Spanish copies.

Mental Mechanics of Shooting: How to Stay Calm at the Center, by Vishnu Karmakar and Thomas Whitney, Littleton, CO, Center Vision, Inc., 2001. 144 pp. Softcover. $19.95

Not only will this book help you stay free of trigger jerk, it will help you in all areas of your shooting.

Model 1911 Automatic Pistol, by Robert Campbell, Accokeek, Maryland, Stoeger Publications, 2004. Hardcover. NEW. $24.95

Modern Law Enforcement Weapons & Tactics, 3rd Edition, by Patrick Sweeney, lola, WI, Krause Publications, 2004. 256 pp. Softcover. NEW. $22.99

The Official 9mm Markarov Pistol Manual, translated into English by Major James Gebhardt, U.S. Army (Ret.), Desert Publications, El Dorado, AR, 1996. 84 pp., illus. Paper covers. $14.95

The information found in this book will be of enormous benefit and interest to the owner or a prospective owner of one of these pistols.

The Operator's Tactical Pistol Shooting Manual; A Practical Guide to Combat Marksmanship, by Erik Lawrence, Linesville, PA, Blackheart Publishing, 2003. 1st edition. 233 pp. Softcover. $24.50

This manual-type book begins with the basics of safety with a pistol and progresses into advanced pistol handling. A self-help guide for improving your capabilities with a pistol at your own pace.

The P08 Luger Pistol, by de Vries & Martens, Alexandria, VA, Ironside International, 2002. 152 pp., illustrated with 200 high quality b&w photos. Hardcover. $34.95

Covers all essential information on history and development, ammunition and accessories, codes and markings, and contains photos of nearly every model and accessory. Includes a unique selection of original German WWII propoganda photos, most never published before.

The P-08 Parabellum Luger Automatic Pistol, edited by J. David McFarland, Desert Publications, Cornville, AZ, 1982. 20 pp., illus. Paper covers. $14.95

Covers every facet of the Luger, plus a listing of all known Luger models.

The P-38 Pistol: Postwar Distributions, 1945-1990. Volume 3, by Warren Buxton, Ucross Books, Los Alamos, MN 1999, plus an addendum to Volumes 1 & 2. 272 pp. with 342 illustrations. $68.50

The P-38 Pistol: The Contract Pistols, 1940-1945. Volume 2., by Warren Buxton, Ucross Books, Los Alamos, MN 1999. 256 pp. with 237 illustrations. $68.50

The P-38 Pistol: The Walther Pistols, 1930-1945. Volume 1, by Warren Buxton, Ucross Books, Los Alamos, MN 1999. $68.50

A limited run reprint of this scarce and sought-after work on the P-38 Pistol. 328 pp. with 160 illustrations.

Pistols of World War I, by Robert J. Adamek, Pittsburgh, Pentagon Press, 2001. 1st edition signed and numbered. Over 90 pistols illustrated, technical data, designers, history, proof marks. 296 pp. with illustrations and photos. Softcover. $45.00

Over 25 pistol magazines illustrated with dimensions, serial number ranges. Over 35 cartridges illustrated with dimensions, manufactures, year of introduction. Weapons from 16 countries involved in WWI, statistics, quantities made, identification.

The Ruger .22 Automatic Pistol, Standard/Mark I/Mark II Series, by Duncan Long, Paladin Press, Boulder, CO, 1989. 168 pp., illus. Paper covers. $16.00

The definitive book about the pistol that has served more than 1 million owners so well.

Ruger .22 Automatic Pistols: The Complete Guide for all Models from 1947 to 2003, Grand Rapids, MI, The Ruger Store, 2004. 74 pp., 66 high-resolution grayscale images. Printed in the U.S.A. with card stock cover and bright white paper. Softcover. NEW. $12.95

Includes 'rare' complete serial numbers and manufacturing dates from 1949-2004.

The Ruger "P" Family of Handguns, by Duncan Long, Desert Publications, El Dorado, AZ, 1993. 128 pp., illus. Paper covers. $14.95

A full-fledged documentary on a remarkable series of Sturm Ruger handguns.

The Semiautomatic Pistols in Police Service and Self Defense, by Massad Ayoob, Police Bookshelf, Concord, NH, 1990. 25 pp., illus. Softcover. $11.95

First quantitative, documented look at actual police experience with 9mm and 45 police service automatics.

Shooting Colt Single Actions, by Mike Venturino, Livingston, MT, 1997. 205 pp., illus. Paper covers. $25.00

A definitive work on the famous Colt SAA and the ammunition it shoots.

Sig Handguns, by Duncan Long, Desert Publications, El Dorado, AZ, 1995. 150 pp., illus. Paper covers. $19.95

The history of Sig/Sauer handguns, including Sig, Sig-Hammerli and Sig/Sauer variants.

Sixgun Cartridges and Loads, by Elmer Keith, reprint edition by The Gun Room Press, Highland Park, NJ, 1984. 151 pp., illus. $24.95

A manual covering the selection, use and loading of the most suitable and popular revolver cartridges.

Sixguns, by Elmer Keith, Wolfe Publishing Company, Prescott, AZ, 1992. 336 pp. Paper covers. $29.95. Hardcover $35.00

The history, selection, repair, care, loading, and use of this historic frontiersman's friend–the one-hand firearm.

Smith & Wesson's Automatics, by Larry Combs, Desert Publications, El Dorado, AZ, 1994. 143 pp., illus. Paper covers. $19.95

A must for every S&W auto owner or prospective owner.

Spanish Handguns: The History of Spanish Pistols and Revolvers, by Gene Gangarosa Jr., Stoeger Publishing Co., Accokeek, MD, 2001. 320 pp., illustrated, b&w photos. Paper covers. $21.95

Standard Catalog of Smith & Wesson, 2nd Edition, by Jim Supica and Richard Nahas, Krause Publications, Iola, WI, 2001. 272 pp., 350 b&w photos, with 16-page color section. Pictorial hardcover. $34.95

Clearly details 775 Smith & Wesson models, knives, holsters, ammunition and police items with complete pricing information, illustrated glossary and index.

Star Firearms, by Leonardo M. Antaris, Davenport, TA, Firac Publications Co., 2002. 1st edition. Hardcover. New in new dust jacket. $119.95

Street Stoppers: The Latest Handgun Stopping Power Street Results, by Evan P. Marshall and Edwin J. Sandow, Paladin Press, Boulder, CO, 1997. 392 pp., illus. Paper covers. $42.95

Compilation of the results of real-life shooting incidents involving every major handgun caliber.

The Tactical 1911, by Dave Lauck, Paladin Press, Boulder, CO, 1999. 152 pp., illus. Paper covers. $22.00

The cop's and SWAT operator's guide to employment and maintenance.

The Tactical Pistol, by Gabriel Suarez, Foreword by Jeff Cooper, Paladin Press, Boulder, CO, 1996. 216 pp., illus. Paper covers. $25.00

Advanced gunfighting concepts and techniques.

The Thompson/Center Contender Pistol, by Charles Tephens, Paladin Press, Boulder, CO, 1997. 58 pp., illus. Paper covers. $14.00

How to tune and time, load and shoot accurately with the Contender pistol.

The Truth About Handguns, by Duane Thomas, Paladin Press, Boulder, CO, 1997. 136 pp., illus. Paper covers. $18.00

Exploding the myths, hype, and misinformation about handguns.

U.S. Handguns of World War II, The Secondary Pistols and Revolvers, by Charles W. Pate, Mowbray Publishers, Lincoln, RI, 1997. 368 pp., illus. $39.00

This indispensable new book covers all of the American military handguns of WWII except for the M1911A1.

ARMS LIBRARY

Walther Pistols: Models 1 Through P99, Factory Variations and Copies, by Dieter H. Marschall, Ucross Books, Los Alamos, NM. 2000. 140 pp., with 140 b&w illustrations, index. Paper covers. $19.95
This is the English translation, revised and updated, of the highly successful and widely acclaimed German language edition. This book provides the collector with a reference guide and overview of the entire line of the Walther military, police, and self-defense pistols from the very first to the very latest Variations, where issued, serial ranges, calibers, marks, proofs, logos, and design aspects in an astonishing quantity and variety are crammed into this very well researched and highly regarded work.

HUNTING

NORTH AMERICA

.577 Snider-Enfield Rifles & Carbines; Australian Service Longarms, by Ian Skennerton, Australia, Arms & Militaria Press, 2003. 1st edition. Hardcover. New in new dust jacket. $39.50

161 Waterfowling Secrets, edited by Matt Young, Willow Creek Press, Minocqua, WI, 1997. 78 pp., Paper covers. $10.95
Time-honored, field-tested waterfowling tips and advice.

A Pheasant Hunter's Notebook: Revised Second Edition, by Larry Brown, Camden, ME, Country Sport Press, 2003. 1st edition. 266 pp. Hardcover. $26.95
Larry Brown has spent a lifetime pursuing America's most colorful and raucous upland game bird, and the advice he presents here, based on written records of his hunts over the decades, is priceless. Particularly valuable are his strategies for hunting different kinds of cover in varying types of weather.

A Varmint Hunter's Odyssey, by Steve Hanson with guest chapter by Mike Johnson, Precision Shooting, Inc. Manchester, CT, 1999. 279 pp., illus. Paper covers. $39.95
A new classic by a writer who eats, drinks and sleeps varmint hunting and varmint rifles.

Advanced Black Powder Hunting, by Toby Bridges, Stoeger Publishing Co., Wayne, NJ, 1998. 288 pp., illus. Paper covers. $21.95
The first modern day publication to be filled from cover to cover with guns, loads, projectiles, accessories and the techniques to get the most from today's front loading guns.

Adventures of an Alaskan–You Can Do, by Dennis W. Confer, Foreword by Craig Boddington. Anchorage, AK, Wiley Ventures, 2003. 1st edition. 279 pp., illus. Softcover. $24.95
This book is about 45% fishing, 45% hunting, & 10% related adventures; travel, camping and boating. It is written to stimulate, encourage and motivate readers to make happy memories that they can do on an average income and to entertain, educate and inform readers of outdoor opportunities.

Aggressive Whitetail Hunting, by Greg Miller, Krause Publications, Iola, WI, 1995. 208 pp., illus. Paper covers. $14.95
Learn how to hunt trophy bucks in public forests, private farmlands and exclusive hunting grounds from one of America's foremost hunters.

Alaska Safari, by Harold Schetzle & Sam Fadala, Anchorage, AK, Great Northwest Publishing, 2002. Revised 2nd edition. 366 pp., illus. with b&w photos. Softcover. $29.95
The author has brought a wealth of information to the hunter and anyone interested in Alaska. Harold Schetzle is a great guide and has also written another book called "Alaska Wilderness Hunter" which is a wonderful book of stories of Alaska hunting taken from many, many years of hunting and guiding. The most comprehensive guide to Alaska hunting.

Alaskan Yukon Trophies Won and Lost, by G.O. Young, Wolfe Publishing, Prescott, AZ, 2002. 273 pp. with b&w photographs and a five-page epilogue by the publisher. Softcover. $35.00
A classic big game hunting tale.

American Duck Shooting, by George Bird Grinnell, Stackpole Books, Harrisburg, PA, 1991. 640 pp., illus. Paper covers. $19.95
First published in 1901 at the height of the author's career. Describes 50 species of waterfowl, and discusses hunting methods common at the turn of the century.

Autumn Passages, compiled by the editors of *Ducks Unlimited* magazine, Willow Creek Press, Minocqua, WI, 1997. 320 pp. $27.50
An exceptional collection of duck hunting stories. Reminiscences of a hunter's life in rural America.

Bare November Days, by George Bird Evans et al, Down East Books, Camden, MA 2002. 136 pp., illus. $39.50
A new, original anthology, a tribute to ruffed grouse, king of upland birds.

The Best of Babcock, by Havilah Babcock, Introduction by Hugh Grey, The Gunnerman Press, Auburn Hills, MI, 1985. 262 pp., illus. $19.95
A treasury of memorable pieces, 21 of which have never before appeared in book form.

Blacktail Trophy Tactics, by Boyd Iverson, Stoneydale Press, Stevensville, MI, 1992. 166 pp., illus. Paper covers. $14.95
A comprehensive analysis of blacktail deer habits, describing a deer's and man's use of scents, still hunting, tree techniques, etc.

Bowhunter's Handbook, Expert Strategies and Techniques, by M.R. James with Fred Asbell, Dave Holt, Dwight Schuh and Dave Samuel, DBI Books, a division of Krause Publications, Iola, WI, 1997. 256 pp., illus. Paper covers. $19.95
Tips from the top on taking your bowhunting skills to the next level.

The Buffalo Harvest, by Frank Mayer as told to Charles Roth, Pioneer Press, Union City, TN, 1995. 96 pp., illus. Paper covers. $12.50
The story of a hide hunter during his buffalo hunting days on the plains.

Call of the Quail: A Tribute to the Gentleman Game Bird, by Michael McIntosh, et al., Countrysport Press, Traverse City, MI, 1990. 175 pp., illus. $35.00
A new anthology on quail hunting.

Calling All Elk, by Jim Zumbo, Cody, WY, 1989. 169 pp., illus. Paper covers. $14.95
The only book on the subject of elk hunting that covers every aspect of elk vocalization.

The Complete Book of Grouse Hunting, by Frank Woolner, The Lyons Press, New York, NY, 2000. 192 pp., illus. Paper covers. $24.95
The history, habits, and habitat of one of America's great game birds–and the methods used to hunt it.

The Complete Book of Mule Deer Hunting, by Walt Prothero, The Lyons Press, New York, NY, 2000. 192 pp., illus. Paper covers. $24.95
Field-tested practical advice on how to bag the trophy buck of a lifetime.

The Complete Book of Wild Turkey Hunting, by John Trout Jr., The Lyons Press, New York, NY, 2000. 192 pp., illus. Paper covers. $24.95
An illustrated guide to hunting for one of America's most popular game birds.

The Complete Book of Woodcock Hunting, by Frank Woolner, The Lyons Press, New York, NY, 2000. 192 pp., illus. Paper covers. $24.95
A thorough, practical guide to the American woodcock and to woodcock hunting.

The Complete Guide To Hunting Wild Boar in California, by Gary Kramer, Safari Press, 2002. 1st edition. 127 pp., 37 photos. Softcover. $15.95
Gary Kramer takes the hunter all over California, from north to south and east to west. He discusses natural history, calibers, bullets, rifles, pistols, shotguns, black powder, and bow and arrows—even recipes.

The Complete Venison Cookbook from Field to Table, by Jim & Ann Casada, Krause Publications, Iola, WI, 1996. 208 pp., Comb-bound. $12.95
More than 200 kitchen-tested recipes make this book the answer to a table full of hungry hunters or guests.

Coveys and Singles: The Handbook of Quail Hunting, by Robert Gooch, A.S. Barnes, San Diego, CA, 1981. 196 pp., illus. $11.95
The story of the quail in North America.

Coyote Hunting, by Phil Simonski, Stoneydale Press, Stevensville, MT, 1994. 126 pp., illus. Paper covers. $12.95
Probably the most thorough "how-to-do-it" book on coyote hunting ever written.

Dabblers & Divers: A Duck Hunter's Book, compiled by the editors of *Ducks Unlimited* magazine, Willow Creek Press, Minocqua, WI, 1997. 160 pp., illus. $39.95
A word-and-photographic portrayal of waterfowl hunter's singular intimacy with, and passion for, watery haunts and wildfowl.

Deer & Deer Hunting, by Al Hofacker, Krause Publications, Iola, WI, 1993. 208 pp., illus. $34.95
Coffee-table volume packed full of how-to-information that will guide hunts for years to come.

The Deer Hunters: The Tactics, Lore, Legacy and Allure of American Deer Hunting, edited by Patrick Durkin, Krause Publications, Iola, WI, 1997. 208 pp., illus. $29.95
More than 20 years of research from America's top whitetail hunters, researchers, and photographers have gone into the making of this book.

Dreaming the Lion, by Thomas McIntyre, Countrysport Press, Traverse City, MI, 1994. 309 pp., illus. $35.00
Reflections on hunting, fishing and a search for the wild. Twenty-three stories by *Sports Afield* editor, Tom McIntyre.

Elk and Elk Hunting, by Hart Wixom, Stackpole Books, Harrisburg, PA, 1986. 288 pp., illus. $34.95
Your practical guide to fundamentals and fine points of elk hunting.

Elk Hunting in the Northern Rockies, by Ed Wolff, Stoneydale Press, Stevensville, MT, 1984. 162 pp., illus. $18.95
Helpful information about hunting the premier elk country of the northern Rocky Mountain states–Wyoming, Montana and Idaho.

Elk Hunting with the Experts, by Bob Robb, Stoneydale Press, Stevensville, MT, 1992. 176 pp., illus. Paper covers. $15.95
A complete guide to elk hunting in North America by America's top elk hunting expert.

Fair Chase in North America, by Craig Boddington, Long Beach, CA, Safari Press, 2004. 1st edition. Hardcover. New in new dust jacket. $39.95

Firelight, by Burton L. Spiller, Gunnerman Press, Auburn Hills, MI, 1990. 196 pp., illus. $19.95
Enjoyable tales of the outdoors and stalwart companions.

Getting a Stand, by Miles Gilbert, Pioneer Press, Union City, TN, 1993. 204 pp., illus. Paper covers. $13.95
An anthology of 18 short personal experiences by buffalo hunters of the late 1800s, specifically from 1870-1882.

Greatest Elk; The Complete Historical and Illustrated Record of North America's Biggest Elk, by R. Selner, Safari Press, Huntington Beach, CA, 2000. 209 pp., profuse color illus. $39.95
Here is the book all elk hunters have been waiting for! This oversized book holds the stories and statistics of the biggest bulls ever killed in North America. Stunning, full-color photographs highlight over 40 world-class heads, including the old world records!

Grouse and Woodcock, A Gunner's Guide, by Don Johnson, Krause Publications, Iola, WI, 1995. 256 pp., illus. Paper covers. $14.95
Find out what you need in guns, ammo, equipment, dogs and terrain.

Gunning for Sea Ducks, by George Howard Gillelan, Tidewater Publishers, Centreville, MD, 1988. 144 pp., illus. $14.95
A book that introduces you to a practically untouched arena of waterfowling.

The Heck with Moose Hunting, by Jim Zumbo, Wapiti Valley Publishing Co., Cody, WY, 1996. 199 pp., illus. $17.95
Jim's hunts around the continent including encounters with moose, caribou, sheep, antelope and mountain goats.

High Pressure Elk Hunting, by Mike Lapinski, Stoneydale Press Publishing Co., Stevensville, MT, 1996. 192 pp., illus. $19.95
The secrets of hunting educated elk revealed.

Horns in the High Country, by Andy Russell, Alfred A. Knopf, NY, 1973. 259 pp., illus. Paper covers. $12.95
A many-sided view of wild sheep and their natural world.

How to Hunt, by Dave Bowring, Winchester Press, Piscataway, NJ, 1982. 208 pp., illus. Hardcover $15.00
A basic guide to hunting big game, small game, upland birds, and waterfowl.

Hunt High for Rocky Mountain Goats, Bighorn Sheep, Chamois & Tahr, by Duncan Gilchrist, Stoneydale Press, Stevensville, MT, 1992. 192 pp., illus. Paper covers. $19.95
The source book for hunting mountain goats.

Hunting Adventure of Me and Joe, by Walt Prothero, Safari Press, Huntington Beach, CA, 1995. 220 pp., illus. $22.50
A collection of the author's best and favorite stories.

Hunting America's Wild Turkey, by Toby Bridges, Stoeger Publishing Company, Pocomoke, MD, 2001. 256 pp., illus. $16.95
The techniques and tactics of hunting North America's largest, and most popular, woodland game bird.

ARMS LIBRARY

Hunting Hard in Alaska, by Marc Taylor, Anchorage, AK, Biblio Distribution, 2003 Softcover. $19.95

Hunting Mature Bucks, by Larry L. Weishuhn, Krause Publications, Iola, WI, 1995. 256 pp., illus. Paper covers. $14.95
One of North America's top white-tailed deer authorities shares his expertise on hunting those big, smart and elusive bucks.

Hunting Open-Country Mule Deer, by Dwight Schuh, Sage Press, Nampa, ID, 1989. 180 pp., illus. $18.95
A guide taking Western bucks with rifle and bow.

Hunting the Rockies, Home of the Giants, by Kirk Darner, Marceline, MO, 1996. 291 pp., illus. $25.00
Understand how and where to hunt Western game in the Rockies.

Hunting Western Deer, by Jim and Wes Brown, Stoneydale Press, Stevensville, MT, 1994. 174 pp., illus. Paper covers. $14.95
A pair of expert Oregon hunters provide insight into hunting mule deer and blacktail deer in the western states.

Hunting Wild Turkeys in the West, by John Higley, Stoneydale Press, Stevensville, MT, 1992. 154 pp., illus. Paper covers. $12.95
Covers the basics of calling, locating and hunting turkeys in the western states.

Hunting with the Twenty-Two, by Charles Singer Landis, R&R Books, Livonia, NY, 1994. 429 pp., illus. $35.00
A miscellany of articles touching on the hunting and shooting of small game.

I Don't Want to Shoot an Elephant, by Havilah Babcock, The Gunnerman Press, Auburn Hills, MI, 1985. 184 pp., illus. $19.95
Eighteen delightful stories that will enthrall the upland gunner for many pleasurable hours.

In Search of the Buffalo, by Charles G. Anderson, Pioneer Press, Union City, TN, 1996. 144 pp., illus. Paper covers. $13.95
The primary study of the life of J. Wright Mooar, one of the few hunters fortunate enough to kill a white buffalo.

In the Turkey Woods, by Jerome B. Robinson, The Lyons Press, N.Y., 1998. 207 pp., illus. $24.95
Practical expert advice on all aspects of turkey hunting–from calls to decoys to guns.

Jaybirds Go to Hell on Friday, by Havilah Babcock, The Gunnerman Press, Auburn Hills, MI, 1985. 149 pp., illus. $19.95
Sixteen jewels that reestablish the lost art of good old-fashioned yarn telling.

Montana–Land of Giant Rams, Volume 2, by Duncan Gilchrist, Outdoor Expeditions and Books, Corvallis, MT, 1992. 208 pp., illus. $34.95
The reader will find stories of how many of the top-scoring trophies were taken.

Montana–Land of Giant Rams, Volume 3, by Duncan Gilchrist, Outdoor Expeditions and Books, Corvallis, MT, 1999. 224 pp., illus. Paper covers. $19.95
All new sheep information including over 70 photos. Learn about how Montana became the "Land of Giant Rams" and what the prospects of the future are.

More Tracks: 78 Years of Mountains, People & Happiness, by Howard Copenhaver, Stoneydale Press, Stevensville, MT, 1992. 150 pp., illus. $18.95
A collection of stories by one of the back country's best storytellers about the people who shared with Howard his great adventure in the high places and wild Montana country.

Mostly Huntin', by Bill Jordan, Everett Publishing Co., Bossier City, LA, 1987. 254 pp., illus. $21.95
Jordan's hunting adventures in North America, Africa, Australia, South America and Mexico.

Mule Deer: Hunting Today's Trophies, by Tom Carpenter and Jim Van Norman, Krause Publications, Iola, WI, 1998. 256 pp., illus. Paper covers. $19.95
A tribute to both the deer and the people who hunt them. Includes info on where to look for big deer, prime mule deer habitat and effective weapons for the hunt.

My Health is Better in November, by Havilah Babcock, University of S. Carolina Press, Columbia, SC, 1985. 284 pp., illus. $24.95
Adventures in the field set in the plantation country and backwater streams of SC.

The North American Waterfowler, by Paul S. Bernsen, Superior Publ. Co., Seattle, WA, 1972. 206 pp. Paper covers. $9.95
The complete inside and outside story of duck and goose shooting. Big and colorful, illustrations by Les Kouba.

The Old Man and the Boy, by Robert Ruark, Henry Holt & Co., New York, NY, 303 pp., illus. $24.95
A timeless classic, telling the story of a remarkable friendship between a young boy and his grandfather as they hunt and fish together.

The Old Man's Boy Grows Older, by Robert Ruark, Henry Holt & Co., Inc., New York, NY, 1993. 300 pp., illus. $24.95
The heartwarming sequel to the best-selling *The Old Man and the Boy.*

One Man, One Rifle, One Land; Hunting all Species of Big Game in North America, by J.Y. Jones, Safari Press, Huntington Beach, CA, 2000. 400 pp., illus. $59.95
Journey with J.Y. Jones as he hunts each of the big-game animals of North America–from the polar bear of the high Arctic to the jaguar of the low-lands of Mexico–with just one rifle.

Outdoor Pastimes of an American Hunter, by Theodore Roosevelt, Stackpole Books, Mechanicsburg, PA, 1994. 480 pp., illus. Paper covers. $18.95
Stories of hunting big game in the West and notes about animals pursued and observed.

The Outlaw Gunner, by Harry M. Walsh, Tidewater Publishers, Cambridge, MD, 1973. 178 pp., illus. $22.95
A colorful story of market gunning in both its legal and illegal phases.

Pheasant Days, by Chris Dorsey, Voyageur Press, Stillwater, MN, 1992. 233 pp., illus. $24.95
The definitive resource on ringnecks. Includes everything from basic hunting techniques to the life cycle of the bird.

Pheasant Hunter's Harvest, by Steve Grooms, Lyons & Burford Publishers, New York, NY, 1990. 180 pp. $22.95
A celebration of pheasant, pheasant dogs and pheasant hunting. Practical advice from a passionate hunter.

Pheasant Tales, by Gene Hill et al, Countrysport Press, Traverse City, MI, 1996. 202 pp., illus. $39.00
Charley Waterman, Michael McIntosh and Phil Bourjaily join the author to tell some of the stories that illustrate why the pheasant is America's favorite game bird.

Pheasants of the Mind, by Datus Proper, Wilderness Adventures Press, Bozeman, MT, 1994. 154 pp., illus. $25.00
No single title sums up the life of the solitary pheasant hunter like this masterful work.

Portraits of Elk Hunting, by Jim Zumbo, Safari Press, Huntington Beach, CA, 2001. 222 pp. illus. $39.95
Zumbo has captured in photos as well as in words the essence, charisma, and wonderful components of elk hunting: back-country wilderness camps, sweaty guides, happy hunters, favorite companions, elk woods, and, of course, the majestic elk. Join Zumbo in the uniqueness of the pursuit of the magnificent and noble elk.

Proven Whitetail Tactics, by Greg Miller, Krause Publications, Iola, WI, 1997. 224 pp., illus. Paper covers. $19.95
Proven tactics for scouting, calling and still-hunting whitetail.

Quest for Dall Rams, by Duncan Gilchrist, Duncan Gilchrist Outdoor Expeditions and Books, Corvallis, MT, 1997. 224 pp., illus. Paper covers. $19.95
The most complete book of Dall sheep ever written. Covers information on Alaska and provinces with Dall sheep and explains hunting techniques, equipment, etc.

Quest for Giant Bighorns, by Duncan Gilchrist, Outdoor Expeditions and Books, Corvallis, MT, 1994. 224 pp., illus. Paper covers. $19.95
How some of the most successful sheep hunters hunt and how some of the best bighorns were taken.

Radical Elk Hunting Strategies, by Mike Lapinski, Stoneydale Press Publishing Co., Stevensville, MT, 1988. 161 pp., illus. $18.95
Secrets of calling elk in close.

Rattling, Calling & Decoying Whitetails, by Gary Clancy, edited by Patrick Durkin, Krause Publications, Iola, WI, 2000. 208 pp., illus. Paper covers. $19.95
How to consistently coax big bucks into range.

Records of North American Big Game 11th Edition, with hunting chapters by Craig Boddington, Tom McIntyre and Jim Zumbo, The Boone and Crockett Club, Missoula, MT, 1999. 700 pp., featuring a 32-page color section. $49.95
Listing over 17,150, of the top trophy big game animals ever recorded. Over 4,000 new listings are featured in this latest edition.

Records of North American Caribou and Moose, Craig Boddington et al, The Boone & Crockett Club, Missoula, MT, 1997. 250 pp., illus. $24.95
More than 1,800 caribou listings and more than 1,500 moose listings, organized by the state or Canadian province where they were taken.

Records of North American Elk and Mule Deer, 2nd Edition, edited by Jack and Susan Reneau, The Boone & Crockett Club, Missoula, MT, 1996. 360 pp., illus. Paper cover, $18.95; hardcover, $24.95
Updated and expanded edition featuring more than 150 trophy, field and historical photos of the finest elk and mule deer trophies ever recorded.

Records of North American Sheep, Rocky Mountain Goats and Pronghorn, edited by Jack and Susan Reneau, The Boone & Crockett Club, Missoula, MT, 1996. 400 pp., illus. Paper cover, $18.95; hardcover, $24.95
The first B&C Club records book featuring all 3941 accepted wild sheep, Rocky Mountain goats and pronghorn trophies.

Reflections on Snipe, by Worth Mathewson, illustrated by Eldridge Hardie, Camden, ME, Country Sport Press, 2003. Hardcover. 144 pp. $25.00
Reflections on Snipe is a delightful compendium of information on snipe behavior and habitats; gunning history; stories from the field; and the pleasures of hunting with good companions, whether human or canine.

Return of Royalty; Wild Sheep of North America, by Dr. Dale E. Toweill and Dr. Valerius Geist, The Boone and Crockett Club, Missoula, MT, 1999. 224 pp., illus. $59.95
A celebration of the return of the wild sheep to many of its historical ranges.

Ringneck; A Tribute to Pheasants and Pheasant Hunting, by Steve Grooms, Russ Sewell and Dave Nomsen, The Lyons Press, New York, NY, 2000. 120 pp., illus. $40.00
A glorious full-color coffee-table tribute to the pheasant and those who hunt them.

Rooster! A Tribute to Pheasant Hunting, by Dale C. Spartas, Riverbend Publishing, 2003. 1st edition. 150+ glorious photos of pheasants, hunting dogs and hunting trips with family and friends. 128 pgs. Hardcover. $39.95
A very special, must-have book for the 2.3 million pheasant hunters across the country!

Rub-Line Secrets, by Greg Miller, edited by Patrick Durkin, Krause Publications, Iola, WI, 1999. 208 pp., illus. Paper covers. $19.95
Based on nearly 30 years' experience. Proven tactics for finding, analyzing and hunting big bucks' rub-lines.

The Season, by Tom Kelly, Lyons & Burford, New York, NY, 1997. 160 pp., illus. $22.95
The delight and challenges of a turkey hunter's spring season.

Secret Strategies from North America's Top Whitetail Hunters, compiled by Nick Sisley, Krause Publications, Iola, WI, 1995. 256 pp., illus. Paper covers. $14.95
Bow and gun hunters share their success stories.

Sheep Hunting in Alaska–The Dall Sheep Hunter's Guide, by Tony Russ, Outdoor Expeditions and Books, Corvallis, MT, 1994. 160 pp., illus. Paper covers. $19.95
A how-to guide for the Dall sheep hunter.

Shots at Big Game, by Craig Boddington, Stackpole Books, Harrisburg, PA, 1989. 198 pp., illus. Softcover $15.95
How to shoot a rifle accurately under hunting conditions.

Southern Deer & Deer Hunting, by Larry Weishuhn and Bill Bynum, Krause Publications, Iola, WI, 1995. 256 pp., illus. Paper covers. $14.95
Mount a trophy southern whitetail on your wall with this firsthand account of stalking big bucks below the Mason-Dixon line.

Spring Gobbler Fever, by Michael Hanback, Krause Publications, Iola, WI, 1996. 256 pp., illus. Paper covers. $15.95
Your complete guide to spring turkey hunting.

Stand Hunting for Whitetails, by Richard P. Smith, Krause Publications, Iola, WI, 1996. 256 pp., illus. Paper covers. $14.95
The author explains the tricks and strategies for successful stand hunting.

The Sultan of Spring: A Hunter's Odyssey Through the World of the Wild Turkey, by Bob Saile, The Lyons Press, New York, NY, 1998. 176 pp., illus. $22.95
A literary salute to the magic and mysticism of spring turkey hunting.

Taking Big Bucks, by Ed Wolff, Stoneydale Press, Stevensville, MT, 1987. 169 pp., illus. $18.95
Solving the whitetail riddle.

ARMS LIBRARY

Tales of Quails 'n Such, by Havilah Babcock, University of S. Carolina Press, Columbia, SC, 1985. 237 pp. $19.95
A group of hunting stories, told in informal style, on field experiences in the South in quest of small game.

They Left Their Tracks, by Howard Coperhaver, Stoneydale Press Publishing Co., Stevensville, MT, 1990. 190 pp., illus. $18.95
Recollections of 60 years as an outfitter in the Bob Marshall Wilderness.

To Heck with Moose Hunting, by Jim Zumbo, Wapiti Publishing Co., Cody, WY, 1996. 199 pp., illus. $17.95
Jim's hunts around the continent and even an African adventure.

Track Pack: Animal Tracks In Full Life Size, by Ed Gray, Mechanicsburg, PA, Stackpole Books, 2003. 1st edition. Spiral-bound, 34 pp. $7.95
An indispensable reference for hunters, trackers, and outdoor enthusiasts. This handy guide features the tracks of 38 common North American animals, from squirrels to grizzlies.

The Trickiest Thing in Feathers, by Corey Ford, compiled and edited by Laurie Morrow, illustrated by Christopher Smith, Wilderness Adventures, Gallatin Gateway, MT, 1998. 208 pp., illus. $29.95
Here is a collection of Corey Ford's best wing-shooting stories, many of them previously unpublished.

The Upland Equation: A Modern Bird-Hunter's Code, by Charles Fergus, Lyons & Burford Publishers, New York, NY, 1996. 86 pp. $18.00
A book that deserves space in every sportsman's library. Observations based on firsthand experience.

Upland Tales, edited by Worth Mathewson, Sand Lake Press, Amity, OR, 1996. 271 pp., illus. $29.95
A collection of articles on grouse, snipe and quail.

Waterfowler's World, by Bill Buckley, Ducks Unlimited, Inc., Memphis, TN, 1999. 192 pp., illustrated in color. $37.50
An unprecedented pictorial book on waterfowl and waterfowlers.

When the Duck Were Plenty, by Ed Muderlak, Safari Press, Inc., Huntington Beach, CA, 2000. 300 pp., illus. $29.95
The golden age of waterfowling and duck hunting from 1840 until 1920. An anthology.

Whitetail: Behavior Through the Seasons, by Charles J. Alsheimer, Krause Publications, Iola, WI, 1996. 208 pp., illus. $34.95
In-depth coverage of whitetail behavior presented through striking portraits of the whitetail in every season.

Whitetail: The Ultimate Challenge, by Charles J. Alsheimer, Krause Publications, Iola, WI, 1995. 228 pp., illus. Paper covers. $14.95
Learn deer hunting's most intriguing secrets–fooling deer using decoys, scents and calls–from America's premier authority.

Whitetails by the Moon, by Charles J. Alsheimer, edited by Patrick Durkin, Krause Publications, Iola, WI, 1999. 208 pp., illus. Paper covers. $19.95
Predict peak times to hunt whitetails. Learn what triggers the rut.

Wildfowler's Season, by Chris Dorsey, Lyons & Burford Publishers, New York, NY, 1998. 224 pp., illus. $37.95
Modern methods for a classic sport.

Wildfowling Tales, by William C. Hazelton, Wilderness Adventures Press, Belgrade, MT, 1999. 117 pp., illustrated with etchings by Brett Smith. In a slipcase. $50.00
Tales from the great ducking resorts of the continent.

Windward Crossings: A Treasury of Original Waterfowling Tales, by Chuck Petrie et al, Willow Creek Press, Minocqua, WI, 1999. 144 pp., 48 color art and etching reproductions. $35.00
An illustrated, modern anthology of previously unpublished waterfowl hunting (fiction and creative nonfiction) stories by America's finest outdoor journalists.

Wings of Thunder: New Grouse Hunting Revisited, by Steven Mulak, Countrysport Books, Selma, AL, 1998. 168 pp. illus. $30.00
The author examines every aspect of New England grouse hunting as it is today–the bird and its habits, the hunter and his dog, guns and loads, shooting and hunting techniques, practice on clay targets, clothing and equipment.

The Woodchuck Hunter, by Paul C. Estey, R&R Books, Livonia, NY, 1994. 135 pp., illus. $25.00
This book contains information on woodchuck equipment, the rifle, telescopic sights and includes interesting stories.

AFRICA/ASIA/ELSEWHERE

A Country Boy in Africa, by George Hoffman, Trophy Room Books, Agoura, CA, 1998. 267 pp., illustrated with over 100 photos. Limited, numbered edition signed by the author. $85.00
In addition to the author's long and successful hunting career, he is known for developing a most effective big game cartridge, the .416 Hoffman.

A Hunter's Africa, by Gordon Cundill, Trophy Room Books, Agoura, CA, 1998. 298 pp., over 125 photographic illustrations. Limited numbered edition signed by the author. $125.00
A good look by the author at the African safari experience - elephant, lion, spiral-horned antelope, firearms, people and events, as well as the clients that make it worthwhile.

A Hunter's Wanderings in Africa, by Frederick Courteney Selous, Alexanders Books, Alexander, NC, 2003. 504 pp., illus. $28.50
A reprinting of the 1920 London edition. A narrative of nine years spent amongst the game of the far interior of South Africa.

A Professional Hunter's Journey of Discovery, by Alec McCallum, Agoura, CA, Trophy Room Books, 2003. Limited edition of 1,000. Signed and numbered. 132 pp. Hardcover. New in new dust jacket. $125.00

A View From A Tall Hill: Robert Ruark in Africa, by Terry Wieland, Bristol, CT, Country Sport Press, 2004. Reprint. 432 pp., Hardcover New in new dust jacket $45.00

African Adventures and Misadventures: Escapades in East Africa with Mau Mau and Giant Forest Hogs, by William York, Long Beach, CA, Safari Press, 2003. A limited edition of 1,000 copies. Signed and numbered. 250 pp., color and b&w photos. Hardcover in a slipcase. $70.00
From his early days in Kenya when he and a companion trekked alone through the desert of the NFD and had to fend off marauding lions that ate his caravan ponies to encountering a Mau Mau terrorist who took potshots at his victims with a stolen elephant gun, the late Bill York gives an entertaining account of his life that will keep you turning the pages. As with York's previous book, the pages are loaded with interesting anecdotes, fascinating tales, and well-written prose that give insight into East Africa and its more famous characters.

African Game Trails, by Theodore Roosevelt, Peter Capstick, Series Editor, St. Martin's Press, New York, NY 1988. 583 pp., illus. $24.95
The famed safari of the noted sportsman, conservationist, and President.

African Hunter, by James Mellon, Safari Press, Huntington Beach, CA, 1996. 522 pp., illus. Paper covers, $75.00
Regarded as the most comprehensive title ever published on African hunting.

African Hunter II, edited by Craig Boddington and Peter Flack, Foreword by Robin Hurt, Introduction by James Mellon, Long Beach, CA, Safari Press, 2004. 1st edition. 606 pp., profuse color and b&w photos. Hardcover. $135.00
James Mellon spent five years hunting in every African country open to hunting during the late 1960s and early 1970s, making him uniquely qualified to write a book of such scope and breadth. Because so much has changed in today's Africa, however, it was necessary to update the original. To start, there is a total of 25 countries covered, with thorough in-depth overviews of their hunting areas, background information, and best times to hunt. Then we cover the game animals: It includes all the Big Five (lion, leopard, buffalo, rhino, and elephant); the nine spiral-horn antelope; game indigenous to only one region; game indigenous to most regions; the rarities; the plains game, and so on–all game animals throughout the entire African continent are given meticulous attention. With over 500 full-color pages, hundreds of photographs, and updated tables on animals and where they are available, this is THE book to consult for the information on Africa today.

African Rifles & Cartridges, by John Taylor, The Gun Room Press, Highland Park, NJ, 1977. 431 pp., illus. $35.00
Experiences and opinions of a professional ivory hunter in Africa describing his knowledge of numerous arms and cartridges for big game. A reprint.

African Twilight, by Robert F. Jones, Wilderness Adventure Press, Bozeman, MT, 1994. 208 pp., illus. $36.00
Details the hunt, danger and changing face of Africa over a span of three decades.

Baron in Africa; The Remarkable Adventures of Werner von Alvensleben, by Brian Marsh, Foreword by Ian Player, Safari Press, Huntington Beach, CA, 2001. 288 pp., illus. $35.00
Follow his career as he hunts lion, goes after large kudu, kills a full-grown buffalo with a spear, and hunts for elephant and ivory in some of the densest brush in Africa. The adventure and the experience were what counted to this fascinating character, not the money or fame; indeed, in the end he left Mozambique with barely more than the clothes on his back. This is a must-read adventure story of one of the most interesting characters to have come out of Africa after WWII.

Big Game and Big Game Rifles, by John "Pondoro" Taylor, Safari Press, Huntington Beach, CA, 1999. 215 pp., illus. $24.95.
Covers rifles and calibers for elephant, rhino, hippo, buffalo and lion.

Buffalo, Elephant, & Bongo (Trade Edition): Alone in the Savannas and Rain Forests of the Cameroon, by Reinald Von Meurers, Long Beach, CA, Safari Press, 2004. Hardcover. New in new dust jacket. $39.50

Cottar: The Exception was the Rule, by Pat Cottar, Trophy Room Books, Agoura, CA, 1999. 350 pp., illus. Limited, numbered and signed edition. $135.00
The remarkable big game hunting stories of one of Kenya's most remarkable pioneers.

Death and Double Rifles, by Mark Sullivan, Nitro Express Safaris, Phoenix, AZ, 2000. 295 pp., illus. $85.00
Sullivan has captured every thrilling detail of hunting dangerous game in this lavishly illustrated book. Full of color pictures of African hunts & rifles.

Death in a Lonely Land, by Peter Capstick, St. Martin's Press, New York, NY, 1990. 284 pp., illus. $22.95
Twenty-three stories of hunting as only the master can tell them.

Death in the Dark Continent, by Peter Capstick, St. Martin's Press, New York, NY, 1983. 238 pp., illus. $22.95
A book that brings to life the suspense, fear and exhilaration of stalking ferocious killers under primitive, savage conditions, with the ever present threat of death.

Death in the Long Grass, by Peter Hathaway Capstick, St. Martin's Press, New York, NY, 1977. 297 pp., illus. $22.95
A big game hunter's adventures in the African bush.

Death in the Silent Places, by Peter Capstick, St. Martin's Press, New York, NY, 1981. 243 pp., illus. $23.95
The author recalls the extraordinary careers of legendary hunters such as Corbett, Karamojo Bell, Stigand and others.

Encounters with Lions, by Jan Hemsing, Trophy Room Books, Agoura, CA, 1995. 302 pp., illus. $75.00
Some stories fierce, fatal, frightening and even humorous of when man and lion meet.

Fodor's African Safari, From Budget to Big Spending Where and How to Find the Best Big Game Adventure In Southern and Eastern Africa, by David Bristow, Julian Harrison, Chris Swiac, New York, Fodor's, 2004. 1st edition. 190 pp. Softcover. NEW. $9.95

From Sailor to Professional Hunter: The Autobiography of John Northcote, Trophy Room Books, Agoura, CA, 1997. 400 pp., illus. Limited edition, signed and numbered. $125.00
Only a handful of men can boast of having a 50-year professional hunting career throughout Africa as John Northcote has had.

Gone are the Days; Jungle Hunting for Tiger and other Game in India and Nepal 1953-1969, by Peter Byrne, Safari Press, Inc., Huntington Beach, CA, 2001. 225 pp., illus. Limited signed, numbered, slipcased. $70.00

Great Hunters: Their Trophy Rooms and Collections, Volume 1, compiled and published by Safari Press, Inc., Huntington Beach, CA, 1997. 172 pp., illustrated in color. $60.00
A rare glimpse into the trophy rooms of top international hunters. A few of these trophy rooms are museums.

Great Hunters: Their Trophy Rooms & Collections, Volume 2, compiled and published by Safari Press, Inc., Huntington Beach, CA, 1998. 224 pp., illustrated with 260 full-color photographs. $60.00
Volume two of the world's finest, best produced series of books on trophy rooms and game collections. 46 sportsmen sharing sights you'll never forget on this guided tour.

ARMS LIBRARY

Great Hunters: Their Trophy Rooms & Collections, Volume 3, compiled and published by Safari Press, Inc., Huntington Beach, CA, 2000. 204 pp., illustrated with 260 full-color photographs. $60.00

At last, the long-awaited third volume in the best photographic series ever published of trophy room collections is finally available. Unbelievable as it may sound, this book tops all previous volumes. Besides some of the greatest North American trophy rooms ever seen, an extra effort was made to include European collections. As before, each trophy room is accompanied by an informative text explaining the collection and giving you insights into the hunters who went to such great efforts to create their trophy rooms. All professionally photographed in the highest quality possible.

Heart of an African Hunter, by Peter Flack, Long Beach, CA, Safari Press, 1999. 266 pp. illustrated with b&w photos. Hardcover. NEW. $35.00

Hemingway in Africa: The Last Safari, by Christopher Ondaatje, Overlook Press, 2004. 1st edition. 240 pp. Hardcover. New in new dust jacket. $37.50

Hi-Standard Sporting Firearms: Dates of Manufacture 1926-1992, by D.R. Morse, Phoenix, AZ, Firing Pin Enterprizes, 2003. 22 pp. Softcover. NEW. $6.95

Covers their pistols, revolvers, rifles, shotguns and commemoratives, plus models & serial numbers.

Horn of the Hunter, by Robert Ruark, Safari Press, Long Beach, CA, 1987. 315 pp., illus. $35.00

Ruark's most sought-after title on African hunting, here in reprint.

Horned Death, by John F. Burger, Safari Press, Huntington Beach, CA, 1992. 343 pp. illus. $35.00

The classic work on hunting the African buffalo.

Hunter, by J.A. Hunter, Safari Press Publications, Huntington Beach, CA, 1999. 263 pp., illus. $24.95

Hunter's best known book on African big-game hunting. Internationally recognized as being one of the all-time African hunting classics.

Hunter's Tracks, by J.A. Hunter, Safari Press Publications, Huntington Beach, CA, 1999. 240 pp., illus. $24.95

This is the exciting story of John Hunter's efforts to capture the shady head man of a gang of ivory poachers and smugglers. The story is interwoven with the tale of one of East Africa's most grandiose safaris taken with an Indian maharaja.

Hunting Adventures Worldwide, by Jack Atcheson, Jack Atcheson & Sons, Butte, MT, 1995. 256 pp., illus. $29.95

The author chronicles the richest adventures of a lifetime spent in quest of big game across the world – including Africa, North America and Asia.

Hunting in Ethiopia, An Anthology, by Tony Sanchez-Arino, Safari Press, Huntington Beach, CA, 1996. 350 pp., illus. Limited, signed and numbered edition. $135.00

The finest selection of hunting stories ever compiled on hunting in this great game country.

Hunting in Kenya, by Tony Sanchez-Arino, Safari Press, Inc., Huntington Beach, CA, 2000. 350 pp., illus. Limited, signed and numbered edition in a slipcase. $135.00

The finest selection of hunting stories ever compiled on hunting in this great game country make up this anthology.

Hunting in the Sudan, An Anthology, compiled by Tony Sanchez-Arino, Safari Press, Huntington Beach, CA, 1992. 350 pp., illus. Limited, signed and numbered edition in a slipcase. $125.00

The finest selection of hunting stories ever compiled on hunting in this great game country.

The Hunting Instinct, by Phillip D. Rowter, Safari Press, Inc., Huntington Beach, CA, 1999. Limited edition signed and numbered and in a slipcase. $50.00

Safari chronicles from the Republic of South Africa and Namibia 1990-1998.

Hunting the Dangerous Game of Africa, by John Kingsley-Heath, Sycamore Island Books, Boulder, CO, 1998. 477 pp., illus. $95.00

Written by one of the most respected, successful, and ethical P.H.'s to trek the sunlit plains of Botswana, Kenya, Uganda, Tanganyika, Somaliland, Eritrea, Ethiopia, and Mozambique. Filled with some of the most gripping and terrifying tales ever to come out of Africa.

Hunting, Settling and Remembering, by Philip H. Percival, Trophy Room Books, Agoura, CA, 1997. 230 pp., illus. Limited, numbered and signed edition. $85.00

If Philip Percival is to come alive again, it will be through this, the first edition of his easy, intricate and magical book illustrated with some of the best historical big game hunting photos ever taken.

In the Salt, by Lou Hallamore, Trophy Room Books, Agoura, CA, 1999. 227 pp., illustrated in b&w and full color. Limited, numbered and signed edition. $125.00

A book about people, animals and the big game hunt, about being outwitted and outmaneuvered. It is about knowing that sooner or later your luck will change and your trophy will be "in the salt."

International Hunter 1945-1999, Hunting's Greatest Era, by Bert Klineburger, Sportsmen on Film, Kerrville, TX, 1999. 400 pp., illus. A limited, numbered and signed edition. $125.00

The most important book of the greatest hunting era by the world's preeminent International hunter.

King of the Wa-Kikuyu, by John Boyes, St. Martin Press, New York, NY, 1993. 240 pp., illus. $19.95

In the 19th and 20th centuries, Africa drew to it a large number of great hunters, explorers, adventurers and rogues. Many have become legendary, but John Boyes (1874-1951) was the most legendary of them all.

Last Horizons: Hunting, Fishing and Shooting on Five Continents, by Peter Capstick, St. Martin's Press, New York, NY, 1989. 288 pp., illus. $19.95

The first in a two-volume collection of hunting, fishing and shooting tales from the selected pages of *The American Hunter, Guns & Ammo* and *Outdoor Life.*

Last of the Ivory Hunters, by John Taylor, Safari Press, Long Beach, CA, 1990. 354 pp., illus. $29.95

Reprint of the classic book "Pondoro" by one of the most famous elephant hunters of all time.

Legends of the Field: More Early Hunters in Africa, by W.R. Foran, Trophy Room Press, Agoura, CA, 1997. 319 pp., illus. Limited edition. $100.00

This book contains the biographies of some very famous hunters: William Cotton Oswell, F.C. Selous, Sir Samuel Baker, Arthur Neumann, Jim Sutherland, W.D.M. Bell and others.

Lives of A Professional Hunting Family, by Gerard Agoura Miller, Trophy Room Books, 2003. A limited edition of 1,000 copies. Signed and numbered. 303 pp., 230 b&w photographic illustrations. Hardcover. $135.00

The Lost Classics, by Robert Ruark, Safari Press, Huntington Beach, CA, 1996. 260 pp., illus. $35.00

The magazine stories that Ruark wrote in the 1950s and 1960s finally in print in book form.

The Lost Wilderness; True Accounts of Hunters and Animals in East Africa, by Mohamed Ismail and Alice Pianfetti, Safari Press, Inc., Huntington Beach, CA, 2000. 216 pp., photos, illus. Limited edition signed, numbered and slipcased. $60.00

Mahonhboh, by Ron Thomson, Hartbeesport, South Africa, 1997. 312 pp., illus. Limited signed and numbered edition. $50.00

Elephants and elephant hunting in South Central Africa.

The Man-Eaters of Tsavo, by Lt. Colonel J.H. Patterson, Peter Capstick, series editor, St. Martin's Press, New York, NY, 1986, 5th printing. 346 pp., illus. $14.95

Maneaters and Marauders, by John "Pondoro" Taylor, Long Beach, CA, Safari Press, 2005. 1st edition, Safari edition. Hardcover. New in new dust jacket. $29.95

McElroy Hunts Asia, by C.J. McElroy, Safari Press, Inc., Huntington Beach, CA, 1989. 272 pp., illus. $50.00

From the founder of SCI comes a book on hunting the great continent of Asia for big game: tiger, bear, sheep and ibex. Includes the story of the all-time record Altai Argali as well as several markhor hunts in Pakistan.

Memoirs of a Sheep Hunter, by Rashid Jamsheed, Safari Press, Inc., Huntington Beach, CA, 1996. 330 pp., illus. $70.00

The author reveals his exciting accounts of obtaining world-record heads from his native Iran, and his eventual move to the U.S. where he procured a grand-slam of North American sheep.

Mundjamba: The Life Story of an African Hunter, by Hugo Seia, Trophy Room Books, Agoura, CA, 1996. 400 pp., illus. Limited, numbered and signed by the author. $125.00

An autobiography of one of the most respected and appreciated professional African hunters.

The Nature of the Game, by Ben Hoskyns, Quiller Press, Ltd., London, England, 1994. 160 pp., illus. $37.50

The first complete guide to British, European and North American game.

On Safari with Bwana Game–Trade Edition, by Eric Balson, Long Beach, CA, Safari Press, 2004. 1st edition. Hardcover. New in new dust jacket. $39.95

On Target, by Christian Le Noel, Trophy Room Books, Agoura, CA, 1999. 275 pp., illus. Limited, numbered and signed edition. $85.00

History and hunting in Central Africa.

One Long Safari, by Peter Hay, Trophy Room Books, Agoura, CA, 1998. 350 pp., with over 200 photographic illustrations and 7 maps. Limited numbered edition signed by the author. $100.00

Contains hunts for leopards, sitatunga, hippo, rhino, snakes and, of course, the general African big game bag.

Optics for the Hunter, by John Barsness, Safari Press, Inc., Huntington Beach, CA, 1999. 236 pp., illus. $24.95

An evaluation of binoculars, scopes, range finders, spotting scopes for use in the field.

Out in the Midday Shade, by William York, Safari Press, Inc., Huntington Beach, CA, 1999. Limited, signed and numbered edition in a slipcase. $70.00

Memoirs of an African hunter 1949-1968.

The Path of a Hunter, by Gilles Tre-Hardy, Trophy Room Books, Agoura, CA, 1997. 318 pp., illus. Limited Edition, signed and numbered. $85.00

A most unusual hunting autobiography with much about elephant hunting in Africa.

The Perfect Shot: Mini Edition for Africa, by Kevin Robertson, Long Beach, CA, Safari Press, 2004. 2nd printing Softcover. NEW. $17.95

The Perfect Shot: Shot Placement for African Big Game, by Kevin "Doctari" Robertson, Safari Press, Inc., Huntington Beach, CA, 1999. 230 pp., illus. $65.00

The most comprehensive work ever undertaken to show the anatomical features for all classes of African game. Includes caliber and bullet selection, rifle selection and trophy handling.

Peter Capstick's Africa: A Return to the Long Grass, by Peter Hathaway Capstick, St. Martin's Press, N. Y., NY, 1987. 213 pp., illus. $35.00

A first-person adventure in which the author returns to the long grass for his own dangerous and very personal excursion.

Pondoro, by John Taylor, Safari Press, Inc., Huntington Beach, CA, 1999. 354 pp., illus. $29.95

The author is considered one of the best storytellers in the hunting book world, and Pondoro is highly entertaining. A classic African big-game hunting title.

The Quotable Hunter, by Jay Cassell and Peter Fiduccia, The Lyons Press, N.Y., 1999. 288 pp., illus. $20.00

This collection of more than three hundred quotes from hunters through the ages captures the essence of the sport, with all its joys, idosyncrasies, and challenges.

Return to Toonaklut–The Russell Annabel Story, by Jeff Davis, Long Beach, CA, Safari Press, 2002. 248 pp., photos, illus. $34.95

Those of us who grew up after WW II cannot imagine the Alaskan frontier that Rusty Annabel walked into early in the twentieth century. The hardships, the resourcefulness, the natural beauty, not knowing what lay beyond the next horizon, all were a part of his existence. This is the story of the man behind the legend, and it is as fascinating as any of the tales Rusty Annabel ever spun for the sporting magazines.

Rifles and Cartridges for Large Game–From Deer to Bear–Advice on the Choice of A Rifle, by Layne Simpson, Long Beach, CA, Safari Press, 2002. Illustrated with 100 color photos, oversize book. 225 pp., color illus. $39.95

Layne Simpson, who has been field editor for *Shooting Times* magazine for 20 years, draws from his hunting experiences on five continents to tell you what rifles, cartridges, bullets, loads, and scopes are best for various applications, and he explains why in plain English. Developer of the popular 7mm STW cartridge, Simpson has taken big game with rifle cartridges ranging in power from the .220 Swift to the .460 Weatherby Magnum, and he pulls no punches when describing their effectiveness in the field.

Rifles for Africa; Practical Advice on Rifles and Ammunition for an African Safari, by Gregor Woods, Long Beach, CA, Safari Press, 2002. 1st edition. 430 pp., illus., photos. $39.95

Invaluable to the person who seeks advice and information on what rifles, calibers, and bullets work on African big game, be they the largest land mammals on earth or an antelope barely weighing in at 20 lbs.!

Robert Ruark's Africa, by Robert Ruark, edited by Michael McIntosh, Countrysport Press, Selma, AL, 1999. 256 pp. illustrated with 19 original etchings by Bruce Langton. $32.00

These previously uncollected works of Robert Ruark make this a classic big-game hunting book.

ARMS LIBRARY

Safari: The Last Adventure, by Peter Capstick, St. Martin's Press, New York, NY, 1984. 291 pp., illus. $22.95

A modern comprehensive guide to the African Safari.

Safari Rifles: Double, Magazine Rifles and Cartridges for African Hunting, by Craig Boddington, Safari Press, Huntington Beach, CA, 1990. 416 pp., illus. $37.50

A wealth of knowledge on the safari rifle. Historical and present double-rifle makers, ballistics for the large bores, and much, much more.

Sands of Silence, by Peter H. Capstick, Saint Martin's Press, New York, NY, 1991. 224 pp., illus. $35.00

Join the author on safari in Nambia for his latest big-game hunting adventures.

Song of the Summits–Hunting Sheep, Ibex, and Markhor in Asia, Europe, and North America, Limited Edition by Jesus Yurén, Long Beach, CA, Safari Press, 2003. Hardcover in a slipcase. NEW. $75.00

Spiral-Horn Dreams, by Terry Wieland, Trophy Room Books, Agoura, CA, 1996. 362 pp., illus. Limited, numbered and signed by the author. $85.00

Everyone who goes to hunt in Africa is looking for something; this is for those who go to hunt the spiral-horned antelope–the bongo, myala, mountain nyala, greater and lesser kudu, etc.

Tales of the African Frontier, by J.A. Hunter, Safari Press Publications, Huntington Beach, CA, 1999. 308 pp., illus. $24.95

The early days of East Africa is the subject of this powerful John Hunter book.

To Heck With It–I'm Going Hunting–My First Eighteen Years as an International Big-Game Hunter–Limited Edition, by Arnold Alward with Bill Quimby, Long Beach, CA, Safari Press, 2003. Deluxe, 1st edition, limited to 1,000 signed copies. NEW. $80.00

Uganda Safaris, by Brian Herne, Winchester Press, Piscataway, NJ, 1979. 236 pp., illus. $24.95

The chronicle of a professional hunter's adventures in Africa.

Under the African Sun, by Dr. Frank Hibben, Safari Press, Inc., Huntington Beach, CA, 1999. Limited edition signed, numbered and in a slipcase. $85.00

Forty-eight years of hunting the African continent.

Under the Shadow of Man Eaters, by Jerry Jaleel, The Jim Corbett Foundation, Edmonton, Alberta, Canada, 1997. 152 pp., illus. A limited, numbered and signed edition. Paper covers. $35.00

The life and legend of Jim Corbett of Kumaon.

Use Enough Gun, by Robert Ruark, Safari Press, Huntington Beach, CA, 1997. 333 pp., illus. $35.00

Robert Ruark on big game hunting.

Warrior: The Legend of Col. Richard Meinertzhagen, by Peter H. Capstick, St. Martins Press, New York, NY, 1998. 320 pp., illus. $23.95

A stirring and vivid biography of the famous British colonial officer Richard Meinertzhagen, whose exploits earned him fame and notoriety as one of the most daring and ruthless men to serve during the glory days of the British Empire.

The Waterfowler's World, by Bill Buckley, Willow Creek Press, Minocqua, WI, 1999. 176 pp., 225 color photographs. $37.50

Waterfowl hunting from Canadian prairies, across the U.S. heartland, to the wilds of Mexico, from the Atlantic to the Pacific coasts and the Gulf of Mexico.

The Weatherby: Stories From the Premier Big-Game Hunters of the World, 1956-2002, edited by Nancy Vokins, Long Beach, CA, Safari Press, 2004. Deluxe, limited, signed edition. 434 pp., profuse color and b&w illus. Hardcover in a slipcase. $200.00

The Wheel of Life–Bunny Allen, A Life of Safaris and Sex, by Bunny Allen, Long Beach, CA, Safari Press, 2004. 1st edition. 300 pp., illus, photos. Hardcover. $34.95

Where Lions Roar: Ten More Years of African Hunting, by Craig Boddington, Safari Press, Huntington Beach, CA, 1997. 250 pp., $35.00

The story of Boddington's hunts in the Dark Continent during the last ten years.

White Hunter, by J.A. Hunter, Safari Press Publications, Huntington Beach, CA, 1999. 282 pp., illus. $24.95

This book is a seldom-seen account of John Hunter's adventures in pre-WWII Africa.

Wind, Dust and Snow, by Robert M. Anderson, Safari Press, Inc., Huntington Beach, CA, 1997. 240 pp., illus. $65.00

A complete chronology of modern exploratory and pioneering Asian sheep-hunting expeditions from 1960 until 1996, with wonderful background history and previously untold stories.

With a Gun in Good Country, by Ian Manning, Trophy Room Books, Agoura, CA, 1996. Limited, numbered and signed by the author. $85.00

A book written about that splendid period before the poaching onslaught which almost closed Zambia and continues to the granting of her independence. It then goes on to recount Manning's experiences in Botswana, Congo, and briefly in South Africa.

Yoshi–The Life and Travels of an International Trophy Hunter, by W. Yoshimoto with Bill Quimby, Long Beach, CA, Safari Press, Inc., 2002. A limited edition of 1,000 copies, signed and numbered. 298 pp., color and b&w photos. Hardcover in a slipcase. $85.00

Watson T. Yoshimoto, a native Hawaiian, collected all 16 major varieties of the world's wild sheep and most of the many types of goats, ibex, bears, antelopes, and antlered game of Asia, Europe, North America, South America, and the South Pacific…as well as the African Big Five. Along the way he earned the respect of his peers and was awarded hunting's highest achievement, the coveted Weatherby Award.

RIFLES

.577 Snider-Enfield Rifles & Carbines; British Service Longarms, by Ian Skennerton. 1866-C.1880. Australia, Arms & Militaria Press, 2003. 1st edition. 240 pp. plus 8 color plates, 100 illustrations. Marking Ribbon. Hardcover. $39.50

The definitive study of Britain's first breech-loading rifle, at first converted from Enfield muskets, then newly made with Mk III breech. The trials, development, rifle and carbine models are detailed; new information along with descriptions of the cartridges.

The '03 Springfield Rifles Era, by Clark S. Campbell, Richmond, VA, privately printed, 2003. 1st edition. 368 pp., 146 illustrations, drawn to scale by author. Hardcover. $58.00

A much-expanded version of this author's famous The '03 Springfield (1957) and The '03 Springfields (1971), representing 40 years of research into all things '03. Part I is a complete and verifiably correct study of all standardized and special-purpose models of the U.S. M1903 Springfield rifle, in both .22 and .30 calibers, including those prototypes which led to standard models, and also all standardized .30 caliber cartridges, including National and International Match, and caliber .22. Part II is the result of the author's five years as a Research and Development Engineer with Remington Arms Co., and will be of inestimable value to anyone planning a custom sporter, whether or not based on the '03.

A Master Gunmaker's Guide to Building Bolt-Action Rifles, by Bill Holmes, Boulder, CO, Paladin Press, 2003. Photos, illus., 152 pp. Softcover. $25.00

Many people today call themselves gunmakers, but very few have actually made a gun. Most buy parts wherever available and simply assemble them. During the past 50 years Bill Holmes has built from scratch countless rifles, shotguns and pistols of amazing artistry, ranging in caliber from .17 to .50.

A Question of Confidence–The Ross Rifle in the Trenches #4 in "Up Close" Series, by Col. A.F. Duguid, Ottawa, Ontario, Service Publications, 2000. 1st edition. 48 pp., 19 illustrations. Softcover, NEW. $29.95

The Accurate Rifle, by Warren Page, Claymore Publishing, Ohio, 1997. 254 pp., illus. Revised edition. Paper covers. $17.95

Provides hunters & shooters alike with detailed practical information on the whole range of subjects affecting rifle accuracy, he explains techniques in ammo, sights & shooting methods. With a 1996 equipment update from Dave Brennan.

The Accurate Varmint Rifle, by Boyd Mace, Precision Shooting, Inc., Whitehall, NY, 1991. 184 pp., illus. $15.00

A long overdue and long needed work on what factors go into the selection of components for and the subsequent assembly of…the accurate varmint rifle.

The AK-47 and AK-74 Kalashnikov Rifles and Their Variations, by Joe Poyer, Tustin, CA, North Cape Publications, 2004. 1st edition. Softcover, NEW. $22.95

The AK-47 Assault Rifle, Desert Publications, Cornville, AZ, 1981. 150 pp., illus. Paper covers. $15.95

Complete and practical technical information on the only weapon in history to be produced in an estimated 30,000,000 units.

American Hunting Rifles: Their Application in the Field for Practical Shooting, by Craig Boddington, Safari Press, Huntington Beach, CA, 1996. 446 pp., illus. Second printing trade edition. Softcover $24.95

Covers all the hunting rifles and calibers that are needed for North America's diverse game.

The American Krag Rifle and Carbine, by Joe Poyer, North Cape Publications, Tustin, CA, 2002. 1st edition. 317 pp., illustrated with hundreds of b&w drawings and photos. Softcover. $19.95

Provides the arms collector, historian and target shooter with a part by part analysis of what has been called the rifle with the smoothest bolt action ever designed. All changes to all parts are analyzed in detail and matched to serial number ranges. A monthly serial number chart by production year has been devised that will provide the collector with the year and month in which his gun was manufactured. A new and complete exploded view was produced for this book.

The American Percussion Schuetzen Rifle, by J. Hamilton and T. Rowe, Rochester, NY, Rowe Publications, 2005. 1st edition. 388 pp. Hardcover. New in new dust jacket. $89.95

The AR-15 Complete Assembly Guide, Volume 2, by Walt Kuleck and Clint McKee. Export, PA, Scott A. Duff Publications, 2002. 1st edition. 155 pp., 164 photographs & line drawings. Softcover. $19.95

This book goes beyond the military manuals in depth and scope, using words and pictures to clearly guide the reader through every operation required to assemble their AR-15-type rifle. You'll learn the best and easiest ways to build your rifle. It won't make you an AR-15 armorer, but it will make you a more knowledgeable owner. You'll be able to do more with (and to) your rifle. You'll also be able to better judge the competence of those whom you choose to work on your rifle, and to discuss your needs more intelligently with them. In short, if you build it, you'll know how to repair it.

The AR-15 Complete Owner's Guide, Volume 1, 2nd Edition, by Walt Kuleck and Scott Duff, Export, PA, Scott A. Duff Publications, 2002. 224 pp., 164 photographs & line drawings. Softcover. $21.95

This book provides the prospective, new or experienced AR-15 owner with the in-depth knowledge he or she needs to select, configure, operate, maintain and troubleshoot his or her rifle. The Guide covers history, applications, details of components and subassemblies, operating, cleaning, maintenance, and future of perhaps the most versatile rifle system ever produced. A comprehensive Colt model number table and pre-/post-ban serial number information are included. This is the book I wish had existed prior to buying my first AR-15!

The AR-15/M16, A Practical Guide, by Duncan Long, Paladin Press, Boulder, CO, 1985. 168 pp., illus. Paper covers. $22.00

The definitive book on the rifle that has been the inspiration for so many modern assault rifles.

Argentine Mauser Rifles 1871-1959, by Colin Atglen, Webster, PA, Schiffer Publications, 2003. 1st edition. 304 pp., over 400 b&w and color photographs, drawings, and charts. Hardcover. $79.95

This is the complete story of Argentina's contract Mauser rifles from the purchase of their first Model 1871s to the disposal of the last shipment of surplus rifles received in the United States in May 2002. The Argentine Commission's relentless pursuit of tactical superiority resulted in a major contribution to the development of Mauser's now famous bolt-action system. The combined efforts of the Belgian, Turkish and Argentine arms commissions between 1889 and 1002 produced the origins of what became the Model 90 bolt-action system that is still in use today over 110 years later.

The Art of Shooting with the Rifle, by Col. Sir H. St. John Halford, Excalibur Publications, Latham, NY, 1996. 96 pp., illus. Paper covers. $12.95

A facsimile edition of the 1888 book by a respected rifleman providing a wealth of detailed information.

The Art of the Rifle, by Jeff Cooper, Paladin Press, Boulder, CO, 1997. 104 pp., illus. $29.95

Everything you need to know about the rifle whether you use it for security, meat or target shooting.

Ballard: The Great American Single Shot Rifle, by John T. Dutcher, Denver, CO, privately printed, 2002. 1st edition. 380 pp., illustrated with b&w photos, with an 8-page color insert. Hardcover. $79.95

Benchrest Actions and Triggers, by Stuart Otteson. Rohnert Park, CA, Adams-Kane Press, July 2003. Limited edition. 64 pp. Softcover. $27.95

Stuart Otteson's Benchrest Actions and Triggers is truly a lost classic. Benchrest Actions and Triggers is a compilation of 17 articles Mr. Otteson wrote. The articles contained are of particular interest to the benchrest crowd. Reprinted by permission of Wolfe Publishing.

ARMS LIBRARY

Black Magic: The Ultra Accurate AR-15, by John Feamster, Precision Shooting, Manchester, CT, 1998. 300 pp., illus. $29.95

The author has compiled his experiences pushing the accuracy envelope of the AR-15 to its maximum potential. A wealth of advice on AR-15 loads, modifications and accessories for everything from NRA Highpower and Service Rifle competitions to benchrest and varmint shooting.

The Black Rifle, M16 Retrospective, R. Blake Stevens and Edward C. Ezell, Collector Grade Publications, Toronto, Canada, 1987. 400 pp., illus. $42.95

Black Rifle II: The M16 into the 21st Century, by Christopher R. Bartocci, Canada, Collector Grade Publications, 2004. 1st edition. 408 pp., 626 illustrations. Hardcover. New in new dust jacket. $69.95

Blitzkrieg!–The MP40 Maschinenpistole of WWII, by Frank Iannamico, Harmony, ME, Moose Lake Publishing, 2003. 1st edition. Over 275 pp., 280 photos and documents. Softcover. $29.95

It's back, now in a new larger 8" x 11" format. Lots of new information and many unpublished photos. This book includes the history and development of the German machine pistol from the MP18.I to the MP40.

Bolt Action Rifles, Expanded 4th Edition, by Frank de Haas and Wayne van Zwoll, Krause Publications, Iola, WI 2003. 696 pp., illustrated with 615 b&w photos. Softcover. $29.95

The Book of the Garand, by Maj. Gen. J.S. Hatcher, The Gun Room Press, Highland Park, NJ, 1977. 292 pp., illus. $26.95

A new printing of the standard reference work on the U.S. Army M1 rifle.

British .22RF Training Rifles, by Dennis Lewis and Robert Washburn, Excaliber Publications, Latham, NY, 1993. 64 pp., illus. Paper covers. $10.95

The story of Britain's training rifles from the early Aiming Tube models to the post-WWII trainers.

Building Double Rifles on Shotgun Actions, by W. Ellis Brown, Ft. Collins, CO, Bunduki Publishing, 2001. 1st edition. 187 pp., including index and b&w photographs. Hardcover. $55.00

Classic Sporting Rifles, by Christopher Austyn, Safari Press, Huntington Beach, CA, 1997. 128 pp., illus. $50.00

As the head of the gun department at Christie's Auction House the author examines the "best" rifles built over the last 150 years.

The Collectable '03, by J.C. Harrison, The Arms Chest, Oklahoma City, OK. 1999. 2nd edition (revised). 234 pp., illustrated with drawings, Spiral bound. $35.00

Valuable and detailed reference book for the collector of the Model 1903 Springfield rifle.

Collecting Classic Bolt Action Military Rifles, by Paul S. Scarlata, Andrew Mowbray, Inc., Lincoln, RI, 2001. 280 pp., illus. $39.95

Over 400 large photographs detail key features you will need to recognize in order to identify guns for your collection. Learn the original military configurations of these service rifles so you can tell them apart from altered guns and bad restorations. The historical sections are particularly strong, giving readers a clear understanding of how and why these rifles were developed, and which troops used them.

Collecting the Garand, by J.C. Harrison, The Arms Chest, Oklahoma City, OK. 2001. 2nd edition (revised). 198 pp., illus. with pictures and drawings. Spiral bound. $35.00

Valuable and detailed reference book for the collector of the Garand.

Collecting the M1 Carbine, by J.C. Harrison, The Arms Chest, Oklahoma City, OK. 2000. 2nd edition (revised). 247 pp., illustrated with pictures and drawings. Spiral bound. $35.00

Valuable and detailed reference book for the collector of the M1 Carbine. Identifies standard issue original military models of M1 and M1A1 Models of 1942, '43, '44, and '45 carbines as produced by each manufacturer, plus arsenal repair, refinish and lend-lease.

The Competitive AR15: The Mouse That Roared, by Glenn Zediker, Zediker Publishing, Oxford, MS, 1999. 286 pp., illus. Paper covers. $29.95

A thorough and detailed study of the newest precision rifle sensation.

The Complete AR15/M16 Sourcebook, Revised and Updated Edition, by Duncan Long, Paladin Press, Boulder, CO, 2002. 336 pp., illus. Paper covers. $39.95

The latest development of the AR15/M16 and the many spin-offs now available, selective-fire conversion systems for the 1990s, the vast selection of new accessories.

The Complete Book of the .22: A Guide to the World's Most Popular Guns, by Wayne van Zwoll, Lyons Press, 2004. 1st edition. 336 pgs. Hardcover. NEW. $26.95

Complete Guide to the M1 Garand and the M1 Carbine, by Bruce Canfield, Andrew Mowbray, Inc., Lincoln, RI, 1999. 296 pp., illus. $39.50

Covers all of the manufacturers of components, parts, variations and markings. Learn which parts are proper for which guns. The total story behind these guns, from their invention through WWII, Korea, Vietnam and beyond! 300+ photos show you features, markings, overall views and action shots. Thirty-three tables and charts give instant reference to serial numbers, markings, dates of issue and proper configurations. Special sections on sniper guns, National Match rifles, exotic variations, and more!

The Complete M1 Garand, by Jim Thompson, Paladin Press, Boulder, CO, 1998. 160 pp., illus. Paper cover. $24.00

A guide for the shooter and collector, heavily illustrated.

Crown Jewels: The Mauser In Sweden; A Century of Accuracy and Precision, by Dana Jones, Canada, Collector Grade Publications, 2003. 1st edition. 312 pp., 691 illustrations. Hardcover. $49.95

Here is the first in-depth study of all the Swedish Mausers: the 6.5mm M/94 carbines, M/96 long rifles, M/38 short rifles, Swedish K98Ks (called the M/39 in 7.92x57mm, then, after rechambering to fire the 8x63mm machine gun cartridge, the M/40); sniper rifles, and other military adaptations such as grenade launchers and artillery simulators. Also covers a wide variety of the micrometer-adjustment rear sight inserts and "diopter" receiver sights which were produced in order to allow shooters to take full advantage of the accuracy and precision of the Swedish Mauser. Full chapters on bayonets and the many accessories, both military and civilian.

Defending the Dominion, Canadian Military Rifles, 1855-1955, by David Edgecombe, Ont. Canada, Service Publications, 2003. 1st edition. 168 pp., with 60+ illustrations. Hardcover. $39.95

The Emma Gees, by Capt. Herbert W McBride, Mt. Ida, AR, Lancer Publishing, 2003. Reprint. 224 pp., b&w photos. Softcover. $19.95

The Emma Gees is the rest of McBride's story. First published in 1918, this was McBride's first book about his service with the machine gun section in WWI. The Emma Gees was even rarer than *A Rifleman Went to War* until this reprint that includes new biographical information from the National Archives of Canada. With chapters such as "A Fine Day for Murder" and "Sniper Barn," this is an excellent companion to his other book.

F.N.-F.A.L. Auto Rifles, Desert Publications, Cornville, AZ, 1981. 130 pp., illus. Paper covers. $18.95

A definitive study of one of the free world's finest combat rifles.

The FAL Rifle, by R. Blake Stevens and Jean van Rutten, Collector Grade Publications, Cobourg, Canada, 1993. 848 pp., illus. $129.95

Originally published in three volumes, this classic edition covers North American, UK and Commonwealth and the metric FAL's.

The Fighting Rifle, by Chuck Taylor, Paladin Press, Boulder, CO, 1983. 184 pp., illus. Paper covers. $25.00

The difference between assault and battle rifles and auto and light machine guns.

Firearms Assembly/Disassembly Part III: Rimfire Rifles, Revised Edition, The Gun Digest Book of, by J.B. Wood, DBI Books, a division of Krause Publications, Iola, WI, 1994. 480 pp., illus. Paper covers. $19.95

Covers 65 popular rimfires plus over 100 variants, all cross-referenced in the index.

The FN-FAL Rifle, et al, by Duncan Long, Delta Press, El Dorado, AR, 1998. 148 pp., illus. Paper covers. $18.95

A comprehensive study of one of the classic assault weapons of all times. Detailed descriptions of the basic models plus the myriad of variants that evolved as a result of its universal acceptance.

Forty Years with the .45-70, Second edition, revised and expanded, by Paul A. Matthews, Wolfe Publishing Co., Prescott, AZ, 1997. 184 pp., illus. Paper covers. $17.95

This book is pure gun lore of the .45-70. It not only contains a history of the cartridge, but also years of the author's personal experiences.

German Sniper 1914-1945, by Peter R. Senich, Paladin Press, Boulder, CO, 1997 8-1/2" x 11", hardcover, photos, 468 pp. $69.95

The complete story of Germany's sniping arms development through both world wars. Presents more than 600 photos of Mauser 98's, Selbstladegewehr 41s and 43s, optical sights by Goerz, Zeiss, etc., plus German snipers in action. An exceptional hardcover collector's edition for serious military historians everywhere.

The Great Remington 8 and Model 81 Autoloading Rifles, by John Henwood, Canada, Collector Grade Publications, 2003. 1st edition. 304 pp., 291 illustrations, 31 in color. Hardcover. $59.95

Greenhill Military Manual: Military Rifles of Two World Wars, by John Walter, London, Greenhill Publishing, 2003. 1st edition. 144 pp., illus. Hardcover. $24.00

Handbook of Military Rifle Marks 1866-1950 (Third Edition), by Richard A. Hoffman and Noel P. Schott, St. Louis, MO, Mapleleaf Militaria Publications, 2002. 3rd edition. NEW. $30.00

The Historic Henry Rifle: Oliver Winchester's Famous Civil War Repeater, by Wiley Sword, Andrew Mowbray, Inc., Lincoln, RI. 2002. Softcover. $29.95

It was perhaps the most important firearm of its era. Tested and proved in the fiery crucible of the Civil War, the Henry Rifle became the forerunner of the famous line of Winchester Repeating Rifles that "Won the West." Here is the fascinating story from the frustrations of early sales efforts aimed at the government to the inspired purchase of the Henry Rifle by veteran soldiers who wanted the best weapon.

Hitler's Garands: German Self-Loading Rifles of World War II, by Darrin W. Weaver, Collector Grade Publications, Canada, 2001. 392 pp., 590 illustrations. $69.95

Hitler's Wehrmacht began WWII armed with the bolt-action K98k, a rifle only cosmetically different from that with which Imperial Germany had fought the Great War a quarter-century earlier. Then in 1940, the Heereswaffenamt (HWaA, the Army Weapons Office) issued a requirement for a new self-loading rifle. Taking their lead from the Russians, Walther copied (and patented) the gas system of the Tokarev SVT self-loader, grafting it onto the flap-locked bolt of the G41 to create the G43, which was only produced during the last nineteen desperate months of WWII.

How-To's for the Black Powder Cartridge Rifle Shooter, by Paul A. Matthews, Wolfe Publishing Co., Prescott, AZ, 1996. 136 pp., illus. Paper covers. $22.50

Practices and procedures used in the reloading and shooting of blackpowder cartridges.

How to Convert Military Rifles, Davidson, MI, Williams Gun Sight Company, 1998. New revised enlarged seventh edition. 76 pp., illus. Softcover. $13.95

Explains the features that make certain models more desirable for conversion. Covers the steps to proper scope mounting, installing triggers and safeties; restocking and finishing. The exploded parts drawings are extremely useful and sight fitting charts can save hours of frustration. Revised and enlarged 7th edition presents information on 14 military and civilian rifles.

The Hunter's Guide to Accurate Shooting, by Wayne van Zwoll, Guilford, CT, Lyons Press, 2002. 1st edition. 288 pp. Hardcover. $29.95

Firearms expert van Zwoll explains exactly how to shoot the big-game rifle accurately. Taking into consideration every pertinent factor, he shows a step-by-step analysis of shooting and hunting with the big-game rifle.

Jaeger Rifles Collected Articles Published in Muzzle Blasts, by George Shumway, York, PA, George Shumway, 2003. Reprint. 108 pp., illus. Stiff paper covers. NEW. $30.00

Johnson Rifles and Machine Guns: The Story of Melvin Maynard Johnson Jr. and his Guns, by Bruce N. Canfield, Lincoln, RI, Andrew Mowbray, Inc., 2002. 1st edition. 272 pp. with over 285 photographs. Hardcover. $49.95

The M1941 Johnson rifle is the hottest WWII rifle on the collector's market today. From invention and manufacture through issue to the troops, this book covers them all!

Kalashnikov: The Arms and the Man, A Revised and Expanded Edition of the AK47 Story, by Edward C. Ezell, Canada, Collector Grade Publications, 2002. 312 pp., 356 illustrations. Hardcover. $59.95

The original edition of The AK47 Story was published in 1986, and the events of the intervening fifteen years have provided much fresh new material. Beginning with an introduction by Dr. Kalashnikov himself, this is a most comprehensive study of the "life and times" of the AK, starting with the early history of small arms manufacture in Czarist Russia and then the Soviet Union.

Know Your M1 Garand, by E.J. Hoffschmidt, Blacksmith Corp., Southport, CT, 1975, 84 pp., illus. Paper covers. $14.95

Facts about America's most famous infantry weapon. Covers test and experimental models, Japanese and Italian copies, National Match models.

ARMS LIBRARY

Know Your Ruger 10/22 Carbine, by William E. Workman, Blacksmith Corp., Chino Valley, AZ, 1991. 96 pp., illus. Paper covers. $14.95

The story and facts about the most popular 22 autoloader ever made.

The Last Enfield: SA80–The Reluctant Rifle, by Steve Raw, Collector Grade Publications, Canada 2003. 1st edition. 360 pp., with 382 illustrations. Hardcover. $49.95

This book presents the entire, in-depth story of its subject firearm, in this case the controversial British SA80, right from the founding of what became the Royal Small Arms Factory (RSAF) Enfield in the early 1800s; briefly through two world wars with Enfield at the forefront of small arms production for British forces; and covering the adoption of the 7.62mm NATO cartridge in 1954 and the L1A1 rifle in 1957.

The Lee Enfield No. 1 Rifles, by Alan M. Petrillo, Excaliber Publications, Latham, NY, 1992. 64 pp., illus. Paper covers. $10.95

Highlights the SMLE rifles from the Mark 1-VI.

The Lee Enfield Number 4 Rifles, by Alan M. Petrillo, Excalibur Publications, Latham, NY, 1992. 64 pp., illus. Paper covers. $10.95

A pocket-sized, bare-bones reference devoted entirely to the .303 WWII and Korean War vintage service rifle.

Legendary Sporting Rifles, by Sam Fadala, Stoeger Publishing Co., So. Hackensack, NJ, 1992. 288 pp., illus. Paper covers. $16.95

Covers a vast span of time and technology beginning with the Kentucky longrifle.

The Li'l M1 .30 Cal. Carbine, by Duncan Long, Desert Publications, El Dorado, AZ, 1995. 203 pp., illus. Paper covers. $19.95

Traces the history of this little giant from its original creation.

M1 Carbine Owner's Manual, M1, M2 & M3 .30 Caliber Carbines, Firepower Publications, Cornville, AZ, 1984. 102 pp., illus. Paper covers. $9.95

The complete book for the owner of an M1 carbine.

The M1 Garand Serial Numbers & Data Sheets, by Scott A. Duff, Scott A. Duff, Export, PA, 1995. 101 pp. Paper covers. $11.95

This pocket reference book includes serial number tables and data sheets on the Springfield Armory, gas trap rifles, gas port rifles, Winchester Repeating Arms, International Harvester and H&R Arms Co. and more.

The M1 Garand: Post World War, by Scott A. Duff, Scott A. Duff Publications, Export, PA, 1990. 139 pp., illus. Softcover. $21.95

A detailed account of the activities at Springfield Armory through this period. International Harvester, H&R, Korean War production and quantities delivered. Serial numbers.

The M1 Garand: World War 2, by Scott A. Duff, Scott A. Duff Publications, Export, PA, 1993. 210 pp., illus. Paper covers. $34.95

The most comprehensive study available to the collector and historian on the M1 Garand of WWII.

The M14 Owner's Guide and Match Conditioning Instructions, by Scott A. Duff and John M. Miller, Duff Publications, Export, PA, 1996. 180 pp., illus. Paper covers. $19.95

Traces the history and development from the T44 through the adoption and production of the M14 rifle.

The M14 Rifle, facsimile reprint of FM 23-8, Desert Publications, Cornville, AZ, 50 pp., illus. Paper $11.95

Well illustrated and informative reprint covering the M-14 and M-14E2.

The M14-Type Rifle: A Shooter's and Collector's Guide, by Joe Poyer, North Cape Publications, Tustin, CA, 1997. 82 pp., illus. Paper covers. $14.95

Covers the history and development, commercial copies, cleaning and maintenance instructions, and targeting and shooting.

M14/M14A1 Rifles and Rifle Marksmanship, Desert Publications, El Dorado, AZ, 1995. 236 pp., illus. Paper covers. $19.95

Contains a detailed description of the M14 and M14A1 rifles and their general characteristics, procedures for disassembly & assembly, operating and functioning of the rifles.

The M16/AR15 Rifle, by Joe Poyer, North Cape Publications, Tustin, CA, 1998. 150 pp., illus. Paper covers. $19.95

From its inception as the first American assault battle rifle to the firing lines of the National Matches, the M16/AR15 rifle in all its various models and guises has made a significant impact on the American rifleman.

Major Ned H. Roberts and the Schuetzen Rifle, edited by Gerald O. Kelver, Brighton, CO, 1998. 3rd edition. 122 pp., illus. $13.95

A compilation of the writings of Major Ned H. Roberts which appeared in various gun magazines.

Mauser Military Rifles of the World, 3rd Edition, by Robert Ball, Iola, WI, Krause Publications, 2003. 304 pp., illus. With 1,000 b&w and 48-page color section. Hardcover. $39.95

This 3rd edition brings more than 200 new photos of these historical rifles and the wars in which they were carried. Mauser military rifles offer collectors almost unlimited variations, and author Bob Ball continues to find rare and interesting specimens. Every detail is presented, from the length and weight of the rifle to the manufacturer's markings. This book shows collectors precisely how to identify every model from 1871 to 1945 and provides production figures and the relative rarity of each model. Because Mauser rifles were produced under contract in so many different nations, the book is organized alphabetically by country and the year of production.

Mauser Smallbore Sporting, Target and Training Rifles, by Jon Speed, Collector Grade Publications, Inc., Cobourg, Ont., Canada, 1998. 372 pp., illus. $67.50

The history of all the smallbore sporting, target and training rifles produced by the legendary Mauser-Werke of Obendorf am Neckar.

Mauser: Original-Oberndorf Sporting Rifles, by Jon Speed, Collector Grade Publications, Inc., Cobourg, Ont., Canada, 1997. 508 pp., illus. $89.95

The most exhaustive study ever published of the design origins and manufacturing history of the original Oberndorf Mauser Sporter.

MG34-MG42 German Universal Machineguns, by Folke Myrvang, Collector Grade Publications, Canada. 2002. 496 pp., 646 illustrations. $79.95

This is the first-ever COMPETE study of the MG34 & MG42. Here the author presents in-depth coverage of the historical development, fielding, tactical use of and modifications made to these remarkable guns and their myriad accessories and ancillaries, plus authoritative tips on troubleshooting.

Military Bolt Action Rifles, 1841-1918, by Donald B. Webster, Museum Restoration Service, Alexander Bay, NY, 1993. 150 pp., illus. $34.50

A photographic survey of the principal rifles and carbines of the European and Asiatic powers of the last half of the 19th century and the first years of the 20th century.

The Mini-14, by Duncan Long, Paladin Press, Boulder, CO, 1987. 120 pp., illus. Paper covers. $17.00

History of the Mini-14, the factory-produced models, specifications, accessories, suppliers, and much more.

The MKB 42, MP43, MP44 and the Sturmgewehr 44, by de Vries & Martens. Alexandria, VA, Ironside International, 2003. 1st edition. 152 pp., illustrated with 200 high quality b&w photos. Hardcover. $39.95

Covers all essential information on history and development, ammunition and accessories, codes and markings, and contains photos of nearly every model and accessory. Includes a unique selection of original German WWII propaganda photos, most never published before.

Modern Sniper Rifles, by Duncan Long, Paladin Press, Boulder, CO, 1997, 8-1/2" x 11", soft cover, photos, illus., 120 pp. $20.00

Noted weapons expert Duncan Long describes the .22 LR, single-shot, bolt-action, semiautomatic and large-caliber rifles that can be used for sniping purposes, including the U.S. M21, Ruger Mini-14, AUG and HK-94SG1. These and other models are evaluated on the basis of their features, accuracy, reliability and handiness in the field. The author also looks at the best scopes, ammunition and accessories.

More Single Shot Rifles and Actions, by Frank de Haas and Mark de Haas, Orange City, IA, 1996. 146 pp., illus. Paper covers. $22.50

Covers 45 different single shot rifles. Includes the history plus photos, drawings and personal comments.

Mr. Single Shot's Book of Rifle Plans, by Frank de Haas and Mark de Haas, Orange City, IA, 1996. 85 pp., illus. Paper covers. $22.50

Contains complete and detailed drawings, plans and instructions on how to build four different and unique breech-loading single shot rifles of the author's own proven design.

The No. 4 (T) Sniper Rifle: An Armourer's Perspective, by Peter Laidler with Ian Skennerton, I.D.S.A. Books, Piqua, OH, 1993. 125 pp., 75 illus. Paper covers. $19.95

A reprint of the 1864 London edition. Captain Heaton was one of the great rifle shots from the earliest days of the Volunteer Movement.

The Official SKS Manual, Translation by Major James F. Gebhardt (Ret.), Paladin Press, Boulder, CO, 1997. 96 pp., illus. Paper covers. $16.00

This Soviet military manual covering the widely distributed SKS is now available in English.

Old German Target Arms: Alte Schiebenwaffen, by Jesse Thompson, C. Ron Dillon, Allen Hallock and Bill Loos, Rochester, NY, Tom Rowe Publications, 2003. 1st edition. 392 pp. Hardcover. $98.00

History of Schueten shooting from the middle ages through WWII. Hundreds of illustrations, most in color. History & Memorabilia of the Bundesschiessen (State or National Shoots), Bird Target rifles, American shooters in Germany. Schutzen rifles such as matchlocks, wheellocks, flintlocks, percussion, bader, bornmuller, rifles by Buchel and more.

Ordnance Tools, Accessories & Appendages of the M1 Rifle, by Billy Pyle, Houston, TX, privately printed, 2002. 2nd edition. 206 pp., illustrated with b&w photos. Softcover. $40.00

This is the new updated second edition with over 350 pictures and drawings, of which 30 are new. Part I contains accessories, appendages, and equipment including such items as bayonets, blank firing attachments, cheek pads, cleaning equipment, clips, flash hiders, grenade launchers, scabbards, slings, telescopes and mounts, winter triggers, and much more. Part II covers ammunition, grenades, and pyrotechnics. Part III shows the inspection gages. Part IV presents the ordnance tools, fixtures, and assemblies. Part V contains miscellaneous items related to the M1 Rifle such as arms racks, rifle racks, clip loading machine, and other devices.

Police Rifles, by Richard Fairburn, Paladin Press, Boulder, CO, 1994. 248 pp., illus. Paper covers. $35.00

Selecting the right rifle for street patrol and special tactical situations.

The Poor Man's Sniper Rifle, by D. Boone, Paladin Press, Boulder, CO, 1995. 152 pp., illus. Paper covers. $18.95

Here is a complete plan for converting readily available surplus military rifles to high-performance sniper weapons.

A Potpourri of Single Shot Rifles and Actions, by Frank de Haas and Mark de Haas, Ridgeway, MO, 1993. 153 pp., illus. Paper covers. $22.50

The author's 6th book on non-bolt-action single shots. Covers more than 40 single-shot rifles in historical and technical detail.

Precision Shooting with the M1 Garand, by Roy Baumgardner, Precision Shooting, Inc., Manchester, CT, 1999. 142 pp., illus. Paper covers. $12.95

Starts off with the ever popular ten-article series on accurizing the M1 that originally appeared in Precision Shooting in the 1993-95 era. There follows nine more Baumgardner-authored articles on the M1 Garand and finally a 1999 updating chapter.

The Remington 700, by John F. Lacy, Taylor Publishing Co., Dallas, TX, 2002. 208 pp., illus. $49.95

Covers the different models, limited editions, chamberings, proofmarks, serial numbers, military models, and much more.

Remington Autoloading And Pump Action Rifles, by Eugene Myszkowski, Tucson, AZ, Excalibur Publications, 2002. 132 pp., with 162 photographs, 6 illustrations and 18 charts. Softcover. $20.95

An illustrated history of Remington's centerfire Models 760, 740, 742, 7400 and 7600. The book is thoroughly researched and features many previously unpublished photos of the rifles, their accessories and accoutrements. Also covers high grade, unusual and experimental rifles. Contains information on collecting, serial numbers and barrel codes.

The Rifle Rules: Magic for the Ultimate Rifleman, by Don Paul, Kaua'i, HI, Pathfinder Publications, 2003. 1st edition. 116 pp., illus. Softcover. $14.95

A new method that shows you how to add hundreds of yards to your effective shooting ability. Ways for you to improve your rifle's accuracy which no factory can do. Illustrations & photos added to make new concepts easy.

The Rifle Shooter, by G. David Tubb, Oxford, MS, Zediker Publishing, 2004. 1st edition. 416 pp softcover, 7x10 size, 400 photos and illustrations, very high quality printing. Softcover. $34.95

This is not just a revision of his landmark "Highpower Rifle" but an all-new, greatly expanded work that reveals David's thoughts and recommendations on all aspects of precision rifle shooting. Each shooting position and event is dissected and taken to extreme detail, as are the topics of ammunition, training, rifle design, event strategies, and wind shooting. You will learn the secrets of perhaps the greatest rifleman ever, and you'll learn how to put them to work for you!

Rifles of the U.S. Army 1861-1906, by John D. McAulay, Lincoln, RI, Andrew Mowbray, Inc., 2003. 1st edition. 278 pp., illus. Hardcover. NEW. $45.89

ARMS LIBRARY

Rifles of the White Death (Valkoisen Kuoleman Kivaarit) A Collector's and Shooter's Guide to Finnish Military Rifles 1918-1944, by Doug Bowser, MS, Camellia City Military Publications, 1998. 1st edition. Stiff paper covers. NEW. $35.00

Rock Island Rifle Model 1903, by C.S. Ferris, Export, PA, Scott A. Duff Publications, 2002. 177 pp., illustrated with b&w photographs. Foreword by Scott A. Duff. Softcover. $22.95

S.L.R.–Australia's F.N. F.A.L., by Ian Skennerton and David Balmer, Arms & Militaria Press, 1989. 124 pp., 100 illus. Paper covers. $24.50

Schuetzen Rifles, History and Loading, by Gerald O. Kelver, Pioneer Press, Union City, TN, 1998. 3rd edition. Illus. $13.95

Reference work on these rifles, their bullets, loading, telescopic sights, accuracy, etc. A limited, numbered ed.

Shooting Lever Guns of the Old West, by Mike Venturino, MLV Enterprises, Livingston, MT, 1999. 300 pp., illus. Paper covers. $27.95

Shooting the lever action type repeating rifles of our American west.

Shooting the .43 Spanish Rolling Block, by Croft Barker, Flatonia, TX, Cistern Publishing, 2003. 1st edition. 137 pp. Softcover. $25.50

The SOURCE for information on .43 caliber rolling blocks. Lots of photos and text covering Remington & Oveido actions, antique cartridges, etc. Features smokless & black powder loads, rifle disassembly and maintenance, 11 mm bullets. Required reading for the rolling block owner.

Shooting the Blackpowder Cartridge Rifle, by Paul A. Matthews, Wolfe Publishing Co., Prescott, AZ, 1994. 129 pp., illus. Paper covers. $22.50

A general discourse on shooting the blackpowder cartridge rifle and the procedure required to make a particular rifle perform.

Single Shot Rifles and Actions, by Frank de Haas, Orange City, IA, 1990. 352 pp., illus. Softcover. $27.00

The definitive book on over 60 single shot rifles and actions.

Small Arms Identification Series, No. 1–.303 Rifle, No. 1 S.M.L.E. Marks III and III*, by Ian Skennerton, I.D.S.A. Books, Piqua, OH, 1981. 48 pp. $10.50

Small Arms Identification Series, No. 2–.303 Rifle, No. 4 Marks I, & I*, Marks 1/2, 1/3 & 2, by Ian Skennerton, I.D.S.A. Books, Piqua, OH, 1994. 48 pp. $10.50

Small Arms Identification Series, No. 3–9mm Austen Mk I & 9mm Owen Mk I Sub-Machine Guns, by Ian Skennerton, I.D.S.A. Books, Piqua, OH, 1994. 48 pp. $10.50

Small Arms Identification Series, No. 4–.303 Rifle, No. 5 Mk I, by Ian Skennerton, I.D.S.A. Books, Piqua, OH, 1994. 48 pp. $10.50

Small Arms Identification Series, No. 5–.303-in. Bren Light Machine Gun, by Ian Skennerton, I.D.S.A. Books, Piqua, OH, 1994. 48 pp. $10.50

The Springfield Rifle M1903, M1903A1, M1903A3, M1903A4, Desert Publications, Cornville, AZ, 1982. 100 pp., illus. Paper covers. $14.95

Covers every aspect of disassembly and assembly, inspection, repair and maintenance.

Still More Single Shot Rifles, by James J. Grant, Pioneer Press, Union City, TN, 1995. 211 pp., illus. $29.95

This is Volume Four in a series of single shot rifles by America's foremost authority. It gives more in-depth information on those single shot rifles which were presented in the first three books.

The Sturm, Ruger 10/22 Rifle and .44 Magnum Carbine, by Duncan Long, Paladin Press, Boulder, CO, 1988. 108 pp., illus. Paper covers. $15.00

An in-depth look at both weapons detailing the elegant simplicity of the Ruger design. Offers specifications, troubleshooting procedures and ammunition recommendations.

Swedish Mauser Rifles, by Steve Kehaya and Joe Poyer, Tustin, CA, North Cape Publications, 2004. 2nd edition, revised. 267 pp., illus. Softcover. $19.95

Every known variation of the Swedish Mauser carbine and rifle is described including all match and target rifles and all sniper versions. Includes serial number and production data.

Swiss Magazine Loading Rifles 1869 to 1958, by Joe Poyer, Tustin, CA, North Cape Publications, 2003. 1st edition. 317 pp., illustrated with hundreds of b&w drawings and photos. Softcover. $19.95

It covers the K-31 on a part-by-part basis, as well as its predecessor models of 1889 and 1911, and the first repeating magazine rifle ever adopted by a military, the Model 1869 Vetterli rifle and its successor models. Also includes a history of the development and use of these fine rifles. Details regarding their ammunition, complete assembly/disassembly instructions as well as sections on cleaning, maintenance and trouble shooting.

The Tactical Rifle, by Gabriel Suarez, Paladin Press, Boulder, CO, 1999. 264 pp., illus. Paper covers. $25.00

The precision tool for urban police operations.

Target Rifle in Australia, by J.E. Corcoran, R&R, Livonia, NY, 1996. 160 pp., illus. $40.00

A most interesting study of the evolution of these rifles from 1860 - 1900. British rifles from the percussion period through the early smokeless era are discussed.

U.S. Marine Corps AR15/M16 A2 Manual, reprinted by Desert Publications, El Dorado, AZ, 1993. 262 pp., illus. Paper covers. $16.95

A reprint of TM05538C-23&P/2, August, 1987. The A-2 manual for the Colt AR15/M16.

U.S. Marine Corps Rifle Marksmanship, by U.S. Marine Corps, Boulder, CO, Paladin Press, 2002. Photos, illus., 120 pp. Softcover. $20.00

This manual is the very latest Marine doctrine on the art and science of shooting effectively in battle. Its 10 chapters teach the versatility, flexibility and skills needed to deal with a situation at any level of intensity across the entire range of military operations. Topics covered include the proper combat mindset; cleaning your rifle under all weather conditions; rifle handling and marksmanship the Marine way; engaging targets from behind cover; obtaining a battlefield zero; engaging immediate threat, multiple and moving targets; shooting at night and at unknown distances; and much more.

U.S. Rifle M14–From John Garand to the M21, by R. Blake Stevens, Collector Grade Publications, Inc., Toronto, Canada, revised second edition, 1991. 350 pp., illus. $49.50

A classic, in-depth examination of the development, manufacture and fielding of the last wood-and-metal ("lock, stock, and barrel") battle rifle to be issued to U.S. troops.

The Ultimate in Rifle Accuracy, by Glenn Newick, Stoeger Publishing Co., Wayne, NJ, 1999. 205 pp., illus. Paper covers. $11.95

This handbook contains the information you need to extract the best performance from your rifle.

War Baby! The U.S. Caliber 30 Carbine, Volume 1, by Larry Ruth, Collector Grade Publications, Toronto, Canada, 1992. 512 pp., illus. $69.95

Volume 1 of the in-depth story of the phenomenally popular U.S. caliber 30 carbine. Concentrates on design and production of the military 30 carbine during WWII.

War Baby Comes Home: The U.S. Caliber 30 Carbine, Volume 2, by Larry Ruth, Collector Grade Publications, Toronto, Canada, 1993. 386 pp., illus. $49.95

The triumphant completion of Larry Ruth's two-volume, in-depth series on the most popular U.S. military small arm in history.

The Winchester Model 52, Perfection in Design, by Herbert G. Houze, Krause Publications, Iola, WI, 1997. 192 pp., illus. $34.95

This book covers the complete story of this technically superior gun.

SHOTGUNS

75 Years with the Shotgun, by C.T. (Buck) Buckman, Valley Publishers, Fresno, CA, 1974. 141 pp., illus. $10.00

An expert hunter and trapshooter shares experiences of a lifetime.

A Collector's Guide to United States Combat Shotguns, by Bruce N. Canfield, Andrew Mowbray Inc., Publishers, Lincoln, RI, 1993. 184 pp., illus. Paper covers. $24.00

Full coverage of the combat shotgun, from the earliest examples to the Gulf War and beyond.

A.H. Fox: "The Finest Gun in the World," revised and enlarged edition, by Michael McIntosh, Countrysport, Inc., New Albany, OH, 1995. 408 pp., illus. $60.00

The first detailed history of one of America's finest shotguns.

Advanced Combat Shotgun: Stress Fire 2, by Massad Ayoob, Police Bookshelf, Concord, NH, 1993. 197 pp., illus. Paper covers. $14.95

Advanced combat shotgun fighting for police.

Best Guns, by Michael McIntosh, Countrysport Press, Selma, AL, 1999, revised edition. 418 pp. $45.00

Combines the best shotguns ever made in America with information on British and Continental makers.

The Best of Holland & Holland, England's Premier Gunmaker, by Michael McIntosh and Jan G. Roosenburg. Long Beach, CA, Safari Press, Inc., 2002. 1st edition. 298 pp., profuse color illustrations. Hardcover. $69.95

Holland & Holland has had a long history of not only building London's "best" guns but also providing superior guns–the ultimate gun in finish, engraving, and embellishment. From the days of old in which a maharaja would order 100 fancifully engraved H&H shotguns for his guests to use at his duck shoot to the recent elaborately decorated sets depicting the Apollo 11 moon landing or the history of the British Empire, all of these guns represent the zenith in the art and craft of gunmaking and engraving. Never before have so many superlative guns from H&H–or any other maker for that matter–been displayed in one book. In addition, many interesting details and a general history of H&H are provided.

The Better Shot, by Ken Davies, Quiller Press, London, England, 1992. 136 pp., illus. $39.95

Step-by-step shotgun techniques with Holland and Holland.

Browning Auto-5 Shotguns: The Belgian FN Production, by H. M. Shirley Jr. and Anthony Vanderlinden, Geensboro, NC, Wet Dog Publications, 2003. Limited edition of 2,000 copies, signed by the author. 233 pp., plus index. Over 400 quality b&w photographs and 24 color photographs. Hardcover $59.95

This is the first book devoted to the history, model variations, accessories and production dates of this legendary gun. This publication is to date the only reference book on the Auto-5 (A-5) shotgun prepared entirely with the extensive cooperation and support of Browning, FN Herstal, the Browning Firearms Museum and the Liege Firearms Museum.

Cogswell & Harrison; Two Centuries of Gunmaking, by G. Cooley and J. Newton, Safari Press, Long Beach, CA, 2000. 128 pp., 30 color photos, 100 b&w photos. $39.95

The authors have gathered a wealth of fascinating historical and technical material that will make the book indispensable, not only to many thousands of "Coggie" owners worldwide, but also to anyone interested in the general history of British gunmaking.

Combat Shotgun and Submachine Gun, "A Special Weapons Analysis" by Chuck Taylor, Paladin Press, Boulder, CO, 1997, soft cover, photos, 176 pp. $25.00

From one of America's top shooting instructors comes an analysis of two controversial, misunderstood and misemployed small arms. Hundreds of photos detail field-testing of both guns, basic and advanced training drills, tactical rules, gun accessories and modifications. Loading procedures, carrying and fighting positions and malfunction clearance drills are included to promote weapon effectiveness.

The Defensive Shotgun, by Louis Awerbuck, S.W.A.T. Publications, Cornville, AZ, 1989. 77 pp., illus. Softcover. $14.95

Cuts through the myths concerning the shotgun and its attendant ballistic effects.

The Ducks Unlimited Guide to Shotgunning, by Don Zutz, Willow Creek Press, Minocqua, WI, 2000. 166 pg. Illustrated. $24.50

This book covers everything from the grand old guns of yesterday to today's best shotguns and loads, from the basic shotgun fit and function to expert advice on ballistics, chocks, and shooting techniques.

Fine European Gunmakers: Best Continental European Gunmakers & Engravers, by M. Nobili, Long Beach, CA, Safari Press, 2002. 250 pp., illustated in color. $69.95

Many experts argue that Continental gunmakers produce guns equally as good or better than British makers. Marco Nobili's new work showcases the skills of the best craftsmen from continental Europe, and the author brings to life in words and pictures their finest sporting guns. The book covers the histories of the individual firms and looks at the guns they currently build, tracing the developments of their most influential models.

Fine Gunmaking: Double Shotguns, by Steven Dodd Hughes, Krause Publications Iola, WI, 1998. 167 pp., illus. $34.95

An in-depth look at the creation of fine shotguns.

Firearms Assembly/Disassembly, Part V: Shotguns, 2nd Edition, The Gun Digest Book of, by J.B. Wood, Krause Publications, Iola, WI, 2002. 560 pp., illus. $24.95

Covers 54 popular shotguns plus over 250 variants. The most comprehensive and professional presentation available to either hobbyist or gunsmith.

Game Shooting, by Robert Churchill, Countrysport Press, Selma, AL, 1998. 258 pp., illus. $30.00

The basis for every shotgun instructional technique devised and the foundation for all wingshooting and the game of sporting clays.

The Greener Story, by Graham Greener, Safari Press, Long Beach, CA, 2000. 231 pp., color and b&w illustrations. $69.95

The history of the Greener gunmakers and their guns.

ARMS LIBRARY

Greenhill Military Manual: Combat Shotguns, by Leroy Thompson, London, Greenhill Publishing, 2002. 1st edition. 144 pp., illus. Hardcover. $24.00

The combat shotgun is one of the most devastating yet most misunderstood close-combat weapons. A great intimidator, the combat shotgun is widely used by military and police units for crowd control. This book traces the history of the combat shotgun, specialized tactics for its usage, the myriad ammunition choices, and the wealth of combat shotguns available to the military or police operator.

Gun Digest Book of Sporting Clays, 2nd Edition, edited by Harold A. Murtz, Krause Publications, Iola, WI, 1999. 256 pp., illus. Paper covers. $21.95

A concise Gun Digest book that covers guns, ammo, chokes, targets and course layouts so you'll stay a step ahead.

The Gun Review Book, by Michael McIntosh, Countrysport Press, Camden, MA, 1997. Paper covers. $19.95

Compiled here for the first time are McIntosh's popular gun reviews from *"Shooting Sportsman: The Magazine of Wingshooting and Fine Shotguns."* The author traces the history of gunmakes, then examines, analyzes, and critiques the fine shotguns of England, Continental Europe and the United States.

Gunsmithing Shotguns: The Complete Guide to Care & Repair, by David Henderson, New York, Globe Pequot, 2003. 1st edition, b&w photos & illus; 6" x 9", 256 pp., illus. Hardcover. $24.95

An overview designed to provide insight, ideas and techniques that will give the amateur gunsmith the confidence and skill to work on his own guns. General troubleshooting, common problems, stocks and woodworking, soldering and brazing, barrel work and more.

The Heyday of the Shotgun, by David Baker, Safari Press, Inc., Huntington Beach, CA, 2000. 160 pp., illus. $39.95

The art of the gunmaker at the turn of the last century when British craftsmen brought forth the finest guns ever made.

Holland & Holland: The "Royal" Gunmaker, by Donald Dallas, London, Safari Press, 2004. 1st edition. 311 pp. Hardcover. $75.00

Donald Dallas tells the fascinating story of Holland & Holland from its very beginnings, and the history of the family is revealed for the first time. The terrific variety of the firm's guns and rifles is described in great detail and set within the historical context of their eras. From punt gun to boy's gun, from rook rifle to elephant gun, Holland & Holland supplied sporting firearms to every corner of the world. The book is profusely illustrated with 112 color and 355 b&w photographs, mostly unpublished. In addition many rare guns and rifles are described and illustrated.

The House of Churchill, by Don Masters, Safari Press, Long Beach, CA, 2002. 512 pp., profuse color and b&w illustrations. $79.95

This marvelous work on the house of Churchill contains serial numbers and dates of manufacture of its guns from 1891 forward, price lists from 1895 onward, a complete listing of all craftsmen employed at the company, as well as the prices realized at the famous Dallas auction where the "last" production guns were sold. It was written by Don Masters, a long-time Churchill employee, who is keeping the flame of Churchill alive.

The Italian Gun, by Steve Smith and Laurie Morrow, Wilderness Adventures, Gallatin Gateway, MT, 1997. 325 pp., illus. $49.95

The first book ever written entirely in English for American enthusiasts who own, aspire to own, or simply admire Italian guns.

The Ithaca Featherlight Repeater; The Best Gun Going, by Walter C. Snyder, Southern Pines, NC, 1998. 300 pp., illus. $89.95

Describes the complete history of each model of the legendary Ithaca Model 37 and Model 87 Repeaters from their conception in 1930 throught 1997.

The Ithaca Gun Company from the Beginning, by Walter C. Snyder, Cook & Uline Publishing Co., Southern Pines, NC, 2nd edition, 1999. 384 pp., illustrated in color and b&w. $90.00

The entire family of Ithaca Gun Company products is described along with new historical information and the serial number/date of manufacturing listing has been improved.

The Little Trapshooting Book, by Frank Little, Shotgun Sports Magazine, Auburn, CA, 1994. 168 pp., illus. Paper covers. $19.95

Packed with know-how from one of the greatest trapshooters of all time.

Lock, Stock, and Barrel, by C. Adams and R. Braden, Safari Press, Huntington Beach, CA, 1996. 254 pp., illus. $24.95

The process of making a best grade English gun from a lump of steel and a walnut tree trunk to the ultimate product plus practical advice on consistent field shooting with a double gun.

Mental Training for the Shotgun Sports, by Michael J. Keyes, Shotgun Sports, Auburn, CA, 1996. 160 pp., illus. Paper covers. $29.95

The most comprehensive book ever published on what it takes to shoot winning scores at trap, skeet and sporting clays.

More Shotguns and Shooting, by Michael McIntosh, Countrysport Books, Selma, AL, 1998. 256 pp., illus. $30.00

From specifics of shotguns to shooting your way out of a slump, it's McIntosh at his best.

Mossberg Shotguns, by Duncan Long, Delta Press, El Dorado, AR, 2000. 120 pp., illus. $24.95

This book contains a brief history of the company and its founder, full coverage of the pump and semiautomatic shotguns, rare products and a care and maintenance section.

The Mysteries of Shotgun Patterns, by George G. Oberfell and Charles E. Thompson, Oklahoma State University Press, Stillwater, OK, 1982. 164 pp., illus. Paper covers. $25.00

Shotgun ballistics for the hunter in non-technical language.

The Parker Gun, by Larry Baer, Gun Room Press, Highland Park, NJ, 1993. 195 pp., illustrated with b&w and color photos. $35.00

Covers in detail, production of all models on this classic gun. Many fine specimens from great collections are illustrated.

Parker Gun Identification & Serialization, by S.P. Fjestad, Minneapolis, MN, Blue Book Publications, 2002. 1st edition. Softcover. $34.95

This new 608-page publication is the only book that provides an easy reference for Parker shotguns manufactured between 1866-1942. Included is a comprehensive 46-page section on Parker identification, with over 100 detailed images depicting serialization location and explanation, various Parker grades, extra features, stock configurations, action types, and barrel identification.

The Parker Story: Volumes 1 & 2, by Bill Mullins, "et al." The Double Gun Journal, East Jordan, MI, 2000. 1,025 pp. of text and 1,500 color and monochrome illustrations. Hardbound in a gold-embossed cover. $295.00

The most complete and attractive "last word" on America's preeminent double gun maker. Includes tables showing the number of guns made by gauge, barrel length and special features for each grade.

Purdey Gun and Rifle Makers: The Definitive History, by Donald Dallas, Quiller Press, London 2000. 245 pp., illus. Signed and numbered. Limited edition of 3,000 copies. With a PURDEY bookplate. $100.00

Re-creating the Double Barrel Muzzle Loading Shotgun, by William R. Brockway, York, PA, George Shumway, 2003. Revised 2nd edition. 175 pp., illus. Includes full size drawings. Softcover. $40.00

This popular book, first published in 1985 and out of print for over a decade, has been updated by the author. This book treats the making of double guns of classic style, and is profusely illustrated, showing how to do it all. Many photos of old and contemporary shotguns.

Reloading for Shotgunners, 4th Edition, by Kurt D. Fackler and M.L. McPherson, DBI Books, a division of Krause Publications, Iola, WI, 1997. 320 pp., illus. Paper covers. $19.95

Expanded reloading tables with over 11,000 loads. Bushing charts for every major press and component maker. All new presentation on all aspects of shotshell reloading by two of the top experts in the field.

Remington Double Shotguns, by Charles G. Semer, Denver, CO, 1997. 617 pp., illus. $60.00

This book deals with the entire production and all grades of double shotguns made by Remington during the period of their production 1873-1910.

The Shotgun Encyclopedia, by John Taylor, Safari Press, Inc., Huntington Beach, CA, 2000. 260 pp., illus. $34.95

A comprehensive reference work on all aspects of shotguns and shotgun shooting.

Shotgun Technicana, by Michael McIntosh and David Trevallion, Camden, ME, Down East Books, 2002. 272 pp., with 100 illustrations. Hardcover $28.00

Everything you wanted to know about fine double shotguns by the nation's foremost experts.

The Shotgun–A Shooting Instructor's Handbook, by Michael Yardley, Long Beach, CA, Safari Press, 2002. 272 pp., b&w photos, line drawings. Hardcover. $29.95

This is one of the very few books intended to be read by shooting instructors and other advanced shooters. He analyzes the components and development of shooting techniques by pointing out the styles of great instructors such as Percy Stanbury and Robert Churchill, as well as the shooting techniques of some of the best-known modern competitors. There is practical advice on gun fit, and on gun and cartridge selection.

Shotgunning: The Art and the Science, by Bob Brister, Winchester Press, Piscataway, NJ, 1976. 321 pp., illus. $18.95

Hundreds of specific tips and truly novel techniques to improve the field and target shooting of every shotgunner.

Shotguns and Shooting, by Michael McIntosh, Countrysport Press, New Albany, OH, 1995. 258 pp., illus. $30.00

The art of guns and gunmaking, this book is a celebration no lover of fine doubles should miss.

Shotguns & Shotgunning, by Layne Simpson, Iola, WI, Krause Publications, 2003. 1st edition. High-quality color photography 224 pp., color illus. Hardcover. $36.95

This is the most comprehensive and valuable guide on the market devoted exclusively to shotguns. Part buyer's guide, part technical manual, and part loving tribute, shooters and hunters of all skill levels will enjoy this comprehensive reference tool. Excellent resource for shooters, gun hunters, and firearms collectors. Comprehensive guide covers the technical aspects of shotguns, hunting with shotguns, the evolution of shotguns, and popular shooting games.

Spanish Best: The Fine Shotguns of Spain, 2nd Edition, by Terry Wieland, Down East Books, Traverse City, MI, 2001. 364 pp., illus. $60.00

A practical source of information for owners of Spanish shotguns and a guide for those considering buying a used shotgun.

Successful Shotgunning; How to Build Skill in the Field and Take More Birds in Competition, by Peter F. Blakeley, Mechanicsburg, PA, Stackpole Books, 2003. 1st edition. 305 pp., illustrated with 119 b&w photos & 4-page color section with 8 photos. Hardcover. $24.95

Successful Shotgunning focuses on wing-shooting and sporting clays techniques.

The Tactical Shotgun, by Gabriel Suzrez, Paladin Press, Boulder, CO, 1996. 232 pp., illus. Paper covers. $25.00

The best techniques and tactics for employing the shotgun in personal combat.

Trap & Skeet Shooting, 4th Edition, by Chris Christian, DBI Books, a division of Krause Publications, Iola, WI, 1994. 288 pp., illus. Paper covers. $21.95

A detailed look at the contemporary world of trap, skeet and sporting clays.

Trapshooting is a Game of Opposites, by Dick Bennett, Shotgun Sports, Inc., Auburn, CA, 1996. 129 pp., illus. Paper covers. $19.95

Discover everything you need to know about shooting trap like the pros.

U.S. Shotguns, All Types, reprint of TM9-285, Desert Publications, Cornville, AZ, 1987. 257 pp., illus. Paper covers. $18.95

Covers operation, assembly and disassembly of nine shotguns used by the U.S. armed forces.

U.S. Winchester Trench and Riot Guns and Other U.S. Military Combat Shotguns, by Joe Poyer, North Cape Publications, Tustin, CA, 1992. 124 pp., illus. Paper covers. $15.95

A detailed history of the use of military shotguns, and the acquisition procedures used by the U.S. Army's Ordnance Department in both world wars.

Uncle Dan Lefever, Master Gunmaker: Guns of Lasting Fame, by Robert W. Elliott, privately printed, 2002. Profusely illustrated with b&w photos, with a 45-page color section. 239 pp. Handsomely bound, with gilt titled spine and top cover. Hardcover. $60.00

The Winchester Model Twelve, by George Madis, Art and Reference House, Dallas, TX, 1982. 176 pp., illus. $26.95

A definitive work on this famous American shotgun.

The World's Fighting Shotguns, by Thomas F. Swearengen, T.B.N. Enterprises, Alexandria, VA, 1998. 500 pp., illus. $59.95

The complete military and police reference work from the shotgun's inception to date, with up-to-date developments.

ARMS ASSOCIATIONS

UNITED STATES

ALABAMA

Alabama Gun Collectors Assn.
Secretary, P.O. Box 70965, Tuscaloosa, AL 35407

ALASKA

Alaska Gun Collectors Assn., Inc.
C.W. Floyd, Pres., 5240 Little Tree, Anchorage, AK 99507

ARIZONA

Arizona Arms Assn.
Don Debusk, President, 4837 Bryce Ave., Glendale, AZ 85301

CALIFORNIA

California Cartridge Collectors Assn.
Rick Montgomery, 1729 Christina, Stockton, CA 95204
209-463-7216 eves.

California Waterfowl Assn.
4630 Northgate Blvd., #150, Sacramento, CA 95834

Greater Calif. Arms & Collectors Assn.
Donald L. Bullock, 8291 Carburton St., Long Beach, CA 90808-3302

Los Angeles Gun Ctg. Collectors Assn.
F.H. Ruffra, 20810 Amie Ave., Apt. #9, Torrance, CA 90503

Stock Gun Players Assn.
6038 Appian Way, Long Beach, CA, 90803

COLORADO

Colorado Gun Collectors Assn.
L.E.(Bud) Greenwald, 2553 S. Quitman St., Denver, CO 80219/303-935-3850

Rocky Mountain Cartridge Collectors Assn.
John Roth, P.O. Box 757, Conifer, CO 80433

CONNECTICUT

Ye Connecticut Gun Guild, Inc.
Dick Fraser, P.O. Box 425, Windsor, CT 06095

FLORIDA

Unified Sportsmen of Florida
P.O. Box 6565, Tallahassee, FL 32314

GEORGIA

Georgia Arms Collectors Assn., Inc.
Michael Kindberg, President, P.O. Box 277, Alpharetta, GA 30239-0277

ILLINOIS

Illinois State Rifle Assn.
P.O. Box 637, Chatsworth, IL 60921

Mississippi Valley Gun & Cartridge Coll. Assn.
Bob Filbert, P.O. Box 61, Port Byron, IL 61275/309-523-2593

Sauk Trail Gun Collectors
Gordell M. Matson, P.O. Box 1113, Milan, IL 61264

Wabash Valley Gun Collectors Assn., Inc.
Roger L. Dorsett, 2601 Willow Rd., Urbana, IL 61801
217-384-7302

INDIANA

Indiana State Rifle & Pistol Assn.
Thos. Glancy, P.O. Box 552, Chesterton, IN 46304

Southern Indiana Gun Collectors Assn., Inc.
Sheila McClary, 309 W. Monroe St., Boonville, IN 47601/812-897-3742

IOWA

Beaver Creek Plainsmen Inc.
Steve Murphy, Secy., P.O. Box 298, Bondurant, IA 50035

Central States Gun Collectors Assn.
Dennis Greischar, Box 841, Mason City, IA 50402-0841

KANSAS

Kansas Cartridge Collectors Assn.
Bob Linder, Box 84, Plainville, KS 67663

KENTUCKY

Kentuckiana Arms Collectors Assn.
Charles Billips, President, Box 1776, Louisville, KY 40201

Kentucky Gun Collectors Assn., Inc.
Ruth Johnson, Box 64, Owensboro, KY 42302/502-729-4197

LOUISIANA

Washitaw River Renegades
Sandra Rushing, P.O. Box 256, Main St., Grayson, LA 71435

MARYLAND

Baltimore Antique Arms Assn.
Mr. Cillo, 1034 Main St., Darlington, MD 21304

MASSACHUSETTS

Bay Colony Weapons Collectors, Inc.
John Brandt, Box 111, Hingham, MA 02043

Massachusetts Arms Collectors
Bruce E. Skinner, P.O. Box 31, No. Carver, MA 02355/508-866-5259

MICHIGAN

Association for the Study and Research of .22 Caliber Rimfire Cartridges
George Kass, 4512 Nakoma Dr., Okemos, MI 48864

MINNESOTA

Sioux Empire Cartridge Collectors Assn.
Bob Cameron, 14597 Glendale Ave. SE, Prior Lake, MN 55372

MISSISSIPPI

Mississippi Gun Collectors Assn.
Jack E. Swinney, P.O. Box 16323, Hattiesburg, MS 39402

MISSOURI

Greater St. Louis Cartridge Collectors Assn.
Don MacChesney, 634 Scottsdale Rd., Kirkwood, MO 63122-1109

Mineral Belt Gun Collectors Assn.
D.F. Saunders, 1110 Cleveland Ave., Monett, MO 65708

Missouri Valley Arms Collectors Assn., Inc.
L.P. Brammer II, Membership Secy., P.O. Box 33033, Kansas City, MO 64114

MONTANA

Montana Arms Collectors Assn.
Dean E. Yearout, Sr., Exec. Secy., 1516 21st Ave. S., Great Falls, MT 59405

Weapons Collectors Society of Montana
R.G. Schipf, Ex. Secy., 3100 Bancroft St., Missoula, MT 59801
406-728-2995

NEBRASKA

Nebraska Cartridge Collectors Club
Gary Muckel, P.O. Box 84442, Lincoln, NE 68501

NEW HAMPSHIRE

New Hampshire Arms Collectors, Inc.
James Stamatelos, Secy., P.O. Box 5, Cambridge, MA 02139

NEW JERSEY

Englishtown Benchrest Shooters Assn.
Michael Toth, 64 Cooke Ave., Carteret, NJ 07008

Jersey Shore Antique Arms Collectors
Joe Sisia, P.O. Box 100, Bayville, NJ 08721-0100

New Jersey Arms Collectors Club, Inc.
Angus Laidlaw, Vice President, 230 Valley Rd., Montclair, NJ 07042/201-746-0939; e-mail: acclaidlaw@juno.com

NEW YORK

Iroquois Arms Collectors Assn.
Bonnie Robinson, Show Secy., P.O. Box 142, Ransomville, NY 14131/716-791-4096

Mid-State Arms Coll. & Shooters Club
Jack Ackerman, 24 S. Mountain Terr., Binghamton, NY 13903

NORTH CAROLINA

North Carolina Gun Collectors Assn.
Jerry Ledford, 3231-7th St. Dr. NE, Hickory, NC 28601

OHIO

Ohio Gun Collectors Assn.
P.O. Box 9007, Maumee, OH 43537-9007/419-897-0861; Fax: 419-897-0860

Shotshell Historical and Collectors Society
Madeline Bruemmer, 3886 Dawley Rd., Ravenna, OH 44266

The Stark Gun Collectors, Inc.
William I. Gann, 5666 Waynesburg Dr., Waynesburg, OH 44688

OREGON

Oregon Arms Collectors Assn., Inc.
Phil Bailey, P.O. Box 13000-A, Portland, OR 97213-0017
503-281-6864; off.: 503-281-0918

Oregon Cartridge Collectors Assn.
Boyd Northrup, P.O. Box 285, Rhododendron, OR 97049

PENNSYLVANIA

Presque Isle Gun Collectors Assn.
James Welch, 156 E. 37 St., Erie, PA 16504

SOUTH CAROLINA

Belton Gun Club, Inc.
Attn. Secretary, P.O. Box 126, Belton, SC 29627/864-369-6767

Gun Owners of South Carolina
Membership Div.: William Strozier, Secretary, P.O. Box 70, Johns Island, SC 29457-0070/803-762-3240; Fax: 803-795-0711; e-mail: 76053.222@compuserve. com

SOUTH DAKOTA

Dakota Territory Gun Coll. Assn., Inc.
Curt Carter, Castlewood, SD 57223

TENNESSEE

Smoky Mountain Gun Coll. Assn., Inc.
Hugh W. Yabro, President, P.O. Box 23225, Knoxville, TN 37933

Tennessee Gun Collectors Assn., Inc.
M.H. Parks, 3556 Pleasant Valley Rd., Nashville, TN 37204-3419

TEXAS

Houston Gun Collectors Assn., Inc.
P.O. Box 741429, Houston, TX 77274-1429

Texas Gun Collectors Assn.
Bob Eder, Pres., P.O. Box 12067, El Paso, TX 79913/915-584-8183

Texas State Rifle Assn.
1131 Rockingham Dr., Suite 101, Richardson, TX 75080-4326

VIRGINIA

Virginia Gun Collectors Assn., Inc.
Addison Hurst, Secy., 38802 Charlestown Height, Waterford, VA 20197/540-882-3543

WASHINGTON

Association of Cartridge Collectors on the Pacific Northwest
Robert Jardin, 14214 Meadowlark Drive KPN, Gig Harbor, WA 98329

Washington Arms Collectors, Inc.
Joyce Boss, P.O. Box 389, Renton, WA, 98057-0389/206-255-8410

WISCONSIN

Great Lakes Arms Collectors Assn., Inc.
Edward C. Warnke, 2913 Woodridge Lane, Waukesha, WI 53188

Wisconsin Gun Collectors Assn., Inc.
Lulita Zellmer, P.O. Box 181, Sussex, WI 53089

WYOMING

Wyoming Weapons Collectors
P.O. Box 284, Laramie, WY 82073/307-745-4652 or 745-9530

NATIONAL ORGANIZATIONS

Amateur Trapshooting Assn.
David D. Bopp, Exec. Director, 601 W. National Rd., Vandalia, OH 45377/937-898-4638; Fax: 937-898-5472

American Airgun Field Target Assn.
5911 Cherokee Ave., Tampa, FL 33604

American Coon Hunters Assn.
Opal Johnston, P.O. Cadet, Route 1, Box 492, Old Mines, MO 63630

American Custom Gunmakers Guild
Jan Billeb, Exec. Director, 22 Vista View Drive, Cody, WY 82414-9606 (307) 587-4297 (phone/fax) Email: acgg@acgg.org Website: www.acgg.org

American Defense Preparedness Assn.
Two Colonial Place, 2101 Wilson Blvd., Suite 400, Arlington, VA 22201-3061

American Paintball League
P.O. Box 3561, Johnson City, TN 37602/800-541-9169

American Pistolsmiths Guild
Alex B. Hamilton, Pres., 1449 Blue Crest Lane, San Antonio, TX 78232/210-494-3063

American Police Pistol & Rifle Assn.
3801 Biscayne Blvd., Miami, FL 33137

American Single Shot Rifle Assn.
Gary Staup, Secy., 709 Carolyn Dr., Delphos, OH 45833

419-692-3866. Website: www.assra.com

American Society of Arms Collectors
George E. Weatherly, P.O. Box 2567, Waxahachie, TX 75165

American Tactical Shooting Assn.(A.T.S.A.)
c/o Skip Gochenour, 2600 N. Third St., Harrisburg, PA 17110
717-233-0402; Fax: 717-233-5340

Association of Firearm and Tool Mark Examiners
Lannie G. Emanuel, Secy., Southwest Institute of Forensic Sciences, P.O. Box 35728, Dallas, TX 75235/214-920-5979; Fax: 214-920-5928; Membership Secy., Ann D. Jones, VA Div. of Forensic Science, P.O. Box 999, Richmond, VA 23208 804-786-4706; Fax: 804-371-8328

Boone & Crockett Club
250 Station Dr., Missoula, MT 59801-2753

Browning Collectors Assn.
Secretary:Scherrie L. Brennac, 2749 Keith Dr., Villa Ridge, MO 63089/314-742-0571

The Cast Bullet Assn., Inc.
Ralland J. Fortier, Editor, 4103 Foxcraft Dr., Traverse City, MI 49684

Citizens Committee for the Right to Keep and Bear Arms
Natl. Hq., Liberty Park, 12500 NE Tenth Pl., Bellevue, WA 98005

Colt Collectors Assn.
25000 Highland Way, Los Gatos, CA 95030/408-353-2658

Contemporary Longrifle Association
P.O. Box 2097, Staunton, VA 24402/540-886-6189 Website: www.CLA@longrifle.ws

Ducks Unlimited, Inc.
Natl. Headquarters, One Waterfowl Way, Memphis, TN 38120 901-758-3937

Fifty Caliber Shooters Assn.
PO Box 111, Monroe UT 84754-0111

Firearms Coalition/Neal Knox Associates
Box 6537, Silver Spring, MD 20906 301-871-3006

Firearms Engravers Guild of America
Rex C. Pedersen, Secy., 511 N. Rath Ave., Lundington, MI 49431 616-845-7695 (Phone/Fax)

Foundation for North American Wild Sheep
720 Allen Ave., Cody, WY 82414-3402; web site: iigi.com/os/non/fnaws/fnaws.htm; e-mail: fnaws@wyoming.com

Freedom Arms Collectors Assn.
P.O. Box 160302, Miami, FL 33116-0302

Garand Collectors Assn.
P.O. Box 181, Richmond, KY 40475

Glock Collectors Association
P.O. Box 1063, Maryland Heights, MO 63043 314-878-2061 Phone/Fax

Glock Shooting Sports Foundation
BO Box 309, Smyrna GA 30081 770-432-1202 Website: www.gssfonline.com

Golden Eagle Collectors Assn. (G.E.C.A.)
Chris Showler, 11144 Slate Creek Rd., Grass Valley, CA 95945

ARMS ASSOCIATIONS

Gun Owners of America
8001 Forbes Place, Suite 102,
Springfield, VA
22151/703-321-8585

Handgun Hunters International
J.D. Jones, Director, P.O. Box 357
MAG, Bloomingdale, OH 43910

Harrington & Richardson Gun Coll. Assn.
George L. Cardet, 330 S.W. 27th
Ave., Suite 603, Miami, FL 33135

High Standard Collectors' Assn.
John J. Stimson, Jr., Pres., 540 W.
92nd St., Indianapolis, IN 46260
Website: www.highstandard.org

Hopkins & Allen Arms & Memorabilia Society (HAAMS)
P.O. Box 187, 1309 Pamela Circle,
Delphos, OH 45833

International Ammunition Association, Inc.
C.R. Punnett, Secy., 8 Hillock Lane,
Chadds Ford, PA 19317
610-358-1285; Fax: 610-358-1560

International Benchrest Shooters
Joan Borden, RR1, Box 250BB,
Springville, PA 18844
717-965-2366

International Blackpowder Hunting Assn.
P.O. Box 1180, Glenrock, WY
82637/307-436-9817

IHMSA (Intl. Handgun Metallic Silhouette Assn.)
PO Box 368, Burlington, IA 52601
Website: www.ihmsa.org

International Society of Mauser Arms Collectors
Michael Kindberg, Pres., P.O. Box
277, Alpharetta, GA 30239-0277

Jews for the Preservation of Firearms Ownership (JPFO) 501(c)(3)
2872 S. Wentworth Ave.,
Milwaukee, WI 53207
414-769-0760, Fax. 414-483-8435

The Mannlicher Collectors Assn.
Membership Office: P.O. Box 1249,
The Dalles, Oregon 97058

Marlin Firearms Collectors Assn., Ltd.
Dick Paterson, Secy., 407 Lincoln
Bldg., 44 Main St., Champaign, IL
61820

Merwin Hulbert Association,
2503 Kentwood Ct., High Point, NC
27265

Miniature Arms Collectors/Makers Society, Ltd.
Ralph Koebbeman, Pres., 4910
Kilburn Ave., Rockford, IL 61101
815-964-2569

M1 Carbine Collectors Assn. (M1-CCA)
623 Apaloosa Ln., Gardnerville, NV
89410-7840

National Association of Buckskinners (NAB)
Territorial Dispatch—1800s
Historical Publication, 4701 Marion
St., Suite 324, Livestock Exchange
Bldg., Denver, CO 80216
303-297-9671

The National Association of Derringer Collectors
P.O. Box 20572, San Jose, CA
95160

National Assn. of Federally Licensed Firearms Dealers
Andrew Molchan, 2455 E. Sunrise,
Ft. Lauderdale, FL 33304

National Association to Keep and Bear Arms
P.O. Box 78336, Seattle, WA 98178

National Automatic Pistol Collectors Assn.
Tom Knox, P.O. Box 15738, Tower
Grove Station, St. Louis, MO 63163

National Bench Rest Shooters Assn., Inc.
Pat Ferrell, 2835 Guilford Lane,
Oklahoma City, OK 73120-4404
405-842-9585; Fax: 405-842-9575

National Muzzle Loading Rifle Assn.
Box 67, Friendship, IN 47021
812-667-5131
Website: www.nmlra@nmlra.org

National Professional Paintball League (NPPL)
540 Main St., Mount Kisco, NY
10549/914-241-7400

National Reloading Manufacturers Assn.
One Centerpointe Dr., Suite 300,
Lake Oswego, OR 97035

National Rifle Assn. of America
11250 Waples Mill Rd., Fairfax, VA
22030/703-267-1000
Website: www.nra.org

National Shooting Sports Foundation, Inc.
Doug Painter, President, Flintlock
Ridge Office Center, 11 Mile Hill
Rd., Newtown, CT 06470-2359
203-426-1320; Fax: 203-426-1087

National Skeet Shooting Assn.
Dan Snyuder, Director, 5931 Roft
Road, San Antonio, TX
78253-9261/800-877-5338
Website: nssa-nsca.com

National Sporting Clays Association
Ann Myers, Director, 5931 Roft
Road, San Antonio, TX
78253-9261/800-877-5338
Website: nssa-nsca.com

National Wild Turkey Federation, Inc.
P.O. Box 530, 770 Augusta Rd.,
Edgefield, SC 29824

North American Hunting Club
P.O. Box 0401, Minnetonka, MN
55343/612-936-9333;
Fax: 612-936-9755

North American Paintball Referees Association (NAPRA)
584 Cestaric Dr., Milpitas, CA
95035

North-South Skirmish Assn., Inc.
Stevan F. Meserve, Exec. Secretary,
507 N. Brighton Court, Sterling, VA
20164-3919

Old West Shooter's Association
712 James Street, Hazel TX 76020
817-444-2049

Remington Society of America
Gordon Fosburg, Secretary, 11900
North Brinton Road, Lake, MI
48623

Rocky Mountain Elk Foundation
P.O. Box 8249, Missoula, MT
59807-8249/406-523-4500;
Fax: 406-523-4581
Website: www.rmef.org

Ruger Collector's Assn., Inc.
P.O. Box 240, Greens Farms, CT
06436

Safari Club International
4800 W. Gates Pass Rd., Tucson,
AZ 85745/520-620-1220

Sako Collectors Assn., Inc.
Jim Lutes, 202 N. Locust,
Whitewater, KS 67154

Second Amendment Foundation
James Madison Building, 12500
NE 10th Pl., Bellevue, WA 98005

Single Action Shooting Society (SASS)
23255-A La Palma Avenue, Yorba
Linda, CA 92887/714-694-1800;
Fax: 714-694-1815
email: sasseot@aol.com
Website: www.sassnet.com

Smith & Wesson Collectors Assn.
Cally Pletl, Admin. Asst.,PO Box
444, Afton, NY 13730

The Society of American Bayonet Collectors
P.O. Box 234, East Islip, NY
11730-0234

Southern California Schuetzen Society
Dean Lillard, 34657 Ave. E.,
Yucaipa, CA 92399

Sporting Arms and Ammunition Manufacturers' Institute (SAAMI)
Flintlock Ridge Office Center, 11
Mile Hill Rd., Newtown, CT
06470-2359/203-426-4358;
Fax: 203-426-1087

Sporting Clays of America (SCA)
Ron L. Blosser, Pres., 9257
Buckeye Rd., Sugar Grove, OH
43155-9632/614-746-8334;
Fax: 614-746-8605

Steel Challenge
23234 Via Barra, Valencia CA
91355
Website: www.steelchallenge.com

The Thompson/Center Assn.
Joe Wright, President, Box 792,
Northboro, MA
01532/508-845-6960

U.S. Practical Shooting Association/IPSC
Dave Thomas, P.O. Box 811, Sedro
Woolley, WA 98284/360-855-2245
Website: www.uspsa.org

U.S. Revolver Assn.
Brian J. Barer, 40 Larchmont Ave.,
Taunton, MA 02780/508-824-4836

U.S.A. Shooting
U.S. Olympic Shooting Center, One
Olympic Plaza, Colorado Springs,
CO 80909/719-578-4670
Website: wwwusashooting.org

The Varmint Hunters Assn., Inc.
Box 759, Pierre, SD 57501
Member Services 800-528-4868

Weatherby Collectors Assn., Inc.
P.O. Box 478, Pacific, MO 63069
Website:
www.weatherbycollectors.com
Email: WCAsecretary@aol.com

The Wildcatters
P.O. Box 170, Greenville, WI 54942

Winchester Arms Collectors Assn.
P.O. Box 230, Brownsboro, TX
75756/903-852-4027

The Women's Shooting Sports Foundation (WSSF)
4620 Edison Avenue, Ste. C,
Colorado Springs, CO 80915
719-638-1299; Fax: 719-638-1271
email: wssf@worldnet.att.net

ARGENTINA

Asociacion Argentina de Coleccionistas de Armes y Municiones
Castilla de Correos No. 28,
Succursal I B, 1401 Buenos Aires,
Republica Argentina

AUSTRALIA

Antique & Historical Arms Collectors of Australia
P.O. Box 5654, GCMC Queensland
9726, Australia

The Arms Collector's Guild of Queensland, Inc.
Ian Skennerton, P.O. Box 433,
Ashmore City 4214, Queensland,
Australia

Australian Cartridge Collectors Assn., Inc.
Bob Bennett, 126 Landscape Dr., E.
Doncaster 3109, Victoria, Australia

Sporting Shooters Assn. of Australia, Inc.
P.O. Box 2066, Kent Town, SA
5071, Australia

BRAZIL

Associaçao de Armaria Coleçao e Tiro (ACOLTI)
Rua do Senado, 258 - 2 andar,
Centro, Rio de Janeiro - RJ -
20231-002 Brazil / tel:
0055-21-31817989

CANADA

ALBERTA

Canadian Historical Arms Society
P.O. Box 901, Edmonton, Alb.,
Canada T5J 2L8

National Firearms Assn.
Natl. Hq: P.O. Box 1779,
Edmonton, Alb., Canada T5J 2P1

BRITISH COLUMBIA

The Historical Arms Collectors of B.C. (Canada)
Harry Moon, Pres., P.O. Box
50117, South Slope RPO, Burnaby,
BC V5J 5G3, Canada
604-438-0950; Fax: 604-277-3646

ONTARIO

Association of Canadian Cartridge Collectors
Monica Wright, RR 1, Millgrove,
ON, L0R 1V0, Canada

Tri-County Antique Arms Fair
P.O. Box 122, RR #1, North
Lancaster, Ont., Canada K0C 1Z0

EUROPE

BELGIUM

European Cartridge Research Association
Graham Irving, 21 Rue Schaltin,
4900 Spa, Belgium
32.87.77.43.40;
Fax: 32.87.77.27.51

CZECHOSLOVAKIA

Spolecnost Pro Studium Naboju (Czech Cartridge Research Association)
JUDr. Jaroslav Bubak, Pod
Homolko 1439, 26601 Beroun 2,
Czech Republic

DENMARK

Aquila Dansk Jagtpatron Historic Forening (Danish Historical Cartridge Collectors Club)
Steen Elgaard Møller, Ulriksdalsvej
7, 4840 Nr. Alslev, Denmark
10045-53846218;
Fax: 0045538462U9

ENGLAND

Arms and Armour Society
Hon. Secretary A. Dove, P.O. Box
10232, London, 5W19 2ZD,
England

Dutch Paintball Federation
Aceville Publ., Castle House 97
High Street, Colchester, Essex C01
1TH, England/011-44-206-564840

European Paintball Sports Foundation
c/o Aceville Publ., Castle House 97
High St., Colchester, Essex, C01
1TH, England

Historical Breechloading Smallarms Assn.
D.J. Penn M.A., Secy., P.O. Box
12778, London SE1 6BX, England

National Rifle Assn.
(Great Britain) Bisley Camp,
Brookwood, Woking Surrey GU24
OPB, England/01483.797777;
Fax: 014730686275

United Kingdom Cartridge Club
Ian Southgate, 20 Millfield, Elmley
Castle, Nr. Pershore,
Worcestershire, WR10 3HR,
England

FRANCE

STAC-Western Co.
3 Ave. Paul Doumer (N.311);
78360 Montesson, France
01.30.53-43-65;
Fax: 01.30.53.19.10

GERMANY

Bund Deutscher Sportschützen e.v. (BDS)
Borsigallee 10, 53125 Bonn 1,
Germany

Deutscher Schützenbund
Lahnstrasse 120, 65195
Wiesbaden, Germany

NORWAY

Scandinavian Ammunition Research Association
c/o Morten Stoen, Annerudstubben
3, N-1383 Asker, Norway

NEW ZEALAND

New Zealand Cartridge Collectors Club
Terry Castle, 70 Tiraumea Dr.,
Pakuranga, Auckland, New Zealand

New Zealand Deerstalkers Association
P.O. Box 6514 TE ARO, Wellington,
New Zealand

SOUTH AFRICA

Historical Firearms Soc. of South Africa
P.O. Box 145, 7725 Newlands,
Republic of South Africa

Republic of South Africa Cartridge Collectors Assn.
Arno Klee, 20 Eugene St.,
Malanshof Randburg, Gauteng
2194, Republic of South Africa

**S.A.A.C.A.
(Southern Africa Arms and Ammunition Assn.)**
Gauteng office:
P.O. Box 7597, Weltevreden Park,
1715, Republic of South Africa/
011-679-1151; Fax: 011-679-1131;
e-mail: saaaca@iafrica.com
Kwa-Zulu Natal office:
P.O. Box 4065, Northway,
Kwazulu-Natal 4065,
Republic of South Africa

SAGA (S.A. Gunowners' Assn.)
P.O. Box 35203, Northway,
Kwazulu-Natal 4065, Republic of
South Africa

SPAIN

Asociacion Espanola de Coleccionistas de Cartuchos (A.E.C.C.)
Secretary: Apdo. Correos No.
1086, 2880-Alcala de Henares
(Madrid), Spain. President: Apdo.
Correos No. 682, 50080 Zaragoza,
Spain

2006
GUN DIGEST
DIRECTORY OF THE
ARMS TRADE

The **Product Directory** contains 84 product categories. The **Manufacturer's Directory** alphabetically lists the manufacturers with their addresses, phone numbers, FAX numbers and Internet addresses, if available.

DIRECTORY OF THE ARMS TRADE INDEX

PRODUCT & SERVICE DIRECTORY

AMMUNITION COMPONENTS, SHOTSHELL

A.W. Peterson Gun Shop, Inc., The
Ballistic Products, Inc.
Blount, Inc., Sporting Equipment Div.
CCI/Speer Div of ATK
Cheddite, France S.A.
Claybuster Wads & Harvester Bullets
Garcia National Gun Traders, Inc.
Gentner Bullets
Guncrafter Industries
Magtech Ammunition Co. Inc.
Precision Reloading, Inc.
Ravell Ltd.
Tar-Hunt Custom Rifles, Inc.
Vitt/Boos

AMMUNITION COMPONENTS– BULLETS, POWDER, PRIMERS, CASES

A.W. Peterson Gun Shop, Inc., The
Acadian Ballistic Specialties
Accuracy Unlimited
Accurate Arms Co., Inc.
Action Bullets & Alloy Inc.
ADCO Sales, Inc.
Alaska Bullet Works, Inc.
Alex, Inc.
Alliant Techsystems, Smokeless Powder Group
Allred Bullet Co.
Alpha LaFranck Enterprises
American Products, Inc.
Ammo Load Worldwide, Inc.
Arizona Ammunition, Inc.
Armfield Custom Bullets
A-Square Co.
Baer's Hollows
Ballard Rifle & Cartridge Co., LLC
Barnes
Barnes Bullets, Inc.
Beartooth Bullets
Bell Reloading, Inc.
Berger Bullets Ltd.
Berry's Mfg., Inc.
Big Bore Bullets of Alaska
Big Bore Express
Bitterroot Bullet Co.
Black Belt Bullets (See Big Bore Express)
Black Hills Shooters Supply
Black Powder Products
Blount, Inc., Sporting Equipment Div.
Blue Mountain Bullets
Brenneke GmbH
Briese Bullet Co., Inc.
Brown Dog Ent.
BRP, Inc. High Performance Cast Bullets
Buck Stix-SOS Products Co.
Buckeye Custom Bullets
Buckskin Bullet Co
Buffalo Arms Co.
Buffalo Bullet Co., Inc.
Buffalo Rock Shooters Supply
Bull-X, Inc.
Butler Enterprises
Cain's Outdoors, Inc.
Calhoon Mfg.
Cambos Outdoorsman
Canyon Cartridge Corp.
Cascade Bullet Co., Inc.
Cast Performance Bullet Company
Casull Arms Corp.
CCI/Speer Div of ATK
Champion's Choice, Inc.
Cheddite, France S.A.
CheVron Bullets
Chuck's Gun Shop

Clean Shot Technologies
Competitor Corp., Inc.
Cook Engineering Service
Corbin Mfg. & Supply, Inc.
Cummings Bullets
Curtis Cast Bullets
Curtis Gun Shop (See Curtis Cast Bullets)
Custom Bullets by Hoffman
D.L. Unmussig Bullets
Dakota Arms, Inc.
Davide Pedersoli and Co.
DKT, Inc.
Dohring Bullets
Eichelberger Bullets, Wm.
Federal Cartridge Co.
Fiocchi of America, Inc.
Firearm Brokers
Forkin Custom Classics
Fowler Bullets
Fowler, Bob (See Black Powder Products)
Freedom Arms, Inc.
Garcia National Gun Traders, Inc.
Gehmann, Walter (See Huntington Die Specialties)
GOEX, Inc.
Golden Bear Bullets
Gotz Bullets
Grayback Wildcats
Grier's Hard Cast Bullets
GTB-Custom Bullets
Gun City
Gun Works, The
Harris Enterprises
Harrison Bullets
Hart & Son, Inc.
Hawk Laboratories, Inc. (See Hawk, Inc.)
Hawk, Inc.
Heidenstrom Bullets
Hercules, Inc. (See Alliant Techsystems Smokeless Powder Group)
Hi-Performance Ammunition Company
Hirtenberger AG
Hobson Precision Mfg. Co.
Hodgdon Powder Co.
Hornady Mfg. Co.
HT Bullets
Hunters Supply, Inc.
Huntington Die Specialties
Impact Case & Container, Inc.
Imperial Magnum Corp.
IMR Powder Co
Intercontinental Distributors, Ltd.
J&D Components
J&L Superior Bullets (See Huntington Die Specialties)
J.R. Williams Bullet Co.
Jamison International
Jensen Bullets
Jensen's Firearms Academy
Jericho Tool & Die Co., Inc.
Jester Bullets
JLK Bullets
JRP Custom Bullets
Ka Pu Kapili
Kaswer Custom, Inc
Keith's Bullets
Keng's Firearms Specialty, Inc./US Tactical Systems
Ken's Kustom Kartridges
Knight Rifles
Knight Rifles (See Modern Muzzleloading, Inc.)
Lawrence Brand Shot (See Precision Reloading, Inc.)
Liberty Shooting Supplies
Lightning Performance Innovations, Inc.
Lindsley Arms Cartridge Co.
Littleton, J. F.
Lomont Precision Bullets
Lyman Products Corp.
Magnus Bullets

Magtech Ammunition Co. Inc.
Marchmon Bullets
Markesbery Muzzle Loaders, Inc.
Marshall Fish Mfg. Gunsmith Sptg. Co.
MAST Technology, Inc.
McMurdo, Lynn
Meister Bullets (See Gander Mountain)
Men-Metallwerk Elisenhuette GmbH
Midway Arms, Inc.
Mitchell Bullets, R.F.
MI-TE Bullets
Montana Precision Swaging
Mulhern, Rick
Murmur Corp.
Nagel's Custom Bullets
Nammo Lapua Oy
National Bullet Co.
Naval Ordnance Works
North American Shooting Systems
North Devon Firearms Services
Northern Precision
Northwest Custom Projectile
Nosler, Inc.
OK Weber, Inc
Oklahoma Ammunition Co.
Old Wagon Bullets
Old Western Scrounger Ammunition Inc.
Ordnance Works, The
Oregon Trail Bullet Company
Pacific Rifle Co.
Page Custom Bullets
Penn Bullets
Petro Explo Inc.
Phillippi Custom Bullets, Justin
Pinetree Bullets
PMC/Eldorado Cartridge Corp.
Polywad, Inc.
Pony Express Reloaders
Power Plus Enterprises, Inc.
Precision Delta Corp.
Prescott Projectile Co.
Price Bullets, Patrick W.
PRL Bullets, c/o Blackburn Enterprises
Professional Hunter Supplies
Proofmark Corp.
PWM Sales Ltd.
Quality Cartridge
Quarton Beamshot
Rainier Ballistics
Ramon B. Gonzalez Guns
Ravell Ltd.
Redwood Bullet Works
Reloading Specialties, Inc.
Remington Arms Co., Inc.
Rhino
Robinson H.V. Bullets
Rubright Bullets
Russ Haydon's Shooters' Supply
SAECO (See Redding Reloading Equipment)
Scharch Mfg., Inc.-Top Brass
Schneider Bullets
Schroeder Bullets
Schumakers Gun Shop
Scot Powder
Seebeck Assoc., R E
Shappy Bullets
Sharps Arms Co., Inc., C.
Shilen, Inc.
Sierra Bullets
SOS Products Co. (See Buck Stix-SOS Products Co.)
Southern Ammunition Co., Inc.
Specialty Gunsmithing
Speer Bullets
Spencer's Rifle Barrels, Inc.
SSK Industries
Stanley Bullets
Star Ammunition, Inc.
Star Custom Bullets
Starke Bullet Company
Starline, Inc.
Stewart's Gunsmithing

Swift Bullet Co.
T.F.C. S.p.A.
Taracorp Industries, Inc.
Tar-Hunt Custom Rifles, Inc.
TCCI
TCSR
Thompson Bullet Lube Co.
Thompson Precision
Traditions Performance Firearms
Trico Plastics
True Flight Bullet Co.
Tucson Mold, Inc.
USAC
Vann Custom Bullets
Vihtavuori Oy/Kaltron-Pettibone
Vincent's Shop
Viper Bullet and Brass Works
Walters Wads
Warren Muzzleloading Co., Inc.
Watson Bullets
Western Nevada West Coast Bullets
Widener's Reloading & Shooting Supply, Inc.
Wildey F. A., Inc.
Winchester Div. Olin Corp.
Woodleigh (See Huntington Die Specialties)
Worthy Products, Inc.
Wyant Bullets
Wyoming Custom Bullets
Zero Ammunition Co., Inc.

AMMUNITION, COMMERCIAL

3-Ten Corp.
A.W. Peterson Gun Shop, Inc., The
Ad Hominem
Air Arms
American Ammunition
Arizona Ammunition, Inc.
Arms Corporation of the Philippines
Arundel Arms & Ammunition, Inc., A.
A-Square Co.
Ballistic Products, Inc.
Benjamin/Sheridan Co., Crosman
Big Bear Arms & Sporting Goods, Inc.
Black Hills Ammunition, Inc.
Blammo Ammo
Blount, Inc., Sporting Equipment Div.
Brenneke GmbH
Buchsenmachermeister
Buffalo Arms Co.
Buffalo Bullet Co., Inc.
Bull-X, Inc.
Cabela's
Cambos Outdoorsman
Casull Arms Corp.
CBC
CCI/Speer Div of ATK
Champion's Choice, Inc.
Cor-Bon Inc./Glaser LLC
Crosman Airguns
Cubic Shot Shell Co., Inc.
Daisy Outdoor Products
Dead Eye's Sport Center
Delta Arms Ltd.
Delta Frangible Ammunition LLC
Dynamit Nobel-RWS, Inc.
Effebi SNC-Dr. Franco Beretta
Eley Ltd.
Elite Ammunition
Ellett Bros.
Estate Cartridge, Inc.
Federal Cartridge Co.
Fiocchi of America, Inc.
Firearm Brokers
Garcia National Gun Traders, Inc.
Garrett Cartridges, Inc.
Garthwaite Pistolsmith, Inc., Jim
Gibbs Rifle Co., Inc.
Gil Hebard Guns, Inc.
Glaser LLC
Glaser Safety Slug, Inc.

GOEX, Inc.
Goodwin's Guns
Gun City
Gun Room Press, The
Gun Works, The
Guncrafter Industries
Hansen & Co.
Hart & Son, Inc.
Hastings
Hi-Performance Ammunition Company
Hirtenberger AG
Hofer Jagdwaffen, P.
Hornady Mfg. Co.
Hunters Supply, Inc.
Intercontinental Distributors, Ltd.
Ion Industries, Inc.
Keng's Firearms Specialty, Inc./US Tactical Systems
Kent Cartridge America, Inc.
Knight Rifles
Lethal Force Institute (See Police Bookshelf)
Lock's Philadelphia Gun Exchange
Lomont Precision Bullets
Magnum Research, Inc.
MagSafe Ammo Co.
Magtech Ammunition Co. Inc.
Mandall Shooting Supply Inc.
Markell, Inc.
Marshall Fish Mfg. Gunsmith Sptg. Co.
Men-Metallwerk Elisenhuette GmbH
Mullins Ammunition
Nammo Lapua Oy
New England Ammunition Co.
Oklahoma Ammunition Co.
Old Western Scrounger Ammunition Inc.
Outdoor Sports Headquarters, Inc.
P.S.M.G. Gun Co.
Paragon Sales & Services, Inc.
Parker & Sons Shooting Supply
Peterson Gun Shop, Inc., A.W.
PMC/Eldorado Cartridge Corp.
Police Bookshelf
Polywad, Inc.
Pony Express Reloaders
Precision Delta Corp.
Pro Load Ammunition, Inc.
Quality Cartridge
R.E.I.
Ravell Ltd.
Remington Arms Co., Inc.
Rucker Dist. Inc.
RWS (See U.S. Importer-Dynamit Nobel-RWS, Inc.)
Sellier & Bellot, USA, Inc.
Southern Ammunition Co., Inc.
Speer Bullets
TCCI
Thompson Bullet Lube Co.
USAC
VAM Distribution Co. LLC
Victory USA
Vihtavuori Oy/Kaltron-Pettibone
Visible Impact Targets
Voere-KGH GmbH
Weatherby, Inc.
Westley Richards & Co. Ltd.
Whitestone Lumber Corp.
Widener's Reloading & Shooting Supply, Inc.
Wildey F. A., Inc.
William E. Phillips Firearms
Winchester Div. Olin Corp.
Zero Ammunition Co., Inc.

AMMUNITION, CUSTOM

3-Ten Corp.
A.W. Peterson Gun Shop, Inc., The
Accuracy Unlimited
AFSCO Ammunition
Allred Bullet Co.
American Derringer Corp.

PRODUCT & SERVICE DIRECTORY

American Products, Inc.
Arizona Ammunition, Inc.
Arms Corporation of the Philippines
Ballard Rifle & Cartridge Co., LLC
Bear Arms
Belding's Custom Gun Shop
Berger Bullets Ltd.
Big Bore Bullets of Alaska
Black Hills Ammunition, Inc.
Blue Mountain Bullets
Brynin, Milton
Buckskin Bullet Co.
Buffalo Arms Co.
CBC
CFVentures
Champlin Firearms, Inc.
Country Armourer, The
Cubic Shot Shell Co., Inc.
Custom Tackle and Ammo
D.L. Unmussig Bullets
Dakota Arms, Inc.
Dead Eye's Sport Center
Delta Frangible Ammunition LLC
DKT, Inc.
Elite Ammunition
Estate Cartridge, Inc.
GDL Enterprises
Gentner Bullets
GOEX, Inc.
Grayback Wildcats
Hawk, Inc.
Hirtenberger AG
Hobson Precision Mfg. Co.
Horizons Unlimited
Hornady Mfg. Co.
Hunters Supply, Inc.
Jensen Bullets
Jensen's Custom Ammunition
Jensen's Firearms Academy
Kaswer Custom, Inc.
L. E. Jurras & Assoc.
L.A.R. Mfg., Inc.
Lethal Force Institute (See Police
    Bookshelf)
Lindsley Arms Cartridge Co.
Linebaugh Custom Sixguns
MagSafe Ammo Co.
Magtech Ammunition Co. Inc.
MAST Technology, Inc.
McMurdo, Lynn
Men-Metallwerk Elisenhuette GmbH
Milstor Corp.
Mullins Ammunition
Oklahoma Ammunition Co.
P.S.M.G. Gun Co.
Peterson Gun Shop, Inc., A.W.
Phillippi Custom Bullets, Justin
Police Bookshelf
Power Plus Enterprises, Inc.
Precision Delta Corp.
Professional Hunter Supplies
Quality Cartridge
R.E.I.
Ramon B. Gonzalez Guns
Sandia Die & Cartridge Co.
SOS Products Co. (See Buck Stix-
    SOS Products Co.)
Specialty Gunsmithing
Spencer's Rifle Barrels, Inc.
SSK Industries
Star Custom Bullets
Stewart's Gunsmithing
TCCI
Vitt/Boos
Vulpes Ventures, Inc., Fox Cartridge
    Division
Warren Muzzleloading Co., Inc.
Watson Bullets
Worthy Products, Inc.
Zero Ammunition Co., Inc.

AMMUNITION, FOREIGN

A.W. Peterson Gun Shop, Inc., The
Ad Hominem
AFSCO Ammunition

Air Arms
Armscorp USA, Inc.
B&P America
Cape Outfitters
CBC
Cheddite, France S.A.
Cubic Shot Shell Co., Inc.
Dead Eye's Sport Center
DKT, Inc.
Dynamit Nobel-RWS, Inc.
E. Arthur Brown Co. Inc.
Fiocchi of America, Inc.
Gamebore Division, Polywad, Inc.
Gibbs Rifle Co., Inc.
GOEX, Inc.
Gunsmithing, Inc.
Hansen & Co.
Heidenstrom Bullets
Hirtenberger AG
Hornady Mfg. Co.
International Shooters Service
Intrac Arms International
Jack First, Inc.
K.B.I. Inc.
MagSafe Ammo Co.
Magtech Ammunition Co. Inc.
Mandall Shooting Supply Inc.
Marksman Products
MAST Technology, Inc.
Mullins Ammunition
Navy Arms Company
Oklahoma Ammunition Co.
P.S.M.G. Gun Co.
Paragon Sales & Services, Inc.
Paul Co., The
Peterson Gun Shop, Inc., A.W.
Petro-Explo Inc.
Precision Delta Corp.
R.E.T. Enterprises
Ramon B. Gonzalez Guns
RWS (See U.S. Importer-Dynamit
    Nobel-RWS, Inc.)
Samco Global Arms, Inc.
Sentinel Arms
Southern Ammunition Co., Inc.
Speer Bullets
Stratco, Inc.
T.F.C. S.p.A.
Vector Arms, Inc.
Victory Ammunition
Vihtavuori Oy/Kaltron-Pettibone
Wolf Performance Ammunition

ANTIQUE ARMS DEALER

Ackerman & Co.
Ad Hominem
Antique American Firearms
Antique Arms Co.
Aplan Antiques & Art
Armoury, Inc., The
Arundel Arms & Ammunition, Inc., A.
Ballard Rifle & Cartridge Co., LLC
Bear Mountain Gun & Tool
Bob's Tactical Indoor Shooting
    Range & Gun Shop
Buffalo Arms Co.
Cape Outfitters
CBC-BRAZIL
Chadick's Ltd.
Chambers Flintlocks Ltd., Jim
Champlin Firearms, Inc.
Chuck's Gun Shop
Cleland's Outdoor World, Inc.
Clements' Custom Leathercraft,
    Chas
Cole's Gun Works
Cousin Bob's Mountain Products
D&D Gunsmiths, Ltd.
David R. Chicoine
Dixie Gun Works
Dixon Muzzleloading Shop, Inc.
Duffy, Charles E. (See Guns Antique
    & Modern DBA)
Ed's Gun House
Enguix Import-Export

Fagan Arms
Flayderman & Co., Inc.
Getz Barrel Company
Glass, Herb
Goergen's Gun Shop, Inc.
Golden Age Arms Co.
Goodwin's Guns
Gun Hunter Books (See Gun Hunter
    Trading Co.)
Gun Hunter Trading Co.
Gun Room Press, The
Gun Room, The
Gun Works, The
Guns Antique & Modern DBA /
    Charles E. Duffy
Hallowell & Co.
Hammans, Charles E.
HandCrafts Unltd. (See Clements'
    Custom Leathercraft)
Handgun Press
Hansen & Co.
Hunkeler, A. (See Buckskin Machine
    Works)
Imperial Miniature Armory
James Wayne Firearms for
    Collectors and Investors
Kelley's
Knight's Manufacturing Co.
Ledbetter Airguns, Riley
LeFever Arms Co., Inc.
Lever Arms Service Ltd.
Lock's Philadelphia Gun Exchange
Log Cabin Sport Shop
Logdewood Mfg.
Mandall Shooting Supply Inc.
Marshall Fish Mfg. Gunsmith Sptg.
    Co.
Martin B. Retting Inc.
Martin's Gun Shop
Michael's Antiques
Mid-America Recreation, Inc.
Montana Outfitters, Lewis E. Yearout
Muzzleloaders Etcetera, Inc.
Navy Arms Company
New England Arms Co.
Olathe Gun Shop
P.S.M.G. Gun Co.
Peter Dyson & Son Ltd.
Pony Express Sport Shop
Powder Horn Ltd.
Ravell Ltd.
Reno, Wayne
Retting, Inc., Martin B.
Robert Valade Engraving
Rutgers Book Center
Samco Global Arms, Inc.
Sarco, Inc.
Scott Fine Guns Inc., Thad
Shootin' Shack
Sportsmen's Exchange & Western
    Gun Traders, Inc.
Steves House of Guns
Stott's Creek Armory, Inc.
Turnbull Restoration, Doug
Vic's Gun Refinishing
Wallace, Terry
Westley Richards & Co. Ltd.
Wild West Guns
Winchester Consultants
Winchester Sutler, Inc., The
Yearout, Lewis E. (See Montana
    Outfitters)

APPRAISER - GUNS, ETC.

A.W. Peterson Gun Shop, Inc., The
Ackerman & Co.
Antique Arms Co.
Armoury, Inc., The
Arundel Arms & Ammunition, Inc., A.
Barta's Gunsmithing
Beitzinger, George
Blue Book Publications, Inc.
Bob's Tactical Indoor Shooting
    Range & Gun Shop

Bonham's & Butterfields
Bullet N Press
Cape Outfitters
Chadick's Ltd.
Champlin Firearms, Inc.
Christie's East
Clark Firearms Engraving
Cleland's Outdoor World, Inc.
Clements' Custom Leathercraft,
    Chas
Cole's Gun Works
Colonial Arms, Inc.
Colonial Repair
Corry, John
Custom Tackle and Ammo
D&D Gunsmiths, Ltd.
David R. Chicoine
DGR Custom Rifles
Dietz Gun Shop & Range, Inc.
Dixie Gun Works
Dixon Muzzleloading Shop, Inc.
Duane's Gun Repair (See DGR
    Custom Rifles)
Ed's Gun House
Eversull Co., Inc.
Fagan Arms
Ferris Firearms
Firearm Brokers
Flayderman & Co., Inc.
Forty-Five Ranch Enterprises
Frontier Arms Co., Inc.
Gene's Custom Guns
Getz Barrel Company
Gillmann, Edwin
Goergen's Gun Shop, Inc.
Golden Age Arms Co.
Griffin & Howe, Inc.
Griffin & Howe, Inc.
Gun City
Gun Hunter Books (See Gun Hunter
    Trading Co.)
Gun Hunter Trading Co.
Gun Room Press, The
Gun Shop, The
Gun Works, The
Guncraft Books (See Guncraft
    Sports, Inc.)
Guncraft Sports, Inc.
Guncraft Sports, Inc.
Gunsmithing, Inc.
Hallowell & Co.
Hammans, Charles E.
HandCrafts Unltd. (See Clements'
    Custom Leathercraft)
Handgun Press
Hank's Gun Shop
Hansen & Co.
Irwin, Campbell H.
Ithaca Classic Doubles
Jackalope Gun Shop
James Wayne Firearms for
    Collectors and Investors
Jensen's Custom Ammunition
JG Airguns, LLC
Kelley's
Ken Eyster Heritage Gunsmiths, Inc.
L.L. Bean, Inc.
Lampert, Ron
LaRocca Gun Works
Ledbetter Airguns, Riley
LeFever Arms Co., Inc.
Lock's Philadelphia Gun Exchange
Log Cabin Sport Shop
Logdewood Mfg.
Long, George F.
Mahony, Philip Bruce
Mandall Shooting Supply Inc.
Marshall Fish Mfg. Gunsmith Sptg.
    Co.
Martin B. Retting Inc.
Martin's Gun Shop
Mathews Gun Shop & Gunsmithing,
    Inc.
McCann Industries
Mercer Custom Guns
Montana Outfitters, Lewis E. Yearout
Muzzleloaders Etcetera, Inc.

Navy Arms Company
New England Arms Co.
Olathe Gun Shop
Orvis Co., The
P&M Sales & Services, LLC
P.S.M.G. Gun Co.
Pasadena Gun Center
Pentheny de Pentheny
Perazone-Gunsmith, Brian
Peterson Gun Shop, Inc., A.W.
Pettinger Books, Gerald
Pony Express Sport Shop
Powder Horn Ltd.
R.A. Wells Custom Gunsmith
R.E.T. Enterprises
Ramon B. Gonzalez Guns
Retting, Inc., Martin B.
Robert Valade Engraving
Russ Haydon's Shooters' Supply
Rutgers Book Center
Scott Fine Guns Inc., Thad
Shootin' Shack
Spencer Reblue Service
Sportsmen's Exchange & Western
    Gun Traders, Inc.
Steven Dodd Hughes
Stott's Creek Armory, Inc.
Stratco, Inc.
Swampfire Shop, The (See Peterson
    Gun Shop, Inc., A.W.)
Ten-Ring Precision, Inc.
Vic's Gun Refinishing
Walker Arms Co., Inc.
Wallace, Terry
Wasmundt, Jim
Weber & Markin Custom Gunsmiths
Werth, T. W.
Whildin & Sons Ltd., E.H.
Whitestone Lumber Corp.
Wild West Guns
Williams Shootin' Iron Service, The
    Lynx-Line
Winchester Consultants
Winchester Sutler, Inc., The
Yearout, Lewis E. (See Montana
    Outfitters)

AUCTIONEER - GUNS, ETC.

"Little John's" Antique Arms
Bonham's & Butterfields
Buck Stix-SOS Products Co.
Christie's East
Fagan Arms
Pete de Coux Auction House
Sotheby's

BOOKS & MANUALS (PUBLISHERS & DEALERS)

"Su-Press-On", Inc.
A.W. Peterson Gun Shop, Inc., The
Alpha 1 Drop Zone
American Gunsmithing Institute
American Handgunner Magazine
Armory Publications
Arms & Armour Press
Ballistic Products, Inc.
Ballistic Products, Inc.
Barnes Bullets, Inc.
Bauska Barrels
Beartooth Bullets
Beeman Precision Airguns
Blacksmith Corp.
Blacktail Mountain Books
Blue Book Publications, Inc.
Blue Ridge Machinery & Tools, Inc.
Boone's Custom Ivory Grips, Inc.
Brownells, Inc.
Buchsenmachermeister
Bullet N Press
C. Sharps Arms Co. Inc./Montana
    Armory

Cain's Outdoors, Inc.
Cape Outfitters
Cheyenne Pioneer Products
Collector's Armoury, Ltd.
Colonial Repair
Corbin Mfg. & Supply, Inc.
David R. Chicoine
deHaas Barrels
Dixon Muzzleloading Shop, Inc.
Excalibur Publications
Executive Protection Institute
F&W Publications, Inc.
Fulton Armory
Galati International
GAR
Golden Age Arms Co.
Gun City
Gun Hunter Books (See Gun Hunter Trading Co.)
Gun Hunter Trading Co.
Gun List (See F&W Publications)
Gun Room Press, The
Gun Works, The
Guncraft Books (See Guncraft Sports, Inc.)
Guncraft Sports, Inc.
Gunnerman Books
GUNS Magazine
Gunsmithing, Inc.
H&P Publishing
Handgun Press
Harris Publications
Hawk Laboratories, Inc. (See Hawk, Inc.)
Hawk, Inc.
Heritage/VSP Gun Books
Hodgdon Powder Co.
Hofer Jagdwaffen, P.
Hornady Mfg. Co.
Huntington Die Specialties
I.D.S.A. Books
Info-Arm
Ironside International Publishers, Inc.
Jantz Supply
Kelley's
King & Co.
Koval Knives
KP Books Division of F&W Publications
L.B.T.
Lebeau-Courally
Lethal Force Institute (See Police Bookshelf)
Lyman Products Corp.
Machinist's Workshop-Village Press
Madis Books
Magma Engineering Co.
Mandall Shooting Supply Inc.
Marshall Fish Mfg. Gunsmith Sptg. Co.
Montana Armory, Inc.
Montana Precision Swaging
Mulberry House Publishing
Nammo Lapua Oy
Navy Arms Company
NgraveR Co., The
Numrich Gun Parts Corporation
OK Weber, Inc.
Outdoor Sports Headquarters, Inc.
Paintball Games International Magazine Aceville
Pansch, Robert F
Pejsa Ballistics
Pettinger Books, Gerald
PFRB Co.
Police Bookshelf
Precision Reloading, Inc.
Precision Shooting, Inc.
Primedia Publishing Co.
Professional Hunter Supplies
Ravell Ltd.
Ray Riling Arms Books Co.
Remington Double Shotguns
Rocky Mountain Wildlife Products
Russ Haydon's Shooters' Supply
Rutgers Book Center

S&S Firearms
Safari Press, Inc.
Saunders Gun & Machine Shop
Scharch Mfg., Inc.-Top Brass
Scharch Mfg., Inc.-Top Brass
Semmer, Charles (See Remington Double Shotguns)
Sharps Arms Co., Inc., C.
Shotgun Sports Magazine, dba Shootin' Accessories Ltd.
Sierra Bullets
Speer Bullets
SPG LLC
Stackpole Books
Star Custom Bullets
Stewart Game Calls, Inc., Johnny
Stoeger Industries
Stoeger Publishing Co. (See Stoeger Industries)
Swift Bullet Co.
Thomas, Charles C.
Track of the Wolf, Inc.
Trafalgar Square
Trotman, Ken
Tru-Balance Knife Co.
Vega Tool Co.
VSP Publishers (See Heritage/VSP Gun Books)
W.E. Brownell Checkering Tools
WAMCO-New Mexico
Wells Creek Knife & Gun Works
Wilderness Sound Products Ltd.
Williams Gun Sight Co.
Winchester Consultants
Winfield Galleries LLC
Wolfe Publishing Co.

BULLET CASTING, ACCESSORIES

A.W. Peterson Gun Shop, Inc., The
Ballisti-Cast, Inc.
Buffalo Arms Co.
Bullet Metals
Cast Performance Bullet Company
CFVentures
Cooper-Woodward Perfect Lube
Davide Pedersoli and Co.
Ferguson, Bill
Hanned Line, The
Huntington Die Specialties
Lee Precision, Inc.
Lithi Bee Bullet Lube
Lyman Products Corp.
MA Systems, Inc.
Magma Engineering Co.
Ox-Yoke Originals, Inc.
Rapine Bullet Mould Mfg. Co.
Redding Reloading Equipment
SPG LLC

BULLET CASTING, FURNACES & POTS

A.W. Peterson Gun Shop, Inc., The
Ballisti-Cast, Inc.
Buffalo Arms Co.
Bullet Metals
Ferguson, Bill
GAR
Gun Works, The
Lee Precision, Inc.
Lyman Products Corp.
Magma Engineering Co.
Rapine Bullet Mould Mfg. Co.
RCBS/ATK
Redding Reloading Equipment
Thompson Bullet Lube Co.

BULLET CASTING, LEAD

A.W. Peterson Gun Shop, Inc., The
Action Bullets & Alloy Inc.
Ames Metal Products
Buckskin Bullet Co.

Buffalo Arms Co.
Bullet Metals
Gun Works, The
Hunters Supply, Inc.
Jericho Tool & Die Co., Inc.
Lee Precision, Inc.
Lithi Bee Bullet Lube
Magma Engineering Co.
Montana Precision Swaging
Ox-Yoke Originals, Inc.
Penn Bullets
Proofmark Corp.
SPG LLC
Splitfire Sporting Goods, L.L.C.
Walters Wads

BULLET PULLERS

A.W. Peterson Gun Shop, Inc., The
Battenfeld Technologies, Inc.
Davide Pedersoli and Co.
Gun Works, The
Hollywood Engineering
Howell Machine, Inc.
Huntington Die Specialties
Royal Arms Gunstocks

BULLET TOOLS

A.W. Peterson Gun Shop, Inc., The
Brynin, Milton
Camdex, Inc.
Corbin Mfg. & Supply, Inc.
Cumberland Arms
Eagan, Donald V.
Hanned Line, The
Holland's Gunsmithing
Hollywood Engineering
Lee Precision, Inc.
Niemi Engineering, W. B.
North Devon Firearms Services
Rorschach Precision Products
Sport Flite Manufacturing Co.
WTA Manufacturing

BULLET, CASE & DIE LUBRICANTS

Beartooth Bullets
Bonanza (See Forster Products)
Buckskin Bullet Co.
Buffalo Arms Co.
Camp-Cap Products
CFVentures
Cooper-Woodward Perfect Lube
CVA
E-Z-Way Systems
Ferguson, Bill
Forster Products, Inc.
GAR
Guardsman Products
Hanned Line, The
Heidenstrom Bullets
Hollywood Engineering
Hornady Mfg. Co.
Imperial (See E-Z-Way Systems)
Knoell, Doug
L.B.T.
Le Clear Industries (See E-Z-Way Systems)
Lee Precision, Inc.
Lithi Bee Bullet Lube
MI-TE Bullets
RCBS Operations/ATK
Reardon Products
Rooster Laboratories
Shay's Gunsmithing
Tamarack Products, Inc.
Uncle Mike's (See Michaels of Oregon, Co.)
Warren Muzzleloading Co., Inc.
Widener's Reloading & Shooting Supply, Inc.
Young Country Arms

CARTRIDGES FOR COLLECTORS

Ackerman & Co.
Ad Hominem
Armory Publications
Cameron's
Campbell, Dick
Cherry Creek State Park Shooting Center
Cole's Gun Works
Colonial Repair
Country Armourer, The
Cubic Shot Shell Co., Inc.
Duane's Gun Repair (See DGR Custom Rifles)
Ed's Gun House
Ed's Gun House
Enguix Import-Export
Forty-Five Ranch Enterprises
Goergen's Gun Shop, Inc.
Grayback Wildcats
Gun City
Gun Hunter Books (See Gun Hunter Trading Co.)
Gun Hunter Trading Co.
Gun Room Press, The
Jack First, Inc.
Kelley's
Liberty Shooting Supplies
Mandall Shooting Supply Inc.
MAST Technology, Inc.
Michael's Antiques
Montana Outfitters, Lewis E. Yearout
Numrich Gun Parts Corporation
Pasadena Gun Center
Pete de Coux Auction House
Samco Global Arms, Inc.
SOS Products Co. (See Buck Stix-SOS Products Co.)
Stone Enterprises Ltd.
Ward & Van Valkenburg
Winchester Consultants
Yearout, Lewis E. (See Montana Outfitters)

CASE & AMMUNITION PROCESSORS, INSPECTORS, BOXERS

A.W. Peterson Gun Shop, Inc., The
Ammo Load, Inc.
Hafner World Wide, Inc.
Scharch Mfg., Inc.-Top Brass

CASE CLEANERS & POLISHING MEDIA

A.W. Peterson Gun Shop, Inc., The
Battenfeld Technologies, Inc.
Buffalo Arms Co.
G96 Products Co., Inc.
Gun Works, The
Huntington Die Specialties
Lee Precision, Inc.
Penn Bullets
Tru-Square Metal Products, Inc.
VibraShine, Inc.

CASE PREPARATION TOOLS

A.W. Peterson Gun Shop, Inc., The
Battenfeld Technologies, Inc.
Forster Products, Inc.
High Precision
Hoehn Sales, Inc.
Huntington Die Specialties
J. Dewey Mfg. Co., Inc.
K&M Services
Lee Precision, Inc.
Match Prep-Doyle Gracey
Plum City Ballistic Range
PWM Sales Ltd.

RCBS Operations/ATK
Redding Reloading Equipment
Russ Haydon's Shooters' Supply
Sinclair International, Inc.
Stoney Point Products, Inc.

CASE TRIMMERS, TRIM DIES & ACCESSORIES

A.W. Peterson Gun Shop, Inc., The
Buffalo Arms Co.
Creedmoor Sports, Inc.
Forster Products, Inc.
Fremont Tool Works
Hollywood Engineering
K&M Services
Lyman Products Corp.
Match Prep-Doyle Gracey
OK Weber, Inc.
PWM Sales Ltd.
RCBS/ATK
Redding Reloading Equipment

CASE TUMBLERS, VIBRATORS, MEDIA & ACCESSORIES

4-D Custom Die Co.
A.W. Peterson Gun Shop, Inc., The
Battenfeld Technologies, Inc.
Berry's Mfg., Inc.
Dillon Precision Products, Inc.
Penn Bullets
Raytech Div. of Lyman Products Corp.
Tru-Square Metal Products, Inc.
VibraShine, Inc.

CASES, CABINETS, RACKS & SAFES - GUN

All Rite Products, Inc.
Allen Co., Inc.
Alumna Sport by Dee Zee
American Display Co.
American Security Products Co.
Americase
Art Jewel Enterprises Ltd.
Bagmaster Mfg., Inc.
Barramundi Corp.
Berry's Mfg., Inc.
Big Spring Enterprises "Bore Stores"
Bison Studios
Black Sheep Brand
Brauer Bros.
Browning Arms Co.
Bushmaster Hunting & Fishing
Cannon Safe, Inc.
Chipmunk (See Oregon Arms, Inc.)
Connecticut Shotgun Mfg. Co.
D&L Industries (See D.J. Marketing)
D.J. Marketing
Dara-Nes, Inc. (See Nesci Enterprises, Inc.)
Deepeeka Exports Pvt. Ltd.
Doskocil Mfg. Co., Inc.
DTM International, Inc.
EMF Co., Inc.
English, Inc., A.G.
Enhanced Presentations, Inc.
Eversull Co., Inc.
Flambeau, Inc.
Fort Knox Security Products
Freedom Arms, Inc.
Frontier Safe Co.
Galati International
GALCO International Ltd.
Gun-Ho Sports Cases
Hall Plastics, Inc., John
Homak
Hoppe's Div. Penguin Industries, Inc.
Hunter Co., Inc.
Hydrosorbent Products
Impact Case & Container, Inc.

Johanssons Vapentillbehor, Bert
Kalispel Case Line
KK Air International (See Impact
    Case & Container Co., Inc.)
Knock on Wood Antiques
Kolpin Outdoors, Inc.
Lakewood Products LLC
Liberty Safe
Mandall Shooting Supply Inc.
Marsh, Mike
McWelco Products
Morton Booth Co.
MPC
MTM Molded Products Co., Inc.
Nalpak
Necessary Concepts, Inc.
Nesci Enterprises Inc.
Oregon Arms, Inc. (See Rogue Rifle
    Co., Inc.)
Outa-Site Gun Carriers
Outdoor Connection, Inc., The
Pflumm Mfg. Co.
Poburka, Philip (See Bison Studios)
Powell & Son (Gunmakers) Ltd.,
    William
Prototech Industries, Inc.
Rogue Rifle Co., Inc.
S.A.R.L. G. Granger
Schulz Industries
Silhouette Leathers
Southern Security
Sportsman's Communicators
Sun Welding Safe Co.
Surecase Co., The
Sweet Home, Inc.
Tinks & Ben Lee Hunting Products
    (See Wellington Outdoors)
Trulock Tool
Universal Sports
W. Waller & Son, Inc.
Whitestone Lumber Corp.
Wilson Case, Inc.
Woodstream
Zanotti Armor, Inc.
Ziegel Engineering

CHOKE DEVICES, RECOIL ABSORBERS & RECOIL PADS

3-Ten Corp.
A.W. Peterson Gun Shop, Inc., The
Action Products, Inc.
Answer Products Co.
Arundel Arms & Ammunition, Inc., A.
Bansner's Ultimate Rifles, LLC
Bartlett Engineering
Battenfeld Technologies, Inc.
Bob Allen Sportswear
Briley Mfg. Inc.
Brooks Tactical Systems-Agrip
Brownells, Inc.
B-Square Company, Inc.
Buffer Technologies
Bull Mountain Rifle Co.
C&H Research
Cation
Chicasaw Gun Works
Clearview Products
Colonial Arms, Inc.
Connecticut Shotgun Mfg. Co.
CRR, Inc./Marble's Inc.
Danuser Machine Co.
Dina Arms Corporation
Gentry Custom LLC
Graybill's Gun Shop
Gruning Precision, Inc.
Harry Lawson Co.
Hastings
Haydel's Game Calls, Inc.
Hogue Grips
Holland's Gunsmithing
I.N.C. Inc. (See Kickeez I.N.C., Inc.)
Jackalope Gun Shop
Jenkins Recoil Pads
JP Enterprises, Inc.

KDF, Inc.
Kickeez I.N.C., Inc.
Lawson Co., Harry
London Guns Ltd.
Lyman Products Corp.
Mag-Na-Port International, Inc.
Mandall Shooting Supply Inc.
Marble Arms (See CRR,
    Inc./Marble's Inc.)
Menck, Gunsmith Inc., T.W.
Middlebrooks Custom Shop
Mobile Area Networks, Inc.
Morrow, Bud
Nu Line Guns
One Of A Kind
Original Box, Inc.
P.S.M.G. Gun Co.
Palsa Outdoor Products
Parker & Sons Shooting Supply
Pro-Port Ltd.
Que Industries, Inc.
Shotguns Unlimited
Simmons Gun Repair, Inc.
Stan Baker Sports
Stone Enterprises Ltd.
Time Precision
Truglo, Inc.
Trulock Tool
Uncle Mike's (See Michaels of
    Oregon, Co.)
Universal Sports
Virgin Valley Custom Guns
Williams Gun Sight Co.
Wilsom Combat
Wise Guns, Dale

CHRONOGRAPHS & PRESSURE TOOLS

Air Rifle Specialists
C.W. Erickson's L.L.C.
Clearview Products
Competition Electronics, Inc.
D&H Precision Tooling
Hege Jagd-u. Sporthandels GmbH
Hutton Rifle Ranch
Mac-1 Airgun Distributors
Oehler Research, Inc.
PACT, Inc.
Romain's Custom Guns, Inc.
Savage Arms, Inc.
Stratco, Inc.
Tepeco

CLEANERS & DEGREASERS

A.W. Peterson Gun Shop, Inc., The
Barnes Bullets, Inc.
Camp-Cap Products
Cubic Shot Shell Co., Inc.
G96 Products Co., Inc.
Gun Works, The
Hafner World Wide, Inc.
Half Moon Rifle Shop
Kleen-Bore, Inc.
Modern Muzzleloading, Inc.
Northern Precision
Parker & Sons Shooting Supply
Parker Gun Finishes
PrOlixr Lubricants
R&S Industries Corp.
Rusteprufe Laboratories
Sheffield Knifemakers Supply, Inc.
Shooter's Choice Gun Care
Sierra Specialty Prod. Co.
Spencer's Rifle Barrels, Inc.
United States Products Co.

CLEANING & REFINISHING SUPPLIES

A.W. Peterson Gun Shop, Inc., The
AC Dyna-tite Corp.
Alpha 1 Drop Zone

American Gas & Chemical Co., Ltd.,
Answer Products Co.
Armite Laboratories
Atlantic Mills, Inc.
Atsko/Sno-Seal, Inc.
Barnes Bullets, Inc.
Battenfeld Technologies, Inc.
Beeman Precision Airguns
Bill's Gun Repair
Birchwood Casey
Blount, Inc., Sporting Equipment
    Div.
Blount/Outers ATK
Blue and Gray Products Inc. (See Ox-
    Yoke Originals)
Break-Free, Inc.
Bridgers Best
Brownells, Inc.
C.S. Van Gorden & Son, Inc.
Cain's Outdoors, Inc.
Cambos Outdoorsman
Cambos Outdoorsman
Camp-Cap Products
CCI/Speer Div of ATK
Connecticut Shotgun Mfg. Co.
Creedmoor Sports, Inc.
CRR, Inc./Marble's Inc.
Custom Products (See Jones
    Custom Products)
Cylinder & Slide, Inc., William R.
    Laughridge
Dara-Nes, Inc. (See Nesci
    Enterprises, Inc.)
Deepeeka Exports Pvt. Ltd.
Dem-Bart Checkering Tools, Inc.
Desert Mountain Mfg.
Du-Lite Corp.
Dykstra, Doug
E&L Mfg., Inc.
Effebi SNC-Dr. Franco Beretta
Ekol Leather Care
Faith Associates
Flitz International Ltd.
Fluoramics, Inc.
Frontier Products Co.
G96 Products Co., Inc.
Golden Age Arms Co.
Guardsman Products
Gunsmithing, Inc.
Hafner World Wide, Inc.
Half Moon Rifle Shop
Hammans, Charles E.
Hoppe's Div. Penguin Industries, Inc.
Hornady Mfg. Co.
Hydrosorbent Products
Iosso Products
J. Dewey Mfg. Co., Inc.
Jantz Supply
Jantz Supply
Jonad Corp.
K&M Industries, Inc.
Kellogg's Professional Products
Kesselring Gun Shop
Kleen-Bore, Inc.
Knight Rifles
Laurel Mountain Forge
Lee Supplies, Mark
Lewis Lead Remover, The (See
    Brownells, Inc.)
List Precision Engineering
LPS Laboratories, Inc.
Lyman Products Corp.
Mac-1 Airgun Distributors
Mandall Shooting Supply Inc.
Marble Arms (See CRR,
    Inc./Marble's Inc.)
Mark Lee Supplies
Micro Sight Co.
Minute Man High Tech Industries
MTM Molded Products Co., Inc.
Muscle Products Corp.
Nesci Enterprises Inc.
Northern Precision
October Country Muzzleloading
Otis Technology, Inc.
Outers Laboratories Div. of ATK
Ox-Yoke Originals, Inc.

Parker & Sons Shooting Supply
Parker Gun Finishes
Paul Co., The
Pendleton Royal, c/o Swingler
    Buckland Ltd.
Pete Rickard, Inc.
Precision Airgun Sales, Inc.
Precision Reloading, Inc.
PrOlixr Lubricants
Pro-Shot Products, Inc.
R&S Industries Corp.
Radiator Specialty Co.
Richards MicroFit Stocks, Inc.
Rooster Laboratories
Rusteprufe Laboratories
Rusty Duck Premium Gun Care
    Products
Saunders Gun & Machine Shop
Schumakers Gun Shop
Shooter's Choice Gun Care
Shotgun Sports Magazine, dba
    Shootin' Accessories Ltd.
Silencio/Safety Direct
Sinclair International, Inc.
Sno-Seal, Inc. (See Atsko/Sno-Seal,
    Inc.)
Southern Bloomer Mfg. Co.
Splitfire Sporting Goods, L.L.C.
Starr Trading Co., Jedediah
Stoney Point Products, Inc.
Svon Corp.
T.F.C. S.p.A.
TDP Industries, Inc.
Tennessee Valley Mfg.
Tetra Gun Care
Texas Platers Supply Co.
Track of the Wolf, Inc.
Tru-Square Metal Products, Inc.
United States Products Co.
Van Gorden & Son Inc., C. S.
Venco Industries, Inc. (See
    Shooter's Choice Gun Care)
VibraShine, Inc.
Volquartsen Custom Ltd.
Warren Muzzleloading Co., Inc.
Watson Bullets
WD-40 Co.
Wick, David E.
Willow Bend
Young Country Arms

COMPUTER SOFTWARE - BALLISTICS

Action Target, Inc.
AmBr Software Group Ltd.
Arms Software
Arms, Programming Solutions (See
    Arms Software)
Ballistic Program Co., Inc., The
Barnes Bullets, Inc.
Corbin Mfg. & Supply, Inc.
Country Armourer, The
Data Tech Software Systems
Gun Works, The
Hodgdon Powder Co.
J.I.T. Ltd.
Jensen Bullets
Oehler Research, Inc.
Outdoor Sports Headquarters, Inc.
PACT, Inc.
Pejsa Ballistics
Powley Computer (See Hutton Rifle
    Ranch)
RCBS Operations/ATK
Sierra Bullets
Tioga Engineering Co., Inc.
W. Square Enterprises

CUSTOM GUNSMITH

A&W Repair
A.A. Arms, Inc.
A.W. Peterson Gun Shop, Inc., The
Acadian Ballistic Specialties
Accuracy Unlimited

Acra-Bond Laminates
Adair Custom Shop, Bill
Ahlman Guns
Aldis Gunsmithing & Shooting
    Supply
Alpha Precision, Inc.
Alpine Indoor Shooting Range
Amrine's Gun Shop
Answer Products Co.
Antique Arms Co.
Armament Gunsmithing Co., Inc.
Arms Craft Gunsmithing
Armscorp USA, Inc.
Artistry in Wood
Art's Gun & Sport Shop, Inc.
Arundel Arms & Ammunition, Inc., A.
Autauga Arms, Inc.
Baelder, Harry
Bain & Davis, Inc.
Bansner's Ultimate Rifles, LLC
Barnes Bullets, Inc.
Baron Technology
Barrel & Gunworks
Barta's Gunsmithing
Bear Arms
Bear Mountain Gun & Tool
Behlert Precision, Inc.
Beitzinger, George
Belding's Custom Gun Shop
Bengtson Arms Co., L.
Bill Adair Custom Shop
Billings Gunsmiths
BlackStar AccuMax Barrels
BlackStar Barrel Accurizing (See
    BlackStar AccuMax)
Bob Rogers Gunsmithing
Bond Custom Firearms
Borden Ridges Rimrock Stocks
Borovnik K.G., Ludwig
Bowen Classic Arms Corp.
Brace, Larry D.
Briese Bullet Co., Inc.
Briganti Custom Gunsmith
Briley Mfg. Inc.
Broad Creek Rifle Works, Ltd.
Brockman's Custom Gunsmithing
Broken Gun Ranch
Brown Precision, Inc.
Brown Products, Inc., Ed
Buchsenmachermeister
Buckhorn Gun Works
Budin, Dave
Bull Mountain Rifle Co.
Bullberry Barrel Works, Ltd.
Burkhart Gunsmithing, Don
Calhoon Mfg.
Cambos Outdoorsman
Cambos Outdoorsman
Campbell, Dick
Carolina Precision Rifles
Carter's Gun Shop
Caywood, Shane J.
CBC-BRAZIL
Chambers Flintlocks Ltd., Jim
Champlin Firearms, Inc.
Chicasaw Gun Works
Chuck's Gun Shop
Clark Custom Guns, Inc.
Clark Firearms Engraving
Classic Arms Company
Classic Arms Corp.
Clearview Products
Cleland's Outdoor World, Inc.
Coffin, Charles H.
Cogar's Gunsmithing
Cole's Gun Works
Colonial Arms, Inc.
Colonial Repair
Colorado Gunsmithing Academy
Colorado School of Trades
Colt's Mfg. Co., Inc.
Competitive Pistol Shop, The
Conrad, C. A.
Corkys Gun Clinic
Cullity Restoration
Custom Shop, The
Custom Single Shot Rifles

PRODUCT & SERVICE DIRECTORY

D&D Gunsmiths, Ltd.
D.L. Unmussig Bullets
Dangler, Homer L.
D'Arcy Echols & Co.
Darlington Gun Works, Inc.
Dave's Gun Shop
David Miller Co.
David R. Chicoine
David W. Schwartz Custom Guns
Davis, Don
Delorge, Ed
Del-Sports, Inc.
DGR Custom Rifles
DGS, Inc., Dale A. Storey
Dietz Gun Shop & Range, Inc.
Dilliott Gunsmithing, Inc.
Don Klein Custom Guns
Donnelly, C. P.
Duane A. Hobbie Gunsmithing
Duane's Gun Repair (See DGR
    Custom Rifles)
Duffy, Charles E. (See Guns Antique
    & Modern DBA)
Duncan's Gun Works, Inc.
E. Arthur Brown Co. Inc.
Eckelman Gunsmithing
Ed Brown Products, Inc.
Eggleston, Jere D.
Entreprise Arms, Inc.
Erhardt, Dennis
Eversull Co., Inc.
Evolution Gun Works, Inc.
FERLIB
Ferris Firearms
Fisher, Jerry A.
Fisher Custom Firearms
Fleming Firearms
Flynn's Custom Guns
Forkin Custom Classics
Forster, Kathy (See Custom
    Checkering)
Forster, Larry L.
Forthofer's Gunsmithing &
    Knifemaking
Fred F. Wells/Wells Sport Store
Frontier Arms Co., Inc.
Fullmer, Geo. M.
Fulton Armory
G.G. & G.
Galaxy Imports Ltd., Inc.
Garthwaite Pistolsmith, Inc., Jim
Gary Reeder Custom Guns
Gator Guns & Repair
Genecco Gun Works
Gene's Custom Guns
Gentry Custom LLC
George Hoenig, Inc.
Gillmann, Edwin
Gilmore Sports Concepts, Inc.
Goens, Dale W.
Gonic Arms North American Arms,
    Inc.
Goodling's Gunsmithing
Grace, Charles E.
Grayback Wildcats
Graybill's Gun Shop
Green, Roger M.
Greg Gunsmithing Repair
Gre-Tan Rifles
Griffin & Howe, Inc.
Griffin & Howe, Inc.
Gruning Precision, Inc.
Gun Doc, Inc.
Gun Shop, The
Gun Works, The
Guncraft Books (See Guncraft
    Sports, Inc.)
Guncraft Sports, Inc.
Guncraft Sports, Inc.
Guns Antique & Modern DBA /
    Charles E. Duffy
Gunsite Training Center
Gunsmithing Ltd.
Hamilton, Alex B. (See Ten-Ring
    Precision, Inc.)
Hammans, Charles E.
Hammerli Service-Precision Mac

Hammond Custom Guns Ltd.
Hank's Gun Shop
Hanson's Gun Center, Dick
Harry Lawson Co.
Hart & Son, Inc.
Hart Rifle Barrels, Inc.
Hartmann & Weiss GmbH
Hawken Shop, The (See Dayton
    Traister)
Hecht, Hubert J., Waffen-Hecht
Heilmann, Stephen
Heinie Specialty Products
Hensley, Gunmaker, Darwin
High Bridge Arms, Inc.
High Performance International
High Precision
High Standard Mfg. Co./F.I., Inc.
Highline Machine Co.
Hill, Loring F.
Hiptmayer, Armurier
Hiptmayer, Klaus
Hoag, James W.
Hodgson, Richard
Hoehn Sales, Inc.
Hofer Jagdwaffen, P.
Holland's Gunsmithing
Huebner, Corey O.
Hunkeler, A. (See Buckskin Machine
    Works)
Imperial Magnum Corp.
Irwin, Campbell H.
Israel Arms Inc.
Ivanoff, Thomas G. (See Tom's Gun
    Repair)
J&S Heat Treat
J.J. Roberts / Engraver
Jack Dever Co.
Jackalope Gun Shop
Jamison's Forge Works
Jarrett Rifles, Inc.
Jarvis, Inc.
Jay McCament Custom Gunmaker
Jeffredo Gunsight
Jensen's Custom Ammunition
Jim Norman Custom Gunstocks
Jim's Precision, Jim Ketchum
John Rigby & Co.
John's Custom Leather
Jones Custom Products, Neil A.
Juenke, Vern
K. Eversull Co., Inc.
KDF, Inc.
Keith's Custom Gunstocks
Ken Eyster Heritage Gunsmiths, Inc.
Ken Starnes Gunmaker
Ketchum, Jim (See Jim's Precision)
Kilham & Co.
King's Gun Works
Kleinendorst, K. W.
KOGOT
Korzinek Riflesmith, J.
L. E. Jurras & Assoc.
LaFrance Specialties
Lampert, Ron
LaRocca Gun Works
Larry Lyons Gunworks
Lathrop's, Inc.
Laughridge, William R. (See Cylinder
    & Slide, Inc.)
Lawson Co., Harry
Lazzeroni Arms Co.
LeFever Arms Co., Inc.
Les Baer Custom, Inc.
Linebaugh Custom Sixguns
List Precision Engineering
Lock's Philadelphia Gun Exchange
Lone Star Rifle Company
Long, George F.
Mag-Na-Port International, Inc.
Mahony, Philip Bruce
Mahony, Philip Bruce
Mahovsky's Metalife
Makinson, Nicholas
Mandall Shooting Supply Inc.
Marshall Fish Mfg. Gunsmith Sptg.
    Co.
Martin's Gun Shop

Martz, John V.
Mathews Gun Shop & Gunsmithing,
    Inc.
Mazur Restoration, Pete
McCann, Tom
McCluskey Precision Rifles
McGowen Rifle Barrels
McMillan Rifle Barrels
MCS, Inc.
Mercer Custom Guns
Michael's Antiques
Mid-America Recreation, Inc.
Middlebrooks Custom Shop
Miller Arms, Inc.
Miller Custom
Mills Jr., Hugh B.
Moeller, Steve
Monell Custom Guns
Morrison Custom Rifles, J. W.
Morrow, Bud
Mo's Competitor Supplies (See MCS,
    Inc.)
Mowrey's Guns & Gunsmithing
Mullis Guncraft
Muzzleloaders Etcetera, Inc.
NCP Products, Inc.
Neil A. Jones Custom Products
Nelson's Custom Guns, Inc.
Nettestad Gun Works
New England Arms Co.
New England Custom Gun Service
Newman Gunshop
Nicholson Custom
Nickels, Paul R.
North American Shooting Systems
Nu Line Guns
Old World Gunsmithing
Olson, Vic
Orvis Co., The
Ottmar, Maurice
Ox-Yoke Originals, Inc.
Ozark Gun Works
P&M Sales & Services, LLC
P.S.M.G. Gun Co.
PAC-NOR Barreling
Pagel Gun Works, Inc.
Parker & Sons Shooting Supply
Parker Gun Finishes
Pasadena Gun Center
Paterson Gunsmithing
Paulsen Gunstocks
Peacemaker Specialists
PEM's Mfg. Co.
Pence Precision Barrels
Pennsylvania Gunsmith School
Penrod Precision
Pentheny de Pentheny
Perazone-Gunsmith, Brian
Performance Specialists
Pete Mazur Restoration
Peterson Gun Shop, Inc., A.W.
Piquette's Custom Engraving
Plum City Ballistic Range
Powell & Son (Gunmakers) Ltd.,
    William
Power Custom, Inc.
Professional Hunter Supplies
Quality Custom Firearms
R&J Gun Shop
R.A. Wells Custom Gunsmith
Ramon B. Gonzalez Guns
Ray's Gunsmith Shop
Renfrew Guns & Supplies
Ridgetop Sporting Goods
Ries, Chuck
RMS Custom Gunsmithing
Robar Co., Inc., The
Robert Valade Engraving
Robinson, Don
Rocky Mountain Arms, Inc.
Romain's Custom Guns, Inc.
Ron Frank Custom Classic Arms
Ruger's Custom Guns
Rupert's Gun Shop
Savage Arms, Inc.
Schiffman, Mike
Schumakers Gun Shop

Score High Gunsmithing
Sharp Shooter Supply
Shaw, Inc., E. R. (See Small Arms
    Mfg. Co.)
Shay's Gunsmithing
Shockley, Harold H.
Shooters Supply
Shootin' Shack
Shotguns Unlimited
Silver Ridge Gun Shop (See Goodwin
    Guns)
Simmons Gun Repair, Inc.
Singletary, Kent
Siskiyou Gun Works (See Donnelly,
    C. P.)
Skeoch, Brian R.
Sklany's Machine Shop
Small Arms Mfg. Co.
Small Arms Specialists
Smith, Art
Snapp's Gunshop
Speiser, Fred D.
Spencer Reblue Service
Spencer's Rifle Barrels, Inc.
Splitfire Sporting Goods, L.L.C.
Sportsmen's Exchange & Western
    Gun Traders, Inc.
Springfield Armory
Springfield, Inc.
SSK Industries
Star Custom Bullets
Steelman's Gun Shop
Steffens, Ron
Steven Dodd Hughes
Stiles Custom Guns
Stott's Creek Armory, Inc.
Sturgeon Valley Sporters
Sullivan, David S. (See Westwind
    Rifles, Inc.)
Swampfire Shop, The (See Peterson
    Gun Shop, Inc., A.W.)
Swann, D. J.
Swenson's 45 Shop, A. D.
Swift River Gunworks
Szweda, Robert (See RMS Custom
    Gunsmithing)
Taconic Firearms Ltd., Perry Lane
Tank's Rifle Shop
Tar-Hunt Custom Rifles, Inc.
Tarnhelm Supply Co., Inc.
Taylor & Robbins
Tennessee Valley Mfg.
Ten-Ring Precision, Inc.
Terry K. Kopp Professional
    Gunsmithing
Theis, Terry
Time Precision
Tom's Gun Repair, Thomas G.
    Ivanoff
Tom's Gunshop
Trevallion Gunstocks
Trulock Tool
Tucker, James C.
Turnbull Restoration, Doug
Upper Missouri Trading Co.
Van Horn, Gil
Van Patten, J. W.
Van's Gunsmith Service
Vest, John
Vic's Gun Refinishing
Virgin Valley Custom Guns
Volquartsen Custom Ltd.
Walker Arms Co., Inc.
Wallace, Terry
Wasmundt, Jim
Weatherby, Inc.
Weber & Markin Custom Gunsmiths
Weems, Cecil
Werth, T. W.
Wessinger Custom Guns &
    Engraving
Westley Richards & Co. Ltd.
Westwind Rifles, Inc., David S.
    Sullivan
White Barn Wor
White Rifles, Inc.
Wichita Arms, Inc.

Wiebe, Duane
Wild West Guns
William E. Phillips Firearms
Williams Gun Sight Co.
Williams Shootin' Iron Service, The
    Lynx-Line
Williamson Precision Gunsmithing
Wilsom Combat
Winter, Robert M.
Wise Guns, Dale
Wiseman and Co., Bill
Wright's Gunstock Blanks
Zeeryp, Russ

CUSTOM METALSMITH

A&W Repair
A.W. Peterson Gun Shop, Inc., The
Ackerman & Co.
Ahlman Guns
Alaskan Silversmith, The
Aldis Gunsmithing & Shooting
    Supply
Alpha Precision, Inc.
Amrine's Gun Shop
Answer Products Co.
Antique Arms Co.
Artistry in Wood
Baron Technology
Barrel & Gunworks
Bear Mountain Gun & Tool
Behlert Precision, Inc.
Beitzinger, George
Bengtson Arms Co., L.
Bill Adair Custom Shop
Billings Gunsmiths
Billingsley & Brownell
Bob Rogers Gunsmithing
Bowen Classic Arms Corp.
Brace, Larry D.
Briganti Custom Gunsmith
Broad Creek Rifle Works, Ltd.
Brown Precision, Inc.
Buckhorn Gun Works
Bull Mountain Rifle Co.
Bullberry Barrel Works, Ltd.
Campbell, Dick
Carter's Gun Shop
Caywood, Shane J.
Checkmate Refinishing
Colonial Repair
Colorado Gunsmithing Academy
Craftguard
Crandall Tool & Machine Co.
Cullity Restoration
Custom Shop, The
Custom Single Shot Rifles
D&D Gunsmiths, Ltd.
D&H Precision Tooling
D'Arcy Echols & Co.
Dave's Gun Shop
Delorge, Ed
DGS, Inc., Dale A. Storey
Dietz Gun Shop & Range, Inc.
Dilliott Gunsmithing, Inc.
Don Klein Custom Guns
Duane's Gun Repair (See DGR
    Custom Rifles)
Duncan's Gun Works, Inc.
Erhardt, Dennis
Eversull Co., Inc.
Ferris Firearms
Fisher, Jerry A.
Forster, Larry L.
Forthofer's Gunsmithing &
    Knifemaking
Fred F. Wells/Wells Sport Store
Fullmer, Geo. M.
Genecco Gun Works
Gentry Custom LLC
Grace, Charles E.
Grayback Wildcats
Graybill's Gun Shop
Green, Roger M.
Gun Shop, The
Gunsmithing Ltd.

PRODUCT & SERVICE DIRECTORY

Hamilton, Alex B. (See Ten-Ring Precision, Inc.)
Harry Lawson Co.
Hartmann & Weiss GmbH
Hecht, Hubert J., Waffen-Hecht
Heilmann, Stephen
High Precision
Highline Machine Co.
Hiptmayer, Armurier
Hiptmayer, Klaus
Hoag, James W.
Holland's Gunsmithing
Ivanoff, Thomas G. (See Tom's Gun Repair)
J J Roberts Firearm Engraver
J&S Heat Treat
J.J. Roberts / Engraver
Jamison's Forge Works
Jay McCament Custom Gunmaker
Jeffredo Gunsight
KDF, Inc.
Ken Eyster Heritage Gunsmiths, Inc.
Ken Starnes Gunmaker
Kilham & Co.
Kleinendorst, K. W.
Lampert, Ron
LaRocca Gun Works
Larry Lyons Gunworks
Lawson Co., Harry
Les Baer Custom, Inc.
List Precision Engineering
Lock's Philadelphia Gun Exchange
Mahovsky's Metalife
Makinson, Nicholas
Mandall Shooting Supply Inc.
Mazur Restoration, Pete
McCann Industries
Mid-America Recreation, Inc.
Miller Arms, Inc.
Morrison Custom Rifles, J. W.
Morrow, Bud
Mullis Guncraft
Nelson's Custom Guns, Inc.
Nettestad Gun Works
New England Custom Gun Service
Nicholson Custom
Noreen, Peter H.
Nu Line Guns
Olson, Vic
Ozark Gun Works
P.S.M.G. Gun Co.
Pagel Gun Works, Inc.
Parker & Sons Shooting Supply
Parker Gun Finishes
Pasadena Gun Center
Penrod Precision
Pete Mazur Restoration
Precision Specialties
Quality Custom Firearms
R.A. Wells Custom Gunsmith
Rice, Keith (See White Rock Tool & Die)
Robar Co., Inc., The
Robinson, Don
Rocky Mountain Arms, Inc.
Romain's Custom Guns, Inc.
Ron Frank Custom Classic Arms
Score High Gunsmithing
Simmons Gun Repair, Inc.
Singletary, Kent
Skeoch, Brian R.
Sklany's Machine Shop
Small Arms Specialists
Smith, Art
Smith, Sharmon
Snapp's Gunshop
Spencer Reblue Service
Spencer's Rifle Barrels, Inc.
Sportsmen's Exchange & Western Gun Traders, Inc.
SSK Industries
Steffens, Ron
Stiles Custom Guns
Taylor & Robbins
Ten-Ring Precision, Inc.
Tom's Gun Repair, Thomas G. Ivanoff

Turnbull Restoration, Doug
Van Horn, Gil
Van Patten, J. W.
Vic's Gun Refinishing
Waldron, Herman
Wallace, Terry
Weber & Markin Custom Gunsmiths
Werth, T. W.
Wessinger Custom Guns & Engraving
White Rock Tool & Die
Wiebe, Duane
Wild West Guns
Williams Shootin' Iron Service, The Lynx-Line
Williamson Precision Gunsmithing
Winter, Robert M.
Wise Guns, Dale
Wright's Gunstock Blanks

DECOYS

A.W. Peterson Gun Shop, Inc., The
Ad Hominem
Belding's Custom Gun Shop
Bill Russ Trading Post
Boyds' Gunstock Industries, Inc.
Carry-Lite, Inc.
Farm Form Decoys, Inc.
Feather, Flex Decoys
Flambeau, Inc.
G&H Decoys, Inc.
Grand Slam Hunting Products
Herter's Manufacturing Inc.
Klingler Woodcarving
Kolpin Outdoors, Inc.
L.L. Bean, Inc.
Murphy, R.R. Co., Inc.
Original Deer Formula Co., The
Quack Decoy & Sporting Clays
Sports Innovations, Inc.
Tanglefree Industries
Tru-Nord Compass
Woods Wise Products

DIE ACCESSORIES, METALLIC

A.W. Peterson Gun Shop, Inc., The
Ammo Load Worldwide, Inc.
High Precision
Howell Machine, Inc.
King & Co.
Rapine Bullet Mould Mfg. Co.
Redding Reloading Equipment
Royal Arms Gunstocks
Sinclair International, Inc.
Sport Flite Manufacturing Co.

DIES, METALLIC

4-D Custom Die Co.
A.W. Peterson Gun Shop, Inc., The
Bald Eagle Precision Machine Co.
Buffalo Arms Co.
Competitor Corp., Inc.
Dakota Arms, Inc.
Dillon Precision Products, Inc.
Dixie Gun Works
Fremont Tool Works
Gruning Precision, Inc.
Jones Custom Products, Neil A.
King & Co.
Lee Precision, Inc.
Montana Precision Swaging
Neil A. Jones Custom Products
Ozark Gun Works
PWM Sales Ltd.
Rapine Bullet Mould Mfg. Co.
RCBS Operations/ATK
RCBS/ATK
Romain's Custom Guns, Inc.
Sinclair International, Inc.
Spencer's Rifle Barrels, Inc.
Sport Flite Manufacturing Co.

SSK Industries
Vega Tool Co.

DIES, SHOTSHELL

A.W. Peterson Gun Shop, Inc., The
Hollywood Engineering
Lee Precision, Inc.
MEC, Inc.

DIES, SWAGE

4-D Custom Die Co.
A.W. Peterson Gun Shop, Inc., The
Ammo Load Worldwide, Inc.
Bullet Swaging Supply, Inc.
Competitor Corp., Inc.
Corbin Mfg. & Supply, Inc.
D.L. Unmussig Bullets
Howell Machine, Inc.
Montana Precision Swaging
Sport Flite Manufacturing Co.

ENGRAVER, ENGRAVING TOOLS

Ackerman & Co.
Adair Custom Shop, Bill
Ahlman Guns
Alaskan Silversmith, The
Alfano, Sam
Allard, Gary/Creek Side Metal & Woodcrafters
Allen Firearm Engraving
Altamont Co.
American Pioneer Video
Baron Technology
Barraclough, John K.
Bates Engraving, Billy
Bill Adair Custom Shop
Billy Bates Engraving
Boessler, Erich
Brooker, Dennis
Buchsenmachermeister
Churchill, Winston G.
Clark Firearms Engraving
Collings, Ronald
Creek Side Metal & Woodcrafters
Cullity Restoration
Cupp, Alana, Custom Engraver
Dayton Traister
Delorge, Ed
Dolbare, Elizabeth
Drain, Mark
Dremel Mfg. Co.
Dubber, Michael W.
Engraving Artistry
Eversull Co., Inc.
Firearms Engraver's Guild of America
Forty-Five Ranch Enterprises
Fountain Products
Frank Knives
Fred F. Wells/Wells Sport Store
Gary Reeder Custom Guns
Gene's Custom Guns
Glimm's Custom Gun Engraving
Golden Age Arms Co.
Gournet Artistic Engraving
Grant, Howard V.
GRS/Glendo Corp.
Gun Room, The
Gurney, F. R.
Half Moon Rifle Shop
Harris Hand Engraving, Paul A.
Hawken Shop, The (See Dayton Traister)
Hiptmayer, Armurier
Hiptmayer, Heidemarie
Hofer Jagdwaffen, P.
J J Roberts Firearm Engraver
J.J. Roberts / Engraver
Jantz Supply
Jeff Flannery Engraving
Jim Blair Engraving
John J. Adams & Son Engravers

Kane, Edward
Kehr, Roger
Kelly, Lance
Ken Eyster Heritage Gunsmiths, Inc.
Kenneth W. Warren Engraver
Klingler Woodcarving
Koevenig's Engraving Service
Larry Lyons Gunworks
LeFever Arms Co., Inc.
Lindsay Engraving & Tools
McCombs, Leo
McDonald, Dennis
McKenzie, Lynton
Mele, Frank
Mid-America Recreation, Inc.
Nelson, Gary K.
New Orleans Jewelers Supply Co.
NgraveR Co., The
Pedersen, C. R.
Pedersen, Rex C.
Peter Hale/Engraver
Piquette's Custom Engraving
Potts, Wayne E.
Quality Custom Firearms
Rabeno, Martin
Ralph Bone Engraving
Reed, Dave
Reno, Wayne
Riggs, Jim
Robert Evans Engraving
Robert Valade Engraving
Robinson, Don
Rohner, Hans
Rohner, John
Rosser, Bob
Rundell's Gun Shop
Sam Welch Gun Engraving
Sampson, Roger
Schiffman, Mike
Sheffield Knifemakers Supply, Inc.
Sherwood, George
Singletary, Kent
Smith, Mark A.
Smith, Ron
Smokey Valley Rifles
SSK Industries
Steve Kamyk Engraver
Swanson, Mark
Theis, Terry
Thiewes, George W.
Thirion Gun Engraving, Denise
Viramontez Engraving
Vorhes, David
W.E. Brownell Checkering Tools
Wagoner, Vernon G.
Wallace, Terry
Warenski Engraving
Weber & Markin Custom Gunsmiths
Wells, Rachel
Wessinger Custom Guns & Engraving
Winchester Consultants

GAME CALLS

A.W. Peterson Gun Shop, Inc., The
African Import Co.
Bill Russ Trading Post
Bostick Wildlife Calls, Inc.
Cedar Hill Game Calls, LLC
Crit'R Call (See Rocky Mountain Wildlife Products)
Custom Calls
D-Boone Ent., Inc.
Deepeeka Exports Pvt. Ltd.
Dr. O's Products Ltd.
Faulhaber Wildlocker
Faulk's Game Call Co., Inc.
Fibron Products, Inc.
Flambeau, Inc.
Glynn Scobey Duck & Goose Calls
Grand Slam Hunting Products
Green Head Game Call Co.
Hally Caller
Haydel's Game Calls, Inc.
Herter's Manufacturing Inc.

Hunter's Specialties Inc.
Keowee Game Calls
Kolpin Outdoors, Inc.
Lohman Mfg. Co., Inc.
Mallardtone Game Calls
Moss Double Tone, Inc.
Oakman Turkey Calls
Original Deer Formula Co., The
Outdoor Sports Headquarters, Inc.
Pete Rickard, Inc.
Philip S. Olt Co.
Primos Hunting Calls
Protektor Model
Quaker Boy, Inc.
Rocky Mountain Wildlife Products
Sceery Game Calls
Sports Innovations, Inc.
Stewart Game Calls, Inc., Johnny
Sure-Shot Game Calls, Inc.
Tanglefree Industries
Tinks & Ben Lee Hunting Products (See Wellington Outdoors)
Tink's Safariland Hunting Corp.
Wellington Outdoors
Wilderness Sound Products Ltd.
Woods Wise Products

GAUGES, CALIPERS & MICROMETERS

Blue Ridge Machinery & Tools, Inc.
Gruning Precision, Inc.
Huntington Die Specialties
JGS Precision Tool Mfg., LLC
K&M Services
King & Co.
Spencer's Rifle Barrels, Inc.
Starrett Co., L. S.
Stoney Point Products, Inc.

GUN PARTS, U.S. & FOREIGN

"Su-Press-On", Inc.
A.A. Arms, Inc.
A.W. Peterson Gun Shop, Inc., The
Ahlman Guns
Amherst Arms
Antique Arms Co.
Armscorp USA, Inc.
Auto-Ordnance Corp.
B.A.C.
Ballard Rifle & Cartridge Co., LLC
Bar-Sto Precision Machine
Bear Mountain Gun & Tool
Billings Gunsmiths
Bill's Gun Repair
Bob's Gun Shop
Briese Bullet Co., Inc.
Brown Products, Inc., Ed
Brownells, Inc.
Bryan & Assoc.
Buffer Technologies
Cambos Outdoorsman
Cambos Outdoorsman
Cape Outfitters
Caspian Arms, Ltd.
CBC-BRAZIL
Century International Arms, Inc.
Chicasaw Gun Works
Chip McCormick Corp.
Cleland's Outdoor World, Inc.
Cole's Gun Works
Colonial Arms, Inc.
Colonial Repair
Colt's Mfg. Co., Inc.
Cylinder & Slide, Inc., William R. Laughridge
Dan Wesson Firearms
David R. Chicoine
Delta Arms Ltd.
DGR Custom Rifles
Dibble, Derek A.
Dixie Gun Works

PRODUCT & SERVICE DIRECTORY

Duane's Gun Repair (See DGR
  Custom Rifles)
Duffy, Charles E. (See Guns Antique
  & Modern DBA)
E.A.A. Corp.
EMF Co. Inc.
Enguix Import-Export
Entreprise Arms, Inc.
European American Armory Corp.
  (See E.A.A. Corp.)
Evolution Gun Works, Inc.
Falcon Industries, Inc.
Felk Pistols, Inc.
Fleming Firearms
Fulton Armory
Gentry Custom LLC
Glimm's Custom Gun Engraving
Granite Mountain Arms, Inc.
Greider Precision
Gre-Tan Rifles
Gun Doc, Inc.
Gun Hunter Books (See Gun Hunter
  Trading Co.)
Gun Hunter Trading Co.
Gun Room Press, The
Gun Shop, The
Gun Works, The
Guns Antique & Modern DBA /
  Charles E. Duffy
Gunsmithing, Inc.
Hawken Shop, The (See Dayton
  Traister)
High Performance International
High Standard Mfg. Co./F.I., Inc.
Irwin, Campbell H.
Jack First, Inc.
Jamison's Forge Works
JG Airguns, LLC
Jonathan Arthur Ciener, Inc.
Kimber of America, Inc.
Knight's Manufacturing Co.
Krico Deutschland GmbH
LaFrance Specialties
Lampert, Ron
LaPrade
Laughridge, William R. (See Cylinder
  & Slide, Inc.)
Leapers, Inc.
List Precision Engineering
Lodewick, Walter H.
Logdewood Mfg.
Lomont Precision Bullets
Long, George F.
Mandall Shooting Supply Inc.
Markell, Inc.
Martin's Gun Shop
MCS, Inc.
Mid-America Recreation, Inc.
Mobile Area Networks, Inc.
Morrow, Bud
Mo's Competitor Supplies (See MCS,
  Inc.)
North Star West
Northwest Arms
Nu Line Guns
Numrich Gun Parts Corporation
Nygord Precision Products, Inc.
Olathe Gun Shop
Olympic Arms Inc.
P S M G Gun Co
Pacific Armament Corp
Perazone-Gunsmith, Brian
Performance Specialists
Peter Dyson & Son Ltd.
Peterson Gun Shop, Inc., A.W.
Ranch Products
Randco UK
Ravell Ltd.
Retting, Inc., Martin B.
Romain's Custom Guns, Inc.
Ruger (See Sturm Ruger & Co., Inc.)
Rutgers Book Center
S&S Firearms
Sabatti SPA
Samco Global Arms, Inc.
Sarco, Inc.
Scherer Supplies

Shockley, Harold H.
Shootin' Shack
Silver Ridge Gun Shop (See Goodwin
  Guns)
Simmons Gun Repair, Inc.
Smires, C. L.
Smith & Wesson
Southern Ammunition Co., Inc.
Southern Armory, The
Sportsmen's Exchange & Western
  Gun Traders, Inc.
Springfield Sporters, Inc.
Springfield, Inc.
Steyr Mannlicher GmbH & Co. KG
STI International
Strayer-Voigt, Inc.
Sturm Ruger & Co. Inc.
Sunny Hill Enterprises, Inc.
Swampfire Shop, The (See Peterson
  Gun Shop, Inc., A.W.)
T&S Industries, Inc.
Tank's Rifle Shop
Tarnhelm Supply Co., Inc.
Taylor's & Co., Inc.
Terry K. Kopp Professional
  Gunsmithing
Tom Forrest, Inc.
VAM Distribution Co. LLC
W. Waller & Son, Inc.
W.C. Wolff Co.
Walker Arms Co., Inc.
Wescombe, Bill (See North Star
  West)
Wild West Guns
Williams Mfg. of Oregon
Winchester Sutler, Inc., The
Wise Guns, Dale
Wisners, Inc.

GUNS & GUN PARTS, REPLICA & ANTIQUE

A.W. Peterson Gun Shop, Inc., The
Ackerman & Co.
Ahlman Guns
Armi San Paolo
Auto-Ordnance Corp.
Ballard Rifle & Cartridge Co., LLC
Bear Mountain Gun & Tool
Billings Gunsmiths
Bob's Gun Shop
Buffalo Arms Co.
Cache La Poudre Rifleworks
Cash Mfg. Co., Inc.
CBC-BRAZIL
CCI Security Products
Chambers Flintlocks Ltd., Jim
Chicasaw Gun Works
Cimarron F.A. Co.
Cogar's Gunsmithing
Cole's Gun Works
Colonial Repair
Colt Blackpowder Arms Co.
Colt's Mfg. Co., Inc.
Custom Single Shot Rifles
Delhi Gun House
Delta Arms Ltd.
Dilliott Gunsmithing, Inc.
Dixie Gun Works
Dixon Muzzleloading Shop, Inc.
Ed's Gun House
Euroarms of America, Inc.
Flintlocks, Etc.
Getz Barrel Company
Golden Age Arms Co.
Gun Doc, Inc.
Gun Hunter Books (See Gun Hunter
  Trading Co.)
Gun Hunter Trading Co.
Gun Room Press, The
Gun Works, The
Hastings
Heidenstrom Bullets
Hunkeler, A. (See Buckskin Machine
  Works)
IAR Inc.

Imperial Miniature Armory
Ithaca Classic Doubles
Jack First, Inc.
JG Airguns, LLC
Ken Starnes Gunmaker
L&R Lock Co.
Leonard Day
List Precision Engineering
Lock's Philadelphia Gun Exchange
Logdewood Mfg.
Lone Star Rifle Company
Lucas, Edward E
Mandall Shooting Supply Inc.
Martin's Gun Shop
Mathews Gun Shop & Gunsmithing,
  Inc.
Mid-America Recreation, Inc.
Mowrey Gun Works
Navy Arms Company
Neumann GmbH
North Star West
Nu Line Guns
Numrich Gun Parts Corporation
Olathe Gun Shop
Parker & Sons Shooting Supply
Pasadena Gun Center
Pecatonica River Longrifle
PEM's Mfg. Co.
Peter Dyson & Son Ltd.
Pony Express Sport Shop
R.A. Wells Custom Gunsmith
Randco UK
Ravell Ltd.
Retting, Inc., Martin B.
Rutgers Book Center
S&S Firearms
Samco Global Arms, Inc.
Sarco, Inc.
Shootin' Shack
Silver Ridge Gun Shop (See Goodwin
  Guns)
Simmons Gun Repair, Inc.
Sklany's Machine Shop
Southern Ammunition Co., Inc.
Starr Trading Co., Jedediah
Stott's Creek Armory, Inc.
Taylor's & Co., Inc.
Tennessee Valley Mfg.
Tiger-Hunt Longrifle Gunstocks
Turnbull Restoration, Doug
Upper Missouri Trading Co.
VTI Gun Parts
Weber & Markin Custom Gunsmiths
Wescombe, Bill (See North Star
  West)
Whitestone Lumber Corp.
Winchester Sutler, Inc., The

GUNS, AIR

A.W. Peterson Gun Shop, Inc., The
Air Arms
Air Rifle Specialists
Air Venture Airguns
AirForce Airguns
Airrow
Allred Bullet Co.
Arms Corporation of the Philippines
BEC, Inc.
Beeman Precision Airguns
Benjamin/Sheridan Co., Crosman
Bryan & Assoc.
BSA Guns Ltd.
Compasseco, Ltd.
Component Concepts, Inc.
Conetrol Scope Mounts
Crosman Airguns
Daisy Outdoor Products
Daystate Ltd.
Domino
Dynamit Nobel-RWS, Inc.
Effebi SNC-Dr. Franco Beretta
European American Armory Corp.
  (See E.A.A. Corp.)
Feinwerkbau Westinger &
  Altenburger

Gamo USA, Inc.
Gaucher Armes, S.A.
Great Lakes Airguns
Gun Room Press, The
Hammerli Service-Precision Mac
IAR Inc.
International Shooters Service
J.G. Anschutz GmbH & Co. KG
JG Airguns, LLC
Labanu Inc.
Leapers, Inc.
List Precision Engineering
Mac-1 Airgun Distributors
Marksman Products
Maryland Paintball Supply
Nationwide Airgun Repair
Nygord Precision Products, Inc.
Olympic Arms Inc.
Pardini Armi Srl
Park Rifle Co., Ltd., The
Precision Airgun Sales, Inc.
Ripley Rifles
Robinson, Don
RWS (See U.S. Importer-Dynamit
  Nobel-RWS, Inc.)
Safari Arms/Schuetzen Pistol Works
Savage Arms, Inc.
Smith & Wesson
Steyr Mannlicher GmbH & Co. KG
Stone Enterprises Ltd.
Tippman Pneumatics, Inc.
Tristar Sporting Arms, Ltd.
Trooper Walsh
UltraSport Arms, Inc.
Visible Impact Targets
Walther GmbH, Carl
Webley and Scott Ltd.
Weihrauch KG, Hermann

GUNS, FOREIGN MANUFACTURER U.S. IMPORTER

A.W. Peterson Gun Shop, Inc., The
Accuracy Internationl Precision
  Rifles (See U.S.)
Accuracy Int'l. North America, Inc.
Ad Hominem
Air Arms
Armas Garbi, S.A.
Armas Kemen S. A. (See U.S.
  Importers)
Armi Perazzi S.P.A.
Armi San Marco (See Taylor's & Co.)
Armi Sport (See Cape Outfitters)
Arms Corporation of the Philippines
Armscorp USA, Inc.
Arrieta S.L.
Astra Sport, S.A.
Atamec-Bretton
AYA (See U.S. Importer-New
  England Custom Gun Serv
B.A.C.
B.C. Outdoors
BEC, Inc.
Benelli Armi S.P.A.
Benelli USA Corp.
Beretta S.P.A., Pietro
Beretta U.S.A. Corp.
Bernardelli, Vincenzo
Bersa S.A.
Bertuzzi (See U.S. Importer-New
  England Arms Co.)
Bill Hanus Birdguns, LLC
Blaser Jagdwaffen GmbH
Borovnik K.G., Ludwig
Bosis (See U.S. Importer-New
  England Arms Co.)
Brenneke GmbH
Browning Arms Co.
Bryan & Assoc.
BSA Guns Ltd.
Buchsenmachermeister
Cabanas (See U.S. Importer-Mandall
  Shooting Supply
Cabela's

Cache La Poudre Rifleworks
Cape Outfitters
CBC
Champlin Firearms, Inc.
Chapuis Armes
Churchill (See U.S. Importer-Ellett
  Bros.)
Collector's Armoury, Ltd.
Conetrol Scope Mounts
Cosmi Americo & Figlio S.N.C.
Crucelegui, Hermanos (See U.S.
  Importer-Mandall)
Cubic Shot Shell Co., Inc.
Dakota (See U.S. Importer-EMF Co.,
  Inc.)
Dakota Arms, Inc.
Daly, Charles/KBI
Davide Pedersoli and Co.
Domino
Dumoulin, Ernest
Eagle Imports, Inc.
EAW (See U.S. Importer-New
  England Custom Gun Serv
Ed's Gun House
Effebi SNC-Dr. Franco Beretta
EMF Co. Inc.
Eversull Co., Inc.
F.A.I.R.
Fabarm S.p.A.
FEG
Feinwerkbau Westinger &
  Altenburger
Felk Pistols, Inc.
FERLIB
Fiocchi Munizioni S.A. (See U.S.
  Importer-Fiocch
Firearms Co. Ltd. / Alpine (See U.S.
  Importer-Mandall
Flintlocks, Etc.
Galaxy Imports Ltd., Inc.
Gamba S.p.A. Societa Armi
  Bresciane Srl
Gamo (See U.S. Importers-Arms
  United Corp., Daisy M
Gaucher Armes, S.A.
Gibbs Rifle Co., Inc.
Glock GmbH
Goergen's Gun Shop, Inc.
Griffin & Howe, Inc.
Griffin & Howe, Inc.
Grulla Armes
Hammerli AG
Hammerli USA
Hartford (See U.S. Importer-EMF Co.
  Inc.)
Hartmann & Weiss GmbH
Heckler & Koch, Inc.
Hege Jagd-u. Sporthandels GmbH
Helwan (See U.S. Importer-
  Interarms)
Hofer Jagdwaffen, P.
Holland & Holland Ltd.
Howa Machinery, Ltd.
I.A.B. (See U.S. Importer-Taylor's &
  Co., Inc.)
IAR Inc.
IGA (See U.S. Importer-Stoeger
  Industries)
Imperial Magnum Corp.
Imperial Miniature Armory
Import Sports Inc.
Inter Ordnance of America LP
International Shooters Service
Intrac Arms International
J.G. Anschutz GmbH & Co. KG
JSL Ltd. (See U.S. Importer-
  Specialty Shooters Supply)
K. Eversull Co., Inc.
Kimar (See U.S. Importer-IAR, Inc.)
Korth Germany GmbH
Krico Deutschland GmbH
Krieghoff Gun Co., H.
Lakefield Arms Ltd. (See Savage
  Arms, Inc.)
Laurona Armas Eibar, S.A.L.
Lebeau-Courally
Lever Arms Service Ltd.

Llama Gabilondo Y Cia
Lomont Precision Bullets
London Guns Ltd.
Mandall Shooting Supply Inc.
Marocchi F.lli S.p.A
Mauser Werke Oberndorf
  Waffensysteme GmbH
McCann Industries
MEC-Gar S.R.L.
Merkel
Mitchell's Mauser
Morini (See U.S. Importers-Mandall
  Shooting Supplies, Inc.)
Nammo Lapua Oy
New England Custom Gun Service
New SKB Arms Co.
Norica, Avnda Otaola
Norinco
Norma Precision AB (See U.S.
  Importers-Dynamit)
Northwest Arms
Nygord Precision Products, Inc.
OK Weber, Inc.
Para-Ordnance Mfg., Inc.
Pardini Armi Srl
Perugini Visini & Co. S.r.l.
Peters Stahl GmbH
Pietta (See U.S. Importers-Navy
  Arms Co, Taylor's
Piotti (See U.S. Importer-Moore &
  Co., Wm. Larkin)
PMC/Eldorado Cartridge Corp.
Powell & Son (Gunmakers) Ltd.,
  William
Prairie Gun Works
Rizzini F.lli (See U.S. Importers-Wm.
  Larkin Moore & Co., N.E. Arms
  Corp.)
Rizzini SNC
Robinson Armament Co.
Rossi Firearms
Rottweil Compe
Rutten (See U.S. Importer-Labanu
  Inc.)
RWS (See U.S. Importer-Dynamit
  Nobel-RWS, Inc.)
S.A.R.L. G. Granger
S.I.A.C.E. (See U.S. Importer-IAR
  Inc.)
Sabatti SPA
Sako Ltd. (See U.S. Importer-
  Stoeger Industries)
San Marco (See U.S. Importers-Cape
  Outfitters-EMF Co., Inc.
Sarsilmaz Shotguns-Turkey (see
  B.C. Outdoors)
Sauer (See U.S. Importers-Paul Co.,
  The Sigarms Inc.)
Savage Arms (Canada), Inc.
SIG
Sigarms Inc.
SIG-Sauer (See U.S. Importer-
  Sigarms, Inc.)
SKB Shotguns
Small Arms Specialists
Societa Armi Bresciane Srl (See U.S.
  Importer-Cape Outfitters)
Sphinx Systems Ltd.
Springfield Armory
Springfield, Inc.
Starr Trading Co., Jedediah
Steyr Mannlicher GmbH & Co. KG
T.F.C. S.p.A
Tanfoglio Fratelli S.r.l.
Tanner (See U.S. Importer-Mandall
  Shooting Supplies, Inc.)
Taurus International Firearms (See
  U.S. Importer Taurus Firearms,
  Inc.)
Taurus S.A. Forjas
Techno Arms (See U.S. Importer-
  Auto-Ordnance Corp.)
Tikka (See U.S. Importer-Stoeger
  Industries)
TOZ (See U.S. Importer-Nygord
  Precision Products, Inc.)
Ugartechea S. A., Ignacio

Ultralux (See U.S. Importer-Keng's
  Firearms Specialty, Inc.)
Valtro USA, Inc.
Verney-Carron
Voere-KGH GmbH
Walther GmbH, Carl
Webley and Scott Ltd.
Weihrauch KG, Hermann
Westley Richards & Co. Ltd.
Yankee Gunsmith "Just Glocks"
Zabala Hermanos S.A.

GUNS, FOREIGN-
IMPORTER

A.W. Peterson Gun Shop, Inc., The
Accuracy International
AcuSport Corporation
Air Rifle Specialists
Auto-Ordnance Corp.
B.A.C.
B.C. Outdoors
Bell's Legendary Country Wear
Benelli USA Corp.
Big Bear Arms & Sporting Goods,
  Inc.
Bill Hanus Birdguns, LLC
Bridgeman Products
British Sporting Arms
Browning Arms Co.
Cape Outfitters
Century International Arms, Inc.
Champion Shooters' Supply
Champion's Choice, Inc.
Cimarron F.A. Co.
CVA
CZ USA
Dixie Gun Works
Dynamit Nobel-RWS, Inc.
E&L Mfg., Inc.
E.A.A. Corp.
Eagle Imports, Inc.
Ellett Bros.
EMF Co. Inc.
Euroarms of America, Inc.
Eversull Co., Inc.
Fiocchi of America, Inc.
Flintlocks, Etc.
Franzen International, Inc. (See U.S.
  Importer-Importer Co.)
G.U. (See U.S. Importer-New
  SKB Arms Co.)
Galaxy Imports Ltd., Inc.
Gamba, USA
Gamo USA, Inc.
Giacomo Sporting USA
Glock, Inc.
GSI, Inc.
Gun Shop, The
Guncraft Books (See Guncraft
  Sports, Inc.)
Guncraft Sports, Inc.
Gunsite Training Center
Hammerli USA
IAR Inc.
Imperial Magnum Corp.
Imperial Miniature Armory
Import Sports Inc.
Intrac Arms International
K. Eversull Co., Inc.
K.B.I. Inc.
Kemen America
Keng's Firearms Specialty, Inc./US
  Tactical Systems
Krieghoff International,Inc.
Labanu Inc.
Legacy Sports International
Lion Country Supply
London Guns Ltd.
Magnum Research, Inc.
Marlin Firearms Co.
Marx, Harry (See U.S. Importer for
  FERLIB)
MCS, Inc.
MEC-Gar U.S.A., Inc.
Mitchell Mfg. Corp.

Navy Arms Company
New England Arms Co.
Nu Line Guns
Nygord Precision Products, Inc.
OK Weber, Inc.
Orvis Co., The
P.S.M.G. Gun Co.
Para-Ordnance, Inc.
Paul Co., The
Perazone-Gunsmith, Brian
Perazzi U.S.A. Inc.
Powell Agency, William
Quality Arms, Inc.
Rocky Mountain Armoury
S.D. Meacham
Safari Arms/Schuetzen Pistol Works
Samco Global Arms, Inc.
Savage Arms, Inc.
Scott Fine Guns Inc., Thad
Sigarms Inc.
SKB Shotguns
Small Arms Specialists
Southern Ammunition Co., Inc.
Specialty Shooters Supply, Inc.
Springfield, Inc.
Stoeger Industries
Stone Enterprises Ltd.
Swarovski Optik North America Ltd.
Taurus Firearms, Inc.
Taylor's & Co., Inc.
Track of the Wolf, Inc.
Traditions Performance Firearms
Tristar Sporting Arms, Ltd.
Trooper Walsh
U.S. Importer-Wm. Larkin Moore
VAM Distribution Co. LLC
Vector Arms, Inc.
VTI Gun Parts
Westley Richards Agency USA (See
  U.S. Importer
Wingshooting Adventures
Yankee Gunsmith "Just Glocks"

GUNS, SURPLUS, PARTS
& AMMUNITION

A.W. Peterson Gun Shop, Inc., The
Ahlman Guns
Alpha 1 Drop Zone
Armscorp USA, Inc.
Arundel Arms & Ammunition, Inc., A.
B.A.C.
Bob's Gun Shop
Cambos Outdoorsman
Century International Arms, Inc.
Cole's Gun Works
Conetrol Scope Mounts
Delta Arms Ltd.
Ed's Gun House
Firearm Brokers
Fleming Firearms
Fulton Armory
Garcia National Gun Traders, Inc.
Gun City
Gun Hunter Books (See Gun Hunter
  Trading Co.)
Gun Hunter Trading Co.
Gun Room Press, The
Hank's Gun Shop
Hege Jagd-u. Sporthandels GmbH
Jackalope Gun Shop
Ken Starnes Gunmaker
LaRocca Gun Works
Lever Arms Service Ltd.
Log Cabin Sport Shop
Martin B. Retting Inc.
Martin's Gun Shop
Navy Arms Company
Northwest Arms
Numrich Gun Parts Corporation
Oil Rod and Gun Shop
Olathe Gun Shop
Paragon Sales & Services, Inc.
Pasadena Gun Center
Power Plus Enterprises, Inc.
Ravell Ltd.

Retting, Inc., Martin B.
Rutgers Book Center
Samco Global Arms, Inc.
Sarco, Inc.
Shootin' Shack
Silver Ridge Gun Shop (See Goodwin
  Guns)
Simmons Gun Repair, Inc.
Sportsmen's Exchange & Western
  Gun Traders, Inc.
Springfield Sporters, Inc.
T.F.C. S.p.A
Tarnhelm Supply Co., Inc.
Taylor's & Co., Inc.
Whitestone Lumber Corp.
Williams Shootin' Iron Service, The
  Lynx-Line

GUNS, U.S. MADE

3-Ten Corp.
A.A. Arms, Inc.
A.W. Peterson Gun Shop, Inc., The
Accu-Tek
Acra-Bond Laminates
Ad Hominem
Airrow
Allred Bullet Co.
American Derringer Corp.
AR-7 Industries, LLC
ArmaLite, Inc.
Armscorp USA, Inc.
Arundel Arms & Ammunition, Inc., A.
A-Square Co.
Austin & Halleck, Inc.
Autauga Arms, Inc.
Auto-Ordnance Corp.
Ballard Rifle & Cartridge Co., LLC
Barrett Firearms Manufacturer, Inc.
Bar-Sto Precision Machine
Benjamin/Sheridan Co., Crosman
Beretta S.P.A., Pietro
Beretta U.S.A. Corp.
Big Bear Arms & Sporting Goods,
  Inc.
Bill Hanus Birdguns, LLC
Bill Russ Trading Post
Bond Arms, Inc.
Borden Ridges Rimrock Stocks
Borden Rifles
Brockman's Custom Gunsmithing
Brown Products, Inc., Ed
Browning Arms Co.
Bryan & Assoc.
Bushmaster Firearms, Inc.
C. Sharps Arms Co. Inc./Montana
  Armory
Cabela's
Cache La Poudre Rifleworks
Calico Light Weapon Systems
Cambos Outdoorsman
Cape Outfitters
Casull Arms Corp.
CCL Security Products
Century Gun Dist. Inc.
Champlin Firearms, Inc.
Charter 2000
Cobra Enterprises, Inc.
Colt's Mfg. Co., Inc.
Competitor Corp., Inc.
Competitor Corp., Inc.
Conetrol Scope Mounts
Connecticut Shotgun Mfg. Co.
Connecticut Valley Classics (See
  CVC, BPI)
Cooper Arms
Crosman Airguns
Cumberland Arms
Cumberland Mountain Arms
CVA
Daisy Outdoor Products
Dakota Arms, Inc.
Dan Wesson Firearms
Dayton Traister
Detonics USA
Dixie Gun Works

Downsizer Corp.
DS Arms, Inc.
DunLyon R&D, Inc.
E&L Mfg., Inc.
E. Arthur Brown Co. Inc.
Eagle Arms, Inc. (See ArmaLite, Inc.)
Ed Brown Products, Inc.
Ellett Bros.
Emerging Technologies, Inc. (See
  Laseraim Technologies, Inc.)
Empire Rifles
Entreprise Arms, Inc.
Essex Arms
Excel Industries, Inc.
Firearm Brokers
Fletcher-Bidwell, LLC
FN Manufacturing
Freedom Arms, Inc.
Fulton Armory
Galena Industries AMT
Garcia National Gun Traders, Inc.
Gary Reeder Custom Guns
Genecco Gun Works
Gentry Custom LLC
George Hoenig, Inc.
Gibbs Rifle Co., Inc.
Gil Hebard Guns, Inc.
Gilbert Equipment Co., Inc.
Goergen's Gun Shop, Inc.
Granite Mountain Arms, Inc.
Grayback Wildcats
Gun Room Press, The
Gun Works, The
Guncrafter Industries
H&R 1871.LLC
Hammans, Charles E.
Hammerli USA
Harrington & Richardson (See H&R
  1871, Inc.)
Hart & Son, Inc.
Hatfield Gun
Hawken Shop, The (See Dayton
  Traister)
Heritage Firearms (See Heritage
  Mfg., Inc.)
Heritage Manufacturing, Inc.
Hesco-Meprolight
High Precision
High Standard Mfg. Co./F.I., Inc.
Hi-Point Firearms/MKS Supply
HJS Arms, Inc.
H-S Precision, Inc.
Hutton Rifle Ranch
IAR Inc.
Imperial Miniature Armory
Israel Arms Inc.
Ithaca Classic Doubles
Ithaca Gun Company LLC
Jim Norman Custom Gunstocks
John Rigby & Co.
John's Custom Leather
JP Enterprises, Inc.
K.B.I. Inc.
Kahr Arms
Kehr, Roger
Kelbly, Inc.
Kel-Tec CNC Industries, Inc.
Keystone Sporting Arms, Inc.
  (Crickett Rifles)
Kimber of America, Inc.
Knight Rifles
Knight's Manufacturing Co.
Kolar
L.A.R. Mfg., Inc.
LaFrance Specialties
Lakefield Arms Ltd. (See Savage
  Arms, Inc.)
Laseraim Technologies, Inc.
Les Baer Custom, Inc.
Lever Arms Service Ltd.
Ljutic Industries, Inc.
Lock's Philadelphia Gun Exchange
Lomont Precision Bullets
Lone Star Rifle Company
Mag-Na-Port International, Inc.
Magnum Research, Inc.
Mandall Shooting Supply Inc.

PRODUCT & SERVICE DIRECTORY

Marlin Firearms Co.
Marshall Fish Mfg. Gunsmith Sptg. Co.
Mathews Gun Shop & Gunsmithing, Inc.
Maverick Arms, Inc.
McCann Industries
Meacham Tool & Hardware Co., Inc.
Mid-America Recreation, Inc.
Miller Arms, Inc.
MKS Supply, Inc. (See Hi-Point Firearms)
MOA Corporation
Montana Armory, Inc.
MPI Stocks
Navy Arms Company
NCP Products, Inc.
New Ultra Light Arms, LLC
Noreen, Peter H.
North American Arms, Inc.
North Star West
Northwest Arms
Nowlin Mfg. Co.
Olympic Arms Inc.
Oregon Arms, Inc. (See Rogue Rifle Co., Inc.)
P&M Sales & Services, LLC
Parker & Sons Shooting Supply
Parker Gun Finishes
Phillips & Rogers, Inc.
Phoenix Arms
Precision Small Arms Inc.
ProWare, Inc.
Rapine Bullet Mould Mfg. Co.
Remington Arms Co., Inc.
Rifles, Inc.
Robinson Armament Co.
Rock River Arms
Rocky Mountain Arms, Inc.
Rogue Rifle Co., Inc.
Rogue River Rifleworks
Rohrbaugh
Romain's Custom Guns, Inc.
RPM
Ruger (See Sturm Ruger & Co., Inc.)
Safari Arms/Schuetzen Pistol Works
Savage Arms (Canada), Inc.
Schumakers Gun Shop
Searcy Enterprises
Sharps Arms Co., Inc., C.
Sigarms Inc.
Sklany's Machine Shop
Small Arms Specialists
Smith & Wesson
Sound Tech Silencers
Spencer's Rifle Barrels, Inc.
Springfield Armory
Springfield, Inc.
SSK Industries
STI International
Stoeger Industries
Strayer-Voigt, Inc.
Sturm Ruger & Co. Inc.
Sunny Hill Enterprises, Inc.
T&S Industries, Inc.
Taconic Firearms Ltd., Perry Lane
Tank's Rifle Shop
Tar-Hunt Custom Rifles, Inc.
Taurus Firearms, Inc.
Taylor's & Co., Inc.
Texas Armory (See Bond Arms, Inc.)
Thompson/Center Arms
Time Precision
Tristar Sporting Arms, Ltd.
U.S. Repeating Arms Co., Inc.
Uselton/Arms, Inc.
Vector Arms, Inc.
Visible Impact Targets
Volquartsen Custom Ltd.
Wallace, Terry
Weatherby, Inc.
Wescombe, Bill (See North Star West)
Wessinger Custom Guns & Engraving
Whildin & Sons Ltd., E.H.
Whitestone Lumber Corp.

Wichita Arms, Inc.
Wildey F. A., Inc.
Wilsom Combat
Winchester Consultants
Z-M Weapons

GUNSMITH SCHOOL

American Gunsmithing Institute
Colorado Gunsmithing Academy
Colorado School of Trades
Cylinder & Slide, Inc., William R. Laughridge
Gun Doc, Inc.
Lassen Community College, Gunsmithing Dept.
Laughridge, William R. (See Cylinder & Slide, Inc.)
Log Cabin Sport Shop
Modern Gun Repair School
Murray State College
North American Correspondence Schools, The Gun Pro
Nowlin Mfg. Co.
NRI Gunsmith School
Pennsylvania Gunsmith School
Piedmont Community College
Pine Technical College
Professional Gunsmiths of America
Smith & Wesson
Southeastern Community College
Spencer's Rifle Barrels, Inc.
Trinidad St. Jr. Col. Gunsmith Dept.
Wright's Gunstock Blanks
Yavapai College

GUNSMITH SUPPLIES, TOOLS & SERVICES

A.W. Peterson Gun Shop, Inc., The
Actions by "T" Teddy Jacobson
Alaskan Silversmith, The
Aldis Gunsmithing & Shooting Supply
Alley Supply Co.
Allred Bullet Co.
Alpec Team, Inc.
American Gunsmithing Institute
Dallard Rifle & Cartridge Co., LLC
Bar-Sto Precision Machine
Battenfeld Technologies, Inc.
Bauska Barrels
Bear Mountain Gun & Tool
Bengtson Arms Co., L.
Bill's Gun Repair
Blue Ridge Machinery & Tools, Inc.
Boyds' Gunstock Industries, Inc.
Briley Mfg. Inc.
Brockman's Custom Gunsmithing
Brown Products, Inc., Ed
Brownells, Inc.
Bryan & Assoc.
B-Square Company, Inc.
Buffer Technologies
Bushmaster Firearms, Inc.
C.S. Van Gorden & Son, Inc.
Cain's Outdoors, Inc.
Carbide Checkering Tools (See J&R Engineering)
Caywood, Shane J.
CBC-BRAZIL
Chapman Manufacturing Co.
Chicasaw Gun Works
Chip McCormick Corp.
Choate Machine & Tool Co., Inc.
Colonial Arms, Inc.
Colorado School of Trades
Colt's Mfg. Co., Inc.
Conetrol Scope Mounts
Corbin Mfg. & Supply, Inc.
Cousin Bob's Mountain Products
CRR, Inc./Marble's Inc.
Cumberland Arms
Cumberland Mountain Arms
Custom Checkering Service, Kathy Forster

Dan's Whetstone Co., Inc.
D'Arcy Echols & Co.
Dem-Bart Checkering Tools, Inc.
Dem-Bart Checkering Tools, Inc.
Dixie Gun Works
Dixie Gun Works
Dremel Mfg. Co.
Du-Lite Corp.
Entreprise Arms, Inc.
Erhardt, Dennis
Evolution Gun Works, Inc.
Faith Associates
FERLIB
Fisher, Jerry A.
Forgreens Tool & Mfg., Inc.
Forster, Kathy (See Custom Checkering)
Forster Products, Inc.
Gentry Custom LLC
Gilmore Sports Concepts, Inc.
Grace Metal Products
Gre-Tan Rifles
Gruning Precision, Inc.
Gun Works, The
Gunline Tools
Half Moon Rifle Shop
Hammond Custom Guns Ltd.
Hastings
Henriksen Tool Co., Inc.
High Performance International
High Precision
Holland's Gunsmithing
Import Sports Inc.
Ironsighter Co.
Israel Arms Inc.
Ivanoff, Thomas G. (See Tom's Gun Repair)
J&R Engineering
J&S Heat Treat
J. Dewey Mfg. Co., Inc.
Jantz Supply
Jenkins Recoil Pads
JGS Precision Tool Mfg., LLC
Jonathan Arthur Ciener, Inc.
Jones Custom Products, Neil A.
Kailua Custom Guns Inc.
Kasenit Co., Inc.
Kleinendorst, K. W.
Korzinek Riflesmith, J.
L. E. Jurras & Assoc.
LaBounty Precision Reboring, Inc
LaFrance Specialties
Laurel Mountain Forge
Lee Supplies, Mark
List Precision Engineering
Lock's Philadelphia Gun Exchange
London Guns Ltd.
Mahovsky's Metalife
Marble Arms (See CRR, Inc./Marble's Inc.)
Mark Lee Supplies
Marsh, Mike
Martin's Gun Shop
McFarland, Stan
Menck, Gunsmith Inc., T.W.
Metalife Industries (See Mahovsky's Metalife)
Micro Sight Co.
Midway Arms, Inc.
MMC
Mo's Competitor Supplies (See MCS, Inc.)
Mowrey's Guns & Gunsmithing
Neil A. Jones Custom Products
New England Custom Gun Service
NgraveR Co., The
Ole Frontier Gunsmith Shop
Olympic Arms Inc.
Parker & Sons Shooting Supply
Parker Gun Finishes
Parker Gun Finishes
Paulsen Gunstocks
PEM's Mfg. Co.
Perazone-Gunsmith, Brian
Peter Dyson & Son Ltd.
Power Custom, Inc.
Practical Tools, Inc.

Precision Specialties
R.A. Wells Custom Gunsmith
Ranch Products
Ransom International Corp.
Reardon Products
Rice, Keith (See White Rock Tool & Die)
Richards MicroFit Stocks, Inc.
Robar Co., Inc., The
Rocky Mountain Arms, Inc.
Romain's Custom Guns, Inc.
Royal Arms Gunstocks
Rusteprufe Laboratories
Score High Gunsmithing
Sharp Shooter Supply
Shooter's Choice Gun Care
Simmons Gun Repair, Inc.
Smith Abrasives, Inc.
Southern Bloomer Mfg. Co.
Spencer Reblue Service
Spencer's Rifle Barrels, Inc.
Spradlin's
Starr Trading Co., Jedediah
Starrett Co., L. S.
Stiles Custom Guns
Stoney Point Products, Inc.
Sullivan, David S. (See Westwind Rifles, Inc.)
Sunny Hill Enterprises, Inc.
T&S Industries, Inc.
T.W. Menck Gunsmith, Inc.
Tank's Rifle Shop
Tar-Hunt Custom Rifles, Inc.
Texas Platers Supply Co.
Theis, Terry
Tom's Gun Repair, Thomas G. Ivanoff
Track of the Wolf, Inc.
Trinidad St. Jr. Col. Gunsmith Dept.
Trulock Tool
Turnbull Restoration, Doug
United States Products Co.
Van Gorden & Son Inc., C. S.
Venco Industries, Inc. (See Shooter's Choice Gun Care)
W.C. Wolff Co.
Warne Manufacturing Co.
Washita Mountain Whetstone Co.
Weigand Combat Handguns, Inc.
Wessinger Custom Guns & Engraving
White Rock Tool & Die
Wilcox All-Pro Tools & Supply
Wild West Guns
Will-Burt Co.
Williams Gun Sight Co.
Williams Shootin' Iron Service, The Lynx-Line
Willow Bend
Windish, Jim
Wise Guns, Dale
Wright's Gunstock Blanks
Yavapai College
Ziegel Engineering

HANDGUN ACCESSORIES

"Su-Press-On", Inc.
A.A. Arms, Inc.
A.W. Peterson Gun Shop, Inc., The
Action Direct, Inc.
ADCO Sales, Inc.
Advantage Arms, Inc.
Aimtech Mount Systems
Ajax Custom Grips, Inc.
Alpha 1 Drop Zone
American Derringer Corp.
Arms Corporation of the Philippines
Astra Sport, S.A.
Autauga Arms, Inc.
Bagmaster Mfg., Inc.
Bar-Sto Precision Machine
Behlert Precision, Inc.
Berry's Mfg., Inc.

Blue and Gray Products Inc. (See Ox-Yoke Originals)
Bond Custom Firearms
Bowen Classic Arms Corp.
Bridgeman Products
Broken Gun Ranch
Brooks Tactical Systems-Agrip
Brown Products, Inc., Ed
Bushmaster Hunting & Fishing
Butler Creek Corp.
Cannon Safe, Inc.
Centaur Systems, Inc.
Central Specialties Ltd. (See Trigger Lock Division)
Charter 2000
Cheyenne Pioneer Products
Chicasaw Gun Works
Clark Custom Guns, Inc.
Classic Arms Company
Concealment Shop, Inc., The
Conetrol Scope Mounts
Crimson Trace Lasers
CRR, Inc./Marble's Inc.
Cylinder & Slide, Inc., William R. Laughridge
D&L Industries (See D.J. Marketing)
D.J. Marketing
Dade Screw Machine Products
Dan Wesson Firearms
Delhi Gun House
DeSantis Holster & Leather Goods, Inc.
Dixie Gun Works
Doskocil Mfg. Co., Inc.
E&L Mfg., Inc.
E. Arthur Brown Co. Inc
E.A.A. Corp.
Eagle Imports, Inc.
Ed Brown Products, Inc.
Essex Arms
European American Armory Corp. (See E.A.A. Corp.)
Evolution Gun Works, Inc.
Falcon Industries, Inc.
Feinwerkbau Westinger & Altenburger
Fisher Custom Firearms
Fleming Firearms
Freedom Arms, Inc.
G.G. & G.
Galati International
GALCO International Ltd.
Garcia National Gun Traders, Inc.
Garthwaite Pistolsmith, Inc., Jim
Gil Hebard Guns, Inc.
Gilmore Sports Concepts, Inc.
Glock, Inc.
Gould & Goodrich Leather, Inc.
Gun Works, The
Gun-Alert
Gun-Ho Sports Cases
H.K.S. Products
Hafner World Wide, Inc.
Hammerli USA
Heinie Specialty Products
Henigson & Associates, Steve
High Standard Mfg. Co./F.I., Inc.
Hill Speed Leather, Ernie
HIP-GRIP Barami Corp.
Hi-Point Firearms/MKS Supply
Hobson Precision Mfg. Co.
Hoppe's Div. Penguin Industries, Inc.
H-S Precision, Inc.
Hume, Don
Hunter Co., Inc.
Impact Case & Container, Inc.
Import Sports Inc.
Jarvis, Inc.
JB Custom
Jeffredo Gunsight
Jim Noble Co.
John's Custom Leather
Jonathan Arthur Ciener, Inc.
JP Enterprises, Inc.
Kalispel Case Line
KeeCo Impressions, Inc.
Keller Co., The

King's Gun Works
KK Air International (See Impact Case & Container Co., Inc.)
Kolpin Outdoors, Inc.
L&S Technologies Inc. (See Aimtech Mount Systems)
Lakewood Products LLC
LaserMax, Inc.
Les Baer Custom, Inc.
Lock's Philadelphia Gun Exchange
Lohman Mfg. Co., Inc.
Mag-Na-Port International, Inc.
Mag-Pack Corp.
Mahony, Philip Bruce
Mandall Shooting Supply Inc.
Marble Arms (See CRR, Inc./Marble's Inc.)
Markell, Inc.
MEC-Gar S.R.L.
Menck, Gunsmith Inc., T.W.
Middlebrooks Custom Shop
Millett Sights
Mobile Area Networks, Inc.
Mogul Co./Life Jacket
MTM Molded Products Co., Inc.
No-Sho Mfg. Co.
Numrich Gun Parts Corporation
Omega Sales
Outdoor Sports Headquarters, Inc.
Ox-Yoke Originals, Inc.
Pachmayr Div. Lyman Products
Pager Pal
Parker & Sons Shooting Supply
Pearce Grip, Inc.
Phoenix Arms
Practical Tools, Inc.
Precision Small Arms Inc.
Protector Mfg. Co., Inc., The
Ram-Line ATK
Ranch Products
Ransom International Corp.
RPM
Simmons Gun Repair, Inc.
Southern Bloomer Mfg. Co.
Springfield Armory
Springfield, Inc.
SSK Industries
Sturm Ruger & Co. Inc.
T.F.C. S.p.A.
Tactical Defense Institute
Tanfoglio Fratelli S.r.l.
Thompson/Center Arms
Trigger Lock Division / Central Specialties Ltd.
Trijicon, Inc.
Triple-K Mfg. Co., Inc.
Truglo, Inc.
United States Products Co.
Universal Sports
Volquartsen Custom Ltd.
W. Waller & Son, Inc.
W.C. Wolff Co.
Warne Manufacturing Co.
Weigand Combat Handguns, Inc.
Wessinger Custom Guns & Engraving
Whitestone Lumber Corp.
Wichita Arms, Inc.
Wild West Guns
Williams Gun Sight Co.
Wilsom Combat
Yankee Gunsmith "Just Glocks"
Ziegel Engineering

HANDGUN GRIPS

A.A. Arms, Inc.
A.W. Peterson Gun Shop, Inc., The
African Import Co.
Ahrends Grips
Ahrends, Kim
Ajax Custom Grips, Inc.
Altamont Co.
American Derringer Corp.
Arms Corporation of the Philippines
Art Jewel Enterprises Ltd.

Baelder, Harry
Big Bear Arms & Sporting Goods, Inc.
Bob's Gun Shop
Boone Trading Co., Inc.
Boone's Custom Ivory Grips, Inc.
Boyds' Gunstock Industries, Inc.
Brooks Tactical Systems-Agrip
Brown Products, Inc., Ed
Clark Custom Guns, Inc.
Claro Walnut Gunstock Co.
Cole-Grip
Colonial Repair
Crimson Trace Lasers
Custom Firearms (See Ahrends, Kim)
Cylinder & Slide, Inc., William R. Laughridge
Dixie Gun Works
Dolbare, Elizabeth
E.A.A. Corp.
Eagle Imports, Inc.
EMF Co. Inc.
Essex Arms
European American Armory Corp. (See E.A.A. Corp.)
Falcon Industries, Inc.
Feinwerkbau Westinger & Altenburger
Fibron Products, Inc.
Fisher Custom Firearms
Garthwaite Pistolsmith, Inc., Jim
Goodwin's Guns
Herrett's Stocks, Inc.
High Standard Mfg. Co./F.I., Inc.
HIP-GRIP Barami Corp.
Hogue Grips
H-S Precision, Inc.
Huebner, Corey O.
International Shooters Service
Israel Arms Inc.
John Masen Co. Inc.
KeeCo Impressions, Inc.
Korth Germany GmbH
Les Baer Custom, Inc.
Lett Custom Grips
Linebaugh Custom Sixguns
Lyman Products Corp.
Mandall Shooting Supply Inc.
Michaels of Oregon Co.
Millett Sights
Mobile Area Networks, Inc.
N.C. Ordnance Co.
Newell, Robert H.
Northern Precision
Pachmayr Div. Lyman Products
Pardini Armi Srl
Parker & Sons Shooting Supply
Pearce Grip, Inc.
Precision Small Arms Inc.
Radical Concepts
Robinson, Don
Rosenberg & Son, Jack A.
Roy's Custom Grips
Spegel, Craig
Stoeger Industries
Sturm Ruger & Co. Inc.
Sunny Hill Enterprises, Inc.
Tactical Defense Institute
Taurus Firearms, Inc.
Tirelli
Tom Forrest, Inc.
Triple-K Mfg. Co., Inc.
Uncle Mike's (See Michaels of Oregon, Co.)
Volquartsen Custom Ltd.
Western Mfg. Co.
Whitestone Lumber Corp.
Wright's Gunstock Blanks

HEARING PROTECTORS

A.W. Peterson Gun Shop, Inc., The
Aero Peltor
Ajax Custom Grips, Inc.
Browning Arms Co.

Creedmoor Sports, Inc.
David Clark Co., Inc.
Dillon Precision Products, Inc.
Dixie Gun Works
E-A-R, Inc.
Electronic Shooters Protection, Inc.
Gentex Corp.
Gun Room Press, The
Gunsmithing, Inc.
Hoppe's Div. Penguin Industries, Inc.
Kesselring Gun Shop
Mandall Shooting Supply Inc.
Mobile Area Networks, Inc.
Parker & Sons Shooting Supply
Paterson Gunsmithing
Peltor, Inc. (See Aero Peltor)
R.E.T. Enterprises
Ridgeline, Inc.
Rucker Dist. Inc.
Silencio/Safety Direct
Tactical Defense Institute
Triple-K Mfg. Co., Inc.
Watson Bullets
Whitestone Lumber Corp.

HOLSTERS & LEATHER GOODS

A.A. Arms, Inc.
A.W. Peterson Gun Shop, Inc., The
Action Direct, Inc.
Action Products, Inc.
Aker International, Inc.
AKJ Concealco
Alessi Holsters, Inc.
Arratoonian, Andy (See Horseshoe Leather Products)
Autauga Arms, Inc.
Bagmaster Mfg., Inc.
Baker's Leather Goods, Roy
Bandcor Industries, Div. of Man-Sew Corp.
Bang-Bang Boutique (See Holster Shop, The)
Beretta S.P.A., Pietro
Bianchi International, Inc.
Bond Arms, Inc.
Brooks Tactical Systems-Agrip
Browning Arms Co.
Bull-X, Inc.
Cape Outfitters
Cathey Enterprises, Inc.
Chace Leather Products
Churchill Glove Co., James
Cimarron F.A. Co.
Classic Old West Styles
Clements' Custom Leathercraft, Chas
Cobra Sport S.R.I.
Collector's Armoury, Ltd.
Colonial Repair
Counter Assault
Delhi Gun House
DeSantis Holster & Leather Goods, Inc.
Dillon Precision Products, Inc.
Dixie Gun Works
Eagle Imports, Inc.
Ekol Leather Care
El Paso Saddlery Co.
Ellett Bros.
EMF Co. Inc.
Faust Inc., T. G.
Freedom Arms, Inc.
Gage Manufacturing
GALCO International Ltd.
Garcia National Gun Traders, Inc.
Gil Hebard Guns, Inc.
Gilmore Sports Concepts, Inc.
GML Products, Inc.
Gould & Goodrich Leather, Inc.
Gun Leather Limited
Gun Works, The
Hafner World Wide, Inc.
HandCrafts Unltd. (See Clements' Custom Leathercraft)

Hank's Gun Shop
Heinie Specialty Products
Henigson & Associates, Steve
Hill Speed Leather, Ernie
HIP-GRIP Barami Corp.
Hobson Precision Mfg. Co.
Hogue Grips
Horseshoe Leather Products
Hume, Don
Hunter Co., Inc.
Import Sports Inc.
Jim Noble Co.
John's Custom Leather
Keller Co., The
Kirkpatrick Leather Co.
Kolpin Outdoors, Inc.
Korth Germany GmbH
Kramer Handgun Leather
L.A.R. Mfg., Inc.
Lawrence Leather Co.
Lock's Philadelphia Gun Exchange
Lone Star Gunleather
Mandall Shooting Supply Inc.
Markell, Inc.
Marksman Products
Michaels of Oregon Co.
Minute Man High Tech Industries
Navy Arms Company
No-Sho Mfg. Co.
Null Holsters Ltd. K.L.
October Country Muzzleloading
Oklahoma Leather Products, Inc.
Old West Reproductions, Inc. R.M. Bachman
Outdoor Connection, Inc., The
Pager Pal
Parker & Sons Shooting Supply
Pathfinder Sports Leather
Protektor Model
PWL Gunleather
Ramon B. Gonzalez Guns
Renegade
Ringler Custom Leather Co.
Rogue Rifle Co., Inc.
S&S Firearms
Safariland Ltd., Inc.
Scharch Mfg., Inc.-Top Brass
Schulz Industries
Second Chance Body Armor
Silhouette Leathers
Smith Saddlery, Jesse W.
Sparks, Milt
Stalker, Inc.
Starr Trading Co., Jedediah
Strong Holster Co.
Stuart, V. Pat
Tabler Marketing
Tactical Defense Institute
Ted Blocker Holsters, Inc.
Tex Shoemaker & Sons, Inc.
Thad Rybka Custom Leather Equipment
Torel, Inc./Tandy Brands Outdoors/AA & E
Triple-K Mfg. Co., Inc.
Tristar Sporting Arms, Ltd.
Uncle Mike's (See Michaels of Oregon, Co.)
Venus Industries
W. Waller & Son, Inc.
Walt's Custom Leather, Walt Whinnery
Watson Bullets
Westley Richards & Co. Ltd.
Whinnery, Walt (See Walt's Custom Leather)
Wild Bill's Originals
Wilsom Combat

HUNTING & CAMP GEAR, CLOTHING, ETC.

A.W. Peterson Gun Shop, Inc., The
Action Direct, Inc.
Action Products, Inc.
Adventure 16, Inc.

All Rite Products, Inc.
Alpha 1 Drop Zone
Armor (See Buck Stop Lure Co., Inc.)
Atlanta Cutlery Corp.
Atsko/Sno-Seal, Inc.
B.B. Walker Co.
Bagmaster Mfg., Inc.
Barbour, Inc.
Bauer, Eddie
Bear Archery
Beaver Park Product, Inc.
Beretta S.P.A., Pietro
Better Concepts Co.
Bill Russ Trading Post
Bob Allen Sportswear
Boonie Packer Products
Boss Manufacturing Co.
Browning Arms Co.
Buck Stop Lure Co., Inc.
Bushmaster Hunting & Fishing
Cambos Outdoorsman
Cambos Outdoorsman
Camp-Cap Products
Carhartt, Inc.
Churchill Glove Co., James
Clarkfield Enterprises, Inc.
Classic Old West Styles
Clements' Custom Leathercraft, Chas
Coghlan's Ltd.
Cold Steel Inc.
Coleman Co., Inc.
Coulston Products, Inc.
Counter Assault
Dakota Corp.
Danner Shoe Mfg. Co.
Deepeeka Exports Pvt. Ltd.
Dr. O's Products Ltd.
Duofold, Inc.
Dynalite Products, Inc.
E-A-R, Inc.
Ekol Leather Care
Flambeau, Inc.
Forrest Tool Co.
Fox River Mills, Inc.
Frontier
G&H Decoys, Inc.
Gerber Legendary Blades
Glacier Glove
Grand Slam Hunting Products
HandCrafts Unltd. (See Clements' Custom Leathercraft)
High North Products, Inc.
Hinman Outfitters, Bob
Hodgman, Inc.
Houtz & Barwick
Hunter's Specialties Inc.
James Churchill Glove Co.
John's Custom Leather
K&M Industries, Inc.
Kamik Outdoor Footwear
Kolpin Outdoors, Inc.
L.L. Bean, Inc.
LaCrosse Footwear, Inc.
Leapers, Inc.
MAG Instrument, Inc.
Mag-Na-Port International, Inc.
McCann Industries
Murphy, R.R. Co., Inc.
Original Deer Formula Co., The
Orvis Co., The
Palsa Outdoor Products
Partridge Sales Ltd., John
Pointing Dog Journal, Village Press Publications
Powell & Son (Gunmakers) Ltd., William
Pro-Mark Div. of Wells Lamont
Ringler Custom Leather Co.
Rocky Shoes & Boots
Scansport, Inc.
Sceery Game Calls
Schaefer Shooting Sports
Servus Footwear Co.
Simmons Outdoor Corp.
Sno-Seal, Inc. (See Atsko/Sno-Seal, Inc.)

PRODUCT & SERVICE DIRECTORY

Swanndri New Zealand
TEN-X Products Group
Tink's Safariland Hunting Corp.
Torel, Inc./Tandy Brands
    Outdoors/AA & E
Triple-K Mfg. Co., Inc.
Tru-Nord Compass
United Cutlery Corp.
Venus Industries
Walls Industries, Inc.
Wideview Scope Mount Corp.
Wilderness Sound Products Ltd.
Winchester Sutler, Inc., The
Wolverine Footwear Group
Woolrich, Inc.
Wyoming Knife Corp.
Yellowstone Wilderness Supply

KNIVES & KNIFEMAKER'S SUPPLIES

A.G. Russell Knives, Inc.
A.W. Peterson Gun Shop, Inc., The
Action Direct, Inc.
Adventure 16, Inc.
African Import Co.
Aitor-Cuchilleria Del Norte S.A.
American Target Knives
Art Jewel Enterprises Ltd.
Atlanta Cutlery Corp.
B&D Trading Co., Inc.
Barteaux Machete
Benchmark Knives (See Gerber
    Legendary Blades)
Beretta S.P.A., Pietro
Beretta U.S.A. Corp.
Big Bear Arms & Sporting Goods,
    Inc.
Bill Russ Trading Post
Boker USA, Inc.
Boone Trading Co., Inc.
Boone's Custom Ivory Grips, Inc.
Bowen Knife Co., Inc.
Brooks Tactical Systems-Agrip
Browning Arms Co.
Buck Knives, Inc.
Buster's Custom Knives
Cain's Outdoors, Inc.
Camillus Cutlery Co.
Campbell, Dick
Case & Sons Cutlery Co., W R
Chicago Cutlery Co.
Claro Walnut Gunstock Co.
Clements' Custom Leathercraft,
    Chas
Cold Steel Inc.
Coleman Co., Inc.
Collector's Armoury, Ltd.
Compass Industries, Inc.
Creative Craftsman, Inc., The
Crosman Blades (See Coleman Co.,
    Inc.)
CRR, Inc./Marble's Inc.
Cutco Cutlery
damascususa@inteliport.com
Dan's Whetstone Co., Inc.
Deepeeka Exports Pvt. Ltd.
Delhi Gun House
DeSantis Holster & Leather Goods,
    Inc.
Diamond Machining Technology Inc.
    (See DMT)
Dixie Gun Works
Dolbare, Elizabeth
EdgeCraft Corp., S. Weiner
Empire Cutlery Corp.
Eze-Lap Diamond Prods.
Flitz International Ltd.
Forrest Tool Co.
Forthofer's Gunsmithing &
    Knifemaking
Fortune Products, Inc.
Frank Knives
Frost Cutlery Co.
Galati International

George Ibberson (Sheffield) Ltd.
Gerber Legendary Blades
Glock, Inc.
Golden Age Arms Co.
Gun Room, The
Gun Works, The
H&B Forge Co.
Hafner World Wide, Inc.
Hammans, Charles E.
HandCrafts Unltd. (See Clements'
    Custom Leathercraft)
Harris Publications
High North Products, Inc.
Hoppe's Div. Penguin Industries, Inc.
Hunter Co., Inc.
Imperial Schrade Corp.
J.A. Blades, Inc. (See Christopher
    Firearms Co.)
J.A. Henckels Zwillingswerk Inc.
Jackalope Gun Shop
Jantz Supply
Jenco Sales, Inc.
Jim Blair Engraving
Johnson Wood Products
KA-BAR Knives
Kasenit Co., Inc.
Kershaw Knives
Knifeware, Inc.
Koval Knives
Lamson & Goodnow Mfg. Co.
Lansky Sharpeners
Leapers, Inc.
Leatherman Tool Group, Inc.
Lethal Force Institute (See Police
    Bookshelf)
Linder Solingen Knives
Mandall Shooting Supply Inc.
Marble Arms (See CRR,
    Inc./Marble's Inc.)
Marshall Fish Mfg. Gunsmith Sptg.
    Co
Matthews Cutlery
McCann Industries
Normark Corp.
October Country Muzzleloading
Outdoor Edge Cutlery Corp.
Plaza Cutlery, Inc.
Police Bookshelf
Queen Cutlery Co.
R&C Knives & Such
R. Murphy Co., Inc.
Randall-Made Knives
Ringler Custom Leather Co.
Robert Valade Engraving
Scansport, Inc.
Schiffman, Mike
Sheffield Knifemakers Supply, Inc.
Smith Saddlery, Jesse W.
Springfield Armory
Spyderco, Inc
T.F.C. S.p.A.
Theis, Terry
Traditions Performance Firearms
Traditions Performance Firearms
Tru-Balance Knife Co.
Tru-Nord Compass
United Cutlery Corp.
Utica Cutlery Co.
Venus Industries
W.R. Case & Sons Cutlery Co.
Washita Mountain Whetstone Co.
Wells Creek Knife & Gun Works
Wenger North America/Precise Int'l.
Western Cutlery (See Camillus
    Cutlery Co.)
Whinnery, Walt (See Walt's Custom
    Leather)
Wideview Scope Mount Corp.
Wyoming Knife Corp.

LABELS, BOXES & CARTRIDGE HOLDERS

Ballistic Products, Inc.
Berry's Mfg., Inc.

Cabinet Mtn. Outfitters Scents &
    Lures
Cheyenne Pioneer Products
Del Rey Products
DeSantis Holster & Leather Goods,
    Inc.
Flambeau, Inc.
Hafner World Wide, Inc.
J&J Products, Inc.
Kolpin Outdoors, Inc.
Liberty Shooting Supplies
Midway Arms, Inc.
MTM Molded Products Co., Inc.
Outdoor Connection, Inc., The
Pendleton Royal, c/o Swingler
    Buckland Ltd.
Ringler Custom Leather Co.
Walt's Custom Leather, Walt
    Whinnery
Ziegel Engineering

LEAD WIRES & WIRE CUTTERS

Ames Metal Products
Big Bore Express
Bullet Swaging Supply, Inc.
D.L. Unmussig Bullets
Liberty Metals
Lightning Performance Innovations,
    Inc.
Montana Precision Swaging
Northern Precision
Sport Flite Manufacturing Co.
Star Ammunition, Inc.

LOAD TESTING & PRODUCT TESTING

Ballistic Research
Bridgeman Products
Briese Bullet Co., Inc.
Buckskin Bullet Co.
Bull Mountain Rifle Co.
CFVentures
Claybuster Wads & Harvester Bullets
Clearview Products
D&H Precision Tooling
Dead Eye's Sport Center
Defense Training International, Inc.
Duane's Gun Repair (See DGR
    Custom Rifles)
Gruning Precision, Inc.
H.P. White Laboratory, Inc.
Hank's Gun Shop
Henigson & Associates, Steve
Hutton Rifle Ranch
J&J Sales
Jackalope Gun Shop
Jensen Bullets
Jonathan Arthur Ciener, Inc.
L. E. Jurras & Assoc.
Liberty Shooting Supplies
Linebaugh Custom Sixguns
Lomont Precision Bullets
MAST Technology, Inc.
McMurdo, Lynn
Middlebrooks Custom Shop
Modern Gun Repair School
Multiplex International
Northwest Arms
Oil Rod and Gun Shop
Plum City Ballistic Range
R.A. Wells Custom Gunsmith
Rupert's Gun Shop
SOS Products Co. (See Buck Stix-
    SOS Products Co.)
Spencer's Rifle Barrels, Inc.
Tar-Hunt Custom Rifles, Inc.
Trinidad St. Jr. Col. Gunsmith Dept.
Vulpes Ventures, Inc., Fox Cartridge
    Division
W. Square Enterprises
X-Spand Target Systems

LOADING BLOCKS, METALLIC & SHOTSHELL

A.W. Peterson Gun Shop, Inc., The
Battenfeld Technologies, Inc.
Buffalo Arms Co.
Huntington Die Specialties
Jericho Tool & Die Co., Inc.
Sinclair International, Inc.

LUBRISIZERS, DIES & ACCESSORIES

A.W. Peterson Gun Shop, Inc., The
Ballisti-Cast, Inc.
Buffalo Arms Co.
Cast Performance Bullet Company
Cooper-Woodward Perfect Lube
Corbin Mfg. & Supply, Inc.
GAR
Hart & Son, Inc.
Javelina Lube Products
Lee Precision, Inc.
Lithi Bee Bullet Lube
Lyman Products Corp.
Magma Engineering Co.
PWM Sales Ltd.
RCBS Operations/ATK
S&S Firearms
SPG LLC
Thompson Bullet Lube Co.
United States Products Co.
WTA Manufacturing

MOULDS & MOULD ACCESSORIES

A.W. Peterson Gun Shop, Inc., The
Ad Hominem
American Products, Inc.
Ballisti-Cast, Inc.
Buffalo Arms Co.
Bullet Swaging Supply, Inc.
Cast Performance Bullet Company
Corbin Mfg. & Supply, Inc.
Davide Pedersoli and Co.
GAR
Gun Works, The
Huntington Die Specialties
Lee Precision, Inc.
Lyman Products Corp.
Magma Engineering Co.
Mobile Area Networks, Inc.
Old West Bullet Moulds
Pacific Rifle Co.
Penn Bullets
Peter Dyson & Son Ltd.
Rapine Bullet Mould Mfg. Co.
RCBS Operations/ATK
S&S Firearms

MUZZLE-LOADING GUNS, BARRELS & EQUIPMENT

A.W. Peterson Gun Shop, Inc., The
Accuracy Unlimited
Ackerman & Co.
Adkins, Luther
Allen Mfg.
Armi San Paolo
Armoury, Inc., The
Austin & Halleck, Inc.
Bauska Barrels
Bentley, John
Big Bore Express
Birdsong & Assoc., W. E.
Black Powder Products
Blount/Outers ATK
Blue and Gray Products Inc. (See Ox-
    Yoke Originals)
Bridgers Best
Buckskin Bullet Co.

Bullberry Barrel Works, Ltd.
Butler Creek Corp.
Cabela's
Cache La Poudre Rifleworks
Cain's Outdoors, Inc.
California Sights (See Fautheree,
    Andy)
Cash Mfg. Co., Inc.
Caywood Gunmakers
CBC-BRAZIL
Chambers Flintlocks Ltd., Jim
Chicasaw Gun Works
Cimarron F.A. Co.
Claybuster Wads & Harvester Bullets
Cogar's Gunsmithing
Colonial Repair
Colt Blackpowder Arms Co.
Conetrol Scope Mounts
Cousin Bob's Mountain Products
Cumberland Arms
Cumberland Mountain Arms
Curly Maple Stock Blanks (See Tiger-
    Hunt)
CVA
Dangler, Homer L.
Davide Pedersoli and Co
Dayton Traister
deHaas Barrels
Delhi Gun House
Dixie Gun Works
Dixie Gun Works
Dixon Muzzleloading Shop, Inc.
Dolbare, Elizabeth
Ellett Bros.
EMF Co. Inc.
Euroarms of America, Inc.
Flintlocks, Etc.
Fort Hill Gunstocks
Fowler, Bob (See Black Powder
    Products)
Frontier
Getz Barrel Company
Goergen's Gun Shop, Inc.
Golden Age Arms Co.
Gonic Arms North American Arms,
    Inc.
Green Mountain Rifle Barrel Co., Inc.
Gun Works, The
H&R 1871.LLC
Hastings
Hawken Shop, The
Hawken Shop, The (See Dayton
    Traister)
Hege Jagd-u. Sporthandels GmbH
Hodgdon Powder Co.
Hoppe's Div. Penguin Industries, Inc.
Hornady Mfg. Co.
House of Muskets, Inc., The
Hunkeler, A. (See Buckskin Machine
    Works)
IAR Inc.
Impact Case & Container, Inc.
Ironsighter Co.
J. Dewey Mfg. Co., Inc.
Jamison's Forge Works
Jones Co., Dale
K&M Industries, Inc.
Kalispel Case Line
Kennedy Firearms
Knight Rifles
Knight Rifles (See Modern
    Muzzleloading, Inc.)
Kolar
L&R Lock Co.
L&S Technologies Inc. (See Aimtech
    Mount Systems)
Lakewood Products LLC
Lodgewood Mfg.
Log Cabin Sport Shop
Lothar Walther Precision Tool Inc.
Lyman Products Corp.
Markesbery Muzzle Loaders, Inc.
Mathews Gun Shop & Gunsmithing,
    Inc.
McCann, Tom
Michaels of Oregon Co.
Millennium Designed Muzzleloaders

PRODUCT & SERVICE DIRECTORY

Modern Muzzleloading, Inc.
Mowrey Gun Works
Navy Arms Company
Newman Gunshop
North Star West
October Country Muzzleloading
Oklahoma Leather Products, Inc.
Olson, Myron
Orion Rifle Barrel Co.
Ox-Yoke Originals, Inc.
Pacific Rifle Co.
Parker & Sons Shooting Supply
Parker Gun Finishes
Pecatonica River Longrifle
Peter Dyson & Son Ltd.
Pioneer Arms Co.
Prairie River Arms
Rossi Firearms
Rusty Duck Premium Gun Care
  Products
S&S Firearms
Selsi Co., Inc.
Simmons Gun Repair, Inc.
Sklany's Machine Shop
Smokey Valley Rifles
South Bend Replicas, Inc.
Southern Bloomer Mfg. Co.
Splitfire Sporting Goods, L.L.C.
Starr Trading Co., Jedediah
Stone Mountain Arms
Sturm Ruger & Co. Inc.
Taylor's & Co., Inc.
Tennessee Valley Mfg.
Thompson Bullet Lube Co.
Thompson/Center Arms
Track of the Wolf, Inc.
Traditions Performance Firearms
Truglo, Inc.
Uncle Mike's (See Michaels of
  Oregon, Co.)
Universal Sports
Upper Missouri Trading Co.
Venco Industries, Inc. (See
  Shooter's Choice Gun Care)
Village Restorations & Consulting,
  Inc.
Virgin Valley Custom Guns
Voere-KGH GmbH
W.E. Birdsong & Assoc.
Warne Manufacturing Co.
Warren Muzzleloading Co., Inc.
Wescombe, Bill (See North Star
  West)
White Rifles, Inc.
William E. Phillips Firearms
Woodworker's Supply
Wright's Gunstock Blanks
Young Country Arms
Ziegel Engineering

PISTOLSMITH

A.W. Peterson Gun Shop, Inc.
A.W. Peterson Gun Shop, Inc., The
Acadian Ballistic Specialties
Accuracy Unlimited
Actions by "T" Teddy Jacobson
Adair Custom Shop, Bill
Ahrends, Kim
Aldis Gunsmithing & Shooting
  Supply
Alpha Precision, Inc.
Alpine Indoor Shooting Range
Armament Gunsmithing Co., Inc.
Arundel Arms & Ammunition, Inc., A.
Bain & Davis, Inc.
Bar-Sto Precision Machine
Behlert Precision, Inc.
Bengtson Arms Co., L.
Bill Adair Custom Shop
Billings Gunsmiths
Bob Rogers Gunsmithing
Bowen Classic Arms Corp.
Broken Gun Ranch
Caraville Manufacturing

Chicasaw Gun Works
Chip McCormick Corp.
Clark Custom Guns, Inc.
Colonial Repair
Colorado School of Trades
Colt's Mfg. Co., Inc.
Corkys Gun Clinic
Custom Firearms (See Ahrends,
  Kim)
Cylinder & Slide, Inc., William R.
  Laughridge
D&D Gunsmiths, Ltd.
D&L Sports
David R. Chicoine
Dayton Traister
Dilliott Gunsmithing, Inc.
Ellicott Arms, Inc. / Woods
  Pistolsmithing
Evolution Gun Works, Inc.
Ferris Firearms
Firearm Brokers
Fisher Custom Firearms
Forkin Custom Classics
G.G. & G.
Garthwaite Pistolsmith, Inc., Jim
Gary Reeder Custom Guns
Genecco Gun Works
Gentry Custom LLC
Greider Precision
Gun Doc, Inc.
Gun Works, The
Guncraft Sports, Inc.
Guncraft Sports, Inc.
Gunsite Training Center
Hamilton, Alex B. (See Ten-Ring
  Precision, Inc.)
Hammerli Service-Precision Mac
Hammond Custom Guns Ltd.
Hank's Gun Shop
Hanson's Gun Center, Dick
Hawken Shop, The (See Dayton
  Traister)
Heinie Specialty Products
High Bridge Arms, Inc.
High Standard Mfg. Co./F.I., Inc.
Highline Machine Co.
Hoag, James W.
Irwin, Campbell H.
Ivanoff, Thomas G. (See Tom's Gun
  Repair)
J&S Heat Treat
Jarvis, Inc.
Jeffredo Gunsight
Jensen's Custom Ammunition
Jungkind, Reeves C.
Kaswer Custom, Inc.
Ken Starnes Gunmaker
Kilham & Co.
King's Gun Works
La Clinique du .45
LaFrance Specialties
LaRocca Gun Works
Lathrop's, Inc.
Lawson, John G. (See Sight Shop,
  The)
Leckie Professional Gunsmithing
Les Baer Custom, Inc.
Linebaugh Custom Sixguns
List Precision Engineering
Long, George F.
Mag-Na-Port International, Inc.
Mahony, Philip Bruce
Mahovsky's Metalife
Mandall Shooting Supply Inc.
Marvel, Alan
Mathews Gun Shop & Gunsmithing,
  Inc.
MCS, Inc.
Middlebrooks Custom Shop
Miller Custom
Mitchell's Accuracy Shop
MJK Gunsmithing, Inc.
Modern Gun Repair School
Mo's Competitor Supplies (See MCS,
  Inc.)
Mowrey's Guns & Gunsmithing
Mullis Guncraft

NCP Products, Inc.
Novak's, Inc.
Nowlin Mfg. Co.
Olathe Gun Shop
Paris, Frank J.
Pasadena Gun Center
Peacemaker Specialists
PEM's Mfg. Co.
Performance Specialists
Peterson Gun Shop, Inc., A.W.
Piquette's Custom Engraving
Power Custom, Inc.
Precision Specialties
Ramon B. Gonzalez Guns
Randco UK
Ries, Chuck
Rim Pac Sports, Inc.
Robar Co., Inc., The
Rocky Mountain Arms, Inc.
RPM
Ruger's Custom Guns
Score High Gunsmithing
Shooters Supply
Shootin' Shack
Sight Shop, The
Singletary, Kent
Springfield, Inc.
SSK Industries
Swenson's 45 Shop, A. D.
Swift River Gunworks
Ten-Ring Precision, Inc.
Terry K. Kopp Professional
  Gunsmithing
Time Precision
Tom's Gun Repair, Thomas G.
  Ivanoff
Turnbull Restoration, Doug
Vic's Gun Refinishing
Volquartsen Custom Ltd.
Walker Arms Co., Inc.
Walters Industries
Wardell Precision Handguns Ltd.
Wessinger Custom Guns &
  Engraving
White Barn Wor
Wichita Arms, Inc.
Wild West Guns
Williams Gun Sight Co.
Williamson Precision Gunsmithing
Wilsom Combat
Wright's Gunstock Blanks

POWDER MEASURES, SCALES, FUNNELS & ACCESSORIES

4-D Custom Die Co.
A.W. Peterson Gun Shop, Inc., The
Battenfeld Technologies, Inc.
Buffalo Arms Co.
Cain's Outdoors, Inc.
Davide Pedersoli and Co.
Dillon Precision Products, Inc.
Fremont Tool Works
Frontier
GAR
High Precision
Hoehn Sales, Inc.
Jones Custom Products, Neil A.
Modern Muzzleloading, Inc.
Neil A. Jones Custom Products
Pacific Rifle Co.
Precision Reloading, Inc.
Ramon B. Gonzalez Guns
RCBS Operations/ATK
RCBS/ATK
Redding Reloading Equipment
Saunders Gun & Machine Shop
Schumakers Gun Shop
Spencer's Rifle Barrels, Inc.
Vega Tool Co.
VibraShine, Inc.
VTI Gun Parts

PRESS ACCESSORIES, METALLIC

A.W. Peterson Gun Shop, Inc., The
Buffalo Arms Co.
Corbin Mfg. & Supply, Inc.
Hollywood Engineering
Huntington Die Specialties
MA Systems, Inc.
R.E.I.
Redding Reloading Equipment
Royal Arms Gunstocks
Thompson Tool Mount
Vega Tool Co.

PRESS ACCESSORIES, SHOTSHELL

A.W. Peterson Gun Shop, Inc., The
Hollywood Engineering
Lee Precision, Inc.
MEC, Inc.
Precision Reloading, Inc.
R.E.I.

PRESSES, ARBOR

A.W. Peterson Gun Shop, Inc., The
Blue Ridge Machinery & Tools, Inc.
Hoehn Sales, Inc.
K&M Services
RCBS Operations/ATK
Spencer's Rifle Barrels, Inc.

PRESSES, METALLIC

4-D Custom Die Co.
A.W. Peterson Gun Shop, Inc., The
Battenfeld Technologies, Inc.
Dillon Precision Products, Inc.
Fremont Tool Works
Hornady Mfg. Co.
Huntington Die Specialties
Lee Precision, Inc.
Meacham Tool & Hardware Co., Inc.
Midway Arms, Inc.
R.E.I.
Ramon B. Gonzalez Guns
RCBS Operations/ATK
RCBS/ATK
Spencer's Rifle Barrels, Inc.

PRESSES, SHOTSHELL

A.W. Peterson Gun Shop, Inc., The
Ballistic Products, Inc.
Dillon Precision Products, Inc.
Hornady Mfg. Co.
MEC, Inc.
Precision Reloading, Inc.
Spolar Power Load, Inc.

PRESSES, SWAGE

A.W. Peterson Gun Shop, Inc., The
Ammo Load Worldwide, Inc.
Bullet Swaging Supply, Inc.
Howell Machine, Inc.

PRIMING TOOLS & ACCESSORIES

A.W. Peterson Gun Shop, Inc., The
Bald Eagle Precision Machine Co.
GAR
Hart & Son, Inc.
Huntington Die Specialties
K&M Services
RCBS Operations/ATK
Simmons, Jerry
Sinclair International, Inc.

REBORING & RERIFLING

Ahlman Guns
Barrel & Gunworks
Bauska Barrels
BlackStar AccuMax Barrels
BlackStar Barrel Accurizing (See
  BlackStar AccuMax)
Buffalo Arms Co.
Champlin Firearms, Inc.
Ed's Gun House
Fred F. Wells/Wells Sport Store
Gun Works, The
Ivanoff, Thomas G. (See Tom's Gun
  Repair)
Jackalope Gun Shop
Jonathan Arthur Ciener, Inc.
LaBounty Precision Reboring, Inc
NCP Products, Inc.
Pence Precision Barrels
Redman's Rifling & Reboring
Rice, Keith (See White Rock Tool &
  Die)
Ridgetop Sporting Goods
Savage Arms, Inc.
Shaw, Inc., E. R. (See Small Arms
  Mfg. Co.)
Siegrist Gun Shop
Simmons Gun Repair, Inc.
Stratco, Inc.
Terry K. Kopp Professional
  Gunsmithing
Time Precision
Tom's Gun Repair, Thomas G.
  Ivanoff
Turnbull Restoration, Doug
Van Patten, J. W.
White Rock Tool & Die

RELOADING TOOLS AND ACCESSORIES

4-D Custom Die Co.
Advance Car Mover Co., Rowell Div.
American Products, Inc.
Ammo Load, Inc.
Armfield Custom Bullets
Armite Laboratories
Arms Corporation of the Philippines
Atsko/Sno-Seal, Inc.
Bald Eagle Precision Machine Co.
Ballistic Products, Inc.
Berger Bullets Ltd.
Berry's Mfg., Inc.
Blount, Inc., Sporting Equipment
  Div.
Blue Mountain Bullets
Blue Ridge Machinery & Tools, Inc.
Bonanza (See Forster Products)
BRP, Inc. High Performance Cast
  Bullets
Brynin, Milton
B-Square Company, Inc.
Buck Stix-SOS Products Co.
Buffalo Arms Co.
Bull Mountain Rifle Co.
C&D Special Products (See
  Claybuster Wads & Harvester
  Bullets)
Camdex, Inc.
Canyon Cartridge Corp.
Case Sorting System
CCI/Speer Div of ATK
CH Tool & Die Co. (See 4-D Custom
  Die Co.)
CheVron Bullets
Claybuster Wads & Harvester Bullets
Cook Engineering Service
Crouse's Country Cover
Cumberland Arms
Curtis Cast Bullets
Custom Products (See Jones
  Custom Products)
CVA
D.C.C. Enterprises
Davide Pedersoli and Co.

PRODUCT & SERVICE DIRECTORY

Davis, Don
Davis Products, Mike
Denver Instrument Co.
Dillon Precision Products, Inc.
Dropkick
E&L Mfg., Inc.
Eagan, Donald V.
Eichelberger Bullets, Wm.
Enguix Import-Export
Euroarms of America, Inc.
E-Z-Way Systems
Federated-Fry (See Fry Metals)
Ferguson, Bill
Fisher Custom Firearms
Flambeau, Inc.
Flitz International Ltd.
Forster Products, Inc.
Fremont Tool Works
Fry Metals
Gehmann, Walter (See Huntington
    Die Specialties)
Graf & Sons
Graphics Direct
Graves Co.
Green, Arthur S.
Greenwood Precision
GTB-Custom Bullets
Gun City
Hanned Line, The
Hanned Precision (See The Hanned
    Line)
Harrell's Precision
Harris Enterprises
Harrison Bullets
Heidenstrom Bullets
High Precision
Hirtenberger AG
Hodgdon Powder Co.
Hoehn Sales, Inc.
Holland's Gunsmithing
Hornady Mfg. Co.
Howell Machine, Inc.
Hunters Supply, Inc.
Hutton Rifle Ranch
Image Ind. Inc.
Imperial Magnum Corp.
INTEC International, Inc.
Iosso Products
J&L Superior Bullets (See
    Huntington Die Specialties)
Jack First, Inc.
Javelina Lube Products
JLK Bullets
Jonad Corp.
Jones Custom Products, Neil A.
Jones Moulds, Paul
K&M Services
Kapro Mfg. Co. Inc. (See R.E.I.)
Knoell, Doug
Korzinek Riflesmith, J.
I A R Mfg , Inc
L.E. Wilson, Inc.
Le Clear Industries (See E-Z-Way
    Systems)
Lee Precision, Inc.
Liberty Metals
Liberty Shooting Supplies
Lightning Performance Innovations,
    Inc.
Lithi Bee Bullet Lube
Littleton, J. F.
Lock's Philadelphia Gun Exchange
Lortone Inc.
Lyman Instant Targets, Inc. (See
    Lyman Products Corp.)
Lyman Products Corp.
MA Systems, Inc.
Magma Engineering Co.
Match Prep-Doyle Gracey
Mayville Engineering Co. (See MEC,
    Inc.)
MCS, Inc.
MEC, Inc.
Midway Arms, Inc.
MI-TE Bullets
Montana Armory, Inc.

Mo's Competitor Supplies (See MCS,
    Inc.)
MTM Molded Products Co., Inc.
MWG Co.
Nammo Lapua Oy
Navy Arms Company
Newman Gunshop
North Devon Firearms Services
Old West Bullet Moulds
Original Box, Inc.
Outdoor Sports Headquarters, Inc.
Paragon Sales & Services, Inc.
Pinetree Bullets
Ponsness, Warren
Prairie River Arms
Prime Reloading
Professional Hunter Supplies
Pro-Shot Products, Inc.
Protector Mfg. Co., Inc., The
R.A. Wells Custom Gunsmith
R.E.I.
Rapine Bullet Mould Mfg. Co.
Redding Reloading Equipment
Reloading Specialties, Inc.
Rice, Keith (See White Rock Tool &
    Die)
Rochester Lead Works
Rooster Laboratories
Rorschach Precision Products
SAECO (See Redding Reloading
    Equipment)
Sandia Die & Cartridge Co.
Saunders Gun & Machine Shop
Saville Iron Co. (See Greenwood
    Precision)
Seebeck Assoc., R.E.
Sharp Shooter Supply
Sharps Arms Co., Inc., C.
Sierra Specialty Prod. Co.
Silver Eagle Machining
Skip's Machine
Sno-Seal, Inc. (See Atsko/Sno-Seal,
    Inc.)
SOS Products Co. (See Buck Stix-
    SOS Products Co.)
Spencer's Rifle Barrels, Inc.
SPG LLC
SSK Industries
Stalwart Corporation
Star Custom Bullets
Starr Trading Co., Jedediah
Stillwell, Robert
Stoney Point Products, Inc.
Stratco, Inc.
Tamarack Products, Inc.
Taracorp Industries, Inc.
TCCI
TCSR
TDP Industries, Inc.
Tetra Gun Care
Thompson/Center Arms
Vega Tool Co.
Venco Industries, Inc. (See
    Shooter's Choice Gun Care)
VibraShine, Inc.
Vibra-Tek Co.
Vihtavuori Oy/Kaltron-Pettibone
Vitt/Boos
W.B. Niemi Engineering
W.J. Riebe Co.
WD-40 Co.
Webster Scale Mfg. Co.
White Rock Tool & Die
Widener's Reloading & Shooting
    Supply, Inc.
Wise Custom Guns
Woodleigh (See Huntington Die
    Specialties)
Yesteryear Armory & Supply
Young Country Arms

RESTS BENCH, PORTABLE AND ACCESSORIES

A.W. Peterson Gun Shop, Inc., The

Adventure 16, Inc.
Armor Metal Products
B.M.F. Activator, Inc.
Bald Eagle Precision Machine Co.
Bald Eagle Precision Machine Co.
Bartlett Engineering
Battenfeld Technologies, Inc.
Blount/Outers ATK
Browning Arms Co.
B-Square Company, Inc.
Clift Mfg., L. R.
Desert Mountain Mfg.
Greenwood Precision
Harris Engineering Inc.
Hart & Son, Inc.
Hidalgo, Tony
Hoehn Sales, Inc.
Hoppe's Div. Penguin Industries, Inc.
J&J Sales
Keng's Firearms Specialty, Inc./US
    Tactical Systems
Kolpin Outdoors, Inc.
Kramer Designs
Midway Arms, Inc.
Millett Sights
Outdoor Connection, Inc., The
Protektor Model
Ransom International Corp.
Russ Haydon's Shooters' Supply
Saville Iron Co. (See Greenwood
    Precision)
Sinclair International, Inc.
Stoney Point Products, Inc.
Thompson Target Technology
Tonoloway Tack Drives
Torel, Inc./Tandy Brands
    Outdoors/AA & E
Varmint Masters, LLC
Wichita Arms, Inc.
York M-1 Conversion
Zanotti Armor, Inc.
Ziegel Engineering

RIFLE BARREL MAKER

Airrow
American Safe Arms, Inc.
Barrel & Gunworks
Bauska Barrels
BlackStar AccuMax Barrels
BlackStar Barrel Accurizing (See
    BlackStar AccuMax)
Border Barrels Ltd.
Buchsenmachermeister
Bullberry Barrel Works, Ltd.
Bushmaster Firearms, Inc.
Carter's Gun Shop
Christensen Arms
Cincinnati Swaging
D.L. Unmussig Bullets
deHaas Barrels
Dilliott Gunsmithing, Inc.
DKT, Inc.
Donnelly, C. P.
Douglas Barrels, Inc.
Fred F. Wells/Wells Sport Store
Gaillard Barrels
Getz Barrel Company
Getz Barrel Company
Granite Mountain Arms, Inc.
Green Mountain Rifle Barrel Co., Inc.
Gruning Precision, Inc.
Gun Works, The
Half Moon Rifle Shop
Hart Rifle Barrels, Inc.
Hastings
Hofer Jagdwaffen, P.
H-S Precision, Inc.
Jackalope Gun Shop
Krieger Barrels, Inc.
Les Baer Custom, Inc.
Lilja Precision Rifle Barrels
Lothar Walther Precision Tool Inc.
McGowen Rifle Barrels
McMillan Rifle Barrels
Mid-America Recreation, Inc.

Modern Gun Repair School
Morrison Precision
N.C. Ordnance Co.
Obermeyer Rifled Barrels
Olympic Arms Inc.
Orion Rifle Barrel Co.
PAC-NOR Barreling
Pence Precision Barrels
Perazone-Gunsmith, Brian
Rogue Rifle Co., Inc.
Sabatti SPA
Savage Arms, Inc.
Schneider Rifle Barrels, Inc.
Shaw, Inc., E. R. (See Small Arms
    Mfg. Co.)
Shilen, Inc.
Siskiyou Gun Works (See Donnelly,
    C. P.)
Small Arms Mfg. Co.
Specialty Shooters Supply, Inc.
Spencer's Rifle Barrels, Inc.
Steyr Mannlicher GmbH & Co. KG
Strutz Rifle Barrels, Inc., W. C.
Swift River Gunworks
Terry K. Kopp Professional
    Gunsmithing
Turnbull Restoration, Doug
Verney-Carron
Virgin Valley Custom Guns
William E. Phillips Firearms
Wilson Arms Co., The
Wiseman and Co., Bill

SCOPES, MOUNTS, ACCESSORIES, OPTICAL EQUIPMENT

A.R.M.S., Inc.
A.W. Peterson Gun Shop, Inc., The
Accu-Tek
Ackerman, Bill (See Optical Services
    Co.)
Action Direct, Inc.
ADCO Sales, Inc.
Aimtech Mount Systems
Air Rifle Specialists
Air Venture Airguns
All Rite Products, Inc.
Alpec Team, Inc.
Apel GmbH, Ernst
ArmaLite, Inc.
Arundel Arms & Ammunition, Inc., A.
B.A.C.
B.M.F. Activator, Inc.
Bansner's Ultimate Rifles, LLC
Barrett Firearms Manufacturer, Inc.
Beaver Park Product, Inc.
BEC, Inc.
Beeman Precision Airguns
Benjamin/Sheridan Co., Crosman
Bill Russ Trading Post
BKL Technologies
Blount, Inc., Sporting Equipment
    Div.
Blount/Outers ATK
Borden Rifles Inc.
Broad Creek Rifle Works, Ltd.
Brockman's Custom Gunsmithing
Brownells, Inc.
Brunton U.S.A.
BSA Optics
B-Square Company, Inc.
Bull Mountain Rifle Co.
Burris Co., Inc.
Bushmaster Firearms, Inc.
Bushnell Sports Optics Worldwide
Butler Creek Corp.
Cabela's
Carl Zeiss Inc.
Center Lock Scope Rings
Chuck's Gun Shop
Clark Custom Guns, Inc.
Clearview Mfg. Co., Inc.
Compass Industries, Inc.
Compasseco, Ltd.
Concept Development Corp.

Conetrol Scope Mounts
Creedmoor Sports, Inc.
Crimson Trace Lasers
Crosman Airguns
D.C.C. Enterprises
D.L. Unmussig Bullets
Daisy Outdoor Products
Del-Sports, Inc.
DHB Products
Dolbare, Elizabeth
E. Arthur Brown Co. Inc.
Eagle Imports, Inc.
Edmund Scientific Co.
Eggleston, Jere D.
Ellett Bros.
Emerging Technologies, Inc. (See
    Laseraim Technologies, Inc.)
Entreprise Arms, Inc.
Euro-Imports
Evolution Gun Works, Inc.
Excalibur Electro Optics, Inc.
Excel Industries, Inc.
Falcon Industries, Inc.
Farr Studio, Inc.
Freedom Arms, Inc.
Fujinon, Inc.
G.G. & G.
Galati International
Gentry Custom LLC
Gil Hebard Guns, Inc.
Gilmore Sports Concepts, Inc.
Goodwin's Guns
GSI, Inc.
Gun South, Inc. (See GSI, Inc.)
Guns Div. of D.C. Engineering, Inc.
Gunsmithing, Inc.
Hakko Co. Ltd.
Hammerli USA
Hart & Son, Inc.
Harvey, Frank
Highwood Special Products
Hiptmayer, Armurier
Hiptmayer, Klaus
Holland's Gunsmithing
Hunter Co., Inc.
Impact Case & Container, Inc.
Ironsighter Co.
Jeffredo Gunsight
Jena Eur
Jerry Phillips Optics
Jewell Triggers, Inc.
John Masen Co. Inc.
John's Custom Leather
Kahles A. Swarovski Company
Kalispel Case Line
KDF, Inc.
Keng's Firearms Specialty, Inc./US
    Tactical Systems
Kesselring Gun Shop
Kimber of America, Inc.
Knight's Manufacturing Co.
Kowa Optimed, Inc.
KVH Industries, Inc.
Kwik-Site Co.
L&S Technologies Inc. (See Aimtech
    Mount Systems)
L.A.R. Mfg., Inc.
Laser Devices, Inc.
Laseraim Technologies, Inc.
LaserMax, Inc.
Leapers, Inc.
Leica USA, Inc.
Les Baer Custom, Inc.
Leupold & Stevens, Inc.
List Precision Engineering
Lohman Mfg. Co., Inc.
Lomont Precision Bullets
London Guns Ltd.
Mac-1 Airgun Distributors
Mag-Na-Port International, Inc.
Mandall Shooting Supply Inc.
Marksman Products
Maxi-Mount Inc.
McMillan Optical Gunsight Co.
MCS, Inc.
MDS
Merit Corp.

Military Armament Corp.
Millett Sights
Mirador Optical Corp.
Mitchell Optics, Inc.
MMC
Mo's Competitor Supplies (See MCS, Inc.)
MWG Co.
Navy Arms Company
New England Custom Gun Service
Nikon, Inc.
Norincoptics (See BEC, Inc.)
Olympic Optical Co.
Op-Tec
Optical Services Co.
Orchard Park Enterprise
Oregon Arms, Inc. (See Rogue Rifle Co., Inc.)
Outdoor Connection, Inc., The
Parker & Sons Shooting Supply
Parsons Optical Mfg. Co.
PECAR Herbert Schwarz GmbH
PEM's Mfg. Co.
Pentax U.S.A., Inc.
PMC/Eldorado Cartridge Corp.
Precision Sport Optics
Premier Reticles
Quarton Beamshot
R.A. Wells Custom Gunsmith
Ram-Line ATK
Ramon B. Gonzalez Guns
Ranch Products
Randolph Engineering, Inc.
Rice, Keith (See White Rock Tool & Die)
Robinson Armament Co.
Rogue Rifle Co., Inc.
Romain's Custom Guns, Inc.
RPM
S&K Scope Mounts
Saunders Gun & Machine Shop
Schmidt & Bender, Inc.
Schumakers Gun Shop
Scope Control, Inc.
Score High Gunsmithing
Segway Industries
Selsi Co., Inc.
Sharp Shooter Supply
Shepherd Enterprises, Inc.
Sightron, Inc.
Simmons Outdoor Corp.
Six Enterprises
Southern Bloomer Mfg. Co.
Spencer's Rifle Barrels, Inc.
Splitfire Sporting Goods, L.L.C.
Sportsmatch U.K. Ltd.
Springfield Armory
Springfield, Inc.
SSK Industries
Stiles Custom Guns
Stoeger Industries
Stoney Point Products, Inc.
Sturm Ruger & Co. Inc.
Sunny Hill Enterprises, Inc.
Swarovski Optik North America Ltd.
Swift Instruments, Inc.
T.K. Lee Co.
Talley, Dave
Tasco Sales, Inc.
Tele-Optics
Thompson/Center Arms
Traditions Performance Firearms
Trijicon, Inc.
Truglo, Inc.
U.S. Optics, A Division of Zeitz Optics U.S.A.
Ultra Dot Distribution
Uncle Mike's (See Michaels of Oregon, Co.)
Unertl Optical Co., Inc.
United Binocular Co.
Virgin Valley Custom Guns
Visible Impact Targets
Voere-KGH GmbH
Warne Manufacturing Co.
Warren Muzzleloading Co., Inc.
Watson Bullets

Weaver Products ATK
Weaver Scope Repair Service
Webley and Scott Ltd.
Weigand Combat Handguns, Inc.
Wessinger Custom Guns & Engraving
Westley Richards & Co. Ltd.
White Rifles, Inc.
White Rock Tool & Die
Whitestone Lumber Corp.
Wideview Scope Mount Corp.
Wilcox Industries Corp.
Wild West Guns
Williams Gun Sight Co.
York M-1 Conversion
Zanotti Armor, Inc.

SHELLHOLDERS

A.W. Peterson Gun Shop, Inc., The
Corbin Mfg. & Supply, Inc.
Fremont Tool Works
GAR
Hart & Son, Inc.
Hollywood Engineering
Huntington Die Specialties
K&M Services
King & Co.
Protektor Model
PWM Sales Ltd.
RCBS Operations/ATK
Redding Reloading Equipment
Vega Tool Co.

SHOOTING/TRAINING SCHOOL

Alpine Indoor Shooting Range
American Gunsmithing Institute
American Small Arms Academy
Auto Arms
Beretta U.S.A. Corp.
Bob's Tactical Indoor Shooting Range & Gun Shop
Bridgeman Products
Chapman Academy of Practical Shooting
Chelsea Gun Club of New York City Inc.
Cherry Creek State Park Shooting Center
Cleland's Outdoor World, Inc.
CQB Training
Defense Training International, Inc.
Executive Protection Institute
Ferris Firearms
Firearm Training Center, The
Front Sight Firearms Training Institute
G.H. Enterprises Ltd.
Gene's Custom Guns
Gentner Bullets
Gilmore Sports Concepts, Inc.
Griffin & Howe, Inc.
Griffin & Howe, Inc.
Gun Doc, The
Guncraft Books (See Guncraft Sports, Inc.)
Guncraft Sports, Inc.
Gunsite Training Center
Henigson & Associates, Steve
High North Products, Inc.
Jensen's Custom Ammunition
Jensen's Firearms Academy
Kemen America
L.L. Bean, Inc.
Lethal Force Institute (See Police Bookshelf)
Long, George F.
McMurdo, Lynn
Mendez, John A.
Midwest Shooting School, The
NCP Products, Inc.
North American Shooting Systems

North Mountain Pine Training Center (See Executive Protection Institute)
Nowlin Mfg. Co.
Paxton Quigley's Personal Protection Strategies
Pentheny de Pentheny
Performance Specialists
Police Bookshelf
Protektor Model
SAFE
Shoot Where You Look
Shooter's World
Shooters, Inc.
Shooting Gallery, The
Sigarms Inc.
Smith & Wesson
Specialty Gunsmithing
Starlight Training Center, Inc.
Tactical Defense Institute
Thunden Ranch
Western Missouri Shooters Alliance
Yankee Gunsmith "Just Glocks"
Yavapai Firearms Academy Ltd.

SHOTSHELL MISCELLANY

A.W. Peterson Gun Shop, Inc., The
American Products, Inc.
Ballistic Products, Inc.
Bridgeman Products
Gun Works, The
Lee Precision, Inc.
MEC, Inc.
Precision Reloading, Inc.
R.E.I.
RCBS Operations/ATK
T&S Industries, Inc.
Vitt/Boos
Ziegel Engineering

SIGHTS, METALLIC

100 Straight Products, Inc.
A.W. Peterson Gun Shop, Inc., The
Accura-Site (See All's, The Jim Tembelis Co., Inc.)
Ad Hominem
Alley Supply Co.
All's, The Jim J. Tembelis Co., Inc.
Alpec Team, Inc.
Andela Tool & Machine, Inc.
AO Sight Systems
ArmaLite, Inc.
Aspen Outfitting Co.
Axtell Rifle Co.
B.A.C.
Ballard Rifle & Cartridge Co., LLC
BEC, Inc.
Bob's Gun Shop
Bo-Mar Tool & Mfg. Co.
Bond Custom Firearms
Bowen Classic Arms Corp.
Brockman's Custom Gunsmithing
Brooks Tactical Systems-Agrip
Brown Dog Ent.
Brownells, Inc.
Buffalo Arms Co.
Bushmaster Firearms, Inc.
C. Sharps Arms Co. Inc./Montana Armory
California Sights (See Fautheree, Andy)
Campbell, Dick
Cape Outfitters
Cape Outfitters
Cash Mfg. Co., Inc.
Center Lock Scope Rings
Champion's Choice, Inc.
Chip McCormick Corp.
C-More Systems
Colonial Repair
CRR, Inc./Marble's Inc.
Davide Pedersoli and Co.
DHB Products

Dixie Gun Works
DPMS (Defense Procurement Manufacturing Services, Inc.)
E. Arthur Brown Co. Inc.
Effebi SNC-Dr. Franco Beretta
Evolution Gun Works, Inc.
Farr Studio, Inc.
G.G. & G.
Garthwaite Pistolsmith, Inc., Jim
Goergen's Gun Shop, Inc.
Gun Doctor, The
Guns Div. of D.C. Engineering, Inc. Gunsmithing, Inc.
Hank's Gun Shop
Heidenstrom Bullets
Heinie Specialty Products
Hesco-Meprolight
Hiptmayer, Armurier
Hiptmayer, Klaus
Innovative Weaponry Inc.
International Shooters Service
J.G. Anschutz GmbH & Co. KG
JP Enterprises, Inc.
Keng's Firearms Specialty, Inc./US Tactical Systems
Knight Rifles
Knight's Manufacturing Co.
L.P.A. Inc.
Leapers, Inc.
Les Baer Custom, Inc.
List Precision Engineering
London Guns Ltd.
Lyman Instant Targets, Inc. (See Lyman Products Corp.)
Mandall Shooting Supply Inc.
Marble Arms (See CRR, Inc./Marble's Inc.)
MCS, Inc.
MEC-Gar S.R.L.
Meprolight (See Hesco-Meprolight)
Merit Corp.
Mid-America Recreation, Inc.
Middlebrooks Custom Shop
Millett Sights
MMC
Modern Muzzleloading, Inc.
Montana Armory, Inc.
Montana Vintage Arms
Mo's Competitor Supplies (See MCS, Inc.)
Navy Arms Company
New England Custom Gun Service
Newman Gunshop
Novak's, Inc.
OK Weber, Inc.
One Ragged Hole
Parker & Sons Shooting Supply
PEM's Mfg. Co.
Perazone-Gunsmith, Brian
RPM
Sharps Arms Co., Inc., C.
Slug Site
STI International
T.F.C. S.p.A.
Talley, Dave
Tank's Rifle Shop
Trijicon, Inc.
Truglo, Inc.
U.S. Optics, A Division of Zeitz Optics U.S.A.
Warne Manufacturing Co.
Weigand Combat Handguns, Inc.
Wichita Arms, Inc.
Wild West Guns
Williams Gun Sight Co.
Wilsom Combat
Wilsom Combat
XS Sight Systems

STOCK MAKER

Acra-Bond Laminates
Amrine's Gun Shop
Antique Arms Co.
Artistry in Wood
Aspen Outfitting Co.

Bain & Davis, Inc.
Bansner's Ultimate Rifles, LLC
Baron Technology
Belding's Custom Gun Shop
Billings Gunsmiths
Bob Rogers Gunsmithing
Boltin, John M.
Borden Ridges Rimrock Stocks
Bowerly, Kent
Boyds' Gunstock Industries, Inc.
Brace, Larry D.
Briganti Custom Gunsmith
Broad Creek Rifle Works, Ltd.
Brown Precision, Inc.
Bull Mountain Rifle Co.
Bullberry Barrel Works, Ltd.
Burkhart Gunsmithing, Don
Cambos Outdoorsman
Cambos Outdoorsman
Campbell, Dick
Caywood, Shane J.
Chicasaw Gun Works
Chuck's Gun Shop
Claro Walnut Gunstock Co.
Coffin, Charles H.
Colorado Gunsmithing Academy
Custom Shop, The
Custom Single Shot Rifles
D&D Gunsmiths, Ltd.
Dangler, Homer L.
D'Arcy Echols & Co.
David W. Schwartz Custom Guns
DGR Custom Rifles
DGR Custom Rifles
DGS, Inc., Dale A. Storey
Don Klein Custom Guns
Erhardt, Dennis
Eversull Co., Inc.
Fieldsport Ltd.
Fisher, Jerry A.
Forster, Larry L.
Fred F. Wells/Wells Sport Store
Gary Goudy Classic Stocks
Genecco Gun Works
Gene's Custom Guns
Gillmann, Edwin
Grace, Charles E.
Great American Gunstock Co.
Gruning Precision, Inc.
Gunsmithing Ltd.
Hank's Gun Shop
Harper's Custom Stocks
Harry Lawson Co.
Heilmann, Stephen
Hensley, Gunmaker, Darwin
Heydenberk, Warren R.
High Tech Specialties, Inc.
Huebner, Corey O.
Jack Dever Co.
Jamison's Forge Works
Jay McCament Custom Gunmaker
Jim Norman Custom Gunstocks
John Rigby & Co.
K. Eversull Co., Inc.
Keith's Custom Gunstocks
Ken Eyster Heritage Gunsmiths, Inc.
Larry Lyons Gunworks
Marshall Fish Mfg. Gunsmith Sptg. Co.
Mathews Gun Shop & Gunsmithing, Inc.
McGowen Rifle Barrels
Mercer Custom Guns
Mid-America Recreation, Inc.
Mike Yee Custom Stocking
Mitchell, Jack
Modern Gun Repair School
Morrow, Bud
Nelson's Custom Guns, Inc.
Nettestad Gun Works
Nickels, Paul R.
Paul and Sharon Dressel
Paul D. Hillmer Custom Gunstocks
Paulsen Gunstocks
Pawling Mountain Club
Pecatonica River Longrifle
Penteny de Pentheny

Quality Custom Firearms
R&J Gun Shop
R.A. Wells Custom Gunsmith
Ralph Bone Engraving
Richards MicroFit Stocks, Inc.
RMS Custom Gunsmithing
Robinson, Don
Ron Frank Custom Classic Arms
Royal Arms Gunstocks
Royal Arms Gunstocks
Ruger's Custom Guns
Six Enterprises
Skeoch, Brian R.
Smith, Art
Smith, Sharmon
Speiser, Fred D.
Steven Dodd Hughes
Stott's Creek Armory, Inc.
Sturgeon Valley Sporters
Taylor & Robbins
Tennessee Valley Mfg.
Tiger-Hunt Longrifle Gunstocks
Treebone Carving
Trico Plastics
Tucker, James C.
Turnbull Restoration, Doug
Vest, John
Walker Arms Co., Inc.
Weber & Markin Custom Gunsmiths
Wenig Custom Gunstocks
Wiebe, Duane
Wild West Guns
Williamson Precision Gunsmithing
Winter, Robert M.

STOCKS (COMMERCIAL)

A.W. Peterson Gun Shop, Inc., The
Accuracy Unlimited
Acra-Bond Laminates
African Import Co.
Ahlman Guns
Aspen Outfitting Co.
B.A.C.
Baelder, Harry
Balickie, Joe
Bansner's Ultimate Rifles, LLC
Barnes Bullets, Inc.
Battenfeld Technologies, Inc.
Beitzinger, George
Belding's Custom Gun Shop
Bell & Carlson, Inc.
Blount, Inc., Sporting Equipment Div.
Blount/Outers ATK
Bob's Gun Shop
Borden Ridges Rimrock Stocks
Borden Rifles Inc.
Bowerly, Kent
Boyds' Gunstock Industries, Inc.
Brockman's Custom Gunsmithing
Buckhorn Gun Works
Bull Mountain Rifle Co.
Butler Creek Corp.
Cali'co Hardwoods, Inc.
Cape Outfitters
Caywood, Shane J.
Chambers Flintlocks Ltd., Jim
Chicasaw Gun Works
Claro Walnut Gunstock Co.
Coffin, Charles H.
Colonial Repair
Colorado Gunsmithing Academy
Colorado School of Trades
Conrad, C. A.
Curly Maple Stock Blanks (See Tiger-Hunt)
Custom Checkering Service, Kathy Forster
D&D Gunsmiths, Ltd.
D&G Precision Duplicators (See Greenwood Precision)
Davide Pedersoli and Co.
DGR Custom Rifles
Duane's Gun Repair (See DGR Custom Rifles)

Duncan's Gun Works, Inc.
Effebi SNC-Dr. Franco Beretta
Eggleston, Jere D.
Erhardt, Dennis
Eversull Co., Inc.
Falcon Industries, Inc.
Falcon Industries, Inc.
Fibron Products, Inc.
Fieldsport Ltd.
Fisher, Jerry A.
Folks, Donald E.
Forster, Kathy (See Custom Checkering)
Forthofer's Gunsmithing & Knifemaking
Game Haven Gunstocks
George Hoenig, Inc.
Gervais, Mike
Gillmann, Edwin
Goens, Dale W.
Golden Age Arms Co.
Great American Gunstock Co.
Green, Roger M.
Greenwood Precision
Gun Shop, The
Guns Div. of D.C. Engineering, Inc.
Hammerli USA
Hanson's Gun Center, Dick
Harper's Custom Stocks
Harry Lawson Co.
Hecht, Hubert J., Waffen-Hecht
Hensley, Gunmaker, Darwin
High Tech Specialties, Inc.
Hiptmayer, Armurier
Hiptmayer, Klaus
Hogue Grips
H-S Precision, Inc.
Huebner, Corey O.
Israel Arms Inc.
Ivanoff, Thomas G. (See Tom's Gun Repair)
Jackalope Gun Shop
Jarrett Rifles, Inc.
Jim Norman Custom Gunstocks
John Masen Co. Inc.
Johnson Wood Products
KDF, Inc.
Keith's Custom Gunstocks
Kelbly, Inc.
Kilham & Co.
Klingler Woodcarving
Lawson Co., Harry
Mandall Shooting Supply Inc.
McDonald, Dennis
McMillan Fiberglass Stocks, Inc.
Michaels of Oregon Co.
Mid-America Recreation, Inc.
Miller Arms, Inc.
Mitchell, Jack
Mobile Area Networks, Inc.
Morrison Custom Rifles, J. W.
MPI Stocks
MWG Co.
NCP Products, Inc.
Nelson's Custom Guns, Inc.
New England Arms Co.
New England Custom Gun Service
Newman Gunshop
Oil Rod and Gun Shop
Old World Gunsmithing
One Of A Kind
Orvis Co., The
Ottmar, Maurice
Pagel Gun Works, Inc.
Paragon Sales & Services, Inc.
Parker & Sons Shooting Supply
Paul and Sharon Dressel
Paul D. Hillmer Custom Gunstocks
Paulsen Gunstocks
Pawling Mountain Club
Pecatonica River Longrifle
PEM's Mfg. Co.
Perazone-Gunsmith, Brian
Powell & Son (Gunmakers) Ltd., William
Precision Gun Works
R&J Gun Shop

R.A. Wells Custom Gunsmith
Ram-Line ATK
Rampart International
Richards MicroFit Stocks, Inc.
RMS Custom Gunsmithing
Robinson, Don
Robinson Armament Co.
Robinson Firearms Mfg. Ltd.
Romain's Custom Guns, Inc.
Ron Frank Custom Classic Arms
Royal Arms Gunstocks
Saville Iron Co. (See Greenwood Precision)
Schiffman, Mike
Score High Gunsmithing
Simmons Gun Repair, Inc.
Six Enterprises
Speiser, Fred D.
Stan De Treville & Co.
Stiles Custom Guns
Swann, D. J.
Swift River Gunworks
Szweda, Robert (See RMS Custom Gunsmithing)
T.F.C. S.p.A.
Tecnolegno S.p.A.
Tiger-Hunt Longrifle Gunstocks
Tirelli
Tom's Gun Repair, Thomas G. Ivanoff
Track of the Wolf, Inc.
Treebone Carving
Trevallion Gunstocks
Tuttle, Dale
Vic's Gun Refinishing
Virgin Valley Custom Guns
Volquartsen Custom Ltd.
Walker Arms Co., Inc.
Weber & Markin Custom Gunsmiths
Weems, Cecil
Wenig Custom Gunstocks
Werth, T. W.
Western Mfg. Co.
Wild West Guns
Williams Gun Sight Co.
Windish, Jim
Wright's Gunstock Blanks
Zeeryp, Russ

STUCK CASE REMOVERS

A.W. Peterson Gun Shop, Inc., The
GAR
Huntington Die Specialties
Redding Reloading Equipment
Tom's Gun Repair, Thomas G. Ivanoff

TARGETS, BULLET & CLAYBIRD TRAPS

A.W. Peterson Gun Shop, Inc., The
Action Target, Inc.
Air Arms
American Target
Autauga Arms, Inc.
Beeman Precision Airguns
Benjamin/Sheridan Co., Crosman
Birchwood Casey
Blount, Inc., Sporting Equipment Div.
Blount/Outers ATK
Blue and Gray Products Inc. (See Ox-Yoke Originals)
Brown Precision, Inc.
Bull-X, Inc.
Caswell International
Champion Target Co.
Creedmoor Sports, Inc.
Crosman Airguns
D.C.C. Enterprises
Daisy Outdoor Products
Diamond Mfg. Co.
Federal Champion Target Co.

G.H. Enterprises Ltd.
H-S Precision, Inc.
Hunterjohn
J.G. Dapkus Co., Inc.
Kennebec Journal
Kleen-Bore, Inc.
Lakefield Arms Ltd. (See Savage Arms, Inc.)
Leapers, Inc.
Littler Sales Co.
Lyman Instant Targets, Inc. (See Lyman Products Corp.)
Marksman Products
Mendez, John A.
Mountain Plains Industries
MSR Targets
N.B.B., Inc.
National Target Co.
North American Shooting Systems
Outers Laboratories Div. of ATK
Ox-Yoke Originals, Inc.
Palsa Outdoor Products
Passive Bullet Traps, Inc. (See Savage Range Systems, Inc.)
PlumFire Press, Inc.
Precision Airgun Sales, Inc.
Protektor Model
Quack Decoy & Sporting Clays
Remington Arms Co., Inc.
Rockwood Corp.
Rocky Mountain Target Co.
Savage Range Systems, Inc.
Schaefer Shooting Sports
Seligman Shooting Products
Shooters Supply
Shoot-N-C Targets (See Birchwood Casey)
Target Shooting, Inc.
Thompson Target Technology
Trius Traps, Inc.
Universal Sports
Visible Impact Targets
Watson Bullets
Woods Wise Products
World of Targets (See Birchwood Casey)
X-Spand Target Systems

TAXIDERMY

African Import Co.
Bill Russ Trading Post
Kulis Freeze Dry Taxidermy
World Trek, Inc.

TRAP & SKEET SHOOTER'S EQUIPMENT

American Products, Inc.
Bagmaster Mfg., Inc.
Ballistic Products, Inc.
Beretta S.P.A., Pietro
Blount/Outers ATK
Bob Allen Sportswear
Bridgeman Products
C&H Research
Cape Outfitters
Claybuster Wads & Harvester Bullets
Danuser Machine Co.
Fiocchi of America, Inc.
G.H. Enterprises Ltd.
Gun Works, The
Hoppe's Div. Penguin Industries, Inc.
Jamison's Forge Works
Jenkins Recoil Pads
Jim Noble Co.
Kalispel Case Line
Kolar
Lakewood Products LLC
Ljutic Industries, Inc.
Mag-Na-Port International, Inc.
MEC, Inc.
Moneymaker Guncraft Corp.
MTM Molded Products Co., Inc.
NCP Products, Inc.
Pachmayr Div. Lyman Products

Palsa Outdoor Products
Pro-Port Ltd.
Protektor Model
Quack Decoy & Sporting Clays
Remington Arms Co., Inc.
Rhodeside, Inc.
Shotgun Sports Magazine, dba Shootin' Accessories Ltd.
Stan Baker Sports
T&S Industries, Inc.
TEN-X Products Group
Torel, Inc./Tandy Brands Outdoors/AA & E
Trius Traps, Inc.
Truglo, Inc.
Universal Sports
Warne Manufacturing Co.
Weber & Markin Custom Gunsmiths
X-Spand Target Systems
Ziegel Engineering

TRIGGERS, RELATED EQUIPMENT

A.W. Peterson Gun Shop, Inc., The
Actions by "T" Teddy Jacobson
B&D Trading Co., Inc.
B.M.F. Activator, Inc.
Behlert Precision, Inc.
Bond Custom Firearms
Boyds' Gunstock Industries, Inc.
Broad Creek Rifle Works, Ltd.
Bull Mountain Rifle Co.
Chicasaw Gun Works
Dayton Traister
Dolbare, Elizabeth
Eversull Co., Inc.
Feinwerkbau Westinger & Altenburger
Gentry Custom LLC
Gun Works, The
Hart & Son, Inc.
Hastings
Hawken Shop, The (See Dayton Traister)
High Performance International
Hoehn Sales, Inc.
Holland's Gunsmithing
Impact Case & Container, Inc.
Jewell Triggers, Inc.
John Masen Co. Inc.
Jones Custom Products, Neil A.
JP Enterprises, Inc.
K. Eversull Co., Inc.
KK Air International (See Impact Case & Container Co., Inc.)
Knight's Manufacturing Co.
L&R Lock Co.
Les Baer Custom, Inc.
List Precision Engineering
London Guns Ltd.
M.H. Canjar Co.
Mahony, Philip Bruce
Master Lock Co.
Miller Single Trigger Mfg. Co.
NCP Products, Inc.
Neil A. Jones Custom Products
Nowlin Mfg. Co.
PEM's Mfg. Co.
Penrod Precision
Perazone-Gunsmith, Brian
Robinson Armament Co.
Sharp Shooter Supply
Shilen, Inc.
Simmons Gun Repair, Inc.
Spencer's Rifle Barrels, Inc.
Tank's Rifle Shop
Target Shooting, Inc.
Watson Bullets
York M-1 Conversion

MANUFACTURER'S DIRECTORY

A

A Zone Bullets, 2039 Walter Rd., Billings, MT 59105 / 800-252-3111; FAX: 406-248-1961

A&W Repair, 2930 Schneider Dr., Arnold, MO 63010 / 617-287-3725

A.A. Arms, Inc., 4811 Persimmont Ct., Monroe, NC 28110 / 704-289-5356; or 800-935-1119; FAX: 704-289-5859

A.B.S. III, 9238 St. Morritz Dr., Fern Creek, KY 40291

A.G. Russell Knives, Inc., 1920 North 26th Street, Lowell, AR 72745-8489 / 800-255-9034; FAX: 479-636-8493 ag@agrussell.com agrussell.com

A.R.M.S., Inc., 230 W. Center St., West Bridgewater, MA 02379-1620 / 508-584-7816; FAX: 508-588-8045

A.W. Peterson Gun Shop, Inc., 4255 W. Old U.S. 441, Mt. Dora, FL 32757-3299 / 352-383-4258; FAX: 352-735-1001

A.W. Peterson Gun Shop, Inc., The, 4255 West Old U.S. 441, Mount Dora, FL 32757-3299 / 352-383-4258

AC Dyna-tite Corp., 155 Kelly St., P.O. Box 0984, Elk Grove Village, IL 60007 / 847-593-5566; FAX: 847-593-1304

Acadian Ballistic Specialties, P.O. Box 787, Folsom, LA 70437 / 504-796-0078 gunsmith@neasolft.com

Accuracy Den, The, 25 Bitterbrush Rd., Reno, NV 89523 / 702-345-0225

Accuracy International, Foster, P.O. Box 111, Wilsall, MT 59086 / 406-587-7922; FAX: 406-585-9434

Accuracy Internationl Precision Rifles (See U.S.)

Accuracy Int'l. North America, Inc., P.O. Box 5267, Oak Ridge, TN 37831 / 423-482-0330; FAX: 423-482-0336

Accuracy Unlimited, 7479 S. DePew St., Littleton, CO 80123

Accuracy Unlimited, 16036 N. 49 Ave., Glendale, AZ 85306 / 602-978-9089; FAX: 602-978-9089 fglenn@cox.net www.glenncustom.com

Accura-Site (See All's, The Jim Tembelis Co., Inc.)

Accurate Arms Co., Inc., 5891 Hwy. 230 West, McEwen, TN 37101 / 931-729-4207; FAX: 931-729-4211 burrensburg@aac-ca.com www.accuratepowder.com

Accu-Tek, 4510 Carter Ct., Chino, CA 91710

Ackerman & Co., Box 133 U.S. Highway Rt. 7, Pownal, VT 05261 / 802-823-9874 muskets@togsther.net

Ackerman, Bill (See Optical Services Co.)

Acra-Bond Laminates, 134 Zimmerman Rd., Kalispell, MT 59901 / 406-257-9003; 903; 406-257-9003 merlins@digisys.net www.acrabondlaminates.com

Action Bullets & Alloy Inc., RR 1, P.O. Box 189, Quinter, KS 67752 / 785-754-3609; FAX: 785-754-3629 bullets@ruraltel.net

Action Direct, Inc., P.O. Box 770400, Miami, FL 33177 / 305-969-0056; FAX: 305-256-3541 www.action-direct.com

Action Products, Inc., 22 N. Mulberry St., Hagerstown, MD 21740 / 301-797-1414; FAX: 301-733-2073

Action Target, Inc., P.O. Box 636, Provo, UT 84603 / 801-377-8033; FAX: 801-377-8096 www.actiontarget.com

Actions by "T" Teddy Jacobson, 16315 Redwood Forest Ct., Sugar Land, TX 77478 / 281-277-4008; FAX: 281-277-9112 tjacobson@houston.rr.com www.actionsbyt.us

AcuSport Corporation, 1 Hunter Place, Bellefontaine, OH 43311-3001 / 513-593-7010; FAX: 513-592-5625

Ad Hominem, 3130 Gun Club Lane, RR #3, Orillia, ON L3V 6H3 CANADA / 705-689-5303; FAX: 705-689-5303

Adair Custom Shop, Bill, 2886 Westridge, Carrollton, TX 75006

ADCO Sales, Inc., 4 Draper St. #A, Woburn, MA 01801 / 781-935-1799; FAX: 781-935-1011

Adkins, Luther, 1292 E. McKay Rd., Shelbyville, IN 46176-8706 / 317-392-3795

Advance Car Mover Co., Rowell Div., P.O. Box 1, 240 N. Depot St., Juneau, WI 53039 / 414-386-4464; FAX: 414-386-4416

Advantage Arms, Inc., 25163 W. Ave. Stanford, Valencia, CA 91355 / 661-257-2290

Adventure 16, Inc., 4620 Alvarado Canyon Rd., San Diego, CA 92120 / 619-283-6314

Aero Peltor, 90 Mechanic St., Southbridge, MA 01550 / 508-764-5500; FAX: 508-764-0188

African Import Co., 22 Goodwin Rd., Plymouth, MA 02360 / 508-746-8552; FAX: 508-746-0404 africanimport@aol.com

AFSCO Ammunition, 731 W. Third St., P.O. Box L, Owen, WI 54460 / 715-229-2516 sailers@webtv.net

Ahlman Guns, 9525 W. 230th St., Morristown, MN 55052 / 507-685-4243; FAX: 507-685-4280 www.ahlmans.com

Ahrends Grips, Box 203, Clarion, IA 50525 / 515-532-3449; FAX: 515-532-3926 ahrends@goldfieldaccess.net

Ahrends, Kim, Box 203, Clarion, IA 50525 / 515-532-3449; FAX: 515-532-3926

Aimtech Mount Systems, P.O. Box 223, Thomasville, GA 31799 / 229-226-4313; FAX: 229-227-0222 mail@aimtech-mounts.com www.aimtech-mounts.com

Air Arms, Hailsham Industrial Park, Diplocks Way, Hailsham, E. Sussex, BN27 3JF ENGLAND / 011-0323-845853; FAX: 1323 440573 general.air-arms.co.uk. www.air-arms.co.uk.

Air Rifle Specialists, P.O. Box 138, 130 Holden Rd., Pine City, NY 14871-0138 / 607-734-7340; FAX: 607-733-3261 ars@stny.rr.com www.air-rifles.com

Air Venture Airguns, 9752 E. Flower St., Bellflower, CA 90706 / 562-867-6355

AirForce Airguns, P.O. Box 2478, Fort Worth, TX 76113 / 817-451-8966; FAX: 817-451-1613 www.airforceairguns.com

Airrow, 11 Monitor Hill Rd., Newtown, CT 06470 / 203-270-6343

Aitor-Cuchilleria Del Norte S.A., Izelaieta, 17, 48260, Ermua, SPAIN / 43-17-08-50 info@aitor.com www.ailor.com

Ajax Custom Grips, Inc., 9130 Viscount Row, Dallas, TX 75247 / 214-630-8893; FAX: 214-630-4942

Aker International, Inc., 2248 Main St., Suite 6, Chula Vista, CA 91911 / 619-423-5182; FAX: 619-423-1363 aker@akerleather.com www.akerleather.com

AKJ Concealco, P.O. Box 871596, Vancouver, WA 98687-1596 / 360-891-8222; FAX: 360-891-8221 Concealco@aol.com www.greatholsters.com

Alana Cupp Custom Engraver, P.O. Box 207, Annabella, UT 84711 / 801-896-4834

Alaska Bullet Works, Inc., 9978 Crazy Horse Drive, Juneau, AK 99801 / 907-789-3834; FAX: 907-789-3433

Alaskan Silversmith, The, 2145 Wagner Hollow Rd., Fort Plain, NY 13339 / 518-993-3983 sidbell@capital.net www.sidbell.cizland.com

Aldis Gunsmithing & Shooting Supply, 502 S. Montezuma St., Prescott, AZ 86303 / 602-445-6723; FAX: 602-445-6763

Alessi Holsters, Inc., 2465 Niagara Falls Blvd., Amherst, NY 14228-3527 / 716-691-5615

Alex, Inc., 3420 Cameron Bridge Rd., Manhattan, MT 59741-8523 / 406-282-7396; FAX: 406-282-7396

Alfano, Sam, 36180 Henry Gaines Rd., Pearl River, LA 70452 / 504-863-3364; FAX: 504-863-7715

All American Lead Shot Corp., P.O. Box 224566, Dallas, TX 75062

All Rite Products, Inc., 9554 Wells Circle, Suite D, West Jordan, UT 84088-6226 / 800-771-8471; FAX: 801-280-8302 info@allriteproducts.com www.allriteproducts.com

Allard, Gary/Creek Side Metal & Woodcrafters, Fishers Hill, VA 22626 / 540-465-3903

Allen Co., Inc., 525 Burbank St., Broomfield, CO 80020 / 303-469-1857; or 800-876-8600; FAX: 303-466-7437

Allen Firearm Engraving, P.O. Box 155, Camp Verde, AZ 86322 / 928-567-6711 rosebudmulgco@netzero.com rosebudmulgco@netzero.com

Allen Mfg., 6449 Hodgson Rd., Circle Pines, MN 55014 / 612-429-8231

Alley Supply Co., P.O. Box 848, Gardnerville, NV 89410 / 775-782-3800; FAX: 775-782-3827 jetalley@aol.com www.alleysupplyco.com

Alliant Techsystems, Smokeless Powder Group, P.O. Box 6, Rt. 114, Bldg. 229, Radford, VA 24141-0096 www.alliantpowder.com

Allred Bullet Co., 932 Evergreen Drive, Logan, UT 84321 / 435-752-6983; FAX: 435-752-6983

All's, The Jim J. Tembelis Co., Inc., 216 Loper Ct., Neenah, WI 54956 / 920-725-5251; FAX: 920-725-5251

Alpec Team, Inc., 201 Ricken Backer Cir., Livermore, CA 94550 / 510-606-8245; FAX: 510-606-4279

Alpha 1 Drop Zone, 2121 N. Tyler, Wichita, KS 67212 / 316-729-0800; FAX: 316-729-4262 www.alpha1dropzone.com

Alpha LaFranck Enterprises, P.O. Box 81072, Lincoln, NE 68501 / 402-466-3193

Alpha Precision, Inc., 3238 Della Slaton Rd., Comer, GA 30629-2212 / 706-783-2131 jim@alphaprecisioninc.com www.alphaprecisioninc.com

Alpine Indoor Shooting Range, 2401 Government Way, Coeur d'Alene, ID 83814 / 208-676-8824; FAX: 208-676-8824

Altamont Co., 901 N. Church St., P.O. Box 309, Thomasboro, IL 61878 / 217-643-3125; or 800-626-5774; FAX: 217-643-7973

Alumna Sport by Dee Zee, 1572 NE 58th Ave., P.O. Box 3090, Des Moines, IA 50316 / 800-798-9899

Amadeo Rossi S.A., Rua: Amadeo Rossi, 143, Sao Leopoldo, RS 93030-220 BRAZIL / 051-592-5566 rossi.firearms@pnet.com.br

Amato, Jeff. See: J&M PRECISION MACHINING

AmBr Software Group Ltd., P.O. Box 301, Reistertown, MD 21136-0301 / 800-888-1917; FAX: 410-526-7212

American Ammunition, 3545 NW 71st St., Miami, FL 33147 / 305-835-7400; FAX: 305-694-0037

American Derringer Corp., 127 N. Lacy Dr., Waco, TX 76705 / 800-642-7817; or 254-799-9111; FAX: 254-799-7935

American Display Co., 55 Cromwell St., Providence, RI 02907 / 401-331-2464; FAX: 401-421-1264

American Gas & Chemical Co., Ltd.,, 220 Pegasus Ave., Northvale, NJ 07647 / 201-767-7300

American Gunsmithing Institute, 1325 Imola Ave. #504, Napa, CA 94559 / 707-253-0462; FAX: 707-253-7149 www.americangunsmith.com

American Handgunner Magazine, 12345 World Trade Dr., San Diego, CA 92128 / 800-537-3006; FAX: 858-605-0204 www.americanhandgunner.com

American Pioneer Video, P.O. Box 50049, Bowling Green, KY 42102-2649 / 800-743-4675

American Products, Inc., 14729 Spring Valley Road, Morrison, IL 61270 / 815-772-3336; FAX: 815-772-8046

American Safe Arms, Inc., 1240 Riverview Dr., Garland, UT 84312 / 801-257-7472; FAX: 801-785-8156

American Security Products Co., 11925 Pacific Ave., Fontana, CA 92337 / 909-685-9680; or 800-421-6142; FAX: 909-685-9685

American Small Arms Academy, P.O. Box 12111, Prescott, AZ 86304 / 602-778-5623

American Target, 1328 S. Jason St., Denver, CO 80223 / 303-733-0433; FAX: 303-777-0311

American Target Knives, 1030 Brownwood NW, Grand Rapids, MI 49504 / 616-453-1998

Americase, P.O. Box 271, 1610 E. Main, Waxahachie, TX 75165 / 800-880-3629; FAX: 214-937-8373

Ames Metal Products, 4323 S. Western Blvd., Chicago, IL 60609 / 773-523-3230; or 800-255-6937; FAX: 773-523-3854

Amherst Arms, P.O. Box 1457, Englewood, FL 34295 / 941-475-2020; FAX: 941-473-1212

Ammo Load Worldwide, Inc., 815 D St., Lewiston, ID 83501 / 208-743-7418; FAX: 208-746-1703 ammoload@microwavedsl.com

Ammo Load, Inc., 1560 E. Edinger, Suite G, Santa Ana, CA 92705 / 714-558-8858; FAX: 714-569-0319

Amrine's Gun Shop, 937 La Luna, Ojai, CA 93023 / 805-646-2376

Amsec, 11925 Pacific Ave., Fontana, CA 92337

Analog Devices, Box 9106, Norwood, MA 02062

Andela Tool & Machine, Inc., RD3, Box 246, Richfield Springs, NY 13439

Anderson Manufacturing Co., Inc., 22602 53rd Ave. SE, Bothell, WA 98021 / 206-481-1858; FAX: 206-481-7839

Andres & Dworsky KG, Bergstrasse 18, A-3822 Karlstein, Thaya, AUSTRIA / 0 28 44-285; FAX: 0 28 44-28619 andres.dnorsky@wvnet.as

Angelo & Little Custom Gun Stock Blanks, P.O. Box 240046, Dell, MT 59724-0046

Answer Products Co., 1519 Westbury Drive, Davison, MI 48423 / 810-653-2911

Antique American Firearms, P.O. Box 71035, Dept. GD, Des Moines, IA 50325 / 515-224-6552

Antique Arms Co., 1110 Cleveland Ave., Monett, MO 65708 / 417-235-6501

AO Sight Systems, 2401 Ludelle St., Fort Worth, TX 76105 / 888-744-4880; or 817-536-0136; FAX: 817-536-3517

Apel GmbH, Ernst, Am Kirschberg 3, D-97218, Gerbrunn, GERMANY / 0 (931) 707192 info@eaw.de www.eaw.de

Aplan Antiques & Art, James O., HC 80, Box 793-25, Piedmont, SD 57769 / 605-347-5016

AR-7 Industries, LLC, 998 N. Colony Rd., Meriden, CT 06450 / 203-630-3536; FAX: 203-630-3637

Arizona Ammunition, Inc., 21421 No. 14th Ave., Suite E, Phoenix, AZ 85027 / 623-516-9004; FAX: 623-516-9012 www.azammo.com

ArmaLite, Inc., P.O. Box 299, Geneseo, IL 61254 / 800-336-0184; or 309-944-6939; FAX: 309-944-6949

Armament Gunsmithing Co., Inc., 525 Rt. 22, Hillside, NJ 07205 / 908-686-0960; FAX: 718-738-5019 armamentgunsmithing@worldnet.att.net

Armas Garbi, S.A., 12-14 20.600 Urki, 12, Eibar (Guipuzcoa), SPAIN / 943 20 3873; FAX: 943 20 3873 armosgarbi@euskalnet.n

Armas Kemen S. A. (See U.S. Importers)

Armfield Custom Bullets, 10584 County Road 100, Carthage, MO 64836 / 417-359-8480; FAX: 417-359-8497

Armi Perazzi S.P.A., Via Fontanelle 1/3, 1-25080, Botticino Mattina, ITALY / 030-2692591; FAX: 030-2692594

Armi San Marco (See Taylor's & Co.)

Armi San Paolo, 172-A, I-25062, via Europa, ITALY / 030-2751725

Armi Sport (See Cape Outfitters)

Armite Laboratories, 1560 Superior Ave., Costa Mesa, CA 92627 / 213-587-7768; FAX: 213-587-5075

Armoloy Co. of Ft. Worth, 204 E. Daggett St., Fort Worth, TX 76104 / 817-332-5604; FAX: 817-335-6517

Armor (See Buck Stop Lure Co., Inc.)

Armor Metal Products, P.O. Box 4609, Helena, MT 59604 / 406-442-5560; FAX: 406-442-5650

Armory Publications, 2120 S. Reserve St., PMB 253, Missoula, MT 59801 / 406-549-7670; FAX: 406-728-0597 armorypub@aol.com www.armorypub.com

Armoury, Inc., The, Rt. 202, Box 2340, New Preston, CT 06777 / 860-868-0001; FAX: 860-868-2919

Arms & Armour Press, Wellington House, 125 Strand, London, WC2R 0BB ENGLAND / 0171-420-5555; FAX: 0171-240-7265

Arms Corporation of the Philippines, Bo. Parang Marikina, Metro Manila, PHILIPPINES / 632 941 6243; or 632-941-6244; FAX: 632-942-0682

Arms Craft Gunsmithing, 1106 Linda Dr., Arroyo Grande, CA 93420 / 805-481-2830

Arms Software, 4851 SW Madrona St., Lake Oswego, OR 97035 / 800-366-5559; or 503-697-0533; FAX: 503-697-3337

Arms, Programming Solutions (See Arms Software)

Armscor Precision, 5740 S. Arville St. #219, Las Vegas, NV 89118 / 702-362-7750

Armscorp USA, Inc., 4424 John Ave., Baltimore, MD 21227 / 410-247-6200; FAX: 410-247-6205 info@armscorpusa.com www.armscorpusa.com

Arratoonian, Andy (See Horseshoe Leather Products)

Arrieta S.L., Morkaiko 5, 20870, Elgoibar, SPAIN / 34-43-743150; FAX: 34-43-743154

Art Jewel Enterprises Ltd., Eagle Business Ctr., 460 Randy Rd., Carol Stream, IL 60188 / 708-260-0400

Artistry in Wood, 134 Zimmerman Rd., Kalispell, MT 59901 / 406-257-9003; FAX: 406-257-9167 merlins@digisys.net www.acrabondlaminates.com

Art's Gun & Sport Shop, Inc., 6008 Hwy. Y, Hillsboro, MO 63050

Arundel Arms & Ammunition, Inc., A., 24A Defense St., Annapolis, MD 21401 / 410-224-8683

Aspen Outfitting Co., Jon Hollinger, 9 Dean St., Aspen, CO 81611 / 970-925-3406

A-Square Co., 205 Fairfield Ave., Jeffersonville, IN 47130 / 812-283-0577; FAX: 812-283-0375

Astra Sport, S.A., Apartado 3, 48300 Guernica, Espagne, SPAIN / 34-4-6250100; FAX: 34-4-6255186

Atamec-Bretton, 19 rue Victor Grignard, F-42026, St.-Etienne (Cedex 1, FRANCE / 33-77-93-54-69; FAX: 33-77-93-57-98

Atlanta Cutlery Corp., 2143 Gees Mill Rd., Box 839 CIS, Conyers, GA 30207 / 800-883-0300; FAX: 404-388-0246

Atlantic Mills, Inc., 1295 Towbin Ave., Lakewood, NJ 08701-5934 / 800-242-7374

Atsko/Sno-Seal, Inc., 2664 Russell St., Orangeburg, SC 29115 / 803-531-1820; FAX: 803-531-2139 info@atsko.com www.atsko.com

Auguste Francotte & Cie S.A., rue du Trois Juin 109, 4400 Herstal-Liege, BELGIUM / 32-4-248-13-18; FAX: 32-4-948-11-79

Austin & Halleck, Inc., 2150 South 950 East, Provo, UT 84606-6285 / 877-543-3256; or 801-374-9990; FAX: 801-374-9998 www.austinhallek.com

Austin Sheridan USA, Inc., P.O. Box 577, 36 Haddam Quarter Rd., Durham, CT 06422 / 860-349-1772; FAX: 860-349-1771 swalzer@palm.net

Autauga Arms, Inc., Pratt Plaza Mall No. 13, Prattville, AL 36067 / 800-262-9563; FAX: 334-361-2961

Auto Arms, 738 Clearview, San Antonio, TX 78228 / 512-434-5450

Auto-Ordnance Corp., P.O. Box 220, Blauvelt, NY 10913 / 914-353-7770

Autumn Sales, Inc. (Blaser), 1320 Lake St., Fort Worth, TX 76102 / 817-335-1634; FAX: 817-338-0119

Avnda Otaola Norica, 16 Apartado 68, 20600, Eibar, SPAIN

AWC Systems Technology, P.O. Box 41938, Phoenix, AZ 85080-1938 / 623-780-1050; FAX: 623-780-2967 awc@awcsystech.com www.awcsystech.com

Axtell Rifle Co., 353 Mill Creek Road, Sheridan, MT 59749 / 406-842-5814

AYA (See U.S. Importer-New England Custom Gun Serv

B

B&D Trading Co., Inc., 3935 Fair Hill Rd., Fair Oaks, CA 95628 / 800-334-3790; or 916-967-9366; FAX: 916-967-4873

B&P America, 12321 Brittany Cir., Dallas, TX 75230 / 972-726-9069

B.A.C., 17101 Los Modelos St., Fountain Valley, CA 92708 / 435-586-3286

B.B. Walker Co., P.O. Box 1167, 414 E Dixie Dr., Asheboro, NC 27204 / 910-625-1380; FAX: 910-625-8125

B.C. Outdoors, Larry McGhee, PO Box 61497, Boulder City, NV 89006 / 702-294-3056; FAX: 702-294-0413 jdalton@pmcammo.com www.pmcammo.com

B.M.F. Activator, Inc., 12145 Mill Creek Run, Plantersville, TX 77363 / 936-894-2397; FAX: 936-894-2397 bmf25years@aol.com

Baelder, Harry, Alte Goennebeker Strasse 5, 24635, Rickling, GERMANY / 04328-722732; FAX: 04328-722733

Baer's Hollows, P.O. Box 603, Taft, CA 93268 / 719-438-5718

Bagmaster Mfg., Inc., 2731 Sutton Ave., St. Louis, MO 63143 / 314-781-8002; FAX: 314-781-3363 sales@bagmaster.com www.bagmaster.com

Bain & Davis, Inc., 307 E. Valley Blvd., San Gabriel, CA 91776-3522 / 626-573-4241; FAX: 323-283-7449 baindavis@aol.com

Baker, Stan. See: STAN BAKER SPORTS

Baker's Leather Goods, Roy, P.O. Box 893, Magnolia, AR 71754 / 870-234-0344 pholsters@ipa.net

Bald Eagle Precision Machine Co., 101-A Allison St., Lock Haven, PA 17745 / 570-748-6772; FAX: 570-748-4443 bepmachine@aol.com www.baldeaglemachine.com

Balickie, Joe, 408 Trelawney Lane, Apex, NC 27502 / 919-362-5185

Ballard, Donald. See: BALLARD INDUSTRIES

Ballard Industries, Donald Ballard Sr., P.O. Box 2035, Arnold, CA 95223 / 408-996-0957; FAX: 408-257-6828

Ballard Rifle & Cartridge Co., LLC, 113 W. Yellowstone Ave., Cody, WY 82414 / 307-587-4914; FAX: 307-527-6097 ballard@wyoming.com www.ballardrifles.com

Ballistic Products, Inc., 20015 75th Ave. North, Corcoran, MN 55340-9456 / 763-494-9237; FAX: 763-494-9236 info@ballisticproducts.com www.ballisticproducts.com

Ballistic Program Co., Inc., The, 2417 N. Patterson St., Thomasville, GA 31792 / 912-228-5739 or 800-368-0835

Ballistic Research, 1108 W. May Ave., McHenry, IL 60050 / 815-385-0037

Ballisti-Cast, Inc., P.O. Box 1057, Minot, ND 58702-1057 / 701-497-3333; FAX: 701-497-3335

Bandcor Industries, Div. of Man-Sew Corp., 6108 Sherwin Dr., Port Richey, FL 34668 / 813-848-0432

Bang-Bang Boutique (See Holster Shop, The)

Bansner's Ultimate Rifles, LLC, P.O. Box 839, 261 E. Main St., Adamstown, PA 19501 / 717-484-2370; FAX: 717-484-0523 bansner@aol.com www.bansnersrifle.com

Barbour, Inc., 55 Meadowbrook Dr., Milford, NH 03055 / 603-673-1313; FAX: 603-673-6510

Barnes, 4347 Tweed Dr., Eau Claire, WI 54703-6302

Barnes Bullets, Inc., P.O. Box 215, American Fork, UT 84003 / 801-756-4222; or 800-574-9200; FAX: 801-756-2465 email@barnesbullets.com www.barnesbullets.com

Baron Technology, 62 Spring Hill Rd., Trumbull, CT 06611 / 203-452-0515; FAX: 203-452-0663 dbaron@baronengraving.com www.baronengraving.com

Barraclough, John K., 55 Merit Park Dr., Gardena, CA 90247 / 310-324-2574 johnbar120@aol.com

Barramundi Corp., P.O. Drawer 4259, Homosassa Springs, FL 32647 / 904-628-0200

Barrel & Gunworks, 2601 Lake Valley Rd., Prescott Valley, AZ 86314 / 928-772-4060 www.cutrifle.com

Barrett Firearms Manufacturer, Inc., P.O. Box 1077, Murfreesboro, TN 37133 / 615-896-2938; FAX: 615-896-7313

Bar-Sto Precision Machine, 73377 Sullivan Rd., P.O. Box 1838, Twentynine Palms, CA 92277 / 760-367-2747; FAX: 760-367-2407 barsto@eee.org www.barsto.com

Barta's Gunsmithing, 10231 U.S. Hwy. 10, Cato, WI 54230 / 920-732-4472

Barteaux Machete, 1916 SE 50th Ave., Portland, OR 97215-3238 / 503-233-5880

Bartlett Engineering, 40 South 200 East, Smithfield, UT 84335-1645 / 801-563-5910

Bates Engraving, Billy, 2302 Winthrop Dr. SW, Decatur, AL 35603 / 256-355-3690 bbrn@aol.com www.angelfire.com/al/billybates

Battenfeld Technologies, Inc., 5885 W. Van Horn Tavern Rd., Columbia, MO 65203 / 573-445-9200; FAX: 573-447-4158 battenfeldtechnologies.com

Bauer, Eddie, 15010 NE 36th St., Redmond, WA 98052

Baumgartner Bullets, 3011 S. Alane St., W. Valley City, UT 84120

Bauska Barrels, 105 9th Ave. W., Kalispell, MT 59901 / 406-752-7706

Bear Archery, RR 4, 4600 Southwest 41st Blvd., Gainesville, FL 32601 / 904-376-2327

Bear Arms, 374-A Carson Rd., St. Mathews, SC 29135

Bear Mountain Gun & Tool, 120 N. Plymouth, New Plymouth, ID 83655 / 208-278-5221; FAX: 208-278-5221

Beartooth Bullets, P.O. Box 491, Dept. HLD, Dover, ID 83825-0491 / 208-448-1865 bullets@beartoothbullets.com beartoothbullets.com

Beaver Park Product, Inc., 840 J St., Penrose, CO 81240 / 719-372-6744

BEC, Inc., 1227 W. Valley Blvd., Suite 204, Alhambra, CA 91803 / 626-281-5751; FAX: 626-293-7073

Beeks, Mike. See: GRAYBACK WILDCATS

Beeman Precision Airguns, 5454 Argosy Dr., Huntington Beach, CA 92649 / 714-890-4808; FAX: 714-890-4808

Behlert Precision, Inc., P.O. Box 288, 7067 Easton Rd., Pipersville, PA 18947 / 215-766-8681; or 215-766-7301; FAX: 215-766-8681

Beitzinger, George, 116-20 Atlantic Ave., Richmond Hill, NY 11419 / 718-847-7661

Belding's Custom Gun Shop, 10691 Sayers Rd., Munith, MI 49259 / 517-596-2388

Bell & Carlson, Inc., Dodge City Industrial Park, 101 Allen Rd., Dodge City, KS 67801 / 800-634-8586; or 620-225-6688; FAX: 620-225-6688 email@bellandcarlson.com www.bellandcarlson.com

Bell Reloading, Inc., 1725 Harlin Lane Rd., Villa Rica, GA 30180

Bell's Gun & Sport Shop, 3309-19 Mannheim Rd., Franklin Park, IL 60131

Bell's Legendary Country Wear, 22 Circle Dr., Bellmore, NY 11710 / 516-679-1158

Benchmark Knives (See Gerber Legendary Blades)

Benelli Armi S.P.A., Via della Stazione, 61029, Urbino, ITALY / 39-722-307-1; FAX: 39-722-327427

Benelli USA Corp., 17603 Indian Head Hwy., Accokeek, MD 20607 / 301-283-6981; FAX: 301-283-6988 benelliusa.com

Bengtson Arms Co., L., 6345-B E. Akron St., Mesa, AZ 85205 / 602-981-6375

Benjamin/Sheridan Co., Crosman, Rts. 5 and 20, E. Bloomfield, NY 14443 / 716-657-6161; FAX: 716-657-5405 www.crosman.com

Bentley, John, 128-D Watson Dr., Turtle Creek, PA 15145

Beretta S.P.A., Pietro, Via Beretta, 18, 25063, Gardone Vae Trompia, ITALY / 39-30-8341-1 info@benetta.com www.benetta.com

Beretta U.S.A. Corp., 17601 Beretta Dr., Accokeek, MD 20607 / 301-283-2191; FAX: 301-283-0435

Berger Bullets Ltd., 5443 W. Westwind Dr., Glendale, AZ 85310 / 602-842-4001; FAX: 602-934-9083

Bernardelli, Vincenzo, P.O. Box 460243, Houston, TX 77056-8243 www.bernardelli.com

Bernardelli, Vincenzo, Via Grande, 10, Sede Legale Torbole Casaglia, Brescia, ITALY / 39-30-8912851-2-3; FAX: 39-030-2150963 bernardelli@bernardelli.com www.bernardelli.com

Berry's Mfg., Inc., 401 North 3050 East St., St. George, UT 84770 / 435-634-1682; FAX: 435-634-1683 sales@berrysmfg.com www.berrysmfg.com

Bersa S.A., Benso Bonadimani, Magallanes 775 B1704 FLC, Ramos Mejia, ARGENTINA / 011-4656-2377; FAX: 011-4656-2093+ info@bersa-sa.com.dr www.bersa-sa.com.ar

Bert Johanssons Vapentillbehor, S-430 20 Veddige, SWEDEN,

Bertuzzi (See U.S. Importer-New England Arms Co.)

Better Concepts Co., 663 New Castle Rd., Butler, PA 16001 / 412-285-9000

Beverly, Mary, 3201 Horseshoe Trail, Tallahassee, FL 32312
Bianchi International, Inc., 100 Calle Cortez, Temecula, CA 92590 / 909-676-5621; FAX: 909-676-6777
Big Bear Arms & Sporting Goods, Inc., 1112 Milam Way, Carrollton, TX 75006 / 972-416-8051; or 800-400-BEAR; FAX: 972-416-0771
Big Bore Bullets of Alaska, P.O. Box 521455, Big Lake, AK 99652 / 907-373-2673; FAX: 907-373-2673 doug@mtaonline.net ww.awloo.com/bbb/index.
Big Bore Express, 2316 E. Railroad St., Nampa, ID 83651 / 800-376-4010 FAX: 208-466-6927 info@powerbeltbullets.com bigbore.com
Big Spring Enterprises "Bore Stores", P.O. Box 1115, Big Spring Rd., Yellville, AR 72687 / 870-449-5297; FAX: 870-449-4446
Bilal, Mustafa. See: TURK'S HEAD PRODUCTIONS
Bilinski, Bryan. See: FIELDSPORT LTD.
Bill Adair Custom Shop, 2886 Westridge, Carrollton, TX 75006 / 972-418-0950
Bill Austin's Calls, Box 284, Kaycee, WY 82639 / 307-738-2552
Bill Hanus Birdguns, LLC, P.O. Box 533, Newport, OR 97365 / 541-265-7433; FAX: 541-265-7400 www.billhanusbirdguns.com
Bill Russ Trading Post, William A. Russ, 25 William St., Addison, NY 14801-1326 / 607-359-3896
Bill Wiseman and Co., P.O. Box 3427, Bryan, TX 77805 / 409-690-3456; FAX: 409-690-0156
Billeb, Stephen. See: QUALITY CUSTOM FIREARMS
Billings Gunsmiths, 1841 Grand Ave., Billings, MT 59102 / 406-256-8390; FAX: 406-256-6530 blgsgunsmiths@msn.com www.billingsgunsmiths.net
Billingsley & Brownell, P.O. Box 25, Dayton, WY 82836 / 307-655-9344
Bill's Gun Repair, 1007 Burlington St., Mendota, IL 61342 / 815-539-5786
Billy Bates Engraving, 2302 Winthrop Dr. SW, Decatur, AL 35603 / 256-355-3690 bbrn@aol.com www.angelfire.com/al/billybates
Birchwood Casey, 7900 Fuller Rd., Eden Prairie, MN 55344 / 800-328-6156; or 612-937-7933; FAX: 612-937-7979
Birdsong & Assoc., W. E., 1435 Monterey Rd., Florence, MS 39073-9748 / 601-366-8270
Bismuth Cartridge Co., 3500 Maple Ave., Suite 1650, Dallas, TX 75219 / 214-521-5880; FAX: 214-521-9035
Bison Studios, 1409 South Commerce St., Las Vegas, NV 89102 / 702-388-2891; FAX: 702-383-9967
Bitterroot Bullet Co., 2001 Cedar Ave., Lewiston, ID 83501-0412 / 208-743-5635 brootbil@lewiston.com
BKL Technologies, P.O. Box 5237, Brownsville, TX 78523
Black Belt Bullets (See Big Bore Express)
Black Hills Ammunition, Inc., P.O. Box 3090, Rapid City, SD 57709-3090 / 605-348-5150; FAX: 605-348-9827
Black Hills Shooters Supply, P.O. Box 4220, Rapid City, SD 57709 / 800-289-2506
Black Powder Products, 67 Township Rd. 1411, Chesapeake, OH 45619 / 614-867-8047
Black Sheep Brand, 3220 W. Gentry Pkwy., Tyler, TX 75702 / 903-592-3853; FAX: 903-592-0527
Blacksmith Corp., P.O. Box 280, North Hampton, OH 45349 / 937-969-8389; FAX: 937-969-8399 sales@blacksmithcorp.com www.blacksmithcorp.com
BlackStar AccuMax Barrels, 11501 Brittmoore Park Drive, Houston, TX 77041 / 281-721-6040; FAX: 281-721-6041
BlackStar Barrel Accurizing (See BlackStar AccuMax)
Blacktail Mountain Books, 42 First Ave. W., Kalispell, MT 59901 / 406-257-5573
Blammo Ammo, P.O. Box 1677, Seneca, SC 29679 / 803-882-1768
Blaser Jagdwaffen GmbH, D-88316, Isny Im Allgau, GERMANY
Blount, Inc., Sporting Equipment Div., 2299 Snake River Ave., P.O. Box 856, Lewiston, ID 83501 / 800-627-3640; or 208-746-2351; FAX: 208-799-3904
Blount/Outers ATK, P.O. Box 39, Onalaska, WI 54650 / 608-781-5800; FAX: 608-781-0368
Blue and Gray Products Inc. (See Ox-Yoke Originals)
Blue Book Publications, Inc., 8009 34th Ave. S., Ste. 175, Minneapolis, MN 55425 / 952-854-5229; FAX: 952-853-1486 bluebook@bluebookinc.com www.bluebookinc.com
Blue Mountain Bullets, 64146 Quail Ln., Box 231, John Day, OR 97845 / 541-820-4594; FAX: 541-820-4594
Blue Ridge Machinery & Tools, Inc., P.O. Box 536-GD, Hurricane, WV 25526 / 800-872-6500; FAX: 304-562-5311 blueridgemachine@worldnet.att.net www.blueridgemachinery.com
BMC Supply, Inc., 26051 - 179th Ave. SE, Kent, WA 98042

Bob Allen Co., P.O. Box 477, 214 SW Jackson, Des Moines, IA 50315 / 800-685-7020; FAX: 515-283-0779
Bob Allen Sportswear, 220 S. Main St., Osceola, IA 50213 / 210-344-8531; FAX: 210-342-2703 sales@bob-allen.com www.bob-allen.com
Bob Rogers Gunsmithing, P.O. Box 305, 344 S. Walnut St., Franklin Grove, IL 61031 / 815-456-2685; FAX: 815-456-2685
Bob's Gun Shop, P.O. Box 200, Royal, AR 71968 / 501-767-1970; FAX: 501-767-1970 gunparts@hsnp.com www.gun-parts.com
Bob's Tactical Indoor Shooting Range & Gun Shop, 90 Lafayette Rd., Salisbury, MA 01952 / 508-465-5561
Boessler, Erich, Am Vogeltal 3, 97702, Munnerstadt, GERMANY
Boker USA, Inc., 1550 Balsam Street, Lakewood, CO 80214 / 303-462-0662; FAX: 303-462-0668 sales@bokerusa.com bokerusa.com
Boltin, John M., P.O. Box 644, Estill, SC 29918 / 803-625-2185
Bo-Mar Tool & Mfg. Co., 6136 State Hwy. 300, Longview, TX 75604 / 903-759-4784; FAX: 903-759-9141 marykor@earthlink.net bo-mar.com
Bonadimani, Benso. See: BERSA S.A.
Bonanza (See Forster Products), 310 E. Lanark Ave., Lanark, IL 61046 / 815-493-6360; FAX: 815-493-2371
Bond Arms, Inc., P.O. Box 1296, Granbury, TX 76048 / 817-573-4445; FAX: 817-573-5636
Bond Custom Firearms, 8954 N. Lewis Ln., Bloomington, IN 47408 / 812-332-4519
Bonham's & Butterfields, 220 San Bruno Ave., San Francisco, CA 94103 / 415-861-7500; FAX: 415-861-0183 arms@butterfields.com www.butterfields.com
Boone Trading Co., Inc., P.O. Box 669, Brinnon, WA 98320 / 800-423-1945; or 360-796-4330; FAX: 360-796-4511 sales@boonetrading.com boonetrading.com
Boone's Custom Ivory Grips, Inc., 562 Coyote Rd., Brinnon, WA 98320 / 206-796-4330
Boonie Packer Products, P.O. Box 12517, Salem, OR 97309-0517 / 800-477-3244; or 503-581-3244; FAX: 503-581-3191 customerservice@booniepacker.com www.booniepacker.com
Borden Ridges Rimrock Stocks, RR 1 Box 250 BC, Springville, PA 18844 / 570-965-2505; FAX: 570-965-2328
Borden Rifles Inc., RD 1, Box 250 #BC, Springville, PA 18844 / 717-965-2505; FAX: 717-965-2328
Border Barrels Ltd., Riccarton Farm, Newcastleton, SCOTLAND UK
Borovnik K.G., Ludwig, 9170 Ferlach, Bahnhofstrasse 7, AUSTRIA / 042 27 24 42; FAX: 042 26 43 49
Bosis (See U.S. Importer-New England Arms Co.)
Boss Manufacturing Co., 221 W. First St., Kewanee, IL 61443 / 309-852-2131; or 800-447-4581; FAX: 309-852-0848
Bostick Wildlife Calls, Inc., P.O. Box 728, Estill, SC 29918 / 803-625-2210; or 803-625-4512
Bowen Classic Arms Corp., P.O. Box 67, Louisville, TN 37777 / 865-984-3583 www.bowenclassicarms.com
Bowen Knife Co., Inc., P.O. Box 590, Blackshear, GA 31516 / 912-449-4794
Bowerly, Kent, 710 Golden Pheasant Dr., Redmond, OR 97756 / 541-923-3501 jkbowerly@aol.com
Boyds' Gunstock Industries, Inc., 25376 403 Rd. Ave., Mitchell, SD 57301 / 605-996-5011; FAX: 605-996-9878 www.boydsgunstocks.com
Brace, Larry D., 771 Blackfoot Av., Eugene, OR 97404 / 541-688-1278; FAX: 541-607-5833
Brauer Bros., 1520 Washington Ave., St. Louis, MO 63103 / 314-231-2864; FAX: 314-249-4952 www.brauerbros.com
Break-Free, Inc., 13386 International Pkwy., Jacksonville, FL 32218 / 800-428-0588; FAX: 904-741-5407 contactus@armorholdings.com www.break-free.com
Brenneke GmbH, P.O. Box 1646, 30837, Langenhagen, GERMANY / +49-511-97262-0; FAX: +49-511-97262-62 info@brenneke.de brenneke.com
Bridgeman Products, Harry Jaffin, 153 B Cross Slope Ct., Englishtown, NJ 07726 / 732-536-3604; FAX: 732-972-1004
Bridgers Best, P.O. Box 1410, Berthoud, CO 80513
Briese Bullet Co., Inc., 3442 42nd Ave. SE, Tappen, ND 58487 / 701-327-4578; FAX: 701-327-4578
Brigade Quartermasters, 1025 Cobb International Blvd., Dept. VH, Kennesaw, GA 30144-4300 / 404-428-1248; or 800-241-3125; FAX: 404-426-7726
Briganti, A.J. See: BRIGANTI CUSTOM GUNSMITH
Briganti Custom Gunsmith, A.J. Briganti, 512 Rt. 32, Highland Mills, NY 10930 / 845-928-9573

Briley Mfg. Inc., 1230 Lumpkin, Houston, TX 77043 / 800-331-5718; or 713-932-6995; FAX: 713-932-1043
Brill, R. See: ROYAL ARMS INTERNATIONAL
British Sporting Arms, RR 1, Box 130, Millbrook, NY 12545 / 914-677-8303
Broad Creek Rifle Works, Ltd., 120 Horsey Ave., Laurel, DE 19956 / 302-875-5446; FAX: 302-875-1448 bcrw4guns@aol.com
Brockman's Custom Gunsmithing, P.O. Box 357, Gooding, ID 83330 / 208-934-5050
Broken Gun Ranch, 10739 126 Rd., Spearville, KS 67876 / 316-385-2587; FAX: 316-385-2597 nbowlin@ucom.net www.brokengunranch
Brooker, Dennis, Rt. 1, Box 12A, Derby, IA 50068 / 515-533-2103
Brooks Tactical Systems-Agrip, 279-C Shorewood Ct., Fox Island, WA 98333 / 253-549-2866 FAX: 253-549-2703 brooks@brookstactical.com www.brookstactical.com
Brown Dog Ent., 2200 Calle Camelia, 1000 Oaks, CA 91360 / 805-497-2318; FAX: 805-497-1618
Brown Precision, Inc., 7786 Molinos Ave., Los Molinos, CA 96055 / 530-384-2506; FAX: 916-384-1638 www.brownprecision.com
Brown Products, Inc., Ed, 43825 Muldrow Trl., Perry, MO 63462 / 573-565-3261; FAX: 573-565-2791 edbrown@edbrown.com www.edbrown.com
Brownells, Inc., 200 S. Front St., Montezuma, IA 50171 / 800-741-0015; FAX: 800-264-3068 orderdesk@brownells.com www.brownells.com
Browning Arms Co., One Browning Place, Morgan, UT 84050 / 801-876-2711; FAX: 801-876-3331 www.browning.com
Browning Arms Co. (Parts & Service), 3005 Arnold Tenbrook Rd., Arnold, MO 63010 / 617-287-6800; FAX: 617-287-9751
BRP, Inc. High Performance Cast Bullets, 1210 Alexander Rd., Colorado Springs, CO 80909 / 719-633-0658
Brunton U.S.A., 620 E. Monroe Ave., Riverton, WY 82501 / 307-856-6559; FAX: 307-857-4702 info@brunton.com www.brunton.com
Bryan & Assoc., R. D. Sauls, P.O. Box 5772, Anderson, SC 29623-5772 / 864-261-6810 bryanandac@aol.com www.huntersweb.com/bryanandac
Brynin, Milton, P.O. Box 383, Yonkers, NY 10710 / 914-779-4333
BSA Guns Ltd., Armoury Rd. Small Heath, Birmingham B11 2PP, ENGLAND / 011-021-772-8543; FAX: 011-021-773-0845 sales@bsagun.com www.bsagun.com
BSA Optics, 3911 SW 47th Ave., Ste. 914, Ft. Lauderdale, FL 33314 / 954-581-2144; FAX: 954-581-3165 4info@basaoptics.com www.bsaoptics.com
B-Square Company, Inc., P.O. Box 11281, 2708 St. Louis Ave., Ft. Worth, TX 76110 / 817-923-0964 or 800-433-2909; FAX: 817-926-7012
Buchsenmachermeister, Peter Hofer Jagdwaffen, A-9170 Ferlach, Kirchgasse 24, Kirchgasse, AUSTRIA / 43 4227 3683; or 43 664 3200216; FAX: 43 4227 368330 peterhofer@hoferwaffen.com www.hoferwaffen.com
Buck Knives, Inc., 1900 Weld Blvd., P.O. Box 1267, El Cajon, CA 92020 / 619-449-1100; or 800-326-2825; FAX: 619-562-5774
Buck Stix-SOS Products Co., Box 3, Neenah, WI 54956
Buck Stop Lure Co., Inc., 3600 Grow Rd. NW, P.O. Box 636, Stanton, MI 48888 / 989-762-5091; FAX: 989-762-5124 buckstop@nethawk.com www.buckstopscents.com
Buckeye Custom Bullets, 6490 Stewart Rd., Elida, OH 45807 / 419-641-4463
Buckhorn Gun Works, 8109 Woodland Dr., Black Hawk, SD 57718 / 605-787-6472
Buckskin Bullet Co., P.O. Box 1893, Cedar City, UT 84721 / 435-586-3286
Budin, Dave, 817 Main St., P.O. Box 685, Margaretville, NY 12455 / 914-568-4103; FAX: 914-586-4105
Budin, Dave. See: DEL-SPORTS, INC.
Buenger Enterprises/Goldenrod Dehumidifier, 3600 S. Harbor Blvd., Oxnard, CA 93035 / 800-451-6797; or 805-985-5828; FAX: 805-985-1534
Buffalo Arms Co., 660 Vermeer Ct., Ponderay, ID 83852 / 208-263-6953; FAX: 208-265-2096 www.buffaloarms.com
Buffalo Bullet Co., Inc., 12637 Los Nietos Rd., Unit A, Santa Fe Springs, CA 90670 / 800-423-8069; FAX: 562-944-5054
Buffalo Gun Center, 3385 Harlem Rd., Buffalo, NY 14225 / 716-833-2581; FAX: 716-833-2265 www.buffaloguncenter.com

Buffalo Rock Shooters Supply, R.R. 1, Ottawa, IL 61350 / 815-433-2471
Buffer Technologies, P.O. Box 104930, Jefferson City, MO 65110 / 573-634-8529; FAX: 573-634-8522
Bull Mountain Rifle Co., 6327 Golden West Terrace, Billings, MT 59106 / 406-656-0778
Bullberry Barrel Works, Ltd., 2430 W. Bullberry Ln., Hurricane, UT 84737 / 435-635-9866; FAX: 435-635-0348 fred@bullberry.com www.bullberry.com
Bullet Metals, Bill Ferguson, P.O. Box 1238, Sierra Vista, AZ 85636 / 520-458-5321; FAX: 520-458-1421 info@theantimonyman.com www.bullet-metals.com
Bullet N Press, 1210 Jones St., Gastonia, NC 28052 / 704-853-0265 bnpress@quik.com www.oldwestgunsmith.com
Bullet Swaging Supply, Inc., P.O. Box 1056, 303 McMillan Rd., West Monroe, LA 71291 / 318-387-3266; FAX: 318-387-7779 leblackmon@colla.com
Bull-X, Inc., 411 E. Water St., Farmer City, IL 61842-1556 / 309-928-2574 or 800-248-3845; FAX: 309-928-2130
Burkhart Gunsmithing, Don, P.O. Box 852, Rawlins, WY 82301 / 307-324-6007
Burnham Bros., P.O. Box 1148, Menard, TX 78659 / 915-396-4572, FAX. 915-396-4574
Burris Co., Inc., P.O. Box 1747, 331 E. 8th St., Greeley, CO 80631 / 970-356-1670; FAX: 970-356-8702
Bushmaster Firearms, Inc., 999 Roosevelt Trail, Windham, ME 04062 / 800-998-7928; FAX: 207-892-8068 info@bushmaster.com www.bushmaster.com
Bushmaster Hunting & Fishing, 451 Alliance Ave., Toronto, ON M6N 2J1 CANADA / 416-763-4040; FAX: 416-763-0623
Bushnell Sports Optics Worldwide, 9200 Cody, Overland Park, KS 66214 / 913-752-3400 or 800-423-3537; FAX: 913-752-3550
Buster's Custom Knives, P.O. Box 214, Richfield, UT 84701 / 435-896-5319; FAX: 435-896-8333 www.warenskiknives.com
Butler Creek Corp., 2100 S. Silverstone Way, Meridian, ID 83642-8151 / 800-423-8327 or 406-388-1356; FAX: 406-388-7204
Butler Enterprises, 834 Oberting Rd., Lawrenceburg, IN 47025 / 812-537-3584
Buzz Fletcher Custom Stockmaker, 117 Silver Road, P.O. Box 189, Taos, NM 87571 / 505-758-3486

C

C&D Special Products (See Claybuster Wads & Harvester Bullets)
C&H Research, 115 Sunnyside Dr., Box 351, Lewis, KS 67552 / 316-324-5445; or 888-324-5445; FAX: 620-324-5984 info@mercuryrecoil.com www.mercuryrecoil.com
C. Palmer Manufacturing Co., Inc., P.O. Box 220, West Newton, PA 15089 / 412-872-8200; FAX: 412-872-8302
C. Sharps Arms Co. Inc./Montana Armory, 100 Centennial Dr., P.O. Box 885, Big Timber, MT 59011 / 406-932-4353; FAX: 406-932-4443
C.S. Van Gorden & Son, Inc., 1815 Main St., Bloomer, WI 54724 / 715-568-2612 vangorden@bloomer.net
C.W. Erickson's L.L.C., 530 Garrison Ave. NE, P.O. Box 522, Buffalo, MN 55313 / 763-682-3665; FAX: 763-682-4328 www.archerhunter.com
Cabanas (See U.S. Importer-Mandall Shooting Supply
Cabela's, One Cabela Drive, Sidney, NE 69160 / 308-254-5505; FAX: 308-254-8420
Cabinet Mtn. Outfitters Scents & Lures, P.O. Box 766, Plains, MT 59859 / 406-826-3970
Cache La Poudre Rifleworks, 140 N. College, Ft. Collins, CO 80524 / 920-482-6913
Cain's Outdoors, Inc., 1832 Williams Hwy., Williamstown, WV 26187 / 304-375-7842; FAX: 304-375-7842 muzzleloading@cainsoutdoor.com www.cainsoutdoor.com
Calhoon Mfg., 4343 U.S. Highway 87, Havre, MT 59501 / 406-395-4079 www.jamescalhoon.com
Cali'co Hardwoods, Inc., 3580 Westwind Blvd., Santa Rosa, CA 95403 / 707-546-4045; FAX: 707-546-4027 calicohardwoods@msn.com
Calico Light Weapon Systems, 1489 Greg St., Sparks, NV 89431
California Sights (See Fautheree, Andy)
Cambos Outdoorsman, 532 E. Idaho Ave., Ontario, OR 97914 / 541-889-3135; FAX: 541-889-2633

Cambos Outdoorsman, Fritz Hallberg, 532 E. Idaho Ave., Ontario, OR 97914 / 541-889-3135; FAX: 541-889-2633
Camdex, Inc., 2330 Alger, Troy, MI 48083 / 810-528-2300; FAX: 810-528-0989
Cameron's, 16690 W. 11th Ave., Golden, CO 80401 / 303-279-7365; FAX: 303-568-1009 ncnoremac@aol.com
Camillus Cutlery Co., 54 Main St., Camillus, NY 13031 / 315-672-8111; FAX: 315-672-8832
Campbell, Dick, 196 Garden Homes Dr., Colville, WA 99114 / 509-684-6080; FAX: 509-684-6080 dicksknives@aol.com
Camp-Cap Products, P.O. Box 3805, Chesterfield, MO 63006 / 866-212-4639; FAX: 636-536-6320 www.langenberghats.com
Cannon Safe, Inc., 216 S. 2nd Ave. #BLD-932, San Bernardino, CA 92400 / 310-692-0636; or 800-242-1055; FAX: 310-692-7252
Canyon Cartridge Corp., P.O. Box 152, Albertson, NY 11507 FAX: 516-294-8946
Cape Outfitters, 599 County Rd. 206, Cape Girardeau, MO 63701 / 573-335-4103; FAX: 573-335-1555
Caraville Manufacturing, P.O. Box 4545, Thousand Oaks, CA 91359 / 805-499-1234
Carbide Checkering Tools (See J&R Engineering)
Carhartt, Inc., P.O. Box 600, 3 Parklane Blvd., Dearborn, MI 48121 / 800-358-3825; or 313-271-8460; FAX: 313-271-3455
Carl Walther GmbH, B.P. 4325, D-89033, Ulm, GERMANY
Carl Zeiss Inc., 13005 N. Kingston Ave., Chester, VA 23836 / 800-441-3005; FAX: 804-530-8481
Carolina Precision Rifles, 1200 Old Jackson Hwy., Jackson, SC 29831 / 803-827-2069
Carrell, William. See: CARRELL'S PRECISION FIREARMS
Carrell's Precision Firearms, William Carrell, 1952 W.Silver Falls Ct., Meridian, ID 83642-3837
Carry-Lite, Inc., P.O. Box 1587, Fort Smith, AR 72902 / 479-782-8971; FAX: 479-783-0234
Carter's Gun Shop, 225 G St., Penrose, CO 81240 / 719-372-6240 rlewiscarter@msn.com
Cascade Bullet Co., Inc., 2355 South 6th St., Klamath Falls, OR 97601 / 503-884-9316
Cascade Shooters, 2155 N.W. 12th St., Redwood, OR 97756
Case & Sons Cutlery Co., W R, Owens Way, Bradford, PA 16701 / 814-368-4123; or 800-523-6350; FAX: 814-768-5369
Case Sorting System, 12695 Cobblestone Creek Rd., Poway, CA 92064 / 619-486-9340
Cash Mfg. Co., Inc., P.O. Box 130, 201 S. Klein Dr., Waunakee, WI 53597-0130 / 800-648-5004; FAX: 608-849-5664
Caspian Arms, Ltd., 14 North Main St., Hardwick, VT 05843 / 802-472-6454; FAX: 802-472-6709
Cast Bullet Association, The, 12857 S. Road, Hoyt, KS 66440-9116 cbamemdir@castbulletassoc.org www.castbulletassoc.org
Cast Performance Bullet Company, P.O. Box 153, Riverton, WY 82501 / 307-857-2940; FAX: 307-857-3132 castperform@wyoming.com castperformance.com
Casull Arms Corp., P.O. Box 1629, Afton, WY 83110 / 307-886-0200
Caswell International, 720 Industrial Dr. No. 112, Cary, IL 60013 / 847-639-7666; FAX: 847-639-7694 www.caswellintl.com
Cathey Enterprises, Inc., P.O. Box 2202, Brownwood, TX 76804 / 915-643-2553; FAX: 915-643-3653
Cation, 2341 Alger St., Troy, MI 48083 / 810-689-0658; FAX: 810-689-7558
Caywood, Shane J., P.O. Box 321, Minocqua, WI 54548 / 715-277-3866
Caywood Gunmakers, 18 Kings Hill Estates, Berryville, AR 72616 / 870-423-4741 www.caywoodguns.com
CBC, Avenida Humberto de Campos 3220, 09400-000, Ribeirao Pires, SP, BRAZIL / 55 11 4822 8378; FAX: 55 11 4822 8323 export@cbc.com.bc www.cbc.com.bc
CBC-BRAZIL, 3 Cuckoo Lane, Honley, Yorkshire HD7 2BR, ENGLAND / 44-1484-661062; FAX: 44-1484-663709
CCG Enterprises, 5217 E. Belknap St., Halton City, TX 76117 / 800-819-7464
CCI/Speer Div of ATK, P.O. Box 856, 2299 Snake River Ave., Lewiston, ID 83501 / 800-627-3640 or 208-746-2351
CCL Security Products, 199 Whiting St., New Britain, CT 06051 / 800-733-8588
Cedar Hill Game Calls, LLC, 238 Vic Allen Rd., Downsville, LA 71234 / 318-982-5632; FAX: 318-982-2031

Centaur Systems, Inc., 1602 Foothill Rd., Kalispell, MT 59901 / 406-755-8609; FAX: 406-755-8609
Center Lock Scope Rings, 9901 France Ct., Lakeville, MN 55044 / 952-461-2114; FAX: 952-461-2194 marklee55044@usfamily.net
Central Specialties Ltd. (See Trigger Lock Division)
Century Gun Dist. Inc., 1467 Jason Rd., Greenfield, IN 46140 / 317-462-4524
Century International Arms, Inc., 430 S. Congress Ave. Ste. 1, Delray Beach, FL 33445-4701 / 800-527-1252; FAX: 561-998-1993 support@centuryarms.com www.centuryarms.com
CFVentures, 509 Harvey Dr., Bloomington, IN 47403-1715 paladinwilltravel@yahoo.com www.caversam16.freeserve.co.uk
CH Tool & Die Co. (See 4-D Custom Die Co.), 711 N Sandusky St., P.O. Box 889, Mt. Vernon, OH 43050-0889 / 740-397-7214; FAX: 740-397-6600
Chace Leather Products, 507 Alden St., Fall River, MA 02722 / 508-678-7556; FAX: 508-675-9666 chacelea@aol.com www.chaceleather.com
Chadick's Ltd., P.O. Box 100, Terrell, TX 75160 / 214-563-7577
Chambers Flintlocks Ltd., Jim, 116 Sams Branch Rd., Candler, NC 28715 / 828-667-8361; FAX: 828-665-0852 www.flintlocks.com
Champion Shooters' Supply, P.O. Box 303, New Albany, OH 43054 / 614-855-1603; FAX: 614-855-1209
Champion Target Co., 232 Industrial Parkway, Richmond, IN 47374 / 800-441-4971
Champion's Choice, Inc., 201 International Blvd., LaVergne, TN 37086 / 615-793-4066; FAX: 615-793-4070 champ.choice@earthlink.net www.champchoice.com
Champlin Firearms, Inc., P.O. Box 3191, Woodring Airport, Enid, OK 73701 / 580-237-7388; FAX: 580-242-6922 info@champlinarms.com www.champlinarms.com
Chapman Academy of Practical Shooting, 4350 Academy Rd., Hallsville, MO 65255 / 573-696-5544; FAX: 573-696-2266 hq@chapmanacademy.com chapmanacademy.com
Chapman, J. Ken. See: OLD WEST BULLET MOULDS
Chapman Manufacturing Co., 471 New Haven Rd., P.O. Box 250, Durham, CT 06422 / 860-349-9228; FAX: 860-349-0084 sales@chapmanmfg.com www.chapmanmfg.com
Chapuis Armes, Z1 La Gravoux, BP15, 42380 P.O. Box 15, St. Bonnet-le-Chatea, FRANCE / (33)477.50.06.96; FAX: (33)477 50 10 70 info@chapuis.armes.com www.chapuis-armes.com
Charter 2000, 273 Canal St., Shelton, CT 06484 / 203-922-1652
Checkmate Refinishing, 370 Champion Dr., Brooksville, FL 34601 / 352-799-5774; FAX: 352-799-2986 checkmatecustom.com
Cheddite, France S.A., 99 Route de Lyon, F-26501, Bourg-les-Valence, FRANCE / 33-75-56-4545; FAX: 33-75-56-3587 export@cheddite.com
Chelsea Gun Club of New York City Inc., 237 Ovington Ave., Apt. D53, Brooklyn, NY 11209 / 718-836-9422; or 718-833-2704
Cherry Creek State Park Shooting Center, 12500 E. Belleview Ave., Englewood, CO 80111 / 303-693-1765
CheVron Bullets, RR1, Ottawa, IL 61350 / 815-433-2971
Cheyenne Pioneer Products, P.O. Box 28425, Kansas City, MO 64188 / 816-413-9196; FAX: 816-455-2859 cheyennepp@aol.com www.cartridgeboxes.com
Chicago Cutlery Co., 1536 Beech St., Terre Haute, IN 47804 / 800-457-2665
Chicasaw Gun Works, 4 Mi. Mkr., Pluto Rd., Box 868, Shady Spring, WV 25918-0868 / 304-763-2848; FAX: 304-763-3725
Chip McCormick Corp., P.O. Box 1560, Manchaca, TX 78652 / 800-328-2447; FAX: 512-280-4282 www.chipmccormick.com
Chipmunk (See Oregon Arms, Inc.)
Choate Machine & Tool Co., Inc., P.O. Box 218, 116 Lovers Ln., Bald Knob, AR 72010 / 501-724-6193; or 800-972-6390; FAX: 501-724-5873
Christensen Arms, 192 East 100 North, Fayette, UT 84630 / 435-528-7999; FAX: 435-528-7494 www.christensenarms.com
Christie's East, 20 Rockefeller Plz., New York, NY 10020-1902 / 212-606-0406 christics.com
Chu Tani Ind., Inc., P.O. Box 2064, Cody, WY 82414-2064
Chuck's Gun Shop, P.O. Box 597, Waldo, FL 32694 / 904-468-2264

MANUFACTURER'S DIRECTORY

Churchill (See U.S. Importer-Ellett Bros.)
Churchill, Winston G., 2838 20 Mile Stream Rd., Proctorville, VT 05153 / 802-226-7772
Churchill Glove Co., James, P.O. Box 298, Centralia, WA 98531 / 360-736-2816; FAX: 360-330-0151
CIDCO, 21480 Pacific Blvd., Sterling, VA 22170 / 703-444-5353
Cimarron F.A. Co., P.O. Box 906, Fredericksburg, TX 78624-0906 / 830-997-9090; FAX: 830-997-0802 cimgraph@koc.com www.cimarron-firearms.com
Cincinnati Swaging, 2605 Marlington Ave., Cincinnati, OH 45208
Clark Custom Guns, Inc., 336 Shootout Lane, Princeton, LA 71067 / 318-949-9884; FAX: 318-949-9829
Clark Firearms Engraving, 6347 Avon Ave., San Gabriel, CA 91775-1801 / 818-287-1652
Clarkfield Enterprises, Inc., 1032 10th Ave., Clarkfield, MN 56223 / 612-669-7140
Claro Walnut Gunstock Co., 1235 Stanley Ave., Chico, CA 95928 / 530-342-5188; FAX: 530-342-5199 wally@clarowalnutgunstocks.com www.clarowalnutgunstocks.com
Classic Arms Company, Rt 1 Box 120F, Burnet, TX 78611 / 512-756-4001
Classic Arms Corp., P.O. Box 106, Dunsmuir, CA 96025-0106 / 530-235-2000
Classic Old West Styles, 1060 Doniphan Park Circle C, El Paso, TX 79936 / 915-587-0684
Claybuster Wads & Harvester Bullets, 309 Sequoya Dr., Hopkinsville, KY 42240 / 800-922-6287; or 800-284-1746; FAX: 502-885-8088
Clean Shot Technologies, 21218 St. Andrews Blvd. Ste 504, Boca Raton, FL 33433 / 888-866-2532
Clearview Mfg. Co., Inc., 413 S. Oakley St., Fordyce, AR 71742 / 501-352-8557; FAX: 501-352-7120
Clearview Products, 3021 N. Portland, Oklahoma City, OK 73107
Cleland's Outdoor World, Inc., 10306 Airport Hwy., Swanton, OH 43558 / 419-865-4713; FAX: 419-865-5865 mail@clelands.com www.clelands.com
Clements' Custom Leathercraft, Chas, 1741 Dallas St., Aurora, CO 80010-2018 / 303-364-0403; FAX: 303-739-9824 gryphons@home.com kuntaoslcat.com
Clenzoil Worldwide Corp., Jack Fitzgerald, 25670 1st St., Westlake, OH 44145-1430 / 440-899-0482; FAX: 440-899-0483
Clift Mfg., L. R., 3821 Hammonton Rd., Marysville, CA 95901 / 916-755-3390; FAX: 916-755-3393
Clymer Mfg. Co., 1645 W. Hamlin Rd., Rochester Hills, MI 48309-3312 / 248-853-5555; FAX: 248-853-1530
C-More Systems, P.O. Box 1750, 7553 Gary Rd., Manassas, VA 20108 / 703-361-2663; FAX: 703-361-5881
Cobra Enterprises, Inc., 1960 S. Milestone Drive, Suite F, Salt Lake City, UT 84104 FAX: 801-908-8301 www.cobrapistols@networld.com
Cobra Sport S.R.I., Via Caduti Nei Lager No. 1, 56020 San Romano, Montopoli v/Arno Pi, ITALY / 0039-571-450490; FAX: 0039-571-450492
Coffin, Charles H., 3719 Scarlet Ave., Odessa, TX 79762 / 915-366-4729; FAX: 915-366-4729
Cogar's Gunsmithing, 206 Redwine Dr., Houghton Lake, MI 48629 / 517-422-4591
Coghlan's Ltd., 121 Irene St., Winnipeg, MB R3T 4C7 CANADA / 204-284-9550; FAX: 204-475-4127
Cold Steel Inc., 3036 Seaborg Ave. Ste. A, Ventura, CA 93003 / 800-255-4716; or 800-624-2363; FAX: 805-642-9727
Cole-Grip, 16135 Cohasset St., Van Nuys, CA 91406 / 818-782-4424
Coleman Co., Inc., 3600 N. Hydraulic, Wichita, KS 67219 / 800-835-3278; www.coleman.com
Cole's Gun Works, Old Bank Building, Rt. 4 Box 250, Moyock, NC 27958 / 919-435-2345
Collector's Armoury, Ltd., Tom Nelson, 9404 Gunston Cove Rd., Lorton, VA 22079 / 703-493-9120; FAX: 703-493-9424 www.collectorsarmoury.com
Collings, Ronald, 1006 Cielta Linda, Vista, CA 92083
Colonial Arms, Inc., P.O. Box 636, Selma, AL 36702-0636 / 334-872-9455; FAX: 334-872-9540 colonialarms@mindspring.com www.colonialarms.com
Colonial Repair, 47 Navarre St., Roslindale, MA 02131-4725 / 617-469-4951
Colorado Gunsmithing Academy, RR 3 Box 79B, El Campo, TX 77437 / 719-336-4099; or 800-754-2046; FAX: 719-336-9642
Colorado School of Trades, 1575 Hoyt St., Lakewood, CO 80215 / 800-234-4594; FAX: 303-233-4723
Colt Blackpowder Arms Co., 110 8th Street, Brooklyn, NY 11215 / 718-499-4678; FAX: 718-768-8056

Colt's Mfg. Co., Inc., P.O. Box 1868, Hartford, CT 06144-1868 / 800-962-COLT; or 860-236-6311; FAX: 860-244-1449
Compass Industries, Inc., 104 East 25th St., New York, NY 10010 / 212-473-2614 or 800-221-9904; FAX: 212-353-0826
Compasseco, Ltd., 151 Atkinson Hill Ave., Bardtown, KY 40004 / 502-349-0910
Competition Electronics, Inc., 3469 Precision Dr., Rockford, IL 61109 / 815-874-8001; FAX: 815-874-8181
Competitive Pistol Shop, The, 5233 Palmer Dr., Fort Worth, TX 76117-2433 / 817-834-8479
Competitor Corp., Inc., 26 Knight St. Unit 3, P.O. Box 352, Jaffrey, NH 03452 / 603-532-9483; FAX: 603-532-8209 competitorcorp@aol.com competitor-pistol.com
Component Concepts, Inc., 530 S. Springbrook Road, Newberg, OR 97132 / 503-554-8095; FAX: 503-554-9370 cci@cybcon.com www.phantomonline.com
Concealment Shop, Inc., The, 3550 E. Hwy. 80, Mesquite, TX 75149 / 972-289-8997; or 800-444-7090; FAX: 972-289-4410 info@theconcealmentshop.com www.theconcealmentshop.com
Concept Development Corp., 16610 E. Laser Drive, Suite 5, Fountain Hills, AZ 85268-6644
Conetrol Scope Mounts, 10225 Hwy. 123 S., Seguin, TX 78155 / 830-379-3030; or 800-CONETROL; FAX: 830-379-3030 email@conetrol.com www.conetrol.com
Connecticut Shotgun Mfg. Co., P.O. Box 1692, 35 Woodland St., New Britain, CT 06051 / 860-225-6581; FAX: 860-832-8707
Connecticut Valley Classics (See CVC, BPI)
Conrad, C. A., 3964 Ebert St., Winston-Salem, NC 27127 / 919-788-5469
Cook Engineering Service, 891 Highbury Rd., Vict 3133, 3133 AUSTRALIA
Cooper Arms, P.O. Box 114, Stevensville, MT 59870 / 406-777-0373; FAX: 406-777-5228
Cooper-Woodward Perfect Lube, 4120 Oesterle Rd., Helena, MT 59602 / 406-459-2287 cwperfectlube@mt.net cwperfectlube.com
Corbin Mfg. & Supply, Inc., 600 Industrial Circle, P.O. Box 2659, White City, OR 97503 / 541-826-5211; FAX: 541-826-8669 sales@corbins.com www.corbins.com
Cor-Bon Inc./Glaser LLC, P.O. Box 173, 1311 Industry Rd., Sturgis, SD 57785 / 605-347-4544; or 800-221-3489; FAX: 605-347-5055 email@corbon.com www.corbon.com
Corkys Gun Clinic, 4401 Hot Springs Dr., Greeley, CO 80634-9226 / 970-330-0516
Corry, John, 861 Princeton Ct., Neshanic Station, NJ 08853 / 908-369-8019
Cosmi Americo & Figlio S.N.C., Via Flaminia 307, Ancona, ITALY / 071-888208; FAX: 39-071-887008
Coulston Products, Inc., P.O. Box 30, 201 Ferry St. Suite 212, Easton, PA 18044-0030 / 215-253-0167; or 800-445-9927; FAX: 215-252-1511
Counter Assault, 120 Industrial Court, Kalispell, MT 59901 / 406-257-4740; FAX: 406-257-6674
Country Armourer, The, P.O. Box 308, Ashby, MA 01431-0308 / 508-827-6797; FAX: 508-827-4845
Cousin Bob's Mountain Products, 7119 Ohio River Blvd., Ben Avon, PA 15202 / 412-766-5114; FAX: 412-766-9354
CP Bullets, 1310 Industrial Hwy #5-6, South Hampton, PA 18966 / 215-953-7264; FAX: 215-953-7275
CQB Training, P.O. Box 1739, Manchester, MO 63011
Craftguard, 3624 Logan Ave., Waterloo, IA 50703 / 319-232-2959; FAX: 319-234-0804
Crandall Tool & Machine Co., 19163 21 Mile Rd., Tustin, MI 49688 / 616-829-4430
Creative Craftsman, Inc., The, 95 Highway 29 N., P.O. Box 331, Lawrenceville, GA 30246 / 404-963-2112; FAX: 404-513-9488
Creedmoor Sports, Inc., 3052 Industry St. #103, Oceanside, CA 92054 / 767-757-5529; FAX: 760-757-5558 shoot@creedmoorsports.com www.creedmoorsports.com
Creek Side Metal & Woodcrafters, Fishers Hill, VA 22626 / 703-465-3903
Creighton Audette, 19 Highland Circle, Springfield, VT 05156 / 802-885-2331
Crimson Trace Lasers, 8090 S.W. Cirrus Dr., Beverton, OR 97008 / 800-442-2406; FAX: 503-627-0166 www.crimsontrace.com
Crit'R Call (See Rocky Mountain Wildlife Products)
Crosman Airguns, Rts. 5 and 20, E. Bloomfield, NY 14443 / 716-657-6161; FAX: 716-657-5405
Crosman Blades (See Coleman Co., Inc.)

Crouse's Country Cover, P.O. Box 160, Storrs, CT 06268 / 860-423-8736
CRR, Inc./Marble's Inc., 420 Industrial Park, P.O. Box 111, Gladstone, MI 49837 / 906-428-3710; FAX: 906-428-3711
Crucelegui, Hermanos (See U.S. Importer-Mandall)
Cubic Shot Shell Co., Inc., 98 Fatima Dr., Campbell, OH 44405 / 330-755-0349
Cullity Restoration, 209 Old Country Rd., East Sandwich, MA 02537 / 508-888-1147
Cumberland Arms, 514 Shafer Road, Manchester, TN 37355 / 800-797-8414
Cumberland Mountain Arms, P.O. Box 710, Winchester, TN 37398 / 615-967-8414; FAX: 615-967-9199
Cummings Bullets, 1417 Esperanza Way, Escondido, CA 92027
Cupp, Alana, Custom Engraver, P.O. Box 207, Annabella, UT 84711 / 801-896-4834
Curly Maple Stock Blanks (See Tiger-Hunt)
Curtis Cast Bullets, 527 W. Babcock St., Bozeman, MT 59715 / 406-587-8117; FAX: 406-587-8117
Curtis Gun Shop (See Curtis Cast Bullets)
Custom Bullets by Hoffman, 2604 Peconic Ave., Seaford, NY 11783
Custom Calls, 607 N. 5th St., Burlington, IA 52601 / 319-752-4465
Custom Checkering Service, Kathy Forster, 2124 S.E. Yamhill St., Portland, OR 97214 / 503-236-5874
Custom Firearms (See Ahrends, Kim)
Custom Products (See Jones Custom Products)
Custom Shop, The, 890 Cochrane Crescent, Peterborough, ON K9H 5N3 CANADA / 705-742-6693
Custom Single Shot Rifles, 9651 Meadows Lane, Guthrie, OK 73044 / 405-282-3634
Custom Tackle and Ammo, P.O. Box 1886, Farmington, NM 87499 / 505-632-3539
Cutco Cutlery, P.O. Box 810, Olean, NY 14760 / 716-372-3111
CVA, 5988 Peachtree Corners East, Norcross, GA 30071 / 770-449-4687; FAX: 770-242-8546 info@cva.com www.cva.com
Cylinder & Slide, Inc., William R. Laughridge, 245 E. 4th St., Fremont, NE 68025 / 402-721-4277; FAX: 402-721-0263 bill@cylinder-slide.com www.clinder-slide.com
CZ USA, P.O. Box 171073, Kansas City, KS 66117 / 913-321-1811; FAX: 913-321-4901

D

D&D Gunsmiths, Ltd., 363 E. Elmwood, Troy, MI 48083 / 248-583-1512; FAX: 248-583-1524
D&G Precision Duplicators (See Greenwood Precision)
D&H Precision Tooling, 7522 Barnard Mill Rd., Ringwood, IL 60072 / 815-653-4011
D&L Industries (See D.J. Marketing)
D&L Sports, P.O. Box 651, Gillette, WY 82717 / 307-686-4008
D.C.C. Enterprises, 259 Wynburn Ave., Athens, GA 30601
D.J. Marketing, 10602 Horton Ave., Downey, CA 90241 / 310-806-0891; FAX: 310-806-6231
D.L. Unmussig Bullets, 7862 Brentford Dr., Richmond, VA 23225 / 804-320-1165; FAX: 804-320-4587
Dade Screw Machine Products, 2319 N.W. 7th Ave., Miami, FL 33127 / 305-573-5050
Daisy Outdoor Products, P.O. Box 220, Rogers, AR 72757 / 479-636-1200; FAX: 479-636-0573 www.daisy.com
Dakota (See U.S. Importer-EMF Co., Inc.)
Dakota Arms, Inc., 130 Industry Road, Sturgis, SD 57785 / 605-347-4686; FAX: 605-347-4459 info@dakotaarms.com www.dakotaarms.com
Dakota Corp., 77 Wales St., P.O. Box 543, Rutland, VT 05701 / 802-775-6062; or 800-451-4167; FAX: 802-773-3919
Daly, Charles/KBI, P.O. Box 6625, Harrisburg, PA 17112 / 866-DALY GUN
Da-Mar Gunsmith's, Inc., 102 1st St., Solvay, NY 13209
damascususa@inteliport.com, 149 Deans Farm Rd., Tyner, NC 27980 / 252-221-2010; FAX: 252-221-2010 damascususa@inteliport.com
Dan Wesson Firearms, 5169 Rt. 12 South, Norwich, NY 13815 / 607-336-1174; FAX: 607-336-2730 danwessonfirearms@citlink.net danwessonfirearms.com
Dangler, Homer L., 2870 Lee Marie Dr., Adrian, MI 49221 / 517-266-1997
Danner Shoe Mfg. Co., 12722 N.E. Airport Way, Portland, OR 97230 / 503-251-1100; or 800-345-0430; FAX: 503-251-1119

Dan's Whetstone Co., Inc., 418 Hilltop Rd., Pearcy, AR 71964 / 501-767-1616; FAX: 501-767-9598 questions@danswhetstone.com www.danswhetstone.com

Danuser Machine Co., 550 E. Third St., P.O. Box 368, Fulton, MO 65251 / 573-642-2246; FAX: 573-642-2240 sales@danuser.com www.danuser.com

Dara-Nes, Inc. (See Nesci Enterprises, Inc.)

D'Arcy Echols & Co., P.O. Box 421, Millville, UT 84326 / 435-755-6842

Darlington Gun Works, Inc., P.O. Box 698, 516 S. 52 Bypass, Darlington, SC 29532 / 803-393-3931

Dart Bell/Brass (See MAST Technology Inc.)

Darwin Hensley Gunmaker, P.O. Box 329, Brightwood, OR 97011 / 503-622-5411

Data Tech Software Systems, 19312 East Eldorado Drive, Aurora, CO 80013

Dave Norin Schrank's Smoke & Gun, 2010 Washington St., Waukegan, IL 60085 / 708-662-4034

Dave's Gun Shop, P.O. Box 2824, Casper, WY 82602-2824 / 307-754-9724

David Clark Co., Inc., P.O. Box 15054, Worcester, MA 01615 / 508-756-6216; FAX: 508-753-5827 sales@davidclark.com www.davidclark.com

David Condon, Inc., 109 E. Washington St., Middleburg, VA 22117 / 703-687-5642

David Miller Co., 3131 E. Greenlee Rd., Tucson, AZ 85716 / 520-326-3117

David R. Chicoine, 1210 Jones Street, Gastonia, NC 28052 / 704-853-0265 bnpress@quik.com www.oldwestgunsmith.com

David W. Schwartz Custom Guns, 2505 Waller St., Eau Claire, WI 54703 / 715-832-1735

Davide Pedersoli and Co., Via Artigiani 57, Gardone VT, Brescia 25063, ITALY / 030-8915000; FAX: 030-8911019 info@davidepedersoli.com www.davide_pedersoli.com

Davis, Don, 1619 Heights, Katy, TX 77493 / 713-391-3090

Davis Industries (See Cobra Enterprises, Inc.)

Davis Products, Mike, 643 Loop Dr., Moses Lake, WA 98837 / 509-765-6178; or 509-766-7281

Daystate Ltd., Birch House Lanee, Cotes Heath Staffs, ST15.022, ENGLAND / 01782-791755; FAX: 01782-791617

Dayton Traister, 4778 N. Monkey Hill Rd., P.O. Box 593, Oak Harbor, WA 98277 / 360-679-4657; FAX: 360-675-1114

D-Boone Ent., Inc., 5900 Colwyn Dr., Harrisburg, PA 17109

Dead Eye's Sport Center, 76 Daer Rd., Shickshinny, PA 18655 / 570-256-7432 deadeyeprizz@aol.com

Deepeeka Exports Pvt. Ltd., D-78, Bakel, Meerut-250-006, INDIA / 011-91-121-640363 or ; FAX: 011-91-121-640988 deepeeka@poboxes.com www.deepeeka.com

Defense Training International, Inc., 749 S. Lemay, Ste. A3-337, Ft. Collins, CO 80524 / 303-482-2520; FAX: 303-482-0548

deHaas Barrels, 20049 W. State Hwy. Z, Ridgeway, MO 64481 / 660-872-6308

Del Rey Products, P.O. Box 5134, Playa Del Rey, CA 90296-5134 / 213-823-0494

Delhi Gun House, 1374 Kashmere Gate. New Delhi 110 006, INDIA / 2940974; or 394-0974; FAX: 2917344 dgh@vsnl.com

Delorge, Ed, 6734 W. Main, Houma, LA 70360 / 985-223-0206 delorge@triparish.net www.eddelorge.com

Del-Sports, Inc., Dave Budin, P.O. Box 685, 817 Main St., Margaretville, NY 12455 / 845-586-4103; FAX: 845-586-4105

Delta Arms Ltd., P.O. Box 1000, Delta, VT 84624-1000

Delta Enterprises, 284 Hagemann Drive, Livermore, CA 94550

Delta Frangible Ammunition LLC, P.O. Box 2350, Stafford, VA 22555-2350 / 540-720-5778; or 800-339-1933; FAX: 540-720-5667 dfa@dfanet.com www.dfanet.com

Dem-Bart Checkering Tools, Inc., 1825 Bickford Ave., Snohomish, WA 98290 / 360-568-7356 walt@dembartco.com www.dembartco.com

Denver Instrument Co., 6542 Fig St., Arvada, CO 80004 / 800-321-1135; or 303-431-7255; FAX: 303-423-4831

DeSantis Holster & Leather Goods, Inc., 431 Bayview Ave., Amityville, NY 11701 / 631-841-6300; FAX: 631-841-6320 www.desantisholster.com

Desert Mountain Mfg., P.O. Box 130184, Coram, MT 59913 / 800-477-0762; or 406-387-5361; FAX: 406-387-5361

Detonics USA, 53 Perimeter Center East #200, Atlanta, GA 30346 / 866-759-1169

DGR Custom Rifles, 4191 37th Ave. SE, Tappen, ND 58487 / 701-327-8135

DGS, Inc., Dale A. Storey, 1117 E. 12th, Casper, WY 82601 / 307-237-2414; FAX: 307-237-2414 dalest@trib.com www.dgsrifle.com

DHB Products, 336 River View Dr., Verona, VA 24482-2547 / 703-836-2648

Diamond Machining Technology Inc. (See DMT)

Diamond Mfg. Co., P.O. Box 174, Wyoming, PA 18644 / 800-233-9601

Dibble, Derek A., 555 John Downey Dr., New Britain, CT 06051 / 203-224-2630

Dietz Gun Shop & Range, Inc., 421 Range Rd., New Braunfels, TX 78132 / 210-885-4662

Dilliott Gunsmithing, Inc., 657 Scarlett Rd., Dandridge, TN 37725 / 865-397-9204 gunsmithd@aol.com dilliottgunsmithing.com

Dillon Precision Products, Inc., 8009 East Dillon's Way, Scottsdale, AZ 85260 / 480-948-8009; or 800-762-3845; FAX: 480-998-2786 sales@dillonprecision.com www.dillonprecision.com

Dina Arms Corporation, P.O. Box 46, Royersford, PA 19468 / 610-287-0266; FAX: 610-287-0266

Dixie Gun Works, P.O. Box 130, Union City, TN 38281 / 731-885-0700; FAX: 731-885-0440 info@dixiegunworks.com www.dixiegunworks.com

Dixon Muzzleloading Shop, Inc., 9952 Kunkels Mill Rd., Kempton, PA 19529 / 610-756-6271 dixonmuzzleloading.com

DKT, Inc., 14623 Vera Dr., Union, MI 49130-9744 / 800-741-7083 orders; FAX: 616-641-2015

DLO Mfg., 10807 SE Foster Ave., Arcadia, FL 33821-7304

DMT-Diamond Machining Technology, Inc., 85 Hayes Memorial Dr., Marlborough, MA 01752 FAX: 508-485-3924

Dohring Bullets, 100 W. 8 Mile Rd., Ferndale, MI 48220

Dolbare, Elizabeth, P.O. Box 502, Dubois, WY 82513-0502 / 307-450-7500 edolbare@hotmail.com www.scrimshaw-engraving.com

Domino, P.O. Box 108, 20019 Settimo Milanese, Milano, ITALY / 1-39-2-33512040; FAX: 1-39-2-33511587

Don Klein Custom Guns, 433 Murray Park Dr., Ripon, WI 54971 / 920-748-2931 daklein@charter.net www.donkleincustomguns.com

Donnelly, C. P., 405 Kubli Rd., Grants Pass, OR 97527 / 541-846-6604

Doskocil Mfg. Co., Inc., P.O. Box 1246, 4209 Barnett, Arlington, TX 76017 / 817-467-5116; FAX: 817-472-9810

Douglas Barrels, Inc., 5504 Big Tyler Rd., Charleston, WV 25313-1398 / 304-776-1341; FAX: 304-776-8560 www.benchrest.com/douglas

Downsizer Corp., P.O. Box 710316, Santee, CA 92072-0316 / 619-448-5510 www.downsizer.com

DPMS (Defense Procurement Manufacturing Services, Inc.), 13983 Industry Ave., Becker, MN 55308 / 800-578-DPMS; or 763-261-5600; FAX: 763-261-5599

Dr. O's Products Ltd., P.O. Box 111, Niverville, NY 12130 / 518-784-3333; FAX: 518-784-2800

Drain, Mark, SE 3211 Kamilche Point Rd., Shelton, WA 98584 / 206-426-5452

Dremel Mfg. Co., 4915-21st St., Racine, WI 53406

Dri-Slide, Inc., 411 N. Darling, Fremont, MI 49412 / 616-924-3950

Dropkick, 1460 Washington Blvd., Williamsport, PA 17701 / 717-326-6561; FAX: 717-326-4950

DS Arms, Inc., P.O. Box 370, 27 West 990 Industrial Ave., Barrington, IL 60010 / 847-277-7258; FAX: 847-277-7259 www.dsarms.com

DTM International, Inc., 40 Joslyn Rd., P.O. Box 5, Lake Orion, MI 48362 / 313-693-6670

Duane A. Hobbie Gunsmithing, 2412 Pattie Ave., Wichita, KS 67216 / 316-264-8266

Duane's Gun Repair (See DGR Custom Rifles)

Dubber, Michael W., P.O. Box 312, Evansville, IN 47702 / 812-424-9000; FAX: 812-424-6551

Duffy, Charles E. (See Guns Antique & Modern DBA), Williams Ln., P.O. Box 2, West Hurley, NY 12491 / 914-679-2997

Du-Lite Corp., 171 River Rd., Middletown, CT 06457 / 203-347-2505; FAX: 203-347-9404

Dumoulin, Ernest, Rue Florent Boclinville 8-10, 13-4041, Votten, BELGIUM / 41 27 78 92

Duncan's Gun Works, Inc., 1619 Grand Ave., San Marcos, CA 92069 / 760-727-0515

DunLyon R&D, Inc., 52151 E. U.S. Hwy. 60, Miami, AZ 85539 / 928-473-9027

Duofold, Inc., RD 3 Rt. 309, Valley Square Mall, Tamaqua, PA 18252 / 717-386-2666; FAX: 717-386-3652

Dybala Gun Shop, P.O. Box 1024, FM 3156, Bay City, TX 77414 / 409-245-0866

Dykstra, Doug, 411 N. Darling, Fremont, MI 49412 / 616-924-3950

Dynalite Products, Inc., 215 S. Washington St., Greenfield, OH 45123 / 513-981-2124

Dynamit Nobel-RWS, Inc., 81 Ruckman Rd., Closter, NJ 07624 / 201-767-7971; FAX: 201-767-1589

E

E&L Mfg., Inc., 4177 Riddle Bypass Rd., Riddle, OR 97469 / 541-874-2137; FAX: 541-874-3107

E. Arthur Brown Co. Inc., 4353 Hwy. 27 E., Alexandria, MN 56308 / 320-762-8847; FAX: 320-763-4310 www.eabco.com

E.A.A. Corp., P.O. Box 1299, Sharpes, FL 32959 / 407-639-4842; or 800-536-4442; FAX: 407-639-7006

Eagan, Donald V., P.O. Box 196, Benton, PA 17814 / 717-925-6134

Eagle Arms, Inc. (See ArmaLite, Inc.)

Eagle Grips, Eagle Business Center, 460 Randy Rd., Carol Stream, IL 60188 / 800-323-6144; or 708-260-0400; FAX: 708-260-0486

Eagle Imports, Inc., 1750 Brielle Ave., Unit B1, Wanamassa, NJ 07712 / 732-493-0333; FAX: 732-493-0301 gsodini@aol.com www.bersa-llama.com

E-A-R, Inc., Div. of Cabot Safety Corp., 5457 W. 79th St., Indianapolis, IN 46268 / 800-327-3431; FAX: 800-488-8007

EAW (See U.S. Importer-New England Custom Gun Serv

Eckelman Gunsmithing, 3125 133rd St. SW, Fort Ripley, MN 56449 / 218-829-3176

Ed Brown Products, Inc., P.O. Box 492, Perry, MO 63462 / 573-565-3261; FAX: 573-565-2791 edbrown@edbrown.com www.edbrown.com

Edenpine, Inc. c/o Six Enterprises, Inc., 320 D Turtle Creek Ct., San Jose, CA 95125 / 408-999-0201; FAX: 408-999-0216

EdgeCraft Corp., S. Weiner, 825 Southwood Rd., Avondale, PA 19311 / 610-268-0500; or 800-342-3255; FAX: 610-268-3545 www.edgecraft.com

Edmisten Co., P.O. Box 1293, Boone, NC 28607

Edmund Scientific Co., 101 E. Gloucester Pike, Barrington, NJ 08033 / 609-543-6250

Ed's Gun House, Ed Kukowski, P.O. Box 62, Minnesota City, MN 55959 / 507-689-2925

Effebi SNC-Dr. Franco Beretta, via Rossa, 4, 25062, ITALY / 030-2751955; FAX: 030-2180414

Eggleston, Jere D., 400 Saluda Ave., Columbia, SC 29205 / 803-799-3402

Eichelberger Bullets, Wm., 158 Crossfield Rd., King Of Prussia, PA 19406

Ekol Leather Care, P.O. Box 2652, West Lafayette, IN 47906 / 317-463-2250; FAX: 317-463-7004

El Paso Saddlery Co., P.O. Box 27194, El Paso, TX 79926 / 915-544-2233; FAX: 915-544-2535 info@epsaddlery.com www.epsaddlery.com

Electro Prismatic Collimators, Inc., 1441 Manatt St., Lincoln, NE 68521

Electronic Shooters Protection, Inc., 15290 Gadsden Ct., Brighton, CO 80603 / 800-797-7791; FAX: 303-659-8668 esp@usa.net espamerican.com

Eley Ltd., Selco Way Minworth Industrial Estate, Minworth Sutton Coldfield, West Midlands, D70 1DA ENGLAND / 44 0 121-313-4567; FAX: 44 0 121-313-4568 www.eley.co.uk

Elite Ammunition, P.O. Box 3251, Oakbrook, IL 60522 / 708-366-9006

Ellett Bros., 267 Columbia Ave., P.O. Box 128, Chapin, SC 29036 / 803-345-3751; or 800-845-3711; FAX: 803-345-1820 www.ellettbrothers.com

Ellicott Arms, Inc. / Woods Pistolsmithing, 8390 Sunset Dr., Ellicott City, MD 21043 / 410-465-7979

EMAP USA, 6420 Wilshire Blvd., Los Angeles, CA 90048 / 213-782-2000; FAX: 213-782-2867

Emerging Technologies, Inc. (See Laseraim Technologies, Inc.)

EMF Co. Inc., 1900 E. Warner Ave., Suite 1-D, Santa Ana, CA 92705 / 949-261-6611; FAX: 949-756-0133

MANUFACTURER'S DIRECTORY

Empire Cutlery Corp., 12 Kruger Ct., Clifton, NJ 07013 / 201-472-5155; FAX: 201-779-0759

Empire Rifles, P.O. Box 406, Meriden, NH 03770 info@empirerifles.com www.empirerifles.com

English, Inc., A.G., 708 S. 12th St., Broken Arrow, OK 74012 / 918-251-3399 www.agenglish.com

Engraving Artistry, 36 Alto Rd., Burlington, CT 06013 / 860-673-6837 bobburt44@hotmail.com

Enguix Import-Export, Alpujarras 58, Alzira, Valencia, SPAIN / (96) 241 43 95; FAX: (96) 241 43 95

Enhanced Presentations, Inc., 5929 Market St., Wilmington, NC 28405 / 910-799-1622; FAX: 910-799-1078

Enlow, Charles, Box 895, Beaver, OK 73932 / 405-625-4487

Ensign-Bickford Co., The, 660 Hopmeadow St., Simsbury, CT 06070

Entreprise Arms, Inc., 5321 Irwindale Ave., Irwindale, CA 91706-2025 / 626-962-8712; FAX: 626-962-4692 www.entreprise.com

EPC, 1441 Manatt St., Lincoln, NE 68521 / 402-476-3946

Erhardt, Dennis, 4508 N. Montana Ave., Helena, MT 59602 / 406-442-4533

Essex Arms, P.O. Box 363, Island Pond, VT 05846 / 802-723-6203; FAX: 802-723-6203

Estate Cartridge, Inc., 900 Bob Ehlen Dr., Anoka, MN 55303-7502 / 409-856-7277; FAX: 409-856-5486

Euber Bullets, No. Orwell Rd., Orwell, VT 05760 / 802-948-2621

Euroarms of America, Inc., P.O. Box 3277, Winchester, VA 22604 / 540-662-1863; FAX: 540-662-4464 www.euroarms.net

Euro-Imports, 2221 Upland Ave. S., Pahrump, NV 89048 / 775-751-6671; FAX: 775-751-6671

European American Armory Corp. (See E.A.A. Corp.)

Eversull Co., Inc., 1 Tracemont, Boyce, LA 71409 / 318-793-8728; FAX: 318-793-5483 bestguns@aol.com

Evolution Gun Works, Inc., 48 Belmont Ave., Quakertown, PA 18951-1347 www.egw-guns.com

Excalibur Electro Optics, Inc., P.O. Box 400, Fogelsville, PA 18051-0400 / 610-391-9105; FAX: 610-391-9220

Excalibur Publications, P.O. Box 89667, Tucson, AZ 85752 / 520-575-9057 excallibureditor@earthlink.net

Excel Industries, Inc., 4510 Carter Ct., Chino, CA 91710 / 909-627-2404; FAX: 909-627-7817

Executive Protection Institute, P.O. Box 802, Berryville, VA 22611 / 540-554-2540; FAX: 540-554-2558 ruk@crosslink.net www.personalprotecion.com

Eze-Lap Diamond Prods., P.O. Box 2229, 15164 W. State St., Westminster, CA 92683 / 714-847-1555; FAX: 714-897-0280

E-Z-Way Systems, P.O. Box 4310, Newark, OH 43058-4310 / 614-345-6645; or 800-848-2072; FAX: 614-345-6600

F

F&W Publications, Inc., 700 E. State St., Iola, WI 54990 / 715-445-2214; FAX: 715-445-4087

F.A.I.R., Via Gitti, 41, 25060 Marcheno Bresc, ITALY / 030 861162-8610344; FAX: 030 8610179 info@fair.it www.fair.it

Fabarm S.p.A., Via Averolda 31, 25039 Travagliato, Brescia, ITALY / 030-6863629; FAX: 030-6863684 info@fabarm.com www.fabarm.com

Fagan Arms, 22952 15 Mile Rd., Clinton Township, MI 48035 / 810-465-4637; FAX: 810-792-6996

Faith Associates, P.O. Box 549, Flat Rock, NC 28731-0549 FAX: 828-697-6827

Falcon Industries, Inc., P.O. Box 1690, Edgewood, NM 87015 / 505-281-3783; FAX: 505-281-3991 shines@ergogrips.net www.ergogrips.net

Far North Outfitters, Box 1252, Bethel, AK 99559

Farm Form Decoys, Inc., 1602 Biovu, P.O. Box 748, Galveston, TX 77553 / 409-744-0762; or 409-765-6361; FAX: 409-765-8513

Farr Studio, Inc., 17149 Bournbrook Ln., Jeffersonton, VA 22724-1796 / 615-638-8825

Farrar Tool Co., Inc., 11855 Cog Hill Dr., Whittier, CA 90601-1902 / 310-863-4367; FAX: 310-863-5123

Faulhaber Wildlocker, Dipl.-Ing. Norbert Wittasek, Seilergasse 2, A-1010 Wien, AUSTRIA / 43-1-5137001; FAX: 43-1-5137001 faulhaber1@utanet.at

Faulk's Game Call Co., Inc., 616 18th St., Lake Charles, LA 70601 / 337-436-9726; FAX: 337-494-7205

Faust Inc., T. G., 544 Minor St., Reading, PA 19602 / 610-375-8549; FAX: 610-375-4488

Fautheree, Andy, P.O. Box 4607, Pagosa Springs, CO 81157 / 970-731-5003; FAX: 970-731-5009

Feather, Flex Decoys, 4500 Doniphan Dr., Neosho, MO 64850 / 318-746-8596; FAX: 318-742-4815

Federal Cartridge Co., 900 Ehlen Dr., Anoka, MN 55303 / 612-323-2300; FAX: 612-323-2506

Federal Champion Target Co., 232 Industrial Pkwy., Richmond, IN 47374 / 800-441-4971; FAX: 317-966-7747

Federated-Fry (See Fry Metals)

FEG, Budapest, Soroksariut 158, H-1095, HUNGARY

Feinwerkbau Westinger & Altenburger, Neckarstrasse 43, 78727, Oberndorf a. N., GERMANY / 07423-814-0; FAX: 07423-814-200 info@feinwerkbau.de www.feinwerkbau.de

Felk Pistols, Inc., P.O. Box 33, Bracey, VA 23919 / 434-636-2537; FAX: 208-988-4834

Ferguson, Bill, P.O. Box 1238, Sierra Vista, AZ 85636 / 520-458-5321; FAX: 520-458-9125

Ferguson, Bill. See: BULLET METALS

FERLIB, Via Parte 33 Marcheno/BS, Marcheno/BS, ITALY / 00390308610191; FAX: 00390308966882 info@ferlib.com www.ferlib.com

Ferris Firearms, 7110 F.M. 1863, Bulverde, TX 78163 / 210-980-4424

Fibron Products, Inc., P.O. Box 430, Buffalo, NY 14209-0430 / 716-886-2378; FAX: 716-886-2394

Fieldsport Ltd., Bryan Bilinski, 3313 W. South Airport Rd., Traverse City, MI 49684 / 616-933-0767

Fiocchi Munizioni S.A. (See U.S. Importer-Fiocch

Fiocchi of America, Inc., 5030 Fremont Rd., Ozark, MO 65721 / 417-725-4118; or 800-721-2666; FAX: 417-725-1039

Firearm Brokers, 4143 Taylor Blvd., Louisville, KY 40215 / 502-366-0555 firearmbrokers@aol.com www.firearmbrokers.com

Firearm Training Center, The, 9555 Blandville Rd., West Paducah, KY 42086 / 502-554-5886

Firearms Co. Ltd. / Alpine (See U.S. Importer-Mandall

Firearms Engraver's Guild of America, 3011 E. Pine Dr., Flagstaff, AZ 86004 / 928-527-8427 fegainfo@fega.com

Fisher, Jerry A., 631 Crane Mt. Rd., Big Fork, MT 59911 / 406-837-2722

Fisher Custom Firearms, 2199 S. Kittredge Way, Aurora, CO 80013 / 303-755-3710

Fitzgerald, Jack. See: CLENZOIL WORLDWIDE CORP.

Flambeau, Inc., 15981 Valplast Rd., Middlefield, OH 44062 / 216-632-1631; FAX: 216-632-1581 www.flambeau.com

Flayderman & Co., Inc., P.O. Box 2446, Fort Lauderdale, FL 33303 / 954-761-8855 www.flayderman.com

Fleming Firearms, 7720 E. 126th St. N., Collinsville, OK 74021-7016 / 918-665-3624

Fletcher-Bidwell, LLC, 305 E. Terhune St., Viroqua, WI 54665-1631 / 866-637-1860 fbguns@netscape.net

Flintlocks, Etc., 160 Rossiter Rd., P.O. Box 181, Richmond, MA 01254 / 413-698-3822; FAX: 413-698-3866 flintetc@berkshire.rr.com

Flitz International Ltd., 821 Mohr Ave., Waterford, WI 53185 / 414-534-5898; FAX: 414-534-2991

Fluoramics, Inc., 18 Industrial Ave., Mahwah, NJ 07430 / 800-922-0075; FAX: 201-825-7035

Flynn's Custom Guns, P.O. Box 7461, Alexandria, LA 71306 / 318-455-7130

FN Manufacturing, P.O. Box 24257, Columbia, SC 29224 / 803-736-0522

Folks, Donald E., 205 W. Lincoln St., Pontiac, IL 61764 / 815-844-7901

Foothills Video Productions, Inc., P.O. Box 651, Spartanburg, SC 29304 / 803-573-7023; or 800-782-5358

Foredom Electric Co., Rt. 6, 16 Stony Hill Rd., Bethel, CT 06801 / 203-792-8622

Forgett, Valmore. See: NAVY ARMS COMPANY

Forgreens Tool & Mfg., Inc., P.O. Box 955, Robert Lee, TX 76945 / 915-453-2800; FAX: 915-453-2460

Forkin Custom Classics, 205 10th Ave. S.W., White Sulphur Spring, MT 59645 / 406-547-2344

Forrest Tool Co., P.O. Box 768, 44380 Gordon Ln., Mendocino, CA 95460 / 707-937-2141; FAX: 717-937-1817

Forster, Kathy (See Custom Checkering)

Forster, Larry L., Box 212, 216 Hwy. 13 E., Gwinner, ND 58040-0212 / 701-678-2475

Forster Products, Inc., 310 E. Lanark Ave., Lanark, IL 61046 / 815-493-6360; FAX: 815-493-2371 info@forsterproducts.com www.forsterproductscom

Fort Hill Gunstocks, 12807 Fort Hill Rd., Hillsboro, OH 45133 / 513-466-2763

Fort Knox Security Products, 1051 N. Industrial Park Rd., Orem, UT 84057 / 801-224-7233; or 800-821-5216; FAX: 801-226-5493

Forthofer's Gunsmithing & Knifemaking, 5535 U.S. Hwy. 93S, Whitefish, MT 59937-8411 / 406-862-2674

Fortune Products, Inc., 205 Hickory Creek Rd., Marble Falls, TX 78654 / 210-693-6111; FAX: 210-693-6394 randy@accusharp.com

Forty-Five Ranch Enterprises, Box 1080, Miami, OK 74355-1080 / 918-542-5875

Foster, . See: ACCURACY INTERNATIONAL

Fountain Products, 492 Prospect Ave., West Springfield, MA 01089 / 413-781-4651; FAX: 413-733-8217

Fowler Bullets, 806 Dogwood Dr., Gastonia, NC 28054 / 704-867-3259

Fowler, Bob (See Black Powder Products)

Fox River Mills, Inc., P.O. Box 298, 227 Poplar St., Osage, IA 50461 / 515-732-3798; FAX: 515-732-5128

Frank Knives, 13868 NW Keleka Pl., Seal Rock, OR 97376 / 541-563-3041; FAX: 541-563-3041

Frank Mittermeier, Inc., P.O. Box 1, Bronx, NY 10465

Franzen International, Inc. (See U.S. Importer-Importer Co.)

Fred F. Wells/Wells Sport Store, 110 N. Summit St., Prescott, AZ 86301 / 928-445-3655 www.wellssportstore@cableone.net

Freedom Arms, Inc., P.O. Box 150, Freedom, WY 83120 / 307-883-2468; FAX: 307-883-2005

Fremont Tool Works, 1214 Prairie, Ford, KS 67842 / 316-369-2327

Front Sight Firearms Training Institute, P.O. Box 2619, Aptos, CA 95001 / 800-987-7719; FAX: 408-684-2137

Frontier, 2910 San Bernardo, Laredo, TX 78040 / 956-723-5409; FAX: 956-723-1774

Frontier Arms Co., Inc., 401 W. Rio Santa Cruz, Green Valley, AZ 85614-3932

Frontier Products Co., 2401 Walker Rd., Roswell, NM 88201-8950 / 614-262-9357

Frontier Safe Co., 3201 S. Clinton St., Fort Wayne, IN 46806 / 219-744-7233; FAX: 219-744-6678

Frost Cutlery Co., P.O. Box 22636, Chattanooga, TN 37422 / 615-894-6079; FAX: 615-894-9576

Fry Metals, 4100 6th Ave., Altoona, PA 16602 / 814-946-1611

Fujinon, Inc., 10 High Point Dr., Wayne, NJ 07470 / 201-633-5600; FAX: 201-633-5216

Fullmer, Geo. M., 2499 Mavis St., Oakland, CA 94601 / 510-533-4193

Fulton Armory, 8725 Bollman Place No. 1, Savage, MD 20763 / 301-490-9485; FAX: 301-490-9547 www.fulton.armory.com

Furr Arms, 91 N. 970 West, Orem, UT 84057 / 801-226-3877; FAX: 801-226-3877

G

G&H Decoys, Inc., P.O. Box 1208, Hwy. 75 North, Henryetta, OK 74437 / 918-652-3314; FAX: 918-652-3400

G.C. Bullet Co., Inc., 40 Mokelumne River Dr., Lodi, CA 95240

G.G. & G., 3602 E. 42nd Stravenue, Tucson, AZ 85713 / 520-748-7167; FAX: 520-748-7583 ggg&3@aol.com www.ggg&3.com

G.H. Enterprises Ltd., Bag 10, Okotoks, AB T0L 1T0 CANADA / 403-938-6070

G.U., Inc. (See U.S. Importer-New SKB Arms Co.)

G96 Products Co., Inc., 85 5th Ave., Bldg. #6, Paterson, NJ 07544 / 973-684-4050; FAX: 973-684-3848 g96prod@aol

Gage Manufacturing, 663 W. 7th St., A, San Pedro, CA 90731 / 310-832-3546

Gaillard Barrels, Box 68, St. Brieux, SK S0K 3V0 CANADA / 306-752-3769; FAX: 306-752-5969

Galati International, P.O. Box 10, 616 Burley Ridge Rd., Wesco, MO 65586 / 636-584-0785; FAX: 573-775-4308 support@galatiinternational.com www.galatiinternational.com

Galaxy Imports Ltd., Inc., P.O. Box 3361, Victoria, TX 77903 / 361-573-4867; FAX: 361-576-9622 galaxy@cox-internet.com

GALCO International Ltd., 2019 W. Quail Ave., Phoenix, AZ 85027 / 623-474-7070; FAX: 623-582-6854 customerservice@usgalco.com www.usgalco.com

Galena Industries AMT, 5463 Diaz St., Irwindale, CA 91706 / 626-856-8883; FAX: 626-856-8887

Gamba S.p.A. Societa Armi Bresciane Srl, Renato, Via Artigiani 93, ITALY / 30-8911640; FAX: 30-8911648

Gamba, USA, P.O. Box 60452, Colorado Springs, CO 80960 / 719-578-1145; FAX: 719-444-0731

Game Haven Gunstocks, 13750 Shire Rd., Wolverine, MI 49799 / 616-525-8257

Gamebore Division, Polywad, Inc., P.O. Box 7916, Macon, GA 31209 / 478-477-0669; or 800-998-0669
Gamo (See U.S. Importers-Arms United Corp., Daisy M
Gamo USA, Inc., 3911 SW 47th Ave., Suite 914, Fort Lauderdale, FL 33314 / 954-581-5822; FAX: 954-581-3165 gamousa@gate.net www.gamo.com
Gander Mountain, Inc., 12400 Fox River Rd., Wilmont, WI 53192 / 414-862-6848
GAR, 590 McBride Ave., West Paterson, NJ 07424 / 973-754-1114; FAX: 973-754-1114 garreloading@aol.com www.garreloading.com
Garcia National Gun Traders, Inc., 225 SW 22nd Ave., Miami, FL 33135 / 305-642-2355
Garrett Cartridges, Inc., P.O. Box 178, Chehalis, WA 98532 / 360-736-0702 www.garrettcartridges.com
Garthwaite Pistolsmith, Inc., Jim, 12130 State Route 405, Watsontown, PA 17777 / 570-538-1566; FAX: 570-538-2965 www.garthwaite.com
Gary Goudy Classic Stocks, 1512 S. 5th St., Dayton, WA 99328 / 509-382-2726 goudy@innw.net
Gary Reeder Custom Guns, 2601 7th Ave. E., Flagstaff, AZ 86004 / 928-526-3313; FAX: 928-527-0840 gary@reedercustomguns.com www.reedercustomguns.com
Gator Guns & Repair, 7952 Kenai Spur Hwy., Kenai, AK 99611-8311
Gaucher Armes, S.A., 46 rue DesJoyaux, 42000, Saint-Etienne, FRANCE / 04-77-33-38-92; FAX: 04-77-61-95-72
GDL Enterprises, 409 Le Gardeur, Slidell, LA 70460 / 504-649-0693
Gehmann, Walter (See Huntington Die Specialties)
Genco, P.O. Box 5704, Asheville, NC 28803
Genecco Gun Works, 10512 Lower Sacramento Rd., Stockton, CA 95210 / 209-951-0706; FAX: 209-931-3872
Gene's Custom Guns, P.O. Box 10534, White Bear Lake, MN 55110 / 651-429-5105; FAX: 651-429-7365
Gentex Corp., 5 Tinkham Ave., Derry, NH 03038 / 603-434-0311; FAX: 603-434-3002 sales@derry.gentexcorp.com www.derry.gentexcorp.com
Gentner Bullets, 109 Woodlawn Ave., Upper Darby, PA 19082 / 610-352-9396 dongentner@rcn.com www.gentnerbullets.com
Gentry Custom LLC, 314 N. Hoffman, Belgrade, MT 59714 / 406-388-GUNS gentryshop@earthlink.net www.gentrycustom.com
George & Roy's, P.O. Box 2125, Sisters, OR 97759-2125 / 503-228-5424; or 800-553-3022; FAX: 503-225-9409
George Hoenig, Inc., 6521 Morton Dr., Boise, ID 83704 / 208-375-1116; FAX: 208-375-1116
George Ibberson (Sheffield) Ltd., 25-31 Allen St., Sheffield, S3 7AW ENGLAND / 0114-2766123; FAX: 0114-2738465 sales@egginton groupco.uk www.eggintongroup.co.uk
Gerber Legendary Blades, 14200 SW 72nd Ave., Portland, OR 97223 / 503-639-6161; or 800-950-6161; FAX: 503-684-7008
Gervais, Mike, 3804 S. Cruise Dr., Salt Lake City, UT 84109 / 801-277-7729
Getz Barrel Company, P.O. Box 88, 426 E. Market St., Beavertown, PA 17813 / 570-658-7263; FAX: 570-658-4110 www.getzbrl.com
Giacomo Sporting USA, 6234 Stokes Lee Center Rd., Lee Center, NY 13363
Gibbs Rifle Co., Inc., 219 Lawn St., Martinsburg, WV 25401 / 304-262-1651; FAX: 304-262-1658 support@gibbsrifle.com www.gibbsrifle.com
Gil Hebard Guns, Inc., 125 Public Square, Knoxville, IL 61448 / 309-289-2700; FAX: 309-289-2233
Gilbert Equipment Co., Inc., 960 Downtowner Rd., Mobile, AL 36609 / 205-344-3322
Gillmann, Edwin, 33 Valley View Dr., Hanover, PA 17331 / 717-632-1662 gillmaned@superpa.net
Gilmore Sports Concepts, Inc., 5949 S. Garnett Rd., Tulsa, OK 74146 / 918-250-3810; FAX: 918-250-3845 info@gilmoresports.com www.gilmoresports.com
Glacier Glove, 4890 Aircenter Circle, Suite 210, Reno, NV 89502 / 702-825-8225; FAX: 702-825-6544
Glaser LLC, P.O. Box 173, Sturgis, SD 57785 / 605-347-4544; or 800-221-3489; FAX: 605-347-5055 email@corbon.com www.safetyslug.com
Glaser Safety Slug, Inc., P.O. Box 8223, Foster City, CA 94404 / 800-221-3489; FAX: 510-785-6685 safetyslug.com

Glass, Herb, P.O. Box 25, Bullville, NY 10915 / 914-361-3021
Glimm, Jerome. See: GLIMM'S CUSTOM GUN ENGRAVING
Glimm's Custom Gun Engraving, Jerome C. Glimm, 19 S. Maryland, Conrad, MT 59425 / 406-278-3574 jandlglimm@mcn.net www.gunengraver.biz
Glock GmbH, P.O. Box 50, A-2232, Deutsch, Wagram, AUSTRIA
Glock, Inc., P.O. Box 369, Smyrna, GA 30081 / 770-432-1202; FAX: 770-433-8719
Glynn Scobey Duck & Goose Calls, Rt. 3, Box 37, Newbern, TN 38059 / 731-643-6128
GML Products, Inc., 394 Laredo Dr., Birmingham, AL 35226 / 205-979-4867
Goens, Dale W., P.O. Box 224, Cedar Crest, NM 87008 / 505-281-5419
Goergen's Gun Shop, Inc., 17985 538th Ave., Austin, MN 55912 / 507-433-9280
GOEX, Inc., P.O. Box 659, Doyline, LA 71023-0659 / 318-382-9300; FAX: 318-382-9303 mfahringer@goexpowder.com www.goexpowder.com
Golden Age Arms Co., 115 E. High St., Ashley, OH 43003 / 614-747-2488
Golden Bear Bullets, 3065 Fairfax Ave., San Jose, CA 95148 / 408-238-9515
Gonic Arms North American Arms, Inc., 134 Flagg Rd., Gonic, NH 03839 / 603-332-8456; or 603-332-8457
Goodling's Gunsmithing, 1950 Stoverstown Rd., Spring Grove, PA 17362 / 717-225-3350
Goodwin, Fred. See: GOODWIN'S GUNS
Goodwin's Guns, Fred Goodwin, Silver Ridge, ME 04776 / 207-365-4451
Gotz Bullets, 11426 Edgemere Ter., Roscoe, IL 61073-8232
Gould & Goodrich Leather, Inc., 709 E. McNeil St., Lillington, NC 27546 / 910-893-2071; FAX: 910-893-4742 info@gouldusa.com www.gouldusa.com
Gournet Artistic Engraving, Geoffroy Gournet, 820 Paxinosa Ave., Easton, PA 18042 / 610-559-0710 www.geoffroygournet.com
Gournet, Geoffroy. See: GOURNET ARTISTIC ENGRAVING
Grace, Charles E., 718 E. 2nd, Trinidad, CO 81082 / 719-846-9435 chuckgrace@sensonics.org
Grace Metal Products, P.O. Box 67, Elk Rapids, MI 49629 / 616-264-8133
Graf & Sons, 4050 S. Clark St., Mexico, MO 65265 / 573-581-2266; FAX: 573-581-2875 customerservice@grafs.com www.grafs.com
Grand Slam Hunting Products, Box 121, 25454 Military Rd., Cascade, MD 21719 / 301-241-4900; FAX: 301-241-4900 rlj6call@aol.com
Granite Mountain Arms, Inc., 3145 W. Hidden Acres Trail, Prescott, AZ 86305 / 520-541-9758; FAX: 520-445-6826
Grant, Howard V., Hiawatha 15, Woodruff, WI 54568 / 715-356-7146
Graphics Direct, P.O. Box 372421, Reseda, CA 91337-2421 / 818-344-9002
Graves Co., 1800 Andrews Ave., Pompano Beach, FL 33069 / 800-327-9103; FAX: 305-960-0301
Grayback Wildcats, Mike Beeks, 5306 Bryant Ave., Klamath Falls, OR 97603 / 541-884-1072; FAX: 541-884-1072 graybackwildcats@aol.com
Graybill's Gun Shop, 1035 Ironville Pike, Columbia, PA 17512 / 717-684-2739
Great American Gunstock Co., 3420 Industrial Drive, Yuba City, CA 95993 / 800-784-4867; FAX: 530-671-3906 gunstox@hotmail.com www.gunstocks.com
Great Lakes Airguns, 6175 S. Park Ave., Hamburg, NY 14075 / 716-648-6666; FAX: 716-648-6666 www.greatlakesairguns.com
Green, Arthur S., 485 S. Robertson Blvd., Beverly Hills, CA 90211 / 310-274-1283
Green, Roger M., P.O. Box 984, 435 E. Birch, Glenrock, WY 82637 / 307-436-9804
Green Head Game Call Co., RR 1, Box 33, Lacon, IL 61540 / 309-246-2155
Green Mountain Rifle Barrel Co., Inc., P.O. Box 2670, 153 W. Main St., Conway, NH 03818 / 603-447-1095; FAX: 603-447-1099 info@gmriflebarrel.com www.gmriflebarrel.com
Greenwood Precision, P.O. Box 407, Rogersville, MO 65742 / 417-725-2330
Greg Gunsmithing Repair, 3732 26th Ave. N., Robbinsdale, MN 55422 / 612-529-8103
Greg's Superior Products, P.O. Box 46219, Seattle, WA 98146

Greider Precision, 431 Santa Marina Ct., Escondido, CA 92029 / 760-480-8892; FAX: 760-480-9800 greider@msn.com
Gre-Tan Rifles, 29742 W.C.R. 50, Kersey, CO 80644 / 970-353-6176; FAX: 970-356-5940 www.gtrtooling.com
Grier Hard Cast Bullets, P.O. Box 41, Tillamook, OR 97141-0041 / 503-963-8796
Grier's Hard Cast Bullets, 1107 11th St., LaGrande, OR 97850 / 503-963-8796
Griffin & Howe, Inc., 340 W. Putnam Ave., Greenwich, CT 06830 / 203-618-0270 info@griffinhowe.com www.griffinhowe.com
Griffin & Howe, Inc., 33 Claremont Rd., Bernardsville, NJ 07924 / 908-766-2287; FAX: 908-766-1068 info@griffinhowe.com www.griffinhowe.com
Grifon, Inc., 58 Guinam St., Waltham, MS 02154
Groenewold, John. See: JG AIRGUNS, LLC
GRS/Glendo Corp., P.O. Box 1153, 900 Overlander St., Emporia, KS 66801 / 620-343-1084; or 800-836-3519; FAX: 620-343-9640 glendo@glendo.com www.glendo.com
Grulla Armes, Apartado 453, Avda Otaloa 12, Eiber, SPAIN
Gruning Precision, Inc., 7101 Jurupa Ave., No. 12, Riverside, CA 92504 / 909-289-4371; FAX: 909-689-7791 gruningprecision@earthlink.net www.gruningprecision.com
GSI, Inc., 7661 Commerce Ln., Trussville, AL 35173 / 205-655-8299
GTB-Custom Bullets, 482 Comerwood Court, S. San Francisco, CA 94080 / 650-583-1550
Guarasi, Robert. See: WILCOX INDUSTRIES CORP.
Guardsman Products, 411 N. Darling, Fremont, MI 49412 / 616-924-3950
Gun City, 212 W. Main Ave., Bismarck, ND 58501 / 701-223-2304
Gun Doc, Inc., 5405 NW 82nd Ave., Miami, FL 33166 / 305-477-2777; FAX: 305-477-2778 www.gundoc.com
Gun Doctor, The, 435 E. Maple, Roselle, IL 60172 / 708-894-0668
Gun Hunter Books (See Gun Hunter Trading Co.), 5075 Heisig St., Beaumont, TX 77705 / 409-835-3006; FAX: 409-838-2266 gunhuntertrading@hotmail.com
Gun Hunter Trading Co., 5075 Heisig St., Beaumont, TX 77705 / 409-835-3006; FAX: 409-838-2266 gunhuntertrading@hotmail.com
Gun Leather Limited, 116 Lipscomb, Fort Worth, TX 76104 / 817-334-0225; FAX: 800-247-0609
Gun List (See F&W Publications), 700 E. State St., Iola, WI 54990 / 715-445-2214; FAX: 715-445-4087
Gun Room Press, The, 127 Raritan Ave., Highland Park, NJ 08904 / 732-545-4344; FAX: 732-545-6686 gunbooks@rutgersgunbooks.com www.rutgersgunbooks.com
Gun Room, The, 1121 Burlington, Muncie, IN 47302 / 765-282-9073; FAX: 765-282-5270 bshstleguns@aol.com
Gun Shop, The, 62778 Spring Creek Rd., Montrose, CO 81401
Gun Shop, The, 5550 S. 900 East, Salt Lake City, UT 84117 / 801-263-3633
Gun South, Inc. (See GSI, Inc.)
Gun Vault, 7339 E. Acoma Dr., Ste. 7, Scottsdale, AZ 85260 / 602-951-6855
Gun Works, The, 247 S. 2nd St., Springfield, OR 97477 / 541-741-4118; FAX: 541-988-1097 gunworks@worldnet.att.net www.thegunworks.com
Gun-Alert, 1010 N. Maclay Ave., San Fernando, CA 91340 / 818-365-0864; FAX: 818-365-1308
Guncraft Books (See Guncraft Sports, Inc.), 10737 Dutchtown Rd., Knoxville, TN 37932 / 865-966-4545; FAX: 865-966-4500 findit@guncraft.com www.guncraft.com
Guncraft Sports, Inc., 10737 Dutchtown Rd., Knoxville, TN 37932 / 865-966-4545; FAX: 865-966-4500 findit@guncraft.com www.usit.net/guncraft
Guncraft Sports, Inc., Marie C. Wiest, 10737 Dutchtown Rd., Knoxville, TN 37932 / 865-966-4545; FAX: 865-966-4500 findit@guncraft.com www.guncraft.com
Guncrafter Industries, 171 Madison 1510, Huntsville, AR 72740 / 479-665-2466 www.guncrafterindustries.com
Gun-Ho Sports Cases, 110 E. 10th St., St. Paul, MN 55101 / 612-224-9491
Gunline Tools, 2950 Saturn St., "O", Brea, CA 92821 / 714-993-5100; FAX: 714-572-4128
Gunnerman Books, P.O. Box 81697, Rochester Hills, MI 48308 / 248-608-2856 gunnermanbks@att.net

MANUFACTURER'S DIRECTORY

Guns Antique & Modern DBA / Charles E. Duffy, Williams Lane, West Hurley, NY 12491 / 914-679-2997
Guns Div. of D.C. Engineering, Inc., 8633 Southfield Fwy., Detroit, MI 48228 / 313-271-7111; or 800-886-7623; FAX: 313-271-7112 guns@rifletech.com www.rifletech.com
GUNS Magazine, 12345 World Trade Dr., San Diego, CA 92128-3743 / 619-297-5350; FAX: 619-297-5353
Gunsight, The, 1712 N. Placentia Ave., Fullerton, CA 92631
Gunsite Training Center, P.O. Box 700, Paulden, AZ 86334 / 520-636-4565; FAX: 520-636-1236
Gunsmithing Ltd., 57 Unquowa Rd., Fairfield, CT 06824 / 203-254-0436; FAX: 203-254-1535
Gunsmithing, Inc., 30 W. Buchanan St., Colorado Springs, CO 80907 / 719-632-3795; FAX: 719-632-3493 www.nealsguns.com
Gurney, F. R., Box 13, Sooke, BC V0S 1N0 CANADA / 604-642-5282; FAX: 604-642-7859

H

H&B Forge Co., Rt. 2, Geisinger Rd., Shiloh, OH 44878 / 419-895-1856
H&P Publishing, 7174 Hoffman Rd., San Angelo, TX 76905 / 915-655-5953
H&R 1871.LLC, 60 Industrial Rowe, Gardner, MA 01440 / 508-632-9393; FAX: 508-632-2300 hr1871@hr1871.com www.hr1871.com
H. Krieghoff Gun Co., Boschstrasse 22, D-89079, Ulm, GERMANY / 731-401820; FAX: 731-4018270
H.K.S. Products, 7841 Founion Dr., Florence, KY 41042 / 606-342-7841; or 800-354-9814; FAX: 606-342-5865
H.P. White Laboratory, Inc., 3114 Scarboro Rd., Street, MD 21154 / 410-838-6550; FAX: 410-838-2802 info@hpwhite.com www.hpwhite.com
Hafner World Wide, Inc., P.O. Box 1987, Lake City, FL 32055 / 904-755-6481; FAX: 904-755-6595 hafner@isgroupe.net
Hakko Co. Ltd., 1-13-12, Narimasu, Itabashiku Tokyo, JAPAN / 03-5997-7870/2; FAX: 81-3-5997-7840
Half Moon Rifle Shop, 490 Halfmoon Rd., Columbia Falls, MT 59912 / 406-892-4409 halfmoonrs@centurytel.net
Hall Manufacturing, 142 CR 406, Clanton, AL 35045 / 205-755-4094
Hall Plastics, Inc., John, P.O. Box 1526, Alvin, TX 77512 / 713-489-8709
Hallberg, Fritz. See: CAMBOS OUTDOORSMAN
Hallowell & Co., P.O. Box 1445, Livingston, MT 59047 / 406-222-4770; FAX: 406-222-4792 morris@hallowellco.com www.hallowellco.com
Hally Caller, 443 Wells Rd., Doylestown, PA 18901 / 215-345-6354; FAX: 215-345-6354 info@hallycaller.com www.hallycaller.com
Hamilton, Alex B. (See Ten-Ring Precision, Inc.)
Hammans, Charles E., P.O. Box 788, 2022 McCracken, Stuttgart, AR 72160-0788 / 870-673-1388
Hammerli AG, Industrieplaz, a/Rheinpall, CH-8212 Neuhausen, SWITZERLAND info@hammerli.com www.haemmerliich.com
Hammerli Service-Precision Mac, Rudolf Marent, 9711 Tiltree St., Houston, TX 77075 / 713-946-7028 rmarent@webtv.net
Hammerli USA, 19296 Oak Grove Circle, Groveland, CA 95321 FAX: 209-962-5311
Hammond Custom Guns Ltd., 619 S. Pandora, Gilbert, AZ 85234 / 602-892-3437
HandCrafts Unltd. (See Clements' Custom Leathercraft), 1741 Dallas St., Aurora, CO 80010-2018 / 303-364-0403; FAX: 303-739-9824 gryphons@home.com kuntaoslcat.com
Handgun Press, P.O. Box 406, Glenview, IL 60025 / 847-657-6500; FAX: 847-724-8831 handgunpress@comcast.net
Hank's Gun Shop, Box 370, 50 W. 100 South, Monroe, UT 84754 / 435-527-4456 hanksgs@compuvision.com
Hanned Line, The, 4463 Madoc Way, San Jose, CA 95130 smith@hanned.com www.hanned.com
Hanned Precision (See The Hanned Line)
Hansen & Co., 244-246 Old Post Rd., Southport, CT 06490 / 203-259-6222; FAX: 203-254-3832
Hanson's Gun Center, Dick, 233 Everett Dr., Colorado Springs, CO 80911
Harford (See U.S. Importer-EMF Co., Inc.)
Harper's Custom Stocks, 928 Lombrano St., San Antonio, TX 78207 / 210-732-7174
Harrell's Precision, 5756 Hickory Dr., Salem, VA 24153 / 540-380-2683

Harrington & Richardson (See H&R 1871, Inc.)
Harris Engineering Inc., Dept. GD54, 999 Broadway, Barlow, KY 42024 / 270-334-3633; FAX: 270-334-3000
Harris Enterprises, P.O. Box 105, Bly, OR 97622 / 503-353-2625
Harris Hand Engraving, Paul A., 113 Rusty Ln., Boerne, TX 78006-5746 / 512-391-5121
Harris Publications, 1115 Broadway, New York, NY 10010 / 212-807-7100; FAX: 212-627-4678
Harrison Bullets, 6437 E. Hobart St., Mesa, AZ 85205
Harry Lawson Co., 3328 N. Richey Blvd., Tucson, AZ 85716 / 520-326-1117; FAX: 520-326-1117
Hart & Son, Inc., Robert W., 401 Montgomery St., Nescopeck, PA 18635 / 717-752-3655; FAX: 717-752-1088
Hart Rifle Barrels, Inc., P.O. Box 182, 1690 Apulia Rd., Lafayette, NY 13084 / 315-677-9841; FAX: 315-677-9610 hartrb@aol.com hartbarrels.com
Hartford (See U.S. Importer-EMF Co. Inc.)
Hartmann & Weiss GmbH, Rahlstedter Bahnhofstr. 47, 22143, Hamburg, GERMANY / (40) 677 55 85; FAX: (40) 677 55 92 hartmannundweiss@t-online.de
Harvey, Frank, 218 Nightfall, Terrace, NV 89015 / 702-558-6998
Hastings, P.O. Box 135, Clay Center, KS 67432 / 785-632-3169; FAX: 785-632-6554
Hatfield Gun, 224 N. 4th St., St. Joseph, MO 64501
Hawk Laboratories, Inc. (See Hawk, Inc.), 849 Hawks Bridge Rd., Salem, NJ 08079 / 609-299-2700; FAX: 609-299-2800
Hawk, Inc., 849 Hawks Bridge Rd., Salem, NJ 08079 / 609-299-2700; FAX: 609-299-2800 info@hawkbullets.com www.hawkbullets.com
Hawken Shop, The, P.O. Box 593, Oak Harbor, WA 98277 / 206-679-4657; FAX: 206-675-1114
Hawken Shop, The (See Dayton Traister)
Haydel's Game Calls, Inc., 5018 Hazel Jones Rd., Bossier City, LA 71111 / 318-746-3586; FAX: 318-746-3711 www.haydels.com
Hecht, Hubert J., Waffen-Hecht, P.O. Box 2635, Fair Oaks, CA 95628 / 916-966-1020
Heckler & Koch GmbH, P.O. Box 1329, 78722 Oberndorf, Neckar, GERMANY / 49-7423179-0; FAX: 49-7423179-2406
Heckler & Koch, Inc., 21480 Pacific Blvd., Sterling, VA 20166-8900 / 703-450-1900; FAX: 703-450-8160 www.heckler-koch-usa.com
Hege Jagd-u. Sporthandels GmbH, P.O. Box 101461, W-7770, Ueberlingen a. Boden, GERMANY
Heidenstrom Bullets, Dalghte 86-3660 Rjukan, 35091818, NORWAY, olau.joh@online.tuo
Heilmann, Stephen, P.O. Box 657, Grass Valley, CA 95945 / 530-272-8758; FAX: 530-274-0285 sheilmann@jps.net www.metalwood.com
Heinie Specialty Products, 301 Oak St., Quincy, IL 62301-2500 / 217-228-9500; FAX: 217-228-9502 rheinie@heinie.com www.heinie.com
Helwan (See U.S. Importer-Interarms)
Henigson & Associates, Steve, P.O. Box 2726, Culver City, CA 90231 / 310-305-8288; FAX: 310-305-1905
Henriksen Tool Co., Inc., 8515 Wagner Creek Rd., Talent, OR 97540 / 541-535-2309; FAX: 541-535-2309
Henry Repeating Arms Co., 110 8th St., Brooklyn, NY 11215 / 718-499-5600; FAX: 718-768-8056 info@henryrepeating.com www.henryrepeating.com
Hensley, Gunmaker, Darwin, P.O. Box 329, Brightwood, OR 97011 / 503-622-5411
Heppler, Keith. See: KEITH'S CUSTOM GUNSTOCKS
Hercules, Inc. (See Alliant Techsystems Smokeless Powder Group)
Heritage Firearms (See Heritage Mfg., Inc.)
Heritage Manufacturing, Inc., 4600 NW 135th St., Opa Locka, FL 33054 / 305-685-5966; FAX: 305-687-6721 infohmi@heritagemfg.com www.heritagemfg.com
Heritage/VSP Gun Books, P.O. Box 887, McCall, ID 83638 / 208-634-4104; FAX: 208-634-3101 heritage@gunbooks.com www.gunbooks.com
Herrett's Stocks, Inc., P.O. Box 741, Twin Falls, ID 83303 / 208-733-1498
Herter's Manufacturing Inc., 111 E. Burnett St., P.O. Box 518, Beaver Dam, WI 53916-1811 / 414-887-1765; FAX: 414-887-8444
Hesco-Meprolight, 2139 Greenville Rd., LaGrange, GA 30241 / 706-884-7967; FAX: 706-882-4683
Hesse Arms, Robert Hesse, 1126 70th St. E., Inver Grove Heights, MN 55077-2416 / 651-455-5760; FAX: 612-455-5760
Hesse, Robert. See: HESSE ARMS

Heydenberk, Warren R., 1059 W. Sawmill Rd., Quakertown, PA 18951 / 215-538-2682
Hickman, Jaclyn, Box 1900, Glenrock, WY 82637
Hidalgo, Tony, 12701 SW 9th Pl., Davie, FL 33325 / 954-476-7645
High Bridge Arms, Inc., 3185 Mission St., San Francisco, CA 94110 / 415-282-8358
High North Products, Inc., P.O. Box 2, Antigo, WI 54409 / 715-627-2331; FAX: 715-623-5451
High Performance International, 5734 W. Florist Ave., Milwaukee, WI 53218 / 414-466-9040; FAX: 414-466-7050 mike@hpirifles.com hpirifles.com
High Precision, Bud Welsh, 80 New Road, E. Amherst, NY 14051 / 716-688-6344; FAX: 716-688-0425 welsh5168@aol.com www.high-precision.com
High Standard Mfg. Co./F.I., Inc., 5200 Mitchelldale St., Ste. E17, Houston, TX 77092-7222 / 713-462-4200; or 800-272-7816; FAX: 713-681-5665 info@highstandard.com www.highstandard.com
High Tech Specialties, Inc., P.O. Box 839, 293 E Main St., Rear, Adamstown, PA 19501 / 717-484-0405; FAX: 717-484-0523 bansner@aol.com www.bansmersrifle.com/hightech
Highline Machine Co., Randall Thompson, Randall Thompson, 654 Lela Place, Grand Junction, CO 81504 / 970-434-4971
Highwood Special Products, 1531 E. Highwood, Pontiac, MI 48340
Hill, Loring F., 304 Cedar Rd., Elkins Park, PA 19027
Hill Speed Leather, Ernie, 4507 N 195th Ave., Litchfield Park, AZ 85340 / 602-853-9222; FAX: 602-853-9235
Hinman Outfitters, Bob, 107 N Sanderson Ave., Bartonville, IL 61607-1839 / 309-691-8132
Hi-Performance Ammunition Company, 484 State Route 366, Apollo, PA 15613 / 304-674-9000; FAX: 304-675-6700
HIP-GRIP Barami Corp., P.O. Box 252224, West Bloomfield, MI 48325-2224 / 248-738-0462; FAX: 248-738-2542 hipgripja@aol.com www.hipgrip.com
Hi-Point Firearms/MKS Supply, 8611-A North Dixie Dr., Dayton, OH 45414 / 877-425-4867; FAX: 937-454-0503 www.hi-pointfirearms.com
Hiptmayer, Armurier, RR 112 750, P.O. Box 136, Eastman, PQ J0E 1P0 CANADA / 514-297-2492
Hiptmayer, Heidemarie, RR 112 750, P.O. Box 136, Eastman, PQ J0E 1P0 CANADA / 514-297-2492
Hiptmayer, Klaus, RR 112 750, P.O. Box 136, Eastman, PQ J0E 1P0 CANADA / 514-297-2492
Hirtenberger AG, Leobersdorferstrasse 31, A-2552, Hirtenberg, AUSTRIA / 43(0)2256 81184; FAX: 43(0)2256 81808 www.hirtenberger.ot
HJS Arms, Inc., P.O. Box 3711, Brownsville, TX 78523-3711 / 956-542-2767; FAX: 956-542-2767
Hoag, James W., 8523 Canoga Ave., Suite C, Canoga Park, CA 91304 / 818-998-1510
Hobson Precision Mfg. Co., 210 Big Oak Ln., Brent, AL 35034 / 205-926-4662; FAX: 205-926-3193 cahobbob@dbtech.net
Hodgdon Powder Co., 6231 Robinson, Shawnee Mission, KS 66202 / 913-362-9455; FAX: 913-362-1307
Hodgman, Inc., 1750 Orchard Rd., Montgomery, IL 60538 / 708-897-7555; FAX: 708-897-7558
Hodgson, Richard, 9081 Tahoe Lane, Boulder, CO 80301
Hoehn Sales, Inc., 2045 Kohn Road, Wright City, MO 63390 / 636-745-8144; FAX: 636-745-7868 hoehnsal@usmo.com
Hofer Jagdwaffen, P., A9170 Ferlach, Kirchgasse 24, Kirchgasse, AUSTRIA / 43 4227 3683; or 43 664 3200216; FAX: 43 4227 368330 peterhofer@hoferwaffen.com www.hoferwaffen.com
Hoffman New Ideas, 821 Northmoor Rd., Lake Forest, IL 60045 / 312-234-4075
Hogue Grips, P.O. Box 1138, Paso Robles, CA 93447 / 800-438-4747 or 805-239-1440; FAX: 805-239-2553
Holland & Holland Ltd., 33 Bruton St., London, ENGLAND / 44-171-499-4411; FAX: 44-171-408-7962
Holland's Gunsmithing, P.O. Box 69, Powers, OR 97466 / 541-439-5155; FAX: 541-439-5155
Hollinger, Jon. See: ASPEN OUTFITTING CO.
Hollywood Engineering, 10642 Arminta St., Sun Valley, CA 91352 / 818-842-8376; FAX: 818-504-4168 cadqueenel1@aol.com
Homak, 350 N. La Salle Dr. Ste. 1100, Chicago, IL 60610-4731 / 312-523-3100; FAX: 312-523-9455
Hoppe's Div. Penguin Industries, Inc., P.O. Box 1690, Oregon City, OR 97045-0690 / 610-384-6000
Horizons Unlimited, P.O. Box 426, Warm Springs, GA 31830 / 706-655-3603; FAX: 706-655-3603

MANUFACTURER'S DIRECTORY

Hornady Mfg. Co., P.O. Box 1848, Grand Island, NE 68802 / 800-338-3220 or 308-382-1390; FAX: 308-382-5761

Horseshoe Leather Products, Andy Arratoonian, The Cottage Sharow, Ripon, ENGLAND U.K. / 44-1765-605858 andy@horseshoe.co.uk www.holsters.org

House of Muskets, Inc., The, PO Box 4640, Pagosa Springs, CO 81157 / 970-731-2295

Houtz & Barwick, P.O. Box 435, W. Church St., Elizabeth City, NC 27909 / 800-775-0337; or 919-335-4191; FAX: 919-335-1152

Howa Machinery, Ltd., Sukaguchi, Shinkawa-cho Nishikasugai-gun, Aichi 452-8601, JAPAN / 81-52-408-1231; FAX: 81-52-401-4999 howa@howa.co.jp http://www.howa.cojpl

Howell Machine, Inc., 815 D St., Lewiston, ID 83501 / 208-743-7418; FAX: 208-746-1703

H-S Precision, Inc., 1301 Turbine Dr., Rapid City, SD 57701 / 605-341-3006; FAX: 605-342-8964

HT Bullets, 244 Belleville Rd., New Bedford, MA 02745 / 508-999-3338

Hubert J. Hecht Waffen-Hecht, P.O. Box 2635, Fair Oaks, CA 95628 / 916-966-1020

Huebner, Corey O., P.O. Box 564, Frenchtown, MT 59834 / 406-721-7168 bugsboys@hotmail.com

Huey Gun Cases, 820 Indiana St., Lawrence, KS 66044-2645 / 785-842-0062; FAX: 785-842-0062 hueycases@aol.com www.hueycases.com

Hume, Don, P.O. Box 351, Miami, OK 74355 / 800-331-2686; FAX: 918-542-4340 info@donhume.com www.donhume.com

Hunkeler, A. (See Buckskin Machine Works), 3235 S 358th St., Auburn, WA 98001 / 206-927-5412

Hunter Co., Inc., 3300 W. 71st Ave., Westminster, CO 80030 / 303-427-4626; FAX: 303-428-3980 debbiet@huntercompany.com www.huntercompany.com

Hunterjohn, P.O. Box 771457, St. Louis, MO 63177 / 314-531-7250 www.hunterjohn.com

Hunter's Specialties Inc., 6000 Huntington Ct. NE, Cedar Rapids, IA 52402-1268 / 319-395-0321; FAX: 319-395-0326

Hunters Supply, Inc., P.O. Box 313, Tioga, TX 76271 / 940-437-2458; FAX: 940-437-2228 hunterssupply@hotmail.com www.hunterssupply.net

Huntington Die Specialties, 601 Oro Dam Blvd., Oroville, CA 95965 / 530-534-1210; FAX: 530-534-1212 buy@huntingtons.com www.huntingtons.com

Hutton Rifle Ranch, P.O. Box 170317, Boise, ID 83717 / 208-345-8781 www.martinbrevik@aol.com

Hydrosorbent Products, P.O. Box 437, Ashley Falls, MA 01222 / 800-448-7903; FAX: 413-229-8743 orders@dehumidify.com www.dehumidify.com

I

I.A.B. (See U.S. Importer-Taylor's & Co., Inc.)

I.D.S.A. Books, 1324 Stratford Drive, Piqua, OH 45356 / 937-773-4203; FAX: 937-778-1922

I.N.C. Inc. (See Kickeez I.N.C., Inc.)

I.S.W., 106 E. Cairo Dr., Tempe, AZ 85282

IAR Inc., 33171 Camino Capistrano, San Juan Capistrano, CA 92675 / 949-443-3642; FAX: 949-443-3647 sales@iar-arms.com iar-arms.com

Ide, Ken. See: STURGEON VALLEY SPORTERS

IGA (See U.S. Importer-Stoeger Industries)

Image Ind. Inc., 11220 E. Main St., Huntley, IL 60142-7369 / 630-766-2402; FAX: 630-766-7373

Impact Case & Container, Inc., P.O. Box 1129, Rathdrum, ID 83858 / 077 007 2452; FAX: 208 007 0002 bradk@icc-case.com www.icc-case.com

Imperial (See E-Z-Way Systems), P.O. Box 4310, Newark, OH 43058-4310 / 614-345-6645; FAX: 614-345-6600 ezway@infinet.com www.jcunald.com

Imperial Magnum Corp., P.O. Box 249, Oroville, WA 98844 / 604-495-3131; FAX: 604-495-2816

Imperial Miniature Armory, 1115 FM 359, Houston, TX 77035-3305 / 800-646-4288; FAX: 832-595-8787 miniguns@houston.rr.com www.1800miniature.com

Imperial Schrade Corp., 7 Schrade Ct., Box 7000, Ellenville, NY 12428 / 914-647-7601; FAX: 914-647-8701 csc@schradeknives.com www.schradeknives.com

Import Sports Inc., 1750 Brielle Ave., Unit B1, Wanamassa, NJ 07712 / 732-493-0302; FAX: 732-493-0301 gsodini@aol.com www.bersa-llama.com

IMR Powder Co., 1080 Military Turnpike, Suite 2, Plattsburgh, NY 12901 / 518-563-2253; FAX: 518-563-6916

Info-Arm, P.O. Box 1262, Champlain, NY 12919 / 514-955-0355; FAX: 514-955-0357 infoarm@qc.aira.com

Innovative Weaponry Inc., 2513 E. Loop 820 N., Fort Worth, TX 76118 / 817-284-0099 or 800-334-3573

INTEC International, Inc., P.O. Box 5708, Scottsdale, AZ 85261 / 602-483-1708

Inter Ordnance of America LP, 3305 Westwood Industrial Dr., Monroe, NC 28110-5204 / 704-821-8337; FAX: 704-821-8523

Intercontinental Distributors, Ltd., P.O. Box 815, Beulah, ND 58523

International Shooters Service, P.O. Box 185234, Ft. Worth, TX 76181 / 817-595-2090; FAX: 817-595-2090 is_s_@sbcglobal.net

Intrac Arms International, 5005 Chapman Hwy., Knoxville, TN 37920

Ion Industries, Inc., 3508 E Allerton Ave., Cudahy, WI 53110 / 414-486-2007; FAX: 414-486-2017

Iosso Products, 1485 Lively Blvd., Elk Grove Village, IL 60007 / 847-437-8400; FAX: 847-437-8478

Iron Bench, 12619 Bailey Rd., Redding, CA 96003 / 916-241-4623

Ironside International Publishers, Inc., P.O. Box 1050, Lorton, VA 22199

Ironsighter Co., P.O. Box 85070, Westland, MI 48185 / 734-326-8731; FAX: 734-326-3378 www.ironsighter.com

Irwin, Campbell H., 140 Hartland Blvd., East Hartland, CT 06027 / 203-653-3901

Israel Arms Inc., 5625 Star Ln. #B, Houston, TX 77057 / 713-789-0745; FAX: 713-914-9515 www.israelarms.com

Ithaca Classic Doubles, Stephen Lamboy, No. 5 Railroad St., Victor, NY 14564 / 716-924-2710; FAX: 716-924-2737 ithacadoubles.com

Ithaca Gun Company LLC, 901 Rt. 34 B, King Ferry, NY 13081 / 315-364-7171; FAX: 315-364-5134 info@ithacagun.com

Ivanoff, Thomas G. (See Tom's Gun Repair)

J

J J Roberts Firearm Engraver, 7808 Lake Dr., Manassas, VA 20111 / 703-330-0448; FAX: 703-264-8600 james.roberts@angelfire.com www.angelfire.com/va2/engraver

J&D Components, 75 East 350 North, Orem, UT 84057-4719 / 801-225-7007 www.jdcomponents.com

J&J Products, Inc., 9240 Whitmore, El Monte, CA 91731 / 818-571-5228; FAX: 800-927-8361

J&J Sales, 1501 21st Ave. S., Great Falls, MT 59405 / 406-727-9789 mtshootingbench@yahoo.com www.j&jsales.us

J&L Superior Bullets (See Huntington Die Specialties)

J&M Precision Machining, Jeff Amato, RR 1 Box 91, Bloomfield, IN 47424

J&R Engineering, P.O. Box 77, 200 Lyons Hill Rd., Athol, MA 01331 / 508-249-9241

J&R Enterprises, 4550 Scotts Valley Rd., Lakeport, CA 95453

J&S Heat Treat, 803 S. 16th St., Blue Springs, MO 64015 / 816-229-2149; FAX: 816-228-1135

J. Dewey Mfg. Co., Inc., P.O. Box 2014, Southbury, CT 06488 / 203-264-3064; FAX: 203-262-6907 deweyrods@worldnet.att.net www.deweyrods.com

J. Korzinek Riflesmith, RD 2, Box 73D, Canton, PA 17724 / 717-673-8512

J.A. Blades, Inc. (See Christopher Firearms Co.)

J.A. Henckels Zwillingswerk Inc., 9 Skyline Dr., Hawthorne, NY 10532 / 914-592-7370

J.G. Anschutz GmbH & Co. KG, Daimlerstr. 12, D-89079 Ulm, Ulm, GERMANY / 49 731 40120; FAX: 49 731 4012700 JGA-info@anschuetz-sport.com www.anschuetz-sport.com

J.G. Dapkus Co., Inc., Commerce Circle, P.O. Box 293, Durham, CT 06422 www.explodingtargets.com

J.I.T. Ltd., P.O. Box 230, Freedom, WY 83120 / 708-494-0937

J.J. Roberts / Engraver, 7808 Lake Dr., Manassas, VA 20111 / 703-330-0448 jjrengraver@aol.com www.angelfire.com/va2/engraver

J.R. Williams Bullet Co., 2008 Tucker Rd., Perry, GA 31069 / 912-987-0274

J.W. Morrison Custom Rifles, 4015 W. Sharon, Phoenix, AZ 85029 / 602-978-3754

Jack A. Rosenberg & Sons, 12229 Cox Ln., Dallas, TX 75234 / 214-241-6302

Jack Dever Co., 8520 NW 90th St., Oklahoma City, OK 73132 / 405-721-6393 jbdever1@home.com

Jack First, Inc., 1201 Turbine Dr., Rapid City, SD 57703 / 605-343-8481; FAX: 605-343-9420

Jack Jonas Appraisals & Taki, 13952 E. Marina Dr., #604, Aurora, CO 80014

Jackalope Gun Shop, 1048 S. 5th St., Douglas, WY 82633 / 307-358-3441

Jaffin, Harry. See: BRIDGEMAN PRODUCTS

Jagdwaffen, Peter. See: BUCHSENMACHERMEISTER

James Churchill Glove Co., PO Box 298, Centralia, WA 98531 / 360-736-2816; FAX: 360-330-0151 churchillglove@localaccess.com

James Wayne Firearms for Collectors and Investors, 2608 N. Laurent, Victoria, TX 77901 / 361-578-1258; FAX: 361-578-3559

Jamison International, Marc Jamison, 3551 Mayer Ave., Sturgis, SD 57785 / 605-347-5090; FAX: 605-347-4704 jbell2@masttechnology.com

Jamison, Marc. See: JAMISON INTERNATIONAL

Jamison's Forge Works, 4527 Rd. 6.5 NE, Moses Lake, WA 98837 / 509-762-2659

Jantz Supply, 309 West Main Dept HD, Davis, OK 73030-0584 / 580-369-2316; FAX: 580-369-3082 jantz@brightok.net www.knifemaking.com

Jarrett Rifles, Inc., 383 Brown Rd., Jackson, SC 29831 / 803-471-3616 www.jarrettrifles.com

Jarvis, Inc., 1123 Cherry Orchard Lane, Hamilton, MT 59840 / 406-961-4392

Javelina Lube Products, P.O. Box 337, San Bernardino, CA 92402 / 909-350-9556; FAX: 909-429-1211

Jay McCament Custom Gunmaker, Jay McCament, 1730-134th St. Ct. S., Tacoma, WA 98444 / 253-531-8832

JB Custom, P.O. Box 6912, Leawood, KS 66206 / 913-381-2329

Jeff Flannery Engraving, 11034 Riddles Run Rd., Union, KY 41091 / 859-384-3127; FAX: 859-384-2222 engraving@fuse.net http://home.fuse.net/engraving/

Jeffredo Gunsight, P.O. Box 669, San Marcos, CA 92079 / 760-728-2695

Jena Eur, P.O. Box 319, Dunmore, PA 18512

Jenco Sales, Inc., P.O. Box 1000, Manchaca, TX 78652 / 800-531-5301; FAX: 800-266-2373 jencosales@sbcglobal.net

Jenkins Recoil Pads, 5438 E. Frontage Ln., Olney, IL 62450 / 618-395-3416

Jensen Bullets, RR 1 Box 187, Arco, ID 83213 / 208-785-5590

Jensen's Custom Ammunition, 5146 E. Pima, Tucson, AZ 85712 / 602-325-3346; FAX: 602-322-5704

Jensen's Firearms Academy, 1280 W. Prince, Tucson, AZ 85705 / 602-293-8516

Jericho Tool & Die Co., Inc., 121 W. Keech Rd., Bainbridge, NY 13733-3248 / 607-563-8222; FAX: 607-563-8560 jerichotool.com www.jerichotool.com

Jerry Phillips Optics, P.O. Box LG32, Langhorne, PA 19047 / 215-757-5037; FAX: 215-757-7097

Jesse W. Smith Saddlery, 0499 County Road J, Pritchett, CO 81064 / 509-325-0622

Jester Bullets, Rt. 1 Box 27, Orienta, OK 73737

Jewell Triggers, Inc., 3620 Hwy. 123, San Marcos, TX 78666 / 512-353-2999; FAX: 512-392-0543

JG Airguns, LLC, John Groenewold, P.O. Box 830, Mundelein, IL 60060 / 847-566-2365; FAX: 847-566-4065 jgairguns@jgairguns.com www.jgairguns.com

JGS Precision Tool Mfg., LLC, 60819 Selander Rd., Coos Bay, OR 97420 / 541-267-4331; FAX: 541-267-5996 jgstools@harborside.com www.jgstools.com

Jim Blair Engraving, P.O. Box 64, Glenrock, WY 82637 / 307-436-8115 jblairengrav@msn.com

Jim Noble Co., 204 W. 5th St., Vancouver, WA 98660 / 360-695-1309; FAX: 360-695-6835 jnobleco@aol.com

Jim Norman Custom Gunstocks, 14281 Cane Rd., Valley Center, CA 92082 / 619-749-6252

Jim's Precision, Jim Ketchum, 1725 Moclips Dr., Petaluma, CA 94952 / 707-762-3014

JLK Bullets, 414 Turner Rd., Dover, AR 72837 / 501-331-4194

Johanssons Vapentillbehor, Bert, S-430 20, Veddige, SWEDEN

MANUFACTURER'S DIRECTORY

John Hall Plastics, Inc., P.O. Box 1526, Alvin, TX 77512 / 713-489-8709

John J. Adams & Son Engravers, 7040 VT Rt 113, Vershire, VT 05079 / 802-685-0019

John Masen Co. Inc., 1305 Jelmak, Grand Prairie, TX 75050 / 817-430-8732; FAX: 817-430-1715

John Partridge Sales Ltd., Trent Meadows Rugeley, Staffordshire, WS15 2HS ENGLAND

John Rigby & Co., 500 Linne Rd. Ste. D, Paso Robles, CA 93446 / 805-227-4236; FAX: 805-227-4723 jrigby@calinet www.johnrigbyandco.com

John's Custom Leather, 523 S. Liberty St., Blairsville, PA 15717 / 724-459-6802; FAX: 724-459-5996

Johnson Wood Products, 34897 Crystal Road, Strawberry Point, IA 52076 / 563-933-6504 johnsonwoodproducts@yahoo.com

Jonad Corp., 2091 Lakeland Ave., Lakewood, OH 44107 / 216-226-3161

Jonathan Arthur Ciener, Inc., 8700 Commerce St., Cape Canaveral, FL 32920 / 321-868-2200; FAX: 321-868-2201 www.22lrconversions.com

Jones Co., Dale, 680 Hoffman Draw, Kila, MT 59920 / 406-755-4684

Jones Custom Products, Neil A., 17217 Brookhouser Rd., Saegertown, PA 16433 / 814-763-2769; FAX: 814-763-4228 njones@mdul.net neiljones.com

Jones, J. See: SSK INDUSTRIES

Jones Moulds, Paul, 4901 Telegraph Rd., Los Angeles, CA 90022 / 213-262-1510

JP Enterprises, Inc., P.O. Box 378, Hugo, MN 55038 / 651-426-9196; FAX: 651-426-2472 www.jprifles.com

JP Sales, Box 307, Anderson, TX 77830

JRP Custom Bullets, RR2 2233 Carlton Rd., Whitehall, NY 12887 / 518-282-0084 or 802-438-5548

JSL Ltd. (See U.S. Importer-Specialty Shooters Supply)

Juenke, Vern, 25 Bitterbush Rd., Reno, NV 89523 / 702-345-0225

Jungkind, Reeves C., 509 E. Granite St., Llano, TX 78643-3055 / 325-247-1151

Jurras, L. See: L. E. JURRAS & ASSOC.

Justin Phillippi Custom Bullets, P.O. Box 773, Ligonier, PA 15658 / 412-238-9671

K

K&M Industries, Inc., Box 66, 510 S. Main, Troy, ID 83871 / 208-835-2281; FAX: 208-835-5211

K&M Services, 5430 Salmon Run Rd., Dover, PA 17315 / 717-292-3175; FAX: 717-292-3175

K. Eversull Co., Inc., 1 Tracemont, Boyce, LA 71409 / 318-793-8728; FAX: 318-793-5483 bestguns@aol.com

K.B.I. Inc., P.O. Box 6625, Harrisburg, PA 17112 / 717-540-8518; FAX: 717-540-8567

Ka Pu Kapili, P.O. Box 745, Honokaa, HI 96727 / 808-776-1644; FAX: 808-776-1731

KA-BAR Knives, 200 Homer St., Olean, NY 14760 / 800-282-0130; FAX: 716-790-7188 info@ka-bar.com www.ka-bar.com

Kahles A. Swarovski Company, 2 Slater Rd., Cranston, RI 02920 / 401-946-2220; FAX: 401-946-2587

Kahr Arms, P.O. Box 220, 630 Route 303, Blauvelt, NY 10913 / 845-353-7770; FAX: 845-353-7833 www.kahr.com

Kailua Custom Guns Inc., 51 N. Dean Street, Coquille, OR 97423 / 541-396-5413 kailuacustom@aol.com www.kailuacustom.com

Kalispel Case Line, P.O. Box 267, Cusick, WA 99119 / 509-445-1121

Kamik Outdoor Footwear, 554 Montee de Liesse, Montreal, PQ H4T 1P1 CANADA / 514-341-3950; FAX: 514-341-1861

Kane, Edward, P.O. Box 385, Ukiah, CA 95482 / 707-462-2937

Kapro Mfg. Co. Inc. (See R.E.I.)

Kasenit Co., Inc., 39 Park Ave., Highland Mills, NY 10930 / 845-928-9595; FAX: 845-986-8038

Kaswer Custom, Inc., 13 Surrey Drive, Brookfield, CT 06804 / 203-775-0564; FAX: 203-775-6872

KDF, Inc., 2485 Hwy. 46 N., Seguin, TX 78155 / 830-379-8141; FAX: 830-379-5420

KeeCo Impressions, Inc., 346 Wood Ave., North Brunswick, NJ 08902 / 800-468-0546

Kehr, Roger, 2131 Agate Ct. SE, Lacy, WA 98503 / 360-491-0691

Keith's Bullets, 942 Twisted Oak, Algonquin, IL 60102 / 708-658-3520

Keith's Custom Gunstocks, Keith M. Heppler, 540 Banyan Circle, Walnut Creek, CA 94598 / 925-934-3509; FAX: 925-934-3143 kmheppler@hotmail.com

Kelbly, Inc., 7222 Dalton Fox Lake Rd., North Lawrence, OH 44666 / 216-683-4674; FAX: 216-683-7349

Keller Co., The, P.O. Box 4057, Port Angeles, WA 98363-0997 / 214-770-8585

Kelley's, P.O. Box 125, Woburn, MA 01801-0125 / 800-879-7273; FAX: 781-272-7077 kels@star.net www.kelsmilitary.com

Kellogg's Professional Products, 325 Pearl St., Sandusky, OH 44870 / 419-625-6551; FAX: 419-625-6167 skwigton@aol.com

Kelly, Lance, 1723 Willow Oak Dr., Edgewater, FL 32132 / 904-423-4933

Kel-Tec CNC Industries, Inc., P.O. Box 236009, Cocoa, FL 32923 / 407-631-0068; FAX: 407-631-1169

Kemen America, 2550 Hwy. 23, Wrenshall, MN 55797 / 218-384-3670 patrickl@midwestshootingschool.com midwestshootingschool.com

Ken Eyster Heritage Gunsmiths, Inc., 6441 Bisop Rd., Centerburg, OH 43011 / 740-625-6131; FAX: 740-625-7811

Ken Starnes Gunmaker, 15940 SW Holly Hill Rd., Hillsboro, OR 97123-9033 / 503-628-0705; FAX: 503-443-2096 kstarnes@kdsa.com

Keng's Firearms Specialty, Inc./US Tactical Systems, 875 Wharton Dr., P.O. Box 44405, Atlanta, GA 30336-1405 / 404-691-7611; FAX: 404-505-8445

Kennebec Journal, 274 Western Ave., Augusta, ME 04330 / 207-622-6288

Kennedy Firearms, 10 N. Market St., Muncy, PA 17756 / 717-546-6695

Kenneth W. Warren Engraver, P.O. Box 2842, Wenatchee, WA 98807 / 509-663-6123; FAX: 509-665-6123

Ken's Kustom Kartridges, 331 Jacobs Rd., Hubbard, OH 44425 / 216-534-4595

Kent Cartridge America, Inc., P.O. Box 849, 1000 Zigor Rd., Kearneysville, WV 25430

Keowee Game Calls, 608 Hwy. 25 North, Travelers Rest, SC 29690 / 864-834-7204; FAX: 864-834-7831

Kershaw Knives, 18600 SW Teton Ave., Tualatin, OR 97062 / 503-682-1966; or 800-325-2891; FAX: 503-682-7168

Kesselring Gun Shop, 4024 Old Hwy. 99N, Burlington, WA 98233 / 360-724-3113; FAX: 360-724-7003 info@kesselrings.com www.kesselrings.com

Ketchum, Jim (See Jim's Precision)

Keystone Sporting Arms, Inc. (Crickett Rifles), 8920 State Route 405, Milton, PA 17847 / 800-742-2777; FAX: 570-742-1455

Kickeez I.N.C., Inc., 301 Industrial Dr., Carl Junction, MO 64834-8806 / 419-649-2100; FAX: 417-649-2200 kickeez@gbronline.com www.kickeez.net

Kilham & Co., Main St., P.O. Box 37, Lyme, NH 03768 / 603-795-4112

Kimar (See U.S. Importer-IAR, Inc.)

Kimber of America, Inc., 1 Lawton St., Yonkers, NY 10705 / 800-880-2418; FAX: 914-964-9340

King & Co., P.O. Box 1242, Bloomington, IL 61702 / 309-473-3964; or 800-914-5464; FAX: 309-473-2161

King's Gun Works, 1837 W. Glenoaks Blvd., Glendale, CA 91201 / 818-956-6010; FAX: 818-548-8606

Kirkpatrick Leather Co., P.O. Box 677, Laredo, TX 78040 / 956-723-6631; FAX: 956-725-0672 mike@kirkpatrickleather.com www.kirkpatrickleather.com

KK Air International (See Impact Case & Container Co., Inc.)

Kleen-Bore, Inc., 16 Industrial Pkwy., Easthampton, MA 01027 / 413-527-0300; FAX: 413-527-2522 info@kleen-bore.com www.kleen-bore.com

Kleinendorst, K. W., RR 1, Box 1500, Hop Bottom, PA 18824 / 717-289-4687

Klingler Woodcarving, P.O. Box 141, Thistle Hill, Cabot, VT 05647 / 802-426-3811 www.vermartcrafts.com

Knifeware, Inc., P.O. Box 3, Greenville, WV 24945 / 304-832-6878

Knight Rifles, 21852 Hwy. J46, P.O. Box 130, Centerville, IA 52544 / 515-856-2626; FAX: 515-856-2628 www.knightrifles.com

Knight Rifles (See Modern Muzzleloading, Inc.)

Knight's Manufacturing Co., 701 Columbia Blvd., Titusville, FL 32780 / 321-607-9900; FAX: 321-268-1498 civiliansales@knightarmco.com www.knightarmco.com

Knock on Wood Antiques, 355 Post Rd., Darien, CT 06820 / 203-655-9031

Knoell, Doug, 9737 McCardle Way, Santee, CA 92071 / 619-449-5189

Knopp, Gary. See: SUPER 6 LLC

Koevenig's Engraving Service, Box 55 Rabbit Gulch, Hill City, SD 57745 / 605-574-2239 ekoevenig@msn.com

KOGOT, 410 College, Trinidad, CO 81082 / 719-846-9406; FAX: 719-846-9406

Kolar, 1925 Roosevelt Ave., Racine, WI 53406 / 414-554-0800; FAX: 414-554-9093

Kolpin Outdoors, Inc., P.O. Box 107, 205 Depot St., Fox Lake, WI 53933 / 414-928-3118; FAX: 414-928-3687 cdutton@kolpin.com www.kolpin.com

Korth Germany GmbH, Robert Bosch Strasse, 11, D-23909, 23909 Ratzeburg, GERMANY / 4541-840363; FAX: 4541-84 05 35 info@korthwaffen.de www.korthwaffen.de

Korth USA, 437R Chandler St., Tewksbury, MA 01876 / 978-851-8656; FAX: 978-851-9462 info@kortusa.com www.korthusa.com

Korzinek Riflesmith, J., RD 2 Box 73D, Canton, PA 17724 / 717-673-8512

Koval Knives, 5819 Zarley St., Suite A, New Albany, OH 43054 / 614-855-0777; FAX: 614-855-0945 koval@kovalknives.com www.kovalknives.com

Kowa Optimed, Inc., 20001 S. Vermont Ave., Torrance, CA 90502 / 310-327-1913; FAX: 310-327-4177 scopekowa@kowa.com www.kowascope.com

KP Books Division of F&W Publications, 700 E. State St., Iola, WI 54990-0001 / 715-445-2214

Kramer Designs, P.O. Box 129, Clancy, MT 59634 / 406-933-8658; FAX: 406-933-8658

Kramer Handgun Leather, P.O. Box 112154, Tacoma, WA 98411 / 800-510-2666; FAX: 253-564-1214 www.kramerleather.com

Krico Deutschland GmbH, Nurnbergerstrasse 6, D-90602, Pyrbaum, GERMANY / 09180-2780; FAX: 09180-2661

Krieger Barrels, Inc., 2024 Mayfield Rd, Richfield, WI 53076 / 262-628-8558; FAX: 262-628-8748

Krieghoff Gun Co., H., Boschstrasse 22, D-89079 Elm, GERMANY / 731-4018270

Krieghoff International,Inc., 7528 Easton Rd., Ottsville, PA 18942 / 610-847-5173; FAX: 610-847-8691

Kukowski, Ed. See: ED'S GUN HOUSE

Kulis Freeze Dry Taxidermy, 725 Broadway Ave., Bedford, OH 44146 / 216-232-8352; FAX: 216-232-7305 jkulis@kastaway.com kastaway.com

KVH Industries, Inc., 110 Enterprise Center, Middletown, RI 02842 / 401-847-3327; FAX: 401-849-0045

Kwik-Site Co., 5555 Treadwell St., Wayne, MI 48184 / 734-326-1500; FAX: 734-326-4120 kwiksiteco@aol.com

L

L&R Lock Co., 2328 Cains Mill Rd., Sumter, SC 29154 / 803-481-5790; FAX: 803-481-5795

L&S Technologies Inc. (See Aimtech Mount Systems)

L. Bengtson Arms Co., 6345-B E. Akron St., Mesa, AZ 85205 / 602-981-6375

L. E. Jurras & Assoc., L. E. Jurras, P.O. Box 680, Washington, IN 47501 / 812-254-6170; FAX: 812-254-6170 jurras@sbcglobal.net www.leejurras.com

L.A.R. Mfg., Inc., 4133 W. Farm Rd., West Jordan, UT 84088 / 801-280-3505; FAX: 801-280-1972

L.B.T., Judy Smith, HCR 62, Box 145, Moyie Springs, ID 83845 / 208-267-3588

L.E. Wilson, Inc., Box 324, 404 Pioneer Ave., Cashmere, WA 98815 / 509-782-1328; FAX: 509-782-7200

L.L. Bean, Inc., Freeport, ME 04032 / 207-865-4761; FAX: 207-552-2802

L.P.A. Inc., Via Alfieri 26, Gardone V.T., Brescia, ITALY / 30-891-14-81; FAX: 30-891-09-51

L.R. Clift Mfg., 3821 Hammonton Rd., Marysville, CA 95901 / 916-755-3390; FAX: 916-755-3393

La Clinique du .45, 1432 Rougemont, Chambly, PQ J3L 2L8 CANADA / 514-658-1144

Labanu Inc., 2201-F Fifth Ave., Ronkonkoma, NY 11779 / 516-467-6197; FAX: 516-981-4112

LaBoone, Pat. See: MIDWEST SHOOTING SCHOOL, THE

LaBounty Precision Reboring, Inc, 7968 Silver Lake Rd., PO Box 186, Maple Falls, WA 98266 / 360-599-2047; FAX: 360-599-3018

LaCrosse Footwear, Inc., 18550 NE Riverside Parkway, Portland, OR 97230 / 503-766-1010; or 800-323-2668; FAX: 503-766-1015

LaFrance Specialties, P.O. Box 87933, San Diego, CA 92138 / 619-293-3373; FAX: 619-293-0819 timlafrance@att.net lafrancespecialties.com

Lake Center Marina, P.O. Box 670, St. Charles, MO 63302 / 314-946-7500

Lakefield Arms Ltd. (See Savage Arms, Inc.)

MANUFACTURER'S DIRECTORY

Lakewood Products LLC, 275 June St., Berlin, WI 54923 / 800-872-8458; FAX: 920-361-7719 lakewood@centurytel.net www.lakewoodproducts.com

Lamboy, Stephen. See: ITHACA CLASSIC DOUBLES

Lampert, Ron, Rt. 1, 44857 Schoolcraft Trl., Guthrie, MN 56461 / 218-854-7345

Lamson & Goodnow Mfg. Co., 45 Conway St., Shelburne Falls, MA 03170 / 413-625-6564; or 800-872-6564; FAX: 413-625-9816 www.lamsonsharp.com

Lansky Levine, Arthur. See: LANSKY SHARPENERS

Lansky Sharpeners, Arthur Lansky Levine, P.O. Box 50830, Las Vegas, NV 89016 / 702-361-7511; FAX: 702-896-9511

LaPrade, P.O. Box 250, Ewing, VA 24248 / 423-733-2615

LaRocca Gun Works, 51 Union Place, Worcester, MA 01608 / 508-754-2887; FAX: 508-754-2887 www.laroccagunworks.com

Larry Lyons Gunworks, 110 Hamilton St., Dowagiac, MI 49047 / 616-782-9478

Laser Devices, Inc., 2 Harris Ct. A-4, Monterey, CA 93940 / 831-373-0701; FAX: 831-373-0903 sales@laserdevices.com www.laserdevices.com

Laseraim Technologies, Inc., P.O. Box 3548, Little Rock, AR 72203 / 501-375-2227

Laserlyte, 2201 Amapola Ct., Torrance, CA 90501

LaserMax, Inc., 3495 Winton Place, Bldg. B, Rochester, NY 14623-2807 / 800-527-3703; FAX: 716-272-5427 customerservice@lasermax-inc.com www.lasermax.com

Lassen Community College, Gunsmithing Dept., P.O. Box 3000, Hwy. 139, Susanville, CA 96130 / 916-251-8800; FAX: 916-251-8838 staylor@lassencollege.edu www.lassencommunitycollege.edu

Lathrop's, Inc., 5146 E. Pima, Tucson, AZ 85712 / 520-881-0266; or 800-875-4867; FAX: 520-322-5704

Laughridge, William R. (See Cylindor & Slide, Inc.)

Laurel Mountain Forge, P.O. Box 52, Crown Point, IN 46308 / 219-548-2950; FAX: 219-548-2950

Laurona Armas Eibar, S.A.L., Avenida de Otaola 25, P.O. Box 260, Eibar 20600, SPAIN / 34-43-700600; FAX: 34-43-700616

Lawrence Brand Shot (See Precision Reloading, Inc.)

Lawrence Leather Co., P.O. Box 1479, Lillington, NC 27546 / 910-893-2071; FAX: 910-893-4742

Lawson Co., Harry, 3328 N Richey Blvd., Tucson, AZ 85716 / 520-326-1117; FAX: 520-326-1117

Lawson, John. See: SIGHT SHOP, THE

Lawson, John G. (See Sight Shop, The)

Lazzeroni Arms Co., P.O. Box 26696, Tucson, AZ 85726 / 888-492-7247; FAX: 520-624-4250

Le Clear Industries (See E-Z-Way Systems)

Leapers, Inc., 7675 Five Mile Rd., Northville, MI 48167 / 248-486-1231; FAX: 248-486-1430

Leatherman Tool Group, Inc., 12106 NE Ainsworth Cir., P.O. Box 20595, Portland, OR 97294 / 503-253-7826; FAX: 503-253-7830

Lebeau-Courally, Rue St. Gilles, 386 4000, Liege, BELGIUM / 042-52-48-43; FAX: 32-4-252-2008 info@lebeau-courally.com www.lebeau-courally.com

Leckie Professional Gunsmithing, 546 Quarry Rd., Ottsville, PA 18942 / 215-847-8594

Ledbetter Airguns, Riley, 1804 E Sprague St., Winston Salem, NC 27107-3521 / 919-784-0676

Lee Precision, Inc., 4275 Hwy. U, Hartford, WI 53027 / 262-673-3075; FAX: 262-673-9273 info@leeprecision.com www.leeprecision.com

Lee Supplies, Mark, 9901 France Ct., Lakeville, MN 55044 / 612-461-2114

LeFever Arms Co., Inc., 6234 Stokes, Lee Center Rd., Lee Contor, NY 13063 / 315 007 0722; FAX: 315-337-1543

Legacy Sports International, 206 S. Union St., Alexandria, VA 22314 / 703-548-4837 www.legacysports.com

Leica USA, Inc., 156 Ludlow Ave., Northvale, NJ 07647 / 201-767-7500; FAX: 201-767-8666

Leonard Day, 3 Kings Hwy., West Hatfield, MA 01027-9506 / 413-337-8369

Les Baer Custom, Inc., 29601 34th Ave., Hillsdale, IL 61257 / 309-658-2716; FAX: 309-658-2610 www.lesbaer.com

LesMerises, Felix. See: ROCKY MOUNTAIN ARMOURY

Lethal Force Institute (See Police Bookshelf), P.O. Box 122, Concord, NH 03301 / 603-224-6814; FAX: 603-226-3554

Lett Custom Grips, 672 Currier Rd., Hopkinton, NH 03229-2652 / 800-421-5388; FAX: 603-226-4580 info@lettgrips.com www.lettgrips.com

Leupold & Stevens, Inc., 14400 NW Greenbrier Pky., Beaverton, OR 97006 / 503-646-9171; FAX: 503-526-1455

Lever Arms Service Ltd., 2131 Burrard St., Vancouver, BC V6J 3H7 CANADA / 604-736-2711; FAX: 604-738-3503 leverarms@leverarms.com www.leverarms.com

Lew Horton Dist. Co., Inc., 15 Walkup Dr., Westboro, MA 01581 / 508-366-7400; FAX: 508-366-5332

Lewis Lead Remover, The (See Brownells, Inc.)

Liberty Metals, 2233 East 16th St., Los Angeles, CA 90021 / 213-581-9171; FAX: 213-581-9351 libertymfgsolder@hotmail.com

Liberty Safe, 999 W. Utah Ave., Payson, UT 84651-1744 / 800-247-5625; FAX: 801-489-6409

Liberty Shooting Supplies, P.O. Box 357, Hillsboro, OR 97123 / 503-640-5518; FAX: 503-640-5518 info@libertyshootingsupplies.com www.libertyshootingsupplies.com

Lightning Performance Innovations, Inc., RD1 Box 555, Mohawk, NY 13407 / 315-866-8819; FAX: 315-867-5701

Lilja Precision Rifle Barrels, P.O. Box 372, Plains, MT 59859 / 406-826-3084; FAX: 406-826-3083 lilja@riflebarrels.com www.riflebarrels.com

Lincoln, Dean, Box 1886, Farmington, NM 87401

Linder Solingen Knives, 4401 Sentry Dr. #B, Tucker, GA 30084 / 770-939-6915; FAX: 770-939-6738

Lindsay Engraving & Tools, Steve Lindsay, 3714 W. Cedar Hills, Kearney, NE 68845 / 308-236-7885 steve@lindsayengraving.com www.handgravers.com

Lindsay, Steve. See: LINDSAY ENGRAVING & TOOLS

Lindsley Arms Cartridge Co., P.O. Box 757, 20 College Hill Rd., Henniker, NH 03242 / 603-428-3127

Linebaugh Custom Sixguns, P.O. Box 455, Cody, WY 82414 / 307-645-3332 www.sixgunner.com

Lion Country Supply, P.O. Box 480, Port Matilda, PA 16870

List Precision Engineering, Unit 1 Ingley Works, 13 River Road, Barking, ENGLAND / 011-081-594-1686

Lithi Bee Bullet Lube, 1728 Carr Rd., Muskegon, MI 49442 / 616-788-4479 lithibee@att.net

"Little John's" Antique Arms, 1740 W. Laveta, Orange, CA 92668

Littler Sales Co., 20815 W. Chicago, Detroit, MI 48228 / 313-273-6889; FAX: 313-273-1099 littlersales@aol.com

Littleton, J. F., 275 Pinedale Ave., Oroville, CA 95966 / 916-533-6084

Ljutic Industries, Inc., 732 N. 16th Ave., Suite 22, Yakima, WA 98902 / 509-248-0476; FAX: 509-576-8233 ljuticgun@earthlink.net www.ljuticgun.com

Llama Gabilondo Y Cia, Apartado 290, E-01080, Victoria, SPAIN

Lock's Philadelphia Gun Exchange, 6700 Rowland Ave., Philadelphia, PA 19149 / 215-332-6225; FAX: 215-332-4800 locks.gunshop@verizon.net

Lodewick, Walter H., 2816 NE Halsey St., Portland, OR 97232 / 503-284-2554 wlodewick@aol.com

Lodgewood Mfg., P.O. Box 611, Whitewater, WI 53190 / 262-473-5444; FAX: 262-473-6448 lodgewd@idcnet.com www.lodgewood.com

Log Cabin Sport Shop, 8010 Lafayette Rd., Lodi, OH 44254 / 330-948-1082; FAX: 330-948-4307 logcabin@logcabinshop.com www.logcabinshop.com

Logan, Harry M., Box 745, Honokaa, HI 96727 / 808-776-1644

Logdewood Mfg., P.O. Box 611, Whitewater, WI 53190 / 262-473-5444; FAX: 262-473-6448 lodgewd@idcnet.com www.lodgewood.com

Lohman Mfg. Co., Inc., 4500 Doniphan Dr., P.O. Box 220, Neosho, MO 64850 / 417-451-4438; FAX: 417-451-2576

Lomont Precision Bullets, 278 Sandy Creek Rd., Salmon, ID 83467 / 208-756-6819; FAX: 208-756-6824 www.klomont.com

London Guns Ltd., Box 3750, Santa Barbara, CA 93130 / 805-683-4141; FAX: 805-683-1712

Lone Star Gunleather, 1301 Brushy Bend Dr., Round Rock, TX 78681 / 512-255-1805

Lone Star Rifle Company, 11231 Rose Road, Conroe, TX 77303 / 936-856-3363; FAX: 936-856-3363 dave@lonestar.com

Long, George F., 1402 Kokanee Ln., Grants Pass, OR 97527 / 541-476-0836

Lortone Inc., 2856 NW Market St., Seattle, WA 98107

Lothar Walther Precision Tool Inc., 3425 Hutchinson Rd., Cumming, GA 30040 / 770-889-9998; FAX: 770-889-4919 lotharwalther@mindspring.com www.lothar-walther.com

LPS Laboratories, Inc., 4647 Hugh Howell Rd., P.O. Box 3050, Tucker, GA 30084 / 404-934-7800

Lucas, Edward E, 32 Garfield Ave., East Brunswick, NJ 08816 / 201-251-5526

Lupton, Keith. See: PAWLING MOUNTAIN CLUB

Lyman Instant Targets, Inc. (See Lyman Products Corp.)

Lyman Products Corp., 475 Smith St., Middletown, CT 06457-1541 / 800-423-9704; FAX: 860-632-1699 lymansales@cshore.com www.lymanproducts.com

M

M.H. Canjar Co., 6510 Raleigh St., Arvada, CO 80003 / 303-295-2638; FAX: 303-295-2638

MA Systems, Inc., P.O. Box 894, Pryor, OK 74362-0894 / 918-824-3705; FAX: 918-824-3710

Mac-1 Airgun Distributors, 139/4 Van Ness Ave., Gardena, CA 90249-2900 / 310-327-3581; FAX: 310-327-0238 mac1@mac1airgun.com www.mac1airgun.com

Machinist's Workshop-Village Press, P.O. Box 1810, Traverse City, MI 49685 / 800-447-7367; FAX: 616-946-3289

Madis Books, 2453 West Five Mile Pkwy., Dallac, TX 75233 / 214-330-7168

Madis, George. See: WINCHESTER CONSULTANTS

MAG Instrument, Inc., 1635 S. Sacramento Ave., Ontario, CA 91761 / 909-947-1006; FAX: 909-947-3116

Magma Engineering Co., P.O. Box 161, 20955 E. Ocotillo Rd., Queen Creek, AZ 85242 / 602-987-9008; FAX: 602-987-0148

Mag-Na-Port International, Inc., 41302 Executive Dr., Harrison Twp., MI 48045-1306 / 586-469-6727; FAX: 586-469-0425 email@magnaport.com www.magnaport.com

Magnum Power Products, Inc., P.O. Box 17768, Fountain Hills, AZ 85268

Magnum Research, Inc., 7110 University Ave. NE, Minneapolis, MN 55432 / 800-772-6168 or 763-574-1868; FAX: 763-574-0109 info@magnumresearch.com

Magnus Bullets, P.O. Box 239, Toney, AL 35773 / 256-420-8359; FAX: 256-420-8360 bulletman@mchsi.com www.magnusbullets.com

Mag-Pack Corp., P.O. Box 846, Chesterland, OH 44026 / 440-285-9480 magpack@hotmail.com

MagSafe Ammo Co., 4700 S US Highway 17/92, Casselberry, FL 32707-3814 / 407-834-9966; FAX: 407-834-8185 www.magsafeonline.com

Magtech Ammunition Co. Inc., 6845 20th Ave. S., Ste. 120, Centerville, MN 55038 / 651-762-8500; FAX: 651-429-9485 www.magtechammunition.com

Mahony, Philip Bruce, 67 White Hollow Rd., Lime Rock, CT 06039-2418 / 860-435-9341 filbalony-redbeard@snet.net

Mahovsky's Metalife, R.D. 1, Box 149a Eureka Road, Grand Valley, PA 16420 / 814-436-7747

Makinson, Nicholas, RR 3, Komoka, ON N0L 1R0 CANADA / 519-471-5462

Mallardtone Game Calls, 10406 96th St., Court West, Taylor Ridge, IL 61284 / 309-798-2481; FAX: 309-798-2501

Mandall Shooting Supply Inc., 5442 E. Cambridge Ave., Phoenix, AZ 85008-1721 / 602-952-0097; FAX: 480-949-0734

Marble Arms (See CRR, Inc./Marble's Inc.)

Marchmon Bullets, 6502 Riverdale Rd., Whitmore Lake, MI 48189

Marent, Rudolf. See: HAMMERLI SERVICE-PRECISION MAC

Mark Lee Supplies, 9901 France Ct., Lakeville, MN 55044 / 952-461-2114; FAX: 952-461-2194 marklee55044@usfamily.net

Markell, Inc., 422 Larkfield Center 235, Santa Rosa, CA 95403 / 707-573-0792; FAX: 707-573-9867

Markesbery Muzzle Loaders, Inc., 7785 Foundation Dr., Ste. 6, Florence, KY 41042 / 606-342-5553 or 606-342-2380

Marksman Products, 5482 Argosy Dr., Huntington Beach, CA 92649 / 714-898-7535; or 800-822-8005; FAX: 714-891-0782

Marlin Firearms Co., 100 Kenna Dr., North Haven, CT 06473 / 203-239-5621; FAX: 203-234-7991 www.marlinfirearms.com

Marocchi F.lli S.p.A, Via Galileo Galilei 8, I-25068 Zanano, ITALY

Marsh, Mike, Croft Cottage, Main St., Derbyshire, DE4 2BY ENGLAND / 01629 650 669

Marshall Enterprises, 792 Canyon Rd., Redwood City, CA 94062

MANUFACTURER'S DIRECTORY

Marshall Fish Mfg. Gunsmith Sptg. Co., 87 Champlain Ave., Westport, NY 12993 / 518-962-4897; FAX: 518-762-4897

Martin B. Retting Inc., 11029 Washington, Culver City, CA 90232 / 213-837-2412 retting@retting.com

Martini & Hagn, 1264 Jimsmith Lake Rd., Cranbrook, BC V1C 6V6 CANADA / 250-417-2926; FAX: 250-417-2928

Martin's Gun Shop, 937 S. Sheridan Blvd., Lakewood, CO 80226 / 303-922-2184

Martz, John V., 8060 Lakeview Lane, Lincoln, CA 95648 FAX: 916-645-3815

Marvel, Alan, 3922 Madonna Rd., Jarretsville, MD 21084 / 301-557-6545

Marx, Harry (See U.S. Importer for FERLIB)

Maryland Paintball Supply, 8507 Harford Rd., Parkville, MD 21234 / 410-882-5607

MAST Technology, Inc., 14555 US Hwy. 95 S., P.O. Box 60969, Boulder City, NV 89006 / 702-293-6969; FAX: 702-293-7255 info@masttechnology.com www.bellammo.com

Master Lock Co., 2600 N. 32nd St., Milwaukee, WI 53245 / 414-444-2800

Match Prep-Doyle Gracey, P.O. Box 155, Tehachapi, CA 93581 / 661-822-5383; FAX: 661-823-8680 gracenotes@csurpers.net www.matchprep.com

Mathews Gun Shop & Gunsmithing, Inc., 10224 S. Paramount Blvd., Downey, CA 90241 / 562-928-2129; FAX: 562-928-8629

Matthews Cutlery, 4401 Sentry Dr. #B, Tucker, GA 30084 / 770-939-6915

Mauser Werke Oberndorf Waffensysteme GmbH, Postfach 1349, 78722, Oberndorf/N., GERMANY

Maverick Arms, Inc., 7 Grasso Ave., P.O. Box 497, North Haven, CT 06473 / 203-230-5300; FAX: 203-230-5420

Maxi-Mount Inc., P.O. Box 291, Willoughby Hills, OH 44096-0291 / 440-944-9456; FAX: 440-944-9456 maximount454@yahoo.com

Mayville Engineering Co. (See MEC, Inc.)

Mazur Restoration, Pete, 13083 Drummer Way, Grass Valley, CA 95949 / 530-268-2412

McCament, Jay. See: JAY MCCAMENT CUSTOM GUNMAKER

McCann, Tom, 14 Walton Dr., New Hope, PA 18938 / 215-862-2728

McCann Industries, P.O. Box 641, Spanaway, WA 98387 / 253-537-6919; FAX: 253-537-6919 mccann.machine@worldnet.att.net www.mccannindustries.com

McCluskey Precision Rifles, 10502 14th Ave. NW, Seattle, WA 98177 / 206-781-2776

McCombs, Leo, 1862 White Cemetery Rd., Patriot, OH 45658 / 740-256-1714

McDonald, Dennis, 8359 Brady St., Peosta, IA 52068 / 319-556-7940

McFarland, Stan, 2221 Idella Ct., Grand Junction, CO 81505 / 970-243-4704

McGhee, Larry. See: B.C. OUTDOORS

McGowen Rifle Barrels, 5961 Spruce Lane, St. Anne, IL 60964 / 815-937-9816; FAX: 815-937-4024

Mchalik, Gary. See: ROSSI FIREARMS

McKenzie, Lynton, 6940 N. Alvernon Way, Tucson, AZ 85718 / 520-299-5090

McMillan Fiberglass Stocks, Inc., 1638 W. Knudsen Dr. #102, Phoenix, AZ 85027 / 623-582-9635; FAX: 623-581-3825 mfsinc@mcmfamily.com www.mcmfamily.com

McMillan Optical Gunsight Co., 28638 N. 42nd St., Cave Creek, AZ 85331 / 602-585-7868; FAX: 602-585-7872

McMillan Rifle Barrels, P.O. Box 3427, Bryan, TX 77805 / 409-690-3456; FAX: 409-690-0156

McMurdo, Lynn, P.O. Box 404, Afton, WY 83110 / 307-886-5535

MCS, Inc., 166 Pocono Rd., Brookfield, CT 06804-2023 / 203-775-1013; FAX: 203-775-9462

McWelco Products, 6730 Santa Fe Ave., Hesperia, CA 92345 / 619-244-8876; FAX: 619-244-9398 products@mcwelco.com www.mcwelco.com

MDS, P.O. Box 1441, Brandon, FL 33509-1441 / 813-653-1180; FAX: 813-684-5953

Meacham Tool & Hardware Co., Inc., 37052 Eberhardt Rd., Peck, ID 83545 / 208-486-7171 smeacham@clearwater.net www.meachamrifles.com

Measurement Group Inc., Box 27777, Raleigh, NC 27611

Measures, Leon. See: SHOOT WHERE YOU LOOK

MEC, Inc., 715 South St., Mayville, WI 53050 reloaders@mayvl.com www.mecreloaders.com

MEC-Gar S.R.L., Via Madonnina 64, Gardone V.T. Brescia, ITALY / 39-030-3733668; FAX: 39-030-3733687 info@mec-gar.it www.mec-gar.it

MEC-Gar U.S.A., Inc., Hurley Farms Industr. Park, 115, Hurley Road 6G, Oxford, CT 06478 / 203-262-1525; FAX: 203-262-1719 mecgar@aol.com www.mec-gar.com

Mech-Tech Systems, Inc., 1602 Foothill Rd., Kalispell, MT 59901 / 406-755-8055

Meister Bullets (See Gander Mountain)

Mele, Frank, 201 S. Wellow Ave., Cookeville, TN 38501 / 615-526-4860

Menck, Gunsmith Inc., T.W., 5703 S 77th St., Ralston, NE 68127

Mendez, John A., 1309 Continental Dr., Daytona Beach, FL 32117-3807 / 407-344-2791

Men-Metallwerk Elisenhuette GmbH, P.O. Box 1263, Nassau/Lahn, D-56372 GERMANY / 2604-7819

Meprolight (See Hesco-Meprolight)

Mercer Custom Guns, 216 S. Whitewater Ave., Jefferson, WI 53549 / 920-674-3839

Merit Corp., P.O. Box 9044, Schenectady, NY 12309 / 518-346-1420 sales@meritcorporation.com www.meritcorporation.com

Merkel, Schutzenstrasse 26, D-98527 Suhl, Suhl, GERMANY FAX: 011-49-3681-854-203 www.merkel-waffen.de

Metal Merchants, P.O. Box 186, Walled Lake, MI 48390-0186

Metalife Industries (See Mahovsky's Metalife)

Michael's Antiques, Box 591, Waldoboro, ME 04572

Michaels of Oregon Co., P.O. Box 1690, Oregon City, OR 97045 www.michaels-oregon.com

Micro Sight Co., 242 Harbor Blvd., Belmont, CA 94002 / 415-591-0769; FAX: 415-591-7531

Microfusion Alfa S.A., Paseo San Andres N8, P.O. Box 271, Eibar 20600, 20600 SPAIN / 34-43-11-89-16; FAX: 34-43-11-40-38

Mid-America Recreation, Inc., 1328 5th Ave., Moline, IL 61265 / 309-764-5089; FAX: 309-764-5089 fmilcusguns@aol.com www.midamericarecreation.com

Middlebrooks Custom Shop, 7366 Colonial Trail East, Surry, VA 23883 / 757-357-0881; FAX: 757-365-0442

Midway Arms, Inc., 5875 W. Van Horn Tavern Rd., Columbia, MO 65203 / 800-243-3220; FAX: 800-992-8312 www.midwayusa.com

Midwest Gun Sport, 1108 Herbert Dr., Zebulon, NC 27597 / 919-269-5570

Midwest Shooting School, The, Pat LaBoone, 2550 Hwy. 23, Wrenshall, MN 55797 / 218-384-3670 shootingschool@starband.net

Midwest Sport Distributors, Box 129, Fayette, MO 65248

Mike Davis Products, 643 Loop Dr., Moses Lake, WA 98837 / 509-765-6178; or 509-766-7281

Mike Yee Custom Stocking, 29927 56 Pl. S., Auburn, WA 98001 / 253-839-3991

Military Armament Corp., P.O. Box 120, Mt. Zion Rd., Lingleville, TX 76461 / 817-965-3253

Millennium Designed Muzzleloaders, P.O. Box 536, Routes 11 & 25, Limington, ME 04049 / 207-637-2316

Miller Arms, Inc., P.O. Box 260 Purl St., St. Onge, SD 57779 / 605-642-5160; FAX: 605-642-5160

Miller Custom, 210 E. Julia, Clinton, IL 61727 / 217-935-9362

Miller Single Trigger Mfg. Co., 6680 Rt. 5-20, P.O. Box 471, Bloomfield, NY 14469 / 585-657-6338

Millett Sights, 7275 Murdy Circle, Adm. Office, Huntington Beach, CA 92647 / 714-842-5575 or 800-645-5388; FAX: 714-843-5707

Mills Jr., Hugh B., 3615 Canterbury Rd., New Bern, NC 28560 / 919-637-4631

Milstor Corp., 80-975 Indio Blvd. C-7, Indio, CA 92201 / 760-775-9998; FAX: 760-775-5229 milstor@webtv.net

Minute Man High Tech Industries, 10611 Canyon Rd. E., Suite 151, Puyallup, WA 98373 / 800-233-2734

Mirador Optical Corp., P.O. Box 11614, Marina Del Rey, CA 90295-7614 / 310-821-5587; FAX: 310-305-0386

Mitchell, Jack, c/o Geoff Gaebe, Addieville East Farm, 200 Pheasant Dr., Mapleville, RI 02839 / 401-568-3185

Mitchell Bullets, R.F., 430 Walnut St., Westernport, MD 21562

Mitchell Mfg. Corp., P.O. Box 9295, Fountain Valley, CA 92728 / 714-444-2220

Mitchell Optics, Inc., 2072 CR 1100 N, Sidney, IL 61877 / 217-688-2219; or 217-621-3018; FAX: 217-688-2505 mitchell@attglobal.net

Mitchell's Accuracy Shop, 68 Greenridge Dr., Stafford, VA 22554 / 703-659-0165

Mitchell's Mauser, P.O. Box 9295, Fountain Valley, CA 92728 / 714-979-7663; FAX: 714-899-3660

MI-TE Bullets, 1396 Ave. K, Ellsworth, KS 67439 / 785-472-4575; FAX: 785-472-5579

Mittleman, William, P.O. Box 65, Etna, CA 96027

Mixson Corp., 7635 W. 28th Ave., Hialeah, FL 33016 / 305-821-5190; or 800-327-0078; FAX: 305-558-9318

MJK Gunsmithing, Inc., 417 N. Huber Ct., E. Wenatchee, WA 98802 / 509-884-7683

MKS Supply, Inc. (See Hi-Point Firearms)

MMC, 2700 W. Sahara Ave. Ste. 440, Las Vegas, NV 89102-1703 / 817-831-9557; FAX: 817-834-5508

MOA Corporation, 2451 Old Camden Pike, Eaton, OH 45320 / 937-456-3669 www.moaguns.com

Mobile Area Networks, Inc., 2772 Depot St., Sanford, FL 32773 / 407-333-2350; FAX: 407-333-9903 georgew@mobilan.com

Modern Gun Repair School, P.O. Box 846, Saint Albans, VT 05478 / 802-524-2223; FAX: 802-524-2053 jfwp@dlilearn.com www.mgsinfoadlilearn.com

Modern Muzzleloading, Inc., P.O. Box 130, Centerville, IA 52544 / 515-856-2626

Moeller, Steve, 1213 4th St., Fulton, IL 61252 / 815-589-2300

Mogul Co./Life Jacket, 500 N. Kimball Rd., Ste. 109, South Lake, TX 76092

Monell Custom Guns, 228 Red Mills Rd., Pine Bush, NY 12566 / 914-744-3021

Moneymaker Guncraft Corp., 1420 Military Ave., Omaha, NE 68131 / 402-556-0226

Montana Armory, Inc., 100 Centennial Dr., P.O. Box 885, Big Timber, MT 59011 / 406-932-4353; FAX: 406-932-4443

Montana Outfitters, Lewis E. Yearout, 308 Riverview Dr. E., Great Falls, MT 59404 / 406-761-0859; or 406-727-4560

Montana Precision Swaging, P.O. Box 4746, Butte, MT 59702 / 406-494-0600; FAX: 406-494-0600

Montana Rifleman, Inc., 2593A Hwy. 2 East, Kalispell, MT 59901 / 406-755-4867

Montana Vintage Arms, 2354 Bear Canyon Rd., Bozeman, MT 59715

Morini (See U.S. Importers-Mandall Shooting Supplies, Inc.)

Morrison Custom Rifles, J. W., 4015 W Sharon, Phoenix, AZ 85029 / 602-978-3754

Morrison Precision, 6719 Calle Mango, Hereford, AZ 85615 / 520-378-6207 morprec@c2i2.com

Morrow, Bud, 11 Hillside Lane, Sheridan, WY 82801-9729 / 307-674-8360

Morton Booth Co., P.O. Box 123, Joplin, MO 64802 / 417-673-1962; FAX: 417-673-3642

Mo's Competitor Supplies (See MCS, Inc.)

Moss Double Tone, Inc., P.O. Box 1112, 2101 S. Kentucky, Sedalia, MO 65301 / 816-827-0827

Mountain Plains Industries, 3720 Otter Place, Lynchburg, VA 24503 / 800-687-3000; FAX: 434-845-6594 MPItargets@verizon.com

Mowrey Gun Works, P.O. Box 246, Waldron, IN 46182 / 317-525-6181; FAX: 317-525-9595

Mowrey's Guns & Gunsmithing, 119 Fredericks St., Canajoharie, NY 13317 / 518-673-3483

MPC, P.O. Box 450, McMinnville, TN 37110-0450 / 615-473-5513; FAX: 615-473-5516 thebox@blomand.net www.mpc-thebox.com

MPI Stocks, P.O. Box 83266, Portland, OR 97283 / 503-226-1215; FAX: 503-226-2661

MSR Targets, P.O. Box 1042, West Covina, CA 91793 / 818-331-7840

MTM Molded Products Co., Inc., 3370 Obco Ct., Dayton, OH 45414 / 937-890-7461; FAX: 937-890-1747

Mulberry House Publishing, P.O. Box 2180, Apache Junction, AZ 85217 / 888-738-1567; FAX: 480-671-1015

Mulhern, Rick, Rt. 5, Box 152, Rayville, LA 71269 / 318-728-2688

Mullins Ammunition, Rt. 2 Box 304N, Clintwood, VA 24228 / 276-926-6772; FAX: 276-926-6092 mammo@extremeshockusa.com www.extremeshockusa.com

Mullis Guncraft, 3523 Lawyers Road E., Monroe, NC 28110 / 704-283-6683

Multiplex International, 26 S. Main St., Concord, NH 03301 FAX: 603-796-2223

Multipropulseurs, La Bertrandiere, 42580, FRANCE / 77 74 01 30; FAX: 77 93 19 34

Mundy, Thomas A., 69 Robbins Road, Somerville, NJ 08876 / 201-722-2199

Murmur Corp., 2823 N. Westmoreland Ave., Dallas, TX 75222 / 214-630-5400

Murphy, R.R. Murphy Co., Inc. See: MURPHY, R.R. CO., INC.

Murphy, R.R. Co., Inc., R.R. Murphy Co., Inc. Murphy, P.O. Box 102, Ripley, TN 38063 / 901-635-4003; FAX: 901-635-2320

Murray State College, 1 Murray Campus St., Tishomingo, OK 73460 / 508-371-2371 darnold@mscol.edu

Muscle Products Corp., 112 Fennell Dr., Butler, PA 16002 / 800-227-7049; or 724-283-0567; FAX: 724-283-8310 mpc@mpc_home.com www.mpc_home.com

Muzzleloaders Etcetera, Inc., 9901 Lyndale Ave. S., Bloomington, MN 55420 / 952-884-1161 www.muzzleloaders-etcetera.com

MWG Co., P.O. Box 971202, Miami, FL 33197 / 800-428-9394; or 305-253-8393; FAX: 305-232-1247

N

N.B.B., Inc., 24 Elliot Rd., Sterling, MA 01564 / 508-422-7538; or 800-942-9444

N.C. Ordnance Co., P.O. Box 3254, Wilson, NC 27895 / 919-237-2440; FAX: 919-243-9845

Nagel's Custom Bullets, 100 Scott St., Baytown, TX 77520-2849

Nalpak, 1937-C Friendship Drive, El Cajon, CA 92020 / 619-258-1200

Nammo Lapua Oy, P.O. Box 5, Lapua, FINLAND / 358-6-4310111; FAX: 358-6-4310317 info@nammo.ti www.lapua.com

Nastoff, Steve. See: NASTOFFS 45 SHOP, INC.

Nastoffs 45 Shop, Inc., Steve Nastoff, 1057 Laverne Dr., Youngstown, OH 44511

National Bullet Co., 1585 E. 361 St., Eastlake, OH 44095 / 216-951-1854; FAX: 216-951-7761

National Target Co., 3958-D Dartmouth Ct., Frederick, MD 21703 / 800-827-7060; FAX: 301-874-4764

Nationwide Airgun Repair, 2310 Windsor Forest Dr., Louisville, KY 40272 / 502-937-2614; FAX: 812-637-1463 shortshoestring@insightbb.com

Naval Ordnance Works, 467 Knott Rd., Sheperdstown, WV 25443 / 304-876-0998; FAX: 304-876-0998 nvordfdy@earthlink.net

Navy Arms Co., 219 Lawn St., Martinsburg, WV 25401 / 304-262-9870; FAX: 304-262-1658

Navy Arms Company, Valmore J. Forgett Jr., 815 22nd Street, Union City, NJ 07087 / 201-863-7100; FAX: 201-863-8770 info@navyarms.com www.navyarms.com

NCP Products, Inc., 3500 12th St. N.W., Canton, OH 44708 / 330-456-5130; FAX: 330-456-5234

Necessary Concepts, Inc., P.O. Box 571, Deer Park, NY 11729 / 516-667-8509; FAX: 516-667-8588

NEI Handtools, Inc., 10960 Gary Player Dr., El Paso, TX 79935

Neil A. Jones Custom Products, 17217 Brookhouser Road, Saegertown, PA 16433 / 814-763-2769; FAX: 814-763-4228

Nelson, Gary K., 975 Terrace Dr., Oakdale, CA 95361 / 209-847-4590

Nelson, Stephen. See: NELSON'S CUSTOM GUNS, INC.

Nelson's Custom Guns, Inc., Stephen Nelson, 7430 Valley View Dr. N.W., Corvallis, OR 97330 / 541-745-5232 nelsons-custom@attbi.com

Nesci Enterprises Inc., P.O. Box 119, Summit St., East Hampton, CT 06424 / 203-267-2588

Nesika Bay Precision, 22239 Big Valley Rd., Poulsbo, WA 98370 / 206-697-3830

Nettestad Gun Works, 38962 160th Avenue, Pelican Rapids, MN 56572 / 218-863-1338

Neumann GmbH, Am Galgenberg 6, 90575, GERMANY / 09101/8258; FAX: 09101/6356

New England Ammunition Co., 1771 Post Rd. East, Suite 223, Westport, CT 06880 / 203-254-8048

New England Arms Co., Box 278, Lawrence Lane, Kittery Point, ME 03905 / 207-439-0593; FAX: 207-439-0525 info@newenglandarms.com www.newenglandarms.com

New England Custom Gun Service, 438 Willow Brook Rd., Plainfield, NH 03781 / 603-469-3450; FAX: 603-469-3471 bestguns@adelphia.net www.newenglandcustom.com

New Orleans Jewelers Supply Co., 206 Charters St., New Orleans, LA 70130 / 504-523-3839; FAX: 504-523-3836

New SKB Arms Co., C.P.O. Box 1401, Tokyo, JAPAN / 81-3-3943-9550; FAX: 81-3-3943-0695

New Ultra Light Arms, LLC, P.O. Box 340, Granville, WV 26534

Newark Electronics, 4801 N. Ravenswood Ave., Chicago, IL 60640

Newell, Robert H., 55 Coyote, Los Alamos, NM 87544 / 505-662-7135

Newman Gunshop, 2035 Chester Ave. #411, Ottumwa, IA 52501-3715 / 515-937-5775

NgraveR Co., The, 67 Wawecus Hill Rd., Bozrah, CT 06334 / 860-823-1533; FAX: 860-887-6252 ngraver98@aol.com www.ngraver.com

Nicholson Custom, 17285 Thornlay Road, Hughesville, MO 65334 / 816-826-8746

Nickels, Paul R., 4328 Seville St., Las Vegas, NV 89121 / 702-435-5318

Niemi Engineering, W. B., Box 126 Center Rd., Greensboro, VT 05841 / 802-533-7180; FAX: 802-533-7141

Nikon, Inc., 1300 Walt Whitman Rd., Melville, NY 11747 / 516-547-8623; FAX: 516-547-0309

Noreen, Peter H., 5075 Buena Vista Dr., Belgrade, MT 59714 / 406-586-7383

Norica, Avnda Otaola, 16 Apartado 68, Eibar, SPAIN

Norinco, 7A Yun Tan N, Beijing, CHINA

Norincoptics (See BEC, Inc.)

Norma Precision AB (See U.S. Importers-Dynamit)

Normark Corp., 10395 Yellow Circle Dr., Minnetonka, MN 55343-9101 / 612-933-7060; FAX: 612-933-0046

North American Arms, Inc., 2150 South 950 East, Provo, UT 84606-6285 / 800-821-5783; or 801-374-9990; FAX: 801-374-9998

North American Correspondence Schools, The Gun Pro, Oak & Pawney St., Scranton, PA 18515 / 717-342-7701

North American Shooting Systems, P.O. Box 306, Osoyoos, BC V0H 1V0 CANADA / 250-495-3131; FAX: 250-495-3131 rifle@cablerocket.com

North Devon Firearms Services, 3 North St., Braunton, EX33 1AJ ENGLAND / 01271 813624; FAX: 01271 813624

North Mountain Pine Training Center (See Executive Protection Institute)

North Star West, P.O. Box 488, Glencoe, CA 95232 / 209-293-7010 northstarwest.com

Northern Precision, 329 S. James St., Carthage, NY 13619 / 315-493-1711

Northside Gun Shop, 2725 NW 109th, Oklahoma City, OK 73120 / 405-840-2353

Northwest Arms, 26884 Pearl Rd., Parma, ID 83660 / 208-722-6771; FAX: 208-722-1062

Northwest Custom Projectile, P.O. Box 127, Butte, MT 59703-0127 www.customprojectile.com

No-Sho Mfg. Co., 10727 Glenfield Ct., Houston, TX 77096 / 713-723-5332

Nosler, Inc., P.O. Box 671, Bend, OR 97709 / 800-285-3701; or 541-382-3921; FAX: 541-388-4667 www.nosler.com

Novak's, Inc., 1206 1/2 30th St., P.O. Box 4045, Parkersburg, WV 26101 / 304-485-9295; FAX: 304-428-6722 www.novaksights.com

Nowlin Mfg. Co., 20622 S 4092 Rd., Claremore, OK 74017 / 918-342-0689; FAX: 918-342-0624 nowlinguns@msn.com nowlinguns.com

NRI Gunsmith School, P.O. Box 182968, Columbus, OH 43218-2968

Nu Line Guns, 8150 CR 4055, Rhineland, MO 65069 / 573-676-5500; FAX: 314-447-5018 nlg@ktis.net

Null Holsters Ltd. K.L., 161 School St. N.W., Resaca, GA 30735 / 706-625-5643; FAX: 706-625-9392 ken@klnullholsters.com www.klnullholsters.com

Numrich Gun Parts Corporation, 226 Williams Lane, P.O. Box 299, West Hurley, NY 12491 / 866-686-7424; FAX: 877-GUNPART info@gunpartscorp.com www.@-gunparts.com

Nygord Precision Products, Inc., P.O. Box 12578, Prescott, AZ 86304 / 928-717-2315; FAX: 928-717-2198 nygords@northlink.com www.nygordprecision.com

O

O.F. Mossberg & Sons, Inc., 7 Grasso Ave., North Haven, CT 06473 / 203-230-5300; FAX: 203-230-5420

Oakman Turkey Calls, RD 1, Box 825, Harrisonville, PA 17228 / 717-485-4620

Obermeyer Rifled Barrels, 23122 60th St., Bristol, WI 53104 / 262-843-3537; FAX: 262-843-2129 www.obermeyerbarrels.com

October Country Muzzleloading, P.O. Box 969, Dept. GD, Hayden, ID 83835 / 208-772-2068; FAX: 208-772-9230 ocinfo@octobercountry.com www.octobercountry.com

Oehler Research, Inc., P.O. Box 9135, Austin, TX 78766 / 512-327-6900; or 800-531-5125; FAX: 512-327-6903 www.oehler-research.com

Oil Rod and Gun Shop, 69 Oak St., East Douglas, MA 01516 / 508-476-3687

OK Weber, Inc., P.O. Box 7485, Eugene, OR 97401 / 541-747-0458; FAX: 541-747-5927 okweber@pacinfo www.okweber.com

Oker's Engraving, P.O. Box 126, Shawnee, CO 80475 / 303-838-6042

Oklahoma Ammunition Co., 3701A S. Harvard Ave., No. 367, Tulsa, OK 74135-2265 / 918-396-3187; FAX: 918-396-4270

Oklahoma Leather Products, Inc., 500 26th NW, Miami, OK 74354 / 918-542-6651; FAX: 918-542-6653

Olathe Gun Shop, 716-A South Rogers Road, Olathe, KS 66062 / 913-782-6900; FAX: 913-782-6902 info@olathegunshop.com www.olathegunshop.com

Old Wagon Bullets, 32 Old Wagon Rd., Wilton, CT 06897

Old West Bullet Moulds, J. Ken Chapman, P.O. Box 519, Flora Vista, NM 87415 / 505-334-6970

Old West Reproductions, Inc. R.M. Bachman, 446 Florence S. Loop, Florence, MT 59833 / 406-273-2615; FAX: 406-273-2615 rick@oldwestreproductions.com www.oldwestreproductions.com

Old Western Scrounger Ammunition Inc., 50 Industrial Parkway, Carson City, NV 89706 / 775-246-2091; FAX: 775-246-2095 www.ows-ammunition.com

Old World Gunsmithing, 2901 SE 122nd St., Portland, OR 97236 / 503-760-7681

Ole Frontier Gunsmith Shop, 2617 Hwy. 29 S., Cantonment, FL 32533 / 904-477-8074

Olson, Myron, 989 W. Kemp, Watertown, SD 57201 / 605-886-9787

Olson, Vic, 5002 Countryside Dr., Imperial, MO 63052 / 314-296-8086

Olympic Arms Inc., 620-626 Old Pacific Hwy. SE, Olympia, WA 98513 / 360-456-3471; FAX: 360-491-3447 info@olyarms.com www.olyarms.com

Olympic Optical Co., P.O. Box 752377, Memphis, TN 38175-2377 / 901-794-3890; or 800-238-7120; FAX: 901-794-0676

Omega Sales, P.O. Box 1066, Mt. Clemens, MI 48043 / 810-469-7323; FAX: 810-469-0425

One Of A Kind, 15610 Purple Sage, San Antonio, TX 78255 / 512-695-3364

One Ragged Hole, P.O. Box 13624, Tallahassee, FL 32317-3624

Op-Tec, P.O. Box L632, Langhorn, PA 19047 / 215-757-5037; FAX: 215-757-7097

Optical Services Co., P.O. Box 1174, Santa Teresa, NM 88008-1174 / 505-589-3833

Orchard Park Enterprise, P.O. Box 563, Orchard Park, NY 14127 / 616-656-0356

Ordnance Works, The, 2969 Pigeon Point Rd., Eureka, CA 95501 / 707-443-3252

Oregon Arms, Inc. (See Rogue Rifle Co., Inc.)

Oregon Trail Bullet Company, P.O. Box 529, Dept. P, Baker City, OR 97814 / 800-811-0548; FAX: 514-523-1803

Original Box, Inc., 700 Linden Ave., York, PA 17404 / 717-854-2897; FAX: 717-845-4276

Original Deer Formula Co., The, P.O. Box 1705, Dickson, TN 37056 / 800-874-6965; FAX: 615-446-0646 deerformula1@aol.com www.deerformula.com

Orion Rifle Barrel Co., RR2, 137 Cobler Village, Kalispell, MT 59901 / 406-257-5649

Orvis Co., The, Rt. 7, Manchester, VT 05254 / 802-362-3622; FAX: 802-362-3525

Otis Technology, Inc., RR 1 Box 84, Boonville, NY 13309 / 315-942-3320

Ottmar, Maurice, Box 657, 113 E. Fir, Coulee City, WA 99115 / 509-632-5717

Outa-Site Gun Carriers, 219 Market St., Laredo, TX 78040 / 210-722-4678; or 800-880-9715; FAX: 210-726-4858

Outdoor Connection, Inc., The, 7901 Panther Way, Waco, TX 76712-6556 / 800-533-6076; FAX: 254-776-3553 info@outdoorconnection.com www.outdoorconnection.com

Outdoor Edge Cutlery Corp., 4699 Nautilus Ct. S. Ste. 503, Boulder, CO 80301-5310 / 303-530-7667; FAX: 303-530-7020 www.outdooredge.com

Outdoor Enthusiast, 3784 W. Woodland, Springfield, MO 65807 / 417-883-9841

Outdoor Sports Headquarters, Inc., 967 Watertower Ln., West Carrollton, OH 45449 / 513-865-5855; FAX: 513-865-5962

Outers Laboratories Div. of ATK, Route 2, P.O. Box 39, Onalaska, WI 54650 / 608-781-5800; FAX: 608-781-0368

Ox-Yoke Originals, Inc., 34 Main St., Milo, ME 04463 / 800-231-8313; or 207-943-7351; FAX: 207-943-2416

Ozark Gun Works, 11830 Cemetery Rd., Rogers, AR 72756 / 479-631-1024; FAX: 479-631-1024 ozarkgunworks@cox.net www.geocities.com

MANUFACTURER'S DIRECTORY

P

P&M Sales & Services, LLC, 4697 Tote Rd. Bldg. H-B, Comins, MI 48619 / 989-848-8364; FAX: 989-848-8364 info@pmsales-online.com

P.S.M.G. Gun Co., 10 Park Ave., Arlington, MA 02174 / 781-646-1699; FAX: 781-643-7212 psmg2@aol.com

Pachmayr Div. Lyman Products, 475 Smith St., Middletown, CT 06457 / 860-632-2020; or 800-225-9626; FAX: 860-632-1699 lymansales@cshore.com www.pachmayr.com

Pacific Armament Corp, 4813 Enterprise Way, Unit K, Modesto, CA 95356 / 209-545-2800 gunsparts@att.net

Pacific Rifle Co., P.O. Box 841, Carlton, OR 97111 / 503-852-6276 pacificrifle@aol.com

PAC-NOR Barreling, 99299 Overlook Rd., P.O. Box 6188, Brookings, OR 97415 / 503-469-7330; FAX: 503-469-7331 info@pac-nor.com www.pac-nor.com

PACT, Inc., P.O. Box 535025, Grand Prairie, TX 75053 / 972-641-0049; FAX: 972-641-2641

Page Custom Bullets, P.O. Box 25, Port Moresby, NEW GUINEA

Pagel Gun Works, Inc., 2 SE 1st St., Grand Rapids, MN 55744

Pager Pal, 200 W Pleasantview, Hurst, TX 76054 / 800-561-1603; FAX: 817-285-8769 www.pagerpal.com

Paintball Games International Magazine Aceville, Castle House 97 High St., Essex, ENGLAND / 011-44-206-564840

Palsa Outdoor Products, P.O. Box 81336, Lincoln, NE 68501 / 402-488-5288; FAX: 402-488-2321

Pansch, Robert F, 1004 Main St. #10, Neenah, WI 54956 / 920-725-8175

Paragon Sales & Services, Inc., 2501 Theodore St., Crest Hill, IL 60435-1613 / 815-725-9212; FAX: 815-725-8974

Para-Ordnance Mfg., Inc., 980 Tapscott Rd., Scarborough, ON M1X 1E7 CANADA / 416-297-7855; FAX: 416-297-1289

Para-Ordnance, Inc., 1919 NE 45th St., Ste 215, Ft. Lauderdale, FL 33308 info@paraord.com www.paraord.com

Pardini Armi Srl, Via Italica 154, 55043, Lido Di Camaiore Lu, ITALY / 584-90121; FAX: 584-90122

Paris, Frank J., 17417 Pershing St., Livonia, MI 48152-3822

Park Rifle Co., Ltd., The, Unit 6a Dartford Trade Park, Power Mill Lane, Dartford DA7 7NX, ENGLAND / 011-0322-222512

Parker & Sons Shooting Supply, 9337 Smoky Row Road, Strawberry Plains, TN 37871 / 865-933-3286; FAX: 865-932-8586

Parker Gun Finishes, 9337 Smokey Row Rd., Strawberry Plains, TN 37871 / 865-933-3286; FAX: 865-932-8586 parcraft7838@netzero.com

Parsons Optical Mfg. Co., PO Box 192, Ross, OH 45061 / 513-867-0820; FAX: 513-867-8380 psscopes@concentric.net

Partridge Sales Ltd., John, Trent Meadows, Rugeley, ENGLAND

Pasadena Gun Center, 206 E. Shaw, Pasadena, TX 77506 / 713-472-0417; FAX: 713-472-1322

Passive Bullet Traps, Inc. (See Savage Range Systems, Inc.)

Paterson Gunsmithing, 438 Main St., Paterson, NJ 07502 / 201-345-4100

Pathfinder Sports Leather, 2920 E. Chambers St., Phoenix, AZ 85040 / 602-276-0016

Patrick W. Price Bullets, 16520 Worthley Drive, San Lorenzo, CA 94580 / 510-278-1547

Pattern Control, 114 N. Third St., P.O. Box 462105, Garland, TX 75046 / 214-494-3551; FAX: 214-272-8447

Paul A. Harris Hand Engraving, 113 Rusty Lane, Boerne, TX 78006-5746 / 512-391-5121

Paul and Sharon Dressel, 209 N. 92nd Ave., Yakima, WA 98908 / 509-966-9233; FAX: 509-966-3365 dressels@nwinfo.net www.dressels.com

Paul Co., The, 27385 Pressonville Rd., Wellsville, KS 66092 / 785-883-4444; FAX: 785-883-2525

Paul D. Hillmer Custom Gunstocks, 7251 Hudson Heights, Hudson, IA 50643 / 319-988-3941

Paul Jones Moulds, 4901 Telegraph Rd., Los Angeles, CA 90022 / 213-262-1510

Paulsen Gunstocks, Rt. 71, Box 11, Chinook, MT 59523 / 406-357-3403

Pawling Mountain Club, Keith Lupton, P.O. Box 573, Pawling, NY 12564 / 914-855-3825

Paxton Quigley's Personal Protection Strategies, 9903 Santa Monica Blvd., 300, Beverly Hills, CA 90212 / 310-281-1762 www.defend-net.com/paxton

Payne Photography, Robert, Robert, P.O. Box 141471, Austin, TX 78714 / 512-272-4554

Peacemaker Specialists, P.O. Box 157, Whitmore, CA 96096 / 530-472-3438 www.peacemakerspecialists.com

Pearce Grip, Inc., P.O. Box 40367, Fort Worth, TX 76140 / 817-568-9704; FAX: 817-568-9707 info@pearcegrip.com www.pearcegrip.com

PECAR Herbert Schwarz GmbH, Kreuzbergstrasse 6, 10965, Berlin, GERMANY / 004930-785-7383; FAX: 004930-785-1934 michael.schwart@pecar-berlin.de www.pecar-berlin.de

Pecatonica River Longrifle, 5205 Nottingham Dr., Rockford, IL 61111 / 815-968-1995; FAX: 815-968-1996

Pedersen, C. R., 2717 S. Pere Marquette Hwy., Ludington, MI 49431 / 231-843-2061; FAX: 231-845-7695 fega@fega.com

Pedersen, Rex C., 2717 S. Pere Marquette Hwy., Ludington, MI 49431 / 231-843-2061; FAX: 231-845-7695 fega@fega.com

Peifer Rifle Co., P.O. Box 220, Nokomis, IL 62075

Pejsa Ballistics, 1314 Marquette Ave., Apt 906, Minneapolis, MN 55403 / 612-332-5073; FAX: 612-332-5204 pejsa@sprintmail.com pejsa.com

Peltor, Inc. (See Aero Peltor)

PEM's Mfg. Co., 5063 Waterloo Rd., Atwater, OH 44201 / 216-947-3721

Pence Precision Barrels, 7567 E. 900 S., S. Whitley, IN 46787 / 219-839-4745

Pendleton Royal, c/o Swingler Buckland Ltd., 4/7 Highgate St., Birmingham, ENGLAND / 44 121 440 3060; or 44 121 446 5898; FAX: 44 121 446 4165

Pendleton Woolen Mills, P.O. Box 3030, 220 N.W. Broadway, Portland, OR 97208 / 503-226-4801

Penn Bullets, P.O. Box 756, Indianola, PA 15051

Pennsylvania Gun Parts Inc., RR 7 Box 150, Mount Pleasant, PA 15666

Pennsylvania Gunsmith School, 812 Ohio River Blvd., Avalon, Pittsburgh, PA 15202 / 412-766-1812; FAX: 412-766-0855 pgs@pagunsmith.com www.pagunsmith.com

Penrod, Mark. See: PENROD PRECISION

Penrod Precision, Mark Penrod, 312 College Ave., P.O. Box 307, N. Manchester, IN 46962 / 260-982-8385; FAX: 260-982-1819 markpenrod@kconline.com

Pentax U.S.A., Inc., 600 12th St. Ste. 300, Golden, CO 80401 / 303-799-8000; FAX: 303-460-1628 www.pentaxlightseeker.com

Pentheny de Pentheny, c/o H.P. Okelly, 321 S. Main St., Sebastopol, CA 95472 / 707-824-1637; FAX: 707-824-1637

Perazone-Gunsmith, Brian, Cold Spring Rd., Roxbury, NY 12474 / 607-326-4088; FAX: 607-326-3140 bpgunsmith@catskill.net www.bpgunsmith@catskill.net

Perazzi U.S.A. Inc., 1010 West Tenth, Azusa, CA 91702 / 626-334-1234; FAX: 626-334-0344 perazziusa@aol.com

Performance Specialists, 308 Eanes School Rd., Austin, TX 78746 / 512-327-0119

Perugini Visini & Co. S.r.l., Via Camprelle, 126, 25080 Nuvolera, ITALY / 30-6897535; FAX: 30-6897821 peruvisi@virgilia.it

Pete de Coux Auction House, 14940 Brenda Dr., Prescott, AZ 86305-7447 / 928-776-8285; FAX: 928-776-8276 pdbullets@commspeed.net

Pete Mazur Restoration, 13083 Drummer Way, Grass Valley, CA 95949 / 530-268-2412; FAX: 530-268-2412

Pete Rickard, Inc., 115 Roy Walsh Rd, Cobleskill, NY 12043 / 518-234-2731; FAX: 518-234-2454 rickard@telenet.net www.peterickard.com

Peter Dyson & Son Ltd., 3 Cuckoo Lane, Honley, Holmfirth, West Yorkshire, HD9 6AS ENGLAND / 44-1484-661062; FAX: 44-1484-663709 peter@peterdyson.co.uk www.peterdyson.co.uk

Peter Hale/Engraver, 997 Maple Dr., Spanish Fork, UT 84660-2524 / 801-798-8215

Peters Stahl GmbH, Stettiner Strasse 42, D-33106, Paderborn, GERMANY / 05251-750025; FAX: 05251-75611

Peterson Gun Shop, Inc., A.W., 4255 W. Old U.S. 441, Mt. Dora, FL 32757-3299 / 352-383-4258; FAX: 352-735-1001

Petro-Explo Inc., 7650 U.S. Hwy. 287, Suite 100, Arlington, TX 76017 / 817-478-8888

Pettinger Books, Gerald, 47827 300th Ave., Russell, IA 50238 / 641-535-2239 gpettinger@lisco.com

Pflumm Mfg. Co., 10662 Widmer Rd., Lenexa, KS 66215 / 800-888-4867; FAX: 913-451-7857

PFRB Co., P.O. Box 1242, Bloomington, IL 61702 / 309-473-3964; or 800-914-5464; FAX: 309-473-2161

Philip S. Olt Co., P.O. Box 550, 12662 Fifth St., Pekin, IL 61554 / 309-348-3633; FAX: 309-348-3300

Phillippi Custom Bullets, Justin, P.O. Box 773, Ligonier, PA 15658 / 724-238-2962; FAX: 724-238-9671 jrp@wpa.net http://www.wpa.net~jrphil

Phillips & Rogers, Inc., 852 FM 980 Rd., Conroe, TX 77320 / 409-435-0011

Phoenix Arms, 4231 Brickell St., Ontario, CA 91761 / 909-937-6900; FAX: 909-937-0060

Piedmont Community College, P.O. Box 1197, Roxboro, NC 27573 / 336-599-1181; FAX: 336-597-3817 www.piedmont.cc.nc.us

Pietta (See U.S. Importers-Navy Arms Co, Taylor's

Pine Technical College, 1100 4th St., Pine City, MN 55063 / 800-521-7463; FAX: 612-629-6766

Pinetree Bullets, 133 Skeena St., Kitimat, BC V8C 1Z1 CANADA / 604-632-3768; FAX: 604-632-3768

Pioneer Arms Co., 355 Lawrence Rd., Broomall, PA 19008 / 215-356-5203

Piotti (See U.S. Importer-Moore & Co., Wm. Larkin)

Piquette, Paul. See: PIQUETTE'S CUSTOM ENGRAVING

Piquette's Custom Engraving, Paul R. Piquette, 511 Southwick St., Feeding Hills, MA 01030 / 413-789-4582 ppiquette@comcast.net www.pistoldynamics.com

Plaza Cutlery, Inc., 3333 Bristol, 161 South Coast Plaza, Costa Mesa, CA 92626 / 714-549-3932

Plum City Ballistic Range, N2162 80th St., Plum City, WI 54761 / 715-647-2539

PlumFire Press, Inc., 30-A Grove Ave., Patchogue, NY 11772-4112 / 800-695-7246; FAX: 516-758-4071

PMC/Eldorado Cartridge Corp., P.O. Box 62508, 12801 U.S. Hwy. 95 S., Boulder City, NV 89005 / 702-294-0025; FAX: 702-294-0121 kbauer@pmcammo.com www.pmcammo.com

Poburka, Philip (See Bison Studios)

Pointing Dog Journal, Village Press Publications, P.O. Box 968, Dept. PGD, Traverse City, MI 49685 / 800-272-3246; FAX: 616-946-3289

Police Bookshelf, P.O. Box 122, Concord, NH 03301 / 603-224-6814; FAX: 603-226-3554

Polywad, Inc., P.O. Box 7916, Macon, GA 31209 / 478-477-0669; or 800-998-0669 FAX: 478-477-0666 polywadmpb@aol.com www.polywad.com

Ponsness, Warren, 7634 W. Ohio St., Rathdrum, ID 83858 / 800-732-0706; FAX: 208-687-2233 www.reloaders.com

Pony Express Reloaders, 608 E. Co. Rd. D, Suite 3, St. Paul, MN 55117 / 612-483-9406; FAX: 612-483-9884

Pony Express Sport Shop, 23404 Lyons Ave., PMB 448, Newhall, CA 91321-2511 / 818-895-1231

Potts, Wayne E., 1580 Meade St. Apt. A, Denver, CO 80204-5930 / 303-355-5462

Powder Horn Ltd., P.O. Box 565, Glenview, IL 60025 / 305-565-6060

Powell & Son (Gunmakers) Ltd., William, 35-37 Carrs Lane, Birmingham, B4 7SX ENGLAND / 121-643-0689; FAX: 121-631-3504 sales@william-powell.co.uk www.william-powell.co.uk

Powell Agency, William, 22 Circle Dr., Bellmore, NY 11710 / 516-679-1158

Power Custom, Inc., 29739 Hwy. J, Gravois Mills, MO 65037 / 573-372-5684; FAX: 573-372-5799 rwpowers@laurie.net www.powercustom.com

Power Plus Enterprises, Inc., P.O. Box 38, Warm Springs, GA 31830 / 706-655-2132

Powley Computer (See Hutton Rifle Ranch)

Practical Tools, Inc., 7067 Easton Rd., P.O. Box 133, Pipersville, PA 18947 / 215-766-7301; FAX: 215-766-8681

Prairie Gun Works, 1-761 Marion St., Winnipeg, MB R2J 0K6 CANADA / 204-231-2976; FAX: 204-231-8566

Prairie River Arms, 1220 N. Sixth St., Princeton, IL 61356 / 815-875-1616; or 800-445-1541; FAX: 815-875-1402

Pranger, Ed G., 1414 7th St., Anacortes, WA 98221 / 206-293-3488

Precision Airgun Sales, Inc., 5247 Warrensville Ctr Rd., Maple Hts., OH 44137 / 216-587-5005; FAX: 216-587-5005

Precision Cast Bullets, 101 Mud Creek Lane, Ronan, MT 59864 / 406-676-5135

Precision Delta Corp., P.O. Box 128, Ruleville, MS 38771 / 662-756-2810; FAX: 662-756-2590

Precision Firearm Finishing, 25 N.W. 44th Avenue, Des Moines, IA 50313 / 515-288-8680; FAX: 515-244-3925

Precision Gun Works, 104 Sierra Rd., Dept. GD, Kerrville, TX 78028 / 830-367-4587

Precision Reloading, Inc., P.O. Box 122, Stafford Springs, CT 06076 / 860-684-7979; FAX: 860-684-6788 info@precisionreloading.com www.precisionreloading.com

MANUFACTURER'S DIRECTORY

Precision Shooting, Inc., 222 McKee St., Manchester, CT 06040 / 860-645-8776; FAX: 860-643-8215 www.theaccuraterifle.com or precisionshooting.com
Precision Small Arms Inc., 9272 Jeronimo Rd., Ste. 121, Irvine, CA 92618 / 800-554-5515; or 949-768-3530; FAX: 949-768-4808 www.tcbebe.com
Precision Specialties, 131 Hendom Dr., Feeding Hills, MA 01030 / 413-786-3365; FAX: 413-786-3365
Precision Sport Optics, 15571 Producer Lane, Unit G, Huntington Beach, CA 92649 / 714-891-1309; FAX: 714-892-6920
Premier Reticles, 920 Breckinridge Lane, Winchester, VA 22601-6707 / 540-722-0601; FAX: 540-722-3522
Prescott Projectile Co., 1808 Meadowbrook Road, Prescott, AZ 86303
Preslik's Gunstocks, 4245 Keith Ln., Chico, CA 95926 / 916-891-8236
Price Bullets, Patrick W., 16520 Worthley Dr., San Lorenzo, CA 94580 / 510-278-1547
Prime Reloading, 30 Chiswick End, Meldreth, ROYSTON UK / 0763-260636
Primedia Publishing Co., 6420 Wilshire Blvd., Los Angeles, CA 90048 / 213-782-2000; FAX: 213-782-2867
Primos Hunting Calls, 604 First St., Flora, MS 39071 / 601-879-9323; FAX: 601-879-9324 www.primos.com
PRL Bullets, c/o Blackburn Enterprises, 114 Stuart Rd., Ste. 110, Cleveland, TN 37312 / 423-559-0340
Pro Load Ammunition, Inc., 5180 E. Seltice Way, Post Falls, ID 83854 / 208-773-9444; FAX: 208-773-9441
Professional Gunsmiths of America, Rt 1 Box 224, Lexington, MO 64067 / 660-259-2636
Professional Hunter Supplies, P.O. Box 608, 468 Main St., Ferndale, CA 95536 / 707-786-9140; FAX: 707-786-9117 wmebride@humboldt.com
PrOlixr Lubricants, P.O. Box 1348, Victorville, CA 92393 / 760-243-3129; FAX: 760-241-0148 prolix@accex.net www.prolixlubricant.com
Pro-Mark Div. of Wells Lamont, 6640 W. Touhy, Chicago, IL 60648 / 312-647-8200
Proofmark Corp., P.O. Box 357, Burgess, VA 22432 / 804-453-4337; FAX: 804-453-4337 proofmark@direzway.com www.proofmarkbullets.com
Pro-Port Ltd., 41302 Executive Dr., Harrison Twp., MI 48045-1306 / 586-469-6727; FAX: 586-469-0425 e-mail@magnaport.com www.magnaport.com
Pro-Shot Products, Inc., P.O. Box 763, Taylorville, IL 62568 / 217-824-9133; FAX: 217-824-8861 www.proshotproducts.com
Protector Mfg. Co., Inc., The, 443 Ashwood Pl., Boca Raton, FL 33431 / 407-394-6011
Protektor Model, 1-11 Bridge St., Galeton, PA 16922 / 814-435-2442 mail@protektormodel.com www.protektormodel.com
Prototech Industries, Inc., 10532 E Road, Delia, KS 66418 / 785-771-3571 prototec@grapevine.net
ProWare, Inc., 15847 NE Hancock St., Portland, OR 97230 / 503-239-0159
PWL Gunleather, P.O. Box 450432, Atlanta, GA 31145 / 800-960-4072; FAX: 770-822-1704 covert@pwlusa.com www.pwlusa.com
PWM Sales Ltd., N.D.F.S., Gowdall Lane, Pollington DN14 0AU, ENGLAND / 01405862688; FAX: 01405862622 Paulwelburn9@aol.com
Pyramyd Stone Inter. Corp., 2447 Suffolk Lane, Pepper Pike, OH 44124-4540

Q

Quack Decoy & Sporting Clays, 4 Ann & Hope Way, P.O. Box 98, Cumberland, RI 02864 / 401-723-8202; FAX: 401-722-5910
Quaker Boy, Inc., 5455 Webster Rd., Orchard Parks, NY 14127 / 716-662-3979; FAX: 716-662-9426
Quality Arms, Inc., Box 19477, Dept. GD, Houston, TX 77224 / 281-870-8377 arrieta2@excite.com www.arrieta.com
Quality Cartridge, P.O. Box 445, Hollywood, MD 20636 / 301-373-3719 www.qual-cart.com
Quality Custom Firearms, Stephen Billeb, 22 Vista View Dr., Cody, WY 82414 / 307-587-4278; FAX: 307-587-4297 stevebilleb@wyoming.com
Quarton Beamshot, 4538 Centerview Dr., Ste. 149, San Antonio, TX 78228 / 800-520-8435; FAX: 210-735-1326 www.beamshot.com
Que Industries, Inc., P.O. Box 2471, Everett, WA 98203 / 425-303-9088; FAX: 206-514-3266 queinfo@queindustries.com

Queen Cutlery Co., P.O. Box 500, Franklinville, NY 14737 / 800-222-5233; FAX: 800-299-2618

R

R&C Knives & Such, 2136 CANDY CANE WALK, Manteca, CA 95336-9501 / 209-239-3722; FAX: 209-825-6947
R&D Gun Repair, Kenny Howell, RR1 Box 283, Beloit, WI 53511
R&J Gun Shop, 337 S. Humbolt St., Canyon City, OR 97820 / 541-575-2130 rjgunshop@highdesertnet.com
R&S Industries Corp., 8255 Brentwood Industrial Dr., St. Louis, MO 63144 / 314-781-5169 ron@miraclepolishingcloth.com www.miraclepolishingcloth.com
R. Murphy Co., Inc., 13 Groton-Harvard Rd., P.O. Box 376, Ayer, MA 01432 / 617-772-3481 www.r.murphyknives.com
R.A. Wells Custom Gunsmith, 3452 1st Ave., Racine, WI 53402 / 414-639-5223
R.E. Seebeck Assoc., P.O. Box 59752, Dallas, TX 75229
R.E.I., P.O. Box 88, Tallevast, FL 34270 / 813-755-0085
R.E.T. Enterprises, 2600 S. Chestnut, Broken Arrow, OK 74012 / 918-251-GUNS; FAX: 918-251-0587
R.F. Mitchell Bullets, 430 Walnut St., Westernport, MD 21562
R.T. Eastman Products, P.O. Box 1531, Jackson, WY 83001 / 307-733-3217; or 800-624-4311
Rabeno, Martin, 530 The Eagle Pass, Durango, CO 81301 / 970-382-0353 fancygun@aol.com
Radack Photography, Lauren, 21140 Jib Court L-12, Aventura, FL 33180 / 305-931-3110
Radiator Specialty Co., 1900 Wilkinson Blvd., P.O. Box 34689, Charlotte, NC 28234 / 800-438-6947; FAX: 800-421-9525 khrossell@gunk.com www.gunk.com
Radical Concepts, P.O. Box 1473, Lake Grove, OR 97035 / 503-538-7437
Rainier Ballistics, 4500 15th St. East, Tacoma, WA 98424 / 800-638-8722; FAX: 253-922-7854 sales@rainierballistics.com www.rainierballistics.com
Ralph Bone Engraving, 718 N. Atlanta St., Owasso, OK 74055 / 918-272-9745
Ram-Line ATK, P.O. Box 39, Onalaska, WI 54650
Ramon B. Gonzalez Guns, P.O. Box 370, Monticello, NY 12701 / 914-794-4515; FAX: 914-794-4515
Rampart International, 2781 W. MacArthur Blvd., B-283, Santa Ana, CA 92704 / 800-976-7240 or 714-557-6405
Ranch Products, P.O. Box 145, Malinta, OH 43535 / 313-277-3118; FAX: 313-565-8536
Randall-Made Knives, P.O. Box 1988, Orlando, FL 32802 / 407-855-8075
Randco UK, 286 Gipsy Rd., Welling, DA16 1JJ ENGLAND / 44 81 303 4118
Randolph Engineering, Inc., Ranger Shooting Glasses, 26 Thomas Patten Dr., Randolph, MA 02368 / 800-541-1405; FAX: 781-986-0337 sales@randolphusa.com www.randolphusa.com
Randy Duane Custom Stocks, 7822 Church St., Middletown, VA 22645-9521
Range Brass Products Company, P.O. Box 218, Rockport, TX 78381
Ransom International Corp., 1027 Spire Dr., Prescott, AZ 86305 / 928-778-7899; FAX: 928-778-7993 ransom@cableone.net www.ransomrest.com
Rapine Bullet Mould Mfg. Co., 9503 Landis Lane, East Greenville, PA 18041 / 215-679-5413; FAX: 215-679-9795
Ravell Ltd., 289 Diputacion St., 08009, Barcelona, SPAIN / 34(3) 4874486; FAX: 34(3) 4881394
Ray Riling Arms Books Co., 6844 Gorsten St., Philadelphia, PA 19119 / 215-438-2456; FAX: 215-438-5395 sales@rayrilingarmsbooks.com www.rayrilingarmsbooks.com
Ray's Gunsmith Shop, 3199 Elm Ave., Grand Junction, CO 81504 / 970-434-6162; FAX: 970-434-6162
Raytech Div. of Lyman Products Corp., 475 Smith Street, Middletown, CT 06457-1541 / 860-632-2020 or 800-225-9626; FAX: 860-632-1699 raysales@cshore.com www.raytech-ind.com
RCBS Operations/ATK, 605 Oro Dam Blvd., Oroville, CA 95965 / 530-533-5191 or 800-533-5000; FAX: 530-533-1647 www.rcbs.com
RCBS/ATK, 605 Oro Dam Blvd., Oroville, CA 95965 / 800-533-5000; FAX: 916-533-1647
Reardon Products, P.O. Box 126, Morrison, IL 61270 / 815-772-3155

Red Diamond Dist. Co., 1304 Snowdon Dr., Knoxville, TN 37912
Redding Reloading Equipment, 1089 Starr Rd., Cortland, NY 13045 / 607-753-3331; FAX: 607-756-8445 techline@redding-reloading.com www.redding-reloading.com
Redfield Media Resource Center, 4607 N.E. Cedar Creek Rd., Woodland, WA 98674 / 360-225-5000; FAX: 360-225-7616
Redman's Rifling & Reboring, 189 Nichols Rd., Omak, WA 98841 / 509-826-5512
Redwood Bullet Works, 3559 Bay Rd., Redwood City, CA 94063 / 415-367-6741
Reed, Dave, Rt. 1, Box 374, Minnesota City, MN 55959 / 507-689-2944
Reimer Johannsen, Inc., 438 Willow Brook Rd., Plainfield, NH 03781 / 603-469-3450; FAX: 603-469-3471
Reloaders Equipment Co., 4680 High St., Ecorse, MI 48229
Reloading Specialties, Inc., Box 1130, Pine Island, MN 55463 / 507-356-8500; FAX: 507-356-8800
Remington Arms Co., Inc., 870 Remington Drive, P.O. Box 700, Madison, NC 27025-0700 / 800-243-9700; FAX: 910-548-0700
Remington Double Shotguns, 7885 Cyd Dr., Denver, CO 80221 / 303-429-6947
Renato Gamba S.p.A.-Societa Armi Bresciane Srl., Via Artigiani 93, 25063 Gardone, Val Trompia (BS), ITALY / 30-8911640; FAX: 30-8911648
Renegade, P.O. Box 31546, Phoenix, AZ 85046 / 602-482-6777; FAX: 602-482-1952
Renfrew Guns & Supplies, R.R. 4, Renfrew, ON K7V 3Z7 CANADA / 613-432-7080
Reno, Wayne, 2808 Stagestop Road, Jefferson, CO 80456
Republic Arms, Inc. (See Cobra Enterprises, Inc.)
Retting, Inc., Martin B., 11029 Washington, Culver City, CA 90232 / 213-837-2412
RG-G, Inc., P.O. Box 935, Trinidad, CO 81082 / 719-845-1436
RH Machine & Consulting Inc., P.O. Box 394, Pacific, MO 63069 / 314-271-8465
Rhino, P.O. Box 787, Locust, NC 28097 / 704-753-2198
Rhodeside, Inc., 1704 Commerce Dr., Piqua, OH 45356 / 513-773-5781
Rice, Keith (See White Rock Tool & Die)
Richards MicroFit Stocks, Inc., P.O. Box 1066, Sun Valley, CA 91352 / 800-895-7420; FAX: 818-771-1242 sales@rifle-stocks.com www.rifle-stocks.com
Ridgeline, Inc., Bruce Sheldon, P.O. Box 930, Dewey, AZ 86327-0930 / 800-632-6000; FAX: 520-632-5000
Ridgetop Sporting Goods, P.O. Box 306, 42907 Hilligoss Ln. East, Eatonville, WA 98328 / 360-832-6422; FAX: 360-832-6422
Ries, Chuck, 415 Ridgecrest Dr., Grants Pass, OR 97527 / 503-476-5623
Rifles, Inc., 3580 Leal Rd., Pleasanton, TX 78064 / 830-569-2055; FAX: 830-569-2297
Riggs, Jim, 206 Azalea, Boerne, TX 78006 / 210-249-8567
Riley Ledbetter Airguns, 1804 E. Sprague St., Winston Salem, NC 27107-3521 / 919-784-0676
Rim Pac Sports, Inc., 1034 N. Soldano Ave., Azusa, CA 91702-2135
Ringler Custom Leather Co., 31 Shining Mtn. Rd., Powell, WY 82435 / 307-645-3255
Ripley Rifles, 42 Fletcher Street, Ripley, Derbyshire, DE5 3LP ENGLAND / 011-0773-748353
Rizzini F.lli (See U.S. Importers-Wm. Larkin Moore & Co., N.E. Arms Corp.)
Rizzini SNC, Via 2 Giugno, 7/7Bis-25060, Marcheno (Brescia), ITALY
RLCM Enterprises, 110 Hill Crest Drive, Burleson, TX 76028
RMS Custom Gunsmithing, 4120 N. Bitterwell, Prescott Valley, AZ 86314 / 520-772-7626 www.customstockmaker.com
Robar Co., Inc., The, 21438 N. 7th Ave., Suite B, Phoenix, AZ 85027 / 623-581-2648; FAX: 623-582-0059 info@robarguns.com www.robarguns.com
Robert Evans Engraving, 332 Vine St., Oregon City, OR 97045 / 503-656-5693
Robert Valade Engraving, 931 3rd Ave., Seaside, OR 97138 / 503-738-7672
Robinett, R. G., P.O. Box 72, Madrid, IA 50156 / 515-795-2906
Robinson, Don, Pennsylvania Hse, 36 Fairfax Crescent, W Yorkshire, ENGLAND / 0422-364458 donrobinsonuk@yahoo.co.uk www.guns4u2.co.uk

MANUFACTURER'S DIRECTORY

Robinson Armament Co., P.O. Box 16776, Salt Lake City, UT 84116 / 801-355-0401; FAX: 801-355-0402 zdf@robarm.com www.robarm.com

Robinson Firearms Mfg. Ltd., 1699 Blondeaux Crescent, Kelowna, BC V1Y 4J8 CANADA / 604-868-9596

Robinson H.V. Bullets, 3145 Church St., Zachary, LA 70791 / 504-654-4029

Rochester Lead Works, 76 Anderson Ave., Rochester, NY 14607 / 716-442-8500; FAX: 716-442-4712

Rock River Arms, 101 Noble St., Cleveland, IL 61241

Rockwood Corp., Speedwell Division, 136 Lincoln Blvd., Middlesex, NJ 08846 / 800-243-8274; FAX: 980-560-7475

Rocky Mountain Armoury, Mr. Felix LesMerises, 610 Main Street, P.O. Box 691, Frisco, CO 80443-0691 / 970-668-0136; FAX: 970-668-4484 felix@rockymountainarmoury.com

Rocky Mountain Arms, Inc., 1813 Sunset Pl., Unit D, Longmont, CO 80501 / 800-375-0846; FAX: 303-678-8766

Rocky Mountain Target Co., 3 Aloe Way, Leesburg, FL 34788 / 352-365-9598

Rocky Mountain Wildlife Products, P.O. Box 999, La Porte, CO 80535 / 970-484-2768; FAX: 970-484-0807 critrcall@larinet.com www.critrcall.com

Rocky Shoes & Boots, 294 Harper St., Nelsonville, OH 45764 / 800-848-9452; or 614-753-1951; FAX: 614-753-4024

Rogue Rifle Co., Inc., 1140 36th St. N., Ste. B, Lewiston, ID 83501 / 208-743-4355; FAX: 208-743-4163

Rogue River Rifleworks, 500 Linne Road #D, Paso Robles, CA 93446 / 805-227-4706; FAX: 805-227-4723 rrrifles@calinet.com

Rohner, Hans, 1148 Twin Sisters Ranch Rd., Nederland, CO 80466-9600

Rohner, John, 186 Virginia Ave., Asheville, NC 28806 / 828-281-3704

Rohrbaugh, P.O. Box 785, Bayport, NY 11705 / 631-363-2843; FAX: 631-363-2681 API380@aol.com

Romain's Custom Guns, Inc., RD 1, Whetstone Rd., Brockport, PA 15823 / 814-265-1948 romwhetstone@penn.com

Ron Frank Custom Classic Arms, 7131 Richland Rd., Ft. Worth, TX 76118 / 817-284-9300; FAX: 817-284-9300 rfrank3974@aol.com

Rooster Laboratories, P.O. Box 414605, Kansas City, MO 64141 / 816-474-1622; FAX: 816-474-7622

Rorschach Precision Products, 417 Keats Cir., Irving, TX 75061 / 214-790-3487

Rosenberg & Son, Jack A., 12229 Cox Ln., Dallas, TX 75234 / 214-241-6302

Ross, Don, 12813 West 83 Terrace, Lenexa, KS 66215 / 913-492-6982

Rosser, Bob, 2809 Crescent Ave., Suite 20, Homewood, AL 35209 / 205-870-4422; FAX: 205-870-4421 www.hand-engravers.com

Rossi Firearms, Gary Mchalik, 16175 NW 49th Ave., Miami, FL 33014-6314 / 305-474-0401; FAX: 305-623-7506

Rottweil Compe, 1330 Glassell, Orange, CA 92667

Roy Baker's Leather Goods, P.O. Box 893, Magnolia, AR 71754 / 870-234-0344

Royal Arms Gunstocks, 919 8th Ave. NW, Great Falls, MT 59404 / 406-453-1149 royalarms@lmt.net www.lmt.net/~royalarms

Royal Arms International, R J Brill, P.O. Box 6083, Woodland Hills, CA 91365 / 818-704-5110; FAX: 818-887-2059 royalarms.com

Roy's Custom Grips, 793 Mt. Olivet Church Rd., Lynchburg, VA 24504 / 434-993-3470

RPM, 15481 N. Twin Lakes Dr., Tucson, AZ 85739 / 520-825-1233; FAX: 520-825-3333

Rubright Bullets, 1008 S. Quince Rd., Walnutport, PA 18088 / 215-767-1339

Rucker Dist. Inc., P.O. Box 479, Terrell, TX 75160 / 214-563-2094

Ruger (See Sturm Ruger & Co., Inc.)

Ruger, Chris. See: RUGER'S CUSTOM GUNS

Ruger's Custom Guns, Chris Ruger, 1050 Morton Blvd., Kingston, NY 12401 / 845-336-7106; FAX: 845-336-7106 rugerscustom@outdrs.net rugergunsmith.com

Rundell's Gun Shop, 6198 Frances Rd., Clio, MI 48420 / 313-687-0559

Rupert's Gun Shop, 2202 Dick Rd., Suite B, Fenwick, MI 48834 / 517-248-3252 17rupert@pathwaynet.com

Russ Haydon's Shooters' Supply, 15018 Goodrich Dr. NW, Gig Harbor, WA 98329 / 877-663-6249; FAX: 253-857-7884 info@shooters-supply.com www.shooters-supply.com

Russ, William. See: BILL RUSS TRADING POST

Rusteprufe Laboratories, 1319 Jefferson Ave., Sparta, WI 54656 / 608-269-4144; FAX: 608-366-1972 rusteprufe@centurytel.net www.rusteprufe.com

Rusty Duck Premium Gun Care Products, 7785 Foundation Dr., Suite 6, Florence, KY 41042 / 606-342-5553; FAX: 606-342-5556

Rutgers Book Center, 127 Raritan Ave., Highland Park, NJ 08904 / 732-545-4344; FAX: 732-545-6686 gunbooks@rutgersgunbooks.com www.rutgersgunbooks.com

Rutten (See U.S. Importer-Labanu Inc.)

RWS (See U.S. Importer-Dynamit Nobel-RWS, Inc.), 81 Ruckman Rd., Closter, NJ 07624 / 201-767-7971; FAX: 201-767-1589

S

S&K Scope Mounts, RD 2 Box 21C, Sugar Grove, PA 16350 / 814-489-3091; or 800-578-9862; FAX: 814-489-5466 comments@scopemounts.com www.scopemounts.com

S&S Firearms, 74-11 Myrtle Ave., Glendale, NY 11385 / 718-497-1100; FAX: 718-497-1105 info@ssfirearms.com ssfirearms.com

S.A.R.L. G. Granger, 66 cours Fauriel, 42100, Saint Etienne, FRANCE / 04 77 25 14 73; FAX: 04 77 38 66 99

S.C.R.C., P.O. Box 660, Katy, TX 77492-0660 FAX: 281-492-6332

S.D. Meacham, 1070 Angel Ridge, Peck, ID 83545

S.I.A.C.E. (See U.S. Importer-IAR Inc.)

Sabatti SPA, Via A Volta 90, 25063 Gandome V.T.(BS), Brescia, ITALY / 030-8912207-831312; FAX: 030-8912059 info@sabatti.it www.sabatti.com

SAECO (See Redding Reloading Equipment)

Safari Arms/Schuetzen Pistol Works, 620-626 Old Pacific Hwy. SE, Olympia, WA 98513 / 360-459-3471; FAX: 360-491-3447 info@olyarms.com www.olyarms.com

Safari Press, Inc., 15621 Chemical Lane B, Huntington Beach, CA 92649 / 714-894-9080; FAX: 714-894-4949 info@safaripress.com www.safaripress.com

Safariland Ltd., Inc., 3120 E. Mission Blvd., P.O. Box 51478, Ontario, CA 91761 / 909-923-7300; FAX: 909-923-7400

SAFE, P.O. Box 864, Post Falls, ID 83877 / 208-773-3624; FAX: 208-773-6819 staysafe@safe-llc.com www.safe-llc.com

Sako Ltd. (See U.S. Importer-Stoeger Industries)

Sam Welch Gun Engraving, Sam Welch, HC 64 Box 2110, Moab, UT 84532 / 435-259-8131

Samco Global Arms, Inc., 6995 NW 43rd St., Miami, FL 33166 / 305-593-9782; FAX: 305-593-1014 samco@samcoglobal.com www.samcoglobal.com

Sampson, Roger, 2316 Mahogany St., Mora, MN 55051 / 612-679-4868

San Marco (See U.S. Importers-Cape Outfitters-EMF Co., Inc.

Sandia Die & Cartridge Co., 37 Atancacio Rd. NE, Albuquerque, NM 87123 / 505-298-5729

Sarco, Inc., 323 Union St., Stirling, NJ 07980 / 908-647-3800; FAX: 908-647-9413

Sarsilmaz Shotguns-Turkey (see B.C. Outdoors)

Sauer (See U.S. Importers-Paul Co., The Sigarms Inc.)

Sauls, R. See: BRYAN & ASSOC.

Saunders Gun & Machine Shop, 145 Delhi Rd., Manchester, IA 52057 / 563-927-4026

Savage Arms (Canada), Inc., 248 Water St., P.O. Box 1240, Lakefield, ON K0L 2H0 CANADA / 705-652-8000; FAX: 705-652-8431 www.savagearms.com

Savage Arms, Inc., 100 Springdale Rd., Westfield, MA 01085 / 413-568-7001; FAX: 413-562-7764

Savage Range Systems, Inc., 100 Springdale Rd., Westfield, MA 01085 / 413-568-7001; FAX: 413-562-1152 snailtraps@savagearms.com www.snailtraps.com

Saville Iron Co. (See Greenwood Precision)

Scansport, Inc., P.O. Box 700, Enfield, NH 03748 / 603-632-7654

Sceery Game Calls, P.O. Box 6520, Sante Fe, NM 87502 / 505-471-9110; FAX: 505-471-3476

Schaefer Shooting Sports, P.O. Box 1515, Melville, NY 11747-0515 / 516-643-5466; FAX: 516-643-2426 robert@robertschaefer.com www.schaefershooting.com

Scharch Mfg., Inc.-Top Brass, 10325 Co. Rd. 120, Salida, CO 81201 / 800-836-4683; FAX: 719-539-3021 topbrass@scharch.com www.handgun-brass.com

Scherer, Liz. See: SCHERER SUPPLIES

Scherer Supplies, Liz Scherer, Box 250, Ewing, VA 24248 FAX: 423-733-2073

Schiffman, Mike, 8233 S. Crystal Springs, McCammon, ID 83250 / 208-254-9114

Schmidt & Bender, Inc., P.O. Box 134, Meriden, NH 03770 / 603-469-3565; FAX: 603-469-3471 scopes@adelphia.net www.schmidtbender.com

Schmidtke Group, 17050 W. Salentine Dr., New Berlin, WI 53151-7349

Schneider Bullets, 3655 West 214th St., Fairview Park, OH 44126

Schneider Rifle Barrels, Inc., 1403 W. Red Baron Rd., Payson, AZ 85541 / 602-948-2525

School of Gunsmithing, The, 6065 Roswell Rd., Atlanta, GA 30328 / 800-223-4542

Schroeder Bullets, 1421 Thermal Ave., San Diego, CA 92154 / 619-423-3523; FAX: 619-423-8124

Schulz Industries, 16247 Minnesota Ave., Paramount, CA 90723 / 213-439-5903

Schumakers Gun Shop, 512 Prouty Corner Lp. A, Colville, WA 99114 / 509-684-4848

Scope Control, Inc., 5775 Co. Rd. 23 SE, Alexandria, MN 56308 / 612-762-7295

Score High Gunsmithing, 9812-A, Cochiti SE, Albuquerque, NM 87123 / 800-326-5632; or 505-292-5532; FAX: 505-292-2592 scorehi@scorehi.com www.probed2000.com

Scot Powder, Rt. 1 Box 167, McEwen, TN 37101 / 800-416-3006; FAX: 615-729-4211

Scott Fine Guns Inc., Thad, P.O. Box 412, Indianola, MS 38751 / 601-887-5929

Searcy Enterprises, P.O. Box 584, Boron, CA 93596 / 760-762-6771; FAX: 760-762-0191

Second Chance Body Armor, P.O. Box 578, Central Lake, MI 49622 / 616-544-5721; FAX: 616-544-9824

Seebeck Assoc., R.E., P.O. Box 59752, Dallas, TX 75229

Segway Industries, P.O. Box 783, Suffern, NY 10901-0783 / 914-357-5510

Seligman Shooting Products, Box 133, Seligman, AZ 86337 / 602-422-3607 shootssp@yahoo.com

Sellier & Bellot, USA, Inc., P.O. Box 27006, Shawnee Mission, KS 66225 / 913-685-0916; FAX: 913-685-0917

Selsi Co., Inc., P.O. Box 10, Midland Park, NJ 07432-0010 / 201-935-0388; FAX: 201-935-5851

Semmer, Charles (See Remington Double Shotguns), 7885 Cyd Dr., Denver, CO 80221 / 303-429-6947

Sentinel Arms, P.O. Box 57, Detroit, MI 48231 / 313-331-1951; FAX: 313-331-1456

Servus Footwear Co., 1136 2nd St., Rock Island, IL 61204 / 309-786-7741; FAX: 309-786-9808

Shappy Bullets, 76 Milldale Ave., Plantsville, CT 06479 / 203-621-3704

Sharp Shooter Supply, 4970 Lehman Road, Delphos, OH 45833 / 419-695-3179

Sharps Arms Co., Inc., C., 100 Centennial, Box 885, Big Timber, MT 59011 / 406-932-4353

Shaw, Inc., E. R. (See Small Arms Mfg. Co.)

Shay's Gunsmithing, 931 Marvin Ave., Lebanon, PA 17042

Sheffield Knifemakers Supply, Inc., P.O. Box 741107, Orange City, FL 32774-1107 / 386-775-6453; FAX: 386-774-5754

Sheldon, Bruce. See: RIDGELINE, INC.

Shepherd Enterprises, Inc., Box 189, Waterloo, NE 68069 / 402-779-2424; FAX: 402-779-4010 sshepherd@shepherdscopes.com www.shepherdscopes.com

Sherwood, George, 46 N. River Dr., Roseburg, OR 97470 / 541-672-3159

Shilen, Inc., 205 Metro Park Blvd., Ennis, TX 75119 / 972-875-5318; FAX: 972-875-5402

Shiloh Rifle Mfg., P.O. Box 279, Big Timber, MT 59011

Shockley, Harold H., 204 E. Farmington Rd., Hanna City, IL 61536 / 309-565-4524

Shoot Where You Look, Leon Measures, Dept GD, 408 Fair, Livingston, TX 77351

Shooters Arms Manufacturing, Inc., Rivergate Mall, Gen. Maxilom Ave., Cebu City 6000, PHILIPPINES / 6332-254-8478 www.shootersarms.com.ph

Shooter's Choice Gun Care, 15050 Berkshire Ind. Pkwy., Middlefield, OH 44062 / 440-834-8888; FAX: 440-834-3388 www.shooterschoice.com

Shooter's Edge Inc., 3313 Creekstone Dr., Fort Collins, CO 80525

Shooters Supply, 1120 Tieton Dr., Yakima, WA 98902 / 509-452-1181

Shooter's World, 3828 N. 28th Ave., Phoenix, AZ 85017 / 602-266-0170

Shooters, Inc., 5139 Stanart St., Norfolk, VA 23502 / 757-461-9152; FAX: 757-461-9155 gflocker@aol.com

Shootin' Shack, 357 Cypress Drive, No. 10, Tequesta, FL 33469 / 561-842-0990; FAX: 561-545-4861

Shooting Gallery, The, 8070 Southern Blvd., Boardman, OH 44512 / 216-726-7788

Shoot-N-C Targets (See Birchwood Casey)

Shotgun Sports, P.O. Box 6810, Auburn, CA 95604 / 530-889-2220; FAX: 530-889-9106 custsrv@shotgunsportsmagazine.com shotgunsportsmagazine.com

Shotgun Sports Magazine, dba Shootin' Accessories Ltd., P.O. Box 6810, Auburn, CA 95604 / 916-889-2220 custsrv@shotgunsportsmagazine.com shotgunspotsmagazine.com

Shotguns Unlimited, 2307 Fon Du Lac Rd., Richmond, VA 23229 / 804-752-7115

Siegrist Gun Shop, 8752 Turtle Road, Whittemore, MI 48770 / 989-873-3929

Sierra Bullets, 1400 W. Henry St., Sedalia, MO 65301 / 816-827-6300; FAX: 816-827-6300

Sierra Specialty Prod. Co., 1344 Oakhurst Ave., Los Altos, CA 94024 FAX: 415-965-1536

SIG, CH-8212 Neuhausen, SWITZERLAND

Sigarms Inc., 18 Industrial Dr., Exeter, NH 03833 / 603-772-2302; FAX: 603-772-9082 www.sigarms.com

Sight Shop, The, John G. Lawson, 1802 E. Columbia Ave., Tacoma, WA 98404 / 253-474-5465 parahellum9@aol.com www.thesightshop.org

Sightron, Inc., 1672B Hwy. 96, Franklinton, NC 27525 / 919-528-8783; FAX: 919-528-0995 info@sightron.com www.sightron.com

SIG-Sauer (See U.S. Importer-Sigarms, Inc.)

Silencio/Safety Direct, 56 Coney Island Dr., Sparks, NV 89431 / 800-648-1812; or 702-354-4451; FAX: 702-359-1074

Silent Hunter, 1100 Newton Ave., W. Collingswood, NJ 08107 / 609-854-3276

Silhouette Leathers, 8598 Hwy. 51 N. #4, Millington, TN 38053 sllhouetteleathers@yahoo.com silhouetteleathers.com

Silver Eagle Machining, 18007 N. 69th Ave., Glendale, AZ 85308

Silver Ridge Gun Shop (See Goodwin Guns)

Simmons, Jerry, 715 Middlebury St., Goshen, IN 46528-2717 / 574-533-8546

Simmons Gun Repair, Inc., 700 S. Rogers Rd., Olathe, KS 66062 / 913-782-3131; FAX: 913-782-4189

Simmons Outdoor Corp., 6001 Oak Canyon, Irvine, CA 92618 / 949-451-1450; FAX: 949-451-1460 www.meade.com

Sinclair International, Inc., 2330 Wayne Haven St., Fort Wayne, IN 46803 / 260-493-1858; or 800-717-8211; FAX: 260-493-2530 sales@sinclairintl.com www.sinclairintl.com

Singletary, Kent, 4538 W. Carol Ave., Glendale, AZ 85302 / 602-526-6836 kent@kscustom www.kscustom.com

Siskiyou Gun Works (See Donnelly, C. P.)

Six Enterprises, 320-D Turtle Creek Ct., San Jose, CA 95125 / 408-999-0201; FAX: 408-999-0216

SKB Shotguns, 4325 S. 120th St., Omaha, NE 68137 / 800-752-2767; FAX: 402-330-8040 skb@skbshotguns.com www.skbshotguns.com

Skeoch, Brian R., P.O. Box 279, Glenrock, WY 82637 / 307-436-9655 skeochbrian@netzero.com

Skip's Machine, 364 29 Road, Grand Junction, CO 81501 / 303-245-5417

Sklany's Machine Shop, 566 Birch Grove Dr., Kalispell, MT 59901 / 406-755-4257

Slug Site, Ozark Wilds, 21300 Hwy. 5, Versailles, MO 65084 / 573-378-6430 john@ebeling.com john.ebeling.com

Small Arms Mfg. Co., 5312 Thoms Run Rd., Bridgeville, PA 15017 / 412-221-4343; FAX: 412-221-4303

Small Arms Specialists, 443 Firchburg Rd., Mason, NH 03048 / 603-878-0427; FAX: 603-878-3905 miniguns@empire.net miniguns.com

Smires, C. L., 5222 Windmill Lane, Columbia, MD 21044-1328

Smith & Wesson, 2100 Roosevelt Ave., Springfield, MA 01104 / 413-781-8300; FAX: 413-731-8980

Smith, Art, P.O. Box 645, Park Rapids, MN 56470 / 218-732-5333

Smith, Mark A., P.O. Box 182, Sinclair, WY 82334 / 307-324-7929

Smith, Michael, 2612 Ashmore Ave., Red Bank, TN 37415 / 615-267-8341

Smith, Ron, 5869 Straley, Fort Worth, TX 76114 / 817-732-6768

Smith, Sharmon, 4545 Speas Rd., Fruitland, ID 83619 / 208-452-6329 sharmon@fmtc.com

Smith Abrasives, Inc., 1700 Sleepy Valley Rd., Hot Springs, AR 71902-5095 / 501-321-2244; FAX: 501-321-9232 www.smithabrasives.com

Smith, Judy. See: L.B.T.

Smith Saddlery, Jesse W., 0499 County Road J, Pritchett, CO 81064 / 509-325-0622

Smokey Valley Rifles, E1976 Smokey Valley Rd., Scandinavia, WI 54977 / 715-467-2674

Snapp's Gunshop, 6911 E. Washington Rd., Clare, MI 48617 / 989-386-9226 snapp@glccomputers.com

Sno-Seal, Inc. (See Atsko/Sno-Seal, Inc.)

Societa Armi Bresciane Srl (See U.S. Importer-Cape Outfitters)

SOS Products Co. (See Buck Stix-SOS Products Co.), Box 3, Neenah, WI 54956

Sotheby's, 1334 York Ave. at 72nd St., New York, NY 10021 / 212-606-7260

Sound Tech Silencers, Box 391, Pelham, AL 35124 / 205-664-5860 silenceio@wmconnect.com www.soundtechsilencers.com

South Bend Replicas, 61650 Oak Rd., South Bend, IN 46614 / 219-289-4500

Southeastern Community College, 1015 S. Gear Ave., West Burlington, IA 52655 / 319-752-2731

Southern Ammunition Co., Inc., 4232 Meadow St., Loris, SC 29569-3124 / 803-756-3262; FAX: 803-756-3583

Southern Armory, The, 25 Millstone Rd., Woodlawn, VA 24381 / 703-238-1343; FAX: 703-238-1453

Southern Bloomer Mfg. Co., P.O. Box 1621, Bristol, TN 37620 / 615-878-6660; FAX: 615-878-8761

Southern Security, 1700 Oak Hills Dr., Kingston, TN 37763 / 423-376-6297; FAX: 800-251-9992

Sparks, Milt, 605 E. 44th St. No. 2, Boise, ID 83714-4800

Spartan-Realtree Products, Inc., 1390 Box Circle, Columbus, GA 31907 / 706-569-9101; FAX: 706-569-0042

Specialty Gunsmithing, Lynn McMurdo, P.O. Box 404, Afton, WY 83110 / 307-886-5535

Specialty Shooters Supply, Inc., 3325 Griffin Rd., Suite 9mm, Fort Lauderdale, FL 33317

Speer Bullets, P.O. Box 856, Lewiston, ID 83501 / 208-746-2351 www.speer-bullets.com

Spegel, Craig, P.O. Box 387, Nehalem, OR 97131 / 503-368-5653

Speiser, Fred D., 2229 Dearborn, Missoula, MT 59801 / 406-549-8133

Spencer Reblue Service, 1820 Tupelo Trail, Holt, MI 48842 / 517-694-7474

Spencer's Rifle Barrels, Inc., 4107 Jacobs Creek Dr., Scottsville, VA 24590 / 804-293-6836; FAX: 804-293-6836 www.spencersriflebarrels.com

SPG LLC, P.O. Box 1625, Cody, WY 82414 / 307-587-7621; FAX: 307-587-7695 spg@cody.wtp.net www.blackpowderspg.com

Sphinx Systems Ltd., Gesteigtsrasse 12, CH-3800, Matten, BRNE, SWITZERLAND

Splitfire Sporting Goods, L.L.C., P.O. Box 1044, Orem, UT 84059-1044 / 801-932-7950; FAX: 801-932-7959 www.splitfireguns.com

Spolar Power Load, Inc., 17376 Filbert, Fontana, CA 92335 / 800-227-9667

Sport Flite Manufacturing Co., 637 Kingsley Trl., Bloomfield Hills, MI 48304-2320 / 248-647-3747

Sporting Clays Of America, 9257 Bluckeye Rd., Sugar Grove, OH 43155-9632 / 740-746-8334; FAX: 740-746-8605

Sports Afield Magazine, 15621 Chemical Lane B, Huntington Beach, CA 92649 / 714-894-9080; FAX: 714-894-4949 info@sportsafield.com www.sportsafield.com

Sports Innovations, Inc., P.O. Box 5181, 8505 Jacksboro Hwy., Wichita Falls, TX 76307 / 817-723-6015

Sportsman Safe Mfg. Co., 6309-6311 Paramount Blvd., Long Beach, CA 90805 / 800-266-7150; or 310-984-5445

Sportsman's Communicators, 588 Radcliffe Ave., Pacific Palisades, CA 90272 / 800-538-3752

Sportsmatch U.K. Ltd., 16 Summer St. Leighton, Buzzard Beds, Bedfordshire, LU7 1HT ENGLAND / 4401525-381638; FAX: 4401525-851236 info@sportsmatch-uk.com www.sportsmatch-uk.com

Sportsmen's Exchange & Western Gun Traders, Inc., 813 Doris Ave., Oxnard, CA 93030 / 805-483-1917

Spradlin's, 457 Shannon Rd., Texas Creek Cotopaxi, CO 81223 / 719-275-7105; FAX: 719-275-3852 spradlins@prodigy.net www.spradlins.net

Springfield Armory, 420 W. Main St., Geneseo, IL 61254 / 309-944-5631; FAX: 309-944-3676 sales@springfield-armory.com www.springfieldarmory.com

Springfield Sporters, Inc., RD 1, Penn Run, PA 15765 / 412-254-2626; FAX: 412-254-9173

Springfield, Inc., 420 W. Main St., Geneseo, IL 61254 / 309-944-5631; FAX: 309-944-3676

Spyderco, Inc., 820 Spyderco Way, Golden, CO 80403 / 800-525-7770; or 800-525-7770; FAX: 303-278-2229 sales@spyderco.com www.spyderco.com

SSK Industries, J. D. Jones, 590 Woodvue Lane, Wintersville, OH 43953 / 740-264-0176; FAX: 740-264-2257 www.sskindustries.com

Stackpole Books, 5067 Ritter Rd., Mechanicsburg, PA 17055-6921 / 717-796-0411; or 800-732-3669; FAX: 717-796-0412 tmanney@stackpolebooks.com www.stackpolebooks.com

Stalker, Inc., P.O. Box 21, Fishermans Wharf Rd., Malakoff, TX 75148 / 903-489-1010

Stalwart Corporation, P.O. Box 46, Evanston, WY 82931 / 307-789-7687; FAX: 307-789-7688

Stan Baker Sports, Stan Baker, 10000 Lake City Way, Seattle, WA 98125 / 206-522-4575

Stan De Treville & Co., 4129 Normal St., San Diego, CA 92103 / 619-298-3393

Stanley Bullets, 2085 Heatheridge Ln., Reno, NV 89509

Star Ammunition, Inc., 5520 Rock Hampton Ct., Indianapolis, IN 46268 / 800-221-5927; FAX: 317-872-5847

Star Custom Bullets, P.O. Box 608, 468 Main St., Ferndale, CA 95536 / 707-786-9140; FAX: 707-786-9117 wmebridge@humboldt.com

Star Machine Works, P.O. Box 1872, Pioneer, CA 95666 / 209-295-5000

Starke Bullet Company, P.O. Box 400, 605 6th St. NW, Cooperstown, ND 58425 / 888-797-3431

Starkey Labs, 6700 Washington Ave. S., Eden Prairie, MN 55344

Starkey's Gun Shop, 9430 McCombs, El Paso, TX 79924 / 915-751-3030

Starlight Training Center, Inc., Rt. 1, P.O. Box 88, Bronaugh, MO 64728 / 417-843-3555

Starline, Inc., 1300 W. Henry St., Sedalia, MO 65301 / 660-827-6640; FAX: 660-827-6650 info@starlinebrass.com http://www.starlinebrass.com

Starr Trading Co., Jedediah, P.O. Box 2007, Farmington Hills, MI 48333 / 810-683-4343; FAX: 810-683-3282

Starrett Co., L. S., 121 Crescent St., Athol, MA 01331 / 978-249-3551; FAX: 978-249-8495

Steelman's Gun Shop, 10465 Beers Rd., Swartz Creek, MI 48473 / 810-735-4884

Steffens, Ron, 18396 Mariposa Creek Rd., Willits, CA 95490 / 707-485-0873

Stegall, James B., 26 Forest Rd., Wallkill, NY 12589

Steve Henigson & Associates, P.O. Box 2726, Culver City, CA 90231 / 310-305-8288; FAX: 310-305-1905

Steve Kamyk Engraver, 9 Grandview Dr., Westfield, MA 01085-1810 / 413-568-0457 stevek201@comcast.net

Steven Dodd Hughes, P.O. Box 545, Livingston, MT 59047 / 406-222-9377; FAX: 406-222-9377

Steves House of Guns, Rt. 1, Minnesota City, MN 55959 / 507-689-2573

Stewart Game Calls, Inc., Johnny, P.O. Box 7954, 5100 Fort Ave., Waco, TX 76714 / 817-772-3261; FAX: 817-772-3670

Stewart's Gunsmithing, P.O. Box 5854, Pietersburg North 0750, Transvaal, SOUTH AFRICA / 01521-89401

Steyr Mannlicher GmbH & Co. KG, Mannlicherstrasse 1, 4400 Steyr, Steyr, AUSTRIA / 0043-7252-896-0; FAX: 0043-7252-78620 office@steyr-mannlicher.com www.steyr-mannlicher.com

STI International, 114 Halmar Cove, Georgetown, TX 78628 / 800-959-8201; FAX: 512-819-0465 www.stiguns.com

Stiles Custom Guns, 76 Cherry Run Rd., Box 1605, Homer City, PA 15748 / 712-479-9945 glstiles@yourinter.net www.yourinter.net/glstiles

Stillwell, Robert, 421 Judith Ann Dr., Schertz, TX 78154

Stoeger Industries, 17603 Indian Head Hwy., Suite 200, Accokeek, MD 20607-2501 / 301-283-6300; FAX: 301-283-6986 www.stoegerindustries.com

Stoeger Publishing Co. (See Stoeger Industries)

Stone Enterprises Ltd., 426 Harveys Neck Rd., P.O. Box 335, Wicomico Church, VA 22579 / 804-580-5114; FAX: 804-580-8421

Stone Mountain Arms, 5988 Peachtree Corners E., Norcross, GA 30071 / 800-251-9412

Stoney Point Products, Inc., P.O. Box 234, 1822 N. Minnesota St., New Ulm, MN 56073-0234 / 507-354-3360; FAX: 507-354-7236 stoney@newulmtel.net www.stoneypoint.com

MANUFACTURER'S DIRECTORY

Storm, Gary, P.O. Box 5211, Richardson, TX 75083 /
214-385-0862
Stott's Creek Armory, Inc., 2526 S. 475W, Morgantown, IN
46160 / 317-878-5489; FAX: 317-878-9489
sccalendar@aol.com www.Sccalendar.aol.com
Stratco, Inc., P.O. Box 2270, Kalispell, MT 59901 /
406-755-1221; FAX: 406-755-1226
Strayer, Sandy. See: STRAYER-VOIGT, INC.
Strayer-Voigt, Inc., Sandy Strayer, 3435 Ray Orr Blvd., Grand
Prairie, TX 75050 / 972-513-0575
Strong Holster Co., 39 Grove St., Gloucester, MA 01930 /
508-281-3300; FAX: 508-281-6321
Strutz Rifle Barrels, Inc., W. C., P.O. Box 611, Eagle River, WI
54521 / 715-479-4766
Stuart, V. Pat, Rt. 1, Box 447-S, Greenville, VA 24440 /
804-556-3845
Sturgeon Valley Sporters, Ken Ide, P.O. Box 283, Vanderbilt,
MI 49795 / 989-983-4338 k.ide@mail.com
Sturm Ruger & Co. Inc., 200 Ruger Rd., Prescott, AZ 86301
/ 928-541-8820; FAX: 520-541-8850 www.ruger.com
Sullivan, David S. (See Westwind Rifles, Inc.)
"Su-Press-On", Inc., P.O. Box 09161, Detroit, MI 48209 /
313-842-4222
Sun Welding Safe Co., 290 Easy St. No. 3, Simi Valley, CA
93065 / 805-584-6678; or 800-729-SAFE; FAX:
805-584-6169 sunwelding.com
Sunny Hill Enterprises, Inc., W1790 Cty. HHH, Malone, WI
53049 / 920-795-4722; FAX: 920-795-4822
Super 6 LLC, Gary Knopp, 3806 W. Lisbon Ave., Milwaukee,
WI 53208 / 414-344-3343; FAX: 414-344-0304
Surecase Co., The, 233 Wilshire Blvd., Ste. 900, Santa
Monica, CA 90401 / 800-92ARMLOC
Sure-Shot Game Calls, Inc., P.O. Box 816, 6835 Capitol,
Groves, TX 77619 / 409-962-1636; FAX: 409-962-5465
Svon Corp., 2107 W. Blue Heron Blvd., Riviera Beach, FL
33404 / 508-881-8852
Swampfire Shop, The (See Peterson Gun Shop, Inc., A.W.)
Swann, D. J., 5 Orsova Close, Eltham North Vic., 3095
AUSTRALIA / 03-431-0323
Swanndri New Zealand, 152 Elm Ave., Burlingame, CA 94010
/ 415-347-6158
Swanson, Mark, 975 Heap Avenue, Prescott, AZ 86301 /
928-778-4423
Swarovski Optik North America Ltd., 2 Slater Rd., Cranston,
RI 02920 / 401-946-2220; or 800-426-3089; FAX:
401-946-2587
Sweet Home, Inc., P.O. Box 900, Orrville, OH 44667-0900
Swenson's 45 Shop, A. D., 3839 Ladera Vista Rd., Fallbrook,
CA 92028-9431
Swift Bullet Co., P.O. Box 27, 201 Main St., Quinter, KS
67752 / 913-754-3959; FAX: 913-754-2359
Swift Instruments, Inc., 952 Dorchester Ave., Boston, MA
02125 / 617-436-2960; FAX: 617-436-3232
Swift River Gunworks, 450 State St., Belchertown, MA 01007
/ 413-323-4052
Szweda, Robert (See RMS Custom Gunsmithing)

T

T&S Industries, Inc., 1027 Skyview Dr., W. Carrollton, OH
45449 / 513-859-8414; FAX: 937-859-8404
keith.tomlinson@tandsshellcatcher.com
www.tandsshellcatcher.com
T.F.C. S.p.A., Via G. Marconi 118, B, Villa Carcina 25069,
ITALY / 030-881271; FAX: 030-881826
T.G. Faust, Inc., 544 Minor St., Reading, PA 19602 /
610-375-8549; FAX: 610-375-4488
T.K. Lee Co., 1282 Branchwater Ln., Birmingham, AL 35216
/ 205-913-5222 odonmich@aol.com
www.scopedot.com
T.W. Menck Gunsmith, Inc., 5703 S. 77th St., Ralston, NE
guntools@cox.net
http://llwww.members.cox.net/guntools
Tabler Marketing, 2554 Lincoln Blvd., Suite 555, Marina Del
Rey, CA 90291 / 818-386-0373; FAX: 818-386-0373
Taconic Firearms Ltd., Perry Lane, P.O. Box 553, Cambridge,
NY 12816 / 518-677-2704; FAX: 518-677-5974
Tactical Defense Institute, 2174 Bethany Ridges, West Union,
OH 45693 / 937-544-7228; FAX: 937-544-2887
tdiohio@dragonbbs.com www.tdiohio.com
Talley, Dave, P.O. Box 369, Santee, SC 29142 /
803-854-5700; or 307-436-9315; FAX: 803-854-9315
talley@diretway www.talleyrings.com
Talon Industries Inc. (See Cobra Enterprises, Inc.)
Tamarack Products, Inc., P.O. Box 625, Wauconda, IL 60084
/ 708-526-9333; FAX: 708-526-9353

Tanfoglio Fratelli S.r.l., via Valtrompia 39, 41, Brescia, ITALY
/ 011-39-030-8910361; FAX: 011-39-030-8910183
info@tanfoglio.it www.tanfoglio.it
Tanglefree Industries, 1261 Heavenly Dr., Martinez, CA
94553 / 800-982-4868; FAX: 510-825-3874
Tank's Rifle Shop, P.O. Box 474, Fremont, NE 68026-0474 /
402-727-1317 jtank@tanksrifleshop.com
www.tanksrifleshop.com
Tanner (See U.S. Importer-Mandall Shooting Supplies, Inc.)
Taracorp Industries, Inc., 1200 Sixteenth St., Granite City, IL
62040 / 618-451-4400
Target Shooting, Inc., P.O. Box 773, Watertown, SD 57201 /
605-882-6955; FAX: 605-882-8840
Tar-Hunt Custom Rifles, Inc., 101 Dogtown Rd.,
Bloomsburg, PA 17815 / 570-784-6368; FAX:
570-389-9150 www.tar-hunt.com
Tarnhelm Supply Co., Inc., 431 High St., Boscawen, NH
03303 / 603-796-2551; FAX: 603-796-2918
info@tarnhelm.com www.tarnhelm.com
Tasco Sales, Inc., 2889 Commerce Pkwy., Miramar, FL
33025
Taurus Firearms, Inc., 16175 NW 49th Ave., Miami, FL 33014
/ 305-624-1115; FAX: 305-623-7506
Taurus International Firearms (See U.S. Importer Taurus
Firearms, Inc.)
Taurus S.A. Forjas, Avenida Do Forte 511, Porto Alegre, RS
BRAZIL 91360 / 55-51-347-4050; FAX: 55-51-347-3065
Taylor & Robbins, P.O. Box 164, Rixford, PA 16745 /
814-966-3233
Taylor's & Co., Inc., 304 Lenoir Dr., Winchester, VA 22603 /
540-722-2017; FAX: 540-722-2018
info@taylorsfirearms.com www.taylorsfirearms.com
TCCI, P.O. Box 302, Phoenix, AZ 85001 / 602-237-3823;
FAX: 602-237-3858
TCSR, 3998 Hoffman Rd., White Bear Lake, MN 55110-4626
/ 800-328-5323; FAX: 612-429-0526
TDP Industries, Inc., P.O. Box 249, Ottsville, PA 18942-0249
/ 215-345-8687; FAX: 215-345-6057
Techno Arms (See U.S. Importer- Auto-Ordnance Corp.)
Tecnolegno S.p.A., Via A. Locatelli, 6 10, 24019 Zogno,
ITALY / 0345-55111; FAX: 0345-55155
Ted Blocker Holsters, Inc., 9396 S.W. Tigard St., Tigard, OR
97223 / 800-650-9742; FAX: 503-670-9692
www.tedblocker.com
Tele-Optics, 630 E. Rockland Rd., P.O. Box 6313, Libertyville,
IL 60048 / 847-362-7757; FAX: 847-362-7757
Tennessee Valley Mfg., 14 County Road 521, Corinth, MS
38834 / 601-286-5014 tvm@avsia.com
www.avsia.com/tvm
Ten-Ring Precision, Inc., Alex B. Hamilton, 1449 Blue Crest
Lane, San Antonio, TX 78232 / 210-494-3063; FAX:
210-494-3066
TEN-X Products Group, 1905 N. Main St., Suite 133,
Cleburne, TX 76031-1305 / 972-243-4016; or
800-433-2225; FAX: 972-243-4112
Tepeco, P.O. Box 342, Friendswood, TX 77546 /
713-482-2702
Terry K. Kopp Professional Gunsmithing, Rt 1 Box 224,
Lexington, MO 64067 / 816-259-2636
Testing Systems, Inc., 220 Pegasus Ave., Northvale, NJ
07647
Tetra Gun Care, 8 Vreeland Rd., Florham Park, NJ 07932 /
973-443-0004; FAX: 973-443-0263
Tex Shoemaker & Sons, Inc., 714 W. Cienega Ave., San
Dimas, CA 91773 / 909-592-2071; FAX: 909-592-2378
texshoemaker@texshoemaker.com
www.texshoemaker.com
Texas Armory (See Bond Arms, Inc.)
Texas Platers Supply Co., 2453 W. Five Mile Parkway, Dallas,
TX 75233 / 214-330-7168
Thad Rybka Custom Leather Equipment, 2050 Canoe Creek
Rd., Springvale, AL 35146-6709
Thad Scott Fine Guns, Inc., P.O. Box 412, Indianola, MS
38751 / 601-887-5929
Theis, Terry, 21452 FM 2093, Harper, TX 78631 /
830-864-4438
Thiewes, George W., 14329 W. Parada Dr., Sun City West, AZ
85375
Things Unlimited, 235 N. Kimbau, Casper, WY 82601 /
307-234-5277
Thirion Gun Engraving, Denise, P.O. Box 408, Graton, CA
95444 / 707-829-1876
Thomas, Charles C., 2600 S. First St., Springfield, IL 62704 /
217-789-8980; FAX: 217-789-9130
books@ccthomas.com ccthomas.com
Thompson Bullet Lube Co., P.O. Box 409, Wills Point, TX
75169 / 866-476-1500; FAX: 866-476-1500
thompsonbulletlube.com www.thompsonbulletlube.com

Thompson Precision, 110 Mary St., P.O. Box 251, Warren, IL
61087 / 815-745-3625
Thompson, Randall. See: HIGHLINE MACHINE CO.
Thompson Target Technology, 4804 Sherman Church Ave.
S.W., Canton, OH 44710 / 330-484-6480; FAX:
330-491-1087 www.thompsontarget.com
Thompson Tool Mount, 1550 Solomon Rd., Santa Maria, CA
93455 / 805-934-1281 ttm@pronet.net
www.thompsontoolmount.com
Thompson/Center Arms, P.O. Box 5002, Rochester, NH
03866 / 603-332-2394; FAX: 603-332-5133
tech@tcarms.com www.tcarms.com
Thunden Ranch, HCR 1, Box 53, Mountain Home, TX 78058 /
830-640-3138
Tiger-Hunt Longrifle Gunstocks, Box 379, Beaverdale, PA
15921 / 814-472-5161 tigerhunt4@aol.com
www.gunstockwood.com
Tikka (See U.S. Importer-Stoeger Industries)
Time Precision, 4 Nicholas Sq., New Milford, CT 06776-3506
/ 860-350-8343; FAX: 860-350-6343
timeprecision@aol.com
Tinks & Ben Lee Hunting Products (See Wellington
Outdoors)
Tink's Safariland Hunting Corp., P.O. Box 244, 1140
Monticello Rd., Madison, GA 30650 / 706-342-4915;
FAX: 706-342-7568
Tioga Engineering Co., Inc., P.O. Box 913, 13 Cone St.,
Wellsboro, PA 16901 / 570-724-3533; FAX:
570-724-3895 tiogaeng@epix.net
Tippman Pneumatics, Inc., 2955 Adams Center Rd., Fort
Wayne, IN 46803
Tirelli, Snc Di Tirelli Primo E.C., Via Matteotti No. 359,
Gardone V.T. Brescia, ITALY / 0039-030-8912819; FAX:
0039-030-832240 tirelli@tirelli.it www.tirelli.it
TM Stockworks, 6355 Maplecrest Rd., Fort Wayne, IN 46835
/ 219-485-5389
Tom Forrest, Inc., P.O. Box 326, Lakeside, CA 92040 /
619-561-5800; FAX: 888-GUN-CLIP info@gunmag.com
www.gunmag.com
Tombstone Smoke`n' Deals, PO Box 31298, Phoenix, AZ
85046 / 602-905-7013; FAX: 602-443-1998
Tom's Gun Repair, Thomas G. Ivanoff, 76-6 Rt. Southfork
Rd., Cody, WY 82414 / 307-587-6949
Tom's Gunshop, 3601 Central Ave., Hot Springs, AR 71913 /
501-624-3856
Tonoloway Tack Drives, HCR 81, Box 100, Needmore, PA
17238
Torel, Inc./Tandy Brands Outdoors/AA & E, 208 Industrial
Loop, Yoakum, TX 77995 / 361-293-6366; FAX:
361-293-9127
TOZ (See U.S. Importer-Nygord Precision Products, Inc.)
Track of the Wolf, Inc., 18308 Joplin St. NW, Elk River, MN
55330-1773 / 763-633-2500; FAX: 763-633-2550
Traditions Performance Firearms, P.O. Box 776, 1375 Boston
Post Rd., Old Saybrook, CT 06475 / 860-388-4656; FAX:
860-388-4657 info@traditionsfirearms.com
www.traditionsfirearms.com
Trafalgar Square, P.O. Box 257, N. Pomfret, VT 05053 /
802-457-1911
Trail Visions, 5800 N. Ames Terrace, Glendale, WI 53209 /
414-228-1328
Trax America, Inc., P.O. Box 898, 1150 Eldridge, Forrest City,
AR 72335 / 870-633-0410; or 800-232-2327; FAX:
870-633-4788 trax@ipa.net www.traxamerica.com
Treadlok Gun Safe, Inc., 1764 Granby St. NE, Roanoke, VA
24012 / 800-729-8732; or 703-982-6881; FAX:
703-982-1059
Treebone Carving, P.O. Box 551, Cimarron, NJ 87714 /
505-376-2145 treebonecarving.com
Treemaster, P.O. Box 247, Guntersville, AL 35976 /
205-878-3597
Trevallion Gunstocks, 9 Old Mountain Rd., Cape Neddick, ME
03902 / 207-361-1130
Trico Plastics, 28061 Diaz Rd., Temecula, CA 92590 /
909-676-7714; FAX: 909-676-0267
ustinfo@ustplastics.com www.tricoplastics.com
Trigger Lock Division / Central Specialties Ltd., 220-D
Exchange Dr., Crystal Lake, IL 60014 / 847-639-3900;
FAX: 847-639-3972
Trijicon, Inc., 49385 Shafer Ave., P.O. Box 930059, Wixom,
MI 48393-0059 / 248-960-7700; or 800-338-0563
Trilby Sport Shop, 1623 Hagley Rd., Toledo, OH 43612-2024
/ 419-472-6222
Trilux, Inc., P.O. Box 24608, Winston-Salem, NC 27114 /
910-659-9438; FAX: 910-768-7720
Trinidad St. Jr. Col. Gunsmith Dept., 600 Prospect St.,
Trinidad, CO 81082 / 719-846-5631; FAX: 719-846-5667

MANUFACTURER'S DIRECTORY

Triple-K Mfg. Co., Inc., 2222 Commercial St., San Diego, CA 92113 / 619-232-2066; FAX: 619-232-7675 sales@triplek.com www.triplek.com
Tristar Sporting Arms, Ltd., 1814 Linn St. #16, N. Kansas City, MO 64116-3627 / 816-421-1400; FAX: 816-421-4182 tristar@blitz-it.net www.tristarsportingarms
Trius Traps, Inc., P.O. Box 25, 221 S. Miami Ave., Cleves, OH 45002 / 513-941-5682; FAX: 513-941-7970 triustraps@fuse.net www.triustraps.com
Trooper Walsh, 2393 N. Edgewood St., Arlington, VA 22207
Trotman, Ken, 135 Ditton Walk, Unit 11, Cambridge, CB5 8PY ENGLAND / 01223-211030; FAX: 01223-212317 www.kentrolman.com
Tru-Balance Knife Co., P.O. Box 140555, Grand Rapids, MI 49514 / 616-647-1215
True Flight Bullet Co., 5581 Roosevelt St., Whitehall, PA 18052 / 610-262-7630; FAX: 610-262-7806
Truglo, Inc., P.O. Box 1612, McKinna, TX 75070 / 972-774-0300; FAX: 972-774-0323 www.truglosights.com
Trulock Tool, P.O. Box 530, Whigham, GA 31797 / 229-762-4678; FAX: 229-762-4050 trulockchokes@hotmail.com trulockchokes.com
Tru-Nord Compass, 1504 Erick Lane, Brainerd, MN 56401 / 218-829-2870; FAX: 218-829-2870 www.trunord.com
Tru-Square Metal Products, Inc., 640 First St. SW, P.O. Box 585, Auburn, WA 98071 / 253-833-2310; or 800-225-1017; FAX: 253-833-2349 t-tumbler@qwest.net
Tucker, James C., P.O. Box 366, Medford, OR 97501 / 541-664-9160 jctstocker@yahoo.com
Tucson Mold, Inc., 930 S. Plumer Ave., Tucson, AZ 85719 / 520-792-1075; FAX: 520-792-1075
Turk's Head Productions, Mustafa Bilal, 908 NW 50th St., Seattle, WA 98107-3634 / 206-782-4164; FAX: 206-783-5677 info@turkshead.com www.turkshead.com
Turnbull Restoration, Doug, 6680 Rts. 5 & 20, P.O. Box 471, Bloomfield, NY 14469 / 585-657-6338; FAX: 585-657-6338 turnbullrest@mindspring.com www.turnbullrestoration.com
Tuttle, Dale, 4046 Russell Rd., Muskegon, MI 49445 / 616-766-2250

U

U.S. Importer-Wm. Larkin Moore, 8430 E. Raintree Ste. B-7, Scottsdale, AZ 85260
U.S. Optics, A Division of Zeitz Optics U.S.A., 5900 Dale St., Buena Park, CA 90621 / 714-994-4901; FAX: 714-994-4904 www.usoptics.com
U.S. Repeating Arms Co., Inc., 275 Winchester Ave., Morgan, UT 84050-9333 / 801-876-3440; FAX: 801-876-3737 www.winchester-guns.com
U.S. Tactical Systems (See Keng's Firearms Specialty, Inc.)
Ugartechea S. A., Ignacio, Chonta 26, Eibar, SPAIN / 43-121257; FAX: 43-121669
Ultra Dot Distribution, P.O. Box 362, 6304 Riverside Dr., Yankeetown, FL 34498 / 352-447-2255; FAX: 352-447-2266
Ultralux (See U.S. Importer-Keng's Firearms Specialty, Inc.)
UltraSport Arms, Inc., 1955 Norwood Ct., Racine, WI 53403 / 414-554-3237; FAX: 414-554-9731
Uncle Bud's, HCR 81, Box 100, Needmore, PA 17238 / 717-294-6000; FAX: 717-294-6005
Uncle Mike's (See Michaels of Oregon, Co.)
Unertl Optical Co., Inc., 103 Grand Avenue, P.O. Box 895, Mars, PA 16046-0895 / 724-625-3810; FAX: 724-625-3819 unertl@nauticom.net www.unertloptics.net
UniTec, 1250 Bedford SW, Canton, OH 44710 / 216-452-4017
United Binocular Co., 9043 S. Western Ave., Chicago, IL 60620
United Cutlery Corp., 1425 United Blvd., Sevierville, TN 37876 / 865-428-2532; or 800-548-0835; FAX: 865-428-2267 www.unitedcutlery.com
United States Products Co., 518 Melwood Ave., Pittsburgh, PA 15213-1136 / 412-621-2130; FAX: 412-621-8740 sales@us-products.com www.usporepaste.com
Universal Sports, P.O. Box 532, Vincennes, IN 47591 / 812-882-8680; FAX: 812-882-8680
Upper Missouri Trading Co., P.O. Box 100, 304 Harold St., Crofton, NE 68730-0100 / 402-388-4844

USAC, 4500-15th St. East, Tacoma, WA 98424 / 206-922-7589
Uselton/Arms, Inc., 842 Conference Dr., Goodlettsville, TN 37072 / 615-851-4919
Utica Cutlery Co., 820 Noyes St., Utica, NY 13503 / 315-733-4663; FAX: 315-733-6602

V

V. H. Blackinton & Co., Inc., 221 John L. Dietsch, Attleboro Falls, MA 02763-0300 / 508-699-4436; FAX: 508-695-5349
Valdada Enterprises, P.O. Box 773122, 31733 County Road 35, Steamboat Springs, CO 80477 / 970-879-2983; FAX: 970-879-0851 www.valdada.com
Valtro USA, Inc., 1281 Andersen Dr., San Rafael, CA 94901 / 415-256-2575; FAX: 415-256-2576
VAM Distribution Co. LLC, 1141-B Mechanicsburg Rd., Wooster, OH 44691 www.rex10.com
Van Gorden & Son Inc., C. S., 1815 Main St., Bloomer, WI 54724 / 715-568-2612
Van Horn, Gil, P.O. Box 207, Llano, CA 93544
Van Patten, J. W., P.O. Box 145, Foster Hill, Milford, PA 18337 / 717-296-7069
Vann Custom Bullets, 2766 N. Willowside Way, Meridian, ID 83642
Van's Gunsmith Service, 224 Route 69-A, Parish, NY 13131 / 315-625-7251
Varmint Masters, LLC, Rick Vecqueray, P.O. Box 6724, Bend, OR 97708 / 541-318-7306; FAX: 541-318-7306 varmintmasters@bendcable.com www.varmintmasters.net
Vecqueray, Rick. See: VARMINT MASTERS, LLC
Vector Arms, Inc., 270 W. 500 N., North Salt Lake, UT 84054 / 801-295-1917; FAX: 801-295-9316 vectorarms@bbscmail.com www.vectorarms.com
Vega Tool Co., c/o T. R. Ross, 4865 Tanglewood Ct., Boulder, CO 80301 / 303-530-0174 clanlaird@aol.com www.vegatool.com
Venco Industries, Inc. (See Shooter's Choice Gun Care)
Venus Industries, P.O. Box 246, Sialkot-1, PAKISTAN FAX: 92 432 85579
Verney-Carron, 54 Boulevard Thiers-B.P. 72, 42002 St. Etienne Cedex 1, St. Etienne Cedex 1, FRANCE / 33-477791500; FAX: 33-477790702 email@verney-carron.com www.verney-carron.com
Vest, John, 1923 NE 7th St., Redmond, OR 97756 / 541-923-8898
VibraShine, Inc., P.O. Box 577, Taylorsville, MS 39168 / 601-785-9854; FAX: 601-785-9874 rdbeke@vibrashine.com www.vibrashine.com
Vibra-Tek Co., 1844 Arroya Rd., Colorado Springs, CO 80906 / 719-634-8611; FAX: 719-634-6886
Vic's Gun Refinishing, 6 Pineview Dr., Dover, NH 03820-6422 / 603-742-0013
Victory Ammunition, P.O. Box 1022, Milford, PA 18337 / 717-296-5768; FAX: 717-296-9298
Victory USA, P.O. Box 1021, Pine Bush, NY 12566 / 914-744-2060; FAX: 914-744-5181
Vihtavuori Oy, FIN-41330 Vihtavuori, FINLAND, / 358-41-3779211; FAX: 358-41-3771643
Vihtavuori Oy/Kaltron-Pettibone, 1241 Ellis St., Bensenville, IL 60106 / 708-350-1116; FAX: 708-350-1606
Viking Video Productions, P.O. Box 251, Roseburg, OR 97470
Village Restorations & Consulting, Inc., P.O. Box 569, Claysburg, PA 16625 / 814-239-8200; FAX: 814-239-2165 www.villagerestoration@yahoo.com
Vincent's Shop, 210 Antoinette, Fairbanks, AK 99701
Viper Bullet and Brass Works, 11 Brock St., Box 582, Norwich, ON N0J 1P0 CANADA
Viramontez Engraving, Ray Viramontez, 601 Springfield Dr., Albany, GA 31721 / 229-432-9683 sgtvira@aol.com
Viramontez, Ray. See: VIRAMONTEZ ENGRAVING
Virgin Valley Custom Guns, 450 E 800 N. #20, Hurricane, UT 84737 / 435-635-8941; FAX: 435-635-8943 vvcguns@infowest.com www.virginvalleyguns.com
Visible Impact Targets, Rts. 5 & 20, E. Bloomfield, NY 14443 / 716-657-6161; FAX: 716-657-5405
Vitt/Boos, 1195 Buck Hill Rd., Townshend, VT 05353 / 802-365-9232
Voere-KGH GmbH, Untere Sparchen 56, A-6330 Kufstein, Tirol, AUSTRIA / 0043-5372-62547; FAX: 0043-5372-65752 voere@aon.com www.voere.com

Volquartsen Custom Ltd., 24276 240th Street, P.O. Box 397, Carroll, IA 51401 / 712-792-4238; FAX: 712-792-2542 vcl@netins.net www.volquartsen.com
Vorhes, David, 3042 Beecham St., Napa, CA 94558 / 707-226-9116; FAX: 707-253-7334
VSP Publishers (See Heritage/VSP Gun Books), P.O. Box 887, McCall, ID 83638 / 208-634-4104; FAX: 208-634-3101 heritage@gunbooks.com www.gunbooks.com
VTI Gun Parts, P.O. Box 509, Lakeville, CT 06039 / 860-435-8068; FAX: 860-435-8146 mail@vtigunparts.com www.vtigunparts.com
Vulpes Ventures, Inc., Fox Cartridge Division, P.O. Box 1363, Bolingbrook, IL 60440-7363 / 630-759-1229

W

W. Square Enterprises, 9826 Sagedale Dr., Houston, TX 77089 / 281-484-0935; FAX: 281-464-9940 lfdw@pdq.net www.loadammo.com
W. Waller & Son, Inc., 2221 Stoney Brook Rd., Grantham, NH 03753-7706 / 603-863-4177 www.wallerandson.com
W.B. Niemi Engineering, Box 126 Center Road, Greensboro, VT 05841 / 802-533-7180; or 802-533-7141
W.C. Wolff Co., P.O. Box 458, Newtown Square, PA 19073 / 610-359-9600; or 800-545-0077 mail@gunsprings.com www.gunsprings.com
W.E. Birdsong & Assoc., 1435 Monterey Rd., Florence, MS 39073-9748 / 601-366-8270
W.E. Brownell Checkering Tools, 9390 Twin Mountain Cir., San Diego, CA 92126 / 858-695-2479; FAX: 858-695-2479
W.J. Riebe Co., 3434 Tucker Rd., Boise, ID 83703
W.R. Case & Sons Cutlery Co., Owens Way, Bradford, PA 16701 / 814-368-4123; or 800-523-6350; FAX: 814-368-1736 jsullivan@wrcase.com www.wrcase.com
Wagoner, Vernon G., 2325 E. Encanto St., Mesa, AZ 85213-5917 / 480-835-1307
Waldron, Herman, Box 475, 80 N. 17th St., Pomeroy, WA 99347 / 509-843-1404
Walker Arms Co., Inc., 499 County Rd. 820, Selma, AL 36701 / 334-872-6231; FAX: 334-872-6262
Wallace, Terry, 385 San Marino, Vallejo, CA 94589 / 707-642-7041
Walls Industries, Inc., P.O. Box 98, 1905 N. Main, Cleburne, TX 76033 / 817-645-4366; FAX: 817-645-7946 www.wallsoutdoors.com
Walters Industries, 6226 Park Lane, Dallas, TX 75225 / 214-691-6973
Walters, John. See: WALTERS WADS
Walters Wads, John Walters, 500 N. Avery Dr., Moore, OK 73160 / 405-799-0376; FAX: 405-799-7727 www.tinwadman@cs.com
Walther America, P.O. Box 22, Springfield, MA 01102 / 413-747-3443 www.walther-usa.com
Walther GmbH, Carl, B.P. 4325, D-89033 Ulm, GERMANY
Walt's Custom Leather, Walt Whinnery, 1947 Meadow Creek Dr., Louisville, KY 40218 / 502-458-4361
WAMCO-New Mexico, P.O. Box 205, Peralta, NM 87042-0205 / 505-869-0826
Ward & Van Valkenburg, 114 32nd Ave. N., Fargo, ND 58102 / 701-232-2351
Ward Machine, 5620 Lexington Rd., Corpus Christi, TX 78412 / 512-992-1221
Wardell Precision Handguns Ltd., P.O. Box 391, Clyde, AZ 79510-0391 / 602-465-7995
Warenski Engraving, Julie Warenski, 590 E. 500 N., Richfield, UT 84701 / 435-896-5319; FAX: 435-896-8333 julie@warenskiknives.com
Warenski, Julie. See: WARENSKI ENGRAVING
Warne Manufacturing Co., 9057 SE Jannsen Rd., Clackamas, OR 97015 / 503-657-5590; or 800-683-5590; FAX: 503-657-5695 info@warnescopemounts.com www.warnescopemounts.com
Warren Muzzleloading Co., Inc., Hwy. 21 North, P.O. Box 100, Ozone, AR 72854 / 501-292-3268
Washita Mountain Whetstone Co., P.O. Box 20378, Hot Springs, AR 71903 / 501-525-3914 www.hsnp.com
Wasmundt, Jim, P.O. Box 130, Powers, OR 97466-0130
Watson Bros., 39 Redcross Way, London Bridge SE1 1H6, London, ENGLAND FAX: 44-171-403-336
Watson Bullets, 231 Allies Pass, Frostproof, FL 33843 / 863-635-7948 cbestbullet@aol.com
Wayne Specialty Services, 260 Waterford Drive, Florissant, MO 63033 / 413-831-7083

MANUFACTURER'S DIRECTORY

WD-40 Co., 1061 Cudahy Pl., San Diego, CA 92110 / 619-275-1400; FAX: 619-275-5823

Weatherby, Inc., 3100 El Camino Real, Atascadero, CA 93422 / 805-466-1767; FAX: 805-466-2527 www.weatherby.com

Weaver Products ATK, P.O. Box 39, Onalaska, WI 54650 / 800-648-9624; or 608-781-5800; FAX: 608-781-0368

Weaver Scope Repair Service, 1121 Larry Mahan Dr., Suite B, El Paso, TX 79925 / 915-593-1005

Webb, Bill, 6504 North Bellefontaine, Kansas City, MO 64119 / 816-453-7431

Weber & Markin Custom Gunsmiths, 4-1691 Powick Rd., Kelowna, BC V1X 4L1 CANADA / 250-762-7575; FAX: 250-861-3655 www.weberandmarkinguns.com

Webley and Scott Ltd., Frankley Industrial Park, Tay Rd., Birmingham, B45 0PA ENGLAND / 011-021-453-1864; FAX: 0121-457-7846 guns@webley.co.uk www.webley.co.uk

Webster Scale Mfg. Co., P.O. Box 188, Sebring, FL 33870 / 813-385-6362

Weems, Cecil, 510 W. Hubbard St., Mineral Wells, TX 76067-4847 / 817-325-1462

Weigand Combat Handguns, Inc., 1057 South Main Rd., Mountain Top, PA 18707 / 570-868-8358; FAX: 570-868-5218 sales@jackweigand.com www.jackweigand.com

Weihrauch KG, Hermann, Industriestrasse 11, 8744 Mellrichstadt, Mellrichstadt, GERMANY

Welch, Sam. See: SAM WELCH GUN ENGRAVING

Wellington Outdoors, P.O. Box 244, 1140 Monticello Rd., Madison, GA 30650 / 706-342-4915; FAX: 706-342-7568

Wells, Rachel, 110 N. Summit St., Prescott, AZ 86301 / 928-445-3655 wellssportstore@cableone.net

Wells Creek Knife & Gun Works, 32956 State Hwy. 38, Scottsburg, OR 97473 / 541-587-4202; FAX: 541-587-4223

Welsh, Bud. See: HIGH PRECISION

Wenger North America/Precise Int'l., 15 Corporate Dr., Orangeburg, NY 10962 / 800-431-2996; FAX: 914-425-4700

Wenig Custom Gunstocks, 103 N. Market St., P.O. Box 249, Lincoln, MO 65338 / 660-547-3334; FAX: 660-547-2881 gustock@wenig.com www.wenig.com

Werth, T. W., 1203 Woodlawn Rd., Lincoln, IL 62656 / 217-732-1300

Wescombe, Bill (See North Star West)

Wessinger Custom Guns & Engraving, 268 Limestone Rd., Chapin, SC 29036 / 803-345-5677

West, Jack L., 1220 W. Fifth, P.O. Box 427, Arlington, OR 97812

Western Cutlery (See Camillus Cutlery Co.)

Western Mfg. Co., 550 Valencia School Rd., Aptos, CA 95003 / 831-688-5884 lotsabears@eathlink.net

Western Missouri Shooters Alliance, P.O. Box 11144, Kansas City, MO 64119 / 816-597-3950; FAX: 816-229-7350

Western Nevada West Coast Bullets, P.O. BOX 2270, DAYTON, NV 89403-2270 / 702-246-3941; FAX: 702-246-0836

Westley Richards & Co. Ltd., 40 Grange Rd., Birmingham, ENGLAND / 010-214722953; FAX: 010-214141138 sales@westleyrichards.com www.westleyrichards.com

Westley Richards Agency USA (See U.S. Importer

Westwind Rifles, Inc., David S. Sullivan, P.O. Box 261, 640 Briggs St., Erie, CO 80516 / 303-828-3823

Weyer International, 2740 Nebraska Ave., Toledo, OH 43607 / 419-534-2020; FAX: 419-534-2697

Whildin & Sons Ltd., E.H., RR 2 Box 119, Tamaqua, PA 18252 / 717-668-6743; FAX: 717-668-6745

Whinnery, Walt (See Walt's Custom Leather)

White Barn Wor, 431 County Road, Broadlands, IL 61816

White Pine Photographic Services, Hwy. 60, General Delivery, Wilno, ON K0J 2N0 CANADA / 613-756-3452

White Rifles, Inc., 234 S. 1250 W., Linden, UT 84042 / 801-932-7950 www.whiterifles.com

White Rock Tool & Die, 6400 N. Brighton Ave., Kansas City, MO 64119 / 816-454-0478

Whitestone Lumber Corp., 148-02 14th Ave., Whitestone, NY 11357 / 718-746-4400; FAX: 718-767-1748 whstco@aol.com

Wichita Arms, Inc., 923 E. Gilbert, Wichita, KS 67211 / 316-265-0661; FAX: 316-265-0760 sales@wichitaarms.com www.wichitaarms.com

Wick, David E., 1504 Michigan Ave., Columbus, IN 47201 / 812-376-6960

Widener's Reloading & Shooting Supply, Inc., P.O. Box 3009 CRS, Johnson City, TN 37602 / 615-282-6786; FAX: 615-282-6651

Wideview Scope Mount Corp., 13535 S. Hwy. 16, Rapid City, SD 57702 / 605-341-3220; FAX: 605-341-9142 wvdon@rapidnet.com www.wideviewscopemount.com

Wiebe, Duane, 5300 Merchant Cir. #2, Placerville, CA 95667 / 530-344-1357; FAX: 530-344-1357 wiebe@d-wdb.com

Wiest, Marie. See: GUNCRAFT SPORTS, INC.

Wilcox All-Pro Tools & Supply, 4880 147th St., Montezuma, IA 50171 / 515-623-3138; FAX: 515-623-3104

Wilcox Industries Corp., Robert F. Guarasi, 53 Durham St., Portsmouth, NH 03801 / 603-431-1331; FAX: 603-431-1221

Wild Bill's Originals, P.O. Box 13037, Burton, WA 98013 / 206-463-5738; FAX: 206-465-5925 wildbill@halcyon.com billcleaver@centurytel.net

Wild West Guns, 7521 Old Seward Hwy., Unit A, Anchorage, AK 99518 / 800-992-4570; or 907-344-4500; FAX: 907-344-4005 wwguns@ak.net www.wildwestguns.com

Wilderness Sound Products Ltd., 4015 Main St. A, Springfield, OR 97478

Wildey F. A., Inc., 45 Angevin Rd., Warren, CT 06754-1818 / 860-355-9000; FAX: 860-354-7759 wildeyfa@optonline.net www.wildeyguns.com

Wildlife Research Center, Inc., 1050 McKinley St., Anoka, MN 55303 / 763-427-3350; or 800-USE-LURE; FAX: 763-427-8354 www.wildlife.com

Will-Burt Co., 169 S. Main, Orrville, OH 44667

William E. Phillips Firearms, 38 Avondale Rd., Wigston, Leicester, ENGLAND / 0116 2886334; FAX: 0116 2810644 william.phillips2@tesco.net

William Powell Agency, 22 Circle Dr., Bellmore, NY 11710 / 516-679-1158

Williams Gun Sight Co., 7389 Lapeer Rd., Box 329, Davison, MI 48423 / 810-653-2131; or 800-530-9028; FAX: 810-658-2140 williamsgunsight.com

Williams Mfg. of Oregon, 110 East B St., Drain, OR 97435 / 503-836-7461; FAX: 503-836-7245

Williams Shootin' Iron Service, The Lynx-Line, Rt. 2 Box 223A, Mountain Grove, MO 65711 / 417-948-0902; FAX: 417-948-0902

Williamson Precision Gunsmithing, 117 W. Pipeline, Hurst, TX 76053 / 817-285-0064; FAX: 817-280-0044

Willow Bend, P.O. Box 203, Chelmsford, MA 01824 / 978-256-8508; FAX: 978-256-8508

Wilsom Combat, 2234 CR 719, Berryville, AR 72616-4573 / 800-955-4856; FAX: 870-545-3310

Wilson Arms Co., The, 63 Leetes Island Rd., Branford, CT 06405 / 203-488-7297; FAX: 203-488-0135

Wilson Case, Inc., P.O. Box 1106, Hastings, NE 68902-1106 / 800-322-5493; FAX: 402-463-5276 sales@wilsoncase.com www.wilsoncase.com

Wilson Combat, 2234 CR 719, Berryville, AR 72616-4573 / 800-955-4856

Winchester Consultants, George Madis, P.O. Box 545, Brownsboro, TX 75756 / 903-852-6480; FAX: 903-852-5486 gmadis@earthlink.net www.georgemadis.com

Winchester Div. Olin Corp., 427 N. Shamrock, E. Alton, IL 62024 / 618-258-3566; FAX: 618-258-3599

Winchester Sutler, Inc., The, 270 Shadow Brook Lane, Winchester, VA 22603 / 540-888-3595; FAX: 540-888-4632

Windish, Jim, 2510 Dawn Dr., Alexandria, VA 22306 / 703-765-1994

Winfield Galleries LLC, 748 Hanley Industrial Ct., St. Louis, MO 63144 / 314-645-7636; FAX: 314-781-0224 info@winfieldgalleries.com www.winfieldgalleries.com

Wingshooting Adventures, 0-1845 W. Leonard, Grand Rapids, MI 49544 / 616-677-1980; FAX: 616-677-1986

Winter, Robert M., P.O. Box 484, 42975-287th St., Menno, SD 57045 / 605-387-5322

Wise Custom Guns, 1402 Blanco Rd., San Antonio, TX 78212-2716 / 210-828-3388

Wise Guns, Dale, 1402 Blanco Rd., San Antonio, TX 78212 / 210-734-9999

Wiseman and Co., Bill, P.O. Box 3427, Bryan, TX 77805 / 409-690-3456; FAX: 409-690-0156

Wisners, Inc., P.O. Box 58, Adna, WA 98522 / 360-748-4590; FAX: 360-748-6028 parts@wisnersinc.com www.wisnersinc.com

Wolf Performance Ammunition, 2201 E. Winston Rd., Ste. K, Anaheim, CA 92806-5537 / 702-837-8506; FAX: 702-837-9250

Wolfe Publishing Co., 2625 Stearman Rd., Ste. A, Prescott, AZ 86301 / 928-445-7810; or 800-899-7810; FAX: 928-778-5124

Wolverine Footwear Group, 9341 Courtland Dr. NE, Rockford, MI 49351 / 616-866-5500; FAX: 616-866-5658

Woodleigh (See Huntington Die Specialties)

Woods Wise Products, P.O. Box 681552, Franklin, TN 37068 / 800-735-8182; FAX: 615-726-2637

Woodstream, P.O. Box 327, Lititz, PA 17543 / 717-626-2125; FAX: 717-626-1912

Woodworker's Supply, 1108 North Glenn Rd., Casper, WY 82601 / 307-237-5354

Woolrich, Inc., Mill St., Woolrich, PA 17701 / 800-995-1299; FAX: 717-769-6234/6259

World of Targets. (See Birchwood Casey)

World Trek, Inc., 7170 Turkey Creek Rd., Pueblo, CO 81007-1046 / 719-546-2121; FAX: 719-543-6886

Worthy Products, Inc., RR 1, P.O. Box 213, Martville, NY 13111 / 315-324-5298

Wright's Gunstock Blanks, 8540 SE Kane Rd., Gresham, OR 97080 / 503-666-1705 doyal@wrightsguns.com www.wrightsguns.com

WTA Manufacturing, P.O. Box 164, Kit Carson, CO 80825 / 719-962-3570; or 719-962-3570 wta@rebeltec.com http://www.members.aol.com/ductman249/wta.html

Wyant Bullets, Gen. Del., Swan Lake, MT 59911

Wyoming Custom Bullets, 1626 21st St., Cody, WY 82414

Wyoming Knife Corp., 101 Commerce Dr., Fort Collins, CO 80524 / 303-224-3454

X

XS Sight Systems, 2401 Ludelle St., Fort Worth, TX 76105 / 888-744-4880; FAX: 800-734-7939

X-Spand Target Systems, 26-10th St. SE, Medicine Hat, AB T1A 1P7 CANADA / 403-526-7997; FAX: 403-528-2362

Y

Yankee Gunsmith "Just Glocks", 2901 Deer Flat Dr., Copperas Cove, TX 76522 / 817-547-8433; FAX: 254-547-8887 ed@justglocks.com www.justglocks.com

Yavapai College, 1100 E. Sheldon St., Prescott, AZ 86301 / 520-776-2353; FAX: 520-776-2355

Yavapai Firearms Academy Ltd., P.O. Box 27290, Prescott Valley, AZ 86312 / 928-772-8262; FAX: 928-772-0062 info@yfainc.com www.yfainc.com

Yearout, Lewis E. (See Montana Outfitters)

Yellowstone Wilderness Supply, P.O. Box 129, West Yellowstone, MT 59758 / 406-646-7613

Yesteryear Armory & Supply, P.O. Box 408, Carthage, TN 37030

York M-1 Conversion, 12145 Mill Creek Run, Plantersville, TX 77363 / 936-894-2397; FAX: 936-894-2397 bmf25years@aol.com

Young Country Arms, William, 1409 Kuehner Dr. #13, Simi Valley, CA 93063-4478

Z

Zabala Hermanos S.A., P.O. Box 97, Elbar Lasao, 6, Elgueta, Guipuzcoa, 20600 SPAIN / 34-943-768076; FAX: 34-943-768201 imanol@zabalahermanos.com www.zabalahermanos.com

Zander's Sporting Goods, 7525 Hwy. 154 West, Baldwin, IL 62217-9706 / 800-851-4373; FAX: 618-785-2320

Zanotti Armor, Inc., 123 W. Lone Tree Rd., Cedar Falls, IA 50613 / 319-232-9650 www.zanottiarmor.com

Zeeryp, Russ, 1601 Foard Dr., Lynn Ross Manor, Morristown, TN 37814 / 615-586-2357

Zero Ammunition Co., Inc., 1601 22nd St. SE, P.O. Box 1188, Cullman, AL 35056-1188 / 800-545-9376; FAX: 205-739-4683 zerobulletco@aoz.com www.zerobullets.com

Ziegel Engineering, 1390 E. Bunnett St. "F", Signal Hill, CA 90755 / 562-596-9481; FAX: 562-598-4734 ziegel@aol.com www.ziegeleng.com

Zim's, Inc., 4370 S. 3rd West, Salt Lake City, UT 84107 / 801-268-2505

Z-M Weapons, 203 South St., Bernardston, MA 01337 / 413-648-9501; FAX: 413-648-0219

Numbers

100 Straight Products, Inc., P.O. Box 6148, Omaha, NE 68106 / 402-556-1055; FAX: 402-556-1055

3-Ten Corp., P.O. Box 269, Feeding Hills, MA 01030 / 413-789-2086; FAX: 413-789-1549 www.3-ten.com

4-D Custom Die Co., 711 N. Sandusky St., P.O. Box 889, Mt. Vernon, OH 43050-0889 / 740-397-7214; FAX: 740-397-6600 info@ch4d.com ch4d.com